ISBN 978-0-331-49731-1
PIBN 11199582

JOURNAL

OF THE

ROYAL HORTICULTURAL SOCIETY

ESTABLISHED
A.D. 1804

ROYAL CHARTERS
A.D. 1809, 1860, 1899

PART I

EDITED BY

GEO. S. SAUNDERS, F.L.S., F.E.S.

PART II

BY

F. J. CHITTENDEN, F.L.S.

VOL. XXXIII.

1908

LONDON

Printed for the Royal Horticultural Society

BY

SPOTTISWOODE & CO. LTD., NEW-STREET SQUARE, E.C.

R - 5.1

Part I. published March 3, 1908.
Part II. published July 8, 1908.

18 · 2

CONTENTS OF VOL. XXXIII.

DIRECTIONS TO BINDER.

Vol. XXXIII. has been issued in two numbers, each containing the "Journal" proper, paged with Arabic figures, and "Extracts from the Proceedings," paged with Roman figures. This title and contents sheet should be placed first, and be followed by pages 1 to 328 and then by pages 329 to 628. After that should come the "Extracts from the Proceedings," pages i to cxxviii and cxxix to ccxlvi, concluding with the two Indexes.

Price (to Non-Fellows) 7s. 6d.   JANUARY 1908

Vol. XXXIII.   Part I.

THE
JOURNAL
OF THE
Royal Horticultural Society

EDITED BY
G. S. SAUNDERS, F.L.S., F.E.S.

CONTENTS.

R.H.S. Office for Advertisements and all Communications,
VINCENT SQUARE, S.W.

Printed for the Royal Horticultural Society
BY
SPOTTISWOODE & CO. LTD., NEW-STREET SQUARE, LONDON.

Entered at Stationers' Hall.]

TESTED SEEDS.

Carters' "Guinea" Box of Vegetable Seeds.

21s. **21s.**

Packing and Carriage Free.

CONTAINS

14 pints Peas, best for succession.
4 pints Broad Beans, in variety.
1 pint Runner Beans, Carter's Champion.
1 pint French Beans, Canadian Wonder.
1 pkt. Beet, Carters' Perfection.
1 pkt. Kale, Half Tall Curled.
1 pkt. Brussels Sprouts, Perfection.
3 pkts. Broccoli, for succession.
3 pkts. Cabbage, Heartwell, Beefheart, &c.
1 pkt. Savoy, Dwarf Curled.
1 pkt. Colewort, Hardy Green.
2½ ozs. Carrot, Intermediate, Early Horn, Surrey.
1 pkt. Cauliflower, Autumn Giant.
2 pkts. Celery, Crimson and White.
3 ozs. } Cress, for Salad.
1 pkt. }
2 pkts. Cucumber, Carters' Telegraph, &c.

1 pkt. Endive, Green Curled.
1 pkt. Leek, Holborn Model.
4 pkts. Lettuce, Giant White Cos and Cabbage.
4 ozs. Mustard, for Salads.
1 pkt. Melon, Blenheim Orange.
4 pkts. Onion, including Long-keeping.
1 pkt. Parsley, Covent Garden.
1 oz. Parsnip, Carters' Maltese.
3½ ozs. Radish, Long, Oval, and Extra Early, Turnip.
1 pkt. Scorzonera.
1 pkt. Salsafy, Carters' Mammoth.
4 ozs. Spinach, Summer and Winter.
3 ozs. Turnip, Summer and Winter.
1 pkt. Tomato, Carters' Perfection.
1 pkt. Vegetable Marrow.
3 pkts. Herbs, Sweet and Pot.

Carters' Complete Box of Flower Seeds.

10s. 6d. **10s. 6d.**

Packing and Postage Free.

12 choicest varieties Pæony-flowered Aster.
6 ,, ,, Dwarf Stock.
2 oz. best mixed var. Sweet Peas.
1 oz. ,, ,, Tom Thumb Nasturtium.
1 oz. finest selected Crimson Giant Mignonette.
1 oz. ,, mixed Flower Seeds for Shrubberies, &c.
6 choice selected var. Hardy Perennials.
3 varieties Everlasting Flowers.

25 beautiful Hardy and Half-hardy Annuals, such as—
Nasturtium, Scarlet King.
Poppy, all sorts, mixed.
Choice Balsam.
Gaillardia.
Phlox Drummondi.
Sunflower.

Silene Compacta.
Convolvulus major.
Petunia.
Salpiglossis, mixed.
Star Zinnia.
Marguerites, &c.

A detailed list of other Collections of Vegetable and Flower Seeds from 2/6 to 105/- each, free on application.

Write for Carters' Illustrated Catalogue for 1908. Post free to Members of R.H.S.

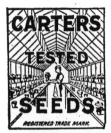

James Carter & Co

Seedsmen by Special Appointment —to His Majesty the King.

Head Office : 237-8 & 97 HIGH HOLBORN, LONDON.

City Branch: 53A QUEEN VICTORIA STREET, E.C.

JOURNAL

OF THE

ROYAL HORTICULTURAL SOCIETY.

VOL. XXXIII. 1907.

THE TRUE DARWINISM.

By Rev. Professor G. HENSLOW, M.A., V.M.H.

[Lecture given on March 5, 1907.]

UP to the middle of the last century we all thought that each species of animal and plant was created by a direct *fiat*, somewhat as Milton so graphically described in his "Paradise Lost." Darwin, however, revived the doctrine of Evolution, about which philosophers had speculated in times past; but he put it forward in a more attractive form, so that it was soon accepted, not only by biologists, but by all the world as well.

Darwin, however, went further, and propounded a theory of the method of Evolution. This is called "Darwinism," and is defined by the title of his book, "The Origin of Species by Means of Natural Selection" (1859).

Darwin based this theory upon the following, partly true and partly hypothetical statements:

1. Variability, or the capacity of varying, which, under changed conditions of life, produces new structures.

2. The production of seeds is enormous; but only the usual average of adults occurs in nature; the majority die.

3. All plants show "Individual Differences"; and when a number of seedlings of the same species grow up under new conditions of life or environment, Darwin *assumed* that of their individual differences some would or might, *by* chance, be "favourable," *i.e.* structures *adapted* to the new surroundings; while others, the majority, would be "injurious," *i.e. inadapted*, and consequently *fatal* variations; as Weismann observes of even slight variations, they may be a matter of life or death to the individual—a pure assumption, based on no evidence.

This mixture of good and bad seedlings Darwin called the "Indefinite Results of the Direct Action of the New Conditions of Life."

4. Presuming the preceding to be true, Darwin now introduced "Natural Selection"; by which he meant that, in the struggle for life, the individuals with favourable, *i.e.* adaptive variations, would survive;

while all those with " injurious " or inadaptive structures would perish. This he termed the " Survival of the Fittest."

5. Lastly, the survivors must leave offspring with the new structural characters ; for unless they be hereditary, the new variety or species could not be certain of a continued existence.   Then through several generations, the slight and favourable variations begun in the first generation would accumulate till they would be recognised as constituting a " variety " ; and a variety Darwin regarded as an " incipient species."

Turning now to the " Origin of Species, &c.," we find his theory based on the preceding facts and suppositions thus expressed :—" Can it be thought improbable . . . that variations useful in some way to each being in the great and complex battle of life should occur in the course of many successive generations ?   If such do occur, can we doubt . . . that the individuals having any advantage, however slight, over others, would have the best chance of surviving and of procreating their kind ?   On the other hand, we may feel sure that any variation in the least degree injurious would be rigidly destroyed ?   This preservation of favourable individual differences and variations and the destruction of those which are injurious I have called Natural Selection, or the Survival of the Fittest." *   This passage may be called the Foundation of Darwinism.   In order to make the theory clear to his readers, he gives the following illustration : " If an architect were to rear a noble and commodious edifice without the use of cut stone, by selecting from the fragments at the base of a precipice wedge-formed stones for his arches, elongated stones for his lintels, and flat stones for his roof, we should admire his skill and regard him as a paramount power.

" Now the fragments of stone, though indispensable to the architect, bear to the edifice built by him the same relation [as a matter of fact there is *no* relationship at all] which the fluctuating variations of each organic being bear to the varied and admirable structures ultimately acquired by its modified descendants." †

With regard to the stones, Darwin says : " their shape may be strictly said to be accidental " ; moreover, he overlooked two important facts. First, it is *quite impossible* to build a " noble and commodious edifice " out of unhewn and unprepared stones, and without any unprepared mortar.   Secondly, *What takes the place of the architect's and builder's skill* in the construction of a living organism ?   Prof. A. H. Church invented the word " Directivity " to account for the fact that nature can make many products in plants which he, as a chemist, can construct in the laboratory, and so suggested this word as representing that property of life which takes his place within the plant.   Or, the question may be put in Darwin's words : " If the architect would be a ' paramount power ' in constructing the house, *What is the paramount power* in the Evolution of animals and plants ? "

In the above illustration Darwin is considering the result of " favourable " variations represented by adaptable stones.   To complete the parallel, suppose the builder is careless and takes up stones at random, using inadaptive as well as adaptive ones, what would happen ?   He tries

* *Origin of Species, &c.,* 6th ed., p. 62.
† *An. and Pl. under Dom.* ii. p. 430.

to build his arches, &c., with them ; but the insecurity of the walls would be an obvious result, and unstable equilibrium would be the consequence. So that, as soon as the weight of the first floor was sufficient, the whole would come down with a crash like a house built of cards, and it would perish in its "development." The unsuitable stones here stand for Darwin's "injurious" individual variations, which thus involve the death of the plant itself. If that be so, why need there be any struggle for existence and natural selection at all ? The struggle may hasten the death, but it would happen in any circumstances. Natural selection really and only means that "some live, but more die."

Darwinism, in point of fact, stands upon, or falls with, the one word "injurious" being true or otherwise. Thus Weismann maintains : "The minutest change in the least important organ may be enough to render the species incapable of existence." *

We have seen that variations of structure are produced through the "direct action of changed conditions of life " ; and, according to the theory, the result is a mixture of many individuals with injurious, and a fewer number with (perchance) favourable, or adaptive variations. This Darwin called "Indefinite Results." But he also observed that "Definite Results " sometimes occurred ; by this he meant that *all* the individuals of a batch of seedlings might vary alike in the same favourable or adaptive manner, there being *no* injurious or inadaptive variations at all. Hence, there would be no mixture for natural selection to deal with, and *all* would survive, provided each individual could secure enough nourishment and light ; but, as a matter of fact, the younger individuals would be overshadowed by the older, &c. ; so that the many might perish in the struggle, though they would have thriven if there had been no struggle at all. Such is what I have elsewhere described as the *true meaning and application of Natural Selection.*†

It may be observed that those who accept Darwinism always speak of adaptive characters, but regard them as due to natural selection. Thus, Dr. D. H. Scott writes : "The word *adaptive* is used here simply for characters newly developed under the influence of Natural Selection, as distinguished from those which were so developed earlier in the history of the race, and have been transmitted for many generations by inheritance. Personally, I regard all characters alike as adaptive at their origin." ‡ The last sentence is undoubtedly correct, and is the true explanation of all specific and generic characters ; but to attribute the "development " of "adaptive characters " to the "influence " of natural selection is a mis-interpretation of *facts.*

Darwin cautions his readers against supposing natural selection to have any influence, agency, or powers of any kind. He says : "It implies only the preservation of such variations as arise and are beneficial to the being under its conditions of life." § "It may *metaphorically* be said that natural selection is daily and hourly scrutinising, throughout the world, the slightest variations ; rejecting those that are bad, preserving and adding up all that are good." ‖ Since, however, there never are any " injurious "

* *Essays*, p. 265. † *Journ. R. Hort. Soc.* vol. xxxi.
‡ *Studies in Fossil Botany*, p. 524, note.
§ *Origin, &c.*, 6th ed., p. 63. ‖ *Ibid.* p. 65.

variations, as he calls them, natural selection—in Darwin's application of
the term—has no place in nature.

When Darwin wrote his book (1859) he was, to a limited extent,
acquainted with this fact; but he thought it was very exceptional, and
certainly not the rule. He gives us a hint, even so early as in the Introduction to the first edition of the " Origin, &c." He thus wrote : " Natural
selection is the main, but not the exclusive, means of modification." This
is explained on the eleventh page, wherein he adds : " Some slight amount
of change may, I think, be attributed to the direct action of the conditions
of life ; " i.e. by the plant responding by making adaptive structures.

When we turn to his " Animals and Plants under Domestication "
(1868), we find that he is much more positive about it. His words
are : " The direct action of changed conditions of life leads to definite or
[assumed] indefinite results. By the term ' Definite Action,' I mean an
action of such a nature that when many individuals of the same variety
are exposed during several generations to any change in their physical
conditions of life, all, or nearly all, the individuals are modified in the
same manner. A new sub-variety would then be produced without the
aid of selection." *

The reader will now perceive that " Indefinite " and " Definite "
results must be mutually exclusive. A batch of seedlings cannot all vary
alike (i.e. definitely) and at the same time have the majority with injurious
variations (i.e. indefinitely). In 1859, however, Darwin seemed to have
thought that natural selection was somehow aided by " definite action "
of the environment ; but he evidently came to the conclusion that such a
combination was quite inadmissible in 1868.

In another passage in his " Animals and Plants under Domestication "
he speaks yet more strongly, for he observes : " The direct and definite
action of changed conditions, in contradistinction to the accumulation of
indefinite variations, seems to me to be so important that I will give a large
additional body of miscellaneous facts " ; and he adds about thirty more
to the one only which previously he had regarded as " the most remarkable case known to me, namely, that in Germany several varieties of maize
brought from the hotter parts of America were transformed in the course
of only two or three generations." †

By the year 1876 we find that Darwin had become even more thoroughly
convinced of the importance of " Definite Action," by which he means,
" Direct action of new or changed conditions of life producing definite
results, or adaptive variations "—for he wrote to Professor Moritz Wagner
as follows : ‡—" The greatest mistake I made was, I now think, I did not
attach sufficient weight to the direct influence of food, climate, &c., quite
independently of natural selection. When I wrote my book, and for some
years later, I could not find a good proof of the direct action of the environment on the species. Such proofs are now plentiful."

After this, one is not surprised to read in the sixth edition of the
" Origin of Species," published two years afterwards (1878) : " There can
be little doubt that the tendency to vary in the same manner has often

---

* Animals and Plants under Domestication, vol. ii. p. 271 ; see also Origin, &c.,
pp. 6, 72, 80, &c. (6th ed.).
† An. and Pl. under Dom. ii. pp. 277–281.   ‡ Life, vol. iii. p. 159.

been so strong that all the individuals of the same species have been similarly modified without the aid of any form of selection." *

By " tendency to vary," he evidently means " Response to the direct action of the new conditions of life."

To judge from the past, had Darwin lived until to-day, he would have become assured that "Definite Results" are not only "plentiful" but *universal*; and that "Indefinite Results"—among which the majority are "Injurious" variations—do not occur at all under any new conditions of life in nature ; so that "New sub-varieties," and we may add varieties, species, and genera, are, in fact, *always* produced "without the aid of natural selection."

The reader will perceive that, unlike "Darwinism," Darwin himself conclusively shows that this alternative interpretation of the Origin of Species is *no theory* at all, but represents the true Natural Law of Evolution.

Half a century has well-nigh passed away, and thirty years since Darwin wrote that letter to Wagner have elapsed : how do we stand now ? Not a single wild species, whether of animals or plants, has ever been scientifically *proved*, either by induction or experiment, to have had its origin by "means of natural selection." Dr. Wallace said : "It is, of course, admitted that direct proof of the action of natural selection is wanting." If a theory cannot be substantiated in fifty years, why is it retained ? Especially since Darwin's alternative solution of the Method of Evolution, or the production of "definite" varieties, by means of the response of the organism itself, to the new influences of changed conditions of life, has been long since *proved* to be the invariable law of nature.

Let us now see what are the opinions of many eminent botanists at the present day, who study plants as they grow and change in nature. They are now called "Ecologists" for that reason.†

There are three things which every Ecologist at once perceives. The *first* is the struggle for existence. This prevails everywhere, and accounts largely for the *Distribution* of species, by *the survival of the better adapted in the circumstances*. *Secondly*, there are obvious adaptations in the structures of plants to their environments, whether the locality be dry or moist, cold or hot, &c. *Thirdly*, whenever one and the same species finds its way into a different set of external conditions, it at once, as it grows, puts on more or less the same adaptive characteristic structures, both morphological and histological, of the natives of the place. This is brought about by means of the inherent *responsive power* residing in the living protoplasm and nuclei of the plant.

I will now quote a few observations by eminent Ecologists on " Adaptation."

Mr. J. A. Thompson, writing on "Synthetic Summary of the Influence of the Environment upon the Organism," says : "No attempt to explain the adaptation of the organism to its environment can be complete without recognition that external influences, in the widest sense and in various degrees of directness, have, and have had, an important transforming and adaptive action." This is exactly what Darwin meant

* *Origin, &c.*, p. 72 ; see also p. 421.
† *I.e.* " The study " of plants " at home."

by "the Direct Action of the conditions of Life producing Definite Results." *

Professor Warming, of Copenhagen, in describing adaptations among "xerophytic" plants, *i.e.* of dry countries, as Mexico, &c., says : "I answer briefly to the question which arises—namely, whether these adaptations to the medium should be regarded as a result of natural selection, or whether they owe their origin to the action, in modifying forms, *exercised directly* by the conditions of the medium. *I adopt this latter view . . .* the characters of adaptation thus directly acquired have become fixed." †

M. Costantin, speaking of Arctic plants, says : "We are led to think, so to say, invincibly, that one can only explain the general characters of Arctic plants by adaptation—*e.g.*, if all Arctic plants are perennials, it is because they live near the Pole. It is the conditions of life which have created this hereditary character." ‡

As another illustration, Professor Warming, of Copenhagen, and Fritz Müller, in Brazil, have both recorded the fact that certain species which are non-climbing herbs when living in the open, become climbers when growing in the semi-darkness of adjacent forests.

Lastly, aquatic plants will often grow better and stronger in air than when submerged ; but the whole anatomical structure is at once altered to suit aërial conditions.

The preceding are just a few cases ; but the reader must understand that *the Power of Responding to New Conditions of Life, and of forming Structures in direct adaptation to them, is a Universal Natural Law.*

The reader will now realise why I call this Responsive power with Adaptation the "True Darwinism," for Darwin suggested it. Of course, it is more or less of the nature of a revival of Lamarck's theory, but it has the advantage of excluding his errors, and is based on an infinite amount of facts, as far as plants are concerned.

It is not my province to carry it into the animal kingdom ; though, as far as inductive evidence goes, it is precisely the same, *e.g.* it is infinitely more probable that all animals with paddle-like limbs, *in adaptation to water*, acquired them by response with modification in adapting themselves to it, than that the same mechanical structures should have arisen accidentally, according to Darwinism, and never out of water. For such structures are found in the invertebrata in insects, also in fishes, amphibia, reptiles, birds, and mammals.

Experimental evidence may not be so easy to procure with animals as with plants, but Nature is not likely to adopt two different methods of Evolution. Semper,§ Pascoe,‖ and Eimer,¶ however, have attacked the problem from the zoological side, and the reader is referred to their works.**

* Royal Phys. Soc. Edin. (1888).
† *Lagoa Santa*, p. 465 (1892).
‡ *Les Végétaux et les Milieux cosmiques*, p. 85 (1898).
§ *The Natural Conditions of Existence, as they Affect Animal Life* (Nat. Sc. Ser., vol. xxxi.).
‖ *The Darwinian Theory of the Origin of Species.*
¶ *Organic Evolution.* (Translated by Cunningham.)
** Since the above was written, Mr. B. B. Woodward has shown that the lungs of molluscs are the direct result of adaptation (*Presidential Address to the Malacological Society*, 1907).

An objector observed that " Weismann had *proved* " that any effects on the *soma*, *i.e.* the vegetative system in plants, by external agencies could not be hereditary. Not to press the fact that it is impossible " to prove a negative," plants entirely *disprove* Weismann's assertion, which was only a supposition to support his theory of germ-plasm. Thus our garden varieties of root-crops are hereditary ; but they arose by modifications on the *soma* long before any reproductive organs existed, as they are biennials. According to Weismann, only those effects of the direct action of the external conditions of life can be hereditary which can reach the reproductive organs. Yet round and long-rooted forms of turnips and rape, of the carrot, and of the radish, arose from sowing the seed in stiff and loose soils respectively, and are due to varying degrees of mechanical obstruction ; yet they are now hereditary, and " true " by seed.

What, then, is the conclusion of the whole matter? It is that Darwinism, or " The Origin of Species by means of Natural Selection," must be replaced by " The Origin of Species by means of Response with Adaptation to the Direct Action of New Conditions of Life." This is the real basis of Evolution.

BRITISH GUIANA.

By J. A. Barbour James.

[Lecture given on March 19, 1907.]

I do not think it necessary for me to refer to the geographical position which British Guiana occupies in South America, considering that it has been under British rule for over a hundred years (it celebrated the centenary of its occupation in 1903), but I am afraid that the British public, as a rule, has but a very vague idea of the constituent parts of the Empire, and that British Guiana is frequently confused with Guinea, in Africa, and British New Guinea. This, no doubt, is to be accounted for, to a great extent, by the similarity of the names. The area of British Guiana is 90,277 square miles, or nearly twice the size of England and Wales.

It is a part of the mainland portion of South America, and is divided into three counties, viz. Demerara, Berbice, and Essequibo, each called after the river of the same name. It extends from Venezuela to the river Corentyn, which divides it from Dutch Guiana (or Surinam).

Very little was known of the country until the search for the golden city of Manoa and the wonderful Eldorado allured many adventurous spirits to explore its great forests.

From reports gleaned out of Spanish letters found in captured vessels, Sir Walter Raleigh was induced by the accounts of this fabulous city to undertake the disastrous expedition which cost him his life.

The climate of British Guiana now compares most favourably with that of most tropical countries, and though a little hot at a certain season it is far from being unhealthy, as is generally supposed by persons who have not visited its shores.

There are instances of longevity among settlers on the banks of the rivers Demerara, Berbice, and Essequibo which can be readily quoted, the natural drainage being so perfect that all impurities of the air are washed away by the torrents of rain which fall, and the purity of the air is so great that the planets Venus and Jupiter may at times be seen during the daylight.

The year is divided into two wet and two dry seasons. The long wet season commences about the middle of April, and with westerly winds prevailing lasts until August. The long dry season then begins, and continues until November. December and January constitute the short wet and February and March the short dry seasons.

The temperature seldom falls below 75° Fahr. or rises above 90°. The mean annual temperature of Georgetown, the capital, is 80°, and the average rainfall is about 85 inches.

The diversity of altitudes in British Guiana accounts for variety of indigenous productions, while many vegetables and floral exotics have been from time to time introduced and have readily adapted themselves to the climate and soil. The growth of vegetation is perpetual, and the never-failing verdure is of surprising brilliancy. The grandeur of Nature's gigantic efforts displayed in the vast size, varied forms, and extraordinary rapidity of growth of the vegetable kingdom has often filled the stranger, accustomed, perhaps, only to the less luxuriant aspect of colder climes, with astonishment and delight.

For example, the promenade as well as the Botanic Gardens, the former situate in the centre of the city and the latter at the back, are lovely spots, and greatly impress the stranger at first sight. Their charming and varied scenery and vast amount of rich, shady foliage render them delightful places of resort.

The Botanic Gardens occupy a strip of land in the form of a parallelogram of about 160 acres in extent, nearly five times as long as it is wide. A portion of it is a flower garden, occupying the part nearest the town, and has an area of between thirty and forty acres on the left of the ample carriage drive which passes through the centre, and parallel with it is a series of lakes linked together by narrow underground connections by which they are supplied with water from a common source (a large reservoir called the Lamaha Canal).

There are several nurseries of considerable proportions, containing hundreds of thousands of young plants of all descriptions. These are sold, or in many cases given away free of charge for cultivation.

As an example to the general public most Government buildings are rendered very picturesque by being surrounded with flower gardens, the Alms House, Orphan Asylum, Onderneeming Reformatory, Town Hall, Government House, Victoria Law Courts, &c. being particularly well kept. The following are some of the flowering and foliage plants cultivated :—

Asparagus ferns.	Ginger lily.
Bay trees.	Hollyhocks.
Begonias.	Honeysuckles.
Camellias.	Hyacinths.
Cannas.	Lilies of the valley.
Carnations.	Nasturtiums.
Chrysanthemums.	Oxalis.
Coleus.	Palms.
Crotons.	Pansies.
Dahlias.	Primroses.
Daisies.	Rhododendrons.
Eucharis lily.	Roses.
Evergreens.	Selaginellas.
Ferns.	Stephanotis.
Foxgloves.	Sunflowers.
Fuchsias.	Sweet peas.
Geraniums.	

There had been held for some considerable time previously at stated periods, varying from three to five years, Agricultural Exhibitions in the colony, which were more or less restricted, or rather were taken advantage of by only a limited class. About fifteen years ago, however, horticulture began to come into fashion, and as it was found that it encouraged a better taste in the community, the Band of Hope held a Horticultural Show with results which far exceeded all anticipations, and at present every well-to-do inhabitant either cultivates his flower garden or, if he should not have the facilities which a plot of land would afford, his window boxes. No lady in the colony to-day thinks her home complete without flowering or foliage plants forming part of its decoration. This applies chiefly to the city, but a more substantial development resulted in some of the rural districts, where there are in existence Horticultural and Agricultural Associations, which arrange Shows periodically, under the direction of the Department of Science and Agriculture, over which Professor J. B. Harrison, C.M.G., presides. Professor Harrison has taken the same interest in these matters as the late Mr. G. S. Jarman did, to whom the colony is much indebted for the splendid public gardens of which it now boasts.

The Government of the colony has warmly responded to the wish of the people, and, since the creation of the Imperial Department of Agriculture at Barbados by Sir Daniel Morris, Commissioner of Agriculture for the West Indies, has evolved a scheme by which the schoolmasters have been taught the science of agriculture. With a view to imparting the same to the scholars, School gardens have in several places been established. Some of the scholars are thereby brought practically in touch with the subject. Field lecturers visit these schools, and their services are also available to all farmers in the neighbourhood.

I need not apologise for referring to the subject of Agriculture, considering that the Council of the Royal Horticultural Society wish to become the means of exhibiting colonial agricultural and other economic products.

The following are some of the vegetables cultivated in the colony: the plantain, yam, squash, cassava (sweet and bitter), tannia, eddoe, pumpkin, cucumber, breadfruit, egg cup, tomatos, cabbage, corn, beans (various), shallot, onions, pea, ochroe, sweet potatos, pepper, carrot, parsnip, cress, turnip, radish, lettuce, celery, spinach, thyme, mint, &c.

Fruits: the cocoanut, gooseberry, mamee apple, mango, sapodilla, sugar apples, custard apples, grapes, water melons, oranges (sweet and Seville), musk melon, lemon, citron, pear, shaddock, granadilla, pineapple, water lemon, guava, pawpaw, sour sop, banana, figs (various), plum, cherry, nut, pomegranate, &c.

Coffee, cocoa, rice, corn meal, cassava bread, cassava meal, arrowroot starch, cassava starch, honey, ginger, tobacco, pickles, sauces, guava jelly, chutney—in very many cases these products are only cultivated for home use, but should the growers be able to secure a remunerative market for their produce I am certain they will take every opportunity of availing themselves of it. Perhaps it may be interesting to recount one or two instances in connection with the agricultural development of the colony, which make me anticipate a large foreign trade.

It was while opening one of the exhibitions of the Victoria Belfield Agricultural Society that I, as President, had the pleasure of accepting the offer of three prizes spontaneously made by Sir Cavendish Boyle for the best essay on agriculture, which might be of help to the Government in popularising that enterprise in the colony. These were forthcoming, and

I believe assisted the Government considerably in carrying out subsequent schemes. A most gratifying feature in the agricultural life of the colony, so far as it affects district organisation, is the periodical meeting of a conference, when views regarding the agricultural outlook are discussed.

The following are the Societies (District) in the colony: Victoria Belfield, Buxton Farmers', Bagotville, and Wakenaam.

The statistics given below may be of interest:

The population of the colony in 1904, according to the census, was 301,923, of whom 10,000 were aboriginal Indians, viz. Accuvoi, Carib, and Waren. The population of Georgetown in 1905 was estimated at 48,802.

The birth rate of the colony in 1905 was 33·6 per 1,000 and the death rate 27·4 per 1,000. The colony can boast of 535 miles of telegraph wires and 814 miles of telephone wires, with an exchange capable of accommodating 500 subscribers (450 of whom are connected), 72 post offices, 24 submarine cables connect various parts of the colony.

The exports in the six years 1900 to 1906 were:

Sugar, valued at	£1,208,155
Rum	126,739
Gold, 95,043 oz.	352,021
Diamonds, 4,202 carats	5,045
Timber	24,989
Balata	40,312
Other items	1,831,479

THE RELATION OF METEOROLOGY TO HORTICULTURE.

By R. H. Curtis, F.R.Met.Soc.

[Lecture given on April 16, 1907.]

Rainfall.

In a previous lecture on the relation of Meteorology to Horticulture which I gave last year (Journ. R. Hort. Soc. vol. xxxii. p. 104) I dealt chiefly with the subject of temperature, but in explaining the use of the wet-bulb thermometer I then referred at some length to the fact that water is a large and most important constituent of the atmosphere, in which it is always present in the form of an invisible gas or vapour, although the quantity varies greatly in different parts of the world, and changes also in the same region almost from hour to hour with variations of the temperature of the air and of other conditions.

I showed that in certain circumstances, which almost invariably involve the cooling of the air, this vapour may be condensed, and that it then becomes visible as a cloud or fog consisting of numberless particles of water each of extreme minuteness—so minute indeed as to be quite invisible individually.

To understand the formation of these minute particles of water we must regard the invisible steam from which they are derived as being itself composed of still more minute atoms, each of which is separate and distinct from its neighbours. When the air becomes sufficiently cooled to produce condensation these molecules of steam coalesce with those immediately adjoining, forming themselves into groups, or minute drops of water, which occupy in their new form very much the same position as they had previously filled as atoms of gas. There is, however, another constituent of the atmosphere which plays a very important part in the formation of these water particles—namely, the excessively minute atoms of dust which are everywhere present to a greater or less degree, and which exert a very material influence upon other phenomena besides the formation of rain-drops. These dust particles form nuclei upon which the vapour molecules condense, each atom of dust forming the foundation of a separate mass of water, so that, speaking generally, we may say that, other conditions being favourable, the greater the dustiness of the air the more numerous will be the particles of water formed, and the greater will be the density of the resulting fog or cloud.

A good deal of thought has been expended in trying to explain how it is that these particles of water, forming large clouds, float in the air instead of at once falling to the ground, because water, being heavier than air, is as little able to float in the atmosphere as iron is able to float in water. An explanation which used to be very generally accepted was that the drops were hollow, like a soap bubble, and therefore floated because of their relatively large displacement. But if the centre of the drop be a solid particle of dust it is clear that that explanation cannot be a correct one ; and indeed it is not strictly correct to speak of the drops of water as floating in the air, because in reality they are always gravitating slowly towards the earth, and therefore the explanation we require is one which will account for the slowness of their fall rather than one to account for their not falling at all.

The rate at which the water particles descend is not uniform for all the particles alike, but is proportional to their size ; and in this fact we find the explanation of the further fact that in their descent the particles grow and form the relatively large rain-drops with which we are all familiar. The weight of the particles is proportional to the cube of their diameters, and therefore by doubling the diameter of a drop its weight will become increased eightfold. The rate of descent of the smallest drops is very small because their diameters and weight are very small, and if the drops were all of uniform size they should all descend at the same rate and without increase of size. But their size is not uniform, and therefore the larger and heavier drops will fall more quickly than the others, and overtaking those smaller ones which are in their path will collide with them and combine to form larger drops. These enlarged particles of water will then fall at a still faster rate, and by overtaking yet other particles the process of augmentation will be again and again repeated, and at an ever increasing rate.

The ultimate size of the rain-drop is, however, governed by another set of phenomena. The aggregation of water particles is held together by their cohesive force, the surface of the drop forming a kind of skin, which is capable of resisting a certain amount of strain before it will break. But when a drop has attained the size and weight at which this limit is reached it will break up into smaller drops, and this explains why, although a rain cloud may be of enormous thickness and density, the rain-drops which fall from it never exceed a certain size—probably not more than one-twentieth, or perhaps in extreme cases one-sixteenth, of an inch in diameter.

In my previous lecture I explained that there is a definite maximum amount of vapour which a given volume of air, at a given temperature, can contain in the gaseous state. When that amount has been reached, any further vapour which may be added will be deposited as water, unless at the same time the temperature of the air be raised, when its capacity for holding vapour will be at once increased. On the other hand, if without changing the amount of vapour the temperature of the air were to be lowered, the cooled air would no longer be able to retain all the vapour present, and therefore some of it would become condensed into water.

Cooling of the air is, therefore, the primary cause of condensation and of the formation of fog or cloud, and we may, therefore, consider briefly how such cooling may be brought about in nature.

There are more ways than one in which it may be effected. Air may be sufficiently cooled to produce condensation by coming into contact with colder ground which has been chilled by radiation on a clear, quiet night, and the ground mists and fogs, which commonly occur after a warm day, particularly in autumn, are generally caused in that way.

But so far as the formation of rain clouds is concerned we need only consider the dynamical cooling of the air caused by its expansion, because it is in that way that nearly all such clouds are formed.

Air, like all gases, expands when it is relieved of pressure, and in doing so it becomes cooled in accordance with definite and well understood laws ; and a body of air which from any cause is made to ascend to a higher level in the atmosphere must necessarily become cooled in this way, because of its expansion as it passes into air whose density is less than its own.

Now let us imagine a body of warm moist air blowing across the surface of the earth and meeting in its path a range of high hills. The horizontal movement of the air in front becomes checked by the mountains, but being pressed on by the moving mass behind it is forced up the mountain slopes to flow over their summits. At that higher level the pressure may be two or three pounds per square foot less than it was at the level of the sea, and owing to its being subject to this reduction in pressure the air would expand considerably, the expansion would be accompanied by a large fall of temperature to below the dew point, and a dense cloud would necessarily be formed.

Those who live in the neighbourhood of high hills are perfectly familiar with the result of this dynamical cooling, although possibly they do not always attribute it to its real cause, but they see it in the covering of cloud with which the flanks and summits of the hills are frequently hid.

But away from mountains the process of cloud-making may often be watched on a warm summer day when the ground has become heated by the sun. The warm ground radiates its heat into the layers of air immediately above it, and the air thus warmed rises in a stream to higher levels, causing the process of expansion, and consequent cooling, to take place in the same way as when the air is forced up the slope of a mountain. When the temperature of the air has fallen to that of the dew point, or, in other words, to the temperature at which it can no longer carry all the vapour it then contains, condensation will begin, and will be shown by the formation of a tiny cloudlet, which will continue to grow in size as fresh supplies of air arrive from below, and will presently form one of those large cumulus clouds which, when lighted by the sun's rays, are often objects of surpassing grandeur and beauty as they slowly sail across the sky. Very often the bases of these clouds appear as if they had all been cut off at a given level, which marks, indeed, the point at which the condensation took place and the formation of the cloud began.

As the evening comes on the reverse of this process may sometimes be seen. With the declining sun the earth's surface begins to cool, and consequently the supply of warm ascending air is first of all checked, and then entirely ceases. The clouds then sink slowly to a lower level, where the air is warmer, and there they again dissolve into vapour and gradually disappear, till soon the sky again becomes cloudless.

Very often, however, instead of dispersing in this way condensation proceeds, and the cloud particles increase in number and size till they fall to the earth as rain.

Meteorology is less concerned with the part which water plays in the phenomena of plant and animal life than with questions concerning its supply and the amount of rain which may be expected to fall, under average conditions, in a particular district or country: the question of the adequacy of the supply to the requirements of any particular species or phase of plant life belongs to the domain of the horticultural physicist.

To obtain the required data for answering questions respecting this important factor of the climate of any region the meteorologist regularly measures the fall of rain, in order to find the average fall and also its distribution as regards time. His measurements are made by means of a rain gauge, which is a very simple instrument, consisting of a cylindrical vessel, generally either 8 inches or 5 inches in diameter, which is placed in the ground at an exposed spot, with its rim 1 foot above the ground level. The water which falls into it is measured in a graduated glass vessel of much smaller diameter, so that a fall of rain which, spread over the area of the gauge, would measure, say, but a tenth of an inch would fill the glass to the depth of perhaps an inch, and thus make it possible to read with accuracy falls of rain which, spread over the surface of the ground, would not be more than a hundredth of an inch deep. Such a gauge is read daily, and usually at 9 o'clock each morning.

There are several patterns of rain gauge in use, but all of them do not fulfil the requirements of a reliable instrument. The aperture of the gauge should, of course, be true in shape, and it should have a sharp rim, so as to prevent splashing of rain-drops falling upon it. Besides this the aperture should be sufficiently deep to prevent rain from splashing out, or snow from being blown out, when once it has fallen into the gauge; and finally the receptacle for the water should be protected against loss by evaporation by the gauge being sunk to a fair depth in the ground, and by causing the water to pass into the receiver through a small aperture and pipe, with which the inverted cone-shaped opening of the gauge terminates.

It is, however, for many purposes desirable to know something of the rate at which rain falls, and frequently it becomes important to know the precise time at which a fall of rain occurred, or the distribution of the fall over the day.

For these purposes a self-recording gauge is used, in which the rain as it falls is made to actuate a pen, which marks the rate of fall by a line traced upon a piece of paper, the paper being made to turn at a uniform rate by means of a clock.

There are several forms of recording gauge in use. In some the rain passes into a balanced bucket, which, when filled to a certain point, tips over and empties itself at the same time that it moves the pen by turning a toothed wheel one notch; simultaneously another bucket is brought up on the opposite side to be filled, the two buckets thus alternating in a kind of see-saw movement.

In another gauge, known as Beckley's gauge, the rain passes into a receiver which floats in a vessel filled with mercury. As the receiver fills it sinks, and carries down with it a pen attached to it by a strip of metal, which, as before, makes a mark upon a clock-turned strip of paper.

When two-tenths of an inch of rain has passed into the receiver a syphon comes into action, by which the receiver is emptied and the pen brought back to the top of the paper to begin another descent.

Almost the newest form of self-registering gauge is Halliwell's, in which the trace is on a more open scale, and the action of the pen is controlled in a very ingenious way. Here again the water passes into a receiver, and in this case raises a float contained within it. As the float rises it pushes upwards a pen, which moves freely between a couple of guides, to keep it upright. At a given point in its rise the rod attached to the float upsets a balanced hammer, which, falling upon a small catch, liberates a syphon and allows it to fall into the receiver. The syphon discharges the water in a couple of seconds or so into another and lower chamber, from which it can run away somewhat less quickly; but before its escape has been accomplished the pen will have fallen again to its zero, and another float in the second chamber will have had time to lift the syphon back into its place, ready for its next liberation.

Now let us turn to some of the results which have been obtained from the systematic measurements of the fall of rain which have been made in various places in the way I have just described, and first as regards the British Islands.

Rather more than forty years ago the late Mr. G. J. Symons, F.R.S., began the "British Rainfall Organisation," which to-day consists of an army of more than 4,200 observers, who daily record the fall of rain in all parts of the kingdom, and forward their observations to Dr. H. R. Mill, the present director of the Organisation, by whom they are collated and arranged. Dr. Mill is thus able to supply us with information of the most complete kind respecting the rainfall of the British Islands. .

The wettest parts of Great Britain and Ireland are the hilly districts of our western coasts. . The reason for this I have already referred to. It is due to the uplifting of the moist air coming from the ocean into higher levels by its encountering the hills in the west of Ireland, in Wales, the Lake District, and the north-west of Scotland. The average fall of rain in and around London is only about 24 inches per annum, but to the south of London, on the hills of Surrey and Sussex, it amounts to 35 inches. On the Devon and Cornwall moors it rises to 60 inches, and in North Wales, the Lake region, and the Western Highlands of Scotland to 100 inches.

To show the way in which the contour of a district may affect its rainfall, take as an example a portion of Sussex of which Chichester is roughly the centre, where the rainfall varies from 25 and 30 inches over the lower part of the region bordering upon the coast to between 30 and 35 inches over the greater part of the Downs, and to between 35 and 40 inches in the neighbourhood of the highest and steepest summits.

The difference between the rainfall in different years is sometimes very large. The driest year of recent times was 1887, when all over the kingdom there was a shortage of rain, and large areas had less than 20 inches in the year. 1903 was, on the contrary, the wettest year.

Pride of place in the matter of heavy rainfall in Great Britain belongs to Seathwaite, in Cumberland, where the daily fall has once at least slightly exceeded 8 inches, and on several occasions has amounted to

6 inches, whilst the average yearly fall is rather more than 137 inches. However, a week without rain is not unknown even at Seathwaite. This place affords an excellent illustration of the way in which rainfall is produced through the cooling of air by its expansion. The moist air, which reaches the southern part of Westmoreland from off the sea, sweeps upwards towards the hills, and in the neighbourhood of the Styehead Pass is driven through a deep valley up the pass to a considerable height, and this results in the copious condensation and fall of rain at Seathwaite, which is just beyond. Last year the largest fall recorded in Great Britain was above 205¼ inches at Gleslyn, on Snowdon, whilst the least was but little more than 19 inches at Boyton in Suffolk.

A still more striking instance of this kind is to be found in India at Cherrapungee, on the slope of the Khasia Hills, where the average annual fall of rain amounts to 500 inches, and occasionally exceeds 600 inches, the air in that case being the vapour-laden south-west monsoon from off the Bay of Bengal. We sometimes are inclined to think that our rainfall is excessive, but compared with that of Cherrapungee even a Snowdon fall of 205 inches becomes very insignificant indeed.

As an example of a less favoured region I might mention Egypt, where the rainfall does not exceed a couple of inches in a year, but where, under the strong sun and parched air, the evaporation exceeds 100 inches in the year. What this amount of evaporation means may be inferred from the fact that, in connexion with the Nile Dam, in summer about 400,000 tons of water has to be held up daily to balance the loss by evaporation.

In the driest parts of our own country the rainfall in summer is about balanced by the evaporation, and therefore the water required to supply springs and underground water has to be drawn from the winter falls; but in the wettest districts the rain which falls is, all the year round, far in excess of the amount evaporated. It may happen, however, that although the surface soil may be well saturated the reserves in the earth may at the same time be very limited, and this condition might very well lead to stagnation in plant growth in the drier seasons of the year.

The conservation of rain water is a matter of practical importance to horticulturists, who grow plants under glass covering a large area, especially in the neighbourhood of towns. These glass roofs collect large quantities of water, which might be stored in tanks underground and pumped by wind power to supply the houses as required. Where water has to be purchased from the water companies the saving in cost which would result from such a plan carefully thought out should suffice to pay interest and to form a sinking fund on the capital expenditure needed to carry it out.

The amount of the rainfall has an important influence upon the character of the plant life of a district or of a country. A few slides will indicate this clearly and briefly. The first shows a ravine in the side of a hill-slope above Loch Fyne, eroded by the action of the water draining the hills and running down to the loch. The course of the ravine is plainly seen by the vegetation which covers its sides, whilst the *débris* which has been carried down by the stream has formed a fertile delta extending some distance into the loch itself. Other slides will give us an idea of the characteristic vegetation of other regions, humid and dry, and of the results obtained in arid districts by means of irrigation.

From measurements which have been made of the hourly falls of rain as recorded by self-registering gauges it is possible to find out what are the most rainy hours of the day in many places. The most rainy hours are in the morning, somewhere near 6 A.M., and there are indications of a second maximum in the afternoon, the driest part of the day being about noon. The quantity of rain measured in each hour is also greatest in the morning, except at Kew, at which place the afternoon hours get the largest falls.

I have already mentioned the limitations of the part played by the meteorologist in dealing with the supply of water, and pointed out that it is the botanical physicist who has to deal with the effect of the supply upon plant life. But there is one important point bearing upon those effects to which I should like to call attention, and that is the relation which Dr. Shaw, the director of the Meteorological Office, has found to exist between the amount of rainfall in the autumn and the yield of wheat in the succeeding harvest; and he has deduced a formula by which he can calculate the probable character of the ensuing harvest from the amount of rainfall, and he finds that the calculated amounts for the same district compared with the actual yield per acre each year are remarkably similar.

I have not the time left to say anything about snow or hail, except to mention that the first is formed of minute particles of frozen vapour in hexagonal crystals, adhering to one another and forming flakes of beautiful form. It only falls in cold weather, whilst hail, on the other hand, seldom falls in winter but generally in the hot weather, and frequently in connection with thunderstorms. The cause of the formation of hail is not very well known, but it is most probably due to the sudden chilling of vapour which has already been condensed into water and which by a sudden further fall of temperature becomes frozen into pellets of ice. It is not necessary to remind a gathering of horticulturists that sometimes hailstorms may be productive of much damage to crops and to gardens.

I said just now that we in this country are much favoured in the matter of rain. At times, however, we get more than we appreciate, and those who dwell by the sides of rivers have sometimes ample reason for an appearance of ingratitude. A rainfall of less than about 18 inches per annum is probably too small for the requirements of agriculture without the aid of irrigation, and an excessive rainfall is doubtless less hurtful to vegetation than a deficient one.

But occasionally long-continued wet weather combined with modern methods of draining land leads to heavy floods, the rivers receiving more water than they can readily carry away, and it is quite easy to understand how dwellers by their banks should fail to consider rain an unmixed blessing.

During one flood, in 1894, the gauging at Teddington Lock showed that the quantity of water which passed over the weir in one day was fifteen times the normal quantity, and amounted to twenty thousand one hundred and thirty-five and a quarter million gallons. Well, that is a quantity which the mind cannot grasp. But I have calculated that if the entire surface of Middlesex were enclosed with a wall 4½ feet high the excess of water passing over the weir in that one day would have sufficed to fill the enclosure to the top of the wall. Or, taking the area of Hyde Park and Kensington Gardens together as 700 acres, if the same amount of water had been turned into that space a wall nearly the height of the Eiffel Tower, or exactly 978 feet high, would have been needed to retain it.

A fall of one inch of rain does not appear at first sight to be much; but spread over an area of two square feet such a fall would measure one gallon and weigh ten pounds ; and over an acre its weight would be 100 tons, and over a square mile 60,000 tons !

These figures will enable us to form some idea of the quantity of water which the earth receives from a shower of rain, and to understand better the extent of the refreshment which even a gentle shower brings to the parched ground after a spell of summer heat.

NOTE.—The lecture was illustrated by a large number of photographic slides and maps, which are not reproduced.

THE AMATEUR AND HORTICULTURAL LAW.

By H. Morgan Veitch, Solicitor.

[Lecture given on April 30, 1907.]

In considering the rules of Horticultural Law as they affect our present subject it is necessary to bear in mind that a very wide distinction has to be drawn between the rights of the amateur and the professional grower. One has to remember that practically none of the Acts of Parliament in force for the benefit of agriculture or market-gardening have anything to do with the amateur gardener. For present purposes these must be entirely dismissed from our minds, and it is equally necessary to follow the same rule with regard to the judicial decisions which we find in the Law Reports. But having got so far, there are still other considerations to be borne in mind if one is to avoid being hopelessly confused by reports of cases which at first sight appear to contradict each other. Many reported decisions with regard to trees (either timber trees or those of smaller growth, such as fruit trees) go back to a very early period of legal history, and one has to remember the varying conditions of land tenure which were in force at that time. For instance, in the case of land held under what is called copyhold tenure (that is to say, land held by the tenant from the lord of the manor) the copyhold tenant had various rights and duties, which varied according to the custom in different localities. These local customs, though in many instances still surviving, do not necessarily represent the general law of the land relating to free-hold property let on lease, and, as many legal authors have not sufficiently emphasised this distinction, considerable confusion has sometimes been created in the mind of the casual reader.

Again, it is necessary to recollect that many reported judgments deal only with the question of what a tenant may or may not do in the case of "settled land"—that is to say, land which under the trusts of a will or settlement is given to one person for life, and on the death of that person goes to someone else called the reversioner. Disputes with regard to the right to cut either timber or seasonable wood or underwood often arise between the person who is enjoying the property during his life and the person who expects to come into that property when the tenant for life dies. The tenant for life naturally wishes to get as much profit as possible out of the property during his own lifetime, whereas the person entitled in reversion is equally anxious that the tenant for life should take away as little as possible, so as to leave all the more for him when he comes into his inheritance. In these disputes the main point very often turns upon whether or not the tenant is what is called "impeachable for waste," and it would be highly misleading if one were to assume that the rights, which in these cases the Court declares to belong to a tenant for life, are necessarily the same rights as those which belong to a tenant who is merely holding under a lease for a term of years. Finally, in the case of such decisions of the Courts as deal only with the rights of the private lessee one has still to make a further distinction, because these rights vary according to the nature of the property itself. Where a house and grounds of considerable extent, including woods and undergrowth, are held on lease it by no means follows that because a tenant has been held entitled to cut down or lop certain trees in the woods therefore he is entitled to cut down or even lop similar trees which are growing in the private ornamental garden surrounding the house. If, therefore, this paper is to be kept within reasonable limits we must deal only with that part of the law which affects the ordinary private garden attached to a house, and we must eliminate all those cases which deal with the rights of any other class of limited owner.

Private Gardens.

Bearing these considerations in mind let us first consider the rights of the private lessee with regard to the trees in his garden. It is sometimes stated in text-books that a tenant (unless restrained by express stipulation) is entitled " to cut down and appropriate all trees on his holding except timber and fruit trees and such trees as have been planted or left standing for ornament, shelter, or shade." This covers most things growing in a private garden, but to secure strict accuracy one must slightly extend this rule. If accepted without qualification it would lead to the conclusion that a tenant may with impunity cut down all trees outside the above definition—for instance, trees planted as curiosities, or for the purpose of botanical and scientific interest, quickset hedges planted to serve the purpose of a fence, and trees planted as landmarks or to commemorate some event, or to mark the site of a grave of a favourite animal. In my humble opinion the tenant is bound to respect all trees such as those just enumerated, and therefore the rule as stated in the text-books requires some modification. In fact it appears to me that the common-law rule would be more correctly stated as follows : A tenant may *not* cut down timber or fruit trees, nor trees planted or left standing by his landlord with the intention that they should form a permanent feature of the property, nor any trees whatever planted by the tenant himself ; all such trees come under the head of " fixtures " and must be respected accordingly.

Any trees which do not fall within any of the above categories (self-sown trees, for instance) might possibly be cut down by the tenant (thus forming an exception to the rule that everything affixed to the land constitutes a fixture), but the class of trees to which this exception applies must obviously be very limited and need only be referred to for the sake of strict accuracy.

According to the text-books the tenant is also entitled (in the absence of stipulation to the contrary) to *lop* those trees which are " timber " for necessary repairs of hedges and husbandry implements, and for fuel ; and it is said that he may even cut down the timber trees themselves provided they are required for necessary repairs to houses and principal buildings. These rights to cut wood for repair and firing are known as the tenant's " botes " and are distinguished as house botes, plough botes, hay botes, &c. It is interesting to note that they represent general customs which have survived from the old times when the tenant was usually dependent on his lord for the necessaries of this kind, *i.e.* before railways and other means of transit for building materials were in existence. It will be observed, however, that the rights in question are really matters of agricultural necessity, and with all due diffidence I venture to suggest that the ordinary private householder would find it difficult to assert any rights of this kind in the present day.

It will be seen therefore that unless our amateur makes a special bargain with his landlord he is bound almost hand and foot. He must not cut down, nor, strictly speaking, may he even transplant the trees, even those which he may himself plant during his tenancy. He must not cut down or remove the plants or bushes, and in short he must do nothing but take those steps which are calculated to improve the growth of whatever he may find growing in the garden or afterwards plant there. For instance, it has been held that a tenant must not grub up or destroy a quickset hedge of white thorn even if he replaces it with something else; though, on the other hand, he may cut a quickset hedge and may keep the trimmings, "because the hedge will grow better by reason thereof." (Although this is good husbandry one must remember that the agricultural rules as to "good husbandry" do not apply to private gardens, and it was held a hundred years ago that they do not even affect nursery gardens.) The tenant has, however, the right to windfalls of decayed timber and of such trees as are not timber; but sound timber which has fallen belongs to the landlord, "because it is useful for building."

Timber.

It frequently happens that in a lease of a house with ornamental grounds the landlord reserves all rights in respect of timber and timber-like trees. This should be objected to by the tenant if possible, because it would enable the landlord to enter and cut down such trees as he thought fit without paying the tenant any compensation. In certain old cases it has even been held that a landlord may erect saw-pits on the tenant's land, so as to cut up this timber, provided he does not take an unreasonable time in so doing; but I confess I should not care to advise the landlord of the present day to attempt to take liberties of this kind with his tenant's garden. Where, however, the landlord reserved the right to timber trees, but the tenant expended money with the knowledge and consent of the landlord in laying out and improving the grounds on the assumption that certain trees, on which the beauty of the scheme of improvement depended, should be left standing, the Court interfered to prevent the landlord from cutting down those trees, thus making a useful exception to the general rule.

This brings us to the question, " What is timber in the eyes of the law ? " and at once we are carried back to a very ancient period of history. In the ancient feudal times of which I have already spoken one must remember that houses were not made of brick, but of wood. Consequently trees which were suitable for building purposes were extremely valuable and were jealously guarded by the law, so that although a tenant was entitled to his " botes," or right to take wood in order to repair his dwelling, he was not allowed to cut timber trees unless no other kind was available. What trees were meant by timber varied in different parts of the country. The oak, ash, and elm were everywhere regarded as timber, and those exceeding twenty years of age were practically sacred, but in many localities certain other trees (if more than two feet in girth) seem to have been considered legal timber, this probably being accounted for by the fact that in some parts of the country there were not enough oak, ash, or elm trees available for building. For instance, in some parts horse-chestnuts, limes, birch, beech, ash, and walnut trees were regarded as timber. In the county of York birch trees have been held by the Court to be timber, because they are used in that county for building sheephouses, cottages, and such other small buildings. At Mottesfont, in Hampshire, and in Berkshire and Yorkshire willows have also been recognised as timber by the custom of the county. Where beech is admitted to be "timber by custom" it has been held that the general rule of law applicable to timber trees in general attaches, so as to give beech the properties and the privileges of "timber" at twenty years' growth. Beech has been held to be timber by custom of the county in the following places : Buckinghamshire, Buriton in Hampshire, Whitmead in Bedfordshire, Mickleham in Surrey, and Whitcomb Magna and Minchinhampton, both in Gloucestershire. One of the Judges (Lord King) was disposed to think pollards might be deemed timber, provided their bodies were good and sound, but other authorities have sometimes taken a different view. There are various other questions arising with regard to what is known as seasonable wood (technically called *silva cædua*), and also underwood, but this leads us into considera- tion of that fascinating branch of law which relates to woods and forests rather than that affecting an ordinary garden, and we must therefore pass it by.

It may be interesting to note that the word "trees," when used in a lease, is as a rule confined by the Court to wood applicable to buildings and does not include orchard trees. In one case a landlord reserved to himself "all timber trees and other trees, but not the fruit thereof." The Court held that this reservation did not cover fruit trees, for in legal language "fruit" may apply to the produce of timber trees without necessarily dragging in any other kind of fruit. Even an exception in favour of the landlord of "all trees &c., of what kind soever," has been held not to include fruit trees where the surrounding circumstances showed that they were meant to apply to trees only useful for their wood.

Before leaving the question of ornamental trees it may be well to mention that in deciding the question of "what is an ornamental tree" the sole point is whether the person who planted it intended it to be (or thought it would be) ornamental. In one old case involving the rights of a tenant for life Lord Eldon made some scathing remarks on what he considered to be the execrable taste of a tenant who had cut his yew trees into the shape of peacocks, the matter being made worse by the fact that they were in sight of the road and could be seen by passers-by ! "

In connection with ornamentation of a garden there is judicial authority for saying that a tenant may build a fishpond in his garden. The reason given by the Court in this old case was a quaint one. It was not a question of ornamentation, but because "fish are a matter of profit and increase of victuals." At the same time I should not advise anyone to rely on this case to the extent of putting a fishpond in the middle of a tennis or croquet lawn !

DAMAGE.

Finally, one might discuss for a moment the question of how far a tenant is obliged to keep his garden in good repair at the expiration of his tenancy. Unless the tenancy agreement contains a distinct provision on the point, the outgoing tenant need take no active steps to put the garden into good condition before leaving it, but on the other hand he must take no active steps to do it harm. We have already seen that he must not remove the trees, plants, and bushes, and it has been held that he must not maliciously grub up a strawberry bed before leaving. So far as injury to trees &c. is concerned, the tenant who does wilful damage for the purpose of spiting his landlord incurs a double liability.

Going back as far as the Magna Charta we find a clause forbidding waste (*i.e.* damage) in the case of gardens and orchards—"in boscis et gardenis," as the language of that day puts it—and the landlord can still obtain compensation from the tenant for damage done. Furthermore the Malicious Injury to Property Act of 1861 makes it a criminal offence to destroy or damage trees or shrubs in a park, garden, orchard, or ground belonging to any dwelling-house, the maximum penalty being, if the damage exceeds £1, three years' penal servitude or two years' hard labour. In small cases where the injury exceeds one shilling, on summary conviction before the local magistrate the maximum penalty is a fine of £5 or three months' imprisonment for the first offence, and twelve months' hard labour for the second offence. Of course this only applies to malicious injury. When the damage is caused other than maliciously the proper remedy is to sue for damages in the Civil Courts.

From all the foregoing remarks it will be seen that if one desires to have a free hand in connection with the transformation of a garden it is necessary to see that one's lease contains special power to take liberties in this respect, and, on the other hand, any rights reserved to the landlord in respect of timber or timber-like trees should also be carefully watched.

By-the-by, there is a popular fallacy with regard to the stamp on the agreement for lease. It is not sufficient to use a 6*d.* agreement stamp (except where the rent does not exceed £5 and the term does not exceed thirty-five years or is indefinite). In all other cases the amount of the stamp duty varies according to amount of rent payable. It is also a mistake to assume that a lease or other legal document is not valid unless it is stamped. With very few exceptions every legal document is valid although not stamped, the only difficulty being that an unstamped document cannot be used as evidence in Court without paying the necessary stamp duty and interest in addition to a penalty for non-stamping. Agreements for lease not under seal have to be stamped within fourteen days after execution, but in the case of deeds under seal, such as a lease, thirty days is allowed for stamping.

ANCIENT LIGHTS.

Perhaps the question of ancient lights is one which affects the amateur horticulturist as much, or even more, than his professional brother, because usually the amateur conducts his operations in a much more confined space. The general rule of law is that where a person has enjoyed the right of light to his buildings for twenty years he is entitled to restrain his neighbour from interfering with this light, but it must be borne in mind that this right of ancient light applies only to the light coming to the windows of a house and does not apply to light which merely filters into a garden.

Recently I saw it suggested in an agricultural paper that a person might have the right to restrain his neighbour from shutting off the sunlight from his garden, on the ground that this would constitute a nuisance, but I confess I should be very reluctant to advise anyone to institute litigation with this object at the present day. During the last few months the Law Lords have considerably restricted even the right of windows in a building to the enjoyment of ancient lights. In a recent case the Courts have held that it is no longer sufficient to show that the light to one's windows has been interfered with by a neighbour. If one seeks for the protection of an injunction one must go still further and prove that the interference with the light is of such a serious nature as to diminish the rental value of the building. This does not mean merely the value to the person who is in occupation at the moment (who would naturally miss the slightest amount of light of which he might be deprived), because the next tenant might notice nothing particularly wrong, not being aware of the additional advantage enjoyed by his predecessor, and in that case the rental value might not be diminished.

OVERHANGING TREES.

The subject of interference by neighbours leads us up to consideration of the remedies available when trees overhang a boundary wall.

If the trees are of such a poisonous nature as to injure a neighbour's horses or cattle which may be likely to feed upon them (in the case of yew trees &c.), an injunction can be obtained against the person on whose land the trees stand, compelling him to cut the trees back to his own boundary, even if the trees have overhung for more than twenty years. Again, the Courts recently granted an injunction against a landowner who allowed his elm and ash trees to overhang a boundary fence in such a way as to interfere with the growth of his neighbour's crops. The Court held that the neighbour was entitled to protection, and compelled the owner of the trees to cut back the overhanging branches. It will be noticed that in this last case the Court interfered expressly because the overhanging trees caused actual damage to the person owning the land on the opposite side of the boundary fence. The Court would not have been so willing to interfere if the trees caused no damage, or were unsightly, or because some capricious objection was taken to the overhanging. Even in cases where no damage results there is, however, a legal remedy, because if your neighbour's trees overhang your land you are entitled to cut off the overhanging branches, and it has been held that one may cut a Virginian creeper which overreaches in the same way. If you cannot do this without going on to your neighbour's land for the purpose you must be careful to notify your neighbour beforehand of your intention to go on his land with this special object. I must warn you, however, that if you cut off any more than what actually overhangs you may incur heavy penalties. There is another reported case where a grower allowed thistles to multiply on his property to such an extent as to blow on to his neighbour's land and damage his crops. In this case the grower was restrained by the Court from permitting the nuisance to continue.

In exercising one's rights to cut the overhanging branches of a neighbour's trees it is necessary to bear in mind that the boughs when cut off still belong to the owner of the tree, and it would therefore be wiser to ascertain whether he wishes them to be returned to him. On the same principle it has been held that if trees growing in a hedge overhang another man's land, and the fruit of them falls on the other's land, the owner of the fruit may go in and retake it if he makes no longer stay than is convenient and does not break the hedge. The owner of the trees has the same right if they are blown down by the wind or fall over by any other inevitable accident. Before going on to one's neighbour's land, however, in order to take back fruit or branches which have fallen in this way it is necessary first to ask for permission to enter on the adjoining land, but if the request be refused then the owner of the fruit may enter and take his fruit without permission. Of course it often happens that it would be very unwise to exercise one's strict rights in this respect, because if friction were to arise the owner of the adjoining land might have the trees cut back by way of reprisal, and one therefore comes back to the point that the wise man is he who acts reasonably towards his neighbour without casting round to see what may be his strict rights or how far the law may permit him to cause annoyance.

With regard to trees overhanging highways, it has been said that if the occupier of land suffers his trees so to protrude over the highway as to inconvenience passers-by, it is a public or common nuisance, and the trees may be lopped sufficiently to avoid the evil by any of the public passing that way, for anyone may justify the removal of a public or common nuisance which is so remediable; it has indeed been stated that by the old law nobody was bound to cut his trees that overhung the road, and therefore anyone might do it.

It is, however, extremely doubtful whether this can now be taken to be an accurate statement of the law, and I should advise you to be very cautious about accepting it. But even if it be correct, any person who proposes to act as a public benefactor in this matter would do well to bear in mind that the person who abates a public nuisance in this way must show special damage arising from the nuisance, and can only interfere with the nuisance so far as is necessary to the exercise of his own right of passing along the highway, and he must not do any unnecessary damage. Probably the safest plan, therefore, is to invoke the aid of the highway surveyor, who in a proper case can obtain a justice's order under the Highway Acts directing the owner of the offending trees to lop the overhanging branches. If this notice is neglected for ten days the owner is liable to a penalty, and the surveyor is authorised to cut or trim any offending trees or hedges himself, the expenses of so doing being made recoverable from the defaulter ; so that a complaint to the local authorities is by far the cheapest and most convenient way to obtain redress.

It is, however, worth noticing that these powers only apply in the case of carriage-ways or cart-ways and not in the case of footpaths. Moreover, trees planted for ornament and for shelter to any hop ground, house, building, or courtyard of the owner thereof are exempted from the operation of this enactment, and it is expressly provided that no person shall be compelled nor any surveyor permitted to cut or prune any hedge at any other time than between the last day of September and the last day of March.

A question sometimes arises as to who is the owner of a tree standing near a boundary line where this tree grows and expands so as to encroach on to the neighbour's land. If the tree is only growing near the confines of the land of the two parties, then, although the roots may extend into the neighbour's soil, the tree still continues to belong to the owner of that land in which the tree was first sown or planted ; but one learned author lays down that a distinction must be made where a man plants a tree upon the extreme limit of his land so that the tree in the ordinary course will necessarily grow on to the neighbour's land. In this case—that is to say, where the tree is planted on the boundary line itself—the trunk must in the natural course of growth stand and grow on the land of both the man who plants it and on the land of his neighbour, and the roots in such case will inevitably penetrate into the soil of each. It is therefore reasonable to assume that the man who planted the tree must have anticipated and intended this result; consequently the tree must be deemed to be the common property of the two adjoining owners. The same author is of opinion that it has yet to be judicially decided beyond any question of doubt whether one proprietor can in the absence of an agreement compel another to have his land burdened with the roots of his neighbour's tree. A right of this kind could only be acquired adversely by an enjoyment which was open and as of right. Still, the law not requiring impossibilities but recognising the course of nature, it seems reasonable to suppose that the right in question may be legally acquired by prescription, i.e. adverse enjoyment, and the author in question remained of this opinion although in one reported case the contrary was suggested by one of the Judges. However, this suggestion was by way of obiter dictum only and the point was not actually decided.

DITCHES.

It may perhaps be of interest to state what is the rule of law with regard to the ownership of ditches where two adjacent fields are separated by a hedge or a ditch. For instance, supposing you have a garden in the country, and at the end of your garden there is a hedge, and beyond the hedge there is a ditch. If there is no evidence to show who is the owner of the ditch the law would assume that you are the owner of it, although it is on the other side of your hedge. At first sight this judgment seems curious, but the rule is arrived at by the following argument : No man making a ditch can cut into his neighbour's soil, but usually he cuts it to the very extremity of his own land. He is of course bound to throw the soil which he digs up on to his own land and not on to his neighbour's. Therefore having thrown the soil backwards on to his own land he often chooses to plant a hedge on the top of it. Consequently it is reasonable to suppose that the ditch is included in his land.

WALLS AND FENCES.

In the case of walls and fences, if there is no evidence to show to whom they belong the law assumes they belong equally to the owners on each side ; that is to say, these owners are said to hold as tenants in common ; but one owner may lose his rights if he " stands by " and allows the other to exercise acts of ownership, such as coping the edge or building or repairing the wall for a considerable length of time, and in this connection a case was decided which may perhaps prove interesting to those who may build a greenhouse against a dividing wall. In the case in question a tenant who owned a wall in common with the owner on the other side took the coping stones off the wall and heightened it, and built a washhouse against it (presumably the result would have been the same if he had built a greenhouse). The roof of this washhouse occupied the whole width of the top of the wall, and the tenant who built the washhouse also let a stone into the wall with an inscription on it stating that the wall and land on which it stood belonged to him. Upon these facts it was held that the builder of the washhouse had ousted his co-tenant, who had made no protest at the time, and it was declared that the wall belonged to the builder.

As to the repair of dividing fences, if there is no evidence to show who is responsible, then the only obligation on each is, that he must so maintain the fence as to prevent his beasts from straying on to the land of his neighbour.

Speaking of fences and ditches reminds one that there is a popular belief in some country districts that the owner of a boundary fence, consisting of a bank with a ditch on the outside of it, is entitled to four feet in width from the base of the bank and four feet in width for the ditch. It is true that there may be some local custom in certain places according to which eight feet in all, to be taken from the owner's own land, are commonly allowed for a bank and a ditch, but there would seem to be no general rule of law to that effect.

FIXTURES.

I mentioned in the early part of this paper that for present purposes we must clear our minds of all those special laws relating to nurserymen and market gardeners. In considering garden fixtures we must follow the same rule, because although a nurseryman on one side of the street may have certain special privileges it does not follow that the amateur neighbour on the other side has any similar rights.

First, it may be well to remind ourselves what fixtures really are. A fixture is an article actually attached by some visible means to the soil or to some building on the soil. If it is not so attached it is not a fixture at all, and anyone, even a private tenant, can remove it. It does not matter how large or how heavy the article may be; if it merely rests on the surface of the land by reason of its own weight it is not a fixture. If, however, the article is attached to the land, or to some building on the land, then it is a fixture, and we have to consider whether it is a landlord's or a tenant's fixture. The first test to apply is whether the article can be removed without causing serious injury to the freehold. If it cannot be removed without such injury then it is usually a landlord's fixture; if it can be removed without such injury it is usually a tenant's fixture, and it is for this reason that tenants are generally advised to employ screws instead of nails when putting up fixtures for their own use.

But even in the case of what would ordinarily be construed to be landlord's fixtures a tenant who is a professional grower has certain special rights under the common law, because these rights are in fact necessary to the carrying on of his trade. For instance, the nurseryman is entitled to remove nursery trees and shrubs, although growing in the ground and therefore fixed to the soil; and he is also entitled at the expiration of his tenancy to remove his greenhouses, although it is still doubtful whether under English law he may remove the low brick walls on which the green-houses are usually raised. But the private owner has no such right, because the garden is maintained, and the greenhouses are erected, for his own pleasure and not by way of trade. It has been held, for instance, that the private tenant must not remove fruit trees even though they have been planted by himself, nor, strictly speaking, can he take away other things which he may have planted, such as hedges, plants, or a border of box. Possibly some of those present may have read a short article of mine on this subject which appeared in the " Gardeners' Chronicle " last year, in which I mentioned that whatever may be the actual law on the subject I had been given to understand that amateurs often " pot " a few of their favourite plants before their tenancy comes to an end. It is of course quite clear that private owners may remove plants standing in pots or growing in a detachable window-box.

Of course, we are now considering what are the strict legal rights of the private owner, and in practice one knows that a good deal of latitude is taken by tenants; unless the matter assumes serious proportions the English landlord usually does not interfere with a tenant who takes an interest in his garden even if he sometimes exceeds his strict legal rights.

Before leaving the subject of fixtures it may be useful to quote a few lines from the article to which I have just referred:—

"It has been held that a non-trading tenant cannot take away a conservatory erected on a brick foundation affixed to and communicating by windows and doors with rooms in his dwelling-house even where he has put it up at his own expense, neither can he remove a verandah the lower part of which is attached to posts fixed in the ground. Further-more, the non-trading tenant cannot take away greenhouses constructed of wooden frames fixed with mortar to foundation walls or brickwork, and some learned writers have even doubted whether he can take them away although only resting on the foundation walls or ground by reason of their own weight. However, this seems to carry the doctrine rather far in favour of the landlord, and there is certainly one decided case where a rector was held entitled to remove his hothouses without incurring liability for dilapidations. A private tenant cannot remove a boiler built into the masonry of a greenhouse, but on the other hand it has been held that he is entitled to remove the pipes with heating apparatus connected with such boiler by screws."

IMPROVEMENTS.

The same distinction as I have already quoted between the rights of the professional and the amateur grower extends also in other directions, such as compensation for improvements made by a tenant during his tenancy.

The market gardener is entitled to compensation for such improvements as the following :—

Planting of standard or other fruit trees or fruit bushes permanently set out.

Planting of strawberry plants ; also asparagus, rhubarb, and other vegetable crops which continue productive for two or more years.

Erection or enlargement of buildings ; and

The application to the land of purchased artificial or other manure.

The private owner has no rights whatever in this respect. If he chooses to spend money on another person's property he must at the expiration of his tenancy leave all improvements of this kind behind him for the benefit of his landlord, and can claim no compensation. It is, indeed, a curious anomaly that even a nurseryman does not enjoy the protection afforded by the Market Gardeners' Compensation Act, being left to derive such comfort as he may from his common law right to remove nursery trees or plants and his greenhouses. Strong efforts have, however, recently been made to get this anomaly rectified, and there seems good reason to hope that before many months have passed steps will have been taken to place the nursery trade on a better footing in this respect. It is understood to be the intention of the Government to bring in, as soon as pressure of public business will permit, a new Market Gardeners' Compensation Act, and the opportunity will then be found—and, one may hope, seized—of putting the matter right. But it is impossible to hold out any prospect of relief to the amateur grower in this respect. Before leaving the subject of fixtures it may interest nurserymen present to know that although their growing trees are part of their stock in trade it was decided nearly a hundred years ago that their landlord cannot distrain on these trees for arrears of rent.

ERECTION OF GREENHOUSES.

With regard to notices to be given to a local authority before the erection of conservatories or greenhouses much will depend upon the by-laws of the particular town where the premises are situated. These by-laws, of course, vary according to different localities. Before erecting a greenhouse it is, therefore, always wiser to make inquiry of the local authority on the point. It sometimes happens that a greenhouse may be deemed a building for one purpose although not for another purpose.

For instance, in a recent case a town had a by-law requiring the walls of any new building to be made of incombustible material, and the question arose as to whether a greenhouse was "a building" for this purpose. Lord Esher held that a conservatory made of wood and glass was not "a building" within the meaning of this particular by-law, although he was not prepared to say that it would be impossible to frame some by-law in such a way as to include greenhouses. On the other hand, a case was heard not long ago in which a photographer had placed outside his house a wood and glass structure measuring 9 feet 6 inches by 3 feet 7 inches, this erection being used for the purpose of exhibiting photographs. The local authority contended that this wood and glass structure came within those sections of the Public Health Acts which provide that "in an Urban District it shall not be lawful to bring forward any house or building in any street or any part of such house or building beyond the main front wall of the house or building on either side in the same street, unless the written consent of the Urban authority is first obtained." The Court held that this photographer's show case was "a building" within the meaning of the section in question ; so that, if a show case of this kind is a building, then it seems obvious that a greenhouse must be a building also within this particular section. Consequently one realises the curious position that sometimes a greenhouse is a building in the eyes of the law and sometimes it is not, and each case must depend on the particular facts and on the particular statute or by-law under which the point arises for consideration.[1] Perhaps the most curious point which appears in the Law Reports with regard to conservatories arose in a case where a greenhouse had been turned into a bedroom. A by-law in that particular locality laid down special rules with regard to the making of any addition to an existing "Building" by raising part thereof. The Court held that the conversion of a conservatory (made of wood and glass) into a bedroom by adding brick walls came within the meaning of the by-law in question, although the bedroom only occupied the same space as that which the conservatory had previously occupied.

Finally, in a case under the Agricultural Rates Acts 1896 the glass houses of a market gardener were deemed to be "buildings" within the special wording of the Act in question, and were therefore not entitled to the privilege of paying half-rates under that Act. On the other hand, nursery grounds have been held to be none the less nursery grounds, and therefore entitled to quarter-rating under the Public Health Act 1875, although consisting of land covered with glass houses. However, neither of these two Acts applies to greenhouses occupied otherwise than for the purposes of trade, and for the purposes of the present subject they are only useful as bearing on the question, "When is a conservatory a building, and when is it not?"

NUISANCES.

The question of nuisances caused by a neighbour cannot adequately be dealt with outside a volume of considerable size, but the following extract

---

[1] Since this lecture was delivered the Divisional Court has held that a show-case similar to that described above is *not* a "building" within the London Building Act, thus reversing the previous decision and removing an anomaly.

from a judgment delivered many years ago sums up in somewhat quaint language the general principle affecting the subject :—

" We think that the true rule of law is, that a person who, for his own purposes, brings on his land and collects and keeps there anything likely to do mischief if it escapes, must keep it in at his peril ; and if he does not do so he is *prima facie* answerable for all the damage which is the natural consequence of its escape. He can excuse himself by showing that the escape was owing to the plaintiff's default ; or, perhaps, that the escape was the consequence of *vis major*, or the act of God. The general rule, as above stated, seems on principle just. The person whose grass or corn is eaten down by the escaping cattle of his neighbour, or whose mine is flooded by the water from his neighbour's reservoir, or whose cellar is invaded by the filth from his neighbour's privy, or whose habitation is made unhealthy by the fumes and noisome vapours of his neighbour's alkali works, is damnified without any fault of his own ; and it seems but reasonable and just that the neighbour who has brought something on his property (which was not naturally there) harmless to others so long as it is confined to his own property, but which he knows will be mischievous if it gets on to his neighbour's, should be obliged to make good the damage which ensues if he does not succeed in confining it to his own property. But for his act in bringing it there no mischief could have accrued, and it seems but just that he should at his peril keep it there, so that no mischief may accrue, or answer for the natural and anticipated consequence. And upon authority this, we think, is established to be the law, whether the things so brought be beasts, or water, or filth, or stenches."

In connexion with the subject of nuisances I have been asked to deal with the question of damage to gardens caused by a neighbour's birds or animals. Unfortunately the reported cases are in many instances very conflicting, and the law on the subject is distinctly vague. The owner of horses, cattle, or poultry is liable for any damage they may do when trespassing, as the law requires him to take steps to keep them in by maintaining reasonably sufficient fences or hedges. So far as dogs are concerned, it would seem that an owner is not liable for the damage done by his dog trespassing, unless done by his consent or incitement, or unless he knows the animal's mischievous propensities and does not take reasonable steps to prevent indulgence in them. (I am, of course, dealing here with damage which may be caused to a garden and not damage caused to cattle, the latter being specially protected by statute.) The gardener who suffers from the depredations of a neighbour's pigeons is in a position of considerable difficulty, and he may possibly find comfort in an old case which decided that although it is not a nuisance to erect a dovecote, yet the owner of the doves can be sued for damage done by them to a neighbour's crops. There is also a reported case in which an owner was held liable for damage done by his tame rabbits, which he had allowed to stray. But on the other hand there are reported cases which were to the opposite effect. The general opinion nowadays seems to amount to this : a man is liable for the *trespasses* of his tame animals, such as cattle, horses, and poultry, but is not liable for the trespasses of his wild animals or birds, such as pigeons. But he is liable if he causes a legal *nuisance,* provided it can be shown that the damage threatened is substantial and such as could be reasonably contemplated. This involves really the question of "degree." The law would not interfere when a man keeps a few pigeons (*de minimis non curat lex*), but might possibly do so when such vast numbers were kept as to involve a legal nuisance, especially if they were not supplied by the owner with sufficient food. There is at all events one decided case where a man was restrained from so overstocking his land with game as seriously to damage his neighbour's crops. The above remarks with regard to pigeons may possibly also apply to tame rabbits, but one is naturally reluctant to indulge in prophecy as to what view the Court might take at the present day.

Stray animals which trespass and are caught doing damage "red-handed," or "damage feasant," as the law terms it, can be impounded; but the right to impound gives only a lien on the animal, and so far as pigeons are concerned it is to be feared that even the most active of gardeners might find considerable difficulty in impounding the culprit. Animals trespassing may be entrapped by merciful means, but may not be killed (a case to the contrary effect having been questioned by later authorities), though perhaps if a gardener were to see a pigeon doing considerable damage, and happened to have an air-gun handy, he would not stay to consider his legal rights, especially if he felt assured that the owner of the pigeon was not looking.

It is a punishable offence to put down poisoned seeds or flesh on the land, though poison for rats may be put down if placed where other animals cannot suffer injury. If traps are used they must not be of a nature likely to involve pain and suffering.

TRESPASSERS.

Perhaps a few words with regard to trespassers may be of some practical use. One often sees notice boards exhibited to the effect that "Trespassers will be prosecuted," but as a matter of fact you cannot prosecute a man *criminally* merely because he trespasses on your land. You can only do so if, while trespassing, he wilfully damages the land or any cultivated roots or plants on it. Grass does not come within this definition, so that it would be useless to prosecute merely on the ground that while running or walking over the land damage had been done to it by reason of the grass being trodden down. If only uncultivated roots or plants, such as wild mushrooms, blackberries, primroses, or wild plants, are trodden down there can be no criminal prosecution. On the other hand, if you scatter mushroom spawn over your field the mushrooms are legally looked upon as being cultivated plants, and a trespasser could be criminally prosecuted for damaging them.

A well-known Judge used to find a special delight in trespassing wherever he saw a warning to trespassers. If the owner or keeper came up to stop him the Judge would solemnly asseverate, "I claim no right, I have done no damage, but in case I have inadvertently done damage I hereby tender you the sum of one shilling in settlement." It may be as well perhaps to point out here that one is not entitled to shoot at a burglar when found on private premises, although one often comes across a mistaken idea to the contrary. The punishment for burglary is imprisonment and not death or maiming ; consequently the only occasion on which one is justified in shooting a burglar is when it is necessary in self-defence.   Probably, however, where a burglar has any offensive weapon handy it would not be difficult to convince a jury on very slight evidence that the shooting had been done in self-defence, and possibly this is how the misunderstanding of the law on this point has arisen. Neither is one justified in setting one's dog on to a trespasser, and here one may mention another legal fallacy which is somewhat widespread. It is not true that "every dog is entitled to his first bite." If you are injured by a dog all you have to prove is that the owner knew, or ought to have known, that his dog was of savage propensity.   Of course where a dog has bitten anyone before that is the best evidence of savageness, but it is quite sufficient to show that the dog had a savage reputation—if, for instance, he has been known to fly at people before, even though he may not have succeeded in biting anyone.

Of course there are other remedies for trespass in addition to the one of criminal prosecution.   For instance, if a person walks on to your land without having any right to do so you can, after going through one important formality, proceed to eject him ; but one has to bear in mind that an owner is not justified in forthwith assaulting a trespasser for the purpose of ejecting him from his land.   The owner must first go through the formality of requesting the trespasser to leave, and then, if he will not do so, the owner can proceed to eject him ; but this remedy has to be used with great caution, inasmuch as the owner is only allowed to use just as much force as is necessary to eject the trespasser, and if the least force is used over and above what is necessary, then the owner is guilty of an assault, and can be prosecuted or sued for damages accordingly.

An owner can also bring an action in the Civil Courts against a trespasser and can claim damages on account of the trespass, and in this case (which, it will be observed, is quite distinct from a criminal prosecution) the owner need not show that he has suffered any damage by reason of the trespass.   In an ordinary case of trespass, however, only nominal damages would be given by the Court to the owner, but the trespasser might be ordered to pay the owner's costs, which in a High Court case might be heavy.   Recently the Judges have shown a marked inclination to discourage actions for merely technical trespassing.   Where there are any special circumstances which aggravate the offence, or where the offender has trespassed after receiving notice not to trespass, then the Court has power to award heavy or vindictive damages irrespective of whether the owner has really suffered actual damage or not.

However, the main difficulty which lies in the way of owners who wish to protect themselves from trespass is that the persons trespassing frequently do not cause damage of such a nature as would justify a criminal prosecution under the circumstances above set forth, while, on the other hand, if the owner brings an action in the Civil Courts claiming damages for the trespass it frequently happens that the offender is a person of no means, so that the owner is unable to get any damages out of him, or even recover legal expenses to which he had been put.

One learned writer has suggested that the best means of keeping impecunious persons off one's lands is always to have two or three fierce little Welsh bulls on the property, but unfortunately this cuts both ways. Bulls have little discrimination, and after the owner had been tossed off his own property he might consider that even the points of a lawsuit were preferable to those of a bull's horns.

Before leaving the subject of trespass it may be remarked that the law recognises certain acts as constituting a technical trespass as distinct from an actual trespass. For instance, it is a trespass to throw stones or rubbish on to a person's land, or for a householder to let his chimney or any other part of his house fall on to his neighbour's land, or to erect a spout on his own land which discharges water on his neighbour's property. Also if a man lets his cattle stray from his own land on to his neighbour's estate it is a trespass (provided the case is one where the neighbour is under no legal obligation to fence his property). Is it a trespass or even a legal nuisance for an orchid-grower to unwittingly import mosquitoes, with the result that they escape into his neighbour's house? I doubt if any action would lie, as anyone may grow orchids and no one would willingly encourage mosquitoes; but this point has yet to be judicially settled.

The notice " Beware of spring guns and man traps " is of course an absurdity in these days, as it is a criminal offence for any person to set or allow to be set on his lands any spring gun, man trap, or other engine calculated to destroy life with the intent of destroying or doing bodily harm to trespassers. Finally, if land adjoining a highway is fenced off with barbed wire, so as to be a nuisance to the highway, the local authority has power to compel its removal.

PHYLLOTAXIS; OR, THE ARRANGEMENTS OF LEAVES IN ACCORDANCE WITH MATHEMATICAL LAWS.

By the Rev. Professor G. HENSLOW, M.A., F.L.S., V.M.H., &c.

[Lecture given on June 25, 1907.]

WE all know that the motions of the heavenly bodies are subject to strict mathematical laws ; that the formation of crystals in the inorganic world is likewise in accordance with laws which can be represented mathematically ; but when we turn to the organised world we do not, somehow, expect to find structures of animals and plants reducible to any representation by mathematical formulæ. Yet this is very often quite possible. The animal frame is composed of bones and muscles, which form levers of various kinds. The flight of birds is strictly in accordance with certain muscular actions, which counteract gravity and can be represented mathematically ; while the bee has practically solved the problem of making cells with the least amount of material, but combined with the greatest capacity and strength. When we turn to the vegetable kingdom we are again amongst organic forces, and we look about almost in vain for results which can be tested by mathematics or which can be represented by their formulæ. The most remarkable instance is probably the arrangement of leaves, and which forms the subject of the present lecture.

If several leafy shoots from different plants be taken, it will be observed that many, probably the majority, have their leaves placed one at a time on the stem, or, as botanists say, *alternately* ; *e.g.* the Garden Flag, a Sedge, the Oak, and the Holly. Others will almost always have two leaves at the same position (or *node*), but situated on *opposite* sides of the stem ; *e.g.* Lilac, Privet, and Horse-chestnut. Of the latter it will be also noticed that *each pair of leaves stands at right angles to those above and below it.* Such series of pairs of opposite leaves constitute what has been called the *decussate* arrangement. Extended observations will only strengthen the conclusion that leaves are for the most part *alternate* or *opposite*.[*]

Alternate Leaves.—If I take a branch of the May or Oak, and hold it vertically with any selected leaf before me, and then pass my finger upwards along the stem from that leaf to the next, and thence to the third, fourth, fifth, and sixth leaf in succession, I find that the one last reached (sixth) is exactly over, or in the same vertical line with, the first ; and if I proceed further I shall find the seventh is vertically over the second, the eighth over the third, and so on, the eleventh being, therefore, over both the sixth and first.

The following observations will result from this examination :—
Obs. 1. All the leaves on the branch are arranged in *five* vertical rows :

---

[*] Leaves will occasionally be found grouped in threes or some higher number ; they are then said to be *whorled* or *verticillate*.

from this fact such an arrangement has been called *pentastichous*. Obs. 2. The imaginary line traced by the finger in passing from leaf to leaf successively is *a spiral line*. Obs. 3. This spiral line *coils twice* round the stem before arriving at the sixth leaf ; the portion of the spiral intercepted between the first and sixth leaf is called a *cycle*. Obs. 4. A cycle *contains five leaves*, the sixth being the first leaf of the succeeding cycle.

The method adopted to represent this arrangement is by means of the fraction $\frac{2}{5}$. The numerator (2) indicates *the number of coils in a cycle*. The denominator (5) *shows the number of leaves in a cycle*.

Let a complete cycle be projected on a plane surface, and represented by a " helix " (a spiral line like a watch-spring) having two complete coils, and let the corresponding positions of the leaves be marked upon it. Then if radii be drawn from the centre to the positions of the leaves, the angle between those drawn to any two successive leaves will be two-fifths of a whole circumference, or of 360° ; *i.e.* it will contain 144 degrees. From this fact the fraction $\frac{2}{5}$ is called the *angular divergence* of the pentastichous arrangement of leaves. An observation of some importance may be here conveniently made, viz. that each coil (*i.e.* the circumference of a circle) contains *three* leaves ; this same number is invariably true for all other arrangements of the " primary " series (with one exception only, viz. the $\frac{1}{2}$ arrangement), as will be hereafter described.

Let another example be taken. Suppose it to be a Sedge (*Carex*). Here the fourth, seventh, tenth, &c. leaves will all be found arranged vertically over the first ; the fifth, eighth, eleventh, &c. over the second ; and the sixth, ninth, twelfth, &c. over the third. Hence there will be only *three* vertical rows of leaves, and the name given to this arrangement is consequently *tristichous*. Moreover, it will be observed that there are but *three* leaves in each cycle, and that the cycle completes but *one* coil or circle passing from any leaf to the next immediately over it ; so that by adopting the method given above, of representing this arrangement by a fraction, the fraction will be $\frac{1}{3}$, and the angular divergence will be $\frac{1}{3}$ of 360°, or 120 degrees.

By extending such observations as these we should soon discover other arrangements of leaves to exist in nature ; and we should find that their angular divergences are equally capable of being represented by fractions. Thus in the Garden Flag (*Iris*) the leaves are on opposite sides of the stem, but are "alternately" arranged, as no two stand at the same level. This, therefore, will be represented by $\frac{1}{2}$, because in passing from one leaf to the next an entire semicircle is traced, and from the second to the third another complete semicircle ; so that the third leaf (which commences the next cycle) is over the first. This arrangement is consequently called *distichous*, as all the leaves on the stem will be in two vertical rows, and on opposite sides of the stem. In another kind a cycle will coil *thrice* round the stem, and contain *eight* leaves ; hence $\frac{3}{8}$ will represent the angular divergence. Another is found to be $\frac{5}{13}$, and several more exist.

If the fractions thus constructed from actual examination of plants be written down in succession according as the numerators and denominators increase, they will be seen to form a series with remarkable connections between its component fractions. It will be as follows : $\frac{1}{2}$, $\frac{1}{3}$, $\frac{2}{5}$, $\frac{3}{8}$, &c. ; such I have elsewhere* proposed to call the primary series. It cannot fail to be noticed that the sum of any two successive numerators, or of any two successive denominators, forms that of the next fraction respectively, so that we might extend this series indefinitely ; thus : $\frac{1}{2}$, $\frac{1}{3}$, $\frac{2}{5}$, $\frac{3}{8}$, $\frac{5}{13}$, $\frac{8}{21}$, $\frac{13}{34}$, $\frac{21}{55}$, $\frac{34}{89}$, &c. It will be also observed that the numerator of any fraction is the same number as the denominator next but one preceding it. There yet remains one more remarkable connection between them, viz. that these fractions are the *successive convergents* of the *continued fraction*

$$\cfrac{1}{2+\cfrac{1}{1+\cfrac{1}{1+ \&c.}}}$$

That is to say, if we reduce, by the ordinary rules for simplifying fractions, the portions

$$\frac{1}{2}, \quad \cfrac{1}{2+\cfrac{1}{1}}, \quad \cfrac{1}{2+\cfrac{1}{1+\cfrac{1}{1}}}, \qquad \&c.$$

and so on, the resulting fractions will be the same as those given above.

I have said that the above series of fractions represent the arrangements which exist in nature, and it is not usual to find any species departing from the arrangement which may be characteristic of it ; in other words, the phyllotaxis of any species is, as a rule, constant to that species. The following are illustrations :—

$\frac{1}{2}$. *Iris*, or Flag. The glumes (chaff) of all grasses. Some " orchids."

$\frac{1}{3}$. *Carex*, or Sedge. Leaves of several grasses.

$\frac{2}{5}$. Oak, Hawthorn. This is one of the commonest arrangements.

$\frac{3}{8}$. *Yew*, Greater Plantain. A common arrangement amongst mosses.

$\frac{5}{13}$. Fruits of Pineapple and many Fir-cones.

$\frac{8}{21}$. Scales of Spruce fir-cones.

If, now, a semicircle be described, and one extremity of its diameter represent the position of any leaf, assumed as the first (in the diagram), and if a radius be drawn at the angular distance of 120° from this point, then the point where the radius meets the circumference will be the position of the second leaf of the tristichous arrangement. The opposite extremity of the diameter will be that of the second leaf of the distichous arrangement. And these points form the extreme positions for the second leaves of spirals of the primary series, corresponding to the fractions $\frac{1}{3}$ and $\frac{1}{2}$ respectively. No *second leaf* ever lies nearer to the first than 120°, nor further than 180°.† The positions of all the second leaves are upon the arc included between those extreme points (viz. 120 and 180 degrees from the extremity of the diameter corresponding to the position of the

---

* " On the Variations of the Angular Divergences of the Leaves of *Helianthus tuberosus*," by the Rev. George Henslow, *Transactions of the Linnean Society*, vol. xxxi. p. 647.

† If the second leaf be at a greater distance than 180, and not less than 240 degrees from the first, it will be seen that the conditions are simply reversed, and the spiral will then run round in the opposite direction.

assumed first leaf). Thus: for the pentastichous, as we have seen, it is at an angular distance of 144°; for the $\frac{3}{8}$ divergence the second leaf is at an angular distance of 135°, while the positions of the second leaves of the spirals, represented by the consecutive fractions $\frac{5}{13}$, $\frac{8}{21}$, $\frac{13}{34}$, &c. gradually approximate to some intermediate point on the arc, but which no known example ever reaches. That point will be understood by mathematicians to represent the "limiting" value of the continued fraction given above, or $\frac{3-\sqrt{5}}{2}$ of 360°, or 187° 30′ 28″ +.

Occasionally other fractions must be constructed to indicate peculiar arrangements, and which cannot be represented by any one of the fractions of the primary series. I discovered the Jerusalem Artichoke to be a plant which, unlike most species having their own peculiar

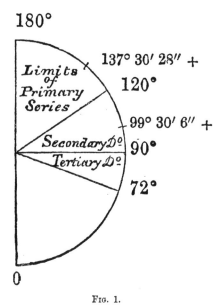

Fig. 1.

arrangements constantly the same, offered the most singular varieties. Not only were some leaves *opposite*, i.e. in pairs at right angles, but also in *threes*, all on the same level; and when this was the case they followed the same law regulating their positions, as already mentioned in the case of opposite or decussate leaves, viz. that the leaves of each group of three *alternate in position* with those of the groups above and below them; I have called * this arrangement *tricussate*. But besides these two kinds the leaves on many stems were arranged *alternately*, and could be represented by the fractions $\frac{1}{3}$, $\frac{2}{5}$, $\frac{3}{8}$, &c. But more than this; for I found that the fractions $\frac{2}{7}$, $\frac{3}{11}$, $\frac{5}{13}$, and others were likewise to be frequently obtained. Now these latter are obviously part of an analogous or *secondary* series; and if continued would stand thus: $\frac{1}{3}$, $\frac{1}{4}$, $\frac{2}{7}$, $\frac{3}{11}$, $\frac{5}{18}$, $\frac{8}{29}$, &c.

* *Op. cit.*

This secondary series will be seen, on comparing it with the primary, to differ in commencing with the fractions $\frac{1}{3}$, $\frac{1}{4}$, &c. in place of $\frac{1}{2}$, $\frac{1}{3}$, &c.; but afterwards each successive fraction may be written down as in the primary series by simply adding the two successive numerators and denominators respectively.

If, now, we project on a plane a cycle of any one of the spiral arrangements represented by a fraction of this secondary series, as in the case of $\frac{2}{7}$, we shall find that *a complete circumference will invariably contain four leaves instead of three*. And, moreover, the angular divergence of any leaf from the next in succession will be found in a similar manner to be *that* fractional part of 360°. Similarly, just as all angular divergences of the leaves of the primary series lie between 120° and 180° inclusively, all those of the leaves of the secondary series lie between 90° and 120°, the limiting point being at an angular distance from the first leaf of 99° 30′ 6″ +. Lastly, it must be observed that the fractions of the secondary series are the successive convergents of the continued fraction :

$$\cfrac{1}{3 + \cfrac{1}{1 + \cfrac{1}{1 + \&c.}}}$$

In a manner analogous to the above, we might construct a *tertiary series*, commencing with the fractions $\frac{1}{4}$, $\frac{1}{5}$, and which would then appear as follows: $\frac{1}{4}$, $\frac{1}{5}$, $\frac{2}{9}$, $\frac{3}{14}$, $\frac{5}{23}$, $\frac{8}{37}$, &c. Such a series, moreover, does exist in nature, as well as others, in *Lycopodium*; e.g. the fractions $\frac{2}{7}$, $\frac{3}{8}$, $\frac{2}{11}$ corresponding to the series $\frac{1}{3}$, $\frac{1}{4}$, &c.; $\frac{1}{4}$, $\frac{1}{5}$, &c.; $\frac{1}{5}$, $\frac{1}{6}$, &c. respectively. Though these series are rarely to be met with now, it is interesting to find that of the trees of the Coal period several of the family allied to our existing *Lycopodium*, or Club-moss, illustrated them. Indeed, I have found $\frac{2}{7}$ on *Araucaria imbricata* on one branch, but the usual arrangement belongs to the usual series, $\frac{1}{2}$, $\frac{1}{3}$, &c. This conifer is a living representative of a very ancient type. Having, then, before us three analogous series, it is obvious that we might construct any number of such series, and finally all would be represented by the algebraical forms, where a is any number :—

$$\frac{1}{a} \qquad \frac{1}{a + 1} \qquad \frac{2}{2a + 1} \qquad \frac{3}{3a + 2} \qquad \frac{5}{5a + 3} \quad \&c.$$

These fractions being the successive convergents of the continued fraction

$$\cfrac{1}{a + \cfrac{1}{1 + \cfrac{1}{1 + \&c.}}}$$

In all the preceding investigations I have supposed the *space* between any two successive leaves on the stem to have been sufficiently developed to enable me to trace an imaginary spiral line through the leaves. But it sometimes happens that such spaces, called *internodes*, are so short, or are practically wanting, that the leaves become crowded together, so that it is quite impossible to say which is the second leaf after having fixed upon some one as the first. This is especially apparent in the case of fir-cones, where the scales may be considered as the representatives of leaves, and which, though crowded, are arranged in a strictly mathematical order.

If a cone of the Norway spruce fir be held vertically, the scales upon it will be observed to run in a series of parallel spirals both to the left hand and to the right. This is a result of their being crowded together, as well as of their definite arrangement. It is the object of the observer to detect and represent that order by some arithmetical symbol. This

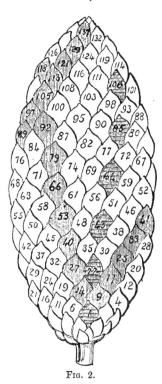

Fig. 2.

may be done by attending closely to the following directions:—Obs. 1. Fix upon any scale as No. 1, and mark the scales which lie in as *nearly a vertical line over it as possible*, viz. numbered at 22, 43, 64, &c. Obs. 2. Note the scales which are *below, nearest to*, and *overlap* that scale (No. 22). Obs. 3. Run the eye along the two *most elevated* spirals, one to the right hand, the other to the left; and passing through the scales which overlap the scale numbered 22.* Obs. 4. Count the number of spirals (called secondary) which run round the cone parallel to these two

* These spirals are shaded in the figure, so as to render them more conspicuous viz. the spiral 1, 9, 17, 25, &c. to the right; and 1, 14, 27, 40, &c. to the left. I have said *the most elevated spirals*, because had I chosen the spiral passing through the scales 1, 6, 11, 16, &c. the object of search would not have been obtained.

spirals just observed; there will be found to be eight such parallel spirals to the right, and thirteen to the left, inclusive respectively of the two first noticed.

From these observations a rule has been deduced for obtaining the fraction which represents the angular divergence of the so-called "generating" spiral which takes in every scale on the cone, in a manner similarly to those described above. Rule: The sum of the two numbers of parallel secondary spirals, viz. $13+8$, or 21, forms the denominator, and the lowest, 8, supplies the numerator; so that $\frac{8}{21}$ represents the angular divergence of the generating spiral. From this it is obvious that the scale immediately over No. 1 will be the 22nd, and this must commence a new cycle.

If the object of our search be only the discovery of this representative fraction $\frac{8}{21}$, or the angular divergence of the generating spiral, then all that is required will have been done; but in order to prove the truth of the rule given above, we must proceed to affix numbers to every scale, and so put it to a rigid test. We have, then, to show that the first cycle of the spiral line passes through *twenty-one* scales before arriving at No. 22, which stands almost immediately over No. 1. Secondly, the cycle must coil *eight* times, or complete eight entire circumferences in so doing.

Method of Numbering the Scales. — Assuming there have been 8 parallel secondary spirals to the *right*, and 13 to the *left*, as in fig. 2, the process of affixing a proper number to each scale on the cone is as follows: Commencing with No. 1, affix the numbers 1, 9, 17, 25, 33, 41, 89, 97, 105, &c. on the scales of the secondary spiral passing through it to the right; these numbers being in arithmetical progression, the common difference being 8, or the number of such parallel spirals; thus all the scales on one of the secondary (shaded) spirals will have numbers allotted to them. In a similar manner, affix the numbers 1, 14, 27, 40, 53, &c. on the successive scales of the secondary spiral *to the left*, using the common difference 13. Thus we shall have two secondary spirals intersecting at No. 1, and again at No. 105, with every scale properly numbered. From these two spirals all other scales can have proper numbers affixed to them. Thus, add 8 to the number of any scale, and affix the sum to the adjacent scale, *on the right hand of it*. Similarly, add 13 to the number of any scale, and affix the sum to the adjacent scale, *on the left hand of it*; e.g. if 8 be added to 40, 48 will be the number of the scale to the *right* of it, so that 40 and 48 are consecutive scales of a secondary spiral parallel to that passing through the scale 1, 9, 17, &c.; or if 13 be added to 25, 38 will be the number of the adjacent scale; *i.e.* on the spiral parallel to that passing through 1, 14, 27, &c. By this process it will be easily seen that every scale on the cone can have a number assigned to it. When this has been done, if the cone be held vertically and caused to revolve, the observer can note the positions of each scale in order (1, 2, 3, 4, &c.); and he will then find that the cone will have revolved *eight* times before the eye will rest upon the 22nd scale, which lies immediately over the first.

This experiment, then, proves the rule for the artificial method of discovering the fraction $\frac{8}{21}$, which represents the angular divergence of the "generating" spiral.

We may also remember that there must be 21 vertical rows of leaves. These may generally be seen without much difficulty by holding the cone horizontally, and looking parallel with its axis, when the twenty-one rows of vertical scales will be observed on revolving it, somewhat in appearance like the rows of grains in a head of Indian corn.

I have said that the 22nd scale will be found almost immediately above, but not accurately in the same vertical line, with the one selected as No. 1. That it cannot be precisely so is obvious from the fact that $\frac{8}{21}$ of 360°, or 137° 31′+, is not an aliquot part of a circumference; the consequence is that the 22nd leaf must stand a little out of the vertical line, and of course the 43rd will be double that distance, and the 64th treble the amount, and so on. Hence it results that this *supposed vertical line* is in reality a highly-elevated spiral line, and instead of there being 21 actually vertical rows of scales there will be 21 very elevated spirals (see fig. 2).

That the rows of leaves on any stem may be strictly vertical, the arrangement must be represented by some fraction the denominator of which measures 360°, such as $\frac{1}{2}$, $\frac{1}{3}$, $\frac{2}{5}$, and $\frac{3}{8}$; whereas $\frac{5}{13}$, $\frac{8}{21}$, &c. represent spirals in which no two leaves are ever in the same vertical line exactly.

As a general rule, all leaf-arrangements on stems with well-developed internodes can be represented by some one of the fractions $\frac{1}{2}$, $\frac{1}{3}$, $\frac{2}{5}$, and $\frac{3}{8}$; whereas those with undeveloped internodes, as in the scales of cones, thistle-heads, &c., are represented by higher members of the series, such as $\frac{5}{13}$, $\frac{8}{21}$, $\frac{13}{34}$, &c.

I must now turn to the other condition under which leaves are arranged, namely *opposite*. When this is the case, each pair of leaves, as has been stated above, stands at right angles to the pairs above and below it. Some plants have, either normally or occasionally, three or more leaves on the same level. When this occurs, the leaves of each group stand over the intervals of the group below it; *i.e.* they alternate with the leaves of the groups both above and below it.

This kind of arrangement is best seen in the parts of flowers, all of which are homologous with, or partake of, the same essential nature as leaves, and which, when complete in number, are separable into four sets of *organs*, called the four *floral whorls*; viz. *calyx* of *sepals*, *corolla* of *petals*, *stamens*, and *pistil* of *carpels*. It appears to be an invariable law that the parts of each whorl should alternate with those of the whorls above and below them. Indeed, so impressed are botanists with the persistency of this law, that when the parts of any one of the floral whorls stand immediately in front of the parts of a preceding external whorl, they at once infer that an intermediate whorl has disappeared. This is conspicuously the case in all primroses and cowslips, and other members of the family to which they belong; wherein it will be noticed that each stamen is affixed or adherent to the tube of the corolla, but immediately in *front* of a petal, and not *between* two petals. That this idea of the suppression of another whorl of stamens is not without foundation, it may be observed that the flowers of a little denizen of damp meadows, *Samolus Valerandi*, and akin to a primrose, have rudimentary stump-like organs which stand affixed to the corolla, and alternate with the petals; while the true stamens alternate with the former; and therefore, as in the

Primrose, stand immediately in the front of the petals.   In the Primrose itself no trace of any such suppressed whorl of stamens is ever apparent. In a large number of plants which are habitually—normally—without a corolla, the stamens, as would be expected, stand in front of, and not alternating with, the sepals.

Although the organs of flowers are usually grouped in distinct whorls, yet in many are they spirally arranged ; and when this is the case they can be represented by some fraction of the series given for alternate leaves.*

A point now to be particularly observed is that these two arrangements, viz. the "spiral" and the " verticillate " (or " whorled," including the " opposite "), appear to be due to forces acting independently of each other ; for it is rare to find whorls passing into spirals, and still rarer for spirals to pass into whorls—if, indeed, it ever occurs.

The Jerusalem Artichoke, however, furnishes many illustrations of the former process, and in some instances of the latter, though no *gradual* transition from a spiral to "verticillate" or opposite conditions ever occurred in the cases examined.

The following will enable it to be understood how a passage from opposite or verticillate leaves into spiral arrangements can be effected : The change from the opposite (decussate) leaves into the $\frac{2}{5}$ divergence occurred somewhat frequently as follows : A pair of leaves slightly converge to one side, the angular distance between them being about 150°. The succeeding pair likewise converge, but have a somewhat less angle, one of the leaves in each case becoming slightly elevated by the development of an internode ; so that the sixth leaf now appears over the first, or the lowest leaf of the first pair that converged to one side.   It must be noted that the angles between the radii drawn to the position of the converging leaves do not accurately contain 144°, or $\frac{2}{5} \times 360°$.   But as the spiral arrangement is continued up the stem and into the terminal bud, the leaves seem to " right " themselves, as it were ; so that the appearance of the spiral in the neighbourhood of the summit is more accurate than at the point of departure from the highest pair of opposite leaves.

The change from opposite and decussate leaves to the $\frac{2}{5}$th arrangement will be seen by the following diagram.   The leaves are represented as still standing in their original positions ; but in becoming alternate one leaf of each pair stands at a higher level than that of its companion. Now the *order* in which the leaves are raised above their fellows is seen by the numbers, lying on a long spiral line (fig. 3).

The passage from opposite and decussate positions to the $\frac{2}{5}$ arrangement is effected by three processes.   *First,* the second pair of leaves is not quite at right angles to the first chosen.   Similarly the third pair is not at right angles to the second ; a slight twist, as it were, has been given to both in the same direction.   *Secondly,* the order of uplifting of one leaf of each pair to a higher level than that of its companion is in a definite and constant order, as shown in fig. 3.   This causes a short internode to

---

* A point worthy of note is, that the *free portions* of the corolla of a primrose *overlap* one another in just such a way as corresponds to the $\frac{2}{5}$ arrangement of spiral leaves ; though, of course, they are now actually verticillate.

be developed between the leaves of each pair. It subsequently becomes equal to the longer intervals between the pairs. *Thirdly*, each pair grows at an obtuse angle of about 150°, finally becoming between later pairs of leaves 144°, when the $\frac{2}{5}$ arrangement is established.

Returning to fig. 3, it will be observed that if a spiral line be drawn through the numbers 1 to 6 it will make 2 coils or circles : 1 to 9 will make 3, 1 to 14 5 coils, and so on.

It will be noted that $\frac{1}{2}$ and $\frac{1}{3}$ are not provided for : yet these two represent the commonest arrangements in Monocotyledons, just as the preceding do in Dicotyledons. The reason for this is that in the latter class alternate leaves follow on a pair of opposite cotyledons ; and the usual plan is $\frac{2}{5}$, as may be well seen in a germinating acorn.

When there is only one cotyledon the next leaf may be either at a distance of 180°, that supplies the $\frac{1}{2}$; or 120°, which results in the $\frac{1}{3}$ arrangement : because (with the exception of $\frac{1}{2}$) in no case is there ever

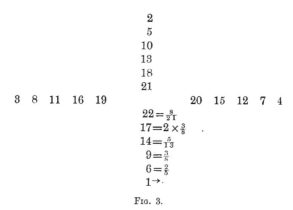

$$2$$
$$5$$
$$10$$
$$13$$
$$18$$
$$21$$

3   8   11   16   19   20   15   12   7   4

$$22 = \tfrac{8}{21}$$
$$17 = 2 \times \tfrac{3}{8}$$
$$14 = \tfrac{5}{13}$$
$$9 = \tfrac{3}{8}$$
$$6 = \tfrac{2}{5}$$
$$1 \rightarrow$$

Fig. 3.

more or less than *three* leaves in any part of the spiral which completes a circle.*

Species of Pondweed (*Potamogeton*) have their leaves distichous, but not infrequently they are in pairs, *apparently* opposite *without* being decussate ; but one leaf of each pair really overlaps the other. They may be distichous with internodes well developed between each leaf (*P. lucens*) ; or there may be some in pairs, others alone (*P. prælongus, perfoliatus*, and *crispus*) ; or they may all be in pairs (*P. densus*).

It is an interesting fact that *Ranunculus Ficaria*, which has *one* cotyledon only, also has its leaves distichous in a similar manner. But when we arrive at the flowers we find the phyllotaxis suddenly changed to $\frac{1}{3}$ arrangement in the 3-sepalled calyx, and $\frac{3}{8}$ in the 1-petalled corolla. This will be explained below.

That Monocotyledons are descended from Dicotyledons is borne out by the fact that it is not infrequent to find the embryo of the former provided with a rudimentary second cotyledon. Thus, *Tamus communis*, the

---

* In the series $\frac{1}{3}, \frac{1}{4}$, &c. there are always 4 leaves &c.

Black Briony, and *Asparagus* are both provided with it.   Several grasses appear to have such a rudiment.*

Changes from the tricussate arrangement, *i.e.* decussating whorls of threes, into the $\frac{3}{7}$ divergence of the secondary series were frequent.   It takes place in the following manner : The first step is to cause the three leaves of the different whorls to separate slightly by a development of their internodes.   Then, if any two consecutive whorls be examined, the order of succession of the six leaves (No. 1 being the lowest) is thus :—

$$
\begin{array}{ccc}
 & 6 & \\
3 & & 2 \\
 & 7\ \ 9 & \\
4 & 8\ \ 5 & \\
 & 1 & \\
\end{array}
$$

Fig. 4.

In which it will be noticed that the fourth leaf, instead of being over the interval between the first and second, is over that between the third and first, so that the angle between the first and second leaf, or between the second and third, is *double* that between the third and fourth.   These latter, it will be remembered, are separated by a long internode.   The same order obtains with the succeeding whorls ; the nodes, however, are now much more widely separated, while a true spiral arrangement, with the same angular distance between all its leaves, is ultimately secured, and is henceforth continued uninterruptedly into the terminal bud, and represented by the fraction $\frac{3}{7}$.

The method by which this is secured is much the same as for the $\frac{2}{5}$ from opposite and decussate leaves, for in order to *reduce* the angle between 1 and 2 from 120° to 103° (nearly), and to *enlarge* the angle between 3 and 4 from 60° to 108°, Nos. 1 and 3 approach No. 2, Nos. 4 and 6 approach No. 5, and Nos. 7 and 9 approach No. 8.   By this means the larger angles are reduced and the smaller, *i.e.* between Nos. 3 and 4, 6 and 7, 8, and 9, are increased till they all reach 103°.

From very many observations on stems of the Jerusalem Artichoke, it appears that to resolve opposite and decussate leaves into spirals of the primary series and tricussate verticils into those of the secondary series is more easily accomplished than any other kinds of transition.   To reverse the process, or to bring back spirals into verticils, seems quite contrary to all nature's tendencies to change, except in flowers.   Stems of the Jerusalem Artichoke occasionally had their leaves arranged spirally below, and verticillate above; but then the change was abrupt.   The spiral suddenly terminated, and the last leaf was succeeded by three in a whorl. The extra third leaf is often " thrown out," as it were, as a supernumerary member.

Leaf arrangements are usually pretty constant to any species ; but this is not absolutely so ; because plants have the power to change it if it be desirable to secure light in different ways.   Thus the common laurel,

* For further particulars the reader is referred to my paper on " A Theoretical Origin of Endogens from Exogens through Self-Adaptation to an Aquatic Habit " (*Journ. Linn. Soc.* vol. xxix. p. 485).

which has its leaves distichous on the lateral boughs, so as to expose their upper surfaces to the light from above, will produce vertical shoots from the top of the bulb, having their leaves arranged on the ⅖ plan. The same occurs with the free branches of the ivy compared with those climbing up a wall, on which the leaves are distichous.

The Yew *seems* to have its leaves distichous, but a closer inspection reveals the fact they are not so, but on the ⅜ plan : each leaf, however, is *twisted* at its base, so as to make the whole horizontal. The young shoots, which may stand more nearly vertical, reveal the true order. As this habit is retained in the Irish Yew the leaves are never distichous on that variety.

Floral Phyllotaxis.—As the parts of flowers are all identical in origin with leaves it is natural to suppose that they will follow the same laws. This they do, with certain modifications, in order to adapt them for their new functions. We have seen why 3's prevail in monocotyledons, and in dicotyledons 5's. The reason is that 5's are cycles of the ⅖ arrangement and 3's of the ⅓. But, instead of each cycle, *i.e.* floral whorl, being *exactly* over the preceding, the "law of alternation" now intervenes ; so that each whorl alternates, *i.e.* in a "decussate" manner, with the next. Hence when a whorl happens to be suppressed this alternation appears to be violated, as stated in the case of the five stamens of a Primrose. If 2's or 4's occur in flowers of dicotyledons, they generally result from opposite leaves, as in Lilac.

By the way the petals are folded in the bud various modifications become revealed. If the reader draw a plan of the ⅖ arrangement on a spiral containing two coils, and place the Nos. 1, 2, 3 at an angular distance of 144°, he will find that by a slight alteration the second petal (represented by a crescent) may have one edge *underlying* the third petal. Then, if the fourth similarly underlies the fifth, we get the so-called imbricate whorl, *i.e.* each petal overlaps the next. But when the first is also underneath the third then the convolute or "contorted" condition is reached, characteristic of mallows, flax, convolvulus, &c.

Various modifications are to be seen in papilionaceous flowers of the Pea family, and especially in flowers with coherent petals, as the Snapdragon, &c., but for details of these I must refer the reader to my paper elsewhere.*

Elaborate calculations as to the number of parts of flowers in many different individuals of the same species have been made to ascertain their relative sequence. Thus on counting the rays or pedicles of umbels of *Torilis Anthriscus* the maxima were 5, 8, 10 (=2×5); while the number of ray petals of *Chrysanthemum segetum* gave 13, 21, 26 (=2×13), 34. In the case of the stigmatic rays of poppies 13 is the maximum. With the ray flowers of the ox-eye Daisy, 21 far outstripped the others. In the Cowslip, 3, 5, 8, 10(=2×5), 13 were the maxima, 5 being the chief.

It will be at once seen that these maxima correspond with the different phyllotactical arrangements; but why, in fixing the number of parts in a whorl, Nature should endeavour to retain what may be called "cycular" numbers is unknown. The above experiments in calculations

* "On the Origin of Floral Æstivations," *Trans. Linn. Soc.* vol. i. 1876, p. 177.

only illustrate what may be observed in nature. A composite with ray florets often has eight only. This was the case with the wild Dahlia and Zinnia, but under cultivation the number rapidly increased. *Chrysocoma* has regularly five only, thereby mimicking a five-petalled flower. One common by road-sides near Cape Town, and in a semi-starved condition, always bore *three* ray florets only. A correspondent informs me that in counting the ray florets of a South European marigold the maxima were 21 and 34, being correlated with their habitats. Thus 21 is the usual or typical number; but near the sea the first maximum rose to 26 (=2×13) and 34. " The ox-eye daisy has generally 21 florets at the level of Lake Como; but at a height of 400 to 500 feet on the mountain a form is developed *during the height of the flowering season* with 34 rays, reverting at the end of the season to 21. The number of ray florets in different composites varies with the environment."

With regard to the 3 sepals and 8 petals of *Ranunculus Ficaria*, the former arise from the fact that the plant is monocotyledonous, as stated above, but the change from 3 sepals to 8 petals is due to the fact that the angle of 120° ($\frac{1}{3}$) is nearer to 135° ($\frac{3}{8}$) than 144° ($\frac{2}{5}$), so that the change is easier from the $\frac{1}{3}$ to $\frac{3}{8}$ arrangement than to the $\frac{2}{5}$.

Conclusion.—I have now endeavoured to give a brief and as clear account as I can of the main facts and principles of Phyllotaxis. But, if we venture to search for a *cause* of such definite and exact arrangements of leaves, it will probably be fruitless, for as yet no satisfactory explanation has ever been given. It is not enough to say that it is a wise arrangement that leaves should not all be over one another, so as to exclude the light and air, and impede one another's functions; but why are there so many different ways of doing it, as represented by the fractions $\frac{1}{2}$, $\frac{1}{3}$, $\frac{2}{5}$, &c.?

ARCHES, PILLARS, AND PERGOLAS.

By Mr. WALTER P. WRIGHT.

[Summary of a lecture delivered on July 11, 1907.]

THIS subject could be dealt with from the descriptive, the artistic, or the practical point of view. I might merely give particulars of existing examples, say what I think they ought to be, or describe how to construct and clothe them. But it would be of little real value to speak at length of the pretty arches or beautiful pergolas in various parts of the country, and I will pay most attention to practical matters.

First, however, let me say that the word "art" is used in far too loose a way in connection with flower gardening. Most people seem to think that they get an artistic garden if they simply leave out "geraniums," and that when they have stuck in some arches, in however incongruous a way, their handiwork is complete. Often the arches are of wire; I prefer my ironmongery in the form of spades and hoes.

As an example of a modern artistic garden I recently saw a straight walk spanned with a series of disconnected wire arches, each with an anæmic and decrepit example of Crimson Rambler Rose. Why arches in such a place? The natural and appropriate use of arches is to mark divisions of gardens. The proper thing for a straight walk is a pergola. Arches out of place, of the wrong material, and with unhealthy plants upon them are ugly and incongruous.

When we have made up our mind that wooden structures are more suitable than metal ones we bring ourselves to practical questions. What is the best material? Where are we to look for it? What may we expect to have to pay for it? The best natural material is larch, because it is straight and is a recognised market commodity. Timber merchants in country districts often stock larch poles about 22 feet long, which, when cut into two, will make two uprights of suitable length. It is the truest economy to purchase a supply of long poles and cut them up. Do not let the vendor peel them; the bark is best left on, as the poles then have a more natural appearance. Larch is not a durable wood naturally, but if 3 feet at the bottom of the pole be peeled and treated with some preservative it would last for a very long time. Some might ask, Why treat 3 feet? Will not half that length suffice? Arches, pillars, and pergolas must be constructed properly, and in order to have them firm and secure from being swayed by the wind, which is very bad for the plants, the upright should be sunk into the ground nearly or quite 3 feet. With an 11-foot pole there will be 3 feet in the ground and 8 feet out of it, which is the orthodox height.

A common preservative is creosote. This should not be used for green wood, as the latter will absorb too much. Seasoned poles should be secured. The creosote should be used cold, as then it has no deleterious action on the tissues of the wood. It is better to soak the

E

ends of the poles in it for two or three weeks rather than to paint it on, and when treated thus the poles are well-nigh imperishable, but it is not innocent of causing root injury. A safer plan is to get ordinary coal tar, ready boiled, paint it on the bottoms of the poles, and dust with sand. This answers well, and is considerably cheaper than creosote, enough for a considerable number of poles being obtainable for 5s. A third and still more economical way is to char the ends of the poles in the garden fire.

The question now arises : Where shall we get the material ? Obtaining poles is not so serious a business as is generally supposed. They can often be got at timber yards in the larger country towns where good nurseries exist. Or they may be obtained at timber sales, which are held in many districts in autumn. For a 15-foot to 18-foot larch pole, rough, one might pay 6d. at a sale, and for a 22-foot pole at the timber merchant's 2s. to 3s. Even at the higher price, viz. 3s., one cannot say it is dear, as two 11-foot poles are thus obtained for 1s. 6d. each. In districts where there are woods, dead spruce may often be obtained cheaply by getting into touch with the forester, and it can be made good use of. So far as durability is concerned oak is undoubtedly the best, but it is very expensive, 11-foot posts costing 3s. to 4s. each. Even an oak post needs the base dressing. When putting arches together one wants a certain amount of short, gnarled, crooked, rough material for the upper part. This is often difficult to get, but it can be obtained at many wood yards in districts where there are large gardens.

A special word should be said about pillars. They form a most valuable feature in flower gardens. Clothed with Clematises, as at Kew, they are exceedingly beautiful, and for giving variety they are splendid. An excellent plan is to have three good pillars in a rough triangle, 3 feet to 4 feet apart, of good, stout material.

Pergolas are annually becoming more popular. I might describe a pergola as a connected series of arches. It may be constructed in various ways, and one of the most solid and attractive that I know of may be briefly described. It is in the garden of the mayor of Canterbury, Mr. Bennett Goldney. On the top of each of the upright poles that form the supports for the pergola is laid a stout piece of unpeeled larch, about 18 inches long. On this meet the ends of three horizontal poles—two forming the continuation of the top side lines and the other connecting the two sides of the pergola across the walk. These three ends abut. On them lie the ends of two more poles—namely, the top diagonals. All these are securely spiked together, forming an absolutely taut, substantial, and homogeneous erection.

The ordinary pergola has the upright poles 8 feet out of the ground and 8 feet apart, but of course this can be varied considerably to suit individual requirements. The upright poles on each side of the path are connected by two lines of horizontal poles, and these in turn are connected with cross poles of lighter weight ; 6-inch material for uprights and 3-inch or 4-inch for cross poles are generally used, but of course much more substantial structures are erected where cost is not the first consideration.

We now come to the important question of the most appropriate kind of plants for arches pillars, and pergolas. One cannot recommend the same

ind of plants for all. For arches the first essential is plants that produce
ong canes, 'Crimson Rambler' Rose being a good example. For pillars

FIG. 5.—A PERGOLA AT BLYTHEWOOD.

we want something that throws out vigorous lateral growths, a typical
plant being the old but beautiful rose 'Félicité-Perpétue.' For pergolas

E 2

we require a blend of both. Of roses suitable for arches we have 'Crimson Rambler,' 'Euphrosyne,' a splendid variety, 'Carmine Pillar' (an almost ideal arch rose), 'Cheshunt Hybrid,' and 'Ards Rover.' Roses suitable for pillars are 'Félicité-Perpétue,' the beautiful white-flowered variety 'Rampant,' which is not half enough known, and 'Dundee Rambler' among the oldest sorts, whilst among the newer varieties 'Hiawatha,' 'Paradise Rambler,' 'Lady Gay,' 'Stella,' and 'Kathleen,' should provide almost ideal material. 'Penzance Briers' are usually looked upon as hedge roses, but they are valuable for pillars if the strongest varieties are selected and well cultivated. 'Lucy Ashton,' 'Lucy Bertram,' and 'Meg Merrilies' are three of the best. By growing in deep, rich soil one gets many long canes, and I deal with some of these in a somewhat heterodox manner. Selecting two or three of the strongest and best ripened canes, I cut them down in the spring to within eighteen inches of the ground; I cut others to within a yard of the soil, and leave the rest uncut, tying in their long laterals in a line with them. One thus gets masses of bloom from bottom to top. 'Lord Penzance' and 'Lady Penzance' are too weak growers to treat like this.

Among the Clematises we have splendid material for covering arches, pillars, and pergolas. A few of the best are 'Miss Bateman,' 'The Queen,' and 'Fair Rosamond,' of the patens type, which need little pruning in spring, and 'Jackmanni,' its white variety, and the red 'Madame Edouard André,' all of which need hard pruning in spring. There are, of course, a large number of other kinds of plants suitable for pergolas, such as Ceanothus, Eccremocarpus, Kerria, Honeysuckle, Jasmine, and the Vitises.

A word in conclusion about cultivation. No matter how well we construct our arches and pergolas we shall never get them well clothed unless we give the plants proper care and attention. Too often the framework is everything, the culture nothing. The soil should be worked two to three spits deep and well manured. Vigorous growth is then insured.

THE JAPANESE DWARF TREES: THEIR CULTIVATION IN JAPAN AND THEIR USE AND TREATMENT IN EUROPE.

By Monsieur Albert Maumerné.

[Abstracts from a pamphlet published in Paris in 1902.]

THE matter contained in the following paper is derived partly from original observation and partly from consultation of the undermentioned works:

Bing, S. Dwarf Trees of Japan: Catalogue of a collection of. (Paris, 1902, with 10 plates.)

Carrière, E.-A. Articles on Japanese Horticulture. (*Rev. hort.*, Paris, 1878, p. 271.)

— — Japanese Gardens. (*Rev. hort.*, Paris, 1899, p. 374.)

Dybowski. The Japanese Garden. (*Nature*, Paris, 1889, II., p. 239.)

Maury. On the Japanese Methods of Dwarfing Trees. (*Bull. Soc. Bot. France.* Paris, 1899, p. 290.)

The Yokohama Nursery. How the Japanese grow Dwarf Trees in Jardinières. (*Gard. Chron.*, London 1899, II., p. 466.)

Vallot, J. Physiological Causes which produce the Stunted Formation of Trees under Japanese Cultivation. (*Bull. Soc. Bot. France*, Paris, 1889, p. 284.)

MM. Carrière and Vallot do not treat the subject in a detailed manner. They do not advance any very intelligent suppositions, and confine themselves principally to facts.

The paper on the Yokohama nursery is by no means a description of the methods of dwarfing adopted by the Japanese, but simply of the treatment bestowed by them on trees already trained or in course of formation.

The art of restricting the growth of even the largest trees, so that they only attain to a mere fraction of their normal size, is, like every other Japanese idea, both original and curious; and it enables us to place on our tables a fir 200 years old or an octogenarian plum tree. To a Japanese the dwarf trees are works of art, equal in value to pictures by true artists. This art of dwarfing forest trees is part of the education of the Japanese gentry. It has its schools and its old masters. The young persons of the wealthy classes devote to this art the time which young European ladies spend in music, drawing, &c. This shows that the Japanese views on many points are very different from ours. To the Japanese the garden is the outdoor salon, and the salon is the indoor garden. They always like to have before them the illusion of a natural landscape. To admire these works in default of special education in this matter, one must learn to appreciate such curved lines as will charm the eye at first sight.

The art of the Japanese gardeners does not consist in simply growing and flowering beautiful plants. Their ambition is far greater: the trees cultivated in china pots must recall and reproduce by their appearance those which grow on the mountain slope or on the edge of the ravine, and although dwarf, they must preserve their majestic shapes and natural outlines.

Next to the artistic part, the treatment of these trees is all a matter of time, and it needs the skilful fingers of the Japanese, their light and accurate manipulation, and their sense of what is necessary to bend, twist, and tie down those frail branches from the offspring of giants, and to make lilliputian trees which will live to 100 years or more.

Fig. 6.—Maple, 250 years old. (*J. Carter & Co.*)

Japanese Æsthetics.—The Japanese, who have invented the art of dwarfing things, prefer the tiny trees and lilliputian forests (which seem so odd to our eyes), rather than the lofty forest trees, venerable shades, and the free growth of plant life. These tiny trees, when planted in little jardinières or in very shallow trays or pans, have all the appearance and the characteristics in miniature of their congeners growing freely in the open; and the majority bear the marks of time as well as such obvious traces of their treatment as knotted and deformed trunks, twisted and deformed branches, and scanty, limited foliage.

The aspirations and tastes of Orientals are different from our own; they hold fast to their national traditions, and particularly to those of an æsthetic nature. Generally speaking, the Japanese men are small, and their houses also, the latter are built with a view to resisting the elements and earthquakes better. Tiny gardens of delicate scenery surround them, in which big trees would appear to be out of proportion and harmony.

It may easily be imagined what pains, patience, and constant attention are necessary to obtain such results, and to arrest the growth of what

Fig. 7.—Pomegranate, 150 years old. (*J. Carter & Co.*)

would become a large tree, so that it only attains very dwarf proportions, is no easy task. For if the dwarf tree lose one of its branches, or characteristics, by a bough being badly trained, it is no longer of any value. It has been said that these plants might be compared to monstrosities or to deformed people; but this reproach is not merited, for their cultivation consists of a real restraint applied to a tree, which, unrestrained in its development, would have grown freely; [and much determination, patience, and tenacity of purpose are required to meet the circumstances of each case.

It would not be accurate to compare dwarf plants obtained by European cultivation with those miniature trees in the treatment of which .the Japanese excel. Whilst the "dwarfing" of plants is carried on by us principally in the direction of "hybridisation" and selection, to which certain cultural operations are added, notably "pinching," in order to render the plants useful for certain purposes, in Japan it is the result of a special and consistent treatment, and we may add that more than one of these dwarfed trees put into the open ground did not take long to break away from the narrow limits in which they had been forced to grow.

We consider, on the other hand, that there is no comparison between the plants treated by the Chinese, and the Japanese dwarf trees, so different are the objects aimed at, and the methods employed. Monsieur Albert Tissandier, who has seen these trees at home, has explained in "Nature" (1891, p. 360, and 1902, p. 86) the manner in which the Chinese prepare them. Their system is to use a framework of iron wire representing various persons, an animal, or other object, being placed on the vase, on which were trained the branches of the plant, when it was wished to represent people, the head, hands, and feet being painted on earthenware. In other cases, yews are cut and twisted in the form of mandarins or other persons. One can thus see that the Japanese plants have no more than a distant resemblance to those of China, as they are treated in an entirely different manner.

PHYSIOLOGICAL CAUSES OF DWARFING AND OF DEFORMITY IN VEGETATION.—Dwarfing, or, to be more exact, the atrophy of these plants, is due to physiological causes, which are themselves the result either of the methods of cultivation employed, or of the conditions amidst which they grow. We can even see both in the formation of the lilliputian Japanese trees, as the climate of that country predisposes the plants to remain dwarf.

Altitude, dry heat, constant chills, lack of nourishment, confined space for the roots, want of nourishment during the youth of the plants, and strong winds, are among the elements which contribute to stunting the plants. Anyone making an excursion among the mountains on their sunny slopes and in dry places, the details of which cannot be now given, may notice how a conifer which has lost its head is checked for a time, and if, after the tree has begun to grow again, this injury is repeated from time to time, the check will be felt more and more at each repetition, and the tree will remain stunted, knotted, and deformed. All the cultural operations bear on these points—want of nourishment, frequent pruning, twisting and bending the branches, the use of small pots, root pruning; and anything which can paralyse the vitality of the plant, by impeding the circulation of the sap and diminishing the nourishment, tends to check the growth and leads to a very noticeable change in the aspect of the plant so treated, and renders it capable of being dwarfed, which is then only a matter of time and perseverance.

That is why the same subjects, but less exaggerated in their growth, may be met with in every pass on the mountain side, in fissures in the rocks, and in all places where the plants have to struggle for their existence, against the natural surroundings. The methods adopted by the

Japanese are not so unnatural as has been often stated. That is, one must not forget, that they are clever and adroit imitators rather than creators in the full sense of the word ; everything in Japanese arts and industries demonstrates this most fully.

The raising of dwarf trees has been practised for centuries in both Japan and China with a true artistic passion. These productions of the

Fig. 8.—Thuya.

collaboration of man and of time are handed down from generation to generation, and plants grown to perfection exhibit either a certain shape obtained according to an initial plan, or else present the same outline in miniature as they have when growing naturally.

This form of Japanese art has its schools and its acknowledged masters, both amateur and professional, just as in Europe in the case of painting and sculpture. Eséki, Chokarô, Murano, Oesopé, Magoyémon,

who were experts in the treatment of pines, the family Ito, who preferred
to work on *Chamaecyparis* and *Thuya*, have educated at Tokio and other
centres renowned pupils: Nishé of Idéka, Také of Denchu, Tanaka,
Takaghè, Terano of Yamamoto. Each of these artists has signed these
·vegetable masterpieces which have attained and kept a high value,
equal at times to that of a great picture. These trees are always taken
particular care of, as the least fault in the shape is regarded as a grave
blemish.

FIG. 9.—THUYA.

THE DIFFERENT FORMS OF TREES AND THEIR CLASSIFICATION.—
Independently of efforts made to preserve the natural features in
dwarfed trees, attempts are made to get forms which follow definite
theories of lines which· conform to the æsthetic canons of Japanese
floral art, the best proof of which is that the dwarf trees are classed in
seven well-defined principal groups, which are recognised under the
following names :

BONSAÏ.—Miniature trees preserving their natural shape and characteristics (figs. 14, 16, 18).

MIKOSHI.—Dwarf trees in which the base is bare (fig. 8).

KENGAÏ.—Trees overhanging a rising ground, or which appear to throw their branches over a rock (fig. 9).

NAZASHI.—Dwarf trees with weeping or downward growing branches (fig. 10).

JIKKI.—With formal arrangement of the branches (figs. 11, 12).

NEAZARI.—Trees or shrubs in which the bare roots above ground are regarded as of most importance (figs. 12, 15, 17).

BONKAÏ.—The arrangement in the same vase of several dwarf plants, forming a group or a picturesque scene.

This classification could be considerably simplified by dividing the plants into two main groups :

(a) Those trees which are only dwarfed and keep their shape and general appearance so exactly that they seem to be photographic reductions of natural-sized plants ; or, to use another comparison, they resemble the natural-sized trees if the latter are looked at through the wrong end of an opera-glass.

(b) Those which have undergone a modification of shape in their treatment, according to a certain theory of lines.

SCENES AND MINIATURE GARDENS.—We must add that the same principles inspire the formation in a simple tray some few inches square, produced by a happy arrangement of various plants on a miniature hillock, sometimes flanked by a rock, the whole generally well proportioned, and showing in miniature various scenes in celebrated Japanese gardens. These are made on a certain preconceived idea, nothing being left to chance. They are made with a real knowledge of the law of proportion, and give the idea of a real piece of country.

We have seen in a tray a miniature reproduction of the Isle of Misaka made by a twisted pine, a loose-growing cryptomeria, a kirisima and a bamboo with their branches entangled, and sheltering under their foliage little houses of bronze, in front of which little china figures appear to be moving. In a second tray was another miniature garden dominated by the curious and twisted form of a pine growing above a Thuya which reared its knotty trunk over a rock, clasping it with its red string-like roots, which somewhat resembled serpents, whilst a dwarf maple overshadowed a little porch with its branches of different coloured leaves.

After having modelled the foundation of a garden in clay, so as to accurately represent the contour of the ground it is wished to portray, the gardener adds fragment of rocks, if the scene requires them, always in proportion to the size of the whole. Then he puts the selected plants, which have been arranged beforehand, in the positions chosen for them, after which he adds the models of dwellings, porticoes and other erections, and finally places in position the figures which serve to give life to the scene. There is nothing artificial in this arrangement, and if a rocky escarpment or other natural rugged scene is shown, everything that would be artificial is omitted, even those groups of plants which might, by one growing out beyond the others, show in time the difference between uncultivated nature and the carefully tended garden.

THE PLANTS MOST SUITABLE FOR DWARFING.—It is evident that the Japanese excel in selecting the species which are best adapted for dwarfing and for the treatment which they have to undergo, at the same time preserving the whole of their natural characteristics.

Conifers are the favourite plants, and among them *Thuya obtusa*, and var. *breviramea* (which the Japanese call the green variety), and

Fig. 10.—Prunus Mume.

var. *filicoides aurea* (the golden variety); *Pinus densiflora* and var. *albiflora, P. parviflora* and var. *brevifolia, P. Massoniana, P. Thunbergii, Podocarpus Nageia* and var. *variegata, P. macrophylla, P. okina; Larix leptolepis ; Juniperus rigida, J. recurva, J. chinensis, J. sabina ; Crypto-meria japonica, Cupressus Corneyana* ; *Sciadopitys verticillata ; Thuya orientalis, Tsuga Sieböldii, Ginko biloba,* &c., are the best adapted for dwarfing for many reasons ; they can live with but little nourishment without any risk of the plant dying suddenly, their roots grow quickly and enable the trunk to carry the crown of foliage at a considerable distance from the pot.

Generally speaking, deciduous plants are not so useful ; the leaves have a tendency to become as large as when the plants grow naturally, and all proportion is lost. Conifers, on the other hand, always appear

FIG. 11.—PINE, CHAMAECYPARIS.

as true representations of the larger trees, and the size of the leaves is in perfect harmony with the size of the plants.

The plants other than Conifers which are most used are : *Negundo aceroides, Acer palmatum, A. trifidum,* and other cut-leaved varieties ; *Rhyncospermum japonicum, Zelkova crenata, Quercus cuspidata,* and *Q. phylliraeoides* ; plum trees (*Prunus Mume* and *P. kaïdo*), *Styrax japonica, Lagerstroemia indica, Cycas revoluta, Crataegus cuneata, Azalea indica* and varieties, honeysuckle, *Wistaria,* bamboos, *Zelkova acuminata, Euonymus Thunbergianus,* Ivy, *Cydonia japonica,* · pome-granate, flowering cherries, *Ficus nipponica, Pittosporum, Trachelo-spermum jasminoides,* &c., *Ternstroemia japonica,* &c.

IMPORTATIONS OF DWARF TREES.—M. Kasavara showed a collection of dwarf trees at the Exposition Universelle in 1878, which was the first importation into France.

English people seem to be particularly fond of these trees, which explains the large and numerous importations which have reached that country during the past few years. His Majesty King Edward VII. himself possesses some unique examples, in which he is greatly interested.

FIG. 12.—PINE.

THE VARIOUS METHODS ADOPTED IN JAPAN FOR DWARFING TREES.—The best way of obtaining these trees is perhaps from seed, but it is also the slowest. The seeds, chosen from among the smallest and poorest of each kind, are sown in small pots and in poor soil. As soon as the young plants have appeared, their heads are taken off just above the two cotyledons with the view of encouraging the formation of two shoots which are much less vigorous than one central shoot, and of which only the weaker is preserved. The development of this shoot takes place very slowly when in a vessel of small size, deprived of nourishment, and only watered sufficiently to prevent the young plant from perishing. As soon as it is long enough, this shoot is made to take the form of a letter **S**, or it is bent in different shapes, or when it has become woody, and has been rendered very pliant by being deprived of water until it begins to droop, it is tied as a string might be into several knots. This operation, which is especially practised on pines, checks their development and makes them grow in an unusual manner at the collar. When the branches are developed, those which are not cut off are twisted, and in due time and in proportion to their length so fastened to the trunk as to make them take an irregular growth, sinuous, zigzag, either vertical, horizontal, or oblique, according to the idea aimed at.

Fig. 13.—Oak, 150 years old, showing Brick embedded in Trunk.
(*J. Carter & Co.*)

Arrangement of the Branches.—The frequent nipping-off of buds, and the use of numerous, almost invisible, fastenings of brass wire or of very fine slips of bamboo, assist considerably in keeping the plant in the form which it is desired it should have.

When a branch dies, another is selected or it may be replaced by grafting.

In many cases, and especially among conifers, the trunk of a young tree is twisted round a support as if it were a climbing plant. This explains the spiral form of certain trunks of *Thuya*, and especially those of pines. The support employed is either a stout length of bamboo, which is subsequently taken away, or the trunk of a tree fern, or again a fragment of porous rock, of coral or madrepore, the outline of which is in harmony with that of the trees, which is allowed to remain. Many of the pigmy trees imported into Europe have been trained in this manner, and their branches have grown on to the rock or the piece of fern trunk which formed their support. One can understand that by this operation the cells become wasted, and the circulation of the sap is hindered. Thus the young tree becomes deformed, or rather assumes the distorted shape which is wished for.

SUPPRESSION AND MUTILATION OF THE ROOTS.—Stunted vegetation is greatly due to lack of nourishment and to the very limited space in which the roots are placed, and which they quickly fill as they grow, in their effort to escape downwards. The pots should be changed at intervals of several years, but the new ones should be but little larger; the plants do not resent this treatment in any way. The entire or partial cutting of the taproot, and mutilations of the principal roots, have a considerable influence in the final result. Even if nothing were done for the suppression of roots, the tap (or principal) root, restricted in its development, soon becomes weak or dies; the rootlets, also restrained in their growth, are unable to develop rapidly enough or in sufficient quantities to draw from the soil the nutritive elements required for the normal nourishment of the plant.

The result of this treatment is a general, very noticeable, alteration in the habit of the plant, which continues, nevertheless, to live, but in a sorry and miserable manner. This fact is observable, but in a less marked degree, in plants in European gardens which have not been repotted at the right time.

TREATMENT OF OLD TREES.—Notwithstanding the perseverance and patience which they bring to bear on the formation of trees which they have raised from seed, the Japanese often wish to gain the same result more quickly. So they search the mountains, the sides of cliffs, and wooded districts, for plants already stunted, twisted, and deformed, or laid low by storms, and to which the situation where they grow has already added a curious, irregular, and picturesque appearance. Or, again, they select in the nurseries subjects whose appearance suggests that they would be susceptible to the intended treatment. As the roots of these plants are far too plentifully developed for them to be kept in the small vessels for which they are intended, all the large roots are cut off and only a few small ones left just to prevent the tree perishing, and for this purpose short roots are the most suitable. The result of this operation is to hinder very considerably the growth of the plant.

In repotting, if the subject is suitable, part of the stock is left out of the earth in the small vases, and the trees are kept in positions similar to those which they have been accustomed to. As to the formation of the branches, those which are twisted are kept, and those that are not required, and which spoil the general effect, are suppressed. Others are bent down and contorted in order to fill places devoid of foliage, so as to be in keeping with the picturesque appearance, and the effect which is desired. Then twistings are practised, bending those which are too vigorous or which take a bad direction, just as is done with seedlings. The trees remain puny and stunted, from the roots having but a limited space to develop in, the supply both of nourishment and water being scanty, and from the trees, moreover, being exposed to the broiling rays of the sun.

TREES WITH AËRIAL ROOTS.—In many plants, the roots, on being confined in the very limited space of a vase, are forced to rise above the soil. To encourage this bareness of the roots, the earth is removed gradually, and the trunk finds itself raised above the ground and

FIG. 14.—CYCAS REVOLUTA ; 15, CHAMAECYPARIS ; 16, CRYPTOMARIA.

supported from four to thirteen inches in height above the vase by its roots like an epiphytic plant or a Pandanus (figs. 15 and 17).

But in the majority of cases these long, frail, aërial roots are obtained by a different treatment, which commences on the sowing of the seed. Each seed is placed in the midst of a small space in a receptacle with firm walls, in which is a mixture of cocoa-nut fibre, moss, torn-up rags,

F

and powdered charcoal. The seed germinates and the little plant appears ; as the roots grow they describe several twists and turns in the limited space. Water is only given when it is necessary. As nutritive matter is very scanty, the young tree grows but slowly, and its branches become twisted spirally or are directed by numberless ties and bands, or restrained by fastenings. This does not prevent the roots from stretching out in search of nourishment, or in branching at their extremities. When the Japanese gardeners consider they are sufficiently long, the young plant is lifted, its roots are laid out, and the lower parts are replanted in a pot of small size. Thus growing upwards and kept in position by props, the roots carry the delicate branches to a certain height above the pot. Subsequently the air, winds, and want of water harden them, causing the circulation of liquids more difficult in the shrunken cells, which are

FIG. 17.—CHAMAECYPARIS OBTUSA.

rendered still more useless owing to the numerous contortions which give to the tree a more rugged aspect, and an appearance scarcely less fantastic than if it were some unreal and mythical object.

The more vigorous the plants are the more numerous and severe are the cuttings and restrictions of the principal roots and the other methods of treatment, also the supply of water and nourishment is curtailed.

The pines retain their vigour notwithstanding the numerous cuttings and bendings to which the branch which is allowed to remain is subjected : this explains the presence of gouty stumps and excrescences from which springs a weak branch with spreading foliage, which grows spirally after having been twisted several times upon itself, tied, and kept in this position by many fine fastenings made of brass or fibres of bamboo.

The Japanese also endeavour, in certain trees, to change the normal distribution of the branches, by favouring the development of the large branches in the upper part, and in not preserving the weaker ones near the base.

GRAFTING.—Grafting plays a great part in the formation of pigmy trees, as in the grafting of two different kinds together. When certain of the branches die from the twisting and contortions they have been subjected to, these are replaced by grafting. Often, indeed, all the branches are cut off, and a certain number of grafts are inserted in the trunk, in order that they may be trained in accordance with preconceived ideas.

But it is principally in training the *Podocarpus* that grafting is largely resorted to. The grafts give this tree a somewhat flattened

FIG. 18.—RETINOSPORA; 19, PINE TRAINED TO RESEMBLE A BOAT.

pyramidal shape. With this object, plants of *Podocarpus macrophyllus* the trunks of which are 2 or 3 inches in diameter, are repotted in small vases, and cut down to a height of from 15 inches to 24 inches. On the top of this bare trunk are placed five or six grafts, and for almost the whole of its height grafts are inserted on the sides at convenient distances apart, of a different species, and especially of those with variegated foliage. The weak branches are fastened together in proportion to their length, nipped and interlaced in the form of a more or less regular pyramid or of a cocked hat.

Maples are the most interesting subjects for grafting. Two maples of different varieties are placed in the same vase and grafted together about six inches below the surface of the soil. When these young trees have arrived at a certain height, the Japanese insert a series of grafts of several other varieties, and so obtain a great diversity in the form and the coloration of the foliage of the same tree.

THE IMITATION OF GRAFTING.—Japanese gardeners and amateurs are wont to conceal the normal grafts ; but, on the other hand, they give as much prominence as possible to the apparently abnormal-looking grafts which, to the uninitiated, have the appearance of being real, but which represent anomalies and monstrosities. That is, as one can see in some examples, where pines appear grafted on maples, and *vice versâ*, which in reality are simply the result of a pretence of grafting.

Two plants are often planted side by side in the same vase and grafted by being in close proximity to each other. As one of the two has usually more strength than the other, it partly surrounds and hides the other, and they grow so that the result appears to be a true graft. In other cases the trunk of a maple is twisted with that of a very flexible young pine, and both are trained together. After a time the trunk of the pine encases that of the maple and completely hides it. The same method is followed with two different kinds of conifers.

DECORATIVE USE.—Without comparing the ornamental part which these curious plants can play in the decoration of rooms and gardens to that which is filled by plants generally used for that purpose, they can produce in most cases very quaint effects.

A little Japanese scene can be easily arranged in one corner of the garden, in which the outline harmonises perfectly with the other objects employed ; or, instead of a scene of this kind, the trees can be placed on the grass where the effect of some of them crowning a rock after the manner of rock-plants, would have somewhat of an Oriental appearance. But it is principally in the decoration of the house that their bizarre elegance is seen to the best effect.

We may now consider whether these plants can live in Europe. Our climate, although different from that of Japan, should be no obstacle to keeping these lilliputian trees in good condition. In England there are numerous speciméns of these trees, growing as they would in Japan. King Edward VII. possesses superb specimens at Sandringham, and in France M. de Montesquiou has a collection of magnificent Thuyas, which since 1889 have grown considerably, but which, on the other hand, are models of vigour and grace.

Many people consider that these trees are only suitable for houses, and this mistake has led to the loss of a great number. On the contrary, the trees for the most part should be grown in the open air, and should be placed in a semi-shaded position, either in the garden or on the terrace. This need not prevent them from being brought into the rooms from time to time as curiosities or to take their part in decoration, but they should be taken into the open air afterwards.

In order to keep these trees to their original form it is necessary every spring to practise pruning rigorously, and during the summer to severely nip off the buds, particularly in the case of those with deciduous foliage, for often some buds are inclined to grow away to the detriment of the others, which spoils the beauty of the shape of the trees.

Maples and other plants with deciduous foliage should be trimmed rigorously in the month of February; afterwards, during their growth, the shoots are pinched back (the more severely the stronger they are), according to the shape of the plant, and the shoots which develop afterwards are treated in the same manner.

The vigorous branches of peaches, plums, cherries, and pomegranates, *Lagerstroemia indica*, &c., are shortened in February, because then the floriferous shoots will not appear until after the flowering season. *Wistaria*, which is very vigorous, is pinched back to four or five leaves, so as to induce it to remain longer in flower. The honeysuckle is treated in the same manner. Conifers generally, with the exception of pines (the buds of which are not pinched back), have all their shoots pinched back during the growing season. Other evergreen shrubs, such as azaleas, are pinched back and shortened after flowering, when that has taken place in the spring; and as early as the month of February if the blossoming of the flowers is very late.

Dwarf trees should not be repotted in too large pans or pots with the idea of providing them with more nourishment, still less should they be planted out in the ground. Nature will always rapidly reassert her rights. To keep trees in a dwarf state it is necessary to restrain their roots in a very limited space.

The soil may be changed every three to five years, and the same pot or vase, or one only very slightly larger, employed. The tree having been lifted, the old earth is loosened all round the bole, as is done in the majority of plants cultivated in pots. It is useful to cut away any roots which are developing too vigorously. The vase having been well drained, the plant is replaced exactly in the proper position on a little fresh compost. Then a little compost is filled in round the edge of the pot, and with the aid of a stick is pressed into all interstices. The same precautions should be taken as in moving heaths and Australian plants. The compost should be a mixture of leaf-mould, peat, and garden soil. February and March are the best months for repotting, as vegetation has not then begun. Plants cultivated in shallow dishes, basins, or pots should have the old top soil removed annually and replaced by new. A copious watering should follow each repotting or re-surfacing to facilitate the union of the old with the new soil. It is desirable to apply some mild manure annually to trees which are not to be repotted. This should be done twice a month from March till June, avoiding the hot months and those of autumn and winter. The most suitable manure is finely powdered oilcake and burnt bones. The quantity to give is about three teaspoonfuls per pot of 12 inches diameter, and half a teaspoonful for those of 4 to 5 inches. The powder should be scattered on the soil and watered in.

Generally the trees, whether evergreen or deciduous, can withstand the temperature outdoors even in the coldest seasons. It is, however, more prudent to keep them in a well-lighted place without artificial heat but well ventilated. It is very desirable to avoid the late spring frosts, which nip the plants just when the buds are swelling.

During the spring and summer *Thuya orientalis* should be placed in a light airy position and watered just sufficiently to keep the soil moist, but avoid too much moisture or dryness, excess or want of water being equally harmful.   Waterings during the winter should be less frequent.

The trees can be used with excellent effect to decorate a terrace, a flight of steps, or a balcony, provided only that they are not continually exposed to a brilliant sun.   The different pines, being less susceptible to external conditions, can also be similarly treated, but their leaves fall more quickly, and they suffer more from being kept too long in a room. Azaleas and other foliage shrubs endure the same treatment as *Chamaecyparis* very well, if placed in a position less exposed to the sun.

The foregoing remarks also apply to deciduous plants.   Maples endure the climate very well in sheltered places.

Figs. 6, 7, and 13 were kindly supplied by Messrs. Jas. Carter & Cc.

MISTLETOE.

By WALTER SMYTH.

THIS " quaint and mystic plant that grows 'twixt earth and heaven " is annually drawn attention to as the festive season of Christmas comes round in the sequence of the events of the year. The mistletoe grows in quite an extraordinary way, never sending its roots into the ground, but drawing its nourishment from other trees, where its berries or its seeds within same have been placed either by the agency of man or birds. I do not think there is any other way in which the mistletoe is likely to be conveyed to the bark of a tree save as before mentioned. The berries might, of course, be carried by mice in the case of ivy growing on an oak tree, or by squirrels to whose feet they may have become attached, but I have never seen these means suggested. Growing as it does in such a different way from the immense majority of plants, mistletoe has always been an object of interest ; but in the olden times it was more than this, it was also an object of veneration. So much was this the case that when the ancient order of priests called Druids found it growing on an oak tree—a tree on which it is rarely found—they held a service under the tree in its honour, as it was considered to be a forerunner of good fortune to the people or tribe. At this service the priest, attired in a white robe, cut away a portion of the mistletoe with a golden knife, letting the severed part fall into the lap of a white-robed attendant who waited beneath the tree. There are many other superstitions connected with mistletoe. In Sweden a ring made from its wood is considered to be a charm against evil. It is also called " the branch of spectres," as it was said to enable the holder to see ghosts and familiar spirits when they came about, which was, perhaps, a safe virtue, considering the rarity of the latter. A decoction from the wood was said to be a cure for strained sinews, toothache, hydrophobia, and poisons.

In Worcestershire there is a popular belief that farmers were in the habit of cutting a bough of mistletoe and giving it to the cow that first calved after New Year's Day to eat, as this act was supposed to avert ill-luck from the dairy. In the West of England there is also a tradition that the Cross was made of mistletoe, which until that time had been a fine forest tree, but was henceforth as a punishment condemned to lead a parasitical existence, and never to draw sustenance from the earth again. The mistletoe was always cut at a particular age of the moon at the beginning of the year, and it was only sought for when the Druids pretended to have had visions directing them to seek it. If the mistletoe fell to the ground without being touched it was considered to be an omen of misfortune. The old and popular custom of kissing under the mistletoe is one of its attractions at Christmas time. And who does not look back to childhood with memories of those happy early days when, like the mistletoe, life was evergreen? The custom seems to have been derived from the

Scandinavian myth which narrates that one of their most beautiful, bright, and good-natured gods was killed by an arrow of mistletoe which an earth-god had shot at·him.   The goddess Friga wove a spell whereby mistletoe was prevented from growing cn the earth again ; hence its growth on trees ; and she decreed that it must be suspended from mid-air, and under it the kiss of peace was to be exchanged ; and this is why we have the mistletoe in our houses at Christmas.   The old mistletoe should be allowed to hang until the new is put up at the following Yuletide, when the old branch should be burnt.

The propagation of mistletoe is very simple, and I have seen many fine clumps raised by merely rubbing the berry and pressing it on to the bark of the tree on which it is desired it should grow.   Some persons, however, make a V-shaped cut underneath the branch, and then raise the bark and insert the berry under it ; but this is quite unnecessary ; others graft the plant into another tree in the many ways in which grafting is done ; while others tie pieces of cotton, wool, or fine linen over it to keep off the birds.   The progress of germination seems to be on this wise. The viscid gum-like substance surrounding the seed dries up and forms a crust, and gradually the radical pierces the bark and throws out rootlets, which draw out the sap of the tree for the nourishment of the plant.   At the end of the first year after the berry is attached to the tree a little green curved piece of mistletoe may be observed containing two tiny leaves ; but it grows very slowly, and it is not until the end of the second year that a full leaf appears.   The progress of growth is more rapid after this, and eventually a fine clump is the result.   April or May is said to be the best month for propagation, but from March onwards, when the seeds are quite ripe, propagation should be tried, and, I think, would be followed by success.

Mistletoe, being a true parasitical plant, breaks out in different places near to the original plant, and so gets well established on the host tree. On a thorn bush in the garden here it has broken out in about twenty different places, and I am sure that three or four berries at the most were placed there at first.   Mistletoe does not grow readily on the oak, but it has been found there.   It may, however, be grown successfully on the apple, mountain ash, thorn, willow, sycamore, white beam, true service tree, and elm.   On the poplars (*Populus alba* and *P. nigra*) it is also not uncommon, and has been noted on *Acer campestre* and *Robinia Pseud-acacia*, and on the true service tree and sweet chestnut.   It does not grow readily on the pear tree in this neighbourhood, (County Down).   It may be seen growing on the oak in Hackwood Park, but I have not seen it on this tree in this neighbourhood.   It is considered very lucky to find it growing on the oak tree, and should be reported when found.

There is a species of mistletoe (*Viscum minimum*) which grows on the Euphorbia, a tree in South Africa, and is possessed of handsome red berries ; and there is another beautiful species which grows in Morocco, and is called *Viscum cruciatum*.   It is at present, I understand, growing on the above tree, Euphorbia, in several greenhouses in England.

The question, " Does it harm the tree ? " is often asked, and has certainly been answered in the affirmative by the French Government, who ordered it to be exterminated in their orchards in the sunny plains and valleys of Normandy. But on the whole one is led to believe that no great harm can arise from its growth. I would also suggest that in the case of apple trees being too luxuriant mistletoe might be very beneficial in drawing off the superabundant sap, and thus bring the tree into fruitful condition. It might also act beneficially on trees affected with canker, and, like the leech, draw away the poisoned sap from the stricken tree. The fact that the sap circulates through the entire tree backwards and forwards would also tend to show that it does not harm the tree to any serious extent. On the whole I think the trees are seldom much injured by it, and its beautiful yellowish green foliage and soft pearl-like berries are very handsome during the barren season of winter.

A curious incident, showing that the berries if taken in large quantities are not suitable food for birds, was told me some time ago by a friend and naturalist. He had been walking in a garden about Christmas time, when the mistletoe was covered with berries and looking at its best, giving a beautiful display to the seeing. eye. During the evening the barometer fell, and a snowstorm came on, covering the ground and trees with snow. On the following morning my friend visited the same garden, and found that all the berries had disappeared, and on looking closely at the foot of some of the trees found them in clusters of eight to a dozen, all more or less burst, showing that they had been swallowed by missel thrushes and other birds, and had acted as an emetic, proving indigestible. The sexes are represented in the mistletoe by different plants, one bearing the male and the other the female flowers. The latter may readily be distinguished from the former, it being the plant which produces the berries. It does not take very long to make a clump in an orchard. There is one in this neighbourhood where mistletoe berries were attached to the trees some four years ago. In many cases large clumps may now be seen. There is another shrub which appears to be very akin to mistletoe, and which in the South of Europe is seen very frequently on oak trees, and is called *Loranthus europaeus*. *L. odoratus* is another species which is possessed of very fragrant flowers. Also in America there are many different species which go under the name of *Phoradendron*.

The derivation of the word "mistletoe" is said to arise from the Anglo-Saxon *mistel*=*gloom*, and Webster noted the Saxon word *mistelta*, and states that it is a plant or shrub which grows in trees, and was held in great veneration by the Druids; but F. A. B. (Mrs. Boyle) in the "Garden" notes that the Anglo-Saxon word must have meant "dropped," namely, dropped by a bird on a tree, and thus propagated; while some modern writer translates "mist" into "glue," which seems to be the most probable of all. The mistletoe tribe contains about four hundred species, which mostly inhabit the tropical regions. One of these, named *Nuytsia floribunda*, which grows in the neighbourhood of King George's Sound, and bears an abundance of bright orange-coloured flowers, is said to look like a tree on fire, from which it is called the "fire-tree." It is, however, not a parasite like the majority of the species referred to. The mistletoe is not now used, I believe, for medicinal purposes, but a species of *Loranthus* is used in Chili as a dye.

GESNERACEAE

WITH ANNOTATED LIST OF THE GENERA AND SPECIES WHICH HAVE
BEEN INTRODUCED TO CULTIVATION.

By COL. R. H. BEDDOME, F.L.S.

A VERY beautiful order, almost every plant of which grows most readily from cuttings, chiefly represented in the western tropics of America and the adjacent islands. In the East, however, we have the beautiful genus **Aeschynanthus,** besides **Chirita, Didymocarpus, Jerdonia, Agalmyla, Stauranthera, Lysionotus,** and **Boea;** also other genera not referred to here, as they are not showy enough to find a place in our conservatories. Africa yields **Saintpaulia, Streptocarpus,** and **Acanthonema;** Australia, **Fieldia;** New Zealand, **Rhabdothamnus;** Chili, **Mitraria** and **Sarmienta,** greenhouse plants; the mountains of Europe, the well-known hardy plants **Haberlea** and **Ramondia;** and finally Japan, **Conandron.**

The plants of this order are mostly herbaceous perennials, many of which adorn our stoves all the year round ; a few only are shrubby.

Amateurs wishing to make a collection of this order should consult Continental catalogues (Lemoine, Van Houtte, Roozen, and others), as it there receives far more attention than in England ; and the hybridising of such genera as **Gesnera, Achimenes, Isoloma,** and **Naegelia,** &c. has received much attention for many years, though it does not seem to have been taken up in this country—why I have often wondered, for they evidently hybridise very readily, and few plants could be more charming than some of the Gesneras, Naegelias, and Isolomas, which often combine very lovely foliage with beautiful flowers, can be had in flower nearly all the year round, and. are most easily grown even by amateurs. Many of our nurserymen fill houses with different-coloured varieties of *Sinningia speciosa* (so-called Gloxinias) and almost entirely neglect all other gesneraceous plants, **Streptocarpus** being an exception, as this has been hybridised with splendid results. Through many years that I have been growing these plants I have taken notes which I here condense for. the benefit of lovers of the order, and I hope that the result of this catalogue may be that more attention will be given to the order in this country. Some genera, such as the lovely **Trichonantha** ("Bot. Mag." 5428) and many species of various genera, are, I fear, now lost to cultivation here— at least I have not been able to trace them.

It may be here stated that many species of Isoloma and Columnea, as well as Dolichoderia and others, come from considerable elevations on mountains, and will stand or indeed require cooler treatment than is generally given.

Acanthonema strigosum (fig. "Bot. Mag." 5339).—Fernando Po ; 4,000-5,000 feet elevation. On rocks and epiphytic on trees in the way of *Streptocarpus*; a solitary leaf, a short panicle of small purple flowers, a perennial stove plant, rare in cultivation.

Achimenes.—A large genus of beautiful plants, all from tropical America.

atrosanguinea = **foliosa.**

candida = **Dicyrta candida.**

coccinea (fig. " Bot. Mag." 374).—Peru, Jamaica. Flowers axillary, small, crimson; a very pretty pot plant, often sent out under the name of ' Dazzler.'

Georgeana = **longiflora.**

grandiflora (fig. " Bot. Reg." 1845, 11).—Mexico. Corolla tube saccate and spurred at the base; flowers axillary, solitary, crimson, smaller than *longiflora*; pedicel leafy. See also " Rev. Hort." ser. ii., ii. 372 ; " Fl. des Serres," i. 3, 245 (as *patens*).

heterophylla (fig. " Bot. Mag." 4871). — Mexico; peduncles axillary, longer than the petioles, 1-flowered; flowers medium size, scarlet, tube cylindric, saccate at the base.

foliosa (fig. " Ann. Soc. Gand." ii. [1846], 403, t. 91).—Guatemala, Mexico. Plant hirsute; peduncles axillary, solitary, 1-flowered; calyx lobes ovate, spreading, small, corolla tube infundibuliform, pubescent, gibbous at the base, orange-crimson, streaked in the mouth.

Ghiesbrechtii (fig. " Jour. Roy. Hort. Soc." 5, 194).—Hybrid ? Stems erect, purplish-brown, with a few scattered hairs ; leaves oblong-lanceolate, rugose, convex, serrate ; peduncles axillary, solitary, slender, twice the length of petioles ; calyx small, lobes 5, equal; corolla tube deflexed, tube cylindric, gibbous at the base. The corolla tube is not spurred at the base, and it differs otherwise from grandiflora, where it has been located in the " Index Kewensis."

gloxiniaeflora = **Plectopoma glabratum.**

hirsuta (fig. " Bot. Mag." 4144).—Guatemala. Aërial bulbils in the axils of the leaves and branches ; flowers large, rose-red, blotched in the mouth, tube saccate at the base ; peduncles elongate, terminal, or axillary, 1-flowered, or forked and 2-flowered. See also " Bot. Reg." 1843, p. 55 ; Paxton, " Mag." 12, 7 (as *grandiflora*), a straggling species.

ichthyostoma (fig. " Hook. Ic." 472).—Brazil. Very like *multiflora*, but peduncles 1-flowered. See Hanst. in " Linn." xxxiv. (1865), 434.

ignescens, " Fl. des Serres " = **heterophylla.**

Jauregnia = **longiflora.**

Kleei (Paxton, " Mag." 16, 289) = **longiflora.**

longiflora (fig. " Bot. Mag." 19 and 3980).—Guatemala and South Mexico. See also " Bot. Reg." 1842, t. 19, and var. *alba* " Fl. des Serres," 536, and " Bot. Mag." 4012 (as *grandiflora*), fine crimson-flowered variety. This species, with its varieties and hybrids, is much the largest flowered and finest in the genus, and should be grown in every collection ; in a hanging basket it is glorious.

magnifica (fig. "Fl. des Serres," 1013) = **Isoloma magnifica.**

multiflora (fig. "Hook. Ic. Pl." 468 ; " Bot. Mag." 3993).—Brazil. Plant hairy; peduncles axillary, 3–5-flowered ; flowers medium-sized, pale purple.

ocellata.—" Fl. des Serres," 336 ; " Bot. Mag." 4359 = **Isoloma ocellata.**

patens.—" Fl. des Serres," i. 3, 245 = **grandiflora.**

pedunculata (fig. "Bot. Mag." 4077). — Guatemala. Aërial · bulbils in the axils of the leaves and branches ; flowers orange and yellow blotched, dark crimson in the mouth, tube saccate at the base ; peduncles leafy, very long, axillary, 1–3-flowered. A beautiful species. See also " Bot. Reg." (1842), 31.

picta = **Isoloma picta.**

pyropoea (" Journ. Hort. Soc." 2, 4) = **coccinea.**

rosea (fig. "Bot. Reg." [1841], 65).—Guatemala. Peduncles axillary, several-flowered ; flowers medium size, scarlet. The plant sent out by florists as ' Harry Williams ' does not appear to differ from this species.

rupestris (fig. "Hook. Ic. Pl." 480).—Brazil. Leaves ternately verticelled ; peduncles axillary, solitary, 1-flowered ; flowers rather large, pale-purple.

Skinneri (" Jour. Hort. Soc." 2, 4) = **hirsuta.**

The hybrids in this genus are too numerous to be mentioned here. In " The Garden," 1882, ii. 198, there is a long list of those grown for trial at Chiswick Gardens. All are very pretty and well worth growing. One hybrid I must mention, that is, *margarittae* (Valleraud), a very beautiful white flowering variety, with the flowers of thick texture, not very often seen in England, but one of the very best for hanging baskets or pots. To show amateurs how very easily this genus is propagated and increased I may mention here that I received two small tubers of *margarittae* from the Continent in January some years ago ; when these grew, the tops were taken off several times and rooted in sand in the propagating frame, and the tops again off these ; they all soon grew into flowering plants, and in the same summer I had several hanging baskets and pots of it in full flower.

(Scheeria.—" Seem. Bot. Her." 184. The two species, *mexicana* and *lanata*, are now referred to **Achimenes ;** the name " Scheeria " may be dropped.)

Scheerii (fig. "Bot. Mag." 4743).—Mexico. Flowers large, purplish-blue, solitary in the axils of the leaves, funnel-shaped, hairy outside; stem erect, hairy (*olim* " *Scheeria mexicana* ").

lanata (fig. "Bot. Mag." 4963 as " Scheeria ").—The Western Cordillera, Mexico. Plant more or less whitish, hairy ; peduncles long, axillary, 1-flowered; flowers lilac with purple veins, the tube swelling upwards, the lobes denticulate. Syn. *Eucodonia Ehrenbergi.*

Continental establishments advertise hybrid Scheerias.

Plectopoma.—Hanst. in " Linnæa " xxvi. 201. This genus is now placed as a sub-genus or section under *Achimenes* in the last monograph of the order (see remarks under *Gloxinia*). It is closely allied to Scheeria, and is intermediate between *Gloxinia* and *Achimenes*. In " Gen. Pl." Bentham has referred *Plect. sarmentiana*, " Hook. Ic. Pl." t. 378, to both *Achimenes* and *Gloxinia*. For horticultural purposes the name " Plectopoma " may, I think, be kept up.

Taller and more robust plants than *Achimenes*, bearing large Gloxinia-like blooms produced on axillary peduncles ; the root (corms) is similar to *Achimenes* in both the species ; the calyx lobes are large and leafy.

Plectopoma sarmentiana (fig. " Hook. Ic. Pl." 378).—Oeiras, Brazil. Calyx leafy, deeply 5-cleft ; flowers large, purplish-blue, axillary, solitary ; peduncles much shorter than the leaves.

glabrata (fig. " Bot. Mag." 4430 as *fimbriata*).—Mexico. Peduncles axillary, solitary, longer than the petioles ; calyx lobes leafy ; corolla declinate, white or yellowish, dotted with purple, tube infundibuliform. *Plectopoma fimbriata*, Hanst. in " Linnæa," xxvi. 201 ; *Achimenes gloxiniaeflora*, " Fl. des Serres," 318. A very fine plant.

naegelioides and its beautifully coloured varieties (fig. " Fl. des Serres," 1745, 1847, 1867) are very old and well-known hybrids. I do not know its origin and I do not think it has ever been given. It has not the large calyx lobes of *sarmentiana* and *glabrata* ; it is very probably a cross between *Ach. Scheerii* and *Naeglia zebrina*.

Continental establishments discourse in glowing terms on some new hybrid Plectopomas, but do not give their origin. From the description they must be very similar to *naegelioides*, and are, I have no doubt, very beautiful plants ; instead of the inflorescence being a bare pyramid above the foliage, as in *Naegelia* and some Gesneras, the flowers are from the axils of all the upper leaves, forming a head of foliage and flowers.

Eucodonia (Hanst. in " Linnæa," xxvi. 201). This supposed genus is now amalgamated with *Achimenes*. It was originally proposed for a plant called *Eucodonia Ehrenbergii*, which has been proved to be the same as *Scheeria*, now *Achimenes lanata*. A second plant was afterwards referred to the genus, viz. *E. naegelioides lilacina* (fig. " Fl. des Serres," xvii. [1867], 1757), but this is a hybrid form, and I do not see how it differs from the hybrids figured under the name of *Plectopoma naegelioides*. Roozen advertises hybrids between *Achimenes lanata* (i.e. *Eucodonia Ehrenbergii* of foreign catalogues) and *Naegelia zebrina* : these are said to have very beautiful foliage. The name " Eucodonia " may well disappear. I may here state that a plant received by me from a Continental firm as *Plectopoma Rollinsoni* is the same as the old *Scheeria mexicana*.

Aeschynanthus.—Very beautiful flowering plants, which in their natural habitats are epiphytic on trees. In hothouses in which there is a very moist atmosphere they can be grown pinned on to rough blocks of wood or on the stumps of tree ferns, but it is not always easy to find these conditions or to cultivate them in this manner : **grandiflora, longiflora, bracteata,** and **speciosa,** four of the finest, are of straggling habit ; they are best grown in pots (with ample drainage) in a mixture of fibrous peat, a little sphagnum, and plenty of crocks of various sizes, and lumps of charcoal, constant watering is necessary when growth is going on ; the long shoots should be trained up sticks.

All the other species are best grown in hanging baskets in orchid soil. **Hildebrandii** is a small pot plant.

The following are the best, and are, or have been, in cultivation :—

bracteata (fig. " Hook. Ill. Him. Pl." t. 17).—Sikkim and Khasia, 2,000–8,000 feet elevation ; peduncles 1 inch long, 1–7-flowered, with scarlet bracts 1 inch long ; calyx lobes red, $\frac{2}{3}$ of an inch long ; corolla $1\frac{1}{3}$ inch long, nearly glabrous, scarlet ; a very fine species.

cordifolia (fig. " Bot. Mag." 5131).—Borneo. Peduncles short, 2–3-flowered ; calyx green, subturbinate, $\frac{1}{4}$ length of corolla ; flowers crimson and black blotched ; cordate leaves ; a fine species.

fulgens (" Wall. Cat." 797) (not figured). — Tavoy. Leaves narrow, lanceolate, pedicels terminal, clustered ; calyx tubular, $\frac{1}{2}$ inch ; nearly glabrous, corolla 2 inches, pubescent, narrow tubular, funnel-shaped, scarlet, mouth mottled with purple.

grandiflora (fig. " Bot. Mag." 3843).—Khasia Mountains, India, from 1 foot up to 3,500 feet. Flowers clustered at the ends of the branches ; calyx small with short lobes ; corolla $1\frac{1}{2}$ inch long, orange scarlet marked with black ; one of the finest of the genus.

Hildebrandii (fig. " Bot. Mag." 7365).—Burma, near Fort Stedman. A dwarf species ; leaves small, ovate ; flowers few from the upper axils ; calyx very small ; corolla 1 inch, orange and scarlet, much curved ; a charming little plant, but rather difficult to grow well and keep in good health ; it is said to be subterrestrial ; it requires cooler treatment than the others.

javanica (fig. " Bot. Mag." 4503).—Java. Corymbs terminal ; calyx downy, more than $\frac{1}{3}$ the corolla, wide at its reddish coloured apex ; flowers scarlet, yellow in mouth ; a beautiful species.

Lamponga (fig. " Nich. Dict. Gard." i. p. 3, as *boschianus*).—Java. Calyx tubular, smooth purple-brown, nearly $\frac{1}{2}$ as long as corolla ; flowers large, axillary, clustered, corolla tubular, wide at the mouth. See also Paxton, " Fl. Gard." iii. p. 14.

Lobbiana (fig. " Bot. Mag." 4260).—Java. Corymbs terminal ; calyx dark purple, more than $\frac{1}{2}$ length of corolla ; flowers scarlet, yellow in the mouth ; very much grown in our stoves.

longiflora (fig. " Bot. Mag." 4328).—Java. Very like *speciosus*, only flowers uniform crimson, and the mouth more contracted.

maculata (fig. "Bot. Reg." 1841, 28).—Himalayas ; up to 8,000 feet elevation ; peduncles clustered, generally terminal ; calyx ⅓ length of corolla, lobes lanceolate, acute ; flowers large, scarlet and yellow.

marmorata.—F. Moore in Paxt., "Fl. Garden" iii. 56 (not figured). Java. Leaves banded zebra-like ; flowers axillary, green and brown ; generally found under the name of " zebrina."

miniata (fig. "Bot. Reg." 32, t. 61).—Java. Peduncles axillary, 3-flowered ; calyx short, spreading, cyathiform, green ; flowers hairy, crimson ; a very pretty species.

obconica (fig. "Bot. Mag." 7336).—Malay Peninsula and Borneo. Calyx large, obconic sub-entire, red ; flowers red and yellow, villous, two on each peduncle, axillary ; introduced by Messrs. Veitch.

pulchra (fig. "Bot. Mag." 4264).—Java. Corymbs terminal ; calyx green, with short lobes about ⅓ length of corolla ; flowers large, crimson, yellow in mouth ; pedicels short, rather thick ; leaves ovate, obscurely toothed ; much grown in our stoves.

speciosa (fig. "Bot. Mag." t. 4320).—Java. Flowers nearly 4 inches long, orange and scarlet, tube narrow, curved towards the apex ; in terminal fascicles of 6–20 ; one of the very best, and should be grown in every stove.

tricolor (fig. "Bot. Mag." 5031).—Borneo. Umbels 2-3-flowered, axillary and terminal ; calyx purplish, short, cup-shaped, with 5 very shallow lobes ; flowers 1½ inch long, scarlet streaked with black and yellow ; very pretty species, introduced by Messrs. Low ; rare in cultivation.

Horsfieldii (fig. "Gartenfl." 297) and **purpurescens** (fig. "Bot. Mag." 4236), both from Java, have also been introduced, but are only of botanical interest.

There are numerous other species in India, the Malay Peninsula, Borneo, and Java which have not been introduced.

Agalmyla staminea (fig. "Bot. Mag." t. 5747).—Java, mountain woods. A climbing plant ; flowers in large axillary sessile fascicles, 8–14, scarlet, 2 inches long ; leaves 8 inches long ; a brilliant stove plant, generally grown in a hanging basket in orchid soil ; rarely seen out of botanical gardens.

Var. longistyla.

Alloplectus.—A genus of scandent, often more or less epiphytic plants, emitting aërial roots all along the stems which cling to rocks and trees ; sometimes met with under the name of **Crantzia.**

dichrous (fig. "Bot. Mag." 4371 as "concolor "). — Brazil. Flowers axillary, aggregate, nearly sessile ; calyx and the hairy corolla scarlet.

discolor=**Lynchii.**

Lynchii (fig. "Bot. Mag." 7271).—Colombia. A rather handsome erect stove plant, chiefly grown for its beautiful purplish foliage ; flowers yellow, calyx reddish, in axillary clusters, not showy ; this is the species generally met with in our stoves.

The following species have been introduced, and may all still be in cultivation, but they are not popular plants—more adapted, it may be said, for botanical than private gardens :—

bicolor (not figured).—Brazil and Colombia. An erect plant; peduncles axillary, 1-flowered; flowers pilose, yellow and purple.

capitatus (fig. "Bot. Mag." 4452).—Brazil. Very large species; flowers silky, capitate; calyx leafy red.

cristatus (fig. Plum. "Ic. Burm." 50).—West Indies. Climbing shrub; peduncles axillary, solitary, 1-flowered; corolla yellowish, hairy; bracts cordate, toothed, sessile, scarlet.

peltatus (fig. "Bot. Mag." 6333).—Central America. Scarlet calyx; yellowish flowers; a handsome plant.

repens (not figured).—West Indies. Trailing plant; peduncles axillary, solitary; flowers yellow.

Schlimii (fig. "Fl. des Serres" 827).—Colombia. Peduncles axillary, twin or few; calyx large, reddish, green-spotted; flowers scarlet, yellow, and violet.

sparsiflorus (fig. "Bot. Mag." 4216 as *dichrous*).—Brazil. A climbing shrub; flowers purple and yellow, nearly sessile, crowded in the axils.

tigrinus (fig. "Bot. Mag." 4774).—Colombia, Caracas. A large ungainly species; peduncles axillary; calyx large, red-tinged; corolla white, pink-spotted.

vittatus (fig. "Rev. Hort." 1870, p. 227).—Peru. Erect fleshy plant; flowers terminal and fasciculate; bracts red, foliaceous; calyx crimson; flowers yellow.

zamorensis (fig. "Ill. Hort." 1870, t. 83).—Colombia. Flowers yellow; calyx orange red.

Besleria coccinea.—Aublet, "Hist. des Pl. Guiana" (not figured). Guiana. Peduncles axillary; flowers yellow, 3-6, umbellate; bracts 2 at the division of the common peduncle, orbicular, cordate-toothed, sessile, scarlet; a climbing stove shrub.

grandiflora.—H. B. and K., "Nov. Gen. et Sp." ii. 401 (not figured). Brazil. Peduncles axillary, elongated, many-flowered; flowers large, campanulate, red-spotted; this is the species generally grown.

Imray (fig. "Bot. Mag." 6341).—Dominica. Flowers small, yellow, ventricose, solitary or fascicled in the axils, herbaceous, perennial; of botanical interest only.

incarnata.—Aub., "Pl. Guiana," ii. 635 (not figured). Guiana. Peduncles axillary, solitary 1-flowered; corolla purplish; tube very long, ventricose; lobes reflexed, fringed; herbaceous perennial.

leucostoma (fig. "Bot. Mag." 4310).—Colombia. Erect, peduncles, axillary, solitary or several together; flowers small, tubular, orange; of botanical interest only.

lutea.—Linn., "Sp. Pl." 619 (fig. Plumier, "Ic. Burm." 49) West Indies. Flowers yellow, small, in axillary clusters; of botanical interest only.

violacea (fig. Aub., "Pl. Gui." ii. 630, t. 254).—Guiana. Peduncles terminal, panicled ; flowers small, purple ; tube curved, limb spreading ; fruit purple, edible (see also fig. "Buchoz Herb." p. 31).

Boea.—A genus of small stove herbs, with the spirally twisted fruit of *Streptocarpus*, but shortly tubed, broadly campanulate small flowers in lax, few-flowered cymes. From the Malay Peninsula, India, and Eastern parts.

Commersonii (fig. "Bull. L'Herb. Boiss." vi. t. 7).—New Britain. A low herb ; peduncles axillary, solitary, umbellately few-flowered, nearly equalling the leaves ; flowers small, pale blue ; of botanical interest only.

hygrometrica (fig. "Bot. Mag." 6468). — Pekin mountains. Leaves radical ; scapes few-flowered ; flowers pedicelled, nodding, $\frac{3}{4}$ inch in diameter ; calyx very small ; corolla blue, throat yellow ; rather a pretty little pot plant.

Campanea grandiflora (fig. "Rev. Hort." 1849, ser. iii., iii. 241).— Santa Fé de Bogota. Flowers few, tufted at the end of a long axillary or terminal peduncle, large, Gloxinia-like, white, red-dotted, plant hairy ; a fine climbing stove plant, easily raised from seed.

Humboldtii (fig. Hanst. in "Linnæa," xxvi. 214, t. 1, fig. 24).— Costa Rica. Peduncles 2-3-flowered ; flowers densely hairy, spotted within, the tube inflated and curved.

Oerstedii.—Oerst. in "Viden. Selsk. Skr." V. v. 108 (not figured). Costa Rica. Peduncles twice as long as the leaves, 3-5-flowered ; flowers greenish, violet-spotted, large, Gloxinia-like.

picturata (fig. "Bot. Gazette," 1890, xv. t. 3).—Alta Verapaz forests 6,000 feet elevation. Peduncles long, axillary, few-flowered, hairy ; flowers like those of *grandiflora*, but smaller and very hairy.

Chirita depressa (fig. "Bot. Mag." 7213).—China. A dwarf greenhouse plant, forming a dense mass of foliage ; cymes few-flowered, shortly peduncled ; flowers violet, $1\frac{1}{2}$ inch long ; tube inflated.

hamosa (fig. "Rev. Hort." 1896, p. 184).—India. Peduncles connate and adnate to the petiole ; flowers $\frac{2}{3}$ inch long ; tube slender, whitish, mouth blue or rose ; much in cultivation, easily grown, flowers freely.

Horsfieldii (fig. "Bot. Mag." 4315).—Java. Peduncles aggregate ; flowers drooping, yellowish, with a purple tinge at base, tubular ; herbaceous, 1-2 feet tall.

lilacina (fig. Lem., "Ill. Hort." 1869, t. 608).—Chiriqui. Flowers pale blue ; tube white, base of tube with large yellow blotch ; a very beautiful species with numerous flowers.

Moonii (fig. "Bot. Mag." 4405).—Ceylon. A tall stove plant ; peduncles axillary, solitary or twin, flowers very large, purple and yellow ; a magnificent plant, but very rare in cultivation.

primulacea.—Hook., "Fl. Brit. Ind." Sikkim, 2,000-3,000 feet elevation (not figured). Almost stemless, villous ; peduncles

G

numerous, short, many-flowered ; calyx densely villous ; corolla yellow-white.

pumila.—Don., "Prod." 90 (not figured). Himalaya, 1,000–6,000 feet elevation. Erect, nearly 2 feet ; peduncles 2 inches long, few-flowered ; corolla funnel-shaped, 1¼ inch long, pubescent, purplish, yellow below.

sinensis (fig. "Bot. Mag." 4284).—China. A very pretty tuberous rooted, stove perennial, Gloxinia-like pale lilac flowers in corymbs ; leaves radical, clouded with white very easily grown and flowered ; common in stoves.

speciosa (fig. "Bot. Mag." 4315).—Java. Peduncles axillary and terminal, cymose, few-flowered ; tube violet ; mouth white ; a lovely species, rare in cultivation.

Walkeri (fig. "Bot. Mag." 4327).—Ceylon. Peduncles axillary, solitary, slender, bearing 2–3 drooping flowers ; calyx ½ length of corolla, teeth subulate ; corolla subcampanulate, large, deep purple.

zeylanica (fig. "Bot. Mag." 4182).—Ceylon. Peduncles axillary, longer than leaves, forming a 3-branched panicle ; flowers large, deep purplish-blue.

Codonanthe Devosiana (Lem. "Ill. Hort." ii. 1855, t. 56).—Brazil. A pretty basket plant (syn. *C. picta*, "Ill. Hort." 1856, 144). Very nearly allied to *gracilis*.

gracilis (fig. "Bot. Mag." 4531).—Organ Mountains, Brazil. Peduncles short, red, single or twin, 1-flowered ; corolla tubular, decurved, cream-coloured, orange-spotted inside ; epiphytic, like *Columnea* (syn. *C. Hookeri* Lem.). A pretty basket plant.

Columnea.—Stove perennials, often scandent or epiphytic, sometimes erect ; they require the same treatment as **Aeschynanthus ;** *glabra, magnifica,* and *crassifolia* are the best and easiest to grow.

crassifolia (fig. "Bot. Mag." 4330).—Mexico ? Shrubby, erect, fibrous roots at the joints ; leaves narrow, lanceolate, 4–5 inches long ; peduncles axillary, short, 1-flowered ; flowers erect, very large ; calyx 1 inch long, cut down to base ; corolla 4 inches long, bright scarlet, yellow in the mouth, covered with long red hairs. This is a very beautiful species, much in the way of *magnifica* ; it requires the same treatment as that species and *glabra*. I do not know if it is still in cultivation.

erythrophaea (fig. "Rev. Hort." 1867, 170).—Mexico. Leaves small, lanceolate ; flowers large, solitary, axillary, long-tubular, vermilion ; calyx lighter in colour, the lobes cordate and much toothed. One of the finest species, very rare in cultivation.

glabra (fig. Oerst. in "Danske Viden. Selsk. Skript." v., t. 11, fig. 18–33).—Costa Rica Mountains, 6,000–7,000 feet. A very fine, shrubby, erect species, emitting aërial roots ; leaves fleshy, glabrous ; flowers very large, axillary, scarlet. It requires cool treatment. It grows well in a compost of leaf-mould and coarse sand in equal parts, with a good allowance of small pea-like crocks over ample drainage topped by moss.

magnifica (Oerst. in " Viden. Selsk. Skript." V. v. 1861, 134) (not figured). From the same locality as *glabra*, and of shrubby habit, requiring the same treatment; it is very similar to that species, except that the leaves are downy. They have both been lately introduced to cultivation by Lemoine, and should become popular, as they are very showy plants and easy to grow.

ovata (fig. Cav. "Icon." iv. 62, t. 391).—Chili. Leaves small, oval, serrated; flowers large, terminal, solitary, crimson. A very pretty species.

rotundifolia (Hook. " Parad. Lond." t. 29).—Isle Trinidad. Leaves small, broadly oval, hairy; flowers large, crimson, axillary, solitary or rarely twin. A beautiful basket plant, in cultivation at Kew and elsewhere.

scandens (fig. " Bot. Reg." 10, 805).—Guiana. Flowers axillary, solitary, hairy, scarlet, calycine lobes toothed. A showy plant when in flower. This and the following, *Scheideana*, are the species generally met with in our stoves.

Scheideana (fig. "Bot. Mag." 4045).—Mexico, at Misantla. Epiphytic on trees. Large, beautiful brown and yellow, very curious flowers, calycine lobes entire.

speciosa (" Wendl. ex Stand. Nom." edit. 2, i. 399) = **Rhytidophyllum prasinatum.**

speciosa (" Presl. Bern." 145) = **Columnea rotundifolia.**

Tulae, var. *flava* (Urban, "Symb. Antill." i. 409) (not figured). —West Indies. Epiphytic climber, with numerous aërial roots; flowers bright yellow, hairy, on axillary 1-flowered peduncles, which are shorter than the leaves; calyx-lobes ovate-acute, entire, hirsute; fruit round, snow-white, copiously produced. A pretty stove species for a hanging basket, very free-flowering either as a basket plant or a small rooted cutting.

The following have been introduced to cultivation; they are inferior to the above, and rarely met with except in botanical gardens.

aurantiaca (fig. " Fl. des Serres," 352).—Colombia. Flowers orange-yellow, axillary, long-peduncled. Generally grown in a hanging basket.

aureonitens (" Bot. Mag." 4294).—Colombia. A large species; flowers orange-red; leaves densely hairy.

hirsuta ("Bot. Mag." 8081).—Jamaica. A large species; flowers axillary, solitary or twin, 1 inch long, hairy, scarlet and yellow.

Kalbreyeriana (" Bot. Mag." 6633).—Antioquia. A very large species; flowers axillary, yellow; calyx lighter-coloured; lobes cordate, acuminate, with toothed margins. A very fine plant.

picta (fig. Karst. " Fl. Colombia," 11, 105, t. 154).—Colombia. Flowers axillary, cymose, mixed with large membranaceous coloured bracts.

rutilans ("Sw. Prod. Veg. Nad. Occ." 94) (not figured).—Jamaica. Calyx villous, the lobes jagged; flowers villous, reddish-yellow.

Oerstediana (fig. Oerst. "Gesneraceae Cent. Amer." t. viii.).—
Costa Rica. Nearly glabrous ; leaves fleshy, very small, ovate ; peduncles slender, about length of leaves, axillary, 1-flowered ; calyx
segments long, acuminate, dentate ; corolla scarlet, 2½ inches
long. A very beautiful small species, which, I believe, has never
been introduced.

Conandron ramondioides (fig. "Bot. Mag." 6484).—Japan. Greenhouse herbaceous perennial ; flowers white or pink, purple-eyed,
in leafless cymes. A well-known plant, nearly hardy.

Cyrtandra.—This genus is only of botanical interest.

> **pendula** ("Fl. d. Jard." iv. p. 161) (not figured).—Java. A curious
> plant. Peduncle axillary, recurved, 3–5-flowered ; flowers pinkish
> white.
>
> **Pritchardii** (fig. " Seem. Fl. Vit." t. 39).—Fiji. Flowers small,
> white, on 3-flowered peduncles.

Diastema Lehmannii (Regel in "Act. Hort. Petros." x. 1889, 695) (not
figured).—Colombia. Glandularly hairy ; pedicels shorter than
the leaves ; flowers white, violet, mottled. Stove perennial, in
the way of *Isoloma picta*.

> **Ochroleucum** (fig. "Bot. Mag." 4254).—Colombia. Terminal
> head of pretty white flowers with yellow throats.
>
> **quinquevulnerum** (fig. "Fl. des Serres," 832). — Colombia.
> Racemes terminal, or in the upper axils lax, many-flowered ;
> flowers small, white, blotched with pink.

Dichrotrichum ternateum (fig. "Belg. Hort." 1871, t. 22).—Isle
Ternate. Peduncle very long, erect ; flowers numerous, subumbellate at the apex ; leaves opposite, very unequal in size ; of
straggling habit.

Dicyrta candida (fig. Lind. "Jour. Hort. Soc." iii. 317, p. 36).—Guatemala. Peduncles axillary, 3-flowered ; flowers white, spotted.

Didymocarpus crinita (fig. "Bot. Mag." 4554).—Malay Peninsula. A
pretty stemless stove plant ; flowers white, tinged with purple
and yellow ; leaves purple underneath.

> **cyanea** (not figured).—Malay Peninsula. A lovely stove species ;
> flowers bright blue. In cultivation at Kew.
>
> **Humboldtiana** (fig. "Bot. Mag." 4757).—Ceylon ; 4,000–5,000
> feet elevation. Leaves radical ; flowers light blue with yellow
> throat, on long scapes. *Primulaefolia* ("Bot. Mag." 5161) is
> only a variety of this species; it requires intermediate temperature.
>
> **lacunosa** (fig. "Bot. Mag." 7236).—Malay Peninsula ; North of
> Penang, on damp rocks. Flowers deep blue, on long few-flowered
> peduncles.
>
> **malayana** (fig. "Bot. Mag." 7526).—Penang. A lovely stove
> plant, with yellow flowers.
>
> **Mortoni** (Hook. "Fl. Ind." iv. 348) (not figured).—Sikkim ; 5,000–
> 8,000 feet elevation. Leaves ovate, serrate, villous above ; calyx
> cut down nearly to the base into narrow oblong lobes ; corolla
> tube linear, limb very oblique, wide-spreading.

This genus is not nearly so much grown as it deserves. There are
numerous species in the tropical and subtropical damp shady .

mountainous tracts in British India which have never been introduced to cultivation ; nearly all are worth growing ; they are easily raised from' seed. *Rottlera* Vahl is a synonym, the genus *Chirita* is very closely allied, and is joined with *Didymo-carpus* by Fritsch, who adopts Vahl's name.

Dolichoderia tubiflora (fig. " Bot. Mag." t. 3971).—Buenos Ayres. Very long-tubed white fragrant flowers, like those of **Achimenes,** but very large tuberous roots, like **Sinningia,** increasing very rapidly. It requires intermediate or greenhouse .treatment after the first stage to induce sturdy growth ; it then flowers well and is a lovely object. If grown in much heat with little air, lanky growth results, and it does not flower at all, or very sparsely ; it also requires feeding. It has been placed in *Gesnera* and in *Gloxinia.* Bentham in " Gen. Pl." places it in *Achimenes,* as it has similar flowers, but its large tuberous roots are very different from the caterpillar-like corms of that genus. Fritsch, in the latest monograph of the order, places it under *Sinningia,* with which it is much at variance in its flowers. It may well stand as a genus by itself, as it does in " Linnæa," xxvi. p. 205. There is a very good figure of it in " The Garden," 1888, pl. 644, drawn from a plant that flowered in my houses.

Dolichoderia hybrid.—*Gloxinia gesnerioides* (" Fl. des Serres," 2, tab. 12) is a very curious hybrid between *Dolichoderia tubiflora* and *Gesnera Cooperi.* It has a terminal raceme of large pink flowers, in shape much like those of *D. tubiflora.* I do not know whether it is still in cultivation ; certainly the most interesting hybrid in the order.

Drymonia.—Scandent stove shrubby plants, climbing by the aid of aërial roots. Only of botanical interest ; rarely seen except in botanical gardens.

bicolor (fig. " Bot. Reg." 1838, 4).—West Indies. Peduncles axillary, solitary ; flowers yellowish ; calyx large, green ; climbing shrub.

marmorata (fig. " Bot. Mag." 6763).—Guiana (?). Peduncles axillary ; few-flowered ; calyx large, rose-coloured ; flowers yellow. Large scandent species.

Turialvae (fig. " Ill. Hort." 1869, 603).—Costa Rica. Racemes axillary ; calyx red ; flowers large, white, pendulous.

Episcia.—Beautiful stove herbaceous plants, requiring shade, as their name implies ; chiefly grown for their beautiful foliage, though the flowers are also rather showy. *Cyrtodeira* is a synonym.

chontalensis (fig. "Bot. Mag." 5925).—Nicaragua. Very beautiful leaves ; flowers axillary, solitary, large, whitish or pale lilac ; requires the same treatment as *fulgida.*

cupreata (fig. " Bot. Mag." 5195).—Colombia. Large scarlet axillary flowers, beautifully coloured bullate hairy leaves, a broad band of reddish and silvery marking down the centre.

fulgida (fig. " Bot. Mag." 6136).—Colombia. Leaves bullate, the main veins silvery ; flowers axillary, crimson. Cuttings of this and *cupreata* rooted in sand make lovely little foliage plants for small pots. I have grown large-flowering plants in hanging baskets and pots very successfully in nothing but fertilising moss. If in soil, plenty of sand, tiny crocks and charcoal should be added, and ample drainage must be given. They are beautiful basket plants.

Luciani (fig. " Ill. Hort." xxiv. 236).—Colombia. Very lovely foliage ; an indispensable foliage stove plant.

mellitifolia (fig. " Bot. Mag." 4720).—Dominica and Brazil. A very pretty erect species ; crimson flowers.

The following have also been introduced. They are inferior to the above, being mostly of large and straggling growth ; seldom met with outside botanical or very large establishments.

bicolor (fig. "Bot. Mag." 4890).—Colombia. A procumbent plant. Flowers white, purple-spotted within, tube rather short ; pedicels axillary, slender.

bractescens (fig. "Bot. Mag." 4675, as *Centrosolenia*).—Colombia. - Erect, 2 feet ; leaves very large ; a pair of large, short-peduncled orbicular bracts, within which are several tubular flowers.

ciliosa (Hanst. in "Mart. Fl. Braz." viii. 403) (not figured).— Tropical America. Stems prostrate and rooting on trees ; leaves 1 foot long ; flowers axillary, aggregate ; calyx-lobes subulate, purple ; corolla 1 inch, tubular, subcampanulate, pubescent, yellowish.

densa (fig. " Bot. Mag." 7481).—Demerara. Stem short, erect ; leaves red beneath ; racemes very short, crowded in the axils ; corolla 2 inches long, straw-coloured.

erythropus (fig. " Bot. Mag." 6219).—Colombia. Stem short, stout ; leaves subradical, very large, red beneath ; flowers fascicled in the axils, pale pink.

Hookeri (fig. " Bot. Mag." 4552, as *Centrosolenia glabra*).—La Guayra. Erect, about 1 foot ; pedicels aggregate in the axils ; calyx-lobes linear, purple ; flowers yellowish, tubular, 1½ inch long, lower lobes of limb fringed.

maculata (fig. " Bot. Mag." 7131).—British Guiana. Scandent flowers in axillary cymes ; calyx ½ length of corolla ; corolla 2 inches long, yellow.

picta (fig. " Bot. Mag." 4611, as *Centrosolenia*).—Amazon. A creeping plant ; leaves velvety ; peduncles axillary, short, aggregate, 1-flowered ; flowers hirsute, large, white.

punctata (fig. " Bot. Mag." 4089).—Guatemala. A creeping hairy succulent plant ; peduncles solitary, 1-flowered ; flowers rather large, yellow, copiously purple-dotted.

splendens (Hanst. in " Linn." xxxiv [1865], 34) (not figured).— Colombia. Nearly allied to *cupreata*.

tessellata (fig. " Ill. Hort." 607 as *Centrosolenia bullata*).—Peru. Leaves very large, bullate, olive-green above, red beneath ; flowers yellowish, crowded in the axils.

villosa (fig. "Bot. Mag." 4866).—Surinam. Subherbaceous; branches thick, woolly; flowers axillary, ternate, large, Gloxinia-like, whitish, purple-flaked.

Fieldia australis (fig. "Bot. Mag." 5089).—New South Wales, on the Blue Mountains. Straggling, shrubby; leaves ovate-lanceolate; flowers yellow, long, tubular, on solitary axillary peduncles. A very pretty plant when in flower.

Gesnera.—Stove perennials, generally with tuberous roots; flowers very showy. *Gesneria* is the name given in the Kew List; the *i* is quite superfluous, and I do not think this name will be generally accepted.

Blassii (fig. "Fl. des Serres," t. 1140, 1).—Brazil. Flowers scarlet, in drooping panicles from the upper axils. A beautiful plant.

bulbosa (fig. "Bot. Reg." t. 343).—Brazil. Tuber large; leaves fleshy, ovate-cordate, on short thick petioles; panicles terminal, numerous, spreading, distant; peduncles corymbosely many-flowered, much shorter than the pedicels, which are 1-flowered; calyx very small; corolla scarlet, pubescent, clavately tubular, tube rather narrow, lobes very unequal, the upper one large, elongated.

cardinalis (fig. "Garden," Sept. 10, 1892, p. 874).—Habitat? Leaves velvety-green; flowers cymose, bright red, velvety, large; very large tuberous roots. Often grown under the name of "macrantha." Very beautiful plant; should be in every stove.

cinnabarina, see **Naegelia cinnabarina.**

cochlearis (fig. "Bot. Mag." 3787).—Brazil. Flowers scarlet, terminal in a racemose head. Very fine species.

Cooperi (Paxton, "Mag. Bot." 1, 1835, 224) (fig. "Bot. Mag." 3041 as *bulbosa*).—Brazil. Tuber large; stem erect, downy, 2-3 feet; panicle terminal; flowers numerous, large, scarlet; calyx small, segments short, linear; corolla tubular, 3 inches long, enlarged upward, contracted just above the base, the base inflated into yellow lobes.

Donkelaeriana (fig. "Bot. Mag." t. 5070).—Colombia. Flowers vermilion, in terminal heads; large tubers. One of the finest of the genus, but rare.

elliptica (fig. "Bot. Mag." 4242).—Colombia mountains. A fine species in the way of *rutila*. Flowers axillary, yellow.

exoniensis (fig. "Floral Mag." 127, 381).—Garden hybrid, probably with *Naegelia*. Leaves very beautiful, velvety, dark reddish; flowers orange-scarlet, in a terminal head. Should be in every stove. It would be better classed probably under *Naegelia* than *Gesnera*.

faucialis (fig. "Bot. Mag." 1785 and 3659, *fascialis* in error).—Rio de Janeiro. Whole plant downy; flowers in terminal racemes, large, handsome, velvety, scarlet.

laterita (fig. "Bot. Mag." t. 1950).—Brazil. Large crimson flowers, much in the way of *cardinalis*.

Leopoldi (fig. "Fl. des Serres," 7, 704, 5).—Brazil. Flowers vermilion, in terminal umbels. Beautiful compact dwarf free-flowering species (see "Garden," 1898, 1, p. 542, t. 1176). Allied to *cardinalis*. Continental establishments advertise variously coloured varieties.

Lindleyi (fig. "Bot. Mag." 3602).—Brazil. Much in the way of **rutila**, but flowers in a terminal raceme.

magnifica (fig. "Bot. Mag." 3886).—Brazil. Tuber large ; leaves downy, short-petioled, ovate-cordate ; panicles terminal, ample, crowded ; cymes opposite, bearing 6–10 scarlet flowers on a common peduncle ; calyx rather small, covered with red glandular tomentum ; corolla 3 inches long, downy. Nearly allied to *Cooperi*, but the calyx very different.

refulgens (fig. Nicholson, "Dict. of Gardening," vol. ii. 66).—A fine hybrid with a large head of red flowers ; leaves velvety with reddish hairs, in the way of *exoniensis*.

rutila (fig. "Bot. Reg." xiv. 1158).—Brazil. A tall handsome species with reddish axillary flowers. Must be given plenty of air and not kept too hot, or lanky growth and few flowers result. Much grown as a stove plant.

Sceptrum (fig. "Bot. Mag." 3576).—Brazil. Flowers dull reddish-yellow, large, in terminal leafless racemes.

Suttoni (fig. "Bot. Reg." t. 1637).—Brazil. Much in the way of *cardinalis*.

tuberosa (fig. "Bot. Mag." 3664).— Brazil. Leaves subradical ; peduncles numerous, subradical ; 2 inches long, erect, 1–3-flowered ; flowers crimson ; tube curved. A very distinct, curious and beautiful species.

The following species are scarcely of more than botanical interest :—

aggregata (fig. "Bot. Mag." 2725).—Rio. Peduncles 2–4, aggregate in the axils, 1-flowered ; flowers cylindric, small, dull red.

allagophylla (fig. "Bot. Reg." 1767).—Brazil. Tuber round ; terminal spike of small flowers.

discolor (fig. "Bot. Mag." 3995 as *polyantha* ; "Bot. Reg." 27, 63). Brazil. A large ungainly species with a large terminal panicle of flowers.

latifolia (fig. "Bot. Mag." 1202 as *macrostachya*).—Brazil. A large coarse species with a terminal head of small flowers, lately reintroduced by Mr. Ledger of Wimbledon.

maculata (fig. "Bot. Mag." 5115 as *purpurea* ; "Bot. Mag." 3612 as *Douglasii* ; "Bot. Mag." 2776 as *verticellata*).—Brazil. A very large ungainly species.

pendulina (fig. "Bot. Mag." 3744 as *Marchii*).—Mexico. Leaves 3-whorled, ovate, crenate ; flowers many, in whorls, scarlet ; corolla cylindric, gibbous at top.

spicata (fig. "H.B.K." ii. 188).—Mexico. A terminal spike of small flowers ; a poor species. See "Rev. Hort. ser." iii., ii. 465.

stricta (fig. "Bot. Mag." 3738).—Rio. Tall species, 3–6 feet ; large terminal head of axillary large reddish flowers.

The following species have been, and may still be, in cultivation ; they have not been figured and I have never seen them :—

caracasana (Otto and Diétr., "Allg. Gart." vi. [1838], 346).—Venezuela. Velvety, pubescent, axillary, solitary, 1-flowered peduncles ; flowers red and yellow.

Claussiniana (Brong. ex Decne "Rev. Hort." ser. iii., i. 363).—Brazil. Racemes terminal, simple ; flowers long-pedicelled, orange-red.

Sellovii (Mart., "Nov. Gen. et Sp." iii. 36).—Brazil. Flowers scarlet, in terminal cymes ; leaves tomentose, whitish underneath.

umbellata (Decne, "Fl. des Serres," ser. i., vii. 167).—Brazil. Plant velvety ; flowers reddish dotted, in a terminal umbel.

Gloxinia maculata (fig. "Bot. Mag." t. 1191).—South America at Cartagena. An erect plant, with knobbed rootlets ; peduncles axillary, solitary, 1-flowered ; flowers large, purplish-blue.

var. *pallidiflora* (fig. "Bot. Mag." 4213).—Flowers very pale blue.

var. *insignis.*—Flowers lilac and crimson.

var. *sceptrum.*—Flowers clear lilac (hybrid).

Very common in gardens in the plains of Southern India, where it grows like a weed and flowers all the year round ; a beautiful plant when well grown ; it requires a good deal of heat and moisture, and is not often seen in really good condition in our stoves.

The species referred to *Plectopoma*, Hanst. in "Linnæa," xxvi. 206, xxvii. 700, and xxxiv. 434, are placed by Bentham in "Gen. Pl." under this genus on account of the leafy calyx lobes ; in the last treatise on the order (by Fritsch) they are placed rightly, I think, under *Achimenes*, and I have followed this arrangement.

Haberlea rhodopensis (fig. "Bot. Mag." 6651).—Mt. Rhodope. Radical leaves ; flowers lilac, drooping, umbellate ; a well-known hardy plant.

Houttea.—These may be called shrubby Isolomas.

Gardneri (fig. "Bot. Mag." 4121).—Organ Mts., Brazil. Herbaceous perennial ; peduncles long, axillary, solitary, 1-flowered ; flowers red, tubular, downy ; leaves thick, fleshy, elm-like, scarcely distinct from *pardina.*

pardina (fig. "Bot. Mag." 4348).—Brazil. Peduncles axillary, solitary, 1-flowered ; flowers orange-red, the tube curved, the spreading limb spotted. See also "Rev. Hort." ser. iii., ii. (1848), 462.

Hypocyrta glabra (fig. "Bot. Mag." 4346).—South America. Very swollen scarlet flowers.

gracilis = **Codonanthe gracilis.**

pulchra (fig. "Bot. Mag." 7468).—Colombia. Beautiful foliage ; calyx scarlet ; flowers yellow, much swollen ; a curious plant.

strigillosa (fig. "Bot. Mag." 4047).—Brazil. Short, tubular, much swollen, scarlet and yellow flowers ; a very curious plant, common in cultivation.

Isoloma.—This genus now includes *Tydaea* and *Sciadocalyx*. · "Sciado-calyx" is a name given to Tydaeas which have an umbrella-like expansion of the cup-like calyx; there is no other difference; and as some of the Tydaeas (true) have a calyx nearly approaching this form, I do not see why "Sciadocalyx" should be kept up even by horticulturists; besides it is not very generally in use, so I hope the name may be allowed to lapse. *Digitaliflorum* and *Warszeviczii* are the types of *Sciadocalyx*.

Tydaea has a corolla much dilated at the mouth of the tube, the lobes spreading and copiously dotted and flaked. *Isoloma* has a more cylindric tube, more or less contracted at the mouth, the lobes small, the colour of the flower nearly uniform crimson, scarlet, or orange, with slight flaking about the mouth; Tydaea is an old well-established name, and will not, I think, be readily given up by horticulturists, particularly as it is easily distinguished from Isoloma.

Tydaeas are easily raised from seed, and many coloured varieties result from this mode of propagation, though to perpetuate any variety a cutting or offshoot must be taken.

Tydaea Section :

amabile (fig. "Bot. Mag." 4999).—Colombia; 8,000–9,000 feet elevation. An erect hairy plant, 1–2 feet; peduncles axillary, solitary, as long as or longer than the leaves, 1-flowered; flowers large, villous, dark rose, copiously dotted and blotched; this is one of the oldest of the Tydaeas, and is, I believe, the parent of most of the hybrids sent out by Continental growers; these are very numerous and all pretty and worth growing. 'Madame Heine' (fig. "The Garden," xxxiv. 440) and 'Robert le Diable' (fig. "The Garden," xv. 376), two of the oldest of the hydrids, are still, I think, about the best. For other plates of beautiful hybrid Tydaeas see "Fl. des Serres" x. 975 (*gigantea*), xi. 1181 (*ortgiesii*), a hybrid between *Tydaea Warszeviczii* and *magnifica*, xii. 1190 (*eeckhautii*); "Ill. Hort." 1858, 160, and 1859, 198, "Gartenflora," vi. 181–2, vii. 218. There is a section of hybrid Tydaeas in which the corolla lobes are much cut and jagged round the edges. Examples, 'Vaca de Castro' (fig. "Garden" [1899], i. 348) and 'Marquis de Guadiano.' Mr. M. B. Roezl in Mexico has largely hybridised the Isolomas.

bogotense (fig. "Bot. Mag." 4126 as *picta*).—Bogota. A slightly hairy plant with lovely clouded leaves; peduncles much longer than the leaves, axillary, solitary, 1-flowered; corolla orange and yellow, much spotted. See also "Bot. Reg." 1845, 42; "Fl. des Serres," ser. i., vi. (1850), 165; "Gartenflora," iii. (1854), 110. As there is another *Isoloma picta* which belongs to the Isoloma section the name of this has been changed in Nicholson's "Dict. Gard." from *picta* to *bogotense*—a very beautiful species.

Ceciliae (fig. "Ill. Hort." 1876, vol. xxiii. t. 178).—Colombia. Plant pilose; leaves dark velvety, rotund, cordate at base, coarsely crenate; peduncles 1–3 in the axils of the leaves, furnished with bracts at the base, 1-flowered; flowers large, rose, spotted darker. Fine species.

digitaliflorum (fig. " Ill. Hort." xvii. p. 95, t. xvii.).—Colombia, at Antioquia. (*Sciadocalyx digitaliflora* of Continental catalogues.) Stems very pilose; panicles short, terminal; flowers very large, deflexed, tube white and purple, the lobes green, purple-dotted. Curious on account of its green flowers; common in many collections. There are many hybrids off this species.

Lindenianum (fig. " Gartenfl." t. 589).—Tropical America. A pretty little pot-plant; leaves prettily clouded; peduncles long, axillary, solitary, 1-flowered; flowers rather large, pale lilac. Easily raised from seed; common in cultivation.

Luciani (fig. " Ill. Hort." 1874, vol. xxi. 182) (hybrid).—Stems, peduncles and flowers villous, with crimson hairs; peduncles erect, solitary, axillary, bracteolate, about 2–3-flowered at apex; flowers large, crimson, copiously spotted; calyx spreading, umbraculiform. (*Sciadocalyx* of some catalogues.) A magnificent plant. It is a hybrid between *digitaliflorum* and *pardinum*, a very rapid and strong grower; it flowered well in my stoves last year.

magnifica (fig. " Fl. des Serres," 1013).—Colombia. Peduncles long axillary, 1-flowered; flowers crimson-black streaked (syn. *Locheria magnifica*).

ocellatum (fig. " Bot. Mag." 4359).—Panama. A small free-flowering pretty little stove pot-plant; peduncle axillary, solitary, bracteate, much shorter than the leaves, 1-flowered; flowers small, tube crimson, short, mouth yellow-spotted. Very common in cultivation.

pardinum (fig. " Ill. Hort." xx. 152). — Mexico. Peduncles axillary, $\frac{1}{2}$–$\frac{3}{4}$ inch long, bracteate at the apex, with 3–4 subumbellate flowers, corolla scarlet with dark spots over the lobes. Must not be confounded with *Houttea pardina*, which has Isoloma-shaped flowers.

pyramidale (fig. " Trans. Russ. Hort. Soc." 1861, t. 54) (hybrid).— A strong tall species; stems densely covered with red hairs; peduncles axillary, 8–9 flowered; nearly allied to *Luciani*, differs chiefly in having more flowers in the umbel; is in cultivation at Kew.

venosum (fig. " L'Hortic. Franç." sér. iii., ii. 1861, 248, t. 20).— Colombia. Leaves purplish underneath; peduncles about 3 inches long, axillary, solitary, 1-flowered; calyx rather large; flowers pink, yellow in the mouth. A well-known and very pretty species.

Warszeviczii (fig. " Bot. Mag." 4843).—Colombia. Plant villoso-hirsute; leaves long-petioled; peduncles axillary, bracteolate, 3–8-flowered at the apex; pedicels longer than the peduncles; flower-tube swollen, scarlet, mouth yellow, crimson-spotted. *Sciadocalyx* of some catalogues. See also " Fl. des Serres," 9, 941.

Continental establishments send out many hybrid *Sciadocalyx*, crosses, I believe, between this species and *digitaliflorum*; *gigantea*, "Fl. des Serres," x. 975, is a hybrid between this species and *bogotense*.

Isoloma Section:

erianthum (Hanst. in "Linnæa," xxiv. 573, as *Brachyloma erianthum* (fig. "Bot. Mag." 7907).—Colombia, up to 8,000 feet elevation. This is the species which has been grown for many years in our stoves under the name of "*hirsutum.*" It was introduced to cultvation by the late Mr. Bull. *Vide* "The Garden," 1883, ii. 264. Mr. Bull's son informs me that it was collected and sent home by Mr. E. Shuttleworth in 1875, and that the late Mr. Moore named it "*hirsutum.*" It is not, however, the *hirsutum* of Humboldt and Bonpland (vol. ii. tab. 189), which is quite a different species that has apparently never been introduced into England, and of which there are good specimens in the Kew Herbarium. The flowers are solitary in the axils or several from a short peduncle. The figure in "Bot. Mag." is exaggerated in the colouring. This is one of the commonest species of the genus in our stoves ; besides being one of our most useful stove plants, it grows as well or even better in a warm greenhouse (even throughout the winter), as it then has sturdy short growth. It can easily be had in flower all the year round if strong tops are continuously rooted in the propagating frame; they make much better plants than the corms ; the old plants should be thrown away after flowering, or when they get shabby. It is the "*hirsutum*" of Continental catalogues, and some of the foreign establishments advertise many hybrids from it. As far as I have received these, they differ very slightly from the type, and show no marked improvement, in fact nothing but a slight difference in the colour of the flowers.

hypocyrtiflorum (fig. "Bot. Mag." 5655).—Andes of Quito. Very curious globular much swollen scarlet flowers on long peduncles, which are solitary or twin in the axils of the ovate-rotund leaves. A very striking plant.

longipedunculatum (fig. "Ill. Hort." 287 as *Kohleria lanata*).— Mexico. Whole plant densely silky-villose ; leaves ternate, elliptic, nearly sessile; peduncles erect, nearly as long as the leaves, solitary or twin in the axils, 1-flowered; calyx rather large, segments oval, spreading ; flowers orange-scarlet, spotted in the mouth, tube 1–1½ inch long. A very handsome species.

pictum (fig. "Bot. Mag." 4431).—Colombia. A tall velvety hirsute plant; leaves reddish underneath ; flowers in a large terminal head; peduncles short, 1–3 in the axils of the small upper leaves ; corolla orange and yellow, tube swollen, very contracted at the mouth. A very fine species, rare in cultivation.

Trianaei (fig. "Gartenfl." [1854], 82).—Colombia. Peduncles thick, long, axillary, umbellate, and bracteolate at the apex, 1–4·

flowered; flowers large, crimson, tube contracted near the mouth, which is yellow, lobes rather more dilated than is usual in **Isoloma**. See also "Fl. des Serres," 10, 1057.

The following Isolomas are inferior to what are recorded above, and are not recommended except for very large establishments or botanical gardens, or where the order is made a speciality.

Deppeanum (fig. "Bot. Mag." 3725).—Mexico. Peduncles very long, axillary, umbellate, bracteolate; flowers 3–4, on pedicels 1½ inch long, small, tubular, orange-red. *Gesnera oblongata* and *G. elongata* are synonyms.

elegans (fig. "Fl. des Serres," t. 489 as *formosa*).—Guatemala. Plant softly hairy; leaves longish-petioled, ovate, from an unequal base; peduncles axillary, solitary, 3 inches long, umbellate and bracteolate at the apex; flowers 3–4-pedicelled, corolla tube scarlet, yellow in the mouth. See also "Gartenfl." 1854, t. 101.

hondense (fig. "Bot. Mag." 4217). — Honda, in Colombia. Peduncles 1–3 in the axils, longer than the petioles; flowers small, hairy, crimson and yellow, tube about 1 inch long, subventricose, contracted at the mouth.

ignoratum (fig. "Gartenfl." 1852, f. 1).—Mexico. Stem pilose; flowers small, tubular, reddish, villous, on 1-flowered peduncles, which are solitary or twin in the axils of the small upper leaves, forming a terminal head.

Jaliscanum ("Proc. Amer. Acad." xxv. [1890], 159) (not figured).—Mexico. Stem pubescent; peduncles axillary, 1 inch long, bearing an umbel of 2–4 flowers on 1-inch pedicels; calyx-lobes acuminate; corolla tube 1 inch long, scarlet, pubescent, funnel-shaped, contracted at the mouth.

longifolium (fig. "Bot. Reg." 28 [1842], t. 40). — Guatemala. Peduncles whorled in the upper axils, much longer than the petioles, forming a terminal head of small dull orange-red flowers. See also "Rev. Hort." ser. iii., ii. (1848), 465.

molle (fig. "Bot. Mag." 3815).—Caracas. Shrubby, 1½ feet, hairy; leaves clothed with long silky hairs; flowers densely hairy, red, funnel-shaped, 3–5, long-pedicelled, in an umbel on very short axillary peduncles.

rubricaule (fig. "Gartenfl." 1852, 7).—Venezuela. Leaves elliptic; peduncles axillary, solitary, a little longer than the petioles, 1-flowered; calyx-lobes long, acute; flowers rather small, tubular, scarlet. . Allied to *hirsutum* of Humb. and Bonpl.

rupestre ("Gard. Chron." 1871, 611).—Nicaragua. Stem woolly, whitish; peduncles 1-flowered, fasciculate in the upper axils, forming a terminal head of flowers; corolla villous, tube cylindric. Allied to *Seemanni*.

Scheideanum (fig. "Bot. Mag." 4152).—Mexico. Leaves softly downy, in whorls of 3; peduncles aggregate in the upper axils, shorter than the leaves, 1–3-flowered; flowers scarlet, hairy, tube between campanulate and funnel-shaped; calyx short, turbinate.

Seemannii (fig. "Bot. Mag." 4504).—Panama. Peduncles 3–4 in the axils of the upper small leaves, forming a terminal head of flowers ; corolla small, reddish-orange, tube short, cylindrical, hairy. Allied to *longifolium*.

triflorum (fig. "Bot. Mag." 4342).—Colombia. Peduncles very short, axillary, umbellate, bracteolate ; pedicels about 3, much longer than the peduncles ; corolla small, yellowish, covered with reddish hair, tube ventricose ; calyx hemispherical, woolly.

tubiflorum (fig. "Cav. Ic." vi. tab. 584).—Colombia. Whole plant hairy ; leaves ovate, short-petioled ; peduncles twin in the axils, twice as long as the petioles ; flowers erect ; calyx small ; corolla funnel-shaped, contracted at the mouth, lobes very small. Closely allied to *hondense*.

Jerdonia indica (fig. "Bot. Mag." 5814).—Sispara Ghat, on the Nilgiri Hills. Pale lilac flowers. A pretty plant for small pots, much in the way of *Sinningia concinna*. It was flowered at Kew from seeds I sent home from the Sispara Ghat, but is, I believe, lost to cultivation, though it could easily be reintroduced.

Klugia zeylanica (fig. "Bot. Mag." 4620).—South India and Ceylon. Only of botanical interest, and not very easy to grow ; it is a very common weed in swampy places in subalpine forests in India.

Koellikeria argyrostigma (fig. "Bot. Mag." 4175).—Peru. A pretty little pot-plant for the stove ; leaves white-spotted ; flowers cream-coloured, red-spotted, in long spikes.

Lietzia brasiliensis (fig. "Gartenfl." t. 1005).—Brazil. A very curious tuberous-rooted stove-plant ; flowers green, brown-mottled, tubular, wide gaping, in terminal racemes. It must not be kept in a high temperature, except at first starting, and plenty of air must be given, as it will not flower unless the growth is sturdy ; it also requires feeding.

Lysionotus carnosa (Hemsley in "Gard. Chron." 1900, ii. 849) (not figured).—China. Thick fleshy leaves ; flowers 1¾ inch long, white, tinged with lilac, Didymocarpus-like, in pairs in the axils of the upper leaves. Rare in cultivation. It is in the Kew collection.

pauciflora (fig. Makino, "Ill. Fl. Jap." t. 2).—Japan. Leaves lanceolate, roughly toothed ; flowers short-pedicelled, axillary large, infundibuliform, campanulate.

serrata (fig. "Bot. Mag." 6538).—Khasya Hills, India. Leaves large ; flowers in drooping long-peduncled axillary corymbs ; calyx small ; corolla 1½ inch long, funnel-shaped, pale lilac veined. Can be grown from seed as well as cuttings.

Mitraria coccinea (fig. "Bot. Mag." t. 4462).—Chili. A beautiful greenhouse shrubby plant ; scarlet flowers with swollen tubes. Very common in cultivation.

Monophyllaea glauca.—Borneo. Small flowers in unilateral scorpioid racemes. Is a plant of only botanical interest.

Monopyle racemosa (fig. "Bot. Mag." 6233).—Colombia. Herbaceous stove perennial ; racemes stout, erect, terminal ; flowers large, white, Gloxinia-like. Much in the way of *Gloxinia maculata*.

Naegelia.—This genus is allied to *Achimenes* and has similar caterpillar-like corms, but the flowers are arranged in a terminal leafless raceme. Many of the species have very beautiful velvety crimson or mottled plush-like leaves ; they require a good deal of heat ; water should not be given over the leaves. The Continental hybrids off *zebrina* are very numerous, differing in the colour of the flowers and leaves ; of these the best are ' Amabilis,' ' Prince de Bulgaria,' and ' Sirius.' The genus has also been crossed with *Achimenes*, the progeny being called *Naegelo-Achimenes*, very pretty stove plants ; the best I have grown being ' Madame Jehenna.' It has also been crossed with *Gesnera*, and *Gesnera refulgens* is, I believe, from this source ; it comes under *Naegelia* rather than *Gesnera*.

    cinnabarina (fig. " Bot. Mag." 5036).—Guatemala. Terminal head of brilliant orange flowers. Very much grown.

    multiflora (fig. " Bot. Mag." 5083).—Oaxaca ; 2,000–3,000 feet elevation. Flowers whitish with yellow throat, in a large terminal head. (*Amabilis* fig. " Fl. des Serres," 1192.)

    zebrina (fig. " Bot. Mag." 3940).—Guatemala and Mexico. Beautiful highly coloured velvety leaves ; large terminal raceme of orange-yellow drooping bell-shaped flowers. Common in cultivation.

Naegelia zebrina and probably the other two species have been crossed with the *Plectopomas* and *Scheerias*, the result being the hybrid *Plectopomas* and *Eucodonias*. See under **Achimenes.**

Nematanthus.—A genus of straggling, climbing or epiphytic plants, seldom seen out of botanical gardens.

    corticicola (fig. " Bot. Mag." 4460 as *ionema*).— Tropical America. Blood-red flowers on long stalks ; straggling habit.

    longipes (fig. " Bot. Mag." 4015).—Brazil. Very long-petioled axillary scarlet flowers ; very straggling habit, generally grown in and trained round a basket. *Chloronema* (" Bot. Mag." 4080) is a shorter-petioled variety of this.

Niphaea oblonga (fig. " Bot. Reg." 28, 5).—Tropical America, Colombia. Pretty white flowers. A nice little pot-plant. *Niphaea rubida*, " Fl. des Serres," iii. 251, *Phinaea rubida* Fritsch., are synonyms.

    Roezli (fig. " Gartenfl." 896).—Of botanical interest only.

Paliavana prasinata (fig. " Bot. Reg." 428).—Brazil. Flowers in a terminal head on short axillary peduncles, greenish, dark-dotted, villous, tube short, much dilated towards the mouth. A very curious plant.

Pentarhaphia catalpaeflora (Decne in " Ann. Sc. Nat." ser. iii., vi. [1846], 100) (not figured).—West Indies. Leaves oblong, crenulate ; peduncles twice as long as the petioles, 2–3-flowered ; pedicels elongate ; calyx-sepals subulate ; corolla-tube ventricose, campanulate. A woody plant.

    craniolaria (Decne, *l.c.* 99) (not figured).—San Domingo. Flowers greenish-yellow, black-dotted, 5–6 on a long peduncle. A shrub.

cubensis (fig. "Bot. Mag." 4829).—Cuba. Leaves small; peduncles axillary, 1-flowered; flowers long, tubular, curved, scarlet, yellow at the base. A shrubby plant for a warm greenhouse. See also " Fl. des Serres,' 3, 297.

floribunda (fig. "Rev. Hort." [1878], 30)—Cuba. A dwarf bushy reddish downy species; flowers axillary, numerous, reddish; the tube distended above the middle, the limb shortly 3-lobed. Very near *libonensis*.

libonensis (fig. "Bot. Mag." 4380 as *Gesnera*).—West Indies. A very pretty little plant, with long crimson tubular flowers and spathulate leaves. Cuttings root rapidly in sand, and flower much more freely than the old plants, and are fascinating in tiny pots. It is sent out from foreign nurseries under the name of *Ophianthe libonensis*. See also " Fl. des Serres," 178.

longiflora (fig. "Bot. Mag." 7339).—West Indies. A beautiful small shrubby plant; supra-axillary peduncles with several fine scarlet flowers.

neglecta (Hanst. in " Linn." xxxiv. [1865], 305) (not figured).— Jamaica. Shrubby; peduncles short, 1-flowered; corolla tube broadly campanulate.

verrucosa (fig. Paxt., " Fl. Garden," iii. 30, t. 250).—Cuba. A rigid greenhouse shrub; flowers tubular, scarlet, solitary in the axils, on long peduncles. In the way of *cubensis*.

Phinaea.—Dwarf stove-herbs allied to *Niphaea*, of scarcely more than botanical interest. Rhizomes like *Achimenes*.

albolineata (fig. " Bot. Mag." 4282).—Colombia. Leaves beautifully streaked with white; peduncles axillary, umbellate; flowers small, white. "Bot. Mag." 5043, *P. reticulata*, is a variety only of this species.

rubida (Nicholson, "Dict. Gard." iii. 99) = **Niphaea oblonga.**

Phylloboea Henryi (Duthie, MS. Herb. Kew).—Yunan, 4,600 feet elevation on rocks. A pretty little pot plant, in the way of *Didymocarpus*; leaves with dense white tomentum beneath; cymes axillary; flowers broadly campanulate, whitish. In cultivation at Kew.

Plectopoma. See under **Achimenes.**

Ramondia pyrenaica (fig. " Bot. Mag." 236).—Pyrenees. A well-known hardy plant; scapes 1–many-flowered; flowers purple or white; scarcely any tube to the corolla.

Rhabdothamnus Solandri (fig. " Bot. Mag." 8019).—New Zealand, Wellington, N. Island. A small shrubby greenhouse plant; flowers tubular, campanulate, sub-bilabiate, orange-scarlet; Tydaea-like, on axillary solitary pedicels; leaves small, round, scabrous, deeply toothed. Lately introduced and sent out by Lemoine.

serbica, DC. "Mon.'" v. 168 (not figured).—Thessaly. Scapes 1–3-flowered; flowers yellow, with scarcely any tube to the corolla; leaves crenato-serrate.

Heldreichii, Hook. " Gen. Pl." ii. p. 1024 (not figured).—Mount Olympus, Thessaly, up to 3,000 feet elevation. Leaves nearly entire, densely silky, peduncles 1–2-flowered ; corolla distinctly campanulate, the tube longer than the lobes, smooth within.

Rhynchoglossa zeylanicum (fig. "Bot. Mag." 4198).—Ceylon. Of botanical interest only.

Rhytidophyllum auriculatum (fig. "Bot. Mag." 3562), Brazil, **prasinatum** and **tomentosum** (fig. "Bot. Mag." 1028), West Indies, are only of botanical interest.

Rosanovia. See under **Sinningia.**

Saintpaulia ionanthe (fig. "Bot. Mag." t.7408).—Tropical East Africa (hilly regions). A well-known lovely little stove plant, easily grown from seed or from a leaf; always in flower. There are four varieties : flowers pale lilac (type) ; flowers very dark-blue (*violacea*) ; flowers white, violet-tinted (*albescens*) ; flowers reddish ; leaves much larger and on longer petioles (*purpurea*).

Sarmienta repens (fig. "Fl. des Serres," 1646).—"Fl. Mag." ii. t. 112. A charming greenhouse, creeping, wiry-stemmed plant ; flowers large crimson, tube swollen ; it should be grown in a cool, quite shaded place in the greenhouse (near water if possible), orchid soil with an ample allowance of small crocks ; it is useless to attempt it under other conditions ; it is in any case a difficult plant to grow well.

Sciadocalyx. See **Isoloma.**

Seemannia Benaryi (fig. "Gartenfl." t. 814).—Peru. Leaves verticelled ; peduncles axillary, several together ; flowers scarlet, bell-shaped, slightly lobed at the apex ; a pretty plant.

Sinningia.—All plants of this genus have tuberous roots (*Gloxinia* has knobbed rootlets).

> **barbata** (fig. "Bot. Mag." 5623).—Brazil. Leaves pilose above, crimson beneath ; peduncles up to $1\frac{1}{2}$ inch long, axillary, solitary or twin ; calyx 1 inch deep ; corolla much swollen at base, curved, white, red-blotched ; a pretty species. "Fl. Mag." 336 as *carolinae* ; "Fl. des Serres," 1847.

> **concinna** (fig. "Bot. Mag." 5253).—Brazil. · A delicate little plant with small round tubers and pretty very small Gloxinia-like flowers, charming for small pots ; flowers all the year round, sometimes called ' Stenogastra concinna.' There is a variety called ' multiflora,' "L'Ill. Hort." (1864), 390. The pots should be filled $\frac{3}{4}$ up with crocks, over which a soil of 1 part leaf mould, 1 part loam, 2 parts sand.

> **diversiflora** (fig. Nicholson, "Dict. Gard." ii. 75).—A pretty dwarf hybrid off *speciosa*. See "Rev. Hort." (1883), 247, f. 45.

> **gesnerioides** (fig. Nicholson, "Dict. Gard." ii. 76).—A handsome erect branched hybrid off *speciosa*, raised by Messrs. Carter ; flowers fiery scarlet. · ' Gloxinia gesnerioides,' its original name, was unfortunate, as this was occupied. See under **Dolichoderia.**

> **guttata** (fig. "Bot. Reg." 1112).—Brazil. Stems, ascending, leafy slender ; flowers pale green, purple-spotted ; calyx large, campanulate, 5-winged, inflated ; corolla a little longer than calyx. See also Paxton, "Mag. Bot." ii. 4.

H

Helleri (fig. "Bot. Reg." 997 and "Bot. Mag." 4212 as *velutina*).—
Brazil. A purple-tinted plant with a stem only a few inches
high; peduncles erect, about 1 inch long; flowers white, throat
greenish, red-spotted, nearly 3 inches long; calyx red, large,
about 2 inches long; a curious plant.

hirsuta (fig. "Bot. Mag." 2690).—Rio. Leaves radical; peduncles
glomerate or subracemose, radical shorter than the leaves;
flowers lilac, violet-dotted; calyx red, very villous.

maxima (Paxt., "Mag. Bot." v. [1838], 219).—A fine hybrid off
speciosa, and not differing much from that species; flowers very
large, drooping, whitish, with purple centre.

regina (fig. "Gartenfl." [1904], 525).—Brazil. A very pretty
recently introduced species; leaves richly coloured; flowers
large purplish. Easily grown from seed or from a leaf;
hybrids have already been raised between this species and
speciosa.

speciosa (fig. "Bot. Mag." 1937 and 3206).—Brazil. All the
so-called Gloxinias, with erect and pendulous flowers, so largely
grown in many establishments, are hybrids or varieties of this
species, which is now called 'Sinningia,' though it will probably
be long before horticulturists give up the old name. See also
"Bot. Reg." 1127 and "Bot. Mag." 3934.

Var. **Menziesiana** (fig. "Bot. Mag." 4943).

variabilis (fig. "Rev. Hort." [1877], 70).—Habitat (?). Peduncles
very long; flowers very large, white, copiously pink-spotted, not
very distinct from *speciosa*; if a species and not a hybrid itself it
is probably the origin of all the spotted forms of *speciosa*.

velutina (fig. Loddig. "Bot. Cat." 1898).—Brazil. Stem purple,
erect, leafy, 1½ foot high; peduncle shorter than calyx; calyx
sub-campanulate, 1 inch long, segments triangular; corolla pale
green, nearly 2 inches long.

villosa (fig. "Bot. Reg." 1134).—Brazil. Stem erect, thick,
1 foot high; peduncles shorter than leaves, aggregate in the
axils; calyx campanulate, spreading; corolla yellowish-green,
2 inches long.

Youngeana (fig. "Bot. Mag." 4954).—Hybrid between *speciosa*
and *velutina*; peduncles three times length of petioles; flowers
axillary or terminal, solitary; corolla large, deep violet.

Rosanovia.—"Gartenfl." xxi. 33. This genus is now referred by
botanists to **Sinningia,** but for horticultural purposes the
former name may remain in use; they are handsome stove
plants, with tuberous roots; large flowers, almost always some
shade of yellow, borne on axillary peduncles.

conspicua (fig. "Gartenflora," 712).—Brazil. Peduncles axillary,
solitary, long; flowers yellow, marbled and dotted with purple
inside the tube. Var. *ornata*, "Fl. des Serres," 2423–4,
is a hybrid; flowers whitish or very pale buff, mottled rose.

Continental establishments have hybridised here very largely,
and many varieties are offered; as far as I have seen them they
are all very similar to *conspicua*; they are very easily grown,

but the tubers must be carefully looked after in the winter or after the plant dies down, and not be allowed to get too dry or too wet.

Sorenophora endlicheriana (fig. "Fl. des Serres," 546).—Mexico. Flowers bell-shaped, hairy outside, 3 inches long, orange, blotched purple, solitary, or in fascicles.

Stauranthera grandiflora (fig. "Bot. Mag." 5409).—Moulmein. Flowers paniculate, bell-shaped, white, tinged with purple and yellow, 1 inch long.

Streptocarpus caulescens (fig. "Bot. Mag." 6814).—Tropical Africa. Hairy plant; peduncle axillary, much longer than the leaves, dichotomously branched into a cyme at the apex; flowers small, white, lilac-streaked, allied to *Kirkii*; a stove species.

Fanninii, Harv. ex C. B. Clark in DC., "Mon. Phan." v. 150 (not figured).—Natal. Leaf solitary, elongate-oblong; cymes long-peduncled, many-flowered; calyx large; corolla tube curved.

Galpinii (fig. "Bot. Mag." 7230).—Transvaal. A fine species with terminal racemes of large blue flowers; leaf radical, solitary.

Gardenii (fig. "Bot. Mag." 4862).—Natal. A fine species, allied to *Rexii*; leaves radical.

Holstii (fig. "Engl. Bot. Jahrb." xviii. t. 4, 5).—Tropical East Africa. A pretty, delicate, erect-branched stove plant; flowers bright blue; stems succulent, dark purple, "Bot. Mag." 8150.

Kirkii (fig. "Bot. Mag." 6782).—Tropical East Africa. Small stove species; fleshy stems; flowers small lilac, in axillary loose cymes; a pretty, small pot plant.

parviflorus (fig. "Bot. Mag." 7036).—South Africa. A greenhouse species; leaves radical; scapes 6–10 inches high, racemose; flowers $\frac{2}{3}$ inch long, slightly recurved, white and violet.

polyanthus (fig. "Bot. Mag." 4850).—Natal. Greenhouse species; leaves few, radical, close to the soil; scapes 1–3, about 12 inches high, panicled; flowers pale blue, rather large; a pretty pot plant.

Rexii (fig. "Bot. Mag." 3005).—"Bot. Reg." 1173. South Africa. A well-known species, but improved out of existence by the hybrids. Nearly all the garden hybrids raised so largely in nearly all nurseries and in many private establishments are off this species and its hybrids crossed with *Dunnii, Saundersonii, Wendlandii, polyanthus*, and others; they are too numerous and well known to require much notice here. They are very useful and beautiful plants; they should be raised every January or February from seed, as the old plants should seldom be kept for more than two years; they require a shaded situation in a greenhouse and plenty of water when growing; except when young difficult to keep in health through the winter. *Achemeniflora* and *grata* are particularly good hybrids, raised at Veitch's. The following are large, rather ungainly species, more adapted for botanical than private gardens:—**Dunnii** (fig. "Bot. Mag." 6903). Transvaal. Large leaves, reddish flowers; **grandis** (fig. "Bot. Mag." 8042). South Africa, a large species, large solitary leaf ; small pale blue paniculate flowers. **Saundersii** (fig. "Bot. Mag." 5251). South Africa. A coarse species with large leaves ; flowers pale blue. **Wendlandii** (fig. "Bot. Mag." 7447). Natal, in the way of **Dunnii**, but with blue flowers ; these have all been used for hybridising.

Trichantha minor (fig. "Bot. Mag." 5428).—Guayaquil. . Lovely stove climber ; calyx ciliate, deeply 5-cut, the lobes pinnatifid ; flower long, tubular, crinite, tube blackish-purple, mouth yellow, on 1-flowered peduncles, which are aggregate in the axils ; leaves opposite, very unequal in size.

Tussacia pulchella (fig. "Bot. Mag." 1146).—West Indies. A pretty stove plant ; calyx red ; lobes deltoid, serrate ; corolla 1½ inch long, yellow, erect, cylindrical ; an easily grown and rather common plant in our stoves.

semiclausa (fig. "L'Ill. Hort." ser. ii. 28).—Brazil. Calyx red, campanulate, truncate ; corolla yellow, striped crimson, in short terminal umbels ; a showy plant.

Tydaea. See **Isoloma.**

A BUNDLE OF HERBS.

By Miss H. C. PHILBRICK, F.R.H.S.

TIME was when every well-regulated garden grew its quota of herbs ; now they are rarely found save and except in the gardens of the old-fashioned country mansion and here and there in the garden of the cottager. Probably the ease with which dried herbs can be obtained in packets has had most to answer for in the decline of the herb in popular favour, but certain it is that our gardens are the poorer for the absence of such sweet old-time favourites as rue and rosemary, mint and marjoram, thyme and tarragon, sage and savoury, balm and basil, chervil and chamomile. I purpose taking the most useful and familiar herbs as the subject matter of my paper, and give an account as best I can of their properties, their uses, their native homes, the mode of growing them, and the part they have played in science, art, literature, history, poetry, and the drama.

I take the familiar garden parsley first. It is a hardy biennial, a native of Sardinia, and was introduced into this country about the middle of the sixteenth century. There are three varieties, two of which are well known and commonly used as pot herbs and for garnishing, namely, the common or plain-leaved, the curled, and the Hamburg large- or carrot-rooted, which last is cultivated only for its roots, which are used occasionally like young carrots. The curled variety is by far the most useful, and from its beautiful foliage cannot be mistaken for the 'fool's parsley,' a poisonous plant somewhat resembling the plain-leaved variety. Their cultivation, as all gardeners know far better than I can tell them, is that of sowing, usually in the spring, in shallow drills about a foot apart, or in single rows along the borders of the kitchen garden. 'Myatt's garnishing' is a good sort to grow. The Hamburg or carrot-rooted variety requires a light soil, such as would suit the carrot, and you may safely give it the same treatment. Parsley was formerly used for garlands, and is mentioned by both Virgil and Horace. In winter, sometimes, the demand is great and the supply very small ; it is therefore well to cover some plants for winter use with hand glasses, so as not to be without it. I may here mention that our friends and neighbours of la belle France have a great penchant for field parsley and in midwinter parsley often fetches a high price for this reason.

Hares and rabbits find it a very choice and toothsome morsel, and will travel a long way to get it ; if the garden be near a wood or at all exposed they will come and rob you of it all, as gardeners know only too well. On the other hand, should you ever by chance want to entice rabbits into a meadow, all you need do is to plant some parsley.

Chervil is another plant of the same nature as parsley : its leaves are valuable to add to salads, or to flavour soups. The seed, however, does not keep well and should be sown as soon as ripe. It likes a moist, shady situation. If not sown when the seed falls it may be sown at the same time as parsley and lightly covered with earth ; only a small patch of it will be required.

Thyme (*Thymus vulgaris*).—Common or garden thyme is a native of the south-west parts of Europe, in dry plains and on hills and uncultivated places free from woods. The plant is very much branched and has purplish flowers. This species is cultivated for flavouring purposes, and many varieties of it are to be met with in gardens. It has a pungent, aromatic odour and taste, which depend upon an essential oil, an ounce of which can be extracted from thirty pounds of the plant. One of the varieties, *Thymus citratus*, is known by the name of ' lemon thyme ' on account of the scent somewhat resembling that of the lemon. The best mode of propagating thyme is by means of cuttings.

Sage (*Salvia*), perhaps from *salvus*, healthy. — The best-known species in this country, and that which is most frequently used, is the *Salvia officinalis*, the garden sage. It is a native of various parts of the south of Europe. It is a low, straggling shrub, with erect branches, hoary with down and leafy at the base. It is much used in cookery, and is supposed to assist in digesting fat and luscious foods. Sage-tea is also commended as a stomachic and slight stimulant. It is said that the Chinese prefer an infusion of sage-leaves to that of their own delicious tea, and that the Dutch at one time carried on a profitable traffic by carrying sage leaves to China and bringing back four times their weight in tea. Sage-tea, with the addition of a small quantity of vinegar, is a valuable remedy as a gargle for sore throat. I need hardly mention that sage is used also for sauce and stuffing to flavour pork, ducks, and geese.

Lavender.—A hoary, narrow-leaved fragrant plant or bush growing in the south of Europe, the Canaries, Barbary, Egypt, Persia, and the west of India, with generally blue flowers, though there is a white variety. I prefer to spell its name as its colour, and call it lavender. The flowers are arranged in close terminal simple or branched spikes. Twelve species are described, of which only two are of general interest, viz. the common lavender and French *L. spica* : both are natives of sterile hills in the south of Europe and Barbary. The former yields the fragrant oil of lavender so extensively employed in perfumery, and the latter "oil of spike," employed by painters on porcelain, and in the preparation of varnishes for artists. Our great-grandmothers delighted to put sprigs of lavender among their napery and fine linen, and in many houses the custom continues to the present time. It has of late been used considerably in table decorations—a new use for it—and the effect was very good when the colours harmonised.

Rue.—The plant is known botanically as *Ruta graveolens.* The ancients probably used also another species, common in Palestine, Malta, &c. The former is a native of the Mediterranean regions, and was formerly eaten as well as highly valued as a drug ; indeed Pliny mentions eighty-four remedies attributable to it. It has long been cultivated in our gardens as a domestic medicine, as it was formerly held in England in great repute, and it is still included in our " Pharmacopœia." It was thought, doubtless from its powerful odour, to be strongly antiseptic in resisting contagions as well as to be an antidote to poisons. Rue leaves and salt are said to have been the antidote which Mithridates took to guard himself against being poisoned. Though usually, if not always, considered nauseous by us moderns, Pliny tells us that "the ancients held rue in peculiar esteem, for I find that honeyed wine flavoured with rue was distributed to the people in his consulship. Rue was called 'herb o' grace' in the sixteenth century. Thus Ophelia says in the play of "Hamlet," "There's rue for you, and here's some for me, we may call it the herb of grace o' Sundays." It is said to be still called 'Ave grace' in Sussex, apparently a remnant from the common invocation "Ave Maria, gratia plena." Jeremy Taylor refers to an employment of rue in "exorcisms," which plant, he says, thence, as we suppose, came to be called 'herb of grace.' Others have suggested different sources for the expression. Thus, as the word "rue" means repentance, and requires God's grace, it became the basis of a play upon words in the older dramatists, as in "King Richard II.": "Ill set a bank of rue, sour herb of grace," &c. And again from "Winter's Tale" come these words: "For you there's rosemary and rue, these keep seeming and savour all the winter long." Cimaruta, sprig of rue (herb of grace), forms part of one of the amulets or charms worn by Neapolitans against the evil eye, and dates from pagan times.

Rosmarinus officinalis, the common rosemary, is a native of the southern parts of France, Spain, and Italy, and the basin of the Mediterranean, growing to the height of three or four feet on the hills. The cultivated and garden plants differ very much in the shape and number of their leaves, on which account Millar describes them as two species. The size of the leaves varies with the soil and situation in which the plant grows. It is generally observed that the broader and longer the leaves the more vigorous is the plant. The rosemary is a very desirable plant for the garden, both on account of its evergreen character and its flowers, which appear from January to April. There are three varieties known in gardens—the green or common, the gold-striped, and the silver-striped—which are distinguished principally by the colour of their leaves. The green variety is the hardiest and the most generally used. It may be propagated by seeds, or cuttings of the young shoots. The striped varieties may be propagated by layers of the young wood: they should be planted in a warm situation, as they are far more tender than the green, and are only cultivated as ornamental plants on account of their variegated leaves. The rosemary abounds in the district of Narbonne, in France, where it is used to form hedges for gardens &c.; and it is supposed to be the aroma of this plant, gathered by the bees, that gives to the honey of this district its peculiarly fine flavour. Rosemary was formerly held in high esteem, especially on the Continent, and in the songs of the troubadours it is frequently mentioned as an emblem of constancy and devotion to the fair sex. It was thought to be a comforter of the brain and a strengthener of the memory, and on the latter account used as a sign of fidelity between lovers. Shakespeare makes Ophelia say, "There's rosemary; that's for remembrance." In some parts of Germany rosemary is grown in large quantities in pots, for the purpose of selling small sprigs of it, when in flower in winter and early spring, for religious purposes. Rosemary possesses valuable stimulant and carminative properties, but it is chiefly employed as a perfume, entering into the composition of "The Queen of Hungary Water," eau-de-Cologne, and aromatic vinegar. It is also said to promote the growth of the hair, and is frequently used in hair-washes, and is supposed to prevent baldness.

Balm, a contraction of ' Balsam.'—There are several plants known under this name. The ordinary balm (*Melissa officinalis*) is one of the most fragrant of aromatic herbs : it is a perennial, a native of France and Switzerland, and grows in any good garden soil, and should be divided every spring to keep up a good stock of young plants. It is used in cooling "cups" and dainty drinks. Another variety—Balm of Gilead—belongs to the genus *Balsamodendron*. Its leaves when bruised yield a strong aromatic scent, and from this plant it is that the balm of Gilead of the shops, or balsam of Mecca, or of Syria, is obtained. It has a yellowish greenish colour, a warm, bitterish, aromatic taste, and an acidulous, fragrant smell. It is valued as a cosmetic by the Turks, who possess the country of its growth, and who adulterate it for the market. It is also used for the high purposes of anointing, and recalls the glorious and undying words of the immortal bard :

> " Not all the water in the rough, rude sea
> Can wash the balm from an anointed king."
>
> *King Richard II.*, act iii. sc. 2.

Basil.—There are two useful varieties, bush, and sweet basil : the bush form is a native of the East Indies, and is raised from seed sown in a pot towards the end of March. It is an annual and rather tender. The sweet basil, of kitchen fame, requires similar treatment. It also is a native of the East Indies, and is quite as tender as the preceding, but is somewhat larger. Both plants flower about July, when they should be taken up and dried in an airy shed for winter use. It is the proper herb for flavouring turtle soup and for " cups."

Chamomile.—Either the double- or single-flowered form may be used ; both like a sandy soil, and may be propagated by stripping off the side-shoots, with a few roots attached, in April or May. Formerly growers always used to tread over chamomile when growing to strengthen the plants. The flowers used for chamomile-tea are gathered in July and dried in slight sunshine. The single- is better flavoured than the double-flowered form.

Mint is such an indispensable adjunct of new potatoes and green peas (though very many cooks spoil the peas by putting too much mint with them) that room should be found for a few roots in every garden. It likes a moist situation and rather a " holding " soil ; cuttings strike easily when the stock is short, or the old roots may be divided. It is never advisable to allow a mint bed to remain more than three years without breaking it up, or the mint-rust may attack it and destroy the plants. *Mentha viridis* (the spearmint) is the best species for garden cultivation. It is a native of Great Britain, and its poetic meaning is the warmth of sentiment. Pennyroyal is another species of mint, and is used for the same purpose as peppermint.

I should like to mention Burnet (*Poterium Sanguisorba*); wild thyme, and water-mints. Burnet is grown in some gardens, especially where the owner has lived in France : it is wild in some districts of England ; its leaves are used in salads, and give to them a peculiar cucumber flavour. Let me quote from Bacon, where he speaks of these herbs : " But those that perfume the air most delightfully, not passed by as the rest, but being trodden upon and crushed, are three—that is, burnet, wild thyme, and water-mints. Therefore you are to set whole alleys of them, to have the pleasure when you walk or tread." And again, from " A Midsummer Night's Dream," we almost catch the fragrance :

> " I know a bank whereon the wild thyme blows,
> Where oxlips and the nodding violet grows."

Marjoram (*Origanum vulgare*).—There are three varieties, one an aromatic pot herb, native of Portugal, used largely both in France and England for flavouring soups. It is sometimes represented in gardens by a wilding form. It should be planted in a sandy soil and divided in March. It likes a hot sunny spot, and runs rampant on chalk hills, being the best beloved of butterflies. It may be planted in patches in gardens or shrubberies, where bees are kept, for the fragrance of the flowers and the delight which the bees appear to have in them. Sweet marjoram (*O. Marjorana*), though really a perennial, is always treated as an annual, as it will not stand frost.

Tarragon.—Its leaves are used for flavouring soups, and just a suspicion of it is a great improvement to salad. It is also used extensively in making the piquant Tarragon vinegar our French friends are so fond of. It is a somewhat delicate plant and cannot always brave our cold winters ; therefore wise gardeners will make a little new plantation every spring, if needed.

Marigold (*Calendula officinalis*), pot marigold.—An interesting old hardy biennial ; one of the best for autumn and winter flowering in almost every garden. The petals were formerly used to flavour dishes in old English cookery, hence its name. A number of varieties are now offered by the seed houses. For late blooming, seed should be sown in July. The plants usually sow themselves freely, and may be sown in the open ground in spring and autumn. Canaries are very fond of the blossoms, and it greatly improves and deepens the colour of their plumage. Shakespeare speaks of it in " A Winter's Tale " thus :

> " Here's flowers for you ;
> Hot lavender, mints, savory, marjoram,
> And marigold that goes to bed with the sun,
> And with him rises weeping : these are flowers
> Of middle summer, and I think they are given
> To men of middle age."

Before I conclude I should like to add my mite, by way of an expression of gratitude, to the memory of the monks of old—those grand old gardeners who loved their gardens, and who brought to England so many plants the benefit of which we are all of us reaping in these twentieth-century days. They give us a fascinating peep into the past and a practical realisation in the present. Surely such "actions" as these, as James Shirley puts it, "smell sweet and blossom in the dust."

> "God of the granite and the rose,
>   Soul of the lily and the bee,
>   The mighty tide of being flows
>   In countless channels, Lord, from Thee.
>   It springs to life in grass and flowers,
>   Through every stage of being runs,
>   And from creation's mighty towers
>   Its glory flames in stars and suns."

ORNAMENTAL GRASSES (*GRAMINEAE*).

By WALTER SMYTH.

THE title is not altogether a popular one, for the ordinary mind treats the subject of ornamental grasses in much the same way as the gentleman who was invited by a lady to come and see her collection. Looking at the beautiful graceful grasses, he said "Yes, they are lovely, but what a splendid place this would be for a donkey." "Yes, indeed," replied his hostess, slily, and, after a short pause, "I do hope you feel quite at home."

The culture of these graceful plants, considering their beauty and attractiveness, is far too limited, I think, in our gardens of to-day. So it may be of interest and use to describe some of the most beautiful of them ; but before doing so it would be desirable to mention something about our natural grasses, and one finds on studying this subject that there are forty-two genera in all, represented by such names as *Festuca*, *Bromus*, *Briza*, *Hordeum*, *Poa*, *Melica*, and *Arundo*. Many of these would be entirely useless, if not pernicious, in our gardens, but from them and foreign grasses and sedges the ornamental varieties which do so much to decorate our gardens to-day have sprung. I prefer myself to cultivate the perennial varieties, as, being permanent growers, they give a lasting result to the initial trouble taken in raising them ; but there are many handsome annual varieties, which are most useful for association with other flowers in the decoration and adornment of our home. The grasses which one finds in our country meadows are in a degree pretty, and children should be encouraged to observe the difference in them ; but one must go abroad for noble specimens ; for instance, the so-called Pampas grass was originally introduced from the banks of the Parana and other rivers in South America. The Arundos come from the South of Europe, the Elymuses from North America, the Panicums from the East and West Indies, and *Achnodonton Bellardii* from the sea coast of Mesopotamia.

The Pampas grasses are such favourite plants on lawn and hardy borders that the following notes on their culture and qualities, which were written about fifty years ago, are so concise that they are worthy of notice and perusal now : "The seeds must be sown in pots, and covered very lightly with sandy loam and peat. Then the pots must be placed in a slight heat until the blades are developed. The young plants must then be separated, and only a few put into each pot ; a cool frame is best adapted to them at this stage, and they require to be well watered. On being finally put out, the place must be prepared for them with plenty of mellow loam and must be in a moist situation. This grass has the male and the female blossoms on different plants. The latter is the one generally preferred as being best suited to our climate. It soon develops a large circular tuft of leaves, which attains a length of several feet and bends upwards in the style so much admired in the colonial ferns, until the abundance of arching foliage resembles the graceful streams of a fountain. From the centre of this group arise a number of perpendicular culms, the apices at first seeming only thickened, but shortly developing a folded sheath, within which rest the closely packed flower-buds; these culms shoot up with such rapidity that they have been known to grow an inch in twenty-four hours, and they attain their full length of from five to seven feet in September. Then the sheath opens gradually, and the inflorescence emerges by degrees, at first as a closely packed head, then exhibiting its complex structure of branches and buds, and by the end of October developing its full glory of a spreading panicle a foot long, and numerous feathery flowers, so white and glossy as to shine like silver, and so lightly mounted on their slender branches that they wave and tremble with every zephyr. The male plant differs in the foliage, being less graceful, and the inflorescence later in opening. The latter habit unfits the plant for out-door culture in Britain, as it leaves little chance of the flowers being perfected before the early frost, and the culms being then full of sap are unable to stand the cold and so perish before the flower can expand. The best way of utilising the beauty of the male plant is to cut the unopened panicles before the coming of frost. The heads should then be carefully dried and the sheaths stripped off; the young florets lying snug within seem made of frosted silver, but so closely packed that they present the appearance of a solid body. But when this compressed cloud of silver blossoms is gently and repeatedly shaken they separate, and the true form of the branching rachis soon becomes developed. Thus treated, the heads which some night would have perished, leaving their latent beauty un-developed and almost unsuspected, become the most lovely objects for drawing-room decoration possible."

The propagation of ornamental grasses is much the same as that of other plants—that is to say, when one wants them early, as in the case of annuals, it is necessary to sow in a slight heat under glass. This treat-ment must be resorted to in the case of perennials in order to get some flowers the same year, otherwise sowing in April or May in the open air will give fine plants for flowering the following season.

The best and most elegant of the annuals are: *Agrostis laxiflora,* *A. nebulosa,* *A. gracilis,* *Briza gracilis,* *B. geniculata,* *Eragrostis elegans,* *E. namaquensis,* *E. papposa,* *Hordeum jubatum,* *Lagurus ovatus,* *Tricholaena rosea*; and the best perennial grasses are, the Gyneriums, the Arundos, *Apera arundinacea*; the Eulalias and the Phormiums (New Zealand Flax) also may be added. A more complete list of the best annuals and perennials which from time to time have been introduced into this country is given at the end of this paper. Ornamental grasses, like yuccas, bamboos, silver birch, and other ornamental plants and shrubs, give an air of refinement and as it were the finishing touch to the gardener's art, and they are quite unsurpassed on the verge of a lake where such varieties are chosen as the Gyneriums, the Phormiums and the Arundos, the Poas, and the new grass *Glyceris aquatica variegata*; these in company with the Japanese Iris, the tall Spireas, and Gunneras and other strong plants of these classes, look at their best and are very attractive, and what can be prettier by the side of a rippling stream or by the broad bosom of a river, shining in its depths on a summer's day than the tall plumes of the Pampas grasses making the surroundings look like fairyland ? In the rock garden also the dwarf varieties, such as *Bromus Brizaeformis, Lasiogrostis argentea,* are seen to advantage when judiciously placed, and along the verge of walks some may be used to advantage—*Festuca glauca, Dactylis elegantissima* for example. At the base of a post or of an arch they are also useful, and here *Stipa pennata* may be used. The old and well-known custom of gathering these grasses for winter decorations is a popular one, and for this purpose they should be well dried in the autumn and utilised with everlasting flowers and the silver moons of *Lunaria biennis* and the tall spikes of the giant reed. The well-known names of garden quaker's ribbon grass, feather grass, ladies' lace windle straw, love grass, Job's tears, quaking grass, pear grass, dog's tail grass, and others bring to memory old-fashioned gardens in which hours of content have been spent.

The derivation of the names of some of these grasses is very interesting ; for instance, the Brizas or quaking grasses come from the Greek "Brizo," to nod, so one may infer that these grasses decorated the artistic homes of ancient Greece and Rome. Eragrostis, the love grass, is also derived from the Greek 'Eros,' Love, and 'agrostis,' a kind of grass. There are many other interesting derivations worthy of notice and thought.

ANNUALS.

Agrostis nebulosa · · · ·	Very fine for bouquets.
„ *laxiflora* · · ·	Pretty.
„ *pulchella* · · ·	Pretty dwarf species.
„ *Stevenii* · · ·	Tall, beautiful.
„ *gracilis* · · ·	Very elegant.
Anthoxanthum gracile · ·	Pretty, graceful.
Asprella Hystrix	
Avena sterilis · · · ·	The animated oat.
Briza geniculata · · ·	A spreading species.
„ *gracilis* · · · ·	Small quaking grass.
„ *maxima* · · · ·	Large quaking grass.
„ *compacta* · · ·	Compact habit, very fine and pretty.
„ *rotundata*	
„ *minima* dwarf	
Brizopyrum siculum · · ·	Very ornamental.
Bromus Brizaeformis · ·	A beautiful grass with elegant hanging ears.
„ *macrostachys* · · ·	Useful for decoration.
„ *lanuginosus* · · ·	Very pretty.
„ *madritensis* · · ·	Charming, very fine for dyeing.
„ *patulus nanus* (new) ·	Very pretty.
Chloris barbata (Finger-grass) ·	Bearded spikes.
„ *elegans* · · · · ·	Elegant and slender.
Chrysurus aurea · · · ·	Dense golden spikes.
Coix lacryma-Jobi (Job's tears) · ·	Curious.
Cryptopyrum Richardsoni · · · · ·	

Diplachne fascicularis . .	Fine border grass.
Eleusine barcinonensis	
„ *coracana* . . .	Spreading habit.
„ *indica*	A dwarf Chinese species curiously horned.
„ *oligostachya* . .	Pretty.
Eragrostis amabilis capillaris .	Very pretty, from Abyssinia.
„ *elegans* (Love grass)	
„ *maxima*, from Abyssinia	
„ *namaquensis* . .	Dwarf spreading
„ *papposa* . . .	Very graceful.
Hordeum vulgare	
Lagurus ovatus (Hare's tail grass)	
Leptochloa gracilis	
Lamarckia aurea	
Melica ciliata	
„ „ *alba*	
Miscanthus sinensis . . .	Very striking.
Panicum altissimum	
„ *colonum*	
„ *spectabile* . . .	Of enormous size.
„ *teneriffae* . . .	Has very pretty beautiful rosy spikes.
Paspalum elegans . . .	Pretty for borders.
Pennisetum fimbriatum .	Very distinct.
„ *longistylum* .	Charming, very graceful.
„ *macrourum* .	Grows to a height of $4\frac{1}{2}$ feet, with white and silk-like panicles.
„ *ruppellii* . .	A very fine miniature Pampas grass; one of the most graceful of grasses.
Setaria macrochaeta .	With drooping plumes of a graceful appearance.
Stipa lagascae . . .	The prettiest feather grass.
Tricholaena rosea	
Triticum violaceum	
Urachne parviflorum .	A very graceful species.
Zea Curagua (Giant maize)	
„ *gracillima* (Miniature maize)	Very pretty.
„ „ *variegata* . .	Very pretty.
„ *japonica foliis variegatis* (Striped maize)	
„ *tunicata variegata*	

PERENNIALS.

Agrostis stolonifera	
Ammophila brevispilis	
Andropogon argenteus . .	A fine border grass.
„ *macrourus* . .	Has silky plumes 2 feet high.
Apera arundinacea . . .	Pheasant's tail grass, and most elegant of all grasses, with elegant arching plumes.

Arrhenathrum bulbosum fol. var.   A neat and very graceful silvery variegated grass.

Arundo Donax

   ,,   *conspicua*   .   .   .   Similar to Pampas grass, but earlier.

   ,,   *Donax variegata*

   ,,   ,,   *macrophylla*

Asperella Hystrix

Briza media

Bromus Brizaeformis   .   .   Elegant Briza-like.

   ,,   *macrostachys*   .   .   Useful for decoration.

Calamagrostis brevispila

   ,,   *Nuttalii*   .   .   Handsome.

Carex alba

   ,,   *Buchanani*   .   .   .   A pretty grass with narrow, purple tinted leaves.

   ,,   *elegantissima*

   ,,   *gallica variegata*   .   .   Two pretty grasses of dwarf habit.

   ,,   *marginata*   .   .   .   A strong golden variegated species.

Cryptopyrum Richardsoni

Dactylis glomerata variegata

   ,,   ,,   *elegantissima*   Dwarf silver-striped grass; lovely for edging purposes.

Deschampsia flexuosa

   ,,   *caespitosa*

Deyenxia Nuttaliana   .   .   Handsome.

Digitaria sanguinale

Diplachne fascicularis

Elymus arenarius   .   .   .   Lime grass; a good plant for a wild garden, quickly forming masses of bluish foliage.

   ,,   *giganteus*   .   .   .   A noble grass with huge wheat-like heads.

   ,,   *glaucus*

   ,,   *hystrix*

Eragrostis grandiflora

   ,,   *pectinata spectabilis*

Erianthus Ravennae .   .   .   Resembles the Pampas grass.

Festuca ovina   .   .   .   Fine for edgings; colour, a lovely tint of bluish grey.

   ,,   *rigida*

   ,,   *clavata*

Gynerium argenteum (Pampas grass)   Good plants; like a well-drained rich soil.

   ,,   *Bertinii*

   ,,   *elegans*   .   .   .   A lovely new grass.

Gymnotherix latifolia   .   .   Gynerium-like.

Glyceria aquatica variegata   .   A lovely new grass; useful for moist situation and lakeside.

White-plumed Varieties.

Gynerium argenteum . .	Marabout : The finest of all the white-flowered varieties.
. .	Monstrum : A form which produces immense snow-white plumes.
. .	Soyeux.

Rosy-plumed Varieties.

.. · ,,   Carmineum Rendalteri.
,,   Gloire du Muséum.
,,   Louis Carrière. .
,,   Roi des Roses : Pyramidal plumes of deep rose.

Variegated Varieties.

,,   albo-lineatum
,,   aureo-lineatum
,,   variegatum novum : Narrow white stripe.
,,   ,,   Wesselingii variegatum
,,   *jubatum*

Hordeum jubatum . . .	Is generally treated as an annual.
Isolepis gracilis . . .	: Suitable for pot culture.
Lasiagrostis argentea . .	Silver panicles.
Melica altissima . . .	A very pretty grass.
,, ,, *atropurpurea* . .	Exceedingly useful for bouquets and decorative purposes.
Miscanthus sinensis . . .	A very elegant grass indeed ; it has narrow leaves, 3–5 feet long, and makes a splendid clump.
Molinia caerulea variegata .	A very pretty dwarf variegated grass.
Panicum virgatum . . .	A very distinct and handsome plant, 4–6 feet high, with purplish drooping and curiously twisted flower heads.
,, *plicatum* . . .	Very beautiful.
,, *sulcatum*	Palm-like, very elegant, suitable for pots.
Pennisetum compressum	
,, *macrourum*	
,, *orientale*	
Phalaris arundinacea variegata	The old variegated ribbon grass ; invaluable for massing in a wild garden or by the waterside.
Phormium tenax (New Zealand flax)	A most distinct and striking plant, with long and broad leaves, 5–8 feet high, and making a clump of fine glaucous green foliage.

Phormium tenax variegatum .	A fine variegated form of *tenax*, with broad linear markings of yellow; perfectly hardy, has withstood a temperature of 28° Fahr. without the slightest injury.
Phragmites communis aurea variegata	A handsome variegated form of the lakeside reed.
Pollinia gracillima	
Saccharum Maddeni	
Sorghum halepense perenne .	In a warm situation will grow up to 10 feet.
Stipa pennata (Feather grass)	
„ *elegantissima* . . .	A very graceful grass.
„ *gigantea* (Giant) .	
Trichloris verticillata . .	With rose-coloured ears.
Uniola latifolia	Useful for bouquets ; very pretty.

The following names are included in the above list; though they are not to be found in the "Index Kewensis," they are known in the trade :—

Agrostis Stevenii.

Apera arundinacea.

Briza compacta.

Brizopyrum siculum.

Bromus lanuginosus.

Carex elegantissima.

„ *gallica variegata.*

Cryptopyrum Richardsonii.

Erianthus Ravennae.

Eragrostis pectinata.

Gymnotherix latifolia.

Gynerium Bertinii.

Panicum sulcatum.

Pasopalum elegans.

Pennisetum fimbriatum.

Saccharum Maddeni.

Zea gracillima.

„ „ *variegata.*

„ *japonica foliis variegatis.*

„ *tunicata variegata.*

NATURAL SELECTION.

By CHARLES T. DRUERY, V.M.H., F.L.S.

ON perusing the several articles by Professor Henslow in your Journal of December 1906 I find that his observations on the Darwinian theory are based throughout on definite assertions which so utterly clash with my own personal experiences in the study of variation, both under wild and cultivated conditions, that I venture to claim the privilege of the same channel of publication in order to put forward the facts, not the theories, which to my mind utterly controvert them. In order that as a preliminary the nature of my experience may be properly weighed it may be well for me to mention that for the last thirty years I have made a special study of variation in our native ferns, hunting for varieties in many parts of the kingdom and being successful in finding a considerable number. In this way I have naturally become intimately acquainted with the conditions under which these marked varieties occur, and as I have subsequently bred from them culturally, I am also practically familiar with that side of the subject. In addition to my individual experience this pursuit has brought me into communication with a number of gentlemen who had, and have, the same hobby and represent the pioneers and their successors in continuous and well-recorded varietal research extending now over considerably more than half a century. The result of all this is that our few species of native ferns constitute a plant family entirely unique among the plants of the world in having been most attentively studied by a large number of intelligent persons from the point of view of spontaneous wild variation of which fully two thousand cases are recorded.

They are unique, too, in another sense, since not only have records been kept throughout that period, and nature prints taken of the most marked forms, but the identical plants themselves largely survive in a living state, leaving thus nothing to the imagination as regards their character or their constancy. With this preliminary I will now quote seriatim those assertions of Professor Henslow to which I have alluded, numbering them for simplicity of reference and following them up with the facts which appear to my mind to confute them entirely.

1. "Plants and animals do not die in consequence of slight variation of structure. Darwin's theory therefore falls to the ground" (p. 90, R.H.S. JOURNAL, December 1906).

2. "But, apart from abnormal monstrosities, nature has never been known to make ' ill-adapted types ' " (p. 90, December 1906).

These are both unqualified assertions incapable of proof, but on the contrary easily disproved. With reference to No. 2 I have in a previous article alluded to the disadvantage of dwarfing variation to the individual plant, but as a recognisable instance of nature making an ill-adapted type (i.e. of course in the struggle for existence) I will take the dwarf specimen of humanity, General Tom Thumb, and ask, what chance of survival would he have had had he been born into a community of savages whose individual existence depended entirely upon their own strength, speed, and ability to defend themselves against wild animals and antagonistic tribes? Granted this case, the assertion is confuted, but anyone who raises variable plants from seed and spore knows full well that some of the varieties vary very much the wrong way, dwarfed, depauperate, and altogether unfitted for the battle of life. What are these but "ill-adapted varieties"? And where will be found a selective cultivator who does not suffer from them, and why are we to assume that such misfits do not occur under wild conditions as well? Furthermore what must we say of such variations as involve sterility, such as perfectly double flowers which bear no seed? Surely these from the natural point of view are ill-adapted variations, yet they occur under wild conditions, and a number of perfectly barren fern sports have been found. Returning now to No. 1 is it not reasonable to impute the "miffiness" of many plants which outwardly resemble their robust relatives to "slight variations of structure"? Constitution and structure are presumably correlated, and liability to disease or defective assimilation is equally presumably due to subtle differences in the cell structure which is the basis of the plant. A very slight difference in human structure facilitating appendicitis may also be fatal. This to my mind disposes of No. 1 and No. 2.

3. "There is no question of *origin* but only of the *distribution* of existing species by means of natural selection" (p. 91). "But in originating new varieties and species the struggle for life is really not required at all. Indeed, new varieties arise much better without it, as every horticulturist knows and takes care that it should be so ". (p. 91).

Considering that Darwin's whole theory is based on the fact that existing species differ from old and extinct ones, on gradational lines, and that he set himself to account for their origin by evolution the one from the other, it is extremely curious that Professor Henslow should say, " There is no question of *origin* but only of the *distribution* of *existing* [my italics here] species by means of natural selection." He ignores the very pith of Darwin's doctrines. Then with regard to the last clause of No. 3 : " But in originating new varieties and species the struggle for life is really not required at all. Indeed, new varieties arise much better without it, as every horticulturist knows and takes care that it should be so." What on earth has this to do with *natural* selection, where the plants have to fight their own battle and survive or perish according as they are best or least fitted for the struggle? In point of fact, however, the horticulturist by weeding out the imperfect ones according to his ideal and selecting the best or fittest in that connection introduces a struggle for existence on quite parallel lines, and he only arrives at his successes as a rule after ruthless slaughter. As a selective fern cultivator I can assert it is this weeding-out which is one of the most painful processes in the cult.

4. Replying to Professor Darwin's remarks implying ill-adapted as well as well-adapted variations, Professor Henslow says :—

" This has been long shown to be erroneous. Experiments prove that *all* the seedlings of a plant *vary alike* and in direct response to the new conditions "; he then continues : " This fact puts natural selection, as a means in the origin of species, out of court, for there are no different or ' indefinite ' variations.".

This is really extraordinary, especially the assertion that "experience proves that *all* the seedlings of a plant *vary alike* and in direct response to the new conditions," and in this particular connection I very much fear that Professor Henslow will have a difficulty in finding any practical plant grower who will endorse his so-called "fact," and until he can do so I need not dispute the very broad assertion based upon it. As a case in point I have recently seen at Messrs. Sutton's, at Reading, a number of potato seedlings all raised from seed contained in one berry, and no two plants were alike in haulm or tuber, each presenting, not slight, but very marked differences ; and this is the rule with the seed of variable cultivated plants generally.

5. "No instance of indefinite variation has ever been known to exist in nature, whereas all experimental evidence favours definite variation, *i.e.* in direct adaptation to the environment " (p. 91).

6. "Natural selection therefore has nothing to do with the origin of species " (p. 96). " The weight of experience proves that it is the changed conditions of life which first stimulate the organism to vary, the hereditary feral constancy is broken, and then responsive action on the part of the being follows" (p. 161, *re* critique on Morgan's " Evolution and Adaptation ").

7. " Both in Darwin's and Dr. Morgan's theories it is maintained that variations *arise without* any correlation to the environment being provided for. In the Neo-Lamarckian view the variation does not arise unless the new conditions of life excite the variability of the organism. This arouses the plant, *i.e.* the seedling, as it grows, develops new structures in response to the new conditions. . . . While Darwin's and Morgan's views are both *unproven hypotheses*, adaptation by response is based upon an infinite amount of actual proof, both in nature and cultivation " (p. 163).

These three I will take together, as they embody Professor Henslow's favourite theory that variation is always due to change of environment and is sympathetically responsive thereto. Darwin's theory, it may be remembered, is that variation occurs in all directions. This obviously permits a plant which scatters its seeds far afield to produce progeny fitted for a different environment from its own, so that in this way the chances of successful dissemination are increased. The idea that a plant only varies *in situ* in response to its present environment involves a much narrower issue, limiting its progeny to a similar one. I will, however, put forward a few facts involving to my mind flat contradictions to both No. 6 and No. 7. I visit the Lake districts and wander away from the beaten track until I reach the soaring flanks of, say, the Long Sleddale mountains. At their feet are a scattered farm or two, but a few hundred feet up we are practically in an environment which is the same now as it has been from time immemorial. The soil is mingled boulder, steep rock, or slopes of bracken and coarse grass, and amid this chaos of débris are innumerable ferns ; here and there are thousands of these waist-high, while in the gullies, worn deep by mountain streams, we find other species large and small. This is an ideal hunting-ground for varieties, and on the self-same flank, with self-same aspect, we may and do find extra foliose varieties, dwarfed varieties, crested varieties, and depauperate varieties. We find these intricately intermingled with the normals and have usually to dig up a clump and sort the "find" out of the tangle. Hundreds of distinct varieties have been found under such circumstances, and exist in proof at any rate of their discovery. How is it possible, then, I ask, to reconcile such facts with Professor Henslow's theory that variation only occurs when a change of environment takes place, and then only varies to fit the altered conditions?

The conditions obviously have not altered, and the divergent forms of variation prove that they have not varied in sympathy with any recognisable factor. Moreover, why is it the rule that such plants are either solitary or few in number and closely associated? Why did their normal relatives mingling with their roots and fronds not respond too if any environmental influence were at work?

Finally in No. 7 Professor Henslow implies that a seedling may and does begin normally, and subsequently adopts the new characters in sympathy with the environmental impulse. I have never seen a case of this sort; the varietal character of a fern is usually shown by an unusual shape of the primary frond, leading me to believe that the varietal tendency is already in the spore when shed.

It seems to me that Professor Henslow confounds the difference of form assumed by wild plants (let us say the cabbage) when brought under culture with variation proper. The cabbage is obviously a highly variable plant, but it must not be forgotten that under cultivation it is always under the eye of a searcher for varieties, and it is due to this fact and the immense numbers raised annually many of them on lines of definite selection for improvement and enhancement of type that we have such a multitude of different forms of it. That these forms are responsive to environment is beyond proof; their extra size and vigour undoubtedly are obvious enough and plainly due to high culture; but that is all that is demonstrable. Take a wild cabbage and "fatten" it up by high culture, and having done so plant it out on its native cliff; and if it survive it will resume its old wild form. Not so a "sport," and that is the vital difference.

In view of the above, and much more that I could add, I fail to believe that Professor Henslow will do much to detract from the world's estimate of Darwin's "unproven hypothesis" unless he can adduce at least an instalment of that "infinite amount of actual proof" which he alleges to exist to the contrary, and ceases to put forward as such the cases with which I have dealt.

Since writing the above I have heard Professor Henslow's lecture at the R.H.S. Hall on March 5 on the True Darwinism, which has given me, I think, a clue to the conflict between the facts I have cited and Professor Henslow's statements. With the exception of a passing allusion to Professor De Vries's experiments with *Œnothera* there was not the slightest reference to true variations, i.e. *inheritable differentiations of plan.* The whole of the pictures and dried specimens dealing with variation as shown by him exemplified merely the fact that, by high culture and feeding, plants can be induced to assume robuster forms, and that the seed may partake of this vigour, and consequently enable larger and larger types to be acquired. This, however, is not natural selection at all, and the differentiation thus induced is fundamentally different from those spontaneous departures from the parental type, embracing "sports" or "mutations" and all grades of subvariation such as Darwin undoubtedly had in view.

Of course if Professor Henslow confines himself to highly cultivated plants, he is naturally confirmed in his idea that variation is induced by change of environment, and only occurs when that occurs, being always sympathetically responsive thereto. When, however, he applies such a deduction to the wild and constant varieties of which I treat, or even to "sports" under culture, it becomes necessary to combat such a contention and to indicate the fallacy upon which it is based.

NOTES ON RECENT RESEARCH

AND

SHORT ABSTRACTS FROM CURRENT PERIODICAL LITERATURE, BRITISH AND FOREIGN,

AFFECTING

HORTICULTURE

AND

HORTICULTURAL AND BOTANICAL SCIENCE.

JUDGING by the number of appreciative letters received, the endeavour commenced in volume xxvi. to enlarge the usefulness of the Society's Journal, by giving an abstract of current Horticultural and Botanical periodical literature, has met with success. It has certainly entailed vastly more labour than was anticipated, and should therefore make the Fellows' thanks to those who have helped in the work all the more hearty.

The Editor desires to express his most grateful thanks to all who co-operate in this work for the very large measure of success already attained, and he ventures to express the hope that they will all strictly adhere to the general order and scheme of working, as the observance of an identical *order* can alone enable the Editor to continue to cope with the work. The order agreed on was as follows :—

1. To place first the name of the plant, disease, pest, &c., being noticed ; and in this, the prominent governing or index word should always have precedence.

2. To place next the name, when given, of the author of the original article.

3. Then, the abbreviated form of the name of the journal &c. in which the original article appears, taking care to use the abbreviation which will be found on pp. 121, 122.

4. After this, a reference to the number, date, and page of the journal in question.

5. If an illustration be given, to note the fact next, as "fig.," "tab.," or "plate."

6. After these preliminary necessities for making reference to the original possible for the reader, the abstract or digest should follow, ending up with the initials of the contributor affixed at the close of each Abstract or Note.

NAMES OF THOSE WHO HAVE KINDLY CONSENTED TO HELP
IN THIS WORK.

Baker, F. J., A.R.C.S., F.R.H.S.
Boulger, Professor G. S., F.L.S., F.R.H.S.
Bowles, E. A., M.A., F.L.S., F.E.S., F.R.H.S.
Chapman, H., F.R.H.S.
Chittenden, F. J., F.R.H.S.
Cook, E. T., F.R.H.S.
Cooke, M. C., M.A., LL.D., A.L.S., F.R.H.S., V.M.H.
Cotton, A. D., F.L.S.
Cox, H. G., F.R.H.S.
Druery, C. T., V.M.H., F.L.S., F.R.H.S.
Farmer, Professor J. B., M.A., F.R.H.S.
Goldring, W., F.R.H.S.
Groom, Professor Percy, M.A., D.Sc., F.L.S., F.R.H.S.
Hartog, Professor Marcus, D.Sc., M.A., F.L.S., F.R.H.S.
Hawes, E. F., F.R.H.S.
Henslow, Rev. Professor Geo., M.A., F.L.S., F.R.H.S., V.M.H.
Hodgson, M. L., F.R.H.S.
Hooper, Cecil H., M.R.A.C., F.R.H.S.
Houston, D., F.L.S., F.R.H.S.
Hurst, C. C., F.L.S., F.R.H.S.
Kent, A. H., A.L.S., F.R.H.S.
Long, C. H., F.R.H.S.
Massee, Geo., F.L.S., F.R.H.S.
Mawley, Ed., F.M.S., F.R.H.S.
Moulder, Victor J., F.R.H.S.
Newstead, R., A.L.S., F.E.S., F.R.H.S.
Rendle, A. B., M.A., D.Sc., F.L.S., F.R.H.S.
Reuthe, G., F.R.H.S.
Saunders, Geo. S., F.L.S., F.E.S., F.R.H.S.
Scott-Elliot, G. F., M.A., B.Sc., F.L.S., F.R.H.S., F.R.G.S.
Shea, Charles E., F.R.H.S.
Shinn, C. H., F.R.H.S.
Smith, William G., B.Sc., Ph.D., F.R.H.S.
Veitch, Harry J., F.L.S., F.Z.S., F.R.H.S.
Webster, A. D., F.R.H.S.
Welby, F. A., F.R.H.S.
Worsdell, W. C., F.L.S., F.R.H.S.

JOURNALS, BULLETINS, AND REPORTS

from which Abstracts are made, with the abbreviations used
for their titles.

Journals &c.	Abbreviated title.
Agricultural Gazette of New South Wales . . .	Agr. Gaz. N.S.W.
Agricult. Journal, Cape of Good Hope	Agr. Jour. Cape G.H.
Annales Agronomiques	Ann. Ag.
Annales de la Soc. d'Hort. et d'Hist. Naturelle de l'Hérault	Ann. Soc. Hé.
Annales de la Soc. Nantaise des Amis de l'Hort. .	Ann. Soc. Nant. des Amis Hort.
Annales des Sciences Naturelles	Ann. Sc. Nat.
Annales du Jard. Bot. de Buitenzorg . . .	Ann. Jard. Bot. Buit.
Annals of Botany	Ann. Bot.
Boletim da Real Sociedade Nacional de Horticultura	Bol. R. Soc. Nac. Hort.
Boletim da Sociedade Broteriana	Bol. Soc. Brot.
Botanical Gazette	Bot. Gaz.
Botanical Magazine	Bot. Mag.
Bulletin de la Société Botanique de France . .	Bull. Soc. Bot. Fr.
Bulletin de la Soc. Hort. de Loiret . . .	Bull. Soc. Hort. Loiret.
Bulletin de la Soc. Mycologique de France . .	Bull. Soc. Myc. Fr.
Bulletin Department of Agricult. Brisbane . .	Bull. Dep. Agr. Bris.
Bulletin Department of Agricult. Melbourne .	Bull. Dep. Agr. Melb.
Bulletin of the Botanical Department, Jamaica .	Bull. Bot. Dep. Jam.
Bulletin of Bot. Dep. Trinidad	Bull. Bot. Dep. Trin.
Bulletino della R. Società Toscana d' Orticultura .	Bull. R. Soc. Tosc. Ort.
Canadian Reports, Guelph and Ontario Stations .	Can. Rep. G. & O. Stat.
Centralblatt für Bacteriologie	Cent. f. Bact.
Chronique Orchidéenne	Chron. Orch.
Comptes Rendus	Comp. Rend.
Department of Agriculture, Victoria . . .	Dep. Agr. Vict.
Department of Agriculture Reports, New Zealand .	Dep. Agr. N.Z.
Dictionnaire Iconographique des Orchidées . .	Dict. Icon. Orch.
Die Gartenwelt	Die Gart.
Engler's Botanische Jahrbücher	Eng. Bot. Jah.
Gardeners' Chronicle	Gard. Chron.
Gardeners' Magazine	Gard. Mag.
Gartenflora	Gartenflora.
Journal de la Société Nationale d'Horticulture de France	Jour. Soc. Nat. Hort. Fr.
Journal Dep. Agricult. Victoria	Jour. Dep. Agr. Vict.
Journal Imperial Department Agriculture, West Indies .	Jour. Imp. Dep. Agr. W.I.
Journal of Botany	Jour. Bot.
Journal of Horticulture	Jour. Hort.
Journal of the Board of Agriculture . . .	Jour. Bd. Agr.
Journal of the Linnean Society	Jour. Linn. Soc.
Journal of the Royal Agricultural Society . .	Jour. R.A.S.
Journal S.E. Agricultural College, Wye . . .	Jour. S.E. Agr. Coll.
Kaiserliche Gesundheitsamte	Kais. Ges.
Le Jardin	Le Jard.
Lindenia	Lind.
Naturwiss. Zeitschrift Land und Forst . . .	Nat. Zeit. Land-Forst.
Notizblatt des Königl. Bot. Gart. und Museums zu Berlin .	Not. Könin. Bot. Berlin.
Orchid Review	Orch. Rev.
Proceedings of the American Pomological Society .	Am. Pom. Soc.
Queensland Agricultural Journal	Qu. Agr. Journ.
Reports of the Missouri Botanical Garden . .	Rep. Miss. Bot. Gard.
Revue de l'Horticulture Belge	Rev. Hort. Belge.
Revue générale de Botanique	Rev. gén. Bot.
Revue Horticole	Rev. Hort.

Journals &c.	Abbreviated title.
The Garden	Garden.
Transactions Bot. Soc. Edinburgh	Trans. Bot. Soc. Edin.
Transactions of the British Mycological Soc. . .	Trans. Brit. Myc. Soc.
Transactions of the Massachusetts Hort. Soc. .	Trans. Mass. Hort. Soc.
U.S.A. Department of Agriculture, Bulletins . .	U.S.A. Dep. Agr.*
U.S.A. Experimental Station Reports . . .	U.S.A. Exp. Stn.†
U.S.A. Horticultural Societies' publications . .	U.S.A. Hort. Soc.†
U.S.A. State Boards of Agriculture and Horticulture .	U.S.A. St. Bd.†
Woburn Experiment Farm Report	Woburn.
Zeitschrift für Pflanzenkrankheiten . . .	Zeit. f. Pflanz.

* The divisions in which the U.S.A. Government publish Bulletins will be added when necessary.
† The name of the Station or State will in each case be added in full or in its abbreviated form.

NOTES AND ABSTRACTS.

Abies Mariesii. By M. T. Masters (*Bot. Mag.* tab. 8098).—Japan. Nat. ord. *Coniferae*; tribe *Abietineae*. A tall pyramidal tree; younger branches scaly; leaves adpressed, 1 inch long; cones erect, $3\frac{1}{2}$-5 inches long, $1\frac{1}{2}$-2 inches wide, dull purple, cask-shaped; male flowers unknown.—*G. H.*

Adenostemma viscosum, Fruit-dispersal in. By R. H. Yapp (*Ann. Bot.* xx. July 1906, pp. 311–316; 1 plate).—A biological account of the sticky fruits of this plant.

In Compositae the protective function of the calyx is performed by the involucre, and the calyx proper being reduced frequently becomes a highly modified pappus. *Adenostemma* is a composite peculiar in possessing a glandular pappus. The inferior ovary is crowned with a projecting ring of tissue, upon which are situated three glandular setae (stalked glands).

During the ripening of the fruits of the capitulum the corolla and styles fall off *en masse*, at which time the pappus excretes an exceedingly viscid liquid which forms a drop at the tip of each seta. In this condition the setæ bear a marked resemblance to the leaf " tentacles " of a *Drosera*. At the same time the setæ gradually move from a vertical into a horizontal position, and during this process the swellings formally present at their bases disappear. The tiny fruits are now fully exposed and are ready to attach themselves to any passing animal.

The swelling at the base of each pappus seta is in reality a pulvinus. It is composed of large thin-walled motor cells, which probably act by losing water during the drying and ripening of the fruit.

In view of the fact that the feathery pappus of many Composites executes similar movements, several British species were examined, with the result that, in a number of instances, a mechanism resembling the pulvinus described above was found. In the cases examined the downward movement of the hairs was found to be effected by means of a continuous annular pulvinus, on the edge of which the pappus hairs were borne.—*A. D. C.*

Alpine Garden at Samoëns. By Hortulus (*Le Jardin*, vol. xxi. No. 480, p. 52; with 3 figs.; February 20, 1907).—The fine Alpine station of La Jaysinia, at Samoëns, Haute-Savoie, was established in the autumn of 1906 for the purpose of collecting together, in twenty-five divisions, the mountain flora from all regions of the globe. The names and geographical habitat of many of the species now acclimatised in the garden are cited in this interesting article.—*F. A. W.*

Amaryllis (Hippeastrum). By Le Texnier (*Le Jardin*, vol. xxi. No. 478, p. 26; January 20, 1907).—Historical account of the genus with description of hybrids.—*F. A. W.*

Anemone japonica crispa (Lady Gilmour). By S. Mottet (*Rev. Hort.*, February 1, 1906, pp. 71–2; fig.).—A description of this very handsome form of *A. japonica* as regards abnormal development of the foliage, which, instead of completing the individual leaf growth on normal lines, continues it through the season, the margins constantly extending and expanding until each leaf becomes à dense mass of over-lapping curls and fringes. The flowers are not appreciably affected, and are rosy pink.—*C. T. D.*

Anemone, The Wood. By W. Irving (*Garden*, No. 1797, p. 233; April 28, 1906; fig.).—Of all our·native plants there are few more beautiful than the common wood anemone. In woods under the shade of trees, and among short grass on hedge banks, it is frequently met with in many parts of this country. Towards the end of March it may be seen opening its snow-white flowers in bright sunny weather, while it may be considered at its best during the first weeks of April. A very easy plant to please, it will thrive well in somewhat light soils, and large groups may be formed quickly, for when established it increases freely by means of its spreading underground roots. In transplanting, these roots should not be kept out of the ground long enough to get dry, as such a check is liable to prevent their flowering in the following spring. They should be planted about 3 inches below the surface in rich loamy soil and well-decayed vegetable mould where it is never likely to become dry.—*E. T. C.*

Aphides affecting the Apple. By A. L. Quaintance (*U.S.A. Dep. Agr., Bur. Ent., Circ.* 81; March 1907; 8 figs.).—The aphides found attacking the apple are: (1) The European grain aphis (*Siphocoryne avenae*, Fab.) which affects also the pear, quince, plum, and rye, oats and wheat, the aphides migrating to the cereals in June or July, and returning to the apple in autumn, when the sexually produced winter eggs are laid near the tips of the shoots; (2) the apple aphis (*Aphis mali*, Fitch) occurring on apple (and in Europe on hawthorn and crab), which it infests throughout the year (See JOURN. R.H.S. vol. xxvi. p. 498); (3) rosy apple aphis (*A. malifoliae*, Fitch) feeds on apple and pear, and in Europe on hawthorn, mountain ash, &c. The life-history is imperfectly known, but the apple is deserted after the third generation, and the return migrants appear in autumn giving rise to the true sexual forms, after which the eggs are deposited. The enemies of the aphides mentioned are species of ladybird, larvæ of *Chrysopidae* (lace-wings) and *Hemerobiidae*, and the larvæ of the hover flies (*Syrphidae*). Small hymenopterous parasites also destroy the aphides, while entire colonies are sometimes swept off by fungous diseases. The aphides are to be kept under control by pruning off shoots on which the little black eggs appear and destroying the prunings; by winter spraying to some extent, though the eggs appear to be largely resistant to the action of such sprays as are not so strong as to injure the trees; the use of the lime-sulphur wash has, however, been attended by good results; by spring and summer spraying with paraffin emulsion or with tobacco decoction.—*F. J. C.*

Apple and Pear Mites. By P. J. Parrott, H. E. Hodgkiss, and W. J. Schoene (*U.S.A. Exp. Stn. Geneva, Bull.* 283; December 1906;

10 plates).—Five species of mites have been recognised on apple and pear leaves in America, *Eriophyes malifoliae*, Parr (sp. nov.), *E. pyri*, Nal., *E. pyri*, var. *variolata*, Nal., *Phyllocoptes schlechtendali*, Nal., and *Epitrimerus pyri*, Nal. With the exception of the first, all of these are known in Europe. The leaf blister-mite (*Eriophyes pyri*) is the most abundant, and is responsible for damage to the leaves of apples as well as pears. It is a "small, vermiform, four-legged animal, about $\frac{1}{125}$ inch in length. . . . It hibernates in the buds, and with the maturing of the bud-scales seeks the tender leaves, which it punctures, producing light green and reddish pimples. These develop into galls or blisters of a blackish or reddish-brown colour, depending on the kind and the variety of fruit." The service berry, cotoneaster, white beam, and mountain ash, are all attacked by the mite. The perpetuation of the mite in nurseries is due to propagation with infected buds, and it is believed that the pest can be eliminated from the nursery by the selection of buds from clean stock and by the fumigation of the stocks. The mite may be kept under on pear trees by careful pruning and by spraying during the late, full, or early spring, with paraffin emulsion, miscible oils, or sulphur washes. It appears much easier to keep the mite under on pear than on apple trees. The bulletin gives a useful account of the group to which these mites belong and a full description of the species mentioned above.—*F. J. C.*

Apple Bitter Rot (*U.S.A. Dep. Agr., Farm. Bull.* 267 ; 1906).—This trouble, which is due to the fungus now known as *Glomerella rufomaculans*, is estimated to have caused the loss of about $10,000,000 in 1900. Varieties differ much in susceptibility, " Yellow Newtown " or " Albemarle " being very susceptible. The fungus is very dependent on high temperature and moisture for its development, and the outbreak may be checked if the temperature falls to or remains at about 70° F. for a few days. The application of Bordeaux mixture of the strength, 5 lb. copper sulphate, 5 lb. lime, 50 gallons water, five or six weeks after the trees bloom, followed by three more at intervals of two weeks, has proved an effective check upon the spread of the disease.—*F. J. C.*

Apples in Oregon. By E. R. Lake (*U.S.A. Exp. Stn. Oregon, Bull.* 82 ; 1904 ; 29 figs.).—An excellent account of apple-growing, with much sound general advice and many hints of local importance.—*F. J. C.*

Apple-leaf Miner. By C. D. Jarvis (*U.S.A. Exp. Stn. Stores, Conn., Bull.* 45 ; December 1906 ; 17 figs.).—The insect described has been known for a considerable time, but has not until last year become a serious pest. It is known throughout the eastern part of the States and in Canada, and injures the tree by mining beneath the epidermis of the leaf. When many mines occur on the leaf it rolls up, and its functions cease. Two broods occur in the year. The pest is usually kept in check by parasites and by unfavourable weather conditions. It is recommended to plough the fallen leaves in, as a means of destroying the pest, which pupates within the tunnel it has made in the leaf. The insect (*Tischeria malifoliella* Clemens) is one of the *Tineideae*, and affects not only the apple, but the hawthorns, *Pyrus coronaria*, *Rubus villosus*, and *R. occidentalis*.

Its attacks are characterised by yellowish or brownish blotches on the upper surface of the leaf,· and often these blotches are very numerous, as many as sixty-eight full-grown caterpillars having been taken from one leaf. The eggs are laid in June, and the caterpillars reach their full size about the middle of July, remaining as pupæ only about eight to ten days, and the larvæ hatched from the eggs laid by this generation reach maturity about September 1. This brood lines its burrows with a dense layer of fine white silk, and hibernates therein, either as pupæ or larvæ, until about May. The perfect insect has a dark-brown shining head and upper wings, the latter being purplish and dusted with pale yellow; the hind wings are dark grey. It measures about 8 mm. in length, and about 8 mm. across the expanded wings. The insect has been found in Germany by Frey and Boll (*Stett. Ent. Zeit.* xxxix. p. 254) on leaves of imported apples.—*F. J. C.*

Arachnanthe annamensis. By R. A. Rolfe (*Bot. Mag.* tab. 8062).—Annam. Nat. ord. *Orchidaceae*; tribe *Vandeae.* A stout, erect plant, 18 inches high. Flowers large, ground colour, bright red-brown and yellow bands; sepals and petals long and narrow.—*G. H.*

Aristolocia elegans. By Ad. van den Heede (*Le Jardin,* vol. xx. No. 471, p. 294; October 5, 1906).—This variety has small leaves and sweet-scented flowers of a dull purple colour blotched with cream. Easily cultivated in cool greenhouse, and remarkably free from insects. This ·species was introduced in 1885, but has been overlooked in favour of the well-known *A. Sipho,* which is rampant in most gardens.

F. A. W.

Asparagus Miner and Beetles. By F. H. Chittenden (*U.S.A. Dep. Agr., Bur. Ent., Bull.* 66, pt. i.; March 1907; 2 figs.).—The larva of a minute black two-winged fly (*Agromyza simplex* Loew) mines under the epidermis of the asparagus stalk, feeding there until the pupa state is reached, when the skin bursts and the presence of the insect is revealed. It is generally found near the base of the stalk, penetrating to 7 or 8 inches below ground. It occurs mostly in the Eastern States and is native in America. Two methods of control offer themselves : (1) trapping by allowing a few stray asparagus plants to grow and so attract the insects; and (2) by pulling old affected stems as soon as the trouble is discovered. Co-operation will be necessary over a considerable area if this remedy is to prove effective.

Good results have followed the use of arsenate of lead as a spray against asparagus beetle (*Ciroceris asparagi*), in some experiments 90 to 100 per cent. of the insects having been killed. The twelve-spotted asparagus beetle has been found to develop and to feed where possible exclusively on the asparagus berry.—*F. J. C.*

Asparagus Sprengeri. By C. H. Wright (*Bot. Mag.* tab. 8052).— Natal. Nat. ord. *Liliaceae*; tribe *Asparageae.* A climbing shrub. Leaf-spines 1–2 lines long; phyllocladia solitary or 2-4 together, flat, linear; fruit globose, crimson.—*G. H.*

Bacteria and Leguminosae (*U.S.A. Dep. Agr. Bur. Pl. Ind., Bulls.* 71 and 72; *Farmers' Bull.* 214; *Exp. Stn. Oklahoma, Bull.* 68; *New York, Geneva, Bull.* 270; *Virginia, Bull.* 154; *Michigan, Bulls.* 224 and 225).—The practice of inoculating seed or soil with cultures of bacteria capable of producing nodules on the roots of leguminous plants is becoming more and more widespread. Experiments seem to show that only one species of micro-organism (*Pseudomones radicicola*) is concerned, and that there are many races the differences between which can be readily broken down by cultivation. The new method of cultivation devised by the American Board of Agriculture experts on media free from nitrogen ensures the infective power of the bacteria being undiminished. Various external conditions, such as heat, moisture, alkalinity, amount of nitrogen in the soil, and so on, all influence the development of the bacteria. The view is taken in the first of the publications cited, that the bacteria which invade the tubercles are dissolved and absorbed by the plant, and it is only the branching forms of the bacterium which are capable of being overcome by the plant and destroyed to its benefit; the rod forms are not able to be dissolved by the host. The relationship between the bacillus and the leguminous plant is precisely that between a parasite and its host. An interesting point discovered is that nitrogen-fixing bacteria are able to penetrate the roots of plants, and be of decided benefit, without the formation of nodules or any external evidence of their presence: this was found to be the case in soy beans and lucerne. Inoculation, it is pointed out, can only be of benefit when the soil does not already contain the particular bacteria, although there are some exceptions to this rule; and where a soil is very rich in nitrogen the development of nitrogen-fixing organisms is inhibited. "Inoculation is necessary—(1) on a soil low in organic matter that has not previously borne leguminous crops; (2) if the legumes previously grown on the same land were devoid of nodules or 'nitrogen knots,' showing the need for supplying the nodule-forming bacteria; (3) when the legume to be sown belongs to a species not closely related to one previously grown on the same soil."

The Oklahoma Bulletin points out that liquid cultures give better results than dried cultures, and that light is fatal to the organisms; cultures and inoculated seed should therefore be kept in the dark. The New York Experiment Station found that the dried cultures distributed on cotton-wool failed to give satisfactory results; that they, indeed, contained no living nodule-making germs—a statement corroborated by some other investigators. The Virginia Bulletin deals with the cultivation of alfalfa (lucerne, *Medicago sativa*) and the inoculation of the soil with the germ proper to that plant. In Michigan it was found that the plants on which nodules were developed were much richer in protein than those from which they were absent, and this was true, not only of the growing plant, but also of the seed produced by it.—*F. J. C.*

Bacterial Rot, A, of the Potato caused by *Bacillus solanisaprus.* By F. C. Harrison (*Centralblatt für Bakteriologie, Parasitenkunde und Infektionskrankheiten*, Abteilung ii. Band xvii. 1906).—The author draws attention to the great confusion which exists among cultivators generally, and even trained observers, in the employment of the terms "rot" and "blight" as applied to diseases of the potato; and it is therefore necessary to insist upon the distinction between the disease produced by the fungus *Phytophthora infestans*, termed "blight," and the soft or wet "rot" caused by bacteria of several different species. The inability to distinguish between the different types of disease gives rise to error in combating them, and renders remedial measures frequently ineffective because applied under a misconception as to the nature of the disease under treatment. For instance, the Bordeaux mixture has been used in the treatment of bacterial rot, to which it was manifestly inapplicable, as the bacteria, being confined to the interior tissues of the stem and tubers, could not be affected by external spraying.

This bacterial rot of potatoes is distributed widely in Canada and the United States, in Great Britain and other European countries.

In the majority of cases the first symptoms of the disease appear when the plants are in full vigour. The leaves droop and become discoloured, while the stems lose their erect appearance and gradually sink to the ground. Black areas are to be noted on the attacked stems and leaves and sections, though these spots show the vascular bundles brown or black according to the progress of the disease. In the tubers this disease first appears as a reddish-brown discoloration of the skin and subjacent tissues; these at first are firm, but afterwards they become soft, and there is frequently a black line of demarcation between the healthy and diseased portions. As the rot progresses the flesh softens to a white watery pulp with a highly offensive odour, and in the final stage the potato becomes a mere mass of black pulp.

The author considers that the natural infection is chiefly to be attributed to the diseased condition of the seed potato, but the possibility of the parasite maintaining its existence in the soil and entering a healthy tuber through a wound is also admitted. The progress of the disease is materially influenced by the amount of moisture in the soil, and a large rainfall, followed by warm weather, presents the most favourable conditions for the spread of the epidemic.

Cultivations have been made of the *Bacillus*, and artificial inoculations have shown that the following plants are liable to attack:—Jerusalem artichoke, cucumber, carrot, radish, parsnip, cauliflower, cabbage, celery, swede, turnip, mangelwurzel, salsify, tomato, and onion.

The parasite is a *Bacillus* with slightly rounded ends, varying from 1·5 to 4 μ by ·6 to ·9 μ. It is actively motile with a varying number of flagella.—*M. C. P.*

Bag Method of Keeping Grapes. By J. Balsacq (*Le Jardin*, vol. xx. No. 473, p. 324; November 5, 1906).—Another general article on the advantages of this method. Suggests the advisability of experimenting with blue bags, on the lines of M. Flammarion's conclusions as to the influence of coloured light on ripening of fruits.—*F. A. W.*

Bag Method of Keeping Grapes. By F. Charmeux (*Le Jardin*, vol. xx. No. 465, p. 204; with 3 figs.; July 5, 1906).—Under favourable conditions (absence of birds, wasps, &c.) the bags now recommended at

Thomery are completely open at the base (see fig. 16), which also shows how the paper curtain can be delicately cut away as the grapes mature.

F. A. W.

Bag Method of Keeping Grapes. By F. Charmeux (*Le Jardin*, vol. xx. No. 468, p. 218; 2 figs.; August 20, 1906).—Insists on the advantage of putting the grapes in bags at the beginning of June, *before they ripen*. The bunches thus enclosed are at least ten days ahead of the exposed bunches. If sent to market in their bags the grapes are kept clean and perfect, the latest model, the "Preserver," being fitted with a little spring by which it can be opened or closed at will.—*F. A. W.*

Bag Method of Keeping Grapes. By A. Pirlot (*Le Jardin*, vol. xxi. No. 486, p. 154; May 30, 1907).—A valuable *résumé* of the subject, giving the rationale of many failures (from over-heating, enclosing the grapes, apples, or pears too late, &c.), and pointing out that with the "Bell" or "Preserver" model, described in previous abstract, the bag can be left open as much as is desired in fine weather and drawn together after the middle of September, thus rendering possible the cultivation of grapes in the open air in many places where the climate is otherwise prohibitive. It should also be noted that these bags are very durable and will last for years.—*F. A. W.*

Banana, The Cultivated (*Rev. Hort.* May 16, 1906, p. 222).— Mr. Otto Kuntze stated that the cultivated banana was known in America 500 years ago, and as it produces no seeds and is only propagated by suckers, he doubts De Candolle's idea that it was introduced into America from Africa and the Pacific Islands; despite its infertility it is not considered to be a variety, as it is found where the so-called wild banana does not exist.—*C. T. D.*

Barberries, The. By W. F. Bean (*Garden*, No. 1810, p. 37; July 28, 1906).—While the total number of species of Berberis in cultivation is now about forty, it may safely be said that one-fourth of these are all that are needed adequately to represent the genus in an ordinary garden. To those who have only a limited space at command I would recommend the following ten sorts :—

Evergreen—*aquifolium* (W. N. America), *Darwinii* (Chili), *japonica* (China and Japan), *stenophylla* (hybrid), and *wallichiana* (Himalayas and China).

Deciduous—*aristata* (Himalayas), *buxifolia* (Chili), *sinensis* (China), *Thunbergi* (Japan), and *vulgaris* (Europe and North Asia).

Several of these, of course, are quite common, and none can be described as rare. Of the evergreen barberries there is not the least doubt but that the most valuable one is *B. stenophylla*. As is now well known, this is a hybrid raised in the famous Handsworth Nurseries, near Sheffield, I suppose, forty or fifty years ago. Its parents are *B. Darwinii* and *B. empetrifolia*. To my mind it represents one of the greatest achievements of the hybridist, for it is not only very different from both its parents, but as a garden plant it is a great improvement on both.

E. T. C.

K

Beans. By L. C. Corbett (*U.S.A. Dep. Agr., Farm. Bull.* 289; 10 figs.; April 1907).—Deals with this important group of plants, including broad beans, kidney beans, lima or sugar beans, dolichos beans, soy beans, scarlet runner beans, velvet beans (*Mucuna utilis*) and cow peas (*Vigna sinensis*). The preparation of the soil, planting, cultivation (when dew is not on the plants), harvesting, cleaning and grading, fertilisers suitable, and diseases are all dealt with.—*F. J. C.*

Beans, Mildew of Lima. By G. P. Clinton, Sc.D. (*U.S.A. Exp. Stn. Conn.*; 13 plates; May 1906).—This annual report of the botanist for 1905 is concerned chiefly with the downy mildew of the Lima bean, and potato (*Phytophthora*), the former of which is recorded for the first time as producing oospores, of which there is a detailed account; and the question of oospores in the potato mildew is discussed in about twenty-four pages. The other fungous diseases reported upon are of less importance, and include a fruit-speck on apple, cause undetermined; pod and leaf blight of Lima bean, *Phoma subcircinata* (E. and E.); leaf spot of Japanese catalpa, *Macrosporium catalpae*; leaf scorch of sugar maple, not yet identified; brown rot of the nectarine *Sclerotinia fructigena*; wilt of okra, *Neocosmospora vasinfecta*; brittle of onion, *Fusarium* sp.; bacterial black spot on plum, *Pseudomonas pruni*; and a damping-off of tobacco, *Sclerotinia* sp.—*M. C. C.*

Beet Seed : Development of Single Germ. By C. O. Townsend and E. C. Rittue (*U.S.A. Dep. Agr., Bur. Pl. Ind., Bull.* 73; 8 plates and 6 figs.; 1905).—An endeavour is being made to produce beet "seed" containing only a single germ, as it is believed that such will materially lessen the labour of thinning. An account is given here of the methods of selection and cross-pollination adopted with this end in view.—*F. J. C.*

Begonia Rex, Some curious Results of Layering. By Max Garnier (*Rev. Hort.*, February 1, 1906, p. 61).—Leaves taken with their entire stalks, the bases of which are inserted a short distance in the soil, support being afforded by sticks, root, and develop buds on the summit, forming tufts of leaves, standard fashion. The stem, however, does not thicken or become woody, and requires continued support. It has also been found that the original leaf, even if developed already to full normal size, will resume growth and become of exceptional dimensions.—*C. T. D.*

Begonias, New (*Le Jardin*, vol. xxi. No. 480, p. 60; 2 figs.; February 20, 1907), *Begonia Cayeuxi* (Cayeux and Leclerc).—Fine decorative hybrid from *B. semperflorens gracilis rosa* crossed with *B. lucida*, the fertile hybrid obtained being crossed in its turn with *B. gracilis rubra*. Hardy plant with abundant flowers, a little taller than *B. semperflorens*.

Begonia hybrida gigantea 'Princesse Royale' (Heinemann).—New hybrid with magnificent carmine flowers and white centres.

B. semperflorens 'Gloire de Chatelaine' (Rivoire).—New variety; one of the finest *sempervirens* ever produced. Resembles 'Gloire de

Lorraine. Very free growth, a mass of bright rosy flowers, equally good in sun or shade. Unequalled for pot culture.—*F. A. W.*

Blakea gracilis. By S. A. Skau (*Bot. Mag.* tab. 8099).—Costa Rica. Nat. ord. *Melastomaceae*; tribe *Blakeae.* A glabrous, much-branched shrub, 9–13 feet high. Leaves opposite, subcoriaceous, 2½–4 inches long, 1¼–1½ inch broad; flowers 1½ inch across; petals 6, whitish rose; stamens 12.—*G. H.*

Blue Glass, Influence of, on Vegetation (*Rev. Hort.* March 16, 1906, p. 128).—Mr. V. A. Clark, at the Horticultural Society, New Orleans, reported that transplanted leafy seedlings are greatly benefited by the use of blue glass on the frames, transpiration being thus checked.—*C. T. D.*

Boronia fastigiata. By T. A. Sprague (*Bot. Mag.* tab. 8089).—Western Australia. Nat. ord. *Rutaceae*; tribe *Boronieae.* A bush 6 feet high; leaves small, obovate; cymes several-flowered; flowers ½ inch broad, rose-coloured.—*G. H.*

Bulbophyllum Ericssoni. By R. A. Rolfe (*Bot. Mag.* tab. 8088).—Malay Archipelago. Nat. ord. *Orchidaceae*; tribe *Epidendreae.* An epiphytic herb; flowers umbellate, large, green, spotted with purple-brown, and red-brown markings; sepals elongated with curled spurs.

G. H.

Cabbage : Club Root. By T. W. Kirk, F.L.S., and A. H. Cockayne (*Dep. Agr. N.Z., Bull.* No. 11, 3 plates ; November 1905).—This disease to cabbages, turnips, and cauliflowers appears to be considerably on the increase in many districts of New Zealand. After a slight description of the disease, which is much assisted by the plates, the report is concerned with preventive measures, which are numerous and explicit. 1. All diseased material, wherever practicable, should be burnt, and should not be fed to pigs, as ground has become badly infected through pig manure. 2. Careful rotation of crops is necessary for the suppression of the disease. 3. Neglect of keeping the ground clear of cruciferous weeds contributes to the spread of club root. 4. Club root is rarely found on land rich in lime ; application of heavy dressings, of lime, four to seven tons per acre, is the most effective preventive. 5. Gas-lime has little or no effect on club root, and acid manures, such as superphosphate of lime, encourage it.—*M. C. C.*

Cacao Disease in Ceylon. By Herbert Wright (*Jour. Imp. Dep. Agr. W.I.* vol. vi. No. 3 ; 1905).—The canker disease of cacao, which has proved a very serious menace to cacao cultivation in Ceylon, is met with in Trinidad, Grenada, and Dominica. This article shows that the fungus causing this disease can be successfully kept in check by rational agricultural methods. These are briefly as follows :—

1. Letting in sunlight.
2. Excision and burning of diseased tissues in the stem.
3. Frequent collecting and burning of diseased fruits, or burying with lime.

4. Spraying with chemical compounds known to be poisonous to the spores of fungi.

It is proved that when the fungus has developed almost to its maximum it can still be attacked with a prospect of being reduced to a minimum within three years, at an expenditure which is made good within that period.—*M. C. C.*

Cacao, Fungoid Diseases of. By L. Lewton-Brain, B.A., F.L.S. (*Jour. Imp. Dep. Agr. W.I.* vol. vi. No. 1; 1905).—This communication summarises the chief facts with regard to the fungi causing these diseases, and mentions the chief methods of dealing with them. These are stem diseases, "canker," due to *Nectria*, and "die back" due to *Diplodia cacaoicola*.

Pod diseases, of which the two principal are "brown rot," caused by the same fungus as the "die back" of the stem; the other is the rot caused by *Phytophthora omnivora*.

"Thread blight" in India is said to be caused by *Stillum nanum*, and a similar disease, distinguished as "horsehair blight," caused by *Marasmius sarmentosus*. The chief information is concentrated on the last two diseases, which are of most recent occurrence, and still under investigation.—*M. C. C.*

Caladiums and their Culture. By L. Duval (*Le Jardin*, vol. xxi. No. 477, p. 4; with 4 figs.; January 5, 1907).—Useful article on the culture of Caladiums.—*F. A. W.*

Calceolarias, Herbaceous. By A. Zogheb (*Le Jardin*, vol. xx. No. 466, p. 219; July 20, 1906).—To avoid degeneration, cross-fertilisation is recommended. Select three or four plants as nearly alike in height and general appearance as possible. Remove stamens from flowers intended for seed-bearing before their pollen is dispersed. Fertilise the pistils of these with pollen from the other flowers, using small tweezers for the purpose. Mark the fertilised flowers with raphia to distinguish them. Water in moderation during the ripening of the plant. Gather the capsules when dry—when the valves are splitting. Keep in dry place. As regards cultivation, sow in July–August, taking care not to bury the seed, which is extremely fine. Cover the pot with glass, and place in a shaded frame or greenhouse. Prick out the seedlings as early as possible (extreme youth is essential), using a pointed match as dibble. When rooted, prick out again into small pots, transplanting subsequently to larger ones. Water with caution, and look out for grubs.

The compost used in repotting should be leaf-mould and manure mixed with a little sand.—*F. A. W.*

Callopsis Volkensii. By N. E. Brown (*Bot. Mag.* tab. 8071).— German East Africa. Nat. ord. *Aroideae*; tribe *Zomicarpeae* (?). A stemless perennial herb, with a short branching underground root-stock. Leaves with a blade 3-5 inches long, 2-3 inches broad; spathe 1 inch long, ¾-1 inch broad, pure white; spadix yellow.—*G. H.*

Camphor, Production of (*Jour. Imp. Dep. Agr. W.I.* vol. vii. No. 2; 1906).—In the present scarcity and rise in the price of camphor this article will probably possess an interest which it would not otherwise have had. We are introduced to a knowledge of camphor monopolies, camphor cultivation in Ceylon, general propagation and cultivation, distillation, with suggestions as to improvement.—*M. C. C.*

Canker of Fruit Trees. By T. W. Kirk, F.L.S., and A. H. Cockayne (*Dep. Agr. N.Z.*, No. 10 ; with 7 plates ; December 1905).—This bulletin includes reports of two cankers of fruit trees—(1) apple and pear canker, *Nectria ditissima* ; (2) apricot coral spot, *Nectria* sp. The first of these diseases is but too well known, and the other is very similar, if not caused by the same fungus. The apricot coral spot has caused considerable losses in the last few years to Nelson fruit growers owing to the large number of apricot trees that have died through the attacks of the apricot canker or apricot coral spot. This disease is a true wound parasite, and can only infect healthy trees through cuts or wounds. Once having gained a foothold it grows rapidly, and soon the fructification bursts through the bark. All trees which show signs of this disease should be heavily cut back, and all the cut surfaces coated with tar and the prunings removed and burnt.—*M. C. C.*

Carduus Keneri (*Le Jardin*, vol. xx. No. 467, p. 227 ; August 5, 1906).—Introduced from Bulgaria by Leichtlin, 60-70 cm. (2-3 feet) in height. Its large heads, borne on long peduncles, are striking before their full development, on account of the reddish-purple bracts. The florets are pinker, resembling *C. cernuus.—F. A. W.*

Carnation 'Colosse Mantais' (*Le Jardin*, vol. xx. No. 472, p. 310).— Derived from Flemish strain of *Camelliaeflora*. Remarkably vigorous, resembling but superior to 'Malmaison,' since the calyx never bursts. Flowers rose-colour flecked with white, and as large as camellias—15-20 on each plant. Invaluable for pot culture.—*F. A. W.*

Carnations, American. By L. Maillard (*Le Jardin*, vol. xx. No. 464, p. 185 ; with 5 figs.; June 20, 1907).—Gives minute description of soil and sterilisation methods, frames employed (with subterranean irrigation), technique of taking cuttings and striking them, diseases to which these are especially liable, and appropriate remedies, with a list of the finest varieties.—*F. A. W.*

· Carnations, Manuring of, in the Riviera. By M. Calvin (*Bull. R. Soc. Tosc. Ort.* 2, February 1906).—Among the plants most extensively cultivated in the Riviera besides the rose is the carnation. In addition to dung, dried blood, and other manures, an excess of ammoniacal manures is employed. If rational manuring is used the above organic manures are not employed, but after improving the ground with large quantities of dung, nitrogenous compounds and phosphoric anhydride and potash are used. One cultivator tried with success the following mixture to each square metre :

Triple hyperphosphate with 45 per cent. of phosphoric anhydride	100 parts
Potassic sulphate	100 ,,

Ammonium sulphate . . . . 200 parts
Sulphate of iron . . . . . . 50 „
Sulphate of lime . . . . . . 50 „

Two plots of ground were manured : one according to the ordinary method with dried blood, &c., the other by the rational method as above. The latter in August was full of flourishing and well-conditioned carnations, the former were very poorly developed and backward. The importance of this latter fact is that if the plants have not set flower-buds by September, the flowering remains backward until March and April, hence the flowers are dear in December, January, and February.

The mineral manure can be directly utilised by the plants, whilst the organic manures require the aid of micro-organisms to render them assimilable, and this process is a slow one during winter.—*W. C. W.*

Catalpas, The. By W. (*Garden*, No. 1832, p. 315 ; December 29, 1906).—Those who know anything at all of hardy exotic trees do not need to be told that the Catalpa is one of the finest ornamental trees we have, but there must be many to whom even such an old tree as this is unknown, seeing how seldom one finds it planted, especially in gardens of modern make. Those who know the American Catalpa will recognise in *C. bignonioides* one of our most handsome trees for garden planting, even when not in flower. There is, in fact, no finer object on an English garden lawn than an old Catalpa, as it is beautiful in leaf and highly attractive throughout harvest time, when, as a rule, it is covered with a profusion of loose white flower clusters, which in warm climates are succeeded by a crop of long seed-pods, which look like attenuated French beans ; hence the name Indian bean tree. Apart from its peculiar growth, its large foliage, and showy flowers, the Catalpa is an important tree in garden landscapes on account of its colour, it being one of the lightest greens we have among big trees ; and therefore a fine Catalpa always stands out prominently among others, both in colour and outline.—*E. T. C.*

Catasetum galeritum, var. **pachyglossum.** By R. A. Rolfe (*Bot. Mag.* tab. 8093).—Brazil. Nat. ord. *Orchidaceae*; tribe *Vandeae*. Epiphyte 1½ foot high ; sepals and petals lanceolate, green blotched with purple ; lip three-lobed ; 1–1¼ inch long, deep red-brown at margin, green spotted, with brown below.—*G. H.*

Celery. By W. R. Beattie (*U.S.A. Dep. Agr., Farm. Bull.* 282 ; 16 figs. ; April 1907).—An account of the cultivation of celery intended to replace that in Bulletin 148, of which it is a revision and extension. Celery can be grown in the summer months in the north United States ; but not in the middle region, as the summer weather is too warm, the atmosphere too moist, and the winter too cold ; while in the south it may be grown in the winter. The ideal conditions for its growth are bright sunshine, pure air, cool nights, and a well-distributed rainfall of about 8 inches during the growing season. The best soil is said to be a sandy loam, and it is stated that there is no manure equal to farmyard manure at about 10 to 20 tons per acre for this crop.—*F. J. C.*

Cerasus laurocerasus schipkaensis. By H. Martinet (*Le Jardin*, vol. xxi. No. 484, p. 115; with 1 fig.; April 20, 1907).—A new variety of cherry-laurel from the Balkans; extremely hardy and of graceful habit.—*F. A. W.*

Cereus Scheerii. By N. E. Brown (*Bot. Mag.* tab. 8096).—Mexico. Nat. ord. *Cactaceae*; tribe *Echinocacteae.* Stems erect, 6 inches high; angles acute, with 8–10 spines radiating outwards; flowers carmine-rose, 4 inches across.—*G. H.*

Ceropegia fusca. By N. E. Brown (*Bot. Mag.* tab. 8066).—Grand Canary. Nat. ord. *Asclepiadaceae.* A bushy succulent, almost leafless, from 1–6 feet high; flowers in fascicles; corolla 1⅓ inch long, dull reddish-brown.—*G. H.*

Chamaebatiaria (Spirea) millefolium. By S. Mottet (*Le Jardin*, vol. xxi. No. 482, p. 84; fig.; March 20, 1907).—A curious plant resembling *Achillea* so much more than *Spirea* that it has often been proposed to place it in a new genus (*Chamaebatiaria*). A shrub about 3 feet high. Flowers best in a sunny position in light soil. The branches are covered with minute white blossoms.—*F. A. W.*

Cherry with Proliferous Double Flowers. By J. Gérôme (*Rev. Hort.*, pp. 249, 250; fig.; June 1, 1906).—Description and illustration of double-flowered cherry, an old tree in the garden of the Natural History Museum (where not stated). The flowers are pure white, very large and very persistent, the tree remaining in flower long after the normal period. In the centre of each flower originates a second one and sometimes several on a smaller scale: the first is naturally barren, but the succeeding one is perfect, the supplementary ones defective. It is a form of the 'Grottier' variety.—*C. T. D.*

Chillies or Capsicums. By W. R. Buttenshaw, M.A., B.Sc. (*Jour. Imp. Dep. Agr. W.I.* vol. vii. No. 3; 1906).—This article is written to illustrate the uses of the "red peppers," the variety of the cultivated forms, the production of capsicums, their consumption, their cultivation in the island of Zanzibar, in British Central Africa, in the West Indies; the market for capsicums, their cultivation, drying and preservation. It is intimated that only two fungoid pests cause any serious trouble, and these are the "pink anthracnose," *Gloeosporium piperatum*, and the "dark anthracnose," *Colletotrichum nigrum.*—*M. C. C.*

Chinese Plants, New. By S. Mottet (*Le Jardin*, vol. xxi. No. 479, p. 36; with 4 figs.; February 5, 1907).—Summary of the recent discoveries of the expeditions promoted by the Museum of Paris and M. Vilmorin; by Kew and Messrs. Veitch; and by the American Universities, with which the author associates the names of Professor Sargent and Miss Willmott.

Part II. (*Le Jardin*, vol. xxi. No. 486, p. 150; with 8 figs.; May 20, 1907).—This part of M. Mottet's article deals more particularly with the Chinese plants introduced by MM. Vilmorin and the house of Vilmorin, Andrieux et Cie. A long list is cited.—*F. A. W.*

Chloræa virescens. By R. A. Rolfe (*Bot. Mag.* tab. 8100).—Chili. Nat. ord. *Orchidaceae*; tribe *Neottieae*. A deciduous terrestrial herb 1-1½ foot high; scape erect; raceme dense, 4-6 inches long; flowers large, yellow, veined with green.—*G. H.*

Chrysanthemum Disease. By G. Derbonn and G. Mingaud (*Le Jardin*, vol. xxi. No. 477, p. 12; January 5, 1907).—*Phytoecia pustulata*, a minute black coleopterous insect; deposits its eggs in the terminal buds of chrysanthemums from April–July. When hatched the larvae burrow into the shoots of the plant, and even reach the roots. Hardy, outdoor varieties only are attacked, and these should be protected, looked over, watered, &c., as carefully as the choicer varieties. From April to June the grub may be picked off by hand, and all shoots already pierced should be cut off 2 inches and more below the injury and burned. Sulphur dressings are advantageous in May and June.—*F. A. W.*

Chrysanthemums. By Le Texnier (*Le Jardin*, vol. xx. No. 473, pp. 329, 345, 359, 474, 478; November 5, 1906).—An interesting historical account of the chrysanthemum since its introduction into Europe. Recapitulates the development and names of the many varieties successively cultivated.—*F. A. W.*

Clematis montana rubens. By A. Pirlot (*Le Jardin*, vol. xx. No. 475, p. 360; with coloured plate; December 5, 1906).—Recently introduced from China by Wilson. Very free grower and strongly recommended.—*F. A. W.*

Clematis Tangutica. By S. Mottet (*Le Jardin*, vol. xx. No. 472, p. 308; fig.; Oct. 20, 1906).—Recently introduced from St. Petersburg. Has glabrous leaves and pendulous yellow flowers, a form highly superior to *C. orientalis*. Flowers July–August; very hardy and decorative. Can be propagated by seeds or cuttings.—*F. A. W.*

Cocoa-nut Palm, Bud-rot, Disease of (*Jour. Imp. Dep. Agr. W.I.* vol. vi. No. 3; 1905).—The bud-rot disease has been known in some localities by the name of " Fever." As the result of recent investigations its origin has been traced to the fungus *Pestalozzia palmarum* (Cooke), but the foul smell of the diseased parts seems to indicate also some bacteriological influence, when the palm is already weakened by fungus. The consensus of opinion appears to be, that when the trees are attacked it is hopeless to dream of their recovery, and the only course to be adopted is to fell diseased trees and burn or properly disinfect with sulphate of copper the terminal bud. Only the most energetic action is likely to avail.—*M. C. C.*

Codlin Moth and Apple Scab. By C. L. Marlatt and W. A. Orton (*U.S.A. Dep. Agr., Farm. Bull.* 247; 9 figs.; 1906).—Summarises the means of control suggested in other papers and already reviewed in these abstracts.—*F. J. C.*

Codonopsis Tangshen. By S. A. Skau (*Bot. Mag.* tab. 8090).— China. Nat. ord. *Campanulaceae*; tribe *Campanuleae*. Perennial herb, stems twining to 10 feet in length ; corolla 1½ inch long, greenish, purple-spotted, and striped inside.—*G. H.*

Colchicum crociflorum. By C. H. Wright (*Bot. Mag.* tab. 8055).— Turkestan. Nat. ord. *Liliaceae* ; tribe *Colchiceae.* Perianth 3-4 inches, white, with an external purple band.—*G. H.*

Coloured Glass : Effect on Fruit (*Le Jardin,* vol. xxi. No. 477, p. 12 ; January 5, 1907).—According to the Bulletin of Agricultural Information, pots of ripe strawberries when placed respectively under red and blue glass show a marked difference. Those beneath red glass were completely spoiled in two days, those beneath blue remained good for a week (see abstract on p. 257, vol. xxxii., June 1907, JOURNAL R.H.S.).

F. A. W.

Coloured Glass : Effect on Vegetation (*Le Jardin,* vol. xx. No. 470, p. 273 ; September 20, 1906).—Pursuing his researches on the action of coloured radiation upon growth, M. Camille Flammarion finds that *Impatiens hostii* presents a remarkable exception to the general rule. Under green glass it grew about 40 cm. (16 inches), under blue glass 36 cm. (14½ inches), under red 28 cm. (11 inches), while under white glass only 36 cm. (14½ inches). There were no symptoms of etiolation. Male fern under similar conditions grew very slowly, but remained green till the end of January in the blue house, and till March in the green.—*F. A. W.*

Coreopsis 'Tom Thumb,' 'Rayon d'Or.' (Rivoire, Denaiffe) (*Le Jardin,* vol. xxi. No. 478, p. 28 ; with fig. ; January 20, 1907).— New variety, highly recommended.—*F. A. W.*

Corn Selection. By F. W. Card (*U.S.A. Exp. Stn. Rhode I., Bull.* 116 ; 9 figs. ; October 1906).—A continuation of the work in selecting corn with the object of increasing the number of ears produced is here reported upon (see JOURN. R.H.S. vol. 29, p. 892). A steady increase in the number of ears per plant has been obtained, over 90 per cent. of the plants now bearing more than one ear, against 35 per cent. in 1901. One plant produced thirteen ears. Selection from the upper ears gave the best results, this being probably due to their better nutrition.—*F. J. C.*

Cotton, Fungoid Diseases of. By L. Lewton-Brain, B.A., F.L.S. (*Jour. Imp. Dep. Agr. W.I.* vol. vi. No. 2 ; 1905).—There are three chief leaf diseases of cotton in the West Indies, none of which can be described as serious at present, though they might become so.

"Rust," due to *Uredo Gossypii.*

"Leaf spot," caused by *Cercospora gossypina.*

"Leaf mildew," cause not identified.

Boll diseases are : "Anthracnose," probably caused by *Colletotrichum Gossypii.*

"Black boll" appears under all conditions, and is probably associated with bacteria,

Stem diseases seem to be confined to a kind of wilt disease, which is probably caused by a species of *Fusarium*, equally with a similar disease in the United States.—*M. C. C.*

Cotton, Insect Pests of. By Henry A. Ballou, B.Sc. (*Jour. Imp. Dep. Agr. W.I.* vol. vi. No. 2 ;. 1905).

The following are enumerated :—The cotton worm (*Aletia argillacea*), cotton stainers (*Dysdercus andreae*; *D. annuliger*), the red maggot (*Diplosis* sp.), cotton-leaf blister mite (*Eriophyes Gossypii*).

Other insect pests :—Cotton boll weevil (*Anthonomus grandis*), cotton aphis (*Aphis Gossypii*), scale insects (*Lecanium nigrum; Chionaspis minor; Dactylopius sacchari*).

Subsequently, in an appendix, the insect whose larvæ is named above as "red maggot" is described and named *Porricondyla* (*Epidosis*) *Gossypii*) Coq.—*M. C. C.*

Cotton Stainers. By H. A. Ballou, B.Sc. (*Jour. Imp. Dep. Agr. W.I.* vol. vii. No. 1 ; 1906).—This is a concise and descriptive enumeration of the species of cotton stainers, belonging to the genus *Dysdercus*, which are known to occur in the Lower Antilles and Trinidad, and in tropical and subtropical America; with notes on their habits and life-histories. Their chief interest consists in their reputation as pests of the cotton plant.—*M. C. C.*

Cottony Maple Scale. By C. Bues (*U.S.A. Exp. Stn. Wisconsin, Ann. Rep.* 1905, pp. 315–321).—This insect attacks maples and does considerable damage. It is recommended to—(1) cut out all dead wood ; (2) head back the tree in winter ; (3) spray the tree with 40 per cent. kerosene emulsion or with caustic wash ; (4) paint large wounds with a thick paste of tar ; (5) scrape off rough bark of trees.—*F. J. C.*

Cover Crops for Young Orchards. By R. A. Emerson (*U.S.A. Exp. Stn. Nebraska, Bull.* 92 ; 12 figs.; June 1906).—Cover crops in orchards are much used in parts of the States. Generally the crop is sown in late summer, allowed to remain on the ground all the winter, and worked into the soil in spring. The object of the cover crop is mainly to dry the ground so that the trees finish up their summer growth early and ripen their wood, rendering them immune from frost attacks ; the frosts should kill the crop so that the light autumn rains are conserved ; at the same time it should be thick enough to prevent freezing of the ground as much as possible in winter. The digging in of the crop will improve the physical condition of the soil, and if a leguminous crop is used the soil is enriched in nitrogen. Cow-peas and soy beans give the best result if sown in the latter part of June ; maize and German millet are also satisfactory cover crops.—*F. J. C.*

Cranberry Investigations. By A. R. Whitson, O. G. Malde, and C. B. Hardenberg (*U.S.A. Exp. Stn. Wisconsin*; 23rd *Annual Rep.*, pp. 135–159 ; October 1906).—A long account of experiments carried out to ascertain the influence of various conditions on the cultivation of the cranberry and the eradication of insects. Flooding is frequently resorted o, and it is found that the plants will withstand long flooding if the water is of a low temperature, but if it be above 65 degrees the flooding must be of short duration.—*F. J. C.*

Crossing Experiments with Sweet Corn. By B. D. Halstead and J. A. Kelsey (*U.S.A. Exp. Stn. New Jersey, Bull.* 170; February 1904).— An historical account of corn (maize) is given, with some botanical notes concerning the plant; then follows a general account of the experiments in cross- and in-breeding corn.—*F. J. C.*

Cynorchis compacta. By R. A. Rolfe (*Bot. Mag.* tab. 8053).— Natal. Nat. ord. *Orchidaceae*; tribe *Ophrydeae*. A dwarf terrestrial herb. Scape 4–7 inches, many-flowered; flowers white, with red-spotted lip.

G. H.

Cypripedium tibeticum. By R. A. Rolfe (*Bot. Mag.* tab. 8070).— Eastern Tibet and Western China. Nat. ord. *Orchidaceae*; tribe *Cypripedieae*. A terrestrial herb ½–1 foot high. Leaves 2–5 inches long; flowers solitary, 4 inches across, striped and reticulated with reddish-purple on a paler ground; front of lip suffused with dark purple.—*G. H.*

Cytisus Andreanus. By L. Mottet. (*Rev. Hort.* June 16, 1906, pp. 313, 314).—Description of several varieties of this pretty bloom raised by Smith, of Newry, Ireland. Planting on own roots is advised, as although development is more rapid when grafted on the laburnum as usual, the latter only last a few years.—*C. T. D.*

Daffodil Yellow Stripe Disease. By Fanny W. Currey (*Garden,* No. 1797, p. 230; April 28, 1906).—With regard to this malady I venture to make a suggestion which I think may possibly be of use. I believe the stripe may be a result of over-division of bulbs. I have never seen it in old-established clumps. I rarely see it among first-sized bulbs, or even among first-sized offsets. I once had a stock of which the foliage was absolutely perfect as to first- and second-sized bulb, but the third and fourth sizes were streaky. They were replanted to grow on, and next year there was not a trace of streakiness among them. Division of bulbs, except when it occurs by a natural falling asunder of the parts, produces some bleeding, and it appears to me possible that the smaller portion of the divided bulb does not retain sufficient colouring matter.—*E. T. C.*

Dahlia, The. By Charles Baltet (*Rev. Hort.* pp. 209–212; 2 figs.; May 1, 1906).—An interesting article on the origin of the dahlia and its introduction from Mexico, with a description of the various distinct groups into which it has sported. The illustration of the wild type is particularly interesting as a contrast.—*C. T. D.*

Dahlias, Cuttings of. By Rivoire *père et fils* (*Le Jardin,* vol. xxi. No. 481, p. 70; 3 figs.; March 5, 1907).—Take last year's tubers in March — not before. Clean well and wipe off all mould &c. Bury in frame, with good soil mixed with sand, up to the neck of the tuber. Water lightly and cover at night. In about three weeks the shoots will be ready for cutting, *i.e.* when they are 2-4 inches high.   Cut them off with a sharp knife, including a small bit of the tuber (fig. 42).   Fresh shoots will develop, which can be taken off, after a couple of months.   Plant in thumb-pots in good sandy leaf-mould.   Mark each parent tuber and corresponding cuttings with name or number of variety.   Put all the pots close together in a hotbed, 15°-20° C. (60°-70° Fahr.) ; keep moist and shaded ; the cuttings will strike in about three weeks.   Repot in 3-inch pots in a cooler frame; when rooted again cool off by gradually opening the frame.—*F. A. W.*

Dahlias : Grafting to obtain Multicoloured Blooms.   By

M. Lombartrix (*Le Jardin*, vol. xxi. No. 483, p. 103 ; April 5, 1907).—Rivoire's method of grafting (as described below) can be modified in various directions—notably for the production of multicoloured dahlias—by inserting a number of grafts from different varieties into one tuber. One plant of ' Etoile du Diable ' in this way bore nine varieties of blooms, of distinct colours, flowering from August to October.   This particular plant was kept under a shaded bell-glass for some days till the grafts had struck.   The rest were plunged in a cold house, and shaded and watered till well rooted in twenty to twenty-five days, and subsequently potted or planted out.   These grafts were made in March ; the method succeeds perfectly in the open air in August if shaded.—*F. A. W.*

Dahlias, Grafts of.   By Rivoire *père et fils* (*Le Jardin*, vol. xxi.

No. 482, p. 85 ; 1 fig. ; March 20, 1907).—Strongly recommended for pot culture.   Choose large tubers of previous year.   Slice off top to remove all eyes, and make V-shaped slit on one side.   Take a cutting prepared as above but trimmed into a wedge to fit the groove.   Bind with raphia, cover with putty.   Put in hot frame and shade well, even when the plants are cooled off.   These plants make roots but no tubers, so they cannot be utilised a second year.   If tubers should be formed they do not come true to the variety.—*F. A. W.*

Dahlias : Propagation by Seed and Division.   By Rivoire

(*Le Jardin*, xxi. No. 480, p. 55 ; February 20, 1907).—The seed of single dahlias should be sown February–April in a hot-bed or cool house. Use clean pots with plenty of drainage, and fill up to $\frac{1}{2}$ inch from the top.   Sow the seeds at this level, not more than $\frac{1}{4}$ in. deep.   Keep the pots moist, watering with a fine rose so as not to disturb the seedlings. Germination takes place in about twelve days, according to temperature. When the seedlings produce four leaves they must be pricked out separately into 3-inch pots, with good soil, and treated as described in the next abstract on cuttings.   Division of tubers is not advisable, since it leads to rapid degeneration, and accounts for much disappointment when the choice varieties purchased lose their characteristics.   When resorted to, large tubers from the previous year should be planted in the hottest part of the garden at the end of April or early in May.   Bury, but let the neck project just beyond the soil.   Keep a mat handy to throw over in case of frost.   Take up about the middle of May and divide off each shoot with its proportion of root and tuber ; then plant out.—*F. A. W.*

Dahlias, Sexual Reproduction of. By Professor R. Gérard (*Le Jardin*, vol. xxi. No. 479, p. 42,; with 3 figs.; February 5, 1907. Also summary and more practical details on p. 46).—A minute scientific description of the structure of the dahlia flower, and mechanism of pollination, with the intention of assisting practical experiment.—*F. A. W.*

Davidia Involucrata. By S. Mottet (*Le Jardin*, vol. xx. No. 466, p. 216; with 3 figs.; July 20, 1906).—Gives the history of the discovery of this remarkable tree, with full botanical description.

F. A. W.

Deutzia scabra Thunb., *not* Hort. By S. Mottet (*Le Jardin*, vol. xx. No. 464, p. 180; with fig.; June 20, 1906).—The characteristics of the true *Deutzia scabra* vs. *D. crenata*, with which it is often confused, are enumerated, with a list of other new species, notably the hybrids of M. Lemoine.—*F. A. W.*

Deutzia Wilsoni. By T. F. Duthie (*Bot. Mag.* tab. 8083).—Western China. Nat. ord. *Saxifragaceae*; tribe *Hydrangeae*. A handsome shrub. Branches reddish-brown; leaves 3-4½ inches long; flowers ⅞ inch across, pure white.—*G. H.*

" Droppers" of Tulipa and Erythronium, The. By Agnes Robinson (*Ann. Bot.* vol. xx. p. 429-440; 2 plates; October 1906).— It is pointed out that the vegetative reproduction characteristic cf bulbous plants possesses a great drawback in that it tends to over-crowding. Various methods are adopted by plants to overcome this disadvantage; these have been classed together as " lateral migration movements." Similarly when the depth in the soil does not appear to be appropriate to the plant, an effort is made to rectify the defect, and for " descending movements " the peculiar stolons known as " droppers " are particularly well adapted. The authoress deals with the subject from an anatomical as well as a morphological standpoint. It is shown that, in the plants mentioned in the title, the immature bulb produces each year a single foliage leaf continued at its base into a hollow tube " the dropper," enclosing a bulb at its tip. The anatomy confirms the view that the dropper is partly axial and partly foliar; the region of greatest growth is, however, immediately behind the apex, showing that this foliar-axial organ has become root-like in more than mere externals.—*A. D. C.*

Eichornea crassipes, Wintering of. By E. Courtois (*Rev. Hort.*, November 16, 1906, pp. 525, 526).—Difficult to preserve in winter in water unless the temperature is maintained; but if the stolons be potted in well-drained sandy peat at end of October, kept in a warm house for a short time, and then transferred to a cool one (under or on the staging with geranium cuttings), they will start into healthy growth the following May when replaced in water, flowering even in the open.—*C. T. D.*

Elm Leaf Beetle. By W. E. Britton (*U.S.A. Exp. Stn. Conn.; Bull.* 155; 6 figs.; May 1907).—The English Elm (*Ulmus campestris*) is most affected by this beetle, which is a native of Europe, where, however, it never assumes the character of a pest, but *U. montana, U. alata, U. fulva, U. suberosa,* and *U. racemosa* are all attacked. The mature beetles eat holes in the leaves, but the main damage is done by the larvæ, which eat away the under surface of the leaves. The worst affected trees usually drop their foliage in the middle of July, a second crop being produced, which is sometimes devoured by a second brood of beetles, there being at least two broods during the year. The trees are naturally greatly weakened by this defoliation. The larvae are black and about ½ inch long when mature, the pupa is bright orange yellow and is found at the base of the tree, and the beetle is light yellow at first, finally darkening to a dull olive green with a distinct black stripe down each wing case. The most important natural enemy is a fungus (*Sporotrichum globuliferum,* Speg.), and the praying mantis and some bugs feed upon it. Spraying with arsenate of lead 3-5 lb., water 50 gals., as soon as the leaves expand, or thoroughly over the under surface of the leaves about June 1, is followed by good results. If arsenate of lead cannot be obtained, Paris green may be used.—*F. J. C.*

Entomology, Economic. By H. A. Gossard (*U.S.A. Exp. Stn. Ohio, Bull.* 164 ; 12 figs.; July 1905).—Under the title of "Winter Manual of Practice in Economic Zoology" the author outlines the treatment which may be adopted in winter in dealing with a large number of garden pests, giving a table showing the "crop affected," "name of insect," "stage in which the winter is passed," "recognition marks," "treatment," and "when to treat." The methods advocated in specific cases include encouragement of birds, clean culture, spraying, grease banding, pruning, destruction of hiding places, and the collection and burning of the pests themselves.—*F. J. C.*

Entomology, Economic, in Connecticut. By W. E. Britton, Ph.D. (*U.S.A. Exp. Stn. Conn., 6th Ann. Rep.* 1906, Part IV.; pp. 219-306 ; 16 plates, 13 figs.).—A large part of this report is occupied by an account of the work done towards the suppression of the gipsy moth in the State, against which a determined onslaught is being made. The spiny elm caterpillar (*Euvanessa antiopa* Linn.) did considerable damage to elm, poplar, and willow in the early part of the year, and a spray of Paris green is recommended in the spring. An account of the insect enemies of the tobacco occupies pages 263–279, following which are details of spraying experiments against San José scale. The lime-sulphur mixtures (*q.v.*) are recommended, and failing these the commercial miscible oils. Other insects of less importance are mentioned.

F. J. C.

Erica, A Wild Serviceable. By G. Ugolini (*Bull. R. Soc. Tosc. Ort.* 5, p. 147 ; 1907).—During a winter sojourn on the Brenta Canal in the Alps, near the Italian frontier, the author observed a charming Erica which he believed to be *E. multiflora nana compacta,* which grows in great masses on the slopes and steep declivities of that region, in soil formed by the detritus of rocks fallen from the top of high precipices. The plants form a beautiful sight with their myriads of tubular flowers emerging from the axils of the small leaves forming spikes 5–10 centimetres (2–10 inches) long, and of a whitish-rose colour. They make red carpets in those alpine solitudes where in March and April ice and snow reign supreme. It could be grown in small pots and could be used for cut flowers, the latter being very resistant and persistent at a season when flowers are scarce. It is not new, but a plant which might be made use of.—*W. C. W.*

Erica terminalis. By S. A. Skau (*Bot. Mag.* tab. 8063).—Southern Europe. Nat. ord. *Ericaceae* ; tribe *Ericeae.* A shrub not exceeding 5 feet in height. Flowers rose-coloured.—*G. H.*

Eryngium. By Ad. Van den Heede (*Le Jardin*, vol. xx. No. 472, p. 309 ; October 20, 1906).—General article, enumerating eighteen varieties besides *E. amethystinum* and *E. Zabelinum*, which is one of the most intensely blue.—*F. A. W.*

Eucomis punctata. By A. Van den Heede (*Le Jardin*, vol. xx. No. 475, p. 358 ; December 5, 1906).—Liliaceous plant introduced from the Cape in 1783. About 10 inches high, with twenty-five to thirty little starry flowers, cream-coloured, with purple ovary. Strongly recommended for window culture.—*F. A. W.*

Eulophia nuda. By R. A. Rolfe (*Bot. Mag.* tab. 8057).—India and China. Nat. ord. *Orchidaceae* ; tribe *Vandeae.* A terrestrial herb. Leaves 4–12 inches long ; flowers variable in colour, rose-purple to pink or yellow-green ; petals $\frac{3}{4}$–1 inch long ; lip with yellow centre.—*G. H.*

Euphorbia heterophylla. By Feuillat (*Le Jardin*, vol. xxi. No. 480, p. 55 ; February 20, 1907).—A new and characteristic species, with bicoloured red and green bracts. Flowers August–September.

F. A. W.

Euphorbia Jacquiniaeflora. By A. van den Heede (*Le Jardin*, vol. xxi. No. 478, p. 27 ; January 20, 1907).—A valuable greenhouse plant that has dropped out of cultivation undeservedly ; characterised by brilliant scarlet bracts.

Euphorbia lophogona. By O. Stapf (*Bot. Mag.* tab. 8076).—Madagascar. Nat. ord. *Euphorbiaceae* ; tribe *Euphorbieae.* A small erect shrub. Stem woody at base, succulent above ; the five angles crested by the large, vertical, almost confluent, deeply lacerate stipules ; leaves in terminal tufts, 8 inches long ; flowers in cymes ; bracts white, opposite.—*G. H.*

Euphorbia procumbens. By N. E. Brown (*Bot. Mag.* tab. 8082).—South Africa. Nat. ord. *Euphorbiaceac* ; tribe *Euphorbieae.* A dwarf succulent herb. Branches numerous, 6 inches long ; leaves $\frac{1}{8}$–$\frac{1}{3}$ inch long, spreading, fleshy ; glands yellow, changing to orange and bright red.

G. H.

Ficus Krishnae. By D. Prain (*Bot. Mag.* tab. 8092).—India. Nat. ord. *Urticaceae*; tribe *Artocarpeae*. A small tree. Leaves cup-shaped, upper surface outside; receptacles axillary, globose, 6–7 lines diameter.—*G. H.*

Flower Preservation by Cold (*Rev. Hort.* June 16, 1906, p. 271).—Pæony flowers preserved several months and subsequently exhibited in fine condition by being cut at stages near the opening period, the stems placed in water, and the buds then stored in refrigerating chambers, full development resulting when desired on removal to warmth. Details of procedure.—*C. T. D.*

Flowers by Artificial Light. By Emily E. Williamson (*Garden*, No. 1828, p. 257; December 1, 1906).—In arranging flowers for evening use, the first consideration should be their capabilities for lighting up well. This is a subject which well repays careful study, for colours change so when artificial light is used, some losing all their brilliancy and failing to harmonise with their surroundings, others deepening in intensity. Much disappointment may be avoided if these changes are carefully noted beforehand.

As a general rule, blues should be avoided, for although some charming schemes may be worked out with cornflowers, pale blue Delphiniums (these make a delightful decoration, using the small side shoots only), plumbago, &c., by daylight, they should not be employed for evening purposes. Mauve is also an unsatisfactory colour on the whole, but some mauve flowers which have a decided tinge of pink light up well, among others certain sweet peas, such as 'Admiration,' 'Lady Grisel Hamilton,' and the darker 'Emily Eckford.'—*E. T. C.*

Freesias. By S. G. Smallridge (*Garden*, No. 1808, p. 19; July 14, 1906).—I know of nothing that gives a better return for little trouble, more especially in the amateur's small greenhouse, than the Freesia. My plan of growing Freesias is to pot up the bulbs early in August in a rich soil, three parts loam, one part leaf-soil, and some sand, with a 6-inch potful of soot to a barrow of soil. Place ten bulbs in a 5-inch pot and cover with about 1 inch of soil. Place out of doors in a sunny place, say, until the end of September. Then bring into a cool house, placing them near the glass. See that they do not suffer from want of water. When the flower spikes appear about February, the plants should have a little manure water once or twice a week.

After flowering, the faded flowers should be pinched off and the plants put in the sunniest place available, and kept well supplied with water until the foliage begins to turn yellow; then reduce the water gradually until all the leaves are dead. The bulbs can be shaken out and stored away in a dry and cool place until it is time to pot them up again. Anyone who cares to carry out these simple instructions will be rewarded with plenty of flowers.—*E. T. C.*

Freesias, Pink (*Le Jardin*, vol. xxi. No. 484, p. 123; April 20, 1907).—Signor Raggioneri, of Florence, has produced a number of hybrid freesias, ranging in colour from pink to violet. The first crosses were between *F. refracta* and *Leichtlinii*, resulting in the *F. Giardino Corso Salviati*, which, again, crossed with *F. Armstrongi*, has yielded these colours.—*F. A. W.*

Fruit Growing in Maryland (*U.S.A. Peninsula, Hort. Soc.,* 19*th Ann. Rep.*, 1906).—This report, though it contains no new observations, gives an excellent account of the fruit-growing industry in Maryland and of the activities of those engaged in horticulture in that State. Articles on peach growing, insect enemies of crops, apples, pears, grapes, strawberries, and other matters all find a place in the journal.

F. J. C.

Fruit Growing in Oregon (*U.S.A. Stn. Bd. Hort. Oregon, Ann. Rep.* 1905).—This excellent report deals in a series of articles, plainly written and splendidly illustrated, with the various aspects of fruit-growing in Oregon. The article on the apple is particularly worthy of mention.—*F. J. C.*

Fruits, New. By M. Houssy (*Le Jardin,* vol. xx. No. 476, p. 371; fig.; December 20, 1906).—Gives list of several new pears, peaches (notably 'Le Vainqueur'), apples, and plums.—*F. A. W.*

Genista cinerea. By O. Stapf (*Bot. Mag.* tab. 8086).—Western Mediterranean region. Nat. ord *Leguminosae*; tribe *Genisteae*. A shrub 1–3 feet high. Leaves small, flowers yellow.—*G. H.*

Genista dalmatica. By O. Stapf (*Bot. Mag.* tab. 8075).—North-West Balkan Peninsula. Nat. ord. *Leguminosae*; tribe *Genisteae*. A small rigid shrub with spiny branches; flowers ½ inch across, yellow.

G. H.

Gerbera aurantiaca. By N. E. Brown (*Bot. Mag.* tab. 8079).—Natal and Transvaal. Nat. ord. *Compositae*; tribe *Mutisiaceae*. Herb with radical leaves 5–10 inches long, 1–2 inches broad; peduncle 4½––16 inches long, white tomentose; flower-head 2–3 inches diameter; ray florets blood-red; disk brownish purple.—*G. H.*

Gipsy, and Brown-Tail Moths. By Dr. L. O. Howard (*U.S.A. Exp. Stn. New Hampshire, Bull.* 128; January 1907).—These pests are steadily spreading over New Hampshire. Not only are trees frequently completely defoliated and often killed by the insects referred to, but the hairs from the caterpillars of the brown-tail moth frequently cause great annoyance and irritation to the skin of human beings. Many of the towns are aiding property owners within their district in destroying the caterpillars, the most effective means of controlling the pests being soaking the eggs of the gipsy moth, which are usually laid in clusters on the bark of trees, this work being done during the autumn, winter, or spring, and removing the webs in which the young caterpillars of the brown-tail moth hibernate during the winter, these webs being formed near the tips of the branches of the affected trees.—*F. J. C.*

Gladiolus carmineus. By C. H. Wright (*Bot. Mag.* tab. 8068).—
South Africa. Nat. ord. *Irideae*; tribe *Ixieae*. Stem 1½ foot long;
flowers 3 inches across; perianth carmine, two lower with a paler
purplish spot surrounded by a dark-red border.—*G. H.*

Gladiolus primulinus. By C. H. Wright (*Bot. Mag.* tab. 8080).—
Tropical Africa. Nat. ord. *Irideae*; tribe *Ixieae*. Leaves 18 inches long,
1 inch broad; perianth uniformly primrose-yellow, 2½ inches across.

G. H.

Gloxinia. By Le Texnier (*Le Jardin*, vol. xx. No. 464, p. 189;
June 20, 1906).—Useful historical account of the genus *Gloxinia* and
its development in different countries.—*F. A. W.*

Gonioscypha eucomoides. By O. Stapf (*Bot. Mag.* tab. 8078).—
Eastern Himalaya. Nat. ord. *Liliaceae*; tribe *Aspidistreae*. Perennial
herb, with a short rhizome. Leaves 10–15 inches long, 5-6 inches broad;
spike 3-4 inches long, with dense green flowers, ⅓ inch diameter; petals
broad, with crisped margins.—*G. H.*

Gourds, Ornamental. By Y. (*Garden*, No. 1821, p. 178; fig.;
October 13, 1906).—Whenever it is seen and however it is grown, the ornamental gourd in its various forms always attracts considerable attention.
There is such a wide range of form and size in the fruits produced that an
extensive collection like that shown at the recent meeting of the Royal
Horticultural Society comprised an infinite variety of shapes, some
resembling oranges, pears, custards, eggs, clubs, and even snakes; in
fact, the fruits range in size from that of a gooseberry up to the mammoth pumpkin, which attains to enormous proportions, sometimes
approaching 200 lb. in weight. In addition, the rich colouring possessed
by many makes them very attractive; and as they retain this for a considerable time when cut, they are valuable for house decoration in the
autumn and winter, but they should not be cut until quite ripe. They
dry best when suspended from rafters in a dry shed.

Gourds are readily grown in this country when planted in open, sunny
positions, and they may be used in a number of different ways. A very
effective method is to train them up poles.—*E. T. C.*

Graft, Influence of, on Rooting of Stock. By Pierre Passy
(*Rev. Hort.* September 16, 1906, p. 432).—It has been observed that the
nature of the roots of grafted pears appears to determine to some extent
the nature of those subsequently developed by the stock as regards extent
of ramification.—*C. T. D.*

**Grapes East of the Rocky Mountains: Insect and Fungous
Enemies.** By A. L. Quaintance and C. L. Shear (*U.S.A. Dep. Agr., Farm.
Bull.* 284; 35 figs.; May 1907).—The principal insects and fungi attacking
the grape are briefly described and illustrated, and appropriate methods of
treatment are mentioned.—*F. J. C.*

Greenhouses: New System.—By G. T. Gregnan (*Rev. Hort.*
April 1, 1906, pp. 162-3; 2 figs.).—Provision is made for two ranges

of plants, one above the other, the upper one arranged on long, box-like shelves (with provision against drip), which are suspended in such a way as to be easily elevated or lowered, by means of pulleys—elevated to bring the plants nearer the light, and lowered for watering and tending purposes. The lower plants are on the ground level and are amply lighted by lateral glazing, extending nearly to the ground and consisting of large panes about 5 feet by 2½ feet. The roof is very slightly inclined and glazed similarly.—*C. T. D.*

Guavas: "Ripe Rot" or Mummy Disease. By John L. Shelton (*U.S.A. Exp. Stn. W. Va., Bull.* 104 ; 4 plates ; April 1906).—The "ripe rot" or mummy disease has been reported from Mexico, Porto Rico, Florida, and Australia, being often very destructive to the crop. Brown spots appear on the ripening fruit, increasing until the entire fruit becomes affected, the decaying fruits finally falling off or the "mummies" remaining on the trees. The fungus causing the disease is *Gloeosporium Psidii* (Delacroix). An ascigerous stage, very similar to that of *Glomerella*, was obtained by artificial cultures. The writer was not able to find any great difference between the fungus and that causing bitter rot of the apple.—*M. C. C.*

Gurania Malacophylla. By T. A. Sprague (*Bot. Mag.* tab. 8085).—Upper Amazons. Nat. ord. *Cucurbitaceae* ; tribe *Cucumerineae*. A tall climber ; leaves broadly ovate, 3–5-lobed ; male flowers in a globose head ; corolla of five linear crimson petals ; female flower unknown.

G. H.

Haricots, Threadless. By J. Barsac (*Le Jardin*, vol. xxi. No. 477, p. 10 ; January 5, 1907).—Seven new varieties of threadless haricot beans have recently been introduced by Sluis & Gruit, Enkhuysen, Holland, of which the dwarf kidney bean (*H. flageolet hâtif, jaune, pâle, sans fil*) is specially recommended.—*F. A. W.*

Hedysarum multijugum. By T. A. Sprague (*Bot. Mag.* tab. 8091).—Central Asia. Nat. ord. *Leguminosae* ; tribe *Hedysareae*. A shrub 4 feet high. Leaves pinnate, 6 inches long ; 8–13 pairs of leaflets ; racemes 6–12 inches long, with 9–25 flowers ; flowers ¾ inch across ; rose-red.—*G. H.*

Heliotropes, New Varieties of. By Max Garnier (*Rev. Hort.* June 16, 1906, pp. 288–9 ; 2 figs.).—The illustrations represent two very fine forms from M. Bruant Poictier's ' Camia ' and ' Marie Ollanesco,' while several others are described ' Ciel poitevin,' ' Ruskin,' ' Madame Mathilde Cremieux,' ' L'Aquitaine,' ' Frida,' ' Alexandre Myrial,' and ' Phenomenal.'—*C. T. D.*

Hollies, The Sea (Eryngium). By G. B. Mallett (*Garden*, No. 1806, p. 341 ; June 30, 1906).—The Eryngiums that owe their value as garden plants to the rich blue or silvery colouring of the stems and inflorescences have always been the more popular of the family. They are vigorous plants, of bushy habit, more refined than ornamental thistles, and of a distinctly decorative type, suggesting the vegetable inhabitants

of deserts in their spiny, drought-resisting character more than any
other type of garden plants. Those kinds that take the form of various
sub-tropical plants—such as yuccas, agaves, and bromeliads generally
—though now tolerably well known, have not been planted to any extent;
the preference is generally, and I think rightly, given to the more hardy
kinds that develop the colouring of amethyst and silver; for not only are
they more effective as border plants, but much easier to grow and, with
one exception, more lasting. They prefer a light soil, and if the position
is the warmest the garden affords one can rely upon excellent colouring
of stem and involucrum. All save one hybrid are easily raised from seeds
if procurable, and most will grow from root-cuttings freely if· divided
when the plants start to grow.—*E. T. C.*

Hollyhock Rust. By T. W. Kirk, F.L.S. (*Dep. Agr. N.Z., Bull.* No. 12;
December 1905).—This rust has been noted in New Zealand on seven
species of malvaceous plants, and the present bulletin is chiefly directed
to suggestions of preventive means. It recommends that all young
hollyhock plants should be carefully sprayed with Bordeaux mixture,
which will generally be found quite effective. If the disease appears
when the plants are on the point of flowering, the use of soda Bordeaux
mixture is recommended, owing to the fact that this spray does not in
any way stain the leaves and render them unsightly. All fading, diseased
leaves should be carefully collected and burnt. It is not considered
advisable to save seed from diseased plants.—*M. C. C.*

Horticultural Society, Transactions of the Iowa. Vol. xl.
Plates.—To quote the letter of transmittal to his Excellency the Governor
of Iowa, which is printed as a preface to this volume, "it contains the
fortieth annual report of the State Horticultural Society . . . also supplementary papers and discussions on horticulture, including the proceedings
of the four auxiliary societies, the whole showing the condition of horticulture in the State for the year 1905." The following were among the
subjects touched upon in the papers read before the societies and in the
subsequent discussions:—Strawberry Growing and Marketing; Apple
Choosing, Rearing, Planting, Cultivating, Harvesting, Marketing, and
Storing, all considered with reference to the conditions in Iowa; Propagation of Shrubs; American Wild Flowers as Garden Plants; the History
of the Chrysanthemum; Nature Study as a Part of Education; School
Gardens; Vineyards; Orchard Spraying; the Work of the State Experi-
mental Stations; Co-operation in Marketing Fruit; Top-grafting; the
Sweet Potato; Pollination of Flowers; Forest Survey of Iowa; Phenology
of Plants, with Tables giving Average Monthly Temperatures in Ames,
Iowa, during 1905, and the blooming periods of various plants and trees;
Potato Diseases and their Remedies; some Bacterial Diseases, including
Cabbage Rot, Soft Rot of Calla Lily, Wilt Disease of Tobacco, Crown
Gall and Hairy Root Diseases, Rust and Blight in all their Forms,
some Powdery Mildew Diseases; the Planting and Care of Woods;
Women's Work in Horticulture; Seedling Fruit Trees raised in South-
Eastern Iowa; New Fruits; Peach Growing; Orchard Troubles and
Treatment; the Control of Insects; the Preparation of Spray Mixtures;

Bees and their Relation to Horticulture ; Fruit in our Dietary ; American Native Shrubs ; Stone Fruits ; Small Fruits for the Farm ; Evergreens ; the Evolution of the Apple ; a List of Recommended Varieties of Several Sorts of Fruits ; the Greenhouse. It is evident, after reading all these various papers and discussions, that the culture of the apple is what comes nearest to the heart of all good American horticulturists. No time or trouble seems to be spared by State departments, by nurserymen, and by many private individuals to produce remunerative crops of apples in spite of the unfavourable climate of Iowa, either for export, the home market, or domestic consumption. Paper after paper on this subject was read, and no other seems to have produced so much interested discussion. We read first of the evolution of the *Pyrus baccata* from the *Pyrus malus*, native of Western Europe from the Caucasus to the Mediterranean and the Atlantic, and probably allied to the two sorts of wild crab whose charred remains are found among the Lake Dwellings of Switzerland. This was crossed with the little pear-like apple which is native to Eastern Siberia. According to Pliny, there were twenty-nine varieties of apple in cultivation about the beginning of the Christian era, but it was only, apparently, at the beginning of the nineteenth century that pomology began to attract wide attention.

In America it has been proved that to secure the best results it is better to rely upon varieties raised from home-grown seedlings than those from Russian parents, even some having their origin in the Atlantic States being failures in the severe climate of the more northerly States. In an account of his experiments in cross-breeding, Mr. C. G. Patten gives evidence of the marked influence of the male parent in determining the habit of growth of the young tree and the colour of its fruit, and he quotes some results as giving great encouragement in the attempt to produce fruit trees hardy enough to withstand the most rigorous North-Western winter.

The situation of the orchard, the preparation of the soil, the arrangement of the trees, the choice of varieties, and the subsequent care of the orchard were all described by successive speakers, as well as the business side of the industry. Cold storage as a means of equalising the price and regulating the supply of apples was advocated, and a co-operative association of fruit-growers, which has successfully negotiated with the railway companies in the matter of rapid and punctual carriage, and has thereby enormously increased the export of fruit from its own centre, was described.

The question of spraying occupied a large part of the attention of the societies, and members were almost unanimously in favour of it. Some few dissentients protested that it was too troublesome and unpleasant a job rather than that it was a useless one. On the whole the treatment most in favour seemed to consist of three or four sprayings with Bordeaux mixture and some arsenic compound—one just as the buds are swelling, one after the petals fall, one about ten days later, and the last ten days later still. One or two papers give the natural history of various orchard pests, and explain why different poisons must be used to control the ravages of different orders of insects. The eating insects, for instance, may be poisoned by some arsenic compound such as Paris green, scattered on the leaves ;

the sucking insects, which feed merely on the sap of the plant, may be smothered by clogging the delicate breathing apparatus at the side of their bodies with soap or kerosene emulsion ; and the scale insects must be dealt with by salt lime and sulphur washes. The most detailed of these natural history papers urges farmers to acquire, with or without the help of a small magnifying glass, an acquaintance with the different orders of insects, which will·enable them to determine what is the best way to extinguish the particular enemy they may be called on to fight.

The general opinion of the meetings was that liquid spraying was infinitely more effective than the dust spray which is sometimes recommended, but good results from dust spraying were recorded in cases where the water supply was deficient or too far away to be used profitably.

In certain cases winter spraying was recommended, though some objectors urged that it might prove to have been a mere waste of time and material. They mentioned cases where the dormant blossom was really killed by frost during the late autumn or winter, and either did not open at all or eventually proved unfertile. The following are the cases in which winter spraying was advised :—

For peach leaf curl, which is caused by a parasitic fungus, spray with Bordeaux mixture in March.

For leaf blister, spray before the buds open with whale-oil soap, kerosene emulsion, or salt lime and sulphur mixture.

For early leaf-eating insects, spray in winter with salt lime and sulphur wash.

It must be remembered that in any case winter spraying is not to be looked upon as a substitute for spraying foliage and fruit. Girdling fruit trees to make them bear was suggested in cases where the trees made rampant growth without blooming ; and one speaker advised planting a young orchard twice as thick as the trees were eventually to stand, and cutting out the intermediate ones when more space was required. *Wagner* was mentioned as an excellent nurse-tree, from its precocity and from its manner of growth.

The dewberry was much recommended as a paying crop, 100 bushels to the acre having been picked by one reporter. *Bartel* was the variety recommended, being free from spines. The plants should be protected in winter (in Iowa) and well cultivated, and pruning should be carefully attended to. As soon as the stems are 2 feet long they should be cut back, when they will throw out laterals and flower on these, and the plants should be gone over two or three times during the growing season. The dewberry roots deep and is not affected by drought.

The papers on grape-culture are interesting and enthusiastic, and contain lists of perfectly hardy varieties.

Several papers bewail the thriftless fashion in which many parts of the United States have been denuded of trees, thereby affecting the climate in some districts, reducing the water supply and causing the destruction of valuable land through erosion during heavy spates. Judicious replanting under expert advice is earnestly urged to reduce these evils, and the actual money benefit to the farmer of such plantations is also insisted upon.—*M. L. II.*

Hyacinths, The Grape. By W. T. (*Garden*, No. 1801, p. 283; fig.; May 26, 1906).—Many names have been applied to the various members of this charming family of early spring-flowering bulbs, but the greater number possess so great a resemblance that it is somewhat difficult to distinguish them from one another. Some of the more distinct kinds, however, are exceedingly useful for planting in groups on the borders of shrubberies and in open places in the wild garden. Seen in a mass on grassy banks nothing can exceed the beautiful effect produced by the numbers of racemes of bright violet-blue flowers of *M. conicum*. The large, handsome flower-heads stand up well above the green grassy foliage, and they last in perfection for a considerable period. Among the easiest of bulbs to grow, they increase very freely, and large masses may soon be obtained by lifting the bulbs every two or three years and dividing the clumps. They make excellent pot plants, and for the cold house they come in very useful during the month of April. Almost any soil suits the Grape Hyacinths, although the most suitable is a deeply worked and well-drained sandy loam.—*E. T. C.*

Insects, New or Unusual, in Michigan. By R. H. Pettit (*U.S.A. Exp. Stn. Michigan, Bull.* 244; 23 figs.; December 1906).— Records, with notes of the occurrence of the strawberry louse (*Aphis Forbesi*), cut-worms in beet, little grain moth (*Tinea granella*), flour moth (*Ephestia kuehniella*), greenhouse leaf-tier (*Phlyctaenia rubigalis*), wheat midge (*Diplosis tritici*), raspberry byturus (*Byturus unicolor*), straw-berry root-worm (*Scelodonta nebulosus*), bean weevil (*Bruchus quadri-maculatus*), powder-post beetles (*Lyctus* sp.), strawberry crown girdler (*Otiorhynchus ovatus*), strawberry weevil (*Anthonomus signatus*), cabbage curculio (*Ceutorhynchus rapae*), and the wheat joint-worm (*Isosoma tritici*).—*F. J. C.*

Insects of Orchard and other Fruits. By C. F. Adams (*U.S.A. Exp. Stn. Arkansas, Bull.* 92; 21 figs.; 1907).—Several common insect pests are dealt with briefly in this bulletin.—*F. J. C.*

Ipomoea purpurea, Fertilisation of. By A. Vigier (*Rev. Hort.* June 1, 1906, pp. 254–5).—An interesting note on the function of the corolla of flowers generally, and description of the manner in which in this case it is the inrolling of the edges of the fading flower which, coupled with its subsequent fall, brings the pollen into contact with the stigma mechanically and independently of insect aid.—*C. T. D.*

Iris bucharica. By W. Irving (*Garden*, No. 1798, p. 243; fig.; May 5, 1906).—One of the new plants of the year 1902, this handsome species was awarded a first-class certificate at a meeting of the Royal Horticultural Society on April 8 of that year. Since then it has become an inmate of many gardens, and has fully justified the distinction con-ferred on it, proving to be a plant of robust habit and very free flowering. A member of the Juno section of the genus *Iris*, it is closely allied to the well-known and beautiful yellow-flowered *I. orchioides*, from which it differs in having almost sessile flowers of a lighter colour. It was introduced into cultivation by Messrs. Van Tubergen, of Haarlem, from Eastern Bokhara, where it is found on mountain slopes at an elevation of 5,000 feet to 6,000 feet, growing on the edges of mountain streams. Of erect habit, with stems about 18 inches high, clothed with shining green, arching leaves, it is an admirable plant for a warm, sheltered border. It requires when in full growth an abundance of moisture and deep, loamy soil, which should be well mixed with plenty of mortar rubbish.—*F. T. C.*

Iris sicheana. By C. H. Wright (*Bot. Mag.* tab. 8059).—Asia Minor. Nat. ord. *Irideae*; tribe *Moraceae*. Leaves 3½ inches long; scape short; one-flowered; outer segments of perianth 2 inches long, silvery-grey striped with reddish-purple; crest yellow.—*G. H.*

Ixias and Sparaxis. By T. B. Field (*Garden*, No. 1795, p. 210; April 14, 1906).—These both require the same kind of cultivation, as they differ but little from each other. They are natives of South Africa, and need more sunshine than we can supply them with. They do not succeed as hardy bulbs in any part of Great Britain, but it is easy to ensure a fine bloom of them as of hyacinths or tulips. It follows, therefore, that they are better adapted for pot culture than in the open ground. The surest way to enjoy them is to get a new stock of bulbs, or, more properly speaking, corms, every year, as by such means a brilliant display at a small cost of money and labour may be ensured. For a good display of Ixias and Sparaxis potting should be done in the month of September, using a mixture of good leaf-mould one part, fibrous peat three parts, and rough silver sand two parts, or where a good sandy peat containing a reasonable amount of fibre can be procured this will suffice without any admixture whatever. And for all general purposes 5-inch pots, three to five roots in a pot, will as a rule be best as to size and numbers; but large pans, if somewhat shallow, are quite as suitable. In any case, it is folly to spread the roots over a large space, and five in a 5-inch pot will be none too many for a good head of bloom.—*E. T. C.*

Ixora macrothyrsa. By Ad. Van den Heede (*Le Jardin*, vol. xx. No. 468, p. 244; with fig.; August 20, 1906).—Gives description of the whole genus, with names and synonyms, notes on cultivation.

Julianaceae, a new Order of Flowering Plants. By W. Botting Hemsley (*Ann. Bot.* vol. xx., October 1906, pp. 467–471).—An abstract of a paper read at the Royal Society; the full account appears in the Proc. Roy. Soc. Series B. lxxvii. pp. 145, 158.

Two genera and five species are known. The plants are resiniferous, deciduous, dioecious, shrubs or small trees, with alternate, exstipulate, imparipinnate leaves. The flowers are small, green, and the males very different from the females: the former resembles in appearance that of the oak, the latter that of the sweet chestnut. The compound fruits are samaroid in form. The author compares the new order with Anarcardiaceae and Cupuliferae, and states that he believes the most natural position for it to be placed is between Juglandaceae and Cupuliferae.—*A. D. C.*

Kitchen Garden, How to Crop a small. By W. H. Morton (*Garden*, No. 1800, p. 265 ; May 19, 1906).—November and December are the best months for preparing the land, and the work should be carried out with due reference to the weather. On frosty days the manure required for use may be wheeled on to the land, which should be deeply dug or trenched. If the land be laid up in ridges to remain during the winter, the soil becomes thoroughly friable.

ROTATION OF CROPS.

This is a most important matter for consideration, and a proper system of rotation in cropping should be strictly carrried out. Never allow the same kind of vegetable to occupy the same piece of ground two years in succession, except in such cases as asparagus, rhubarb, seakale, &c., which occupy the ground for several seasons. Although the same plot may produce for several years in succession good crops of the same kind, such as onions, for instance, by being well and judiciously manured, yet it is not by any means a good practice. In the end the land would become so exhausted that no system of manuring would again fit it for a similar crop until a rigid system of rotation had been practised. Crops, such as cabbages and potatoes, which are of an exhaustive nature, should be relegated to different soil each year. Tap-rooted plants should be succeeded by those having fibrous roots ; thus beet, carrots, and parsnips may be followed by the cabbage tribe, which may also succeed beans and peas.—*E. T. C.*

Lantanas. By Le Texnier (*Le Jardin*, vol. xx. No. 470, p. 276 ; 2 figs. ; September 20, 1906).—Historical sketch of the genus in general.
F. A. W.

Lantanas, Dwarf. By E. Saget (*Le Jardin*, vol. xx. No. 470, p. 277 ; 2 figs. ; September 20, 1906).—Classification, with two figures, of the *Bruant* varieties, some fifty of these being enumerated.—*F. A. W.*

Larkspurs, Annual. By A. N. (*Garden*, No. 1813, p. 79; fig.; August 18, 1906).—Annual larkspurs, varieties of *Delphinium Ajacis*, are very showy hardy annuals. This remark is especially true of the double dwarf German rocket (hyacinth-flowered) varieties. The seeds are sold in separate colours or mixed. As there are upwards of a dozen different shades of colour, growers can select the particular shades they prefer. Light and dark blue, brick-red, rose, white, and lilac are the most distinct. If the soil is light the seeds may be sown where the plants are to flower. This may be done in late autumn or spring ; generally plants from the former sowing give the better results. Where the soil is heavy the seeds should be sown in boxes and the seedlings transferred to their flowering quarters in April or early in May. Clumps of separate colours on a border or in separate beds are very effective. The plants grow 18 inches to 2 feet in height. The spikes are densely packed with flowers.
E. T. C.

Legume Inoculation : Value of Commercial Cultures. By M. J. Prucha and H. A. Harding (*U.S.A. Exp. Stn. Geneva, Bull.* 282 ; December 1906).—The authors found in previous years that the inoculation material sent out dry on absorbent cotton was useless for the purpose for which it was intended, and now report similarly upon cultures which had been protected by being enclosed in tin boxes. It had been claimed for these that as the cultures were kept dry they would remain uninjured for a long time.—*F. J. C.*

Lemon Rot. By R. E. Smith.(*U.S.A. Exp. Stn. California, Bull.* 184; 3 figs.; January 1907).—The trouble dealt with is known as "brown rot," and spreads very rapidly through lemons in the packing-house and marketing box. The loss in one season amounted to 75,000 dollars. The rot has been found to be due to a hitherto undescribed fungus, *Pythiacystis citrophthora*, the spores of which are developed in the soil beneath the trees. Some fruit becomes infected in wet weather on the trees, but the chief source of infection is the water in the washing tank, which soon contains numbers of spores from the dust and dirt of the orchard. The fungus spreads from fruit to fruit through contact between them, but no spores are developed upon the fruits.—*F. J. C.*

Lilac, Double. By Georges Bellair (*Rev. Hort.* June 16, 1906, pp. 321–324; 3 illustrations).—An interesting article describing some very fine forms raised by M. Lemoine, and figuring two of the finest, 'Alphonse Lavallée' and 'Docteur Masters,' both white. A list of early and late forms is given, many of which by their description merit a place in our gardens and are of value for forcing purposes.— *C. T. D.*

Lilács, The. By W. J. Bean (*Garden*, No. 1799, p. 253; May 12, 1906).—Garden varieties of lilac, which now constitute one of the most beautiful groups of hardy shrubs, are derived from two species of *Syringa* only. These are the common lilac (*S. vulgaris*) and the Persian lilac (*S. persica*). It is to the former of these that the finest of the garden varieties owe their origin, although some of the hybrids between it and the Persian lilac are very delightful, notably, the old Rouen lilac.

Lilac-time, of which the poets sing, is a time of fragrance and colour in the garden, for it comes in later May; but there is nothing sweeter in its perfume or more alluring in its beauty even then than a flower-laden lilac. Although the common lilac is not a native of Britain, it has for over 300 years been an inmate of our gardens, and is as closely associated with rural scenery as almost any native plant. It is even doubtful if it be a native of Europe, for, although it has been found apparently wild in the region of the Danube, it was not till 1828 that it was admitted into the European flora. This seems a very late date for so noticeable a plant to have been discovered. Some authorities believe that it is, like the Persian lilac, of Asiatic—probably Chinese—origin. However this may be, the common lilac reached Western Europe about the middle of the sixteenth century, and the Persian lilac about the beginning of the seventeenth.

The first variety or hybrid of which we have any record is the Rouen lilac: this is said to have been raised in the Botanic Garden at Rouen near the end of the eighteenth century.—*E. T. C.*

Lilium Brownii. By H. P. (*Garden*, No. 1797, p. 234; coloured plate; April 28, 1906).—The typical *Lilium Brownii*, that is to say, the form the name of which first occurred in the catalogue of Mr. F. E. Brown, nurseryman, of Windsor, about the year 1838, has since that time been cultivated by the Dutch. While different works of reference give *Lilium Brownii* as a native of China, the fact remains that, much as that country has been explored of late, it has not, to my knowledge, been found there. Various allied forms have been imported, but not the Dutchman's *Lilium Brownii*. This last is a very beautiful lily that flowers, as a rule, in June. In the first place the bulbs are very distinct, having a narrow base from which they gradually widen upwards to an almost flat top. They are usually more or less tinged with reddish brown. The lower part of the stem, which is of a purplish hue, is leafless for some little distance, the leaves which clothe the upper portion being long, narrow, sharp-pointed, of a deep green tint, and recurving in a graceful manner. The large trumpet-shaped flowers are of an unusually thick, wax-like texture ; inside they are ivory-white, but heavily suffused with chocolate on the outside of the three outer segments, so that the un-opened buds are entirely of a reddish-brown hue, that is, when they have been grown in a spot fully exposed to the sun. The dark-brown anthers are very conspicuous against the white interior of the flower, which in showery weather is quickly discoloured thereby.—*E. T. C.*

Lilium candidum, Bulbil Generation on. By A. Vigier (*Rev. Hort.* September 1, 1906, p. 406).—The flowering stems of *Lilium candidum* if severed just above the soil and treated as cuttings in sand, the floral bud being suppressed, produce numerous bulbils in the axils both in the soil and in the air. It is suggested that rarer lilies might lend themselves to propagation in the same way.—*C. T. D.*

Lilium candidum, Fertility of. By Paul Passy (*Rev. Hort.* November 1, 1906, p. 506).—Author reports that the white lily in his locality (not named) fruits freely and regularly, and under varied conditions of soil and exposure.—*C. T. D.*

Lilium candidum, Fructification of. By L. Henry (*Rev. Hort.* April 1, 1906, pp. 158–160 ; fig.).—Some interesting remarks on the rarity of seed production in the species and modes of inducing it. The theory is advanced that the reproductive system is not at fault and the seeds are duly fertilised, the requisite energy, however, is subsequently diverted to form buds on the bulbs and the seed consequently fails. Seed may be fully developed if the stalks be severed at the base and suspended upside down, or the bulb may be exposed and all the scales and bulbils removed, leaving the stalks attached to the roots. By either of these means the reproductive energy becomes concentrated and seeds capable of germination are produced. The vicinity of *L. testaccum* to spontaneously fertile examples of *L. candidum* has been remarked, but no evidence of crossing is given.—*C. T. D.*

Lilium Duchartri. By C. H. Wright (*Bot. Mag.* tab. 8072).— Western and Central China. Nat. ord. *Liliaceae* ; tribe *Tulipeae*. Herb, about 3 feet high. Flowers nodding, 3 inches across, white, tinged with rose externally, finely spotted with rose inside.—*G. H.*

Ligustrum strongylophyllum. By S. A. Skan (*Bot. Mag.* tab. 8069).—China. Nat. ord. *Oleaceae*; tribe *Oleineae*. An evergreen small tree. Flowers white. (The illustration shows the corolla as very pale-yellow.)—*G. H.*

Lime-Sulphur-Salt Wash and its Substitutes. By J. K. Haywood (*U.S.A. Dep. Agr., Bur. Chem., Bull.* 101; February 1907).—This bulletin contains an account of a chemical study of this important wash so much used as a winter spray against various species of scale in the States. It was found that from 45 to 60 minutes' boiling was necessary in order to dissolve all the sulphur contained in a wash of the following composition : lime 30 lb., sulphur 20 lb., salt 15 lb., water 60 gals. Longer boiling resulted in some loss of sulphur. At the end of the boiling the sulphur is in the form of thiosulphates ·84 gr., sulphides 2·91 grs., sulphates and sulphites ·01 gr.; total 3·76 grs. (Total sulphur in the amount used 8·89 grs.) The thiosulphates and sulphates are somewhat increased by more prolonged boiling. Salt was found to have no influence on the composition of the wash so far as the sulphur was concerned. It was found that one part of lime to one of sulphur gives more than enough lime to cause all the sulphur to go into solution, and it is suggested that a wash containing 20 to 22·5 lb. lime and 22 lb. sulphur to 50 gallons of water should be experimented with. Slaked lime gives a wash of almost the same constitution as quicklime, but if the lime has become converted into carbonate it is, of course, of no use. Experiments demonstrated that a satisfactory wash *cannot be made with the heat generated only by quicklime.* Flowers of sulphur and flour sulphur gave washes practically identical in composition, but " crystalline " sulphur gave very variable results, and even when ground to a very fine powder it dissolves much more slowly than either of the other forms. It appears from a consideration of the changes taking place in the wash after its application that only in a dry climate will it be of great effectiveness ; in a wet or damp one most of the soluble compounds of sulphur will be lost and the insecticidal value of the wash very greatly reduced. Investigation showed that when lime 30 lb., sulphur 20 lb., salt 15 lb., caustic soda 10 lb., water 60 gallons, are boiled together, practically all the sulphur goes into solution as salts of sodium of a similar nature to those of lime in the first case, and more oxide of calcium will remain than in that giving with the caustic soda a more caustic wash ; the best wash is made by adding the ingredients in the order—sulphur, caustic soda, lime. But in a damp climate the sodium wash would be even more easily washed off than the lime wash. It is recommended, on purely theoretical grounds, that a trial should be given in dry districts to a wash made by making 19 lb. of powdered sulphur into a paste with not more than 5½ gallons of boiling water, add 10 lb. caustic soda, and stir occasionally for half an hour, then add 44½ gallons of water, stir, and the wash is ready for use.—*F. J. C.*

Linospadix Micholitzii. By C. H. Wright (*Bot. Mag.* tab. 8095).— New Guinea. Nat. ord. *Palmeae*; tribe *Areceae.* A stemless palm. Leaves 2-3½ feet long, 7 inches wide; spadices slender, unisexual, 1½-2½ feet long ; flowers small greenish.—*G. H.*

Linum corymbiferum and Linum corymbulosum. By
J. Paquet (*Le Jardin*, vol. xxi. No. 488, p. 182 ; June 20, 1907).—The
' Golden Flax ' and the ' Yellow Flax ' are two valuable plants, rivalling the
Gypsophyllas for table decoration. The former is an annual about
18 inches high, with small golden flowers ; the latter is taller and has
larger yellow flowers. Indigenous to France, they are not on the market.
Autumn sowing is recommended, the seedlings being kept under glass
through the winter and planted out in spring.—*F. A. W.*

Liriodendron tulipifera L. By A. Bedène (*Bull. R. Soc. Tosc.
Ort.* 10, 1906, p. 301).—Native of North America, where it occurs in
damp spots and along rivers. It is easily naturalised in France and in
a large part of Europe. It prefers a light, loamy and deep soil, a
temperate climate, and an open, damp spot. It is usually multiplied by
seed sown in spring in a position having a northern aspect, or in autumn
in a spot with a southern aspect. They are sown in a light soil ; during
the winter the seed beds are covered with a layer of leaves or straw
manure ; during the summer they are watered, and this attention must
continue for two or three years. In colder countries the seeds are sown
in pots, which are taken under cover in the winter.

In the third or fourth year the seedlings are planted in the open
ground, 30 cm. (1 foot) apart.

It bears transplanting with difficulty, and is not easy to establish after
a certain age. It is best planted on reaching a height of about two metres
(6 feet about) ; it should be transplanted in spring. After five or six
years there is no danger to be feared from cold It does not get attacked
by insects, but will not stand much pruning What moderate pruning
in the later life of the plant takes place should be done always in March.
It grows rapidly, the annual shoots often being more than a metre (3 feet)
long. Some individuals reach 30 metres (100 feet) in height, with a trunk
diameter of a metre (3 feet). In America there are specimens having a
height of 45 metres (150 feet) and diameter of trunk of 3 metres. It has
a white alburnum, rather like that of the white poplar, but heavier and
compacter. As it rapidly decomposes in the open air it should only be
used indoors. The central wood is lemon-yellow in colour, more durable
than the alburnum, and may be employed for many purposes.

There appear to be two types : one with yellow, soft, and fragile
wood ; the other with hard, heavy, white wood. This probably depends
on local influences and varied development of the wood in plants of
varying age. Very varied articles are made from the wood ; the natives
make boats out of a single piece of the trunk.

The bark, especially that of the roots, is more odorous than the
wood and has a very bitter taste ; it is used in the manufacture of beer
for giving taste and smell to the latter ; it has also medicinal properties.

This plant has two distinct varieties : the one (*L. t. marginata
aurea*) has fine broad leaves, having white margins in spring and yellow
in autumn ; the other (*L. t. pyramidalis*) has an erect habit in the form
of a pyramid and is very vigorous.

The tulip-like flowers are well known.—*W. C. W.*

Listrostachys hamata. By R. A. Rolfe (*Bot. Mag.* tab. 8074).— Tropical West Africa. Nat. ord. *Orchidaceae* ; tribe *Vandeae.* An epiphyte, under a foot high. Flowers white, with a green spur ; sepals recurved, linear ; petals smaller but similar.—*G. H.*

Lonicera pileata. By L. Farmar (*Bot. Mag.* tab. 8060).—Central and Western China. Nat. ord. *Caprifoliaceae* ; tribe *Lonicerae.* An evergreen shrub, 1 foot high. Leaves ½–1 inch long ; flowers sessile, pale yellow, ½ inch diameter.—*G. H.*

Lonicera tragophylla. By S. A. Skau (*Bot. Mag.* tab. 8064).— China. Leaves sessile ; papery ; 2½–4 inches long ; flowers 10–20 ; corolla bright orange or yellow, 2–3 inches long.—*G. H.*

Magnolia hypoleuca. By S. A. Skau (*Bot. Mag.* tab. 8077).— Japan and China. Nat. ord. *Magnoliaceae* ; tribe *Magnolieae.* A large tree, 50–80 feet. Leaves in tufts at end of branches, 8–15 inches long, 6–8 inches broad ; flowers creamy-white, highly fragrant, 6–8 inches in diameter ; filaments bright reddish-purple with yellow anthers.—*G. H.*

Malus Niedzwetzkiana. By Louis Tillier (*Rev. Hort.* May 16, 1906, p. 232 ; coloured plate).—A very beautiful, deep rosy-flowered apple, the leaves when young are red, and as they mature and turn dark green, the veins retain their colour, and even the wood is suffused with red.—*C. T. D.*

Marigolds, The Marsh.—By W. T. (*Garden,* No. 1800, p. 268 ; fig. ; May 19, 1906).—Most of the members of this small family of plants greatly resemble one another in habit and flowers. They are spread all over the north temperate regions, usually growing in damp meadows and waterside places. In our native marsh marigold we possess one of the brightest and best of early-flowering bog plants, and those who are considering the formation of a bog garden will do well to make free use of this when planting. Its favourite position, where it grows most luxuriantly and produces the largest flowers, is in valley bottoms of black muddy soil on the edges of streams or often partly submerged. Under these conditions the golden yellow flowers are particularly attractive, and fully justify a prominent position in the bog garden. Calthas should also be employed in beautifying the edges of lakes and other ornamental waters by being planted in large groups. Once established, the plants increase freely by means of self-sown seeds, which germinate readily. Plants may also be increased by division of the root in autumn or spring. There are now six recognised species in cultivation.—*E. T. C.*

Masdevallia muscosa. By A. Van der Heede (*Le Jardin,* vol. xx. No. 467, p. 236 ; August 5, 1906).—A sensitive orchid, native of Colombia. Peduncles covered with long granulated hairs, which are absent in the petiole of the leaf. Flowers solitary and abundant, greenish-yellow, about 3 cm. (1¼ inches) across. The label, marked with two little reddish dots, is sensitive to the touch, and closes sharply upon the flower. Insects when caught become covered with pollen in their struggles to escape, and in forcing their way out carry it to other flowers. No other orchid is known to be sensitive.—*F. A. W.*

Melon Culture. By F. Garcia (*U.S.A. Exp. Stn. New Mexico, Bull.* 63; 10 figs; 1907).—The outdoor culture of water-melons and musk-melons in New Mexico is detailed.—*F. J. C.*

Melon, Wild: Culture in Central Asia. By J. Balsacq (*Le Jardin*, vol. xx. No. 466, p. 213; July 20, 1906).—An exhaustive classification of twenty-nine varieties of melon, with notes on their cultivation.—*F. A. W.*

Morphological Notes, Protective Adaptations, I. By W. T. Thiselton-Dyer. (*Ann. Bot.* xx. April 1906, pp. 123–127; 3 plates).— No. xi. of this series concerns remarkable cases of mimicry.

Mesembryanthemum Bohesii is first described, a plant which is practically composed of a pair of leaves. The leaves, known technically as trigonously hemispherical, simulate in general appearance the angular rock fragments amongst which the plant grows. Nor is the mimicry confined to form, but the weathering of the stones is also imitated by the pustular spots on the surface of the leaves.

Another remarkable case of protective adaptation is found in *M. truncatum.* Here the plant is reduced to a small succulent ball, which, in colour and appearance, bears the closest resemblance to the pebbles between which it is found. So much is this the case, that the plant was picked up by its original discoverer in mistake for a stone. The weathering on the stone is in this case reproduced by mottling on the surface of the leaves.

Concerning this species the author remarks:—" The *Mesembryanthemum* had two problems to face: (1) How to minimise the loss of water by transpiration: this is achieved by assuming the spheroidal form with its minimum surface. But (2) as soon as it became a succulent blob it was exposed to the danger of being eaten, and it only escaped this by pretending to be an inedible pebble."

A third case, *Anacampseros papyracea*, is also described.—*A. D. C.*

Movement of Soil Moisture, Studies on the. By E. Buckingham (*U.S.A. Dep. Agr., Bur. Soils, Bull.* 38; 23 figs.; February 1907).—A technical paper tending towards the development of a theory regarding the distribution of moisture in the soil analogous to the theory of electrical and thermal potentials. The analogy is not perfect, however, since the electrical and thermal resistance is practically independent of the amount of current and heat passing, whereas the capillary potential and resistance to flow are dependent upon the moisture contents of the soil.

F. J. C.

Musa, The Genus. By A. Pucci (*Bull. R. Soc. Tosc. Ort.* 8, 1906, p. 235).—According to Dr. Sagot's work, " Les différentes espèces dans le genre *Musa*," it can be divided into three groups :—

1. Giant Musas, e.g. *M. Ensete.*
2. Those with fleshy, edible fruits, e.g. *M. sapientum.*

3. Ornamental ones, on account of the flowers and fruit, e.g. *M. coccinea* and *M. rosacea*.

Baker in his "Synopsis of the Genera and Species of Museae" takes as a basis the height of the leaf-stalks, the number of the flowers within each bract, the shape of the floral leaves, &c. He divided the species into three sub-genera. Another English work, "Species and principal Varieties of *Musa*," deals chiefly with the history, origin, geographical area, and economic uses of the plants. A brief description of all the species is given by the present author.—*W. C. W.*

Muscari, Note on a Monstrous. By P. Baccarini (*Bull. R. Soc. Tosc. Ort.* 6, p. 179 ; 1906).—The bulbs of this *M. comosum*, Willd., came from the gardens of Catania, where it is frequently grown. Not being very prolific, it is not widely diffused. The bulbs obtained by the author originated from wild plants in the neighbourhood of Aci San Antonio. It was known to the botanists of the first half of the seventeenth century. At the time of Colonna it was cultivated in Rome in the garden of Cardinal Sannesio, in honour of whom it was called *Hyacinthus Sannesius panicula comosa.* Boerhaave also speaks of it ; as indeed most of the pre-Linneans. Linnæus gives a *résumé* of their observations and gives it his own name of *H. monstrosus*, expressing a doubt as to whether it is a monstrous variety of *M. comosum*. In "Hort. Cliff." p. 126, he observes : "Hyacinthus floribus paniculatis monstrosis. Nullum florem magis monstrosum me vidisse fateor, hinc nec de genere, nec specie certus. Monstrosa est planta, quænam ideo mater sit me nescire fateor, cum nulla pars fructificationis sana persistat." And in "Spec. Plant." ed. 1, p. 818, he adopts the name *H. monstrosus*, and adds to the synonym and the habitat (Pavia and Boran) the phrase, "An sequentis sola varietas?" and the following species is *H. comosus.*

There was a time when it was widely diffused in botanic gardens and would seem to have since become lost, to judge by the silence of horticultural journals with regard to such a distinctive form. Its disappearance must be very recent, for it has been a subject for morphological study by Engelmann, Morren, Magnus, and even De Vries.

It is quite sterile, all the flowers being resolved into a dense truss of curved and slightly clavate filaments, often hollow internally, reminding one, especially before the buds unfold, of a cabbage.

As regards the causes of the strange anomaly we are quite in the dark ; it may be due to parasitic action on the part of fungi, mites, or insects, but it may also be a case of a mutation in the sense of De Vries. In support of this view is the fact of its rarity, and its repeated and independent appearance in localities so far apart as Sicily, Lombardy, and Borgogna. A rather obscure photograph of this plant is given.—*W. C. W.*

Mushrooms in the Open (*Garden*, No. 1798, p. 219 ; May 5, 1906).—It does not matter very much, as regards the position of the proposed mushroom-beds, whether they are in the sun or in shade, but they must be placed in a sheltered position, well protected from north and east winds. It is too late now to make the beds up. (They never do well in hot weather during the height of summer.) The best time to start forming the beds is any time in September, and in succession afterwards, as manure is available any time up to the middle of March following.

As regards manure, no other than fresh horse manure, with half the strawy litter mixed with it, will do. That from corn-fed animals is the best. Until sufficient manure is collected, say, to make a cartload, it should be spread out thinly and preserved from too much wet. When a cartload has been collected it should be made into a heap and left so until it is well heated, which will be in about nine days. It should then be turned over and left to cool for an hour, when it should be put up again to heat in the same way, for the same time, when it must be turned over again and allowed to cool. It will then be ready to form the bed.

E. T. C.

Nectarine 'Lily Baltet.' By Charles Baltet (*Rev. Hort.* March 1, 1906, pp. 112–113; coloured plate).—The plate represents a very beautiful nectarine, and the letterpress gives the pedigree, embracing some very interesting facts relating to peaches, nectarines (non-adherent stones) and brugnons (adherent stones), which occurred apparently indiscriminately in the crops and trees concerned.—*C. T. D.*

Nepenthes Phyllamphora. By W. B. Hemsley (*Bot. Mag.* tab. 8067).—Eastern Tropical Asia and Western Polynesia. Nat. ord. *Nepenthaceae.* A vigorous species. Pitchers 3–7 inches long, green and red outside.—*G. H.*

Nicandra violacea. By Henri Lemoine (*Rev. Hort.* May 1, 1906, pp. 208–9; coloured plate).—A very handsome annual which appeared as a seedling in the Botanic Garden of Tours in 1900. The plant is of vigorous habit, somewhat on the lines of physalis, with bright blue flowers, rather mallow-like, two inches across, the seeds occupying a large berry-like fruit, swathed in curiously enlarged sepals mottled with purple. Sow March–April and plant out end May.—*C. T. D.*

Nympheas. By C. Giernier (*Le Jardin*, vol. xx. No. 467, p. 228; coloured plate and 4 figs.; August 5, 1906).—An exhaustive article on the employment of nympheas for the ornamentation of gardens. Deals with the botanical characters, types, varieties, culture, &c. of the group of water-lilies.—*F. A. W.*

Odontoglossum naevium. By R. A. Rolfe (*Bot. Mag.* tab. 8097).—Colombia. Nat. ord. *Orchidaceae*; tribe *Vandeae.* An epiphyte 1–1½ foot high; flowers white, with dark-purple blotches and a bright-yellow disk to the lip; sepals and petals very acuminate, undulate, 1½ inch long; lip with a broad yellow claw.—*G. H.*

Oidiopsis Laurica (Lév.): **An endophytic member of the Erysiphaceae.** By E. S. Salmon (*Ann. Bot.* vol. xx. April 1906, pp. 187–199; 2 plates).—The author gives a full account of the

M

morphology and life-history of *Erysiphe Laurica* Lév., a member of the Erysiphaceae, which he last year recorded as being endoparasitic. On account of its endophytic habit he separates the plant as a distinct genus, *Oidiopsis Scalia* emend., belonging to a new sub-family, *Oidiopsideae*. In the new genus the mycelium is at first wholly endophytic, producing conidiophores, which are sent up through the stomata; the perithecia are produced externally on the hyphae of a superficial mycelium.

The synonomy of *O. Laurica*, Salm. and its distribution and host plants are added.—*A. D. C.*

Orchard Cultivation, Experiments in. By R. A. Emerson (*U.S.A. Exp. Stn. Nebraska, Bull.* 79; 8 figs.; March 1903).—Experiments on orchard cultivation are reported at length in this bulletin, and it is concluded that the best method of culture is to cultivate thoroughly in early summer and follow with a cover crop in the fall. Straw mulch is good early in the year, but it results in frost killing the tender, unripened shoots later on, as well as in inducing shallow rooting, which the author considers may result in disaster later on. Good culture in early summer prevents shallow rooting and protects against drought, while the use of a tender cover crop later brings about that drying of the soil which results in good ripening of the newly formed wood.—*F. J. C.*

Orchard Culture, Grass Mulch Method (*U.S.A. Dep. Agr., Farm. Bull.* 267; 1906).—In the Eastern United States the usual method of cultivation followed in orchards is to clean cultivate from early spring to the middle of summer, and then to sow a cover crop. It is contended that this method tends to evaporate the moisture from the soil, checking the growth of the trees, and hastening the ripening of the wood, so that the trees enter the winter in a well-matured, frost-resistant condition. The Ohio Experiment Station has conducted comparative trials with this method and the method of laying the orchard down to grass and cutting the grass over and leaving it on the ground as a mulch. It was found that the trees made a better growth and gave double the yield by the latter method of treatment than by any other.—*F. J. C.*

Orchard Management in New England, Experiments in (*U.S.A. Exp. Stn. New Hampshire, Bull.* 110; 6 figs.; March 1904).— Gives a general account in a small space (twenty pages) of the more important problems in fruit growing.—*F. J. C.*

Ornamental Trees, Shrubs, and Herbaceous Plants. By S. B. Green (*U.S.A. Exp. Stn. Minnesota*; *14th Ann. Rep.* pp. 232-351; 108 figs.).—An alphabetical list of trees, shrubs, and herbaceous plants, suitable for planting in Minnesota, is given, together with rules and plans for planting, and lists of trees and shrubs, &c., grouped according to their uses.—*F. J. C.*

Orobus, Species of. By Jules Rudolph (*Rev. Hort.* January 16, 1906, pp. 49, 50; 6 woodcuts).—Several species are described and recom-mended as pretty spring flowering hardy plants for borders. The species mentioned and figured are *O. vernus, O. flaccidus, O. variegatus, O. lathyroides, O. luteus,* and *O. niger,* all varying greatly in habits from each other. Flowers pea-like, in smaller or larger clusters.

C. T. D.

Osier, Parasite of (*Le Jardin,* vol. xxi. No. 479, p. 35 ; February 5, 1907).—*Phyllodacta* or *Phratora vulgatissima.*—A small coleopterous insect, which feeds more particularly on yellow osiers. That red osiers, as well as the variety known as ' Grisette Jaune,' are far less liable to the pest illustrates the fact of the varying resistance offered to the same parasite by different varieties of one plant.—*F. A. W.*

Oxalis adenophylla. By L. Farmar (*Bot. Mag.* tab. 8054).— Chili. Nat. ord. *Geraniaceae* ; tribe *Oxalideae.* A stemless herb. Leaves with 12–22 digitate leaflets ; flowers heterostyled, 1½–2 inches diameter, deep rose-coloured with a purple base.—*G. H.*

Paeony Culture. By P. Saveau (*Le Jardin,* vol. xxi. No. 479, p. 39 ; February 5, 1907).—Practical notes on the culture of herbaceous paeonies, with list of varieties best suited for cutting.—*F. A. W.*

Paeonies, Tree.—*Classification,* with coloured plate and 2 figs., by Hortulus ; *Culture,* by P. Savreau (*Le Jardin,* vol. xxi. No. 485, p. 136 ; May 5, 1907).—Tree paeonies are best propagated by grafting on roots of ordinary herbaceous paeony at the end of August. Choose the grafts from shoots that flowered in the spring, leaving two to three eyes at the base, and trim into a wedge from lowest eye to fit groove in root, which has previously been sliced across horizontally, leaving 3 to 4 inches in length. Pot the grafts in frame or bell-glass. Leave for a month in northerly exposure with full light and air. Tree paeonies are easy to force. Select plants that have been reared in pots with well-formed buds, bringing them into a cool house, 15°–20° C. (60°-68° Fahr.), in December or January. In the open they require protection in the spring. They should be looked over each spring, cutting out the dead wood, lopping the bigger branches, and thoroughly pruning what are left, leaving only a certain number of flowering buds, and encouraging the lower eyes at the expense of those borne on the old wood.—*F. A. W.*

Paphiopedilum glaucophyllum. By R. A. Rolfe (*Bot. Mag.* tab. 8084).—Java. Nat. ord. *Orchidaceae* ; tribe *Cypripedieae.* Leaves glaucous, unmarked, 6–9 inches long ; dorsal sepal suborbicular, 1¼ inch across, yellowish green, with a primrose-yellow margin ; petals twisted and undulate, 1¾ inch long, white, with bright red-purple blotches ; lip 1½ inch long, light rose-purple, with darker spots and a light-green margin.—*G. H.*

Passiflora punctata. By T. A. Sprague (*Bot. Mag.* tab. 8101).— South America. Nat. ord. *Passifloraceae* ; tribe *Passifloreae.* Leaves nearly lunate, variegated with purple ; sepals and petals pale yellow : corona segments with purple heads.—*G. H.*

Pea, Powdery Mildew. By J. M. Van Hook (*U.S.A. Exp. Stn. Ohio*, No. 173; April 1906).—This section of the report on pea blight is devoted to the powdery mildew of the pea, *Erysiphe communis*. It is ordinarily recognised by the whitish or greyish coating on all parts of the pea plant, especially late in the season. The mildew fungus lives over the winter on the seed. On account of the habits of the powdery-mildew fungus it is easily prevented by applications of the Bordeaux mixture. The vegetative part of the mildew fungus grows mostly on the exterior of the host plant. Hence the fungicide is not only a preventive, but actually kills the fungus in great part, when sprayed upon it. On account of this manner of growing, many of the powdery mildews are controlled by the use of sulphur alone.—*M. C. C.*

Peas, Blighting of Field and Garden. By J. M. Van Hook (*U.S.A. Exp. Stn. Ohio*, No. 173; with 12 figs.; April 1906).—This report on blighting of peas is accentuated in interest by the assurance that the blight is chiefly due to seed infection. The fungus causing the disease is *Ascochyta pisi* (Lib.), well known as a pest in Europe. Perhaps the most important feature is that the mycelium grows through the husk of infected pods into the seed, and often produces spores there by the time the peas are mature. More frequently the peas are mature and dry before fruit bodies of the fungus develop, though discoloured areas may appear. Seed treatment by immersion in liquid fungicides failed to produce good results. Heating the seed also failed. Tying up the plants and spraying increased the crop only slightly, but produced peas much freer from this and other fungi. Planting such healthy peas in soil free from the fungus is recommended as the best means of reducing the loss from blight.—*M. C. C.*

Peaches, Studies on. By W. D. Bigelow and H. C. Gore (*U.S.A. Dep. Agr. Bur. Chem., Bull.* 97; 1905).—A review of the study of the chemical analysis of peaches is followed by an account of the varieties selected for analysis in this instance. Tables are given showing the composition of the peaches at different stages of ripening and an account of the changes which take place during the time the fruit may be kept in cold storage.—*F. J. C.*

Pears, Bergamot. By C. Maheut (*Le Jardin*, vol. xx. No. 465, p. 199; July 5, 1906).—The best of the sixty varieties of bergamot pears are enumerated, with synonyms and various etymologies—from Bergamo in Lombardy, Pergamus in Asia Minor, or from the Turkish *beg* and *armoudi*, which signifies 'Pear of the Sovereign.'—*F. A. W.*

Pear Blight. By R. E. Smith (*U.S.A. Exp. Stn. California, Bull.* 184; January 1907).—This virulent disease, which is due to the attacks of a bacterium, has since 1904 (previous to which it was unknown in California) been rife in various parts of the State, and by its attacks has seriously threatened the pear-growing industry. Vigorous means are being taken to combat it by the station staff acting with the central government. Since the bacteria are carried from tree to tree by insects, including bees visiting the flowers, special stress is laid upon the necessity of eradicating the blight in large districts rather than by single efforts in individual orchards. The treatment consists in inspecting the trees during winter, removing all affected growths by cutting below the point of infection, afterwards disinfecting the cut surfaces and tools with an antiseptic solution. Trees in which the trunk is affected are to be completely destroyed. All the sprouts and fruit spurs on the trunk and main limbs are to be removed, and cultivation and irrigation resorted to as little as possible, since rapid growth is conducive to the spread of the disease. Unfortunately "the inability, disinclination, or actual refusal of some growers to do the work at times convenient to our limited force of inspectors, or in some cases to do it at all," seriously interfered with the systematic and thorough accomplishment of the work. Some 700,000 trees have been inspected individually so far, and in Sacramento County 3·8 per cent. had to be condemned.—*F. J. C.*

Pear-Melon, The. By P. Baccarini (*Bull. R. Soc. Tosc. Ort.* 7, 1906, p. 193).—This fruit appears in the Italian markets in the winter not infrequently. It comes from the Peruvian Andes, and is there grown in several varieties at an altitude of 2,000 to 2,400 metres (6,600 to 7,900 feet). The natives call it *Pepino* or *Pepino de terra*, *Pepo*, &c. It appears to be common in the markets of Chili, Peru, and Bolivia. Ancient travellers all sing its praises, but warn Europeans against eating it in too great quantities as it produces colic and visceral troubles. It is a half-shrub, with branches rooting at the base, probably stoloniferous, with lanceolate, entire, pubescent leaves, and very floriferous. The "Journal des Observ. Phys. et Mathém.," Paris, 1714, described and figured it first ; then Aiton, a little later in the "Hortus Kewensis," gave it the name of *Solanum muricatum*. The figure given by Héritier in "Stirpes Novæ, &c.," Plate cvi., agrees exactly with the imported form. Lowe found it cultivated in 1867 in the Canaries in great abundance, and described it under the name of *Solanum insigne* in the "Journ. Hort. Soc." i. p. 178. In his manual, "Flora of Madeira," he states that he introduced it there from the Canaries. Webb and Berthelot, the natural historians of the Canaries, make no mention of it. It is not unlikely that this subtropical plant could be grown in the maritime region of Italy.

W. C. W.

Peperomia : the Morphology and Seedling Structure of the Geophilous Species of; together with some views on the Origin of Monocotyledons. By Arthur W. Hill (*Ann. Bot.* vol. xx. October 1906, pp. 395–427 ; 2 plates).—The comparative examination of the morphology of the geophilous Peperomias, by the author, brings to light some points of exceptional interest. At the conclusion of the paper theoretical considerations of wide bearing are discussed.

The early history of the embryo follows the usual course, but in germination there are striking aberrations from the dicotyledonous type common to the majority of species, for the seedling is in appearance monocotyledonous. One cotyledon remains more or less enclosed in the seed and performs the function of absorption, the other supplements this reserve supply by performing the function of carbon assimilation.

For details as to the degrees of specialisation the original paper must be consulted.   It is suggested that this remarkable division of labour has been brought about by the necessity of making an underground storage as rapidly as possible, and that the different forms of biological adaptation which are found represent the response to the peculiar xerophytic conditions of the several localities.   Adaptation to new conditions, says the author, must have appeared first in the adult structure of the plant, and the tendency to bulb production must be due to the shortening of the internodes ; with further advances towards geophily the modifications of the adult would be thrown back more and more into the early stages of the plant's development, until finally the structure of the embryo itself would become involved.

It is suggested that the geophilous Peperomias may represent a recent attempt, by a fairly simple group of Dicotyledons, to attain to the geophilous conditions reached by Monocotyledons.—*A. D. C.*

Phaseolus multiflorus papilio (Benary) (*Le Jardin*, vol. xxi. No. 478, p. 28 ; January 1, 1907).—New haricot bean ; large white wings, with salmon-pink standard.   Beans white, flecked with brown.   Equally valuable in kitchen and flower garden.—*F. A. W.*

Phosphates, Availability of, in relation to Soil Acidity. By A. R. Whitson and C. W. Stoddart (*U.S.A. Exp. Stn. Wisconsin,* 23rd Ann. Rep. pp. 171–186 ; October 1906).—The authors conclude from a comparison of analyses with the known requirements of soils that if a soil gives an acid reaction with litmus that soil will benefit by a dressing of a phosphatic manure.—*F. J. C.*

Pinks, Mule.   By C. Blair (*Garden*, No. 1798, p. 248 ; May 5, 1906). Few dwarf border plants make a finer show than these hardy Dianthuses. True they do not possess the delicious fragrance of the ordinary garden pinks, but their brilliant and freely produced flowers make up, in part at least, for the want of perfume.   Probably the finest variety is the brilliant crimson-scarlet 'Napoleon III.'   I am aware that there is great difficulty in some localities in keeping this variety in health.   It has the annoying habit of suddenly dying off in the most unexpected manner.   After careful study of the plant, I find that the reason for this lies in the fact that it literally flowers itself into such a weak state that it is unable to survive ordinary hardy plant treatment.   To overcome this I propagate annually in August.   The difficulty of procuring cuttings may be got over by planting a few good young plants on a north border, or by keeping a few of the plants from flowering.   I have been successful with these Dianthuses on stiff clay soil by simply making a hole about six inches deep, and as much across, at planting time, and filling in with good light soil, in which a good quantity of wood ashes was mixed.—*E. T. C.*

Pinks, The Wild (*Garden*, No. 1811, p. 51 ; fig. ; August 4, 1906).— The beauty and fragrance of the Dianthus family render them one of the most valuable groups of hardy plants that we have.   Some of the taller-growing kinds, like *D. Carthusianorum* and *D. cruentus,* are useful for the herbaceous border, not to mention such a well-known favourite as the Chinese pink (*D. chinensis*) and its innumerable varieties. Others of low-growing and spreading growth form one of the chief ornaments of the rock garden during the late spring and early summer. There is a wide range of kinds to choose from, some suitable for almost any position and aspect. Some are at home on sunny ledges, where their glaucous foliage forms a curtain over the face of the rocks, making a pleasing picture even when not in flower. Others may be planted while very small in the rocky fissures or in cracks of old walls, where they quickly make themselves at home and soon form beautiful evergreen tufts.

For a shady position others may also be found which will thrive under those conditions. The chief requirement of the pink family is thorough drainage, anything in the nature of stagnant moisture being fatal to their well-being.

For the great majority plenty of mortar rubbish mixed with the soil is beneficial ; but, of course, there are exceptions which dislike lime in any form, and these should be supplied with plenty of broken sandstone and grit.—*E. T. C.*

Piptanthus nepalensis. By J. M. Duvenay (*Le Jardin*, vol. xx. No. 467, p. 234).—This plant, introduced 1821, has been almost forgotten. A leguminous papilionaceous species, with abundance of short racemes of golden flowers, produced at the end of May. These, however, as the name implies (*pipto*, I fall ; *anthos*, flower), drop off very quickly, and the chief value of the shrub, which is of rapid growth, lies in the fact that its leaves are almost evergreen. Another species not yet introduced is *P. tomentosus*, from Tonkin, a shrub 3-6 feet, covered in all its parts with a soft, silvery down.—*F. A. W.*

Plane Disease. By Hortulus (*Le Jardin*, vol. xx. No. 467, p. 236 ; 2 figs. ; August 5, 1906).—The plane trees of France have lately been ravaged by a cryptogamic disease, due to *Glocosporium nervisequum.* The fungus attacks the young leaves, covering them with dry, scaly patches, which run inwards from edge to petiole, after which the leaf drops off. The shoots, branches, and trunks are attacked as well. Fumigation and spraying with fungicides are the remedies recommended.—*F. A. W.*

Plant Diseases in California. By R. E. Smith (*U.S.A. Exp. Stn. California, Bull.* 184 ; January 1907).—A list of the chief fungal diseases of plants in California is given, with brief recommendations for their treatment.—*F. J. C.*

Plums in Georgia. By H. N. Starnes (*U.S.A. Exp. Stn. Georgia, Bull.* 67 ; December 19, 1904).—A brief but complete account of the culture of the plum in Georgia is given under the heads of Soil, Propagation, Planting, Manuring, Pruning (pruning of the roots to within 5 inches of the main root being recommended), Cultivation, Thinning, Defective Pollination, Premature Blooming (whitewashing trees to prevent this is recommended), and Marketing. Then follows an account of the variety of plums cultivated in Georgia, viz. Japan plums (*Prunus triflora*), " hybrids " generally having *P. triflora* for one parent; Americana group (*P. americana*), the variety "Hanson" only being found of any use in Georgia, all the others lacking in constitution; Hortulana group (*P. hortulana*), to which belong the only plums (excepting Japan) worthy of cultivation commercially; Chicasaw group (*P. chicasa* and *P. angustifolia*); Myrobalan group (*P. myrobalana* or *P. cerasifera*) containing few of commercial value, but good as nursery stock; European group (*P. domestica*), all of which rot quickly and are worthless in Georgia; dwarf plums (*P. pumila*), merely curiosities. Insect enemies and fungoid diseases are described. A list of varieties is given, with popular descriptions of each.—*F. J. C.*

Plums, Japanese and Hybrid. By H. N. Starnes (*U.S.A. Exp. Stn. Georgia, Bull.* 68; August 1905).—The superiority of the Japanese over the native plums for cultivation in Georgia is pointed out and descriptions of a large number of varieties (which are figured natural size) are given in simple language.—*F. J. C.*

Poisonous Plants, Larkspur and other. By G. H. Clover (*U.S.A. Exp. Stn. Colorado, Bull.* 113; 8 plates; June 1906).—A number of weeds poisonous to cattle occurring in Colorado are mentioned, including *Delphinium bicolor, D. Nelsonii, D. glaucum, D. elongatum, Zygadenus venenosus, Cicuta occidentalis, Lupinus sericeus, Aconitum columbianum,* and *Hymenoxys floribunda.*—*F. J. C.*

Polygala apopetala. By T. A. Sprague (*Bot. Mag.* tab. 8065).—Lower California. Nat. ord. *Polygalaceae.* Shrub or tree from 2-15 feet high. Leaves lanceolate, 1½-3 inches long; flowers about 1 inch across, purple.—*G. H.*

Poplar and Willow Borer. By W. J. Schoene (*U.S.A. Exp. Stn. Geneva, Bull.* 286; 6 plates; February 1907).—A beetle (*Cryptorhynchus lapathi* L.) which has been introduced from Europe (and which occurs in England) has been doing much damage to nursery stock and basket willows, and now threatens ornamental poplars and willows. The eggs hatch about September, and the larva bores into the tree and feeds near the cambium, later penetrating more deeply into the tree. It is whitish and shining, and is ready to pupate about the beginning of July, the pupal stage lasting about fourteen days. The adult beetle is about ⅓ to ¾ inch long, dull black with white scales here and there on the body. The female eats holes in bark in which to deposit her eggs, and this gives an opportunity of destroying the pest by spraying with arsenical poisons, taking care to wet the twigs as well as the trunk. Infested trees or portions of trees should be burnt, and young plantations should not be made near old ones.—*F. J. C.*

Potato Diseases. By T. W. Kirk, F.L.S. (*Dep. Agr. N.Z.* No. 7; with 6 plates; October 1905).—This bulletin includes reference to all the potato diseases of New Zealand, viz. (1) Irish blight, *Phytophthora infestans*; (2) early blight, *Macrosporium solani*; (3) bacteriosis, *Bacillus solanacearum*; (4) scab, *Oospora scabies*; (5) dry rot,

Fusarium oxysporum ; (6) wet rot ; and (7) brown spot. These several diseases are described and the various preventive measures recommended. "Wet rot," found in land which is badly drained, is now considered to be caused by bacteria, but whether one or more separate organisms are primarily responsible has not yet been ascertained. "Brown spot" affects the tubers, but up to the present no signs of any parasitic organism has been discovered.—*M. C. C.*

Potato Diseases. By A. Nelson (*U.S.A. Exp. Stn. Wyoming, Bull.* 71 ; 11 figs. ; January 1907).—It is estimated that a loss of at least $100,000 resulted from the partial failure of the potato crop in Wyoming in 1906. The bulletin discusses the diseases due to *Alternaria solani* (=*Macrosporium solani*), early blight; *Phytophthora infestans,* causing late blight; *Corticium vagum solani* (=*Rhizoctonia*), causing, according to the virulence of the attack, a girdling of the stem, often resulting in increased vigour or a wet rot of the stem ; and *Oospora scabies,* causing potato scab. The first two are controlled by the application of Bordeaux mixture at the proper season ; the last two by proper rotation of crops and treatment of the seed potatoes with corrosive sublimate or formalin. The latter is probably the better, and is carried out as follows : The seed potatoes are soaked for two hours in a solution of fifteen gallons of water and half-pint of formalin. The seed is dried and planted as usual.—*F. J. C.*

Potato Experiments. By R. A. Emerson (*U.S.A. Exp. Stn. Nebraska, Bull.* 97 ; April 1907).—Seed potatoes were grown beneath a mulch of litter and on cultivated ground in 1904, with the result that in 1905 and 1906 respectively, cultivated seed produced 384 lb. and 123 lb., while mulched seed produced 563 lb. and 174 lb. from the same weights of seed. Soft, sprouted tubers were found to give a less yield than firm tubers, as is shown in the following table :—

	First test. lb.	Second test. lb.	Third test. lb.
Soft, sprouted seed	129	225	212
Firm seed .	229	320	321

giving an advance of 56 per cent. in favour of the firm seed. Treatment with formalin was found to be excellent as a remedy against scab in potatoes. The percentage of small tubers in a crop appears to depend more upon the size of the seed pieces than upon the distance apart of the plants, being greatest where large seed pieces were used. The yield and value of the crop increased with the quantity of seed planted up to a certain limit, while the yield and value of the crop increased with the distance between the plants when a given quantity of seed was used, and the yield depends much less upon the size of the pieces planted than upon the quantity of seed per acre and the distance apart. Deep planting up to 4 inches gave better results than shallow planting, probably on account of the moisture and temperature varying less at that depth.—*F. J. C.*

Potato Leaf Blotch. By L. R. Jones and O. S. Pomeroy (*U.S.A. Exp. Stn. Vermont,* 19*th Rep.* pp. 236-257).—A fungus, *Cercospora* *concors,* has been found attacking leaves of potatoes in Vermont and producing rather obscurely defined pale spots, from ⅛ to ⅜ inch across, bearing on the lower surface a pale violet-grey fungus growth. This disease seems most abundant in old gardens and in the northern parts of the district in which the potato is cultivated It has been recorded from parts of Germany, Russia, Sweden, and Switzerland. The characters of growth of the fungus on various media are described, and the results of inoculation experiments are given. Spraying with Bordeaux mixture, as for Phytophthora, is recommended.—*F. J. C.*

Potato-spraying Experiments in 1905. By F. C. Stewart, H. J. Eustace, and F. A. Sirrine (*U.S.A. Exp. Stn. Geneva, Bull.* 279, 5 plates, 1 map; May 1906).—In 1902 a ten-year course of potato-spraying experiments was planned, of which four years are now completed. Summaries of the results obtained in previous years are given, and full details concerning the soil, planting, cultivation, &c., of the crops experimented upon. Objections have been raised concerning the Station experiments—viz. that $\frac{3}{10}$ acre is too small a plot, that spraying is done more thoroughly than farmers would do it, that it is difficult to ascertain the cost, and that extra good care is given to the crop at the Station in order to obtain large yields. These objections have been met by instituting experiments on ordinary farms, carrying out the spraying as it would be done by farmers, and the results are detailed here. In all, the results of seventy experiments are dealt with. In these "business" experiments in 1905, 160⅔ acres were sprayed, with an average increase in yield of 46½ bushels, at an average cost of spraying per acre of $4.25, or for each spraying of 98 cents, and an average profit per acre of $20.04. In addition to this fifty volunteer experiments were carried out on 407 acres. The average increase in yield was 59 bushels 32 lb., the average cost of spraying per acre (twenty-nine experiments) $4.57, the average cost of each spraying 92 cents, and the average profit per acre $29.85. The general conclusions are as follows :—(1) Soda Bordeaux is not superior to Lime Bordeaux for potatoes ; (2) Paris green, at the rate of 1 lb. to 2 lb. per acre, may be added to Bordeaux mixture without interfering with its efficiency or injuring the potato plants, and either this or arsenite of soda may be used as a remedy against the potato flea beetle ; (3) potato foliage is not injured by spraying on hot summer days with a solution at 40°-54° F. ; (4) spraying tends to prevent rot caused by *Phytophthora infestans* ; (5) the yield of marketable potatoes is always largely increased ; and (6) spraying should be begun when the plants are from 6 inches to 8 inches high, and repeated at intervals of ten to fourteen days.—*F. J. C.*

Primula Cockburniana. By S. A. Skau (*Bot. Mag.* tab. 8073).— China. Nat. ord. *Primulaceæ* ; tribe *Primuleæ.* Perennial herb. Leaves 2-5 inches long ; corolla rich orange-red, ½ inch diam.—*G. H.*

Primula hazarica. By P. Hariot (*Le Jardin,* vol. **xx.** No. 466, p. 212 ; July 20, 1906).—Discovered in the Western Himalayas and Cashmere by Duthie. Belongs to the section *Callianthae,* which consists of sixteen species indigenous to China and the Himalayas, one only being known in Turkestan. *P. hazarica* is the only species cultivated in Europe. It has a purple corolla and mealy leaves of graceful habit and easy to cultivate.—*F. A. W.*

Primula obconica superba. By G. T. Grignan (*Rev. Hort.* October 1, 1906, pp. 448–449; coloured plate and 1 fig.).—A very handsome primula, flowers bright red and resembling *P. sinensis* in size. Raised from sport by M. Nonin.—*C. T. D.*

Primula verticillata sinensis (?). By S. Mottet (*Rev. Hort.* November 1, 1906, p. 504).—" sinensis " is a misnomer for " simensis," indicating an Abyssinian origin and not a Chinese one, the name being derived from " Semen," a plain in Abyssinia.—*C. T. D.*

Prunus triloba. By O. Stapf (*Bot. Mag.* tab. 8061).—China. Nat. ord. *Rosaceae*; tribe *Pruneae*. Shrub or small tree, flowering before the leaves; flowers pink, 1 inch diameter.—*G. H.*

Raspberry, Billard's Framboise Perpetuelle. By Alfred Nomblot (*Rev. Hort.* April 1, 1906, pp. 160–161; coloured plate).— Descriptive of a highly recommended variety with deep crimson fruit, bearing from July until the autumnal frosts; cultural directions.

C. T. D.

Rhododendron Vaseyi. By S. A. Skau (*Bot. Mag.* tab. 8081).— North and South Carolina. Nat. ord. *Ericaceae*; tribe *Rhodoreae.* A shrub 18 feet in height. Leaves lanceolate; flowers precocious, odourless, 4–8 in an umbel; corolla bright rose or purple, stamens extending beyond the corolla.—*G. H.*

Rhodostachys pitcairniifolia. By C. H. Wright (*Bot. Mag.* tab. 8087).—Chili. Nat. ord. *Bromeliaceae*; tribe *Bromelieae.* Stem short, thick; leaves crowded, uniform from an ovate base, inner ones crimson, with purplish base; flowers on a dense head; petals blue.—*G. H.*

Ribes viburnifolium. By S. A. Skau (*Bot. Mag.* tab. 8094).— Lower California and Santa Catalina Island. Nat. ord. *Saxifragaceae*; tribe *Ribesieae.* An evergreen shrub. Leaves $\frac{3}{4}$–$1\frac{3}{4}$ inch long; racemes terminal; calyx rose-coloured, $\frac{1}{12}$ inch diameter; petals very small, greenish; berries oval, scarlet.—*G. H.*

Rosa rugosa: for Perfume. By H. Lebrun (*Le Jardin,* vol. xx. No. 468; p. 264, August 20, 1906).—The substitution of *R. rugosa* for all other varieties in the making of perfumes is urged. It appears from the report of M. Gravereaux (addressed to the Minister of Agriculture, December 31, 1905) that France imports over a third of the essence of roses made in Bulgaria. M. Lebrun points out that the soil and climate of France are particularly favourable to the culture of roses and manu-facture of the essence. It would be desirable to replace all other varieties by *R. rugosa*, the sweetest of all. Seeing that this rose was introduced in 1845, it is surprising that more attention has not been paid to it commercially. A dozen or more of the principal varieties are enumerated.—*F. A. W.*

Rosa sericea (*Garden*, No. 1802, p. 294 ; coloured plate ; June 2, 1906).—Of the wild roses there are few that equal *Rosa sericea* in simple grace and beauty ; yet it is one of the least common in gardens. It was introduced from Gossam Than, a mountain in Northern Nepal, about ninety years ago, and was first described by Lindley in his " Monograph of Roses," published in 1820. Its flowers are distinct from those of other roses in having nearly always but four petals, which are arranged in the form of a Maltese cross. They are of a creamy-white, and the flower is about 2 inches across. One great charm of this rose is its beautiful foliage ; the leaflets are small and rich green, giving to the plant as a whole a soft, fern-like aspect. There is a fine bush at Kew measuring 15 feet through and 9 feet high. It is almost the earliest rose to flower in the open—usually during the last week of May—and its wide-spreading, arching branches, laden with blossom, make a lovely picture.—*E. T. C.*

Rose ' Maurice Fournet,' Sport from ' Soleil d'Or.' By H. Lebrun (*Le Jardin*, vol. xx. No. 465, p. 203 ; July 5, 1906).—A new variety, pale pink with copper tinge. M. Lebrun writes an interesting note on dichroism in roses, to which this hybrid is due. When two species as distinct as *R. lutea* (from which ' Persian Yellow,' one parent of ' Soleil d'Or ' is derived) and *R. gallica* (whence comes ' Antoine Duchet,' the other parent) are blended, new sports are apt to arise by throwing back to one of the two ancestors in some definite feature without altering the general character of the rose. In this case ' Maurice Fournet ' reverts to the hybrid perpetual parent in the colour of its flower only, being otherwise an Austrian briar.—*F. A. W.*

Roses, Christmas. By W. T. (*Garden*, No. 1831, p. 297 ; December 22, 1906).—Towards the end of the year the winter hellebore (*H. niger*) throws up its ever-welcome flowers, and is certainly one of the finest hardy winter-flowering plants we have. A large clump in good condition, with its broad, dark green foliage some 2 feet or 3 feet in diameter, overtopped by a quantity of big white blossoms, is exceedingly attractive, especially in the dull winter months. Flowers outside at this season are so scarce that it is worth a little trouble to provide a suitable place for the Christmas roses. Most important of all, they like a deep and somewhat rich soil, and, while they will do well in a rather sunny place, their favourite situation is among other low-growing plants like ferns, sheltered from the east by trees, and also shaded during the greater part of the day from the sun. In getting a border ready for these plants it should be trenched to a depth of over 2 feet. If the soil is poor or light, a layer of rotten cow manure should be worked in with the lower spit of soil. With regard to the best time for planting, there is no doubt that as soon as they have done flowering is a most favourable period. This would be in February or March, and the plants would then have plenty of time to establish themselves and develop their leaves during the following summer. They may also be moved successfully in the autumn after they have finished their growth.

E. T. C.

Roses: Origin of 'Leuchstern' and 'Frau Karl Druschki.'

By Cochet-Cochet (*Le Jardin*, vol. xxi. No. 480, p. 56; with 3 figs.; February 20, 1907).—'Leuchstern' (C.P.), distributed by J. C. Schmidt, 1898, was a sport from Turner's 'Crimson Rambler.' 'Frau Karl Druschki' (H.P.), distributed by Peter Lambert, 1901, was produced by fertilization of 'Merveille de Lyon' by 'Mlle. Caroline Testout.' One of the three resulting seeds was raised, and flowered for the first time in 1897. It was first known as 'Schnee-Königin.'—*F. A. W.*

Salvia cyanea (*Le Jardin*, xxi. No. 486, p. 146; May 20, 1907).— Recently introduced from Central America. Discovered at Costa Rica by M. C. Wercklé. Has quadrangular winged stems, with oboval, dentate, bright green, glabrous leaves. Close panicles of brilliant sky-blue flowers resembling *Coleus thyrsoideus.* Blooms from December all through the winter. Invaluable for the greenhouse.—*F. A. W.*

San José, or Chinese Scale. By C. L. Marlatt (*U.S.A. Dep. Agr., Bur. Entom., Bull.* 62; December 1906).—A most important bulletin, authoritatively summarising all the information concerning this pest, which was introduced to America about 1875 from China, and has now to be reckoned with in all culture of deciduous fruit trees in all the principal fruit-growing areas of the States, and has proved by far the worst of the many troublesome scale insects infesting cultivated plants. Full notes on its life-history, native home, insect and fungus enemies, and means of control are given, and the bulletin is well illustrated by figures, maps, and plates.—*F. J. C.*

San José Scale. By J. S. Houser (*U.S.A. Exp. Stn. Ohio, Bull.* 169; 6 plates; January 1906).—This scale insect appears to be steadily spreading, and to well merit its name "*perniciosus.*" Numerous experiments with sprays have been tried with more or less success, and the two most advocated at the present time are kerosene and sulphur sprays. As the result of experiments a spray fluid composed of 15 lb. to 20 lb. lime and 15 lb. sulphur boiled together in sufficient water to make a thick liquid for at least forty-five minutes, and afterwards diluted to fifty gallons, was found to be the most effective and practicable remedy. The best time to apply the wash is in the spring, but in cases of extreme infestation it may be advisable to make both a fall and a spring spraying. It is important to strain the solution, so that no large particles get into the sprayer strainers, and all the working parts of the pumps and nozzles should be made of brass. The spray should be applied as quickly as possible after it is made, and all the articles used should be thoroughly washed with clean water at the end of each day's work.—*F. J. C.*

San José Scale. By E. A. Popenoe (*U.S.A. Exp. Stn. Kansas, Press-Bull.* 150; April 1906).—The San José scale has just been found in Kansas, where, in the gardens of Dodge City, it is now infesting apple, pear, peach, plum (both wild and cultivated), cherry, apricot, plumcot, grape, currant, rose, Osage orange, cottonwood, and Russian mulberry. The use of kerosene emulsion is recommended on the growing trees, and during the resting season the lime sulphur-salt wash.—*F. J. C.*

San José Scale : Test of Different Sprays. By W. E. Rumsey and F. E. Brooks (*U.S.A. Exp. Stn. W. Virginia, Bull.* 107 ; June 1906).— Concentrated soluble oils gave the best results, almost all the scale being killed when the best of them were used.—*F. J. C.*

San José Scale : Use of Miscible Oils for Treatment of. By P. J. Parrott, H. E. Hodgkiss, and F. A. Sirrine (*U.S.A. Exp. Stn. Geneva, Bull.* 281 ; December 1906).—These oils, which are emulsions of kerosene put on the market by various firms and sold under proprietary names, have been tested against San José scale, and have been found useless in the proportion in which they are recommended, viz. one part of oil to twenty or twenty-five of water. They should be used at the rate of about one part to ten or fifteen of water, and even then their use is not followed by such good results as spraying with the boiled lime-sulphur-salt solution.—*F. J. C.*

Saxifraga scardica. By T. A. Sprague (*Bot. Mag.* tab. 8058).— Balkan Peninsula. Nat. ord. *Saxifragaceae* ; tribe *Saxifrageae.* A tufted plant. Leaves $\frac{1}{4}$-$\frac{1}{2}$ inch long, ciliate ; flowering stems 3 inches long, with 1-11 flowers ; petals $4\frac{1}{2}$ lines long, white.—*G. H.*

Sequoia, A Weeping (*Sequoia gigantea pendula*).— By Georges Bellair (*Rev. Hort.* September 1, 1906, pp. 394, 395 ; 1 fig.). — Description and photograph of very markedly weeping form in the park of Trianon ; branches absolutely lax and pendulous and very long. Dislikes lime and drought, needs deep loamy soil.—*C. T. D.*

Shading, Effects of, on Soil Conditions. By J. B. Stewart (*U.S.A. Dep. Agr., Bur. of Soils, Bull.* 39 ; 7 figs., 4 plates ; February 1907).— The cultivation of tobacco, pineapples, and certain market garden crops under the shade of a tent or slat cover is steadily growing in the States. The experiments recorded here prove that the tent conserves the moisture in the soil to a marked degree by checking evaporation, resulting in great benefit to the crop during prolonged drought. The temperature in the tent was from 1° to 3° above the normal throughout the season, the variation being greatest during the heat of the day, and the relative humidity was considerably greater. These differences in atmospheric conditions result largely from the low velocity of the wind inside the tent as compared with that outside. The average growth of the plants in the tent was much greater than that outside, and maturity was reached earlier ; but the weight produced was less per acre by from 100 lb. to 300 lb. inside the tent, probably owing to the fact that while the surface exposed was larger the leaves were thinner.—*F. J. C.*

Soil Bacteria and Decomposition of Nitrogenous Compounds.

By Conrad Hoffmann (*U.S.A. Exp. Stn. Wisconsin*, 23rd *Ann. Rep.*; October 1906).—The author finds that the numbers and character of the bacterial flora of the soil are largely influenced by the nature of the fertilisers used and by the character of the soil itself, the number being smallest in sand and greatest in black marsh soil. The degree of nitrogenous decomposition is, in a general way, directly dependent on the total number of bacteria present, and the progress of the decomposition is marked by numerous fluctuations, corresponding with the fluctuations in the numbers of bacteria present. Large amounts of ammonia are formed before nitrification becomes active without interfering in any way with the subsequent development of the nitrifying organisms. Blood and bran are much more easily decomposed than bone meal and peat, and decomposition is most complete in black marsh land, followed by clay, sandy loam and sand in the order named.—*F. J. C.*

Soil Sterilisation.

By A. D. Selby (*U.S.A. Exp. Stn. Ohio, Circ.* 59; October 1906).—Recommends drenching the old beds in which tobacco has been grown with formalin at the rate of 2 lb. of formalin (40 per cent.) to fifty gallons of water in order to destroy the fungi *Rhizoctonia*, which causes " bed rot " and *Thielavia*, which causes " black rot." The formalin must be allowed to evaporate before the seed is sown.—*F. J. C.*

Solanum Commersonii and S. C. Violet.

By Labergerie (*Rev. Hort.* June 16, 1906, pp. 303–307; coloured plate).—A detailed account of the appearance of the violet form and the result of subsequent culture by M. Labergerie and others; of interest to those who have followed the recent controversy in connection with these potatoes as practically forming its starting-point.—*C. T. D.*

Specific Names for Garden Varieties.

By S. Mottet (*Rev. Hort.* February 16, 1906, pp. 97-99).—A much-needed protest against the naming of new varieties as if they were species, the name of the species proper being ignored, leading to great confusion.—*C. T. D.*

Spinach, Mercury or Perennial.

By G. Wythes (*Garden*, No. 1796, p. 219; April 21, 1906).—In many parts of the country the above plant is little known, yet few are cultivated more easily. In Lincolnshire this plant is found in most gardens grown under the names of Mercury and Lincolnshire spinach, but in the adjoining counties it is called '.Good King Henry' (*Chenopodium Bonus Henricus*). The plants are usually propagated at this season (March or early April). It may also be raised from seed sown thinly in the spring, as it is a quick grower, the seedlings being planted out in dull weather in the early autumn in rich land in rows 18 inches apart, half that distance between the plants. Grown thus there will be good cutting material the next spring. It is propagated by division early, and in well-manured deeply dug land.—*E. T. C.*

Spraying Notes.

By E. Walker (*U.S.A. Exp. Stn. Arkansas, Bull.* 95; 1907).—Spraying has frequently been disregarded, but the recurrence of short apple crops has awakened greater zeal in its application.   Spraying often fails, and the author points out as among the causes of failure :—(1) No agitator to the pump ; (2) poor nozzles, throwing a shower instead of a mist ; (3) insufficient and variable pressure ; (4) lack of thoroughness ; (5) failure to do the work at the right time on account of unfavourable weather ; (6) use of wrong materials for the pest being fought ; (7) use of impure materials ; (8) improper mixing of ingredients ; (9) neglect of later spraying ; (10) too large orchards for the spraying facilities ; (11) interference of winds or rains with timely and thorough work ; (12) expecting spraying to compensate for neglect of the usual good care of which spraying is only one feature.   A full list of fungicides and insecticides is given, with recipes and notes as to when and what to use in various cases.   The recipes have been several times given in these columns.—*F. J. C.*

Strawberries, Perpetual Fruiting.   By A. Pirlot (*Le Jardin,* vol. xx. No. 470, p. 284 ; 3 figs. ; September 20, 1906).—New varieties of perpetual-fruiting strawberries are 'Prof. Battenchon,' a hybrid from ' Constante Féconde ' and ' Sensation,' with large, deep-red berries, growing on short stalks sheltered by the leaves ; ' La Perle,' which is most fertile and vigorous, keeping the flavour and rigid stems of the parent wild strawberry ; and ' Perle Rouge,' derived from ' Perle,' perhaps the best of all.   Plant between July and April, preferably August–September, choosing runners from specially prepared plants of the previous autumn. These should be set widely apart, care being taken that the runners have space and plenty of water given them, the parent plants not being allowed to flower.—*A. W. F.*

Sugar Cane, Insect Pests of.   By H. A. Ballou, B.Sc. (*Jour. Imp. Dep. Agr. W.I.* vol. vi. No. 1 ; 1905).—This is assumed to be a concise summary of what has been published up to date on this subject, and includes the following :—The moth borer (*Diatraea saccharalis*), hard back (*Ligyrus tumulosus*), the weevil-borer (*Sphenophorus sericeus*), the root-borer (*Diaprepes abbreviatus*), the cane fly (*Delphax saccharicora*), scale insects (*Dactylopius sacchari*) (*Dactylopius calceolariae*) (*Aspidiotus sacchari*), the shot-borer (*Xyleborus perforans*), the larger moth-borer (*Castnia licus*).   Each with life-history, description, observations, and remedies.—*M. C. C.*

Summer Pruning.   By A. Dickens (*U.S.A. Exp. Stn. Kansas, Press Bull.* 142 ; June 1905).—The conclusion is arrived at as the result of experiments that summer pruning of fruit, timber and shade trees, consisting in the cutting back of new wood and the thinning out of heavy growth during early summer and late spring, leads to better results than pruning during autumn and winter.—*F. J. C.*

Sweet Potatoes, Diseases of.   By E. Mead Wilcox, Ph.D. (*U.S.A. Exp. Stn. Alabama,* No. 135 ; June 1906).—The present bulletin assumes to enumerate all the principal diseases which affect the sweet potato crop in Alabama.

" Black rot" may be recognised by the formation on the root of olive-brown or greenish spots, which become larger as the disease progresses, until the entire root may turn black. The same disease attacks also the young sprouts, and is then called " black shank." This disease is caused by a fungus known as *Ceratocystis fimbriata*.

" Dry rot " appears only on the underground portions of the plant. The whole upper end of the root becomes wrinkled and covered with small pimples, which progresses until the whole root is diseased. This condition is caused by *Phoma Batatae*.

" Scurf " attacks the root only, and appears first as a small brownish speck; this enlarges, and large areas of the root become affected, assume a dark colour, sometimes shrivelling to a considerable extent. It is caused by *Monilochaetes injuscans*.

" Soft rot " is strictly confined to the roots, and is largely a storage trouble, caused by *Rhizopus nigricans*. The root soon acquires a most disagreeable and characteristic odour.

" Soil rot " is a strict field disease. The first indication of the disease will be found generally about the base of one of the small rootlets, and it seems that the fungus can gain entrance to the main root only through these young delicate rootlets. The disease is caused by the fungus *Acrocystis batatas*. Kainit and sulphur sown broadcast is recommended, at the rate of 300 lb. or 400 lb. per acre.

" Stem rot " first appears in that portion of the stem at the surface of the ground, and proceeds thence in both directions. It is caused by *Nectria Ipomoeae*.

" White rot " attacks the roots only, and changes the tissues into a granular whitish substance. The spores are produced in immense numbers, and are greenish blue in colour. The fungus would appear to be a mould allied to the common " blue mould."—*M. C. C.*

Tellima affinis (Rivoire) (*Le Jardin*, vol. xxi. No. 478, p. 28, fig.; January 20, 1907).—New bulbous plant with long rigid stems and white flowers. Very useful for bouquets; will grow in a frame or cold house. The minute bulbs should be planted three and four together in a 5-inch pot.—*F. A. W.*

Teratology, Experimental. By L. Daniel (*Le Jardin*, vol. xx. No. 469, p. 260; with 6 figs.; September 5, 1906).—An interesting scientific article. Discusses the etiology of monstrosities, and suggests that they arise from nutritive plethora, or the disequilibrium of absorption predominating over consumption, with the ratio $\frac{Cv}{Ca} < 1$

The author refers to a number of recent publications on this subject.

F. A. W.

Thyrsacanthus rutilans. By H. P. (*Garden*, No. 1795, p. 209; fig.; April 14, 1906).—Among the plants available for indoor gardening there is not one that would be, even by the beginner, confounded with the *Thyrsacanthus*, that is, when in flower, for it owes its chief distinctive features to the beauty of its inflorescence. To the cultivator who endeavours to form this into a neat, shapely plant its beauty is altogether lost, as the flowers are borne in very long drooping racemes, and are consequently seen to the best advantage on tall stems. The object aimed at should be good, strong growth, the main shoot being. allowed to grow without pinching. Even if the result is a plant 4 feet to 5 feet in height, it will be found that this is by no means too tall for the long racemes pushed out from the upper part. It is in no way a novelty, for it was introduced from Colombia in 1851, *Thyrsacanthus rutilans* is one of the fine old plants which are coming more prominently forward after many years of comparative neglect.—*E. T. C.*

Tobacco Breeding. By A. D. Shamel and W. W. Cobey (*U.S.A. Dep. Agr., Bur. Pl. Ind., Bull.* 96 ; 14 figs., 10 plates ; March 1907).— Great variability is found among tobacco plants in what is reputed the same variety on the same field. The causes of variation include crossing, change of soil and change of climatic conditions, while individual varia- tions are due to such causes as inherent tendency to variability, methods of soil fertilisation and cultivation, maturity of seed, and various local conditions. Instances of these variations are given. The tobacco flower is self-fertile, and plants from self-fertilized seed are always stronger than those from cross-fertilized ; but there is danger of cross-fertilization by bees &c. The objects in view in the experiments have been the improve- ment in the shape of the leaf, modification of size, control of number of leaves, production of non-suckering types and of early varieties, and improvement of burning qualities. Then follow descriptions of the methods of saving seed, of seed separation, of a variety raised by seed selection, and of others raised by cross-fertilization.—*F. J. C.*

Tobacco, Experiments with Fertilisers on. By Chas. E. Thorne (*U.S.A. Exp. Stn. Ohio, Bull.* 172 ; March 1906).—The average yield for the three years 1902–1905 on the unfertilized plots was 522 lb., on the fertilized 986 lb., while the quality was much better on the latter than the former. Farmyard manure is found to be the best material for use, while sodium nitrate appears the best form for use in supplying nitrogen.—*F. J. C.*

Tobacco Thrips. By W. A. Hooker (*U.S.A. Dep. Agr., Bur. Ent., Bull.* 65, April 1907 ; 2 plates, 2 text figs.).—Under shade cultivation tobacco enemies appear to be found at their worst, and a new pest is here described. The injury wrought by this species of thrips leads to the pro- duction of a white coloration on the veins, which shows in the fermented leaf, at times about 20 per cent. of the crop being affected. The insect appears to be widely distributed and a general feeder in the States, and a description and figure of the insect, which proves to be a new species, are given. Rains act as a great check, and it is advised to raise the seed- lings away from the general bed, to cultivate cleanly, not to plant cereals next to shade-grown tobacco, and to apply kerosene emulsion (1 part to 10 parts of water) with a knapsack sprayer twice a week regularly, com- mencing when the plants are in the seed bed.—*F. J. C.*

Tomatoes, Excessive Feeding as a Factor in Producing. By E. P. Sandsten (*U.S.A. Exp. Stn. Wisconsin, Ann. Rep.* 1905, pp. 300–314 ; 11 figs.).—The writer found that scarcely two plants in a bed of ninety-six were alike when the amount of manure applied was excessive. The seed used was obtained from a seed firm. Some seedless fruits were obtained.—*F. J. C.*

Trachycarpus. By C. D'Ancona (*Bull. R. Soc. Tosc. Ort.*, March-April, p. 102 ; 1906).—The botanist Beccari lately published a very accurate study of the species of this genus, of which there are three, viz. : *T. excelsa*, H. Wendl., *T. Takil*, Becc., and *T. Martiana*, H. Wendl. All are natives of Eastern Extra-tropical Asia, and of Central, Eastern, and Western Himalayas, in distinct localities ; this is enough to show that they can live in the open in Southern and Central Italy.

T. excelsa.—This is the most commonly grown one in Europe and the hardiest of all, even more so than *Chamaerops humilis.* It is very variable, Beccari regarded *T. Fortunei* as a synonym of *T. excelsa*, and not, as some have supposed, a distinct species. A description and sketches of the flowers are given. · The fibres attached to the leaf-bases are used in the manufacture of many objects in China. In Italy it flowers in April and May, and the fruits mature in the following March. The fruits are at first yellowish, when mature blackish-violet, like dark purple grapes, and pruinose, globose-reniform across, 12–13 mill. broad, 9 mill. long. The seeds are the same shape as the fruit.

T. Takil, Becc., sp. n.—This species is called by Duthie in the "Gardeners' Chronicle" of April 10, 1886, p. 457, *Chamaerops Martiana.* The stem of the young plant grows obliquely at first. It begins to flower when it is about 1 metre (3 feet 3 inches) high. It only occurs in the Western Himalayas on Mount Takil in Kumaon about 2,000 to 2,380 metres (6,600 to 7,700 feet) above the level of the sea ; Sir J. Hooker reports it as being annually covered with snow. According to Gamble, it prefers the cool, narrow valleys, with a north-west aspect. According to Beccari, it is closely allied to *T. excelsa*, which it represents in the Western Himalayas, but it is hardier. Duthie reports it as growing to a greater height than *T. excelsa.* Trees planted in the neighbourhood of Florence resisted well the severe winters there ; they appear to dislike heat more than cold. The fibrous covering of the leaf-bases is not so dense as in *T. excelsa ;* the crown of leaves is more diffuse, graceful, and elegant. A sketch of the apical portion of the trunk is given, also of the flowers and fruit.

T. Martiana.—It grows in Central and Eastern Himalayas, in Assam, Northern Burma, and it is very abundant in Nepaul, at Bunipa, at a height of 1,500 metres above the sea, and fairly frequent in the hills of Khasia, in Assam, at from 1,000 to 1,500 metres (3,300 to 4,900 feet). Synonyms of this plant are : *T. khasiana*, Wend., *Chamaerops Martiana*, Wall., *C. khasiana*, Griff., *C. Griffithii*, Verl., and *C. tomentosa*, Morr. The first mention of this palm was by Wallich in his " Plantae Asiaticae Rariores," under the name of *Chamaerops Martiana.* The plant grown in the Jardin des Plantes at Paris, under the name of *T. Griffithii*, is the same as this species, according to Beccari. It was figured in the "Revue Horticole" of 1879, p. 212, fig. 43. It was about 6 metres (20 feet) high and had flowered twice, producing female flowers, and was sent to that garden by Wallich. Others exist at the Jardin d'Acclimatation in Paris, and two large ones occur in Kew Gardens, one of which latter, which produced male flowers, was figured by Sir J. Hooker in the " Botanical Magazine," plate 7128, under the name of *T. khasianus.* This species is quite distinct from, yet closely allied to, the other two species. It is distinguished by having its leaves regularly divided into segments half-way along the limb ; they are deciduous as the trees get old, so that a large part of the trunk is bare ; the fruits are olive-shaped, resembling that of small species of *Phoenia.* Figures of the fruit and seed are given. The endocarp is formed of curious colonies of sclerotic cells. A magnified portion of a section of the pericarp is given. Finally, a brief distinguishing description of each of the three species of *Trachycarpus* is afforded.—*W. C. W.*

Two-winged Flies, Affecting Farm, Garden, Stock, and Household. By F. L. Washburn (*U.S.A. Exp. Stn. Minnesota, 14th Ann. Rep.* pp. 19-164 ; 2 plates, 159 figs.; 1906).—An excellent and well-illustrated account of the Diptera of economic importance in Minnesota. Appropriate methods of dealing with the pests are mentioned in all cases where such are called for.—*F. J. C.*

Valeriana pyrenaica, Linn. By S. Mottet (*Le Jardin,* vol. xxi. No. 485, p. 132; with fig.; May 5, 1907).—The most remarkable and decorative of all the valerians, it has been too much neglected ; grows about 4 feet high, with handsome leaves and deep rose-coloured flowers. Lasts well in water.—*F. A. W.*

Verbascums, The. By E. H. Jenkins (*Garden,* No. 1814, p. 90, fig.; August 25, 1906).—The Verbascums, or mulleins, are in their way among the more showy of garden plants, and as such deserve attention at the hands of the gardener. To say that this somewhat extensive genus is an important one would be perhaps ascribing praise to it not wholly merited. There are, however, certain species that demand more than ordinary attention by reason of their boldness when well grown, and their adaptability for forming groups of an attractive or even an imposing character. Regarded generally these plants are better suited to woodland gardening or to those other parts of the garden where bold effects or vistas may be used with advantage. The large shrubbery border, for example, frequently affords an excellent opening for such plants as these, and if kept away from the radius of hungry tree roots and their requirements liberally catered for in other ways, a scene of great beauty and attractiveness will result.—*E. T. C.*

Veronica Hulkeana. By G. T. Grignan (*Rev. Hort.* January 16, 1906, pp. 40-41 ; coloured plate and woodcuts).—The coloured plate depicts two spikes of flowers of a delicate lilac tint, and much resembling that of the lilac, though less dense. The woodcut shows a handsome, compact, and very floriferous shrub, which is described as very hardy and of easy cultivation. The flowers last long and appear in May.—*C. T. D.*

Veronica, Parasite of (*Le Jardin*, vol. xx. No. 472, p. 318; Oct. 20, 1906).—*Septoria exotica*, a new cryptogamic parasite recorded from the Argentine Republic, Italy, Berlin, and Moravia, where it has caused great ravages. It forms greyish-white spots, bearing black sporangia. The leaves attacked curl up and drop off till the plant is almost defoliated. Treat with ammonia solution, adding crystals of soda.—*F. A. W.*

Vervain. By Le Texnier (*Le Jardin*, vol. xx. No. 471, p. 301; October 5, 1906).—Historical article, enumerating all the varieties of this plant.—*F. A. W.*

Vine Culture, Houses for. By Numa Schneider (*Rev. Hort.* April 16, 1906, pp. 185--189; 7 figs.).—A very interesting article on various types of vineries with details of their construction and arrange-ments.—*C. T. D.*

Violet, Cultivation of, at Hyères. By E. Tschaen (*Rev. Hort.* August 1, 1906, pp. 353-355; 4 figs.).—A very interesting descrip-tion of the method of growing violets for the market at Hyères, on ridges affording some protection, and in conjunction with vegetables.

C. T. D.

Vitis Voinieriana. By H. Martinet (*Le Jardin*, vol. xx. No. 465, p. 200; 3 figs.; July 5, 1906).—A plea for *Vitis Voinieriana*, introduced in 1889 from China, as a free-growing and vigorous greenhouse climber. A note on p. 239, No. 467, by Dybowski, director of the Colonial Garden, Nogent-sur-Marne, points out that this plant should, properly speaking, be called *Cissus Voinieriana* Viala.—*F. A. W.*

Walnut Blight. By R. E. Smith (*U.S.A. Exp. Stn. California, Bull.* 184; 3 figs.; January 1907).—This disease, which is at present restricted to the Pacific coast, is due to the attack of a bacterium called *Pseudomonas juglandis.* The disease is characterised by black, cankered spots on the young nuts, causing them to fall prematurely or spoiling the kernel. Similar spots appear on the youngest, green, new shoots, but do not continue down the twig. In bad years, however, a large portion of the terminal twigs are destroyed by this means, and with them the next year's crop. Spraying with Bordeaux mixture greatly diminishes the loss, but the cost is almost prohibitive. Immune varieties are feasible and are to be sought.—*F. J. C.*

Walnut Trees in Oregon. By C. J. Lewis (*U.S.A. Exp. Stn. Oregon, Bull.* 92; 23 plates; December 19, 1906).—Walnut-growing appears to be becoming an important industry in Oregon, and the present bulletin gives an account of the propagation and treatment of the trees and of the harvesting and marketing of the nuts. The "Cali-fornian growers believe that the beating of the trees does more harm than good, as it often seems to knock off a great many buds." The late-flowering French varieties, 'Mayette' and 'Franquette,' are the ones most generally grown. It is interesting to note that in 1905 the United States imported over 20,000,000 lb. of walnuts.—*F. J. C.*

Water-cress Pests. By F. A. Chittenden (*U.S.A. Dep. Agr. Bur. Ent., Bull.* 66, pt. ii.; 5 figs.; April 1907).—Two pests are described : the water-cress sowbug (*Mancasellus brachyurus*, Harger), which is a strictly aquatic species, feeding exclusively on cress and attacking the roots and lower leaves and stems, cutting off the last so as to cause the plants to float away ; and the beetle (*Phaedon aeruginosa*, Suffr.) which attacks the leaves, feeding on their lower surfaces. Methods of control are suggested.—*F. J. C.*

Willows for Basket-making. By A. D. Webster (*Garden*, No. 1798, p. 241 ; May 5, 1906).—The best willows to plant are *Salix purpurea* (the purple osier), *S. viminalis*, and *S. triandra* ; but there are many hybrids, as willows cross freely. Probably the most valuable is *S. viminalis*, the rods being produced freely, while they are remarkably thin and flexible ; but those of the others named are very good for basket-making. They produce exceedingly lithe and tough wands. After the soil has been got into good tilth, planting the sets or cuttings should take place. These should be from 12 inches to 15 inches long and formed of well-ripened rods of one year's growth, the cleanest and straightest portions only being used. In planting the cuttings great caution should be exercised to prevent the bark becoming loosened or removed from the wood. The rows may be 50 inches from each other, and the individual cuttings about 15 inches apart. Much depends upon the kind of willow and the quality of soil. The cuttings may be inserted about 9 inches into the ground, leaving about 3 inches exposed for the future stool.

Cutting may begin after the second or third year, and should take place when the crop is dormant, or not later than the middle of February. The following short rules might be observed in willow culture for basket-making :—

1. Willows will not succeed well in peaty, sandy, or waterlogged soil—rich, well-drained loam that can be flooded at will being most suitable.

2. Prepare the ground by trenching or ploughing, and thoroughly cleanse it from weeds.

3. Plant only the best kinds, avoiding a mixed crop.—*E. T. C.*

Wistarias, The. By W. J. Bean (*Garden*, No. 1802, p. 289 ; June 2, 1906).—Among the stronger-growing climbers that are hardy in Britain—and the Wistarias are, perhaps, the most robust of them—none equal the best members of this genus in the gorgeousness of their flower beauty. The old *Wistaria chinensis*, a denizen of our gardens now for ninety years, is, of course, the best known of them all ; but, beautiful as it is, I am inclined to think that it is surpassed by the best forms of *W. multijuga*. In recent years some very charming varieties of this latter species have been introduced.

Like so many other genera of plants, Wistarias are represented on both the American and Asiatic continents, although but one species—*W. frutescens*—is found in America. At present five species are known, no new one having been added to our collections for over thirty years, and

I have not heard that the explorations of Dr. Henry, Mr. E. H. Wilson, or other travellers have brought any new Wistaria to light.

Whilst Wistarias are not particular in their requirements, a few conditions are requisite if they are to be seen at their best. They like a rich soil, plenty of moisture, and abundant sunlight. *W. chinensis*, the only species that has, as yet, obtained a really wide foothold in gardens, is usually grown on the south side of a house or wall; and in no other position can it be seen to better advantage. It is, however, very attractive trained in other ways, as, for instance, on a pergola.—*E. T. C.*

Wittmackia lingulata. By C. H. Wright (*Bot. Mag.* tab. 8056).— West Indies. Nat. ord. *Bromeliaceae*; tribe *Bromelieae*. Leaves forming a rosette, 2 feet long, 2½ inches wide; sepals white, petals yellow, one line long.—*G. H.*

ASTERS AT WISLEY, 1906-07.

A TRIAL of Michaelmas daisies was held at Wisley during 1906 and 1907 in which 525 stocks were planted, representing 300 distinct varieties. The collection included 134 varieties from the Society's Gardens at Chiswick, which contained the nucleus of the trials of 1892 and 1902, reported upon in vols. xv. and xxvii. of the JOURNAL. The genus comprises not less than 250 species, of which more than one-half are North American. Of those reported on in the trial, with the exception of *acris, Amellus, canus,* and *Linosyris,* which lack the Michaelmas daisy habit, all are from North America, and the great majority of them from the Eastern United States. As a rule, those species having the widest natural distribution have proved most amenable to cultivation; but it is to the species *laevis* and *Novi-Belgii* that our gardens are most indebted, it having been estimated that considerably more than one-third of the varieties cultivated have resulted from distinct crosses between these species. So hopelessly have the specific characters become mingled that it has been a continued source of difficulty to botanists to determine to which species many of the garden forms should be referred. In the report the varieties have been entered under their proper names simply, but for convenience of reference the names of the species under which the varieties have been classed are inserted in brackets at the end of the description. It will be seen that in many cases the same variety has been referred to two or more species (*e.g.* Calliope); that in others, varieties very similar in habit and flower have been referred to different species (*e.g. densus* and *decorus*); and that a variety is sometimes referred to a species to which it has no apparent resemblance (*e.g.* Alice, Jessie Crum).

Most of the Michaelmas daisies prefer a deep, well-manured, strong soil, inclined to be wet rather than dry. All varieties that show a tendency to become rampant should be lifted every year, only two or three of the outside growths being replanted to furnish the fresh clump, this work being preferably carried out in spring as soon as fresh growth begins. For the purposes of the trial the plants were grown in rows 4 feet apart, with 4 feet between each plant in the row.

It must be borne in mind when examining the report that collected forms of many of the species show great variation, and that the periods of flowering and heights recorded represent the results of only one set of observations, which soil, season, and climate might considerably modify.

The following is a list of the best species and varieties selected at the trials of 1892, 1902, and 1907. The names of the most decorative varieties at Wisley, 1907, are printed in italics.

Commencing to flower in August:—

> *White,* 3 feet or less: *corymbosus,* Perseus, Sensation, *vimineus perfectus,* White Queen of the Dwarfs.
>
> 3-5 feet: Albion, Dot, White Queen.

Pink to lilac-pink, 3 feet or less : Miss Stafford.

    3-5 feet : Edna Mercia, Elsie Perry, Mavourneen.

Pale-blue to lilac-white, 3 feet or less : *Lindleyanus*, Ophir, *sagitti-folius*, *undulatus*.

    3-5 feet : Dorothy, *puniceus lucidulus*.

Lilac, 3 feet or less : Aurora, *Curtisii*, *lilacinus*, *paniculatus laxus*, *prenanthoides*.

    3-5 feet : Argus, Discolor, Janus, *paniculatus*, *patulus*, Ravennae.

Mauve to dark blue, 3 feet or less : *acris*, *eminens*, Mrs. Davis Evans, *puniceus*, Pygmalion.

    3-5 feet : *D. B. Crane, Vice-President.*

Commencing in September :—

Rayless, 3 feet or less : *Linosyris*.

White, 3 feet or less : Cassiope, Collerette blanche, Daisy Peters, Delight, *ericoides superbus*, Evening Star, Freedom, Mrs. W. Peters, *ptarmicoides*, Vesta, *vimineus*.

    3-5 feet : Antigone, Decima, Harpur Crewe, John Wood, *multi-florus*, Norah Peters, Peters' White, *polyphyllus*, Purity, Thora, W. J. Grant.

    Over 5 feet : Ceres, Fairfield, *umbellatus*, White Spray.

Pink to lilac-pink, 3 feet or less : Alice, Captivation, Esther, Hon. Vicary Gibbs, St. Egwin.

    3-5 feet : Clio, Collerette rose, Mrs. Rayner, Mrs. Twinam, N.A. *ruber*.

    Over 5 feet : Lil Fardell, N.A. roseus, Ryecroft Pink.

Pale-blue to lilac-white, 3 feet or less : Catulus.

    3-5 feet : *cordifolius*, *C. albulus*, *C. major*, Edwin Beckett, *grandis*, Ideal, King Edward VII., *litoreus*, Nancy, *paniculatus blandus*, St. Patrick.

    Over 5 feet : Cora, *cordifolius giganteus*, Mrs. C. W. Earle, *puniceus pulcherrimus*.

Lilac, 3 feet or less : *decorus*, *dumosus*, Irene, *Shortii*.

    3-5 feet : Archer Hind, Berenice, Brightness, Coombe Fishacre, Cordelia, Diana, Fanny, F. W. Burbidge, Hilda Morris, Horace, Minerva, Photograph, Proserpine, Top-Sawyer, Warley semi-plena.

    Over 5 feet : Robert Parker, Virgil.

Mauve to dark blue, 3 feet or less : *acris nanus*, Amellus, and vars. Celestial, *densus*, Distinction, Gloriosa, *laevigatus*, Stella.

    3-5 feet : Apollo, Arcturus, Ariadne, Beauty of Colwall, N.A. *praecox*, *splendens*, *turbinellus*, W. Marshall.

    Over 5 feet : Mrs. S. T. Wright, Ryecroft Purple, W. Bowman.

Commencing in October :—

White, 3 feet or less : *diffusus horizontalis*, *ericoides*.

    Over 5 feet : *diffusus pendulus*.

Pink to lilac-pink, 3 feet or less : *gracillimus*, Tresserve.

    3-5 feet : Flora, Fortuna.

    Over 5 feet : Thirza.

Pale-blue to lilac-white, 3-5 feet : Amethystinus, Enchantress, Hon. E. Gibbs.

    Over 5 feet : *cordifolius magnificus*.

Lilac, 3 feet or less : Osprey.

3–5 feet : Calliope, *Drummondii*, Sappho, T. Wilks.

Mauve to dark blue, 3 feet or less : *grandiflorus*, Juno.

3–5 feet : *floribundus, formosissimus*, Jessie Crum, *N.A. pulchellus*, Pluto.

Over 5 feet : *laevis*, and *Harvard var.*, Miss Southall.

The varieties latest in flower were *diffusus pendulus, Drummondii, gracillimus, grandiflorus*, Little Gem, *Tradescanti*, and Tresserve,

F.C.＝First-class Certificate.

A.M.＝Award of Merit.

XXX＝Highly Commended.

XX＝Commended.

Fl.＝Flower-head.

Hab.＝Habitat.

Infl.＝Inflorescence.

1. *acris* (Barr, Dobbie, Chiswick), **XXX** 1892, 1907.—Two and a half feet ; infl. densely flowered, corymbose ; fl. 1½ inch across, stellate ; rays mauve ; disc lemon yellow.   Flowering for seven weeks from August 31 ; leaves linear-lanceolate, pale green.   Hab. South Europe.

2. *acris dracunculodes* (Barr, Dobbie, Chiswick).—Less valuable than the type, from which it differs in its taller habit (3½ feet) and in its narrower and paler ray florets.

3. *acris nanus* (Barr, Dobbie), **A.M.** October 13, 1902.—Three to four weeks later than the type ; fl. smaller.   Habit dwarfer, more compact and pyramidal ; 1½ feet.

4. Admiration (Beckett).—One and a half feet ; infl. dense-flowered, pyramidal ; fl. 1 inch across, mauve-pink, full-rayed, neat.   Flowering for five weeks from September 13.

5. Alan Peters (Peters).—Four feet ; infl. a loose open pyramid ; fl. 1½ inches across, pure white, becoming pinkish with age ; rays broad, loose. Habit erect, but rather lacking vigour.   Flowering for five weeks from September 30.

6. Albion (Chiswick collection), **XX** 1892.—Four and a half feet ; stem rigid, dark ; infl. a loosely flowered round-headed panicle ; flowering almost to the ground ; fl. 1 inch across, white, becoming pinkish ; growth rampant.   Flowering for four weeks from August 31 (*Novi-Belgii*).

7. Alice (Barr).—Two feet ; infl. densely flowered, corymbose ; fl. ¾ inch across, flesh-pink, becoming deeper, full-rayed ; disc rich yellow. Habit very vigorous ; stems and heath-like foliage, bright green. Flowering for four weeks from September 13.   Somewhat similar to Esther, with *ericoides* habit, but quite distinct from *Novi-Belgii*, to which Messrs. Barr refer it.

8. *Amellus* (Dobbie), **XXX** 1892.—One and a half feet ; infl. loosely corymbose ; fl. 1½ inches across, purple.   Habit loose ; leaves rough, the lower ones spathulate.   Flowering for six weeks from September 30. Hab. South Europe, &c.

9. *Amellus bessarabicus* (Dobbie), **A.M.** October 1, 1902.—Two feet ; much finer than the type ; fl. 2 inches across, stellate, rich purple-mauve.

Flowering for five weeks from September 13. A much inferior variety, flowering a month later, was received from another source under this name.

10. *Amellus elegans* (Barr).—Neater than the type ; fl. full-rayed ; disc bright yellow, rays violet. Flowering for four weeks from September 13.

11. *Amellus fastigatus.*—Under this name plants were grown from the Chiswick collection and from Messrs. Dobbie which proved to belong to *Boltonia,* a genus closely allied to Aster, but without the capillary bristles to the pappus. Three and a half feet ; infl. a freely branched loose panicle ; fl. 1¾ inches across, full-rayed, lilac-white ; leaves lanceolate, coarsely toothed, veins deeply sunk. A showy plant flowering from the latter part of July well into September.

12. *Amellus Framfieldii* (Barr, Dobbie).—Weaker than the type, at Wisley. Flowering scantily for four weeks from November 2.

13. *Amellus ibericus* (Barr).—Fl. larger ; rays more numerous than in the type. The wild form has more downy stems, more entire leaves, and smaller flowers than the type.

14. *Amellus major* (Dobbie), **XXX**, 1892.—Two and a half feet ;· more vigorous and dense than the type ; fl. 2 inches across, rich mauve. A very fine variety flowering for eight weeks from September 13. Another firm sent an inferior variety under the same name.

For other varieties of Amellus see Distinction, Little Gem *and* Stella. ·

15. amethystinus (Barr, Chiswick), **XX**, 1892.—Three and a half to five and a half feet ; infl. a much-branched, dense panicle ; stems downy, weak, forming loosely arching sprays ; fl. ¾ inch across, lilac-blue ; disc brown-yellow ; the spreading bracts give a mossy appearance to the plant. Flowering for three weeks from October 28. Lower leaves sessile, half amplexicaul, linear-oblong, roughly downy. Hab. Eastern United States, in moist soil.

16. Amy (Chiswick collection).—Four feet ; infl. a long, loose pyramid with dark wiry stems ; fl. 1 inch across, white, becoming lilac. Flowering for three weeks from September 13.

17. Andromeda (Barr).—Four and a half feet ; infl. a densely flowered pyramid ; fl. 1½ inches across, pale mauve-lilac, paler towards the disc ; rays full, flat ; disc golden-yellow, becoming rosy ; growth rampant. Flowering for four weeks from September 13 (*Novi-Belgii*).

18. Annie (Barr).—One foot. The plant was too weak to show its proper form ; fl. pale mauve. Flowering for three weeks from October 19 (*Novi-Belgii*).

19. Antigone (Barr), **XXX** 1892.—Four and a half feet ; infl. broadly pyramidal with rigid branches ; fl. 1 inch across, white, becoming pink with age ; rays broad, full ; disc yellow, becoming crimson. Flowering for four weeks from September 21. A good variety, but susceptible to mildew (*versicolor*).

20. A 1 (Chiswick collection).—Height 3½ feet ; infl. a rather densely flowered broad pyramid ; fl. 1¼ inches across, pale mauve, full-rayed ; disc large. Habit very vigorous. Flowering for four weeks from September 21.

21. Apollo (Barr, Dobbie, Chiswick), **XXX** 1892.—Four and a half feet ; infl. a much-branched, loose, oblong panicle with brown slender stems ;

fl. 1¼ inches across, mauve ; subject to mildew.   Flowering for four weeks from September 6.   Similar but inferior to Ariadne (*laevis*).

22. Archer Hind (Barr, Dobbie, Chiswick), **XXX** 1892.—Five feet ; infl. a dense, much branched, rounded pyramid ; fl. 1½ inches across, pale lilac, rather stellate. 'Flowering for five weeks from September 18.· Growth very vigorous (*Novi-Belgii*).

23. The variety received from 'Messrs. Barr under the above name was 2½ feet ; smaller, mauve fl. ; three weeks later in bloom and less lasting.

24. Arcturus (Barr), **XXX** 1892.—Two feet [4] ; infl. loosely sub-corymbose with dark stems ; fl. 1¼ inches across, rich mauve, rays rough. The plant was a weak one and failed to do itself justice.   Flowering for four weeks from September 13 (*laevis*).

25. Argus (Chiswick collection), **XX** 1892.—Three and a half feet ; infl. sub-corymbose with dark-stemmed, rigid branches ; fl. 1¼ inches, full-rayed, pale lilac.   Flowering for five weeks from August 24.   Habit rather rampant (*Novi-Belgii*).

26. Ariadne (Barr, Chiswick), **A.M.** October 13, 1902.—Four and a half feet ; infl. a long, loose, oblong panicle with dark brown wiry stems ; fl. 1¼ inches across, mauve.   Flowering for four weeks from September 7 (*laevis, Novi-Belgii*).

27. Ashley Smith (Dobbie).—Two and a half feet ; infl. a round-headed, densely flowered pyramid ; fl. 1¼ inches across, almost white.   A weak plant, flowering for two weeks from September 13 (*Novi-Belgii*).

28. Aurora (Chiswick collection), **XXX** 1892.—Three feet ; infl. a sparsely branched, open panicle with dark-stemmed rigid branches ; fl. 1¼ inches across, lilac.   Habit very vigorous.   Flowering for four weeks from August 31 (*Novi-Belgii*).   The variety received from Messrs. Dobbie under this name was identical with Flora, *q.v.*

29. Autumn Glory (Barr).—Four and a half feet ; infl. a wiry, loose, oblong panicle ; fl. 1¼ inches across, mauve.   A weak plant, flowering for two weeks from September 30 (*Novi-Belgii*).

30. Barrosa (Notcutt).—Three feet ; infl. dense, leafy, sub-corymbose ; fl. 1½ inches across, mauve-blue, full-rayed.   Flowering for four weeks from September 13 (*Novi-Belgii*).

31, 32. Beatrice.—Two distinct varieties were grown under this name. That from Messrs. Barr, 5 feet ; infl. a wiry, erect, oblong panicle ; fl. 1¼ inches across, mauve ; subject to mildew ; flowering for four weeks from September 13 ; and that from the Chiswick collection 3½ feet ; infl. sub-corymbose ; fl. 1¼ inches across ; white, becoming pinkish, full-rayed.   Plant weak, flowering three weeks from September 21.

33. Beauty (Barr).—Five feet.   Very similar to Berenice, *q.v.*   Very subject to mildew (*Novi-Belgii*).

34. Beauty of Colwall (Ballard), **F.C.** September 26, 1907.—Five feet ; infl. a fine rigidly branched pyramid ; fl. 1¾ inches across, bluish-mauve, very double.   In full flower September 24.   The bold habit and numerous rays mark this out as quite the finest variety of recent introduction. Warley semi-plena is the only other double variety in the collection.

35. Beauty of Tywardreath (Barr).—Two feet ; infl. a round-headed, densely flowered pyramid ; fl. white, suffusing with pink ; disc cream,

becoming bright purplish-rose, Habit weak, flowering for four weeks from September 30.

36. Berenice (Barr, Chiswick), **XXX** 1892.—Five feet; infl. a long, loose, oblong panicle, with dark wiry stems; fl. 1¼ inches, purplish-lilac, rays full; very subject to mildew. Habit of Ariadne. Flowering for three weeks from September 20 (*Novi-Belgii*).

37. Betty (Chiswick collection).—Five-and-a-half feet; infl. a loosely branched oblong panicle with wiry, rather weak stems; fl. 1½ inches across, rosy-mauve, with two to three rows of ray-florets. Flowering for four weeks from September 21.

38. Blue Gem (Barr).—Three feet; infl. a wiry, erect, oblong panicle; fl. 1¼ inches, mauve, full-rayed. Plant weak, subject to mildew. Flowering three weeks from September 21 (*Novi-Belgii*).

39. Breydon (Jones).—Four feet; infl. a round-headed panicle, green-stemmed; fl. 1¼ inches, pale lilac-blue, full-rayed, flat, disc becoming dark crimson and conspicuous. Flowering for three weeks from September 21.

40. Brightness (Barr), **A.M.** October 13, 1902.—Four and a half feet; infl. a pyramidal to oblong, full-flowered, red-stemmed panicle; fl. 1¼ inches across, rosy-lilac; disc large, yellow, becoming rosy; ray florets in three rows, giving the flower a flat and very neat appearance. Flowering for four weeks from September 21. (A variety of Coombe Fishacre.)

41. Broton (Chiswick collection).—Two feet; infl. a loose branching panicle with rigid brown stems and little foliage; fl. 1½ inches across, rather stellate, almost white, fading to blue-lilac; disc small. Flowering for four weeks from August 31.

42. Caeruleus (Chiswick collection).—One foot; a round-headed dense little bush; fl. 1 inch across, mauve-lilac, full-rayed. Flowering for three weeks from September 13.

43. Calliope (Barr, Dobbie, Chiswick), **A.M.** October 13, 1902.—Five feet; infl. a densely flowered, much and rigidly branched, leafy pyramid; fl. over 1½ inches across, full-rayed, mauve-lilac; disc large. Flowering for four weeks from October 5. Foliage dark green, broad. Habit erect, very vigorous (*laevis, Novi-Belgii*).

44. Candida (Barr).—Three and a half feet; infl. a small densely flowered pyramid; fl. 1¼ inches across, white; rays very full and narrow. Habit erect but plant weak. Flowering four weeks from September 13 (*Novi-Belgii*).

45. *canus* (Barr).—Two and a half feet; infl. densely flowered, sub-corymbose; fl. 1 inch across, stellate, rosy-mauve; disc bright yellow. Flowering for four weeks from September 21. Fl. and habit very much those of *acris*, to which, however, as a garden plant this is much inferior. Leaves shorter and broader. Hab. Europe.

46. Capricornus (Chiswick collection).—Three feet; infl. a much and rigidly branched densely flowered pyramid; fl. 1¼ inches across, lilac; rays very full. Flowering for four weeks from August 31. Habit very vigorous.

47. Captivation (Barr, Dobbie, Chiswick), **A.M.** October 9, 1900.— Three feet; infl. a densely flowered pyramid; fl. 1 inch across, whitish

suffusing with pink ; full-rayed. Habit rather weak, but very pretty. Flowering for four weeks from September 21 (*Novi-Belgii*).

48. ˙Cassiope (Barr, Notcutt), **XX** 1892.—Two feet. A variety of *vimineus*, q.v., which it closely resembles. Branched to the ground and covered with small stellate fl., ¾ inch across, white, both ray and disc becoming rosy. Flowering for three weeks from September 21.

49. Catulus (Barr), **XX** 1892.—Three feet ; infl. a broad wiry pyramid with dark stems and foliage ; fl. 1¼ inches across, lilac-white, rays narrow. Flowering for three weeks from September 13. Habit vigorous (*Novi-Belgii*).

50. Celestial (Chiswick collection), **A.M.** September 24, 1902.—Three feet ; infl. a sparsely flowered pyramid ; fl. 1¼ inches across, rose-mauve ; rays very full, in four or more rows ; growth weak. Flowering for three weeks from September 21 (*Novi-Belgii*).˙

51. Ceres (Chiswick collection), **XX** 1892.—Five and a half feet˙; infl. a loose, very long, oblong panicle ; fl. 1¼ inches across, white, stellate. Flowering for three weeks from September 13 (*Novi Belgii*).

52. Charming (Barr).—Three feet ; infl. a much-branched, wiry pyramid ; general appearance mossy or heathlike ; fl. 1 inch across, white aging to pink, full-rayed ; disc large. Flowering for four weeks from September 13 (*versicolor*).

53. Clio (Barr), **XX** 1892.—Three and a half feet ; infl. a close mass of oblong, mossy panicles ; fl. creamy-pink, becoming white, rays full, narrow ; disc remaining yellow. Flowering for five weeks from September 13. Habit very vigorous, rapidly forming a dense flat-topped bush ; foliage and stems light green (*ericoides*).

54. Collerette blanche (Barr).—Three feet ; infl. a densely flowered, rounded pyramid ; fl. 1¼ inches across, white, rays full. Flowering for five weeks from September 13. A good variety (*Novi-Belgii*).

55. Collerette rose (Barr), **XXX** 1907.—Four feet ; infl. pyramidal ; fl. very neat and distinct, 1¼ inches across, mauve-rose, rays very full (in three rows) ; disc large in proportion, rich yellow. Flowering for three weeks from September 13. Habit almost rampant (*Novi-Belgii*).

56. *commutatus* (Barr).—Two feet. Habit dense but weak, producing strong runners ; leaves linear, oblong, downy ; fl. 1 inch across, white, rays curled. Flowering for three weeks from October 19. Nearly related to *multiflorus*, but of no value as a garden plant. The White Prairie Aster of Western N. America.

57. Constance (Chiswick collection).—Three feet ; infl. a round-headed, rather dense panicle ; fl. 1 inch across, mauve-lilac, full-rayed. Flowering for two weeks from September 21.

58. Coombe Fishacre (Barr, Dobbie).—Three and a half feet ; infl. a spreading, rigidly branched, broad panicle, flowering loosely almost to the ground ; fl. 1 inch across, rays full, pink-lilac ; disc cream,˙but rapidly becoming rosy. Flowering for five weeks from September 21. A distinct and pretty variety.

59. Coombe Fishacre Brightness.—*See* Brightness.

60. Coombe Fishacre White (Barr).—Failed.

61. Cora ..(Barr, Chiswick), **XX** 1892.—Five feet ;. infl. a sparsely branched loose pyramid with dark stems ; fl. ⅞ inch across, white-lilac ;

disc cream, rapidly becoming purplish-rose. Habit erect, not running at the base; lower leaves cordate. Flowering for four weeks from September 21 (*Drummondii*.)

62. Cordelia (Chiswick collection), **A.M.** October 13, 1902.—Four feet; infl. a dark-stemmed, densely branched pyramid; fl. 1 inch across, stellate, mauve-lilac, rays broad and loose; disc small, becoming crimson. Flowering for four weeks from September 13 (*laevis*).

63. *cordifolius* (Barr, Jones), **XXX** 1892.—Three and a half feet; infl. a dark-stemmed long loose pointed panicle; fl. very numerous, stellate, $\frac{3}{4}$ inch across, pale blue or lilac-white (the wild form varies from violet to white); disc small, cream-coloured, becoming crimson. Flowering for four weeks from September 21. Leaves thin, more or less hairy, the lower ones cordate, slender-petioled, finely serrate. Habit light and graceful. The Common Blue Wood Aster of Eastern United States; enjoys a little shade.

64. *cordifolius albulus* (Barr, Jones), **XXX** 1892.—Four feet; very similar to the type; infl. denser; fl. $\frac{1}{2}$ inch across, with few loose rays of the palest blue, almost white. Flowering for four weeks from September 13.

65. *cordifolius elegans* (Barr, Dobbie, Jones), **A.M.** October 13, 1902. Four and a half feet. Habit graceful and loose as in the type; fl. $\frac{5}{8}$ inch across; rays few, but broad, mauve-lilac. Flowering for five weeks from September 13. Very similar to Diana.

66. *cordifolius giganteus* (Jones), **XXX** 1907.—Over five feet. Habit of type; fl. over $1\frac{1}{4}$ inches across, lilac-white. Flowering for five weeks from September 13. Very similar to Dandy, than which it is later and taller, and the fl. are simpler.

67. *cordifolius magnificus* (Barr, Notcutt).—Five feet. Habit of type; fl. 1 to $1\frac{1}{4}$ inches across, pale lilac-blue. Flowering for three weeks from October 19. The variety Edwin Beckett received an award of merit under this name September 24, 1902, but Edwin Beckett is much earlier. *cordifolius magnificus* is one of the best late Asters.

68. *cordifolius major* (Barr, Dobbie, Jones), **XXX** 1907.—Four and a half feet. Habit of type; fl. $\frac{7}{8}$ inch across, lilac-white, rays broad, stellate, the creamy disc rapidly becoming rosy. Flowering for three weeks from September 21. Very similar to Photograph, but a week earlier.

For other varieties of cordifolius see Dandy, Diana, Ideal, and Photograph.

69. *corymbosus* (Barr), **XXX** 1892.—Two feet; infl. much branched, spreading, corymbose, with dark slender, brittle stems; fl. $\frac{3}{4}$ inch across, stellate, rays few, white. Flowering for three weeks from August 24. Leaves very thin, light green, lower ones slender-stalked, cordate acute, dentate. The White Wood Aster of Eastern North America.

70. *corymbosus paniculatus* (Notcutt).—One and a half feet. Similar to type; infl. much denser; fl. stellate 1 inch across with eight or nine broad white rays. Flowering for five weeks from August 31. Free and pretty.

See also Perseus.

71. Cottage Maid (Barr).—Four feet; infl. round-headed, densely flowered; fl. 1½ inches across, lilac-pink, very full-rayed. Flowering for two weeks from September 13. Pretty, but subject to mildew and of rampant habit (*Novi-Belgii*).

72. Councillor W. Watters (Barr).—Four and a half feet; infl. a loose pyramid rigidly branched; fl. 1½ inches across, very pale lilac, full-rayed, rather rough. Flowering for four weeks from September 13 (*laevis*).

73. *Curtisii* (Barr, Dobbie, Chiswick), **XX** 1892.—Two to three and a half feet; infl. round-headed, leafy, densely flowered with brown-green rigid stems and branches; fl. 1¼ inches, very full-rayed, lilac. Flowering for four weeks from August 31. The variety under this name from Messrs. Dobbie flowered a fortnight earlier, and was of a deeper colour. That from Messrs. Barr was identical with St. Patrick, *q.v.* The type has large deep violet flowers clustered in loose panicles, growing in dry soil in woodlands in the Alleghany mountains.

74. Daisy Hill (Barr).—Three feet; infl. pyramidal, round-topped; fl. 1½ inches across, pale lilac; rays full, but rather ragged. Flowering for two weeks from September 13 (*Novi-Belgii*).

75. Daisy Peters (Dobbie, Chiswick), **A.M.** September 24, 1902.—Three feet; infl. densely flowered, bushy; fl. 1½ inches across, full-rayed, white, becoming pinkish with age. Flowering for two weeks from September 13. A pretty but not a vigorous variety (*Novi-Belgii*).

76. Dandy (Barr, Jones), a variety of *cordifolius* of which it has the light graceful wiry habit; fl. 1¼ inches across, lilac-white, becoming darker, many of the rays quilled. Flowering for four weeks from September 13.

77. Daphne (Barr).—Four feet; infl. a long oblong loose panicle with dark wiry stems; fl. 1½ inches across, mauve-lilac. Flowering for four weeks from September 13. Habit stiff and erect, but lacking vigour (*Novi-Belgii*).

78. D. B. Crane (Barr, Jones).—Three and a half feet; infl. pyramidal, round-topped, densely flowered, with brown rigid branches; fl. more than 1½ inches across, bright mauve, full-rayed. Flowering for four weeks from August 31. A handsome variety (*Novi-Belgii*).

79. Decima (Notcutt), **XXX** 1907.—Four and a half feet; infl. pyramidal, round-topped; fl. 1½ inches across, white, becoming pinkish, disc bright yellow turning rosy purple. Flowering for three weeks from September 30. The upper half of the plant richly covered with flowers. Habit vigorous. The variety from the Chiswick collection under this name was weak and poor.

80. *decorus* (Barr), **XXX** 1892.—Three feet; infl. broad, bushy; fl. 1½ inches, mauve-lilac, rays very full, disc large. Flowering for three weeks from September 13 (*laevis, Novi-Belgii*).

81. Delicata (Barr, Notcutt).—Three and a half feet; infl. pyramidal, full-flowered; fl. 1¼ inches, pale lilac, rays ragged. Flowering for three weeks from September 21. Of no value (*Novi-Belgii*).

82. Delight (Barr, Notcutt), **A.M.** October 13, 1902.—Three feet. This is the best variety of *vimineus*, of which it has the bushy habit. The fl. are much whiter than in the type; disc creamy-yellow. Flowering for

four weeks from September 30. A fine variety, clothed to the ground with its small stellate flowers.

83. *densus* (Barr), **XXX** 1892.—Three feet; infl. densely flowered, bushy, sub-corymbose; fl. 1¼ inches across, bright mauve-blue, full-rayed; disc bright yellow. Flowering for three weeks from September 30. Vigorous (*Novi-Belgii*).

84. Diadem (Barr).—Three and a half feet; infl. densely flowered, leafy, round-headed, dark-stemmed; fl. 1 inch across, pink, full-rayed, flat. The buds are tinted with deep rose, and give a pleasing contrast with the pink of the open flower. Flowering for four weeks from September 21.

85. Diana (Barr, Dobbie, Jones), **XXX** 1892, originally named Photograph, but see No. 222.—Three and a half feet. A variety of *cordifolius*, of which it has the habit, with graceful oblong, loosely branched panicles; fl. ⅝ inch across, stellate; rays broad but few, pale mauve-lilac; disc small, cream-yellow, becoming rosy-crimson. Flowering for five weeks from September 30. Almost identical with *cordifolius elegans*, but later and a little paler.

86. *diffusus horizontalis* (Barr), **XXX** 1892.—Two feet; infl. broad, bushy, stiffly branched almost to the base, the branches at right angles to the stem; fl. distichously arranged, ½ inch across; rays white, strongly recurved; disc rosy purple. Flowering for four weeks from October 12. Unique in habit and flower. Hab. Eastern United States.

87. *diffusus pendulus* (Barr, Notcutt, Chiswick), **XX** 1892.—Over 6 feet; infl. loose, much branched, with long wiry spreading and arching dark stems; fl. ½ inch across, white; disc purplish. Flowering for four weeks from October 28. (Another firm sent *Tradescantii* under this name.)

See also The Prince.

88. Discolor (Chiswick), **XX** 1892.—Four and a half feet; infl. pyramidal, round-topped, dark-stemmed; fl. 1½ inches across, rosy lilac, full-rayed. Flowering for four weeks from August 31. Similar but inferior to F. W. Burbidge (*Novi-Belgii*). *discolor* is an old synonym of *versicolor*, having white and pale-lilac flowers.

89. Distinction (Barr), **A.M.** October 10, 1899.—A variety of *Amellus*. Failed to flower.

90. Dorothy (Chiswick collection), **A.M.** September 24, 1902.—Four and a half feet; infl. pyramidal, round-topped, open, with dark rigid stems; fl. numerous, 1½ inches across, pale lavender; rays full, rather incurved. Flowering for five weeks from August 31. Pretty. Habit running at the base.

91. Dot (Barr), **XX** 1892.—Four and a half feet; infl. densely flowered, paniculate; fl. ⅞ inch across, pinkish-white. Flowering for four weeks from August 31. Habit vigorous, rampant, and, unless unsparingly thinned, throwing up a mass of flowering stems which form a loose corymb. Loses its lower leaves except in moist situations (*paniculatus*, q.v.).

92. *Drummondii* (Dobbie, Chiswick), **XXX** 1892.—Four feet; infl. a broad but little-branched panicle; stems rigid, wiry, branching at right angles; fl. few, more or less distichously arranged, 1 inch across, lilac. Flowering sparingly in October and November. Lower leaves cordate to

hastate on long stalks ; upper leaves broad, shortly stalked.   Hab. United States, dry soil.   Of no value at Wisley.   (*For varieties of Drummondii see* Cora, grandis, *and* Sappho.)

93. Duchess of Albany (Beckett).—Five feet ; infl. loosely pyramidal, dark-stemmed ; fl. 1½ inches across, mauve-lilac, becoming paler, very full-rayed.   Flowering for four weeks from September 30.   Subject to mildew, rather poor.

94. *dumosus* (Barr, Dobbie).—One foot ; infl. bushy, dense, leafy, flowered to the ground ; fl. 1 inch across, pale lilac ; disc pale yellow, but rapidly becoming rosy and giving a rosy hue to the plant.   Flowering for five weeks from September 21.   Habit densely cushioned, suitable for rockery.   This is distinct from the typical North American species, *A. dumosus.*

95. E. C. Buxton (Chiswick).—One foot ; infl. bushy, densely cushioned ; fl. 1¼ inches, pale lilac, full-rayed.   Flowering for five weeks from August 31.

96. Edith (Barr).—Three and a half feet ; infl. densely branched and flowered, leafy ; fl. 1¼ inches across, lilac, full-rayed ; disc pale yellow but suffusing with lilac.   Flowering for four weeks from September 21.   A variety under this name from the Chiswick collection proved a different Aster ; 5 feet ; infl. pyramidal, rigidly branched, dark-stemmed ; fl. 1½ inches across, pale mauve.   Flowering for two weeks from October 5 (*Novi-Belgii*).

97. Edna Mercia (Barr), **XXX** 1902.—Three and a half feet ; infl. thin, pyramidal, round-topped, dark-stemmed ; fl. ¾ inch across, very full-rayed, deep pink.   Flowering for two weeks from August 31.   The specimen was a weak one with scanty foliage (*Novi-Belgii*).

98. Edwin Beckett (Barr, Notcutt, Chiswick), **A.M.** September 24, 1902.—Four feet ; infl. loosely pyramidal, with dark glossy wiry stems ; fl. 1 inch across, stellate, pale lilac-blue ; disc small, soft yellow to crimson.   Flowering for four weeks from September 7 (*paniculatus*).   Habit and appearance of *cordifolius magnificus* but earlier.

99. E. G. Lowe (Barr).—Three feet ; infl. paniculate, loosely branched, broad, dark-stemmed ; fl. 1¼ inches across, mauve-lilac, full-rayed ; disc large, rich yellow.   Flowering for three weeks from September 30.   A dwarf Robert Parker, but inferior (*Novi-Belgii*).

100. Ella (Barr, Dobbie, Chiswick).—Identical with Robert Parker, *q.v.*

101. Elsie Perry (Barr), **A.M.** October 13, 1902.—Four feet ; infl. densely branched, bushy, dark-stemmed ; fl. 1 inch across, pink, very full-rayed.   Flowering for five weeks from August 31.   Subject to mildew. The value of the variety is reduced by the conspicuousness of the dead among the fresh flowerheads.

102. *eminens* (Barr, Chiswick), **XX** 1892.—One and a half feet ; infl. a much-spreading, open panicle with very stiff, brown, wiry, and almost leafless branches ; fl. very few, 1 inch across, mauve ; disc large in pro-portion.   A few fl. appearing from August 31 onwards.   Growth rampant. Subject to mildew.

103. Enchantress (Barr), **A.M.** October 15, 1901.—Three and a half feet ; infl. broadly paniculate, much-branched, gracefully arching ; fl. ½ inch across, pale lilac, becoming white ; rays full, a little reflexed.

Flowering for six weeks from October 5. This is a seedling from Hon. E. Gibbs, of which it has much of the grace, with a stiffer habit.

104. *ericoides* (Barr), **XX** 1892.—Two to four feet; habit light, bushy, with bright green wiry stems and heath-like, spreading foliage; infl. broadly panicled, sub-secund, spreading; fl. $\frac{1}{2}$–1 inch across, white, stellate; rays narrow and few; involucre squarrose. Flowering for five weeks from October 19. Lower leaves spathulate with margined petioles, often ciliate; upper, linear to subulate, firm. Propagation comparatively slow. The White Heath Aster of N. America, in dry soil: often confused with *Tradescanti*, q.v.

105. *ericoides Middlewick* var. (Barr), identical with *Tradescanti*, q.v.

106. *ericoides superbus* (Barr).—Three feet; infl. broadly pyramidal, densely branched and flowered to the ground, bushy; fl. $\frac{1}{2}$ inch across, white, becoming rosy with age, stellate. Flowering for four weeks from September 21. Very similar to Sensation, but fl. a little larger and later. Habit near *vimineus*.

The reputed varieties of ericoides show a wide range in habit, form, and colour. For other varieties see Clio, Hon. Edith Gibbs, Ophir, and Sensation.

107. Esme (Barr).—The plant was a very weak one and scarcely flowered (*Novi-Belgii*).

108. Esther (Barr, Beckett), **XXX** 1907.—Two feet; infl. densely branched, panicled; fl. very numerous, $\frac{3}{4}$ inch, flesh-pink; rays full; disc pale yellow and darkening but little. Flowering for six weeks from September 13. Habit vigorous; foliage and stems light green, heath-like.

109. Ethel (Barr).—Three and a half feet; infl. round-headed to sub-corymbose, densely branched and flowered; fl. $1\frac{1}{4}$ inches across, white, fading pink; rays full, a little incurved. Flowering for three weeks from September 13 (*Novi-Belgii*). The variety from the Chiswick collection under the same name proved distinct; $3\frac{1}{2}$ feet; infl. broadly pyramidal, full-flowered; fl. $1\frac{1}{4}$ inches across, stellate, rich mauve, pretty. Flowering for three weeks from September 30 (*Novi-Belgii*).

110. Eva (Chiswick collection).—Two and a half feet; infl. densely flowered, small, oblong; fl. $1\frac{1}{4}$ inches, mauve-lilac. Flowering for three weeks from September 21. Weak.

111. Evening Star (Barr).—Three feet. A variety of *vimineus*, which it much resembles, but the habit is less stiff and the fl. are larger; infl. loose arching sprays; fl. $\frac{1}{2}$ inch across, stellate, white, distichously arranged on stiff branchlets. Flowering for five weeks from September 30. A very pretty variety.

112. Fairfield (Barr), **XXX** 1907.—Over 6 feet; infl. a strong branching panicle, flowering almost to the ground; fl. $1\frac{1}{4}$ inches across, white, full-rayed. Flowering for five weeks from September 30. Habit erect.

113. Fanny (Barr, Dobbie, Chiswick), **XX** 1892.—Four feet; infl. densely flowered, pyramidal; fl. $1\frac{1}{4}$ inches across, lilac, full-rayed, flat. Flowering for three weeks from September 21 (*Novi-Belgii*).

114. Flora (Dobbie, Chiswick), **XX** 1892.—Five feet; infl. much branched, densely flowered, broadly pyramidal, the stems and foliage light green; fl. $1\frac{1}{4}$ inches across, mauve-pink; rays full, narrow; disc

large, yellow to brown. Flowering for three weeks from October 12. Habit very vigorous (*laevis, Novi-Belgii*).

115. *floribundus* (Barr, Dobbie, Chiswick), **XXX** 1892.—Four feet; infl. a dense, stiffly branched, leafy, round-topped pyramid ; fl. 1¾ inches across, mauve, full-rayed. Flowering for four weeks from October 5. Subject to mildew ; foliage very dark green. Habit stiffly erect. Hab. North America (*laevis*).

116. *formosissimus* (Barr, Dobbie, Chiswick), **XXX** 1892.—In habit, height, and flowering period quite like the last. Fl. rosy-mauve (*laevis, Novi-Belgii*).

117. Fortuna (Chiswick collection), **XX** 1892.—Five feet ; infl. densely flowered, broadly pyramidal ; fl. 1¼ inches across, lilac-pink, full-rayed. Flowering for three weeks from October 12. Foliage dark green. Habit running (*Novi-Belgii*).

118. Fox's Blush (Notcutt).—Three feet ; infl. loose, sub-corymbose ; fl. 1¾ inches across, lilac-white ; rays loose, stellate. Plant weak, flowering for three weeks from October 5.

119. Freedom (Barr, Dobbie), **XXX** 1902.—A variety of *vimineus* which it closely resembles, perhaps a little more vigorous and pretty ; fl. creamy white, but yellowish compared with Delight. Flowering for four weeks from September 21.

120. F. W. Burbidge (Barr, Dobbie, Notcutt, Chiswick), **A.M.** September 24, 1902.—Four to five feet ; infl. densely flowered, pyramidal, round-topped with dark stems and foliage ; fl. 1½ inches across, mauve-lilac with a shade of pink ; rays very full, broad and flat. Flowering for four weeks from September 13. A bold and handsome variety (*Novi-Belgii*).

121. *glaucus* (Barr, Chiswick).—One foot ; a sparsely branched straggling bush with oblong glaucous leaves ; fl. very few, 1¼ inches, mauve, stellate. Flowering for two weeks from August 31. Hab. Western North America. Of no value as a garden plant. The variety from one source was not true to name.

122. Gloriosa (Barr).—One and a half feet ; a dense rigid bushy little plant with very heath-like foliage ; fl. ¾ inch across, rosy-mauve, intensifying with age ; disc golden brown. Flowering for three weeks from September 30. One of the most distinct varieties.

123. Gorgeous (Barr).—One and a half feet ; infl. densely flowered, bushy with mossy foliage ; fl. ¾-1 inch across, bright rosy-mauve ; disc orange. Flowering for four weeks from September 30 (*Novi-Belgii*).

124. Grace (Barr).—Three and a half feet ; infl. a densely branched oblong green-stemmed panicle ; fl. 1¼ inches across, lilac-mauve, full-rayed, rather rough. Flowering for four weeks from September 13 (*Novi-Belgii*).

125. Grace Darling (Barr).—Three feet ; infl. a round-topped, densely flowered panicle with very rigid stems ; fl. ¾ inch across, pale lilac ; rays full, but rough. Flowering for two weeks from September 21 (*Novi-Belgii*).

126. Gracillimus (Barr).—Three to four feet. This is a coloured form of *ericoides*, of which it has the light habit and soft green mossy foliage. Fl. 1 inch across, white, rapidly tinting with rose ; rays narrow,

stellate. Flowering for five weeks from October 19. The white, pink, and rose fl. of different age on the same plant give it a lively and distinct appearance ; one of the latest varieties to flower.

127. *grandiflorus* (Barr), **A.M.** November 10, 1891.—Two and a half feet. Habit bushy, with rigid, hairy stems ; fl. terminating the branches, 2 inches across, rich violet. Flowering for five weeks from October 28. The spreading and leafy bracts of the involucre, the large buds, the small reflexed linear upper leaves, and stiff stems render this one of the most distinct species. Hab. dry soil in Eastern United States.

128. Grandis (Barr, Chiswick).—Five feet ; fl. distichously arranged on graceful long arching sprays ; stems downy, dark red ; fl. 1 inch across, pale rose-lilac or lilac-white ; rays narrow, stellate. Flowering for three weeks from September 30 (*Drummondii*, but basal leaves lanceolate).

129. Harpur Crewe (Dobbie), **XXX** 1892.—Four feet ; infl. loosely branched, pyramidal ; fl. 1 inch across, white. Flowering for three weeks from September 21. Habit running at the base (*Novi-Belgii*).

130. *Herveyi* (Barr).—Two and a half feet ; infl. stiffly branched, corymbose ; fl. 1½ inches across, mauve, stellate. Flowering for about three weeks from August 14. Lower leaves ovate, rough, slender-stalked. Habit erect, stiff. An interesting rather than a showy species. Hab. dry soil of Eastern United States.

131. Hilda (Barr).—Three and a half feet ; infl. pyramidal with dark rigid stems ; fl. ¾ inch across, blush-white ; rays full, reflexed ; disc cream, becoming rosy-crimson, distinct. Flowering for four weeks from September 13. Foliage dark, stiff.

132. Hilda Morris (Jones), **A.M.** September 26, 1907.—Four feet. The upper half of the plant a dense pyramid of bloom ; fl. 1½ inches across, lilac, full-rayed, flat. Flowering for two weeks from September 21.

133. Hon. Edith Gibbs (Notcutt, Chiswick), **A.M.** October 9, 1900.— Four feet ; fl. arranged distichously on graceful arching, dark-stemmed sprays reaching almost to the ground, ¾ inch across, pale lilac, stellate. Flowering for five weeks from October 5 (*ericoides*).

134. Hon. Vicary Gibbs (Notcutt), **A.M.** October 9, 1900.—Two and a half feet ; infl. weak, scattered ; fl. 1 inch across, pink with an almost white band round the disc, full-rayed. Flowering for four weeks from September 21.

135. Horace (Chiswick collection), **XX** 1892.—Four feet ; infl. a loose, wiry panicle ; fl. 1¼ inches, mauve-lilac. Flowering for four weeks from September 21. Subject to mildew (*laevis, Novi-Belgii*).

136. Ianthe (Barr).—Two and a half feet ; infl. an oblong, rather densely flowered, dark-stemmed panicle ; fl. 1 inch across, mauve. Flowering for two weeks from September 13 (*Novi-Belgii*).

137. Ida (Chiswick collection).—Two feet ; infl. sub-corymbose, densely flowered ; fl. 1½ inches across, whitish, becoming lilac. Flowering for three weeks from September 13.

138. Ideal (Barr, Beckett), **XXX** 1902, 1907.—Four feet ; fl. ¾ inch across, pale blue, stellate, distichously arranged on graceful, broad, arching sprays ; disc very small, creamy-yellow, becoming rosy. Flowering for five weeks from September 30. Somewhat similar to Hon. Edith Gibbs

and King Edward VII., but fl. larger, denser, bluer, and smaller disc (*cordifolius*).

139. Imogen (Chiswick collection).—Three and a half feet; infl. a densely flowered, round-topped pyramid, green-stemmed; fl. 1¼ inches across, lilac. Flowering for two weeks from September 13. Habit running at the base.

140. Irene (Barr, Chiswick), **XX** 1892.—Three feet; infl. a long, loose panicle with dark stiffly branched, wiry stems; fl. 1¼ inches across, bright lilac, stellate; disc small. Flowering for four weeks from September 13 (*Novi-Belgii*).

141. Iris (Chiswick collection).—Five feet; infl. rigidly branched, open panicle; fl. 1¼ inches across, mauve; rays full, broad. Flowering for four weeks from September 21.

142. Isabel (Barr).—Four feet; infl. a loose, sparse panicle with dark wiry stems; fl. 1 inch across, whitish, becoming lilac, stellate. Flowering for three weeks from September 21 (*Novi-Belgii* of Barr, but basal leaves and habit of *cordifolius*). The variety from the Chiswick collection under this name was distinct, but of no value.

143. Janus (Chiswick collection), **XXX** 1892.—This name was given to the old *versicolor* of gardens; white turning pink, distinct from the variety now cultivated. Three and a half feet; infl. a densely flowered, leafy, round-headed panicle; fl. 1¼ inches across, pale rose-lilac, full-rayed, flat. Flowering for four weeks from August 31. Habit very vigorous, but a good variety.

144. Jessie Crum (Barr, Dobbie, Chiswick), **XXX** 1902.—Five feet; infl. a dark-stemmed, loose wiry panicle; fl. 1¼ inches across, mauve; disc small, creamy-yellow, becoming crimson. Flowering for five weeks from October 5 (*laevis*, *Novi-Belgii*, but basal leaves, habit, and fl. rather of *cordifolius*). A fine variety.

145. John Henshaw (Barr).—Three and a half feet. After Robert Parker, but poorer; panicle more pointed. Fl. 1½ inches across, mauve-lilac. Flowering for four weeks from October 5 (*Novi-Belgii*).

146. John Wood (Barr, Dobbie, Chiswick), **XXX** 1892.—Four feet; infl. a broad open leafy panicle; fl. 1¼ inches across, white, becoming pink, very full-rayed. Flowering for four weeks from September 21 (*Novi-Belgii*).

147. Juno (Barr, Chiswick), **XX** 1892.—Three feet; infl. a dark green, rigid leafy panicle; fl. 1¼ inches across, mauve-blue; disc large. Flowering for three weeks from October 5. Similar to *floribundus* (*laevis Novi-Belgii*).

148. Katie (Chiswick collection).—Two feet; infl. sub-corymbose, dense, leafy; fl. 1½ inches across, mauve; disc small. Flowering for seven weeks from August 31, but not of much decorative value.

149. King Edward VII. (Beckett), **XXX** 1907.—Four feet; fl. on long arching sprays, clothing the plant to the ground, ¾ inch across, pale lilac-blue; rays narrow, stellate; disc small. Flowering for five weeks from September 30. Very similar to Hon. Edith Gibbs; a little stiffer and better.

150. Lady Trevelyan (Chiswick collection).—Four and a half feet; infl. a loose, rounded pyramid; fl. 1¾ inches across, white, stellate.

Flowering for three weeks from September 13. Good, but subject to mildew.

151. *laevigatus* (Barr), **A.M.** September 24, 1902.—Two and a half feet. Very weak, scarcely flowered; fl. 1 inch across, rose-mauve; subject to mildew (*Novi-Belgii*).

152. *laevis* (of Barr, Dobbie, Chiswick), **XXX** 1892.—Six feet; infl. a very loose, gracefully spreading, wiry, dark-stemmed panicle, with scanty foliage; fl. arranged distichously, 1 inch across, full-rayed, pale mauve-blue. Flowering for three to four weeks from October 5. Leaves sub-amplexicaul. Hab. North America, but the plants distributed under this name and here described differ considerably from the typical American plant.

153. *laevis, Harvard var.* (Barr), **XXX** 1892.—Identical with the above.

The varieties of laevis are very numerous : the best in the collection are Ariadne, Calliope, formosissimus, Jessie Crum, Psyche, *and* Pygmalion.

154. *lanceolatus* (Barr).—Five feet; infl. a long pointed panicle with dark downy stems; fl. $\frac{3}{4}$ inch across, white; rays full, but very narrow. Flowering for three weeks from October 12. A rampant grower, of no value in the garden.

155. Laura Cadogan (Barr).—Failed.

156. Leda (Barr).—Three and a half feet; infl. a loose, oblong, wiry panicle; fl. $1\frac{1}{2}$ inches across, bright mauve, full-rayed. Flowering for five weeks from September 13 (*Novi-Belgii*).

157. Lena Peters (Peters).—Two and a half feet; panicle broad, full-flowered, stiff-stemmed; fl. $1\frac{3}{4}$ inches across, pale rosy-lilac, full-rayed; disc large, pale yellow. Flowering for three weeks from September 30. Pretty.

158. Lilacinus (Chiswick collection), **XX** 1892.—Three feet; bushy, free-flowered; fl. $1\frac{1}{4}$ inches across, pale lilac, stellate; rays narrow. Flowering for two weeks from August 31. A strong grower, but pretty (*Novi-Belgii*).

159. Lil Fardell (Jones), **A.M.** September 26, 1907.—Five and a half feet; infl. sub-corymbose; · fl. 2 inches across, rose-pink, full-rayed. Flowering for five weeks from September 13. A fine variety (*Novae-Angliae*).

160. *Lindleyanus* (Barr, Dobbie), **XXX** 1892.—One and a half to three feet; panicle branched, oblong, with stout downy stems; fl. 1 inch across, pale lilac, stellate; disc small. Flowering for about four weeks, August to October. Leaves rather thick, pale green, the lower ones cordate at the base. Hab. North America.

161. *Lindleyanus nanus* (Barr), **XXX** 1892.—Failed.

162. *Linosyris* (Barr), **XX** 1892.—One-half to two feet; infl. densely flowered, corymbose; fl. rayless; disc $\frac{3}{4}$ inch across, bright yellow. Flowering for four weeks from September 13. Leaves linear. The Goldylocks of Europe.

163. Little Gem (Dobbie).—One and a half to two feet.—A variety of *Amellus*, than which it is more compact and bushy. Fl. $1\frac{3}{4}$ inches across, rich mauve, full-rayed. Flowering for seven weeks from October 5.

164. *litoreus* (Chiswick collection), **XX** 1892.—Four and a half feet ; infl. a loose, broad panicle ; fl. 1¼ inches across, lilac-white, stellate ; rays loose. Flowering for three weeks from September 13 (*Novi-Belgii*).

165. *longifolius* (Chiswick collection).—Four and a half feet; habit erect, running at the base; panicle loose, oblong, with dark downy stems ; fl. 1¼ inches across, white suffusing with pink, stellate; disc small. Flowering for four weeks from August 15. Leaves long, lanceolate. The Long-leaved Aster of moist ground and swamps, N. America. The type is purple.

166. Lord Cadogan (Barr).—Four feet ; panicle green-stemmed, broad ; fl. 1½ inches across, lilac ; rays narrow, full. Flowering for four weeks from September 13 (*Novi-Belgii*).

167. Lower Soughton (Barr).—Two and half feet ; panicle loose, oblong, dark-stemmed ; fl. 1 inch across, mauve, full-rayed. Flowering for two weeks from September 13. Habit erect (*Novi-Belgii*).

168. Mabel (Chiswick collection).—Three and a half feet ; infl. a rigid, oblong, much-branched panicle, with dark green stems and foliage ; fl. 1½ inches across, rich mauve, very full-rayed ; disc large. Flowering for five weeks from August 31.

169. Madame Cacheux (Barr, Dobbie).—One and a half feet ; infl. bushy ; fl. 1 inch across, soft pinky-white, full-rayed. Flowering for four weeks from September 30 (*Novi-Belgii*).

170. Madonna (Barr, Dobbie, Notcutt).—Two and a half feet ; infl. much branched, sub-corymbose ; fl. 1¼ inches across, white, fading pink, very full-rayed. Flowering for three weeks from September 13 (*Novi-Belgii*).

171. Magnifica (Barr).—Three feet ; infl. stiffly branched, broad, loosely flowered ; fl. 1¼ inches across, mauve-lilac. Poor. Flowering for three weeks from September 30 (*Novi-Belgii*).

172. Maia (Barr).—Three and a half feet ; infl. rigidly branched, loosely flowered ; fl. 1½ inches across, mauve-lilac, full-rayed ; disc large, rich yellow. Flowering for three weeks from September 30 (*Novi-Belgii*).

173. Maiden's Blush (Barr).—Failed.

174. Margaret (Barr, Chiswick).—Four and a half feet ; habit of Robert Parker, but inferior ; fl. 1½ inches across, lilac, full-rayed. Flowering for four weeks from September 21 (*Novi-Belgii*).

175. Maud (Chiswick collection).—Three and a half feet ; infl. sub-corymbose, densely flowered, stiff-stemmed ; fl. 1¼ inches across, full-rayed, bluish lilac. Flowering for three weeks from August 31.

176. Mavourneen (Jones).—Four and a half feet ; panicle densely branched and flowered ; fl. 1 inch across, lilac-pink, full-rayed. Flowering for four weeks from August 31 (*Novi-Belgii*).

177. May Crum (Barr, Chiswick).—Five feet ; panicle conical, loosely flowered ; habit open and wiry ; fl. 1¼ inches across, very pale lilac, becoming rosy ; full-rayed. Flowering for three weeks from September 30. Subject to mildew (*Novi-Belgii*).

178. Melpomene (Jones).—A variety of *Novae-Angliae*, differing only in the flowers ; fl. violet, 2 inches across, full-rayed. Flowering for five weeks from October 5.

179. Miltonian (Davies).—Three and a half feet; infl. round-topped, densely flowered; fl. 1¼ inches across, light mauve, full-rayed. Flowering for four weeks from September 21.

180. Middlewick. See *ericoides*, Middlewick var.

181. Minerva (Barr, Chiswick), **XXX** 1892.—Three and a half feet; infl. leafy, densely flowered, round-topped; fl. 1½ inches across, mauve-lilac, full-rayed. Flowering for five weeks from September 13 (*Novi-Belgii*).

182. Minnie (Barr, Beckett).—Very similar to Grace Darling, *q.v.* Flowering for three weeks from September 13 (*Novi-Belgii*).

183. Miss Grant (Chiswick collection).—Four feet; infl. an open, rigidly branched oblong panicle; fl. 1 inch across, stellate, lilac-white suffusing with pink; disc creamy yellow. Flowering for four weeks from September 21.

184. Miss Southall (Davies, Chiswick), **A.M.** October 15, 1907.—Five and a half feet; panicle long, pointed, richly flowered, with dark wiry stems; fl. 2 inches across, lilac-mauve, full-rayed. Flowering for three weeks from October 5. A fine variety (*Novi-Belgii*).

185. Miss Stafford (Barr), **A.M.** September 6, 1907.—Three feet; infl. bushy, dense; fl. 1 inch across, pink, very full-rayed, flat and neat; disc large. Flowering for four weeks from August 31. Somewhat similar to Edna Mercia, but better (*Novi-Belgii*).

186. Mrs. C. W. Earle (Barr, Dobbie).—Five feet; infl. broadly pyramidal, dark-stemmed; fl. 1⅜ inches across, lilac-white, stellate, rays loose. Flowering for six weeks from September 30. A good variety (*Novi-Belgii*).

187. Mrs. Davis Evans (Barr), **A.M.** September 6, 1907.—Three feet; infl. rather stiff, bushy, leafy, densely branched and flowered; fl. 1 inch across, heliotrope-blue, full-rayed and flat. Flowering for four weeks from August 23 (*Novi-Belgii*).

188. Mrs. Duncombe Mann (Jones).—Four feet; infl. a broad, much-branched panicle; fl. 1¼ inches across, lilac, stellate. Flowering for three weeks from September 21.

189. Mrs. Huson Morris (Jones).—Failed.

190. Mrs. J. F. Rayner (Barr, Dobbie, Jones), **A.M.** September 26, 1907.—Four feet. A variety of *Novae-Angliae*, dwarfer and earlier than the type and more richly flowered; fl. 1½ inches across, deep rose-pink, full-rayed. Flowering for five weeks from September 13.

191. Mrs. J. G. Day (Jones).—Failed.

192. Mrs. Raynor.—See Mrs. J. F. Rayner.

193. Mrs. S. T. Wright (Jones), **A.M.** September 26, 1907.—Five and a half feet. A variety of *Novae-Angliae*. Fl. 2 inches across, rich rosy-purple, full-rayed, flat; disc golden. Flowering for five weeks from September 30.

194. Mrs. Twinam (Jones).—Five feet; panicle oblong, densely branched and flowered; fl. 1½ inches across, bright pink, very full-rayed. Flowering for three weeks from September 10. A fine variety, but subject to mildew.

195. Mrs. W. Peters (Dobbie), **A.M.** September 7, 1897.—One and a half feet. The plants were weak. Fl. white suffusing with pale pink (*Novi-Belgii*).

196. Mont Blanc (Barr, Chiswick).—Four and a half feet. Habit erect, running at the base ; panicle stiff, oblong ; fl. 1½ inches across white, stellate. Flowering for three weeks from September 21 (*Novi-Belgii*).

197. *multiflorus* (Barr, Chiswick), **XXX** 1892.—Four and a half feet ; infl. a much branched, pyramidal panicle, with rather weak, downy stems, and crowded small, rough linear leaves ; fl. ⅜ inch across, white, full-rayed, not opening flat ; disc large in proportion. Flowering for four weeks from September 30. The White Wreath Aster or Fall Flower of North America.

198. Nancy (Barr, Jones, Notcutt), **XXX** 1907.—Four feet ; panicle densely flowered, pyramidal ; fl. 1½ inches across, pale lilac-blue, full-rayed, flat. Flowering for three weeks from September 30. A vigorous and handsome variety (*Novi-Belgii*).

199. Newry Seedling (Barr).—Two and a half feet ; panicle loosely branched, broad, round-topped ; fl. 1¼ inches across, pale lilac ; rays narrow, rather rough. Flowering for three weeks from September 13 (*Novi-Belgii*).

200. Niveus Barr).—Three feet ; panicle broad, pyramidal, rigidly branched ; fl. 1½ inches across, white, full-rayed. Flowering for four weeks from August 31. A strong grower (*Novi-Belgii*).

201. Norah Peters (Peters), **A.M.** October 1, 1907 (not for the plant at Wisley).—Three and a half feet ; infl. a long-pointed, rigidly branched panicle, with scanty pale-green foliage ; fl. 1½ inches across, white becoming pinkish ; rays narrow and full. Flowering for three weeks from September 30. A fine variety, but not vigorous. The narrow rays quite suggestive of Erigeron, which is reputed to be the pollen parent.

202. *Novae-Angliae* (Dobbie).—Six feet ; infl. densely flowered, sub-corymbose, with downy, leafy stems ; fl. 1–2 inches across, typically violet-purple, rarely pink, red, or white ; rays full, very narrow, loose. Flowering August to October. Leaves downy, oblong, lanceolate, stem-clasping. Hab. North America. The variety from Messrs. Dobbie was identical with var. *roseus*, q.v. ' A very fine species, though excelled in beauty by several named varieties, preferring a moist situation and comparatively slow to increase. The foliage is fragrant.

203. *N.-A. coccineus* (Barr).—Very similar to *N.-A. ruber*, but flowering for three weeks from October 12.

204. *N.-A. praecox* (Barr, Jones, Notcutt), **XXX** 1892.—Five feet. Habit of type ; fl. 2 inches across, purple. Flowering for four or five weeks from September 13.

205. *N.-A. pulchellus* (Barr, Dobbie, Jones, Chiswick), **XXX** 1892.— Four and a half feet. Habit of type ; fl. 2–2½ inches across, violet-purple, very full-rayed. Flowering for five weeks from October 5. Handsome.

206. *N.-A. roseus* (Barr, Jones, Chiswick), **XXX** 1892.—Six feet. Habit of type ; fl. 1¼ inches across, rose-pink ; disc small. Flowering for four weeks from September 21. Lil Fardell, of the same colour, is much superior.

207. *N.-A. ruber* (Barr, Jones, Chiswick), **XXX** 1892.—Four and a half feet. Habit of type ; fl. 1¼ inches across, deep rose ; rays flat.

Flowering for three weeks from September 30. Inferior to Mrs. J. F. Rayner.

For other varieties of Novae-Angliae see Lil Fardell, Melpomene, Mrs. J. F. Rayner, Mrs. S. T. Wright, Précocité, Ryecroft Pink, Ryecroft Purple, Treasure, *and* W. Bowman.

208· *Novi-Belgii.*—This is the type from which most of the garden varieties have sprung. Stems slender, branched ; infl. corymbose-paniculate ; fl. numerous, 1 inch across, violet. Flowering August to October. The New York Aster, of swampy ground in the Eastern maritime States.

209. *N.-B. semi-plena.*—See Warley semi-plena.

210. Ophir (Barr), **A.M.** October 1, 1902.—Two and a half feet. Habit, bushy, with rigid, spreading branches and rather oblong panicles ; stems and foliage pale green ; fl. very numerous, $\frac{1}{2}$ inch across, pale lilac-white ; rays narrow, stellate. Flowering for four weeks from August 31 (*ericoides*).

211. Osprey (Barr), **XXX** 1907.—Three feet. A variety of *vimineus,* of which it has the bushy habit, free-flowering qualities, and pale green foliage ; fl. $\frac{1}{2}$ inch across, lilac; rays narrow, stellate. Flowering for five weeks from October 5. A pretty variety, studded with flower to the ground.

212. *paniculatus* (Chiswick collection), **XX** 1892.—Three and a half feet ; infl. a densely branched and full-flowered panicle, stems rigid ; fl. $\frac{3}{4}$ inch across, pale pink-lilac; rays reflexing a little ; disc large. Flowering for four weeks from August 31. Very vigorous. Leaves oblong-lanceolate, the lower ones 6 × $\frac{3}{4}$ inches, sub-serrate. The Tall White Aster of the United States, in moist soil.

213. *paniculatus blandus* (Chiswick collection), **XX** 1892.—Four feet ; habit dense ; fl. 1 inch across, lilac-white, stellate. Flowering for four weeks from September 13.

214. *paniculatus laxus* (Barr).—Two and a half feet ; infl. a much-branched loosely spreading panicle, with stems and leaves so slight as to give the flowers the appearance of being suspended in air ; fl. 1 inch across, pale lilac, stellate. Flowering for six weeks from August 31. Growth rather rampant, but habit loose, wiry, and pretty.

For other varieties of paniculatus see Dot, Edwin Beckett, Rev. E. W. Badger, Triumph, W. J. Grant, *and* W. J. Grant Improved.

215. Panope (Chiswick collection).—Three and a half feet ; infl. stiffly and densely branched, round-topped ; fl. $1\frac{1}{4}$ inches across, lilac-mauve, full-rayed. Flowering for three weeks from September 21.

216. *patens* (Barr).—Growth thin and weak ; infl. a sparsely branched leafy panicle, bearing a few fl. at the tips of the loose, wiry branches ; fl. $1\frac{1}{4}$ inches across, pale mauve ; rays narrow, stellate. Flowering for about a week from October 5. Leaves thick, downy, netted, oblong, stem-clasping. The Late Purple Aster of the United States, in dry open places.

217. *patulus* (Dobbie, Chiswick), **XXX** 1892.—Three and a half feet ; infl. a freely branched, loose, pointed panicle with reddish stems ; fl. 1 inch across, pale rose-lilac (violet-purple typically), stellate. Flowering for four weeks from August 31. Habit rampant at the base,

but free-flowering and pretty.   The Spreading Aster of the Eastern States.

218. Perle Lyonnaise (Barr).—Two and a half feet; infl. sub-corymbose, densely flowered; fl. 1⅛ inches. across, white suffusing pink, flat, very full-rayed. Flowering for five weeks from August 31 (*Novi-Belgii*).

219. Perry's Pink (Barr, Notcutt).—Three and a half feet; habit thin and wiry, dark-stemmed, but denser and stronger than Edna Mercia, which it much resembles; fl. 1 inch across, pink, full-rayed. Flowering for four weeks from September 6 (*Novi-Belgii*).

220. Perseus (Barr), **XXX** 1892.—Two feet. A fine variety of *corymbosus*, with darker, firmer, and more wrinkled foliage; infl. more densely flowered, with brown wiry stems; later; fl. 1 inch across, white, stellate, with nine or ten broad rays. Flowering for five weeks from August 31.

221. Peters' White (Peters), **A.M.** September 26, 1907.—Three and a half feet; infl. a loosely branched, bushy panicle, clothing the plant with flower almost to the base; fl. 2 inches across, white, full-rayed; rays broad but pointed, giving a stellate appearance; bracts squarrose. Flowering for five weeks from September 13. A magnificent variety, the best white in the collection.

222. Photograph (Barr, Jones).—Four feet. A variety of *cordifolius*. This name was originally applied to Diana, but the varieties received under these names at Wisley were distinct. Fl. ¾ inch across, whitish-lilac, stellate. Flowering for three weeks from September 30.

223. Phyllis (Chiswick collection).—Five feet; infl. a broad, loose pyramidal panicle, with the terminal flowerhead curiously distant from the rest; fl. 1½ inches across, lilac, very full-rayed. Flowering for three weeks from September 13.

224. Pink Gem (Jones).—Failed.

225. Pleiad (Barr), **XX** 1892.—Failed.

226. Pluto (Chiswick collection), **XX** 1892.—Three and a half feet; infl. a rigidly branched, leafy, long-pointed panicle; fl. 1½ inches across, light mauve, full-rayed and flat. Flowering for two weeks from October 5 (*laevis, Novi-Belgii*).

227. *polyphyllus* (Barr, Chiswick), **XXX** 1892.—Five feet; panicle loosely pyramidal; habit vigorous and rampant; fl. 1 inch across, white; rays loose, with a noticeable and persistently yellow disc. Flowering for three weeks from September 30. Faxon's Aster of the Eastern States, on moist cliffs.

228. Précocité (Jones).—Six feet. A variety of *Novae-Angliae*, near *N.-A. praecox*. Fl. 2 inches across, rich rose-purple, very full-rayed. Flowering for four weeks from September 21.

229. *prenanthoides* (Chiswick collection), **XXX** 1892.—Two and a half feet; infl. much branched, loosely sub-corymbose; fl. 1 inch across, pale lilac (typically violet), stellate; rays reflexed a little. Flowering for seven weeks from August 10. Lower leaves spathulate, upper stem-clasping, thin, light green, sharply serrate. The Crooked-stem Aster of the United States, in moist soil.

230. Proserpine (Barr, Dobbie, Chiswick), **XXX** 1892.—Five to six feet; habit vigorous; infl. a broad, densely flowered, stiffly branched panicle; fl. 1¼ inches across, rosy-lilac; rays narrow. Flowering for three weeks from September 30 (*Novi-Belgii*).

231. Psyche (Barr, Dobbie), **XX** 1892.—The varieties received under this name were distinct. That of Messrs. Barr, three feet, flowering for six weeks from August 31; a stiff panicle; fl. 1½ inches across, bright lilac-mauve; rays full. That of Messrs. Dobbie, flowering for five weeks from October 5, of looser habit. Both varieties good (*laevis*).

232. *ptarmicoides* (Barr), **XXX** 1892.—One and a half feet; infl. densely branched, sub-corymbose; fl. ¾ inch across, white, stellate, with creamy disc. Flowering for four weeks from September 13. Leaves linear-lanceolate, pale green. The Upland White Daisy of the United States, in dry or rocky soil.

233. *ptarmicoides major* (Barr).—One and a quarter feet; darker foliage, dwarfer habit, earlier flowering, larger flowerheads with broader rays than the type, but not prettier. Flowering for six weeks from August 31.

234. *puniceus* (Dobbie, Chiswick), **XXX** 1892.—Three feet; panicle broad, leafy, densely branched and flowered; fl. 1¾ inches, reddish-mauve (typically violet-purple), stellate; rays narrow; disc small. Flowering for four weeks from August 13. Stems stout, reddish, hairy; leaves sessile, oblong-lanceolate, large, puckered—both stems and foliage rather coarse. The Red-stalked Aster of the Eastern States of North America, in swamps.

235. *puniceus lucidulus* (Chiswick collection), **XXX** 1892.—Three and a half feet; panicle very sparsely branched; less leafy and the foliage less coarse than in the type; fl. 1 inch across, pale heliotrope. Flowering for three weeks from August 31.

236. *puniceus pulcherrimus* (Barr, Dobbie, Chiswick), **XXX** 1892.—Six feet; rigid, hairy; red stems, as in the type, but the panicle is long, open, and sparsely branched; fl. aggregated at the tips of the branchlets, 2 inches across, lilac-white to white, stellate; rays loose and twisted. Flowering for four weeks from September 10. A very handsome variety, comparatively slow to increase, requiring a moist position.

237. Purity (Dobbie, Chiswick), **XX** 1892.—Four feet; panicle round-headed, dense; fl. 1¼ inches across, white, becoming pinkish. Flowering for four weeks from September 13 (*Novi-Belgii*).

238. Pygmalion (Chiswick collection), **XXX** 1892.—One and a half feet; infl. densely branched, leafy, corymbose; fl. 1⅜ inches across, pale mauve, full-rayed; disc large. Flowering for seven weeks from August 10. A dense mound of flower and foliage; pretty (*laevis*).

239. Ravennae (Chiswick collection), **XXX** 1892.—Three and a half feet; infl. much branched, loose, panicled, with slender stems; fl. 1¼ inches, lilac, stellate. Flowering for four weeks from August 31. Growth very rampant (*Novi-Belgii*).

240. Rev. Egles (Barr).—Three and a half feet; infl. loosely pyramidal, densely flowered at the top; fl. 1¼ inches across, mauve-lilac; rays very full, but not flat. Flowering for three weeks from September 30. Of no value (*Novi-Belgii*).

241. Rev. E. W. Badger (Barr, Dobbie).—Three and a half to five feet; panicle loose, oblong; fl. 1½ inches across, lilac-white, stellate. Fowering for three weeks from September 21. Poor (*paniculatus* of Barr, *Novi-Belgii* of Dobbie).

242. Robert Parker (Barr, Dobbie, Chiswick), **XXX** 1892.—Five and a half feet; panicle broad, pyramidal, round-topped, and leafy, open; fl. 1¾ inches across, mauve-lilac, full-rayed, flat. Flowering for four weeks from September 21. Vigorous and handsome (*Novi-Belgii*).

243. Robert Parker *nanus*.—See Vice-President.

244. Rosalie (Barr).—Five feet; infl. much branched, broadly pyramidal, green-stemmed; fl. 1½ inches across, pale mauve-lilac; rays narrow and full. Flowering for three weeks from September 13. Vigorous (*Novi-Belgii*).

245. Rosy Blue (Barr).—Four feet; panicle oblong, brown-stemmed; growth very dense; fl. 1¼ inches across, light mauve, full-rayed; disc large. Flowering for four weeks from September 30 (*Novi-Belgii*).

246. Rosy Grey (Barr).—Four feet; panicle densely branched, round-topped; fl. 1¼ inches across, very pale lilac, full-rayed. Flowering for four weeks from September 30 (*Novi-Belgii*).

247. Rosy Morn (Barr).—Four feet; infl. loosely branched, wiry, dark-stemmed, densely flowered; fl. 1 inch across, rich rosy-mauve; rays dense. Flowering for four weeks from August 31 (*Novi-Belgii*).

248. Royalty (Beckett).—Two feet; a weak plant; infl. pyramidal, densely flowered; fl. 1¼ inches across, lilac, deepening with age. Flowering for four weeks from September 13.

249. Ryecroft Pink (Barr, Jones, Chiswick).—Five and a half feet; a variety of *Novae-Angliae*, of which it has the habit; fl. 1¾ inches across, rich pink, flat, stellate; rays narrow, pretty. Flowering for five weeks from September 13.

250. Ryecroft Purple (Barr, Jones), **XXX** 1907.—Five feet; a variety of *Novae-Angliae*, of which it has the habit; fl. 1¾ inches, rich blue-purple; rays narrow, double-rowed; disc dark orange. Flowering for five weeks from September 21.

251. *sagittifolius* (Barr, Chiswick), **XX** 1892.—Two and a half to three feet; infl. a freely branched, open panicle, flowering to the ground, with rigid, dark-purple waved stems; branches ascending; fl. 1 inch across, pale lilac-blue, stellate (10–15 rays); disc small. Flowering for four to five weeks from August 10. Lower leaves ovate to sagittate, long-stalked. The Arrow-leaved Aster of North America, in dry soil.

252, 253. St. Brigid.—Two varieties were grown under this name. From Messrs. Barr.—Three feet. Habit vigorous; infl. sub-corymbose, densely branched; fl. 1½ inches across, lilac. Flowering for four weeks from September 13. From Messrs. Dobbie and Chiswick collection.— Three and a half feet; panicle rather oblong, loose; fl. 1¼ inches across, lilac-white, very full-rayed. Flowering for four weeks from September 21 (*Novi-Belgii*).

254. St. Egwyn (Pollard), **A.M.** September 26, 1907.—Three feet; infl. very densely branched, sub-corymbose, green-stemmed; fl. 1⅜ inches across, pure pink, flat, full-rayed; fl. for four weeks from September 13. Habit bushy; a fine variety.

255. St. Patrick (Barr, Notcutt).—Three and a half feet; infl. loosely pyramidal; fl. 2 inches across, lilac-white; rays narrow, full, a little incurved. Flowering for four weeks from September 13. Pretty (*Novi-Belgii*).

256. *salicifolius* (Chiswick collection).—Four and a half feet; a weak plant; infl. broadly pyramidal; fl. 1 inch across, very pale lilac (typically violet), poor. Flowering for three weeks from September 30. Near *paniculatus*. The Willow Aster of the United States, in moist soil.

See also Tresserve.

257. Sappho (Chiswick collection, **XX** 1892.—Three and a half feet; a variety of *Drummondii* with the cordate lower leaves and sparsely and rigidly branched, open panicle of that species; fl. 1 inch across, lilac poor. Flowering scantily in mid-October.

258. Sensation (Barr), **A.M.** October 1, 1902.—Three feet. Habit densely bushy, with light green foliage; panicle much branched; fl. very numerous, ½ inch across, creamy-white suffusing with pink, stellate; rays narrow. Flowering for six weeks from August 31 (*ericoides*).

259. *Shortii* (Barr, Dobbie, Chiswick), **XXX** 1902.—Three feet; stems green, wiry, arching; infl. much branched, spreading; fl. 1¼ inches across, mauve-lilac (typically violet-blue), stellate; disc small, creamy-yellow, becoming rosy. Flowering for four weeks from September 13. Lower leaves cordate at the base, upper leaves often shortly stalked, sage green, closely netted. Hab. United States, on banks and edges of woods.

260. Snowflake (Barr).—Four feet; panicle oblong; fl. 1½ inches, white, shading to lilac, stellate; rays broad. Flowering for five weeks from September 13 (*Novi-Belgii*).

261. Splendens (Davies), **XXX** 1907.—Four feet; panicle rather oblong, densely flowered; fl. 1½ inches across, mauve, full-rayed. Flowering for four weeks from September 13 (*Novi-Belgii*).

262. Starlight (Barr, Notcutt).—Four and a half feet; infl. long, loosely pyramidal, open, with dark, thin, wiry stems; fl. 1¼ inches across, mauve; disc small, becoming crimson. Flowering for five weeks from September 21 (*Novi-Belgii*).

263. Stella (Barr).—Two feet; a pretty and distinct variety of *Amellus*; infl. loosely corymbose, with dark wiry stems; fl. 2 inches across, mauve, rays narrow; very stellate. Flowering for six weeks from September 30. A variety of *Novi-Belgii* also bears this name, **XX** 1892, but no longer in the collection.

264. Stellatus (Notcutt).—Two and a half feet; infl. sub-corymbose, much-branched, spreading; fl. 1¾ inches across, rich lilac, becoming paler; rays narrow, stellate. Flowering for 8 weeks from August 10, but not of much value. Habit, running at the base (*Novi-Belgii*).

265. Superbus (Barr).—Four feet. Habit erect, rigid; panicle bushy and dense; fl. 1¼ inches across, mauve, very full-rayed. Flowering for four weeks from September 13. Leaves dark green, thick; appearance rather spoiled by presence of bright and faded flowers together (*Novi-Belgii*).

266. Themis (Barr).—Four feet; infl. pyramidal, bushy; habit vigorous; fl. 1¾ inches across, mauve-lilac; rays narrow, numerous stellate, and pretty. Flowering for four weeks from September 13. This

plant appears to have been incorrectly sent out under this name, the true Themis being a variety of *versicolor*, white-flowered and dwarf, **XXX** 1892.

267. Theodore (Barr, Chiswick).—Four and half feet. Very similar to Robert Parker, flatter-headed. Flowering for three weeks from September 30 (*Novi-Belgii*).

268. The Pearl (Barr, Beckett).—Two feet; bushy, panicled, becoming sub-corymbose, densely flowered, with light mossy foliage; fl. 1 inch across, pale lilac-pink, full-rayed. Flowering for four weeks from September 20.

269. The Prince (Barr).—Three and a half feet; a broad open panicle with dark wiry stems; fl. 1½ inches across, mauve; rays rather narrow and stellate; disc bright yellow, becoming crimson. Flowering for five weeks from September 13 (*diffusus* of Barr, but apparently *Novi-Belgii*).

270. Thirza (Jones, Notcutt), **XXX** 1907.—Six feet; infl. a long, open, well-branched panicle; fl. 1¼ inches across, lilac-pink, stellate. Flowering for three weeks from October 5. A fine variety (*Novi-Belgii*).

271. Thomas Hemming (Notcutt).—Two and a half feet; infl. stiff, broadly pyramidal, full-flowered; fl. 1½ inches across, rosy-lilac, full-rayed. Flowering for four weeks from September 30. A dwarf Robert Parker (*Novi-Belgii*).

272. Thora (Barr).—Three and a half feet. In habit and colour similar to *vimineus*. Flowering for three weeks from September 30. Pretty.

273. Top Sawyer (Barr, Dobbie, Chiswick), **A.M.** September 24, 1902. Five feet; panicle open, rather oblong; fl. 1½ inches across, mauve-lilac very full-rayed, flat. Flowering for two to three weeks from September 30. Habit of Robert Parker. In 1902 thought to be superior to that variety, but in 1907 inferior (*Novi-Belgii*).

274. T. Smith (Barr, Dobbie, Chiswick).—Four feet; infl. dark-stemmed, sub-corymbose, much branched; fl. 1¼ inches across, mauve-lilac; rays curled. Flowering for four weeks from August 31. Subject to mildew (*Novi-Belgii*).

275. T. S. Ware (Jones).—Five feet; infl. broadly pyramidal, densely flowered; fl. 1½ inches across; rays very full, lilac. Flowering for three weeks from September 21. Subject to mildew (*Novi-Belgii*).

276. T. Wilkes (Chiswick collection), **XXX** 1907.—Five feet; infl. a pointed, leafy, rigidly branched, and densely flowered panicle; fl. 1½ inches across, mauve-lilac, very full-rayed; disc large. Flowering for three weeks from October 5. A handsome variety.

277. *Tradescanti* (Barr, Dobbie, Chiswick).—Four feet; habit slender, graceful, bushy, with bright-green stems and foliage; infl. a spreading panicle; fl. numerous, ½ inch across, white, full-rayed; involucral bracts appressed. Flowering for four weeks from October 28. Leaves thin, strongly running at the base. Tradescant's Aster of N. America, in fields and swamps. *ericoides* is often sent out under this name, but typically *ericoides* is later to flower and dwarfer in habit, with less numerous and smaller flower heads, which have squarrose bracts.

278. Treasure (Jones).—Five feet. A variety of *Novae-Angliae*, of

which it has the habit; fl. 2 inches across, purple, very full-rayed. Flowering for four weeks from September 21.

279. Tresserve (Barr).—One and a half feet; panicle broad, pointed, full-flowered ; branches ascending ; habit spreading, bushy ; fl. ¾ inch across, mauve-rose ; rays full, pointed. Flowering for five weeks from October 28. Very distinct and pretty, and one of the latest to flower (*salicifolius*).

280. *trinervis* (Notcutt).—Failed to flower.

281. Triumph (Barr).—Five feet ; panicle dark-stemmed, wiry, large and loose ; fl. 1¼ inches across, rosy-lilac, full-rayed, but rather rough ; disc lemon-yellow, becoming rosy. Flowering for four weeks from October 5 (*paniculatus, Novi-Belgii*).

282. *turbinellus* (Barr, Chiswick), **XXX** 1892.—Four feet ; panicle broad, open, with very thread-like or wiry stems ; fl. few, one to three together, at the ends of the branches, 1 inch across, stellate, typically violet or mauve (white from Messrs. Barr). Flowering for three weeks from September 30. The Prairie Aster of the United States, in dry soil.

283. *turbinellus albus* (Barr).—Five feet ; fl. 1¼ inches across, white, becoming pinkish. Flowering for three weeks from September 30.

284. Ulster Echo (Barr).—Three and a half feet ; infl. a broad, densely flowered, rigidly branched panicle ; fl. 1¼ inches across, almost white, pinkish with age. Specimen weak. Flowering for two weeks from September 30 (*Novi-Belgii*).

285. *umbellatus* (Chiswick collection), **XXX** 1892.—Six and a half feet ; infl. a compound corymb ; fl. ¾ inch across, creamy-white, stellate ; rays a little reflexed ; disc greenish-yellow. Flowering for five weeks from September 13. The Tall Flat-top White Aster of N. America, in moist soil. (Syn. *Doellingeria umbellata*, Nees, from the distinctly double pappus, with long inner bristles.)

286. *undulatus* (Chiswick collection), **XXX** 1892.—Two and a half feet ; stems stiff, rough, and very downy ; panicle leafy, rigid, dense, pyramidal ; fl. 1 inch across, pale lilac-blue (to violet) ; rays reflexed, narrow. Flowering for four weeks from August 31. The Wavy-leaf Aster of Eastern N. America, in dry soil.

287. Venus (Barr, Chiswick).—Three and a half feet ; panicle dense, oblong ; fl. 1 inch across, lilac-pink ; rays very full. Flowering for two weeks from September 30 (*Novi-Belgii*).

288. *versicolor albus* (Barr).—Five feet ; infl. a long, oblong, loose panicle ; fl. 1½ inches across, white suffusing with pink, rather stellate. Flowering for three weeks from September 13.

289. *versicolor albus*, improved (Barr).—Four feet ; fl. larger, more stellate, finer. Flowering for four weeks from September 13.

For other varieties of versicolor see Antigone, Charming, *and* Themis.

290. Vesta (Barr), **XXX** 1892.—Two and a half feet ; infl. densely flowered, bushy ; fl. 1¼ inches across, white, becoming pinkish, rather stellate. Flowering for five weeks from September 13 (*laevis, Novi-Belgii*).

291. Vice-President (Barr).—**A.M.** October 10, 1899, under the name of Robert Parker nanus.—Three and a half feet ; infl. sub-corymbose, densely branched and flowered ; fl. 1¾ inches across, pale mauve.

P

Flowering for four weeks from August 31.   Habit rather rampant (*Novi-Belgii*).

292. *vimineus* (Barr, Dobbie, Chiswick), **XX** 1892.—Two and a half feet (2-5 feet); habit bushy, stems slender, foliage light green, mossy; infl. much branched; branches rigid, divergent; fl. very numerous, short-stalked, and crowded along the branches, ¾ inch across, creamy-white, stellate.   Flowering for four weeks from September 30.   The Small White Aster of N. America, in moist soil.

293. *vimineus nanus* (Barr).—Three feet.   A better white, very free-flowering and pretty, but more vigorous than the last!

294. *vimineus perfectus* (Barr, Notcutt, Chiswick), **A.M.** September 24, 1902.—Two and a half to three and a half feet; habit light and graceful; fl. ⅝ inch across, pinkish-white, very stellate; disc small, becoming rosy. Flowering for six weeks from August 23.   Pretty.

For other varieties of vimineus see Cassiope, Delight (the best), Evening Star, Freedom, *and* Osprey (lilac).

295. Virgil (Barr, Dobbie), **XXX** 1892. Of Barr.—Four and a half feet; very vigorous, bushy; fl. 1 inch across, lilac-white, rather stellate. Flowering four weeks from September 13. Of Dobbie.—Six feet; panicle loose; fl. 1½ inches across, mauve-lilac. Flowering for four weeks from September 21.   That from Messrs. Dobbie would seem to be the variety commended in 1892 (*laevis*).

296. Warley semiplena (Barr, Chiswick), **XXX** 1902.—Five feet; panicle rather oblong, flat-topped; fl. 1¼-1½ inches across, many fl. double, but many with only two to three rows of ray-florets, mauve-lilac. Flowering for three weeks from September 30.   Habit vigorous, rampant. Much inferior to Beauty of Colwall.

297. W. B. Child (Dobbie).—Five feet; infl. pyramidal, with rigid, wiry stems; fl. 1½ inches across, rosy-mauve, stellate. Flowering for three weeks from September 30 (*Novi-Belgii*).

298. White Pet (Barr).—Three and a half feet; weak, subject to mildew; infl. much branched; fl. white suffusing with pink; disc pale. Flowering for three weeks from September 30 (*Novi-Belgii*).

299. White Queen (Barr), **A.M.** September 6, 1907.—Three and a half feet; infl. a much branched, bushy panicle, stiff-stemmed; fl. 1¼ inches across; rays full, pure white. Flowering for four weeks from August 31.   A little subject to mildew, but quite the best early white Aster (*Novi-Belgii*).

300. White Queen of the Dwarfs (Barr).—Two and a half feet. Habit and flower of the last.   Flowering for four weeks from August 23. A good variety (*Novi-Belgii*).

301. White Spray (Barr, Dobbie), **XXX** 1907.—Five and a half feet; panicle loose, oblong, clothing the upper half of the plant; fl. 1½ inches across, white, a little pinkish with age; rays narrow, stellate, a little twisted. Flowering for four weeks from September 13.   Habit very vigorous (*Novi-Belgii*).

302. W. Bowman (Jones, Notcutt, Chiswick), **XXX** 1902.—Six feet; a variety of *Novae-Angliae*, of which it has the habit; branches red; fl. violet-purple, 1¾ inches across. Flowering for three to four weeks from September 30.   Very similar to Ryecroft Purple.

303. W. J. Grant (Barr), **XXX** 1892.—Four and a half feet; infl. a long, much branched, oblong panicle; foliage and stems dark glossy green; fl. 1 inch across, white, becoming lilac; rays loose, stellate. Flowering for four weeks from September 13. Very vigorous (*paniculatus*).

304. W. J. Grant Improved (Barr).—Four feet; very similar to the last, but inferior.

305. William Marshall (Barr), **XXX** 1907.—Four and a half feet; infl. pyramidal, with rigid stems; fl. 1½ inches across, rosy mauve, full-rayed, flat, neat; disc large. Flowering for three weeks from September 30. Vigorous (*Novi-Belgii*).

CANNAS AT WISLEY, 1906–07.

In the spring of 1906, 271 stocks of Cannas were received for trial from growers and raisers in Europe and America. Arriving at different periods, and in various stages of growth and vigour, it was impossible during 1906 to properly compare their merits. They were, therefore, together with twenty-six additional stocks, started in gentle heat under equal conditions in March 1907. The compost used was a turfy loam, intimately mixed with some well-decayed manure and leaves, with sufficient sand to ensure thorough drainage. As vigorous root action proceeded they were rapidly advanced from the 48's, in which they were started, to the 10- and 12-inch pots in which they were flowered. Cannas are gross feeders, and, while in active growth, should receive copious supplies of water with occasional applications of artificial fertilisers. The plants, at intervals of from seven to ten days, received small doses of Peruvian guano—a generous treatment that was amply repaid in the additional wealth of bloom and vigour of foliage. The stocks filled two greenhouses, and with their brilliant flowers and handsome foliage produced a fine display during the months of July to October inclusive ; 220 distinct varieties were represented. These were three times inspected by the Floral Committee, and the following varieties were selected as the best in the collection, receiving awards of merit (**A.M.**), or highly commended (**XXX**) :—

White.—Blanche Wintzer.

Yellow.—Burbank, R. Wallace, Wyoming.

Orange.—Hesperide, Oscar Dannecker, S. T. Wright, Uncle Sam.

Rose.—Duke of York, Frau Philipp Siesmayer, Isabella Breitschwerdt, Melrose, Venus.

Red.—Fürst Wied, Grossherzog Ernst Ludwig, Karl Kirsten, Pluto, Wilhelm Bofinger, Wm. Saunders.

Yellow, spotted with red.—Elizabeth Hoss, Gladiator, J. B. van der Schoot, R. Wallace.

The garden cannas are generally grouped in two sections, though the now evident distinctions between the sections already show signs of breaking down in the newer varieties, such as S. T. Wright and Uncle Sam, the Italian or orchid-flowered section represented by O. in the Report, and the French, Crozy or gladiolus-flowered varieties marked G.

The gladiolus-flowered type was introduced some fifty years ago, though Mme. Crozy and most of the older varieties are now far surpassed by recent introductions. These are derived from intercrossing *Canna iridiflora, C. Warscewiczii* and *C. glauca.* They are characterised by their dwarf habit, free-flowering qualities, fine spike, brilliant colour, and smooth petals.

The orchid-flowered varieties were first raised in 1893, when Mme. Crozy × *C. flaccida* produced Italia and Austria. They are of taller growth and richer foliage than the older varieties, and their flowers are larger and more regular in appearance from the breadth of the stamen-petals, but *Canna flaccida* at the same time has introduced a smaller truss, a softness and fragility of texture of the petals, and a reduction in the brilliance and purity of colour of the flowers.

1. Admiral Schley (Conrad).—G. Orange-red, irregularly spotted with a deeper red and edged yellow; green foliage; growth very weak; 1½ feet.

2. Africa (Dobbie).—O. Apricot to terra-cotta, irregularly shaded with deeper colour; truss rather small; foliage very rich, bronzy-crimson, striped with green; 5 feet.

3. Alemannia (Dammann, Froebel), **A.M.** July 27, 1897.—O. Reddish-orange, mottled with a deeper shade and edged broadly and irregularly with yellow; flowers very large; truss rather small; foliage green, glaucous; 4 feet.

4. Alliance (Cannell).—G. Orange-red fading to rose with the narrowest edging of yellow; petals yellow on the reverse; foliage light green; 2 feet.

5. Alphonse Bouvier (Cannell, Dobbie), **A.M.** January 12, 1892.—G. Dark scarlet with a trace of yellow at the throat; flowers large, smooth petalled but irregular; foliage green, glaucous; 3 feet.

6. Alsace (Dobbie, Froebel).—G. Straw yellow to creamy-white, faintly spotted with pink; flowers small; petals narrow; truss loose; foliage yellowish-green, glaucous; 3 feet.

7. America (Dammann, Froebel), **A.M.** July 27, 1897.—O. Bright orange-red with deeper shadings and yellow markings at the throat; truss very poor; foliage very handsome and broad, crimson and green-striped-crimson; 6 feet.

8. Ami Jules Chrétien (Cannell, Dobbie), **A.M.** July 14, 1896.—G. Orange-salmon to salmon, often with thin yellow edge, margin waved; truss weak; foliage green, glaucous; 2½ feet.

9. Annie Laurie (Cannell).—G. Salmon-pink; petals notched; truss large; foliage dark green; 3 feet.

10. Antoine Barton (Veitch), **XXX** June 20, 1894.—G. Deep yellow, richly spotted with red; flowers rather small but truss good; foliage light grey-green; 3 feet.

11. Aphrodite (Dammann).—O. Orange-red with irregular yellow margin; truss poor; foliage bright green; 4 feet.

12. Arthur William Paul (Dammann).—G. Dark orange, spotted with red; small truss, late flowering; foliage very dark; 4 feet.

13. Asia (Dammann).—Failed.

14. Atalanta (Dammann).—Failed.

15. Attika (Dammann).—Failed.

16. Auguste Chantin (Cannell, Veitch).—G. Orange-red to rose, veined; truss small; foliage green; 2 feet.

17. Aurea (Cannell, Veitch).—G. Yellow, faintly spotted with gold; petals smooth, unnotched, round; foliage light green; 3½ feet.

18. Aurore (Cannell), **A.M.** July 14, 1896.—G. Apricot; 2½ feet.

19. Australia (Dammann).—O. Yellow, striped and overlaid with red; foliage green, with distinct crimson edge; 3 feet.

20. Austria (Dobbie, Froebel), **A.M.** June 9, 1896.—O.   Light yellow, spotted on the inner petals with orange ; foliage light green ; 4 feet.

21. Beauté de Portevine (Cannell).—Failed.

22. Betsy Ross (Conrad).—G.   Yellow, richly spotted with bright red, the petaloid stamen and style bright red ; very distinct ; foliage dark green ; 2½ feet.

23. Black Prince (Conrad, Dobbie, Veitch).—G.   Deep cardinal ; petal long, oblong ; truss very large and handsome ; foliage green ; 3 feet.

24. Black Warrior (Conrad).—G.   Deep velvety-crimson, the darkest red in the collection ; flowers rather small ; petals narrow, margin waved ; foliage grey-green ; 2½ feet.

25. Blanche Wintzer (Conrad), **A.M.** August 13, 1907.—G.   Lemon-white, becoming pure white with scarcely perceptible pale-pink spots ; flowers large, petals broad, waved at the margins ; truss rather small, close-flowered ; foliage green ; 1½ feet.   Quite the best white in the collection.

26. Brandywine (Conrad).—G.   Orange-scarlet to salmon-red with darker blotches ; flowers rather small ; foliage very dark, green and crimson ; 3 feet.

27. Britannia (Dammann).—O.   Reddish-orange, mottled with a deeper shade and edged irregularly with yellow ; flowers very large, a shade deeper in colour than Alemannia ; foliage large, bright green ; 4 feet.

28. Burbank (Cannell, Froebel, Veitch), **A.M.** September 6, 1907.—O.   Yellow, the inner petal much spotted with red ; truss large for the orchid-flowered section ; foliage almost emerald-green with darker markings ; 3 feet.

29. Buttercup (Conrad, Dobbie, Froebel).—G.   Rich pure yellow with a little red at the throat ; petals rather narrow and small, but truss good ; foliage green ; 3 feet.   This is the richest yellow-flowered variety.

30. California (Conrad).—G.   Rich orange, reddish towards the throat, and a little mottled ; truss dense ; foliage green ; 1½ feet.

31. Camille Bernardin (Veitch). — G.   Salmon-rose with deeper mottlings ; flower and truss poor ; foliage green ; 3 feet.

32. Campania (Dammann).—O.   Very similar to Burbank.   Flower and truss large ; foliage green, handsome ; 5 feet.

33. Chameleon (Conrad).—G.   Orange-yellow, spotted and shaded with red ; truss small ; flower rather loose ; foliage green ; 2½ feet.

34. Champion (Froebel).—O.   Yellow ground, heavily run and spotted with apricot ; flowers large ; foliage light green, broad ; 4 feet.

35. Chappaqua (Conrad).—G.   Orange-red with deeper spottings ; flowers and truss weak ; foliage bronzy-green and crimson ; 3 feet.

36. Charles Molin (Cannell, Dammann).—G.   Apricot, fading to rose, lightly spotted in lines with rose ; flower loose ; foliage green ; 2½ feet.

37. Charles Moore (Dobbie).—Failed.

38. Cherokee (Conrad).—G.   Light crimson ; truss small ; foliage green ; 1½–2 feet.

39. Cloth of Gold (Conrad).—G.   Old gold, pinkish at the throat ; flowers and truss poor ; foliage green veined with crimson ; 2 feet.

40. Comte de Bouchard (Veitch), **A.M.** May 26, 1897.—G.   Yellow,

richly and uniformly spotted with red; truss good; flowers smooth; foliage green; 8 feet.

41. Conqueror (Conrad).—G. Orange-red, slightly edged and mottled with yellow; flowers smallish, rather speckled in appearance; truss dense; foliage green; 2½ feet.

42. Conseilleur Heidenreich (Cannell).—G. Orange-scarlet; flowers regular but petals rather narrow; truss very good; foliage dark; 3 feet.

43. Coronet Improved (Conrad).—G. Pale yellow; weak; 1½ feet.

44. Cuba (Cannell).—Very weak; failed; 1 foot.

45. Cyclope (Dammann).—G. Bright red; petals smooth, but rather loose and narrow; foliage rich dark glaucous green; 8½ feet.

46. Czar Alexander III. (Dammann).—Failed.

47. Deutscher Kronprinz (Dammann).—G. Deep scarlet; foliage dark; 8 feet. One of the best varieties, with outstanding large truss and fine flowers; maintains its colour well.

48. Dr. Dock (Veitch).—G. Orange-red to cardinal-red with darker spottings; petals long, narrow, spreading; foliage green; 2-8 feet.

49. Dr. Marcus (Pfitzer).—G. Orange-red, lightly spotted with deeper colour; flowers large; truss small; foliage crimson-purple; 2 feet.

50. Dr. Nansen (Conrad).—G. Clear lemon-yellow with orange-red on the stamen and stigma; petals narrow; truss large, with the flowers neatly arranged in three ranks, well above the foliage; foliage green; 2 feet.

51. Duchess of York (Cannell), **A.M.** August 8, 1893.—G. Yellow spotted with dull red; flowers rather small; foliage light grey-green; 2½ feet.

52. Duke Ernst (Cannell, Veitch).—G. Deep orange to reddish-orange; flowers regular, small; foliage bronzy-crimson and green, glaucous; 4 feet.

53. Duke of Marlborough (Cannell, Conrad, Dobbie, Froebel, Veitch). —G. Rich dark red; petals with waved margin; truss very fine; foliage light grey-green, very glaucous; 2½ feet. A free-flowering variety. The variety from Messrs. Veitch was inferior, with narrow petals; while that from Mr. Froebel belonged to the O. section; yellow, lightly spotted with red.

54. Duke of York (Conrad), **A.M.** September 6, 1907.—G. Rich rose with narrow sulphur-yellow edge; flowers large; petals very smooth; truss not large; foliage green; 2½ feet. A fine distinct variety.

55. Eastern Beauty (Cannell, Conrad).—G. Salmon-pink; flowers good, but truss rather small, round; foliage very distinct, bronze-green and crimson; 2½ feet.

56. Edouard André (Dammann, Dobbie, Froebel).—O. Reddish-orange, mottled and shaded with red; flower large, regular; foliage rich bronzy-crimson and green; 5 feet.

57. Edouard Meig (Cannell), **A.M.** July 27, 1897.—G. Dark orange-scarlet, a little yellow at the throat; petals rounded, smooth, fine; truss good; foliage green; 8 feet.

58. Egandale (Dobbie).—G. Different stocks of this variety were received. (a) Light carmine-red in close oblong truss; foliage dark bronze-green and crimson; 8½ feet; and (b) carmine-red; flowers very

small ; truss long, loose ; foliage erect, narrow, crimson, thickly covered with glaucous bloom ; handsome ; 5 feet.

59. Elizabeth Hoss (Cannell, Veitch), **A.M.** June 4, 1901.—G. Rich yellow, heavily spotted with red ; flowers large, but petals irregular ; foliage green ; 3 feet. Still one of the best spotted varieties.

60. Else (Pfitzer).—G. Cream-buff, suffusing with pink with age ; truss weak ; foliage green ; 2½ feet.

61. Emilia (Cannell, Dobbie).—O. Orange-red with deeper markings ; truss small ; foliage very handsome, bronzy-crimson and green ; 5-6 feet.

62. Emma Bedau (Pfitzer).—G. Intense fiery-scarlet ; flower large, petals long ; truss good ; foliage green ; 2½ feet.

63. Evolution (Conrad).—G. Salmon-pink, deeper at the throat ; truss small ; foliage dark bronze-green ; 2 feet.

64. Floreal (Dammann).—G. Salmon-rose ; flower irregular, rather narrow-petalled ; truss thin ; foliage rich dark crimson ; 3 feet.

65. Florence Vaughan (Dobbie).—G. Yellow, richly spotted with red ; foliage grey-green ; 3-4 feet.

66. Francis Wood (Veitch).—G. Rich orange ; truss dense, long ; smooth, rather small flowers ; foliage green ; 4 feet.

67. Franz Büchner (Cannell).—G. Apricot, lightly mottled with a deeper shade and very thinly edged with yellow ; petals with waved margin ; truss good, but flowers weak ; foliage green ; 2½ feet.

68. Frau Gräfin Ernestine von Thun (Pfitzer).—G. Salmon-pink ; smooth petals ; rather poor truss ; foliage dark ; 3 feet.

69. Fräulein Anna Benary (Veitch).—G. Orange-scarlet with a little yellow at the throat ; margin of petals waved ; rather small truss ; foliage green ; 2 feet. Inferior to Edouard Meig.

70. Frau Philipp Siesmayer (Pfitzer), **XXX** July 30, 1907.—G. Rich salmon-rose ; large flowers, broad petals, and very fine truss ; free-flowering ; foliage dark green ; 3 feet.

71. Fürst Bismarck (Dobbie, Froebel).—G. Fiery orange-scarlet ; margin of petals much waved ; truss dense, large ; flower rather small ; foliage green ; 2½ feet.

72. Fürst Wied (Pfitzer), **A.M.** August 13, 1907.—G. Fiery-red, a little yellow at the throat ; flowers large, petals broad, margin waved ; truss good ; foliage glaucous green ; 3 feet.

73. Gart Stapel (Cannell).—Failed.

74. General Merkel (Pfitzer).—G. Scarlet-orange, edged yellow ; foliage green ; 2 feet. Very similar to Mme. Crozy.

75. George Washington Improved (Conrad).—G. Cardinal, a little yellow at the throat ; foliage green ; 2 feet.

76. Gladiator (Conrad), **A.M.** August 13, 1907.—G. Yellow, heavily spotted and shaded rose-red ; stigma and anther quite red ; truss good ; foliage vigorous, dark green ; 3 feet. A very distinct variety.

77. Gloriosa (Cannell).—G. Scarlet, edged yellow ; truss close ; flowers poor ; foliage green ; 1½ feet.

78. Goliath (Dammann).—G. Red-scarlet ; long-petalled rather loose flowers ; foliage broad, green, markedly edged with crimson ; 1½ feet.

79. Gouverneer von Zimmerer (Froebel).—Failed.

80. Grossherzog Ernst Ludwig (Dammann), **A.M.** June 4, 1901.—G.

Orange-red with deeper spots; flower very large; petals broad; truss large; foliage green and rich crimson; 3 feet. A fine variety, the flower approaching in size and form those of the O. varieties.

81. **Hans Werdmuller** (Cannell).—G. Orange-scarlet, yellow at the throat; foliage dark green, veined and shaded crimson; 3 feet.

82. **Harlequin** (Conrad).—G. Scarlet, yellow edge and throat; 1½ feet.

83. **Heinrich Seidel** (Cannell, Dammann). -O. Red, very broadly and irregularly edged with yellow; flowers and truss large; foliage light grey-green; 4 feet.

84. **Hellas** (Dammann).—O. Yellow, mottled and marked with red; truss poor; foliage light green; 2½ feet.

85. **Herzogin Vera** (Dammann).—Failed.

86. **Hesperide** (Veitch), **A.M.** September 6, 1907.—G. Bright orange, deeper at the throat; petals broad; truss good; foliage green; 2-3 feet. A very showy variety.

87. **H. Guichard** (Veitch).—G. Light rose-red; large flowers with rather pointed narrow petals and good truss; foliage grey-green; 2½ feet.

88. **Hiawatha** (Conrad).—G. Soft salmon-rose; truss rather small, close; smooth, but not broad petals; foliage handsome, dark, bronzed. 3 feet.

89. **Hofgarten-Director Walter** (Dammann).—G. Fiery-red; flowers small; foliage dark green and crimson; 2 feet.

90. **Hofgarten-Director Wendland** (Dammann), **XXX** July 27, 1898.—O. Reddish-orange with darker mottlings, broadly and irregularly edged with yellow; foliage broad, green, striped light green; 3½ feet.

91. **Iberia** (Dammann).—Weak; failed.

92. **Indiana** (Conrad).—Failed.

93. **Isabella Breitschwerdt** (Pfitzer), **A.M.** August 13, 1907.—G. Salmon-rose, very lightly mottled with a deeper shade, yellowish on the reverse; flowers very large; truss large and close-flowered; margins of petals waved; foliage green; 3½ feet.

94. **Italia** (Dobbie), **A.M.** June 23, 1896.—O. Yellow, spotted with red towards the throat; flowers large; foliage emerald green; 3 feet.

95. **J. B. van der Schoot** (Cannell, Dobbie), **A.M.** August 13, 1907.—G. Rich yellow, much spotted with red; free-flowering, large fine truss; smooth scarcely notched petals; foliage green, vigorous; 2½ feet. The red runs a little at the throat, but this is the best spotted yellow variety.

96. **J. D. Eisele** (Veitch).—G. Scarlet, yellow at the throat; flowers rather small but very neat from the roundness of the petals; foliage light green with marked crimson edge; 3 feet.

97. **Jean Tissot** (Veitch), **A.M.** June 4, 1901.—G. Rich orange-scarlet with a little deeper veining; flower and truss both good; foliage green, broad; 3 feet.

98. **John Tulett** (Pfitzer).—G. Very rich yellow, slightly spotted with red at the throat; truss and flowers rather small; foliage green; 2 feet.

99. **Juanita** (Conrad).—G. Rich apricot-yellow, fading to creamy-yellow; truss and flowers large; petals smooth, broad; foliage bronze-green, veined; 2½ feet.

100. Jupiter (Conrad).—Failed.

101. Karl Kirsten (Pfitzer), **XXX** July 30, 1907.—G. Orange-scarlet a little yellow at the throat ; flowers large ; petals broad, rounded ; truss bold ; foliage green, broad ; 3–4 feet. A very handsome variety.

102. Klondyke (Veitch).—G. Orange ; flower small ; truss good ; foliage light green ; 3 feet.

103. Königin Charlotte (Veitch), **A.M.** August 8, 1893.—G. Bright red, edged with yellow ; flowers small ; truss stiff, neat, oblong ; foliage light green, very glaucous ; 2½ feet.

104. Konsul W. Vellnagel (Pfitzer).—G. Yellow, spotted red ; truss very good ; foliage green ; 3–4 feet. Early flowering and one of the best spotted varieties.

105. Kronos (Dobbie).—O. Yellow, richly spotted and mottled with reddish-apricot ; large flowers ; small truss ; foliage green ; 3½ feet.

106. Kronprinzessin Cäcilie (Pfitzer).—G. Salmon-pink, a very delicate colour, but flowers rather small ; truss close, oblong ; foliage dark ; 3 feet.

107. La France (Dammann, Froebel), **XXX** July 27, 1898.—O. Bright orange-red, yellow at the throat ; foliage very handsome, bronzy-crimson and green ; 6 feet.

108. L. E. Bally (Veitch), **A.M.** April 10, 1894.—G. Pale yellow, much spotted with terra-cotta ; flowers rather small ; foliage light green ; 2–3 feet.

109. Léon Vassilière (Cannell).—Failed.

110. Leo Vaughan (Dobbie).—G. Orange-scarlet with faint reddish spots ; foliage green, shaded and veined purple ; 2½ feet.

111. Louisiana (Conrad).—Failed.

112. Louise (Cannell, Dobbie).—G. Salmon-rose with mottlings of a deeper shade ; free-flowering ; truss very fine and large ; foliage dark green ; 3 feet.

113. L. Patry (Dobbie).—Failed.

114. Luray (Conrad, Dobbie).— G. Carmine-rose ; petals rather narrow, but truss handsome ; foliage green ; 3 feet.

115. Madame Chabanne (Dammann).—G. Yellow, lightly spotted with pink ; flowers and truss poor ; foliage green ; 3 feet.

116. Madame Crozy (Dobbie, Veitch), **A.M.** May 28, 1890.—G. Orange-scarlet with narrow yellow edge ; flowers rather small ; truss stiff ; foliage light green ; 2 feet.

117. Madame Legris (Dammann).—G. Pale yellow, much spotted with orange-red ; flowers and truss poor ; foliage green ; 2½ feet.

118. Mlle. Berat (Cannell, Veitch).—G. Carmine-rose ; large open truss ; petals rather narrow with waved margins ; foliage dark green ; 3 feet.

119. Maiden's Blush (Conrad).—G. Salmon-pink ; weak ; 1½ feet.

120. Martha Washington (Conrad, Dobbie).— G. Orange to rosy-red with narrow yellow edge ; truss close ; petals smooth ; flowers rather small ; foliage very light green ; 3 feet.

121. Max Kolb (Dammann).—G. Deep orange ; truss large, dense-flowered ; petals smooth ; foliage very dark ; 3 feet. A very handsome variety.

122. Melrose (Conrad), **A.M.** August 13, 1907.—G. Rose-pink ; truss rather small, but flowers regular and petals rounded ; foliage bronze-green and purple ; 1½-2 feet.

123. Mephisto (Pfitzer).—G. Dark red ; 3 feet.

124. Météore (Cannell, Veitch).—G. Rich orange ; truss large, close-flowered ; flowers large, margin of petal crimped ; foliage glaucous green ; 3 feet.

125. Minerva (Veitch).—G. Reddish-orange with deeper shadings ; truss close-flowered ; foliage green ; 2½ feet.

126. Miss B. Brunner (Cannell).—G. Pale yellow, much spotted with red ; flowers large and truss very fine ; foliage glaucous green ; 3 feet.

127. **Mrs. F. Dreer** (Veitch).—Failed.

128. Mrs. G. A. Strohlein (Cannell, Veitch), **A.M.** August 13, 1901.— G. Carmine-crimson ; truss very fine ; flowers large ; petals smooth, broad, unnotched ; foliage rich dark crimson, glaucous ; 3 feet.

129. Mrs. Kate Gray (Dammann, Veitch), **A.M.** July 2, 1901.— O. Reddish-orange with darker markings, sometimes lightly edged with yellow ; truss good ; flowers large, regular ; margin of petals waved ; foliage green ; 5-6 feet.

130. M. Florent Penwels (Veitch).—G. Orange-scarlet to reddish-orange, yellow at the throat ; flower large, rather loose and irregular ; petals broad, rounded, smooth ; foliage dark green, broad ; 4½ feet.

131-134. Mont Blanc (Conrad).—G. This, with Mont Blanc second generation, and second generations A. and B., are new white seedlings. They are of dwarf habit, with green foliage and creamy-white to white flowers of rather indifferent form.

135. Mont Etna (Conrad).—G. Orange-red to cardinal ; flowers and truss rather small ; margin of petals waved ; foliage bronze-green to bronze ; 2½ feet.

136. Niagara (Conrad).—Failed.

137. Oceanus (Dammann).—O. Apricot-red, broadly edged with yellow and yellow at the throat ;- foliage grey-green ; 5 feet.

138. Olympia (Dobbie).—Failed.

139. Orange Queen (Froebel).—G. Orange, red at the throat ; truss dense ; flowers thin and rather small ; foliage green ; 2 feet.

140. Oscar Dannecker (Cannell, Dammann, Froebel, Veitch), **A.M.** June 4, 1901.—G. Rich orange, shading to yellow at the edge ; truss good ; flowers large, regular ; petal smooth, broad, notched ; foliage dark grey-green with a little crimson ; very glaucous and distinct ; 2½ feet. A very fine variety.

141. Ottawa (Conrad).—G. Rich salmon-rose ; truss good ; flowers large ; petals broad ; foliage green ; 2½ feet.

142. Pandora (Dammann, Dobbie).—O. Reddish-orange, redder towards the edge ; truss large, loose ; foliage bronzy-green and crimson, very glaucous ; 5 feet.

143. Papa Canna (Dammann, Dobbie, Veitch).—G. Orange-scarlet, often with rather patchy markings of a deeper shade, yellow at the throat ; margin of petal waved ; truss good ; foliage light green ; 3 feet.

144. Partenope (Cannell, Froebel), **A.M.** Aug. 16, 1898.—O. Reddish-

orange lightly splashed, with red and running to red at the edge.; flower regular ; truss good ; foliage light green, very glaucous ; 4½ feet.

145. Paul Bruant (Cannell, Veitch).—G. Reddish-orange with patchy markings of a deeper shade ; truss dense ; flowers small ; petals narrow ; foliage green ; 3 feet.

146. Paul Lorenz (Cannell, Froebel).—G. Dark glowing cardinal-red ; neat ; foliage green and purple ; 2½-3 feet.

147. Paul Sigrist (Veitch).—G. Bright red with narrow yellow edge ; flower and truss small ; foliage weak, green ; 1½-2 feet.

148. Pennsylvania (Dobbie).—Failed.

149. Perseus (Dammann).—O. Yellow, lightly spotted with red ; foliage broad, green and yellowish-green ; 3½ feet.

150. Philadelphia Improved (Conrad).—G. Rich orange-scarlet ; truss rather poor ; foliage green ; 2½ feet.

151. Phoebe (Dammann).—Failed.

152. Pillar of Fire (Conrad).—G. Orange-scarlet ; flowers small ; foliage green ; 2½ feet.

153. Pluto (Cannell, Dammann), **A.M.** August 13, 1907.—O. Orange-red, yellow at the throat ; foliage handsome, green and crimson ; 3 feet.

154. Poète (Dammann).—Failed.

155. President Carnot (Dobbie, Veitch).—G. Orange, suffusing with red, then rose ; truss small ; flowers rather small ; petals notched ; foliage dark, very glaucous ; 3 feet.

156. Président de Péronne (Dammann).—G. Reddish-orange with darker spots ; foliage deep green and crimson ; 3-4 feet.

157. President Meyer (Cannell, Dammann, Dobbie).—G. Dark orange-scarlet ; truss good ; flowers large ; petals very smooth and flat ; foliage handsome, dark green and purple, glaucous ; 3 feet. A fine variety.

158. Prince Hohenlohe (Veitch).—G. Salmon-red ; truss long, narrow ; flowers rather small ; foliage light green ; 4 feet.

159. Professor Fr. Róber (Pfitzer).—G. Rich cardinal-red ; truss good ; flowers large ; margin of petals waved ; foliage dark ; 3½ feet.

160. Professor G. Baker (Veitch).—G. Orange-scarlet, yellow at the throat ; flowers and truss good ; petals broad ; foliage green ; 3 feet.

161. Professor Treub (Dammann).—O. Reddish-orange with deeper shadings, yellow at the throat ; flowers comparatively small ; foliage very broad, handsome, deep crimson ; 4 feet.

162. Queen Charlotte (Dobbie).—G. Bright red, edged with yellow ; flowers and truss poor ; foliage green ; 2½ feet.

163. Red Indian (Dammann).—Failed.

164. Reichskanzler Fürst (R. F.) Hohenlohe (Cannell), **A.M.** September 10, 1901.—G. Rich yellow, spotted towards the throat with red ; flowers irregular ; foliage deep green ; 2½ feet.

165. Rhea (Dobbie).—O. Orange-red, mottled ; foliage handsome, crimson, very glaucous ; 4½ feet.

166. Robert Christie (Veitch).—G. Reddish-orange ; truss dense, oblong ; flowers small, irregular ; margin of petals waved ; foliage light green ; 3 feet.

167. Roi des Rouges (Dammann), **A.M.** May 5, 1896.—G. Glowing

orange-scarlet; margin of petals waved; truss good; flowers regular; foliage green; plant weak; 3 feet.

168. Roma (Dammann).—Failed.

169. Rosemawr (Conrad).—G. Rose, flower of good size and form; foliage green; 2 feet.

170. R. Wallace (Cannell, Pfitzer), **A.M.** August 13, 1907.—G. Yellow to cream, faintly spotted in the centre of the petal with rose; truss and flowers large; petals broad, margins waved; foliage light green; 3 feet.

171. Schwabenland (Pfitzer).—G. Dark scarlet, unnotched petal; foliage handsome, rich green and crimson; 3½ feet.

172. Secrétaire Chabanne (Cannell, Veitch), **A.M.** April 24, 1900.— G. Salmon-orange to salmon-rose with darker markings; truss large but rather loose; margin of petals waved; foliage grey-green; 3½ feet.

173. Semaphore (Cannell, Dammann).—G. Rich clear orange; truss good but flowers small; foliage rich dark crimson, very glaucous; 4½ feet.

174. Semeur A. Sannier (Veitch).—G. Rich apricot with darker markings; truss good; flower poor; foliage green; 3 feet.

175. Shenandoah (Conrad).—G. Salmon-rose; truss and flowers rather small; foliage dark, glaucous; 2 feet.

176. Sicilia (Dobbie).—Failed.

177. S. Milland (Cannell).—O. Rich reddish-orange, but very small, narrow, notched petals; foliage dark bronzy-crimson; 5 feet.

178. Solfatara (Cannell).—Failed.

179. Sophie Buchner (Veitch), **A.M.** May 9, 1893.—G. Yellow, splashed at the throat with red; truss good; flowers rather small; margin of petals waved; foliage green; 2 feet.

180. Souvenir d'Antoine Crozy (Dobbie, Veitch).—G. Scarlet with narrow yellow edge; truss good; flowers rather small; margin of petals waved; foliage green; 2½ feet.

181. Souvenir de Madame Crozy (Cannell).—G. Bright red, mottled with red and irregularly edged with yellow; truss very large; flowers of poor form; foliage large, light glaucous green; 3 feet.

182. Stadtrath Heidenreich (Dammann, Dobbie, Froebel), **A.M.** July 27, 1897.—G. Glowing orange-scarlet with a little yellow at the throat; truss large, loose; flowers large, broad-petalled, smooth; foliage dark, handsome, very glaucous; 3½ feet.

183. Striped Beauty (Conrad).—G. Yellow, much dotted in straight lines with red, red-throated; truss dense, flowers small; foliage green; 2½ feet.

184. S. T. Wright (Conrad), **A.M.** August 13, 1907.—G. Rich reddish-orange; truss rather small, globular; flowers very large; petals broad, smooth; foliage bronze-green and crimson; 5 feet.

185. Suevia (Dammann, Froebel).—O. Pale yellow shading to bronzy-red at the throat; flowers long; petals pointed; foliage green; 4½ feet.

186. Trinacria (Dammann).—Failed.

187. Triumph (Conrad, Froebel).—G. Orange-red, mottled with red; truss close-flowered; foliage green; 1½ feet.

188. Uncle Sam (Conrad), **A.M.** August 13, 1907.—O. Rich orange, becoming red; yellow spotted with red at the throat; truss good; flowers

large; petal broad, smooth; foliage very broad, glaucous green with distinct crimson edge. The habit distinctly that of the orchid-flowered varieties, but the smoothness and substance of the petals almost that of the gladiolus section.

189. Venus (Conrad), **A.M.** September 6, 1907.—G. Salmon-rose, paler and mottled towards the throat, edged thinly with creamy-yellow; truss good; petals broad, very smooth; flower irregular; foliage dark green; 2½ feet.

190. Ville de Poitiers (Dammann).—Failed.

191. West Grove (Conrad, Dobbie).—Failed.

192. Wilhelm Beck (Dammann).—O. Red, broadly edged with pale yellow, throat yellow spotted with red; foliage green; 2½ feet.

193. Wilhelm Bofinger (Dammann, Froebel, Veitch), **A.M.** August 13, 1907.—G. Orange-scarlet, yellow at the throat; truss large, fine; flowers large; margin of petals waved; foliage green; 3 feet.

194. Wilhelm Tell (Pfitzer).—G. Salmon-orange, shading to a yellow edge; foliage distinct grey-green a little suffused with crimson, very glaucous; 3 feet. A fine variety, very similar to Oscar Dannecker, a shade deeper in colour.

195. William Bull (Dobbie).—G. Orange-red; truss small, dense; flowers small; margin of petals waved; foliage green; 2½ feet.

196. William Saunders (Conrad), **A.M.** August 13, 1907.—G. Deep red; flower large, regular; petal very broad and smooth, with waved margin; foliage bronzy-crimson and green, very glaucous; 3 feet. A fine variety.

197. William Watson (Pfitzer).—G. Salmon shaded with pink and lightly mottled; petals broad, smooth, not large; foliage very handsome dark, glaucous; 3½ feet.

198. Wyoming (Conrad), **XXX** July 30, 1907.—G. Orange-yellow; flowers of good form; foliage purple; 3 feet.

Several other varieties, received under number only, from Messrs. Conrad and Jones, have not yet been named.

DAHLIAS AT WISLEY, 1907.

In conjunction with the National Dahlia Society, a trial of Cactus Dahlias was held at Wisley in 1907 to test the value of the more recently introduced varieties from the point of view of garden decoration. The ideal aimed at is a vigorous plant, holding its flowers of good cactus form boldly erect, well above the foliage, on stiff stalks. One hundred and ninety-seven stocks, representing 170 distinct varieties, including 137 fresh stocks from the leading nurserymen and raisers, and sixty stocks of the older varieties for comparison, propagated from tubers on trial in the gardens, 1903–1906, were planted out early in June. Owing to the cold, unseasonable weather the plants failed to show their usual vigour and wealth of colour until the autumn. Several varieties were spoiled by the frost of September 23, when 26·8° F. was registered on an adjoining grass plot. The plants were finally cut by the frost on October 24, when 25·6° F. was registered. The trial was twice inspected by a joint committee of the Royal Horticultural Society and National Dahlia Society, and the following varieties were highly commended (**XXX**) :—

> A. D. Stoop—light crimson.
> Beacon—maroon-crimson.
> Eclair—bright scarlet.
> Lustre—bright blood-red.
> Meteor—orange-scarlet.
> Mrs. J. S. Brunton—yellow, and
> Primrose—pale yellow.
>
> **A.M.** = Award of Merit.
> **XXX** = Highly commended.

A number of pæony-flowered varieties were included in the trial (see Nos. 162 *et seq.*).

1. Achievement (Seale).—Reddish-orange ; petals rather broad and thin, stalks not stiff ; growth weak.

2. Acrobat (Hobbies).—White, shaded and edged with red ; flowers rather small, but neat, with twisted quills ; stalks stiff, but flowers drooping.

3. A. D. Stoop (Baxter), **XXX** for garden decoration, September 14, 1906, September 26, 1907.—Light crimson ; petals rather broad, twisted ; free-flowering, with flowers held well on long stiff stalks.

4. Ajax (Hobbies), **A.M.** August 15, 1899.—Bright salmon-apricot ; large flowers on drooping stalks.

5. Albion (Turner), **A.M.** September 23, 1902.—Cream-white ; broad petals, weak centres, erect growth, stiff stalks.

6. Alexander (Dobbie, Hobbies, Mortimer, Turner), **A.M.** September 20, 1904.—Dark crimson ; flowers of good form on stout stalks.

7. Alice Mortimer (Mortimer).—Warm salmon; flower large; quilled, much twisted petals; flowers held well above the foliage, but drooping, from short stalks.

8. Alight (Burrell), **A.M.** September 26, 1905.—Scarlet; full- and narrow-petalled flowers of good form, but stalks rather weak; foliage scanty.

9. Alpha (Hobbies), **A.M.** September 10, 1901.—White, spotted and streaked with crimson; petals broad; stalks long, but not strong.

10. Amos Perry (Turner), **A.M.** September 29, 1903; **XXX** for garden decoration September 28, 1905.—Glowing scarlet; flowers large, broad petalled, held well above the foliage on long stiff stalks.

11. Antelope (Dobbie, Hobbies, Turner), **A.M.** September 20, 1898.— Fawn, buff-yellow at the centre; flowers almost buried in the dense, vigorous foliage.

12. Apricot (Turner).—Apricot to buff; stalks neither long nor strong, and flowers rather buried in foliage.

13. Arab (Dobbie, 1903), **XXX** for garden decoration, September 15, 1905.—Dark crimson; broad-petalled,. straight-quilled, free-flowering; stalks good, but flowers drooping.

14. Aunt Chloe (Baxter, 1905), **A.M.** September 24, 1901; **XXX** for garden decoration September 15, 1905.—Deep crimson; inner petals broad, quills straight; growth weak.

15. Beacon (Hobbies, 1905), **XXX** for garden decoration, September 13, 1907.—Dark maroon-crimson, broad-petalled, straight-quilled; very free flowering, with flowers held well above the foliage on good stalks.

16. Brilliance (Seale).—Orange-scarlet; flowers small, thin, drooping, but pretty.

17. Bute (Dobbie).—Orange-scarlet, broad petals; flowers hidden in dense leafage.

18. Butterfly (Hobbies).—Orange-vermilion tipped with white, the outer petals white lightly edged with red, but the colours very inconstant; petals broad, stalks short.

19. Cannell's Gem (Veitch, 1905), **A.M.** September 12, 1893, **XXX** for garden decoration, September 28, 1905.—Salmon-red, broad-petalled; small-flowered decorative variety, very free-flowering.

20. Caradoc (Hobbies).—Lemon-yellow; flowers large, petals quilled, twisted, of good form; stalks weak and short.

21. Cinderella (Veitch, 1905), **A.M.** September 8, 1896.—Crimson-purple, broad-petalled flowers of poor form; stalks weak.

22. Clara Stredwick (Turner), **A.M.** September 24, 1901.—Salmon-buff; stalks stiff; growth weak.

23. Cockatoo (Hobbies), **A.M.** September 20, 1904.—White, based with yellow; outer petals edged and shaded buff, but colours very.inconstant; quills straight, stems short, very weak.

24. Columbia (Veitch, 1905), **A.M.** September 24, 1901.—White, edged and based with bright red; stalks weak, but flowers held well above the foliage.

25. Coronation (Hobbies), **A.M.** for garden decoration, September 23, 1902.—Vivid scarlet, small, neat, straight-quilled; very free, but stalks rather short.

·26. Countess of Malmesbury (Hobbies).—Pink, tipped with cream, central florets cream ; flowers large, of good form, but rather·buried in foliage.

27. Crayfish (Hobbies).—Orange red, much twisted quills, on very short weak stalks.

28. Crépuscule (Hobbies), **XXX** for garden decoration, September 14, 1906.—Buff, the base of the petals yellow ; flowers large, flat, broad-petalled on poor stalks ; habit, erect.

29. Crespy (Burrell).—Pale mauve-pink, white at the centre ; stalks good ; growth weak.

30. Crimson Beauty (Mortimer), **A.M.** September 9, 1890.—Bright crimson-scarlet ; free-flowering ; flowers held loosely above the foliage on short stalks.

31. Cycle (Veitch, 1905), **A.M.** September 8, 1896.—Carmine-red, large broad-petalled, rather flat flower on long stalks.

32. D. A. Dunbar (Cheal, 1905), **XXX** for garden decoration, September 15, 1905.—Salmon-scarlet, rather broad petals with twisted tips ; very free-flowering, on stiffish stalks held well above the foliage, but flowers drooping.

33. Dainty (Hobbies), **A.M.** September 15, 1903, **XXX** for garden decoration, September 15, 1905.—Petals yellow in the centre, soft pink tipped with yellow towards the outside of the flower ; quills straight ; free-flowering on rather short stalks but free of the foliage.

34. Daisy (Dobbie, Turner), **A.M.** September 12, 1905.—Salmon-pink, yellowish towards the base of petals ; flowers large, of good form, with twisted quills ; growth vigorous.

35. Daisy Staples (Shoesmith), **A.M.** September 25, 1906.—Rose-pink ; quills narrow, much twisted ; growth weak.

36. Day Dream (Hobbies).—Yellow, shading to and tipped with salmon ; flowers of indifferent form on weak stalks.

37. Decima (Baxter, 1905).—Salmon-red, yellowish towards the centre ; stalks weak ; foliage scanty.

38. Diavolo (Stredwick).—Cream, splashed and striped with dark crimson, splashing variable ; stalks stiff ; growth vigorous ; free-flowering, but flowers drooping.

·39. Dorothy Vernon (Hobbies, 1905).—Pale salmon, yellowish towards the centre ; quills straight ; flowers held well above the scanty leafage.

40. Dreadnought (Dobbie).—Reddish-crimson ; flowers very large ; petals flat ; growth vigorous, dense.

41. Eclair (Turner), **XXX** for garden decoration, September 13, 1907.—Light scarlet, broad petal, and rather poor form, but excellent long stiff stalks holding the flower boldly ; free-flowering.

42. Edith Groom (Hobbies).—Creamy-white, the outer florets a little pinkish on the reverse ; flowers of medium size on weak stalks.

43. Ella Kraemar (Hobbies), **A.M.** September 20, 1904.—Bright pink, quills numerous, rather flat ; stalks long but more or less buried in the vigorous leafage.

44. Ethel Pearson (Mortimer).—Pom-cactus variety ; pale salmon-pink, yellowish at the centre ; free-flowering but not of good habit.

Q

45. Etna (Baxter, 1905), **A.M.** September 23, 1902.—Rose-lilac, yellow at the centre ; broad-petalled, rather rough flower on weak stalks.

46. Fairy (Dobbie, Hobbies), **A.M.** September 6, 1904.—White, narrow, twisted, numerous quills ; neat but stalks weak.

47. Floradora (Veitch, 1905), **XXX** for garden decoration, September 15, 1905.—Bright crimson ; flowers large, broad-petalled, held well above the foliage.

48. Gabriel (Veitch, 1905), **A.M.** September 10, 1901.—Cream, inner segments edged carmine-red ; flowers thin, weak ; stalks weak.

49. Garden King (Hobbies).—Salmon ; flowers small and of poor form ; free flowering but short-stalked.

50. Gazelle (Stredwick), **A.M.** September 11, 1906.—Rose-pink, white-tipped ; flowers large and of good form but buried in vigorous leafage.

51. Glow (Burrell).—Salmon-buff, yellow at the centre ; flowers large, of good form, on long but not stout stalks.

52. Good Hope (Dobbie).—Crimson, with long white tips ; colouring inconstant ; petals broad, a little twisted ; flowers large.

53. Gracie (Hobbies, 1905). — Rose-salmon, rather broad-petalled, weak flower ; growth weak.

54. Great Scott (Seale).—Light crimson ; large, broad, loose, twisted petals.

55. Hamlet (Shoesmith), **A.M.** September 11, 1906.—Crimson-vermilion ; flowers of good form, with fine, long, twisted quills, but rather buried in the foliage.

56. Harbour Lights (Hobbies), **A.M.** September 20, 1904.—Reddish, orange ; flowers very large, of good form, but buried in dense foliage.

57. Harlequin (Hobbies).—White, red at the base and edge of florets but colouring inconstant ; quills broad ; flowers held well above foliage.

58. Helen Stephens (Dobbie), **A.M.** September 20, 1904.—Lemon-yellow ; many flowers semi-double ; stalks short.

59. H. J. Jones (Hobbies), **A.M.** September 23, 1902.—Primrose yellow, the outer florets with a delicate cast of pink ; flowers large, of good form, but stalks weak.

60. H. Shoesmith (Shoesmith, Turner), **A.M.** September 12, 1905.—Scarlet, narrow, twisted quills ; flowers buried in foliage.

61. Hyacinth (Stredwick).—Salmon- to mauve-pink, overlaid towards the centre with yellow ; growth vigorous but not free flowering.

62. Imperator (Baxter, 1905), **A.M.** September 11, 1900.—Crimson, broad-petalled ; flowers buried in foliage ; growth weak.

63. International (Mortimer).—Orange-scarlet, broad straight quills ; flowers on long stalks but buried in vigorous foliage.

64. J. B. Riding (Stredwick), **A.M.** September 6, 1904.—Salmon. orange shading to a yellow centre, tips yellow ; flower full-petalled and of show form, but stalks thin and weak.

65. J. C. Newbury (Seale).—Vivid crimson-scarlet, outer florets twisted ; many flowers very rough ; growth weak.

66. Jealousy (Veitch, 1905), **A.M.** September 11, 1900.—Lemon. yellow, broad-petalled ; free-flowering but flowers rather buried in foliage.

67. J. H. Jackson (Veitch, 1905), **XXX** for garden decoration. September 15, 1905.—Deep crimson, very large, broad straight quills on long stalks.

68. J. Kolodeeft (Mortimer).—Crimson-scarlet, large flower but petals few, broad, loose, twisted; stalks stiff but not free from the foliage.

69. John E. Knight (Mortimer).—Salmon, broad incurved petals, buried in dense leafage.

70. Juarezii (Jekyll, 1904), **B.C.** September 16, 1879.—The type from which the Cactus Dahlia has sprung; scarlet, flat-petalled, decorative.

71. Juliet (Hobbies).—Pink, a little white-tipped, and white at the centre, broad-petalled, stout-stalked.

72. Jupiter (Dobbie).—Very similar to ' Juliet,' *q.v.*

73. Lady Nina Balfour (Cheal, 1905).—Crimson-scarlet, stalks weak, short.

74. Lauretta (Turner).—Rose-salmon, yellowish at the centre; flowers large, petals broad, stalks good.

75. Little Albert (Shoesmith).—Salmon, overlaid towards the centre with yellow; flowers small, neat, held well above foliage, free-flowering. Plants weak. (Pom-cactus.)

76. Little Dolly (Dobbie, Shoesmith).—Bright rose-pink; flowers small, broad-petalled; growth vigorous, with but little flower. (Pom-cactus.)

77. Little Fred (Shoesmith), **A.M.** September 26, 1905.—Pale primrose-yellow, deeper towards the centre, broad petals. (Pom-cactus.)

78. Lord of the Manor (Dobbie, 1906), **A.M.** September 20, 1904.—Bright scarlet, twisted quills, weak stalked.

79. Lustre (Burrell), **XXX** for garden decoration, September 13, 1907.—Bright blood-red, full petalled, long twisted quills, on long stiff stalks holding the flowers above the foliage.

80. Maid of Honour (Baxter, 1905).—Rose-pink, rather rough twisted petals.

81. Marcellus (Turner).—Crimson-scarlet, long twisted quills; flowers buried in foliage.

82. Marjorie Caselton (Hobbies).—Soft pink, yellow at the base of petal, stalks short; flowers quite buried in vigorous leafage.

83. Market White (Hobbies).—White, broad-petalled, free-flowering, weak stalked.

84. Mars (Dobbie), **A.M.** September 10, 1901.—Crimson-scarlet; flowers large, broad-petalled on weak stalks.

85. Mavis (Baxter and Hobbies), 1905), **XXX** for garden decoration, September 15, 1905.—Buff-salmon; flowers of good form, with twisted quills, stalks stiff, but short.

86. Mercury (Dobbie).—The variety received under this name proved a semi-double crimson-and-white decorative variety. Valueless.

87–88. Meteor. There are two varieties distributed by the trade under this name — that from Turner, **XXX** for garden decoration, September 26, 1907, orange-scarlet, vigorous grower, with flowers held boldly above the foliage on long, dark, stout stalks—the flowers are very weak-centred; and that from Stredwick, **A.M.** as a show-flower, September 25, 1906, white, shaded and splashed with rose-purple, narrow twisted quills, stalks stout, but flowers buried in vigorous leafage.

89. Miss Dorothy Oliver (Dobbie).—Soft lemon-yellow, straight quilled, free-flowering, and flowers held well above foliage, but stalks weak.

90. Miss Finch (Cheal, 1905), **A.M.** September 21, 1897.—Bright crimson-purple, broad-petalled, flat flower ; free-flowering, and flowers held well above foliage, but stalks short.

91. Mr. Keith (Hobbies).—Bright crimson-scarlet, broad-petalled, free-flowering and showy, but stalks short and weak.

92. Mrs. Charles Scott (Seale).—Warm buff ; flowers large, held well above foliage, but stalks short and flowers drooping.

93. Mrs. D. B. Crane (Cheal, Hobbies, and Veitch, 1905).—White, on long stiff stalks, but not free-flowering, and flowers rather buried in vigorous erect growths.

94. Mrs. de Luca (Cheal and Veitch, 1905), **A.M.** September 10, 1901.— Yellow, shaded buff, dark stalks, free-flowering, and flowers held well above foliage, but stalks weak.

95. Mrs. E. Mawley (Veitch, 1905), **A.M.** September 24, 1901.—Yellow, full petalled, and of good form, on stout stalks, but flowers rather buried in vigorous growths.

96. Mrs. Gaskell (Turner).—Pink, creamy towards the centre ; flower large, of good form, stalks stout, not free-flowering.

97. Mrs. H. A. Needs (Veitch, 1905), **A.M.** September 24, 1901.—Rose-crimson ; flowers rather small, many only semi-double ; free-flowering, and flowers held above foliage, but stalks weak.

98. Mrs. H. L. Brousson (Turner), **A.M.** September 15, 1903.—Buff, free-flowering on stiff stalks, but flowers not held well above foliage.

99. Mrs. H. Shoesmith (Shoesmith), **A.M.** September 12, 1905.— White, rather broad, straight quills, erect stiff stalks. Growths very erect.

100. Mrs. John Barker (Mortimer, 1903), **XXX** for garden decoration, September 28, 1905.—Rosy-salmon ; flowers large on stout stalks well above the foliage ; growth weak.

101. Mrs. J. J. Crowe (Veitch, 1905), **.M.** September 12, 1899.— Lemon-yellow, narrow petals, weak centre ; flowers rather buried in foliage.

102. Mrs. J. S. Brunton (Mortimer, 1905), **XXX** for garden decoration, September 28, 1905, September 26, 1907.—Rich yellow, rather broad petals, but very long stiff stalks holding the flowers well above the foliage ; growth erect.

103. Mrs. Macmillan (Stredwick, Turner), **A.M.** September 12, 1905.— Mauve-pink, white centre ; flowers of good form, held above the foliage, but drooping.

104. Mrs. Reg. Gurney (Hobbies).—Flesh-pink, creamy towards the centre ; many flowers semi-double, flowers drooping on weak stalks.

105. Mrs. Seale (Seale).—Dark crimson, tipped with white ; flowers very large, rather flat-petalled and buried in vigorous foliage.

106. Mrs. Sonnenthal (Cheal, 1905).—Bright rose-crimson tipped with purple ; stalks stiff ; growths erect.

107. Mrs. Stevenson (Turner), **A.M.** September 26, 1905.—Lemon-yellow of good form on long stout stalks, but the flowers are not held well above the vigorous erect growth.

108. Mrs. W. Cash (Cheal, 1905).—Yellow, shaded buff ; free flowering, but flowers of poor form, drooping on short stalks.

109. Mrs. W. H. Raby (Stredwick).—Creamy-white, broad straight quills; flowers rather buried in foliage.

110. Modesty (Dobbie).—Carmine-red, tipped lightly with white, very free-flowering; flowers small, showy, held well above the foliage, but stalks weak. (Pom-cactus.)

111. Molly (Baxter), **XXX** for garden decoration, October 10, 1907.—Yellow, the outer petals a little shaded buff; broad straight quills; free-flowering, but stalks short.

112. Mont Blanc (Dobbie), **XXX** for garden decoration, September 14, 1906.—Creamy-white; broad-petalled, vigorous foliage with but little flower.

113. Morning Glow (Dobbie).—Yellow, outer petals shaded buff; form poor, plant weak.

114. Muriel (Staward).—Bright yellow; flowers of poor form, but the erect habit very fine; stalks long, stiff, well above the foliage, displaying the flowers well.

115. Nelson (Turner), **A.M.** August 29, 1905. — Bright crimson, becoming purplish; large flower, narrow twisted petals; stalks long, but weak.

116. Neptune (Dobbie).—White, edged crimson, but colour variable and form very poor, many flowers almost single.

117. Oscar (Burrell).—Reddish-salmon, narrow quill petals, very poor centre; free-flowering and flowers above the foliage, but drooping from short stalks.

118. Pearl (Turner).—Deep pink, paler at the tips and centre; stalks stiff, but flowers rather buried in vigorous foliage.

119. Pickwick (Hobbies, 1905).—Orange-scarlet, yellow at the base; petals much twisted; flowers drooping from long stalks well above the foliage.

120. Pink Pearl (Hobbies, 1905), **XXX** for garden decoration, September 14, 1906.—Bright pink, lightly tipped with white, and paler at the centre; petals broad; free-flowering, but stalks short.

121. Pink Perfection (Mortimer), **A.M.** August 29, 1905.—Mauve-pink, flowers large, but many of poor form.

122. Primrose (Hobbies, Stredwick), **A.M.** September 12, 1905. **XXX** for garden decoration, September 26, 1907.—Primrose yellow, deeper at the centre; broad straight petals; free-flowering on stout stalks showing well above the foliage.

123. Prince of Orange (Baxter, 1905).—Purplish-rose, rather rough flower, with much twisted petals.

124. Princess Mary (Hobbies), **A.M.** August 28, 1906.—Salmon, very free-flowering and flowers held well above the foliage, but stalks short and weak and flowers drooping.

125. Progenitor (Veitch, 1905), **A.M.** September 20, 1898.—Crimson-scarlet; petals broad, forked at the tips, rough-looking.

126. Queen Alexandra (Hobbies and Mortimer, 1905).—Salmon, a little shaded with orange; rather broad petals and weak stalks, free-flowering.

127. Queenie (Hobbies).—Deep rose-carmine, orange towards the centre; free-flowering, but flowers of poor form and drooping

128. Reliable (Hobbies, 1905), **XXX** for garden decoration, September 15, 1905.—Buff, pink at the tips and yellow at the centre; free-flowering and flowers large, held well above the scanty foliage, but drooping.

129. Rev. Arthur Hall (Stredwick), September 11, 1906.—Light rosy-crimson; flowers large with long twisted narrow quills; rather buried in foliage.

130. Rev. C. T. Digby (Hobbies).—Salmon-pink, very narrow, much twisted quills, well-incurved, but stalks thin and weak, and flowers buried in foliage.

131. Rosine (Veitch, 1905), **A.M.** September 11, 1900.—Carmine-rose, rather broad-petalled, and not held well above the dense foliage.

132. Shrewsbury (Baxter, 1905). — Lemon-yellow, stalks short, but holding the drooping flowers well above the foliage.

133. Silver Wings (Hobbies).—Lemon-white, of good form; quills straight; stalks rigid and long; growth erect.

134. Sir Alex. Lamb (Turner).—Carmine-crimson, the flowers held well above the foliage, but on weak stalks.

135. Sirius (Hobbies, 1905).—Buff, splashed and streaked with red, yellowish at the centre; stalks long and stiff, but flowers buried.

136. Slough Rival (Turner).—Crimson; flowers broad-petalled of poor form, but very free and loosely held well above the foliage.

137. Spotless Queen (Dobbie, Hobbies, 1903), **A.M.** September 10, 1901, **XXX** for garden decoration, September 28, 1905.—White; flowers small, with broad, straight petals; very free-flowering; stalks short and stiff.

138. Standard Bearer (Veitch, 1905), **XXX** for garden decoration, September 28, 1905.—Vivid scarlet; broad-petalled, decorative, free-flowering on good stalks well above the foliage.

139. Star (Dobbie, Hobbies, Turner). — Salmon-buff, yellow at tips and centre; quills narrow; flowers of good form; stalks long and stiff, but rather buried in foliage.

140. Stephen Walker (Baxter).—Rose-scarlet; petals white-tipped, but colour variable; free-flowering, flowers hanging loosely well above the foliage.

141. Sweet Nell (Hobbies), **A.M.** September 15, 1903.—Soft pink; free-flowering, but stalks weak and flowers of very poor form; growth erect.

142. Sybil Green (Hobbies).—White; flowers held well above the foliage, but of very poor form and on short weak stalks.

143. T. A. Havemeyer (Stredwick), **A.M.** August 15, 1905.—Old rose, overlaid towards the centre with orange; petals narrow, twisted; flowers buried in foliage.

144. The Hon. Lady Barrington (Staward). — Salmon-buff; free-flowering, and flowers held well above foliage, but of poor form and drooping.

145. The Pilot (Hobbies, Turner), **A.M.** September 12, 1905.—Salmon-orange; yellow centre; twisted petals; flowers buried in foliage.

146. Thos. Parkin (Dobbie).—Reddish-orange, full petalled, quills twisted; flowers very large, rather buried in dense foliage.

147. Thos. Wilson (Hobbies).—Salmon, flowers large with narrow twisted quills, held well above the foliage, but drooping.

148. Tinted Queen (Mortimer).—Salmon-pink, free-flowering, and flowers well above the foliage, but of poor form and with weak stalks.

149. Titus (Dobbie).—White, the central florets edged with yellow and the outer florets edged and shaded buff, but colouring inconstant; flowers rather small, buried in dense foliage.

150. Tomtit (Stredwick), **A.M.** September 12, 1905.—Pink, small, narrow twisted quills, but flowers of poor form (Pom-Cactus).

151. Uplands (Seale).—Crimson-scarlet, large rather flat flower; stalks short, weak, and flowers rather buried in foliage.

152. W. E. Dickson (Dobbie).—Rich rose-purple, decorative variety, flat-petalled.

153. West Hall Scarlet (Baxter), **XXX** for garden decoration, September 14, 1906.—Scarlet, straight quills, good stalks; growth weak.

154. W. F. Balding (Hobbies), **A.M.** September 10, 1901.—Warm buff, yellow centre; stalks short and weak.

155. White Lady (Shoesmith).—White, full petalled, straight-quilled; stalks short, weak, but flowers well above foliage; growth erect.

156. W. Hopkins (Dobbie), **A.M.** September 6, 1904.—Rich crimson, large straight petals, long stalks.

157. Williamsonii (Hobbies).—Rosy-salmon, flowers large, petals twisted, centre rough; stalks weak. The Latin termination to the name of a garden variety is discouraged by the Committee.

158. Winsome (Hobbies), **A.M.** September 23, 1902.—Cream-white, petals broad, centre weak, stalks stiff not long.

159. W. Marshall (Stredwick), **A.M.** August 15, 1905.—Buff, yellowish towards the centre; flowers large, on drooping stalks.

160. Yellow Gem (Hobbies, 1905).—Primrose-yellow, straight quills, foliage thin; stalks good.

161. Zoë (Turner), **A.M.** September 10, 1895.—Creamy-white, medium size, broad-petalled.

PÆONY-FLOWERED DAHLIAS.

Messrs. Hobbies sent the following varieties :—The flowers of all are large and showy, held well above the foliage on long stalks, but the form is poor, the large yellow disc being surrounded with two or three rows of ray-florets, generally with a number of deformed florets in addition.

162. Dr. van Gorkom.—Soft pink shading to white.

163. Duke Henry.—Glowing vermilion.

164. Germania.—Vermilion, dwarf habit, free flowering.

165. King Leopold.—Primrose yellow.

166. Nicholas II.—Pure white, free.

167. Paul Kruger.—Purplish rose, with paler margin and splashings.

168. Queen Emma.—Salmon, shaded with yellow.

169. Queen Wilhelmina.—White; only one row of ray florets.

170. Solfaterre.—Vermilion to rose, with a yellow band surrounding the disc.

TULIPS AT WISLEY, 1906-07.

THIRTEEN hundred and thirty stocks of bulbs were received in the autumn of 1905, planted in November of that year, and lifted in splendid condition in mid-July 1906. In the autumn of 1906 sixty additional stocks were received, and the whole collection was replanted in November. From mid-April to the end of May in both years the brilliant display of flower attracted considerable attention. Excluding synonyms and duplicates, the 1,890 stocks comprised 895 distinct varieties, including 87 single, 58 double, 7 parrot, 231 May-flowering and species, 65 Rembrandt, and 456 Darwin. In both years the trial was inspected from time to time by the Floral (Tulip) Committee, and several awards were made, but unfortunately in both seasons the appointed visit of the Committee to inspect the later-flowering varieties among the Darwins and May-flowering was frustrated by ill weather. The bulbs have been, however, again lifted in good condition, and will be again replanted ; and it is hoped that the Floral Committee will be able to again inspect the varieties in the spring of 1908. Bulbs were received from English, Irish, and Dutch growers, but no material differences were perceived with regard to their respective vigour and period of flowering, with the exception of the stocks from Messrs. de Graaff. These, owing to a special method of ripening or storing the bulbs, flowered about a week later than other stocks of similar varieties ; but in the second year of planting this difference practically disappeared. Various packing materials were used by the donors ; bulbs packed in buckwheat husk, or cork dust arrived in excellent condition, but a considerable number of stocks packed in sawdust arrived both soft and mildewed, owing to excess of moisture.

The following summary includes all the varieties in the trial that have been certificated or commended by the Floral and Tulip Committees :—

I. EARLY SINGLES (Nos. 1-101).

White.—Brunhilde, David Teniers, Joost van Vondel white, Pottebakker white, Snowdrift, Snowflake.

Rose.—Flamingo, Jenny, La Précieuse, Le Matelas, Pink Beauty, Princess Wilhelmina, Rosamundi, Rose luisante, Rose Queen.

Red.—Artus, Couleur Cardinal, Cramoisi Brillant, Maes, Pottebakker Verboom, Sir Thos. Lipton, Waterloo.

Orange.—Hector, Prince of Austria, Thomas Moore.

Yellow.—Boule d'Or, Canary Bird, Chrysolora, Golden Queen, Mon Trésor.

Red and Yellow.—Duc de Malakoff, Duchesse de Parma, Golden Lion, Keizerskroon, Village Boy.

Other Colours.—Epaminondas Flaked (red and white), Joost van Vondel (crimson), Kohinoor (maroon), Lac d'Asturie (crimson and white), La Reine (white and rose), La Remarquable (claret), Le Rêve (bronze-salmon), Proserpine (carmine), Queen of the Netherlands (white and pink), Stanley (carmine-purple).

II. Doubles (Nos. 102-165).

Pink-Rose.—La Grandesse, Murillo, Queen Emma, Rose d'Amour, Salvator Rosa.

Red.—Don Carlos, Le Matador, Sultan's Favourite, Vuurbaak, William III.

Red and Yellow.—Couronne d'Or, El Toreador, Orange King, Tournesol.

Rose-purple.—Lac d'Haarlem.

III. Parrots (Nos. 166-173).

None.

IV. May-flowering and Species (Nos. 174-431).

White.—Cygnet, Elegans alba, Parisian White, Royal White, Water Lily, White Swan.

Rose and Red.—Elegans, Feu Ardent, Fosteriana, Fulgens, Gesneriana spathulata, Greigi, Inglescombe Pink, Inglescombe Scarlet, Lion d'Orange, Lord Byron, Macrospeila, Maculata globosa grandiflora, Maculata major, Mauriana, Orange Beauty, Ostrowskiana, Praestans, Scarlet Emperor, Stella, Tubergeniana.

Yellow.—Bouton d'Or, Gesneriana lutea, Gesneriana lutea pallida, Ixioides, Kolpakowskiana, Mrs. Moon, Persica, Retroflexa, Strangulata maculata, The Fawn, Vitellina, Yellow Queen.

Red and Yellow.—Billietiana, Columbus, Flamed Crown, Golden Crown, Goldflake, Isabella, Sunset, Striped Beauty, Zomerschoon.

Other Colours.—Jaune d'Œuf (bronze-yellow), John Ruskin (salmonpink and yellow), Picotee (picotee-edged), Rose Royale (cream to crimson), Turenne (purplish-bronze).

V. Rembrandts (Nos. 432-487).

These are broken Darwins, and though often beautifully marked and feathered lack both the brilliance and simplicity of that race. Two varieties were commended by the Committee—Sirène, Vasco da Gama.

VI. Darwins (Nos. 488-961).

Cream, Pale Lilac.—Electra, Lantern, Margaret, Wedding Veil, White Queen.

Pink, Lilac, Rose.—Anthony Roozen, Ascanio, Buffon, Clara Butt, Fanny, Galatea, Gustave Doré, Haarlem, Landelle, L'Ingénue, Mme. Barrois, Mme. Krelage, May Queen, Mrs. Stanley, Prince of the Netherlands, Psyche, Sieraad van Flora, Suzon, The Bride, Yolande, Zephyr.

Carmine-Scarlet, Scarlet.—Calypso, Europe, G. de Cordous, Louis de la Vallière, Phaeacia, Prof. Rawenhoff.

Crimson-Scarlet, Blood-red, Carmine-Crimson.—Ariadne, Claude Gillot, Etna, Feu Brillant, Isis, Pride of Haarlem, Prof. Michael Foster, Rev. H. H. d'Ombrain, Van Poortvliet, Whistler, Wm. Pitt.

Crimson.—Auber, Donders, King Harold, Millet, Minister Roell, Mr. Farncombe Sanders, Paris, Sir Joseph Hooker.

Very Dark Crimson, Maroon.—Allard Pierson, André Doria, Cetewayo, Faust, Fra Angelico, Hecla, Henner, La Tulipe Noire, Leonardo da Vinci, Sultan, Von Jehring, Zulu.

Purple.—Bacchus, Excelsior, Franz Hals, Giant, Godet Parfait, Linnaeus, McOwan, Mme. Bosboom Toussaint, Moucheron, Oliphant (slaty), Valentin.

Blue-Lilac.—Corydon, Erguste, Fräulein Amberg, La Tristesse, Rev. H. Ewbank.

> **F.C.** = First Class Certificate.
> **A.M.** = Award of Merit.
> **XXX** = Highly commended.
> **XX** = Commended.

The average height of the blossom, the date of its opening, and the number of days it remains in flower are given.

I. Early-flowering Single Tulips.

1. Albert Cuyp (Barr).—Deep rose, shading within to white towards the base ; yellow centre ; small whitish flame outside ; average height, 12 inches ; opening April 24, and lasting 16 days in flower.

2. American Lac, *syn.* Le Rêve, *q.v.*

3. Artus (Wüstenhoff), **XX** May 2, 1906.—Dark scarlet with base of yellow, a little suffused with olive ; a good bedding variety ; 13 inches ; April 24, 19 days.

4. Belle Alliance, *syn.* Waterloo, *q.v.*

5. Boule d'Or (Barr), **XXX** May 2, 1906.—Deep yellow, segments pointed and slightly recurved ; a fine long flower of good form, misnamed Boule d'Or ; 12 inches ; April 19, 18 days.

6. Brunhilde (Barr, Hogg & Robertson, Sydenham), **A.M.** May 7, 1901.—White, richly flamed' and based with yellow ; a large globular flower, fine ; 14 inches ; May 17, 22 days. *Syn.* Unique.

7. Canary Bird (Hogg & Robertson), **XX** April 25, 1907.—Yellow ; a fine egg-shaped flower, the earliest yellow ; 12 inches ; April 15, 22 days.

8. Carlisle (Barr).—Deep red with sharply defined base of yellow and olive ; a fine cup-shaped flower, with purplish bloom outside ; 12 inches, 21 days.

9. Chanticleer (Barr, Hogg & Robertson).—Bright red-edged yellow ; flowers small, but bulbs uniform ; *syn.* de Haan ; 6 inches ; April 17, 21 days.

10. Charles V. (Sydenham).—Soft yellow, lightly shaded rose ; stems rather weak, rather similar, but inferior to Village Boy ; 11 inches ; April 24, 19 days.

11. Chrysolora (Wüstenhoff), **XXX** April 19, 1906.—Golden yellow ; flowers large, cup-shaped ; bulbs uniform ; a fine bedder ; 11 inches ; April 19, 23 days.

12. Cochineal (Barr).—Dark scarlet, with yellow centre ; 9 inches : April 8, 15 days. The earliest red, a large fine flower, but lacking substance.

13. Cottage Boy, *syn.* Village Boy, *q.v.*

14. Cottage Maid, *syn.* La Précieuse, *q.v.*

15. Couleur Cardinal (Wüstenhoff), **A.M.** May 2, 1906.—Orange-red with neat yellow base; richly covered outside with purplish bloom; 15 inches; April 25, 17 days. In foliage, form and substance of flower, strong stem, and uniformity of bulbs one of the finest early varieties.

16. Cramoisi Brillant (Barr), **XXX** May 2, 1906.—Deep scarlet with well-defined yellow base; stems rather weak; 16 inches; April 25, 21 days. *Syn.* Sparkler. There is a Parrot variety of this name. See No. 168.

17. Cramoisi Pourpre, *syn.* Stanley, *q.v.*

18. David Teniers (Hogg & Robertson), **XXX** May 9, 1900.—Creamy white, based with yellow; 15 inches; April 22, 24 days. *Syn.* Franz Hals.

19. De Haan, *syn.* Chanticleer, *q.v.*

20. De la Martin (Barr).—Purplish-crimson, broad white edge and yellow base; whitish flame outside; strong-stalked; distinct; 17 inches; April 15, 22 days.

21. Distinction (Barr).—Orange-red shading to orange at the edge, with clear yellow centre; marked bloom outside; 10 inches; April 22, 16 days.

22. Drapeau de France (Barr).—Bright reddish-purple with small yellow centre, dark filaments, purple anthers; 14 inches; April 24, 17 days.

23. Duc de Malakoff (Barr, Hogg & Robertson), **XX** May 2, 1906.—Red with narrow margin, and large base, of yellow; marked bloom outside; flowers large; 12 inches; April 25, 18 days.

24. Duchesse de Parma (Wüstenhoff), **XXX** May 2, 1900.—Bright red shading to a thin yellow edge, large yellow centre; strong conical bud, large broad-shouldered flowers of great substance; stems a little weak; 14 inches; April 24, 19 days.

25. Duc van Thol Scarlet (Wüstenhoff).—Scarlet, yellow base; flowers small, of little substance; 8 inches; April 13, 17 days.

26. Duc van Thol Violet (Wüstenhoff).—Purplish crimson, edge white, base yellow; flowers small; 6 inches; April 13, 21 days.

27. Duke of Gordon (Hogg & Robertson).—Yellow, lightly feathered. red; flowers small, stems weak; 9 inches; April 17, 18 days.

28. Eleanore (Hogg & Robertson).—Purplish crimson, shading to a light edge, yellow centre, marked bloom outside; bulbs regular; flowers of a deeper shade than Duc van Thol Violet; 14 inches; April 25, 16 days.

29. Enchantress (Sydenham).—Bright red, edge cream, base yellow, marked bloom outside; flowers goblet-shaped, very regular; 10 inches; April 24, 17 days.

30. Epaminondas Flaked (Sydenham), **XXX** April 26, 1900.—Carmine red, broadly flaked white; 8 inches; April 26, 19 days. Flowers of a brighter red than in Grandmaster of Malta and Roi Pépin.

31. Fairy Queen (Hogg & Robertson).—White, richly flamed with rose-pink, yellow centre; rather weak-stemmed; 13 inches; April 29, 17 days. See Rose à Merveille.

32. Flamingo (Barr), **XXX** May 8, 1907.—Rose, shading to pink at the edge and to creamy-white at the base, centre yellow, broad creamy flame outside ; a fine egg-shaped flower ; 13 inches ; April 24, 17 days. *Syn.* Rose Hawk.   There is also a Darwin of this name.   See No. 617.

33. Franz Hals, *syn.* David Teniers, *q.v.*

34. Golden Lion (Barr, Bath, Hogg & Robertson), **XXX** May 2, 1906. Yellow, heavily shaded and edged deep orange-red ; stems a little weak, but a very fine flower ; 14 inches ; April 24, 19 days.   *Syn.* Golden Lion of Hillegon.

35. Golden Lion of Hillegon, *syn.* Golden Lion.

36. Golden Queen (Barr, Bath, Hogg & Robertson, Sydenham), **A.M.** May 2, 1906.—Yellow ; flowers a little rough but very large and showy ; bulbs uniform ; 15 inches ; April 18, 25 days.

37. Grace Darling (Bath, Sydenham).—Orange-scarlet with yellow and olive centre, marked bloom outside ; flower rough but very large and showy, bulbs uniform ; 14 inches ; April 15, 23 days.

38. Grandmaster of Malta (Hogg & Robertson). — Creamy-white, variably flaked with crimson ; 11 inches ; April 29, 14 days.

39. Hector (Barr, Hogg & Robertson), **A.M.** May 8, 1900. Orange-red, edged and based with yellow, marked bloom outside ; 14 inches ; April 25, 18 days.   Not so good here as Duchesse de Parma.

40. Jaune Aplatie (Barr).—Lemon-yellow, lightly splashed with red ; flowers small ; 10 inches ; April 24, 14 days.

41. Jenny (Barr), **XXX** May 2, 1906.—Bright rose-carmine, shading to a centre of creamy-white and yellow ; whitish flame outside ; a bright flower of good form, well shouldered ; 11 inches ; April 24, 17 days.

42. Joost van Vondel White (Wüstenhoff), **XXX** May 2, 1900.—Rose-crimson, generally lightly flaked with white ; centre white ; broad whitish flame outside ; flowers large ; 11 inches ; April 22, 19 days.

43. Joost van Vondel White (Barr), **XXX** May 2, 1900.—Satiny-white, small yellow base, outside lightly flamed with sulphur ; a large, long flower, outer segments pointed, recurved ; quite the best white at Wisley ; 11 inches ; April 22, 15 days.

44. Keizerskroon (Wüstenhoff), **XXX** April 26, 1900.—Red, heavy edge and centre yellow ; flowers large, showy ; stalks strong, foliage bold ; 15 inches ; April 22, 20 days.

45. King of Yellows (Hogg & Robertson).—Yellow ; 14 inches ; April 23, 16 days.

46. Kohinoor (Barr, Hogg & Robertson), **XXX** May 2, 1906.—Crimson-maroon, with clear yellow base ; marked bloom outside ; bulbs uniform ; the darkest red variety ; 12 inches ; April 23, 18 days.

47. La Belle Alliance, *syn.* Waterloo, *q.v.*

48. Lac d'Asturie (Barr), **XX** May 8, 1907.—Purplish-crimson, broad white edge, based with white and yellow ; marked bloom outside ; 16 inches ; April 29, 15 days.

49. Lac Dorée (Barr).—Deep purplish-crimson, broad white edge, centre yellow ; 11 inches ; April 22, 16 days.

50. La Laitière (Barr).—White, the outside lightly shaded with the blue of London milk ; flowers small, stems rather weak ; 11 inches ; April 24, 19 days.

51. La Précieuse (Wüstenhoff), **XXX** May 2, 1900.—Bright rose-pink with large yellow centre, broadly flamed outside with white ; 11 inches ; April 24, 19 days. *Syn.* Cottage Maid.

52. La Reine (Wüstenhoff), **XXX** May 2, 1900.—White, with small yellow centre, the edges softly shaded with rose as they age ; 12 inches ; April 24, 18 days. *Syn.* Queen Victoria.

53. La Remarquable (Barr), **XXX** May 2, 1906. Claret-red, shading to pink at the edge, centre yellow, marked bloom outside ; bulbs regular, flowers large, colour unique ; 12 inches ; April 22, 19 days.

54. La Riante (Barr).—Light rose, broadly flamed outside with white, deeper rose within with large white and yellow base ; flower rather rough ; 11 inches ; April 24, 17 days.

55. Le Matelas (Hogg & Robertson), **XXX** April 26, 1900.—Rose edged pink, shading to creamy-white and yellow centre ; a large and beautiful flower, but a poor bedder from the lack of uniformity in the heights of the flower stalks ; 5 to 14 inches.

56. Leonardo da Vinci (Hogg & Robertson).—Orange-scarlet, shading to yellow at the edge, base yellow ; marked bloom outside ; flowers globular, rather rough ; 13 inches ; April 24, 19 days.

57. Le Rêve (Barr, Hogg & Robertson, Sydenham), **A.M.**, May 5, 1903.—Bronze-salmon ; 16 inches ; April 29, 24 days. Flower of good form, large, shouldered ; bulbs regular, stalks strong. One of the best. *Syn.* American Lac, Hobbema.

58. L'Immaculée (Wüstenhoff).—Creamy-white with yellow base ; a rather small, indifferent flower ; 9 inches ; April 22, 16 days.

59. Lord Derby (Barr).—White, small yellow base ; flower rather coarse ; 10 inches ; April 17, 20 days.

60. Maes (Hogg & Robertson), **XXX** April 26, 1900.—Dark scarlet with yellow and olive centre ; flower large but rather rough ; 10 inches ; April 13, 20 days.

61. Mr. Cleveland (Barr).—Creamy-yellow, suffused towards the edges with pink, pale-bluish flame outside ; the rose shade in the flower intensifies with age. Flowers small ; 12 inches ; May 4, 14 days.

62. Mon Trésor (Hogg & Robertson, Wüstenhoff), **XXX** April 26, 1900.—Yellow ; flower showy but rather rough ; 11 inches ; April 17, 20 days.

63. Moucheron (Hogg & Robertson).—Deep red with small, well-defined yellow base, marked bloom outside ; 13 inches ; April 22, 20 days. There is a Darwin of this name.

64. Pink Beauty (Barr, Bath, Hogg & Robertson, Wesstein), **A.M.** May 8, 1900.—Rich rose, with large white centre with yellow base, well-defined white flame outside ; flowers very large, of good form and great substance ; 14 inches ; May 2, 17 days.

65. Pottebakker Verboom (Scarlet) (Wüstenhoff), **XXX** May 2, 1906.—Deep scarlet, large yellow base ; flowers large, fine ; 12 inches ; April 23, 18 days.

66. Pottebakker White (Wüstenhoff), **XXX** April 26, 1900.—White, small yellow base ; large globular flower ; the second best, if not the best, white ; 12 inches ; April 17, 20 days.

67. Potter (Barr). — Deep rose-carmine to purplish-crimson, neat

yellow base, marked bloom outside; flowers of much substance, stalks strong, bulbs uniform ; 14 inches ; April 25, 17 days.

68. President Lincoln (Barr).—Purplish-lilac with creamy-white and yellow centre ; 11 inches ; April 24, 19 days.

69. Primrose Queen (Hogg & Robertson). — Lemon-yellow, paler without ; a few spots and light shades of rose appear with age ; 11 inches April 22, 15 days.

70. Prince de Ligny (Hogg & Robertson).—Yellow ; the richest yellow variety, with long pointed segments ; 14 inches ; April 22, 16 days.

71. Prince of Austria (Hogg & Robertson, Wüstenhoff), **XXX** May 2, 1906.—Orange-scarlet, small yellow base, marked bloom outside; 14 inches ; April 25, 19 days.

72. Princess Ida (Hogg & Robertson).—White ; flamed within and without with yellow ; segments pointed, narrow ; bulbs flowered irregularly ; much inferior to Brunhilde ; 11 inches ; April 22, 17 days.

73. Princess Wilhelmina (Bath), **XXX** April 19, 1906.—Bright rose based with yellow, with broad whitish flame outside; segments pointed, recurved ; very similar to Rose Queen, but of a slightly deeper shade of rose ; 14 inches ; April 24, 17 days. *Syn.* Queen of Pinks.

74. Proserpine (Wüstenhoff), **XXX** April 26, 1900.—Rose-carmine, centre pale-yellow marked with olive, filaments black ; flowers well shouldered, egg-shaped ; bulbs uniform, stems rather weak ; 16 inches ; April 24, 22 days.

75. Queen of Pinks, *syn.* Princess Wilhelmina, *q.v.*

76. Queen of the Netherlands (Barr), **A.M.** May 9, 1900.—White, based yellow, striped and suffused with pink, the pink intensifying with age ; bulbs uniform, flowers globular of fine form ; 12 inches ; April 23, 20 days.

77. Queen Victoria, *syn.* La Reine, *q.v.*

78. Rachel Ruysch (Wüstenhoff).—Pale rose, shading to white, large cream and yellow centre; outer segments pointed, recurved ; 12 inches ; April 23, 17 days.

79. Roi Pépin (Hogg and Robertson).—Creamy-white, variably flaked with crimson ; almost identical with Grandmaster of Malta ; 9 inches ; April 29, 13 days.

80. Rosamundi (Wüstenhoff), **XXX** May 9, 1900.—Rose, broadly flamed without with white ; white and yellow centre ; 13 inches ; April 29, 17 days. *Syn.* Rosamundi Hyychman.

81. Rose à Merveille (Barr). — Practically identical with Fairy Queen, *q.v.*

82. Rose aplatie (Hogg & Robertson).—Cream, variably splashed and shaded with pink, colour intensifying with age ; flowers small ; 13 inches ; April 24, 14 days.

83. Rose gris-de-lin (Wüstenhoff).—Pale rose shading to white, pale-yellow centre, broad white flame outside ; 10 inches ; April 23, 17 days.

84. Rose Hawk, *syn.* Flamingo, *q.v.*

85. Rose luisante (Hogg & Robertson, Wüstenhoff), **XX** May 11, 1906.—Rose, paling towards the edge, a little splashed with white, creamy-yellow centre and flame outside ; 15 inches ; May 4, 16 days.

86. Rose Queen (Barr), **XXX** May 2, 1906.—Bright rose, based with

yellow, flamed outside with white; segments pointed, recurved; stems rather weak; 14 inches; April 24, 17 days.

87. Rose Superbe, *syn.* Stanley, *q.v.*

88. Sir Thomas Lipton (Barr, Sydenham), **A.M.** May 3, 1904.—Dark scarlet with yellow and olive centre, bloom outside; a fine bedder; flowers large, uniform in height and flowering period; 13 inches; April 22, 22 days.

89. Snowdrift (Barr, Hogg & Robertson), **XX** May 2, 1906.—White with small pale-yellow centre; flowers of good form, well shouldered; outer segments pointed, recurving; foliage very grey; bulbs uniform; 10 inches; April 23, 18 days. *Syn.* White Bird.

90. Snowflake (Hogg & Robertson), **XX** May 2, 1906.—White, small yellow centre and faint purplish tinge without; fine conical bud and egg-shaped flower; 12 inches; April 24, 19 days.

91. Sparkler, *syn.* Cramoisi Brillant, *q.v.*

92. Stanley (Barr, Hogg & Robertson), **XX** May 8, 1907. Light carmine-purple with cream-yellow centre; some flowers a little splashed with red, foliage broad, stems crooked; 14 inches; April 26, 18 days. *Syn.* Rose superbe, Cramoisi Pourpre.

93. Thomas Moore (Hogg & Robertson, Wüstenhoff), **XXX** May 2, 1900.—Light orange-red shading to yellow edge, centre yellow bordered with olive, marked bloom outside; bulbs uniform; flowers good, but stems weak and brittle; 16 inches; April 24, 19 days.

94. Unique, *syn.* Brunhilde, *q.v.*

95. Van Berghem (Hogg & Robertson).—Bright rose with light-yellow centre; stems rather weak; 11 inches; April 23, 22 days. *Syn.* Van Berchem, John Bright.

96. Village Boy (Barr, Bath), **XXX** May 2, 1906.—Yellow, heavily shaded and edged reddish-orange; 9 inches; April 22, 17 days. *Syn.* Cottage Boy.

97. Vuurvlam (Barr).—Deep rose-red well-defined yellow centre; 13 inches; May 4, 14 days. Bulbs uniform.

98. Waterloo (Wüstenhoff), **XXX** May 2, 1900.—Dark scarlet, with clear circular yellow base; stems rather weak. Outside very similar in colour to Sir Thomas Lipton, but a shade brighter within; 12 inches; April 23, 20 days. *Syn.* Belle Alliance, but there is a double-flowered variety of this name.

99. White Bird, *syn.* Snowdrift, *q.v.*

100. White Hawk (Barr).—Cream-white, small yellow base, anthers tipped purple; 13 inches; April 23, 16 days. *Syn.* White Falcon.

101. Yellow Prince (Wüstenhoff).—Soft yellow; 9 inches; April 22, 19 days. The flowers develop slight red splashings with age.

II. DOUBLE-FLOWERED TULIPS.

102. Agnes (Barr).—Bright scarlet; 6 inches; April 29, 15 days.

103. Arabella (Barr).—Rose-carmine without, scarlet with yellow base within; scarcely fuller than a single; 11 inches; April 22, 18 days.

104. Belle Alliance (Hogg & Robertson).—White, much flaked with lilac and purple; flowers failed to open properly; 17 inches; May 10, 10 days. *Syn.* Overwinnaar.

105. Blanche hâtive (Hogg & Robertson).—Creamy-white; flowers semi-double, rough; 12 inches; April 22, 17 days.

106. Bleu Céleste (Hogg & Robertson).—Lilac-purple, a little flaked with white; flowers failed to open; 11 inches; May 9, 7 days.

107. Blue Flag (Barr).—Purplish-lilac; flowers hardly opened; 17 inches; May 6, 14 days.

108. Bride of Lammermoor (Barr).—White, lightly marked and flushed with pink; bulbs uniform; 12 inches; May 1, 12 days.

109. Brimstone, *syn.* Safrano, *q.v.*

110. Carmen Sylva (Barr).—Rose-pink; flowers rather small, but very neat; 12 inches; May 1, 16 days.

111. Clothilde (Hogg & Robertson).—Carmine-red; flowers rather thin, inferior to Gladstone; 10 inches; April 24, 19 days. A variety from Messrs. Barr & Sons received under this name proved to be Sultan's Favourite, *q.v.*

112. Count of Leicester, *syn.* Orange King, *q.v.*

113. Couronne de Cerise (Barr).—Rosy-crimson; flowers semi-double only; 12 inches; April 24, 20 days.

114. Couronne des Roses (Hogg & Robertson).—The variety catalogued by nurserymen under this name is said to be " rich pure rose," but the variety received for trial in the garden proved identical with Princess Beatrice, *q.v.*

115. Couronne d'Or (Barr, Hogg & Robertson, Wüstenhoff), **XXX** May 2, 1906.—Yellow, lightly flushed orange-red; 13 inches; April 17, 20 days.

116. Couronne Impériale (Hogg & Robertson).—White, feathered with red and purple; flowers variable, stems rather weak; 18 inches; May 7, 13 days.

117. Don Carlos (Hogg & Robertson), **XXX** May 2, 1906.—Dark scarlet; flowers large, very full; bulbs uniform; 12 inches; April 23, 20 days.

118. Duc van Thol Double (Wüstenhoff).—Red and yellow; flowers small, semi-double only; 9 inches ; April 17, 17 days.

119. Duke of York (Hogg & Robertson).—Red, purplish towards the base and broadly edged with white; flowers large; 15 inches; April 26, 16 days.

120. Eastern Queen (Hogg & Robertson).—Red, broadly flaked with white; bulbs uniform, a double Grandmaster of Malta; 10 inches; April 26, 18 days.

121. El Toreador (Barr), **A.M.** May 9, 1900.—Bright red, broadly edged with orange; flowers large, very full; bulbs uniform; stems a little weak; 11 inches; April 19, 22 days.

122. Epaulette d'Argent (Hogg & Robertson).—The variety received under this name was identical with Don Carlos.

123. Fanny (Barr).—Soft pink, splashed with rose; 10 inches; April 22, 16 days. Flowers semi-double only.

124. Gladstone (Barr, Hogg & Robertson).—Carmine-red; 10 inches; April 22, 21 days. Flowers full, bulbs very uniform.

125. Henry Witte (Barr).—Bright red, shading to orange edge, yellow centre; flowers large, stems rather weak; 13 inches; April 25, 15 days. Similar to El Toreador, but later less full and more yellow.

126. La Candeur (Wüstenhoff).—White, lightly tinged with pink; flowers hardly opened; 9 inches; April 25, 18 days. There is a Darwin of this name.

127. Lac d'Haarlem (Barr), **XXX** May 2, 1906.—Rose-purple; flowers large, full; 11 inches, April 22, 19 days.

128. La Coquette (Barr).—Yellow, flushed with orange-red; flowers rough; 9 inches; April 22, 19 days.

129. Lady Palmerston (Hogg & Robertson).—Creamy-pink, flushed with bright rose; darker in colour than Parmesiano, but lighter than La Grandesse; 11 inches; April 22, 19 days.

130. La Grandesse (Hogg & Robertson), **XXX** May 2, 1906.—Pink, flushed with bright rose; 9 inches; April 24, 18 days.

131. La Parfaite (Barr).—Red, broadly edged pale yellow; 9 inches; April 22, 16 days.

132. L'Argentine (Barr).—Red, splashed and broadly edged with white; bulbs not uniform; 15 inches; April 26, 16 days. Very similar to Duke of York, but the white more splashed.

133. La Vertu (Hogg & Robertson).—Cream, shaded lightly with rose; 11 inches; April 25, 23 days.

134. Le Matador (Barr, Hogg & Robertson), **XXX** May 2, 1906.—Dark scarlet, yellow base; bulbs uniform; 14 inches; April 25, 18 days.

135. Lucretia (Barr, Hogg & Robertson).—Bright rose, paler at the edge, aging to purplish-rose; 10 inches; April 24, 21 days.

136. Mariage de ma Fille (Barr, Hogg & Robertson).—White, much feathered with bright red and purple, blue base; 18 inches; May 7, 9 days.

137. Minnie Hawk (Barr).—Rose; the darkest of the roses, some flowers flaked with pink; 7 inches; April 22, 19 days.

138. Murillo (Wüstenhoff), **XXX** May 2, 1906.—Cream, suffused with soft rose; flowers large; 10 inches; April 24, 20 days.

139. Murillo Yellow, *syn.* Safrano, *q.v.*

140. Orange Brilliant (Barr).—Scarlet shading to orange edge, yellow base; poor doer; 14 inches; May 10, 10 days.

141. Orange King (Barr, Hogg & Robertson), **A.M.** May 19, 1903.—Sulphur-yellow lightly suffused with orange-red; bulbs often two-flowered; flowers neat; *syn.* Count of Leicester; 12 inches; April 29, 17 days.

142. Overwinnaar, *syn.* Belle Alliance, *q.v.*

143. Paeony Gold (Hogg & Robertson).—Dark red; flowers hardly opened; 11 inches; May 8, 12 days.

144. Parmesiano (Barr, Hogg & Robertson).—Rose-pink shaded rose; 8 inches; April 24, 18 days; *syn.* Rose aimable.

145. Prince of Wales (Barr, Hogg & Robertson).—Carmine-crimson, white centre; bulbs uniform; 12 inches; 20 days.

146. Princess Beatrice (Barr, Hogg & Robertson).—White, lightly shaded with rose; stems weak; 12 inches; April 24, 16 days.

147. Queen Emma (Barr), **XXX** May 2, 1906.—Very bright rose-red; 10 inches; April 24, 15 days.

148. Queen of the Whites (Barr).—Creamy-white with yellow base, suffusing with pink as flowers age; flowers small but neat, bulbs uniform; 10 inches; April 23, 14 days.

149. Radamanth (Barr).—Bronze-yellow with reddish tint; flowers small and neat; 15 inches; May 6, 10 days.

150. Raphael (Hogg & Robertson).—The variety received under this name proved identical with La Grandesse, *q.v.*

151. Regina rubrorum (Barr).—Crimson flaked white; practically synonymous with Eastern Queen; 10 inches; April 26, 17 days.

152. Rex rubrorum (Wüstenhoff).—Dark scarlet; bulbs uniform, flowers full; 11 inches; April 25, 18 days.

153. Rose aimable, *syn.* Parmesiano, *q.v.*

154. Rosea perfecta (Barr).—Soft pink striped dark rose and flamed outside with cream; 10 inches; April 24, 16 days. Stems rather weak.

155. Rose d'Amour (Barr, Hogg & Robertson), **XXX** May 2, 1906.— Soft pinkish-rose; flowers small, neat; rather poor doer; 8 inches; April 24, 17 days.

156. Safrano (Barr, Hogg & Robertson).—Soft yellow, gradually suffusing with salmon-pink with age; bulbs uniform, colour distinct, *syn.* Brimstone, Murillo yellow; 11 inches; April 22, 17 days.

157. Salvator Rosa (Salfator Rose) (Hogg & Robertson, Wüstenhoff), **XXX** May 2, 1906.—Bright rose, paler at the edge, later on purplish-rose; bulbs uniform; 13 inches; April 22, 20 days.

158. Sultan's Favourite (Barr), **XX** May 2, 1906.—Dark scarlet; 9 inches; April 25, 16 days. This variety was received as Clothilde, from which it is quite distinct.

159. Tournesol (Wüstenhoff), **XXX** May 2, 1900.—Red, broadly edged, with yellow base; flowers large, full; 10 inches; April 17, 24 days. Received as Tournesol Red and Yellow.

160. Turban Violet (Hogg & Robertson).—Rose-purple, lightly splashed with scarlet and yellow; very similar but rather inferior to Lac d'Haarlem; 11 inches; April 23, 17 days.

161. Violet Suprême (Barr).—Rose-purple; 8 inches; April 24, 19 days. A darker shade than Lac d'Haarlem. Flowers hardly opened.

162. Virgilius (Barr).—Rose shading to pink edge, yellow base; flowers almost single; 10 inches; April 24, 17 days.

163. Vuurbaak (Barr), **XXX** May 9, 1900.—Orange-scarlet; bulbs uniform; 11 inches; April 23, 23 days.

164. William III. (Barr), **A.M.** May 7, 1901.—Fiery red, yellow base flowers large, bulbs uniform; 13 inches; April 25, 18 days.

165. Yellow Rose (Hogg & Robertson).—Bright yellow; stems very weak; 15 inches; May 8, 10 days.

III. Parrot Tulips.

The Parrot or Dragon varieties of Tulips are characterised by their large flowers, with much torn and richly variegated petals. All were weak-stemmed, averaged 16 inches in height, came into flower on May 7, and lasted 13 days.

166. Admiral van Constantinople (Hogg & Robertson).—Orange-red with brownish base ringed with yellow. .

167. Café Brun (Hogg & Robertson).—The bulbs received under this name bore flowers varying from yellow to red, with variable splashings of red.

168. Cramoisi Brillant (Hogg & Robertson).—Crimson, with small brown base ringed yellow. The best.

169. Lutea major (Hogg & Robertson).—Yellow, lightly and variably spotted and splashed with green and red.

170. Mark Graaff (Hogg & Robertson).—Yellow; the inside lightly, the outside deeply shaded with red.

171. Monstre Rouge (Hogg & Robertson).—The variety received under this name proved identical with Cramoisi Brillant.

172. Perfecta (Hogg & Robertson).—Yellow, heavily splashed with red, sometimes also with green.

173. Rubra major (Hogg & Robertson).—Scarlet, with base of yellow and brown.

IV. May-flowering Tulips, including Species, and Cottage and Old-fashioned Border Varieties.

The names of species are printed in italics.

174. Aard Globe (de Graaff).—Creamy-yellow, almost entirely covered with a flaming of rosy-red and light purple; a border bizarre; flowers variable in colour, large; stems rather weak; 22 inches; May 7, 12 days. This name, Anglicised, was attached to a different variety received from Hogg & Robertson; see No. 238. Practically identical with Alexander, *q.v.*

175. *acuminata* (de Graaff).—Yellow edged and much suffused red; petals very long (5 inches), narrow, and pointed, spreading; 17 inches, but very variable; May 1, 11 days. Syn. *cornuta.*

176. Albiflora (de Graaff).—Soft lemon-yellow, becoming creamy-white; small yellow eye; outer petals pointed, recurved; 16 inches; May 4, 12 days.

177. Alexander (Hogg & Robertson).—Primrose-yellow ground, much feathered with bright red and light purple; flowers large, identical with Aard Globe; 23 inches; May 7, 12 days.

178. Annie (Barr).—Rich yellow; 19 inches; May 11, 18 days. Flowers cup-shaped.

179. Apricot (de Graaff, Hogg & Robertson).—Reddish-bronze, yellow and olive base; 26 inches; May 9, 15 days. Flowers cup-shaped, stems much branched, bearing several flowers; foliage broad, light green. Apparently synonymous with Perfection, *q.v.*

180. Archimedes (Hogg & Robertson).—Creamy-white, deeply feathered crimson and purple, light olive base; 16 inches; May 10, 14 days. (Border Bybloemen.)

181. *armena* (Hogg & Robertson).—Bright red, base dark brown, ringed thinly with yellow; 9 inches; May 8, 12 days. Received as *concinna.*

182. Aurora (de Graaff).—Bright yellow, suffused within with a reddish band and variably edged with bright red; 21 inches; May 9, 14 days. Apparently a selection from Billietiana.

183. Aximensis (*a.*) (de Graaff).—Rose-red, flamed outside with white and centred with olive blotches on yellow. (*b.*) (Hogg & Robertson).—Rich rose-red with deep violet eye. 23 inches; May 8, 14 days.

184. Bandmaster (Hartland).—Rich yellow edged and lightly spotted with red, the red running as flower ages ; base, blotched olive ; 18 inches ; May 13, 16 days. Intermediate between Picta octaroon and Picta aurea.

185. Beauty of America (Hogg & Robertson).—Soft lemon-yellow, turning white, small yellow base; pointed, recurved petals ; 15 inches, 13 days. *Syn.* Gilt Crown.

186. *Billietiana* (de Graaff, Hogg & Robertson), **XXX** May 24, 1900.—Yellow, banded within and edged without with red ; pointed, recurved outer petals ; 20 inches ; May 9, 16 days.

187. *Billietiana* l'Eblouissante. See L'Eblouissante.

188. *Billietiana nana* (Hogg & Robertson).—Yellow, edged and shaded with rose, clear yellow centre ; 15 inches, variable ; May 14, 17 days.

189. *Billietiana* Sunset, syn. Sunset, *q.v.*

190. Bishop's Mitre (Hartland).—Yellow, slightly spotted and tipped rose, the base shaded with olive ; 16 inches ; May 14, 16 days. Very similar to *Billietiana.*

191. Bonfire (Hogg & Robertson).—Bright orange-red, with light-brown markings on a yellow base ; uniform and good ; 22 inches ; May 6, 20 days.

192. Bouquet Rigout (Hogg & Robertson).—Rose-purple, heavily marked with crimson, shaded with bronze at the edge ; yellow centre ; 21 inches ; May 13, 13 days.

193. Bouton d'Or (de Graaff, Hogg & Robertson), **XXX** May 16, 1900.—Very fine rich yellow, dark-purple anthers ; goblet-shape ; 16 inches ; May 6, 17 days.

194. Bridesmaid (Hogg & Robertson).—Creamy-white, heavily spotted and flamed with rose ; 18 inches ; May 13, 12 days.

195. Brilliant (Hogg & Robertson).—Pale yellow edged and lightly feathered with bright rose-red ; 14 inches ; May 10, 13 days. Border bizarre. Not synonymous with *maculata* Brilliant, No. 327.

196. Bronze King (Barr, de Graaff, Hogg & Robertson).—Reddish-bronze, shading to a bronze edge, reddish flame outside ; 22 inches ; May 6, 16 days.

197. Bronze Prince (Hartland).—Claret, shading to bronze edge, yellow and olive base ; 17 inches ; May 11, 18 days. Received as Bronze Queen, but now renamed.

198. Bronze Queen (Barr, de Graaff).—Soft bronze, paler towards the edge, with purplish flame outside, yellow base ; flowers large ; 28 inches ; May 6, 18 days.

199. Brunette (Wallace).—Reddish-maroon, small yellowish base ; 23 inches ; May 7, 17 days.

200. Buenaventura (Barr, de Graaff, Hogg & Robertson).—Yellow, richly flaked bright red, many flowers suffused with rose ; pointed, recurved outer petals ; 11 inches ; May 6, 14 days.

201. Caledonia (Barr, de Graaff, Hogg & Robertson).—Orange-scarlet, with olive blotches on the yellow base ; 16 inches ; May 19, 20 days.

202. Calypso. See 548 (Darwin).

203. Canary Cup (Barr).—The variety received under this name proved to be Carinata rubra, *q.v.*

204. Carinata rubra (de Graaff).—Red, broadly flamed with green and with large yellowish-green base ; 18 inches ; May 13, 17 days.

205. Carinata violacea (de Graaff).—Very similar to but greener than the last.

206. Carnation (Tubergen).—Creamy-white, with thin rose edge ; very similar to Parisian White ; the rose colour develops earlier in carnation, but in both varieties intensifies and runs, with age ; 16 inches ; May 9, 16 days.

207. Cassandra (Barr).—Carmine-rose with creamy-buff markings on white base ; 19 inches ; May 6, 12 days.

208. Catafalque (Hogg & Robertson).—Bronze-maroon, clear yellow base ; 25 inches ; May 10, 20 days. (Breeder.)

209. Chameleon (Hogg & Robertson).—Light bronzy-yellow, shaded and splashed with lilac and maroon ; base small, yellow, marked with bluish-green ; 19 inches ; May 7, 16 days.

210. Cherbourg (Hogg & Robertson).—Rich yellow, feathered with maroon ; 17 inches ; May 3, 17 days.

211. Chestnut (de Graaff).—Dark crimson-maroon, with dark olive and yellow centre ; 22 inches ; May 7, 23 days. (Breeder.)

212. Cleopatra (Hogg & Robertson).—Crimson-scarlet, with olive-brown and yellow base ; 15 inches ; May 6, 16 days. A large *maculata globosa grandiflora*.

213. Clio (Hogg & Robertson).—Very similar to Bronze Queen, but with an olive band to the yellow base ; 23 inches ; May 9, 14 days. There is a Rembrandt of this name, No. 440.

214. Cloth of Gold (Hartland).—Yellow, a little suffused and edged with rose ; flowers variable ; similar to Bishop's Mitre ; 15 inches ; May 13, 18 days.

215. *Clusiana* (Hogg & Robertson).—White, with small deep crimson base and filaments, outside broadly flamed rose-red ; flowers and bulbs small, leaves linear ; 9 inches ; April 29, 15 days. A very pretty species.

216. Columbus (de Graaff, Hogg & Robertson), **XXX** May 24, 1900.—Bright yellow, richly flaked deep red ; very showy and uniform ; outer petals pointed and recurved ; 17 inches ; May 10, 16 days.

217. *concinna* (Hogg & Robertson).—The variety received under this name proved to be *armena*, q.v.

218. Coquette de Belleville (Barr, Hogg & Robertson).—Rose-red edged with white ; centre large, white banded with purple, marked bloom outside ; stems slight, rather weak ; 15 inches ; April 25, 17 days.

219. Coquette d'Orange, *syn.* Orange Coquette, *q.v.*

220. *cornuta*, syn. *acuminata*.

221. Corona lutea (Barr, de Graaff, Hogg & Robertson).—Lemon-yellow, lightly splashed with rose ; petals pointed ; 19 inches ; May 6, 14 days.

222. Corona tardiva (Hogg & Robertson).—Soft primrose-yellow with buff base ; outer petals pointed ; 16 inches ; May 13, 18 days.

223. Corydon (Hogg & Robertson).—Yellow, shaded with bronze ; 22 inches ; May 4, 17 days. This variety was received as a Darwin, see No. 569.

224. Cottager (de Graaff).—Carmine-purple, with yellow base blotched with olive ; 15 inches ; May 10, 12 days.

225. Crimson Flame (Barr).—Purplish rose, splashed rose-red, with white base ; 18 inches ; May 13, 14 days.

226. Crimson Globe (Hartland).—Crimson-scarlet, with neat dark-brown base bordered with yellow ; leaves much curled ; 12 inches ; May 9, 15 days.

227. Cyclops (de Graaff).—Orange-scarlet, with clear yellow base ; 21 inches ; May 10, 20 days.

228. Cygnet (de Graaff), **A.M.** May 17, 1904.—White ; flowers small ; 21 inches ; May 11, 20 days.

229. Dainty Maid. See No. 445 (Rembrandt).

230. Dame Blanche, *syn. Didieri alba*, q.v.

231. Dame Elégante (de Graaff, Hogg & Robertson).—Cream, lightly splashed with red, bright yellow base ; flowers goblet-shaped ; 16 inches ; May 3, 18 days.

232. *Didieri* (de Graaff, Hogg & Robertson).—Glowing rose-red, with dark blue on soft yellow base ; petals pointed, recurved ; 19 inches ; May 7, 14 days.

233. *Didieri alba* (de Graaff, Hogg & Robertson).—Creamy-white, with small dull cream base ; flowers small ; outer petals pointed ; 17 inches ; May 10, 15 days.

234. *Didieri lutescens* (de Graaff, Hogg & Robertson).—Lemon-yellow, lightly dotted with red, dark olive-green centre ; flowers small ; outer petals pointed, recurved ; 17 inches ; May 6, 12 days.

235. Don Pedro (Barr, de Graaff, Hogg & Robertson).—Maroon, with darker base ; flowers large, cup-shaped ; bulbs uniform ; 20 inches ; May 6, 16 days. (Breeder.)

236. Doris (Wallace).—Rosy-lilac, shading to a bronzy-salmon edge, base pale yellow, blotched with dark olive ; stems purplish ; 17 inches, May 10, 14 days.

237. Dutch Lion (Hogg & Robertson).—Maroon, striped and splashed with yellow and crimson ; 21 inches ; May 11, 18 days.

238. Earthglobe (Hogg & Robertson).—Purple, feathered with maroon and crimson, and outside with white, yellow base ; 27 inches ; May 10, 15 days. Distinct from Aard Globe, No. 174.

239. *elegans* (de Graaff, Hogg & Robertson), **XXX** May 2, 1906.—Bright crimson, based with yellow ; petals equal, narrow, pointed, recurved ; 16 inches ; April 24, 20 days.

240. *elegans alba* (Barr, de Graaff, Hogg & Robertson), **A.M.** May 14, 1895.—Creamy-white, with fawn base, and a very thin edging of rose ; the stock from de Graaff was very fine ; 20 inches ; May 3, 18 days.

241. *elegans lutea* (de Graaff, Hogg & Robertson).—Rich yellow ; pointed recurved petals ; 18 inches ; May 13, 17 days.

242. *elegans maxima lutea*, *syn.* Golden Spire, *q.v.*

243. *elegans variegata* (Barr, de Graaff).—Bright crimson, variably striped with pale yellow ; 13 inches ; April 24, 20 days.

244. Emerald Gem (Hartland).—Orange, with olive blotches on a small yellow centre, reddish orange without ; very bright ; 22 inches ; May 13, 17 days.

245. Emin Pasha (Hogg & Robertson).—Rosy-crimson, with base of yellow slightly edged with purple ; 15 inches ; April 29, 23 days.

246. Empress of China (Barr).—Deep bronzy-yellow, bronzy-olive base, outside slightly flamed purple ; 23 inches ; May 9, 16 days.

247. Eurasian (Wallace). — Pale bronzy-yellow, olive and bluish blotches at base, outside flamed bluish- to rosy-lilac ; 19 inches ; May 10, 13 days.

248. Eyebright (Hartland).—Rose, shaded buff, centre of yellow and olive ; 16 inches ; May 13, 13 days. Some flowers splashed with yellow. Very near to Firefly.

249. Faerie Queen, *syn.* Fairy Queen, *q.v.*

· 250. Fairy (Tubergen). — Dark orange-red, with large olive-brown base ; bulbs uniform ; 22 inches ; May 8, 22 days.

251. Fairy Queen (Barr, de Graaff, Hogg & Robertson).—Bronzy-yellow, broadly flamed outside with heliotrope, brownish-olive base ; 21 inches ; May 9, 17 days.

252. Fashion (Bath).—Creamy-white, with narrow margin and light spottings of crimson, the whole flower gradually becoming suffused with rose ; 25 inches ; May 10, 14 days. See Rose Royale, No. 385.

253. Feu Ardent (Hogg & Robertson), **A.M.** May 8, 1907.—Dark currant-red, with yellow and olive base, marked bloom outside ; bulbs uniform, stems rather weak ; 21 inches ; April 26, 19 days. (Breeder.)

254. Fire Dragon (Barr).—The variety received under this name was indistinguishable from Goldflake, *q.v.*

255. Firefly (Barr).—Rosy-red, flamed reddish-buff, base olive and yellow ; 17 inches ; May 11, 14 days.

256. Flame (Wallace).—Bright orange-red, centre of yellow and olive ; 18 inches ; May 8, 14 days.

257. Flamed Crown (Hogg & Robertson), **XXX** May 11, 1906.—Bright red, broadly and irregularly marked with orange, dark olive-green base, marked bloom outside ; outer segments pointed, reflexed, larger than in Buenaventura ; 14 inches ; May 6, 14 days.

258. Flava (de Graaff, Hogg & Robertson).—Soft greenish lemon-yellow ; inner segments ovate, outer lanceolate, recurved ; stems stout ; 26 inches ; May 13, 16 days.

259. Flora (Hogg & Robertson).—The variety received under this name was identical with Flava.

260. *Fosteriana* (Tubergen), **F.C.** April 19, 1906.—Glowing scarlet, with well-defined clear yellow centre ; flowers 8 inches across when expanded ; leaves very broad, in one case 9 × 7 inches, and downy, which renders them rather liable to injury from wet. A magnificent tulip and a good doer, but unsuitable for "bedding," from the irregularity in height and period of flowering. There is a variety in commerce with brown markings on the yellow base ; 6–10 inches ; mid-April, 18 days.

261. *fulgens* (de Graaff), **XXX** May 24, 1900.—Rosy-crimson, yellow base ; segments rather narrow, pointed ; 27 inches ; May 6, 13 days.

262. Garibaldi (Hogg & Robertson).—Light purplish-bronze, broadly flamed outside with light purple ; similar to but paler than Bronze Queen ; 26 inches ; May 8, 21 days.

263. General Vetter (de Graaff, Hogg & Robertson).—Soft yellow,

spotted and splashed with rose-red; 21 inches; May 15, 15 days. Practically identical with Irish Beauty.

264. *Gesneriana aurantiaca* (Barr, Hogg & Robertson, de Graaff).—Orange-scarlet, the yellow base shaded with olive; flowers large; 19 inches; May 13, 16 days.

265. *Gesneriana aurantiaca maculata* (Hogg & Robertson).—The variety received under this name was identical with Orange Globe, *q.v.*

266. *Gesneriana* Bouton d'Or (Hogg & Robertson). See Bouton d'Or.

267. *Gesneriana* Bridesmaid (Hogg & Robertson). See Bridesmaid.

268. *Gesneriana ixioides* (de Graaff). See Ixioides.

269. *Gesneriana* Leghorn Bonnet (Hogg & Robertson). See Leghorn Bonnet.

270. *Gesneriana lutea* (Barr, de Graaff, Hogg & Robertson, Hartland), **A.M.** May 15, 1906.—Rich self-yellow; large, open flower, with pointed recurved segments; 15 inches; May 11, 14 days..

271. *Gesneriana lutea pallida* (Barr, de Graaff, Giles, Hartland, Hogg & Robertson, Wallace), **F.C.** May 6, 1902.—Rich self-yellow, large; very similar to the last; 20 inches; May 6, 19 days. *Syn.* Mrs. Keightley. The variety forwarded under this name by Mr. Giles was very pale lemon-yellow.

272. *Gesneriana* Rosalind. See Rosalind.

273. *Gesneriana rosea* (Hogg & Robertson).—Bright rose, with small, neat black base; 14 inches; May 10, 12 days.

274. *Gesneriana rosea* Stella. See Stella.

275. *Gesneriana spathulata* (Barr, de Graaff, Hogg & Robertson), **XXX** May 24, 1900.—Crimson-scarlet, with very rich violet-blue base; 23 inches; May 9, 11 days.

276. *Gesneriana* Stella. See Stella.

277. *Gesneriana* The Fawn. See The Fawn.

278. Gilt Crown (Hogg & Robertson).—The variety received under this name was identical with Beauty of America, *q.v.*

279. Gipsy Queen.—Three varieties were received under this name. (*a*) (de Graaff, Hogg & Robertson), dark crimson, with violet-blue base, banded with white; 32 inches; May 8, 17 days. (*b*) (Barr), rich crimson, flaked with very dark crimson; 22 inches; May 10, 19 days. (*c*) (Hogg & Robertson), yellow, heavily feathered with light and dark shades of marooon; 20 inches; May 6, 17 days.

280. Glare of the Garden (Hartland).—Synonymous with *maculata globosa grandiflora*, q.v.

281. Glau Kopis (Wallace).—Salmon-rose, with neat blue-green base; small but pretty; 14 inches; May 9, 14 days.

282. Globe of Fire (Hartland). Orange-scarlet with olive-brown blotches on yellow base; very near Orange Globe; 15 inches; May 13, 16 days.

283. Gold Cup (Barr, Hogg & Robertson).—Rich yellow, with a few spots of red; dark olive centre; pointed recurved segments; 16 inches; May 8, 15 days.

284. Goldflake (Barr, de Graaff, Hogg & Robertson), **XXX** May 24, 1900. Orange-scarlet, flaked with orange and yellow, centre yellow

lightly marked with olive; a rather variable variety; 17 inches; May 9, 14 days.

285. Golden Crown (Hogg & Robertson), **XXX** May 16, 1900.—Rich yellow, edged and lightly spotted with red; the whole flower suffused with red as it ages; segments pointed, outcurved; 16 inches; May 4, 13 days.

286. Golden Eagle (Hogg & Robertson).—Yellow, outer segments recurved; bulbs uniform, stems weak; 13 inches; April 24, 17 days.

287. Golden Glow (Barr).—Rich yellow, with very small olive centre; 18 inches; May 11, 18 days.

288. Golden Goblet (Hogg & Robertson).—Rich yellow; similar to but larger than *Gesneriana lutea*; 16 inches; May 11, 12 days.

289. Golden Spire (Barr, Hartland).—Yellow, with very narrow rose edge; segments long, pointed; 19 inches; May 13, 16 days.

290. Graaff van Bieren (Hogg & Robertson).—Purplish-crimson lightly splashed and based with yellow; outside creamy-white, heavily spotted and edged with bright crimson; 23 inches; 12 days. (Border Bybloemen.)

291. Grandee (Ware).—Yellow, splashed and margined with red, the red suffusing as it ages; 18 inches; May 13, 17 days. Similar to but a little bolder than Sunset.

292. *Griegi* (Hogg & Robertson), **F.C.** April 18, 1877.—Orange-scarlet with olive-brown blotches on a large yellow centre; the inner considerably broader and larger than the recurved outer segments; leaves spotted purplish-brown; a fine species, but a poor doer, often failing to flower; 8 inches; April 22, 18 days.

293. Grenadier (Hartland).—Rich yellow, edged and slightly spotted with rose, the centre lightly shaded with olive; 16 inches; May 13, 16 days. Bandmaster and Sunset are very similar.

294. Hammer Hales (Wilson).—Rich orange-red, yellow centre shaded with olive; flowers large, near *Gesneriana aurantiaca*; 21 inches; May 13, 16 days.

295. Hatfield Pink (Barr).—Bright rose-pink, cream and yellow centre; segments of the flower rather narrow; 20 inches; May 13, 17 days.

296. Illuminator (Hartland).—Rich yellow, broadly edged and shaded with rose, the rose intensifying with age, centre blotched with rich olive; 17 inches; May 13, 17 days. Very similar to Grandee.

297. Impératrice de Maroc (Hogg & Robertson).—Creamy-white, richly feathered with dark crimson and purple; 22 inches; May 7, 16 days. (Border Bybloemen.)

298. Indian Prince (Hartland).—Claret-red, yellowish at the margin; centre yellow and olive; 16 inches; May 10, 14 days.

299. Inglescombe Pink (Wallace, Ware), **A.M.** May 3, 1904.—Rosy-pink shaded with salmon, centre creamy-white with bright blue-green blotches; 21 inches; May 9, 16 days. A beautiful variety, subtly coloured.

300. Inglescombe Scarlet (de Graaff, Ware), **A.M.** May 20, 1902.—Bright scarlet, with well-defined purplish-black blotches at the centre; a fine regular variety, the petals long and rather narrow; 20 inches May 11, 14 days.

301. Inglescombe Yellow (Ware).—Bright yellow, uniform ; 19 inches ; May 12, 16 days.

302. Innocenza (Tubergen).—Creamy-white, yellow centre ; outer segments pointed, flower open ; 17 inches ; May 6, 15 days.

303. Irish Beauty (Barr).—Yellow splashed, spotted and edged with bright red, based with olive blotches ; 15 inches ; May 14, 15 days. Very near General Vetter.

304. Isabella (Hogg & Robertson), **XXX** May 24, 1900.—Soft yellow lightly splashed and edged with rose ; 11 inches ; May 7, 13 days. See Silver Queen.

305. Ixioides (de Graaff, Hartland), **A.M.** May 22, 1901.—Yellow with small distinct olive-brown base, pointed outcurved segments ; 16 inches ; May 11, 18 days.

306. Jaune d'Œuf (Barr, de Graaff), **XX** May 8, 1907.—Bronzy-yellow, large olive centre, outside shaded with rose ; stems purple ; 21 inches ; May 7, 15 days.

307. John Ruskin (Hartland), **A.M.** May 17, 1904.—Salmon-pink, flushed at the edge with yellow ; base yellow with some olive ; 16 inches ; May 13, 16 days.

308. *Kolpakowskiana* (Hogg & Robertson), **A.M.** May 8, 1900.—Yellow flushed outside with reddish-brown ; 4–7–12 inches ; **May 1,** 14 days. A fine species from Turkestan ; is better left undisturbed in the ground.

309. Koningskroon (Barr, Hogg & Robertson).—Bright-red shading to a broad yellow edge, centre yellow ; outside the yellow edge is narrow ; 17 inches ; May 6, 14 days. *Syn.* Royal Crown.

310. Kroschell (Hogg & Robertson).—Rich yellow much feathered with orange and reddish-maroon ; uniform ; 21 inches ; May 7, 17 days. (Border Bizarre.)

311. La Candeur, *syn.* Parisian White, *q.v.*

312. La Circassienne (Barr).—Creamy-yellow much splashed with light and dark rosy-crimson ; 19 inches ; May 9, 14 days.

313. Lady Roberts (Barr, de Graaff, Hogg & Robertson).—Sulphur-white, but gradually suffusing with rose ; pointed, recurved outer segments ; elegant ; weak stems ; 10 inches ; April 23, 16 days.

314. La Merveille (Barr, Hogg & Robertson).—Orange-scarlet, centre yellow lightly edged with olive ; flower large, open ; 22 inches ; May 13, 16 days.

315. La Panachée (Barr, de Graaff, Hogg & Robertson).—Cream, eavily flaked with bright rose-red ; 13 inches ; May 7, 14 days.

316. La Perle (Hartland).—Soft salmon, rich yellow centre ; outside flushed salmon-lilac ; 18 inches ; May 15, 16 days.

317. La Singulière (Hogg & Robertson).—Cream-yellow shaded with green, spotted and edged with crimson ; 16 inches ; May 9, 13 days.

318. L'Eblouissante (Hogg & Robertson).—Yellow, variably flamed red ; 12 inches ; May 11, 13 days. A variety of *Billietiana.*

319. Leghorn Bonnet (Barr, de Graaff, Hartland, Hogg & Robertson).—Bright yellow, some flowers showing a shade of salmon ; 20 inches ; May 13, 16 days.

320. Lion d'Orange (Barr, Hogg & Robertson), **XX** May 8, 1907.—

Orange-red, clear yellow centre, marked bloom outside, cup-shaped; 21 inches; May 5, 14 days.

321. Little Coquette (Barr), *syn.* Orange Coquette, *q.v.*

322. Lord Byron (de Graaff, Tubergen), **XX** May 11, 1906.—Crimson-red, neat yellow centre, marked purplish bloom without, long oval bud and flower; 21 inches; April 29, 16 days.

323. Lucifer (de Graaff, Hogg and Robertson).—Orange-red, flaked at the base with yellow, centre yellow ringed with olive; 22 inches; April 13, 17 days.

324. *macrospeila* (de Graaff, Hogg & Robertson), **XXX** May 24, 1900.—Bright rose with olive blotches on the yellow centre; outer segments recurved; bulbs uniform; 18 inches; May 11, 14 days.

325. *maculata* (de Graaff).—Crimson-scarlet, with dark olive-brown blotches on the yellow centre; 18 inches; May 11, 14 days.

326. *maculata aurantiaca major* (de Graaff).—Yellow, richly flamed with scarlet and crimson, the flaking olive-brown at the centre; 18 inches; May 11; 18 days.

327. *maculata* Brilliant (Barr, Hogg & Robertson).—Dark crimson-scarlet, with variable dark olive markings on the yellow base; filaments black; 18 inches; May 9, 14 days. Not synonymous with Brilliant, No. 195.

328. *maculata globosa grandiflora* (de Graaff), **A.M.** May 17, 1904.—Dark crimson-scarlet, centre deep olive-brown banded with yellow; 11 inches; May 8, 14 days. *Syn.* Glare of the Garden.

329. *maculata major* (Hogg & Robertson), **XXX** May 24, 1900.—In colour similar to the last; 20 inches; May 9, 14 days.

330. *maculata* The Moor (de Graaff). See The Moor.

331. *maculata* The Nigger (Hogg & Robertson). See The Nigger.

332. Maid of Holland (Hogg and Robertson).—Creamy-yellow, much spotted and flamed rose-red, dark olive-blotched centre; 15 inches; May 13, 14 days.

333. Maid of Honour (Hogg & Robertson).—Pale yellow, lightly marked with rose, pointed recurved outer segments; 17 inches; May 7, 16 days. A form of *Didieri lutescens*.

334. Mandarin (Barr).—Yellow, heavily spotted and suffused with rose, centre dark brown banded with yellow; 13 inches; May 11, 14 days.

335. *Marjoletti* (Barr, de Graaff, Hogg & Robertson, Tubergen).—Soft yellow, lightly suffused at the edges without and banded at the base within with rose; bulbs uniform; 20 inches; May 9, 14 days.

336. Marjorie (Barr).—Yellow, lightly and variably spotted with red, blotched at the centre with olive; 16 inches; May 9, 11 days.

337. Mars (Hartland).—Glowing scarlet with centre of olive-brown blotches, of which three are banded with yellow, marked bloom outside; form similar to *maculata*; 16 inches; May 15, 15 days.

338. *Mauriana* (Barr, Hogg & Robertson, de Graaff), **A.M.** May 22, 1901.—Glowing scarlet with well-defined rich yellow centre; 20 inches; May 11, 18 days.

339. Merry Maid (Barr).—Pale yellow, variably marked with rose; bulbs lack uniformity; 11 inches; May 10, 10 days.

340. Miss Willmott (de Graaff).—Soft lemon-yellow, paler without, anthers dark, pointed recurved segments; 20 inches; May 13, 16 days.

341. Mrs. Jas. Robertson (Hogg & Robertson).—Rich self-yellow, very similar to *Gesneriana lutea*, but at Wisley rather poorer; 14 inches; May 11, 12 days.

342. Mrs. Keightley (Hogg & Robertson).—Syn. *Gesneriana lutea pallida*, q.v.

343. Mrs. Moon (de Graaff, Hartland), **A.M.** May 23, 1900.—Rich self-yellow, similar, but at Wisley inferior, to *Gesneriana lutea*; 14 inches; May 11, 13 days.

344. Nabob (Barr).—Glossy crimson-maroon with yellow filaments but dark anthers, cup-shaped; 20 inches; May 7, 18 days.

345. Narbonensis alba (de Graaff), *syn.* Sweet Nancy, q.v.

346. Nigrette (Hogg & Robertson).—Dark crimson-maroon with slight yellow and olive markings at the centre; 20 inches; May 6, 19 days.

347. Norham Beauty (Barr).—Purplish lilac shading to a bronzy-yellow edge; the centre yellow lightly touched with olive; 14 inches; May 9, 11 days.

348. Nutmeg (Hartland).—Reddish-maroon, small; 17 inches; May 10, 7 days.

349. Orange Beauty (Barr, Hogg & Robertson, Wallace, Ware), **A.M.** May 9, 1905.—Dark orange-red, orange at the edge, centre yellow blotched with dark olive; 21 inches; May 11, 19 days.

350. Orange Coquette (Barr, de Graaff, Hogg & Robertson).—Yellow variably suffused with rose, the rose intensifying with age, pointed segments; 13 inches; May 6, 13 days. *Syn.* Little Coquette, Coquette d'Orange.

351. Orange Globe (Barr, Hartland).—Scarlet-orange, with olive-brown markings on the yellow centre, reddish-orange without; 21 inches; May 11, 18 days.

352. Orlando (Barr).—Rosy-crimson with violet markings on the pale-yellow centre, narrow pointed segments of but little substance; 17 inches; May 4, 14 days.

353. Orpheus (Barr).—Pale yellow, with narrow bright rose margin, the whole flower gradually suffusing with rose; 18 inches; May 7, 15 days.

354. *Ostrowskiana* (Hogg & Robertson, Tubergen), **XXX** May 2, 1906.—Dark scarlet, flushed outside with orange; centre small, yellow and brown; filaments crimson; flowers rather small, with narrow pointed segments; foliage thin; stems sometimes branched; 15 inches; April 29, 14 days.

355. Othello (Hartland, Hogg & Robertson).—Crimson, the centre blotched with dark olive-brown; 18 inches; May 10, 16 days.

356. Parisian White (de Graaff, Hogg & Robertson), **XX** May 11, 1906.—Creamy-white with very light fawn centre; a rose edge and shading suffuse the flower as it ages; 14 inches; May 4, 16 days. *Syn.* La Candeur.

357. Parisian Yellow (Hogg & Robertson).—Rich yellow; pointed recurved segments; 24 inches; May 11, 18 days.

358. Pauline (Barr).—Very soft yellow, slightly spotted with red ; 15 inches ; May 6, 10 days.

359. Perfection (de Graaff, Hogg & Robertson).—Reddish-bronze with centre of yellow and olive; foliage broad, light green ; stems much branched ; 23 inches ; May 10, 14 days.

360. *persica* (Hogg & Robertson), **XXX** May 24, 1900.—Yellow, flamed green outside, with reddish edge, small; leaves twisted, scarcely rising above the ground ; 6 inches ; May 13, 16 days.

361. Philomel (Hogg & Robertson).—White, richly feathered rose and red ; 18 inches ; May 6, 13 days. (Border Bybloemen.)

362. Picotee (de Graaff, Hogg & Robertson), **XXX** May 16, 1900.— Pale lemon-yellow with thin rose edge, the rose gradually suffusing upwards ; pointed, recurved outer segments ; 20 inches ; May 9, 14 days.

363. Picta aurea (Hartland).—Rich yellow, lightly spotted red ; dark olive centre ; 14 inches ; May 11, 13 days.

364. Picta octaroon (Hartland).—Rich yellow, much spotted and edged red ; dark olive centre ; 20 inches ; May 13, 16 days.

365. *planifolia* (de Graaff, Hogg & Robertson).—Crimson-scarlet, centred neatly with olive blotches on yellow ; 18 inches ; May 6, 13 days.

366. *platystigma* (Hogg & Robertson).—The variety received under this name was crimson, with small olive and yellow centre.

367. Plutargus (Hogg & Robertson).—Reddish-bronze with light olive-green centre, broadly flamed outside with purple ; 24 inches; May 9, 18 days.

368. Poison d'Œuf (de Graaff).—Reddish-bronze flaked with crimson and yellow, shading to a bronze edge ; centre small, olive; 17 inches; May 9, 12 days.

369. Pompadour (Hartland).—Crimson, blotched at the centre with blackish-olive ; recurved outer segments ; 12 inches ; May 9, 13 days.

370. *praestans*, **A.M.** April 7, 1903, Regel's variety (Tubergen).— Scarlet, the outer segments with a yellowish flame outside, filaments black, stems 2-flowered, leaves very downy ; 10, 16, 21 inches ; April 17, 17 days.

371. *praestans*, Tubergen's variety (Tubergen).—Light scarlet, filaments red, stems 1- to 4-flowered, leaves downy ; 6–11 inches ; bulbs flowering irregularly between April 8 and May 13. A poor doer.

372. Pride of Inglescombe (Ware).—Creamy-white, edged with rich rose, the rose suffusing upwards ; filaments and centre blue ; 21 inches ; May 13, 16 days.

373. Primrose Beauty (de Graaff, Hogg & Robertson).—Soft primrose yellow ; 14 inches ; May 11, 12 days.

374. Primrose Gem (Wallace).—Pale yellow, segments long, narrow ; 18 inches ; May 11, 14 days.

375. *primulina* (Hogg & Robertson).—Creamy-white, marked lightly outside with green and rose ; each bulb throws up one to three small flowers with narrow pointed segments ; 7 inches ; May 4, 8 days.

376. Prince of Orange (Hogg & Robertson), *syn.* Orange Beauty, *q.v.*

377. Prince of Wales (Hogg & Robertson).—Yellow, deeply marked with maroon ; bulbs uniform ; 17 inches ; May 10, 13 days. (Border Bizarre.)

378. Queen Alexandra (de Graaff).—Bright yellow, shaded on the reverse with bronze ; 14 inches ; May 8, 9 days.

379. Reflexa Mars. See Mars.

380. *retroflexa* (de Graaff, Hogg & Robertson), **XXX** May 2, 1906.—Pale yellow, a little greenish, with narrow tapering recurved segments ; stems slight ; 16 inches ; May 1, 15 days.

381. Rosalind (Hogg & Robertson).—Bright rose with white and cream centre ; 20 inches ; May 11, 18 days.

382. Rose Cornélie (Hogg & Robertson).—White and soft rose ; 17 inches ; May 10, 16 days. (Border Bybloemen.)

383. Rose Mignon (Barr, de Graaff, Hogg & Robertson).—Soft creamy-yellow, a little splashed with rose ; outer segments pointed, recurved ; 16 inches ; May 6, 14 days. The variety forwarded by Messrs. de Graaff had variegated foliage.

384. Rose Pompon (Hogg & Robertson).—Soft yellow, lightly spotted and edged with rose ; semi-double ; 17 inches ; May 8, 12 days.

385. Rose Royale (Ware), **XXX** May 11, 1906.—Cream, thinly edged and a little splashed with crimson, the latter colour gradually suffusing the whole flower ; 23 inches ; May 6, 15 days. Practically synonymous with Fashion, No. 252.

386. Rosetta (Barr).—Creamy-white, much splashed with rose and purplish-rose ; flowers variable, including rose and rose-lilac selfs ; 21 inches ; May 11, 18 days.

387. Rouge éblouissante (Hogg & Robertson).—Purplish-lilac, variably striped with crimson ; centre metallic blue ; 16 inches ; May 4, 16 days.

388. Royal Crown (Barr), *syn.* Koningskroon, *q.v.*

389. Royal White (Barr, Hogg & Robertson), **XXX** May 16, 1900.—Creamy-white, centred with yellow ; soft yellow flame outside ; smooth petals, cup-shaped flowers ; 14 inches ; May 6, 17 days. See also Water Lily.

390. Ruby (Barr, de Graaff, Hogg & Robertson).—Dark ruby-red with bronze-olive centre ; 21 inches ; May 7, 15 days.

391. Sabrina (Hogg & Robertson).—Dark reddish-bronze, paler towards the edge ; olive centre ; 20 inches ; May 7, 14 days.

392. Salmon Queen (de Graaff).—Pink, shading through salmon to a yellow margin, which disappears as the flower ages, salmon-pink without ; 22 inches ; May 10, 15 days. Practically identical with Inglescombe Pink.

393. *Saracenica* (Hogg & Robertson).—The variety received under this name was identical with *planifolia*, q.v.

394. Scarlet Beauty (de Graaff, Hogg & Robertson).—Bright orange-red, with yellow centre slightly touched with olive ; 20 inches ; May 6, 16 days. Apparently identical with Bonfire.

395. Scarlet Emperor (de Graaff, Ware), **A.M.** May 20, 1902 ; **F.C.** May 17, 1904.—Deep glowing scarlet, with yellow centre ; 21 inches ; May 7, 16 days.

396. *Segusiana* (Hogg & Robertson).—Bright red, with well-defined centre of olive banded with yellow ; flowers rather small ; 15 inches ; May 6, 10 days.

397. Shahzada (Barr).—Crimson, with a shade of bronze ; centre yellow, a little edged with olive ; 16 inches ; May 9, 14 days.

398. Shandon Bells (Hartland). — Practically synonymous with Isabella, *q.v.*, perhaps a little more rosy.

399. Silver Queen (Hartland).—Soft yellow, variably shaded and spotted with rose, the rose intensifying with age ; 12 inches ; May 10, 15 days. Shandon Bells is perhaps a little deeper in colour, Isabella and York and Lancaster a little paler, but all are very similar.

400. Snow Queen (de Graaff).—Pure white, with faint yellowish-flame outside, slightly spotted with purple ; long, narrow, pointed segments ; 12 inches ; May 2, 13 days.

401. Stella (Barr, de Graaff, Hogg & Robertson), **XXX** May 24, 1900.—Glowing rose, with buff-white base blotched with blue ; 12 inches ; May 7, 14 days.

402. *strangulata* (Barr, de Graaff).—Lemon-yellow, with dull yellow centre, occasionally marked with olive ; 15 inches ; May 7, 12 days.

403. *strangulata maculata* (Barr), **A.M.** May 19, 1903.—Pale yellow, with a few rose spots ; centre dark olive green ; 15 inches ; May 7 ; 12 days.

404. *strangulata picta* (Barr, de Graaff).—Pale yellow, variably spotted, generally lightly, with red ; sometimes quite suffused with red ; centre dark olive-green ; 14 inches ; May 7, 12 days.

405. *strangulata primulina* (Barr, de Graaff).—Lemon-yellow, with dull-yellow base ; 14 inches ; May 7, 12 days. The variety received from Messrs. de Graaff was based with olive and spotted with red.

406. Striped Beauty (de Graaff), **XXX** May 16, 1900.—Cream, richly suffused with lilac and splashed bright rose-red ; centre light blue ; 16 inches ; May 8, 12 days ; *syn.* Summer Beauty.

407. Summer Beauty (Hogg & Robertson), *syn.* Striped Beauty, *q.v.*

408. Sunset (Barr, de Graaff, Hartland, Hogg & Robertson), **XXX** May 24, 1900.—Yellow, lightly spotted with red ; becoming with age broadly edged and much suffused with red ; richer than Grenadier, to which it is very similar ; leaves very glaucous, with curled margins ; 16 inches ; May 10, 16 days.

409. Sweet Nancy (de Graaff, Hogg & Robertson).—White, lightly bordered with rose ; the centre and filaments touched with blue ; 16 inches ; May 8, 14 days ; *syn.* Narbonensis alba.

410. *sylvestris* (Hogg & Robertson).—The wild Tulip : yellow, filaments woolly at base ; fragrant ; of no value for bedding, but excellent for naturalising ; 18 inches ; April and May.

411. The Fawn (de Graaff, Hartland, Hogg & Robertson), **A.M.** May 19, 1903.—Cream, shaded with fawn, centre yellow ; outside flamed with fawn ; a shade of salmon suffuses the flower as it ages ; 20 inches ; a fine egg-shaped flower ; May 10, 18 days.

412. The Lizard (Hartland).—Bronze-lilac and crimson, with small yellow centre and splashings ; 16 inches ; May 13, 10 days.

413. The Moor (Barr, de Graaff, Hartland).—Crimson-scarlet, with dark-brown centre lightly ringed with yellow ; 18 inches ; May 13 ; 16 days. A variety of *maculata*.

414. The Nigger (Hogg & Robertson).—Crimson, with violet and olive centre ; 14 inches ; May 6, 15 days. A variety of *maculata*.

415. The Zebra (Hartland).—Bronze-lilac and crimson, based and splashed with light yellow; 18 inches; May 11, 18 days.

416. *Tubergeniana* (Tubergen), **A.M.** May 17, 1904.—Scarlet, with six small oval black blotches at the centre; bloom outside; flowers large, leaves downy; irregular in height and in period of flowering, but a fine species; 6, 12, 16 inches; April 17 to May 13.

417. Turenne (de Graaff, Hogg & Robertson), **XX** May 11, 1906.— Purplish-bronze within, heavily flamed purple without; flowers very large, bulbs uniform; 30 inches; May 6, 18 days.

418. Virginalis (Hogg & Robertson).—Creamy-white, edged and spotted with rose; centre and filaments blue; segments recurved; 16 inches; May 7, 12 days. Very similar to Sweet Nancy, but rather more conspicuously coloured.

419. *viridiflora* (Barr, de Graaff, Hogg & Robertson).—Light green, edged yellow; 18 inches; May 13, 16 days.

420. *viridiflora praecox* (de Graaff, Hogg & Robertson).—Similar to the last, but a week earlier; segments spreading.

421. *viridiflora tardiva* (de Graaff, Hogg & Robertson).—The varieties received under this name were not later than the type, and were inferior in vigour.

422. *vitellina* (Barr, Hogg & Robertson), **A.M.** May 5, 1896.—Soft greenish-yellow; a fine flower, bulbs uniform; 24 inches; May 6, 18 days.

423. Vivid (Barr).—Orange-red, with centre of greenish-yellow; 18 inches; May 4, 14 days.

424. Water Lily (de Graaff), **XXX** May 11, 1906.—Pure white, with small yellow centre; petals broad, showing a very few small splashes of red; flower large; 16 inches; April 24, 17 days. Suggestive of Joost van Vondel white. This variety was received under the name of Royal White, but it is much finer than that variety and has been renamed.

425. White Swan (de Graaff, Hogg & Robertson), **XXX** May 2, 1906.—Creamy white, becoming pure white, the centre scarcely touched with yellow; a fine egg-shaped flower, rather weak-stemmed; 16 inches; April 25, 20 days.

426. Yellow Gem (Hogg & Robertson).—Lemon-yellow, centred with rich yellow; long oval segments; 18 inches; May 11, 12 days.

427. Yellow Hammer (Barr).—Rich self-yellow; two flowers slightly spotted with red; 16 inches; May 13, 16 days.

428. Yellow Perfection (de Graaff, Hogg & Robertson).—Bronzy-yellow, darker without, bronze centre; 20 inches; May 8, 15 days.

429. Yellow Queen (Hogg & Robertson), **XXX** May 11, 1906.—Rich yellow, large flower, with long oval segments; 16 inches; May 6, 10 days.

430. York and Lancaster (de Graaff, Hartland).—Cream, with broad rose edge, bluish filaments and centre; 10 inches; May 7, 15 days.

431. Zomerschoon (Hogg & Robertson), **A.M.** May 19, 1903.—Cream heavily flaked with carmine-rose; 19 inches; May 13, 13 days.

V.—REMBRANDT TULIPS.

432. Anne Mary (Krelage).—White, suffused with lilac, splashed with crimson, white centre ; 18 inches ; May 4, 16 days.

433. Apollo (Krelage).—White, heavily marked purplish-lilac and crimson, small white centre ; rather weak-stemmed ; 21 inches ; May 7, 16 days.

434. Beatrice (Krelage).—Rose, slightly marked with red and white, violet centre ; 21 inches ; May 9, 14 days.

435. Bellona (Krelage).—White, very heavily marked with light and dark shades of purplish-crimson ; centre bright blue and white ; 22 inches ; May 8, 15 days.

436. Bougainville (Krelage).—White, boldly marked with purplish-lilac and crimson, blue centre ; good flower ; 22 inches ; May 7, 15 days.

437. Butterfly (Krelage).—Much suffused with lilac and heavily splashed with rich crimson ; centre blue ; stems purple ; 21 inches ; May 8, 15 days.

438. Carolus Duran (Krelage).—White, heavily marked with purple and deep crimson-purple ; 20 inches ; May 4, 15 days.

439. Cincisimodo. See Quasimodo.

440. Clio (Krelage).—White ground, heavily marked with bluish-lilac and violet, light bluish-white centre ; 22 inches ; May 7, 10 days. There is a May-flowering variety of this name.

441. Constable (Krelage).—White, heavily marked with light crimson and splashed with dark crimson ; centre poor, light blue and white ; 22 inches ; May 7, 15 days.

442. Constance (de Graaff, Krelage).—White, richly marked with rosy-purple and crimson, deeper in colour than Lord Beaconsfield ; bluish-white centre ; regular and good ; 20 inches ; May 9, 16 days.

443. Cosette (Krelage).—White, suffused with pale rose to lilac and splashed bright rose ; olive centre ; 20 inches ; May 7, 17 days.

444. Crimson Beauty (Krelage).—White, heavily marked and splashed with dark crimson ; dark olive centre ; 21 inches ; May 8, 15 days.

445. Dainty Maid (Barr, de Graaff, Hogg & Robertson).—White, very heavily marked with purple and light crimson ; pale blue centre ; 22 inches ; May 9, 15 days.

446. Daisy (Krelage).—White, very heavily marked light and dark purplish crimson ; yellowish centre, ringed with blue ; 19 inches ; May 13, 12 days.

447. Diana (Krelage).—White, heavily marked rosy-purple and splashed with crimson ; centre white ; 20 inches ; May 10, 14 days.

448. Ellen (Krelage).—Bright red and crimson heavily marked on white, rich centre of lilac-blue ; 22 inches ; May 9, 14 days.

449. Eros (de Graaff, Krelage).—White, marked and suffused with violet and lightly splashed with crimson ; centre poor, blue and white ; 21 inches ; May 7, 15 days.

450. Fantasy (Krelage).—White and rosy-lilac, with crimson featherings ; white centre banded with blue ; 16 inches ; May 10, 13 days.

451. Hebe (Krelage).—White, purplish-lilac and crimson ; poor, ill-defined centre ; 16 inches ; May 9, 9 days.

452. Henri Jules (de Graaff).—White, boldly marked with lilac and crimson-purple; white centre; 22 inches; May 1, 14 days.

453. Hero (Krelage).—White, much marked with rosy-crimson; centre blue and white; 21 inches; May 7, 10 days.

454. Horace (Krelage).—Heavy markings of purple and deep-crimson-purple almost covering the white ground; 26 inches; May 4, 17 days.

455. Jeanneton (Krelage).—Bright red and light crimson, heavily marked on white; lilac-blue centre; 18 inches; May 7, 10 days. Almost failed to flower at Wisley.

456. La Coquette (Krelage).—White, boldly marked with lilac and crimson-purple; light blue centre.

457. Lantern (Krelage).—White, lilac and crimson, markings lacking vigour; 22 inches; May 6, 15 days. There is a Darwin of this name.

458. Le Faisandoré (de Graaff).—Heavy markings of purplish-crimson and dark crimson on a white ground; dark olive centre; 22 inches; May 7, 14 days.

459. Le Printemps (Krelage).—White, marked with purplish-lilac and crimson; rather weak-stemmed; 21 inches; May 19, 13 days.

460. Le Séduisant (de Graaff).—White, boldly marked lilac and crimson-purple; light blue centre; 22 inches; May 6, 12 days.

461. Lord Beaconsfield (Krelage).—White, rosy-purple and crimson; markings bold but centre ill-defined.

462. Loreley (Krelage).—White and light and dark purplish-crimson; blue centre, large flower; 25 inches; May 6, 15 days.

463. Lydia (Krelage).—White, purple and crimson, blue and white centre; 20 inches; May 9, 13 days.

464. Madame Krelage (Krelage).—White, purplish-rose and crimson, markings bold; centre light blue; 21 inches; May 7, 14 days. There is a Darwin of this name.

465. Marco Spadi (de Graaff, Krelage).—Bright red and light crimson on white ground; centre poor; 22 inches; May 7, 14 days.

466. Margaret (Krelage).—White, suffused soft pink and marked with crimson-red; centre poor; 18 inches; May 8, 14 days. This is the broken form of the Darwin variety of the same name.

467. Mauve Queen (Krelage).—White, brightly marked with mauve and crimson; centre bright blue; 18 inches; May 7, 14 days.

468. May Blossom (Hogg & Robertson).—Creamy-white, lightly marked with purplish-crimson; 15 inches; May 7, 13 days.

469. Meyerbeer (Krelage).—White, heavily marked with bright rose-red and light crimson; blue and white centre. Practically synonymous with Red Prince.

470. Micromegas (Krelage).—Heavy markings of purplish-rose and crimson on white ground; centre banded with blue; 24 inches; May 6, 14 days.

471. Olympe (de Graaff, Krelage).—White, lilac and purplish-crimson, centre banded with blue: 24 inches; May 6, 14 days. *Syn.* Olympia.

472. Palma (Krelage).—White purplish-lilac and crimson; centre poor; 21 inches; May 6, 14 days.

473. Procles (Krelage).—White, heavily marked with bluish-lilac and deep crimson-purple; centre blue and white; 24 inches; May 6, 16 days.

474. Purity (Krelage).—Creamy-white splashed with purple on lilac ; centre poor ; 14 inches ; May 9, 10 days.

475. Quasimodo (de Graaff, Krelage).—White, boldly marked with reddish-purple and crimson; centre blue and white; 26 inches; May 9, 14 days.

476. Red Prince (Krelage).—Practically identical with Meyerbeer, *q.v.*

477. Rosy Gem (Krelage).—White, purplish-rose, and light crimson ; light blue and white centre ; 24 inches ; May 8, 12 days.

478. Salome (Krelage).—White suffused with lilac and splashed with crimson ; centre brown; 16 inches ; May 9, 10 days.

479. Semele (Krelage).—White, variably suffused with lilac-rose and splashed crimson; centre poor, olive and white ; 16 inches ; May 9, 12 days.

480. Sirène (Krelage), **XX** May 8, 1907.—White, lilac and crimson, much feathered ; centre white banded with blue ; stems purplish in upper part ; 20 inches ; May 6, 11 days.

481. Suzanna (Krelage).—White, boldly marked with purplish-lilac and crimson ; centre blue and white ; flower large and of good form ; 21 inches ; May 6, 12 days.

482. Titania (Krelage).—White, heavily marked with rose-purple and crimson ; flower of great substance ; 18 inches ; May 3, 16 days.

483. Triumph (Krelage).—White, heavily marked with dark purple and deep crimson-purple ; centre rough, blue and white ; 21 inches ; May 6, 12 days.

484. Troubadour (Krelage).—White, bluish-lilac and crimson-purple ; centre dark blue ; 25 inches ; May 7, 15 days.

485. Vasco da Gama (de Graaff, Krelage), **XX** May 8, 1907.—White, very heavily marked with crimson-red ; centre and filaments dark blue ; 20 inches ; April 29, 16 days. The stock from Messrs. de Graaff was an inferior one.

486. Vesta (Krelage).—White, heavily marked with lilac and crimson ; centre poor, blue and white; 18 inches ; May 8, 12 days.

487. Victor Hugo (de Graaff, Krelage).—Bright red with crimson markings, similar to Marco Spadi ; the centre larger, white, ringed with blue ; 16 inches ; May 7, 14 days.

VI. DARWIN TULIPS.

488. A. Baltet (Hogg & Robertson).—Violet-purple, blue centre ; 20 inches ; May 6, 16 days.

489. Acaste (Hogg & Robertson).—Rose-purple shading outside to soft lilac edge, white centre ; 25 inches ; May 3, 18 days.

490. Ada (Hogg & Robertson).—Soft blue-lilac with broad cream-lilac edge ; centre white ; 20 inches ; May 6, 15 days.

491. Adèle Barrois (Hogg & Robertson).—Purplish-rose, dull centre, small ; 22 inches ; May 10, 15 days.

492. Adèle Sandrock (Hogg and Robertson).—Deeper purplish-rose, dull white centre banded with blue ; 23 inches ; May 7, 15 days.

493. Adeline Patti (Hogg & Robertson).—Crimson-scarlet, violet centre banded with white ; 21 inches ; May 8, 14 days.

491. Admiral Togo (Hogg & Robertson).—Crimson-rose, purplish outside, blue and white centre ; 23 inches ; May 6, 16 days.

495. Admiral van den Heede (Hogg & Robertson).—Carmine-scarlet, dark red outside, with violet centre ; 21 inches ; May 7, 12 days.

496. Agathon Raven (Hogg & Robertson).—Crimson, blackish centre banded with white ; 21 inches ; May 6, 16 days.

497. Agnes (Wallace).—Rose-purple, light blue and white centre ; thin ; 18 inches ; May 3, 14 days.

498. Alabama (Hogg & Robertson).—Purplish-rose, shading outside to lilac edge, deep violet centre ; 22 inches ; May 7, 14 days.

499. Alex. Bleu (Hogg & Robertson).—Violet-purple, blue and white centre, weak and poor ; 20 inches ; May 3, 14 days.

500. Alex. Dickson (Hogg & Robertson).—Purplish-rose, violet centre ; 22 inches ; May 8, 14 days.

501. Alexis (Hogg & Robertson).—Rose to purplish-rose, dull centre ; 26 inches ; May 8, 17 days.

502. Allard Pierson (Hogg & Robertson, Krelage), **XX** May 8, 1907.— Dark maroon-crimson with large violet centre marked with white ; 24 inches ; May 5, 14 days.

503. Alphonse Daudet (Hogg & Robertson).—Dark crimson, neat black centre ; 28 inches ; May 6, 16 days.

504. André Doria (Hogg & Robertson, Krelage), **XX** May 11, 1906.— Very dark crimson, with black centre ; several stems two-flowered ; 30 inches ; May 4, 18 days.

505. Andromaque (Hogg & Robertson).—Rich purple, large violet-purple centre ; 25 inches ; May 7, 15 days.

506. Angelina (Hogg & Robertson).—Purplish-rose, large blue centre ; 22 inches ; May 7, 9 days.

507. Angeline (de Graaff).—Light blue-lilac, shading to a broad whitish-lilac edge, white centre ; 24 inches ; May 3, 14 days.

508. Anna (Hogg & Robertson).—Purplish-rose, deeper outside, white centre marked with violet ; 25 inches ; May 9, 13 days.

509. Anna Paulowna (de Graaff, Hogg & Robertson).—Purple, whitish centre ringed with blue ; 22 inches ; May 9, 16 days.

510. Anthony de Bary (Hogg & Robertson).—Rose-purple, violet centre ; 24 inches ; May 9, 14 days.

511. Anthony Roozen (Barr, de Graaff, Hogg & Robertson, Krelage, Wallace), **XXX** May 11, 1906.—Bright lilac-rose, deeper rose outside, paler towards the edge ; centre violet and white ; vigorous and fine ; 25 inches ; May 2, 19 days.

512. Antonia (Hogg & Robertson). — Carmine-crimson, dark blue centre ; 24 inches ; May 6, 16 days.

513. Apollos (Hogg & Robertson). — Purplish-lilac, paler outside ; whitish centre ; 21 inches ; May 8, 18 days.

514. Archimedes (Hogg & Robertson).—Purplish-crimson, deep violet centre ; 24 inches ; May 7, 12 days.

515. Ariadne (Barr, de Graaff, Hogg & Robertson, Krelage), **A.M.** May 9, 1905.—Crimson-scarlet, large violet centre ; 24 inches ; May 6, 16 days.

516. Arizona (Hogg & Robertson, Wallace).—Dark crimson, violet-black centre ; 24 inches ; May 12, 14 days.

517. Asa Gray (Hogg & Robertson).—Deep rose, dark blue centre; 24 inches; May 8, 14 days.

518. Ascanio (Hogg & Robertson), **XX** May 11, 1906.—Rosy-lilac with neat white centre; 26 inches; May 9, 16 days. The same variety was also received under the name Asconis.

519. Athalie (Hogg & Robertson).—Light crimson, poor centre; 26 inches; May 2, 19 days.

520. Auber (Barr, Hogg & Robertson), **XXX** May 16, 1900.—Dark purplish-crimson with violet patches on the white centre; 24 inches; May 6, 17 days.

521. Bacchus (Hogg & Robertson), **XXX** April 26. 1900.—Deep purple with violet and white centre; long flower; 24 inches; May 6, 15 days.

522. Barbara (Barr, Hogg & Robertson).—Rose-purple, paler towards the edge, blue and white centre; 21 inches; May 6, 20 days.

523. Baron de Stael (Hogg & Robertson).—Rosy-lilac, white and blue centre; 27 inches; May 9, 16 days.

524. Baronne de la Tonnaye (Barr, de Graaff, Hogg & Robertson, Krelage, Wallace).—Bright carmine-rose, purplish without, paler at the edge; filaments dark blue over a white centre; 30 inches; May 9, 20 days. *Syn.* La Tonnaye.

525. Baron von Goldstein (Hogg & Robertson).—Deep lilac-rose, purplish-red outside; large dull blue centre; foliage very glaucous, with waved margins; 22 inches; May 9, 14 days.

526. Bartigon (Hogg & Robertson, Krelage).—Carmine-crimson, with white centre edged with violet; 21 inches; May 6, 16 days.

527. Beatrice (de Graaff, Hogg & Robertson).—Carmine-scarlet, white and blue centre; 24 inches; May 6, 16 days.

528. Beauty (Wallace).—Carmine-crimson, rich violet centre; 22 inches; May 9, 12 days.

529. Beethoven (Barr, de Graaff, Hogg & Robertson, Krelage).—Rich rose, centre white ringed with violet; a tender variety; 22 inches; May 9, 14 days.

530. Bernard Lami (de Graaff, Hogg & Robertson).—Lilac-purple, with small centre of greenish-white and blue; 20 inches; May 7, 10 days. Also received under the name Bernard.

531. Berthelot (Hogg & Robertson).—Rosy-purple, paler outside, centre poor; 24 inches; May 6, 16 days.

532. Berthold Schwarz (Hogg & Robertson). — Deep rose-purple, centre white edged with blue; broad petals; 24 inches; May 6, 20 days.

533. Beulah (Hogg & Robertson).—Purplish-lilac, paler towards the edge; centre white banded with blue; 18 inches; May 7, 14 days.

534. Beyerinck (Hogg & Robertson).—Light purplish-rose, paler towards the edge; centre pale blue; some stems two-flowered; 24 inches; May 7, 20 days.

535. Black Knight (Hogg & Robertson, Krelage).—Very dark purplish-crimson, violet-black centre; 28 inches; May 5, 16 days.

536. Bloemhof (Hogg & Robertson).—Lilac-purple, centre blue-green; 24 inches; May 2, 16 days.

537. Blushing Bride (Hogg & Robertson).—Purplish-lilac, paler towards the edge, centre poor ; 20 inches ; May 4, 14 days.

538. Bouquet Rigout is sometimes catalogued as a Darwin (May-flowering). See No. 192.

539. Bridesmaid (Hogg & Robertson).—Purplish-rose, pale blue and white centre ; 22 inches ; May 8, 14 days.

540. Bruno. See St. Bruno, No. 894.

541. Buffon (Hogg & Robertson), **XX** May 11, 1906.—Salmon- to lilac-rose, deeper outside, centre light blue-green ; a broad-shouldered flower ; 24 inches ; May 4, 18 days.

542. Burbidgei (Hogg & Robertson).—Dark purplish-rose, blue centre. Short flower, broad segments ; 24 inches ; May 9, 14 days.

543. Burgomaster Fock (Hogg & Robertson).—Deep blood-red with violet, edged white, centre ; 24 inches ; May 8, 14 days.

544. Bussy Rabutin (de Graaff, Hogg & Robertson).—Purplish-rose, blue centre ; 24 inches ; May 7, 14 days.

545. Cabanel (Hogg & Robertson).—Lilac-rose, purplish-rose outside, centre white ; 21 inches ; May 8, 14 days.

546. Calamettei (Hogg & Robertson). — Light purplish-crimson ; flowers failed to open ; 15 inches.

547. Calliope (Hogg & Robertson, Krelage, Wallace).—Bright rose, lilac-rose at the edge ; uniform and strong ; 26 inches ; May 8, 18 days.

548. Calypso (Hogg & Robertson, Krelage), **XXX** May 24, 1900.— Carmine-scarlet, centre dull white banded with blue ; 18 inches ; May 8, 14 days. The variety received under this name from de Graaff was reddish-maroon, with clear yellow centre—not a Darwin.

549. Camille Bernardin (Hogg & Robertson).—Rich crimson, centre dark violet, banded with white ; 24 inches ; May 6, 16 days.

550. Canossa (de Graaff, Hogg & Robertson). — Carmine-scarlet, whitish-blue centre, weak stalks ; 30 inches ; May 6, 18 days.

551. Carl Becker (de Graaff, Hogg & Robertson).—Lilac-rose, shaded with salmon, deeper outside ; centre blue-green and yellow ; stalks weak ; 30 inches ; May 2, 16 days.

552. Carminea (Barr, de Graaff).—Carmine-purple, small dark violet centre ; 22 inches ; May 10, 12 days.

553. Cettiwayo (Hogg & Robertson), **XX** May 8, 1907.—Dark crimson, with small dark violet centre ; 27 inches ; May 4, 18 days.

554. Chapuis (Hogg & Robertson).—Crimson-scarlet, rich blue and white centre ; 21 inches ; May 8, 14 days.

555. Charles Dickens (Hogg & Robertson).—Carmine-purple, large white centre, violet-edged ; 24 inches ; May 9, 14 days.

556. Charles H. Marot (Hogg & Robertson).—Deep purple, white centre, poor ; 20 inches ; May 4, 12 days.

557. Circe (Barr, Hogg & Robertson).—Pale lilac, rosy outside, shading to white edge and centre ; 24 inches ; May 1, 14 days.

558. City of Haarlem (Hogg & Robertson).—Crimson-scarlet, large violet centre ringed with white ; 22 inches ; May 6, 16 days.

559. C. J. Salter (Hogg & Robertson).—Carmine-rose, light blue centre, banded with violet ; 27 inches ; May 10, 14 days.

560. Clara Butt (de Graaff, Hogg & Robertson, Krelage, Wallace,

Ware), **A.M.** May 17, 1904 ; **F.C.** May 9, 1905.—Soft-rose, a shade paler at the margin, with three small olive blotches on the white centre ; uniform ; foliage light green ; 24 inches ; May 8, 18 days.

561. Claude Gillot (de Graaff, Wallace), **A.M.** May 9, 1905.—Crimson-scarlet, centre blue-black, ringed with white ; 21 inches ; May 10, 14 days.

562. Claude Monet (Hogg & Robertson).—Lilac-rose, flamed purplish-rose outside, light blue centre ; 24 inches ; May 9, 14 days.

563. Comte de Fresvan (Hogg & Robertson).—Deep rose, large blue and white centre ; 28 inches ; May 11, 14 days.

564. Coquelin (Hogg & Robertson).—The colours of Feu Brillant, but smaller ; 21 inches ; May 6, 16 days.

565. Coquette (Ba$_{rr}$, Hogg & Robertson).—Bright lilac-rose, deeper outside ; light violet centre ; 20 inches ; May 7, 14 days.

566. Cordelia (Barr, de Graaff, Hogg & Robertson).—Very weak, all three stocks failing to colour or open their flowers, in spite of good foliage ; 12 inches.

567. Corot (Barr, Hogg & Robertson).—Purplish-lilac, paler at the margin ; centre white edged with blue ; 21 inches ; May 6, 16 days.

568. Corridor (Hogg & Robertson).—Purplish-crimson, blue and white centre ; 26 inches ; May 9, 20 days.

569. Corydon (Barr, Hogg & Robertson), **XX** May 11, 1906.—Dark bluish-lilac, paler at the margin ; small white centre ; globular ; 18 inches ; May 6, 16 days. Also received as Coridon and Coridion. A May-flowering variety was received under the same name (see No. 223).

570. Crépuscule (Krelage).—Rosy-lilac, bright blue centre ; 22 inches ; May 8, 18 days.

571. Cupido (Hogg & Robertson).—Bright rose, purplish outside, with small white and violet centre ; 22 inches ; May 10, 14 days.

572. Cyrano de Bergerac (Hogg & Robertson).—Carmine-crimson, violet-blue centre ; 24 inches ; May 7, 14 days.

573. Czar Peter (Wallace).—Rose-purple ; white centre, shaded with blue ; 20 inches ; May 10, 12 days.

574. Dal Ongaro (Hogg & Robertson, Wallace).—Purplish-lilac, paler at the margin ; white and blue centre ; 20 inches ; May 10, 14 days.

575. De Sacey (Hogg & Robertson).—Rich crimson, dark violet centre ; 22 inches ; May 7, 21 days.

576. Descartes (Hogg & Robertson).—Purplish-crimson, blue and olive centre, poor ; 24 inches ; May 6, 14 days.

577. Deschamps (Hogg & Robertson).—Dark crimson, violet centre, poor ; 18 inches ; May 8, 14 days.

578. Diamond (Wallace).—Deep carmine-crimson, violet centre ; 27 inches ; May 10, 14 days.

579. Diana (de Graaff, Hogg & Robertson).—Crimson-scarlet, blackish-violet and white centre ; 20 inches ; May 7, 14 days.

580. Dido (Hogg & Robertson).—Bright crimson, dark violet centre ; 18 inches ; May 7, 14 days.

581. Dr. de Commines. *Syn.* Ph. de Commines, *q.v.*

582. Dr. Wagner (Hogg & Robertson).—Carmine-crimson, bright blue centre ; 24 inches ; May 9, 14 days.

583. Dodaneus (Barr, Hogg & Robertson).—Crimson-scarlet, black-violet centre edged with white ; 20 inches ; May 8, 14 days.

584. Don Carlos (Hogg & Robertson).—Deep rose-purple, yellowish centre ; 30 inches ; May 6, 20 days.

585. Donders ·(Barr, de Graaff, Hogg & Robertson), **XXX** May 16, 1900.—Crimson ; dark violet centre, edged with white ; 24 inches ; May 2, 14 days.

586. Don Fredericio (de Graaff, Hogg & Robertson).—Purplish-lilac, dull base ; 21 inches ; May 11, 12 days.

587. Dora Silberrad (Hogg & Robertson).—Carmine-crimson, rich violet base ; 20 inches ; May 10, 12 days.

588. Dorothy (Barr, Hogg & Robertson, Wallace).—Pale purplish-lilac, softer outside ; whitish centre ; 20 inches ; May 10, 16 days.

589. Dream (Barr, Hogg & Robertson).—Purplish- to bluish-lilac, blue centre ; 24 inches ; May 7, 12 days.

590. Duchesse de Mouchy (Barr, Hogg & Robertson).—Rosy-lilac, large white centre ; weak stems ; 24 inches ; May 8, 14 days.

591. Early Dawn (Barr, de Graaff, Hogg & Robertson, Wallace).—Purplish-rose, paler outside, dark blue centre ; burns badly ; weak foliage ; 20 inches ; May 7, 16 days.

592. Ebony (Krelage).—Dark crimson, violet centre ; 24 inches ; May 7, 20 days. The variety forwarded under this name by Hogg & Robertson was carmine-crimson.

593. Edison (Hogg & Robertson).—Bright purplish-rose, poor centre ; 20 inches ; May 7, 14 days.

594. Edmée (Barr, de Graaff, Hogg & Robertson, Krelage, Wallace).—Rich purplish-rose, paler at the margin, lilac-rose within, centre poor ; 20 inches ; May 8, 14 days.

595. Edmond Rostand (Hogg & Robertson).—Carmine-rose within, deep purplish-rose outside ; rich violet centre ; 22 inches ; May 9, 14 days.

596. Edouard André (Barr, Hogg & Robertson, Krelage).—Bright rosy-purple, shading at the margin to lilac ; centre whitish ; 22 inches ; May 4, 18 days.

597. Electra (Barr, Hogg & Robertson, Krelage), **XXX** May 8, 1907.—Pale lilac shading to a white centre, flamed outside with dark purplish-lilac ; stems dark purple ; 25 inches ; May 4, 18 days.

598. Emerson (Hogg & Robertson).—Light purplish-crimson, dark blue centre ; 24 inches ; May 8, 14 days.

599. Emilie (Krelage, Hogg & Robertson, Wallace).—Also received under the names Emile and Emily. Rosy-crimson, rich violet centre touched with white ; 26 inches ; May 9, 20 days.

600. Emmanuel Sweertz (Barr, de Graaff, Hogg & Robertson).—Rose-purple, large white and blue centre ; 22 inches : May 9, 20 days.

601. Erguste (de Graaff, Hogg & Robertson, Wallace), **XX** May 11, 1906.—Bluish-lilac, paler towards the margin, white centre ; 26 inches ; May 2, 20 days.

602. Esculape (Wallace).—Violet-purple, poor centre ; 22 inches ; May 8, 16 days.

603. Etna (Hogg & Robertson, Krelage), **XXX** May 11, 1906.—Deep carmine-crimson, violet centre ; rather weak stems ; 24 inches ; May 6, 16 days.

604. Eugène Delacroix (Hogg & Robertson, Krelage).—Very dark crimson, violet-black centre ; 26 inches ; May 1, 18 days.

605· Europe (Barr, de Graaff, Hogg & Robertson, Krelage, Wallace), **XXX** ·May 16, 1900.—Scarlet, white centre banded with blue ; good stems, uniform ; 20 inches ; May 6, 16 days.

606. Excelsior (Hogg & Robertson), **XXX** May 11, 1906.—Dark purple with white markings at the centre ; 26 inches ; May 6, 14 days. The variety received from Wallace under this name was light purplish-crimson.

607. Fanny (Barr, Hogg & Robertson, Krelage), **XXX** May 11, 1906.—Lilac-rose, paler outside and flamed with bluish-lilac ; centre light blue on white ; 22 inches ; May 2, 16 days.

608. Farncombe Sanders. See Mr. F. Sanders.

609· Faust (Hogg & Robertson, Krelage), **XX** May 11, 1906.—Very dark purplish-crimson with violet-black base ; very regular and of good form ; 24 inches ; May 6, 18 days.

610. Feu Brillant (Krelage), **XXX** May 11, 1906.— Deep blood-red with violet, edged white, centre ; 28 inches ; May 2, 20 days.

611. Feu d'Artifice (Hogg & Robertson). — Carmine-crimson, poor centre, weak ; 20 inches ; May 7, 14 days.

612. Fille Chérie (Hogg & Robertson).—Rosy-purple within, lilac outside, shading to creamy edge ; 22 inches ; May 8, 14 days.

613. Fireball (Hogg & Robertson).—Deep blood-red ; centre blue, banded with white ; 22 inches ; May 3, 17 days.

614. Firebrand (Hogg & Robertson).—Dark crimson-purple with yellow and white centre ; 22 inches ; May 6, 16 days.

615. Fire King (Hogg & Robertson).—Scarlet, purplish outside ; 18 inches ; May 9, 14 days.

616. Flambeau (Barr, de Graaff, Hogg & Robertson, Wallace).—Dark scarlet, purplish-red outside ; weak ; 18 inches ; May 7, 14 days.

617. Flamingo (Krelage).—The variety received under this name was deep blood-red, not the plant described by the raiser. There is also an early single of this name. See No. 32.

618. Flora's Feast (Hogg & Robertson).—Purplish-rose, blue centre, poor doer ; 21 inches ; May 10, 12 days.

619. Flora's Ornament, *syn.* Sieraad van Flora, *q.v.*

620. Fontanelle (Barr, de Graaff, Hogg & Robertson).—Purplish-crimson, centre olive and blue ; 26 inches ; May 6, 20 days.

621. Fra Angelico (Hogg & Robertson, Krelage, Wallace), **XXX** May 11, 1906.—Very dark purplish-crimson, though not quite so dark as Faust ; dark violet centre ; 22 inches ; April 29, 18 days. Also received as Frau Angelica !

622. François Crepin (Hogg & Robertson).—Carmine-scarlet, centre poor ; 18 inches ; May 8, 14 days.

623. Franz. Hals, (Krelage), **XXX** May 11, 1906.—Dark magenta-purple with large dark violet base ; 26 inches ; May 6, 18 days.

624. Fräulein Amberg (Hogg & Robertson, Wallace), **XXX** May 16, 1900.—Dark bluish-lilac, a little paler towards the margin ; small white centre ; many stalks branched, bearing 2-4 flowers ; 24 inches ; May 1, 20 days.

625. Frosine (Hogg & Robertson).—Lilac-rose, paler outside; dark blue centre ; 24 inches ; May 6, 12 days.

626. Galatea (Barr, Hogg & Robertson, Krelage), **XX** May 11, 1906.— Deep lilac-rose, large dull blue centre ; 26 inches ; May 8, 16 days.

627. Ganymedes (Hogg & Robertson).— Rose-purple, light slate-blue centre ; 20 inches ; May 10, 12 days.

628. Garricoult (Hogg & Robertson).—Purple, poor centre, weak.; 21 inches ; May 8, 10 days.

629. G. de Cordous (Hogg & Robertson, Krelage), **XX** May 11, 1906.— Scarlet, blue centre, stalks rather weak ; 22 inches ; May 1, 14 days.

680. G. de Salelle. (Hogg & Robertson).—Dark purplish-crimson, violet and white centre ; 22 inches ; May 9, 20 days.

631. Geefs (Hogg & Robertson).—Rosy-crimson, blue-white centre ; 82 inches ; May 7, 18 days.

632. General Kohler (Barr, de Graaff, Hogg & Robertson, Krelage).— Deep carmine-crimson, violet-blue centre ; 21 inches ; May 8, 14 days.

633. General van Heutz (Hogg & Robertson).—Crimson-scarlet, violet centre, very poor ; 21 inches ; May 9, 12 days.

634. General Verspyck (Hogg & Robertson).—Carmine-crimson, rich violet centre ; 22 inches ; May 9, 14 days.

635. Georgiana (Hogg & Robertson, Wallace). — Lilac-rose, large white centre, deep purplish-rose outside ; 28 inches; May 9, 16 days.

636. George Maw (de Graaff, Hogg & Robertson).—Lilac- to purplish-rose ; soft sky-blue centre ; 28 inches ; May 9; 16 days.

637. George Sand (Hogg & Robertson, Wallace).—Light crimson, violet and white centre ; 20 inches ; May 8, 14 days.

638. Georgia (Hogg & Robertson).—Light rose-purple, much paler outside, white and blue centre ; 21 inches ; May 6, 12 days.

639. G. F. Wilson (Barr, Hogg & Robertson, Wallace).—Rose-purple, small blue and white centre, small flower ; 28 inches ; May 6, 16 days.

640. Giant (Krelage), **XXX** May 11, 1906.—Received as Goliath, but renamed. Dark crimson-purple, poor centre, huge flower ; 30 inches ; May 6, 16 days.

641. Giovanni (de Graaff, Hogg & Robertson).—Deep rose, dull olive centre ; 24 inches ; May 9, 14 days.

642. Girodet (Hogg & Robertson).—Dark purplish-crimson, violet-black centre ; 24 inches ; May 7, 16 days.

643. Glory (Barr, Hogg & Robertson, Krelage).—Scarlet, bright blue centre, tender ; 18 inches ; May 6, 16 days.

644. Glow (Barr, de Graaff, Hogg & Robertson, Krelage, Wallace).— Fiery-red ; deep violet, edged white, centre ; 24 inches ; May 8, 14 days.

645. Glück (Hogg & Robertson).—Rose-purple, variable ; 20 inches ; May 6, 16 days.

646. Godet Parfait (Barr), **XX** May 11, 1906.—Violet-purple, poor centre ; 24 inches ; May 4, 18 days.

647. Goliath (Hogg & Robertson, Wallace).—Carmine-crimson, violet centre, weak stalks ; 18 inches ; May 6, 14 days. See also ' Giant.'

648. Grandmaster, *syn.* St. Bruno, *q.v.*

649. Grand Monarque (Barr, de Graaff, Hogg & Robertson).—Deep

reddish-purple, with bronzy shade; centre yellow and green; 25 inches; May 7, 16 days. Not a true Darwin variety.

650. Gretchen, *syn.* Margaret, *q.v.*

651. Grimaldus (Hogg & Robertson).—Dark scarlet, with dull purplish-green centre; 24 inches; May 6, 14 days.

652. Grossi (Hogg & Robertson).—Light purplish-crimson, blue centre; 26 inches; May 7, 20 days.

653. Gryphus (Hogg & Robertson, Krelage).—Very dark purple, blue and white centre; 24 inches; May 6, 14 days.

654. Gudin (Barr, de Graaff, Hogg & Robertson, Krelage).—Bluish-lilac, shading to a broad cream edge, centre blue and white; 18 inches; May 9, 14 days.

655. Gustave Doré (Hogg & Robertson, Krelage, Wallace), **XXX** May 16, 1900.—Lilac-rose, deep purplish-rose outside, paler at the margin, blue and white centre; 20 inches; May 7, 14 days.

656. Haarlem (Krelage), **XX** May 11, 1906.—Purplish-rose, darker outside, paler at the margin; pale blue centre; weak stems; 24 inches; May 4, 12 days.

657. Hannibal (Hogg & Robertson).—Carmine-crimson, dull olive-blue centre; 22 inches; May 7, 16 days.

658. Harry Veitch (Hogg & Robertson, Krelage).—Crimson, large violet and white centre; 20 inches; May 6, 16 days.

659. Hecla (Barr, de Graaff, Hogg & Robertson, Wallace), **XXX** May 11, 1906.—Dark crimson, deep violet and white centre; 25 inches; May 4, 18 days.

660. Henner (Hogg & Robertson, Wallace), **A.M.** May 15, 1906.—Reddish-crimson; centre blue-black, edged white; poor doer; 21 inches; May 6, 16 days.

661. Henri Lyte (Hogg & Robertson).—Carmine-crimson, rich violet-blue centre; 21 inches; May 9, 12 days.

662. Henri Vilmorin (Hogg & Robertson).—Carmine-crimson, dull olive-blue centre; 21 inches; May 8, 14 days.

663. Henry Conscience (Hogg & Robertson).—Carmine-crimson, dirty-white centre; 22 inches; May 7, 16 days.

664. Henry Leys (Hogg & Robertson).—Rose-purple, deep blue centre; 26 inches; May 7, 16 days.

665. Herald (Hogg & Robertson).—Light rose-purple, shading to a lilac edge; ill-defined whitish centre; 24 inches; May 4, 18 days.

666. Herschel (Hogg & Robertson, Wallace).—Dark crimson, centre dark violet patches on white; 22 inches; May 6, 18 days.

667. Herta (Hogg & Robertson).—Purplish-crimson, blue and white centre, large; 33 inches; May 4, 20 days.

668. Hesperia (Hogg & Robertson).—Rose, small blue centre; 24 inches; May 4, 16 days.

669. H. G. Elwes (Hogg & Robertson).—Crimson-scarlet; dark violet, edged white, centre; 20 inches; May 9, 12 days.

670. Hippolyte (Wallace).—Rose-purple, blue and white centre, small; 20 inches; May 7, 10 days.

671. Hoola van Nooten (Hogg & Robertson).—Lilac-rose, large blue centre; 24 inches; May 9, 16 days.

672. Hugo de Vries (Hogg & Robertson).—Purplish-rose shading to a rose-lilac edge, paler outside ; light blue centre, large flower ; 22 inches ; May 8, 14 days.

673. H. Witte (Hogg & Robertson).—Deep purplish-rose, dirty-white centre ; 22 inches ; May 9, 14 days.

674. Isis (Krelage, Wallace), **A.M.** May 15, 1906.—Dark-scarlet ; with bluish centre, edged white ; weak stalks ; 20 inches ; May 4, 16 days.

675. James Douglas (Hogg & Robertson).—Purplish-rose, light blue centre, poor doer ; 24 inches ; May 8, 14 days.

676. James McIntosh (Hogg & Robertson, Wallace).—Lilac-rose, violet and light blue centre ; 22 inches ; May 7, 20 days.

677. James Walker (Hogg & Robertson).—Carmine-crimson, rich blue centre ; 22 inches ; May 8, 14 days.

678. Je maintiendrai (Barr, de Graaff, Hogg & Robertson).—Deep purple, creamy-yellow centre ; 28 inches ; May 6, 18 days.

679. Jhr. Schorer (Hogg & Robertson).—Purplish-rose, darker outside, paler at the margin ; blue centre ; weak stems ; 26 inches ; May 2, 14 days.

680. Johanna (Hogg & Robertson).—Deep rose, violet and white centre ; 24 inches ; May 10, 18 days.

681. Johanna de Mathilda (Hogg & Robertson).—Dark purplish-crimson, violet and greenish-yellow centre ; 24 inches ; May 4, 16 days.

682. John Fraser (Barr, Hogg & Robertson, Wallace).—Dark scarlet ; deep blue centre, neatly edged with white ; 24 inches ; May 7, 14 days.

683. John Laing (Hogg & Robertson).—Crimson ; dark violet, edged white, centre ; 20 inches ; May 6, 16 days.

684. John Lee (Hogg & Robertson).—Carmine-scarlet, whitish-blue centre ; 22 inches ; May 9, 14 days.

685. John Malcolm (Hogg & Robertson).—Rose-purple, yellowish centre, edged blue ; 24 inches ; May 4, 18 days.

686. John Swift (Hogg & Robertson).—Dark crimson, violet-black centre ; 24 inches ; May 4, 14 days.

687. Jcos (Hogg & Robertson).—Reddish-purple, poor centre, weak doer ; 21 inches ; May 7, 14 days.

688. Joseph Chamberlain (Barr, de Graaff, Hogg & Robertson).—Crimson, centre blue and white ; 21 inches ; May 5, 16 days.

689. J. Reynault (Hogg & Robertson).—Dark crimson-purple, violet and white centre ; 20 inches ; May 10, 12 days.

690. Julia (Hogg & Robertson).—Purplish-rose, dark blue centre ; 27 inches ; May 9, 16 days.

691. Julie Vinot (Hogg & Robertson).—Purplish rose, with a narrow paler margin, lilac-rose within ; large white centre ; 24 inches ; May 8, 17 days.

692. Kate Greenaway (de Graaff, Hogg & Robertson).—Soft purplish-lilac, shading at the margin to very soft lilac ; bluish centre ; 24 inches, May 10, 18 days.

693. Kentucky (Hogg & Robertson).—Rosy-crimson, deep blue centre, irregular ; 24 inches ; May 6, 16 days.

694. Kepler (Hogg & Robertson).—Very dark crimson, violet-black centre ; 24 inches ; May 10, 12 days.

695. Kern (Hogg & Robertson).—Rose-purple, shading to lilac edge, pale yellow centre ; 24 inches ; May 10, 12 days.

696. King David (Hogg & Robertson).—Crimson-scarlet, blue and white centre ; 24 inches ; May 7, 18 days.

697. King Harold (Barr, de Graaff, Wallace), **A.M.** May 9, 1905.— Rich crimson, violet centre ; 20 inches ; May 7, 18 days.

698. Königin Emma (Krelage).—Purplish-rose, blue and white centre, a little weak-stemmed ; 26 inches ; May 4, 18 days.

699. La Candeur, *syn.* White Queen, *q.v.*

700. L'Admirable (Hogg & Robertson). — Carmine-crimson, small blue centre ; 20 inches ; May 6, 16 days.

701. Lady Kitty Ashe (de Graaff).—Lilac-rose within, outside cream shading to a lilac-rose margin ; 24 inches ; May 4, 14 days.

702. La Grande Duchesse (Hogg and Robertson).—Light purplish-crimson, rich violet centre ; 30 inches ; May 8, 14 days.

703. Landelle (Hogg & Robertson, Wallace), **XXX** May 24, 1900.— Rose within, outside purplish-rose with narrow paler margin ; centre white and violet ; 22 inches ; May 9, 14 days.

704. Lantern (Barr, de Graaff, Hogg & Robertson, Krelage, Wallace), **XX** May 11, 1906.—Soft lilac, paler towards the edge, tipped outside with purplish-rose, white centre ; uniform, vigorous ; 22 inches ; May 7, 20 days. *Syn.* Nezza, Le Petit Blondin. There is a Rembrandt var. of this name.

705. La Tonnaye, *syn.* Baronne de la Tonnaye, *q.v.*

706. La Tristesse (Hogg & Robertson, Krelage), **XX** May 11, 1906.— Within slaty-purple, outside dark blue-lilac, paler towards the edge ; 21 inches ; May 8, 14 days.

707. La Tulipe Noire (Hogg & Robertson, Krelage), **A.M.** May 22, 1901.—Very dark purplish-crimson, deep violet centre ; 24 inches ; May 7, 18 days.

708. Laurentia (Hogg & Robertson).—Carmine-scarlet, violet centre ; 24 inches ; May 7, 16 days.

709. Lawrence (Wallace).—Purplish-rose, violet centre ; 24 inches ; May 7, 16 days.

710. Lawrence Sterne (Hogg & Robertson).—Rose-purple, light blue centre, weak-stemmed ; 22 inches ; May 3, 14 days.

711. Lazaro Peppo (de Graaff, Hogg & Robertson).—Purplish-lilac, darker outside ; white centre ; 28 inches ; May 6, 16 days.

712. Lenotre (Hogg & Robertson).—Deep rose, outside lilac-rose with paler margin ; centre small, bluish ; 22 inches ; May 6, 16 days.

713. Leo XIII. (Hogg & Robertson).—Crimson ; dark violet centre, white-edged ; 22 inches ; May 3, 18 days.

714. Leoncra (Barr, Hogg & Robertson).—Purplish-rose, dirty-white centre ; 18 inches ; May 6, 16 days.

715. Leonardo da Vinci (Barr, de Graaff, Hogg & Robertson, Krelage, Wallace), **XXX** May 11, 1906.—Very dark purplish-crimson, small violet-black centre ; 24 inches ; May 4, 18 days.

716. Leopold de Rothschild (Krelage).—Rich crimson, large violet centre banded with white ; 18 inches ; May 7, 14 days.

717. Le Petit Blondin, *syn.* Lantern, *q.v.*

718. Liberia (Hogg & Robertson).—Dark purple-crimson, dark violet centre ; 28 inches ; May 10, 16 days. *Syn.* Prof. Wittmack.

719. Lilith (Hogg & Robertson).—Deep purplish-rose, light violet centre, thick-stemmed ; 21 inches ; May 8, 14 days.

720. L'Ingénue (Krelage), **XXX** May 11, 1906. — Soft lilac-rose, deeper at the tip ; centre rich blue ; 27 inches ; May 6, 16 days.

721. Linnaeus (Hogg & Robertson), **XX** May 11, 1906.—Dark magenta-purple, poor centre ; 28 inches ; May 3, 14 days.

722. Lisette (Hogg & Robertson).—Lilac-rose, blue centre ; 20 inches ; May 9, 12 days.

723. Liszt (Hogg & Robertson).—Deep reddish-purple, centre greenish-blue and white ; 24 inches ; May 7, 20 days.

724. Longfellow (Hogg & Robertson). — Purplish-rose, dirty-white centre ; 21 inches ; May 7, 16 days.

725. Lord Duncan (Hogg & Robertson).—Carmine-crimson, violet and white centre ; 24 inches ; May 7, 16 days.

726. Lord Peel (Wallace).—Rose-purple, light violet centre ; 24 inches ; May 10, 18 days.

727. Louis Cusin (Hogg & Robertson).—Purplish-rose, bright blue centre ; 22 inches ; May 9, 14 days.

728. Louis de la Vallière (de Graaff, Hogg & Robertson), **XX** May 8, 1907.—Scarlet to deep rose, small violet centre ; 28 inches ; May 7, 18 days.

729. Louise (Hogg & Robertson).—Bluish-lilac, paler at the margin, white centre, small ; 20 inches ; May 8, 14 days.

730. Louis Mimmerel (Hogg & Robertson, Wallace).—Rich purplish-rose, a little paler at the margin ; centre poor ; 21 inches ; May 9, 16 days.

731. Loveliness (Barr, de Graaff, Hogg & Robertson, Wallace).—Soft rose, intensifying with age ; white centre ; bulbs uniform ; 22 inches ; May 7, 20 days.

732. Lyciscus (Hogg & Robertson).—Purplish-lilac, dirty-white centre ; 20 inches ; May 9, 12 days.

733. McOwan (Hogg & Robertson), **XX** May 11, 1906.—Deep purple, centre blue and white ; May 6, 10 days.

734. Madame Barrois (Krelage), **XXX** May 11, 1906.—Rose-pink, paler at the margin ; outside flamed deep lilac-rose ; centre blue and green ; 24 inches ; May 9, 20 days.

735. Madame Bosboom Toussaint (Hogg & Robertson), **XXX** May 24, 1900.—Rose-purple, deep blue centre ; 21 inches ; May 8, 14 days.

736. Mme. de Beynat (Hogg & Robertson).—Lilac-purple, purplish-red outside, large white centre ; 20 inches ; May 9, 16 days.

737. Mme. de Tavernier (Hogg & Robertson).—Carmine-crimson, large white centre ; 27 inches ; May 9, 18 days.

738. Mme. Krelage (Barr, Hogg & Robertson, Krelage, Wallace), **XXX** May 11, 1906.—Soft lilac-rose, much deeper rose outside ; large whitish centre ; 27 inches ; May 6, 16 days. There is also a Rembrandt variety of this name.

739. Mme. Lethierry (Hogg & Robertson). — Lilac-rose, olive and yellow centre, poor, weak stem ; 24 inches ; May 6, 14 days.

740. Mme. Raven (Hogg & Robertson).—Deep purplish-rose, paler at the margin ; white centre banded with blue ; 24 inches ; May 9, 14 days.

741. Mme. Schreiter (Hogg & Robertson).—Deep rose, rich violet centre ; 24 inches ; May 8, 16 days.

742. Mlle. Prevet (Hogg & Robertson).—Lilac-rose, large white centre, small flower ; 22 inches ; May 8, 16 days.

743. Maeterlinck (Hogg & Robertson). — Purplish-rose, light violet centre ; 22 inches ; May 9, 14 days.

744. Magnet (Wallace).—Pale-lilac, outside flamed with rose, centre dull olive and white ; egg-shaped ; 22 inches ; May 9, 20 days.

745. Maharajah (Hogg & Robertson).—Dark purplish-crimson, dark violet and white centre ; 18 inches ; May 6, 16 days.

746. Mahony (Hogg & Robertson).—Rich crimson, violet centre ; 24 inches ; May 8, 16 days.

747. Maiden's Blush (Barr, Hogg & Robertson, Krelage, Wallace).— Bright purplish-rose ; 24 inches ; May 8, 20 days.

748. Major Mason (Hogg & Robertson).—Bright purplish-rose, poor centre ; 24 inches ; May 8, 20 days.

749. Manceau (Barr, Hogg & Robertson, Krelage).—Deep purple, white centre ; 27 inches ; May 2, 20 days.

750. Manitoba (Hogg & Robertson). — Rose-purple, poor centre ; 20 inches ; May 8, 14 days.

751. Marcello (Hogg & Robertson).—Bright crimson ; with neat dark violet centre, edged white ; 20 inches ; May 6, 16 days.

752. Marc Micheli (Krelage).—Lilac-rose, deeper outside ; large violet centre ; 26 inches ; May 6, 18 days.

753. Marconi (Hogg & Robertson, Krelage).—Deep purple with yellow and olive centre ; 28 inches ; May 6, 18 days.

754. Margaret (Barr, de Graaff, Hogg & Robertson, Krelage, Wallace), **A.M.** May 17, 1904.—Soft lilac-rose, shading to cream, with white centre lightly ringed with blue ; 24 inches ; May 8, 16 days. *Syn.* Gretchen.

755. Marianne (de Graaff). — Deep purple, small white centre ; 22 inches ; May 8, 14 days.

756. Marie (Hogg & Robertson, Wallace).—Light scarlet, light blue centre, weak ; 22 inches ; May 6, 12 days.

757. Maria Edgeworth (Hogg & Robertson).—Purplish-rose, white and blue centre, small flower ; 20 inches ; May 10, 14 days.

758. Mark Twain (Hogg & Robertson, Wallace).—Rich purplish-rose, shading to a very pale margin ; white centre ; 22 inches ; May 9, 14 days.

759. Mars (Hogg & Robertson).—Crimson-scarlet ; blue-black centre edged white ; 21 inches ; May 9, 12 days.

760. Martianus Capella (de Graaff, Hogg & Robertson, Wallace).— Crimson-scarlet, blue-green centre ; 22 inches ; May 6, 16 days.

761. Massachusetts (de Graaff, Hogg & Robertson).—Lilac-rose, outside flamed purplish-rose ; pale bluish centre ; 26 inches ; May 3, 16 days.

762. Massenet (de Graaff, Hogg & Robertson).—Rich lilac-rose shading to flesh edge, centre blue and white ; 22 inches ; May 10, 12 days.

763. Mattia (Hogg & Robertson).—Dark carmine-crimson, blue centre ; 26 inches ; May 6, 16 days.

764. Maugiron (Hogg & Robertson).—Deep purple, small dark violet centre ; 26 inches ; May 4, 16 days.

765. Mauve Clair (Krelage). — Rosy-purple within, outside lilac, shading to a creamy edge ; centre dark blue ; 20 inches ; May 7, 16 days.

766. Max Leichtlin (Hogg & Robertson). — Crimson rose, violet centre, short flower ; 24 inches ; May 6, 20 days.

767. May Queen (Barr, de Graaff, Hogg & Robertson, Krelage), **A.M.** May 19, 1903.—Salmon-rose, shaded, especially outside, with lilac ; dark blue-olive centre ; flowers very large ; stalks purplish ; 26 inches ; May 4, 20 days.

768. M. Barrois (Hogg & Robertson).—Rose-purple, lilac-edged ; centre yellow ; 18 inches ; May 8, 10 days.   Not the same as Mme. Barrois.

769. Medusa (Hogg & Robertson, Krelage). — Carmine-scarlet, light blue centre ; 22 inches ; May 9, 12 days.

770. Michael Angelo (Hogg & Robertson).—Light crimson, irregular violet and white centre ; 24 inches ; May 6, 16 days.

771. Michelin (Hogg & Robertson).—Dark scarlet, poor ; 24 inches ; May 4, 16 days.

772. Mignon (de Graaff, Hogg & Robertson).—Violet-purple, poor centre ; 21 inches ; May 4, 14 days.

773. Millet (Hogg & Robertson, Wallace), **A.M.** May 15, 1906.—Light crimson, deep violet centre ; 20 inches ; May 7, 16 days.

774. Mima (Wallace). — Rosy-crimson, violet centre ; 28 inches ; May 8, 14 days.

775. Minister Pearson (Hogg & Robertson).—Crimson, blue centre ; 20 inches ; May 6, 16 days.

776. Minister Roell (Hogg & Robertson, Wallace), **XXX** May 24, 1900.—Crimson, deep violet white-edged centre ; 24 inches ; May 9, 14 days.

777. Minister Tak van Poortvliet.   See Van Poortvliet.

778. Minister van den Berg (Hogg & Robertson).—Crimson-scarlet, slaty-blue centre ; 21 inches ; May 9, 12 days.

779. Minnesota (Hogg & Robertson). — Crimson-scarlet, slaty-blue centre ; 20 inches ; May 9, 12 days.

780. Mississippi (Hogg & Robertson).—Lilac-rose, flamed purplish-rose outside ; light blue and white centre ; 28 inches ; May 7, 18 days.

781. Miss Ormerod (Hogg & Robertson).—Bright rose, paler at the margin, deep purplish-rose outside ; blue-black centre ; 24 inches ; May 7, 18 days.

782. Missouri (Hogg & Robertson, Krelage).—Purplish-rose, dull blue-green centre ; 26 inches ; May 7, 18 days.

783. Miss White (Hogg & Robertson).—Purplish-rose, violet centre ; 20 inches ; May 7, 14 days.

784. Mr. A. F. Barron (Hogg & Robertson).—Purplish-crimson, small olive-green and black centre ; 24 inches ; May 6, 16 days.

785. Mr. Bergoma (Hogg & Robertson).—Very dark crimson, violet-black centre ; 22 inches ; May 6, 16 days.

786. Mr. D. T. Fish (Barr, Hogg & Robertson).—Rich purple, deep violet centre ; 27 inches ; May 9, 18 days.

787. Mr. Farncombe Sanders (Barr, de Graaff, Hogg & Robertson, Krelage, Wallace), **A.M.** May 17, 1904.—Carmine-rose to carmine-crimson, large white centre; 24 inches; May 8, 14 days. Also received as F. Sanders and Mrs. F. Sanders.

788. Mr. J. Douglas (Hogg & Robertson).—Rose-red, purplish-rose outside, blue and white centre; weak stems; 22 inches; May 6, 14 days.

789. Mr. Jeffries (Hogg & Robertson).—Reddish-crimson; small blue, white-edged centre; 22 inches; May 7, 14 days.

790. Mr. J. G. Baker (Hogg & Robertson).—Carmine-scarlet, rich blue centre; 20 inches; May 9, 12 days.

791. Mr. W. Roberts (Hogg & Robertson).—Crimson; dark violet, white-edged centre; weak stalks; 21 inches; May 3, 18 days.

792. Mrs. Cleveland (de Graaff, Hogg & Robertson, Krelage, Wallace).—Soft lilac-rose, a little deeper than Margaret; centre more blue; 26 inches; May 9, 14 days.

793. Mrs. Humphry Ward (Hogg & Robertson).—Crimson-rose, purplish outside; blue and white centre; 18 inches; May 4, 18 days.

794. Mrs. Potter Palmer (Hogg & Robertson, Krelage).—Deep purple, violet and white centre.

795. Mrs. Stanley (Hogg & Robertson, Krelage), **XX** May 11, 1906.—Rose, purplish outside and paler towards the edge; large bright blue centre; 24 inches; May 6, 18 days.

796. Mommsen (Hogg & Robertson).—Light purplish-lilac, poor centre; 22 inches; May 7, 12 days.

797. Monaco (Hogg & Robertson). — Crimson, blackish centre; 24 inches; May 3, 17 days.

798. Monseigneur Bottimanni (Hogg & Robertson).—Rose-purple, white centre; 18 inches; May 9, 12 days.

799. Montana (Hogg & Robertson).—Dark crimson-scarlet; violet centre, white-edged; 24 inches; May 7, 14 days. There is a species of this name.

800. Moralis (Hogg & Robertson, Krelage).—Violet-purple, poor centre; 24 inches; May 7, 14 days.

801. Moucheron (Hogg & Robertson), **A.M.** May 3, 1904.—Deep purple, small violet centre; 24 inches; May 6, 16 days. There is an early single variety of the same name.

802. Muret (Wallace).—Lilac-rose, poor centre; 20 inches; May 9, 14 days.

803. Napoleon, *syn.* Professor Francis Darwin, *q.v.*

804. Nauticas (Barr, Hogg & Robertson, Krelage).—Purplish-rose, blue-green centre; 21 inches; May 9, 12 days.

805. Negro (Barr, Hogg & Robertson, Krelage, Wallace).—Crimson-maroon, darker centre; 24 inches; May 8, 18 days.

806. New Hampshire (Hogg & Robertson).—Purplish-rose, violet and white centre; 24 inches; May 6, 12 days.

807. New York (Hogg & Robertson).—Reddish-purple, dull centre; 22 inches; May 7, 14 days.

808. Nezza, *syn.* Lantern, *q.v.*

809. Night (Hogg & Robertson).—Very dark crimson, violet-black centre; 24 inches; May 7, 14 days.

810. Nora Ware (Barr, de Graaff, Hogg & Robertson, Krelage).—
Lilac, paler outside, shaded in the bud with bronze ; small bluish centre ;
uniform ; 22 inches ; March 7 ; 16 days.

811. Norma (Hogg & Robertson).—Deep rose, softer at the margin ;
small blue-green centre ; 24 inches ; May 12, 16 days.

812. Nova Scotia (Hogg & Robertson).—Carmine-rose, large white
centre ; 22 inches ; May 9, 12 days.

813. Nymph (Barr, de Graaff, Hogg & Robertson, Wallace).—Soft
lilac, flushed outside with bluish-lilac ; large cream centre ; strong and
uniform ; 26 inches ; May 10, 18 days.

814. O'Brien (Wallace).—Rose-purple, bluish centre ; 24 inches ;
May 3, 18 days.

815. Olga (Hogg & Robertson).—Soft-lilac, flamed outside with lilac-
rose ; 20 inches ; May 6, 16 days.

816. Oliphant (Krelage), **XXX** May 8, 1907.—Slaty-purple, paler
towards the margin ; white centre ; unique in colour ; 28 inches ; May 2,
20 days.

817. Oliver Goldsmith (Hogg & Robertson).—Rose-crimson, blue
centre ; 21 inches ; May 3, 18 days.

818. Oregon (Hogg & Robertson).—Purplish-rose, deeper outside ;
violet centre ; 22 inches ; May 8, 14 days.

819. Orgon (Hogg & Robertson).—Very dark purplish-crimson, large
violet centre ; 22 inches ; May 7, 14 days.

820. Orion (Hogg & Robertson).—Dark scarlet, deep blue centre ;
20 inches ; May 6, 16 days.

821. Ouida (Hogg & Robertson, Krelage).—Distinct varieties were
received under this name, that from the latter carmine-rose, from the
former crimson-scarlet ; 24 inches ; May 8, 14 days.

822. Painted Lady (Barr, de Graaff, Hogg & Robertson, Krelage,
Wallace).—Cream, lightly shaded outside with lilac ; dark-olive filaments.;
28 inches ; May 6, 18 days.

823. Pales (Hogg & Robertson).—Lilac, whitish centre ; 22 inches ;
May 7, 14 days. *Syn.* Saas.

824. Palisa (Hogg & Robertson).—Purple, blue and white centre ;
26 inches ; May 7, 14 days.

825. Pallas (Hogg & Robertson).—Bright carmine-crimson, blue
centre ; 21 inches ; May 6, 14 days.

826. Paris (Hogg & Robertson, Krelage), **XX** May 11, 1906.—Rich
crimson, dark violet centre ; 22 inches ; May 3, 18 days.

827. Parkinson (Hogg & Robertson).—Dark scarlet, deep blue white-
edged centre ; 20 inches ; May 8, 14 days.

828. Parthenope (Hogg & Robertson).—Bright rose shading to lilac
edge, purplish outside ; large white centre ; 24 inches ; May 7, 18 days.

829. Passaeus (de Graaff, Hogg & Robertson, Wallace).—Carmine-
crimson, poor centre ; 20 inches ; May 7, 14 days.

830. Pastilla (Wallace).—Reddish-purple, violet and white centre ;
20 inches ; May 9, 16 days.

831. Patrocle (Hogg & Robertson).—Purplish-crimson, violet and
white centre ; 28 inches ; May 7, 18 days.

832. Paul Baudry (Hogg & Robertson).—Deep reddish-purple, dark
blue centre ; 24 inches ; May 6, 14 days.

833. Pauline (Hogg & Robertson).—Lilac-rose,.flushed purplish-rose outside, paler at the margin ; blue and white centre ; 20 inches ; May 7, 12 days.

834. Penelope (Barr, Hogg & Robertson).—Purplish-rose, paler outside and towards the margin ; small white centre, small flower, weak stems ; 20 inches ; May 6, 16 days.

835. Pensée amère (Hogg & Robertson).—Purple, shading to a slaty-blue edge, dark blue-lilac outside ; centre white ; 22 inches ; May 8, 16 days.

836. Peter Barr (Barr).—Very dark purplish-crimson, dark blue centre ; 24 inches ; May 7, 18 days. The variety received from Hogg & Robertson under this name was not true.

837. Phaeacia (Hogg & Robertson), **XXX** May 16, 1900.—Carmine-scarlet, becoming purplish ; deep blue centre ; 22 inches ; May 6, 12 days.

838. Ph. de Commines (Comminet) (Hogg & Robertson, Krelage, Wallace).—Very dark purplish-crimson, centre poor ; 24 inches ; May 6, 18 days.

839. Phyllis (Barr, de Graaff, Hogg & Robertson, Wallace).—Soft-lilac, paler towards the margin ; centre white ; stems purple ; not so good as Lantern ; 24 inches ; May 8, 16 days.

840. Pieneman (Hogg & Robertson).—Bright reddish-crimson ; black centre, white-edged ; 18 inches ; May 7, 14 days.

841. Pierre Loti (Hogg & Robertson).—Deep purple, neat violet-black centre ; 26 inches ; May 6, 16 days.

842. Polyhymnia (Hogg & Robertson).—Rich crimson, poor centre ; 21 inches ; May 3, 18 days.

843. Portails (Hogg & Robertson).—Carmine-crimson, blue centre ; weak ; 20 inches ; May 8, 10 days.

844. Potgieter (Hogg & Robertson). — Deep red, violet centre ; 18 inches ; May 7, 14 days.

845. Premier Noble (de Graaff, Hogg & Robertson).—Rose-purple, yellow centre ; 24 inches ; May 2, 20 days.

846. Pres. Perier (Hogg & Robertson, Wallace).—Carmine-scarlet, deep blue centre ; 21 inches ; May 3, 14 days.

847. Prévost d'Exilles (Hogg & Robertson, Wallace).—Purplish-lilac, light blue centre ; 24 inches ; May 8, 14 days. Similar to Dream.

848. Pride of Haarlem (Barr, de Graaff, Hogg & Robertson, Krelage, Wallace), **A.M.** May 28, 1902.—Carmine-crimson, blue centre, very large flower, strong stalks ; 24 inches ; May 2, 18 days.

849. Prince George (Hogg & Robertson).—Rose, poor centre ; 21 inches ; May 10, 14 days.

850. Prince of the Netherlands (Krelage), **XXX** May 11, 1906.—Deep rose, grey-blue centre, flowers large ; 24 inches ; May 7, 16 days.

851. Princess Alice (Hogg & Robertson).—Lilac-rose, bluish centre, weak stems, poor ; 21 inches ; May 6, 12 days.

852. Princess Amalia (Hogg & Robertson).—Purplish-rose, small bright-blue centre ; 22 inches ; May 8, 16 days.

853. Princess Olga. See Olga.

854. Professor Balfour (Hogg & Robertson).—Reddish-crimson, violet and white centre ; 20 inches ; May 8, 14 days.

T 2

855. Professor Buys Ballot (Hogg & Robertson).—Crimson, dark-violet centre ringed with white; 21 inches; May 9, 12 days.

856. Professor Clurens (Hogg & Robertson).—Crimson-scarlet, violet centre; 20 inches; May 9, 12 days.

857. Professor Francis Darwin (Hogg & Robertson, Krelage, Wallace).—Carmine-crimson, large violet centre, strong-stalked and uniform; 20 inches; May 6, 16 days. *Syn.* Napoleon.

858. Professor Marshall Ward (Hogg & Robertson, Wallace).—Deep rose shaded with lilac, dark blue centre; 24 inches; May 11, 12 days.

859. Professor Michael Foster (Barr, Hogg & Robertson), **XXX** May 16, 1900.—Carmine-crimson, violet and white centre; 24 inches; May 6, 16 days.

860. Professor Michael Wilder (Hogg & Robertson).—Flowers failed to open.

861. Professor Oliver (Hogg & Robertson).—Rich rose-scarlet, deep blue centre; 28 inches; May 10, 18 days.

862. Professor Rawenhoff (Barr, Hogg & Robertson), **XXX** May 8, 1907.—Scarlet, purplish outside, white and violet centre; 24 inches; May 6, 16 days.

863. Professor Sargent (Hogg & Robertson).—Light crimson, small violet centre; 24 inches; May 1, 14 days.

864. Professor Suringar (Hogg & Robertson).—Dark crimson, violet centre; 24 inches; May 7, 20 days.

865. Professor Trelease (Hogg & Robertson).—Identical with Herald, *q.v.*

866. Professor Walkenstein (Hogg & Robertson).—Bright rose purple, dark olive centre; 24 inches; May 6, 12 days.

867. Psyche (Hogg & Robertson, Krelage, Wallace), **A.M.** May 15, 1906.—Soft lilac-rose flushed outside with purple, very pale blue centre; 24 inches; May 6, 16 days.

868. Purple Perfection (Barr, de Graaff, Hogg & Robertson).—Dark crimson-purple, dull centre; 24 inches; May 7, 16 days.

869. Pygmalion (Barr, de Graaff, Hogg and Robertson, Krelage, Wallace).—Rose-purple, bluish-purple outside; white centre; 20 inches; May 7, 16 days.

870. Queen of Brilliants (Barr, de Graaff, Hogg & Robertson).—Carmine-scarlet, centre white ringed with blue; 24 inches; May 9, 14 days.

871. Queen of Roses (Barr, de Graaff, Hogg & Robertson).—Deep rose, dull centre; 24 inches; May 10, 14 days.

872. Queen Wilhelmina. See Reine Wilhelmine.

873. Reine Wilhelmine (Hogg & Robertson, Krelage).—Pale rose-lilac, shaded towards the edges with buff, outside shaded rosy-buff; vigorous; 26 inches; May 6, 16 days.

874. Remembrance (Barr, Hogg & Robertson, Krelage).—Dark bluish-lilac, whitish centre; 24 inches; May 7, 14 days. Also received as Remonstrance!

875. Rev. Bourne (Hogg & Robertson).—Purplish-rose, poor centre; 20 inches; May 9, 12 days.

876. Rev. G. A. Ellacombe (Hogg and Robertson).—Crimson-scarlet, violet and white centre; 20 inches; May 8, 14 days.

877. Rev. Harpur Crewe (Hogg & Robertson).—Deep lilac-rose, bright blue centre : 24 inches ; May 8, 14 days.

878. Rev. H. Ewbank (Barr, de Graaff, Hogg & Robertson, Krelage), **A.M.** May 8, 1907.—Bluish-lilac, much paler towards the margin ; white centre ; uniform ; 20 inches ; May 4, 18 days.

879. Rev. H. H. d'Ombrain (Barr, Hogg & Robertson), **XXX** May 16, 1900.—Crimson-scarlet, large violet and white centre ; 27 inches ; May 7, 14 days.

880. Rider Haggard (Hogg & Robertson).—Rose-crimson, violet centre ; 20 inches ; May 4, 16 days.

881. Ripperda (Hogg & Robertson).—Dark carmine-crimson, violet centre ; 28 inches ; May 6, 16 days.

882. Robert Lindsay (Hogg & Robertson).—Rose-purple, paler towards the edge ; small dark blue centre ; poor ; 22 inches ; May 8, 10 days.

883. Robert Manning (Hogg & Robertson).—Dark carmine-crimson ; 20 inches ; May 7, 14 days.

884. Romano (Hogg & Robertson).—Purplish-rose, blue-green centre ; 20 inches ; May 7, 12 days.

885. Ronald Gunn (Hogg & Robertson).—Blue-lilac. Flowers failed to open in spite of vigorous leafage.

886. Ronner Knip (Hogg & Robertson).—Bright lilac-rose, violet and white centre ; 24 inches ; May 8, 16 days.

887. Roosje (Wallace).—Carmine-crimson, rich violet-blue centre ; 20 inches ; May 9, 12 days.

888. Rosa (Hogg & Robertson, Krelage).—Lilac-rose within, outside purplish-rose with paler margin ; light blue centre ; weak stems ; 26 inches ; May 7, 10 days.

889. Rose Queen (Hogg & Robertson, Krelage, Wallace).—Bright lilac-rose within, outside dark purplish-rose with paler edge ; centre poor ; 22 inches ; May 3, 14 days.

890. Rose Tendre (Krelage).—Soft lilac-rose, flamed outside with deep rose ; large blue centre ; large flower ; 28 inches ; May 7, 20 days.

891. Roxane (Hogg & Robertson).—Lilac-rose, paler towards the edge ; light blue centre ; weak ; 20 inches ; May 4, 12 days.

892. Ruby (Hogg & Robertson, de Graaff).—See No. 390. (May-flower.)

893. Saas, *syn.* Pales, *q.v.*

894. St. Bruno (Hogg & Robertson, Wallace).—Dark purplish-crimson, with deep blue centre ; uniform, vigorous ; 26 inches ; May 6, 16 days. *Syns.* Bruno, Grandmaster.

895. St. Simon (Hogg & Robertson, Krelage).—Purple, dull blue centre ; 24 inches ; May 7, 14 days.

896. Salmonea (Krelage).—Purplish-rose, shading to a bronze-salmon margin ; centre violet and olive ; 24 inches ; May 6, 12 days.

897. Salmon King (Barr, de Graaff, Hogg & Robertson).—Salmon-rose, whitish centre, dark filaments ; 18 inches ; May 8, 10 days.

898. Samiel (Hogg & Robertson).—Very dark crimson, small flower ; 24 inches ; May 10, 12 days.

899. Sam. Richardson (Hogg & Robertson) Rose-purple, white centre ringed with blue.

900. Scylla (Barr, de Graaff, Hogg & Robertson, Krelage).—Carmine-crimson, deep blue centre, rather weak stalks; 24 inches; May 3, 17 days.

901. Shakespeare (Hogg & Robertson).—Dark crimson, neat violet-black centre; 27 inches; May 6, 16 days.

902. Sibella (Hogg & Robertson).—Purplish-lilac, paler towards the edge; dark blue centre; 22 inches; May 6, 16 days.

903. Sieraad van Flora (Hogg & Robertson, Krelage), **XXX** May 11, 1906.—Lilac-rose, paler outside; blue centre; flowers large; bulbs uniform; 24 inches; April 29, 14 days. *Syn.* Flora's Ornament.

904. Sir Joseph Hooker (Barr, Hogg & Robertson, Krelage), **XX** May 8, 1907.—Rich crimson, rather poor centre of violet and white; 20 inches; May 2, 20 days.

905. Sir Walter Scott (Hogg & Robertson).—Deep purplish-rose, small violet centre; 20 inches; May 9, 12 days.

906. Sophrosyne (Krelage).—Rich lilac-rose shading to a soft rose edge, deep violet-blue centre; large, well-shouldered flower; 30 inches; May 10, 18 days. Finer in flower and foliage than Suzon.

907. Souvenir de Carnot (Hogg & Robertson).—Rose-crimson, violet centre; 24 inches; May 7, 16 days.

908. Spohr (Hogg & Robertson).—Violet-purple, weak and poor; 21 inches; May 8, 10 days.

909. Spring Beauty (de Graaff, Hogg & Robertson).—Crimson-scarlet, dark olive and white centre; 27 inches; May 7, 14 days.

910. Stabens (Wallace).—Lilac-rose, purplish outside; light blue and white centre; 24 inches; May 9, 18 days.

911. Sultan (Barr, de Graaff, Hogg & Robertson, Krelage, Wallace), **A.M.** May 5, 1896.—Very dark purplish-crimson, violet-black centre, uniform; smaller and dwarfer than Faust; 20 inches; May 6, 16 days.

912. Suzon (Barr, Hogg & Robertson, Krelage), **A.M.** May 17, 1904.—Rich lilac-rose within, shading to flesh at the edge, outside soft flesh broadly flamed with lilac-rose; rich blue centre; large flower; 27 inches; May 7, 14 days.

913. Sybille Meriana (de Graaff).—Purplish-lilac, large white centre; 24 inches; May 4, 14 days.

914. Tak van Poortvliet. See van Poortvliet.

915. Terpsichore (Hogg & Robertson).—Rose, small white centre, small flower; 20 inches; May 6, 16 days.

916. Texas (Hogg & Robertson).—Lilac-rose, bright blue centre, 27 inches; May 3, 18 days. A clearer rose than Ant. Roozen, but bulbs not uniform.

917. Thackeray (de Graaff, Hogg & Robertson).—Deep rose, poor centre, small; 24 inches; May 6, 16 days.

918. The Bride (Barr, Hogg & Robertson), **XX** May 11, 1906.—Deep lilac-rose, much paler towards the margin; large blue centre; large, broad petals; 27 inches; May 2, 14 days.

919. The Dove (Hogg & Robertson).—Purplish-rose shading to creamy edge, olive and blue centre; 24 inches; May 11, 12 days.

920. The Lilac (de Graaff).—Lilac, whitish centre; 24 inches; May 9, 14 days.

921. Theodore Jorisen (Barr), Theodor Jorrison (Hogg & Robertson).—Rose-purple, deep blue centre ; 26 inches ; May 7, 16 days.

922. Thérèse Schwartze (Hogg & Robertson, Krelage).—Lilac shading to soft lilac and cream at the edge, bluish centre ; 24 inches ; May 9, 16 days.

923. The Shah (Barr, de Graaff, Hogg & Robertson).—Purplish-crimson, blue centre, small flower ; 21 inches ; May 6, 16 days.

924. Thomas Gray (Hogg & Robertson).—Rose, greenish-blue centre ; 24 inches ; May 9, 16 days.

925. Thorbecke (Hogg & Robertson).—Light purplish-crimson, olive and blue centre ; 25 inches ; May 7, 14 days.

926. Tiberius Winckler (Hogg & Robertson).—Rich crimson, purplish-black centre ; 21 inches ; May 7, 14 days.

927. Tolosa (Hogg & Robertson).—Purplish-rose, bright blue centre ; 24 inches ; May 8, 14 days.

928. Torch (Hogg & Robertson).—Carmine-crimson, light violet and white centre ; 24 inches ; May 8, 14 days.

929. Toulon (Hogg & Robertson).—Purplish-crimson, poor centre ; 28 inches ; May 7, 16 days.

930. Uncle Sam (Hogg & Robertson).—Flowers failed to open, weak ; 20 inches.

931. Urania (Hogg & Robertson).—Carmine-crimson, olive-blue-white centre, very weak ; 20 inches ; May 8, 12 days.

932. Valentin (Hogg & Robertson), **XX** May 11, 1906.—Lilac-purple, blue centre ; 28 inches ; May 1, 18 days.

933. Valère (Hogg & Robertson).—Rose-purple, poor centre, weak flower ; 20 inches ; May 3, 14 days.

934. Van der Heyden (Wallace).—Dark scarlet, olive-blue centre ; 22 inches ; May 9, 12 days.

935. Van Dyck (Hogg & Robertson, Wallace).—Rose, light blue and green centre ; 24 inches ; May 7, 14 days.

936. Vanity (Hogg & Robertson).—Crimson, violet centre ; 20 inches ; May 7, 14 days.

937. Van Poortvliet (Barr, de Graaff, Hogg & Robertson, Krelage, Wallace), **A.M.** May 22, 1901.—Bright carmine-crimson, violet centre ; 27 inches ; May 6, 16 days.

938. Van 't Hoff (Hogg & Robertson).—Rose-purple, deeper outside ; white centre ; 24 inches ; May 8, 14 days.

939. Vargas (Hogg & Robertson).—Deep rose, rich violet centre ; 25 inches ; May 9, 16 days.

940. Velvet King (de Graaff, Hogg & Robertson).—Crimson-purple, large dirty-white centre ; 24 inches ; May 8, 15 days.

941. Vermont (Hogg & Robertson).—Rose-purple shading to lilac, light blue centre ; 24 inches ; May 7, 18 days.

942. Vesuvius (Wallace).—Flowers failed to open ; 9 inches.

943. Victoire d'Olivieri (Hogg & Robertson).—Crimson-scarlet, small olive-blue centre broadly ringed with white ; 24 inches ; May 9, 14 days.

944. Violet Queen (Barr, de Graaff, Hogg & Robertson).—Violet-purple, a little paler towards the edge, a little bronzed within ; poor centre ; 24 inches ; May 6, 16 days.

945. Virginia (Hogg & Robertson).—Rose-purple, small white centre ; 22 inches ; May 7, 16 days.

946. Von Jehring (Barr, Hogg & Robertson, Krelage), **XX** May 11 1906.—Very dark purplish-crimson, violet-black centre; 30 inches ; May 4, 22 days.

947. Wally Moes (Krelage).—Lilac shading to a broad creamy edge, white centre ; 20 inches ; May 6, 18 days.

948. Washington (Barr, Hogg & Robertson, Krelage).—Lilac- to purplish-rose, centre whitish, flower large ; 20 inches ; May 3, 14 days. *Syn.* d'Aubigny.

949. Wedding Veil (Barr, de Graaff, Hogg & Robertson, Krelage, Wallace), **XX** May 11, 1906.—Soft lilac, paler outside, white centre ; 24 inches ; May 4, 20 days.

950. W. F. Stead (Hogg & Robertson).—Carmine-crimson, blue-green centre ; 25 inches ; May 9, 14 days.

951. Whistler (Hogg & Robertson, Krelage), **A.M.** May 23, 1905.— Deep blood-red, rich violet centre, white-edged ; 22 inches ; May 7, 14 days.

952. White Queen (Barr, de Graaff, Hogg & Robertson, Krelage, Wallace), **XXX** May 11, 1906.—Creamy-white softly suffused with rose-lilac, centre cream ; 24 inches ; May 3, 20 days. *Syn.* La Candeur, under which name it is perhaps more generally catalogued, but there is a May-flowering variety of this name.

953. Wm. Copeland (de Graaff, Hogg & Robertson).—Rose-purple shading to a lilac edge ; centre blue-white ; 24 inches ; April 29, 16 days.

954. Wm. Goldring (Hogg & Robertson).—Rose-purple, blue centre ; 24 inches ; May 4, 17 days.

955. Wm. Pitt (de Graaff, Hogg & Robertson, Krelage), **XXX** May 11, 1906.—Rose-crimson, light blue centre, uniform ; 18 inches ; May 4, 14 days.

956. Wisconsin (Hogg & Robertson).—Rose-crimson, violet centre ; 22 inches ; May 6, 14 days.

957. Yolande (Krelage), **XXX** May 8, 1907.—Bright rose, olive and yellow centre, rather weak ; 21 inches ; May 7, 14 days.

958. Zanzibar (Hogg & Robertson).—Very dark crimson, poor centre ; 21 inches ; May 7, 15 days.

959. Zephyr (Barr, de Graaff, Hogg & Robertson, Krelage, Wallace), **XX** May 11, 1906.—Rich rose-lilac, paler outside ; small white centre ringed with blue ; a rather tender variety, several flowers failing to open, and variable in height ; 20-26 inches ; May 3, 14 days. Bulbs from de Graaff a May-flowering variety.

960. Zulu (Barr, de Graaff, Hogg and Robertson, Krelage, Wallace), **A.M.** May, 19, 1903.—Very dark crimson-purple, centre white and violet ; 25 inches ; May 7, 18 days.

961. Zulu King (Hogg & Robertson).—Dark purplish-crimson, violet and white centre, poor ; 20 inches ; May 10, 12 days.

MELONS AT WISLEY, 1907.

A TRIAL of fifty-three stocks of melons was made in the Society's gardens, seeds being sent by many of the leading firms. All of them were sown at the end of April, and when the seedlings were large enough they were planted out on mounds of soil consisting of strong loam, with a little well-decayed leaf-mould added to make it porous ; each mound consisted of about one bushel of soil, and as the roots came through a slight surfacing of similar compost was added. This was done about every ten days, until the fruit was nearly its full size. A dressing of Peruvian guano, at the rate of 2 oz. to each plant, was given twice during the growing season. No other manure was used. The results were so good that the Fruit and Vegetable Committee complimented the Superintendent on the admirable condition of the plants, and the heavy crop of fine fruits. The trial filled one span-roofed house, and a frame 100 feet long. In both structures the results were equally satisfactory.

F.C.C. = First-class Certificate.
A.M. = Award of Merit.

1, 2. A 1 (Sutton, Barr).—Fruit large, averaging 5 lb. each, each plant carrying four fruits ; oval ; lemon-yellow colour, heavily netted ; flesh thick, scarlet, melting, and of fine flavour. Constitution strong, free setter, and early in coming to maturity.

3. Algerian (Barr).—A Cantaloupe variety that grew freely, but produced no fruit.

4, 5. Best of All (Sutton, Barr).—Fruit large, averaging 4 lb. each, each plant carrying four fruits ; round ; creamy-yellow skin, heavily netted ; flesh green, thick, very good flavour. Constitution strong, free setter, and early in coming to maturity.

6. Black Portugal (Barr).—Fruits very large, averaging 5 lb. each, each plant bearing four fruits ; skin black, but when ripe spotted with yellow, ribbed, no netting. Good constitution, free setter. Flesh yellow, thick, and of fair flavour. A Cantaloupe variety.

7. Blenheim Orange, **F.C.C.** September 14, 1880 (Barr).—Fruit of medium size, averaging $3\frac{1}{2}$ lb. each, each plant bearing four fruits ; shape deep round ; skin creamy-yellow, heavily netted ; flesh very thick, scarlet, melting, delicious flavour. A strong grower and very free setter, arriving quickly at maturity.

8. Charles Ross, **A.M.** August 9, 1907 (Ross).—Fruit of medium size, averaging about 3 lb. each, each plant carrying four fruits ; shape flattish round ; skin greenish-yellow, well netted. Fine constitution, and free setter. Flesh green, melting, thick, and excellent flavour.

9. Countess of Derby (Barr).—Fruit of medium size, averaging four fruits to a plant, each about 3 lb. ; shape oval ; skin green, marked with patches of yellow ; flesh green, thick, melting, and of good flavour. A strong grower and free setter, moderately early in coming to maturity.

10. Diamond Jubilee, **F.C.C.** August 9, 1907 (Hurst).—Fruit medium, oval, averaging 3 lb. each, and four fruits to a plant ; skin deep orange-yellow, moderately netted, very handsome ; flesh white, thick, melting, and exquisite flavour—in fact, the Committee considered this the finest-flavoured melon in the collection. A strong grower, free setter, and very early in coming to maturity.

11, 12, 13. Duchess of York, **A.M.** August 20, 1907 (Hurst).—Fruit of medium size, roundish oval, averaging three fruits to a plant, each about 3 lb. ; skin deep yellow, heavily netted ; flesh white, thick, very melting, and of delicious flavour. A strong grower, and fairly good setter, and early in arriving at maturity.

14. Early Black Rock (Barr).—Very large, oval, coarse, corrugated ; deep orange colour when ripe ; averaging four fruits to a plant ; flesh thick, yellow, and of very poor flavour. A rampant grower and free-setting Cantaloupe variety.

15, 16, 17. Earl's Favourite, **F.C.C.** September 10, 1895 (J. Veitch, Sydenham).—Fruit rather small, oval ; pale green skin ; averaging four fruits to a plant, each fruit about 2½ lb. ; well netted ; flesh thick, green, melting, of exquisite flavour. Strong constitution, and very free setter, coming to maturity moderately early.

18. Eastnor Castle, **A.M.** August 9, 1907 (Barr).—Fruit very large, averaging 6 lb. each, and each plant bearing four fruits ; oval shape ; skin deep green, changing to a paler colour with age ; no netting, or very little ; flesh thick, green, melting, and of delicious flavour. A strong grower and free setter, arriving at maturity moderately early. A very fine quality, but not so handsome as some.

19. Emerald Gem (Barr).—A Cantaloupe variety of great size, round, corrugated ; skin rough, yellow, slightly netted ; flesh thick, scarlet, fair flavour. Strong grower and free setter. Distinct from 'Emerald Gem' which had an **A.M.** in 1892.

20. Empress, The, **A.M.** August 9, 1907 (Sydenham).—Fruit large, averaging 6 lb. each, each plant bearing three fruits ; oval irregular shape ; skin creamy yellow, well netted ; flesh white, melting, and of very fine flavour. A strong grower and free setter. One of the first to arrive at maturity.

21. Empress (Sutton).—Fruit of medium size, round, averaging 3½ lb. each and four fruits to a plant ; skin deep golden yellow, heavily netted ; flesh scarlet, thick and luscious. A strong grower and free setter, arriving at maturity early. Distinct from No. 20.

22. Frogmore Scarlet, **A.M.** August 24, 1897 (Barr).—Fruit of medium size, about 4 lb. each, and averaging four fruits to a plant ; shape oval, slightly ridged ; skin pale lemon colour, covered with fine netting, handsome ; flesh scarlet, thick, very melting, and of excellent flavour. A strong constitution and free setter, arriving at maturity moderately early.

23, 24. Golden Perfection (Hurst, Barr).—Fruit of medium size, about 4 lb. each, averaging four fruits to a plant ; shape nearly round ; skin bright yellow, covered with well-defined netting, very handsome ; flesh white, melting, and of good flavour. A strong grower and free setter, arriving moderately early at perfection. One of the plants was not true to name.

25. Gunton Scarlet, **A.M.** October 11, 1898 (J. Veitch).—Fruit of medium size, about 3½ lb. each, averaging four fruits to a plant; shape roundish oval, faintly ridged; skin pale yellow, moderately netted; flesh scarlet, thick, fine flavour. Strong grower and free setter, arriving at maturity moderately early.

26, 27, 28. Hero of Lockinge (J. Veitch, Sutton, Barr).—Fruit of medium size, about 4 lb. each, averaging four fruits to a plant; shape round, inclined to oval; skin bright yellow, well netted; flesh white, melting, and of delicious flavour. Strong grower and free setter, arriving at maturity moderately early. This variety is so well known and popular that any description seems superfluous.

29. Highcross Hybrid, **F.C.C.** June 28, 1881 (Barr).—Not true to name.

30. Long Island Beauty (Barr).—A Cantaloupe variety of large size, about 5 lb. each, averaging four fruits to a plant; skin yellow, well netted, ribbed; round; flesh scarlet, thick, and of poor flavour. A stronger grower, free setter, arriving at maturity early.

31. Mauldslie Castle (Barr).—Fruit of medium size, about 3 lb. each, averaging four fruits to a plant; shape nearly round; skin greenish yellow, irregularly netted; flesh green, thick, and of a fair flavour. Strong grower, free setter, arriving at maturity late.

32. Monro's Little Heath, **F.C.C.** May 15, 1872 (Barr).—Fruit medium to large, about 4 lb. each, averaging four fruits to a plant; shape irregular oval, faintly ridged; skin creamy yellow, well netted; flesh scarlet, thick, and of fairly good flavour. Strong grower, free setter, rather late in arriving at maturity.

33. Netted Gem (Barr).—A Cantaloupe variety of rampant growth, refusing to set its fruit.

34. Open Air (Sutton).—Fruit very large, about 6 lb. each, averaging three fruits to a plant; shape flat round, ribbed; skin orange and green, slightly netted; flesh scarlet, fair flavour. A strong grower and free setter, arriving at maturity early. This variety closely resembles ' Hardy Scarlet.'

35. Parisian (Barr).—A Cantaloupe variety of large size, about 5 lb. each, averaging three fruits to a plant; shape flat round, corrugated; skin pale yellow; flesh scarlet, moderate flavour. Strong grower, free setter, arriving at maturity late.

36. Paris Favourite (Sutton).—Fruit very large, averaging over 6 lb. each, and carrying four fruits to a plant; shape round, corrugated; skin yellow with patches of white, no netting; flesh scarlet and of fairly good flavour. Strong grower and free setter, arriving at maturity very early.

37. Perfection, **A.M.** August 20, 1907 (Sutton).—Fruit large, averaging 6 lb. each, four fruits to a plant; shape round; colour green, beautifully netted; flesh green, very thick, and of delicious flavour. A strong grower, and very free setter, arriving at maturity moderately early. The Committee considered this the handsomest melon in the trial.

38, 39, 40. Ringleader (Sutton, Veitch, Barr).—Fruit very large, over 6 lb. each, four fruits to a plant; shape rounded oval, rounded at the ends; skin creamy green, heavily netted; flesh green, thick, very fine flavour. A strong grower and free setter, arriving at maturity early. The heaviest cropper in the trial.

41. Royal Favourite (Sutton).—Fruit of medium size, about 4 lb. each, averaging four fruits to a plant; shape round, with flattened ends; skin pale yellow, moderately netted; flesh white, very thick, melting, excellent flavour.   Strong grower, free setter, arriving at maturity moderately early.

42. Royal Sovereign (Hurst).—Fruit of medium size, about 4 lb. each, averaging four fruits to a plant; skin very deep yellow, irregularly netted; shape round, handsome; flesh white, melting, thick, fine flavour. Strong grower, free setter, very early in arriving at maturity.

43. Superlative (Sutton).—Fruit of medium size, 4 lb. each, averaging four fruits to a plant; shape round, heavily netted; colour greenish-yellow; flesh scarlet, remarkably thick, very good flavour.   Strong grower, free setter, arriving at maturity early.

44. Supreme (J. Veitch).—Fruit large, about 5 lb. each, averaging four fruits to a plant; shape oval; skin orange green, moderately netted; flesh green, very thick, of excellent flavour.   A strong grower and free setter, late in arriving at maturity.

45. Sutton's Scarlet, **F.C.C.** August 9, 1907 (Sutton).—Fruit of medium size, 4 lb. each, averaging four fruits to a plant; shape round, handsome; skin rich golden yellow, beautifully netted; flesh very thick, scarlet, and of most exquisite flavour. Strong grower, very free setter, and early in arriving at maturity.

46. Syon Perfection, **A.M.** July 13, 1897 (J. Veitch).—Fruit medium to large, about $4\frac{1}{2}$ lb. each, averaging three fruits to a plant; shape oval; skin green, well netted; flesh scarlet, thick, and of excellent flavour. A strong grower but not a free setter, rather late in arriving at maturity.

47, 48. The Countess, **F.C.C.** July 9, 1889 (Sydenham, Barr).—Fruit of medium size, about 4 lb. each, averaging four fruits to a plant; shape oval; skin deep orange, moderately netted; flesh white, melting, thick, and of delicious flavour.   Strong grower, free setter, arriving at maturity early.

49. The Paul Rose (Barr).—Fruit rather small, about $2\frac{1}{2}$ lb., averaging four fruits to a plant; shape oval, ribbed deeply; skin yellowish green, heavily netted; flesh scarlet, thick, fair flavour. Strong grower, free setter, arriving at maturity moderately early. A Cantaloupe variety.

50. Triumph (Barr).—Fruit of medium size, about 4 lb. each, averaging four fruits to a plant; shape oval; skin green, well netted; flesh thick, green, good flavour. Strong grower, free setter, arriving at maturity very early.

51. William Tillery, **F.C.C.** June 10, 1879 (Hurst).—Fruit large, about 6 lb. each, averaging three fruits to a plant; shape oval; skin green, tinged with yellow, irregularly netted; flesh green, very thick, and of most delicious flavour.   Strong grower, moderate setter, arriving at maturity early. A very fine old variety.

52, 53. Windsor Castle (Barr, Sutton).—Fruit of medium size, about $3\frac{1}{2}$ lb. each, averaging three fruits to a plant; shape oval; skin greenish yellow, well netted; flesh green, thick, luscious. Strong grower, moderate setter, late in arriving at maturity.

STRAWBERRIES AT WISLEY, 1907.

IN March 1905 thirty-five stocks of strawberries were sent for trial; these were all planted at once on ground that had been deeply trenched and heavily manured. All the stocks made excellent growth, and blossomed profusely in 1906, but the whole crop was destroyed by frost, and the trial was continued in 1907, when they were examined by the Fruit and Vegetable Committee.

F.C.C.=First-class Certificate.
A.M. = Award of Merit.

1. Afrikose (?) (Lloyd).—Fruit of medium size, round, scarlet, with prominent yellow seeds. Light crop, and both foliage and fruit badly infested with mildew. Ripe June 26.

2. Bedford Champion, **A.M.** July 4, 1905 (Laxton).—Fruit of great size, conical or round, bright scarlet, heavy ; good flavour. Very heavy crop. A robust grower, free from mildew. Ripe July 16.

3. British Queen (Laxton).—Fruit of medium size, round, red, flesh firm, and of delicious flavour. Good crop, free from mildew. Ripe July 16. This fine old strawberry is uncertain on most soils, but the light sandy soil at Wisley appears to suit it.

4. Climax (Laxton).—A strong grower and free bearer, but the crop was spoiled by mildew.

5. Dr. Hogg, **F.C.C.** July 3, 1866 (Laxton).—Fruit rather large, round, bright red ; first-rate flavour. Good crop, free from mildew. Ripe July 5. An earlier and more robust form of ' British Queen.'

6. Empress of India, **F.C.C.** May 17, 1892 (Laxton). The soil at Wisley does not suit this variety, as many of the plants die off in winter, and those that survive are weak. It is a delicious fruit where it succeeds, and is a good variety for forcing.

7. Fillbasket, **A.M.** July 23, 1907 (Laxton).—Fruit of medium size, conical, bright red ; flesh firm, very good in flavour. Heavy crop, free from mildew ; strong, vigorous habit. Ripe July 16.

8. Filbert Pine (Laxton).—Fruit of rather small conical or wedge shape, dull red ; flesh firm and of delicious flavour. Moderate crop, free from mildew. Ripe July 16.

9. Givon's Late Prolific, **F.C.C.** July 22, 1902 (Laxton).—Fruit large, cockscomb shape, dark red ; very firm, and of excellent flavour. A strong grower and free bearer ; foliage slightly attacked by mildew. Ripe July 15.

10. Gunton Park, **F.C.C.** July 21, 1891 (Laxton).—Not a success on the light sandy soil at Wisley.

11. Jarles (Lloyd). Fruits rather large, bright red, prominent yellow seeds, round ; flesh firm, and of good flavour. Moderate crop, free from mildew. Ripe June 26.

12. Kentish Favourite (Pierce).   The Committee unanimously decided this to be synonymous with 'Leader.'

13. La France (Laxton).—Fruit medium to large, round, scarlet; flesh firm, good flavour.   Moderate crop; strong grower; free from mildew.   Ripe July 16.

14. La Grosse Sucrée (Laxton).   Fruit large, deep round, very dark red; flesh firm, fine flavour.   Great bearer; vigorous habit; free from mildew.   Ripe June 16.   The earliest variety in the collection.

15. Latest of All, **F.C.C.** July 24, 1894 (Laxton).—Fruit large, round or wedge-shaped, pale red colour; flesh firm, very good flavour.   Very heavy crop, free from mildew.   Ripe July 19.   Raised from 'British Queen' × 'Helene Gloede.'

16. Leader, **F.C.C.** May 14, 1895 (Laxton).—Fruit large, wedge-shaped, bright scarlet; flesh solid, rich and pleasantly acid flavour.   Great crop; free from mildew.   Ripe June 26.   The heaviest cropper in the collection.

17. Lord Suffield, **F.C.C.** July 21, 1891 (Laxton).—Fruit of medium size, wedge-shaped, very dark red; delicious flavour.   Moderate crop; foliage badly infested with mildew.   Ripe July 1.

18. Mentmore, **A.M.** June 29, 1897 (Laxton).   Fruit large, pyriform, bright crimson; flesh solid, brisk pleasant flavour.   Very heavy crop, free from mildew.   Ripe June 25.

19. Monarch, **F.C.C.** June 25, 1895 (Laxton).—Fruit very large, round to conical, bright red; flesh white, and of good flavour.   Moderate crop, free from mildew.

20. Noble, **F.C.C.** July 1, 1886 (Laxton).—A very poor variety at Wisley; flavour bad.   A light crop, and much mildewed.   Ripe July 1.

21. Perpetual (Laxton).—Fruit rather small, round, dark red; flesh bright red, firm and agreeable, sweet flavour.   A good, continuous cropper from June, until stopped by frost; free from mildew.

22. President (Laxton).—Fruit large, roundish or conical, bright red; flesh firm, and of delicious flavour.   Heavy crop, free from mildew.   Ripe July 25.   An old variety, but still one of the best for all purposes.

23. Reward, **A.M.** July 5, 1898 (Laxton).—Fruit large, wedge-shaped; red; flesh solid and of good flavour.   Poor crop, free from mildew.   Ripe July 1.

24. Royal Sovereign, **F.C.C.** June 21, 1892 (Laxton).—This variety is too well known to require any description; it was the finest all-round strawberry in the collection.   Ripe June 26.

25. St. Antoine de Padoue, **A.M.** August 28, 1900 (Laxton).—Fruit small, round, dark red; flesh firm, and of pleasant flavour.   One of the best of the perpetual fruiting varieties; free from mildew.

26. Scarlet Queen (Laxton).—Fruit of medium size, conical, scarlet; flesh firm, good flavour.   Light crop; strong grower; free from mildew.   Ripe July 16.

27. Seedling (Kent & Brydon).—Plants received in 1907, too late to fruit until 1908.

28. St. Joseph, **A.M.** September 20, 1898 (Laxton).—A perpetual fruiting variety, not so good or prolific as No. 25.

29. Sensation (Laxton).—Fruits very large, blunt round, scarlet;

flesh firm and of fair quality. Light crop ; foliage much attacked by mildew. Ripe July 1.

30. The Bedford (Laxton).—Fruit large, unevenly conical, scarlet, with prominent scarlet seeds ; flesh firm, brisk and good flavour. Heavy crop ; strong grower ; free from mildew. Ripe June 26.

31. The Laxton, **F.C.C.** June 18, 1901 (Laxton).—This was raised from 'Royal Sovereign' × 'Sir Joseph Paxton,' and combines the fine flavour, colour, free bearing, and vigorous habit of both parents. Ripe June 25.

32. The Latest, **A.M.** July 12, 1904 (Laxton).—Fruit large, wedge-shaped, scarlet, firm, solid, fine flavour. Moderate crop ; habit weak ; free from mildew. Ripe July 19.

33. The Captain (Laxton).—Crop light, and both fruit and foliage severely attacked with mildew.

34. Trafalgar, **A.M.** June 5, 1900 (Laxton).—A failure on the light soil at Wisley.

35. Vicomtesse Héricart de Thury (Laxton).—Fruit of medium size, conical, bright red ; flesh firm, dark red colour, and of delicious flavour. Heavy crop, free from mildew. Ripe June 24.

FRENCH BEANS AT WISLEY, 1907.

Sixty-six stocks of Beans were sent to Wisley for trial, all of which were sown on April 28, in rows 3 feet apart. Owing to the cold season the germination of some varieties was indifferent, and a second sowing was made. Later on good progress was made, and most of the varieties cropped well, in spite of attacks of black aphis. When at their best, the Committee examined the whole collection.

F.C.C.=First-class Certificate.

A.M.=Award of Merit.

XXX=Highly Commended.

1, 2. Bountiful (Hurst, J. Veitch). — Growth vigorous ; foliage moderate ; pods long, but somewhat irregular ; heavy crop. Flowers white.

3, 4, 5, 6. Canadian Wonder, **F.C.C.**, September 1, 1903 (Barr, J. Veitch, Carter, Dobbie).—Growth vigorous ; foliage large ; pods long, straight, handsome ; heavy crop. Flowers white.

7. Centenary Golden-podded (J. Veitch).—Growth moderate ; foliage large ; pods long, rather curved ; medium crop. Flowers cream.

8. Dun or Cream-coloured (Barr).—Growth very dwarf and compact ; foliage small ; pods long and straight ; good crop. Flowers creamy white.

9. Dutch Stringless (Pearson).—Growth moderately strong ; foliage of medium size ; pods long, straight, stringless ; good crop. Flowers cream.

10. Dwarf Sugar Parisian Long-pod (Barr).—Not a success. Flowers white, shaded with purple.

11. Dwarf Prolific (Barr).—Growth vigorous ; foliage large ; pods long and very straight ; splendid crop. Flowers pale purple.

12. Dwarf Sugar (Sutton).—Growth vigorous ; foliage moderate ; pods long, nearly straight, round, stringless ; heavy crop. Flowers white.

13. Dobbie's, Earliest (Dobbie).—Growth moderate ; foliage rather small ; pods of medium length, straight ; good crop. Flowers white.

14. Early Prolific (Barr).—Growth rather weak ; foliage moderate ; pods of medium length, straight ; light crop. Flowers white.

15. Early Wonder (J. Veitch).—Growth vigorous and compact ; foliage moderate ; pods of average length, straight, handsome ; heavy crop. Flowers purple.

16. Early Pale Dun (Carter).—Not a success. Flowers lilac.

17. Earliest of All (Hurst).—Growth very vigorous ; foliage rather large ; pods long, flat, straight ; heavy crop. Flowers pale purple.

18. Emil Perrier (Hurst).—Growth stunted. Probably the successive cold nights crippled this variety.

19. Every Day (J. Veitch).—Growth moderately vigorous; foliage of medium size; pods long, nearly straight, yellow; great crop. Flowers pale lilac.

20. Evergreen (Sutton).—Growth moderately vigorous; foliage of medium size; pods of average length, thick and very even; heavy crop. Flowers pale lilac.

21· Excelsior (Barr). — Growth sturdy and very compact; foliage rather small; pods long, handsome, straight; very heavy crop. Flowers white, tinged with purple.

22. Extra Early Negro (Nutting).—Growth vigorous and sturdy; foliage large and dark green; pods long and of even size, straight; heavy crop. Flowers lilac.

23. Forcing Stringless (Carter).—Growth vigorous; foliage moderate; pods long, fairly straight; medium crop. Flowers white, shaded with lilac.

24. Fulmer Forcing (Hurst).—Growth tall; foliage large; pods long, flat, straight; very heavy crop. Flowers white, tinted with purple.

25. Goliath (Dobbie).—Growth very vigorous; foliage large; pods very long, handsome, flat, straight; good crop. Flowers not fixed in colour.

26. Golden Butter, **A.M.** August 13, 1895 (Dobbie).—Growth moderately vigorous; foliage rather small; pods long, flat, inclined to curl; medium crop. Flowers pale lilac.

27. Golden Wax, **A.M.** April 27, 1897. A forcing variety (Barr).— Very similar to No. 26. Flowers also similar.

28. Golden Prolific (Barr).—Practically a failure. Flowers white.

29. Golden Scimitar (J. Veitch).—Growth moderate; foliage immense; pods long, flat, curled; fair crop. Flowers pale lilac.

30. Green Haricot (Barr).—Growth moderate; foliage of medium size; pods long and curved; light crop. Flowers white, tinted with purple.

31. Holborn Wonder (Carter).—Growth vigorous; foliage rather large; pods long, straight, flat, good crop. Flowers white, tinted with purple.

32. Improved Bush Lima (R. Veitch).—A failure.

33. Incomparable (Daniel).—Growth vigorous; foliage moderate; pods of medium length, straight, flat, handsome; heavy crop. Flowers pale purple.

34. Kingston Gem, **A.M.** September 1, 1903 (Dobbie).—Growth very vigorous; foliage large; pods long, straight; heavy crop. Flowers white.

35. Longsword (Carter).—Growth stunted. Not a success.

36. Leicester Wonder (Harrison).—Growth vigorous; foliage rather large; pods long, flat, straight; pale green; heavy crop. Flowers white.

37. Magnum Bonum (Sutton).—Growth moderately vigorous; foliage large and pale green; pods very long, straight, handsome; good crop. Flowers white.

38. Monster Negro Longpod (Barr).—Growth vigorous; foliage large; pods long and straight; good crop. Flowers purple. Same as Negro Longpod.

39, 40, 41. Ne Plus Ultra, **A.M.** July 2, 1899 (Barr, J. Veitch, Carter).—Growth moderately vigorous ; foliage large ; pods long, straight ; heavy crop. Flowers very pale lilac.

42. New Century (Hurst).—Growth very sturdy and strong ; foliage moderate ; pods long, straight, flat ; heavy crop. Flowers very pale lilac.

43. Osborn's Forcing, **F.C.C.** August 5, 1873 (J. Veitch).—Growth sturdy and compact ; foliage rather small ; pods of medium length, straight ; good crop. Flowers white, tinted with purple.

44, 45. Perfection, **A.M.** July 25, 1899 (Sutton, Barr).—Growth moderately vigorous ; foliage of medium size ; dark green ; pods long, straight, handsome ; very heavy crop. Flowers white.

46. Plentiful (Sutton).—Growth vigorous ; foliage moderate ; pods long, straight, flat ; heavy crop. Flowers white, tinted with purple.

47. Prolific Negro (Sutton).—Very similar to No. 38.

48. Progress, **A.M.** July 25, 1899 (J. Veitch).—Growth very vigorous ; fine dark medium-sized foliage ; pods of average length, straight ; great crop. Flowers pale purple.

49. Reliance, **A.M.** September 1, 1903 (Sutton).—This may be described as an improved form of Nos. 39, 40, 41.

50. Sir Joseph Paxton (Carter).—Growth tall and vigorous ; foliage large ; pods of medium length, straight ; very heavy crop. Flowers white.

51. Stringless, **A.M.** July 25, 1899 (Carter).—Growth dwarf and sturdy ; foliage large ; pods long, round, fleshy, stringless ; heavy crop. Flowers lilac.

52. Surrey Prolific, **A.M.** August 18, 1901 (Dobbie).—Growth very vigorous ; foliage large and plentiful ; pods long, straight, handsome ; good crop. Flowers white.

53. Superb Early Forcing (J. Veitch).—Not a success.

54. Stringless Canadian Glory (Carter).—Growth vigorous ; foliage large ; pods long, round, inclined to curl ; light crop. Flowers white, tinted lilac.

55. Sword-largest-podded (Carter).—Not a success.

56. Syon House Improved (Carter).—Growth moderately vigorous ; foliage medium ; pods long, straight ; good crop. Flowers white, shaded with lilac.

57. The Duke (Nutting).—A failure.

58. The Treasure (Toogood).—Growth vigorous ; foliage large, dark green ; pods long, straight, handsome, flat ; heavy crop. Flowers purple.

59. Triumph (Sutton).—Not a success.

60. Triumph Forcing (Toogood).—Not a success.

61. Veitch's Hybrid (J. Veitch).—Growth very vigorous ; foliage large, dark, and plentiful ; pods long, straight, handsome ; very heavy crop, but rather late. Flowers very pale purple.

62. Williams's Earliest of All (Nutting).—Growth moderately vigorous ; foliage large, dark, and plentiful ; pods long, uneven in size ; heavy crop. Flowers pale lilac.

63. White Haricot (Sutton).—Growth vigorous ; foliage moderate and rather pale ; pods of great length and somewhat coarse ; heavy crop. Flowers white.

64. White Wonder (J. Veitch).—Growth moderately vigorous; foliage medium; pods long, straight; good crop. Flowers white.

65. Wythes's Early, **A.M.** September 1, 1903 (J. Veitch).—Growth moderate and compact; foliage medium; pods very long, flat and straight; heavy crop. Flowers pink.

66. Staward's Best of All (Staward).—This variety was received late, and was not a success.

Runner Varieties.

1. Champion Scarlet (Sydenham).—Scarlet runner. Growth vigorous and sturdy; pods of moderate length, straight; even in size, handsome; great crop. Flowers scarlet. Seeds black, spotted with violet.

2. Loseley Park Success (Staward).—Very similar to Ne Plus Ultra.

3. Ne Plus Ultra (Sydenham).—Growth very vigorous and of the usual scarlet runner type; pods long, straight, handsome, very crisp; very heavy crop. Flowers scarlet. Seeds black, spotted with violet.

4. Phenomenon (Pearson).—Climbing French. Growth vigorous; foliage moderate; pods long, straight, handsome, very crisp and delicate; very heavy crop. Flowers and seeds white.

5. Sex Bounty (Staward).—Similar to No. 3, but not so vigorous or prolific.

6. Striped Bean (Owen).—Climbing French. Growth only moderately vigorous, about 3 feet high; foliage medium; pods rather short, inclined to curl, striped purple; light crop. Flowers deep lilac.

7. The Admiral (Sydenham).—Climbing French. Growth moderate good foliage; pods long, straight, very handsome, tender; excellent crop. Flower pale lilac. Seeds crimson.

KALES AT WISLEY, 1906-07.

FIFTY-FOUR stocks of kale were received for trial, all of which germinated freely, and, when large enough, were planted out on deeply dug, well-manured land, at a distance of 3 feet apart each way. In spite of the dry summer of 1906 all the stocks made splendid growth, completely covering the ground, and were admired by every one who saw them for their fine, robust, healthy appearance. On September 25, 1906, the thermometer marked 37°, and from that date certain types, such as Buda and Asparagus kales, collapsed, decay setting in, and by the end of the year all of these types were dead, while others of a different character were uninjured. On cutting the dead or dying stems through, a great number were found to be affected by *Pseudomonas campestris*, a bacillus which is said to attack all the Brassica family. Whether the death of the kales was caused by frost or fungus is a difficult question for future research, but the great value of the trial consisted in showing which varieties withstood frost and fungoid attacks and which did not, and were consequently of much less service to the gardener or the market grower, who requires supplies of vegetables in the spring.

F.C.C. = First-class Certificate.
A.M. = Award of Merit.

1. A1 (Sutton).—Height 2½ feet; sturdy; well curled; green; stood frost well. A fine true stock of the Scotch type.
2. Arctic Curled (Sutton).—Height 1 foot; sturdy, compact, green; beautifully curled; uninjured by frost; excellent true stock. May be planted 18 inches apart.
3, 4. Asparagus (J. Veitch, Barr).—All killed.
5. Buda (Barr).—All killed.
6. Brydon's Tall Green Curled (Kent & Brydon).—Same as No. 50.
7. Chou de Milan (Carter).—Height 18 to 20 inches; sturdy; green; foliage broad and bluntly serrated; not injured by frost and stood well; true stock. In the spring a mass of tender sprouts are produced.
8. Chou de Russie, **F.C.C.** March 19, 1907 (Carter).—Height about 20 inches; very sturdy; foliage a pale green; much cut and divided, and serrated at the margins; centre of the plant full, and may be termed 'hearting.' Withstood the winter without the slightest injury, and in the spring months produced a great mass of tender and delicious sprouts; a valuable hardy kale. This is not a new variety, and has long been known as Russian kale, but for some reason or other it has not become much known or grown.
9, 10, 11. Cottager's Kale, **A.M.** March 8, 1907 (J. Veitch, Carter, Barr).—Height about 3 feet; sturdy; foliage green, tinged with purple, and slightly curled. A very hardy and prolific variety, that stood the winter without injury.

12. Couve Tronchuda or Seakale Cabbage (Carter).—Height about 1 foot; foliage green, and forming a loose heart; very hardy and stood the winter well, and has the best flavour after having passed through frost. Although not a kale, this variety was sent to show its hardiness in comparison with kales.

13, 14, 15, 16. Drumhead, **A.M.** November 21, 1905 (J. Veitch, Sutton, Barr, Carter).—Height 1 foot; compact; foliage pale green or white forming good hearts; margins of the leaves curled; handsome; stood the winter well; an excellent early dwarf kale, which will stand through the winter. Very good flavour when cooked.

17. Dwarf Curled (J. Veitch).—Height 18 inches; foliage of moderate size, and well curled; green; stood the winter well. Fine true stock.

18. Dwarf Moss Curled, **A.M.** March 8, 1907 (Carter).—Very dwarf, only about 8 inches high, with long, broad green, beautifully curled foliage; stood the winter well, and produced an abundance of tender sprouts in spring. Excellent true stock.

19. Dwarf Purple (Carter).—See No. 22.

20. Exhibition Kale (J. Veitch).—Height about ·20 inches; foliage green and deeply curled; sturdy habit; stood the winter well. Excellent true stock.

21. Exquisite Dwarf Moss Curled (Barr).—Height 1 foot; sturdy; foliage green, handsome, beautifully curled. Most of the old foliage was killed by frost, but a mass of tender sprouts were produced in spring. Very true stock.

22. Exquisite Dwarf Purple Curled (Barr).—Height 9 inches; foliage of moderate size, dark purple, and heavily curled. Stood the winter well; true stock.

23. Extra Curled Kale (Sutton).—Height 20 inches; sturdy, green, well curled. Some of the older leaves were injured by the winter, but a splendid crop of excellent sprouts were borne in the spring. Fine true stock.

24. Extra Selected Dwarf Green Curled (Hogg and Robertson).—See No. 46.

25. Favourite (Sutton).—One of the asparagus type, and killed by the winter.

26. Green Asparagus (Carter).—All killed.

27. Green Buda (Carter).—All killed.

28. Half-tall Scotch (Carter).—Height 18 inches; foliage of medium size, green, well curled. Somewhat injured by frost, but a moderate quantity of sprouts were produced in spring. True stock.

29. Hardy Sprouting (Sutton).—Height about 20 inches; foliage green, broad, slightly curled; sturdy. Uninjured by the winter, and bearing a mass of very tender sprouts in the spring. A very reliable hardy variety.

30. Imperial Hearting (Carter).—Height 15 inches; sturdy; foliage green, and finely curled, forming good hearts. Uninjured by frost. Fine true stock.

31. Improved Branching (Sutton).—Height 2 feet; very sturdy; foliage green, and crinkled. This may be described as a garden form of the well-known 'Thousand-headed Kale,' combining the hardiness and

exceedingly prolific character of that variety. Not injured by the winter. True stock.

32. Improved Garnishing (Carter).—See No. 52.

33, 34.—Improved Hearting (Sutton, Barr).—Height 20 inches; sturdy; foliage green and deeply curled, forming a small heart. Stood the winter fairly well and produced plenty of tender sprouts in spring.

35. Jersey Tree (Carter).—Height 3 feet; foliage very large, oval at the end, and deep green colour. This plant is of little value as a Kale, and if allowed will grow on for several years, attaining a great height and is more curious than useful. Very hardy, and stood the winter uninjured.

36. Mammoth Tall Scotch (Carter).—See No. 50.

37. New Sprouting (J. Veitch).—Height 1 foot; sturdy; foliage green, of medium size, moderately crimped or curled. Some of the old leaves were injured by frost, but in March a great quantity of very tender sprouts were produced. This variety received an Award of Merit, April 26, 1898, under the name of 'Read's Sprouting.'

38. Paragon Giant Parsley Curled (Barr).—Height 3 feet; sturdy; foliage green and finely curled. Somewhat injured by frost, but plenty of sprouts were produced in March.

39. Phœnix (Carter).—All killed.

40. Purple Asparagus (Carter).—All killed.

41. Purple Buda (Carter).—All killed.

42, 43. Ragged Jack (Barr, Carter).—All killed.

44. Read's Hearting, **F.C.C.** April 24, 1883 (J. Veitch).—Height 18 inches; sturdy; foliage green, well curled and folding in the centre. Stood the winter well and produced abundance of tender sprouts in spring. Fine true stock.

45. Scotch (Barr).—Height 2 feet; foliage green, well curled. Stood the winter fairly well and bore good crops of sprouts in the spring. True stock.

46. Selected Dwarf Curled (Sharpe).—Height 1 foot; sturdy; foliage green and beautifully curled. Stood the winter uninjured, and carried excellent crops of delicate sprouts in spring. True stock.

47. Selected Dwarf Green Curled, **A.M.** March 8, 1907 (Kent and Brydon).—Height, 18 to 20 inches; foliage green and very deeply curled, keeping its foliage fresh and good all through the winter, and bearing a great crop of sprouts in the spring. Fine true stock.

48. Tall Green Curled, **A.M.** March 8, 1907 (J. Veitch).—Height 2½ feet; foliage green, of medium size, beautifully curled, handsome. Stood the winter well and carried great crops of tender sprouts in the spring. Fine true stock.

49. Tall Purple Curled (Carter).—Height 2½ feet; foliage of medium size, purple, well curled. Stood the winter uninjured. The darkest Kale in the trial.

50. Tall Scotch (Barr).—A taller form of No. 48.

51. The Sutton Variegated (Sutton).—See No. 52.

52. Variegated, **A.M.** February 12, 1889 (J. Veitch). — Height 18 inches; foliage beautifully curled, and of many colours, including

purple, red, white, green, &c. mingled and separate. Stood the winter uninjured.

53. Victoria (Dobbie).—Height 18 inches ; sturdy ; foliage green and finely curled. Stood the winter fairly well and produced heavy crops of tender sprouts in spring. A fine true stock of Scotch Kale.

54. Welsh Kale (Carter).—Height 18 inches ; foliage green, well curled, long and narrow. Stood the winter uninjured. Very productive in spring. True stock.

SPRING-SOWN ONIONS AT WISLEY, 1907.

Sixty-six stocks of onions were received for trial in the Society's Gardens, all of which were sown on March 5 on ground that had been trenched 2 feet deep and liberally manured. Plenty of burnt garden refuse was worked into the soil, also a moderate dressing of gas lime to destroy wire-worm, which abounded in the light sandy soil. Germination was generally good, but while quite small the plants were attacked by the larvae of the onion-fly. To check this and to give vigour to the plants a dressing of sulphate of ammonia, at the rate of 1 oz. per square yard, was applied twice, and later on 1 oz. Peruvian guano per square yard. These manures were applied at intervals of one month. The effect was so good that the plants became free of all pests and grew vigorously, only a slight touch of mildew appearing on one or two varieties at the end of the season. The Committee examined the whole collection in due course.

F.C.C.=First-class Certificate.
A.M.=Award of Merit.

1, 2. **A1** (Barr, Sutton).—Size medium; oval; heavy; colour outside dark straw, touched with red; the next skin is a greenish-straw colour. Crop very good, and even in size.

3, 4, 5, 6. **Ailsa Craig** (Barr, Carter, Sutton, Hurst).—Size large; oval or cocoanut-shaped; very heavy; outer skin a brownish straw colour, next skin greenish-white. Crop very heavy, and even in size.

7, 8. **All the Year Round** (Hurst, Nutting).—Size medium; shape somewhat irregular, varying from flat round to globe shape; outer skin brownish-straw colour, next skin green. Crop heavy, but irregular in size.

9. **Barr's Long Keeper** (Barr).—Size uneven and irregular in shape; heavy; outer skin brown, inner skin green. Crop light.

10, 11, 12. **Banbury Cross, A.M.** September 1, 1898 (Barr, Hurst, Harrison).—Size large; flattish-round; heavy; outer skin brown-straw colour, next skin green. Crop very heavy, and even in size.

13, 14, 15. **Bedfordshire Champion** (Carter, Nutting, Barr).—Size fairly large; heavy; flat round; outer skin brown-straw colour, next skin white, tinged with brown. Crop very heavy, and even in size.

16, 17. **Blood Red** (Barr, Carter).—Size somewhat uneven; flat round, and very even in type; heavy; outer and inner skin crimson. Crop heavy.

18, 19. **Brown Globe** (Carter, J. Veitch).—Size medium; deep globular to cocoanut-shaped; heavy; outer skin brown-straw colour, touched with red; next skin yellowish-green. Crop heavy, but rather uneven in size.

20. **Brooks' Extra Long-keeping** (Hurst).—Size medium; flat round; heavy; outer skin dark-straw colour; inner skin yellowish-green. Crop light.

21. Contello's Prize (Cooper-Taber).—Size small to medium ; flat round ; heavy ; outer skin deep-straw colour ; next skin pale yellow. Crop fair, but uneven.

22. Covent Garden Silver-skinned Pickler (Barr).—Size small, but if the crop is thinned the bulbs are of average size ; flat round ; colour china white. Crop thin.

23, 24, 25, 26. Cranston's Excelsior, **A.M.** October 8, 1907 (Barr, Carter, Nutting, J. Veitch).—Size large ; cocoanut-shaped ; very even in type ; heavy ; outer skin pale yellow, next skin greenish-yellow. Crop very heavy, and even in size.

27. Crimson Globe (Barr).—The Committee decided this was the same as Southport Red Globe, which received a **F.C.C.** in 1888.—Size medium to large ; globular ; heavy ; skin dull crimson. Crop heavy, and even in size.

28. Early Golden Gem (Barr).—A failure.

29. Early Wonder (Hurst).—Size small and irregular in shape ; solid ; outer skin dark-straw colour, next skin yellowish-green. Crop plentiful.

30, 31. Exhibition (Sutton, Nutting).—Size large ; flat round ; outer skin pale straw colour, next skin yellowish-green. Crop very heavy, solid, and even in size.

32. Express (Toogood).—A failure.

33. Golden Ball (Nutting).—Size small to medium ; globular or cocoanut-shaped ; heavy ; outer skin pale-straw colour, inner skin pale yellow. Crop fair.

34. Improved Reading (Sutton).—Size medium to large ; very solid flat round ; skin pale-straw colour outside, and the next skin greenish-yellow. Crop very good.

35. Improved Queen (Sutton).—A failure.

36 & 36A. James Keeping (Sutton, J. Veitch).—Size moderate ; cocoanut-shaped ; solid ; outer skin a reddish-brown, next skin white. Fair crop.

37. Long Keeper (Carter).—Size uneven ; cocoanut-shaped ; solid ; outer skin a brown-straw colour, next skin a greenish-yellow. Crop good.

38. Long Keeper (Daniel).—A paler coloured form of No. 36.

39. Losely Gem (Staward).—A failure.

40, 41. Magnum Bonum (Sutton, Barr).—Size large ; deep round, very solid ; outer skin brown-straw colour, next skin green. Heavy crop of fine bulbs.

42. Maincrop (J. Veitch).—Size rather large ; shape flat round, very even, and solid ; outer skin dark-straw colour, next skin pale yellow. Very heavy crop of fine bulbs.

43, 44. Nuneham Park, **A.M.** September 6, 1898 (Barr, Carter).—Size large ; shape flat round, even, solid ; outer skin brownish-straw colour, next skin green. Very heavy crop.

45. Perfection (Sutton).—Size large ; cocoanut-shaped, solid ; outer skin yellow, next skin greenish-white. Good crop.

46. Pearl Pickler (Carter).—Size small ; flat round ; colour china white ; moderately firm. A useful pickling variety if the plants are not thinned in the rows.

47, 48, 49. Rousham Park Hero, **A.M.** September 6, 1898 (Barr, Carter, Hurst).—Size large; shape flat round; very even and solid; outer skin brown, next skin yellowish-green. Very good crop.

50. Record (Carter).—Size very large; cocoanut-shaped; solid; outer skin brown, next skin a rosy-pink shade. Good crop.

50a. Selected Globe (J. Veitch).—A fine strain of Nos. 18 and 19.

51. Silver Globe (Barr).—Very similar to No. 46.

52. The Holborn (Carter).—Size medium; shape irregular; solid; outer skin brown, next skin yellowish-green. Fair crop.

53. The Sutton Globe (Sutton).—Size large, but uneven; cocoanut-shaped; solid; outer skin deep-straw colour, next skin greenish-yellow. Moderate crop.

54. The Giant (Barr).—Size medium to large; shape variable; solid; outer skin brownish-straw colour, next skin greenish-white. Good crop.

55. Trebon, **F.C.C.** August 11, 1876 (Barr).—Size large; shape deep oval; solid, even; outer skin brownish-straw colour, next skin pale green. Very good crop.

56. Tennis Ball (Carter).—Did not germinate well, and was not a success.

57, 58, 59. Up-to-date (Barr, Hurst, Nutting).—Size medium to large; roundish oval shape; very solid; outer skin very dark-straw colour, next skin paler. Very fine crop of even bulbs.

60. White Globe, **F.C.C.** August 30, 1883 (Carter).—Stock not true.

61. White Spanish (Carter).—Size medium, and very even; shape flat round and regular; solid; outer skin very pale-straw colour, next skin white. Very good crop.

62. White Spanish Portugal (J. Veitch).—Very similar to No. 61.

63. White Leviathan (Sutton).—A Tripoli variety of great size; flat round; not very firm; skin china white. Good crop.

64. Zittau Giant, **F.C.C.** 1880 (Barr).—Size and shape very uneven; solid; outer skin reddish-straw colour, inside greenish-yellow. Good crop.

POTATOES AT WISLEY, 1907.

ONE HUNDRED AND TWENTY-EIGHT stocks of potatoes were sent to the Society's Gardens for trial, and, with the exception of a few received late, all were planted on April 9 in rows of 3 feet distant and 18 inches apart in the rows. Nearly all the varieties germinated well and made excellent growth, but more disease appeared than in any previous trial we remember. The soil at Wisley is very sandy and porous, and was deeply dug and liberally manured during the previous winter, making the conditions very favourable for the trial, but the damp cold season was equally favourable for disease, which attacked some varieties very badly, other slightly, and some were quite free, although growing between rows of diseased ones. By reason of their good crop, fine clean appearance, and freedom from disease, the following varieties were ordered to be cooked, viz. :—

Dreadnought.	Massey's Leader.
Favourite.	The Cardinal.
Leonardslee Favourite.	The Colleen.
Longkeeping.	The Forester.
	The Provost.

F.C.C.=First-class Certificate.
A.M.=Award of Merit.
XXX=Highly Commended.

1. Albert Victor (Barr).—White ; round ; eyes shallow to prominent ; rather large ; slightly diseased ; good crop ; haulm moderate ; early to midseason ; white flower.

2. Alpha, A.M. July 28, 1903 (Dobbie).—White ; flat round ; eyes full ; medium to large ; slightly diseased ; heavy crop ; haulm short and sturdy ; early ; white flower.

3. Ashleaf (Massey).—Too well known to need description ; moderate crop ; free from disease : early ; no flower.

4. Beauty of Hebron, A.M. August 14, 1900 (Barr).—Another well-known variety, needing no description ; early ; white flower.

5. British Queen, A.M. August 15, 1905 (Barr).—White ; round, some inclined to kidney shape ; eyes shallow and broad ; rather large ; slightly diseased ; very heavy crop ; haulm moderate and sturdy ; mid-season ; white flower.

6. Cardinal, The (Dobbie).—Red ; kidney ; russety ; eyes shallow ; medium size ; very even ; free from disease ; moderate crop ; haulm short and sturdy ; midseason ; purple flower, with pointed white petals.

7. Cheltonia (Onion).—Yellow ; smooth ; kidney ; eye shallow and almost obscure ; medium size ; slightly diseased ; moderate crop ; haulm weak ; late ; purple flower.

8. Chiswick Favourite, F.C.C. March 30, 1886 (J. Veitch).—White ;

round ; eyes full and very small ; medium size ; diseased ; moderate crop ; haulm rather weak ; late ; white flower.

9. Cigarette, **A.M.** November 21, 1905 (Barr).—Very badly diseased ; purple flower.

10. Clansman, The (Dobbie).—White, tinged with pink, with large pink eyes ; flat round ; medium to large ; heavy crop ; free from disease ; haulm tall and strong ; late ; purple flower.

11. Colleen, The, **A.M.** August 9, 1907 (Williamson).—White ; round ; russety ; eyes shallow ; handsome ; medium size ; free from disease ; great crop ; haulm tall and sturdy ; second early ; white flower.

12. Conquering Hero (Williamson).—Pale-straw colour ; flat round ; eyes large and full ; large ; heavy crop ; slightly diseased ; haulm tall and strong ; midseason ; purple flower.

13. Crofter, The (Dobbie).—White ; flat round ; . eyes prominent ; large ; good crop ; very slightly diseased ; haulm moderate and very sturdy ; late ; white flower.

14, 15. Dalmeny Acme (Dobbie, Massey).—Yellowish-white ; flat kidney ; eyes shallow ; russety ; handsome ; medium size ; heavy crop ; free from disease ; haulm moderate and sturdy ; late ; no flower.

16, 17, 18. Dalmeny Early (Dobbie, Barr, Hurst).—White ; round ; russety ; light crop ; much diseased ; haulm weak ; early ; white flower.

19. Dalmeny Radium (Dobbie).—Very badly diseased ; white flower.

20. Dalmeny Red (Dobbie).—Red ; round ; eyes rather deep ; russety ; medium to large ; heavy crop ; free from disease ; haulm tall and strong ; late ; purple flower.

21. Diamond, The (Barr).—The Committee decided this was too much like ' Abundance ' to be considered distinct.

22. Discovery (Massey).—Not a success.   White flower.

23. Dr. Woollerton (Woollerton).—A failure.

24. D. P. Laird (Staward).—Straw colour ; long flat kidney ; eyes shallow ; rather large ; good crop ; free from disease ; haulm tall and strong ; late ; purple flower.

25. Dreadnought, **XXX** October 8, 1907 (Kirk).—White ; round ; eyes shallow ; handsome ; medium to large ; heavy crop ; free from disease ; haulm tall and strong ; late ; purple flower.   This is distinct from ' Dreadnought ' sent by Mr. Massey in 1906, the latter being a red variety.

26. Duchess of Cornwall, **A.M.** October 24, 1905 (Barr).—White ; round ; eyes full ; russety ; handsome ; medium size ; free from disease ; haulm tall and strong ; late.

27. Early Kidney (Hurst).—White ; kidney ; eyes full ; medium size ; fair crop ; free from disease ; haulm short and sturdy ; early ; white flower.

28. Early Kidney—Somner (Hurst).—A flat pink kidney, too poor to describe ; purple flower.

29. Early Puritan, **A.M.** August 16, 1900 (Barr).—White ; round ; eyes shallow : flesh very white ; medium size ; good crop ; free from disease ; haulm moderate and sturdy ; early ; white flower.

30. Early Regent, **F.C.C.** October 10, 1893 (Barr).—White ; round ; russety ; handsome ; eyes shallow ; good crop ; free from disease ; early ; no flower.   This variety is the same as ' Lady Truscott.'

31. Early Rose (Barr).—Pale pink; flat kidney; eyes rather deep; medium to large; very heavy crop; free from disease; haulm moderate and sturdy; early; white flower.

32. Eightyfold (Dobbie).—Pale purple; round; eyes prominent; medium size; fair crop; slightly diseased; haulm short and sturdy; midseason; purple or pale-blue flower.

33. Eldorado (Massey).—Not a success; further experiments will be made with this variety.

34. England's Glory (Winn).—White; long flat kidney; eyes shallow; russety; medium size: moderate crop; free from disease; haulm weak; midseason or late; purple flower.

35, 36. Ensign Bagley (Dobbie, Hurst).—White; flat round to pebble-shape; eyes shallow; medium size; moderate crop; free from disease; haulm short and weak; early to midseason; white flower.

37, 38. Epicure, **A.M.** August 15, 1905 (Sutton, Barr).—White; flat round; eyes shallow; medium size; very even; heavy crop; free from disease; haulm short and sturdy; early; white flower.

39. Eureka (Dobbie).—Pale-white; round; eyes shallow; medium size; handsome; very good crop; free from disease; haulm short and sturdy; early or midseason; purple flower.

40. Evergood (Massey). Not a success; further experiments will be made with this variety.

41. Factor, The, **F.C.C.** April 25, 1905 (Dobbie).—White; flat round; russety; handsome; eyes shallow; very heavy crop; slightly diseased; medium to large; haulm tall and strong; midseason or late; purple flower.

42. Favourite (Dobbie).—White; round; russety; handsome; eyes shallow; medium size; heavy crop; free from disease; haulm tall and strong; midseason; white flower.

43. First Crop (Ellington).—Very much diseased, and tubers small.

44. Forester, The, **XXX** October 8, 1907 (Sinclair).—Straw colour; flat round to kidney-shape; russety; eyes full; handsome; medium to large; heavy crop; free from disease; late; purple flower.

45. Forest Ruby (Toogood).—Red; kidney; eyes prominent; good crop; free from disease; medium size; haulm tall and very strong; midseason; purple flower.

46. General French, **A.M.** October 1, 1901 (Barr).—White; round; eyes shallow: rather large; moderate crop; much diseased; haulm tall and strong; late; white flower.

47. General Roberts (Barr).—White; round; eyes full; medium size; light crop, slightly diseased; haulm tall and strong; late; purple flower.

48. Gould's Enchantress (Gould).—White; kidney; eyes small and full; light crop; small size; haulm short, and rather weak; early or midseason; purple flower.

49. Great Central (Dobbie).—White; flat round; eyes shallow; medium size; poor crop, slightly diseased; haulm tall and weak; midseason; white flower.

50, 51. Harbinger, **A.M.** August 5, 1897 (Sutton, Barr).—White; flat round; eyes shallow; handsome; russety; medium size; very even;

very heavy crop; free from disease; haulm short and sturdy; very early; no flower. A splendid first-early variety.

52. Haywood Beauty (Clarke).—Red: kidney; eyes small and shallow; medium size; moderate crop; free from disease; haulm moderate and sturdy; midseason; white flower;

53. Ideal, **A.M.** August 15, 1905 (Sutton).—White; flat kidney; eyes shallow; russety; medium size; very heavy crop; slightly diseased; second early or midseason; no flower.

54. Improved Kidney, **A.M.** December 17, 1901 (Dobbie).—White; long flat kidney; eyes prominent; russety; handsome; heavy crop; slightly diseased; haulm tall and strong; midseason or late; purple flower.

55. Improved Snowdrop (Barr).—Yellowish-white; kidney or pebble-shaped; eyes full; small; good crop; free from disease; haulm moderate and study; midseason; white flower. A good selection of ' Snow-drop' which received a **F.C.C.** August 30, 1883.

56. Irish Cobbler (Cooper, Taber).—White; flat round; eyes rather deep; heavy crop; much grown out, and slightly diseased; midseason; haulm moderate and very sturdy; purple flower.

57. Kentish Hero (Wiles).—Practically a failure; white flower.

58. King Edward VII. (J. Veitch).—White ground, marked with pink; eyes prominent; flat kidney; good crop; free from diseased; medium to large; haulm moderate and sturdy; purple flower.

59. Late Round Seedling (Hurst).—A failure.

60. Leonardslee Favourite (Cook).—White; flat round varying to kidney; eyes full; medium and even in size; heavy crop; free from disease; haulm tall and strong; midseason; no flower.

61. Longkeeper, **A.M.** October 15, 1907 (Carter).—Yellowish-white; flat round; eyes shallow; large; heavy crop; free from disease; haulm moderately tall and strong; late; purple flower.

62. Lord Minto (Ross).—A very poor crop, and not worth describing.

63. Lyonian, The (Duke).—White; pebble-shaped; eyes shallow; russety; small to medium size; moderate crop; slightly diseased; haulm short and weak; second early or midseason; purple flower.

64, 65. Maid of Coil, **A.M.** September 11, 1903 (Dobbie, Barr).—White; round; eyes shallow: russety; fair crop; free from disease; haulm moderate; late; white flower.

66. Massey's Leader (Massey).—Pale yellow; flat kidney; eyes prominent; handsome; medium even size; very good crop; slightly diseased; midseason or late; haulm short and sturdy; white flower.

67. May Queen **A.M.** August 15, 1905 (Sutton).—White; kidney; eyes prominent; handsome; large; very heavy crop; free from disease and even in size; haulm moderate and sturdy; a first-rate very early variety; purple flower.

68, 69. Midlothian Early (Dobbie, Hurst).—The Committee decided this to be a fine stock of ' Duke of York.' . Pale-yellow flower.

70. Midsummer Kidney (Ellington).—Too small to be of value.

71. Mr. Ambrose (Dobbie).—Pink or rose coloured; round; eyes rather deep; medium size; very even; heavy crop; free from disease; haulm tall and sturdy; midseason or late; white flower.

72. Monarch (Carter).—White ; pebble-shape ; russety ; eyes rather deep ; light crop ; and rather small ; free from disease ; haulm tall and robust ; late ; white flower.

73. Myatt's Prolific Ashleaf (Barr).—A well-known old favourite early variety ; a fine tree stock which produced an abundant crop ; free from disease.

74, 75. Ninety-fold, **A.M.** July 10, 1900 (Sutton, Barr).—White ; flattish kidney ; eyes full ; large ; very heavy crop ; haulm moderate and sturdy ; early or midseason ; white flower.

76, 77, 78. Noroton Beauty (Dobbie, Barr, R. Veitch).—White with pink eyes ; round ; eyes rather large and deep ; medium size ; moderate crop ; free from disease ; haulm weak ; midseason ; white flower.

79. Northern Star (Massey).—Not a success ; further experiments will be made with this variety.

80. Palm Top (Ellington).—Yellowish-white ; flat kidney ; eyes shallow ; medium size ; poor crop ; free from disease ; haulm weak ; midseason ; purple flower.

81. Pearl, The (Barr).—White ; kidney ; eyes full ; very poor crop ; white flower.

82. Penrhos (Morris).—White ; flat round ; eyes rather deep ; uneven in size ; good crop ; free from disease ; haulm moderate ; midseason or late ; white flower.

83. Pioneer (J. Veitch).—White ; pebble-shaped ; eyes full ; medium and even in size ; fair crop ; slightly diseased ; haulm moderate and sturdy ; midseason ; white flower.

84. Professor Walker (Barr).—White ; round ; deep eyes ; irregular in size ; good crop ; slightly diseased ; haulm moderate ; midseason or late ; purple flower.

85. Provost, The, **A.M.** October 15, 1907 (Dobbie).—White ; round ; eyes shallow ; medium to large ; handsome ; heavy crop ; haulm tall and strong ; midseason or late ; white flower.

86. Quick Lunch (Harrison).—A failure.

87. Recorder (Barr).—White ; kidney ; eyes shallow ; medium size ; fair crop ; free from disease ; haulm moderate and robust ; late ; white flower.

88, 89. Ringleader, **A.M.** July 10, 1900 (Barr, J. Veitch).—White ; pebble-shape ; eyes prominent ; medium size ; russety ; light crop ; slightly diseased ; haulm short and weak ; early ; no flower.

90. Royal Norfolk (Daniel).—White ; round ; irregular shape ; eyes shallow ; rather small ; light crop ; free from disease ; haulm moderate and sturdy ; midseason or late ; purple flower.

91. Royal Purple (Dobbie).—Purple ; pebble-shape ; eyes full ; medium size ; very even ; very good crop ; free from disease ; haulm tall and robust ; midseason ; white flower.

92. Royalty (Carter).—White ; varying from flat round to kidney shape ; russety ; eyes full ; the largest variety in the trial ; heavy crop ; free from disease ; haulm moderate and sturdy ; late ; white flower.

93. Rusty Coat (Ellington).—White ; flat round ; eyes shallow ; very russety ; medium size ; light crop ; free from disease ; haulm weak ; white flower.

94. Satisfaction, **A.M.** September 10, 1895 (Barr).—White; flat round; eyes shallow; russety; medium to large; light crop; much diseased; haulm tall and strong; midseason; white flower.

95. Schoolmaster, **F.C.C.** August 16, 1876 (Barr).—White; round; eyes full; russety; medium size; light crop; diseased and very scabby; haulm moderate; midseason; white flower.

96. Scot, The (Dobbie).—White; flat round; eyes full; medium and even in size; very good crop; free from disease; haulm tall and strong; late; purplish-blue flower.

97. Scottish Triumph (Barr).—The Committee decided this to be the same as Up-to-date.

98. Selected Old Short-top (Barr).—Not a success.

99. Selected Russet (Dobbie).—Red; round; eyes shallow; rough skin; uneven in size; fair crop; free from disease; haulm moderate and sturdy; early or midseason; white flower.

100, 101. Sharpe's Express (Barr, J. Veitch).—White; kidney; eyes full; medium size; uneven and inclined to scab; very good crop; slightly diseased; haulm long and robust; early; light blue flower.

102, 103. Sharpe's Victor, **A.M.** August 14, 1900 (Barr, J. Veitch).—White; flat round; eyes full; handsome; medium size; uneven; good crop; slightly diseased; haulm short and sturdy. A fine early variety. Pale blue or purple flower.

104, 105. Sir John Llewelyn, **A.M.** September 11, 1900 (J. Veitch, Barr).—White; flat oval; eyes shallow; handsome; very heavy crop; free from disease; haulm moderate and sturdy; early or midseason; white flower.

106. Sir Mark Stewart (Barr).—White; flat round; russety; eyes shallow; large; light crop; much diseased; haulm weak; late; purple flower.

107. Snowball (Carter).—White; round; eyes shallow; medium size; light crop: slightly diseased; haulm moderate; midseason.

108. Southern Queen, **A.M.** November 21, 1905 (Dobbie).—White; flat round or oval; russety; eyes shallow; handsome; medium size; heavy crop; free from disease; haulm tall and strong; midseason; white flower.

109, 110. Superlative (Sutton, Ellington).—Both stocks much diseased.

111. Supreme, **A.M.** September 11, 1900 (Barr).—Much diseased.

112. Talisman (Dobbie).—White; long flat kidney; eyes full; russety; light crop; slightly diseased; haulm weak; midseason; purple flower.

113. Twentieth Century (J. Veitch).—White; flat round; eyes shallow; russety; medium size; good crop; diseased; haulm moderate and sturdy; late; white flower.

114. Up-to-date (Barr).—A true stock of the well-known late variety. Good crop; slightly diseased; purple flower.

115. Vicar of Downe (Wiles).—White; flat round; eyes shallow; medium size; light crop; much diseased; haulm weak; midseason or late; light blue flower.

116. Weston Pride (Ellington).—Stock not fixed.

117. W. H. Massie (Staward).—White ; long kidney ; eyes shallow ; medium size ; handsome ; heavy crop ; free from disease ; haulm moderate and sturdy ; late ; purple flower.

118. Windsor Castle, **F.C.C.** September 12, 1893 (Barr).—A failure.

119. Yorkshire Giant (Walton).—White ; long flat kidney ; eyes full ; uneven in size ; good crop ; much diseased ; haulm tall and strong ; late ; purple flower.

Nine seedling varieties under numbers only were received, none of which were of superior merit.

OUTDOOR TOMATOES AT WISLEY, 1907.

Eighty-six stocks of tomatoes were sent for trial in the Society's Gardens, all of which were sown on March 7 in gentle heat, and, when large enough, were potted separately, and after gradually hardening off were all planted out early in June in a very open, exposed position, devoid of any shelter. The season was notoriously a bad one for outdoor tomatoes, as it was damp, cold, and sunless until September. Yet, in spite of the adverse conditions, the trial was a very satisfactory one. The soil had been deeply dug and moderately manured. One stem only was allowed to each plant, and as the fruit formed they had a dressing of 1 oz. muriate of potash and 2 oz. superphosphate per square yard superficial, no other manure being applied. When ready all the stocks were examined by the Fruit and Vegetable Committee.

F.C.C.=First-class Certificate.

A.M.=Award of Merit.

1. Abundance (Sutton).—Fruit large, red, roundish, very slightly corrugated ; a free setter ; foliage and habit sturdy ; early in ripening. Good cropper.

2. Advancer (Laxton).—Fruit of medium size, red, slightly corrugated ; a free setter ; foliage and habit sturdy ; moderately early in ripening. Good cropper.

3. A 1 (Sutton).—Fruit of medium size, round or apple-shape, deep red, smooth. This variety did not set freely, and the foliage suffered on cold nights, curling and turning a bad colour.

4. Bates' Surprise (Bates).—Fruit large, red, smooth, flat round ; a free setter ; foliage and habit sturdy ; early in ripening. Good cropper.

5. Bedfordian (Laxton).—Fruit of medium size, slightly corrugated, red, flat round ; foliage and habit very strong ; late in ripening. Fair crop.

6, 7. Best of All (Sutton, Toogood).—Fruit large, round, smooth, reddish-scarlet ; free setter ; foliage and habit excellent ; moderately early in ripening. Good crop.

8. Blenheim Orange, **A.M.** September 20, 1892 (Carter).—This variety was not fixed.

9. Cascade (Sutton).—Fruit small ; cherry shape ; brilliant crimson ; produced in very long racemes ; a very free setter ; foliage and habit sturdy. Heavy cropper, and ornamental.

10, 11. Challenger (Carter, Hurst).—Fruit of medium size, semi-oval, smooth, red ; a free setter ; moderate foliage and habit ; late in ripening. Moderate crop.

12. Chemin Rouge (J. Veitch).—Fruit of medium size ; deep round ; deep scarlet colour ; smooth ; very free setter ; foliage and habit sturdy. Heavy cropper, ripening early.

13. Cherry Red (J. Veitch).—Fruit small; cherry shape; bright red; borne in moderately long racemes; a free setter; foliage and habit rather weak. Good crop. A pretty ornamental variety.

14. Cherry Yellow (J. Veitch).—A yellow-fruited form of No. 13.

15. Chiswick Peach, **F.C.C.** August 15, 1899 (J. Veitch).—Fruit rather below the average size; deep round; pale yellow or whitish colour; smooth; not a free setter out of doors, and the crop was light. A very fine dessert variety when grown under glass.

· 16. Cooper's First (Cooper, Taber).—Fruit of medium size; nearly round, smooth; bright-red; very free setter; foliage and hiabt mode rately vigorous. Good crop. One of the earliest varieties to ripen.

17. Dedham Favourite, **F.C.C.** July 26, 1881 (Carter).—Fruit very large, smooth; flat round; purplish-red colour; moderate setter; late in ripening. Fair crop.

18. Duke of York, **F.C.C.** July 23, 1895 (Carter).—Fruit medium to large, smooth, flat round; bright scarlet; foliage and habit sturdy; moderate setter. Fair crop; late in ripening.

19. Earliest of All (Sutton).—Fruit of medium size, corrugated, flat round; deep scarlet colour; foliage rather tender; habit sturdy; free setter, and good crop, ripening early.

20. Earliest Outdoor (Cannell).—Fruit of medium size; slightly corrugated, flat round; foliage and habit moderately sturdy; ripening its fruit moderately early; free setter, and good crop.

21. Early Market (Sutton).—Fruit of medium size, round, nearly smooth; red; free setter; foliage and habit sturdy; moderately early in ripening. Light crop.

22, 23. Early Prolific (Barr, Nutting).—Fruit of medium size, slightly corrugated; deep red; free setter; foliage and habit sturdy; early in ripening. Good crop.

24, 25. Early Ruby (Barr, Nutting).—Fruit of medium size, round, slightly corrugated; very free setter; foliage and habit rather weak; early in ripening. Good crop.

26. Favourite (Laxton).—Fruit rather large, nearly smooth; moderate setter; foliage and habit vigorous; inclined to sport; late in ripening. Fair crop.

27. Frogmore Selected, **F.C.C.** April 24, 1894 (J. Veitch).—Fruit large, nearly smooth, bright scarlet; foliage and habit moderately sturdy. This variety did not "set" freely, and the crop was light.

28. Golden Jubilee, **F.C.C.** May 26, 1897 (J. Veitch).—Fruit medium to large, smooth; foliage and habit very vigorous; late in ripening. Fair crop.

29. Golden Nugget, **F.C.C.** August 14, 1894 (Hurst).—Fruit small, round, smooth; a remarkably free setter; early in ripening; foliage and habit excellent. Great crop.

30. Golden Perfection (Sutton).—This variety grew well, but produced very little fruit, and is evidently not suited for outdoor culture in a cold season.

31. Golden Plover (Staward).—Not a success.

32. Golden Queen, **F.C.C.** August 19, 1884 (Hurst).—Fruit large,

round, smooth ; a free setter ; late in ripening ; foliage and habit very sturdy. Good crop.

33. Green Gage (Carter).—Fruit small, round, smooth, orange colour ; free setter ; early in ripening ; foliage and habit sturdy. Good crop.

34. Ham Green Favourite, **F.C.C.** September 21, 1887 (Carter).—Fruit rather large, smooth, bright red ; a free setter ; very early in ripening ; foliage and habit excellent. Heavy crop.

35. Harefield Golden Gem (Carter).—This variety grew vigorously, but set no fruit.

36. Harrowgate Beauty (Hurst).—Stock not fixed.

37. Hero (Laxton).—Fruit medium size, nearly round, smooth, red ; a free setter ; foliage and habit sturdy; early in ripening. Heavy crop.

38. Hillside Comet (Barr).—Very poor crop ; not a success.

39. Hipper's No. 1 (Barr).—A vigorous growing variety, but set its fruit too late to ripen.

40, 41. Holmes Supreme, **A.M.** August 15, 1905 (J. Veitch, Hurst).— Fruit medium size, round, smooth, bright red ; very free setter ; foliage and habit strong ; early in ripening. Very good crop.

42. Hurst Marvel (Hurst).—Fruit large, flat round, smooth, red ; very free setter ; foliage distinct and potato-like ; moderately early in ripening. Good crop.

43. Hybrid Prolific (Allen).—Fruit medium size, round, smooth, red ; free setter ; habit very dwarf and compact ; early in ripening. Good crop.

44. Industry .(Toogood).—Fruit large, flat round, smooth, red ; free setter ; foliage distinct ; sturdy habit ; late in ripening. Good crop.

45. Large Red Italian (Barr).—Fruit large, slightly corrugated ; free setter ; foliage and habit sturdy ; early in ripening. . Good crop.

46. Lawrenson's No. 3 (Nutting).—Very similar to No. 45.

47. Losely Yellow (Staward).—Stock not fixed.

48. Lye's Early Gem, **A.M.** September 25, 1906 (Lye).—Fruit medium size, round, smooth, bright red ; free setter ; foliage and habit excellent ; early in ripening. Heavy crop.

49. Magnum Bonum (Sutton).—Fruit of medium size, red, round, slightly corrugated ; moderate setter ; foliage and habit sturdy. Fair crop.

50. Market Favourite (Carter).—Fruit medium size, round, smooth, bright red or scarlet ; very free setter ; foliage and habit compact and sturdy ; early in ripening. Heavy crop.

51. New Dwarf Red, **A.M.** August 15, 1905 (J. Veitch).—Fruit rather large, bright red, flattish round, nearly smooth ; free setter ; foliage very distinct, and habit dwarf and sturdy ; moderately early in ripening. Fair crop.

52. Northern King (Barr).—Fruit large, round, smooth, orange colour ; free setter ; foliage and habit sturdy ; early in ripening. Good crop.

53. Omega (Lansdell).—This variety did not ripen its fruit.

54, 55, 56. Open Air (Sutton, Daniel, Barr).—Fruit large, roundish oval, bright scarlet ; free setter ; foliage and habit moderately vigorous ; early in ripening. Good crop.

57. Peach Blow (Sutton).—Fruit large, smooth, some faintly corrugated ; did not set well, and the crop was very light.

58, 59, 60. Perfection, **F.C.C.** August 19, 1884 (Sutton, J. Veitch, Carter).—Fruit very large, smooth, flat round, bright scarlet; not a free setter; foliage and habit vigorous ; late in ripening. Light crop of large fruits.

61. Perpetual (Laxton).—Stock not fixed.

62. Princess of Wales, **A.M.** August 15, 1905 (Sutton).—Fruit of medium size, round, smooth, bright scarlet; free setter ; foliage and habit sturdy ; moderately early in ripening. Fair crop.

63. Prolific (Staward).—Fruit large, flattish round, smooth ; free setter ; foliage and habit sturdy. None of the fruit ripened, although it attained a large size. Good crop.

64, 65. Red Currant (J. Veitch, Carter).—Fruit very small and red currant-like, bright red, and borne in long handsome racemes ; a very free setter, and ripening very early. Heavy crop. A handsome ornamental variety.

66. Ryecroft Gem (Hurst).—Fruit of medium size, round, smooth, bright scarlet ; free setter; foliage and habit of great vigour; late in ripening. Good crop.

67. Sandwich Island (Carter).—This variety produced a fair crop, but none of the fruit ripened.

68. Satisfaction (Sutton).—Fruit very large, flat round, smooth, bright scarlet ; a free setter ; foliage and habit sturdy ; moderately early in ripening. Heavy crop.

69. Smith's Queen (Smith).—A very prolific variety, but late, as none of the fruit ripened. A promising variety for a warmer season or under glass.

70, 71. Stirling Castle, **A.M.** September 6, 1898 (Carter, Barr).—Fruit of medium size, round, smooth, scarlet; free setter ; foliage and habit moderately vigorous ; early in ripening. Heavy crop.

72. Sunbeam (Sutton).—Fruit of medium size, oval or plum-shaped, smooth, pale-yellow colour ; moderate setter ; foliage and habit fairly sturdy ; early in ripening. Fair crop.

73. Sunrise, **F.C.C.** July 4, 1905, and confirmed October 8, 1907, as an outdoor variety (Carter).—Fruit of medium size, deep round, smooth, bright red ; very free setter ; foliage and habit robust ; ripening early. Great crop.

74, 75. The Comet, **A.M.** July 25, 1899 (Carter, Hurst).—Same as No. 40.

76. The Hastings (J. Veitch).—Fruit rather large, round, smooth, red ; very free setter ; foliage and habit strong ; early in ripening. Good crop.

77. The Peach (Carter).—Not a success outside.

78, 79. The Trophy, **F.C.C.** August 20, 1877 (Carter, J Veitch).—Fruit large, slightly corrugated, brilliant scarlet ; a free setter ; foliage and habit very sturdy ; moderately early in ripening. Good crop.

80. Topper (Laxton).—This variety did not ripen its fruit, of which there was a good crop.

81. Up-to-Date, **A.M.** October 8, 1907, as an outdoor variety (Hurst).—Fruit large, deep round, smooth, scarlet; free setter; foliage and habit moderately strong; early in ripening. Very heavy crop.

82, 83. Winter Beauty, **A.M.** April 18, 1899 (Sutton, Barr).—Fruit large, flat round, nearly smooth, bright scarlet; very free setter; foliage and habit compact and sturdy; early in ripening. Heavy crop.

84. Wonderful (Laxton).—Very similar to No. 37.

85, 86. Red Peach (Barr).—This variety set no fruit, but grew plenty of foliage.

REPORT ON MANURES, APPLIANCES, &c., 1907.

1. Acha-Kut (Henry).—A powerful chemical manure producing an immediate effect on the growth of wood and foliage, and giving a deep green colour to the growths.

2. Banding Grease (Voss).—A preparation for grease banding fruit trees to catch the female winter moths as they ascend the trees. We found the sample received lacking in consistency and not sufficiently sticky.

3. Cyanamide (Boor).—A new chemical manure received late in 1907, and which we have had no opportunity of testing.

4. Fertiliser (Boor).—A mixture of chemical manures adapted for light soils, and which had a good effect on roses, vegetables, &c.

5. Fertilisers (Voss).—Received too late in 1907 to report upon.

6. Fertiliser (Sun Gas Co.).—This was cyanamide of lime, and proved excellent on vegetable crops.

7. Frame-raiser (De Luca).—A very handy wooden arrangement that can be screwed to the frame for raising the frame lights up to different heights for ventilation.

8. Green Sulphur (Voss).—A green form of the well-known powdered sulphur, and being green it is not so conspicuous as the yellow sulphur when applied.

9. Handy-Andy Hoes (Standard Manufacturing Co.).—Excellent little hoes for small gardens, or for ladies.

10. Hop Manure (Wakeley).—This was tried on pot fruit trees, with very good results, and is a safe and reliable manure.

11. National Knapsack Sprayer (de Luzy Frères).—One of the most useful appliances for spraying roses, fruit trees, &c. in the garden, and should be in every garden, as it is easily carried about, and produces a very fine dense spray that completely covers all insect pests on the trees or plants with the insecticide employed.

12. Nebula Sprayer (Patent Nebula Spray Co.).—An excellent little sprayer for under glass, either for use with insecticides or for spraying delicate flowers or foliage with water.

13. Necrotine Insecticide (The British Nicotine Co.).—A very good and safe insecticide for red spider, aphis, thrip, &c.

14. Necrotine Vaporising Compound (The British Nicotine Co.).— Quite as effective and safe in use as any vaporising insecticide we have tried.

15. Patent Flower Supports (Forster).—A useful appliance if it were more durable. It consists of a wooden stake, with soft metal clips to secure the plant.

16. Patent Tree Fastener (Willis).—Received late for trying in 1907, but so far they are very effective in preventing any movement of the tree, and are reasonable in price, viz. 9d. per dozen.

17. Perpetuated April or Bearded Red Spring Wheat (Raynbird).—This wheat only succeeded moderately well, and did not show any special merits.

18. Phospho-Nicotyl (Voss).—This is said to be destructive to mice, wood-lice, &c., but we did not find it very effectual.

19. Potato Fertiliser (Massey).—A very good manure on the light soil at Wisley for potatoes.

20. Sulphide of Potassium (Voss).—An excellent remedy for mildew on roses or similar plants when used at the rate of $\frac{1}{4}$ oz. dissolved in one gallon of water and applied as a fine spray. In bad cases we used $\frac{1}{2}$ oz. to the gallon of water with no injury to the plants.

21. Syringes (The Compact Manufacturing Co.).—Four syringes were sent for trial. 1 inch × 20 inches is a very handy syringe for delicate things such as choice ferns, orchids, &c., as it sends out a fine mist-like spray. 1$\frac{1}{2}$ inch × 18 inches was too weak in the shaft, and soon broke (ordinary). 1$\frac{1}{2}$ inch × 18 inches : a very useful syringe with an elbowed nozzle, very good for syringing on the under side of foliage, or for ordinary purposes. 1$\frac{1}{2}$ inch × 18 inches : an improvement on the last-named syringe with a special nozzle.

22. Tree Clips (Creak).—Not a success ; the clips break in strong wind, and the sharp edges of the clip cut the tree.

23. Veitch's Horticultural Manure (J. Veitch).—After many years' trial of this, we confirm our previous reports of its value for all plants, fruits, or vegetables.

24. Veitch's Secateurs (J. Veitch).—In our opinion this is the best Secateur on the market.

25. Wellson's Manure (Wellson).—A first-rate manure. Tried on pot fruit trees the results were very satisfactory, likewise on other fruit-bearing plants and trees.

26. Worm-killer (Carter).—Not quite satisfactory.

MISCELLANEOUS FLORAL TRIALS AT WISLEY, 1907,

A.M. = Award of Merit.
XXX = Highly Commended.

DIASCIA.

Barberae (Veitch).—A very pretty half-hardy annual from South Africa. Flowers rose-pink, with double spur. One foot.

DIMORPHOTHECA.

aurantiaca (Barr).—A very fine half-hardy annual from South Africa, producing throughout the summer a profusion of large bright orange flowers. An admirable plant for a sunny spot on the rockery. One foot.

ESCHSCHOLTZIA.

Pink Fluted (Berkeley).—This is a strain with rather small fluted or pleated petals, rosy without and creamy within, but it requires fixing.

Yellow Prince (Berkeley).—Flowers creamy yellow, petals fluted. As with the last variety, some 70 per cent. of the plants proved the common orange smooth-petalled variety.

GLADIOLUS.

Golden West (Dreer).—Flowers not large, but of good form and substance. Bright scarlet, the inner lower petals having a cream-coloured centre-line and throat of the same colour, spotted with scarlet.

LARKSPUR.

Empress Carmine (Veitch), **A.M.** September 6, 1907.—A good strain of *Delphinium Consolida*, quite true from seed ; 4–5 feet. Flowers double, carmine-rose, giving a long succession of bloom.

MARIGOLD.

French, Gold Striped (Forbes).—A very variable strain ; 1½ feet to 2 feet. About 10 per cent. were of good form, very double, with maroon rays marked with a central band of gold.

PANSIES.

Seeds of choice mixed Fancy and Show Varieties (Forbes).—A number of interesting forms raised, but rather a high percentage of Violas.

PENTSTEMONS.

Forbes' Hybrids (Forbes).—A good strain.
Rubicunda (Beckett).—Bright red, with white throat.
The Earl of Minto (Beckett).—Crimson, with white throat margined and blotched with deeper crimson.

Virgin Queen (Beckett).—White, lightly tipped in the bud with rose, and the open flower showing a suffused pink edging. Very free-flowering, with long closely flowered racemes.

These are the best of a number of named varieties raised by Mr. Beckett. The habit of all is vigorous, the bells are of fine size and form. Henry Irving (purplish-rose) and Rachel (creamy-white) are also good.

PHLOX.

Gruppenkönigin (Pfitzer), **A.M.** August 13, 1907.—3–3½ feet. Salmon-pink, with deeper coloured eye. Pip large (1¾ inches in diameter), flat, of good form. Very free-flowering.

SALVIA.

Zurich (Barr, Veitch).—A dwarf, free-flowering form of *S. splendens*.

SCHIZANTHUS.

Veitch's *grandiflora* hybrids (Veitch).

Wisetonensis (Sydenham).

A batch of both varieties was raised under glass and planted out, but the season was unfavourable, and a very poor growth and display of flower followed ; 9 inches to 1 foot ; flowers white, pink, purple, and violet variously blotched at the throat.

STOCKS, EAST LOTHIAN.

Crimson, wallflower-leaved (Forbes).— Fair.

Crimson (Forbes).—Fair.

Purple (Forbes).—A good dwarf strain.

White, wallflower-leaved (Forbes), **A.M.** September 6, 1907.—A very fine strain ; 1 foot, much branched, with densely flowered trusses of double flowers ; 20 per cent. single.

STOKESIA.

cyanea alba (Dreer).—Received in dying condition.

STREPTOCARPUS.

Veitch's improved strain, extra special (Veitch).—A good strain, the flowers giving a wide range of colour.

SWEET PEAS.

Albatross (Dobbie), **XXX** July 30, 1907.—White ; standard erect, bold, unwaved, wings spreading. Flowers four to a stem. Chiefly recommended for its free-flowering qualities.

Baroness W. Schröder (Stark).—A very mixed strain, with white, soft pink, and bright pink varieties predominating.

Blush Queen (Dobbie).—A very mixed strain ; white, suffused with blush-pink.

Brilliant Blue (Sydenham), *syn.* Lord Nelson, **XXX** July 30, 1907.— Deep blue ; standard erect, flat, rather small, with purplish tint. Flowers four to a stem. Burns, the best dark-blue variety.

Enchantress (Stark).—Apparently identical with Paradise, *q.v.*

Eric Hinton (Hinton).—Pink, medium size ; standard erect, waved. Flowers three to a stem. Inferior to Countess Spencer.

Florence Spencer (Sydenham).—Practically identical with Paradise, *q.v.*

George Stark (Stark).—A mixed strain. Deep rose ; standard erect, flat. Flowers three to a stem.

Hannah Dale (Dobbie).—Dark purplish-crimson ; standard erect, flat, unwaved. Flowers three to a stem.

John Ingman (Sydenham).—Carmine-rose ; standard erect. Flowers three to a stem. Inferior to the strain grown in 1906.

Lady Treloar (Dobbie).—A mixed strain. Rosy-purple ; burns badly. Flowers three to a stem.

Lorna Doone (Stark).—Soft pink, suffused in the bud with salmon ; standard erect, waved ; keel white. Flowers three to a stem.

Mrs. Chas. Foster (Sydenham).—A very badly mixed strain. The variety is a fine one ; standard slightly waved, rosy-mauve ; wings mauve to lavender. Flowers large, three to a stem.

Mrs. Collier (Dobbie).—Cream ; standard slightly hooded. Flowers large, on good stalks, three to a stem.

Paradise (Sydenham).—Bright pink ; standard waved, erect. Flowers large, three or four to a stem.

Rosie Sydenham (Sydenham).—A mixed strain. Carmine-rose ; standard waved, erect. Flowers large, three or four to a stem.

The Marquis (Dobbie).—Rosy-mauve ; standard erect, waved. Flowers three to a stem.

White Spencer (Dobbie).—A mixed strain, including three distinct varieties—white, white suffused with pink, and white splashed with pink, Flowers large, four to a stem.

Tropaeolum (Nasturtium).

Dwarf Ryburgh Perfection, variegated (Stark).—One foot. Flowers bright scarlet ; variegated foliage ; not compact in habit.

Leprechaun, or Puck (Hartland).—Yellow, blotched with crimson ; spur red.

Queen of Tom Thumbs (Veitch).—Nine inches. Flowers deep red ; variegated foliage. Habit dwarf and compact.

Tall, variegated, Stark's hybrids (Stark).—Variegated foliage.

The variegation in the foliage of these varieties comes quite true from seed, but as a rule fails to form the desirable green setting to the brilliance of the flowers.

Violas.

Seed of Extra Choice Mixed (Forbes).—A fairly good strain, producing some good cream, yellow, light, and dark blues, but including many of very poor form.

REVIEWS OF BOOKS.

"Practical Botany for Beginners." By F. O. Bower and D. T. Gwynne-Vaughan. 8vo., 307 pp. (Macmillan, London.) 3s. 6d.

"This little book contains, in an abridged form, the elementary and more essential parts of the text of the larger *Course of Practical Instruction in Botany*." It is an admirable epitome of laboratory work ; but the young student must not think he is a botanist when he has worked it throughout. He should have gone through a course in morphology *before* approaching this work. Then using his knowledge of external and internal structure, he must see how *both* are utilised by the living plants in nature. In other words he must study plants ecologically.

"First Lessons in Practical Botany." By C. T. Bettany. 8vo., 103 pp. (Macmillan, London.) 1s.

The title is scarcely a correct one. It is a useful little book on nomenclature, to assist pupils in describing entire plants. At the end are definitions of the principal orders. " Descriptions should be written out twice a week during two years of the school course. If this work is faithfully done, students gain a power over their language, as well as over their faculties of observation, which is far beyond even the gain in their knowledge of botany." We quite agree with the author, and believe the wish of some teachers to abandon plant descriptions to be a grave mistake.

"First Stage Botany." By A. J. Ewart, D.Sc. 8vo., 320 pp. (Clive, London.) 2s.

This little book is designed for the elementary stage of the Board of Education. Morphological structure, and less anatomy than in other books of the same description, are features in accordance with the design of this book. It is a good book of its kind ; but we hope in the future editions more prominence will be given to ecology, or the adaptations of structure to the plant's own requirements as studied in the field.

"Botany for Beginners." By E. Evans. 8vo., 300 pp. (Macmillan, London.) 2s. 6d.

This is not the only book on botany written to meet the requirements of the Board of Education. It consists of the usual combination of morphology, anatomy, and elementary physiology, and is very well done. It is hoped that ecology and the adaptations of plants to their environments will be allowed more prominence in future editions.

"Wild Flowers of the British Isles." Illustrated and written by H. Isabel Adams, F.L.S. ; revised by Jas. E. Bagnell, A.L.S. 4to., 168 pp., 29 plates. (Heinemann, London.) 30s. net.

This large volume contains 29 families only, out of 89 of British flowering plants, terminating with *Compositae* ; so that it can only be called an "incomplete flora." The descriptions of the species are in as simple language as possible ; but instead of giving a brief "description of botanical terms," in which some used (as "dichotomous ") are omitted, it would have been better to have had an index, referring to the page wherein each term is *first* used and explained. The illustrations are carefully and accurately drawn ; but too many are often crowded on the same plate. The Latin names might have been italicised in the index.

"The Principles of Horticulture. A Series of Practical Scientific Lessons." By W. M. Webb, F.L.S. 8½ inches by 6 inches, 136 pp. (Blackie & Son, London.) 2s. net.

This is an excellent book for beginners, with good self-explanatory illustrations. It deals with such subjects as A Sample Plant and its Parts ; Internal structure ; Seed and Embryo ; Food of Plants ; Joint Work of Root, Leaves, and Stem ; Formation and Improvement of Soils &c. ; Flowers and Fertilisation ; Fruits ; and many other things which a learner ought to know.

We note on pp. 17 and 44 no mention of the pericycle, which supplies the "long fibres," and the secondary roots ; while on pp. 40-43 the name is apparently given to the endoderm, the inner boundary of the cortex, the pericycle being the layer within, and in contact with, the endoderm. Some good descriptions and figures of common fungi are added, and a table of fungoid diseases with remedies.

"Flowers of the Field." By the Rev. C. A. Johns. Revised throughout and edited by C. Elliott. With 92 coloured illustrations by E. N. Gwatkin, and 245 cuts in the text. 8vo., 316 pp. (Routledge, London.) 7s. 6d. net.

So far from being "revised throughout," the Introduction contains all the old misstatements of the original edition ; such as embryo being regarded as a seed and confounded with the plumule &c. The editor has struck out several species and the whole of the grasses and sedges. Moreover, he has headed every left-hand page, from 290 to 300, with the word *Glumaceae*, including nine families not one of which belongs to this group ! The families he persistently miscalls "tribes."

We observe that he has struck out all the accents—an important help to young botanists not familiar with Latin. With regard to the illustrations, the plates, we suppose, are intended to attract, but the value of the original large woodcuts of Johns is not enhanced by greatly reducing their size.

As the S.P.C.K. has already issued an edition edited by Prof. Boulger, we naturally compared the two ; and, whereas the former is thoroughly up to date and accurate, the present one is most decidedly not so ; and if any young student use it, he will find he has something to unlearn when he becomes an·advanced botanist. We cannot recommend this edition.

"Indian Trees. An Account of Trees, Shrubs, Woody Climbers, Bamboos, and Palms, indigenous or commonly cultivated, in the British Indian Empire." By Sir Dietrich Brandis, K.C.I.E. 8vo., 767 pp. (Constable, London.) 16s. net.

This most important work gives really complete botanical descriptions of every species, with its Indian distribution or origin in foreign countries.

"The object of this work," writes Sir D. Brandis in the Introduction, "is restricted, and is entirely practical. It is intended for foresters and others who may wish to make themselves acquainted with the immense variety of trees, shrubs, climbers, bamboos, and palms in the British Indian Empire."

"Lessons in Elementary Biology." By T. J. Parker, D.Sc., F.R.S. 8vo., 503 pp. 127 illustrations. (Macmillan, London.) 10s. 6d.

Contrary to Huxley's view that a student should begin with vertebrates, the author adopts the plan of taking the lower forms of life, on the ground that it has "the advantage of logical treatment of proceeding from the simple to the complex." Theoretically this may be true, but it places difficulties before a beginner, which he is not prepared for in "the new and strange region of microscopic life," as Huxley says. This is equally applicable to botany. Balfour's "Text Book" of the middle of last century began with tissues and, as we know, had the effect of repelling and not attracting beginners. Henfrey was the first to reverse the order in his "Elementary Text Book," still one of the best. The present author evidently prefers zoology, occupying 399 pages, only seventy-seven being devoted to botany; and of this, forty-seven are given up to cryptogams, a single chapter (the last) being all that is devoted to Monocotyledons and Dicotyledons, which in our opinion should come first. For advanced students the book is excellent, but for beginners long experience has convinced us that Huxley and Henfrey were right.

"The Teaching Botanist. A Manual of Information upon Botanical Instruction; together with Outlines and Directions for a Comprehensive Elementary Course." By W. F. Ganong. 8vo., pp. 270. (Macmillan, New York and London.) 5s.

This is a valuable book for all concerned in teaching botany in schools and colleges. The following are some of the subjects dealt with. Part I.—Essays on Botanical Pedagogics. These contain:—1. The Place of the Sciences in Education and of Botany. 2. What Botany is of most worth? 3. On things essential to good Botanical Teaching. 4-8. On Drawing and Descriptions, Laboratories, Collections, Books, and Common Errors. Part II.—Outline of an Elementary Course, &c.

An important feature lies in the author's insisting upon the ecological aspect of botanical teaching. Thus, he rightly urges that "topics of ecology should accompany the study of the structures best explained by them." Again, alluding to the natural tendency of students to ask "why," he adds, "For the cultivation of this instinct of causation anatomy and morphology should, from the first, be viewed in the light of the factors determining them; that is, they should be approached through physiology and ecology." So, in giving in detail a lesson on shoots and roots, he describes it as "The Ecology of Shoot and Root." It is this important aspect of botanical teaching in which our English text-books are so deficient. The method of describing entire plants, which has long prevailed in England, does not seem to have been adopted in America to so great an extent.

"An Introduction to Nature-Study." By E. Stenhouse, B.Sc. 8vo., pp. 432. (Macmillan, London.) 3s. 6d.

"The aim of nature-study is not primarily the acquisition of the facts of natural history ; it is rather a training in methods of open-eyed, close and accurate observation, especially of familiar animals and plants, which shall teach the student to *see* what he looks at, and to *think about* what he sees." We quite agree with the author, and his little book is in thorough accord with the above extract from the preface. It is more than many books on nature-study profess to give, for it practically consists of elementary courses on botany and zoology. Not only are all the parts of plants described but experiments are suggested and the *uses* of structures (now called ecology) to the plants themselves are mentioned, though this aspect might be perhaps even more insisted upon. On p. 63 it might have been explained how it is that after the floral axis has fallen off, a *lateral bud* takes the lead, and so assumes a similar or apparently a terminal floral-bud for next year. On p. 92, the author is still under the influence of Darwin in saying "Botanists have proved that a flower produces more and also better seeds when it is fertilised by pollen from another flower of the same species." The mistake arose from Darwin's supposing what was only a temporary stimulus in his experiments to be a general result. Self-fertilising weeds, as groundsel, shepherd's purse, etc., will soon kill out, by smothering them, plants requiring to be crossed. In speaking of the opening of buds in spring, the way the young leaves place themselves vertically to avoid injury by radiation is an object of much interest to be observed. The part on animals is equally good. We can thoroughly recommend this book for what might be called a second stage in nature study.

"Entomology with Special Reference to its Biological and Economic Aspects." By J. W. Folsom, Sc.D. 8vo., 485 pp. (Rebman, London.) 14s. net.

This work by Dr. Folsom fills a place in entomological literature which has not previously been occupied. The title describes very accurately the nature of its contents. It is profusely illustrated. Besides a coloured frontispiece giving examples of "protective mimicry among butterflies," there are no fewer than 500 very good figures given in the text, most of which, however, are more or less diagrammatic. The terminology unfortunately is far from popular ; in fact, it is very technical, and no glossary is given ; this is a great omission in a work of this nature, which is likely to prove of great interest to many whose knowledge of entomology and technical terms is very slight. The book is divided into thirteen chapters ; the first three give a very clear and concise account of the classification, anatomy, physiology, and development of insects. Then follow chapters on coloration, "origin of adaptations and of species." Perhaps the two most interesting chapters to horticulturists are those on "insects in relation to plants " and "insects in relation to man." There is nothing actually new in these chapters, but the subjects are treated in a very terse and interesting manner. The first part (on tropisms) of the chapter on "insect behaviour " is open to much criticism ; in it the author quotes other writers to show that the movements of insects are to a great extent dependent on light and heat, and that they are actuated by them and not by any volition of their own. For instance, to explain why a moth flies to a light, it is suggested that the light shining on one side of the insect causes it to turn until both sides are acted upon equally (much in the same way as the vane of a weathercock is acted upon by the wind) and, this action being kept up, the insect when it flies is bound to fly straight to the light, and that insects which move rapidly like moths " get into the flame before the heat of the flame has time to check them in their flight." Why the heat should check them is not mentioned. The common daddy-long-legs will fly into a flame over and over again and it cannot be considered a rapid mover. In fact, it is sometimes hardly out of the flame before it is in again, so that the light can hardly have time to act in the manner suggested. I cannot but think that the views expressed in this chapter under the head of " Tropisms " are in many cases very fallacious. The second and third heads, on instinct and intelligence respectively, are very interesting. It is, however, difficult to reconcile some of the statements in them with the theories previously mentioned under " tropisms." The last chapter (on " insects in relation to man ") deals chiefly with organisations formed and the means taken for the destruction of insect pests. There is a very extensive bibliography occupying 57 pages, the works mentioned in it are arranged primarily in subjects, and then chronologically. This plan has its merits, but it renders it difficult to find a book if you do not quite realise under which heading you should look for it. There is also a very full index. This is one of the most interesting books on entomology in general which has been published for some years.

"Tree Planting in Natal." By T. R. Sim. 8vo., 354 + xviii pp. (Davis & Sons, Pieter Maritzburg.) 2s. 6d.

This is an interesting and well-written book on the trees suitable for the different districts of Natal, their propagation and general characteristics. There are twenty-six chapters, with over 100 well-executed illustrations of matter contained in the text. The articles on " The Care of Plantations," " The Planting of Trees," and " Urban and Suburban Horticulture " are full of useful information, and, though primarily intended for dwellers in Natal, might be read with advantage by horticulturists in any part of the world. Although not very comprehensive, the list of indigenous trees is of particular interest, and includes several genera that are commonly cultivated in this country, though the species and varieties are quite distinct. The black wattle industry is the most profitable of any carried out in the Natal forests, although considerable knowledge of how to remove and harvest the bark is required, and it is on record that many planters make reasonable fortunes within one decade and reap returns on expenditure that are probably unequalled in forest management.

"Timber and Timber Trees." By the late Thomas Laslett. Edited by Professor Marshall Ward. 8vo., 442 pp. (Macmillan, London.) 8s. 6d.

This valuable work, which extends to fully 400 pages, is divided into thirty-seven chapters, with thirty-four well-executed illustrations, every one of which goes far towards elucidating the text. Particularly valuable are the chapters on " Storing Timber," and on " The Defects of Trees "— the results of many carefully conducted experiments and keen observation, while the description of European and other timber-producing trees is most valuable for reference purposes and full of interesting notes.

There are, however, a few omissions, such as no mention being made of the produce of willow timber in the production of cricket bats, and for which a very high price can be obtained. Neither is poplar timber fully treated on, for its consumption in the making of packing-cases and for stone-carts and barrows is very considerable.

But these are minor omissions, and altogether this work is by far the most valuable of any that has been compiled on timber and timber-producing trees, and is a decided acquisition to all who are engaged in the growing or converting of wood, be it home or foreign.

" British Forest -Trees and their Sylvicultural Characteristics and Treatment." By John Nisbett, D.Œc. 8vo., 352 pp. (Macmillan, London.) 6s. net.

The author tells us that his book "is, and only professes to be, to a considerable extent, a compilation from the best German sources." Though savouring greatly of Continental ideas, in the matter of timber culture at least, there is much within the 352 pages of which the book is composed that will interest and possibly edify the student of forestry in this country.

The criticism on portions of the article on " Woodlands," by Sir Herbert Maxwell, which appeared in the "Nineteenth Century" (July 1891), is severe in the extreme, but only what might be expected from one whose knowledge of Indian and Continental methods of woodland management is extensive as compared with what is practised in this country. Mixed plantations are no doubt good enough, but those who have examined the pure larch or Scotch pine woods of Scotland, or beech woods of parts of England, can only come to the conclusion that, whether for ease of management or readiness with which the produce may be marketed, pure forest is preferable to mixed. The comparison between Thomas Carlyle and our average British forester, in point of knowledge of woodland management, must not be taken as serious, and sounds strange to one who knew well the capabilities of the great writer in that respect. When a new edition of the work is brought out many additions can be made, such as up-to-date information regarding that pest of our beech-woods—*Cryptococcus fagi*; and the reafforesting of waste and unprofitable lands in various parts of the country.

"Game and Game Coverts." By John Simpson. Sm. 4to., 83 pp. (Pawson & Brailsford, Sheffield.) 15s. net.

There are few books dealing exclusively with game coverts, and Mr. Simpson is to be congratulated for giving us a well-written and illustrated work on the subject, though in the matter of trees and shrubs that have been found valuable for game coverts the list is not as comprehensive as could be desired. The formation of game coverts differs so much on various estates that on no two properties do we find either the same plants in use or similar methods of distribution adopted, and what is rightly objected to in one situation is valuable in another, owing mainly to differences in soil and situation. Bracken, which is condemned wholesale by the author, is in some instances, when convenient to pasture land, valuable covert. Our English coppice woods, too, are invaluable game coverts, while thickly grown birches and thorns carpeted with branches and rough-growing grasses are hard to beat—but it should be remembered that open clearances, in dense and far-reaching masses of covert, are desirable. Contrary to the author's opinion we have always found that in order to thicken the exposed side of a plantation early and careful thinning is necessary—far preferable to the killing-out process by the survival of the fittest as sometimes practised.

To the list of shelter-giving trees the evergreen oak might well be added, while the ribes, sea buckthorn, dogwood, viburnum, and shrubby thorns are all useful for particular situations.

The book is nicely got up and printed, and the numerous well-executed illustrations are valuable, and should commend the work to all those who are interested in game and game coverts.

"Introduction to Plant Ecology." By Prof. G. Henslow. 8vo., 130 pp. (Edward Stanford, London.) 2s.

This little book is intended to introduce to teachers and students of botany a point of view which to many may be new. Ecology has been defined as "the study of plants in their natural home," and the author rightly insists that the study of plant-form, of internal structure, and of the functions of the various organs must be pursued before a thorough grasp of the meaning of plant distribution can be obtained. He considers, however, that all botanical teaching should lead up to an accurate appreciation of the influence of external conditions in moulding the form of the plant, and this may be attained by always keeping in view throughout all branches of botany the ecological aspect. The author believes that the final outcome of ecology is evolution, and that the study of plants from an ecological point of view will lead to the conclusion that, "the origin of specific characters . . . is nothing more nor less than the result of response and adaptation to the direct action of the conditions of life." Though all teachers will not be able to follow him so far, few will consider that the ecological point of view of studying botany is not the right one, and this little book will serve to give an idea of the very wide field open for research, and the greatly enhanced value of botany as an educational subject when the ecological aspect of botany is kept in sight. A copious index is given, the print is large and clear, and the text very free from misprints.

"Text-book of Plant-diseases." By G. Massee. Third edition. 8vo., 472 pp. (Duckworth, London.) 6s. net.

Plant diseases caused by the attacks of fungi appear to become more and more common every year, possibly on account of the prevalent methods of massing together large numbers of the same kind of plant. Any book that brings together accounts of these parasitic fungi and describes in a trustworthy manner the diseases they produce should be a welcome addition to the library of every cultivator of plants. In this book all the more common diseases of cultivated plants of the fields and gardens both of this country and of other countries are accurately described in sufficiently simple language so that any gardener may be able generally to ascertain what particular pest is troubling his plants. Excellent figures enhance the value of the descriptions, and preventive measures are described in the majority of cases. A valuable chapter deals with the general methods of treatment in combating fungal diseases, and another gives recipes for the making of various fungicides. In this third edition, twenty pages are inserted near the beginning, describing some of the diseases that have, during the four years that have elapsed since the publication of the first edition, proved more than usually troublesome.

"Getting acquainted with the Trees." By J. H. McFarland. 8vo., 241 pp. (The Outlook Company, New York: Macmillan, London.) 7s. 6d. net.

A pleasant book, written by one who has learned to know and love trees in the hope that others may learn to know and love them too. The more familiar trees of the United States are dealt with in a style easy to read, and while the statements made are accurate, there is no pretence to the writing of a botanical treatise. The trees on which the author discourses are illustrated by many admirably chosen and reproduced photographs and by tinted pictures, over some of which the letterpress is printed. The whole "get-up" of the book is worthy of its contents.

"Physiological Botany." By Professor George L. Goodale, A.M., M.D. 8vo., 499 pp. Appendix 36 pp. (American Book Company: Macmillan, London.) 10s. 6d.

This book, which forms Part II. of "Gray's Botanical Textbook," has already passed through five editions, a fact which speaks much for its value. It contains a full account of the minute structure of flowering plants, such as is necessary for the proper understanding of the way a plant does its work, and gives directions to the student as to how to proceed in verifying the statements made. Then follow chapters on the physiology of flowering plants, written in a clear manner, easy to be understood. To any who wish for some knowledge of the manner of plant growth, the way plants feed and reproduce themselves, this book may be confidently recommended.

"Lectures on Plant Physiology." By Dr. Ludwig Jost, Professor of Botany in the University of Strasburg. Authorised English translation by R. J. Harvey Gibson, M.A., F.L.S., Professor of Botany in the University of Liverpool. (Clarendon Press. 1907.)

The increasing number of compilations on plant physiology gives cause for regret that the subject has not yet been deemed worthy of the treatment now so generally adopted in animal physiology—namely, a series of monographs or memoirs, each written by the authority most competent to deal with the matter in hand—on the plan of Schäfer's "Text-book of Physiology" and other recent publications. In the book before us there are 550 pages of more or less digested matter, lucid and synthetic in some of the earlier chapters on metabolism, assimilation, respiration, &c.—obscure and fragmentary in, for example, such a section as that on electrical currents, where neither author nor translator seems to have an idea of the work that has been done by Waller and others since the publication of Biedermann's "Elektro-Physiologie" (the latest work quoted) in 1895. In these days vegetable physiology can no more than animal physiology be confined to one laboratory or to one author, and little progress will be made in the solution of its countless problems until this development is appreciated. It is, moreover, obvious that with Pfeffer's "Physiology of Plants" to hand, in the scholarly form of its English translation, a new compilation could only be of value if thoroughly up to date and complete in all its details. But in this book the admirable system of footnotes by which the editor of Pfeffer brings his translations of vols. i., ii., and iii. in 1900, 1903, and 1906, respectively, up to date, has not been adopted. The author contents himself with interpolations in square brackets in the text, a method which leads to considerable confusion—on the surface at any rate. The student wants his facts presented in tangible form, without the battledore and shuttlecock of chronological order. As an instance, the argument on pp. 107–110 is difficult to disentangle, as it would certainly appear at first sight as though the conclusions which Molisch drew from assimilation effected by " dried dead cells " were in favour of the modern view that chlorophyll may, apart from the living protoplasmic basis of the choroplast, carry out the photolytic function. Whereas p. 110 shows that he attributes the continuance of the function in " dead " cells to a " survival " of the protoplasm. Surely this debatable ground would, from the student's point of view, be better in a footnote, and clearly differentiated from classical matter.

In this connection, too, it may be remarked that the bibliographies at the end of each chapter—an excellent feature—have not always been brought up to date in accordance with the interpolations. Up to Chapter X. no notice is taken of these, compare pp. 90, 95, 98, 110, 112. In Chapter X., re p. 130, no reference is given to the paper containing the " very careful researches of Brown and Escombe in 1904"; and in Chapter XVII., re p. 214, the bibliography gives no reference to the hand-book by Lafar which the text praises so highly. In this particular the utility of the work is impaired for the student who looks on the bibliography as an indication of what is referred to in the text.

The chemical portions of the book (under Metabolism) are most interesting, and appear to be more fully worked out than in Pfeffer. Such are the classification of proteins and conversion of the products of assimilation (with much that is new on enzyme action), respiration, fermentation, symbiosis, &c. Under the heading Metamorphosis there is a comprehensive account of the external modifications produced by gall-parasites, and of the internal correlations exemplified in the effect of grafts, disturbances of nutrition, injury, and regeneration, &c.—a subject now attracting much interest abroad under the ugly name of "experimental teratology."

In short, a great part of the book is (supplementary to Pfeffer, and, given a certain knowledge of morphology, which is here taken for granted), of extreme interest for the advanced student. The translation, admirably as a whole, contains a few errors that mar its perfection and would puzzle the reader who has not access to the German original. These, like the bibliographical omissions, will presumably be corrected in the next edition. Curiously enough, those we encountered all lie within the same section.

P. 237. "Just *as we have seen* in the case of galls" sends the reader on a vain chase backwards. It should be, "As we shall see" (pp. 320-324), the German being *sehen werden.*

P. 334. "Pollinated with pollen *for*" (read "from," *von*) "*D. barbatus.*"

P. 372. "*Eludicate*"? for elucidate (the German is *nachweisen*).

P. 377, line 9. "The assumption *that* the" (read "of the," *der*) "inheritance."

P. 400, end of last line, there is a serious omission of the words "admixture of fluids, next imbibition, and finally friction" (*die Mischung von Flussigkeiten, ferner die Quellung, u. endlich*).

P. 402. "A positive current will, as a rule, be *generated*" contradicts the point of demonstrating current in uninjured plant organs. The German is "*so findet man.*" And five lines lower down the insertion of "even" (not in original) makes nonsense, the point now being that when no current can be demonstrated on the uninjured plant a difference of electrical potential will be at once set up on wounding the tissue.

In conclusion the book has an excellent index.

"The Nature and Work of Plants." An Introduction to the Study of Botany. By Daniel Trembly Macdougal, Ph.D. (Macmillan & Co. 1900.)

This charming little book would be an invaluable adjunct to a course of Nature Study. It encourages observation and trains the student to notice physiological facts for himself in the fields and garden. Many of the experiments are planned to extend over days or weeks, the answers to the problems proposed being left to the experimenter to discover.

The book treats of the composition and purposes of plants, the functions of their tissues, the physiology of leaves (a most interesting and delightful chapter), stems and buds, the way new plants arise, seeds and fruit, plant energy, and what M. Maeterlinck would term the social life of plants. The index seems good, with a misprint under Sugar Maple: 154, 184 should read 105.

"Soils: How to Handle and Improve Them." By S. W. Fletcher. 8vo., 488 pp.; 114 plates and a frontispiece. (Constable, London.) Price 8s. 6d. net.

This book was written to set forth the important facts about soil in a plain and untechnical manner, and to present the reader with a *résumé* of what is already known upon the subject. Having gone very carefully through this book the feeling that is uppermost in our mind is one of regret that reviewers are too apt to write flatteringly of new books, so that when such a thoroughly excellent work as the present one appears, it is difficult to sufficiently impress the public mind with its many excellent points.

The formation of soils, their nature, variation, and management, receive due attention. Soil water, tillage, drainage, and irrigation occupy over 200 pages. General and special manures with green manuring occupy several chapters. English readers will appreciate the fact that the book is nearly. as well adapted to our soils and crops as to those of America. We do not say that every statement is unimpeachable, but we have seldom, if ever, read a work of this kind with such satisfaction and assurance that the information is sound, concisely and lucidly presented. The gardener or farmer who reads this book and understands it will know a great deal more about the subject than is known by the majority of cultivators.

A book for every library in which it may be justly placed. It is also admirably adapted for presentation as a prize or otherwise. There should be no need for further comment, except to advise every one to get it.

The printing is excellent and the plates charming.

--

JUNIPERUS SABINA.

FROM time to time Fellows are so good as to send us photographs of noteworthy specimens of plants, and here we are able, through the kindness of G. Carter, Esq., F.R.H.S., to give a picture of a striking specimen of the well-known and beautiful Savin, *Juniperus Sabina*. The bush is growing in the gardens of Stourton Court, Stourbridge, the residence of Randle Matthews, Esq., and occupies an isolated position on the edge of the lawn close to a descent of six feet. It forms a striking object in the landscape, standing as it does at the head of a broad valley, which rises on the opposite side to the "Kniver Edge," that famous resort of trippers. The bush measures six feet in height, nineteen feet in length by fifteen feet six inches in width, and fifty-seven feet six inches in circumference. It owes much of its striking appearance to the "hundreds of curly points, somewhat like tongues of flame," that rise above the mass of the bush. The soil in which the bush is growing overlies the Old Red Sandstone, and the position is entirely open to the west and somewhat to the south, but well protected on the north and east by the garden wall and the house.

FIG. 20.—JUNIPERUS SABINA AT STOURTON COURT, STOURBRIDGE.

FELLOWS' PRIVILEGES OF CHEMICAL ANALYSIS

(Applicable only to the case of those Fellows who are not engaged in any Horticultural Trade, or in the manufacture or sale of any substance sent for Analysis.)

THE Council have fixed the following rates of charges for Chemical Analysis to Fellows of the Society being *bonâ fide* Gardeners or Amateurs.

These privileges are applicable only when the Analyses are for *bonâ fide* horticultural purposes, and are required by Fellows for their own use and guidance in respect of gardens or orchards in their own occupation.

The analyses are given on the understanding that they are required for the individual and sole benefit of the Fellow applying for them, and must not be used for the information of other persons, or for commercial purposes.

Gardeners, when forwarding samples, are required to state the name of the Fellow on whose behalf they apply.

The analyses and reports may not be communicated to either vendor or manufacturer, except in cases of dispute.

When applying for an analysis, Fellows must be very particular to quote the number in the following schedule under which they wish it to be made.

No.
1. An opinion on the purity of bone-dust (each sample) .   .   .   . 2s. 6d.
2. An analysis of sulphate or muriate of ammonia, or of nitrate of soda, together with an opinion as to whether it be worth the price charged .   5s.
3. An analysis of guano, showing the proportion of moisture, organic matter, sand, phosphate of lime, alkaline salts and ammonia, together with an opinion as to whether it be worth the price charged   .   .   .   10s.
4. An analysis of mineral superphosphate of lime for soluble phosphates only, together with an opinion as to whether it be worth the price charged   .   .   .   .   5s.
5. An analysis of superphosphate of lime, dissolved bones, &c., showing the proportions of moisture, organic matter, sand, soluble and insoluble phosphates, sulphate of lime and ammonia, together with an opinion as to whether it be worth the price charged .   .   .   .   10s.
6. An analysis of bone-dust, basic slag, or any other ordinary artificial manure, together with an opinion as to whether it be worth the price charged   .   .   .   .   10s.
7. Determination of potash in potash salts, compound manures, &c.   .   . 7s. 6d.
8. An analysis of compound artificial manures, animal products, refuse substances used for manure, &c.   .   .   .   .   .   from 10s. to £1
9. An analysis of limestone, showing the proportion of lime .   .   . 7s. 6d.
10. Partial analysis of a soil, including determinations of clay, sand, organic matter, and carbonate of lime   .   .   .   .   .   .   10s.
11. Complete analysis of a soil £3
12. Analysis of any vegetable product   .   .   .   .   .   .   10s.
13. Determination of the "hardness" of a sample of water before and after boiling .   .   .   .   5s.
14. Analysis of water of land-drainage, and of water used for irrigation   . £1
15. Analysis of water used for domestic purposes   .   .   .   . £1 10s.
16. Consultation by letter   .   .   .   .   5s.

Letters and samples (postage and carriage prepaid) should be addressed to the Consulting Chemist, Dr. J. AUGUSTUS VOELCKER, 22 Tudor Street, New Bridge Street, London, E.C.

The fees for analysis must be sent to the Consulting Chemist at the time of application.

Instructions for selecting, drawing, and sending samples for analysis will be found in the Society's "Book of Arrangements," or can be obtained on application to the Society's Office, Vincent Square, S.W.

JAMES MURRAY

Tenders his Grateful Thanks to the
Nobility, *Ladies* and *Gentlemen*, for
the Great Preference he has experienced
in the *SALE* of his fuperfine

SEEDS *and* Dutch Bulbs,

which have met with the univerfal
approbation of the *Public*.

J. MURRAY hopes to be honoured with their
future commands, and begs to affure them nothing
fhall be wanting in his endeavours to merit a continuance of their favours, as every article fold by him
fhall be *warranted* of the *firft quality*.

ORDERS, *Retail* or *Wholefale*, per Penny or
General Poft, Coach, Carrier, *&c.*, with Orders for
Payment on Delivery, or enclofing *Bank* or *Good Bills*,
executed to exact amount, or *Change* returned with
Goods, and fent as per Order *to any part*, from his

Old-Eftablifhed Warehoufe
at DEPTFORD.

FOR ALL THE
GARDEN OPERATIONS
—— OF 1908 ——

YOU WILL NEED

LAY'S
ERTILIZER

ITS USE ENSURES

The Most Successful Cultivation

AND THE PRODUCTION OF ALL

FLOWERS, FOLIAGE, FRUITS,
AND VEGETABLES

in Profusion and in the Highest Perfection.

CLAY'S FERTILIZER is sold everywhere in

TRADE MARK.

Tins, 6d. and **1/-**; **Sealed Bags:** 7 lbs., **2/6**; 14 lbs., **4/6**;
28 lbs., **7/6**; 56 lbs., **12/6**; 112 lbs., **20/-**

Or direct from the Works carriage paid in the United
Kingdom for Cash with Order
(except **6d.** tins).

☞ *Every TIN, BAG, and SEAL bears the TRADE MARK.*
The only Guarantee of Genuineness.

CLAY & SON, Manure Manufacturers, Bone Crushers, &c.
STRATFORD, LONDON, E.

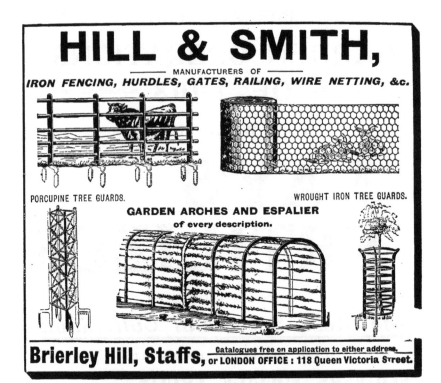

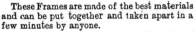

New and Recent Books

LONDON PARKS AND GARDENS. By the Hon. Mrs. Evelyn Cecil (Alicia Amherst, Citizen and Gardener of London). Author of "A History of Gardening in England," "Children's Gardens," &c. With numerous Illustrations in Colour by LADY VICTORIA MANNERS. Imp. 8vo. 21s. net.

In spite of the abundance of books on London, not one existed until the present work was published which told the story of the Parks and Gardens as a whole. Some of the Royal Parks have been dealt with, and most of the Municipal Parks, but in separate works. When Squares are touched on, in guide-books or in volumes to themselves, the Gardens are for the most part left alone, and gossip of the inhabitants forms the centre of the narrative. This is the case also with public buildings and private houses which have gardens attached to them.

THE ART OF LANDSCAPE GARDENING. By Humphry Repton. Revised and Edited by JOHN NOLEN, Member of American Society of Landscape Architects. Fully Illustrated from the Original Plates. Demy 8vo. 12s. 6d. net.

It is generally conceded that the world has not yet produced a designer in the informal or landscape style with the genius and skill of Repton. Therefore landscape architects, the members of allied professions, and laymen who wish first hand and trustworthy information concerning the principles of landscape design must return again and again to the period of Repton, and more especially to the work of Repton himself. It is fortunate for the progress of this art that Repton has left the record of his experience in such convenient, readable and inspiring form. His books embody the best results of his practice.

THE ENGLISH PEASANTRY AND THE ENCLOSURE OF COMMON FIELDS. By Gilbert Slater, M.A., Mayor of Woolwich. With an introduction by EARL CARRINGTON. Demy 8vo. 10s. 6d. net.

The enclosure of common fields and the passing away of the English village community to make room for the agricultural organisation prevailing to-day, is a subject not merely of historical interest, but one which touches very closely some of the most vital national problems of the twentieth century.

THE PRINCIPLES OF MICROSCOPY: being an Introduction to Work with the Microscope. By Sir A. E. Wright, M.D., F.R.S., D.Sc.Dublin, Pathologist to St. Mary's Hospital, Paddington. With many Illustrations and Coloured Plates. Royal 8vo. 21s. net.

The general scope of this important work is *the technique of the microscope*, to the study of which the author has devoted many years.

THE KINGDOM OF MAN. By Sir E. Ray Lankester, M.A., D.Sc., LL.D., F.R.S., &c. Demy 8vo. With about 60 Illustrations. Price 3s. 6d. net.

Traces the history of man and his rebellion against nature, and shows that his destiny is to conquer.

SOILS, How to Handle and Improve Them, By S. W. Fletcher, With more than 100 Illustrations. Demy 8vo. about 350 pages. Price 8s. 6d. net.

The Field.—"The author is thoroughly up-to-date in his knowledge of the different phases of the subject of soil study, and brings his store of knowledge into effective use in the accomplishment of his task. The distinguishing characteristic of the book is the lucid and homely nature of its contents. The author has continued to dispense with technical terms and phraseology without impairing the clearness of his meaning. The volume is handsomely illustrated."

FARM MANAGEMENT. By F. W. Card, Professor of Agriculture. With 66 full-page Illustrations and numerous useful Tables and Returns. Demy 8vo. Price 8s. 6d. net.

This book covers an almost untouched field of agricultural literature; it shows how farms may be turned into solid business undertakings. The purchase of property, the comparative values of crops and stock, marketing, business forms and accounts, are all treated with clearness and good business sense.

FARM ANIMALS, How to Breed, Feed, Care for and Use them. By E. V. Wilcox, Ph.D., M.A., U.S.A. Department of Agriculture. With upwards of 60 Full-Page Illustrations. Demy 8vo. Price 8s. 6d. net.

CONTENTS:—The Horse. The Mule. Beef Cattle. The Dairy Cow. Pigs. Sheep. Goats. Poultry.

FRUIT RECIPES: a Manual of the Food Values of Fruits, and Nine Hundred different ways of Using Them. By Riley M. Fletcher Berry. Illustrated from Photographs. Large crown 8vo. 7s. 6d. net.

WASPS, Social and Solitary. By George W. Peckham and Elizabeth G. Peckham. With an Introduction by JOHN BURROUGHS and Illustrations by JAMES H. EMERTON. Crown 8vo. 6s. net.

LORD AVEBURY, in the *Daily Chronicle.*—"Their whole book is most interesting."

Athenæum.—"This is a book of the fields; it is one of those delightful narratives with which the name of Fabre is associated."

Daily Telegraph.—"This book is at once a delight and a revelation, the most charming monograph on a natural history subject that we have had occasion to notice in recent years."

AMERICAN INSECTS. By Professor Vernon L. Kellogg. With many original Illustrations by MARY WELLMAN. Square 8vo. 21s. net.

The chapters on insects and flowers, colour and pattern and their uses, insects and disease, are of great interest.

Nature.—"The work is probably the best that exists for anyone desiring an introductory work on North American insects compressed into a single volume."

"An admirable work on general entomology that cannot fail to at once arrest the attention and rivet the interest of the merest tyro."

Published by Archibald Constable & Co., Ld.,

10 ORANGE STREET, LEICESTER SQUARE, W.C.

Complete Catalogue sent post free on application.

R.H.S. Advertisement Office:—VINCENT SQUARE, WESTMINSTER, S.W.

FOSTER & PEARSON

LIMITED.

Established 1841.

Estimates on application
for
**RANGES, VINERIES,
ORCHID HOUSES,
IMPROVED FRAMES
&c.,
IN TEAK OR DEAL.**

ECONOMY IN FUEL.

The "ROBIN HOOD" Boiler is most
economical in fuel.
No Brickwork Setting required.
Any section can be quickly replaced.

BEESTON, NOTTs.

R.H.S. Advertisement Office :—VINCENT SQUARE, WESTMINSTER, S.W.

17   b

22

HARKNESS

FOR ALL KINDS OF

ROSES.

SEND FOR

CATALOGUE TO

R. HARKNESS & CO.,

THE ROSE GARDENS,

HITCHIN.

DATES OF THE

ROYAL HORTICULTURAL SOCIETY'S

Examinations in Horticulture 1908.

PUBLIC PARKS EXAMINATION, Monday, January 13th.
JUNIORS' EXAMINATION, Wednesday, March 25th.
GENERAL EXAMINATION, Wednesday, April 8th.
SCHOOL TEACHERS' EXAMINATION, Wednesday, April 29th.

The new SYLLABUS is now ready, and a copy will be sent to
any applicant enclosing a penny stamped envelope.

EXAMINATION PAPERS, 1893–1907.

The SOCIETY'S QUESTIONS, set at the various Examinations
—from 1893 to 1907—are now published in book form, and will
——— prove very useful to intending candidates. ———

TO BE OBTAINED FROM THE SOCIETY'S OFFICES,

VINCENT SQUARE, WESTMINSTER.   Price 2s.

R.H.S. Advertisement Office:—VINCENT SQUARE, WESTMINSTER, S.W.

GRAND
Begonias Double and Single

LIST OF ECKFORD'S GIANT SWEET PEAS FOR 1908.

Only genuine direct from Wem, Shropshire.

	Seeds	Price	Seeds	Price	Seeds	Price
Agnes Eckford, Pink	12	3d.	25	6d.	50	1/-
Agnes Johnston, Blush	50	3d.	100	6d.	200	1/-
*A. J. Cook, Waved Lavender	10	3d.	20	6d.	40	1/-
America, Striped	50	3d.	100	6d.	200	1/-
Aurora, do	do		do		do	
Black Knight, Maroon	do		do		do	
Black Michael, do	do		do		do	
Bolton's Pink, Pink	25	3d.	50	6d.	100	1/-
Brilliant Blue, Blue	12	3d.	25	6d.	50	1/-
Captain of the Blues, Blue	50	3d.	100	6d.	200	1/-
Chancellor, Orange	do		do		do	
Coccinea, Red	do		do		do	
Colonist, Lilac	do		do		do	
Countess Cadogan, Blue	do		do		do	
Countess of Latham, Pink	do		do		do	
Countess of Powis. Orange	do		do		do	
Countess of Radnor, Lavender	do		do		do	
*Countess Spencer (True), Pink	15	6d.	30	1/-		
Dainty, Picotee Edged	50	3d.	100	6d.	200	1/-
David R. Williamson, Indigo	do		do		do	
Dora Breadmore, Creamy Ground Tinted	do		do		do	
Dorothy Eckford, White	do		do		do	
Dorothy Tennant, Mauve	do		do		do	
Duchess of Sutherland, Blush	do		do		do	
Duchess of Westminster, Pink	do		do		do	
Duke of Sutherland, Indigo	do		do		do	
Duke of Westminster, Claret	do		do		do	
Earl Cromer, Crimson	12	3d.	25	6d.	50	1/-
Earliest of all, Pink and White	50	3d.	100	6d.	200	1/-
*E J. Castle, Rose	10	3d.	20	6d.	40	1/-
Eliza Eckford, Blush	50	3d.	100	6d.	200	1/-
Emily Eckford, Blue	do		do		do	
*Enchantress (Syn Paradise), Pink	12	3d.	25	6d.	50	1/-
Evelyn Byatt, Orange	25	3d.	50	6d.	100	1/-
Firefly, Crimson	50	3d.	100	6d.	200	1/-
*Frank Dolby, Lavender	10	3d.	20	6d.	40	1/-
George Gordon, Magenta	50	3d.	100	6d.	200	1/-
*Gladys Unwin, Pink	do		do		do	
Gorgeous, Orange	do		do		do	
Gracie Greenwood, Pink	do		do		do	
Hannah Dale, **Novelty,** Maroon	20	1/-				
*Helen Lewis, Orange	12	3d.	25	6d.	50	1/-
Helen Pierce, Striped	25	3d.	50	6d.	100	1/-
Henry Eckford, Orange	do		do		do	
H. J. R. Digges, **Novelty,** Maroon	20	1/-				
Hon. F. Bouverie, Pink	50	3d.	100	6d.	200	1/-
Hon Mrs. E. Kenyon, Pale Yellow	do		do		do	
Horace Wright, Dark Blue	12	3d.	25	6d.	50	1/-

	Seeds	Price	Seeds	Price	Seeds	Price
James Grieve, **Novelty,** Pale Yellow	15	1/-				
Janet Scott, Pink	50	3d.	100	6d.	200	1/-
Jeanie Gordon, Creamy Ground Tinted ...	do		do		do	
Jessie Cuthbertson, Striped	do		do		do	
*John Ingman, Rose	12	3d.	25	6d.	50	1/-
King Edward VII, Crimson	50	3d.	100	6d.	200	1/-
Lady Beaconsfield, Creamy Ground Tinted	do		do		do	
Lady Grisel Hamilton, Lavender	do		do		do	
Lady Mary Currie, Orange	do		do		do	
Lady M. Ó. Gore, Pale Yellow	do		do		do	
Lady Nina Balfour, Lavender	do		do		do	
Little Dorrit, Pink and White	do		do		do	
Lord Kenyon, Rose	do		do		do	
Lord Rosebery, Rose	do		do		do	
Lottie Eckford, Picotee Edged	do		do		do	
Lottie Hutchings, Creamy Ground Tinted ...	do		do		do	
Lovely, Pink	do		do		do	
Marchioness of Cholmondeley, Creamy Ground Tinted	do		do		do	
Mars, Crimson	do		do		do	
May Perrett, **Novelty,** Blush	15	1/-				
Mima Johnston, **Novelty,** Rose	20	1/-				
Miss Philbrick, Blue	50	3d.	100	6d.	200	1/-
Miss Willmott, Orange	do		do		do	
Mont Blanc, White	do		do		do	
Mrs. Collier, Pale Yellow	10	3d.	20	6d.	40	1/-
Mrs. Dugdale, Rose	50	3d.	100	6d.	200	1/-
Mrs. Fitzgerald, Creamy Ground, tinted ...	do		do		do	
Mrs. G. Higginson, Lavender	do		do		do	
Mrs. Hardcastle Sykes, Pink						
Mrs. J. Chamberlain, Striped	do		do		do	
Mrs. Walter Wright, Mauve	do		do		do	
Navy Blue, Blue	do		do		do	
*Nora Unwin, White	10	3d.	20	6d.	40	1/-
Othello, Maroon	50	3d.	100	6d.	200	1/-
Peach Blossom, Pink	do		do		do	
*Phenomenal, Picotee Edged ...	do		do		do	
*Phyllis Unwin, Rose	25	3d.	50	6d.	100	1/-
Pink Friar, Striped	50	3d.	100	6d.	200	1/-
Prima Donna, Pink	do		do		do	
*Primrose Waved, **Novelty,** Pale Yellow	20	1/-				
Prince Edward of York, Scarlet	50	3d.	100	6d.	200	1/-
Prince Olaf, **Novelty,** Striped	20	1/-				
Prince of Wales, Rose	50	3d.	100	6d.	200	1/-
Princess Beatrice, Pink	do		do		do	
Princess May, Lavender	do		do		do	
*Princess Victoria, **Novelty,** Pink	10	1/-				
Princess of Wales, Striped	50	3d.	100	6d.	200	1/-
Purple King, **Novelty,** Purple	20	1/-				
Queen Alexandra, Scarlet	25	3d.	50	6d.	100	1/-
Queen of Spain, Pink	12	3d.	25	6d.	50	1/-
Queen Victoria, Pale Yellow	50	3d.	100	6d.	200	1/-
Romolo Piazzani, Blue	50	3d.	100	6d.	200	1/-
Royal Rose, Rose	50	3d.	100	6d.	200	1/

	Seeds	Price	Seeds	Price	Seeds	Price
*Saint George, **Novelty,** Orange	5	1/-				
Salopian, Crimson	50	3d.	100	6d.	200	1/-
Scarlet Gem, Scarlet	do		do		do	
Senator, Striped	do		do		do	
Shazada, Indigo	do		do		do	
Sybil Eckford, Blush	25	3d.	50	6d.	100	1/-
*The Marquis, **Novelty,** Heliotrope	12	1/-				
Triumph, Orange	50	3d.	100	6d.	200	1/-
Unique, Striped	12	3d.	25	6d.	50	1/-
Venus, Creamy Ground, tinted	50	3d.	100	6d.	200	1/-
*White Waved, **Novelty,** White	20	1/-				

Those marked with an asterisk are Waved and Slightly Waved Varieties.

SPECIAL OFFER.

Any dozen priced at 3d. per packet, **2s. 9d.**
   ,,   ,,   6d.   ,,   **5s. 6d.**
   ,,   ,,   1s.   ,,   **10s. 6d.**
Post Free for Cash.

This Special Offer does not apply to Novelties.

For SPECIAL OFFER OF NOVELTIES see Catalogue which is Free for the asking.

Before Using Eckford's Seeds.   **After Using!!**

The above amusing sketch was sent in by a delighted customer residing in North London. Although it tells its own tale, it was accompanied by the following extract ftom his letter. We receive thousands of similar letters every year.

Dear Sir,—The above represents my experience with regard to Sweet Pea growing. I had a grand show this year, which I trust will be repeated *fortissimo* next season.

INDEX TO ADVERTISEMENTS

IN THE PRESENT ISSUE.

VOL. XXXIII. PART I.

The figures refer to the pages, which are numbered at the bottom.

R.H.S. Advertisement Office :—VINCENT SQUARE, WESTMINSTER, S.W.

ERRATA.

PAGES 34 AND 35 OF ADVERTISEMENTS.

Bulbs.—J. Murray & Sons (Yellow Inset).
  For facing page 123, *read* facing page 328.
Seeds.—J. Murray & Sons (Yellow Inset).
  For facing page 123, *read* facing page 328.

INDEX TO ADVERTISEMENTS

(Continued).

R.H.S. Advertisement Office : –VINCENT SQUARE, WESTMINSTER, S.W.

85   c 2

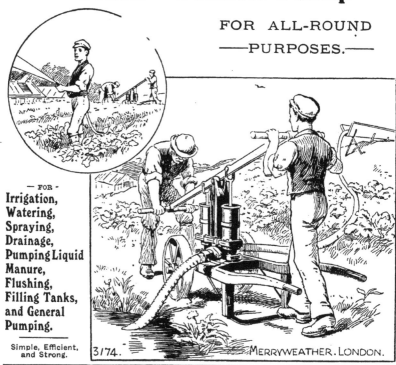

CAMPBELL'S PATENT
SULPHUR VAPORISER.

ABSOLUTELY
BEST REMEDY

FOR

Mildew and all
Diseases of .
Plants and .
Fruit Trees .

IN GREENHOUSES.

Campbell's CAUSTIC ALKALI WASH, for the winter washing of dormant fruit trees, kills all lurking Insects and Eggs, and leaves tree in a healthier and cleaner condition amply repaying cost and labour.

Campbell's NICO SOAP, a mixture of Nicotine and Soft Soap, destroys Aphis and Thrip infesting Plants, Fruit Trees, Hops, &c., far more effectual and cheaper than Quassia, Petroleum and other old-fashioned mixtures.

Campbell's BORDEAUX MIXTURE, instantly soluble in water, free from grit, and altogether both better and cheaper than the home-made article.

Write for Price List and Particulars to

Exors. ROBERT CAMPBELL,

Manufacturers of Nicotine, Weedkillers, Fumigators, Insecticides and Fungicides, Manures, and all Chemicals for use in Horticulture and Agriculture.

Water Street, MANCHESTER.

R.H.S. Advertisement Office:—VINCENT SQUARE, WESTMINSTER, S.W.

38

41

42

44

GEO. JACKMAN & SON,

Woking Nurseries, Surrey,

INVITE INSPECTION OF THEIR LARGE AND VARIED STOCK OF

Fruit Trees, Roses, Ornamental Trees and Shrubs, Forest Trees, Climbers

(including their celebrated Clematis),

Herbaceous and Alpine Plants.

200 ACRES OF STOCK TO SELECT FROM.

CATALOGUES FREE ON APPLICATION.

LANDSCAPE GARDENING A LEADING FEATURE.

R.H.S. Advertisement Office :—VINCENT SQUARE, WESTMINSTER, S.W.

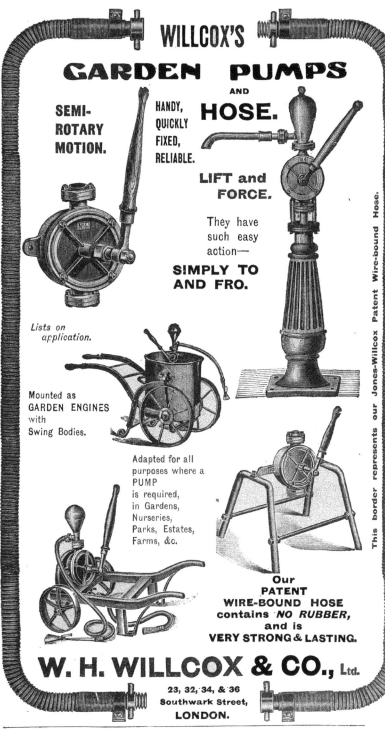

WILLCOX'S

GARDEN PUMPS

AND

HOSE.

SEMI-ROTARY MOTION.

HANDY, QUICKLY FIXED, RELIABLE.

LIFT and FORCE.

They have such easy action—

SIMPLY TO AND FRO.

Lists on application.

Mounted as GARDEN ENGINES with Swing Bodies.

Adapted for all purposes where a PUMP is required, in Gardens, Nurseries, Parks, Estates, Farms, &c.

This border represents our Jones-Willcox Patent Wire-bound Hose.

Our PATENT WIRE-BOUND HOSE contains *NO RUBBER*, and is VERY STRONG & LASTING.

W. H. WILLCOX & CO., Ltd.

23, 32, 34, & 36 Southwark Street, LONDON.

48

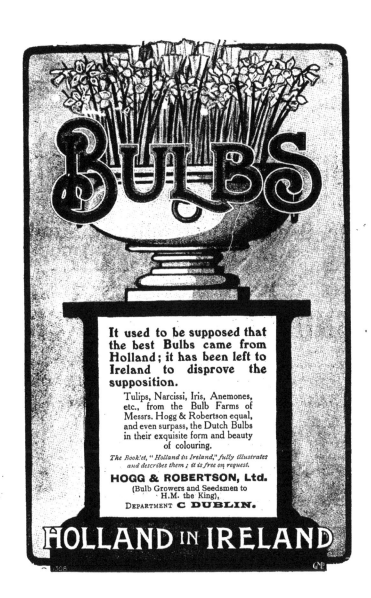

BULBS

It used to be supposed that the best Bulbs came from Holland; it has been left to Ireland to disprove the supposition.

Tulips, Narcissi, Iris, Anemones, etc., from the Bulb Farms of Messrs. Hogg & Robertson equal, and even surpass, the Dutch Bulbs in their exquisite form and beauty of colouring.

The Booklet, "Holland in Ireland," fully illustrates and describes them; it is free on request.

HOGG & ROBERTSON, Ltd.
(Bulb Growers and Seedsmen to H.M. the King),
Department **C DUBLIN.**

HOLLAND IN IRELAND

R.H.S. Advertisement Office :—VINCENT SQUARE, WESTMINSTER, S.W.

49

d

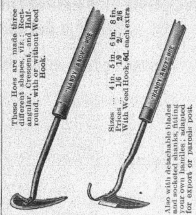
R.H.S. Advertisement Office:—VINCENT SQUARE, WESTMINSTER, S.W.

51   d 2

53

54

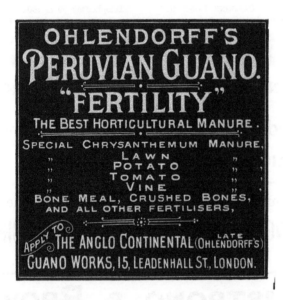

R.H.S. Advertisement Office:—VINCENT SQUARE, WESTMINSTER, S.W.

58

CRISPINS',
= BRISTOL.

FOR ALL CLASSES OF

Horticultural Buildings
AND
HEATING AND VENTILATING APPARATUS.

Erected at Bath and West of England Show, Newport, 1907.

JAMES CRISPIN, F.R.H.S., & SONS,
NELSON STREET,
BRISTOL.

HARTLEY & SUGDEN,
HALIFAX. LTD.

Makers of all Patterns of Heating Apparatus Boilers for

HORTICULTURAL HEATING.

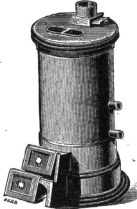

Catalogue

post free

on

application.

For Prices

apply to your

Heating Engineer

or

Horticultural

Builder.

WROUGHT WELDED "STANLEY" BOILER.

Series A.

Series F.

THE "WHITE ROSE"
Cast Iron Sectional Boilers.

R.H.S. Advertisement Office:—VINCENT SQUARE, WESTMINSTER, S.W.

61

R.H.S. Advertisement Office:—VINCENT SQUARE, WESTMINSTER, S.W.

66

THE MOST PERFECT FERTILIZER

for all Horticultural Purposes is

WAKELEY'S

CELEBRATED

HOP MANURE

(PATENTED).

HOP Manure is prepared by scientifically and chemically treating Hops. It is cleanly to use and absolutely free from any unpleasant smell. It enriches the soil with Humus and produces lovely blooms, rich foliage, grand quality vegetables, fruits, &c., also encourages the growth of fine grasses on lawns.

Strongly recommended by the late Mr. F. W. Burbidge, V.M.H., Mr. J. Hudson, V.M.H., and other noted Horticulturists.

Sold in Bags—1 cwt., 6/-; 5 cwt., 28/9; 10 cwt., 55/-
(AND SMALLER SIZES)

Carriage paid to any railway station in England and Wales, or delivered by Carrier in London districts.

To be obtained of Messrs. CARTER'S, King's Seedsmen, Holborn; J. VEITCH & SONS, Ltd., Royal Exotic Nursery, Chelsea; T. RIVERS & SON, Sawbridgeworth; PAUL & SON, Cheshunt; BARR & SONS, Covent Garden, and other leading Nurserymen and Seedsmen. Also the following Stores:—The ARMY & NAVY AUXILIARY CO-OP. SUPPLY; C.S.S.A.; W. WHITELEY'S, Ltd.; HARROD'S, Ltd.; SPIERS & POND, Ltd.; A. W. GAMAGE, Ltd.; or direct from

WAKELEY BROS. & CO., LIMITED,

HONDURAS WHARF, BANKSIDE, LONDON.

R.H.S. Advertisement Office:—VINCENT SQUARE, WESTMINSTER, S.W.

e 2

R.H.S. Advertisement Office:—VINCENT SQUARE, WESTMINSTER, S.W.

73

H. LANE & SON

⅀ The Nurseries, ⅀
BERKHAMSTED.

INTENDING PLANTERS SHOULD INSPECT OUR
MAGNIFICENT STOCK OF

Conifers, Yews, and other Evergreens,
Rhododendrons (grown in loam),
Ornamental Trees and Shrubs,
Fruit Trees of all kinds. Roses.
Forest Trees and Climbers.

WE HAVE THE FINEST STOCK IN ENGLAND OF

GRAPE VINES

A Splendid Selection of
FIGS, &c.

*Gardens planted
and laid
out.*

CATALOGUE ON APPLICATION.

Telephone: BERKHAMSTED 18.   Telegrams: "LANE, BERKHAMSTED."

ESTABLISHED 130 YEARS.

H. LANE & SON

The Nurseries, Berkhamsted, Herts.

R.H.S. Advertisement Office :—VINCENT SQUARE, WESTMINSTER, S.W.

❧ IRISH FRUIT TREES ❧

A grand collection of "native," healthy well-rooted trees for retroduction, and all the best leading English varieties, at very moderate prices.

APPLE "ARD-CAIRN RUSSET." (Colour, Deep Orange and Vermilion.)

For Price and Particulars apply to—

WM. BAYLOR HARTLAND & SONS,

ROYAL SEEDSMEN, NURSERYMEN, AND BULB GROWERS,

ARD-CAIRN, BALLINTEMPLE, CORK.

Established, Co. Cork, 1774.   (See *Gardener's Chronicle*, March 1907.)   Telegrams: "Princeps," Cork.

R.H.S. Advertisement Office :—VINCENT SQUARE, WESTMINSTER, S.W.

GEO. COOLING & SONS,

Rose Growers and Nurserymen,

BATH.

Geo. Cooling & Sons have always made a speciality of **Garden, Old Fashioned,** and **Decorative Roses,** and their collection is a unique one.

❧ ❧ ❧

Roses of all kinds.

Standard Roses.　　**Bedding Roses.**

Bush Roses.　　　 **Pot Roses.**

Climbing Roses.　 **Pillar Roses.**

❧ ❧ ❧

Fruit Trees also a Speciality.

Cooling & Sons' Rose and Fruit Tree Catalogue (one of the most complete and reliable published) is forwarded gratis and post free.

GEO. COOLING & SONS,

BATH.

R.H.S. Advertisement Office:—VINCENT SQUARE, WESTMINSTER, S.W.
84

Kelway's Lovely Delphiniums.

No garden is the perfection of loveliness unless it includes a display of brilliant Delphiniums, planted in borders or beds, alone, or in harmony with other plants. During many years of skilful hybridisation Kelway & Son have produced an immense variety of magnificent kinds ranging through every shade of blue, from rich dark royals to exquisite pale azure. With spikes growing to splendid heights, the size and markings of the blooms never fail to excite admiration wherever grown— in town or country.

Plant them at once for splendid development early in 1908. Prices and lists sent post free to Fellows of R.H.S.

KELWAY & SON, The Royal Horticulturists, LANGPORT, SOMERSET.

R.H.S. Advertisement Office :—VINCENT SQUARE, WESTMINSTER, S.W.

88

Two and a quarter miles of Sweet Peas,

comprising 461 varieties, under comparative trial at our Experimental Grounds during the summer of 1907, attracted large numbers of visitors from all parts of the Kingdom.

GIANT-FLOWERED SWEET PEAS.

The New Sweet Pea, Sutton's Queen.

This is undoubtedly the finest Sweet Pea yet raised, notwithstanding the great number of admirable new varieties recently introduced. The magnificent frilled flowers measure over two inches across, and the unrivalled combination of pure pink on deep cream ground gives the richest and most refined colouring attained in Sweet Peas. Under the provisional names of Mrs. Rothera and Miss Hilda Chamberlain this variety gained an

Award of Merit ... ... National Sweet Pea Society.
First Class Certificate ... ... Wolverhampton Floral Fete, 1907.

Per packet, 2s. 6d.

Sutton's Giant-flowered varieties

include the most effective colours yet introduced. Flowers of immense size, borne three or four on a stem instead of in pairs, as in the older varieties. Plants robust and remain in bloom for a considerable period.

White.	Purple.	Mauve shades.	Primrose yellow.
Sky-blue.	Maroon.	Carmine and white.	Scarlet striped.
Blue.	Delicate pink.	Brilliant scarlet.	Marbled blue.
Dark blue.	Salmon pink.	Cream, flaked pink.	—

We offer the above colours separately, each at 1s. per packet.

Collection of 10 varieties, one packet of each, our selection, 7s. 6d.
Mixed, all Colours, including the finest of the new varieties, per packet, 1s.

SUTTON & SONS, THE KING'S SEEDSMEN, READING.

R.H.S. Advertisement Office:—VINCENT SQUARE, WESTMINSTER, S.W.

Price (to Non-Fellows) 7s. 6d.   JUNE 190

Vol. XXXIII. Part II.

THE
JOURNAL

OF THE

Royal Horticultural Society

EDITED BY

F. J. CHITTENDEN, F.L.S.

CONTENTS.

R.H.S. Office for Advertisements and all Communications,
VINCENT SQUARE, S.W.

Printed for the Royal Horticultural Society

BY

SPOTTISWOODE & CO. LTD., NEW-STREET SQUARE, LONDON.

Beautiful Flowers & Delicious Vegetables are grown from CARTERS TESTED SEEDS

Illustrated Price List post free

James Carter & Co

SEED GROWERS
237/8 HIGH HOLBORN
LONDON W C

JOURNAL

OF THE

ROYAL HORTICULTURAL SOCIETY.

VOL. XXXIII. 1908.

PART II.

OPENING OF THE LABORATORY AND RESEARCH STATION AT THE WISLEY GARDENS BY THE RIGHT HON. LORD AVEBURY, P.C., F.R.S., JULY 19, 1907.

To those closely connected with the Society, July 19, 1907, is a day to be remembered, for it saw the inauguration of a long-wished-for and patiently anticipated scientific Laboratory and Research and Experimental Station, as a new and additional branch of the Society's work at Wisley, under the direct control of the Council.

For many years past the great want at the Society's Garden has been a Laboratory for scientific research, to investigate some of the multitudinous questions which are every day arising, connected with plant diseases, plant pests, and the laws which govern plant life and development. Wisley is an ideal spot for the carrying-on of such research, as it is absolutely in the country, without a house in sight to contaminate the air with its smoke—nothing but open commons and fields stretching away in every direction.

The opening ceremony was performed by the Right Hon. the Lord Avebury, P.C., F.R.S., &c., better known perhaps to students of Natural Science under the name of Sir John Lubbock. Invitations to the ceremony were issued to those whose scientific or educational interests link them with this new work of the Society, with the result that about 100 guests were present. Sir Trevor Lawrence, Bart., President of the Society; occupied the chair, with Lord Avebury on his right hand, and there were also present:—The Right Hon. the Lord Balfour of Burleigh, Lady Lawrence, Sir John Llewelyn, Bart., and Lady Llewelyn, Sir Wm. Vincent, Bart., J.P., Sir Wm. Chance, Bart., J.P., Sir Geo. Watt, C.I.E., the Hon. Mrs. Evelyn-Cecil, Sir Wm. T. Thiselton Dyer, F.R.S., K.C.M.G., Sir Albert Rollit, Sir Thomas H. Elliott, Francis J. Marnham, Esq., M.P., Professor Michael E. Sadler, LL.D., Miss E. Willmott, V.M.H., and Mrs. C. W. Earle, with other Members of the Council of the Royal Horticultural Society and of the Surrey Education Committee, and others.

The building is contained within one story, erected upon a site adjoining the ranges of glass-houses, and is warmed by hot-water radiators and lighted with acetylene gas. The external elevations are finished with rough-cast cement, rising from a plinth of red bricks, and the roof is covered with red tiles. It contains a students' laboratory about 21 feet by 36 feet, a small research laboratory, 14 feet 6 inches by 14 feet 6 inches, with a photographic dark-room attached. There is also a small glass annexe for experiments in plant physiology and diseases; and an office.

For a full hundred years the Society has maintained gardens for the experimental trial of fruits, flowers, and vegetables, and of all other matters and things connected with practical garden work. The Society has introduced hundreds of new plants from abroad of economic or ornamental value; and it has tested many thousands of professed novelties, thus bringing some sort of order out of the otherwise chaos of multitudinous names given to one and the same variety by different growers, seedsmen, and nurserymen. It has also by this means indicated to the general public the best varieties to plant and to grow, thus conferring a far greater benefit on the country at large than the public is at all cognisant of.

Thus :

    (1) By the introduction of new and valuable plants ;

    (2) By the elimination of synonyms ; and

    (3) By pointing out the best varieties,

the Society has rendered an inestimable benefit to—

    (1) The country at large ;

    (2) The trades of nurserymen, market gardeners, greengrocers, and fruit and vegetable sellers ; and

    (3) The private gentleman's garden,

all of which it has vastly enriched.

Besides its work with plants, the Society has always been able to send out a stream—small, it is true, but constant—of trained and more or less skilled gardeners, who, passing away into all parts of the country and to our Colonies, have carried with them the best traditions of the art of gardening. The Society has now extended this work by the erection of this laboratory, which is to be partly devoted to the training of young men in the elements of chemistry, biology, physiology, and kindred sciences as applied to the gardener's art.

The student's part of the laboratory is equipped with the most suitable apparatus that can be secured. There are work-tables and lockers for the use of twenty-four students at a time, gas and water supplies, a fume-chamber, chemical reagent cupboards, herbarium, specimen museum, Fram microscopes (each with two objectives), chemical and physical balances, and other apparatus suited to the study of plants, how they live their lives, and of the soil and air in which they live. A demonstration lantern with screen is also provided for the lecturer.

The Prospectus and Syllabus of Instruction for Students has received the approval and sanction of the Board of Education, under which body this branch of work—viz. the training of students—receives recognition as a technical school. A copy of the terms of the prospectus will be found on pp. 339 to 346.

The smaller laboratory is for experimental and research purposes, and is fitted with a steam and a hot-air steriliser, an incubator for the cultivation of organisms causing diseases in plants, a hot-water oven, paraffin bath, a microtome, and a very powerful microscope with excellent lenses. Here it is intended to investigate some of the difficult and obscure points which, though constantly cropping up in practical gardening, still puzzle and baffle the scientist to assign an approximate cause or suggest an appropriate remedy for.

A camera and other accessories are provided in the dark-room.

An addition to the Society's Garden and to its far-reaching and ever-extending influence is therefore now inaugurated; and the Council rejoices to see still another step forward in the great cause for which it exists.

The cost of the building has been about £1,000, the furniture, fittings, and apparatus representing a further £600.

At the Opening Luncheon to which the Society's guests sat down the following toasts were given :—

1. HIS GRACIOUS MAJESTY THE KING.
   Proposed by The PRESIDENT.

2. THE ROYAL HORTICULTURAL SOCIETY.
   Proposed by The LORD AVEBURY, P.C., F.R.S.
   Responded to by The LORD BALFOUR OF BURLEIGH, K.T.

3. THE BOARD OF AGRICULTURE AND HORTICULTURE.
   Proposed by Sir WILLIAM CHANCE, Bart.
   Responded to by Sir THOMAS H. ELLIOTT, K.C.B.

4. THE SURREY COUNTY COUNCIL.
   Proposed by Professor MICHAEL E. SADLER, LL.D.
   Responded to by Sir WILLIAM VINCENT, Bart., J.P.

5. THE LORD AVEBURY, P.C., F.R.S.
   Proposed by Sir TREVOR LAWRENCE, Bart., K.C.V.O., V.M.H.

6. SIR TREVOR LAWRENCE, Bart., K.C.V.O., V.M.H., President of the Royal Horticultural Society.
   Proposed by Sir JOHN T. DILLWYN-LLEWELYN, Bart., D.L., V.M.H.

The PRESIDENT having given the toast of "The King," which was enthusiastically received,

Lord AVEBURY rose to propose "The Royal Horticultural Society," and said :—

While very sensible of the honour you have done me in inviting me to open this interesting Laboratory I cannot but feel, especially when I look round, that there are others who might have done so much more appropriately. One name especially—that of my friend Sir Trevor Lawrence, your President, who is himself so great an authority, and who has done so much to bring the Society to its present remarkable state of prosperity —will occur to everyone.

As we stand here to-day two men will be in all our thoughts—Mr. G. F. Wilson, whose loving care and horticultural skill originally made the Garden what it was, and Sir Thomas Hanbury, who prevented it from being broken up, and, with his usual liberality, presented it to the Society.

I have now the pleasure of proposing " Prosperity to the Royal Horticultural Society." The Society dates back more than a hundred years. It was founded as long ago as 1804 by Mr. Thomas Andrew Knight, Sir Joseph Banks, and other distinguished botanists, but for many years it vegetated rather than flourished.

When your present President was elected in 1885 the Society had 1,108 Fellows—a goodly number certainly, but not enough—and the Society was in some pecuniary difficulties. Owing largely to his ability and energy it has now nearly 10,000 Fellows, has assets, without counting Wisley, of some £70,000, and an annual income of £18,000.

Your centenary in 1904 was marked by the erection in Vincent Square of an Exhibition Hall and Library, costing £42,000—raised mainly by private subscription—and also by Sir Thomas Hanbury's munificent gift of this Wisley property, one of his many public benefactions. Mr. Wilson, one of our many City men who have taken a warm interest in science, devoted his leisure during twenty-four years to the planting, arrangement, and development of the Garden, which comprises sixty acres.

In adding this Laboratory to the important gift of the Garden you have, I understand, two main objects in view—

1. The improvement of Horticulture by giving the best possible training to a number of young gardeners, and
2. The promotion of horticultural and botanical science by experiment and investigation.

The erection of this Laboratory and Research Station meets a long-felt want in connection with the Society's work. In the United States, and in many of our own Colonies, there are several such stations under Government supervision and maintenance, but in the home country their initiation, direction, and support are left to private enterprise. The good work being done at the Royal Botanic Gardens, Kew, at the Botanic Gardens of Cambridge, Oxford, Edinburgh, and other Universities, is well known and appreciated, as is also the experimental work for some years past undertaken at Rothamsted by the late Sir John Lawes and at Woburn by the Duke of Bedford.

Among "the subjects it is hoped to experiment upon in the near future are soil-sterilisation by steam as a means of destroying pests of plants which live in the soil; an investigation into the influence of sterilisation on the plants cultivated in the soil; study of the bacterial flora of the soil; etherisation of plants; and certain plant diseases. Each of these subjects will entail a large amount of laboratory work, as well as experiments in the Garden." [1]

When we look round us at the endless variety of trees, shrubs, and herbs, no two alike in their form, their leaves, their flowers, their fruit, or their seeds, and when we reflect that for every difference in form and

[1] *Gardeners' Chronicle*, April 13, 1907, p. 233.

texture, in colour or scent, there is some cause and explanation, comparatively few of which are yet known to us, we see what a rich and beautiful field of inquiry horticulturists· have before them. In fact, the range of research and inquiry is so wide as to be practically inexhaustible.

I cannot doubt that, in addition to its other services to the community, the Society will, in connection with this Garden, do much to promote Horticulture in its æsthetic as well as in its scientific aspect, and I have much pleasure in proposing the toast " Prosperity to the Royal Horticultural Society."

Lord BALFOUR, in reply, said :—I shall be astonished if the prevailing feeling in this tent at the present moment is not one of profound surprise that I should be selected to respond to this toast. We can all of us, however, thank Lord Avebury for the honour he has conferred upon us, and upon the object of our gathering, by being present on this memorable occasion, and also for all the kindly words he has said of the Society and its work in the past, and of its opportunities and aspirations for the future. The only justification I can think of for my present position is that I can say one thing which the Chairman could not, namely, that after the twenty-one years of his Presidency the Society has increased so much. I do not give him the whole credit, as I am sure he would desire it to be shared with him by the Council and by the office staff; but, nevertheless, without the judicious and tactful guiding hand of Sir Trevor the Society would not, I venture to think, be in the very enviable position it is to-day.

The progress of the Society, if we look back twenty years, has been very striking. Then there were 1,100 Fellows, and now there are nearly, if not quite, 10,000. The annual income at that time was but £2,800, it now exceeds £18,000; and whilst our investments then consisted of a debt of £1,100, we have now £28,500 invested besides the Vincent Square property. Twenty years ago the Society had to leave South Kensington, and from that time, up to three years ago, it occupied hired offices and a hired hall. Now the Society possesses its own Hall, Library, and offices, valued at £50,000, and several other assets. Twenty years ago the Society had Gardens at Chiswick of but thirteen acres in extent; now you see this beautiful Garden extending over sixty acres. I do not think I need say more upon these points.

I think the predominant feeling to-day is that we are opening up a new era of usefulness and prosperity by making the practice and scientific theory of horticulture go hand in hand for the mutual benefit of both departments. In this I think we are like our sister pursuit of agriculture (with which I am also proud to be connected), for I can remember when there was almost a war between the scientific and the practical agriculturists. Neither would believe *they* had anything to learn from the other. But this is now all changed in agriculture; and if the antipathy and mutual distrust was never so great in horticulture, I think I may say that the practical and scientific horticulturists are now able to see the good points in each other's work which was not the case a dozen years or so ago. If science has proved of use to agriculture, how much more is it of use to horticulture. Agriculture deals with only about a dozen plants and half a dozen kinds of animals, whereas the horticulturist has thousands of plants to deal with from all parts of the world, varying in their requirements of treatment, temperature, and soil; of pruning, light, and shade; and of every influence which contributes to the work of the successful gardener, and therefore I think I may truly say that the scientific side of gardening in the Gardens of the Royal Horticultural Society will make the Society of more use to the practical side than it has ever been before.

The work, however, is not quite new or strange to the Society. In 1864 we invited the co-operation of the Society of Arts in holding examinations in horticulture throughout the country, and in 1892 the Society commenced its present system of General Examinations, for which nearly two thousand candidates have entered. I must also, as the representative of the Council of the Royal Horticultural Society who has been coupled with this toast, acknowledge with pleasure the co-operation we are here now just commencing with the Surrey County Council. At present it is true the benefits seem to be all on one side—the County Council's—but we hope the day is not far distant when the County Council may see its way to affording, as well as to receiving, material assistance. The work we are starting to do is a practical work. Those engaged in practical gardening come from a class who, when they have large families, are often tempted to consider only how soon they can utilise their sons in helping to keep up the home. The temptation is a very great and real one, and if it is indulged in it is calculated to do a greater harm to a young gardener than to a lad in any other similar profession, because a few years' training in the scientific theory of gardening is nowadays so very essential to a thoroughly good gardener's education.

As contrasted with farmers, gardeners are a particularly contented race. They do not complain, although I think they often have (and certainly this year have) very just cause for complaint. A poet of Scotland says something about the "sunny spring," but this year neither spring nor summer has deserved the adjective. However, there is now, I think, a promise of better things in the future, and I hope the gardener's troubles are behind him, and not before him. But, although gardeners are a contented lot, they have their weak points. Few gardeners, I fancy, think they have done their duty to their employer unless they spend at least two-thirds of his annual income on the gardens; all the rest of the establishment they consider as a mere appanage of theirs, which is the primary department. If we want good gardeners, we must not only educate them in practice and theory, we must also be liberal with them in plants and necessaries, and they must turn them to good account.

3. THE BOARD OF AGRICULTURE AND HORTICULTURE.

Proposed by Sir WILLIAM CHANCE, Bart.
Responded to by Sir THOMAS H. ELLIOTT, K.C.B.

Sir WILLIAM CHANCE said :—I notice in the programme that the toast appears as "The Board of Agriculture and Horticulture." This is not the usual title of the Board : they call themselves " The Board of Agriculture and Fisheries." To-day's sunshine and warmth would, perhaps, make us linger on the word "Fisheries," so suggestive of the cool sea. However, the word "agriculture" is always taken to include "horticulture."

The Lord Avebury and Lord Balfour have said almost all about the work of the Society in the past which it is necessary to say to-day. I certainly do think we owe a very great debt to this Society for its invaluable work, the plants it has introduced into the country, and in extending the cause of horticulture generally. Although the Society has at present a good balance in hand, still in the past its resources have been taxed to the utmost to carry on its work. There are, I hope, people who will be willing to come forward to make donations to the Laboratory, because in building and maintaining it the Society is doing a really National work, and I am sure the Society will offer no objection if the Secretary of the Board of Agriculture will bring pressure to bear on the Privy Purse for financial help in forwarding this work. May I express the hope that Sir Thomas Elliott will take back such a good account of these Gardens and the work which the Society is inaugurating to-day that the hard heart of the Chancellor of the Exchequer will be touched? And in anticipation of such a benefit let us drink the toast of " The Board of Agriculture."

Sir Thomas Elliott said :—It is with very special pleasure that I rise to thank you for the hearty manner in which you have drunk this toast. I take the mere fact of the inclusion of this toast in your list as a reminder to the Board of their duty—that we are under obligations to our horticultural clients as well as to our agricultural clients.

We have during the last few days secured the passing of the " Destruction of Insects and Pests Bill," by which Parliament has given to the Board very considerable powers in this direction. We have already commenced a crusade in two parts of England against the gooseberry pest. We had to make a beginning, and we have done what seemed to lie to our hand.

I will say no more, but thank you for the way you have drunk this toast, and express the hope that the mutual goodwill and friendship existing between the Society and the Board of Agriculture will ever continue to be as cordial as it is at present.

4. THE SURREY COUNTY COUNCIL.

Proposed by Professor Michael E. Sadler, LL.D.
Responded to by Sir William Vincent, Bart., J.P.

Professor Michael Sadler said :—I gladly rise to propose a toast which expresses our sense of obligation to the Surrey County Council. Its work is distinguished by public spirit and by practical wisdom.

The connection between the Surrey County Council and these Gardens will, I hope, in the future be a close and a fruitful one. The County Council propose to select year by year a number of suitable boys from elementary schools—boys with promise and aptitude for gardening—who will be received here by the Royal Horticultural Society for a thorough course of training, free at least for one year, and then, if their promise continues, for a second year, with all the benefits of scientific training and scientific education, as has already been admirably explained. The system of practical education begins in September next with a batch of five boys, and we shall all desire to congratulate the Surrey County Council and the Royal Horticultural Society on this plan, which will give wise, practical training in every branch of horticulture. We are met to-day amid many historical associations. Within two miles of us is Ockham, from which village there went forth, more than five hundred years ago, a youth, William of Ockham, who was destined to become one of the three greatest philosophers of mediæval Europe. He must have passed near this place as he journeyed from his home to Oxford. English thought and letters have always been recruited by men of genius born in humble homes. For centuries much has been done, though not in a very systematic way, to provide opportunities by means of which such boys may obtain the education appropriate to their powers. One of the distinctive marks of the educational movement which has done so much for England during the last thirty years has been the development of the scholarship system, the purpose of which is to give effective access to all callings and professions. Our scholarship system in England, however, has been far too exclusively directed to the recruiting of the literary callings. We now need a further development of the scholarship system to enable boys to get the training needed for a favourable start in skilled callings. The scholarships offered by the Surrey County Council and the Royal Horticultural Society are a good example of the new type of scholarship which we need. Our education has been in the past too bookish. Too little has been done to bring school training into close relation with nature and with handicraft. Our aim should be to make education at one and the same time practical and humane, scientific in its grip on facts, and at the same time inspiring through its moral ideals. The County Education Committees have been charged with a great task of educational reform, and we wish them success in the efforts which they are making to accomplish it. Among the English County Councils a particularly honourable place is held by the County Council of Surrey, the health of which I have the honour to propose.

Sir WILLIAM VINCENT said :—The work of the Surrey County Council is an ever-increasing one. The motor traffic—the inconveniences of which we have already experienced on our way to Wisley—is responsible for no small part of this. The Council has 220 miles of main road to up-keep, at a cost of £65,000 last year. This is an increase of £5,000 on the previous year, which was itself £5,000 more than the year before it, and so on.

The Surrey County Council does its duty, not to perfection perhaps, but it has tried to do something for those having special aptitude for horticulture. Last year we spent on special subjects (horticulture being the special subject referred to) £614, and the estimate for the current year for horticulture as a special subject is £750. Last year eighteen lectures on fruit, flowers, and vegetables were given, besides addresses

FIG. 39.—OPENING OF THE WISLEY LABORATORY.

THE RIGHT HON. THE LORD AVEBURY, P.C., F.R.S., SIR TREVOR LAWRENCE, BART., V.M.H.,
AND MR. F. J. CHITTENDEN, DIRECTOR.

(*To face page* 336.)

Fig. 40.—The Wisley Laboratory.

Fig. 41.—The Students' Laboratory (Interior).

at twenty local shows, with an average attendance of twenty-six. Lectures on the science of gardening are also given by Wye College to the members of gardeners' societies, and an average attendance of ninety-five gardeners has been secured. Last year also we had gardens attached to fifty-nine elementary schools in which 993 scholars were having instruction. Also thirty-five teachers spent their vacation at Wye College, and had instruction in botany and horticulture. Further practical horticultural instruction is being given by the Surrey County Council; this year sixty-two elementary day schools, with a total number of 1,250 scholars, are receiving instruction. Though you might wish that we were doing more even than that, still I think you will agree that we are paying some attention to the study and teaching of horticulture in this county.

Then as regards the general work of the Surrey County Council, the reason, I think, why we are to a very large extent successful in the work we are doing is that we are entirely non-political; and I think that as long as we refuse to pay attention to political views and confine ourselves to administration we shall go on with success, and be amongst the foremost of the counties of England for County Council work.

5. THE LORD AVEBURY, P.C., F.R.S.

Proposed by Sir TREVOR LAWRENCE, Bart., K.C.V.O., V.M.H.

Sir TREVOR LAWRENCE said :—It is hardly necessary for me to say how much we appreciate Lord Avebury's presence with us here to-day to open our new Laboratory and Research Station. We have been privileged to listen to very interesting and stirring speeches, and we have, I think, been particularly fortunate in the selection of speakers on this occasion. So far from thinking that Lord Balfour has been trespassing on my province, I think you had from him a speech very full of interest from many aspects, especially as regards the Laboratory.

One great fault which I feel has long existed amongst our fellow-countrymen is that they have shown a disinclination to appreciate the teaching of science in connection with horticulture, whereas in various foreign countries, by the encouragement and endowment of science, many discoveries have been brought to the practical aid of the gardener. The fault is an obvious one, because we have nothing in this country that does not owe an enormous improvement to scientific teaching, and in regard to practical horticulture this Society may claim some little credit. Only a few days ago I received a letter from that eminent and distinguished botanist, Sir Joseph Hooker, which I will read you. It lays stress on this point.

" The Camp, Sunningdale, July 15, 1907.

" MY DEAR SIR TREVOR,—-Your letter of June 25, conveying the hearty congratulations of the President, Council, and Fellows of the Royal Horticultural Society on the approach of my ninetieth birthday has gratified me more than I can express.

" It is not by many times the first instance I have experienced of the friendly and all too liberal estimate of my labours in the cause horticultural that the Society has entertained.

" It has been a source of great regret that I was obliged, when resigning my post of Chairman of the Scientific Committee, to abandon all hope of attending our meetings on account of having to devote my energies to the Directorship of Kew, and to the completion of labours of botanical works I have in progress.

" I had also to endeavour to overtake arrears of work extending over many years, and which are still far from being overtaken.

" As a botanist I have thereby lost much, for since the days of David Douglas the Royal Horticultural Society has contributed more for botanical science, as represented by collections, publications, and experimental research, than any other establishment in Europe.

" I have now to request you, as their President, to accept yourself, and convey to the Council and to my fellow members, my pride and gratitude for this most welcome evidence of their friendship and esteem.

" With every good wish for the continued welfare and renown of the Society,

"Believe me, dear Sir Trevor,

" Sincerely yours,

" Jos. D. Hooker."

That is a letter which needs no comment from me, but it is, I think, a very pleasant testimony to the work and value of our old Society. I am very grateful to Lord Avebury for coming here, and I am sure you are all equally so, and we hope we may see him here often again. I ask you to join with me heartily in drinking the toast to Lord Avebury.

Lord AVEBURY replied :—It seems to me I am receiving this afternoon much more praise than I deserve. I thank Sir Trevor for the kind words he has spoken. I wish for nothing better than the kindly picture he has drawn, so will detain you no longer for fear I should weaken the impression he has made ; but in thanking you I will only say that " my feeling of gratitude is in ' inverse ratio ' to the length of my remarks."

6. SIR TREVOR LAWRENCE, BART., K.C.V.O., V.M.H.,
President of the Royal Horticultural Society.

Proposed by Sir JOHN T. DILLWYN-LLEWELYN, Bart., D.L., F.L.S.

Sir JOHN LLEWELYN said :—It is only those who collaborated with Sir Trevor during the troublous times of twenty years ago, and again at the time when the Society celebrated its centenary in 1904, who will know the difficulties which had to be met with great determination and tact in dealing with the proposals for celebrating our centenary. A new Hall was proposed and a new Garden was proposed, each of which was supported by its own particular section of the Fellows, and each of which was considered to be antagonistic to the other. It is only those who were on the Council at that time who know what it cost to bring the many opposing elements into harmony and the many apparently insurmountable difficulties to a successful issue ; and I venture to say that the happy and harmonious condition of the Society to-day is due very largely to the way Sir Trevor then managed the Society's affairs. I am sure you will all drink with me the health of the President of the Society.

Sir TREVOR LAWRENCE briefly acknowledged the toast.

The following are the terms of the Prospectus of Instruction for Students :—

ROYAL HORTICULTURAL SOCIETY.

SCHOOL OF HORTICULTURE.

PROSPECTUS.

The Society admits a limited number of young men to study the Principles and Operations of Horticulture in their Gardens at Wisley, near Ripley, in Surrey.

CONDITIONS OF ADMISSION.

The following are the principal conditions of admission :—

1. Applicants for admission as working Students into the Royal Horticultural Society's Gardens at Wisley are furnished with a copy of this paper, which, when signed, must be returned to the Secretary, Royal Horticultural Society, Vincent Square, Westminster, accompanied by a letter in the applicant's own handwriting.

2. Applicants must not exceed twenty-two years in age, and they must be healthy, free from physical defect, and not so much below average height as to interfere with their prospects as Gardeners. They must also be prepared to perform all kinds of Gardening work, including the humblest.

3. Two testimonials as to character should accompany the application.

4. The applicant will be informed if his name has been entered for admission, and, on a vacancy occurring, he will receive notice to that effect. Should there be no vacancy within six months, the application must be renewed if admission is still desired. If not renewed, the applicant's name will be removed from the list. The terms begin on the last Monday in September and the last Monday in March, when only can Students be admitted.

5. After any applicant has received notice of his admission, a fee of £5 5s. must be forwarded to the Secretary of the Society before the order for admission can be issued. This payment covers all charges for two years, with the exception of books, stationery, note-books, and suchlike.

6. No wages are given to Students.

7. On appointment the Student will have to sign the following agreement to abide by the rules and regulations of the Gardens, and to stay not less than two years, the Council having full power to terminate the engagement sooner should conditions arise rendering such a course, in their opinion, desirable.

8. Students are required to conform to the following regulations :—

(1) *Obedience.*—Implicit obedience to the Director, Superintendent, Foremen, and others appointed as Instructors, and to conform to the ordinary rules of the Gardens.

(2) *Regularity and Punctuality.*—To observe regularity and punctuality in daily attendance. Hours, 8.45 A.M. to 6 P.M. in summer, and in winter as may be arranged. The Council strongly advise Students to visit the Garden in the early morning in spring and summer for the purpose of making their own observations and taking notes thereof. For this purpose they may enter at 6 A.M. or as soon after as light will permit.

(3) *Holidays.*—Each Student will be allowed the Bank holidays, Sundays, Saturday afternoon (from 1 P.M.), and twenty-one days during the year. The twenty-one days' holidays must be arranged, as to date, with the consent of the Director and Superintendent, and may be taken either one week's holiday at Easter, or Christmas, and two weeks in August or September ; or, if preferred, three weeks in August or September.

(4) Students misconducting themselves or breaking these rules will be subject to instant dismissal.

I agree to the above conditions and regulations and promise to observe them in all things.

Usual Signature _____

{
Applicant's Name (in full) _____
Age _____
Address _____
}

{
Father's Name _____
Address _____
Occupation _____
}

CERTIFICATES.

Certificates of Proficiency are granted to each Student at the end of the two years' course provided that, in addition to fulfilling the foregoing conditions, he—

(1) Pass written and practical examinations in the Principles and Operations of Horticulture upon the syllabus laid down for study.

(2) Present an essay written by himself upon some approved Horticultural or Scientific subject.

(3) Submit a collection of at least 200 properly dried, named, and localised plant specimens collected *outside the Wisley Gardens.*

(4) Submit a collection of Insects either injurious or helpful to Horticulture.

One or two Student demonstratorships or travelling scholarships will be awarded by the Council at their discretion, after considering the reports of the Director, Superintendent, and Examiners, to enable the

Student to acquire special knowledge of some particular branch of Horticulture. Students to whom these awards are made will receive a small remuneration and will be required to assist in demonstrating to the junior students.

COURSES OF INSTRUCTION.

There will be two courses of instruction, an Elementary or first-year, and an Advanced or second-year course. Each course will include Laboratory Instruction in Elementary Science as applied to Horticulture, together with Field work, and Garden Instruction in the Practical Operations of Horticulture. Every Student will have an opportunity of spending part of his two years in each department of the Garden, and the practical work will be supplemented by lectures. Students will have an opportunity of seeing the various trials and experimental work in progress in the Garden. Selected Students have also the advantage of attending certain of the Society's Shows and Lectures in London.

THE LABORATORY.

The Laboratory accommodates twenty-four Students and is well lighted, ventilated, and heated.

Lockers are provided for the use of each Student, so that books and apparatus may be kept under lock and key when not in actual use.

Apparatus.—Each Student is provided with all the instruments and materials needful in the practical work of the Laboratory (except knives, books, and such like). Great care must be taken of these, and they must always be left in good condition. Breakages will have to be paid for by the breaker.

Microscopes.—The microscopes provided must be placed in their proper compartments in the microscope cupboard when not in actual use.

Tables.—Students are expected to keep their work-tables clean and tidy at all times.

Library.—A library of books useful to Horticultural Students is available for general use.

THE GARDEN.

The Garden consists of about sixty acres of land presented to the Society by the late Sir Thomas Hanbury, K.C.V.O., and includes the celebrated wild garden of the late Mr. G. F. Wilson, V.M.H. Several acres of fruit trees have since been planted, and an outdoor vineyard has been started. as an experiment; fine collections of flowering shrubs and of roses have been presented; trials of vegetables and of hardy flowers and plants are continually in progress; and an extensive range of glass-houses, including orchard house, vinery, stove, propagating pits, &c., has been erected, so that all departments of Horticulture are represented. Each Student also has a small plot allotted to him; and a botanical garden in which plants are systematically arranged according to a natural system of classification is in course of formation. A well-equipped Meteorological Station is situated in the Garden.

SHORT SYLLABUS OF INSTRUCTION.

NOTE.—The following outline Syllabuses are not intended to indicate more than broadly the subjects of instruction, and do not show the sequence of instruction, as although arranged under different headings as Plant Life, Physics, Chemistry, Soil, &c., the inter-relation between the parts is not indicated and can only be shown in a very full Syllabus. Almost everything in the following Syllabus will be studied practically by observation and by experiment.

I.—ELEMENTARY SCIENCE COURSE.

A.— Plant Life.   Flowering Plants.

Study of a typical plant.

Study of seeds. Structure, uses of various parts. Conditions of germination. Fate of food-stuff stored in seed. Respiration. Testing of seeds.

Roots. Functions of roots. Fixation. Absorption of water and earth salts. Osmosis. Root pressure. Bleeding of wounds. Study of substances absorbed. Water-culture experiments. Mode of growth of root. Manner in which it is placed in a position to do its work. Transplanting, &c.

Leaves. Structure. Functions. Transpiration. Source of water and course of current. Conditions affecting Transpiration. Reciprocal action of root and foliage. Absorption of carbon dioxide. Influence of light. Phyto-synthesis and conditions affecting the making of starch in the leaf.

Buds and stems. Structure of buds. Growth and development of buds. Growth of stems. Conditions affecting growth of stems. Structure and function of various parts. Healing of wounds. Formation of roots from stems. Effect of pruning, ringing, notching, bending, &c. Grafting and budding. Climbing plants.

Storage of food and water. Parts of plant used for vegetative reproduction. Tubers, corms, runners, &c.

Flowers. Uses of various parts. Pollination. Cross-pollination, natural and artificial. Fertilisation. Formation of seeds.

Fruits. Structure of common fruits. Seed saving.

Study of plant relationships. The more common orders of flowering plants.

Field study of the influence of environment on plant growth. The vegetation typical of certain soils, and so on. Plant societies. Use of a flora.

B.—Physics and Chemistry.

Heat and temperature. Expansion and contraction. Thermometers. Changes of state in matter. Conduction. Radiation and absorption. Chemical change.

Light. Chemical change under. Passage through prism.

Air. Its physical properties (Barometers). Nitrogen, oxygen, carbonic acid gas, water vapour in air (Hygrometer).

Water. Chemical composition of. Physical properties. Hard and soft water. Solution and solubility.

Acids, Alkalis, and Salts.

Carbon and some of its compounds. Carbon monoxide and dioxide, carbonates. Carbon in vegetable and animal matter. Fats and oils, starch, sugar, gluten, and albumen.

C.—Soil.

The origin and composition of soils. Mechanical analysis of soils of various kinds, loams, peats, sands, clays, &c. Physical properties of the constituents, capacity for water, &c., clay, sand, lime, humus. Soluble and insoluble constitutents. Action of acid solutions, &c. Relation of plant to soil. Recognition of some of the more important salts in soil.

II.—More Advanced Course.

A.—Plant Life.

A more advanced treatment of certain subjects in the Elementary Course, particularly with reference to plant physiology and composition, and classification. Life-history and mode of life of ferns. Study of fungi, particularly in relation to plant diseases. Geographical distribution of plants. Origin of races, varieties, &c., hybridisation, selection, and fixing of varieties.

B.—Insect Life, &c.

Insects, with special reference to those injurious and helpful to plants. Life-histories and habits. Treatment to destroy insect pests. Mites, centipedes and millepedes, woodlice, eelworms, earthworms, snails and slugs, &c.

C.—Soils.

Further study of soil physics. " Heavy " and " light " soils. Action of lime on soils, &c. Humus—origin of, and effect on texture of soils. Water in soils. Temperature of soils and source of heat in soils, hot-beds, &c.

Chemistry of soils. Sand, clay, lime, humus. Weathering of soils. Life in the soil. Results of decay. Nitrification and denitrification. Minerals in soil. Fertility of soil. Rotation of crops. Manuring. Changes due to tillage, &c. Source and composition of artificial manures and their effect on plant growth.

D.—Economic Botany. Lectures on.

E.—Horticultural Economics. Lectures on.

III.—Operations of Horticulture.

The Garden affords ample opportunities for instruction in all the practical operations of Horticulture, both outdoors and under glass, and actual work will be done by the Students (who will spend the greater part of their time in the Garden according to the accompanying Syllabus and Time Table) in all the departments. Experiments in the use of insecticides and fungicides will be carried out.

The practical work will be supplemented by lectures and revision in the class-room and by friendly debates and discussions among the

Students themselves under the chairmanship of the Director or Superintendent or other capable person.

For purposes of the instruction of Students the Gardens are divided into two sections:—A, the fruit and vegetable, and B, the floral and arboricultural. For the sake of convenience, A includes the orchid house and the rose border, B the wild garden, the propagating pits and nursery, the collections of herbaceous plants, and the arboretum. Students spend one year in each of these departments, their work being arranged so that they gain experience in all the branches of the subject.

The work of the Botanical Garden is done by the Students collectively. Each Student has also a small plot allotted to him, which he may crop as he desires, and the work of which is done in his spare time.

Students are required to keep a diary of the work done, with full notes on the manner in which it is carried out. The outdoor garden work is supplemented by revision in the class-room, the diaries forming the basis of this revision.

Students also in turn take part in the making of meteorological records, Section C.

The following is a brief Syllabus of the work done in departments A and B throughout the year.

A.—Fruit and Vegetable Department.

1. The cultivation of fruit and vegetables under glass, including the preparation of the borders, their drainage, aëration, and manuring.

The mixing of soils and the values of artificial fertilisers.

The planting or potting and subsequent treatment of vines, peaches, nectarines, plums, apricots, cherries, figs, and other orchard-house fruits in borders and pots.

The cultivation in pits and frames of melons, cucumbers, and tomatos.

Stoking and general attention to boilers ; heating by hot water and by hot-beds.

Ventilation ; watering ; artificial pollination ; the thinning of fruit ; tying-in, training, and pruning.

2. Fruit in the open air, including planting, training, summer and winter pruning, mulching, drainage, and routine work in the orchard.

The gathering, packing, and storing of fruit.

Selection of varieties :—The Gardens contain very extensive collections of apples, pears, plums, damsons, gooseberries, currants, &c., and an experimental outdoor vineyard.

Strawberry cultivation.

3. Vegetables, including the preparation of the ground, trenching, digging, manuring, &c., and the routine work in the cultivation of broccoli, cabbage, cauliflower, celery, kale, onions, potatos, rhubarb, root crops, &c.

Tomatos in the open.

4. Nursery work, including the raising of seedlings, and propagation of fruit trees by buds, eyes, cuttings, grafts.

5. The identification and suppression of insect and fungus pests by fumigation, spraying, washing, &c.

The use of knapsack sprayers, powder bellows.

The preparation of insecticides and fungicides.

6. The choice of site and soil for orchard and kitchen garden.

Intercropping, catch crops, and the rotation of crops.

7. Cultivation of roses. The rose border includes a large collection of bush and climbing varieties of roses, mostly teas and hybrid teas.

Propagation by budding and by cuttings.

Planting, pruning, training, mulching, &c.

8. Cultivation of orchids. The orchid house contains a small representative collection of mainly intermediate and cool-house orchids.

Watering, ventilation, ripening, dividing, repotting, &c.

Hybridisation and the raising of seedlings.

B.—Floral and Arboricultural Department.

1. The preparation and mixing of soils and manures and soil cultivation by trenching, digging, mulching, hoeing, &c.

Seed sowing and the care of seedlings, potting-on, pricking-out, &c.

Watering, ventilation, shading.

2. Propagation of shrubs and herbaceous plants by division, cuttings, budding, grafting, layering, &c.

Planting, transplanting, pruning and staking trees and shrubs.

3. Seed-saving, drying, cleaning, and testing.

4. Florists' flowers and types, selection and seed saving.

5. Garden design. Choice of site and soil, laying out pleasure-grounds.

Arrangement and planting of arboretum and shrubbery.

Design and care of wild garden, rockery, herbaceous borders, flower beds.

The making and maintenance of hedges, paths, roads, lawns, ponds, &c.

The preparation of ornamental and nursery flower beds.

The suppression of insect and fungus pests.

C.—Meteorological Department.

1. The Meteorological Station is of the second order of the international classification, and consists of barometer, Campbell-Stokes sunshine recorder, rain gauge, Stevenson screen with dry and wet bulb and maximum and minimum thermometers, and radiation and earth thermometers at the surface and at one, two, and four feet depth.

2. The Station is under the control and periodical inspection of the Government Meteorological Department.

I I

TIME TABLE FOR STUDENTS.

		MORNING.		1-2.	AFTERNOON.	EVENING.
		8.45-10.	10-1.		2-5.	6.30-8.
MONDAY	1st Year	Attend to Watering, &c.	Garden Work.	Dinner Hour.	Garden Work.	Paper by Student and Discussion.
	2nd Year		Garden Work.		Science.	
TUESDAY	1st Year		Science.		Garden Work.	
	2nd Year		Garden Work or Show.		Garden Work or Show.	
WEDNESDAY	1st Year		Garden Work.		Garden Work.	
	2nd Year		Garden Work.		Science.	
THURSDAY	1st Year		Science.		Garden Work.	
	2nd Year		Garden Work.		*Garden Work and Revision.	
FRIDAY	1st Year		*Garden Work and Revision.		Garden Work.	
	2nd Year		Garden Work.		Science.	
SATURDAY	1st Year		Science.		Holiday.	
	2nd Year		Garden Work.			

* Garden Work 1 hour. Revision 2 hours.

RARE SHRUBS IN THE OPEN AIR.

By the HON. VICARY GIBBS.

[Lecture delivered July 23, 1907.]

I HAVE been asked to read a paper on trees and shrubs growing at Aldenham, in Hertfordshire, with a view to making more widely known how large is the variety which can be successfully cultivated where the conditions are not specially favourable, and where, indeed, a cold clay soil and severe frosts in late spring militate against plant life. To confine this paper within reasonable limits I have found myself compelled to exclude many interesting classes of plants which we have in our garden as follows :—

1. All trees, not merely timber trees, but smaller types, such as *Zanthoxylum, Idesia,* Phellodendron, &c.

2. All shrubs necessitating peat, such as *Pieris, Andromeda, Rhododendron,* &c.

3. All shrubs that in our climate die down every winter, such as *Clerodendron ¦foetidum, Fuchsia reflexa, Bosea Amherstiana, Lespedeza Sieboldii, Desmodium tiliaefolium,* &c.·

4. All Conifers, such as *Saxegothaea, Prumnopitys,* Podocarpus, &c.

5. All Bamboos, *Arundo,* and grasses of any kind.

6. All creepers, such as *Berchemia, Muehlenbeckia,* &c.

7. All rock plants, sub-shrubs, or bushy herbs, such as *Helianthemum,* Hyssop, Wormwood, &c.

Of course I am well aware that there is no scientific distinction between trees and shrubs, and that the tree of one country is the shrub of another; and, further, I have little doubt that I have included some plants, which I only know in their young state, that may, later on, have a claim to be considered as small trees. The distinction between shrubs and shrubby herbs is, I admit, also equally arbitrary. I shall, however, confine myself to the rarer specimens of what are ordinarily looked upon as bushes, with which we succeed, and even so the list will be long enough to try the patience of any but enthusiasts.

Berberis.—We have a great many different species and varieties of this attractive shrub, and all of them, with the exception of *B. Fortunei* and *B. Fremontii,* are absolutely hardy and vigorous. Of the rarer evergreen forms the former has refined foliage but requires a wall, and the latter has an upright growth and long, narrow leaflets, and very distinct appearance. *B. rotundifolia Herveyi* is a round-leaved form of *Mahonia.* *B. fascicularis* is of a glaucous tint, and has seven small leaflets with marked spiny edges and an upright growth; the finest specimen of this which I have ever seen is in Canon Ellacombe's beautiful garden at Bitton. *B. Neuberti,* known to nurserymen as *B. ilicifolia,* is a handsome shrub, also of glaucous tone. *B. nervosa,* an evergreen from North America, is worth having. *B. Knightii* is a large-leaved form of

B. Wallichiana, and is certainly handsomer than the type. *B. congestiflora hakeoides* has a round leaf with spiny edge and a bright yellow flower, and can be recommended as one of the best-looking of the genus. Of deciduous forms *B. vulgaris aur. marg.* and *B. vulgaris spathulata* are varieties of the common barberry, neither of which is worth growing, in my judgment; and the same remark applies to *B. purpurea Egberti,* in which the purple leaves are faintly striped or powdered with white, and, as far as I can see, to *B. canadensis* also. *B. Lycium,* usually sold under the name of *B. elegans,* is a robust, free-growing kind, with grey-green foliage. *B. virescens* is also a strong, upright grower, of which the young canes come a bright red, turning to nut brown as they get older; its foliage in autumn almost equals in brilliancy the well known *B. Thunbergii.* It flowers freely. *B. concinna,* as its name implies, is a neat plant of compact growth; the fruit is in colour and shape like the edible barberry, but grows singly instead of in racemes, and is rather stouter. *B. diaphana* is very like *B. virescens* to look at when in winter dress; its name indicates the diaphanous appearance of the fruit, but it has not yet fruited with us. *B. umbellata* is a strong grower and sub-evergreen, the leaves persisting all through an ordinary winter, but turning from a dark green to a rich purple. *B. sp.,* from the Chilian Andes, unnamed, was given me by Mr. Elwes, the well-known writer on trees; it is evergreen and more like *B. dulcis* than any other of the genus with which I am acquainted. *B. integerrima* might easily be mistaken for *B. vulgaris.* We have also *B. actinacantha, B. dictyophylla,* and *B. pruinosa,* all of which I can recommend, *B. Guimpelii, B. brachybotrys,* a good unnamed species from Yunnan, and others.

Both the golden and the silver variegated forms of *Aralia chinensis,* or, as we used to call it, *Dimorphanthus mandschuricus,* before the Kew handbook taught us different, are very decorative, though rather expensive additions to a shrubbery. *A. chinensis pyramidalis* is not often met with in England, but is quite distinct from the type in appearance. We also grow the closely allied *Acanthopanax spinosum* (*Aralia pentaphylla*), which is an effective shrub, especially when the variety *albo-marginata* is obtained. *Acanthopanax ricinifolium* (*Aralia Maximowiczii*), introduced from Japan in 1874, is an elegant plant with large, deeply cut leaves and erect, spiny stem; it is quite hardy, but is a slow grower, both here and in our London garden. I will conclude my remarks on the Araliaceae by mentioning *Fatsia japonica,* which, though perfectly well known both for sub-tropical bedding-out purposes and in London doctors' and dentists' reception rooms, where it vies with the indiarubber plant, is much more hardy in my experience, both in its green and variegated form, than most people imagine. We have several plants doing quite well in sheltered positions, and in London we have a large fine specimen which went through the awful winter of 1894–5 unprotected and uninjured.

Many varieties of the Box family do well with us, though not, of course, so well as they would on chalk or gravel. I cannot afford the space to discuss them in detail, but will pick out *Buxus latifolia nova, B. salicifolia,* and *B. sempervirens variegata pendula* for favourable mention.

Amorpha fruticosa, ' False Indigo.'—This forms a tall, weedy, sprawling plant, which I do not think worth growing, but its relative, *A. canescens,* the 'lead plant,' has a more compact habit, and a really attractive violet-hued flower, borne in late summer.

Fontanesia Fortunei, from China, and *F. philliraeoides (F. linearis)* are hardy privet-like plants which are hardly sufficiently ornamental to justify their being planted except where a botanical collection is being formed. The above remarks apply also to *Forestiera acuminata (F. ligustrina),* except that this is said to have the additional disadvantage of being tender.

Spiraea.—This, including as it now does the Neillias, is a very large family. Not only are there many species but many hybrids, and the matter is made worse by the same plant being catalogued under many different names ; e.g., the Kew handbook gives twenty-four synonyms for the graceful *S. canescens !* Almost all these plants are free flowerers, and some, such as *S. prunifolia,* take on a grand colour in the fall of the year. I should find no difficulty in writing a paper confined only to the Spiraeas which we possess, but will instead pick out some half a dozen of the rarest and best for special mention. *S. assurgens* has ribbed, hornbeam-like leaves, and erect spikes of white flowers in September. *S. bracteata* (fig. 43), from Japan, bears a flat mass of white flowers at the end of May. We have failed to get cuttings of it to strike, but I should think it would layer. *S. bullata (S. crispa),* a compact dwarf form, covered in July with rosy red corymbs. *S. laevigata,* a Siberian species with glaucous, leathery leaves, recalling a spurge laurel or a Bupleurum rather than any other known Spiraea. *S. Aitchisoni,* a vigorous grower with reddish stems, has showy white flower spikes late in autumn, and resembles in general appearance the old *S. Lindleyana,* though superior to it. Many of the Spiraeas, such as *S. Douglasi, S. chamaedrifolia (S. ulmifolia), S. japonica (S. callosa),* are particularly suited to mass planting, being cut down to the ground every spring, when a level sheet of flowers will be obtained in autumn and a bright effect from the young canes in winter. *S. sibirica* has clustered spikes of white flower early in May. *S. nudiflora* has white corymbs suffused with a pink flush in May and June, and is remarkably pretty. *S. revirescens parviflora,* bearing red corymbs about a fortnight after the last-named, also deserves mention.

Colletia cruciata, from Uruguay.—In spite of its habitat this is hardy with us, and we have a large plant in the open which passed safely through the terrible frost of January 1895. The Kew handbook gives *C. spinosa, ferox, horrida, Bictonensis* as synonyms, and though these may be botanically the same plants we have two forms growing which to the eye are quite distinct, one with very large awl-shaped spines, suggesting a desert plant, such as the cactus, and another, less striking, with small prickles, which might to the casual eye pass for a gorse ; when the last is covered with its pearl-like little white flowers it is, however, impressive, and we were fortunate enough to get an Award of Merit for it some years ago.

Polygala Chamaebuxus.—This is an attractive, hardy, dwarf evergreen with white flowers, and is known as the ' Bastard Box ' ; the variety

P. *Chamaebuxus purpurea* bears a purple flower with yellow centre in early April.

Hibiscus syriacus.—There are many garden varieties of this hardy plant; the best, known to me, are *totus albus*, a pure single white; *celeste*, a clear light blue; and *Hamabou*, a newly introduced form, which I first saw at Canon Ellacombe's; this has a bronzy colour, like a Salpiglossis. All the species of Hibiscus flower very late in autumn, and though on the whole this is an advantage yet in some seasons the blooms wait too long and are spoilt by frost before they can develop.

Cydonia japonica.—We have a great many varieties of this, with all sorts of names. Some of them are very beautiful and they range in colour from the pigeon's blood ruby of var. *Simonii* (for which we were fortunate enough to get an Award of Merit this year) to a clear white; none of them, however, can be depended upon to come true from seed, nor will they strike from cuttings, so the only way to reproduce them satisfactorily is by layering. All these plants enjoy a strong soil, and our largest single plant, aged between 60 and 70 years, is 22 feet through by 8 feet high, and in April of this year was one vivid sheet of scarlet. *Cydonia Maulei superba* is a distinct advance on the type, and *Cydonia Sargentii* is, from its close trailing habit, well suited to a rockery.

We are not very rich in Roses when regarded from a botanical standpoint, but I may mention *R. ferruginea* (almost invariably known as *R. rubrifolia*), whose home is in the mountains of Europe, as a rampant grower which produces a splendid effect when planted in a mass and pegged down over old roots; the foliage is of a rich plum colour, the flower small and pink, single, and the heps in autumn are very showy. *R. nitida* is also admirable for autumn and winter, the leaves and hirsute stems turning a bright red; it is not a very strong grower and is well suited, when pegged down, to carpet a point of a shrubbery, or small bed in a garden. *R. Soulieana* is to be recommended for its glaucous foliage and free, prostrate growth. *R. viridiflora*, with its green flowers, is merely a curiosity. All the above are perfectly hardy, but *R. bracteata*, the well-known Chinese Macartney rose, though always looked upon as tender, has flourished with us for the last ten years on a sheltered bank by water.

Hymenanthera crassifolia is a low-growing evergreen with a spreading habit from New Zealand; it bears small yellowish flowers, and so far has been uninjured by frost. Botanists tell us it belongs to the violet family, and we are bound to believe them.

Eucryphia pinnatifida, from Chile, is said to be hardy, but we have found it difficult to establish. I fancy it likes a peaty soil. Our plant, though quite healthy, has not yet borne any of the large white flowers which ought to ornament it.

We have many species of *Cornus*, some very good and some very indifferent. I have not yet been able to find any horticultural merit in *C. Amomum*, *C. circinata*, *C. asperifolia*, *C. pubescens*, and *C. Purpusii*, all of which are from North America; indeed, I have often been struck with the inferiority in beauty of the North American flora to that of Japan and China. On the other hand, the following species of *Cornus* are, for one reason or another, well worth growing. *C. Hessei* is a

compact grower with a very dark purple leaf, and bears white cymes at
the end of May. *C. stolonifera flaviramea* should be cut down every
spring, when the young wood will turn a bright yellow, like an osier,
in winter. *Cornus mas elegantissima* has tricoloured foliage—green,
white, and pink. *C. candidissima* grows to be a large bush; our plant
is 8 feet by 5 feet; it has a soft purple tone in autumn. *C. brachypoda*
flowers freely in June; the lateral shoots seem always to master the
leader. The variegated form of this species is very bright and effective.
C. macrophylla flowers a month later than the last named, and though
somewhat like it can always be distinguished by the fact that its leaves
are opposite. *C. florida* is a beautiful tree with the finest flowers of any
of the family; we have a pendulous form of it which, when older, should
make a very pretty plant. *C. atrosanguinea*, which is, I imagine, a variety
of *C. alba*, has its wood of a deep red in winter, while the leaves of
C. Nuttallii go red and yellow in the fall. *C. Kousa* is a good thing
where climate and soil suit it, but though it lives with us it does not
thrive. *C. Bretschneideri* is from China, and *C. alternifolia* has yellow
flowers in bud which turn to white as they open in June.

Erythrina cristagalli is strictly a greenhouse plant, but it has lived
with us for twenty-two years in poor ground against the east wall of a
hothouse, being matted over in winter. In July its bright scarlet flowers,
like little cooked lobster's claws, are a sight as quaint as it is brilliant.

Ribes Lobbii is a rare and fine species, having deep red flowers with
a white centre hanging down, something like a fuchsia. *R. lacustre*
has long currant-like racemes of pale yellow with dull red centre.
R. Spathianum is an elegant loose-growing shrub with small round
leaves. *R. leptanthum* has still smaller leaves and a very neat appearance,
but the white flower is inconspicuous. *R. villosum* (*R. chilense*) is the
only evergreen *Ribes* which I know, and, like *R. mogollonicum*, it is
mainly of botanical interest. *R. speciosum* (*R. fuchsioides*) has conspicuous rust-coloured thorns, which are effective in winter. The synonym
given above well indicates its red fuchsia-like flowers, which hang in rows
under the branches from May into July. *R. prostratum* is a weeping
form. *R. alpinum foliis aureis* is a compact, small-leaved plant, with a
soft golden tone. *R. nigrum foliis aureis* is showy but rather coarse,
and apt to revert to the type and to burn in hot summers. We have
also *R. amictum* and *R. oxycanthoides*.

Of deciduous members of the Spindle-wood family we have *Euonymus
verrucosus*, which is chiefly noticeable for its curious bark; *E. latifolius*,
which has large red seed cases, and looks well when grown on a standard;
E. alatus, which is one of the most lovely plants for autumn colour,
every leaf turning rosy red; *E. nanus*, which is pretty in flower, fruit,
and leaf, the last being, as its synonym (*E. rosmarinus*) imports, like that
of rosemary. We also possess the variety *E. nanus Koopmanni*, which
has larger leaves and less dwarf habit than the type. Of the varieties
of *E. europaeus* we have *alb. var.*, with small, delicate silver leaves,
atropurpureus, of which the foliage is green till about July, and then
becomes dark purple, and *aucubaefolius*, with rather conspicuous yellow
splashes. We also have *E. americanus* and its variety *E. americanus
pendulus*, *E. obovatus*, *E. Sieboldianus*, *E. Hamiltonianus*, and

E. Bungeanus, but they have not been with us long enough to enable me to comment on them satisfactorily.

I believe that all the *Cotoneasters* are evergreen or sub-evergreen. Of the rarer kinds we have *C. acutifolia* (*C. lucida*), bearing white flowers tinged with pink in early June and whose foliage has a fine autumn colour ; *C. acuminata*, somewhat like the foregoing in general appearance ; *C. angustifolia*, a free-growing shrub recently introduced by M. de Vilmorin, which I fear will not prove hardy with us. *C. pannosa* has small white flowers in profusion, a silvery under side to the leaves, and red fruits with silky hairs. *C. Franchetii*, not unlike the last to look at. *C. adpressa*, close-growing, dwarfish, and a little like the better known and attractive *C. horizontalis*. *C. thymifolia*, with very tiny leaves. (I hope my readers will realise that the false concords in this paragraph are not due to the fact that I imagine *Cotoneaster* to be feminine, but because I have to follow Kew and the other botanists.)

The varieties of *Broussonetia papyrifera*, the old ' Paper Mulberry,' have distinct and effective foliage ; they grow freely, but do not ripen their wood well. Indeed, were it not that they come into leaf so late I doubt if they would thrive with us at all. *B. papyrifera dissecta* has leaves like hairs. *B. papyrifera macrophylla* has large leaves, about half of which are entire. *B. papyrifera cucullata* has curious-looking foliage. The separate species from Japan, *B. Kazinoki*, has large uncut leaves of a black-purple colour when young and rather pretty creamy flowers.

Maclura aurantiaca, the ' Osage Orange' of South U. S. America, is a free grower, but suffers from spring frosts. I believe it has fruited in this country, though not with us. It is diœcious, so plants of both sexes would have to be obtained before this consummation could be reached. The variety *M. aurantiaca pulverulenta alba* has a very pretty variegation.

Cudrania triloba (*Maclura tricuspidata*), the ' Silkworm Thorn' of China.—We have only a small specimen of this and I cannot properly describe it.

Excluding many beautiful named varieties of the common Lilac, I would mention the following as noticeable :—

Syringa japonica is a big bush, 7 feet high, bearing white flowers in June. *S. Emodi* has white spots on the bark, stout twigs, a large long-stalked leaf, and white flowers with an unpleasant smell. *S. oblata* has large cordiform leaves. *S. Josikaea* has a very dark green leaf and purple, scentless flower in early June. *S. persica laciniata* has very finely cut foliage. *S. vulgaris fol. aur.* is liable to burn and the lilac flowers do not consort well in colour with the golden leaf. We also have *S. pekinensis pendula*, which is sometimes separately classed as *Ligustrina*, and *S. amurensis*, which is hardly worth growing.

Our tree Paeonies (*Paeonia Moutan*) have been very good this year, and some members may have noticed our exhibit of them at the Temple Show in June. They were all imported direct from Yokohama and I only know their Japanese names. Among the finest appear to be Adsumasaki, Akashigata, Konronkoku, Yasookina, Adzumakagama, Nishiki-jima (fig. 44).

Fig. 42.—"The Wrestler's Pond," Aldenham.

(To face page 352.)

FIG. 43.—SPIRAEA BRACTEATA.

Fig. 44.—Paeonia Moutan, 'Nishiki-jina.'

Fig. 45.—Olearia stellulata.

Lycium pallidum has greyish foliage and dull white tubular flowers, quite unlike the bloom of the common Lycium.

Rhamnus Alaternus var.—I have seen charming large shrubs of this in France, but with us it is barely hardy. The leaves are broadly margined with white and it looks at a distance like a silver holly. *R. hybrida* (*R. sempervirens*) bears clusters of brilliant red fruit. *R. davurica* has yellowish flowers and rather remarkable light green foliage. *R. grandifolia* is a handsome deciduous shrub with big, ribbed, leathery leaves. *R. Erythroxylon* bears its little black Cotoneaster-like berries close to the stem in a fashion quite distinct from any other Rhamnus. *R. libanotica* (*Imeritiae*) is a long, large-leaved evergreen from Asia Minor.

Ononis rotundifolia is a charming hardy, low-growing plant, covered with soft, pink, pea-like flowers in May until October; it belongs to the same family as the British 'Rest-barrow'; it is short-lived but is easily reproduced from seed. *O. spinosa* is low-growing and rather weedy-looking, but flowers freely late in July. We have also *O. fruticosa*, which grows bigger than, but of which the pink flowers are not quite so showy as those of, *O. rotundifolia*. *O. aragonensis* and *O. Natrix*, which we do not possess, have yellow flowers.

Dorycnium suffruticosum, a near ally of the same genus, is covered with small white flowers in September; its habitat is South Europe, but it appears to be quite hardy.

Forsythia europaea is a recently discovered plant which has no floral merit beyond *F. intermedia*, *F. suspensa*, and *F. viridissima*, all of which are well known and generally admired. The interesting thing from a botanical point of view is that so close a relative of our old friends should be found in a habitat so distant. Wherever a scarlet Ribes is planted there should be one of the Forsythias in the vicinity, as they flower at the same period, grow with about the same vigour, and furnish a perfect contrast of colour.

Caryopteris Mastacanthus.—This is valuable both for its glaucous, aromatic foliage and its profuse heliotrope-coloured flowers, produced in October, when flowering shrubs have a particular value. It belongs to the same family as the sage and has a peculiar attraction for bees.

The Daphnes find our soil rather heavy, but *D. Laureola purpurea* is to be recommended for its deep-coloured, almost black, foliage, and *D. altaica* (which we owe to the kindness of Messrs. Cutbush) for its brilliant little white flowers, with which it is adorned at the end of May. *D. Blagayana* is a hardy evergreen, with white flowers in April; the curious feature about it is that it requires stones to be laid on the branches for its successful cultivation.

Xanthoceras sorbifolia is a handsome Chinese shrub or small tree, covered in May with ivory, white flowers having a red streak at the base; its fruit is said to resemble that of a Horse Chestnut.

Astragalus tragacantha is a papilionaceous, prickly, grey, slow-growing, dwarf, evergreen plant with pretty pale violet, vetch-like flowers in early June.

Nuttallia cerasiformis is common enough and valuable for its white flowers in early spring, but it is dioecious, and if the purple berries are desired the female plants, of which the flowers are inferior, should be obtained and planted near the males.

Diostea juncea looks just like a *Cytisus*, except that its leaves are opposite ; it has violet flowers and belongs to the *Verbenaceae.*

Osmanthus aquifolium.—We have the type and most of the varieties of this useful Japanese shrub, viz. *ilicifolius purpureus, myrtifolius, rotundifolius,* var. *aureum* and var. *argentea.* Except the golden form they all thrive very well on our heavy soil.

Xanthorrhiza apiifolia might be mistaken for a low-growing Spiraea ; it has brownish purple flowers in April, and is excellent for planting in damp ground in shade.

Prunus nana rosea is a remarkably pretty dwarf shrub in spring. *Prunus japonica flore pleno* and ditto *roseo* are both quite a sight in early May. Unlike others of the family they are much the better for hard pruning directly after they have flowered.

Artemisia tridentata has a fastigiate habit, silver-grey foliage, and the same aromatic smell as the old-fashioned *A. Abrotanum* (southern wood or old man) ; it is, however, much superior to it as an ornamental shrub.

Suaeda fruticosa (*Salsola fruticosa*), a plant of upright growth, is condemned by Nicholson as having "no horticultural value," but any shrub with silvery grey foliage, like this, is useful for contrast in a shrubbery.

Ligustrum Delavayanum is a sub-evergreen of flat-branching habit and has refined grey-green leaves; I fear it will not prove absolutely hardy. This last remark applies also to *L. strongylophyllum,* which is not unlike it in appearance. *L. yunnanense* has an upright growth and light green, deciduous, almond-like leaves ; it is curiously unlike a Privet. *L. vulgare alb. marg.* has a grey effect at a little distance, which reminds one of a Willow. *L. vulgare elegantissimum* is a silver weeping form which should be grown as a standard. *L. lucidum tricolor* is a handsome evergreen having a soft yellow variegation with a rich pink edging. *L. japonicum coriaceum* is a slow-growing evergreen thickly covered with shining leathery, shell-like foliage. The variety *involutum* of this last has the leaves turned every way, like a bottle brush. *L. Quihoui,* a free-growing species, with large loose white panicles of flowers late in the summer, is perhaps the finest bloomer of all the privets. *L. Ibota* (*L. ciliatum*), very distinct, is a pretty shrub from Japan, with thick fleshy leaf and pure white flower in August.

Hamamelis.—We have all the four species, viz., *H. japonica* var. *Zuccariniana, H. arborea, H. mollis,* and *H. virginica.* Flowering as they do in mid-winter gives them a special value, but *virginica* has the least merit and *mollis* the most. Our plant of this last is 5 feet high, and the Kew experts say it is the finest in the country.

Ulex Gallii has the advantage of being in full flower in October, when gorse bloom is scarce. *U. europaeus strictus* is a curiously stiff, erect form.

Olearia stellulata (*Eurybia Gunniana*) is a glaucous, narrow-leaved evergreen with profuse small white, starry flowers in June (fig. 45). *O. macrodonta* (*O. dentata*) is a beautiful grey holly-leaved evergreen from New Zealand, but is not truly hardy with us.

Pittosporum tenuifolium.—We have a large plant 10 feet high by 5 feet acrcss, and of perfect shape, but I am not learned in the New Zealand plants, and it is just conceivable that it may be one of the other Pittosporums ; anyhow, I doubt if there is one of the family so large anywhere else north of London.   We give it shelter in severe winters (fig. 46).

We have many different species of St. John's Wort, and all are worth growing ; the colour of flower in all cases is much the same, and they differ mainly in size of flower and habit of growth. *Hypericum fragile* has minute foliage and is suited for a rock garden. *H. Moserianum* has especially fine large flowers, and the variety *tricolor* has charming foliage. We have also *H. lysimachioides* ; *H. dubium*, of erect growth ; *H. pyramidatum* ; *H. patulum Henryi* ; *H. perfoliatum* ; and *H. Hookerianum* (*oblongifolium*), and others which I cannot spare space to describe.

Jamesia americana (*Stephanomeria americana*) is an erect deciduous shrub with white flowers in May to June, and when grown in a mass, as it may be seen at Kew, it is quite pleasing.

Decaisnea Fargesi is an upright plant with pleasing, Robinia-like foliage and delicate primrose-coloured flowers having a dark base in May to June ; it is said to bear deep blue fruits, but I have never seen them.

Veronicas I shall not discuss, as none of them are truly hardy here, even the old *V. Traversii* having all been killed in January 1895.

Meliosma myriantha is, I believe, a beautiful plant, and rare even in its own habitat (China and Japan), though we have one small plant just alive.   I have failed to grow it more than once, and cannot describe it of my own knowledge.

Purshia tridentata is an upright sub-evergreen shrub or small tree belonging to the Rosaceae ; it has very dark leaves and small yellow flowers in April ; it is a native of North-West America.

The shrubby *Potentillas* are not enough planted in England, considering that they are perfectly hardy, easily grown, and are bright and continuous flowerers.   Besides the type we have P. *Friedrichseni*, which is a strong grower ; P. *salesoviana*, which has a distinct silvery leaf and white flower ; P. *micrandra*, which has a rich yellow flower ; P. *humilis*, which I take to be a dwarf form of P. *fruticosa* ; and lastly P. *davurica*. The plants which we have under this name (bought from different nurserymen abroad) are very squat and close-growing, with yellow flowers ; there is, however, another P. *davurica*, which I have seen exhibited by Messrs. Veitch, of Exeter (but which we do not possess), of much looser growth and with white flowers.   I cannot solve the problem as to which is the true P. *davurica*.

Cytisus leucanthus (*C. schipkaensis*), *C. kewensis*, and *C. albus durus* are all three ornamental white-flowered brooms of more or less dwarf growth.   *C. scoparius fol. var.* is a showy form of common broom with yellow bark and foliage ; it looks very well as a standard.   *C. nigricans* and *C. sessilifolius* are distinguished by foreign botanists and known as *Lembotropis*.   They have certainly this difference from the ordinary *Cytisus* : that they bear moving well, instead of very badly ; they flower freely in late summer, and hold their blossoms, which are of a soft yellow colour, well.

Besides many varieties of the common Holly, such as the brilliant
'Golden King'—of which our plant is over 4 feet high—*Ilex aquifolium
donningtonensis*, with its myrtle-shaped leaves, *I. aquifolium ferox*,
I. aquifolium angustifolia, and various weeping and variegated forms,
we have the following species :—*I. opaca*, with dull leaf and spiny edges.
I. dipyrena, 'Himalayan Holly,' similar to the last, and unlike most
Hollies in its dull, unpolished look ; it has brown berries and no spines.
I. cornuta is a beautiful plant from China, with rich green, striking
foliage.   *I. latifolia* (*I. Tarajo*) has the largest leaf of any of the species,
and I know a very large plant, about seventy years old, near Bristol,
which might be taken at first sight for an evergreen Magnolia ; unfortunately it is not over hardy in Hertfordshire.   *I. crenata microphylla*
(*I. Fortunei* var.), on the other hand, is the smallest-leaved holly which
I know. It makes a neat, attractive shrub. *Ilex glabra* and *I. verticillata*
used to be treated separately, under the heading *Prinos*.   The last named
and *I. decidua*, from the South United States, are the only deciduous
hollies, I believe ; and indeed it requires a botanist to recognise that they
are hollies at all.

We have also *Nemopanthus canadensis*, formerly classed as an Ilex,
which, indeed, on the surface it resembles far more than some of the
true Ilexes which I have mentioned.

Of the more uncommon Sumachs I can recommend *Rhus Osbeckii*,
with erect habit, very large leaves, and general resemblance to some of
the Elders ; *R. copallina*, with fifteen leaflets on a midrib, with irregular
leafy edging and fine autumn colour, in respect of which last it is
surpassed by *R. cotinoides* (' Chittam-wood ') with larger, longer foliage
than the well known *Rhus cotinus*.   *R. vernicifera*, the Japanese lacquer
tree, has lived with us for five or six years, but I cannot pretend that it
has grown materially or shows enough vigour for me to give a fair account
of it.   *R. canadensis trilobata* has distinct cut foliage.

Genista radiata has a peculiar wiry growth.   *G. virgata* has the merit
of seeding itself where the soil is suitable.   *G. pilosa* and *G. decumbens*
are both low, trailing plants, flowering freely in May, and well fitted for
planting in rock gardens or on banks.   *G. tinctoria* is an upright grower
and flowers very prettily in June.

Pachystima Myrsinites is a small-leaved, dwarf evergreen, not
calculated, as far as I can see, to arouse any great enthusiasm.

Sambucus canadensis (otherwise known as *S. pubens maxima*)
requires plenty of room, though it may be cut hard back every year
with advantage ; its creamy white inflorescence, of immense size, and
supported by red stems to the trusses, is most conspicuous.   *S. Thun-
bergiana* has not so fine a flower, but the young growth is a rich
purplish red in early summer, and its scarlet fruits are also decorative.
S. racemosa serratifolia aurea is much more refined and less garish than
the common golden Elder.   *S. racemosa tenuifolia*, with its very finely cut
foliage and pleasing habit, might almost be taken for a Japanese maple ;
unhappily it is unlike most of the Elders in that it does not strike readily
from cuttings.   Of the forms of *S. nigra*, *S. nigra pulverulenta* has quite
a snowy appearance in late summer.   *S. nigra pyramidalis* and *S. nigra
pendula* make an excellent contrast to other plants if judiciously placed.

The comparatively common *S. nigra fol. var.* is wonderfully effective if grown as a standard (see photograph, fig. 47).

Perowskia atriplicifolia is related to the Lavender; it has silvery leaves and delicate lilac-coloured flowers in autumn. It is liable to be killed to the ground in severe winters, but grows again rapidly. I have seen a very fine bush of it in Somersetshire.

Philadelphus.—The name of these is legion, and dozens of named varieties are to be seen in any foreign nurseryman's catalogue. Of those which we grow I would pick out *P. purpureo maculatus* for its very handsome flower, and *P. microphyllus* for its compact form and refined greyish foliage, and both of them, alike, for their delicious scent at even-time.

Bupleurum fruticosum (Hare's Ear).—This, though very common about the Mediterranean, is not often seen in England; it makes a handsome bush if pruned pretty heavily. The flowers are yellow and the foliage sea green.

Hedysarum multijugum, from Mongolia.—This has pretty purple, vetch-like flowers late in the season and finely cut foliage; it is inclined to be a ragged grower, and is the better for being "knifed" in.

Dirca palustris, the "Leather Wood" of North America, bears yellowish flowers in March, but is not especially ornamental.

Sophora viciifolia, though belonging to a family which makes large trees in this country, never itself rises beyond the dignity of a bush; in a wild state in its native habitat, China, it covers the hills in the form of scrub, and here it blooms freely in June, being clothed with pretty blue and white flowers and small foliage.

Symplocos crataegoides.—"Nicholson's Dictionary of Gardening" calls this a greenhouse shrub—I think wrongly, for we have had it for some years in the open, and unprotected, and it appears quite hardy. Indeed, it has stood out at Kew for more than fifteen years. It belongs to the family of *Styraceae*, and has flattened corymbs of white flowers.

Aristotelia Macqui.—This is a very handsome evergreen from Chile with soft red twigs. Our specimen is 7 feet high by 5 feet across. Nicholson says that it is hardy, and the Kew handbook says that it is tender. "Who shall decide when doctors disagree?" But in this case I am inclined to agree with Mr. Nicholson. We have also young plants of the pleasing variegated form with dull gold edging, of which cuttings strike pretty readily under glass. No one would think, to look at an Aristotelia, that it belongs to the same order as the lime tree.

Disanthus cercidifolia, a rare plant belonging to the Hamamelis family, has done very well with us and is now 4 feet high; the round leaves are unsurpassable for rosy colour in autumn.

Chionanthus virginica gains its name of "Fringe Tree" from the drooping, sweet-scented white flowers produced in June. We have long grown it against a wall and latterly in the open; it is one of the *Oleaceae* and succeeds well when grafted on the common ash.

Of the shrubby *Loniceras* which we possess in great variety I can only spare space here for three. *L. spinosa* (*L. Alberti*) has frail, graceful, pendulous branches, and when grown as a half-standard might easily be taken at a short distance for one of the Caraganas.   It has pretty pink flowers in May–June.

L. alpigena has short stout twigs, and when its showy red fruit is not in evidence few would label it as belonging to this family.   The same remark applies to the evergreen *L. pileata*, which bears fruit of a pleasing violet colour, and at a careless glance might easier pass for a *Ligustrum*.

Peraphyllum ramosissimum produces flowers like a small apple blossom in early summer, and is a hardy and desirable member of the family of Rosaceae, with willow-like leaves.

Caesalpinia japonica is of low growth, covered with thorns, and bears bright yellow racemes and elegant foliage.   The finest plant I have seen in this country is in the Bath public gardens.

Abelia chinensis (*A. rupestris*) is not, certainly, very rare, but its mass of pink-flushed white flowers against the dark myrtle-like leaves, blooming as they do as late as October, make it a most valuable acquisition for any garden; it is a pity that our climate is too cold for its congener, *A. floribunda*.

Skimmia japonica Veitchii has a much larger leaf than the type and is decidedly handsome.

Grewia parviflora is a curious Chinese shrub belonging to the same genus as the lime, which it closely resembles in the fruit; its interest is mainly botanical.

Stephanandra flexuosa has very delicate foliage, which at a distance recalls some of the Japanese maples; it is liable, however, to get badly burnt in hot, dry summers.   *S. Tanakae* has bolder, coarser leaves, and attractive red twigs; both plants require plenty of room, as their charm is quite destroyed if they are cut back.

Tamarix Pallasii rosea (usually known as *T. hispida aestivalis*).— This is far the best of all the Tamarisks; it has glaucous foliage and bears its deep pink flowers later in the season than any others of its family.

Fothergilla alnifolia is worth growing for its fine colour in the autumn; it prefers a moist, peaty soil, but does very fairly well with us. It bears conspicuous white, sweet-scented flowers in May before the leaves are out.

Davidia involucrata.—This is quite a new introduction to English gardens, and we have only a small though healthy specimen; it is said to be very striking when its large white bracts are developed, but this only takes place when the plant is ten or twelve years old.

Among laurels we have *Prunus Laurocerasus parvifolia*, which is quite distinct, but a very slow grower, and P. *Laurocerasus Zabeliana*, with sharp pointed leaves and spreading habit, the white flowers in May covering the bush.   This is, I think, superior to either of the varieties *serbica* or *Bruanti*, though they are not without merit.   Of Portugal laurels, *Prunus lusitanica azorica* has very handsome shell-like foliage, and P. *lusitanica myrtifolia* is more refined and elegant than the type.

Photinia serrulata.—We only grow this handsome, shining, half-hardy evergreen and the variety *rotundifolia* against a wall, whilst P. *japonica*, the well-known 'Loquat' of South Europe, will not stand our hard winters, though it does pretty well in our London garden.

Photinia variabilis (*P. villosa*) is a deciduous plant well worth grow-ing for its fine colour in the autumn, but I think it would be more at home in a lighter soil than this is.

Corylopsis spicata, from Japan, bears hanging yellow flowers in April; it closely resembles the Hamamelis, and belongs to that family.

Shepherdia canadensis is very rare in England, and in many places is a very bad doer; it likes lime in the soil. Professor Sargent, at a recent visit, told me that ours was the finest plant he had ever seen. It is a strong shrub with greyish green leaves resembling an *Elaeagnus*. The two families are closely allied and constantly confused, though they may easily be distinguished by the fact that the former have opposite leaves and the latter alternate.

Shepherdia argentea is somewhat more silvery and better looking; it is very rare in English gardens, although it frequently occurs in nursery-men's catalogues; but the plant which they supply under this name is in reality *Elaeagnus argentea*, which has steely, metallic-looking foliage, such as I know of in no other plant, but it is a bad doer on our stiff soil. It is the 'Silver Berry' of North America.

Elaeagnus macrophylla is a handsome shrub, which also has shiny, metallic-looking leaves; it is a better doer with us than *E. argentea*. *E. multiflora* (*E. crispa*, *E. edulis*) has profuse buff, small flowers in May. The other evergreen forms are not really hardy with us.

Cephalanthus occidentalis, the 'Button Bush' of North America, has light brown flowers, borne singly, and of spherical shape, after the style of *Buddleia globosa*.

Stachyurus praecox has yellow-green flowers in February–March before the leaves come out; it is not of much account, except for the fact that it blooms when flowers are scarce.

Trachelospermum crocostomum is a small-leaved evergreen, from China (?), which we have only recently acquired, and of which I can give no particulars.

Neviusia alabamensis.—The 'Alabama Snowwreath' is of erect habit and bears white flowers, which appear to consist exclusively of stamens; it is quite worthless from an ornamental standpoint.

Coronilla glauca has a beautiful yellow flower in early June, but is only half hardy.

Viburnum tomentosum has conspicuous flat, Hydrangea-like flowers in early June. The sterile and finer form, *Viburnum tomentosum plicatum* (fig. 48), is better known with its vivid white, globose cymes. *V. cassinoides*, the 'Withe Rod' of the United States of America, is sometimes classed as a variety of *V. nudum*. *V. bullatum* is a dwarf plant with round leaves, of unknown origin, whose colour is good in autumn. We also grow *V. acerifolium* and the native *V. Lantana*, and *V. macrocephalum*, which has the largest, showiest flowers of the genus.

Ehretia acuminata (*E. serrata*) is a handsome upright, long, smooth-leaved plant, which gets cut back in winter if it has not properly ripened its wood; the foliage when young has a good purple tone.

Euptelea polyandra.—I have not long been acquainted with this rare shrub, and can only say that it has elegant foliage, somewhat like a Stephanandra.

Loropetalum chinense.—We have only a small plant of this, which, however, produced its elegant white flowers this June. It is said to be a splendid sight in its native habitat, where it grows to be a large bush.

Choysia ternata.—This beautiful shrub is well known in the West of England, but it may surprise some gardeners to see it growing as vigorously as it does with us north of London.

Symphoricarpus Heyeri, with glaucous leaves and reddish flowers, and *S. acutus* are neither of them highly-ornamental.

Styrax japonicum.—We had a fine plant of this, which looked lovely when in flower, but the cruel frosts at the end of May 1906, after the sap was up, killed it to the ground. We have only young plants of its large-leaved congener, *S. Obassia*, and these, I imagine, will make trees if our weather will permit. *S. serrulatum*, from the East Indies, is an extremely rare plant in England, and requires the protection of a wall. At the time of writing (July 5) it is just coming into flower.

Atriplex halimus, the 'Tree Purslane,' has grey leaves, is a fast grower, and strikes easily from cuttings. *A. canescens*, its North American cousin, has finer foliage but is not so vigorous, whilst *A. congestiflora* combines both advantages.

Rubus deliciosus is one of the best of the brambles, and, unlike most of them, does not die down biennially. Our best plant is 12 feet high, and at the moment of writing (July 5) is covered with large white flowers like a dog-rose. *R. palmatus* (*R. incisus*) has upright whitish canes. It is hardier than *R. biflorus*, but its bark is not so vivid in colour. *R. trifidus* is a handsome erect, vine-leaved plant, with fine white flowers. *R. illecibrosus*, with ribbed spiraea-like leaves and bright red fruit, resembles *R. xanthocarpus*, except that the latter is of a dwarf habit; both of them have a tendency to spread, like the Polygonums, and they might easily become an almost ineradicable pest in shrubberies. *R. crataegi-folius* has tall red canes, which look very well in winter. *R. villosus*, the 'high blackberry,' attains to 10 feet, and puts on a fine autumn colour. *R. nutkanus* has large white flowers in June.

Daphniphyllum macropodum (*D. glaucescens*) is a handsome hardy evergreen. Through the kindness of the Director of Kew I have recently got a small plant of the rare variety *Jezoense*, but I can give no account of it, except that at present its leaves look more like those of a Skimmia than do those of the type.

Colutea cilicia bullata is a squat-looking plant, with round head and small leaves, suited for the front of a shrubbery.

Rhaphiolepis japonica is a slow-growing, round-leaved, handsome evergreen from Japan; it is said to prefer peat, but is quite healthy with us. When covered with bright white flowers in late June it produces a fine effect.

Halesia diptera.—We have a large bush of this North American plant, and when covered in May with its showy drooping, white flowers it is a fine sight; but I do not know that it is in any way superior to the much better known *H. tetraptera*, the 'Snowdrop Tree.'

Coriaria japonica.—The fruit of this is much finer than that of *C. myrtifolia*, which is fairly well known, while *C. terminalis* has

FIG. 46.—PITTOSPORUM TENUIFOLIUM.

(*To face page* 360.)

FIG. 47.—STANDARD VARIEGATED ELDER, SAMBUCUS NIGRA, FOL. VAR.

Fig. 48.—Viburnum tomentosum plicatum.

FIG. 49.—In the Water Garden, Aldenham.

rounder leaflets and bears its fruit at the end of the branches. Both shrubs are distinct in appearance and are worth growing.

Nandina domestica.—This is one of the many attractive shrubs which we owe to Japan. The young growth is red and amber in colour, and the white flowers, with yellow centre, appear in September; it is, unfortunately, rather tender, and, though it has lived with us a good many years, I cannot pretend that it shows any great vigour.

• *Microglossa albescens* (*Amphiraphis albescens*) bears its aster-like flowers freely about the middle of July, and seems quite hardy.

Nesaea salicifolia is a small-leaved, deciduous shrub, covered with bright little yellow flowers in October, a time of year when any flowering shrub is precious. It really looks superficially much more like a Hypericum than a pomegranate, to which last it is closely allied.

Caragana jubata bears a pretty, clear white pea-flower in May, and again in August, whilst in winter the rich chocolate-coloured pendent twigs, covered with grey hairs, give it a very curious and striking appearance. *C. Chamlagu* has showy yellow flowers in May. I find the pendulous form of the old *C. arborescens, C. aurantiaca, C. pygmaea* (*C. gracilis*), and *C. microphylla* all worth a place; they should be grown as half-standards, and are common enough in Continental gardens, though but seldom seen in England.

Chamaebatia foliolosa has deeply cut leaves and white flowers, resembling some of the Spiraeas; it is a decorative plant, and comes from California, but is, alas! none too hardy.

Of the *Buddleias*, which belong to the same family as the beautiful *Desfontainea spinosa* (a plant unfortunately too tender for anywhere north of London), we have, besides the old-fashioned *B. globosa, B. variabilis Veitchii,* a decided improvement in colour on the type, and *B. Helmsleyana,* a novelty in which I can detect no advantage over *B. variabilis.* The lovely *B. Colvillei,* whose red flowers adorn Italian gardens, requires a more favoured climate than ours.

Exochorda Alberti has proved too shy a flowerer for me to be able to recommend it; the variety *E. Alberti macrantha* is said to be superior in this respect, though I cannot vouch for it, but we have made a large and successful use of the better known *E. grandiflora,* which, if planted in quantity, makes a very fine effect in May.

I must now bring this long list to an end for very shame, and not because I have exhausted the number of shrubs which we grow. I do not suppose that such a lecture, given by a man without botanical knowledge, can be of much value, though it may be of some interest to amateur cultivators and collectors, like myself, and be something of a guide to them when giving their orders to nurserymen. I can fairly claim that almost every opinion expressed is the result of personal observation of growing plants, and that there has been no " cribbing " from books or reports at secondhand of what I myself have never seen.

It will be observed that I have not confined myself, in mentioning rarities, only to those which, in my judgment, are worth growing, for it may be just as useful to a collector who is examining a catalogue and contemplating giving orders to learn that I don't think, say, *Neviusia alabamensis* or *Forestiera acuminata* are particularly ornamental as to find that I highly recommend, say, *Lonicera spinosa* or *Euonymus alatus*.

Wherever I could I have adopted the nomenclature of the Kew handbook, often adding (in brackets) the more common synonym by which it is known in the trade. Although I have taken the greatest pains it is of course possible that, in one or two cases, I may have really described one species when I thought I was describing another.

For years past some of the most eminent experts in shrubs and trees, both English and foreign, have visited our garden, and wherever I was in doubt as to the identification of a plant I have eagerly and humbly sought for their pronouncement. Alas! it is not uncommon for them flatly to contradict one another. We have a rose which, under this process, has changed its name three times: at the moment it is *R. nitida*.

The cheap and excellent Kew handbook of trees and shrubs is invaluable to any collector who wishes to know what he is buying. I can imagine a beginner ordering from a foreign catalogue *Parthenocissus tricuspidata*, and, having expected to secure an interesting rarity, being disgusted to find that he had bought the commonest of creepers. Later on the same man, having got a learned friend to give him the correct names of his plants, might say, pointing to it, " There is one, at any rate, of which I need not ask you the right name, for every one knows that it is *Ampelopsis Veitchii*," to which his friend would reply, " Oh dear, no, that is quite out of date nowadays; it is *Vitis inconstans*! "

No one who has not attempted to make a collection of shrubs and get them correctly named can realise the difficulties involved. Let me point out some of them. The names adopted by Kew and followed in this paper are those which, as far as can be ascertained, were first given to the plants; they are not adopted, I believe, by any other country, nor by the bulk of nurserymen in this. Plants which for fifty years have been popularly known under one name appear in this system under another; *e.g.*, the old Alexandrian laurel, *Ruscus racemosus* is now *Danaea Laurus*, and *Citrus trifoliata* has become *Aegle sepiaria*.

There are very few nurseries indeed where one can be sure of obtaining plants true to name. Of course there may be cases where nurserymen who have not a particular species in stock send out another which they think will do as well, but usually the trouble arises from *bonâ fide* error in identification; *e.g.*, if *Schizophragma hydrangeoides* is asked for *Hydrangea scandens* is almost invariably supplied; if *Deutzia scabra*, a form of *D. crenata*; if *Shepherdia argentea*, then *Elaeagnus argentea*; and I could add many others to this list if it were worth while. Again, plants are often sold under names botanically incorrect and to which they have no title; thus *Bosea Amherstiana* appears in catalogues as a variegated form of *Leycesteria formosa*, and *Rhus toxicodendron* as *Ampelopsis Hoggii*, though it is a Sumach and not a Vine.

In this way confusion arises, and a man who has bought a plant under a wrong name, and learnt for years to identify it wrongly, teaches the wrong name to visitors, and disseminates error when he fancies himself to be enlightening ignorance.

I don't suppose there is a garden in England, including the one at Aldenham, where all plants are rightly named ; even at Kew, the Mecca of botanists, I have certainly seen specimens of the same tree with different names, and of different trees with the same name. A study of the Kew Handbook will show how much excuse there is for errors in nomenclature.

There will be found among the broad-leaved plants alone—eight with eleven synonyms, three with twelve, one with thirteen, three with fourteen, one with sixteen, one with seventeen, one 'with eighteen, one with nineteen, and one (*Spiraea canescens*) with no less than twenty-four synonyms!

Nor is this the worst of it, for there are plenty of cases where the name adopted for a species by Kew is also the synonym adopted by other botanists for a different species ; e.g., *Crataegus flava* is a true N. American species, and is also a synonym for *C. oxyacantha aurea*.

Euonymus atropurpureus is a true N. American species, and is also the name for a variety of *E. europaeus* ; while to make " confusion worse confounded," and darken counsel altogether, the names of two different shrubs are sometimes interchanged ; e.g., the *Ligustrum lucidum* of Kew is the *Ligustrum japonicum* of nurserymen, and the *L. japonicum* of Kew is the *L. lucidum* of nurserymen. Some people might suppose that when one had two similar plants under different names, or *vice versâ*, it would be very easy for an observant eye quickly to detect it, but the reverse is the case ; the newcomer is probably sickly after arrival, and does not assume its true foliage for two years ; it may not flower for three or four years, and may in our climate never fruit at all.

Plants of the same species, when grown under different conditions, and even in different situations in the same garden, may present superficially a very different appearance. In truth a man must be a very expert and studious botanist before he can assure himself with certainty of all the plants in a large collection, and I hope that a consideration of this fact will make my critics leniently view any oversights or blunders into which I have fallen.

NOTE.—The photographs from which the illustrations were made were most kindly taken at Aldenham by Messrs. Carter's resident artist, Mr. G. H. C. Bard.

HARDY NYMPHAEAS.

By Mr. A. BEDFORD, of Gunnersbury House Gardens.

[Lecture delivered on August 6, 1907.]

NYMPHAEAS, or water-lilies, have existed through many ages, and no other class of plants is more widely distributed at the present time. Species are indigenous in almost all parts of the world, and such diversity of flower-colour as white, blue, yellow, red, and many intermediate shades, is found in the genus.

Until the introduction of the coloured hardy hybrid water-lilies, our water-gardens were little thought about, and contained merely a few of our native aquatics, including our own native water-lily *Nymphaea alba*. But with the advent of the coloured water-lilies our garden waters began to improve, and have continued to do so up to the present day. Judging from the many beautiful and marvellous groups of aquatic and water-side plants which have been exhibited at our horticultural shows throughout the country during the past few years, perhaps in no other branch of horticulture have popularity and progress been more rapid than in the cultivation of aquatics. Another proof of this progress is found in the special lists and the many pages of catalogues now devoted to this class of plants by the different nurserymen who make a speciality of them.

Although we have a number of beautiful Nymphaeas from various growers and raisers, it is to M. Latour-Marliac we owe, perhaps, the heaviest debt of gratitude; for he was the first to give us hybrid hardy water-lilies; and, while others have since been introduced, the Marliac hybrids hold their own, and for general utility are still unsurpassed. Now that our lakes and ponds may be studded over with these dainty water-lilies, resembling, as it were, brilliantly coloured stars, swaying to and fro in the breeze, and in brilliance of colour rivalling the Nymphaeas of the tropics, it may be said that no present-day garden is complete without some of these floral gems.

The cultivation of aquatics is of the very simplest: all they require is some good soil or the mud such as is found at the bottom of natural lakes. This is the natural food of Nymphaeas. Given this to grow in and plenty of water above them, they soon establish themselves and grow into handsome specimens, covering the surface of the water with a wealth of beautiful foliage intermixed with star-like flowers. But though the culture of Nymphaeas is so simple, it must not be thought that, once planted, there they are to remain for ever undisturbed or uncared for. No! Just as the perennial asters and sunflowers and other plants of our herbaceous borders require to be dug up and divided when they become too thick or get out of bounds, so with Nymphaeas. After growing for a few years, some, such as the *Marliacea* section, being very vigorous growers, become so crowded, and produce so much foliage, that the leaves grow right out of the water, and so completely hide what flowers are produced. It is only when all the leaves are floating that the true beauty of the plants can be appreciated.

Lakes or ponds exposed to the sun, but sheltered from rough and cold winds, provide the most suitable home for water-lilies, although, failing possession of a natural piece of water, these charming plants may be grown in cement tanks, or even in tubs. A lake for the cultivation of choice aquatics should be free from all coarse weeds, and in all cases the natural mud will be the best soil in which to plant. Where it is impossible to lower the water for planting, this difficulty is soon got over. All that is necessary is to procure shallow baskets of various sizes, and place the plants in these with some soil; then put a few small stones on the surface or a few ties across the basket to keep the plant from floating out. Each plant can then be sunk where it is intended to grow, and before the basket has rotted away the plant will have rooted through and secured itself to the bottom. Large plants may also be planted by fixing a stone or other weight to the root and dropping the whole in where the plant is required to grow. In artificial ponds or tanks a copious inflow of water is not at all desirable; a trickle of water sufficient to keep things wholesome is all that is needed, and is, indeed, far better than a constant inrush. In small tanks a layer of soil, to the depth of 10 or 12 inches, 'might be spread over the bottom, and in larger structures little mounds or hillocks, made by placing a few sods together, should be formed.

When planting, secure the plant with a peg or weight to prevent it floating. The soil in which Nymphaeas are to be planted should be prepared some months before it is required, and should consist of good turfy loam, which has been cut and stacked for at least twelve months, plenty of half-decayed leaves, and some sharp sand, and the compost should be kept dry until it is wanted for use. The use of manures in any form I do not advocate, as they only excite rank leaf growth and predispose to disease.

The best time for dividing or planting Nymphaeas is the spring, about the end of April or beginning of May, although they may be safely moved at a much later period. If planted at the time stated the plants make sufficient progress to give a supply of bloom before the summer is gone. The flowering season for established plants begins early in June, reaches its height in August, and in good years lasts well on into October.

The depth of water required for the culture of Nymphaeas may vary from 18 inches to 4 or 5 feet; but, although I believe some of the stronger growing ones would do in a much greater depth, it is not wise to plant them so deeply, for they could not be got at without a boat or raft, and when it became necessary to divide and transplant them the water would have to be lowered, and this is not always an easy matter. I should therefore never plant choice Nymphaeas in a greater depth of water than I could get at with a pair of wading boots, with the tops made long enough to come well up under the arms. Four feet of water above the crowns of any of the stronger growing varieties is quite enough, and not less than a foot above the lesser growing ones.

A crowded water-garden is often a matter of necessity ; but where space is at command the plants are best in bold groups, and far enough apart, to keep them quite distinct, while allowing for effective contrast in colour. All the *Marliacea* section, being of strong growth, together with similar strong-growing kinds, should be placed in the deepest water, but should not be put so far out that their beauty cannot be seen from the margin of the pond or lake. Drawing nearer to the margin, where the water will naturally be a little more shallow, we may plant the *Laydekeri* section, and some of the American hybrids, which will be admirably suited for this position ; and for planting nearest to the margin we have the lovely *odorata* section and the *pygmaea* forms.

To give a list and description of the Nymphaeas in cultivation at the present day would occupy far too much time and space. They are accurately described by those who make a speciality of them. But a few might be mentioned, which stand out above all others. The first is *N. gloriosa*, which is beyond doubt a grand variety, rich carmine red in colour, with abundance of bright orange stamens, and the only Nymphaea with five sepals. *N. Marliacea chromatella* and *N. odorata sulphurea* are still the best yellow-flowered varieties we possess ; *Ellisiana, atropurpurea, sanguinea*, and ‘ William Falconer ’ are some of our best dark-flowered varieties ; and for rich rosy-crimson we have ‘ James Brydon,’ quite one of the best American varieties ; *lucida* and *Robinsonii* are also good in this shade of colour ; of white-flowered varieties there is none better than *Gladstoniana* and *Marliacea albida*. The *odorata* section, of which *rosacea, rubra*, and *exquisita* are some of the best-known, are all sweetly scented. The last-named section will soon deteriorate if confined in small tanks, and I have sometimes heard of failures with it under such conditions, which can only be attributed to confinement. The *odorata* section is easily distinguished from all others, as the varieties have long wiry-looking rhizomes, or root-stocks, sometimes measuring 4 or 5 feet in length. Where space can be found for them to grow freely on the bottom of large or medium-sized ponds, they are bound to succeed.

Although Nymphaeas are naturally sun-loving plants, yet I have always noticed that the water-garden is seen at its loveliest on dull, showery days, when the water is clear, and the leaves and flowers are thickly set with diamond drops that glisten and sparkle like rubies, topaz, and garnets. The flowers vary as to opening and closing, and, while on bright days, in the beginning of the season, they open in early morning and, unless the weather is dull, mostly close about three or four o’clock in the afternoon, as the season advances just the reverse takes place ; they open later in the day, and sometimes keep open even into the early moonlight of a summer’s night. The varieties also differ as to earliness and length of season. *Alba rosea* is always one of the first to flower, but soon goes to rest ; this is followed by the *Laydekeri* section, all of which are good ; for not only do they begin early, but keep on flowering all the summer, and as late as any in autumn. *Laydekeri rosea prolifera*, lately introduced by Mr. Perry, is one of the best of this section, and quite bears out its name. *Colossea*, quite the giant of all Marliac’s hybrids, together with *Gladstoniana, Robinsonii, gloriosa* and the many other hybrids, are some of the best for effect through a long season. The common white water-lily *Nymphaea alba* is two or three weeks behind the earliest hybrids, showing a gain in length of season which is even more remarkable in autumn. It is the end of June or beginning of July before the forms of the *odorata* section are much seen and *odorata sulphurea* often waits until August; but when once started this class flowers well into the autumn with such others as *pygmaea Helvola* and *Brakleyi rosea*. *Nymphaea odorata sulphurea* I have always noted to be the last in flower, and quite a bold one it is with large yellow vanilla-scented cactus-like flowers, rising well out of the water. In colour some of the Nymphaeas vary from day to day. 'Aurora ' and the *Laydekeri* section open pale in colour and darken each day with age, so that sometimes three distinct colours are seen upon the same plant ; on the other hand, the *Marliacea* section grow paler from day to day.

Not only are these hardy water-lilies valued on account of their beautiful flowers, but for their handsome foliage as well; for in such varieties as ' Arc-en-ciel,' *Andreana, lucida, Robinsonii, chromatella*, and *odorata sulphurea* the leaves are beautifully marbled and spotted.

Though some of the finer hybrids make few side crowns, and thus increase very slowly, others grow very rapidly and may be freely divided, the offsets being cut away with a piece of the old rhizome, or root-stock, attached. Those of the *Laydekeri* section are extremely difficult to propagate, as they make but few offsets ; but some produce seed freely, and are easily increased in that way, the seed being sown as soon as it is ripe. Many are sterile, and can only be increased by division of the roots, which work is best accomplished in the spring, and when new growth is assured.

If a pond or water-garden is impossible many of these charming plants may still be grown in tubs. For this purpose the *Laydekeri* section and *pygmaea* forms will be most suitable, as they are of compact growth. Tubs or half-casks for water-lilies should be as wide as possible and about 2 feet deep, allowing for soil, with not less than a foot of water over the crowns. A very pretty effect can be obtained, if a grass plot is available, by sinking the tubs into the ground, forming a background with Bamboos, Arundos and Eulalias, and other foliage plants, with a few tubs of other aquatics, such as the single and double flowered arrow-head, the flowering rush, *Typha minima*, &c. If it is possible to do so, and for convenience in keeping the tubs filled, a trickle of water might be made to pass from one to another, and so both time and labour might be saved. By sinking the tubs frost is easily kept out by a covering of boards overlaid with straw, reeds, or mats whenever necessary. With regard to the hardiness of all these beautiful hybrid water-lilies, there can be no doubt. I know of places where they are cultivated in tubs not sunk in the ground and without any protection in winter. They have been frozen in solid blocks of ice, yet the plants have not been injured in any way. It would be better, however, not to run this risk with any valuable varieties.

Though free from many enemies of the garden, water-lilies have foes of their own which must be held in check. All waters in which they grow must be kept free from weeds, as they not only choke the lilies, but keep the water cold and too stagnant for the promotion of good growth. Aphides, green and black, will sometimes be found troublesome, and must be washed off with hose or syringe or the leaves dusted with tobacco powder to rid them of these pests. As a rule plants generally outgrow these troubles, and have more to fear from rats and water-fowl at all times. It is impossible to grow Nymphaeas in any water to which swans, ducks, or other water-fowl have access. The water- or moor-hen is also very destructive, both to foliage and flowers, pecking them to pieces and even carrying them off to build their nests. The water-rat and common brown rat will sometimes attack and eat both rhizomes and flower-buds; therefore a sharp look-out must be kept for these pests or they may do considerable damage before one is aware of their presence. From some unknown cause the root-stock, or rhizome, of Nymphaeas will sometimes develop into a flat fasciated-like form, and when growth begins a dense cluster of small leaves, without the sign of a flower, will be the result. So far I have been unable to find any means to prevent it, but when such growth is noticed it is best to lift the plant and cut the rhizome into very small pieces, leaving two or three leaves attached, plant thickly in shallow baskets, and in a few years the majority of them will make flowering plants.

Though we have already such a large number of beautiful hybrid water-lilies, of all sizes and nearly all colours, white, yellow, rose, salmon, peach, flesh, rose purple, and red, in all shades to deepest crimson, there is no doubt that we have by no means come to the end of their development, and before long we shall be hearing of a hardy blue-flowering Nymphaea, which at present we are without. The difficulty of obtaining the blue colouring in the hardy plant is that the blue kinds are natives of the tropics; but there seems good reason to suppose that this difficulty will be got over, for there are also blue Nymphaeas from the Cape and Australia which will no doubt play their part in the production of new garden varieties.

PLANTS FOR TERRACE GARDENING.

By JAS. HUDSON, V.M.H.

[Lecture delivered August 20, 1907.]

BY this title it should be understood that I have in view such plants as are adapted for decorative purposes contiguous to a mansion and its surroundings of terraces, in harmony with the architecture of the house itself. The use of such plants for some years past has fallen off very considerably. Where are now the grand examples, for instance, of standard and other forms of the Orange, the Lemon, and the Citron, which at one time were the ornaments of many a terraced garden ; or, again, of the Agaves, the Yuccas, and other similar plants of fine foliage and distinct characteristics ? These may, in the inordinate demand for what are termed "decorative" plants, have had to be thrust aside, so to speak, to make room for subjects, many of which are but of a transitory character. Possibly, too, the varied styles of buildings that prevailed some years ago, and are still found, as conservatories and winter gardens, in immediate connection with the mansion, compared with what was the ideal of half a century or so back, may have been the cause of their disuse or relegation to less important places in the garden. Conservatories at one time were not so frequently connected to the house ; hence there was room in them for those fine specimens which are now but rarely seen in gardens. These specimen plants have been, like the exhibition specimen Stove and Greenhouse plants, far from prominent objects, for a decade or more now past. Upon the Continent there is still a demand for them, and they are to be found in the best gardens around Paris and other Continental cities, as well as in southern Europe, where many of those that we grow in England are comparatively hardy.

I am glad to see, however, that there is now a growing tendency to revert to their cultivation for this particular purpose in our British gardens, and I trust it will still go on. Any close observer of the effect that is produced by a judicious selection of the best plants for terrace gardening cannot fail to be impressed by their suitability. I was so impressed myself last autumn when viewing a well-known garden in the suburbs of Paris—in the Bois de Boulogne. In this instance the arrangement was simple, yet most effective, the plants in question being luxurious and immense specimens of Oranges grown as standards in huge tubs. Plants that have taken many years to grow to such a size as these were, may not be readily obtainable, but when once a taste is created.the supply will in due course follow. It would also be the very best experience for our rising generation of gardeners to become thus conversant with the careful cultivation of specimen plants ; experience would be gained that cannot be got by growing dozens of one or hundreds of another soft and easily grown plant, which at the same time may be of a decorative character yet not such as to claim attention the season throughout, or which when out of flower and in a shabby condition is relegated to any out of the way corner.

There is a wide field of choice from which some suitable plant or plants may be selected. Some, it is true, take several years to arrive at an effective size; yet when this is attained the reward is ample.

Oranges have been grown for years, and at one time where they received attention, many fine specimens were to be seen. Of late years there has been but little demand for them, hence the stock has not been kept up by the trade growers. It is not an easy matter now to obtain good specimens with well balanced heads. Their growth is comparatively slow, but at the same time it is tolerably sure. Both Oranges and Lemons deserve every attention that can be bestowed upon them. The proof of their scarcity is apparent in the difficulty that is sometimes experienced in obtaining orange blossom.

Myrtles probably stand next to the orange in popular favour. They are of rapid growth on the whole, but in order to make shapely plants some pains must be bestowed upon training them. In doing this any stray shoots will prove of great service (and at the same time durable) in a cut state. The small-leaved, or, as it is commonly known, the Box-leaved myrtle (*Myrtus communis angustifolia*) is of better habit than the type, and is an extremely useful plant, even from a plant in a six-inch pot up to a tall, shapely specimen. There are one or more varied forms of this myrtle, but they all possess a better branching habit. When grown as bushy pyramids they are seen to the best advantage, flowering too in a most profuse manner in the autumn. The ordinary myrtle (*M. communis*) is the better plant to grow as a standard. In 1889 I struck eight cuttings of the Box-leaved variety. These made good progress and all are thriving well; the largest is now ten feet high and six feet wide, with branches that nearly hide the tub, being at the same time both dense and bushy. For some years the best of this set of eight did duty in a London garden until their size became too great. This season I collected some seeds, whilst in Rome, of this small-leaved variety; these already show considerable variation. The variegated form of the common myrtle is also a most distinct plant, so also is the double-blossomed variety (*M. communis flore pleno*). It is the small-leaved Myrtle that is so largely grown in Germany, and for the German market, as standards for use at wedding festivities. The myrtle with us at Gunnersbury needs a cool shelter in the winter; ours are stored in a cold house from the end of November until the end of March, when they are gradually hardened off. Like the Oranges we find that myrtles thrive best in a strong calcareous loam with which is incorporated some old mortar rubble and sharp sand to keep the soil somewhat open. Firm potting is most essential. This fact must be enforced, because the plants have to remain for some years in the same pot or tub. Were the soil not so treated the plants would decline much sooner, owing to the constituents of the soil being rendered all the poorer by the rapid passing away of the water applied. Besides which a firm soil is conducive to a firm and enduring growth, even though it be not quite so luxuriant in all appearance.

Pomegranates (*Punica granata fl. pl.*).—Of this delightfully decorative plant the double varieties are most ornamental. Of these we grow three distinct forms, viz. the ' double scarlet,' which is, I think, the best and most floriferous ; the ' mottled form,' pale scarlet with white, a distinctly pretty plant ; and the double white, which, like some of the carnations, splits its calyx. The first two are beautiful with the young foliage, and again in the autumn, when the plants are resplendent in crimson and golden yellow. Being deciduous the pomegranate is easily stored during the winter. All that we find necessary is to well protect the tubs with dry stable litter as a safeguard against frost, and then put them in a sheltered place. (A note here may not be inopportune. Many plants that are considered to be hardy and would oftentimes be so, if planted out, are, when in tubs or pots, more susceptible to injury resulting from frost from the simple fact that their roots are then frozen, and probably throughout the entire ball. This fact should be patent to all plant cultivators.) I find that we flower the Pomegranates much more satisfactorily by not attempting any pruning whatever. It will be noted by a close observer that the flowers are produced upon the terminals, generally upon the terminal of the previous year, and sometimes upon the terminal of the current season. When first treating these plants I pruned in the winter, but soon found out the mistake. Now, if any pruning is required, it is done in the summer and by pinching the grosser shoots only. The Pomegranates are, I think, seen to the best advantage as standards upon a clear stem ; as bushes they are not quite so compact in habit. The soil required is the same as for myrtles. Our largest pair, standards of the double scarlet Pomegranate, measure 9 feet high by 7 feet in diameter.

Veronicas.—A few of this genus, the shrubby section, are recommended. These are quite uncommon and most attractive for late autumnal display, being oftentimes at their best during October, withstanding the rains and fogs better than many plants. It is as standards that these Veronicas are most effective, but it takes a few years at the least before plants of this form can be obtained. First the stem has to be worked up and then a head formed thereon. When, however, it has been secured such a Veronica will well repay the waiting and the labour expended upon it. I find that, although the shrubby Veronica will break back upon the old wood and send forth shoots, it somewhat resents a moderate pruning. Hence we tie the shoots in once at least in the season—the earlier the better— so that the growth is free by the autumn and not too formal. The best varieties for this purpose are *Veronica* ' La Séduisante,' ' Diamant,' ' Reine des Blanches,' ' Blue Gem,' and *V. Andersoni* ; each of these is quite distinct in colour, and the names are given in order of merit. During the winter we find it is safer to treat them as greenhouse plants, although it is well known that they will stand outside for some few seasons, especially near to the sea-coast. The aphis is somewhat troublesome when under glass, but the usual remedies are effectual. We use a lighter soil for these ; light loam, with either leaf-mould or a small proportion of peat, being a good and durable compost. Our large plant of ' *V.* La Séduisante ' is about twelve years old, and is still as healthy as ever. It measures 8 feet in height, and the head is $3\frac{1}{2}$ feet across and 5 feet in height.

Scented Geraniums.—These are well known as favourite subjects for the sake of their fragrance, but there are only a few that are suitable for growing into large specimens. Those we grow in this manner are *Pelargonium capitatum*, P. *Radula major*, P. ' Clorinda,' P. *crispum*, and P. *quercifolium*. Finding these to be so extremely useful we grow them in varied forms—as fans, as standards, and as pyramids. The first-named are used as screens, being in this form of great service. P. *capitatum* and P. *Radula major* are the best, but P. ' Clorinda ' is almost as good, while for the floral effect produced almost continuously through the season it is even better ; its soft, rosy-pink flowers are most distinct and effective. Our oldest of these fans are P. *capitatum* ; they measure 10 feet across at the base, with a depth at the centre of 8 feet, the tub included. The oldest of these are about thirteen years from the cutting. No pruning is ever done, save to cut a few straggling shoots occasionally to associate with flowers. To this non-pruning I attribute their longevity, our plan being to tie the shoots in ; rarely do we reduce the balls, but top-dress annually with good loam and leaf-mould or decomposed manure. During the winter these large plants are kept very dry, and by this means a thoroughly sweetening process is effected. The standards are chiefly of P. *capitatum* and P. *Radula major* ; they last quite as long as the fans, and are treated in a similar way. They measure 8 feet in height and 4½ feet in depth of the head alone, and 3 feet in width. The pyramids, too, are most serviceable ; they, like the standards, are all round plants, measuring in height about 9½ feet and 3 feet in width. *Pelargonium crispum* is a well known variety, often grown as small plants for decoration. I repeatedly tried to grow it as a large bush, but failed. Then I tried an upright style of growth, and have succeeded in keeping my plants healthy and vigorous. They now measure 8 feet high by 2 feet at the base, and are among the prettiest plants imaginable. It is somewhat curious that the method of training should have affected the vitality of this plant, but it is a fact nevertheless, and an object lesson that might be noted. A selection of these scented Geraniums (or Pelargoniums, to be strictly correct) is made, and after careful hardening off they are sent to the town garden in Hamilton Place, Park Lane, towards the end of May. They remain there until the end of July, doing good service around the mansion—in the open air, of course. As a proof of their adaptability for this purpose it is sufficient to state that the plants invariably come back to Gunnersbury in better health than when they are sent up, being of a darker green colour in the foliage.

Aloysia citriodora, syn. *Lippia citriodora* (or the scented Verbena, or lemon plant), is another plant that I can most strongly recommend for growing as a specimen. Its fragrance is well known, being an almost universal favourite. When it is well cared for the plant will live for years and increase in size, if need be. I started ours as cuttings in 1890, and in order to form a stem as quickly as possible I planted them in the open ground during the summer of that year, and thus secured stems from 4 to 5 feet in length that season. Then, when lifted in the autumn, we kept them steadily growing and commenced to form the head. In this way we saved quite a season, and in three years they were very useful plants. They some time since attained the limit of their size for our use, and now measure 10 feet in height, with a diameter of 3 feet, being of a pyramidal outline. Since the stems became woody we dry them off every winter, keeping them just free from frost. They are, in fact, treated as one would treat old stools of Fuchsias. About once in three years it is a good plan to repot them, reducing the ball to a moderate degree and then replacing them into the same size of tub or pot. For these we use a lighter soil, but always ram it firmly. I have, in order to secure what might be termed an early growth in the spring, started them under glass in a cool house, but I find that it is not so satisfactory as starting them in the open air, where we choose a spot somewhat sheltered and free from any risk of frost. The growth thus made retains its leaves, whereas often that made under glass will cast its leaves during an easterly wind. When the plants begin to show flower we pinch the points out, at least for the first time of their so doing. A more dense habit is thus encouraged. They are somewhat predisposed to attacks of red spider and of black fly, but the well known remedies are found sufficient. There is now in cultivation another variety of *Aloysia*, called *A. Mazonettii*, which is the same in all respects as regard habit of growth, but instead of being *lemon*-scented it is *mint*-scented, and most distinctly so. Of this variety more will soon be heard.

Laurus nobilis—the Sweet Bay.—This well known plant is grown in greater numbers than any other for this and kindred forms of decoration. It is not so much in demand now in England as it was, but upon the Continent, more particularly in Germany, and in the United States, there is still a considerable call for it. It is without doubt one of the best of all tub plants, and when it is well grown is always a conspicuous object. Its cultivation does not always receive the attention it deserves. In many parts it is not quite hardy : this may be the reason. To ensure its safety in the neighbourhood of London it needs a little protection, especially around the tubs during the winter months, and if the plants can be stored, even in an outhouse, they will be all the safer from the end of November until March. The Bay is a gross feeder. This probably explains why it is often seen with pale or sickly foliage instead of with the dark green and lustrous leaves that are characteristic of the plants that are grown in Ghent and Bruges, in Belgium, where it is one of the principal subjects cultivated for export. So far I have not seen any specimens in tubs of *Laurus nobilis regalis*, a narrow-leaved variety, but one in which the fragrance is intensified.

The Bay is one of the finest of terrace plants, but ought not to be too freely used, simply because the larger the plant the better is the effect, and there is not room for too many of that character. Of the styles of growth in which the sweet bay is grown I prefer the standard form. Tall, pyramidal plants are most imposing, but they are rather too dense ; hence I prefer the standard, with a clear length of stem supporting its head.

Agapanthus umbellatus.—This is a very favourite plant with many, and that rightly so. It is of comparatively easy cultivation, and that is much in its favour. To secure large masses in tubs is a question of years. They should not be grown in pots, because of the known tendency for the

root growth to burst the pots. They flower most profusely too when
confined at the root ; hence strong tubs are the best receptacles for them.
When in luxuriant growth the leaf-growth alone is most ornamental,
but when crowned with a profusion of flower trusses they are very imposing. They will last longer in beauty if not fully exposed all the day
to the direct rays of the sun, a partial shade during the earlier part of the
day being preferable. I find that the Agapanthus flowers more profusely
if the plants be kept dry through the winter, and even well forward into the
spring months. Ours are stored where safe from the frost, and are
put outside about the middle of April. Up to that time but little water is
given them. When the flower stems appear water is freely given, to
encourage their development and the leaf-growth also. The Agapanthus
looks well when grouped, or when standing alone, and is particularly
appropriate near to the water. The white variety is spoken of as a suitable companion to the blue, but I have not grown it. I have, however,
tried a ' major ' form which is later in flowering, but thus far it is not
satisfactory. A strong loamy soil suits them well ; they will remain for
years in their tubs, however, without any change, a manurial stimulant
being given them when in active growth.

Hydrangea hortensis.—For the late summer this showy plant, when
in flower, is a fitting companion to the preceding. With generous treatment it is possible to secure quite large specimens. It has a tendency to
form what may be termed a low dense bush, but if a little care is bestowed
upon it the height may be increased, and it is then more imposing. It is
better in all respects if exposed to the sun towards the autumn, in order
to mature the wood. It is also most interesting to watch the development
of the floral trusses with the expectancy of their assuming the blue rather
than the usual pale pink shade. When in tubs it is safer to protect from
frost during the winter.

Bamboos.—When not in too exposed situations these may be used
with distinctly good effect. The best kinds, in my opinion, are P*hyllo-
stachys aurea*, P. *Castilonis*, *Arundinaria nitida*, and *A. anceps*. The
first named is the variety that is chiefly relied upon on the Continent
for this purpose ; its upright and self-supporting style of growth is in
its favour for withstanding a breeze, and it is always attractive with its
light green foliage. P. *Castilonis* is not so well known, but I think it
bids fair to rival it, being very distinct in the marking of the stems, the
nodes being alternately yellow and green. It is of a rather more spreading
habit, but quite as handsome. Both of the Arundinarias are light in
growth, distinctly graceful in habit, and in every way suitable for growing
in tubs. When well supplied with water, and an occasional dose of a
phosphatic manurial stimulant, they will last for some years in the
same tubs. Loam and peat mixed will be found better than all loam
for bamboos in tubs. A sheltered position in the winter is desirable,
or they may be advantageously employed to decorate conservatories.
Bambusa japonica is at times grown in tubs, but I do not recommend
it ; it lacks a distinct character of its own.

Palms.—To associate with bamboos these are most appropriate, but,
as in the case of that family, the choice is limited to a few only. The
most common, and one of the most suitable, is *Chamærops excelsa*,

syn. *C. Fortunei*, which is now relegated to the genus *Trachycarpus*; *Chamærops humilis*, distinct from the preceding, and in every respect a fitting companion to it; and *Cocos australis*, syn. *C. Yatai*, and *C. Bonneti* are three of the best that I know. Each of these palms when well grown possesses a rigid growth, thus withstanding the wind to a considerable degree. *Cocos australis* is not yet apparently so well known as it deserves to be. It is slow in growth, but most durable, being also one of the very few Palms that do not need a liberal supply of water; in fact, it appears to thrive best when only sparingly supplied,

FIG. 50.—TUB OF SLATE AND PITCH PINE.

and also when in pots or tubs of limited size. It is quite distinct in its glaucous grey colour and graceful habit, being also one of the few palms that will thrive in the sunshine. It will take years to form a stem, hence the two species of *Chamærops* I have named are in that respect desirable. These, with well developed stems, have a distinct character of their own. Each will thrive under the same soil treatment as the bamboos.

Phormiums.—These, as large specimens, are highly ornamental, but they appear to be more appreciated upon the Continent than in our own country. They are both hardy and of permanent character, being well suited for exposed situations, and, like the *Agapanthus*, in association with water. In the winter, like the bamboos and palms, they can be turned to a good effect in the conservatory or winter garden. The best are the broad-leaved variety of P. *tenax* (called also the 'Powerscourt' variety), P. *Cookii*, P. *Veitchii*, and P. *Colensoi*; the last three are variegated varieties. Of these three variegated forms P. *Cookii* is the dwarfest, with rather short, upright foliage, being also considered one of the hardiest. P. *Veitchii* is the most distinctly variegated, being brilliantly striped with golden venations.

Clethra alnifolia is more thought of upon the Continent than with us ; it makes a very handsome standard, flowering late in the summer, not unlike a spike of lily of the valley. It is a peat-loving plant.

Fig. 51.—Tub of Slate.

Fuchsias.—Large plants of fuchsias are most ornamental, either as standards or as pyramids, being much better when grown for this purpose than for the cool house. It is not necessary even to give them more than the shelter of a cold greenhouse to start them into growth. Some of the best are 'Ballet Girl,' 'Charming,' 'Mauve Beauty,' 'Scarcity,' 'Mrs. Rundle,' and 'Chilwell Beauty.'

The Rosemary (*Rosmarina officinalis*) makes an excellent dwarf standard.

I have refrained from making any allusion to such plants as can be planted out *en masse* in tubs or large vases, my object being to draw attention rather to permanent plants of ornamental character.

The Tubs.—I have recommended tubs rather than pots for the plants under consideration. Their appearance is all in their favour, being more appropriate to any style of architecture. They are also immune from breakages, and, if properly constructed, are very durable. Ours (fig. 50) are made of slate and pitch pine, being square in shape. The four sides and the bottom are of slate slabs, $\frac{3}{8}$ inch thick, with the sides bevelled, so that they fit closely together, the bottom slate having provision made for drainage by holes drilled therein. The pitch pine forms the framework, which, when fitted together, is tightened at the top and bottom with bolts and screws. No soil comes into contact with the wood by this arrangement; hence there is not the risk of decay. Another very durable form of tub is made of slate only (fig. 51).

LESSER KNOWN ORCHIDS.

By F. W. Moore, V.M.H.

[Lecture given September 3, 1907.]

A mere enumeration of the names of orchids which are uncommon in cultivation, and perhaps also in their native countries, would, I fear, be of little interest in a paper such as this, and even if botanical descriptions and references were added it would only be duplicating information which can be obtained from special lists, floras, and other descriptive works.   On consideration I have decided to confine my remarks to rare or uncommon orchids having some special feature to recommend them, and also to such species that I am able to illustrate by slides made from specimens of the actual living plants, and in each case from plants in the Glasnevin collection.   This will necessarily very much limit the scope of the paper, the more so as I have only had from February to August of the current year, 1907, to get the slides prepared.   All orchid-growers know only too well that orchids will not flower to order, and, in fact, in some cases it is often difficult to get them to flower at all.   They may be hastened by a few weeks, or retarded by a few weeks, but, practically speaking, there the matter ends, and any erratic departure from the usual season of flowering is viewed with suspicion by growers, as probably indicating that all is not well with the plant.

In the definition "special feature" I include a wide range, such as orchid giants, orchid pigmies, orchids with peculiar habit of growth, such as a pendulous habit, orchids of remarkable appearance, orchids requiring special treatment, orchids with peculiar structure of flower, and orchids which have masqueraded in the names of other orchids, and have been generally known under the wrong name.   I find a further difficulty in the fact that almost the identical subject matter has been dealt with some few years ago by one of the ablest orchid-growers of the present generation, and one who had the finest collection in existence to draw on for his material.   On March 26, 1901, Mr. W. H. White read before your Society a paper on "Inconspicuous and Rarely Cultivated Orchids," which is published in the "Journal" for August 1901, p. 136. On carefully reading over that paper I find that Mr. White has gone so fully into uncommon orchids that practically he has left little for me to say, and I found that several slides which I had prepared had to be put aside, as Mr. White has dealt fully with the plants.   No genus of orchids seems to have escaped his vigilance.

My special pets, the Masdevallias, are fully dealt with, and such genera as Bulbophyllum, Cirrhopetalum, Megaclinium, Pleurothallis, and Re-strepia have been abundantly drawn on.

In orchids, generally, there is great variety in the formation of the flower, and although there may be general conformity to a plan, the variations within the limits necessary to bring any one plant into the order, or family, are very marked. These variations are not confined to any one organ or segment; all seem to vary. Frequently we find that the more any one part varies the more strongly the remaining parts or organs adhere to the general plan, so as to leave no doubt as to the

Fig. 52.—Gongora semilis.

affinity of the plant. Some of the most marked differences in type are to be found in the labellum. There is, for instance, the curiously shaped, fleshy labellum of *Stanhopea*. There are several species in which the labellum is heavily fringed, or covered with hairs, as in *Chondrorhyncha*

Chestertoni and *Brassavola Digbyana*. In both these the labellum is fixed. *Chondrorhyncha Chestertoni* may be taken as a type. It is a beautiful species, described by Reichenbach in the "Gardeners' Chronicle" in 1879. The flowers are pale yellow, and very delicate in structure. It is said to come from New Grenada. Further, we have in the well-known *Bulbophyllum barbigerum* an instance of an orchid in which the labellum is not only fringed or covered with hairs, but in which this organ is delicately hinged, and moves with the least current of air. This orchid, a native of Sierra Leone, has been in our collections for about three-quarters of a century, and can, therefore, not be called "uncommon." There are, however, two more recent introductions which are still uncommon.

Fig. 53.—Bulbophyllum miniatum.

Bulbophyllum tremulum.—I got the Glasnevin plant from Mr. O'Brien, who imported it from the Mysore Hills, and I regard it as one of the most striking orchids when in flower. The peculiar heavy fringe of dark hairs gives an irresistibly comical appearance to the flowers when looked at from a certain angle.

Bulbophyllum miniatum (fig. 53) comes from the Congo. It flowered at Glasnevin in August 1903. Here the hairs are white, and instead of being a fringe only they form more or less a beard all over the lip. This organ is extremely vibratile, so much so that when the photograph from which this slide was prepared was being taken the chimney had to be stuffed with paper, as the draught from it kept the flowers constantly moving. While dealing with the genus *Bulbophyllum* reference may be made to one or two species of special interest—for instance, *Bulbophyllum inflatum*. This species is remarkable for the curiously inflated rachis. In every other way it is inconspicuous, as the flowers are small, greenish

FIG. 54.—BULBOPHYLLUM DICHROMUM.

in colour, very hairy, and closely pressed to the rachis. It is a native of West Africa, and was described by Rolfe in 1891 in the "Gardeners' Chronicle." When the flowers have fallen away the persistent rachis strongly resembles a small pickling cucumber, two or three inches in length, three-quarters to one inch in diameter, and quite rough from the scars left by the fallen flowers.

. ˙ Some years ago interesting importations of orchids old and new were constantly being put on the market, such as those from Roraima Mountain, New Guinea, Sumatra, Philippines, &c. For many years there has been no such valuable and interesting importation as that made by Messrs. Sander & Sons from Annam, through their collector Micholitz. I went carefully through this importation shortly after its arrival, and purchased a large number of unnamed plants. The reward has been generous. Already five new species have flowered, three of which I have slides of.

Bulbophyllum dichromum (fig. 54) is one of these. It is a very remarkable plant. The pseudobulbs are far apart on a stout rhizome, and in the Glasnevin plant the inflorescence curiously springs from the base of an old imported and leafless pseudobulb, so that one may reasonably hope for even better results when the new and vigorous growths flower. The inflorescence is very bright and striking. The flowers are crowded near the top, and there is a marked contrast between the colour of the lip and that of the other segments of the perianth, the former being dark purple and the latter light yellow. It flowered at Glasnevin in February last, and was named and described by Mr. Rolfe. It is being figured in the ˊ " Botanical Magazine " for the current year.

Amongst orchids which attain giant size for plants of this family, the members of which are generally of modest dimensions, I have always considered that the two most remarkable I have seen are the huge plant of *Grammatophyllum* at Kew and the wonderful plant of *Arachnanthe Lowii* at Messrs. Sander & Sons', St. Albans. Twenty years ago Herr Wendland presented a plant of *Arachnanthe Lowii* to Glasnevin, and it is still alive and vigorous, though small in comparison with the St. Albans plant. It is one of the most remarkable of all orchids on account of its huge size, the length of its racemes, and the dimorphic flowers. Not only are the flowers different in shape, but they are different in colour, two, three, or four of the lowest flowers on each raceme being different from the others. They seem to be sexually perfect, and a reasonable explanation of this peculiarity has yet to be found. The Glasnevin plant, when photographed, had six inflorescences, each between six and seven feet long.

Eulophiella Peetersiana (fig. 55) may also rank as a giant amongst orchids. Its advent to cultivation created quite a sensation, and before it flowered much incredulity was expressed as to what it really was, and as to whether it really would be worth growing. In the " Orchid Review " for March 1897, notice is given of the sale of a few plants by Messrs. Prothero & Morris, and the collector's description is given, some doubt being expressed as to the identity of the new arrival. But few of these imported plants lived, so that it was distinctly a rare orchid in collections. At the present moment it is still rarer. In the April number for the same year further reference to this plant is made, and extracts from Dr. Kranzlin's description are given. The collector states that the flower stems are a yard high with twenty to twenty-five flowers, 2¾ inches across, leaves about two feet long. All these particulars have been exceeded in the Glasnevin plant which I got from Mr. Peeters of Brussels in 1898. The flowering rachis was 5 feet 6 inches high; it bore twenty-eight flowers, more than three inches across, and had ten leaves, the largest of which was 4 feet 1 inch long and $5\frac{1}{2}$ inches broad. In every respect it was a noble and stately plant. Sir Trevor Lawrence, Bart., had the

FIG. 55.—EULOPHIELLA PEETERSIANA.

satisfaction of first flowering *Eulophiella Peetersiana.* In the "Orchid Review" for April 1898 it was announced that it was in flower at Burford, and ample amends are made for any aspersions which may have been cast on it. The writer, amongst other things, says, "This is a most remarkable and very handsome orchid, and we congratulate Sir Trevor and his

able grower, Mr. White, on their success in flowering it." It may briefly
be stated that the flowers, with the exception of the lip, are bright shining
purple, the lip being white. Curiously, I attribute any success I may
have had in cultivating it to want of space. The stem is thick and
creeping, and there is from eighteen inches to twenty-four inches between
the pseudo-bulbs. In the only available house there was no room for
such a giant to spread, so I kept the young growths tied in, gradually
tightening the tie until I made them coil right round like a snake, and all
the young roots were forced to enter the material in the basket; hence
they remained fresh and sound, and did not die away for two or three
years. On three occasions this plant made two flowering shoots from one
pseudo-bulb, but only one was allowed to develop. It is very difficult to
increase, and there is but the original plant at Glasnevin.

Another large orchid is *Cyrtopodium Andersonii*, from the West
Indies. All the members of this genus are large, and I merely select
this species because I am able to illustrate it by a slide. . From pot to top
of flowers was 4 feet 9 inches. As the pseudo-bulbs are large and solid
they require more substantial diet than that usually accorded to orchids,
and loam and dried cow manure, finely broken up, seem to meet the
requirements.

The last orchid amongst the giants to which I will allude is
Cypripedium Lindleyanum. Compared to some it is small, but amongst
Cypripediums it is a giant, and I cannot admit that it deserves its
reputation of being a bad doer. The Glasnevin plant has been in the
collection since 1885, and it is healthy and vigorous. Writing about it
in February 1891, Mr. O'Brien said, "I like *Cypripedium Lindleyanum*
much, but never saw it of such stature as yours." It comes from
British Guiana, and is, I think, sometimes cultivated in too warm a
temperature. The plant represented had leaves 2 feet 3 inches long,
3½ inches broad, and the inflorescence was 4 feet 9 inches high. I should
have spoken, and written, of this as *Phragmopedilum*, but the name
sounds strange and unfamiliar.

From giants to pigmies is the next step, and amongst orchids these
are abundant. They are generally neglected, or rather were, as there is
a growing taste for them, and collectors are disappointed because there are
not long lists of them in nursery catalogues and because they are
not cheap. How could it be otherwise? For years regulated to the
limbo of what was contemptuously called "botanical stuff," they were
unheeded and unasked for, and to this fact many owe their presence in
the Glasnevin collection. I have often been allowed to pick over new
importations of orchids for such plants in Messrs. Low's, Sander's, and
Veitch's, and fared well. Mr. O'Brien has all along championed their
cause. I have had valuable assistance from him, and feel grateful to
him and to the various nurserymen.

A typical plant in this class is *Pleurothallis asterophora*. I consider
this to be one of the most beautiful of all minute orchids. I got it in
1891, but not for nothing. When I look at this pigmy I have always
felt ashamed of the price I paid for it, but I have never regretted it; it
has given so much pleasure to visitors. The plant when in flower is not
more than 3 inches high, leaves about ¾ inch by ¼ inch. It is very

floriferous; the flowers are numerous, very minute, and bright glistening purple. When held towards the light they seem to sparkle all over.

Three very minute and very rare species of *Pleurothallis* are *Pleuro-thallis hypnicola*, *P. Simmleriana*, and *P. lateritia*. *P. hypnicola* is one of Lindley's species, from Brazil, and is nearly the smallest of all orchids. It grows in dense tufts, the leaves from ¼ inch to ½ inch in length, the flowers pale yellow, with tiny purple lip. They are so inconspicuous that they can hardly be seen.

P. lateritia Reichb. f. from Costa Rica, is a very interesting little species with orange-red flowers. Mr. Rolfe considers that, from descriptions, it cannot be separated from Lindley's *P. tribuloides*. As cultivated plants they seem distinct.

P. Simmleriana is also a very minute species from Costa Rica, even smaller than the last named. It is very slender and delicate in all its parts, but singularly graceful and elegant.

Maxillaria funerea, *Masdevallia nidifica*, and *Megaclinium minutum* are another trio of dwarfs representing other genera.

Maxillaria funerea, named by Lindley from Brazilian material, is remarkable inasmuch as the small dull brown flowers do not rise above the leaves, and stand upright like small open cups. Rolfe described it in the "Orchid Review" for 1903, p. 232.

Megaclinium minutum is figured in "Bot. Mag." t. 7314. It comes from Sierra Leone, and is described as "the smallest species known." It shows the characteristic flattened rachis, which is dull purple, and curiously undulated on the margins.

Masdevallia nidifica is one of Mr. Lehmann's discoveries in Ecuador. It is remarkable only for its insignificance, but it is uncommon.

Every collector occasionally has a slice of luck, and the acquisition of *Arachnanthe annamensis* (fig. 56) was such a slice. The genus *Arachnanthe* is not a large one, but nearly all the species are curious and interesting, as well as beautiful. It may safely be said that *Arachnanthe annamensis* is not the least remarkable. When looking through the importations of orchids sent to Messrs. F. Sander & Sons from Annam I selected one from a number of distichous-leaved plants. I got it in June 1904 and it flowered in June 1905, and it has flowered each year since. The plant is not very vigorous in growth; the leaves are narrow and rather short, but the inflorescence is stout and erect, well elevated above the head of the plant, and the flowers are large and showy. The segments are narrow, the two lateral sepals and the two lateral petals are bent in a falcate manner, giving a rather weird appearance to the inflorescence of eight to ten flowers. Each individual flower is over 5 inches, by 3 to 3½ broad, and, as the ground colour is red, with transverse bars of yellow, the effect is bright and attractive.

It is a well-known fact that many orchids can only be grown in a pendulous position. They absolutely refuse to grow, or even live, in any other position. The first introduced plants of the rare *Masdevallia deorsa* were lost through not understanding this peculiarity. *Brassavola nodosa*, *Cattleya citrina*, *Scutecaria Steelii*, *Lycaste Dyeriana*, and *Epidendrum vesicatum* are other cases in point, and there are other uncommon species with similar idiosyncrasies. *Lycaste Dyeriana* is a remarkable instance of

FIG. 56.—ARACHNANTHE ANNAMENSIS.

an orchid of pendulous habit of growth. This plant clearly indicates by the direction of its pseudo-bulbs, that it must be grown in a hanging position. True, it might be mistaken without leaves for an upright grower, but the mistake would soon be discovered, and it refuses to grow in such a position. In fact it dies in a short time unless grown in the position it likes. If this detail be attended to there is no difficulty in cultivating it, and in getting it to flower regularly. It flowered at Glasnevin in 1896, and each year since then. It is not by any means a showy orchid, but it is curious and striking. I find it does best in an intermediate house temperature. The leaves are very glaucous, lanceolate, and quite a foot

FIG. 57.—EPIDENDRUM VESICATUM.

long. The flowers are produced freely from the bases of the old pseudo-bulbs just before growth commences. They are pale yellowish green. It is a native of Peru.

Lindley's *Epidendrum vesicatum* (fig. 57), from Brazil, is another instance, but in its case cause and effect are quite apparent. The leaves are thick and very glaucous. They are sharply folded inwards at the midrib, united at the base, free above, so that they are almost amplexicaul, and equitant. They are scale-like at the base, gradually becoming larger, the upper pair forming a large open cup in which the flowers are. A series of small tanks is thus formed, and if the stem be kept upright water lodges in these tanks and the leaves damp off, hence the necessity for the pendulous position. The flowers are white to pink, about ¾ inch across.

Mr. Rolfe considers this species very variable as to size, and colour, of flowers. It is a good doer and likes an intermediate house temperature.

By chance I discovered an orchid which, though apparently of creeping habit, would only thrive in an upright position. No one would ever feel surprised at seeing *Vanda tricolor*, *Renanthera coccinea*, or *Sobralia macrantha* growing in an upright position. To put it shortly, "they are built that way," but to see *Coelogyne triplicatula* growing upright is quite another matter. It looks almost uncanny. It has been in the Glasnevin collection over five years, and the slide shows what stupid mistakes may be made. The angle of the imported pseudo-bulb towards the stem spoke eloquently, but I would not heed, and put the stem flat ; it struggled for two years, making poor weak growths, and looking thoroughly unhappy, the pseudo-bulbs keeping at a curious angle. Told to put it any way he liked, my grower put it upright, and the result was magical. It made in a few months a strong growth which flowered, and each year since, further progress. This plant is very scarce. It comes from India (Moulmein), and was described by Reichenbach in 1864. The flowers are brownish yellow, the lip darker with marked keels.

Take now a few orchids with marked peculiarities. Several genera possess species which seem to be highly self-fertile, and in these species the flowers often open imperfectly, and are unattractive. A well-known case is that of *Dendrobium Brymerianum*, of which there are two varieties, one of which is not worth growing. *Cymbidium grandiflorum* of Griffin, more generally known as *C. Hookerianum*, being dedicated to Sir Joseph Hooker, who found it growing wild in the Sikkim Himalayas, is another. It is figured in "Bot. Mag." t. 5574. Orchid-growers know that some forms of this persistently refuse to open their flowers. The ovary begins to swell, the flowers turn yellow and drop off. According to Mr. Seden, Mr. O'Brien, Mr. Rolfe, and others, the Glasnevin variety of this (fig. 58) is the best known. It is free, vigorous, and floriferous, and the flowers open well. This year it had four inflorescences.

In August 1895 Mr. Measures got a botanical certificate for *Pleurothallis immersa*, a very curious and well-named orchid. The flower rachis is literally immersed in the leaf. The midrib becomes hollowed into a channel, or rather tunnel, in which the flower stalk is enclosed, but the edges are not united on the upper surface, and the stalk, which is not visible until it becomes free, can be pulled out. It becomes free about half-way up the leaf, and thus seems to spring from the middle of the surface of the leaf.

We have come to regard the labellum in the position in which we usually see it as the normal position of the flower, but just to keep us right some species flower without any torsion, and then we have the labellum in the upper part of the flower, and apparently upside-down.

Eria globifera, a new species from Annam, described by Rolfe from the Glasnevin plant, illustrates this. It is very happily named, as the small pseudo-bulbs are globose. It flowered last year for the first time.

Let me now turn to the masqueraders. *Dendrobium cymbidioides* is not considered rare or uncommon. It exists, or was thought to exist, in several collections. I got it from Java, and it flowered twenty years ago. It was formally identified for me in 1889, and I had no doubt as to the accuracy. In 1903 another species—which I got from Messrs. Sander—flowered, and the flowers considerably puzzled Mr. Rolfe, who inclined to consider it to be *D. cymbidioides*, but the plants were too distinct for this to be the case. Mr. Rolfe visited Glasnevin in 1903, and saw the plants. When at last I got them to flower together the difference was apparent, and Mr. Rolfe discovered that the plant known as *D. cymbidioides* was in reality *D. triflorum*, and that the true *D. cymbidioides* was this puzzling plant, which had flowered in 1903, and which I do not know in any other collection. The differences between them are well shown in the figure (fig. 59), but there is only one

FIG. 58.—CYMBIDIUM GRANDIFLORUM.

inflorescence remaining on *D. triflorum*. Mr. Rolfe gives the history of these plants in the "Orchid Review," March 1904, p. 69.

There is a fine strong-growing species of *Restrepia*, generally known in gardens as *R. antennifera*. It is a free grower in a cool house; the flowers are richly spotted, and the plant is very variable as to size of flowers, colouring of flowers, and vigour of growth. It is not only a variable plant, it is also an impostor. It is not *R. antennifera*, but *R. maculata* of Lindley. The name had not been questioned until about 1900. In 1889 I flowered a little *Restrepia* with beautifully striped flowers, very bright and charming, which Rolfe named and described in the "Gardeners' Chronicle," January 1891, as *R. striata*. In 1897 another species flowered, also with striped flowers, but much paler and less active than *R. striata*, and the flowers different in shape. Rolfe says it, "*R. antennifera*, H.B.K., not the plant usually so called in dens, which is *R. maculata* Lindl." In the "Orchid Review," August

Fig. 59.—Dendrobium triflorum.
D. cymbidioides.

4, he deals critically with these species of *Restrepia*, and says, "It is ious what confusion has been introduced into the histories of some our garden orchids. *Restrepia antennifera*, the type of the genus, nishes a very good example. This species is supposed to be well known in gardens, though in reality it has been confounded with another species which has usurped the name.' ' Further on, " The true *R. antennifera* is extremely rare in cultivation." Yet another impostor! Until recently the name *Cymbidium Dayanum* conveyed to an orchidist's mind the red-spotted variety of *C. eburneum.* In 1894 I purchased from Messrs. Sander a plant under the name of *C. pulcherrimum.* I sent flowers to Rolfe, who replied, " *C. Dayanum.*" I expostulated mildly, and suggested there was no resemblance between the flowers I sent and those of *C. eburneum.* My ignorance was pointed out to me in a very nice way, but I had the satisfaction of knowing that my ignorance was shared by most orchid-growers. A full history of the confusion will be found in the " Orchid Review " for December 1897. *C. Dayanum* is a pretty species, nearly allied to *C. pendulum*; flowers pale yellow, with red lines or streaks.

Fig. 60.—Dendrobium linguiforme.

.· Mr. Ross, when gardener to Sir G. Macleay, once remarked to me, " It is a pity that young gardeners know what an orchid is, as they immediately seem to think some extraordinary kind of treatment is necessary." There is much force in this remark. The name orchid seems to suggest shade, heat, and moisture, but these conditions are absolutely unsuitable for many species, especially so for most of the Australian orchids, such as *Dendrobium linguiforme* (fig. 60). These plants seem to grow and thrive in the dry airy atmosphere of the bulb house, especially when hung close to the constantly open ventilators. *D. Beckleri,* F. Muller, is a very rare species from Australia which enjoys the conditions described. It differs widely in habit from *D. linguiforme,* being a loose, straggling grower, with terete leaves, far apart from each other on the stem. Professor Henry Dixon, of Trinity College, Dublin, has made some interesting microscopical studies of the leaves of some of these Australian orchids. The slides exhibited to illustrate some of the peculiarities in the leaf structure were kindly prepared by Professor H. Dixon.

Hexisia bidentata, from Colombia, is another uncommon orchid with curious habit of growth. The stems are jointed; at the end of each joint is a pair of leaves which are persistent for several years. The annual growth seems to spring from the axil of one of these leaves, as the inflorescence occupies the central and terminal position. The flowers are bright orange red, somewhat darker than those of *Epidendrum vitellinum*.

Hexadesmia crurigera has been a long time in cultivation, but it is still very uncommon in collections. It, like the preceding species, has a peculiar and distinctive habit of growth. The stems are thin and woody, and are terminated by a pair of narrow hard leaves, at the base of which numerous small white flowers are produced, the purple top of the column appearing like an eye in each flower. It comes from Guatemala, and is illustrated and described in the " Orchid Review" for October 1903, p. 329.

The genus *Maxillaria* contains several species with remarkable flowers, and species which are very uncommon in cultivation, as well as in appearance.

Maxillaria fractiflexa.—This curious species is figured in the "Gardeners' Chronicle," May 31, 1902, from a plant in Sir Trevor Lawrence's collection, and I am indebted to Sir Trevor Lawrence for the Glasnevin plant. The flowers are yellowish brown in colour, and nearly 8 inches across. The two lower sepals are curiously bent, so as to make them point downwards, and the two lateral petals have a remarkable twist like an elegantly curled moustache. It is a native of Ecuador.

Maxillaria macrura, a Venezuelan species, is to me specially interesting, as it was the first orchid named for me by Reichenbach. He wrote that he was glad to get the specimens, but complained that he had to pay $1\frac{1}{2}d.$ extra postage, and politely stated that I must excuse him if he refused to accept the next parcel underpaid. This species has curious long sepals, which hang downwards as shown. There is a variety of it with rather longer sepals which Rolfe has named var. *longisepala*. They are both uncommon in cultivation.

The last genus to which I will allude is *Masdevallia*, and in it there are a number of species which may be classed as uncommon.

Masdevallia velifera (fig. 61) seems to have been fairly common in cultivation some twenty-five years ago, but it is now extremely rare. This can scarcely be wondered at, as it has not much to recommend it. The very colour of the flower—a dull lurid brown, with a shining surface—seems to indicate evil, and as far as the smell is concerned it certainly is evil, even worse than that of *Stapelia*, but not so all-pervading. It seems first to have been introduced by Potin, and subsequently by Shuttleworth, from Colombia, and it was described by Reichenbach in the " Gardeners' Chronicle " in July 1874. The plant at Glasnevin was obtained from Messrs. Veitch in 1883. It is a strong-growing species with thick leaves, and resembles *Masdevallia Mooreana*. It is figured in the " Gardeners' Chronicle," July 4, 1887, and in " The Genus *Masdevallia*," published by the Marquis of Lothian. Writing about it in the " Orchidophile " in 1883, Mr. G. Schneider says, " C'est une plante extrêmement vigoureuse, dont la fleur exhale un doux parfum." There is no accounting for taste!

FIG. 61.—MASDEVALLIA VELIFERA.

Masdevallia trinema.—This is another rare species of *Masdevallia* about which there is much confusion. It was imported by Messrs. H. Low & Co., and is generally known in collections as *M. Lowii.*

Miss Woolward points out in "The Genus *Masdevallia*" that the two names refer to the same plant, and that Reichenbach's name of *trinema* has priority. It comes from the Cauca. Not only is it one of the rarest of Masdevallias, but it is also one of the most beautiful, and one which always attracts the attention of visitors. It thrives in the cool orchid-house, and is quite a free grower.

The very limited section of Masdevallias known as *Echidnae* is now represented in many collections by *M. muscosa*. This curious little plant is interesting on account of the hairy peduncle, the hairy surface being interrupted where the small scale-like bracts lie close round the stem, and the irritable lip, which closes up when touched.

There is a much more uncommon species, namely, *M. Xipheres*, which also has the hairy peduncle and the sensitive lip. In this species the leaves are larger than those of *M. muscosa*, and the surface is rougher. The flowers are brown, not yellow; the lip is rather spathulate than cordate; there are three well-marked raised veins running to each tail, and the tails are spreading, not crossed, as they are in *M. muscosa*. Further, the flowers are curiously compressed, as if they had been squeezed between the finger and thumb. Rolfe deals with this section in the "Orchid Review" for August 1902, p. 228, and gives some very interesting information about it.

Masdevallia triglochin belongs to another section of the genus, *Triaristellae*, which contains several very pretty species with minute flowers, and it certainly is the most uncommon of those in cultivation. It might be confused with *M. gemmata*, but it can readily be distinguished by the curious pouch-like spur which looks like a hump on the back of the flower. It comes from Ecuador.

Lastly, I may draw attention to *M. peruviana*, named by Rolfe in April 1902 from the Glasnevin plant. Rolfe at first considered it identical with *M. auropurpurea*, but when they flowered together he made the new species *M. peruviana*, and described it in the "Kew Bulletin." It is a very distinct and pretty species.

THE CHINESE FLORA.

By E. H. WILSON.

Lecture given Nov. 6, 1906.

THE Chinese flora, like China herself, is a very large subject. The whole flora is estimated to contain not less than 12,000 species, and it is probable that this figure is well under the mark. During the last few years, owing to the enterprise of Messrs. James Veitch, of Chelsea, the Chinese flora has been brought very prominently before the horticultural world, but it must not for one moment be supposed that the Chinese flora can be said to be exhausted in any sense. Large tracts of country, and even whole provinces, such as Hunan, have never had a plant collected in them; and when it is remembered that in China each glen and mountain range has plants peculiar to itself, it will perhaps be recognised that our subject is far from being exhausted. It is, indeed, practically inexhaustible.

Our knowledge of the wonderfully rich flora of China has gradually been built up through the labours of a large number of persons of various occupations—Jesuit priests, Protestant missionaries, travellers, merchants, Consular and Imperial Maritime Customs officials, as well as others, have added to it. I do not propose to give an account of botanical exploration in China, but a few remarks about the part played by the Royal Horticultural Society seem opportune.

Dr. Lindley, writing in 1821, says:

"One of the many objects which occupy the Horticultural Society is the introduction of ornamental plants to gardens of this country, and the free distribution of them when procured. As it is difficult to form a very correct idea of the beauty of the plants from the appearance they assume when dried, it was determined by the Society that a person should be employed in making drawings of the plants in the country where they grew. For several reasons China was selected for a beginning, and particularly as being the residence of John Reeves, Esq., a correspondent and very active member of the Society, under whose immediate superintendence the draughtsmen could be placed."

John Reeves, the gentleman mentioned by Dr. Lindley, was born in 1774, and entered the service of the Honourable East India Company in 1808. In 1812 he proceeded to Canton, finally leaving China in 1831. When Reeves went to China very little was known of the country, its natural productions or its gardens; from the time of his arrival Reeves devoted his leisure to investigating its resources. He made it his principal aim to procure specimens of the natural productions of the country, and transmit them to such individuals or Societies in England as appeared most likely to make good use of them. His principal correspondent for some years was Sir Joseph Banks. During the whole of his residence in China, Reeves contributed largely to English horticulture and to this Society in particular, not only by his own direct shipments, but also by collecting plants during the spring and summer, establishing them well in pots previous to the shipping season, and then commending them to the care of the captains of the Company's ships, to whom he was also able to recommend the most desirable plants for transportation to England, and to whom also he succeeded in communicating some of the enthusiasm with which he himself was animated. Reeves applied himself with indefatigable zeal to sending home all that he found most rare and beautiful among living plants in the Canton Gardens. He was either the immediate or indirect source from which we first derived our varieties of Chinese Azaleas, Camellias, Tree Paeonies, Chrysanthemums, Roses, and numerous other treasures. Not a Company's ship at that time sailed for Europe without her deck being decorated with the little portable green-houses which preceded the Wardian cases of a later date.

The R.H.S. is indebted to Reeves for a fine collection of coloured drawings of Chinese plants executed under his immediate supervision by Chinese draughtsmen. These drawings first brought to us a knowledge of the Chinese Primrose, *Dendrobium nobile*, *Wistaria sinensis*, and other plants which were subsequently introduced into English gardens by Reeves himself.

The good work of the elder Reeves was followed by work of a similar nature on the part of his son, John Russell Reeves. To him we are indebted for such well-known plants as *Deutzia crenata*, *Acer palmatum*, *Prunus japonica* (single form), *Kerria japonica* (single form), and *Spiraea cantonensis*.

In those early days the acquisition of different varieties of Chrysanthemums, Camellias, &c., was an object this Society exerted itself to secure. The first collector sent out by this Society to China was John Potts, in 1821. Potts sailed to China on board the "General Kyd," and returned by the same ship in August 1822. He visited Canton, Macao, and Calcutta, and brought back with him a valuable collection of living plants and herbarium specimens, chiefly from China. In Canton he got together a collection of some forty varieties of Chrysanthemum, but an accident befell these on board and every one was lost. *Hoya Pottsii* and *Pottsia cantonensis* were brought home living and com-memorate this meritorious collector. Unfortunately, Potts died soon after his return to England.

In 1823 our Society despatched John Damper Parks to China. He also made a successful voyage, and returned in 1824, bringing back living plants of twenty distinct varieties of Chrysanthemum, sixteen of which proved to be new and were described by Sabine. In addition to these, he brought over several species and varieties of Camellia, *Rosa Banksiae* var. *lutea* and a distinct variety of *R. indica* and many other plants of lesser interest.

After Parks' trip, owing to the unsettled state of China, nothing further was attempted by our Society until 1843, when Robert Fortune was despatched. The travels and explorations of Fortune in China inaugurate a new era in the history of botanical discoveries in that country. Before that time the Chinese plants introduced into our gardens came from the neighbourhood of Canton and Macao, but Fortune explored new country to the north, in the neighbourhood of Shanghai and Ningpo, and, further, pushed his explorations into Japan. His diary shows that the gardens and nurseries of the Chinese contained a wealth of new and interesting plants, and from these sources he obtained the great majority of his plants.

Fortune visited China four times. The first journey (1843-1845) was only in the interests of our Society. His next two journeys were on behalf of the Honourable East India Company, and had for their object the introduction of the tea plant from China into India. His fourth and last journey was mainly on his own responsibility. Fortune was extremely successful, and we owe many of the commonest and most valued Chinese and Japanese plants in our gardens to-day to his labours.

Among the more important of Fortune's introductions the following may be mentioned :—*Anemone japonica, Dicentra spectabilis, Prunus triloba, Skimmia japonica, Spiraea japonica, Saxifraga sarmentosa, Viburnum ;furcatum, Aucuba japonica* (male), *Diervilla rosea, Platycodon grandiflorum, Rhododendron Fortunei, Jasminum nudiflorum, Forsythia viridissima, Trachelospermum jasminoides,* and, in addition to all these treasures, the double-flowered Peach and many varieties of Chrysanthemum, Camellia, Azalea, and *Paeonia Moutan.*

In each of its ventures into China our Society appears to have been most successful.

Stretching as China does through 20° of latitude, with its southern part just within the tropics and its northern part lying within a very cold region, having a rainfall varying from 30 inches per annum in the north to over 100 inches in the south, and possessing a great diversity of surface, we might expect the country to be a very rich one from a botanical point of view.

One feature of the Chinese flora which makes it of peculiar interest to all garden lovers is that it includes the original type of many of our most familiar garden plants. Ichang, standing just at the beginning of the mountains and at the head of the navigable portion of the river, over 1,000 miles from the sea, is the home of many of these.

The flower of the season—the Chrysanthemum—the Queen of Autumn, is, as you all well know, one of them. It has been cultivated in China and Japan from time immemorial, and up to the middle of the last century (1860) the introduction of new varieties from these countries to Europe was considered of great importance. Now all is changed, for China and Japan are acquiring new varieties raised in this country. It may interest some to know that grafting the Chrysanthemum on a species of Artemisia is frequently practised in China. The plants are more vigorous, it is said, but the real reason is, that the purchaser, unaware of the grafting, having cut down his plant after flowering in the usual way, is unable to perpetuate the stock, and in consequence has to buy afresh from the nurseryman the following year. *Chrysanthemum sinensis* was first cultivated in Europe in the flower gardens of Holland, and we may therefore presume that it had been imported in Dutch ships. As early as 1689, no less than six varieties were to be found in the Dutch gardens ; but they were subsequently lost, and when the plant was again introduced into Europe, in 1789, it was absolutely unknown in Holland.

C. indicum is also a native of China, where it was first gathered in 1751, and was cultivated by Phillip Miller in the Chelsea Physic Gardens in 1764.

Rosa indica, the Chinese monthly Rose and parent of the Tea Rose, is a native of Central China, where wild specimens were discovered by Dr. Henry. It was first introduced into this country by Sir Joseph Banks in 1789.

To illustrate our indebtedness to China in the matter of our national flower, I might mention the following species: *Rosa multiflora, R. Wichuraiana, R. bracteata, R. Banksiae, R. rugosa.* Take away these and their progeny and our Rose gardens would present a very sorry appearance.

There are altogether about thirty species of Roses in China, and Rose bushes are extraordinarily abundant. In warmer parts, *R. laevigata, R. microcarpa, R. Banksiae,* and *R. moschata* hang from cliffs or festoon the trees and bushes, while *R. sericea* in the woods is a wealth of white flowers. The variety *pteracantha* of the last species, on grassy and scrub-clad hills above 4,000 feet, is a mass of white in early summer and a mass of orange or scarlet in early autumn, while its long-winged crimson, translucent prickles make it beautiful from early spring to the fall of the leaf.

To China also we owe *Clematis lanuginosa,* one of the parents of the favourite *C. Jackmannii; C. patens, C. florida, C. hakonensis, C. Sieboldii,* and others. *C. lanuginosa* is a doubtful native of Japan, but both Dr. Henry and myself have collected wild specimens in China.

Rhododendrons like *R. sinense (Azalea mollis)* and *R. indicum (Azalea indica),* which in places clothe the hills with scarlet, Camellias, China Asters (*Callistephus hortensis*), the Chinese Primula, the Sweet Orange, Mandarin Orange, and the Peach, all have their native home in China, and the last was introduced to Persia and Europe in all probability by way of the old trade route from China through Bokhara.

Some idea of the great wealth of plants in China may be gathered from a glance at the following list of the more important genera represented there:—

Senecio.—One hundred and ten species in woodlands and by alpine stream sides.

Clematis.—Sixty-five species in woods and shrubby places, including *C. montana, C. florida, C. heracleaefolia* and its variety *Davidiana, C. tangutica,* and *C. orientalis.*

Berberis.—Thirty species, of which mention may be made of *B. Wallichiana, B. asiatica,* and *B. nepalensis,* found in woods, not in shrubberies.

Prunus.—Fifty species, including the Peach, P. *triloba,* and many Cherries.

Pyrus occupies in China the place filled by *Crataegus* in the United States. The genus is at present in a state of chaos, but at least thirty species are found in China, and probably many more. P. *spectabilis,* P. *Aucuparia,* and several with white fruits, and various species of the section Aria, occurring in woods and shrubberies, deserve mention. Many are remarkable for their ornamental fruits and the autumnal tints of their foliage.

Acer.—Forty species, wonderfully diverse in appearance, including *A. palmatum, A. Henryi,* and *A. Davidii.*

Ilex.—Thirty species, in woods and shrubberies.

Vitis.—Twenty-five species, of which I was able to introduce about twelve, including *V. Thomsonii,* and *V. Henryana.*

Corydalis.—Sixty-six species, with flowers of many different colours. *C. thalictrifolia* and *C. Wilsoni* are worthy of mention, as also are the allied *Dicentra spectabilis* and *D. macrantha,* a species with yellow flowers.

Gentiana.—Ninety species, covering alpine meadows.

Anemone.—Forty species, very variable in appearance, including *A. dentata* and *A. caroliana.*

Rubus.—Seventy species (and good species too), including *R. rosaefolius* and *R. bambusarum. R. parvifolium, R. xanthocarpum,* and *R. rosaefolius* are worth growing for their fruit.

Saxifraga.--Forty-five species, including *S. sarmentosa.*

Amidst this great wealth of plants it is remarkable to notice the absence of Gorse (*Ulex*), Broom (*Cytisus*), Heather (*Erica* and *Calluna*), and Cistus (Rock-rose family). The place of Gorse and Broom is taken by *Forsythia* and *Berberis Wallichiana*; that of the Heathers by very tiny-leaved Rhododendrons, of which there are at least ten species, while the Cistus family is not represented.

The open country, which would compare with our common land, is covered with *Berberis, Spiraea, Sophora viciifolia, Caragana, Rosa, Crataegus Pyracantha, Cotoneaster, Philadelphus,* &c.

As in the Himalaya, so in Western China, Rhododendrons form a special feature of the vegetation; indeed, *Rhododendron* is the largest genus recorded from China, no fewer than 140 species being known. On my second journey I collected about seventy species, and succeeded in introducing about fifty. Of these about twenty are new to science. Rhododendrons begin at about 5,000 feet, but do not become really abundant till 8,000 feet is reached, and they extend up to 15,000 feet, the limit of ligneous vegetation. Rhododendrons are gregarious plants, and nearly every species has a well-defined altitudinal limit. In June the mountains are one mass of colour, and no finer sight can be imagined than miles and miles of these mountain sides covered with Rhododendrons in full bloom. They vary in size from trees 40 feet in height to alpine plants only a few inches high. In colour they range from pure white through clear yellow to the deepest and richest shades of crimson. It is impossible to exaggerate their beauty, and from the altitude and latitude in which they occur there is every reason to believe that they will prove hardier than their Himalayan congeners.

Lilium is another genus well represented in China, thirty-two species having been recorded, seventeen of which are peculiar to the country, including *Henryi, Brownii, microphyllum, formosum, concolor, giganteum, tigrinum, Bakerianum, nepalense. L. sutchuense* I have found growing on the cliffs around Talien-lu at an altitude of upwards of 8,000 feet.

We will now turn our attention to a most interesting problem in plant distribution, namely, the affinity which exists between the flora of China and that of North America, and more particularly of the South-Eastern Atlantic States.

One of the most remarkable results of the extension of our knowledge of the Chinese flora has been the discovery in the heart of China of representatives of genera originally known only from the Atlantic side of the U.S.A. Indeed the headquarters of many genera originally only known from the Southern States of U.S.A. is now known to be China.

The genus *Podophyllum* illustrates this : the first known species was P. *peltatum* from America ; now we have P. *Emodi* from the Himalaya and W. China, P. *pleianthum* from Formosa, P. *versipelle* from South China (Canton), and two new species in Hupeh, and another in W. China. Magnolias also afford a good illustration of this remarkable affinity. The genus is absent from Europe and Western North America, and is represented by six species on the Atlantic side of U.S.A. and eleven species in China and Japan.

Several genera are represented by one species each in China and South-Eastern U.S.A.

CHINA.	UNITED STATES OF AMERICA.
Liriodendron chinensis.	*Liriodendron tulipifera.*
Gymnocladus chinensis.	*Gymnocladus canadensis.*
Stylophorum japonicum.	*Stylophorum diphyllum.*
Nelumbium speciosum.	*Nelumbium luteum.*
Decumaria sinensis.	*Decumaria barbara.*

But even more remarkable than either of the foregoing facts is the occurrence of the same species of plants in China and Japan and in the Alleghany Mountains between Virginia and Georgia (South-Eastern U.S.A.) and nowhere else between. *Diphylleia cymosa* is one such, and no variation is to be seen between the two forms, although they are separated by 140° longitude. *Sassafras Tzumu* occurs only in China and South-Eastern U.S.A., and has similar medicinal use in China and the States, although separated by 150° longitude.

The outstanding features of the Chinese flora may be thus summarised :—

(1) Its richness, particularly in flowering trees, shrubs, herbaceous and alpine plants eminently suitable for outdoor cultivation in Great Britain.

(2) It is the home of the parents of many of our best known garden plants.

(3) The complete absence of the Broom (*Cytisus*), Gorse (*Ulex*), Heather, and the Rock-rose family.

(4) The border line of China and India, that is, the Tibetan-China-Himalayan region, is the headquarters of that wonderful flora which extends from Afghanistan to the Yellow Sea and southwards to Malaya.

(5) The Chinese flora proper is distinct from the floras of Japan and Korea, which have affinities with that of Siberia.

(6) The close affinity between the flora of China and that of the Atlantic States of the U.S.A.

ELECTRIC CULTIVATION IN RELATION TO HORTICULTURE.

By B. H. Thwaite, F.C.S.

(Lecture given October 1, 1907.)

The solution of the problems offered by the many mysteries associated with the growth and development of plants has fascinated many brilliant men of science, and link by link the chain of knowledge has been forged, so that in these days it is possible to construct a chain that, if only approximately, symbolises the cycle of operations which in its grand unity represents life, and, subject to reliance on solar influences, one that also represents the complete cycle of the conservation of energy, the conception of which immortalised the name of Meyer, of Heilbronn.*

The nature of the complete cycle, uniting in its embrace both animal and vegetable life, is the most impressive fact in the whole range of our knowledge of natural causes and effects. Once we examine each link in the chain forming this great cycle, we recognise how deeply we are indebted to the beautiful processes associated with the growth of a plant for our very existence, and the enjoyment of that existence. Each petal and flower of a plant should, indeed, be worshipped by man, not alone for the fruit it foretells, but for the beauty of form, colour, and fragrance it presents to us as elements of its relationship to the other (the animal) branch of organic life, to which it acts as the silent and self-immovable servant.

It is realised, at least by certain French *savants*, that a trait resembling intelligence is possessed by plants. That they may even be imagined to serve as friends in distress is well known to all the readers of Chateaubriand's exquisite literary creation "La Picciola." Let anyone who desires to realise, as in duty bound one ought, the many and wondrous signs of marked intelligence or instinct of flowering plants, carefully read Maurice Maeterlinck's recent work "L'Intelligence des Fleurs."

The omniscient Creator has selected the green leaf, so characteristic of vegetable life, to act as the connecting link between the sun and life, and through this link and by a series of beautiful operations, the wastes of the processes constituting animal life are assimilated, and (as a result of luminous or electrical stimuli) ultimately form foodstuffs for the support of animal life (fig. 62).

The remarkable operations by which the wastes from animal organic processes are absorbed, assimilated, and utilised in supporting plant life may be briefly described as follows:—

The essential food elements of plants are carbon (which the leaves of plants absorb from the ambiant atmosphere, in which it exists as the carbon-dioxide gas exhaled by animals), nitrogen (which the plant by

---

* Herr Meyer died in absolute desperation, his theory completely ignored.

means of its roots derives from the soil, usually in the form of nitrates), earth salts, and water.

Of all the processes that constitute links in the chain of still life, none are more wonderful than those associated with the making of plant food by the plant itself.

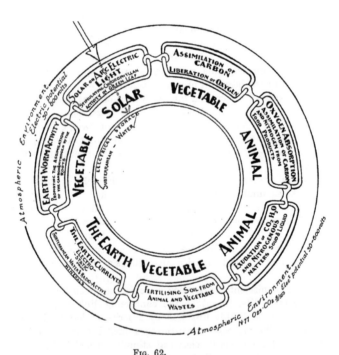

Fig. 62.

The chlorophyll granules embedded in protoplasm, causing the green colour of leaves, form the field of chemical activity. Their function is to find the nutriment for the leaves and, through them, the plant during the active periods of existence; but this function cannot be exercised unless they are receiving the chemically active or actinic (or, shall we say, electrically energising) rays of the sun, or its substitute, the arc electric light.

So soon as these energising rays fall upon the green leaves, the chlorophyll grains commence to act, absorbing the carbon from the carbon-dioxide, and, with the elements of water, producing chemical compounds suitable for assimilation by the plant.

It will be observed that this sequence of operations relies for its inception upon solar, or voltaic arc actinic rays. It might be argued that this solar ray which switches on the action of the chlorophyll grains is the electrical agency: a flash of electric rays from the arc light or from the sun falls on the green leaf and, presto! the leaf is energised and the chlorophyll grains begin their work.

The wet membranes of the leaves allow gaseous exchange; the carbon-dioxide of the air flows through the moist cellulose membranes into the cells of the leaf along with the moisture, and the considerable surface exposed by leaves permits a large attack of the CO_2 on the exposed and moist membranes. The CO_2 is broken up, the carbon is absorbed by the leaf and the oxygen is liberated, escaping back into the air. The permeability of the exposed leafy membrane is seriously reduced if moisture is not present, hence the great importance, in a dual sense, of moisture. The pores of a leaf when dry become contracted, and offer resistance to the passage of the gaseous CO_2 and the moisture which carries electrical energy. By the absence of moisture the process of carbon absorption becomes seriously impeded. We may therefore say that both the electrical energy of the sunlight, and the electrical energy stored in moisture, are necessary for the initiation of the function of the leaf so far referred to.

Independently of the importance of moisture in facilitating gaseous exchange through the leafy membrane, it is important, because the elements of water combine with the carbon to produce within the chlorophyll-bearing cells *carbo-hydrates*, such as starch. The excess oxygen, as we know, escapes back into the air.

The energising effect of the electric light or sun's rays continues so long as the sunlight falls upon the leaf; in fact, it continues a short time after the rays are cut off—a fact of enormous significance, the knowledge of which we owe to the refined investigations of Dr. Waller, F.R.S.

According to Dr. Waller, the living leaf immediately responds to the stimulus of sunlight, and in a lesser degree to the influence of electric arc light.

Diffuse daylight only produces slight response. The effect is clearly illustrated by the diagram (fig. 63). The needle of the galvanometer is *instantly* deflected when the light falls on the leaf, the deflection ranging over − 0·02 volt and + 0·02 volt. When the light rays are cut off the needle slowly falls down to zero, which it reaches after a lapse of thirty minutes from the time the light is removed.

The rays projected from the sun, with potentials of energy beyond calculation, flow into our planet's atmosphere, becoming gradually diffused in the higher strata. Their density or electrical potential enormously exceeds that of the electric potential of, and near to, the earth's surface, and the energising activity is proportionately greater; but when the rays pass into hygrometric or water-carrying strata, it is presumed that the potential is rapidly lowered, because it is by the moisture suspended in the air (or the hygrometrical conditions) that the electric energy flows to or is carried to the earth. The particles of moisture, "the carriers of electricity," constitute nuclei of electrical reception and of electrical storage.

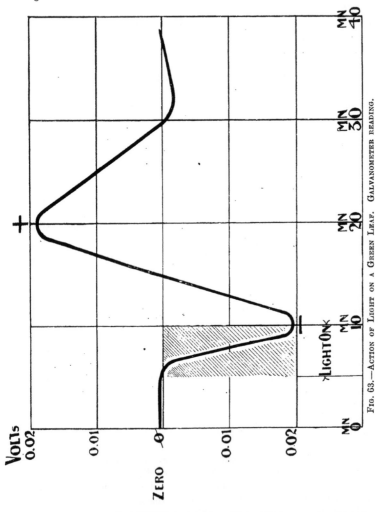

Fig. 63.—Action of Light on a Green Leaf. Galvanometer reading.

When rain falls, the abnormal electrical storage is reduced by the fall of the electrical energy along with the rain to the earth. This electrically charged rain in passing through the soil releases part of the electric potential, the balance being held by the subterranean water, into which the rain finally percolates. This subterranean water (and electrical storage) constitutes a liquid shell that practically envelops the earth. This storage is a compensator, producing dew, &c., by evaporation and condensation effects. The electrical potential of this storage is distributed to the soil and the roots and leafy surfaces of plants.*

Obviously, therefore, the electrical potential of the atmosphere is a function of the amount of water suspended or flowing through the air.

During the time rain falls, bringing down the electrical energy from higher altitudes, it will be found that the electric potential near the earth's surface is increased from, say, 30 volts normal to 600 volts and higher. This electric environment will constitute a highly stimulating influence on vegetation. Volta, over a century ago, discovered with some degree of exactitude that the proportions of the ordinates of the curve or gradient of electric potential increased as the distance from the earth increases, and, more recently, Engel has provided data to calculate the increase. It appears that the electric density increases 38 volts with each metre of altitude above the earth, or, in feet equivalents, 1·19 volts per foot of altitude (fig. 64).

This fact is emphasised, because in future developments of one of the methods of securing the services of electricity for the stimulation of plant growth, it may be desirable to locate the electro-static collecting apparatus at a comparatively high altitude—a principle the author has already adopted in other applications of static electricity.

Even at a height of only 64 feet, the output of a given collector should be twenty times greater than if it were located at the ground level.

It may be mentioned that the late illustrious *savant*, Berthelot, made certain experiments at Meudon to determine the electric potential on the summit of a tower of 28 metres high. In fine weather the electric potential of the air oscillated between 600 and 800 volts. The least fall of rain raised the potential to no less than 12,000 to 15,000 volts.† As will be shown further on, in the historical notes (p. 408), as early as 1783 the Abbé Berthelon suggested the collection of electric energy by raising a conductor with metallic heads and points high into the air.

Referring again to the *rôle* that water plays in the physiology of vegetable and animal life, we recognise that water serves as a carrier of electrical potential. It assists in the process of assimilation of carbon, and constitutes the source of the hydrogen in the carbo-hydrate formation. It attracts the atmospheric electricity. It also constitutes the great storage element for receiving the flow of electricity through the soil, and it returns the electricity to the surface of the earth and to the plants upon it. Doubtless it serves in some equivalent capacity for animal life; it is certainly one of the elements of exchange between plant and animal life.

Even when the water is evaporated, the electric energy is deposited, hence probably the origin of the radio-activity of many minerals.

The electrical energy supplied by the sun is stored under characteristic excess of normal requirements in the water above and beneath the earth's surface. The vastness of the proportions of the stored electrical energy is immeasurably beyond our conception.

* Elster and Geitel say that the source of radio-activity is the soil.
† Vide *Comptes Rendus*, November 12, 1900, page 976.

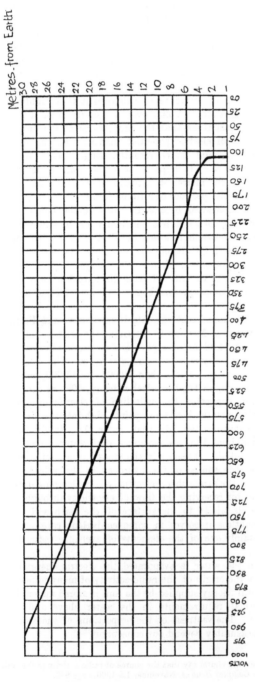

FIG. 64.—ELECTRIC POTENTIAL AT VARYING HEIGHTS ABOVE EARTH'S SURFACE.

Berthelot believes that the limitation of hydrogen in the atmosphere is due to the effects of the electric currents of very high intensity upon the mixture of hydrogen and oxygen constituting aqueous vapour.

Scarcely a week passes without an addition to the list of radioactive substances. Verily the life work of Faraday, Berthelot, Currie, and others has enlarged the vista for those that have eyes to see.

The portentous fact noticeable in a close examination and analysis of natural operations is the excess of supply over the quantitative requirements provided by Nature to effect a given result. The Master Power takes no risks whether in securing germinating results or in the electrical initiation of natural processes, or indeed any other operations. For instance, Becquerel states that the potential energy represented by the organic matter of a culture of sunflower is only $\frac{4}{1000}$ of the available solar energy supplied to the plant.

The power of intellect and the triumphs of research and invention have discovered that the stored results of the excess energy, provided by the sun in prehistoric periods, are available as compensating services during sunless days in our own time. For instance, we take the coal, the result of past periods of solar energy absorbed in the building of vast forests, and convert the carbonaceous residue into a gaseous condition, and burn it with its proper equivalent of air in a motive-power generating engine, the power of which is transformed into electro-static current by a rotary machine or by a gas engine, and by Faraday's dynamo-electric machine into electric-light energy, which the phenomenon of the voltaic arc converts into a near resemblance of the beam of sunlight. This voltaic arc provides the electric energising or actinic rays which initiate and support the activity of the chlorophyll grains of the green leaf.

As we know the same energy also secures, if required, the electro-static current addition to the sum of the atmospheric electric potential environment of the plant.

So far there have been two schools of experimentalists in the science of electric cultivation of plants.

One school has applied itself to the study of the effect of electro-static currents, the other to the study of the effect of the rays of the voltaic electric arc. As one might expect, the investigators of the pre-Faraday period belonged to the static current school. The voltaic-arc experiments followed the results of Faraday's discovery by which the current for the voltaic arc lamp could be produced, without involving the aggregation of a cumbersome mass of batteries.

Before Faraday's time an immense amount of ingenuity was expended in the production of rotary collecting friction or influence machines, which were referred to as electro-static machines. Faraday's discovery diverted attention from the electro-static machine, but in recent years physicists have given some attention to securing improvements in this type of electric machine. Voss, Wimshurst, Pidgoon and Lemström may be mentioned in this connection, and one must not forget the late Lord Armstrong's steam collector.*

---

* Further, very important improvements in induction coils have been made, thanks to the X-ray and Hertz-ray applications, by which the ordinary continuous current can be converted to serve electro-static continuous requirements.

The earliest attempts in electric cultivation were confined more or less to the use of static collectors similar to lightning conductors. Mention has already been made of Abbé Berthelon, who in 1788,[*] using for a collector a lofty pole with cupped points, discharged the collected current into the plants around the base of the pole (fig. 65, 4) : but prior to this, in 1749, Abbé Nollet hung iron trays suspended from a silk cord, and on this insulated plate he placed his plants, which he charged with electro-static current from a primitive kind of rotary electro-static or induction machine (fig. 65, 5). The experiments of both Abbé Nollet and Berthelon were attended with some degree of success. Nollet succeeded in accelerating the germination of maize and mustard. Berthelon's experiments secured an increase in the fertility and growth of the plants, and his plan has, it is said, been in common use in France ever since. In highly electric districts it would not be difficult to advantageously utilise abnormal electric potentials for electric distribution to cultivated areas.

The Russian experimentalist, Speschnew, relied on the flow of electrical current between metals of opposite polarity, and experiments on those lines have been conducted in Massachusetts, U.S.A. Two plates of copper and zinc were sunk in the ground at either end of forcing-beds in greenhouses (fig. 65, 6). The slight current flowing between the plates was found to highly accelerate the growth of lettuce.

Berthelot had been occupied for some time before his death with electric culture experiments. He employed electro-static currents, but the author is not in possession of the actual quantitative results, though Berthelot's electric carrots are not unknown in France. The greatest and most persistent worker in the electro-static school so far was the late Professor Lemström, who also died before his experiments were completed.

The electro-static current passing through the soil energises the micro-organisms whose function it is to convert the nitrogen of the fertilisers into a nitrate condition suitable for assimilation.

The activities of the micro-organisms at the roots of the plant convert the insoluble minerals into soluble ones, as nitrates, &c., in which form they pass into the sap and help to build the structure of the plant. According to Lemström, the electro-static current greatly stimulates the flow of the sap.

Lemström commenced his experiments in the year 1885. Employing a small Holtz electro-static machine, barley, wheat, and rye were sown in separate pots. The results showed 40 per cent. increase over non-electrified grains, and subsequent experiment in a field of barley secured an increase of about 35·1 per cent. The summary of Lemström's results are given in the Appendix.

Generally it may be said that Lemström's applications secured an increased weight of products, whether the electric energy applied was of positive or negative quality, or whether applied during the night or during the daytime, but the success was greatly influenced by the hygrometric condition of the air.

---

[*] It is recorded that Maimberg, a Scotchman, made some tests in the year 1746, on the influence of electricity on two myrtles, but the results were inconclusive.

Lemström discharged the electric current from an overhead wire, as shown by fig. 65, 7. The discharge was effected by well-distributed points

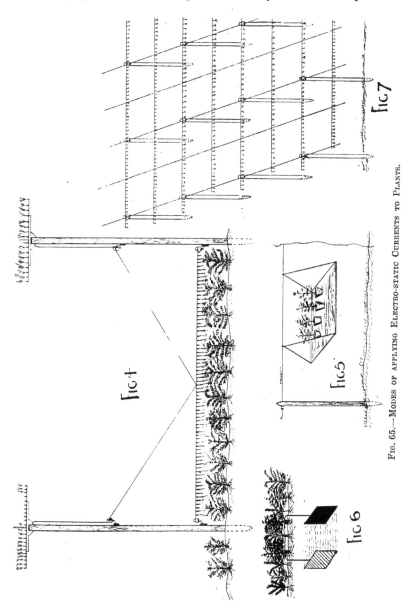

FIG. 65.—MODES OF APPLYING ELECTRO-STATIC CURRENTS TO PLANTS.

along the wires. He employed a special kind of electric collector machine. Lemström has left valuable results as a legacy to his successors, one of which is the fact that in the periods of field growth an accleration, ranging from 10 per cent. to 91 per cent., can be secured by the application of electric stimulus. His investigations and experiments covered nearly all the ordinary vegetable food products, including rye, wheat, oats, barley, peas, potatos, beet-root, carrots, beans, turnips, tobacco, and flax.

Other experimentalists have more or less confirmed Lemström's results. The optimum voltage according to Berthelot is 5 volts ; according to Sir J. Kenny it is 8 volts ; according to the Swedish investigator, Hilfvengren, the optimum voltage varies with different plants and climatic and soil environment,* which is obvious. But to the author the experiments of his friend, Mr. J. E. Newman, appear to constitute the best promise for practical success of any experiments applying only the electro-static stimuli for field work. It is satisfactory to know that the experiments have been applied to the soil of England.

Mr. Newman employs the overhead discharge. According to Mr. Priestley, Mr. Newman's arrangement is as follows :—

Direct current is generated by a dynamo of some 2 h.p. ; the electrical energy developed passes from the dynamo terminals through the primary of a large induction coil with a make and break contact interposed in the circuit ; the high-tension current is passed from the secondary of the coil through rectifiers, one pole being connected to the overhead distributing wires, the other pole being earthed.

Large poles, some 5 yards high and equipped with insulators, and placed in rows, separated by a distance of 102 yards, cause the current to cross wires 12 yards apart, and the current is sent through the wires at such a high tension as to secure a discharge at points all along the line.

Applied to wheat the following results were obtained :—

YEAR 1906.

Bushels per acre.

	Electrified Per cent.	Non-electrified Per cent.	Increase Per cent.
Canadian (Red Fife) .	. 35½	. 25½	. 39
English (White Queen)	. 40	. 31	. 29

The electrified wheat was of a higher quality, containing by analysis ·080 per cent. average dry gluten.

The author has just received from Mr. Newman the following information relating to this year's crops :

Strawberries planted in March.

Electrified	Non-electrified
223½ lb.	293½ lb.
from 11·725 yards.	from 20·850 yards.

* Berthelot claims that a difference of potential of 7 volts is sufficient to initiate the chemical actions forming the basis of plant growth, and this slight potential difference is capable of changing oxygen into ozone, and fixing atmospheric nitrogen upon the carbo-hydrates constituting the tissue of plants. According to this *savant* all these reactions will become so much easier and produce more intense effects in proportion as the stalk of the plant is greater and the agitation of the air is considerable.

Showing an average increase of 85·5 per cent. of productivity per unit of area. Analysis shows 14½ per cent. increase of glucose.

Mr. Priestley gives the following information concerning experiments made at Bristol in 1906 to determine the value of earth-current electric stimuli, employing the Speschnew system of plates embedded in the soil (see fig. 65, 6). Copper and zinc plates were used.

Beans were planted on February 21, 1901, and weighed in June.

	Electrified	Non-electrified
Average volume of bean .	. 2 c.c.	1·5 c.c.
Average weight . .	. 2·26 gr.	1·71 gr.

The plates had an area of 200 square inches and were placed 4 feet apart. A current strength was recorded of ·12 milli-ampère.

THE VOLTAIC ARC STIMULI.

Faraday's laboratory machine was transformed into a practical and fairly efficient machine by a sequence of improvements. The shunting of part of the current on to the magnet is claimed by two inventors, one an Englishman, Cromwell Varley, whose claims for recognition have never yet secured from his countrymen the reward they deserve; the other, Werner Siemens of Berlin.

Gramme also made specific improvements, and the Siemens family of distinguished inventors finally evolved a thoroughly practical machine. Sir William Siemens, a brother of Werner, was probably the first to recognise the full possibilities of the voltaic arc as a supplement to, or substitute in winter time for, the rays of the sun.

It may here be stated that whereas the electro-static application is applicable to field service in the ordinary periods of natural cultivation in summer time, the voltaic arc is available if desired for use all through the winter months.

In the year 1861 Hervé Mangon had noticed the effect of the voltaic arc light in stimulating the growth of plants; but Siemens pioneered the practical application for the specific purpose of cultivating fruit and flowering plants in the glass house in winter months. The results * of these trials have passed into history. Although the apparatus employed by Siemens, compared with those available to-day, were primitive, his papers and the discussions lead the way to the modern attempts to secure results that we all require—viz., electric cultivation associated with profit possibilities.

Objections have been raised on the score of the hard and burning intensity of the fixed electric beam. On the other hand a summary of the

---

* Siemens found that peas sown in October produced a harvest of ripe fruit on February 16; raspberry stalks put into the house on December 16, produced ripe fruit on March 1; strawberry plants put in at the same time, produced ripe fruit of excellent flavour and colour on February 14; vines which broke on December 26 produced ripe grapes of stronger flavour than usual on March 10; peas gathered on February 16 from the plant were replanted on February 18, and vegetated in a few days; bananas and melons were produced of remarkable size and aromatic flavour.

reports of more recent experiments made at the Cornell Experimental Station is given as follows :—

"The stimulus of the electric arc light promotes assimilation and hastens growth and maturity. The electric arc might be employed with profit in certain branches of the forcing industry."

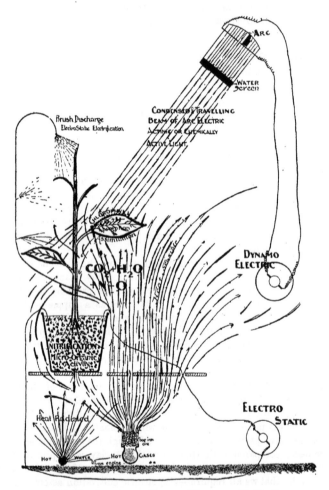

FIG. 66.—SCHEME FOR UTILISING ENERGY.   (*See text.*)

Many years' study of the problem of securing a supply of electric stimuli that would, by giving comparative independence of the sun's rays, permit us to extend the period of cultivation through the winter months if needs be, at a cost of electric energy that would, in all probability, make such cultivation a remunerative operation, has evolved the Thwaite system of May 1905 (fig. 66).

In this system, as far as possible, all the practical methods of electric stimuli are united to secure a common effect, employing the best and most economical methods of generating power.

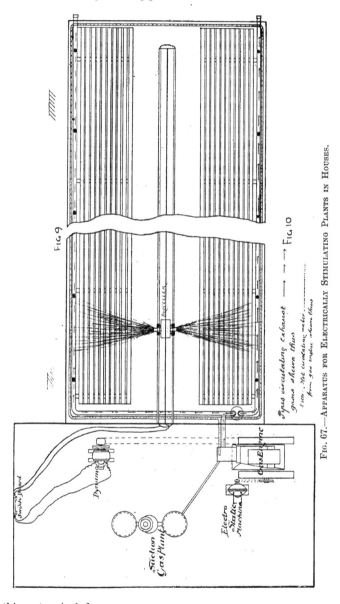

FIG. 67.—APPARATUS FOR ELECTRICALLY STIMULATING PLANTS IN HOUSES.

Briefly this system includes :—

1. The employment of a scheme of economical power production which the author first employed in a Yorkshire factory in 1897, and by which,

with the exception of the heat losses in the gas generator, every available heat source both of exhaust gases (as sensible heat) and of jacket water (as sensible heat) is utilised, securing a useful efficiency of 90 per cent.

The actual programme of the experimental machine includes not only the jacket-water service and the exhaust-gases service for heating the glass house and for adding moisture to the air, but also the air from around the gas plant. The heated air is circulated by an electric fan, which also diffuses the water vapour. The arc light travels on a special electric traveller backwards and forwards along the length of the house, so as to secure as near a resemblance as practicable to actual solar effect. The rays are reflected through a water or double-glass screen, so that the rays are subdued, the red ray effects being modified and allowing freer play for the effect of the violet or actinic rays (fig. 67).

Fig. 68.—Stimulated Plants on right; Normal on left.

A chimney is provided on the hood for removing the oxides of nitrogen that may be produced by the arc. The programme of operations includes as a second stage the *pari passu* application of the electrostatic influence overhead discharge, but intermittently into the lamps and direct to the soil.

The third stage will include the addition of carbon dioxide isolated from the exhaust gases to the extent to increase the proportion to the optimum extent or 3 per cent.

An objection that may be raised is the possibility of the entrance of carbon monoxide into the glass house. According to the interesting experiments of W. B. Bottomley, if CO displaces CO_2 in proportion to their relative solubilities in water, or with twenty times as much CO as CO_2, the plants remain healthy and normal; with a CO environment starch is formed when plants are exposed to sunlight during three days, whereas with a CO_2 gas environment no starch is formed in the three days' period.

It is, of course, too early to measure the results of the experiments during the very short periods of stimulating operation, extending over some three to four hours daily for nineteen days, excluding Saturdays and Sundays, making up sixty-three hours. What is certain is that the stimulating tendency of the system is remarkably striking, as the photograph (fig. 68) clearly shows, and it will probably have to be checked, at least for some of the plants under influence. We have proof that it satisfies to a great measure the conditions that a substitute for solar rays should possess for application during winter months. The temperature that has been maintained in the house from the thermal or heat by-products of the gas-power plant was 70° F., with only 1° of difference in any part of the house.

Of course the periods of application to secure the best results can only be determined by lengthy experience.

The supervision of the plant is well within the capacity of any intelligent labourer, and the apparatus can be safely left for three to four hours without risk.

Obviously the system can be applied throughout the twenty-four hours to *several glass houses* in succession, so that allowing three hours' period on twenty-four hours it will be possible to at least electrify eight houses, 50 feet long by 10 feet in width. It would of course be necessary to employ, as an auxiliary only, the ordinary hot-water heating arrangements in the winter months.

APPENDIX I.

LEMSTRÖM'S EXPERIMENTS.

Strawberries.		*Potatos.*	
England .	. 37·0 per cent. increase	England	. 31 per cent.
Germany	. 50·1 „ „	Germany	. 13·8 „

Watering increases the acceleration enormously.

An increase of 12·3 per cent. is recorded in growth of Carrots,

| | 40·7 | „ | „ | | „ | Oats, |
| | 19·5 | „ | | | | Rye. |

APPENDIX II.

LEMSTRÖM.

1903.

Increase per cent.

Country.	Barley.	Sugar Beets.	Potatos.	Increase per cent. of Sugar Beets.	
				Absolute.	Relative.
	Per cent.	Per cent.	Per cent.	Per cent.	Per cent.
Poland	32·5	79·7	7·6	1·0	7·2
England . . .	—	49·6	65·5	0·7	8·4
Sweden . . .	40·1	6·2	4·8	1·9	13·4

APPENDIX III.

1904. March 7 to July 26, 108 days, 9·3 hours daily=1,004 hours.

Newman's Results.—Bristol Experiments, 1904.

Cucumbers   .   .   .   .   17 per cent. increase.
Strawberries (five-years' plants)   36   ,,   ,,

Gloucester Experiments.

Beet showed 33 per cent. increase and 1·1 per cent. absolute increase per cent. of total sugar.

Carrots showed 50 per cent. increase.

THE ORIGIN AND PRESENT DISTRIBUTION OF THE BRITISH FLORA.

By Rev. Professor G. HENSLOW, M.A., V.M.H., &c.

Lecture given October 15, 1907.

IF anyone were to travel from within the Arctic Circle to the Equator he could not fail to be struck, not only with the vast differences in the appearances of the floras that would come under his observation, but also with their manifest discrepancy in point of numbers. For while in Lapland not more than 500 species of Phaenogams and 600 Cryptogams would be met with, in a tropical country, as the East Indies, there would probably be found more than 12,000 in all. Moreover, if our traveller proceeded southwards along more than one meridian, he would not invariably meet with the same plants on or about the same latitude ; for if they were separated by some great physical barrier, as an ocean or range of mountains, *representative species* would more probably be observed ; *i.e.* not merely other species of the same genera, but also plants possessing very similar aspects, and often the same habit as others of quite different families. Thus the fleshy-stemmed species of the genus *Euphorbia* of Africa *represent* the order Cactaceae of America, and the Epacrideae of Australia represent the Ericaceae of South Africa.

· Again, in ascending a snow-capped mountain in the tropics the same peculiarities would be observed : at the bottom there would be all the luxuriant vegetation of the tropics, and at the limits of vegetation the lichens, like those of Greenland and Iceland ; while the plants of the intermediate stages would be identical with, or representative of, the vegetation of the different latitudes between the Equator and the Arctic Circle.*

The inference naturally drawn from these facts would be that temperature is an important agent in regulating the distribution of plants. Now this to a considerable extent is the case, but there are so many subservient and modifying influences, such as moisture, wind, mountain chains, &c., that the same kind of vegetation is by no means necessarily confined to the same degrees of latitude. Thus, *e.g.*, the extension of tropical forms of plants into lower and cooler latitudes in South America and in Natal than in the northern hemisphere is consequent on the greater abundance of humidity in the atmosphere. Similarly in the northern and eastern hemispheres the descending of temperate plants—such as species of oak, willow, rose, &c.—on the Cassia mountains to nearly the sea coast in latitude 25° in tropical Asia is due to the same cause ; while, on the other hand, tropical forms of laurel, bamboo, &c. rise to 9,000 feet on extra-tropical Himalayan Mountains.

---

* The temperature of the atmosphere about a tropical mountain decreases one degree for every three to four hundred feet in elevation.

Although climate is the most essential element to be taken into account when the distribution of the plants of any flora is to be considered, yet as that of our own country at the present time is so well known it will be superfluous to describe it in detail.* All that will be necessary is to compare it generally, as being insular and maritime, with that of the Continent, and then to see what differences may be expected to exist between the flora of Great Britain and that of Europe.

The chief difference between all maritime or insular, and continental climates, lies in the predominance of moisture in the air of the former and in the greater degree of dryness in that of the latter. The immediate effect of watery vapour is to moderate the heat in summer by arresting its passage from the sun, and similarly to arrest its radiation at night and in winter. The consequence is that maritime and insular climates are far less subject to extremes of temperature, diurnal or annual, than are places situate away from a seaboard and many miles in the interior of a continent. Another very important agent in affecting the climate is the prevalence of aërial and ocean currents ; warm in ameliorating, cold in deteriorating it, as far as the magnitude and vitality of any flora may be concerned. This is particularly the case with the British Isles ; for were it not for the warm currents, both of air and water, sweeping past us in a north-easterly direction across the Atlantic, our climate would be very likely to be as inhospitable as is that in the same latitudes of America.

Perhaps few places could be better chosen to illustrate the above statements than Edinburgh and Moscow. Thus, while the difference between the hottest and coldest months of the year is under 30° for Edinburgh, it amounts to 60° for Moscow ; and it may be added for Nain, on the coast of Labrador, it is 50°, and for Cape Churchill, on the west coast of Hudson's Bay, the difference is even 80°. All the above places are very nearly on the same parallel of latitude. Again, if we take winter and summer temperatures, we find that for July the mean at London is over 62° ; at Berlin, 66° ; at St. Petersburg, 64° ; and at Astrakhan, 77°. While for January at London it is 37° ; at Berlin, 28° ; at St. Petersburg, 16° ; and at Astrakhan it is 13°. Similarly in Cumberland (North America), in the latitude of Edinburgh, the winter temperature is −13°, the summer temperature being + 62°.

If we consider the temperatures of places in the west of Europe, we soon see how important is the influence of warm aërial currents in regulating and ameliorating them ; thus, at Hammerfest (lat. 71°), in Norway, the mean winter temperature is 22°, while in the same latitude in Greenland it is 5° below zero. Again, the temperature at

Caithness	58° N.L. is	36° in January
Labrador	„ „	−4 „
Lisbon	39 „	47 „
Chesapeake Bay	„ „	−36 „

---

* The word *climate* must be taken to represent the aggregate environment of plants included under 1. Latitude ; 2. Elevation above the sea ; 3. Maritime or insular or continental position ; 4. Inclination of land ; 5. Mountainous country or otherwise ; 6. Character of soil ; 7. Condition of soil, wet or dry, &c. ; 8. Degree of cultivation ; 9. Prevalent winds ; 10. Rainfall ; 11. Mean summer and mean winter temperatures, &c.

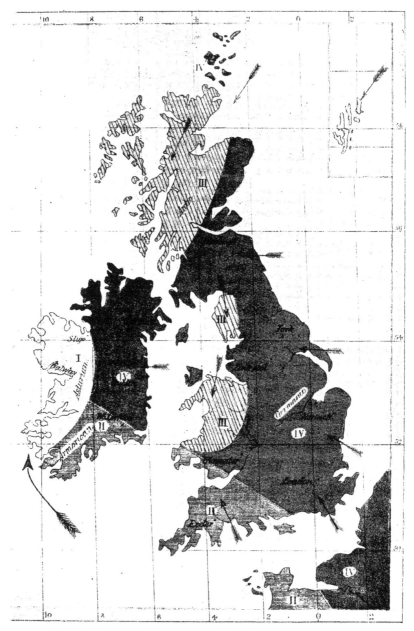

FIG. 69.—PROFESSOR EDWARD FORBES' DISTRIBUTION OF FLOWERING PLANTS IN THE BRITISH ISLES.

(From *Popular Science Review*, vol. iv. p. 28.)

And the temperature at

Edinburgh	56° N.L. is	37°	in January
Bergen (Norway)	60 ,,	32	,,
Yakutsk	62 ,, ·	−36	,,

In the latter group of places we see the great contrast between the temperature of an inland site, such as Yakutsk, and that of the maritime coast of the west of Europe, which is swept by warm currents.

Now, the most obvious effect that such differences of temperature have on plants is that a continental climate is favourable to annuals and a maritime to perennials; for in places where a summer temperature rises high, plants whose whole life-history is comprised in a few months, or even weeks, may easily, therefore, survive; while the intensely cold winters of the same place would annihilate many perennials that would flourish in a less rigorous climate. Hence evergreen shrubs of South Europe, such as the laurustinus and bay laurel, will survive our winters, which are rarely excessive; yet the climate in summer and autumn is quite insufficient in its degree of heat to ripen efficiently the grape or Indian corn; for the summers are as equally tempered as the winters.

The British flora, as might, therefore, be expected, contains a large number of perennials, especially herbaceous ones. Many annuals, being weeds of cultivation only, would be probably more or less exterminated if our arable land should cease to be cultivated.

There are no forms peculiar to Great Britain whatever; with the exception of *Eriocaulon septangulare* every plant may be found on the Continent, or introduced and naturalised.

Although our British plants are almost all European, yet they are not equally or at all uniformly distributed over our territory. They have, consequently, been divided into sub-floras, or *florulae*, each being more or less restricted in area. We are indebted mainly to the labours of the late Professor Edward Forbes and Mr. H. C. Watson for tracing out these districts. The following is a comparative table of the respective results of these eminent botanists, with their nomenclatures :—

WATSON'S.	FORBES'.
1. British corresponds with	
2. English ,,	Germanic. IV.
3. Scottish	
4. Highland ,,	Alpine. III.
5. Germanic (in part) ,,	Kentish. IV.
6. Atlantic ,,	Asturian. I. / Armorican. II.
7. Local or doubtful.	

That entitled *Germanic* by Forbes is so called because it is identical with the German flora, though the latter contains many plants wanting in England. This is subdivided by Watson into (1) the *British*, which includes plants found in all his eighteen "provinces"; (2) the *English*, which includes plants found chiefly in England and not in Scotland; and (3) the *Scottish*, embracing plants found chiefly in Scotland and the north of England only. The *Alpine* of Forbes or the *Highland* of Watson includes a group of arctic plants. The nearest localities where plants of this group are to be found are the Alps, Pyrenees, Scandinavian mountains, and arctic regions generally; though they are mostly or entirely absent from the warmer lowlands which separate such widely ‧ severed districts. Watson's *Germanic* takes in plants found in the east and south-east of England bordering the German Ocean, whence he derives the name, and includes those plants called *Kentish* by Forbes, but which do not seem to be deserving of a special name, as they are chiefly, if nòt always, plants affecting a limestone or chalky soil, and which, in part, occur elsewhere. The *Atlantic* types of Watson embrace plants found in the west and south-west of England and in Ireland. In these are included the *Armorican* of Forbes, which is characterised by a group of plants found in Normandy, the Channel Islands, the south-west of England, extending (in part) some distance along the west and south coasts, ˙and in the south-east of Ireland. This group is in reality South European, reaching Normandy by crossing north of the Pyrenees. The number of peculiar species continually decreases in passing in a north-westerly direction from their original home in South Europe; so that while several which are in the Channel Islands are wanting in the south-west of England, others which reach that corner fail to cross over to Ireland.* A portion of this Atlantic type was separated by Forbes as *Asturian*, because the nearest locality on the Continent whence it was presumed by him that these plants had come was the Asturian mountains of North Spain. They consist of six species of saxifrage: *Saxifraga umbrosa* (cultivated as 'London Pride'), *S. elegans*, *S. hirsuta*, *S. Geum*, *S. hirta*, *S. affinis*; two heaths: *Erica Mackaiana*, *E. mediterranea ; Menziesia polifolia ; Arbutus Unedo* (the " strawberry tree "); and *Arabis ciliata*.†

---

* *Helianthemum polifolium, Tamarix gallica, Polycarpon tetraphyllum, Corrigiola littoralis*, and *Bupleurum aristatum* occur in Devonshire and Cornwall, but do not extend into Ireland. The following are some which are to be found in the Channel Islands, but not in England or Ireland :—*Ranunculus ophioglossifolius, Sinapis incana, Helianthemum guttatum, Silene quinquevulnera, Centaurea aspera, Gnaphalium luteo-album, Cicendia pusilla, Linaria Pelisseriana, Echium plantagineum, Armeria plantaginea, Orchis laxiflora, Scirpus pungens, Lagurus ovatus, Cynosurus cristatus, Bromus maximus, Gymnogramme leptophylla, Ophioglossum lusitanicum.*

† Subjoined are a few selected plants in order to illustrate the sub-floras of Watson:—

1. British type. *Betula alba, Corylus Avellana, Salix ˙Caprea, Rosa canina, Hedera Helix, Calluna vulgaris, Ranunculus acris, Trifolium repens, Lotus corniculatus, Bellis perennis, Myosurus minimus, Urtica dioica, Lemna minor, Poa annua. Pteris aquilina, Polygonum aviculare.*

2. English type. *Rhamnus catharticus, Ulex nana, Tamus communis, Bryonia dioica, Hottonia palustris, Chlora perfoliata, Sison Amomum, Linaria Elatine, Ranunculus parviflorus, Lamium Galeobdolon, Hordeum pratense, Ceterach officinarum.*

3. Scottish type. *Empetrum nigrum, Rubus saxatilis, Trollius europaeus, Geranium sylvaticum, Habenaria albida, Ligusticum scoticum, Lithospermum maritimum.*

4. Highland type. *Azalea procumbens, Cherleria sedoides,⸮Veronica alpina, Alopecurus alpinus, Phleum alpinum, Juncus trifidus, Sibbaldia procumbens, Erigeron alpinum, Gentiana nivalis, Salix herbacea, Silene acaulis, Saxifraga stellaris, Oxyria reniformis, Thalictrum alpinum, Rubus Chamaemorus, Epilobium alsinifolium, Dryas octopetala, Alchemilla alpina.*

5. Germanic type. *Frankenia laevis, Anemone Pulsatilla, Reseda lutea. Silene*

If, however, we now leave Europe, and endeavour to find any British plants elsewhere, we shall discover small groups appearing here and there in many parts of the world. The following numbers will indicate how many British plants have been hitherto found in the several localities, and will also illustrate the fact that the plants of Britain, like his Majesty's dominions and subjects, are world-wide in their dispersion. Travelling eastwards from the Ural Mountains, Siberia contains about 750 British plants, and within the area included between the river Obi and Bering Strait, and bounded southwards by the Arctic Circle (lat. 66½°), there are 111. Kamchatka contains 140. In North-east Asia, including the area from Bering Strait to South Japan, there are 325, of which Japan has 156 British species.

Next, regarding the extension of our plants eastwards along the southern line of mountains, Hooker and Thomson give a list of 222 British plants which reach India.* These appear to have travelled eastwards from Europe, finding means of transit along the Taurus, Caucasus, and western hilly or mountainous regions ; and the above authors remark that "the keystone to the whole system of distribution in Western Asia does not rest so much upon a number of 'representative' species as upon the fact that not only are a large proportion of annual and herbaceous species of each common to Western India and Europe, but of shrubs and trees also. Those of North Europe inhabit the loftier levels of the Himalayas, where they blend with the Siberian types." † It may be added that European types disappear eastwards gradually at first, but rapidly after reaching Kumaon. Few species enter Nepal, and still fewer reach Sikkim. Of the plants which cross the Indian mountains and appear in tropical Asia (i.e. India south of the Himalayas, the Khasia Mountains of Eastern Bengal, together with the mountains of both peninsulas of India, Ceylon, and Java), the number, as might be expected, is much reduced, only twenty-three species being found there.

The next distributions to be considered are along the three greatest lines of extension of land into the southern hemisphere—namely, first, from India, through the East India islands to Australia, Tasmania, New Zealand, and the islands to the south ; secondly, from Europe, through Africa and the islands near the coast to the Cape ; thirdly, from Greenland and arctic America to Cape Horn ; lastly, the isolated spots in Polynesia, which can boast of a few representatives of the British flora.

I. Of the first of these extensions South Australia contains 100 indigenous plants common to Great Britain, in addition to which a large number have become naturalised ; Tasmania contains 56, New Zealand has

---

noctiflora, Silene conica, Pimpinella magna, Pulicaria vulgaris, Atriplex pedunculata, Aceras anthropophora, Ophrys aranifera, Spartina stricta.

6. Atlantic type. Brassica monensis, Matthiola sinuata, Raphanus maritimus, Sedum anglicum, Cotyledon umbilicus, Bartsia viscosa, Euphorbia Peplis, E. portlandica, Sibthorpia europaea, Erica vagans, E. ciliaris, Polycarpon tetraphyllum, Adiantum Capillus-Veneris, Cynodon Dactylon.

* Flora Indica, p. 109 (1855).

† The following British trees and shrubs occur in India :—Berberis vulgaris, Prunus Padus, P. Avium, Rubus fruticosus, R. saxatilis, Crataegus Oxyacantha, Cotoneaster vulgaris, Pyrus Aria, Ribes Grossularia, R. nigrum, Hedera Helix, Buxus sempervirens, Ulmus campestris, Salix purpurea, S. alba, Taxus baccata, and Juniperus communis.

92, and Kerguelen's Land, 8; while Auckland and Campbell Islands possess 6. A curious fact worth notice is that in South-eastern Australia European species form $\frac{1}{27}$th nearly of the whole flora; but in South-western Australia they constitute $\frac{1}{100}$th only; while in Tasmania they amount to $\frac{1}{15}$th. In Tasmania the following British plants occur, which are not found in Australia:—*Ranunculus aquatilis, Montia fontana, Hierochloë borealis.* On the other hand, the Victoria Alps of Australia contain fifteen European species not found in Tasmania, and all but one are British plants.

II. With regard to the extension of British plants from Europe to the Cape, commencing with Morocco we find 344 present there, while in northern Africa generally, which is largely "Mediterranean" in character, there are 420 British plants. North-east Africa and Abyssinia appear to yield about 90 British species. On the west coast of Africa the little island of Fernando Po in the Gulf of Guinea was found to contain, on "Clarence Peak," at above 5,000 feet elevation, 76 species of plants, of which number 56 species of 45 genera belong to a temperate flora. Their affinity is curiously much more with the plants of Abyssinia and of the Mauritius than with those of the adjacent west coast of Africa. Of the temperate flora a large proportion are European, and the following seven are British:—*Oxalis corniculata, Sanicula europaea, Galium Aparine, Limosella aquatica, Luzula campestris, Aira caespitosa, Brachypodium sylvaticum.* Of the South African flora, including the portion of land from the Tropic of Capricorn to the Cape, 27 species are British.

Here, as elsewhere in our colonies, weeds of cultivation are continually being introduced.

III. In the third great extension of land, Greenland contains 210 (Iceland has 335), while British plants abound in arctic British America, as in Siberia, even Parry's Island (76° north latitude) containing 32. The number decreases as the warmer regions are reached; thus Mr. Drummond* records only 40 British plants in the Western States. In tropical America (including the temperate and alpine regions of the Cordillera from Mexico to Peru) there are 35 British plants, of which the following eight are common with tropical Asia:—*Cardamine hirsuta, Stellaria nemorum, S. media, Ceratophyllum demersum, Polygonum Persicaria, Juncus bufonius, Scirpus lacustris, Phragmites communis.* In extra-tropical South America, however, there are no less than 64 British species, while in Fuegia and the Falkland Islands there are 24. Of the British plants common to these three greatest extensions of land there are common to Australia, &c., and Africa 17; common to Australia and South America, 35; common to South Africa and South America, 19; common to all three extensions, 15. Lastly there have been found a few British plants in islands of the Pacific Ocean. Thus, the Society Islands contain 3; the Sandwich, 5; and Fiji, 16 species.

If now we attempt to find an explanation of the fact of so many plants thoroughly establishing themselves in foreign countries, there are two features which strike us as worthy of observance. One peculiarity is that plants do not always flourish best where nature has, so to say, made their home, but in consequence of the struggle for existence they hold

* Hooker' *Journal of Botany,* vol. i. p. 185.

their position as long as they can manage to do so; so that the flora of any locality under normal and existing circumstances has, so to say, long ago arrived at a condition of equilibrium of mutual adjustment. If, however, plants be suddenly transported to other countries, they sometimes at once assume astonishing vigour, and for a long time at least gain great ascendancy over the native vegetable population. This is conspicuously so in New Zealand, where an English watercress (*Nasturtium amphibium*) grows to twelve feet in length, and three-quarters of an inch in thickness; while a single plant of P*olygonum aviculare* will cover several square feet, and the little Dutch clover is driving the huge P*hormium tenax*, or "New Zealand flax," before it! The number of British plants has for years been steadily increasing in New Zealand. Similarly does the Canadian *Elodea canadensis* flourish in England, though we possess the female plant only. It would seem, therefore, that the change of climate has somehow introduced new and invigorating elements into their constitution, which the native flora cannot acquire, having been so long adapted to it. This appears to be one cause of introduced plants so readily establishing themselves. Another is that the sporadic plants, being generally inconspicuous annuals and *wind-* or *self-fertilising*, are independent of insects; so that they survive in the struggle for existence over their more showy brethren, which cannot propagate fully by seed unless habitually visited.

In a paper on the "Self-fertilisation of Plants" [*] I have shown how this was the case as deduced from statistics, and so will not repeat the evidence now, but would just illustrate it by mentioning a few of the most widely dispersed of our British plants. Thus, *e.g.*, the bitter-cress (*Cardamine hirsuta*) is found in north-east Asia, tropical Asia, Hong Kong, Kamchatka, Chili, South Australia, Auckland, and Campbell's Islands, Falkland and Fuegia, Tasmania, South Africa, New Zealand, Madeira, &c. Similarly is *Cerastium vulgatum* dispersed over the same area. *Solanum nigrum* is also found in California, South Australia, Tasmania, New Zealand, Society Islands, Andaman Isles, North China, Japan, Galapagos Islands, &c.

Having now considered the present distribution of the British flora, we have to account for it as far as possible; and here theory must supplement facts. In looking back to discover an historical or rather geological origin of our present flora, we soon find that there have been very remarkable changes in the characters of successive floras that peopled our country. Going no further back than the Eocene period—for attempts at deductions as to climatal conditions become more and more uncertain in proportion as the faunas and floras are more remote in time from and unlike their living representatives—we find tolerably certain evidence that the climate of England at that time was tropical, at least so far as palms, *Mimosae, Nipadites,* on the one hand, and turtles, crocodiles, and large water-snakes on the other, justify us in drawing such a conclusion. This period, then, could not have seen the origin of our present temperate and arctic floras. The next epoch, the Miocene, likewise fails to furnish any members of it. The flora of this period was sub-tropical, but probably became less and less so as the next—the

* *Trans. Lin. Soc.* 1877.

Pliocene epoch—drew near. The Miocene flora is remarkable for its great extent. Not only are remains of plants to be found in England, as at Bovey Tracey in Devonshire, but at many places on the Continent ; and, what is still more remarkable, it is found to have extended all over the Arctic regions—as at Disco Island, Greenland, arctic North America, &c. In all these places such plants as vines, custard apples, figs, cinnamons, *Nelumbium* (the lotus of the East), water-lilies, and the ubiquitous "*Wellingtonia*" * are to be found. This shows, therefore, that there must have been a very different state of things in the northern hemisphere then from what obtains now. The preceding flora had its day, flourished, and then passed away for ever. A colder period drew on. This is signalised in our country by the celebrated Cromer Forest, and the peat or lignite beds on the north coast of Norfolk.† These are overlaid by a steep cliff of "glacial deposits." The flora of these beds is identical with the existing one ; that is to say, the Scotch fir, accompanied by the Norway spruce (now extinct, but reintroduced), both our water-lilies, the buck-bean, alder, &c., then flourished, but with the strange companions of *Elephas meridionalis*, many *Cervi*, the *Rhinoceros*, the great *Bos primigenius*, the Irish elk, and other extinct animals.

The reduction of temperature (for the forest beds indicate as temperate a climate as our own), seen by comparing it with that of the preceding Miocene period, was the antecedent condition to an arctic or glacial state of things shortly to follow, or "the Great Ice Age." The evidence of this, as derived from plants, is seen in the presence of an arctic willow, *Salix polaris*, found in a deposit overlying the sub-tropical Miocene beds at Bovey Tracey.

Now as England is at present temperate, and an arctic flora reigns over high latitudes simultaneously with it, so does it seem probable that such was the state of things, if not before, at least soon after the close of the Glacial epoch ; that when the Cromer Forest flourished, an arctic flora prevailed simultaneous with it in high latitudes. As, however, the ice continued to increase southwards, and the land in all latitudes was encroached upon and rendered unfit for such plants to inhabit, they were driven southwards down every meridian, from the arctic regions. The long line of mountains in America, forming an unbroken bridge of trans-port, enabled many to cross the tropics, and so reach the extra-tropical regions of South America. Mr. Belt discovered signs of "glaciation" in Nicaragua down to 2,000 feet above the sea, apparently showing that

---

* This genus is better known to botanists as *Sequoia*, and the species *S. Couttsiae* is found at Bovey Tracey ; two species only now exist, *S. sempervirens* (red-wood) and *S. gigantea*, both confined to California.

† Whether the temperate period indicated by these plant-beds preceded the " Glacial " epoch, or whether they represent interglacial milder periods, is perhaps at present undecided by geologists. Mr. Clement Reid, F.G.S., has drawn up a list of plants from the Cromer bed, as well as some obtained after storms at Happisburgh, and from Pakefield (*Trans. of the Norfolk and Norwich Naturalists' Society*, vol. iv. p. 189). He enumerates fifty-six determined species besides Charas and mosses. There are twenty terrestrial and fifteen aquatic dicotyledons, including one extinct, *Trapa natans* and two foreign species of *Medicago*. There are seventeen monocotyledons, all being aquatic ; of gymnosperms, besides our Scotch fir and yew, there are the Norway spruce, *Abies excelsa*, and a variety, *A. pectinata*, no longer indigenous ; *Osmunda regalis, Isoëtes lacustris*, and species of *Equisetum* are the only higher cryptogams.

there was a "cooling" going on at least locally in the tropical regions, which would seem to dispose of the difficulty of arctic plants crossing the torrid zone. Similarly in the eastern hemisphere, assuming the land to have been continuous—and there are solid reasons for believing it to have been so—the arctic flora would have been able to find a passage from the Himalayas, through eastern China and the Celebes, to Australia, New Zealand, and Tasmania.

Another suggestion is that the Australian forms came from South America to New Zealand, then Tasmania, and finally Australia; for the New Zealand flora is strangely like that of South America and South Africa in some respects, and it has been shown above that Tasmania has more British types than Australia.[*]

Thus is it supposed that the arctic flora has been driven over all the world, and on the close of the Glacial epoch the plants situated on what are now tropical plains perished, or else retired up the mountains where we now find them, as on Clarence Peak in the island of Fernando Po; while in the northern hemisphere many retreated back again into arctic regions, perhaps accompanied by other plants of the countries they had previously invaded.

With reference to our own islands, there is reason to believe that the Atlantic type of Watson, or the groups including the *Asturian* and *Norman* or *Armorican* of Forbes, are very ancient. This is inferred, first, from their fragmentary character; secondly, from their isolation; and thirdly, from the fact that boulders have been found stranded on the south coast of England, implying that these islands were severed from the Continent, at least on the west and south-west, during the Glacial epoch, and that, therefore, these plants owe their origin to a much earlier connection with the Continent; for, as already remarked, the nearest continental site of the Asturian plants is to be found in Spain; while the Armorican doubtless came from Normandy, both being, as stated, really groups from South Europe or the Mediterranean regions. With regard to the Arctic and common English and Scottish types, many of which are to be found in the Arctic regions, they appear to have travelled from the north, or from the Scandinavian regions across the plain of the German Ocean; [†] but on the subsequent depression of the land below the sea, and with the elevation of temperature to its present state, the more arctic types would be confined to the tops of our mountains, while the rest would people the plains, and the floras would thus be gradually established in our islands in the conditions in which we now find them.

---

[*] A broad belt, only 2,000 fathoms below the sea, surrounds the Antarctic regions, sending northward extensions to Australia, the Cape, South America, and New Zealand.

[†] There appear to have been four well-marked periods at least in the Glacial epoch : (1) a period of elevation at the time of Cromer Forest ; (2) one of great depression, so that Great Britain became an archipelago ; then (3) a re-elevation, when the German Ocean was land ; and finally, a last depression to its present condition.

THE COMMONER BIRDS OF OUR GARDENS: THEIR HABITS AND FOODS.

By CECIL H. HOOPER, M.R.A.C., of the South Eastern Agricultural College, Wye.

Lecture given October 28, 1907.

I PROPOSE to give a brief description of the more striking characteristics from a natural history point of view of the birds most commonly met with, and to endeavour, together with a deep love of birds, to consider in fairness their economic aspect as regards the garden. I do not pretend that all the information is original, or even most of it. I have studied many books to obtain information, including the excellent works of W. Yarrell, Professor A. Newton, Granville Sharpe, Howard Saunders and John Gould; also the Catalogue of English Birds in the Natural History Museum at South Kensington, prepared by W. R. Ogilvie-Grant, from all of which I have in different parts quoted. I have consulted many gardeners and farmers; I have endeavoured during most of my life to observe our native birds, and more recently to verify what I have read about them. I have constructed several tables with the assistance of Mr. F. V. Theobald to show the relation of birds to insect and other pests: these appear towards the end of the Paper.

Some may think I do not give due credit to the birds for the good they do; while others may consider I do not sufficiently emphasise in some cases the injury done.

At the end of my Paper I mention a few methods of modifying harm done by birds.

I have endeavoured to arrange the birds in order of the relative numbers of them that we see, and have consulted several of my friends to get their opinions.

HOUSE SPARROW: *Passer domesticus.*

Starting with the ubiquitous house sparrow, I take its good points first. It eats and feeds its young with a certain number of caterpillars, including those of the cabbage butterfly, some aphides on beans, roses, and plums, and some weed seeds, including those of chickweed; but its food consists mainly of grain, on which its young are fed at a very early age, taking heavy toll from the farmer and poultry keeper. To the fruit grower the sparrow's chief sin is the terrible quantity of buds of gooseberries, red-currants, and plums it destroys during winter time. The hop grower finds it eats his best insect friend, the larva of the lady-bird; and the gardener is disheartened by the destruction of seed and seedlings of turnip, cabbage, spinach, lettuce, &c., and the damage it does to crocuses and some other flowers.

Philip Sparrow rears a large family—two or three batches of five or six eggs, laid in a hastily made untidy nest of hay and feathers.

Sparrows frequently save themselves the trouble of nest building by taking the nest of the house martin. This theft is occasionally revenged by the martin claying up the hole to the nest and making the sparrow a prisoner. The sparrow is a wonderful bird in that it seems to be able to live wherever man can. It can stand the North American cold and the Australian heat. Miss E. A. Ormerod mentions the sparrow as driving away martins and swallows. Mr. F. V. Theobald says he has examined the food in fifty sparrows, of which forty-two had grain in their crops, two no result, six grain and larvæ of winter moth and some aphides.

Starling : Sturnus vulgaris.

This bird, which we so frequently see on the lawns in the early morning and on the house-tops and chimneys later in the day, is seen in huge flocks at some seasons of the year, their evolutions in the air being very wonderful. These birds move from one place to another dependent on the supply of food, and are generally increasing in numbers in England and Scotland, greatly to the detriment of fruit-growers. It very frequently makes its nest on or near houses, and has two broods each of from four to seven young.

It has an unfortunate habit of making its nest in the hole which the woodpecker has made with great pains, and so decreases the numbers of that useful and interesting bird.

In hard weather the starlings are said to migrate to Cornwall and Wales and the Western Counties and other parts of the country where the frosts are not so intense. In the forests of Belgium and Germany, owing to the large number of grubs eaten by this bird, and on which the young are fed, artificial nesting places are made for them. They are valuable on grass land and in forests, but steal most kinds of fruit, being very fond of cherries, and in Essex are very severe on raspberries.

Starlings are frequently seen on sheep eating the " ticks," and around cattle, apparently eating insects disturbed by their feet. Starlings frequently accompany rooks, and attack newly sown corn and seedlings. The Board of Agriculture leaflet gives the following as the food of the starling :—Worms, snails, chafer larvæ, beetles, wireworms, surface-caterpillars, larvæ of Daddy Longlegs, together with pupæ and eggs ; and summarises its habits as chiefly useful to agriculture and garden, but a most serious pest to fruit. Miss Ormerod mentions it as eating the larvæ of the Diamond-back moth (Plutella cruciferarum), Silver Y moth (Plusia gamma), and the garden chafer (Phyllopertha horticola).

Robin : Erithacus rubecula.

This companionable little bird that comes and settles beside one when one digs, devours vast quantities of earthworms and searches among dead leaves under trees and bushes for insects. Yarrell says that they show great attachment for each other, and pair for life ; but they are also the most pugnacious among birds, and maintain their right to a certain limited domain against all intruders ; they are generally distributed over the British Isles.

These birds are largely eaten on the Continent, especially in Rome. The colour of the female is not so bright as that of the male.

The eggs are from five to seven in number, and as many as two or three broods are reared in the year. The old birds drive off the young when able to take care of themselves.

No farmer and few gardeners will say much against this lovable bird, but it is due to record that although its food chiefly consists of worms, insects (including the larvæ of the Swift moth), ground grubs, wood-lice and even earwigs, yet red and white currants suffer from its attacks ; it takes cherries, it damages hot-house grapes, taking one peck at each berry, and so does considerable harm in a very short time. It will sometimes go up a strawberry row and peck at each fruit as it passes along, not like a blackbird or thrush, but just sufficiently to make a very fine specimen of ' Royal Sovereign ' worthless for market purposes.

The robin is an indefatigable singer, and is said to be silent only from about July 17 to August 6 ; it will even sing during rain.

BLACKBIRD : *Turdus merula.*

This sweet singer is a shy bird, generally seen singly or in pairs, very seldom in flocks. It is considered the "prince of fruit thieves," eating green and ripe strawberries, red currants, gooseberries, raspberries, soft, coloured, and best apples, cherries, plums, tomatos, mulberries, figs, loganberries, and more rarely black currants ; it also pecks holes in late pears. The male has a jet-black coat and orange bill ; the female is of a sooty colour and dusky brown bill. In taking fruit from bushes this bird keeps near the ground, and if disturbed gets up with a loud chattering cry of alarm. Yarrell says that in winter it feeds on grain and seed, and in spring and early summer on the larvæ of insects, worms, molluscs ; and as the season advances it exhibits great fondness for fruit. It frequents woods, plantations, and hedges.

He speaks of its song as being powerful rather than with quality of tone, compass, or variety. It is chiefly heard in the early morning or late evening, and never better than during a warm April shower.

From four to six eggs are laid very early in the year. Several broods are raised in a season. Yarrell mentions that the young of the first brood sometimes assist their parents in feeding the young of the second ; Mr. Blyth in 1838 knew a pair raise four broods, in all seventeen birds, in one season ; and Dr. Gordon recorded twenty-five eggs with fourteen birds reared.

The blackbird is a resident species, commonly distributed throughout the British Islands, and though some of our native birds migrate southward in the autumn, their place is taken by numbers of visitors from the Continent. Large numbers arrive on the Northumberland coast and go in a south-westerly direction, a large number of them staying with us during the whole winter. This bird appears to be plentiful at times all over Europe.

It is generally considered that the Wild Birds' Protection Act has had the effect of increasing the blackbird during the last few years. Miss Ormerod mentions it as eating caterpillars of the large white cabbage butterfly (*Pieris brassicae*).

Mr. F. V. Theobald tells me that of twelve blackbirds recently examined, the contents of the stomachs showed vegetable pulp, seeds of raspberries, strawberries, also cabbages, yew, and insects.

CHAFFINCH : *Fringilla coelebs.*

This sprightly and handsome bird is generally distributed throughout the cultivated and wooded portions of the British Islands.

The nest is particularly beautifully constructed, and is said to be made by the female, the male bringing the material.

The eggs are from four to six, and there are two broods. Large numbers of chaffinches arrive in autumn on the East Coast, coming apparently from Norway and Sweden.

The chaffinch associates with the sparrow and greenfinch in the stubbles and farmyard, feeding on corn and other seeds.

In the gardens and the forest nursery it is often very tiresome in picking up seeds and seedlings, and needs to be scared by shot from a long distance ; the seeds of peas may be protected by cotton or other means. In company with the sparrow it eats the buds of gooseberries red currants, and plums. To the credit of the chaffinch it is due to say it eats many caterpillars.

GREENFINCH OR GREEN LINNET : *Ligurinus chloris.*

This sturdily built bird with its strong bill is common everywhere ; it is somewhat shy in summer ; in autumn and winter they travel in large flocks, and are frequently seen with sparrows and chaffinches in fields and farmyards.

Their food consists of seeds, including wild mustard, pink persicaria, grain, and insects, feeding their young largely on caterpillars.

In habits they are very similar to chaffinches except that they themselves eat very few insects, and are if anything more destructive to garden seeds and sprouting crops : they are great weed-seed eaters, but they distribute them as well. They attack plum, pear, and gooseberry buds, and are a terrible pest among hops, picking the cones to pieces for seeds ; they eat turnip, cabbage, and radish seeds, also ripe corn. A Sittingbourne grower wrote me that they eat the seeds off strawberries when ripe.

ROOK : *Corvus frugilegus.*

This bird does not often enter small gardens, but in large gardens and on farms attacks both the newly planted potatos and those that are maturing. On a farm they often do serious damage to newly planted corn, beans, peas, and to the seedlings of the same, and it is absolutely necessary to scare them with the rifle or gun.

On grass land and on newly ploughed land they do valuable service in eating wireworms, leather-jackets, cockchafer, and other grubs and cater-pillars, but in most districts they are too numerous, and they ought to be thinned at nesting time. Careful observations of the food of the rook have been made throughout the year in different parts of Scotland and published in the *Journal of the Highland Agricultural Society* and in a pamphlet entitled "The Rook as an Enemy to Sport and Agriculture."

Small areas of crops as of maize may be protected by strings placed zigzag two or three feet above the ground, the rook being afraid of being entrapped ; but this is rather expensive.

Rooks live in flocks, build their nests in the highest trees, often in elms, preferably in the vicinity of buildings. From three to six eggs are laid. Yarrell observes that early in the morning rooks visit meadows while the grass is yet wet with dew to feed on worms and slugs ; later in the day they search the new-ploughed land for insects exposed, or again visit the pastures for other purposes. Rooks frequently associate with starlings and with gulls.

Miss Ormerod mentions the rook eating surface caterpillars, including *Plusia gamma* (Silver Y moth), *Agrotis exclamationis* (Heart and dart moth), *Agrotis segetum* (Turnip moth) ; also the May bug (*Melolontha vulgaris*).

The Hungarian Central Office of Ornithology in 1905 printed a pamphlet entitled " The Economical Importance of the Rook." It commenced work by sending out query sheets to which a thousand replies were received. It next dealt with the analysis of stomach contents, in order to endeavour to obtain the complete biography of the rook from month to month, so as to arrive at its agricultural significance. For this purpose it examined 470 stomach contents and several thousand castings from several hundred stations in Hungary. The principal points for observation being : " What is its behaviour towards cereals and corn at the time of sowing and maturity ? Is this damage balanced by the destruction of obnoxious insects ? What part does the rook play in stock-raising ? Ought we to protect our smaller birds against its depredations ? Can one prevent him doing damage ? "

It was found that the rook fed in the first place on insects and mice, but that from spring to autumn, and on cold, wet days of the warmer season he eats vegetable food as well.

At sowing and harvest time, unless the cornfields are guarded, it causes every year and everywhere great damage. It, however, particularly in the fall and early spring, consumes many insects (*Gryllotalpa, Cleonus, Otiorhynchus*), just at a period when the large majority of our insectivorous birds are in their winter quarters. To its young it brings enormous quantities of insects and larvæ (including *Melolontha* and its larvæ), of the caterpillar of the common dart—*Agrotis*—of *Curculionidae, Dorcadion*, and *Gryllus*. It pulls up cereals and corn sprouts when attacked by wireworm (*Elateridae*) and white grubs (*Chafers*). At the time of pests of mice, three and even five mice, with an average of two, have been found in every rook's stomach.

Game-raising in Hungary is said to be in no way compromised by the rook ; herein he differs from the carrion-crow (*Corvus corone*) and the hooded crow (*Corvus cornix*). He never attacks young hares, and never destroys birds' eggs.* It has been proved by experience that small game and singing birds multiply undisturbedly even in the neighbourhood of strong colonies.

---

* In England and Scotland they are found to interfere with young poultry and pheasants, and with eggs.

His beneficial work can in no way be compensated, because the preponderating part of the diet of the rook consists of noxious insect larvæ, living under the surface of the soil, against which human power is of hardly any avail.

Concerning the optimal number of rooks, a positive answer cannot yet be given, but in some districts of Hungary it is evident it becomes noxious through excessive increase.

Song Thrush: *Turdus musicus.*

This pleasant singer is a common resident throughout the British Isles. Yarrell says that a considerable number of our native birds migrate in the autumn, their place being taken by visitors from the Continent. I am told in the north of England there are fewer thrushes in winter than in summer, but that they are more numerous in winter in the south.

On the lawn it is characteristic of this bird to run a few steps and halt. It feeds largely on worms and grubs in the grass, and may be often seen with a snail in its mouth, beating the shell against a stone to break it, and so get at the contents. It chooses a special stone to which it brings its victims.

From a gardener's point of view it is the third worst fruit thief, though useful in winter. It destroys large quantities of strawberries, cherries, red currants, and raspberries, but does not, like the blackbird, peck apples and plums on the trees ; the damage is worst in dry weather, when its natural food, consisting of worms, snails, grubs, and slugs, is hard to get. One grower mentions it eating raspberry weevils.

Yarrell says on the Continent this bird feeds largely on grapes in the autumn, and at this time of the year it is found excellent for the table.

Apparently a large proportion of the thrushes migrate before winter.

Its mud-lined nest is very familiar, and the male bird shares in incubating the eggs, which are from four to six in number, and laid early in the season. Two or three broods are reared in a season. The eggs take about thirteen days to hatch.

Miss Ormerod mentions it eating caterpillars of the large white cabbage butterfly (*Pieris brassicae*).

Skylark: *Alauda arvensis.*

The lark is characterised by a very long hind toe which leaves its mark on the earth or mud where it treads. When ascending into the air it rises on a quivering wing. Yarrell says of the lark that its song varies whether ascending, stationary, or descending ; it ceases song as it approaches the ground, and alights with a headlong dart.

It sings at least eight months of the year; in summer the cock begins to sing about two hours before sunrise and continues at intervals till after sunset. Yarrell says its food consists of various seeds, including corn, sometimes a few berries, with many insects and worms. It pairs early in the year, in the southern counties at least ; several broods are produced, three to five eggs, which take fifteen days to hatch, being laid each time. The first brood is hatched about the middle of May. The parents are strongly attached to their young. It nests on the ground, and has a peculiar habit of making two or more hollows before one is found to its liking. Miss Ormerod mentions the lark as probably eating wireworms.

This bird seldom comes into gardens,* but is common in market gardens and on arable land generally, where it is destructive to the seedlings of late-sown wheat, to peas when coming up, to vetches in hard winters, and sometimes strips autumn-planted cabbage and Brussels sprouts. It is a nuisance to early field strawberries, which it pecks, and is hard to scare. The question from a market gardener's standpoint is, Does the good it does in eleven months of the year balance the harm it does in one ?

It seems hard to have to speak so plainly of a bird, otherwise such a general favourite both in the open country and as a cage bird in the less-favoured dingy courts of towns, where it still sings lustily and appears happy, sometimes living for nineteen or twenty years in captivity.

It lives in pairs in spring and summer, but is gregarious in autumn and winter, flitting about from field to field in search of food, flocks of home-bred birds being often increased by arrivals from abroad as the weather becomes more severe : 'these are said to be larger and much darker in colour. From the north of England, on a heavy snow over-whelming the food supply, they are impelled southward : some cross to the Continent, others stay with us through the hard winter, shifting their haunts if the ground is free from snow. They damage autumn-sown wheat and green crops. The return of the emigrants in spring has been noticed. Larks are excellent food and easily caught.

HOUSE MARTIN : *Chelidon urbica.*

The house martin is distinguished from the swallow by the white chin, that of the swallow being chestnut brown. The martin has a white breast and a white patch on back, with dark black head, wings, and tail. The martin is generally distributed throughout the British Isles, arrives about the middle of April, and usually departs in September or October. Its mud nest, shaped like the half of a cup, is common, usually being placed against the wall and under the eaves of houses, and is entered by a hole in the rim. Four or five eggs are laid, and two, or even three, broods are reared in a season. It has at different times been proved that individual martins return year by year to the same nest, or at least the same locality. J. Gould mentions a case in his " Birds of Britain." Unfortunately the martins are often dispossessed of their nests by house sparrows. The martin catches winged aphides, gnats, and almost any other flying pest, including moths, and is therefore very useful.

The Rev. J. G. Wood says in his most attractive book, " Garden Foes and Friends," that the martin is more useful to the garden than the swallow or the swift, because it catches the lower-flying insects, whilst the swift and swallow catch the high-flying beetles, &c.

* Mr. F. V. Theobald tells me in some hard winters larks have come into his garden at Wye and stripped all the greens and winter spinach.

SWALLOW : *Hirundo rustica.*

The swallow has a red chin, a white breast, its back is entirely black, and its tail is more forked than that of the house martin.

The swallow usually arrives about the second week in April, after which it is generally distributed throughout the British Isles until September or October, or even later. Its nest is made of mud, but unlike that of the martin is open at the top, and usually placed upon a joist or on the wall under the roof of a barn or outhouse. The eggs are four to six in number, two broods being usually reared in a season. Mr. F. V. Theobald tells me swallows do enormous good by devouring winged aphis, and may be watched working amongst the hop aphis as they swarm back to the plum trees.

HEDGE SPARROW : *Accentor modularis.*

The hedge sparrow, called in some parts the Shuffle-wing, from its peculiar flight, has somewhat the appearance of the house sparrow, but its habits are quite different, and it is of quite a different family. Its beak is narrow and of a brown colour, and is suited to an insect and worm diet, whilst that of the house sparrow is strong and cone-shaped, suited for eating grain. It is not gregarious, more than two or three seldom being seen together. Yarrell says of it that it is generally diffused over the British Isles, and is resident throughout the year. From spring to autumn it feeds indiscriminately on insects, worms, and seeds, but not on fruit, drawing nearer to the habitations of men as winter approaches to gain such scanty subsistence as chance or kindness may provide. It is seen in woods, hedgerows, and gardens all the year round, and does not appear to be a migratory species, as the numbers do not noticeably diminish during the hardest winters. Early in February the male begins its soft, gentle, sweet song, and sings throughout the year except in moulting time, which is in August.

These birds live in pairs, feeding and moving in company with each other. The female resembles the male closely; it is nearly the first bird to form a nest. Four or five eggs are laid of a pretty bluish colour; and the cuckoo frequently lays or places its egg in the nest of the hedge sparrow, the hedge sparrow becoming the foster-parent. The character given to this bird by both farmer and gardener is "all good and no harm."

PIED WAGTAIL : *Motacilla lugubris.*

This graceful bird, often seen running along a lawn, by the edge of water, or in the plough furrow, is a resident of the British Isles, but some go southward in the winter. Flies, insects, and fresh-water molluscs form its principal food, and on the farm and in the garden its character is " good in every way."

Miss Ormerod mentions wagtails as eating the marsh snail, which is the host of the Liver-fluke, which causes such destruction to sheep.

Wood-pigeon : *Columba palumbus.*

The wood-pigeon is generally distributed throughout the wooded districts of the British Isles, where it is also known as the ring-dove, or queest.

This bird has greatly increased during the last thirty years or so, owing to the close preservation of woods for game and perhaps to the increased cultivation of turnips and other winter forage crops.

Yarrell says large flocks in winter and autumn cross the North Sea from the Continent by an east-to-west flight. It builds chiefly in woods in fir, elm, beech, or holly trees, but preys on the crops of neighbouring farms and gardens, being chiefly a vegetable feeder.

The first clutch is laid early in April, the second early in June, and a third is not infrequent. The eggs are invariably two in number, as with all pigeons. Incubation lasts sixteen to eighteen days; the male shares in the task. The young when hatched are helpless and blind until the ninth day. They are nourished by food supplied from the crops of the parent birds; they are fully fledged by the end of the third week. It is strictly monogamous though gregarious in winter.

Its food in the summer consists of green corn, young clover, the leaves of which they devour by the bushel, and where numerous they are most destructive to ripe peas and tares. It also eats gooseberries, and in winter it eats acorns and beech nuts, and does serious damage to cabbage and similar plants.

Lapwing, Plover, or Peewit: *Vanellus cristatus.*

The plover is a useful bird against which no one has a word to say. It is more often seen in open fields than in gardens. Yarrell says it is a partial migrant southwards in severe weather.

It is decreasing in England, partly owing to the taking of its eggs, but immense flocks come over from the Continent in the autumn, and the spread of cultivation in Scotland seems rather to have favoured its increase.

This bird has a characteristic flight, due to the slow flapping of its rounded wings, and by its cry tries to allure one away from its nest.

From autumn to winter it is an excellent bird for the table, and its eggs are a luxury in spring.* The taking of the eggs involves great loss of birds, as many that are collected are unfit to eat, being partially incubated.

A farmer in Worcestershire wrote me that the bird there was a general favourite, and never shot in those parts; and another gentleman informed me that he had reason to believe that the green plover feeds upon the small black slug which infests strawberry plants. The extensive strawberry fields in that part of Herefordshire are frequented during autumn and winter by enormous flocks of peewits, which are encouraged and are never disturbed by the owners.

---

* Mr. F. V. Theobald, writing in the October number of *Science Progress* on "Economic Ornithology," pp. 261-283, suggests that it should be made illegal, not only to take the eggs of the plover, but to offer them *for sale* in shops (p. 272).

Miss Ormerod mentions it eating larvæ of *Tipula oleracea* (leather-jacket), *Athalia spinarum* (turnip sawfly), and P*lutella maculipennis*.

BLUE TIT: *Parus coeruleus.*

The blue titmouse is a common resident, and generally distributed throughout the greater part of the British Islands. It has been stated that its numbers are largely augmented in autumn by the arrival of flocks from the Continent, but they do not appear to be among the birds picked up at lighthouses of which a record is kept.

Yarrell says the blue tit has no time for singing, but talks much ; is an insect feeder, its diet consisting of caterpillars, scale insects, woolly aphis, and the eggs of other insects, including those of the sawfly. It damages apples and pears by pecking a hole near the stalk. It pulls half-expanded apple and pear bloom to pieces, presumably for insects. The blue tit lays from six to nine eggs. The young are fed almost entirely on caterpillars, mostly collected in fruit trees. Macgillivray in his "British Birds" mentions a pair of blue tits that brought food to their young 475 times in one day. No bird is said to sit closer, be bolder in the defence of its nestlings, or more indefatigable in feeding them, the foraging for food going on in wet or dry weather. The blue tit is very fond of maize, sunflower seed, and fat, and is very spiteful if trapped ; hence its name of "billy biter." The blue tit will often enter a vinery and spoil grapes.

BROWN LINNET: *Linota cannabina.*

This sweet singer is found very destructive to radish and cabbage seed, and in the districts where these are grown for seed this bird is found to be too numerous. Gorse bushes form a favourite nesting place ; four to six eggs are laid, and sometimes a second brood is reared.

In autumn and winter brown linnets assemble in flocks on stubble and open ground. They are said to prefer soft seeds, especially those containing oil, such as flax and hemp ; the seeds of charlock and knotgrass are also largely consumed, while in winter various kinds of berries and often oats are devoured.

Mr. F. V. Theobald says the linnet is a great nuisance on farms ; out of thirty examined all contained vegetable seeds and no insects.

In East Kent this bird is seldom seen in winter.

GREAT TIT: *Parus major.*

The great titmouse is generally distributed, but is nowhere found in numbers ; it is rather a solitary bird, only seen in pairs in summer ; it has strong beak and feet, and, like the blue tit, is a skilled gymnast ; it is not quite as common as the latter, but, like it, attacks apples and pears. Rev. Henry Slater says they eat walnuts and filberts.* They also peck buds ; but as these frequently contain insects, little real damage is done to the tree by them.

---

* "Wild Birds on the Farm," an excellent paper on the subject read before the Farmers' Club in April 1905.

Together with the Cole-tit and Long-tailed tit they help to keep down winter and codlin moths, apple-blossom weevil, and aphides in all stages, from egg upwards. The note of this bird is said to be like the sharpening of a saw. Great tits probably pair for life, or at least for more than one season. A pair keep together during the winter. Yarrell mentions that mixed parties of tits, a dozen or more together, may be seen rummaging about among decayed leaves, most frequently under beech trees.

Gilbert White mentions the great tit as pulling straw out of thatch, apparently in search of insects. It lays from six to twelve eggs in each clutch, and two broods are produced in a season. In the Natural History Museum at South Kensington is a village letter-box from Rowfant, Sussex, in which great tits for several years made their nest and reared their young, although letters were posted daily, and were often found on the back of the sitting bird. The birds entered and left the nest by the slit for the letters.

Mr. Theobald speaks of the long-tailed tit as always common around Wye, in Kent, and most beneficial: it eats scale, woolly aphis, and bud scales ; it pecks buds containing *Eriophyes pruni.*

The long-tailed tit and *cole-tit* eat larvæ and aphides. The long-tailed tit eats caterpillars of Ermine moth and scale on apple, gooseberry, and red currant ; also woolly aphis and insect eggs.

Mr. Theobald says the cole-tit feeds largely in winter on laburnum-leaf miner and lilac-leaf roller caterpillars.

YELLOW HAMMER : *Emberiza citrinella.*

This beautiful and common bird is sometimes seen in gardens, but is more often associated with a dusty country road in summer time, flitting from hedge to hedge as one walks along.

Its note resembles "a little bread and no cheese." In winter it congregates with sparrows, chaffinches, and greenfinches, and visits the stubbles and farmyards, feeding largely on grain and weed seeds, particularly docks ; but in summer it eats insects and caterpillars and feeds its young on the same. This is a resident bird, and Yarrell says that in the Eastern Counties in winter their numbers are much augmented by immigration from the Continent.

In Italy it is fattened for table purposes. Its eggs are four or five in number, and, like the other buntings, are covered with the curious scribble-like markings which serve to distinguish them from those of other British birds.

BULLFINCH : *Pyrrhula europaea.*

This handsome and attractive bird is shy and retiring. The male bird has a pink breast, that of the female is grey ; both have black heads and beaks, and they are usually seen in pairs both in winter and summer; they are seldom seen associating with birds of any other species. In flight the white band across the back is conspicuous, but they are more often heard than seen. Their food consists of the leaves and immature seeds of docks, thistles, ragwort, groundsel, chickweed and plantain, wild fruits and berries, particularly dog-rose and privet ; but their grievous

sin is their terrible destruction of young buds of fruit trees—plums and
cherries, red currants and gooseberries—and there is no redeeming point
in this destruction, for they do not do it to get insects. Mr. F. V.
Theobald told me recently that he had examined the stomachs of
150 bullfinches, in search for insects they had consumed, without finding
any. They are attractive cage-birds, although their piping song is not as
beautiful as the song of many birds, but they are clever imitators.

The bullfinch commences to nest early in the month of May, often
choosing a box or yew tree. It lays from four to six eggs, and allows

Fig. 70.—Two Plum Trees, about twenty years old, in Mr. A. D. Hall's Garden
(Harpenden, Herts), with Buds entirely destroyed by Birds, May 25, 1906.
It will be noted that whilst other trees and plants are in full leaf, these plum
trees are almost leafless, owing to the buds during winter having been eaten out by
bullfinches and sparrows.

close approach when upon its nest. Yarrell says that there is little doubt
that the prevalence of this bird in England, like the nightingale, is due
to game-preservers, who during the critical period of breeding so jealously
protect its woodland retreats from disturbance. The young continue to
associate with their parents through autumn and winter until the following
spring ; and so constant is the attachment of these birds to one another
that they are believed to pair for life.

Yarrell further says that countless dissections have proved that the
remains of insects are so rarely found in the crop or stomach that their

entrance into its diet must be regarded as accidental, while its warmest advocate cannot deny the regular way in which it will at all times set itself to bite off the blossom buds from one bough after another. The bullfinch is a good judge of variety : some trees and bushes will be wholly spared, while others growing among them will be utterly stripped (fig. 70). The buds which produce leaves are said frequently to be passed over, whilst those containing the embryo blossom are eaten. Red currant, gooseberry, cherry, and plum are first attacked, then pear and apple when sufficiently forward, while peach and kindred trees are neglected.

After March they are seldom seen out of deep woodland. They are said to produce only one brood, but this is said to need verification.

Newman asserts that it devours the larvæ of the winter moth.

Swift : *Cypselus apus.*

The swift is larger than the martin or swallow. Its body is of a dark grey-brown colour. The chin is a dull white. The tail is more forked than that of the martin, and less forked than that of the swallow.

Unlike the swallow and martin its nest is a slight structure of straws, cobwebs, and a few feathers, often placed under tiles or slates of roofs of buildings.

It arrives towards the end of April, lays two eggs, and usually produces only one brood, quitting the country at the end of August.

Like the swallow and martin its food consists of insects caught whilst in flight. The bird seems to be in continual motion, rarely resting.

Missel-thrush : *Turdus viscivorus.*

This bird is somewhat larger than the song thrush, and with larger spots on its breast. It is resident all the year round, though some migrate. It is not as abundant as the song thrush, though numerous in Kent ; it is most noticeable in autumn and winter.

The distribution of this bird is increasing ; it is said that it used not to be known in the north of England and Scotland. The males begin to sing very early, often in January, and, if the weather be mild, sometimes in December. It sings generally from the top of some lofty tree, and as it sings in bad weather, regardless of wind, rain, and even snow, it is often called "stormcock." Its flight is rapid, and made in a succession of jerks.

Its food consists chiefly of worms, slugs, and snails, fruit and berries, it being especially fond of those of yew, holly, mountain ash, and mistletoe. In some parts, particularly in Kent, it is very severe on garden and orchard fruit.

It makes its nest early in the year, sometimes as early as February.

It lays four or five eggs and generally rears two broods in a season. Yarrell mentions that the chaffinch builds its nest near to that of the missel-thrush, perhaps for protection.

Greater Whitethroat : *Sylvia cinerea.*

The whitethroat, also called the Nettle-creeper, is one of our commonest summer visitors and generally distributed throughout the British

Isles; it reaches us about the middle of April (the male arriving first), and remains with us until the beginning of September. Its noisy chatter often brings it to our notice, for this bird seems to live in a perpetual state of excitement. It visits the gardens in company with its young and pilfers currants, raspberries, and other ripe fruit. It creates great havoc among peas, and Miss Peggy Whitethroat is fond of sweet cherries, grapes, and figs. It partly compensates for its offences by eating large numbers of Daddy Longlegs in summer, also caterpillars and other insects.

The Lesser Whitethroat and Garden Warbler are offenders in eating ripe raspberries, but they are otherwise insectivorous.

REDSTART : *Ruticilla phoenicurus.*

The redstart is not a common summer visitor, but should be encouraged: it eats worms, beetles and their grubs, flies, spiders, ants and their eggs, fruit, and berries. Mr. F. V. Theobald tells me the redstart is unfortunately often caught in rat-gins in hedges.

JACKDAW : *Corvus monedula.*

The jackdaw is a close companion of the rook, especially in winter. It eats wireworms, leather-jackets and chafer-grubs, and in this it is very useful, but in some districts it is too numerous, as it will clear cherries and walnuts from the trees. It clears nests of small birds of their eggs and young, and destroys the eggs of game and poultry, and the young of both. It is also very destructive to peas and grain crops where very numerous. Otherwise it is an interesting and attractive bird. Mr. Wilmott Yates, of Walton, Hants, wrote me that in May 1906 he shot a male jackdaw taking food to the hen which was sitting; to his surprise he found that the beak contained thirteen wireworms, four grubs, and a few other insects.

SPOTTED FLYCATCHER : *Muscicapa grisola.*

Yarrell says of this bird that it is one the latest, yet one of the most regular of our summer visitors, reaching us about May 20, when oak leaves are partially expanded; it begins its nest almost immediately on its arrival. It frequents woods, orchards, gardens, and lawns. The same birds will return and occupy the same spot for several years in succession.

It is also called the "Beam bird," as it sometimes builds on a beam in an out-house. It is believed the female builds the nest; the male collects and brings her the required material. It lays four to five eggs, and two broods are sometimes reared in a season. White says the female, while sitting on the eggs, is fed by the male even as late as nine o'clock at night. This bird has no power of voice beyond a harsh call note.

The young are hatched about the second week in June. When able to leave the nest they follow the parent birds, who feed them until they can catch insects for themselves. When on the look-out for food they generally take their stand on the top of a post, or the upper bar of a flight of rails, or the extreme end of a branch of a tree, whence they dart off on the approach of an insect, catching it with ease by a short and rapid movement, returning frequently to the same spot they had quitted, to be on the look-out as before.

These birds feed exclusively on winged insects, though they have been accused of eating cherries and raspberries ; and in this belief the species in some parts of Kent goes by the name of the " Cherry-sucker," but they are said to visit fruit trees for the sake of the flies which the ripening pro- duce attracts, since, on examination of the stomachs of flycatchers killed under such circumstances, no remains of the fruit were found.

It is common in all counties of Great Britain during summer, on the Continent, in Palestine, Russia, Arabia, and Africa to Cape Colony. The beak is dark brown and slightly curved towards the tip.

The flycatcher sometimes nests in the London parks.

In autumn they are said to eat berries and in Norway they are caught with mountain-ash berries.

Growers have written me of this bird saying: " wholly beneficial " ; " useful in destroying aphides, gnats, and beetles " ; " have seen it with caterpillars in its beak " ; " saves many a pound of hellebore for killing the gooseberry sawfly caterpillars by eating the fly as it hovers about the bushes."

Macgillivray tells us he watched one summer day a pair of flycatchers feed their young : they began at twenty-five minutes to four and ended at ten minutes to nine, feeding their young 537 times.

Granville Sharp describes their keen power of sight in picking up some tiny creature from the grass many yards off.

WREN : *Anorthura troglodytes.*

This favourite and interesting little bird is resident and generally distributed throughout the British Isles, and its numbers, some people say, are greatly increased by autumnal immigration. It is hardy, active, and strictly insectivorous, constantly picking out insects or eggs on the branches ; it eats aphides and searches for wood-lice and other creatures among fallen trees and at the bottom of hedges. It makes nests which it does not use, perhaps to draw off attention from the real nest. It lays six to nine eggs, and even twenty have been found ; two broods are not uncommon in a season.

Mr. Weir observed the young fed 278 times in the course of the day. In frosty weather wrens roost together in company. The male sings during the greater part of the year.

CUCKOO : *Cuculus canorus.*

The cuckoo arrives about the middle of April from its winter quarters in Africa (the male arriving first) and generally leaves in July or August. During the season it lays from four to eight eggs which it places in different birds' nests. Should the nest be inaccessible or too small to enter, the cuckoo places the egg in the nest with its beak. The eggs take about twelve or thirteen days to hatch. In the Natural History Museum at South Kensington there is a collection of cuckoos' eggs and the eggs among which they were found, showing that the eggs of individuals vary greatly in colour, sometimes resembling those of the foster parent ; even pale blue eggs are occasionally found, like those of the hedge-sparrow and redstart, but not invariably placed in the nests of these birds. The size of the egg is small compared with the size of the bird. The food of the cuckoo consists of insects and their larvæ, among them hairy caterpillars. In the *Journal of the Royal Agricultural Society* of 1862 the following statement is made —" By careful observation it was ascertained that a cuckoo devours one caterpillar every five minutes, or 170 in a long day. If we assume that one-half of the destroyed insects are females, and that each contains about 500 eggs, one single cuckoo daily prevents the reproduction of 42,500 destructive caterpillars." *

W. Swaysland, in " Familiar Wild Birds," says the note " cuckoo " is nearly always uttered while the bird is flying, or immediately after settling, and this circumstance may possibly explain the fact that the cuckoo is silent in captivity. The parent cuckoos have left the country before the young birds are ready to migrate. From a gardener's point of view, except for the fact that it destroys the eggs and young of insectivorous birds, the cuckoo is a useful bird, feeding on the caterpillars of Ermine moths, woolly bears, Magpie moth, and the larvæ of the Gooseberry sawfly. It especially feeds on hairy larvæ, such as those of the Lackey, Vapourer, and Gold and Brown Tail moths.

Turtle Dove : *Turtur communis.*

The turtle dove is sometimes harmful in a garden, especially to peas, but is not very common. In some of the eastern counties (Cambridge, Beds, Hunts), it is fairly abundant, and flocks do harm to field peas and tares. Mr. Frederick Smith says the turtle dove is very fond of fumitory ; and Mr. J. Boorman, that in some districts it feeds largely on chickweed seeds.

Hawfinch : *Coccothraustes vulgaris.*

The Guide to the British Birds of the Natural History Museum says that the hawfinch is a resident throughout Great Britain, and has been known to breed in every county in England, except Cornwall, but its habits are so shy and retiring that it may easily escape detection.

R. B. Lodge says in " The Birds and their Story " that " these birds are increasing, and perhaps this is due to their very silent and wary ways during nesting, but its partiality to green peas endangers its life at the hands of the gardener. This bird is noticeable by its large beak and the white iris of its eye. It eats the kernels of hard seeds and stone fruits (plums, bullaces, cherries), which it is able to crush with its strong bill ; it then rejects the fruit and eats the kernels ; it pecks apples and pears in search for the pips, and it also feeds on nuts. It destroys the buds of plums and pears to a very considerable extent, but in many districts it is rare.

Jay : *Garrulus glandarius.*

This beautiful bird is decreasing, mainly owing to the severe treatment of it by gamekeepers, who detest it as a devourer of eggs and young birds.

* *Destructive Insects and the Immense Utility of Birds,* by Frederic de Tschudi, of Switzerland.

The bird is extremely shy and wary, and difficult to shoot. It feeds largely on acorns, although in the spring the jay devours a large number of chafers and other beetles and grubs. It is, however, a great lover of apples, plums, cherries, and ripe strawberries, and will commit havoc among peas and beans in a garden near a wood. It is useful in destroying young mice and blackbirds' eggs; it is also said to eat many chaffinches' eggs.

BLACKCAP: *Sylvia atricapilla.*

This lovely songster, which likes to sing in the innermost recesses of thick undergrowth, is one of the five fruit-eating warblers arriving about the middle of April. Harting says the males arrive some days before the females. Both birds take their turn in incubation and leave together early in September.

Yarrell says it is common in the south-east of England, attracted by the fruit upon which the parent bird lives to a great extent, and after bringing up its young upon various kinds of insects which infest fruit trees—in which it unquestionably does us good service—it introduces its progeny at length to more palatable pulp upon which it itself has been faring so sumptuously. The female blackcap is larger than the male, a very unusual thing in birds of this family. The top of the head of the male is jet black while that of the female is a grey-brown. Like other fruit-eating warblers, it has a half-hopping, half-creeping motion. It eats all manner of insects; also raspberries, cherries, and figs; around Worthing, owing to the damage it does, it is called the " Fig-bird."

BUTCHER BIRD OR RED-BACKED SHRIKE: *Lanius collurio.*

This summer visitor of strange habits sometimes makes its nest in gardens in the south of England. It seizes the young birds out of neighbouring nests, and, bringing them home, places them in its "larder," which consists of a bough of a thorn-bush on which it impales its prey, whether beetles, bumble-bees, wasps, or birds.

It sometimes gets badly mauled should the parent bird (for example a thrush) whose nest it has ravaged be close at hand. The butcher bird lays from four to six eggs.

BROWN-HEADED SEA-GULL: *Larus ridibundus.*

In stormy weather this bird travels ten or more miles inland, and will sometimes come into a garden and pick up grubs. Mr. F. V. Theobald tells me he examined one bird and found it full of young leather-jackets. This gull is a useful friend to the farmer, feeding for the greater part of the year on grubs and other noxious insects.

TREE-CREEPER: *Certhia familiaris.*

This small bird is a resident, but is not often seen and is difficult to observe. It is found in all parts of the country more or less, chiefly in woods and plantations, and is usually seen diligently searching the bark and branches of trees for spiders, caterpillars and beetles. Its curved beak, sharp pointed claws, and stiff tail feathers render it especially well adapted for such work. The character given to it by a fruit-grower was: "Harmless, a good insect-destroyer." It lays six to nine eggs, and has two broods in a season.

NUTHATCH : *Sitta caesia.*

This interesting little bird is a resident in the southern and central districts of England, but is not often seen.

It runs up and down the bodies of trees like a woodpecker.

Its food consists of beech nuts, acorns, and various kinds of hard seeds; it is extremely partial to hazel nuts. At times it eats beetles, caterpillars, and other insects.

R. B. Lodge says of it in "Birds and their Story" that when it has discovered a suitable and convenient crack in the bark of a tree in which to place the nuts, it will come to the same spot again and again, until there is quite an accumulation of nut shells.

The force with which it delivers its stroke is very surprising, and it can be heard for some distance when boring a hole in a nut.

Another peculiarity of this bird is that, in case the hole into the tree in which it makes its nest is too large, it will plaster up the entrance so as to leave only just sufficient room for entry and exit; on account of this it is sometimes called the "Mud stopper."

It lays from four to seven eggs.

The Rev. Gilbert White took special interest in this bird and mentions it several times in his charming book "The Natural History of Selborne."

GREEN WOODPECKER : *Gecinus viridis.*

The green woodpecker, or yaffle, is the commonest, largest, and handsomest of our three British woodpeckers, and is not uncommon in the wooded districts of England. In some parts it is called the "Rain-bird" because when it makes a louder noise than ordinary it is supposed to foretell rain. Both the feet and the tongue of the woodpecker differ from other birds. The foot consists of two toes before and two behind; the tongue is wound round the skull, and can be protruded $4\frac{1}{2}$ inches; the tip of the tongue is sharply pointed, so that it can get at a grub in a hole in the wood. Besides feeding on insects in the stems it feeds on the ground on ants and their pupæ, and in this the glutinous substance on the tongue must be of great assistance. It makes its nest usually in the decayed trunk or branch of a tree, which hole it excavates with arduous labour. It lays from five to seven eggs. Unfortunately the starling frequently robs it by taking its nesting hole, and the unfortunate woodpecker has to peck itself out another hole elsewhere.

Amongst the insects eaten may be mentioned the goat-moth caterpillar, wood-lice, and aphides. It is a bird, however, that frequents the forest and the wood rather than the garden.

Miss Ormerod mentions the woodpecker as being the special enemy of the puss-moth. Mr. F. V. Theobald tells me that they have been seen pecking out the pupæ from the hard cocoons, but they do not touch the larvæ.

WRYNECK : *Iÿnx torquilla.*

This bird, often called the "Cuckoo's mate," generally arrives a day or two before the cuckoo and quits the country in September. It frequents orchards, and feeds on ants and their larvæ, but it is a bird difficult to observe. It has a peculiar way of turning its neck round and bringing its head over its shoulders, whence its name "Wryneck"; the young birds hiss like snakes, whence its name of "Snake-bird." It does good on old fruit trees owing to its insectivorous habits. Its feet, like those of the woodpecker and cuckoo, have each toes pointing forward and two behind.

MAGPIE : *Pica rustica.*

This bird, which in some districts has been almost exterminated by game preservers from its liability to destroy the eggs of game birds, is fond of cherries, and in search of them may come into the orchard or garden; it also eats peas, beans, and grain, but it is useful in destroying and eating rats, mice, slugs, snails, worms and a large number of insects and grubs. This shy bird of the woods is still said to be plentiful in some of the midland counties; it is generally seen in pairs, but is said to be sometimes seen in flocks of as many as forty.

The number of eggs is given as from six to eight.

BARN OWL : *Strix flammea.*

One might devote an hour to speaking of the usefulness of the various owls and the many points of interest in their habits. That kindly and observant naturalist Waterton has given us the benefit of his study of them in his writings. The Rev. J. G. Wood says the barn owl is worth his weight in gold. Lionel Adams, in examining 1,124 pellets of the barn owl, found the remains of 997 field voles, 726 mice, 469 shrews, 205 rats, 97 sparrows, 81 other birds, 10 water voles, 9 frogs and toads, 5 moles, 2 rabbits, 3 beetles, 1 squirrel, so probably nine-tenths of their food consist of mice of some kind.

KESTREL HAWK : *Falco tinnunculus.*

The Guide to the British Bird Department of the Natural History Museum, South Kensington, says of the Kestrel hawk:—"This useful friend of the agriculturist is the commonest bird of prey in the British Islands, where it is often known as the 'Wind-hover,' from its habit of hovering and hanging almost motionless in the air against the wind, almost in one spot; while it searches the ground for prey." Its food consists chiefly of mice, beetles, and other insects, very seldom touching game unless very severely tempted. Mr. George Smith, of Boughton Monchelsea, near Maidstone, wrote me:

"What we want in this country is to get *strong* protection for our good old friend the *kestrel*, now, I am sorry to say, rapidly disappearing. I have observed him for sixty years, and rarely indeed has he been caught in any mischief; his food is mice and beetles, occasionally a lark or small bird.

The same in regard to the *barn owl* most emphatically. I have always noted that our common birds increase at a great rate till there comes a severe winter, when they are thinned in a wholesale fashion. Thus Nature remedies matters in her usual cruel and relentless fashion."

NIGHTJAR: *Caprimulgus europaeus.*

The nightjar is one of the latest to arrive of our summer migrants. It sometimes frequents gardens. This bird is peculiar in several respects ; it has a very large mouth, lined at the edge with bristles like the swallow, the martin, and the swift, apparently to retain the large moths, cockchafers, and other beetles it catches. It has a light, noiseless flight, coming out at dusk, and making a burring noise like a spinning-wheel. R. B. Lodge says it sometimes claps its wings over its back like a pigeon. Its middle claw has a strange serrated edge like a minute comb, apparently used to clean the bristles of its mouth from the fluff off the moths. This bird, unlike other birds, sits lengthways instead of crossways on a bough, and is consequently more difficult to see. It often lays its two eggs on the ground among the bracken, and is sometimes called the " Fern owl." It is a very useful bird and does no harm.

GOLDFINCH : *Carduelis elegans.*

This bird, " endowed with the fatal gift of beauty," has been becoming scarcer for many years, probably being driven away by the development of towns, and we have to thank the Wild Birds' Protection Act for endeavouring to preserve it from bird-catchers, by whom it is one of the most prized of caged birds. It is seldom seen in the garden, as it prefers waste land, feeding on the seeds of thistle, groundsel, dandelion, and burdock. The " Guide to the British Birds " says :—" It is generally distributed throughout the summer months over England and Ireland, but rarer and local in Scotland. The majority are migratory, leaving Great Britain in October and returning in April, but in mild winters some individuals remain in England. Four to six eggs are laid, two broods are produced."

NIGHTINGALE : *Aëdon luscinia.*

Perhaps a list of garden birds would be considered incomplete without the nightingale. This sweet singer, although it keeps mainly to the woods, occasionally visits the garden, and adds its own peculiar charm to the delights of a summer evening's stroll. It is rather fastidious as to locality, and R. B. Lodge says of it that it is reluctant to visit the west of England and has hardly yet penetrated to Devon, although it goes as far north as York and Lincoln.

The nightingale is, perhaps, the most renowned of all songsters in the world. It is entirely beneficial, being almost entirely insectivorous.

Ireland is avoided by many migratory birds ; the redstart is rare there, the blackcap and warbler uncommon, and the nightingale is said to be unknown. W. Swaysland, in " Familiar Wild Birds," says " the nightingale arrives in England about the early part of April, the males preceding the females by about a week, or at times even a fortnight ;

as a rule they fly to their old retreats, but sometimes they will desert them even for years and then return again in augmented numbers."

Their chief month for singing is in early June, and they migrate in July and August.

A Rough Classification of Birds as to Food.

Insect-eaters.—Swift, swallow, and martins catch flies, gnats, aphides, and moths on the wing in daytime ; nightjar eats beetles and moths flying at dusk ; wren, robin, hedge-sparrow, tits, tree-creeper, and nuthatch eat insects on trees.

Cuckoo eats hairy caterpillars in fruit trees and sometimes gooseberry sawfly larvæ.

Finches and many small birds eagerly search for caterpillars, especially for their young.

Grubs in the soil are probed for by many birds with long bills, the lapwing, or green plover, being the most useful ; the gulls, rook and starling eat leather-jackets, wireworms, and other beetles and their grubs ; the song thrush eats leather-jackets (larvæ of crane-fly).

The wagtails take insects and small snails from fresh water and marshy land, and follow the plough to pick up insects.

Birds of prey.—Hawks and owls eat mice, voles, and rats ; the smaller birds, beetles, and grubs.

Corn and Seed Eaters.—Finches (worst of all, house sparrow, then greenfinch and chaffinch) and buntings, both having short strong conical beaks, eat corn and seed of cultivated and wild plants and seedlings. Rook and starling eat corn and sprouting grain ; lark eats late-sown spring corn ; wood-pigeon eats sown peas, tares, and corn.

Buds.—Eaten by bullfinch, house sparrow, chaffinch, and greenfinch.

Fruit.—Eaten by blackbird, missel and song thrush, starling and blue tit.

Green stuff during winter.—Eaten by wood-pigeon and lark.

Worm-eaters.—Robin, blackbird, song and missel thrush, and starling.

Snails and slugs.—Thrush, blackbird, plover, rook, corncrake, and partridge.

Wild Birds in Relation to the Garden.

Resident all the year round in England :—

House Sparrow	Starling	Robin	Tawny Owl
Bullfinch	Wood Pigeon *	Hedge Sparrow	Woodpeckers
Chaffinch	Rook	Wren	Gulls
Greenfinch	Blue Tit	Tree Creeper	Jay
Hawfinch	Great Tit	Sparrow Hawk	Magpie
Goldfinch	Cole Tit	Kestrel Hawk	Jackdaw
Missel Thrush	Pied Wagtail	Plover	Nuthatch
Skylark	Yellow Hammer	Barn Owl	

Partially Migratory or " Gipsy Migrants," though found in England during the whole year :—

Song Thrush	Blackbird	Tits	Brown Linnet

* Numerous Continental wood-pigeons come over and these do most harm

Migratory, in England during the summer :—

Cuckoo	Blackcap	Swallow	Nightingale
Wryneck	Garden Warbler	Swift	Butcher-bird
White-throats	Martin	Spotted Flycatcher	Nightjar
Redstart	Turtle Dove		

Insects Injurious to Fruit and the Influence of Birds.

Winter moth, Ermine moth, and Lackey moth caterpillars on apple, plum, and cherry — Cuckoo eats hairy caterpillars; house sparrow, chaffinch, and greenfinch occasionally eat caterpillars on apple trees ; so does, more rarely, the rook.

Magpie moth and Sawfly larvæ on gooseberry and red currant — Rarely taken by any bird, not being liked. Cuckoo and house sparrow occasionally eat them.

Codlin moth larvæ . . . . . — Largely devoured by tits, tree-creeper, and nuthatch in winter.

Bud moth caterpillars in apple and plum — Eaten by tits.

Apple-blossom weevil . . . . — Eaten by great tit.

Mite in black currant buds . . . — Not eaten by any bird.

Red spider on gooseberry, plum, and apple — Not eaten by birds.

Apple-sucker, or Psylla . . . . — Not eaten by birds, but the eggs of the insect are eaten by the blue tit.

Woolly aphis on apple . . . . — Eaten largely by tits and occasionally by chaffinch. There is, however, liability of the pest being spread, carried about on the feet of the birds.

Aphis on plum, damson, cherry, apple, red currant, black currant — The aphides are seldom eaten largely by birds ; the wren, robin, spotted flycatcher, and long-tailed tit eat some aphides ; a few are eaten by the house sparrow and chaffinch.

Scale on apple bark . . . . . — Eaten by tits, especially the blue tit.

Scale on goosebery and red currant . . — Not eaten by any bird.

Damage done by Birds to Fruit.

Buds of gooseberry, red currant, damson, plum, cherry, apple, pear, raspberry — Bullfinch eats all these buds, house sparrow eats largely, and the chaffinch and greenfinch to a lesser extent eat the buds of gooseberry, red currant, and damson.

Flowers of gooseberry, cherry, and plum — Are pecked and pulled to pieces by the house sparrow, bullfinch, chaffinch, and greenfinch.

Fruits of strawberry, cherry, apple, pear, damson and plum — Are eaten by blackbird, missel and song thrush, starling (especially cherries), wood-pigeon. Blue tit pecks apples and pears. House sparrow eats a few cherries. Plums are not usually much eaten by birds except in dry weather.

Fruits of red currant . . . . — Are eaten by blackbird, missel and song thrush, starling, and a few by robin.

Fruits of black currant . . . . — Are eaten by blackbird, missel and song thrush, starling, and a few by robin when fully ripe.

Fruits of gooseberry . . . — Are eaten by blackbird, and a few eaten by house sparrow ; also by wood-pigeon.

Fruits of raspberry . . . . . Are eaten by starling and in Scotland by rook.

Fruits of mulberry . . . . . Are eaten by blackbird and thrush.

Fruits of grape in vinery . . . Are eaten by robin and blue tit.

Fruits of cob, filbert, and hazel nut . Are eaten by nuthatch.

Fruits of walnut . . . . . Are eaten by rook.

TABLE OF THE CHIEF INSECTS INJURIOUS TO VEGETABLE CROPS, AND WHETHER EATEN BY BIRDS.

Insect.	Crop.	The birds which destroy them.
Wireworm	Roots of corn and many other crops	Rook, starling, plover, jackdaw, kestrel, partridge, pheasant.
Leather-jacket (grub of crane-fly)	Grass roots	Rook, starling.
Cockchafer grub	Roots of plants, including strawberries	Rook, Royston crow, and gulls.
Turnip flea beetles	Young plants of turnip, swede, and cabbage, &c.	None known to eat these.
Caterpillar of the large and small cabbage butterflies	Cabbages	Occasionally eaten by the sparrow.
Larvæ of celery fly	Between upper and lower surfaces of leaf of celery	Apparently eaten by no bird.
Surface caterpillars, heart and dart and gamma moths	Ground line of cabbages	Thrush, blackbird, rooks, and starlings.
Black aphis	Broad beans and field beans	Sparrow sometimes eats it, very little eaten by any other bird.
Wheat midge	Ears of wheat	No bird known to eat it.
Weevils	Leaves of peas, beans, and sometimes clover	Occasionally eaten by sparrow, also by shrikes.
Earwigs	Young scarlet runner plants and dahlias	None known to eat them except the robin.

METHODS OF MODIFYING THE HARM DONE BY BIRDS.

PROTECTION OF SEEDS.

Peas are less palatable to birds if soaked for a short time in paraffin. I recently went over a flower farm in Somersetshire where a large quantity of sweet peas are grown for Covent Garden. The grower told me that for autumn-sown peas he sprinkled the seed with paraffin and then scattered red lead over them, thereby giving each seed a coat of red lead. This protects the seeds from mice and birds. Seeds to be sown in the forest nursery are also coated with red lead; perhaps this might be applicable for cabbage and such like seeds which are badly attacked by birds. Farmers, in order to protect their wheat, dress it first with copper sulphate to preserve it from fungoid diseases, and often mix the seed afterwards with tar to protect it from rooks and other birds.

Both soot and lime are distasteful to birds, and aid in keeping away insects, birds, and slugs from seedlings. Cotton, preferably black, is used to make a guard for peas and small seeds generally by running it in parallel lines, an inch apart, over the seedling rows, the cotton being attached at either end of the row to tacks nailed on to suitably shaped boards. Galvanized-wire netting makes a splendid protection against birds, but is expensive.

Fish netting is very often largely used for small areas; boughs with plenty of twigs are sometimes used to protect seed beds. The worst seed-eating birds are the sparrow, greenfinch, rook, chaffinch, lark, wood-pigeon, and brown linnet.

PROTECTION OF BUDS.

It seems possible that spraying trees and bushes with lime-wash will deter birds from eating the buds, but the cost and trouble are considerable, as the plants need to be continuously covered with the lime from autumn till spring, which necessitates several sprayings, but is advantageous to the trees and bushes. Lime or soot thrown up into the trees or over bushes when moist with dew, helps in the protection of the buds, checks insects, cleans the trees, and acts as a manure. Gooseberry and currant bushes are in many places cottoned, for which purpose a special tool called "the webber" may be used. My friend Mr. F. Baker, of Meopham, practises and recommends tying the branches of gooseberries closely together, somewhat like a broom, during winter to protect the buds from birds, and releasing them in spring when the danger is over; he has shown me good results from this method. The worst birds, as regards buds, are the bullfinch, house sparrow, greenfinch, and chaffinch.

PROTECTION OF FRUIT.

The most perfect safeguard against birds eating the fruit is to wire in the fruit bushes with wire netting over and at the sides, but this is very expensive; in gardens string netting is largely used, but is not practicable in orchards or fruit plantations, and some form of scaring is necessary either by clappers, bell, or by the gun.

With regard to the damage to apples and pears through the blue and great tits pecking them, Mr. Frederick Smith, of Loddington, near Maidstone, tells us in his excellent paper on " The Fruit-grower and the Birds," read before the Maidstone Farmers' Club in 1906, that from his experience in his own plantations he has found that sunflowers planted in his fruit orchards tend to keep these birds away from the fruit, as they are so fond of sunflower seed, and he recommends their growth as a means of protection.

For persons fond of birds and wishing to know more about them who live near, or come up to London, I would recommend a visit to the South Kensington Natural History Museum to see the superbly mounted cases of British birds in natural surroundings. The Director of the Natural History Museum at South Kensington kindly gave me permission to quote from " The Guide to the Nesting Series of British Birds " if I acknowledged the source. From this useful guide I have quoted most of the numbers of·eggs and the number of broods, and in several cases as to the migration of the birds. I beg to tender my sincere thanks for the privilege. I have also to tender my thanks to others who have very kindly assisted me with information, but whose names are too many, I fear, to mention individually.

SUCCULENT PLANTS.

By R. Irwin Lynch, M.A., A.L.S., V.M.H.

Lecture delivered November 12, 1907.

Succulent plants are a speciality both in nature and in gardens. As a speciality in gardens they have never been forgotten, they have always had some devoted admirers, but they are so much neglected by the great majority of plant lovers that this meeting of to-day should be of the greatest value in stimulating a revival of interest. My remarks in order to assist this revival must be, I think, as comprehensive as possible; and allow me first of all to point out, in the space of one or two minutes, what these plants are in the scheme of Nature, and where they come in the study of Ecology—that interesting department of Natural History which deals with the plant in relation to its environment. In this connection, all these plants are classed with xerophytes— that is to say, they are constructed to grow where water would be deficient for every other kind of plant. In Nature, but for special construction, many plants would often find themselves in great difficulty with regard to water, and xerophytes are those plants that possess some special structure or adaptation for the purpose of maintaining a balance between the absorption of water by the roots on the one hand, and its transpiration or exhalation by aerial surfaces on the other. All xerophytes, I should mention, are not succulent, many are thin and dry. There is great diversity of circumstance, and there are various means of attaining the important end of which I have spoken. We have now to do with succulent xerophytes, and they maintain the balance in question most conspicuously by the storage of water within themselves—hence their succulence and so the popular designation by which they are known.

They attain their highest development in the dry, warm climates of the world, but they grow, as they do in Britain, wherever dry conditions are liable to last for any length of time. They grow in the driest climates of the world, but it is a mistake to suppose that they always disdain water. Water, indeed, is essential to all forms of life that exist on this earth. They sometimes grow under conditions of considerable moisture, and are not rarely given to the habit of absorbing considerable quantities whenever they get the opportunity. They are not unlike the camel of the desert, able to drink a considerable quantity and then able to go a long time without drinking again. But more than this: they have a special power of conserving water. However it may be with the skin of the camel, these plants have a special epidermal or skin structure, which ensures the performance of function with the minimum loss of water, and very often in shape itself they are formed so as to expose the smallest area of external surface to the air.

As might be expected, these plants—especially by storage of water, but also because of the sum total of xerophytic adaptations—have a very special and characteristic appearance. It is really chiefly because of their various xerophytic features that we admire them. They are always curious, sometimes grotesque, very often grand and imposing, or very handsome, and in the Cactaceae we find a special ornamentation of spines sometimes very beautiful. But in addition they very often possess the most gorgeous flowers of the purest and most brilliant tints known in Nature. This is true of many Cactaceae, of many Crassulaceae, of many Mesembryanthemums, and of a number of others. The Phyllocactae exhibited every year by Messrs. Jas. Veitch & Sons at the Temple Show may be remembered, but the various kinds of *Epiphyllum*, now rarely seen, are equally beautiful, and, among the Crassulaceae, *Rochea* (*Kalosanthes*) *coccinea* was once commonly seen at exhibitions, while, among more recent introductions, such plants as *Kalanchoe flammea*, *K. Dyeri*, and *K. kewensis* are unrivalled in point of beauty.

It is a fact I should like to point out that many plants not grown in collections as succulents have good claim to be included. Many orchids have a perfect title to be regarded as succulent plants; orchids and succulents, in fact, are sometimes found growing together under the same conditions. Fortunately there is a conventional limitation to what we grow as a succulent plant, and by this convention I must now be limited.

Succulent plants are frequently found in natural groups occupying different parts of the world, and so I propose to take you in imagination to the countries where these groups are found.*

Britain.

We have not far to go to find our first examples. In Britain we have an interesting set of Sedums, a *Cotyledon* and a *Sempervivum*. What can be more charming in a garden than an edging of *Sedum album*? Or is there anything more splendid than a sheet of golden *Sedum acre*? *Sempervivum tectorum*, the houseleek, is not really native, but is commonly grown on roofs in villages. It is used for the cure of warts and corns, and was once supposed to be good for fevers. For this reason, by an edict of Charlemagne, it is said to have been made common over the whole of Europe.

Continent of Europe.

On the Continent, Sedums and Sempervivums are still the chief succulents, but in this larger area we get greater variety. Neither of these genera has been fully worked out, and forms may still be found that differ in some degree from those that have been already defined. They make very interesting garden collections, and much interest awaits the traveller and tourist, who would find them transmitted quite easily. Hybrid Sedums are not familiar, but Sempervivums hybridise freely in the garden and in a wild state. I have recently received *Sempervivum Thompsonii*, a cross between *S. arachnoideum* and *S. tectorum*.

Sedum amplexicaule drying up to spindle-shaped stems in summer is most curious; *S. glaucum* is commonly used for bedding out;

---

* As the lecturer remarked, he had no means of showing scenery, but a large number of lantern slides of the plants themselves was exhibited.

S. coeruleum, an annual, is extremely pretty with pale-blue flowers, and *S. brevifolium* and *S. dasyphyllum* are well-known rockery plants. Sempervivums are numerous—*S. calcareum,* with dark leaf-tips, is often used for edgings, sometimes under the corrupt name *S. californicum;* *S. arachnoideum* in several varieties is well known, and *S. Reginae-Ameliae* is a choice form found in Greece. It is quite sufficiently distinct from *S. tectorum,* to which botanically it is referred. *S. atlanticum* is an outlier, beyond the Mediterranean, in the Atlas Mountains. One species, *S. arboreum* (fig. 71), is remarkable as a native of Europe; it is frutescent, and as it grows in Sardinia, Sicily, and Crete (as well as on the

1   2   3

4   5

FIG. 71.—(1) SEMPERVIVUM STREPSICLADUM; (2) S. URBICUM ?; (3) S. ARBOREUM; (4) S. CANARIENSE; (5) S. HAWORTHII.

mainland, where it might have been introduced) it seems to suggest that these islands are of oceanic rank and the Mediterranean equal to an ocean. Low herbaceous plants growing on continents are often represented on oceanic islands by shrubby species, and the only other frutescent Sempervivums are found in Madeira and the Canaries. It would be of interest to introduce *S. mutabile,* a native of Crete.

MADEIRA AND THE CANARIES.

In Madeira we find *Sempervivum glutinosum* and the remarkable *S. tabulaeforme,*[*] the leaves of which form a perfectly level disc, and others,

[*] I follow the *Index Kewensis* in referring this plant to Madeira. Lowe, in *Flora Madeira,* p. 334, says it belongs strictly to the Canaries.

besides a few Sedums, including the pretty *S. farinosum* and *Monanthes polyphylla*, a small plant of much interest. The flora of the Canaries is exceedingly interesting, and interest is fully maintained in the succulent plants. Here we find numerous species of the shrubby Sempervivums above alluded to. Among the most interesting (fig. 71) are *S. canariense*; *S. Haworthii*, with roots descending to the ground like those of a Banyan tree; *S. strepsicladum*; and *S. urbicum* ("Bot. Mag." t. 7898).

Darwin ("Origin of Species," p. 350) accounts for the shrubbiness of certain plants native on oceanic islands and closely related to herbaceous continental species, by supposing that an herbaceous plant not able to compete with trees would be able to gain an advantage over other

FIG. 72.—"MIMICRY," CEROPEGIA DICHOTOMA, WITH A PIECE OF
EUPHORBIA SCHIMPERI ON EXTREME LEFT.

herbaceous plants where trees have not to be competed with by growing taller than they.

In the Canaries there is only one *Sedum*—*S. rubens*, found also in the South of Europe. *Euphorbia canariensis* (fig. 86) is quite an imposing species worth growing in any collection of these plants. A *Ceropegia*, *C. dichotoma*, with bright-green stems, is well known in Botanic Gardens, and now, through the energy of Mr. Walter Ledger, we have another species, *C. fusca* ("Bot. Mag." t. 8066), a similar plant with red-brown flowers. It was discovered in 1860 in Grand Canary, and lost sight of for many years till Mr. Ledger, by means of information he forwarded, got it rediscovered. Both these species out of flower might be taken for Euphorbias (see fig. 72). The well-known "Ice-plant," *Mesembryanthemum crystallinum*, is here native, but it grows in widely distant parts of the world. One other plant only need be mentioned, and that is *Kleinia neriifolia*, a shrub of upright-branching habit, with thick stems and narrow leaves, worth growing with other plants of the Canaries.

AMERICA.

We now cross the Atlantic, and here, on the American continent, we find practically all the Cactaceae, only a few unimportant species of *Rhipsalis* being found in Madagascar and Africa. They grow from Manitoba, in Canada, where *Mamillaria vivipara* is found, down to temperate Chile, with their chief centre, no doubt, in Mexico, where several genera of supreme interest are found. They usually consist

FIG. 73.—MAMILLARIA GRACILIS.

of a thick fleshy stem, ranging in height from one or two inches in the smaller Mamillarias to sixty feet in *Cereus giganteus*. They are usually leafless, but have a special development of spines : true leaves are found in *Opuntia*, but of ordinary flat type only in *Pereskia*. In this genus, too, the flowers are sometimes stalked, but almost always the flowers of cacti are sessile. They are often very brilliantly coloured, the tints being clear and transparent. Until we come to *Rhipsalis*, all genera have a calyx tube above the ovary.

Melocactus.—The first genus to which I shall call your attention is *Melocactus*. Schumann counts fourteen species, but one only is commonly seen in cultivation. This is *M. communis*, the first cactus ever seen in this country, having been introduced about the year 1581. The stem is more or less globose, 1-5 feet in diameter, with from twelve to twenty vertical, angular ridges, studded with spines. The remarkable feature of the plant is its inflorescence, on account of which it is called the "Turk's-cap Cactus," "Englishman's Head," and "Pope's Head." It consists of a cylindrical mass of whitish cotton-like substance interspersed with slender red spines, among which the small red flowers appear, succeeded by small red fruits. The plant is difficult to grow, is almost always imported, and dies after flowering for some time. It is native of St. Kitt's and other islands of the West Indies. The other species are similar.

Mamillaria.—This genus is chiefly Mexican and contains some of the most popular of Cactaceae (figs. 73, 74). It is readily recognised by the

FIG. 74. – MAMILLARIA SCHMIDTII, SIXTEEN YEARS FROM SEED.

globose or cylindrical stems closely studded with conical or mamillaeform tubercles, at the apex of each of which there is usually a tuft of radiating spines. This tuft of spines is sometimes wonderfully beautiful—either viewed singly or in the mass—and the ornamental character of the plant is usually determined by them. Schumann makes ninety-nine species, natives of Mexico and the warmer parts of North America, rarely Brazil, Bolivia, and the islands of the West Indies.

Coryphanta is a subgenus with furrowed tubercles. In *Mamillaria* proper they are never furrowed.

Ariocarpus,* Scheidw. (*Anhalonium*, Lemaire) is best regarded as a distinct genus. It is readily distinguished by its triangular or sub-

* *A. Williamsii* and *A. Lewinii* do not belong here. The former is placed in *Echinocactus* (section *Lophophora*) by Schumann, and the latter in the same genus

foliaceous tubercles, smooth or fissured above. The plants are all most curious. *A. fissuratus* is most frequently cultivated, and the tubercles on the upper surface are remarkably fissured; it has rose-coloured flowers. The following key of the genera *Ariocarpus* and *Lophophora* is abridged from the valuable account by Mr. C. H. Thompson in the Ninth Report of the Missouri Botanical Garden :

I. Tubercles evident, triangular, epidermis cartilaginous. *Ariocarpus.*
    Tubercles with wool-bearing groove.
        Tubercles fissured above. *A. fissuratus.*
        Tubercles flat and finely papillose. *A. Kotschubeyanus.*
    Tubercles not grooved above.
        Tubercles reflexed and closely imbricated. *A. furfurascens.*
        Tubercles more open, squarrosely spreading. *A. retusus* (" Bot. Mag.,'
            t. 7279).
II. Tubercles scarcely evident, epidermis flexible. *Lophophora.*
    Ribs, commonly 8, quite regular. *L. Williamsii.*
    Ribs, commonly 13, irregular to much broken. *L. Lewinii.*

A. fissuratus has been given the popular name " Living Rock." The species are natives of Mexico.

Lophophora.—This generic name has not, I believe, been used in gardens, but it usefully separates two plants that are very distinct from any with which they have been associated. [See above.] *L. Lewinii* may prove, I believe, to be only a variety of ·*L. Williamsii.* They have no spines, and, when quite healthy, the flesh is remarkably yielding to the touch and grey in colour. _*L. Lewinii* (and no doubt *L. Williamsii* is quite of the same character) produces a very poisonous fruit which, being dried, is known as Muscale Buttons, and is chewed by the Mexicans and Indians. The result is a feeling of ideal content, the mind remains self-possessed, but there is an intoxicating orgy of glorious visions in which are seen the most marvellous colour effects. An interesting account is given under the heading of " Drug Dreams " in the January number of the " Grand Magazine," 1907. Paragraphs on the drug will be found in the " Pharmaceutical Journal." The popular name " Whiskey Plant " has been used.

Pelecyphora.—A very curious and distinct genus. The stem is club-shaped and covered with short tubercles, each terminated by a scale in the place of spines. There are two species, P. *aselliformis* with flowers tending to carmine but variable in shade, and P. *pectinata* with yellowish flowers. Both are natives of Mexico.

Leuchtenbergia.—This is one of the most remarkable of the genera of Cactaceae. There is only one species, *L. principis* (fig. 75). In developed plants the base of the stem is naked, above are the much-elongated, three-sided tubercles, three to six inches long, and at the apex are several long, flat, awn-like structures. Years ago it was thought that the flowers must be produced as in *Mamillaria*, but now it is well known that the flowers are produced at the apices of the younger tubercles—usually

by Hennings. These plants by Coulter (*Contr. U.S. Nat. Herb.* 3. 131) are established to form the genus *Lophophora*, and as such it should, I think, be maintained. They are quite unlike all other Cactaceae, and a separate genus for them is therefore probably correct.

only one on the plant at a time. They are yellow in colour and about
four inches across. It is a native of Mexico.

Echinocactus.—The stem is short, globose, or elongate, furnished
with spines, sometimes very strong, as in *E. corniger.* The flowers,
which have a campanulate tube, are centrally produced, while in *Cereus*
they are found distinctly below the apex of the stem. *Discocactus,*
Malacocarpus, Lophophora, and *Astrophytum* are regarded by Schumann
as subgenera. *Astrophytum* is worth generic rank, I think, for *A. myrio-*
stigma (fig. 76), known as 'Bishop's Hood,' and *A. Asterias* are both very
distinct plants in adult condition and without spines. The species are
native from Chili to Mexico. *Astrophytum* is Mexican. Besides the above-

Fig. 75.—Leuchtenbergia principis.

mentioned, *E. Emoryi,* the 'Fish-hook Cactus,' *E. texensis,* the 'Devil's
Pincushion,' *E. Grusonii,* and several others are worth growing.

Cereus.—This genus is one of the best known, and among the species
are some of the most imposing of all Cactaceae. It is chiefly marked by
tall-growing, angled stems, in *C. giganteus* of Mexico reaching a height
of 60 feet, but other species are recumbent or trailing, or, if erect, may
reach no more than a few inches in height. In some species the genus
approaches *Echinocactus,* but as a rule it is easily distinguished, and
always so when the stems are elongate, with flowers well below the apex.
Several are night-flowering, and these frequently excite great interest.
Many have large and splendid flowers. *C. peruvianus monstrosus,*
remarkable as a monstrosity, has been called 'Rock of Ages.' The
night-flowering species are very fine ; the principal are *C. triangularis,*

C. Macdonaldiae, and *C. nycticalus*, all with immense white flowers. The "Botanical Magazine" quotes of one species :

> ' Queen of the dark, whose tender glories fade
> In the gay radiance of the noontide hour."

Pilocereus.—This genus has been reduced to *Cereus*, but it may be retained for P. *Houletii* and for P. *senilis* and allied plants. The latter is called by Schumann *Cephalocereus*. Both are natives of Mexico.

Echinopsis.—Regarded as a section of *Cereus* by Hooker and Bentham, this genus may also be conveniently retained for species with the stem as in *Echinocactus*, and flowers having a long floral tube.

FIG. 76. –ASTROPHYTUM MYRIOSTIGMA.

E. Eyriesii, with large white flowers, and *E. multiplex* (fig. 77), with large rose flowers, are successfully grown out of doors. Both are natives of Mexico.

Echinocereus.—To include some forty species, this genus also is worth keeping apart from *Cereus*. They appear to be clearly marked off by having a prickly ovary and thick green stigma.

Phyllocactus.—For the magnificence of its flowers this genus is pre-eminent among Cactaceae, and, with the exception of *Epiphyllum*, which is nearly allied, no other has been so popular within recent years. Annually at the Temple Show a group of hybrids is one of the fine features in the exhibits of Messrs. James Veitch of Chelsea. The stems are flat, though sometimes three-angled and notched, each notch representing a node. The flowers vary from yellowish white to pure white, scarlet, salmon-red, pink, and yellow, often with effects to be compared with that of shot-silk, and ranging from three or four to ten inches in diameter. The species are natives of Mexico and tropical America, and are usually more or less epiphytic on the trunks of large trees, growing with Bromeliads and orchids. P. *biformis*, a native of Honduras, was *Disocactus biformis* of Lindley (" Bot. Reg.," 1845, t. 9).

Epiphyllum is a genus of few species, but all beautiful. As in *Phyllocactus*, the stems are flat; they are composed, however, of short joints, and are quite different from those of P*hyllocactus*. In *E. truncatum* (" Bot. Mag.," t. 2562), of which there are many variations in violet-purples and carmines, the flowers are irregular. In *E. Gaertneri* (" Bot. Mag.," t. 7201) the flowers are more regular, of a beautiful red-orange colour, and on account of the regularity, apparently, Schumann places it in P*hyllocactus*, as he does *E. Russellianum* (" Bot. Mag.," 8717). This is the

Fig. 77.—Echinopsis ʒultiplex in Mr. E. A. Bowles's Garden, Waltham ̄Cross·

plant known as *Schlumbergera epiphylloides*. All are natives of Brazil, where they are common on trees, and they agree in distinction from P*hyllocactus* by the terminal flowers. *E. Gaertneri* is one of the great attractions in the Cambridge Botanic Gardens when in flower.

Rhipsalis.—The plants of this genus are not usually attractive in flower, but the stems are always curious. They are round, sometimes very slender, often angled, or, again, flattened. The flowers are small, regular, with spreading petals, usually white or whitish. In *R. salicornoides* the flowers are orange. *R. paradoxa* (*Lepismium paradoxum*) is the most remarkable in stem character. *R. Cassytha*, having small white berries, is known as the Mistletoe Cactus. A few species of this genus are found in the Old World, in Ceylon, Mauritius, tropical Africa, and Madagascar. *R. madagascariensis* is cultivated in the Botanic Garden

Cambridge. The old *Lepismium commune* is now *R. Mittleri*. *Pfeiffera cereiformis* is *Rhipsalis cereiformis*. Brazil appears to be the head-quarters of the genus.

Opuntia.—This genus is usually recognised at once by its flat-jointed stems and flowers without a tube, but a few species like *O. arborescens*, *O. cylindrica*, and *O. subulata* have round stems. The flat joints, however (in *O. decumana* 20 inches long by 12 inches broad), are very characteristic, and are usually furnished with tufts of spines, each of which very frequently has a barbed point. In *O. tunicata* the spines are covered with a white papery sheath, easily pulled off. *O. cochinellifera* ("Bot. Mag.," 2742) was formerly important as the chief kind used for the support of the cochineal insect. It is one of several species by

FIG. 78.—OPUNTIA CANTABRIGIENSIS AT CAMBRIDGE.

Hooker and Bentham and by Schumann held to form the genus *Nopalea*. The stamens are much longer than in other Opuntias, but there is hardly any other difference. *O. Ficus indica* is the 'Prickly Pear,' fruits of which are frequently imported. The genus appears to be native over the entire range of the order in the New World.

Pterocactus.—This is an interesting genus established by K. Schumann * as a plant closely allied to *Opuntia*, but with dry instead of fleshy fruit and a broadly winged seed. The one species is *P. Kuntzei*, a caespitose plant with short clavate branches bearing yellow flowers. It is a native of the Argentine Andes.

Pereskia.—This is the one genus of Cactaceae which has leaves of the ordinary type with well-developed blades. The best-known species are *P. aculeata* and *P. Bleo*, both largely used as stocks for *Epiphyllum*.

* *Monographia*, p. 753.

P. *aculeata* is the West Indian or 'Barbadoes gooseberry,' but the fruits
are rarely seen in this country. The plant has been said to flower rarely,
but recently in the Cambridge Botanical Gardens fine masses have been
produced with a perfume like that of orange blossom. The flowers are
white and as no fruit has been produced it is probable that pollen must
come from another plant.

Hardy Cactaceae.—Out of doors I grow about 27 species, and by
experiment it would be possible no doubt to find others that are equally
hardy. The finest I have are *Opuntia arborescens* 4 feet wide,
5 feet high and 2 feet 6 inches from front to back ; *O. cantabrigiensis*
(fig. 78) 18 feet × 3 feet, and 6 feet from front to back ; *O. bicolor*

FIG. 79.—(1) OPUNTIA MONACANTHA (IN FRUIT) ; (2) O. ROBUSTA ; (3) AGAVE
UTAHENSIS ; (4) DYCKIA RARIFLORA.

8 feet × 2 feet 6 inches, and 3 feet from front to back ; *O. monacantha*
(fig. 79) 4 feet wide, 4 feet 6 inches high, and 2 feet 6 inches from
front to back ; *O. robusta* (fig. 80) 9 feet wide, 4 feet high, and
4 feet from front to back ; *Echinopsis Eyriesii* does very well and
occasionally flowers freely. All these outdoor Cactaceae must have a hot
position in full sun against a south wall, and the low walls of plant-
houses do exceedingly well. They must have good drainage, and in order
to secure this the borders on which they are planted may be raised by
means of a few stones. When they are growing it should be remembered
that the large quantities of water they contain must be supplied from
some outside source, otherwise even a cactus may be stunted in growth
merely for want of moisture. The soil should be of a porous nature

with some lime in it, and any good loam of this description is likely to answer well. Stones may be interspersed in the soil with advantage. It is advisable to keep off rain in winter by means of glass, but the strong-growing kinds if well ripened may be expected to succeed without this protection.*

Agave.—Next in importance to the Cactaceae on the American Continent are the Agaves or American Aloes. They extend over the whole of tropical America, and are especially abundant in Mexico and the Southern United States. *A. americana*, and, I have no doubt, its allies, produce the celebrated liquor known as Pulque ; and of great economic importance is the fibre known as Sisal Hemp, produced by *A. rigida* var. *sisalana.* To this genus belong some of the most imposing plants that can be grown in the largest of cool garden structures. The finest set perhaps in the

FIG. 80.—OPUNTIA ROBUSTA.

world is that at Kew. A selection might include *A. Victoriae-Reginae, A. Morrisii, A. Elemeetiana, A. schidigera, A. striata* in several forms, and *A. attenuata* with stem several feet long ; but selection is difficult to make. It is marvellous that these fine plants should be so little grown. There are many species, and Mr. Baker in his " Monograph of the *Amaryllideae* " enumerates 188. All are not equally worth growing, but nurserymen when they get orders know very well as a rule how to find the best. With one exception the genus *Agave* is without close relationship in the

---

* The student and grower of Cactaceae will find the following works very useful :
Gesamtbeschreibung der Kakteen (Monographia Cactacearum). By Professor Karl Schumann. Neudam : Verlag von J. Neumann, 1899. This is the latest monograph of the natural order.
Cactus Culture for Amateurs. By W. Watson, Royal Gardens, Kew. L. Upcott Gill, 170 Strand. This book is essential to the amateur in Britain.
Cactaceous Plants : their History and Culture. By Lewis Castle, *Journal of Horticulture* Office, Fleet Street.

order to which it belongs, and stands apart on account of its usually more or less succulent leaves, though not rarely they are hard and dry. The exception is *Furcraea*, commonly known as *Fourcroya*. The flowers of *Agave* have a funnel-shaped perianth with a short tube. The filaments are long and filiform. An *Agave* allied to *A. americana*, 4 feet high, has survived out of doors at Cambridge for several years. *A. utahensis* (fig. 79) is perfectly hardy, so also appears to be *A. Parryi*.

Furcraea.—This genus is distinguished as a rule from *Agave* by its flatter, paler-green leaves. The flowers are white and rotate, while the filaments are strumose at the base. The plants are usually dwarf, as in the case of *Agave*, but, in the subgenus *Roezlia*, *F. longaeva* attains 40 to 50 feet. All are found in tropical America. (For the literature of *Furcraea* with synopsis of known species, see report of the Missouri Botanic Gardens for 1907.)

Echeveria.—Botanically the genus *Echeveria* is not now separated from *Cotyledon*, but it may usually be distinguished by the rosulate arrangement of the leaves, and also by their being alternate; and as they are all Mexican, with the exception of one Peruvian and one Japanese species, I doubt the wisdom of foregoing the advantages of using the name in gardens. *Cotyledon* is native of South Africa, and the leaves are usually opposite. In gardens the genus is popular, and it is represented by the well-known *Echeveria secunda glauca* and the fine *E. gibbiflora metallica*. Of the latter there is a curious monstrous form at Kew. *E. farinosa* and *E. agavoides* are indispensable plants. Mr. Cannell grows *E. edulis*, a rare Californian species. *E. fulgens* is ornamental as a greenhouse flowering plant in winter, and the cut flowers last a long time.

Sedum.—In North America are a few species deserving of note. *S. oxypetalum*, a native of Mexico, is very interesting. It has an erect fleshy trunk, and in the Botanic Garden of Rouen is a specimen about 4 feet high and having a stem several inches thick. *S. obtusatum*, frequently found in gardens, is a native of California. One of the prettiest of Sedums is *S. pulchellum*. *S. ternatum* is well known, and in North-West America we have *S. spathulifolium* and *S. stenopetalum*. *S. ebracteatum* is not very ornamental, but it has a persistency of life in collections worthy of a better plant; it is Mexican. *S. Stahlii*, introduced not long since, is worth cultivation. This is also a native of Mexico.

Fouquieria.—This is a genus of the order *Tamaricaceae* composed of about three species, sometimes represented in succulent collections. The flowers have never been seen in this country, but they are said to be showy. All are native of Mexico.

Pedilanthus.—A curious genus of *Euphorbiaceae*. *P. tithymaloides* of South America, known as the 'Jew-bush,' is sometimes grown. It has red flowers remarkably like a foot, the stems are green, and bear ovate acuminate leaves, with margins wavy. Mr. Cobbold has a curious species in the Alexandra Park collection, Manchester, named *P. macrocuspis*.

Plumeria.—A genus of the order *Apocynaceae*, with thick stems, fleshy leaves, and fine ornamental flowers, sometimes represented in tropical houses. The habit of growth, unfortunately, is not ornamental.

P. *rubra*, a native of Jamaica, is so deliciously scented as to be known as 'Red Jasmine,' or the 'Frangipani Plant.' P. *tricolor*, a native of Peru, is figured in Nicholson's 'Dictionary.'

SOUTH AFRICA.

The flora of South Africa is the richest in the world, and, in addition to many other features, it is remarkable as the richest in succulent plants, apart from the Cactaceae. The genera of succulent plants are here the most numerous and the most interesting. They belong to about eight different natural orders, and are particularly strong in *Crassulaceae*, *Ficoideae* (*Mesembryanthemum*), *Compositae*, *Asclepiadaceae*, *Euphorbiaceae*, and *Liliaceae*.

Portulaceae.—*Portulacaria*.—There is one species only, P. *Afra*, known popularly as 'Elephant's Food,' and with considerable resemblance to *Crassula portulacea*. The flowers are rosy, but in this country are produced with extreme rarity.

Anacampseros.—About nine species of small suffruticose herbs with fleshy leaves compose this genus. *A. arachnoides* ("Bot. Mag.," t. 1868) has white flowers, *A. filamentosa* ("Bot. Mag.," t. 1867), rosy flowers, and *A. ustulata*, is a curious plant with worm-like branches.

Geraniaceae.—Belonging to the genera *Monsonia*, *Sarcocaulon*, *Erodium*, and P*elargonium*, are many plants with fine ornamental flowers, perfectly entitled to be classed among succulents; but, when they are cultivated in this country, it is usual to regard them as a set by themselves. They are rarely seen except in Botanic Gardens.

Crassulaceae.—*Crassula*.—This well-known genus, numbering more than 120 species, is almost confined to the Cape. It is known from allied genera here in question by having free petals, or petals connate at the base only.

The following is a selection of some of the best kinds:—
C. arborescens, substantial in habit and foliage, but not free-flowering; *C. lactea*, flowers white, freely produced, and responding to liberal cultivation; *C. lycopodioides*, a plant with much resemblance to a *Lycopodium*; *C. Cooperi*, a small-growing but pretty, free-flowering plant; *C. quadrifida*, free-flowering, flowers pinkish, the parts in fours; *C. hemispherica*, with shoots, each forming a flat mosaic of leaves; *C. pyramidalis*, an exceedingly curious plant with cylindrical shoots, and leaves tightly superposed so as to show only their edges; *C. cordata* with small and numerous flowers, interspersed with innumerable tiny plantlets; and *C. marginata*, with shoots pendulous.

Rochea.—Nearly allied to *Crassula*, but the petals are connate into a tube. *R. coccinea* ("Bot. Mag.," t. 495) is the old *Kalosanthes* or *Crassula coccinea*, a very ornamental plant deserving of careful culture and formerly much grown for exhibition. *R. jasminea* ("Bot. Mag.," t. 2178) and *R. versicolor* ("Bot. Mag.," t. 2356) are the other two species, the first with white flowers, the second with red and much like *R. coccinea*. The plants universally known in gardens as *Rochea falcata* and *R. perfoliata* are both Crassulas, but form a very distinct group.

Bryophyllum.—A small genus well marked by the inflated calyx. The flowers are usually dull in colour, but by good cultivation the plants may be made ornamental. *B. proliferum* ("Bot. Mag.," t. 5147) is sometimes known as the "air plant," leaves when hung up being capable of producing buds in the crenatures. For that reason, also, the plant is held to illustrate the nature of the carpellary leaf, the young plants appearing at the edge of the leaf in the place of the ovule. *B. calycinum* ("Bot. Mag.," t. 1409), which extends from tropical Africa into Asia, is often found in gardens.

Kalanchoë.—A genus with several good species belonging to South Africa, but with its best horticultural exponents in Somaliland, Abyssinia, and tropical Africa. It differs from *Cotyledon* in having quadripartite flowers, and to no other genus has it any particular resemblance. *K. carnea*, a few years ago, was much grown. *K. thyrsiflora*,

FIG. 81.—COTYLEDON CORUSCANS.

figured from Cambridge in the "Bot. Mag." (t. 7678), has remarkably Cotyledon-like foliage.

Cotyledon.—A large and important genus, including ornamental and also curious species. It is distinguished among allies by having a quinquépartite calyx, often much shorter than the corolla, ten stamens, and five connate petals forming a tube. The leaves are almost always opposite, and all are natives of the Cape. *Echeveria*, which, most inconveniently, I think, has been united with it, is not found at the Cape. The leaves are alternate, very often arranged in a rosulate manner; the calyx is often foliaceous and often longer than the corolla.* Among the most

* When plants are geographically distant, distinct in aspect, and without intermediates, it should be philosophically correct not to rely upon floral difference but to seek for characters in the vegetative organs. Among all the hybrids of *Echeveria* there is not one, I believe, with *Cotyledon*. A systematic arrangement is chiefly for convenience, and no purely scientific interest is interfered with by giving a generic name to every conspicuously distinct set of plants.

ornamental in flower are *C. undulata* (" Bot. Mag.," t. 7931, figured from Cambridge) : the leaves are white with apex undulated ; *C. coruscans* (fig. 81), freely branching, dwarf, each shoot terminating in an inflorescence ; and *C. orbiculata*, erect-branching, leaves white.

Among the curious species are *C. gracilis*, with slender branches and spindle-shaped leaves ; *C. Eckloniana* (fig. 82), *C. tricuspidata*, with narrow white leaves, ending in three points ; *C. teretifolia*, with cylindrical green leaves ; and *C. reticulata* (fig. 83), with short and thick stem, bearing persistent flower stems, flowers small and inconspicuous.

Ficoideae.—*Mesembryanthemum.*—An exceedingly remarkable genus. The order *Ficoideae* and the *Cactaceae* form a group by themselves ; in the *Cactaceae* leaves are usually small or absent, but here the leaves are

FIG. 82.—COTYLEDON ECKLONIANA.

always well developed, and the stem is sometimes much reduced, as in certain kinds which simulate the stones among which the plants grow. The flowers are often very showy though fugacious.

The annual species worth cultivation out of doors are *M. crystallinum*, native also of Greece, the Canaries and California ; *M. pomeridianum*, yellow flowers, plant prostrate ; and *M. pyropeum* (*tricolor*, Hort.), with its white variety illustrated in " Gard. Chron.," Jan. 18, 1908, p. 42.

The following are curious in foliage : *M. Bolusii* (" Bot. Mag.," t. 6664), leaves two, liver-coloured, flower yellow and red ; *M. minutum*, plant stemless, leaves connate, glaucous ; *M. testiculatum*, plant stemless, leaves four to eight, white, flowers yellow ; *M. tigrinum*, leaves with suggestive side teeth.

The following species are brilliant or showy in flower: *M. blandum,* at first white, then pinkish; *M. aureum,* bright orange; *M. coccineum,* scarlet; *M. aurantiacum,* orange; *M. conspicuum,* red; *M. spectabile,* red.

The 'Hottentot Fig,' an edible fruit, is borne by *M. edule.*

Compositae.—Very remarkable in South Africa are some plants of this order. Among succulents they usually belong broadly to the genus *Senecio.* Flowers of a structure quite similar to that of a groundsel are found on plants of a totally different appearance. In suiting themselves to their environment they have attained the succulent habit common to some two dozen genera which, as it were, more exclusively belong to the dry conditions of this part of the world.

Fig. 83.—Cotyledon reticulata.

Senecio.—*S. macroglossus* (" Bot. Mag.," t. 6149) is a very ornamental climbing plant with leaves so ivy-like as to have been mistaken for ivy by a great botanical authority. The flower-heads are large, with yellow rays and decidedly ornamental. Of *S. junceus* a good specimen consists of little more than a few green sticks in a pot, bearing small yellow flower-heads without a ray. *S. oxyriaefolius* is a prostrate plant, with round succulent leaves, and *S. tropaeolaefolius* is similar.

Kleinia.—*K. ficoides* (fig. 84) is one of the most ornamental, with long white sharp-pointed leaves and white flowers. *K. articulata* has round-ended cylindrical stems; this is known as the 'Candle-plant.' *K. Galpini* (" Bot. Mag.," t. 7239) is a dwarf-habited plant with orange flower-heads, worth growing for its colour and ornamental character. *K. Haworthii* (" Bot. Mag.," t. 6063) is a curiosity on account of its white felted, spindle-shaped leaves. *K. radicans* is of pendulous habit; useful for a hanging pot. *K. fulgens* ("Bot. Mag.," t. 5590) grows 2 feet high, has flat glaucous leaves, and bears heads of vermilion-orange flowers.

Othonna.—Two species are worth growing, viz. *O. carnosa* and *O. crassifolia*, both with bright green foliage and yellow flowers.

Apocynaceae.—An order closely allied to *Asclepiadaceae*, but while having two carpels it has only one style.

FIG. 84.—KLEINIA FICOIDES.

Pachypodium tomentosum (P. *succulentum*) is sometimes found in Botanic Gardens. P. *namaquamum* should be introduced.

Asclepiadaceae.—An order of much interest, with pollen agglutinated into masses as in orchids.

Ceropegia.—The flowers are wonderfully curious, and the species differ widely from one another. *C. Sandersonii* ("Bot. Mag.," t. 5792) is a climber, with green flowers provided with a "howdah"-like top delicately fringed. *C. stapeliaeformis* ("Bot. Mag.," t. 3567) is a thick-stemmed rambler with dark mottled stems, the flowers thickly claret-spotted and with spreading segments. *C. Woodii* ("Bot. Mag.," 7704) is a freely growing and free-flowering plant with pendulous stems bearing mottled leaves and brown-red flowers. It bears tubers on the stems like a *Dioscorea*.

Any selection must include the above. Other South African species in cultivation are *C. africana* ("Bot. Reg.," t. 626) ; *C. Barklyi* ("Bot. Mag.," t. 6315) ; *C. Bowkeri* ("Bot. Mag.," t. 5407) ; *C. Monteiroae*, Delagoa Bay ("Bot. Mag.," t. 6927) ; *C. multiflora* ("Ref. Bot.," t. 10) ; *C. radicans*, and *C. Rendallii* (Transvaal).

Ceropegias, though succulent, appear to do much the best, as a rule, in a moist house. This has been found particularly true of *C. Woodii*. *C. geminifera*, recently received, and of which I do not yet know the native country, is a most curious plant ; the stems are slender and not very leafy, but stuck all over with sausage-shaped tubers.

Sarcostemma.—One species, *S. viminale*, is often cultivated in succulent collections, though of little interest. It consists of long green leafless stems the size of a quill which never seem to produce a flower. The flowers are small, produced in cymes. This species grows in the Welwitschia country.

Piaranthus.—This genus is allied to *Boucerosia*, and may be typified by the plant figured in "Bot. Mag.," t. 1648 as *Stapelia pulla*. There are about six species, none of which appears to be in cultivation. The attention of collectors may therefore be called to this genus. It is like *Stapelia*, but with flowers usually in fascicles and with very narrow corolla lobes.

Hoodia.—A most remarkable genus composed of about three species, with low, many-angled leafless stems and large campanulate flowers. In *H. Gordoni* ("Bot. Mag.," t. 6228) of Little Namaqualand, the flowers are 4 in. across, of primrose-yellow colour with a flush of pink in the centre. The vertical angles are not markedly broken up into tubercles. In *H. Bainii* ("Bot. Mag.," t. 6348) the flowers are smaller, of a pinkish-yellow colour, and the angles are broken up into compressed tubercles each bearing a spine. It is only by skill and good fortune that these plants can be kept for any length of time. "Treat as a Phalaenopsis" is advice I received at Kew, and the treatment has been successful ; which illustrates my dictum that a plant should not necessarily be kept dry because it is succulent.

Podanthes.—A genus of *Stapelia*-like plants—often known under the genus *Stapelia*—but with corolla described as broadly campanulate, *Stapelia* being rotate or reflexed. *S. geminata* ("Bot. Mag.," t. 1326) is counted a *Podanthes* in the "Genera Plantarum," so also is *S. verrucosa* ("Bot. Mag.," t. 786). Perhaps too near *Stapelia*.

Duvalia.—*Stapelia*-like plants often referred to that genus, but the corolla has a broadly campanulate lower part with an elevated ring at the throat. It has the scales of the interior corona incumbent, while *Huernia* has the same scales erect, and a tooth in each sinus of the corolla, which *Duvalia* has not. It is of similar interest to *Stapelia*, but the flowers are less striking. *D. reclinata* ("Bot. Mag.," t. 1397) and

D. radiata (" Bot. Mag.," t. 619) are in cultivation. Both have narrower radiating segments, those of the first-mentioned with hairs.

Decabelone.—A very charming genus of dwarf plants with many-angled stems bearing setæ and large tubular campanulate flowers. *D. Barklyi* ("Bot. Mag.," t. 6203) is native of Little Namaqualand. It is an elegant plant 3 to 6 inches high, the stems with ten to twelve angles furnished with processes bearing one erect and two lateral deflexed, slender white spines. The corolla is slightly curved, the ground colour being livid yellow upon which are many red-brown streaks and spots. *D. elegans* will be mentioned under Tropical Africa. Both species are difficult to keep, and grafting on a strong-growing ally should be tried.

FIG. 85.—STAPELIA GIGANTEA.

Huernia.—Much more attractive than *Duvalia*. The flowers are campanulate, the lobes of the corolla short and with a tooth between each. *H. oculata* ("Bot. Mag.," t. 6658), from Damaraland, is remarkable and also extremely pretty on account of the purple-brown flowers with white centres. *H. primulina* is also a nice plant with flowers of a colour indicated by the name. *H. Hystrix* is another species in cultivation from South Africa. The genus is also found in Zanzibar and Somaliland.

Stapelia.—Perhaps the most popular and most frequently cultivated of succulent Asclepiads, and known as Carrion-flowers on account of the smell, which attracts flies for the purpose of cross-pollination, and causes them to lay their eggs in the centre of the flower. The genus belongs to a group with a double corona, and is distinguished from its allies, like *Duvalia* and *Huernia*, which are sometimes included within it, by having a rotate or reflexed corolla. One of the finest is *S. gigantea* ("Bot. Mag.," t. 7068), a native of Zululand (fig. 85). It is curious that this and other largest flowers of the vegetable kingdom should be lurid in colour and of unpleasant odour. A selection might include : *S. clypeatá*; *S. conspurcata*; *S. deflexa* ("Bot. Mag.," t. 1890) ; *S. grandiflora* ("Bot. Mag.," t. 585) ; *S. mutabilis* ("Jacq. Stapel.," t. 42) ; *S. olivacea* ("Bot. Mag.," t. 6212) ; *S. patula*; *S. picta* ("Bot. Mag.," t. 1169) ; *S. Plantii* ("Bot. Mag.," t. 5692) ; *S. sanguinea*; *S. trisulca*; *S. variegata*.

Euphorbiaceae.

Euphorbia.—A highly interesting genus known widely over the world, and, while represented in Britain by annual and perennial herbs,

FIG. 86.—MIMICRY IN EUPHORBIA AND CEREUS. (1) CEREUS SP. ; (2) EUPHORBIA ABYSSINICA ; (3) C. SPACHIANUS ; (4) C. FORBESII ; (5) E. POLYGONA ; (6) E. CANARIENSIS.

in South Africa it becomes succulent, frequently frutescent, and often shaped like a cactus. The sap is always milky, but never so in a cactus. The following are interesting species for cultivation: *E. bupleurifolia*; *E. Caput-Medusae*; *E. globosa* ("Bot. Mag.," t. 2624) ; *E. grandidens*; *E. mamillaris* (fig. 87) ; *E. meloformis*; *E. pentagona*; *E. polygona* (fig. 86) ; *E. procumbens* ("Bot. Mag.," t. 8082) ; *E. virosa* (*coerulescens*, Haw.). The well-known *E. Bojeri* ("Bot. Mag.," t. 3527), *E. splendens* ("Bot. Mag.," t. 2902), *E. xylophylloides* and others are natives of Madagascar.

Synadenium.—A genus closely allied to *Euphorbia,* but of no great importance. *S. arborescens* ("Bot. Mag.," t. 7184) is a shrub 4 feet high, native of Natal. The stems are green, leaves cuneately obovate, 3 or 3½ inches long, fleshy; the flowers are inconspicuous.

Liliaceae.—In America we found succulent Amaryllids, but in South Africa we find a much larger representation of this allied order.

Aloe.—A genus of some 150 species or more, often with imposing foliage and sometimes producing flowers distinctly ornamental. The three following species are arborescent: *A. Bainesii* (*A. Zeyheri*) ("Bot. Mag.," t. 6848) is said to be the finest of the species. It rarely flowers, but is fine in foliage and grows 40 to 60 feet high. *A. plicatilis* ("Bot. Mag.," t. 457) is an old inhabitant of our gardens and distinct in its freely branching habit. It flowers freely. *A. dichotoma* (see "Gard. Chron." 1874, p. 567) is a slow-growing plant, not yet flowered, I believe, in this country. It is known as the "Quiver-tree," and grows 20 to 30 feet high with a trunk 3 to 4 feet diameter. A collection might, include: *A. Thraskii,* the finest in head of foliage; *A. variegata,* a small plant, sometimes seen in windows; *A. Greenii,* with pretty green variegation; *A. tricolor,* a pretty plant, with pretty flowers; *A. ferox,* foliage covered with spines; *A. ciliaris,* one of the prettiest in flower, the perianth being brilliant red, a small-habited plant.

Gasteria.—Quite sufficiently distinct from *Aloe,* with which it has been united. The plants are stemless, of usually olivaceous, deep-green hue, almost always spotted, and bearing pendulous flowers, usually pretty, of some shade of red and with one side of the perianth swollen out—hence its name. *G. verrucosa* is one of the most distinct on account of its numerous white warts. *Aloe Lynchi* is a hybrid between this and *Aloe albocincta,* combining the characters of both plants. *G. Croucheri* ("Bot. Mag.," t. 5812) is a fine plant. *G. pulchra* has distinctly spotted leaves. *G. Vroomii* is the finest of all the species I have seen. Under this name I found it in the Friedrich-Wilhelms-Garten at Magdeburg, with an inflorescence 8 feet across.

Haworthia.—The plants are all small and stemless, with the leaves arranged in a rosulate manner, producing slender scapes with small pale-coloured flowers. There is quite an entertaining variety in the form of the leaf, and all the species obtainable could be grown within the area of a square yard. *H. margaritifera, H. cymbaeformis, H. retusa,* and *H. tessellata* are among the species worth growing.

Apicra.—Very nearly allied to *Haworthia.* The plants are slender and never stemless, though never many inches high. The inflorescences and flowers are similar to those of *Haworthia.*

Bulbine.—An interesting genus with fleshy leaves and with filaments hairy. Two species are sometimes found in collections, *B. latifolia* with broad leaves, and *B. alooides* with narrow leaves. *B. annua,* also native of South Africa, may be grown as an annual out of doors.

Before leaving South Africa, allow me to draw attention to a very remarkable circumstance, never yet accounted for. Numerous plants of this part of the world invariably flower, when artificially cultivated in Europe, according to their time of flowering in South Africa. If only imported plants did this there would be little wonder in it, but plants that have been raised from seed in this country strictly follow the calendar, and that in distinct opposition to British seasons. How do they do this? It happens, for instance, in the case of *Aloe*, and *Nerine*—to mention a plant that is not a succulent. The time of sowing the seed makes no difference, so far as I have yet discovered.

MADAGASCAR.

Didiera.—A marvellous genus of the order *Sapindaceae,* with right to a position among succulent plants by reason of its stems, "which are something like those of the succulent *Euphorbias.*" They are, however, very distinct, and grow to a height of several yards on dry rocky soil. *D. mirabilis*—of which a seedling plant is figured in the "Gardeners' Chronicle," February 19, 1898, p. 110—is cultivated at Kew. Flowers have not yet been produced in this country, but they are described as rose-coloured. There is another species, *D. madagascariensis,* and both are described by Baillon in the "Bulletin of the Natural History Museum," Paris.

Bryophyllum.—A pretty species introduced by Messrs. Vilmorin, Andrieux et Cie. is *B. crenatum.* It is of slender habit, with rather small glaucous leaves, and has flowers of a brick-red colour. It is of easy culture, and flowers the same year when grown from leaves.

Euphorbia.—An interesting species with flat stems is *E. xylophylloides,* worth growing in any collection.

E. splendens is the well-known prickly-stemmed species with coral-red flower bracts, useful for cutting, and produced at all times of the year. *E. Bojeri* is similar but not so good.

Aloe capitata appears to be the one species in cultivation native of Madagascar.

MAURITIUS.

Lomatophyllum.—An interesting genus similar to and closely allied to *Aloe,* differing in the fruit, which, instead of being capsular, is succulent. There are two species in cultivation : *L. borbonicum,* the finer plant, and *L. macrum,* both natives of the Mauritius.

TROPICAL AFRICA.

Going north of the main stream of the Zambesi, but strictly considering garden plants alone, we find that certain genera like *Stapelia, Gasteria,* and *Haworthia* are left behind, and that others like *Aloe* and *Euphorbia* are represented by fewer species. We shall meet with genera that are new to us, however, and in *Kalanchoë,* for instance, we shall discover species that are finer than any we have seen before.

UNLOCALISED TROPICAL AFRICAN SPECIES.

Vitis.—The genus of the common vine is a remarkable one, and from this quarter two remarkable species have been cultivated. One is *V. Baincsii* ("Bot. Mag.," t. 5472), and the other *V. macropus* ("Bot. Mag.," t. 5479). They have very thick fleshy stems, which produce deciduous branches that fall off after flowering. This certainly is true of the last, which is still in cultivation. I have received a plant that seems identical from Somaliland. They have thick fleshy leaves.

Euphorbia.—*E. grandicornis*, the finest of all the species perhaps, is referred to this region. It is essentially tropical and suffers from cold in winter where other species are happy. *Synadenium Grantii* (" Bot. Mag.," t. 5633) is a strong-growing plant with bright green fleshy leaves 3 to 4 inches long, not beautiful in flower, native of Central Africa.

Aloe.—*A. agavaefolia*, *A. Buchananii*, and *A. macrosiphon* may be mentioned.

EAST TROPICAL AFRICA.

Aloe Hildebrandtii (" Bot. Mag. " t. 6981), *A. Kirkii* (" Bot. Mag.," t. 7386), and *A. tenuifolia* are mentioned in the " Kew Hand List.'

WEST TROPICAL AFRICA.

A. Barteri is included in the " Kew Hand List."

NYASSALAND.

Kalanchoë.—One of the very finest of the species, viz. *K. Dyeri* (" Bot. Mag.," t. 7987), is native of this country. It is one of a group found in tropical Africa, and characterised by long-tubed white flowers. This plant grows from 2 to 2½ feet high, it has fine leaves 7½ inches long, and produces an inflorescence from 6 to 9 inches across. It was introduced to Kew, flowered first in 1904, and it is said that plants will soon be offered by the trade.

K. Kirkii, between which and the Indian *K. grandiflora* I have obtained a hybrid, is native of this region.

ZANZIBAR.

Huernia.—For one species, *H. aspera* (" Bot. Mag.," t. 7000), it is worth while to mention this island, though it may be native of the opposite coast. It is interesting as a member of a genus previously known only in South Africa. The stems are straggling, purplish-brown, with divaricate, ascending, green, cylindrical or fusiform branches bearing flowers nearly one inch in diameter of a very dark brown-purple colour.

Aloe.—*A. brachystachys* (" Bot. Mag.," t. 7399), *A. concinna*, and *A. penduliflora*, all in the last " Kew Hand List," are natives of Zanzibar.

SOMALILAND.

Owing to the visits of Mr. and Mrs. Lort-Phillips and Miss Edith Cole, some very fine and interesting plants have been introduced.

Kalanchoë.—One of the finest of all the species is *K. flammea* (" Bot. Mag.," t. 7595), and none can compare with it in the brilliant scarlet colour of the flowers. A hybrid raised between it and *K. Bentii* of South Arabia is the wonderful *K. kewensis*, remarkable in foliage and beautiful with masses of pink flowers.

K. somaliensis, collected and introduced by Sir Edmund Loder, is allied to *K. Dyeri*, and is second only to it among those with white flowers.

Kleinia.—One of the finest is *K. Grantii*, introduced by Miss Edith Cole to the Cambridge Botanic Garden, and figured in the "Bot. Mag.," t. 7691. It has flat glaucous leaves, and heads of scarlet flowers. *K. pendula*—quite a different species, with leafless curving succulent stems, but yet with ornamental scarlet flower-heads—was also figured from the Cambridge Botanic Garden from plants sent by Mrs. Lort-Phillips and Miss Edith Cole ("Bot. Mag.," t. 7689).

Huernia.—A very interesting and pretty plant is *H. concinna*, with yellowish-white campanulate flowers, introduced to Cambridge by Mrs. Lort-Phillips, and figured in the "Bot. Mag.," t. 7905. Almost equally pretty is *H. somalica*, also introduced to Cambridge by Mrs. Lort-Phillips, and figured in the "Bot. Mag.," t. 7730. It has more openly campanulate flowers of ochraceous hue, studded with purple papillae.

Echidnopsis.—The old well-known species is *E. cereiformis*, mentioned under Abyssinia. *E. somaliensis* was introduced to the Botanic Garden, Cambridge, by Mrs. Lort-Phillips, and is figured in the "Bot. Mag.," t. 7929. The two kinds are very similar, but this has brown-purple flowers spotted with yellow.

Edithcolea grandis.—A new genus, and this the one species. It was found by Miss Edith Cole and Mrs. Lort-Phillips in the Henweina Valley, at a height of 3,000 feet. Unfortunately it was not introduced alive, and travellers to Somaliland should make every effort to get it. In habit the plant is similar to *Stapelia gigantea*. It grows a foot high, and the stems are an inch or more in diameter. The genus is allied to *Caralluma*, and has a very large corolla with a small tube. The colour of the flower is not given. The plant is described by Mr. N. E. Brown in the "Kew Bulletin," 1895, p. 220.

Euphorbia.—The new *E. Phillipsiae* is a Cambridge introduction sent by the lady whose name it bears. It has numerous angles and many spines, is of small growth, and is a most interesting plant—one of the rarest of the genus.

ABYSSINIA.

Kalanchoë.—One of the most interesting species is *K. marmorata* ("Bot. Mag.," t. 7333). Its leaves, according to the amount of sun, are either pale glaucous green or spotted with very dark purple-black, or they are almost entirely black. The flowers are large and white.

Echidnopsis.—The common species is *E. cereiformis* (fig. 87), which has cylindrical stems nearly a foot high—a good mimic of those of *Euphorbia mamillaris*—and small yellow flowers produced near their summits. It is figured in the "Bot. Mag.," t. 5930. It is native of Eritrea and Somaliland, as well as Abyssinia.

Aloe.—Several species may be included here. The principal are *A. abyssinica*, *A. Camperi*, *A. elegans*, *A. macrocarpa*, and *A. Schimperi*, all of merit for collections.

NORTH AFRICA.

Sedum.—Nine species are recorded from Morocco alone, but it does not appear that any from this region are of garden importance.

Boucerosia.—This genus and *Caralluma* are very nearly related, and Mr. N. E. Brown, the great authority upon succulent Asclepiads, believes that they should be united. They are *Stapelia*-like plants, but with smaller flowers having a single corona, the *Stapelia* group, including *Duvalia* and *Huernia*, having a double corona. *B. Gussoniana* ("Bot. Mag.," t. 5087, as *Apteranthes*) has been well known as *Stapelia euròpaea*. It is the most interesting member of the group, since it is actually a native of Europe as well as of North Africa, being found in Spain and on one of the Sicilian islands. It has small flowers, of brown-purple colour much barred with yellow, in clusters of eight or ten, at the tips of the branches. *B. maroccana* ("Bot. Mag.," t. 6137) is a species which, though near the last, must be quite distinct. The flowers

FIG. 87.—'MIMICRY.' ECHIDNOPSIS CEREIFORMIS AND EUPHORBIA MAMILLARIS (ON EXTREME RIGHT).

are borne much below the tips of the branches, in clusters of four to five, and though nearly of the same colour they are much less barred with yellow. The flower-stalks are shorter. As the name indicates, it is native of Morocco, and was introduced to Kew by Sir Joseph Hooker. *B. Munbyana,* a native of Algeria, is also in cultivation.

Aloe vera (A. vulgaris) is said to be native of the whole Mediterranean region.

Euphorbia.—The most important North African species is *E. resinifera,* a native of Morocco. The stems are four-angled, and attain a height of a yard and more. *E. Beaumiereana* is also a cactoid species from Morocco, the stem nine- or ten-angled. Still another is *E. Echinus,* with six-angled stems. The last is perhaps not in cultivation.

ARABIA.

This is a most interesting country, and, as it is not well known, plants sent home by travellers must always be acceptable.

Kalanchoë Bentii ("Bot. Mag.," t. 7765) is unlike all others in its leaves, which are compressed but nearly round in section; the flowers are white with pink unexpanded corolla lobes; the tube about 1¼ inch long. The plant is not very free-growing, but the inflorescence is distinctly beautiful, and of all others this species is most noteworthy as being a parent of the wonderful *K. kewensis*. It is native of Southern Arabia.

Adenium.—A genus of the order *Apocynaceae* and rarely met with except in Botanic Gardens. It is represented by *A. obesum* ("Bot. Mag.," t. 5418), a plant with a thick stem and flowers with resemblance to those of Oleander, pink in colour, and darker towards the margin. This species, with several others not in cultivation, is native of Tropical Africa.

Euphorbia Schimperi, which mimics *Ceropegia dichotoma*, is from South Arabia.

Echidnopsis.—This genus has been referred to under Abyssinia and Somaliland. There are two species native of Arabia, one being *E. Bentii* ("Bot. Mag.," t. 7760) with brown flowers, and *E. Dammanniana*, which is nearly allied.

Caralluma.—A genus of the tribe *Stapeliae*, with small flowers. It has a membranous corona, by which it is distinguished from *Boucerosia*. *C. fimbriata*, sometimes found in cultivation, is native of the East Indies as well as of Arabia.

Aloe.—*A. pendens* may here be referred to. It is figured in the " Bot. Mag.," t. 7837, and appears to be distinctly ornamental. It was collected by Schweinfurth and was introduced by the Berlin Botanic Garden. *A. inermis* is also Arabian.

EAST INDIES.

Succulent plants are proportionately uncommon and unimportant in this part of the world, and, with the exception of *Frerea*, we meet only with genera to which we have given attention already. *Frerea* is allied to *Boucerosia*; it has stems scarcely angled, which are provided with thick leaves, and it has a rotate, not campanulate, corolla of a purple colour. It has never been introduced. Other Asclepiads are *Boucerosia umbellata*, *Ceropegia elegans* ("Bot. Mag.," 3015), a slender species with spotted purple flowers, and *C. Decaisneana*.

Kalanchoë grandiflora, an old Botanic Garden plant, is well worth growing for its bright yellow, sweetly scented flowers. There are several Euphorbias, and the most important, perhaps, are *E. Antiquorum* and *E. lactea*, both trigonous species.

CEYLON.

Caralluma campanulata ("Bot. Mag.," t. 7274), with bright red-brown flowers, is distinctly a good plant of its kind from this country.

Ceropegia.—Two species are native in Ceylon, *C. Gardneri* ("Bot. Mag.," t. 5306), with pale purplish-spotted flowers, similar to *C. elegans*, but larger ; and *C. Thwaitesii* (" Bot. Mag.," t. 4758), a distinct plant with pretty flowers. The leaves are ovate acuminate ; the tube of the corolla is slender, of a yellow colour, expanding above, and there sprinkled with blood-red spots ; the segments are connivent into a cone with a band of dark purple and a green tip.

CHINA.

Sedum sarmentosum is well known in the variegated form as *S. carneum variegatum*. Among other new species described by Franchet in the "Journal de Botanique," 1896, *S. nobile* and *S. primuloides* are probably worth introduction.

JAPAN.

Sedum spectabile is distinctly a fine plant from this country, and *S. Sieboldii* is also useful. An outlying *Echeveria* I have noted as worth introduction, and it may be *Cotyledon Sikokiana* of Makino in the " Botanical Magazine " of Tokyo.

From Japan we are but on a return journey, and have little of much interest to meet with. The almost ubiquitous *Sedum* we find on the Amur to be represented by *S. Middendorfianum* and *S. Maximowiczii*, which also grows in Japan. In Siberia among others we meet with *S. hybridum* and *S. Ewersii*. On the Himalayas the last species and a few other Crassulaceae, including *Cotyledon*, occur. The Caucasus have several well-known species, including *S. stoloniferum* and *S. spurium*. In Asia Minor is a section of *Cotyledon* to which no reference has yet been made, viz. *Umbilicus*, and from other sections this appears to be distinguished by having the calyx nearly, if not quite, as long as the corolla, and a corolla tubular or campanulate with a terete tube. The cultivated species we may here meet with are *U. chrysanthus*, not unlike a *Sempervivum*, with yellow flowers, and the not widely different *U. Pestalozzae*. *Sedum sempervivoides*, described by its name and with bright red flowers, is a handsome biennial species also found in Asia Minor. Lastly, if we have friends calling at Crete, may it be asked that they would kindly send us *Sempervivum mutabile*, a plant that has never been introduced ?

Cultivation.

It would be impossible not to include a paragraph on cultivation, but it is to be observed that the great majority of succulent plants are very easily cultivated. Many Cactaceae do require special treatment, and for them every grower should consult Mr. Watson's book, noted under the head of "Bibliography," p. 463. The few other succulent plants which present any difficulty are found chiefly among the Asclepiads. For Stapelias I have my own method, and that is to grow them in pans suspended from the roof as if they were orchids. As much light as possible is essential, and as gritty, loamy soil is the best, pots or pans must be used. I use pans because of the spreading or decumbent habit of many of the species,

though for others pots are suitable. A shelf near the glass is quite satisfactory ; but these pans, or pots even, can be suspended where no shelf is
possible, and space is economised. For small succulents I have miniature
stages standing on ordinary side shelves, and upon these such plants as
Haworthia are very effectively displayed. There is also the advantage
of bringing the plants into better light, and standing space is very largely
increased. Many succulents do well if given liberal treatment, and in
this way *Kalanchoë kewensis, K. Dyeri,* and many others can be grown
in very effective batches for the conservatory. It would be impossible
here to refer to all the schemes that are adopted by succulent-plant
growers, but they will soon be discovered by those who devote themselves
to this class of cultivation. Planting out in frames, or even out of doors,
may often be done with advantage, but discretion must be exercised,
and this can only be attained by practice and experience. Just one remark
must be made on the plan of storing in boxes for the winter such plants
as Echeverias and some Cactaceae that have been planted out for the

FIG. 88.—ORNAMENTAL BED OF SUCCULENT PLANTS IN MR. FIDLER'S GARDEN,
ANERLEY.

summer. It is very easily done, and space is economised. Fig. 88 shows
a handsome bed of Echeverias and other succulents in the garden of
Mr. Fidler, of Anerley, managed upon this plan. Some special hints I
have given when referring to particular plants.

Where to see Succulent Plants.

By far the finest collection in the world is at Kew. Agaves, Aloes,
and numerous other genera are splendidly represented, and many novelties
may always be seen. From the point of view of general representation
the collection at Cambridge probably comes next ; and here, undoubtedly,
are the finest outdoor Cactaceae. A leading collection, especially of
Cactaceae, is that formed by the late Mr. Darrah, of Heaton Mersey, and
now in the Alexandra Park, Manchester, under the skilful care of Mr.
Cobbold. It contains examples not equalled elsewhere, and for splendid
Euphorbias it is remarkable. In the Botanic Gardens of Glasnevin and
Edinburgh the succulent collections are important, and at Oxford is a
collection of many years' reputation.

On the Continent are some leading collections, and one of the finest is in the Friedrich-Wilhelms-Garten at Magdeburg, originally formed by the late Herr Grusson, and this must not be missed in going to Berlin. In the Imperial Botanic Gardens at Dahlem, near Berlin, is a very fine collection. The old collection in the Jardin des Plantes, Paris, must not be forgotten. In some gardens special collections are to be found, as, for instance, that of the species of *Melocactus* at Leyden. On the Riviera are to be seen various Cactaceae and other succulents of a degree of development not elsewhere to be met with in Europe. The collections of Mr. H. Cannell, V.M.H., of Swanley; M. Frantz de Laet, of Contich, near Antwerp; and Herr Hermann Zeissold, of Leipzig, are well worth a visit.*

* [We are desired to thank Mons. Frantz de Laet, of Contich, and Herr Hermann Zeissold, of Leipzig, on behalf of the President and Council of the Society, for their exhibits of Cactaceae to illustrate the lecture. The Council awarded a Silver Banksian Medal to each of them.— ED.]

GARDEN EXPERIMENTS.

By F. J. BAKER, A.R.C.Sc.

Lecture given November 26, 1907.

EVERY gardener is continually having to consider, not only what he shall grow, but what cultural methods he shall adopt. Two persons in charge of adjacent gardens may work very differently, although the same object is sought. Frequently investigations show that practices which have become time-honoured are wrong. Writers and speakers too often obtain their ideas almost exclusively from books, and errors are perpetuated again and again. How is the earnest gardener to ascertain the real facts ? Only by careful experiment.

I desire to show the need for each gardener to be his, or her, own experimenter ; to endeavour to indicate somewhat of the intense interest, as well as the utility, accruing ; and to describe methods which I have adopted for several years, and a few of the results obtained with soils, manures, vegetables, hardy fruit, and flowers.

Many of us are well-nigh daily receiving circulars, pictorial post-cards, and the like, intended to show the wonderful results obtainable by using this or that substance. One sometimes wonders why the writers do not make their fortunes in the way they advise others to do. Alas! these flattering reports are usually selected for purposes of advertisement. A concrete example will illustrate the point. Some years ago a well-known company requested me to undertake sundry manurial experiments. I obtained the necessary substances, and the experiments were made. In due course I was asked that plots which showed the utility of the substance might be selected and photographs taken for publication. It was easy to select isolated plots which apparently showed good results, especially if one conveniently forgot, for the time, any previous manurial treatment, although the experiments as a whole showed that the stuff did not nearly pay expenses. I refused to be a party to such selection, and in consequence, of course, got nothing for the substances used, my time, or anything else. The following and succeeding years a neighbour, quite a novice at practical gardening, did the required experiments, and long reports were published in the general and local press to show the wonderful profits which were obtained. Several of these results are still being republished. If the results had been generally true of the holding, the occupier should have been making a large income. The poor crops he generally obtained were, however, strongly commented upon in the district, and throughout the whole time the man was getting badly into debt, and while the reports were passing through the press the whole of his stock was seized and sold.

The experiments being made by county councils and other public authorities are doubtless more reliable, but many of them are by no means what they should be and what they will be when individual cultivators awake to the real facts, and, having themselves carried their investigations as far as their knowledge and means permit, make definite requests to those who are paid from public funds to do research work. We wish to get the best results from our work. One advises this and another that, while we may from previous observations and experience think something quite different. We must act in the manner we deem best, so far as the greater part of the work is concerned; but at very little trouble, expense, or inconvenience we can usually vary the work on some plots, be they large or small, or even on two or three plants. If careful memoranda be made of such variations in the work, and, as time goes on, observations of the effects of these, the work becomes so intensely fascinating that it is difficult to tear oneself away from the garden even to discuss the results with one's fellows. I speak from experience. So absorbed have I often been in my investigations that I feel something like a second Robinson Crusoe, who has almost forgotten his mother-tongue, and therefore unable properly to express the results of the work.

I have no wish that my results should be taken as indicating, without further investigation, desirable changes in cultural methods. I hope to stimulate cultivators to test these things for themselves, and thereby verify or disprove my results.

For ten years I have been making experiments with peas and other leguminous plants. The general plan of one set of experiments is indicated by the diagram :

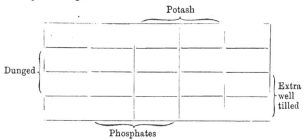

The strips marked " extra well tilled " were deeply worked in autumn, and frequently moved afterwards till seed time. The other half received ordinary tillage. At seed time potash and phosphates were sown broadcast at right angles to the tillage experiments. These experiments show that leguminous plants require a well aërated soil and one in which water can move freely from point to point; and that, given a fairly rich soil, thorough tillage is the most important. A good physical condition, whether chiefly obtained by tillage or dung, is essential to success. An abundance of minerals, such as phosphates, potash, and lime, is of great importance; but only if the soil is in sufficiently good condition to enable the plants to assimilate these will really satisfactory results be obtained. Evidently these plants, particularly peas, require as the first essential a thoroughly well aërated and hence a specially well cultivated soil with an adequate supply of water.

Many gardeners put dung largely into the second, and even the third, spit beneath the surface. Is this desirable? The nitrifying bacteria and other agents which convert the unavailable plant-food into available forms occur most largely in the surface soil. Experiments made with different soils and for different plants have induced me—and others who have seen my results—to apply dung near the surface, but as thoroughly as possible incorporated with the soil. When cultivating, the surface soil rich in humus may, with advantage, be intermixed with that underlying, but the fresh dung should be kept in the first spit.

Underground irrigation has engaged considerable attention, more especially in connection with the disposal and utilisation of house sewage. There can be no doubt that, when possible, this substance should be speedily transmitted to the earth in such a condition and position that it can be promptly changed to innocuous and, indeed, useful forms. Intermittent action is essential and easily obtained. Raspberries form an especially suitable crop for irrigating in the manner indicated, but in no case should sewage be used for irrigating salads and such like. The irrigatory system is composed of ordinary drainage pipes, unglazed and unjointed, is equally available for ordinary watering, and forms a particularly easy, cheap, and effective means of ensuring underground irrigation.

Should hardy fruit trees, such as apples, pears, and the like, be pruned at the time of planting, or after? Most experts have said, " the following season," but recently this view has been modified by many to pruning the first spring after planting. Careful experiments made for a number of years—at first with two or three, later with many trees—clearly indicated the desirability of pruning so as properly to balance a young tree *before* planting. In transplanting a tree many of the roots are unavoidably injured : these require careful pruning, and when doing this necessary operation it is recommended so to prune the top that the whole plant, top and bottom, may be well balanced, with a slight preponderance to the root. Therefore the better root the plant has the less need to prune the top hard, and *vice versa*.

Summer pruning has been much discussed lately, and as it has engaged much of my attention for about fifteen years it may be desirable to make some comments thereon. We prune such trees as dwarf apples and pears, first, to produce a shapely plant and furnish available space with branches; and, secondly, to induce fruitfulness by spur-formation along the whole of each branch. Generally speaking, once a spur is formed it should be maintained. Summer pruning should prevent the formation of useless wood, and in this way conserve energy, which the common methods do not do. Very satisfactory results have sometimes been obtained by pressing the terminal bud of a lateral shoot during the last few days of May sufficiently hard to injure it materially, but not destroy it. This operation has often arrested elongation and induced a swelling of the basal part of the shoot and enlargement of the buds in that part. Frequently the formation of an additional small leaf or two indicates development towards a rosette or young spur. This operation has not by any means invariably been a success; but even the failures have usually indicated that the work was in the right direction, if the operation can be easily and certainly performed so as to bring it within the range of practical gardening. More success attends the spiral twisting of the young laterals during the third or fourth week in June. To do this the shoot must be held with a very firm grip of the thumb and fingers of the left hand, just above, say, the third good bud, and then with the right hand placed close to the top of the left, give the shoot a third or half turn, so as to injure the wood (xylem), but not to completely break it, and certainly not cause the shoot to hang down, as is usually done by those who have heard of the system, but apparently know very little about it. Great care must be taken that the twisting motion does not pass the left hand. One cannot too strongly condemn the unsightly method of breaking, or even twisting, so as to hang down. Many experiments are now being made upon this subject, and much information will soon be forthcoming.

Summer pruning of gooseberries and red and white currants is a subject to which attention should be drawn. Many experiments have been made with these, and show clearly the advantages accruing. It may be noted that when gooseberries have been summer pruned the buds are well formed and well ripened, and then as soon as the leaves fall in autumn the bush may be tied up with a band in such a manner that all the branches are brought as nearly as possible into an upright position and held there until the buds begin to push in spring. This method of tying has been found very effective in protecting buds from bullfinches and other birds. The operation is easily and speedily done in autumn, preferably by two persons. In spring, when the band is removed, the branches readily spread out again, and if there has been permanently induced a slight upward direction it is no disadvantage, but rather the reverse (see p. xxxii).

Experiments with flowers must ever be fascinating. Hybridisation certainly must claim its devotees; and now that it can be pursued along fairly well-defined lines we may expect great developments; it is, however, largely a subject for the specialist. Wonderfully brilliant results will doubtless be obtained and will be duly boomed, the failures of amateurs, &c., will be many, but we shall hear little of these. Some intensely interesting and useful experimental work may, however, be done by all in development by selection of many of the plants we already have. Our native wild plants give us an enormous field for work of assured interest and usefulness. Time and space would fail to tell of one's experiments with the pheasant's eye (*flos Adonis*). This plant, with its finely cut green leaves, its crimson petals, and dark stamens, claims admiration, whether its gorgeous brilliancy be seen in May or from under the frozen snow at Christmas. It is a plant which luxuriates in abundance of lime and phosphates, but an excess of available nitrogen induces a thin, although large petal, which has very little endurance. In this last respect it is wonderfully similar to the evening primrose, a plant which one can admire when growing in woody places, but scarcely when it is seen in cultivated ground with large petals which lack solidity.

In conclusion I desire to record the fact that my observations, experience, and experiments incline me very strongly to the opinion that improved cultural methods are the best safeguards against disease, especially from fungoid attacks.   Fungicides are undoubtedly useful, but the cultivator will do well to strain every nerve to obtain plants of great constitutional vigour, and to develop them by appropriate cultural methods.   High forcing, especially by an unbalanced plant-food containing an excess of available nitrogen, will certainly induce liability to disease, although if the plant be not attacked, a greater amount of vegetative growth will doubtless be produced ; but this increase is often of doubtful advantage.

THE SUMMER PRUNING OF FRUIT TREES.

Papers read at the Scientific Committee meeting, October 15, 1907.

THE Chairman, Mr. E. A. BOWLES, in introducing the matter for discussion, pointed out that the subject of the summer pruning of fruit trees is one upon which there is much difference of opinion and great variety of practice among fruit-growers. It therefore becomes important to collate the experience of the practical grower and the results obtained by those who have made the matter a subject of careful experiment, in order that a rational system of procedure may be laid down for the benefit of the fruit-growing industry in the country, and that those points which are still obscure may be defined, so that they may the better be made the objects of future experiment. The principal points upon which it seems desirable to obtain evidence are the bearing upon the question of (1) the form of the tree dealt with, (2) the nature of the stock upon which it is grafted, (3) the nature of the root system developed, (4) the nature of the variety, (5) the method of pruning adopted in the winter, (6) the age of the tree, (7) the character of the soil, and (8) the character of the season both before and after the pruning is done.

Mr. H. SOMERS RIVERS, of Sawbridgeworth, said :

There would not appear at first sight to be much connection between the summer pruning of fruit trees and salmon fishing with a fly, yet there is this similarity in that there is a diversity of opinion about each.

In the fishing some maintain that the salmon takes a fly with the laudable desire of feeding on it, others that it is merely out of curiosity or play. Since whenever the fish is examined after being killed in our rivers no food is found in him, the latter theory would seem to be correct, but it was a long time before this was established.

In the same way with fruit trees, summer pruning is said to be beneficial because it induces the formation of dwarf shoots or fruit spurs.

As the fisherman has his book full of gaudy flies to choose from according to the state of the water, so the pruner advises earlier or later summer pinching or pruning, or even the twisting only of the shoots, the partially snapped ends of which are left hanging down, showy and attractive to the eye as a salmon-fly.

Whether an apple or pear tree be summer and winter pruned, or winter-pruned only, makes not a particle of difference, as far as I can see, to the buds at the base of the current year's shoots. They are not changed from long into dwarf shoot-producers because the shoot on which they are borne has been shortened a few weeks earlier or later.

Summer pruning is beneficial because it lets the light and air into a tree, exposing the fruit to the evening dews and the summer sun, enabling it to develop its full colour and beauty.

The root system and branch system are closely correlated, and in their mutual relations the former is the dominant partner.

By using dwarfing stocks, which develop a multitude of small fibrous roots, we obtain trees with a diminished growth-vigour and a corresponding increase of dwarf shoots.

Root-pruning has the same object and effect. Fed by the roots of the sturdy crab or pear stock, the apple or pear builds up a larger framework, and the tree devotes its energies more or less to this until its vegetative vigour slackens and it has attained its full size. An old orchard standard is usually somewhat like an open umbrella, boughs and branches answering to the supports and ribs, leaves and fruits to the silk envelope, each of the latter exposed as fully as possible to the light.

Nature summer-prunes. In a cold, sunless period aphides multiply amazingly, especially on the shoot-tips. The tree cannot grow away from them. They curl up the leaves, reducing their breathing and shade area ; they appropriate to themselves the sap which the tree sends up for the further development of the shoots and leaves.

Most fruit-growers know Du Breuil's book on the training of fruit trees, illustrated with a hundred and one diagrams of the various geometrical patterns, pleasing to the eye, which trees may be made to assume.

My father called on M. Du Breuil one day, but, as he was unfortu-nately away from home, was shown round by the old gardener. The place was full of trees, varied in shape and trained geometrically, exactly as the drawings of the book. " Wonderful ! " said my father, after he had been round, "wonderful ! but where do you get your fruit ? " The man's eyes twinkled as he threw open the door in a wall of the garden leading to an old but well-cared-for orchard in which the trees were laden. " Here, Monsieur," he said ; " here the master does not come ! "

Trees do not lend themselves well to mathematical treatment.

This was a case of both summer and winter pruning carried to excess : continually stimulated, the trees continuously tried to grow more naturally. They had no time for the formation of fruit buds.

Ordinary summer pruning makes the trees in a garden look neater, and, as has been said before, lets in the light and air to the fruit. It is possible there may be a result something analogous to root pruning in the suppression of so many leaves and the ensuing check to, or rather diversion of, the activities of the tree. This could no doubt be ascer-tained by direct experiment during a number of years.

With peaches and nectarines, which bear their fruits along shoots the year after they have been formed, the case is different.

These trees are always necessarily subjected to a much more artificial treatment than the hardier fruit trees. For them, too, we have as yet no dwarfing stocks.

The shoots must be stopped ; the buds behind this point then get the benefit of the food which would otherwise be employed in the lengthening of the shoot.

Mr. SPENCER PICKERING, F.R.S. (Director of the Woburn Experimental Fruit Farm), said :

Such remarks as I may make in contribution to the discussion on this subject must be prefaced by the statement that it is a subject on which no very complete experiments have yet been made at

Woburn, and it is one, therefore, on which I wish to speak with considerable diffidence. It is true that two or three of our experimental plots, of eighteen bush apple trees each, have been subject to summer pruning for the last thirteen years ; but two or three experiments are quite inadequate for any complete examination of the subject; whilst other more extensive experiments have not been in progress long enough to admit of any conclusions being drawn from them. The results, however, which have been obtained at the farm, on the subject of pruning in general, are calculated to throw some light on the more special question of summer pruning.

One of the general conclusions from our pruning experiments (which have been dealt with at length in the Seventh Report) * is that, in opposition to the popular opinion on the subject, the pruning of a healthy, growing tree results in a diminution of the amount of new wood formed, as measured either by the increase in size or weight of the tree, or by the length or weight of the new shoots. The harder the pruning, the greater is this diminution. As compared with moderately pruned trees, those which had been continuously hard-pruned were nearly 20 per cent. smaller, whereas those which had been left unpruned were about 20 per cent. larger. It certainly cannot be a matter of surprise that the removal of any essential portion of an organism should, under normal conditions, result in a check to the natural growth of that organism, and this check should be all the greater if the part is removed while it is still functioning actively—*i.e.* if the pruning is practised in summer. Such evidence as exists, indicates that this is so, and shows that pruning in summer checks the growth of the tree much more than pruning at any other time of the year. The experiments which illustrate this point most clearly are some in which very hard pruning, or cutting back, was done on similar trees at different times in the year (see Seventh Report, p. 37). Trees cut back at various dates during the dormant season, November to April, all behaved similarly as regards their subsequent growth, but when cut back in summer (the middle of July) the amount of growth made by the end of the season was only one-fifth of that of the other trees ; and the evil effects were not confined to the one season only, for in the succeeding season these trees still produced only three-quarters of the wood produced by those which had been cut back while dormant, and they were otherwise deficient in health and vigour. Cutting back quite early in the summer (middle of May) produced similar but much less serious results. Other experiments on cutting back young freshly planted trees are leading to like conclusions, but the actual figures cannot yet be given.

Ample evidence has been brought forward in our Seventh Report to show that branch-pruning generally, when done in autumn, is inimical to heavy cropping, but it does not follow that this will be so with summer pruning ; indeed, the object of summer pruning is to increase cropping ; and, on account of the check produced by it on wood formation, it is easy to see that such a result should, or may, follow. The removal of a portion of any shoot which is in a state of activity will divert the

---

* Eyre & Spottiswoode. 1907. The Fifth Report, p. 36, deals more fully with the results up to that date from the summer-pruned plots.

flow of sap to the buds on that portion of the shoot left, and these, in consequence, will start developing. This development may take one of two directions : it may proceed only sufficiently far to nourish the dormant buds and convert them into future fruit buds, or it may proceed far enough to force the buds into growth. The latter effect is, of course, the reverse of what is desired, since it will result in the formation of numerous small shoots, which will not have time to ripen, and which will have to be cut away in the following autumn.

Whether summer pruning will bring about the desirable or the undesirable result would appear to depend on so many circumstances that any general statement on the matter, or the prediction of the event, would seem to be an impossibility; and this would account for the diversity of opinion which is held on the subject. Clearly the vigour with which a tree is growing at the time will determine whether the buds at the base of the shoots will be forced into activity or not, and the vigour of growth depends on many things : on the variety of the tree dealt with, the nature of its root-stock, and the age and character of the individual tree; also on the position and sturdiness of the branch pruned, the extent to which the pruning has been carried, and the time at which the pruning has been done, as well as on the condition as to moisture of the soil in which the tree is growing, and the character of the weather following the operation. This last circumstance, above all others, would appear to render the results of summer pruning uncertain, even in the hands of the most skilful.

It would seem that the summer pruning of any shoots which are growing vigorously should be avoided, if the object in view is the formation of fruit buds; and the operation, therefore, should be confined to the weaker shoots, which will generally be side shoots. Such pruning is more appropriately termed summer pinching ; and, as it is desirable to have the fruit spurs as near the base of the shoots as possible, it seems clear that the pinching should be close, leaving not more than three or four buds on the shoot; for it is only the buds nearest to the cut which appear to be affected by the pruning. To avoid starting the basal buds into growth, the pinching should evidently be done late in the season, though the actual time at which it will be most successful must vary very much with the character of the trees, and of that of the season in question.

In the experiments which have recently been started at Woburn the influence of the date of summer pruning is being investigated on a number of different varieties of apples and pears, the dates selected ranging from the middle of July to the beginning of September. In the few experiments which have been in progress there since 1894 the summer pruning has been done in August, and the general results obtained are entirely negative in character, neither the size of the trees nor the weight of the crops showing any appreciable difference when compared with similar trees which have been subjected to moderate autumn pruning only (*loc. cit.*). In 1906, however, the crops from the summer-pruned plots were very much below the average, but only one of the three varieties under investigation (Bramley) fruited that year. Although the present size of the summer-pruned and winter-pruned trees is the same, it is not possible to affirm that the wood formation has been identical, for the prunings have not been weighed. From the results obtained with very severe pruning and cutting back in summer, it would appear that even moderate summer pruning must decrease somewhat the wood-formation.

In illustration of the great variation of results produced by differences in soil I may quote a letter received some time ago from Mr. F. W. Moore, of the Botanic Gardens, Glasnevin. He says :

"Within a radius of fifteen miles from this the conditions are quite different. Here, if I do not summer-prune—or, I should say, summer-pinch, for I never remove more than two eyes in summer—I get a number of blind eyes at the base ; and if I cut hard enough in spring to make these eyes break, I only get growths and not spurs. The soil here is a poor light loam, shallow, and resting on limestone gravel. At Straffan, about fifteen miles from this, on a cool stiff clay near the river, Mr. Bedford finds that if he summer-prunes he gets too much rank growth, and that the eyes break well even after a light winter pruning. We have often compared results. He suffers from too much moisture as a rule ; I suffer from too much drought."

The more serious operation of summer pruning proper, as contrasted with summer pinching, may doubtless have some inhibitory effect on the growth of the tree similar to that which followed from the hard pruning in summer in the case of the Woburn experiments already quoted. It can only be in exceptional cases that such stunting of a tree can ever be desirable ; and, whatever the immediate effect on the fruiting may be, it is probable that it will result in a diminution of the total crop borne by the tree in its lifetime. It is clear, too, that with such summer pruning there is always a great risk of getting a thicket of useless growth and a considerable reduction of fruit. It would seem, therefore, that summer pruning proper should only be applied to vigorously growing branches in cases where it is desirable to check their growth for the sake of improving the balance of the tree.

Perhaps it is legitimate to raise the question as to how far summer pruning, even when it accomplishes all that is expected of it, is really desirable. All that it can do is to increase the blossom buds on a tree, but that does not necessarily increase the fruiting, and it may even have the opposite effect. Probably, in nine cases out of ten, a deficiency of crop, in the case of a tree which has come to maturity, is not due to deficiency of flowering, but to the destruction of the blossoms by frost or living pests, or to the imperfect fertilisation, or setting, of the fruit. Numerous cases may be noticed every year in which trees which seemed rather deficient in flower have yielded as much fruit as they could well carry, and others in which there has been excessive flowering followed by little or no fruit. Excessive flowering also often leads to reduction in the value of a crop by the strain which it puts on the resources of the tree. This is very noticeable with 'Lord Grosvenor' and some other apples. A row of twenty large bush trees of this variety, which have been under my immediate observation, have offered a conspicuous example in point this year. About half of them had very little blossom, but yielded eventually a good paying crop of fine fruits, the trees being

s s 2

throughout the season in a good, healthy condition; the other half of the trees flowered so profusely, and the fruit set so well, that the trees have been quite exhausted and almost killed; and, in spite of the most ruthless thinning, the apples never swelled and the crop was worthless. In fact, with many varieties it is a reduction, and not an increase, of the blossom-buds which is required to assure a paying crop; and this is recognised in the case of trained trees, where persistent summer pruning often multiplies the fruit buds to such an extent that disbudding has to be resorted to.

Mr. A. H. PEARSON, of Lowdham, Notts, wrote:

In accepting your invitation to write a short paper upon "summer pruning of fruit trees" I fear I have done wrong, for science, it would seem, asks for a large number of data which the ordinary practical pruner has not made himself familiar with; and the facts accepted by science have frequently to be demonstrated by a long and wide series of experiments, which many of us have not the leisure to undertake. However, if any remarks of mine are likely to be of the least service, I shall only be too pleased to give them.

At the onset I would say that summer pruning, as it is often under-stood, is, I think, perhaps the most mischievous practice which fruit growers undertake, and the cause of more dismal failures than any other operation in the fruit garden. What I advocate is summer *pinching*, which is done by taking off the points of growing shoots when they have made some five or six leaves, or, say, from four to six inches of wood. When the shoots break again from the top bud, pinch back to two more leaves, which will be all that is necessary in an ordinary season; but in a wet summer a third pinching may be required.

The shoots treated in this way are, of course, side shoots; the leading shoots will in many cases need no stopping in the summer. The object of this pinching is to keep the side growths from becoming too strong and to cause the basal buds to plump up, and subsequently develop into fruit buds. The word "subsequently" applies to such fruits as pears, apples, &c.; for in the case of small fruits, gooseberries, and currants the buds will develop the first season. The winter pruning of these side shoots depends much upon the age and condition of the tree; but on all young and vigorous trees every side shoot should be left from four to five buds in length, according to the habit of the tree and whether the variety has buds placed far apart or more closely together. If pruned in this way the top bud, and probably the second, will make growth, thus providing an outlet for the vigorous sap of the tree, whilst the lower buds will remain almost dormant and will make the little rosette of leaves which plainly foretells a bloom bud next season. *When* bloom buds are formed and fully developed at the lower part of the shoot, and *not before*, the shoots may be shortened back to such bloom buds in order to keep the spurs close to the leading branches, and so ensure a full supply of sap and also to prevent overcrowding.

Summer pruning as often practised consists in letting all side shoots grow wild and then in cutting them back to within two or three buds of the leading branch which carries them: by this method all the side shoots get very strong, and the vast majority of the buds left after pruning make vigorous growth either in the following spring, or, as is quite as often the case during a growing season, the growth is made the same autumn. The result is much the same as that obtained by clipping a hawthorn hedge in July and again at Christmas. I believe there is a Scotch saying, " Saw ye ever haws on a clippit hedge ? " and most certainly one rarely sees fruit on the thousands of almost solid pyramid apple and pear trees which are to be seen in British gardens, almost as handsome as the Continental bay trees, and quite as useful to form nesting shelters for blackbirds.

Summer pinching as described is proper for all kinds of fruit trees which form fruiting spurs—apples, pears, plums, and cherries with the exception of the Morello class—and also for cordon and trained goose-berries and red and white currants, whilst peaches, nectarines, apricots, and Morello cherries fruit on the young wood, and the pinching of these is confined to stopping hard those shoots which will not be required for laying in, or any which threaten to upset the balance of the tree by too vigorous growth. If pinching be practised, the knife will only be required to cut out the wood which has carried a crop of fruit, and gumming will be much less seen than where the knife is used more freely. This is most marked in the case of young trees ; it was formerly the custom of nursery-men to grow their one-year trees of these fruits, which are termed maidens, in a natural manner, and they made upright bushes three or four feet in height, which when required for training were cut back the following season to some 12 or 15 inches from the soil in order to make them branch out from the lower buds. This severe pruning often caused gumming, and to avoid this we now pinch out the lead of the trees which are wanted for training, and so cause the buds to break the first season ; the resulting shoots are tied out, and the foundation of a trained tree is secured the first season, which is a gain ; but the great point is that gumming is almost unknown upon trees treated in this manner.

Now as to the form of tree which should be summer-pinched : one naturally turns first to the single cordon as an example of the tree which *must* be so treated ; then we take all wall and espalier trees of those fruits which bear on spurs, and we say that the side branches of horizontally trained trees are only cordons growing laterally from the main stem ; double cordons, palmettes, and palmette verries are of course only multiplications of the single cordon ; and, lastly, true pyramids are only single cordons springing from the central axis of the main stem. Such pyramids one rarely sees in this country, where skilled pruners are scarce and their labour dear ; but in Belgium, where I learned my pruning, every decent fruit garden can show grand specimens of this style of pruning, especially of pears, trees of many years' standing, and carrying crops of grand fruit to old age. In many gardens in Britain one finds apple trees trained in basin-shape and all the branches treated as cordons, which carry fine exhibition fruit ; and in Worcestershire there are hundreds of acres so pruned ; but as the trees get older and carry heavy crops they are only pruned once a year.

The great majority of growers for market do very little pruning upon either standard or bush fruit trees after the first three or four years, beyond cutting out any dead or crossing branches, but allow the trees to follow their own inclinations.

With regard to the value of summer pinching, one has only to walk into the young quarters of a fruit-tree nursery and see three-year apples which have been pinched for cordons carrying full crops of fruit, whilst the bushes amongst which they are standing, and under precisely similar conditions otherwise, have only odd fruits here and there. At the last R.H.S. meeting Messrs. Veitch showed some two-year-old cordon apples with ten large fruit on each : they could not carry more because there was no space to stick them on. Again, how frequently one goes into gardens where the wall trees run wild, with summer growths from one to two feet long smothering the trees, and fruit conspicuous by its absence, or only to be found at the extreme end of the extension-shoots. This is often because the head gardener delights more in glass than in hardy fruits, but more often because in these days large gardens are terribly under-staffed and there is no one to do the work at the proper time. In these cases I always say, as soon as the rush of early summer work—bedding and what not—is over, run round the walls and espaliers and break the side shoots back to six or eight inches, leaving the broken portion hanging on. This broken part will absorb a small amount of sap, and so prevent the lower buds from breaking into growth ; but at the same time there will be a sufficient check to throw the sap into these lower buds and plump them up ready for forming fruit buds the following season. If the owner of the trees should object to the untidy appearance of hundreds of broken shoots hanging on the trees, the obvious remedy is to provide labour to do the pinching earlier.

I fear I have failed to answer many of the questions put to me, but it will, I think, be clear that young trees, especially those growing in rich soil and upon free stocks, will need more attention in the way of summer pinching than those which are older and less vigorous or worked upon dwarfing stocks or growing in less fertile soil.

In conclusion, I may say that pinching may be too severe, as well as pruning : healthy trees must have some outlet for the sap ; the extension-shoots will not take all the roots send up, and if one *will* pinch or prune too closely, the remaining buds *must* make wood growth instead of bloom. I was once asked to see the trees of an amateur who said he could obtain no fruit, and after looking round his walls and espaliers I told him I had never seen trees better pruned. He thought I was joking, and said that was only his first pruning to allow the wood to ripen off, and that he intended to go over them again and shorten every side growth to two buds, under which treatment only complete exhaustion of the trees would produce fruit buds.

Too close pinching or pruning, especially the latter, is the great cause of our gardens being fruitless ; and the next great fault is allowing bunches of spurs to remain on older trees. After fruit spurs are fully developed they should be pruned closely ; two or three bloom buds on a side shoot, each bud capable of producing a bunch of flowers and leaves, should suffice ; but many old trees will be found with a dozen or more fruit buds on a side growth, the result being that they smother one another out of existence.

Mr. W. SEABROOK, of Springfield, Chelmsford, said that he had learned to grow good fruit by making mistakes and correcting them.

Thirty years ago, when he had first begun to grow fruit, he read all there was to be read in books upon the subject of pruning, and found much diversity of statement ; a condition of things that persisted to this day. As a result of his experience he had formed the opinion that if first-class fruit was to be grown—and that was the only kind for which there was a continual demand at remunerative prices, and the only kind that was worth growing—severe pruning, both in winter and summer, must be resorted to. Dwarfing stocks *must* be used, and then fruit will be formed and grow well early in the life of the tree, and the tree will keep on fruiting. He had been told that the trees on dwarfing stocks would not last long, but he thought it better to have twenty years' fruit to start with, even if after that time the trees required to be renewed, rather than to wait fifteen years while the trees were growing before he had any fruit at all. He had at one time tried the method of breaking down the laterals, and had come to the conclusion that it was far better to remove them altogether, because if they were left hanging they shaded the rest of the shoots, and a considerable part of the benefit that was to be derived from summer pruning was lost. Many people advocated summer pruning back to within six buds of the base of the shoot, but he considered that not to be sufficiently far, as the fruit buds that would develop on the shoot as the result of that treatment would be too far from the branch. He found that the basal buds were quite unaffected if the shoots were left as long as that. They should be pruned back to three buds ; then usually the highest of these would develop into a vegetative bud, the middle one would remain dormant, and the basal one would either in the same season or in the succeeding one become a fruit bud. If the tree was in too vigorous a condition, the second bud might develop into a shoot bud ; then, he thought, was the time to root-prune the trees. The subsequent development of the shoot left after pruning gave a good indication of the state of the root system, and showed well when root pruning was necessary. Summer pruning should consist of cutting back all new wood to three leaves, *except the leader* of the branch. This leader is shortened back half-way in winter. The end of July and August is usually the best time for summer pruning. Pinching out the points of lateral shoots of wall plum trees, when they have attained to six leaves (generally in June), will cause fruit buds to form along the entire shoot. He considered that the best form of tree for growing good fruit on this system, apart from wall trees, was the open bush, or the single cordon when space was a greater consideration. The late Dr. Bartrum had, during the closing years of his life, resorted greatly to severe summer·and winter pruning, dealing even with his standard trees in this way ; but Mr. Seabrook thought that would be probably carrying the application of the method too far. In the first six or seven years of their life, however, even standard trees would benefit greatly by the treatment.

Mr. F. W. MOORE, of Glasnevin, followed, and upheld most of what had been said about summer pruning. He thought that this particular subject was one that was peculiarly fitted to come up for discussion before the Scientific Committee of the Society, as it was a subject that was intimately connected with both the practical and scientific aspects

of plant physiology, and much good should arise from the wedding of
the scientific inquiry with the experiences of the practical man. He
thought that a considerable amount of the difference of opinion expressed
upon the subject by growers arose from the fact that the expression
"summer pruning" was often misconstrued, and many had insisted
upon the term "summer pinching" as being the more accurate one.
He considered, however, that the process was properly called pruning,
and that all such operations as this, and thinning of shoots, should be
included under the same term. He insisted upon the fact that no
general rule could be laid down for the treatment of all trees, but that
several things should be taken into consideration. The nature of the
stock should be considered, the variety of fruit grown should also be
considered. For instance, certain varieties behave very differently on the
Crab and on the Paradise stocks. 'Early Victoria,' 'Stirling Castle,'
and 'Beauty of Bath' on the Paradise stock were inclined to fruit
very freely in quite a young state, and to make too little wood, so that
they appeared stunted. In such cases no summer pruning was necessary ;
on the contrary, every encouragement had to be given the trees to make
as free growth as possible. On the Crab stock these varieties grow much
more vigorously, and summer pruning had often to be resorted to. On
the other hand, 'Bismarck' and 'Blenheim Orange' grow freely on both
stocks, and summer pruning was beneficial to the trees, whether on the
Crab stock or the Paradise stock. The question of soil had also to be
considered. On a light dry soil pruning might be unnecessary in many
cases, whereas on a deep, cool soil careful summer pruning often gained
a year in the formation of fruit spurs. He spoke in eulogistic terms of
the Belgian system of pruning, and advocated the open bush as the best
form of tree for giving the greatest amount of first-class fruit from the
smallest space. He thought that judicious summer pruning would go a
long way to avoid the necessity of heavy winter pruning.

Mr. SMITH, of Loddington, was the next speaker. He said he could
add very little to the remarks that had been made by the previous
speakers, but he would like to emphasize the advice that had been given
to thin the trees out well and to shorten the lateral shoots back to three
buds in the summer. He thought, too, that each variety should be considered separately, and that each required different pruning from the others,
giving as instances of this the fact that 'Bismarck' should be severely
pruned while 'Worcester Pearmain' should only be thinned out. He
pointed out the necessity for admitting all the light and air possible into
the tree, and said that the pruning should be done from all round the
tree, not from one side only.

Mr. F. J. BAKER, A.R.C.S., thought that there was need to investigate
the conditions under which the bud may be made to form a fruit instead
of a shoot, and suggested that the presence of a considerable amount of
nitrogenous manure in the soil would tend rather to the formation of
shoot buds than to that of fruit buds. He considered that many of the
previous speakers had suggested the carrying-out of the operation under
discussion at a period too late in the year, and thought that twisting the
shoot some little distance above its point of origin was a better practice
than actually removing the whole of the portion of the shoot that was

considered undesirable. He had found that by carrying out this operation in the first week in June there was an unmistakable development of fruit buds at the base of the shoot operated upon towards the end of July.

Mr. CHAS. FOSTER, of Reading, considered that the balance between the root and branch system could be better kept up by lifting the tree at frequent intervals than by doing so much pruning. Each variety should be treated upon its merits, but he thought that severe summer pruning was not to be advocated.

Mr. W. H. DIVERS sent a branch of an apple tree, of the variety Bismarck,' heavily laden with somewhat small fruits, showing the result of omitting both summer and winter pruning in 1906. The tree was bearing a heavy crop on the top, so that it was really breaking down with the weight. Several of the speakers referred to the branch in the course of their remarks, and regarded it as a good illustration of an undesirable state of things, since many small fruits had been secured, instead of a few of much better quality, and these in a part of the tree that was not easily dealt with, and where they were greatly exposed to the wind.

*   *   *   *   *   *   *   *

At a subsequent meeting of the Committee the following report upon a series of experiments on the summer pruning of fruit trees was read. The experiments were carried out by Mr. C. Wakely, F.R.H.S., at the Essex County School of Horticulture, Chelmsford. Mr. Wakely wrote :

" The general results of the summer-pruning experiments agree well with my conclusions of past years, but there is evidently much to be learnt as to the behaviour of different varieties, and therefore as to the time of pruning. Stocks, too, are of great importance in this connection.

"Many men have an idea that the basal buds of the pruned shoot are developed into blossom buds, but my observations are entirely contrary to this notion, and go to show that only those buds nearest to the cut are influenced to any extent, and these are the buds that develop into blossom buds, if any change occurs.

" The apple has a greater tendency to secondary growth than the plum. Hence it is absolutely useless to give any *general* directions for summer pruning. There is great need of experimental work with an evenly started set of trees, so that the results obtained may be more accurately compared ; but the following table calls attention to a few of the important factors in the case.

" It may be noted that gooseberry and red currant bushes pruned on June 4 both refrained from making secondary growth, but they seem to have plumped up their lower buds a good deal. Close pruning is the plan to be adopted with these.

" The soil in which the trees experimented with are growing is a somewhat heavy loam overlying boulder clay, and the rainfall during the year was distributed as follows : January, 1·29 in. ; February, 0·93 in. ; March, 0·91 in. ; April, 2·34 ins. ; May, 2·02 ins. ; June, 1·98 in. ; July, 1·96 in. ; August, 1·48 in. ; September, 0·60 in. ; October, 2·85 ins. ; November, 2·47 ins.—giving a total during the first six months of the year of 9·47 ins., and during the period July to November 9·36 ins."

The tables on the next two pages show the results of summer pruning in Pears, Apples, and Plums.

SUMMER PRUNING OF PEARS.

Variety.	Form of tree.	Stock.	Years from graft.	Vigour of individual.	Cropping or not.	Time.	Method.	Results by Autumn.
Conference	Half Standard	Pear	12	Strong	A fair crop	June 4	Pruned to fifth leaf from base	No ... 15 ... of ... growth, 12—
"	"	"	12	"	"	July 8	"	A few ... rather plump, 12-15 ... of secondary growth.
"	Bush	Quince	9	"	Heavy crop	July 18	"	Some fair ...
Emile d'Heyst	...	"	8	Moderate	Light crop	July 8	"	Some good blossom ...
"	Espalier	"	8	"	Fair crop	June 25	"	Some fair ...
"	...	"	8	"	Heavy ...	July 8	"	Some good ... at ... making
Josephine de Malines	Pyramid	"	9	Strong	A good crop	June 4	"	Gd buds, probably blossom. 12-18 ins. of secondary growth.
"	Espalier	"	8	"	No crop	June 26	"	some attempts at ...
"	Vase-shaped	"	8	Moderate	A good crop	Aug. 6	"	A few ... rather pl ... no ... growth.
Marie Louise d'Ucele	Cordon	"	8	"	A fair crop	July 8	"	Gd ..., probably blossom.
"	"	"	4	"	"	June 27	"	No ... 12-15 ins. of ... growth.
Pitmaston Duchess	Pyramid	"	9	Strong	A heavy crop	June 4	"	Gd ... buds developed.
"	Espalier	"	8	"	No crop	June 26	"	Gd ... and also ... at same.
Williams' Bon Chrétien	Pyramid	"	9	"	A heavy crop	Aug. 6	"	A few ... plump.
"	Cordon	"	8	"	A light crop	July 8	"	Gd attempts at ... buds.
"	Espalier	"	8	"	"	June 26	"	Some ... and at same, 12-15 ins. of ... growth.
"	Pyramid	"	9	Moderate	A fair crop	Aug. 6	"	Slight attempts at bl ... buds, no ... growth.
"	Cordon	"	8	"	A light crop	July 8	"	Slight attempts at blossom ...
Beurré Diel	"	"	4	"	No crop	June 27	"	no ...; Gd ...
Duchesse d'Angoulême	"	"	4	"	"	"	"	Good ...
Vicar of Winkfield	"	"	4	"	"	"	"	No ..., 12-15 ins. of ... growth.

SUMMER PRUNING OF APPLES.

Variety.	Form of tree.	Stock.	Years from graft.	Vigour of individual.	Cropping or not.	Time.	Method.	Results by Autumn.
Beauty of Bath	Espalier	Paradise	9	Strong	No crop	June 4	Pruned to 5th leaf from base	Slight plumping of 3rd bds, 12–20 ins. of growth. 2nd and 4th dry
Beauty of Kent	Cordon	,,	8	Moderate	Good crop	June 27	,,	Gd blossom bds devel pd.
Hoary Morning	Pyramid	,,	9	,,	,,	July 15	,,	Gd bdm bds devel pd.
James Grieve	Cordon	,,	4	,,	Light crop	June 27	,,	Gd bdm bds devel pd.
Lady Sudeley	Half Standard	,,	4	Moderate	,,	June 4	,,	Gd bdm bds devel pd.
Worcester Pearmain	,,	Crab	12	,,	,,	,,	,,	Fair gwth. bdm bds on 6 ins. of
,,	,,	,,	12	,,	,,	,,	,,	Small gwth. bdm bds on 6 ins. of
,,	Cordon	Paradise	8	Strong	No crop	,,	,,	Fair bdm bds on 18 ins. of growth.

SUMMER PRUNING OF PLUMS.

Variety.	Form of tree.	Stock.	Years from graft.	Vigour of individual.	Cropping or not.	Time.	Method.	Results by Autumn.
Czar	Bush	?	8	Strong	Heavy crop	June 26	Pruned to 5th leaf from base	Buds well pl growth. no secondary
Monarch	Half Standard	?	12	,,	,,	June 4	,,	Buds well pd, 3 ins. of secondary growth.
,,	,,	Mussel	12	,,	,,	June 27	,,	Buds well pd, 6 ins. of secondary growth.
,,	,,	?	12	,,	,,	Aug. 6	,,	Buds well pd, no secondary growth.
,,	Pyramid	?	8	Moderate	Fair crop	,,	,,	Buds fairly pl pd, no secondary growth.
Rivers' Early Prolific	Bush	Mussel	8	Weak	Heavy crop	June 4	,,	Buds well plumped, 6 ins. of secondary growth.
,,	Half Standard	?	12	Strong	,,	June 26	,,	Buds well pd, 3–6 ins. of secondary growth.
,,	,,	?	12	,,	,,	Aug. 6	,,	Buds well plumped, no secondary growth.

CONTRIBUTIONS FROM THE WISLEY LABORATORY.

I. Apple-leaf Spot.

By Fred. J. Chittenden, F.L.S.

The occurrence of brown dead spots on the leaves of the apple was more than usually frequent during the summer of 1907, and specimens have been received at the laboratory from a considerable number of widely separated localities. At the same time there have been repeated references to the blotching and death of apple leaves and the consequent lessening of the crop, particularly as regards weight, in the horticultural Press, thus emphasising the fact that the trouble has been met with in nearly all parts of the country.

Many different reasons have been assigned by growers as the cause of the appearance of the leaf-spot, *e.g.* the prevalence of adverse weather conditions during the growing season, particularly of frost or of excessively low temperatures closely approaching the freezing-point; the use of certain spray fluids against the attacks of aphides and similar pests; the attacks of insects themselves; and, very rarely indeed, the attack of a fungus, which was actually the direct cause of the trouble.

In every case of apple-leaf spot brought to our notice (and some hundreds of leaves have been examined)—with the exception of a very few in which the spot had been caused by a small burrowing larva feeding on the soft tissue between the two skins of the leaf, leaving the skins intact—the spot was associated with the presence of a fungus. This form of trouble in apple culture appears to merit greater attention than it has hitherto received in this country, as it is capable of causing considerable damage both in the year of the attack and in the years subsequent to it, even if it should not recur with equal virulence in those years.

Description of the Spots.—As a rule the spots on the apple leaves are more or less rounded (fig. 89, A); but as their growth is limited by the main veins, they may have one or more straight sides. They never include large veins. They vary considerably in size, being from 1 mm. to 6 mm. in diameter (*i.e.* from one-twelfth to half an inch), but the largest of these measurements is very rarely attained. They are brown in colour, and each is surrounded by a narrow purplish line. The tissue of the part of the leaf attacked is perhaps a little thinner than the rest of the leaf and is brittle.* Several spots frequently occur near together on a leaf, and, where they meet, run together, so that a considerable area of the leaf is killed. In the worst instances the leaf appears as if scorched with fire.

---

* Spots very similar in appearance to these are produced by the fungus *Phyllosticta prunicola*, and the microsclerotia on the spots bear a superficial resemblance to the perithecia of that fungus, so that at first the spots might be attributed to it; but spots caused by *P. prunicola* lack the narrow purple margin and are surrounded by a line of the same colour as the spot. Injury to the leaves of apples very similar to that here described has been caused in severe attacks of *Fusicladium dendriticum*, the fungus producing the too well-known apple-scab.

Frequently, too, the dead tissue of the spot drops out and·leaves a hole in the leaf, in the same way as the tissue killed by the 'shot-hole' fungus in peaches. In very bad cases the leaves themselves drop prematurely, so that a branch may become defoliated for a great part of its length. The first indication of the attack is the appearance of a purplish tinge on the affected area.

The part of the tree most usually affected in the past year was the first 9 to 12 inches of the growth made in the early part of the season, but later on in the autumn it frequently happened that the greater part of the foliage became more or less affected.

The Injury to the Trees.—As all the food upon which the tree depends for its existence and growth is made in the green leaves, and there

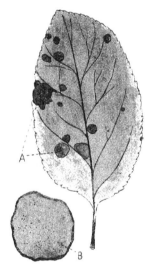

FIG. 89.

A, Apple leaf showing spots (natural size); B, One of the spots enlarged; the dots are microsclerotia.

only, it is obvious that anything that interferes to the destruction of the tissues of these organs, reducing their effective area, must seriously handicap the tree, not only in the season of the attack, but also in those immediately following. For in each season a certain amount of the food made in the leaves is sent into the stem, where it forms a reserve of food to serve for the start of growth in the next year, and upon this reserve depends to a large extent the power of the tree to withstand adverse conditions during the early part of the growing season; and the same factor largely determines the weight of fruit that may be borne without materially weakening the tree. When the attack follows weakening from any other cause, the result may be little short of disastrous. In the train of such reduction of effective leaf area, particularly if the attack be recurrent, must come lessened vitality, inability to recoup losses due to the attacks of aphides and other insects, lessened crops (though, perhaps, not for some time in the actual number of fruits produced), and general ill-health. The trees will be neither things of beauty nor capable of yielding profitable crops.

A further source of damage to the tree may arise from the fact that when the first foliage is destroyed early in the season the terminal buds of the shoot may be induced to grow out instead of going to rest at the normal time. This extra growth entails a further call upon the reserves laid by, and must be detrimental to the general well-being of the tree. Further, the growth made will probably be made too late to ripen properly, and the foliage near the tips of the shoots will persist for a considerable time after the greater part has fallen. In the present season many leaves were to be seen on such shoots at Christmas.

The Cause of the Attack.—It will be instructive, first, to see how far the suggestions put forward by different growers as to the cause of the spotting are upheld by actual facts.

The use of spray fluids too strong for the foliage to bear, may be at once dismissed ; for the trouble appeared both on trees that had been sprayed with such sprays as quassia and soft soap, or with paraffin emulsion against the attacks of aphides, &c., and on those that had not been sprayed ; not only in different plantations, but in the same plantation where one portion had been sprayed and another had not, trees in both were attacked indiscriminately.

In the same way the appearance of these spots on the leaves cannot be laid to the charge of insects, as these pests were frequently entirely absent from the plants showing the leaf spotting.

There remains the question of the prevalence of adverse weather conditions.

Usually an examination into the truth or falsity of accusations against the weather is very difficult to make. Temperature and the other factors that go to make climate often vary materially within the space of even a few hundred yards,* so that no reasoning from the temperature recorded a short distance away from the place where the injury to plant growth has occurred can be accepted without some shadow of suspicion. Fortunately, however, thanks to the well-equipped meteorological station in the Wisley Garden, and the extreme care and accuracy with which the records are kept, the difficulty is in this case reduced to a minimum.

The apples over the whole of the fruit plantation at Wisley suffered severely, and as the meteorological station stands in the midst of the apple trees, and practically on a level with the whole of the plantation, exact comparisons of the temperatures at certain periods, and the amount of injury done, may be made with a close approximation to the drawing of just inferences.

The climatic conditions which appear capable of causing the death of certain portions of leaves of such a hardy tree as the apple, so that spots somewhat similar to those described above are produced, while other portions of the leaves remain healthy and green, are : (1) the occurrence of frosts, or (2) temperatures closely approaching freezing-point, and

* For instance, two thermometers placed about 350 yards apart in different parts of the Wisley Garden often record minimum temperatures varying from 8° to 10°.

(3) the scorching of the foliage through the hot sun shining directly upon it after rain or heavy dew.

As pointed out above, the portions of the shoots that suffered most from the attacks of the fungus were usually the first nine inches to twelve inches of the growth. This being so, we may assume that if this spotting were directly due to adverse climatic conditions, these must have occurred during the time when the growth was made, that is, during the latter end of April or the month of May. The screen in which the maximum and minimum thermometers are kept is about the height of the branches of many of the bushes from the ground, and we may take the minimum recorded in the screen as the minimum to which the vast majority of the bushes were exposed. An examination of the temperature chart which accompanies this paper (fig. 90) shows that the minimum temperature during these six weeks *did not once reach the* '*freezing-point*. Even on the grass, where the radiation is intense (and the trees are in cultivated ground), the thermometer only six times touched freezing-point and only twice fell a little below 30°. It is inconceivable that the spotting of the leaves of such a hardy plant as the apple should be due to such a small amount of frost. The justice of this inference is upheld by the fact that in previous years, of which we have any record here, the trouble was not nearly so rife; when it was, indeed, so slight as to call for no remark, frosts were much more prevalent. The thermometer in the screen during the same period in 1904 did not touch freezing-point, in 1905 it fell to 32° once, while in the same period in 1906 seven frosts were recorded. The difference on the grass is more marked; for while in 1907 the thermometer reached the freezing-point six times, frost was recorded during the same period in 1904 nine times, in 1905 fourteen times, and in 1906 twelve times. It would seem, then, reasonable to conclude that frost could not have been the direct cause of the trouble.

If we turn to the prevalence of low temperatures we find a similar state of things. The minimum temperature in the screen fell during the period of six weeks four times below 36°; in 1904 it fell to that temperature five times; in 1905 six times; and in 1906 ten times. On the grass, a temperature of 36°, or below, was recorded twelve times during the period; in 1904, however, fifteen times; in 1905 twenty times; and in 1906 sixteen times. Here again, therefore, the season of 1907 does not seem to have been worse than the few preceding ones, as far as temperature goes; and it would not appear just to ascribe the prevalence of the leaf spotting to the direct action of low temperatures.

The question of sun scorching is less easy to investigate after a short period of time than the foregoing; but as the leaves affected were quite as frequently on the north side of the tree, as on the other sides where they would be directly exposed to the sun, and perhaps more frequently in the middle of the tree than on the outside (but that partly arises from the fact that the earlier part of the growth was usually most injured), it would appear that sun scorching had little to do with the question. In another garden at Cobham, where the trees were better protected from changes of temperature and sheltered from cold winds from north and east, but exposed to the same amount of rain and sunshine, and, therefore, scorching, the leaf spotting could not be found.

The suggestion, therefore, that climatic conditions were directly responsible for the trouble seems to be put entirely out of court; and this being so, it is obvious that the fungus was not growing upon already dead tissue, but attacked living tissue and caused its death.

This somewhat long discussion of the direct connection between the injury to the leaves and the weather, seems called for on account of the frequency of the ascription to this cause of injuries to plants that are directly attributable to other, and often preventable, causes.

The question next arises as to whether there were any climatic conditions prevailing during the period that might contribute to the weakening of the foliage, and so lay it open to the attacks of a fungus.

Climatic conditions apt to lead to abnormal or weak development include—

(1) Too little moisture in the soil; and

(2) the converse, a water-logged condition of the soil ;

(3) a low soil temperature, preventing the ready absorption of water by the roots ;

(4) too great a degree of direct sunshine on the young leaves ;

(5) too little sunshine, checking transpiration ;

(6) too great a degree of moisture in the air, checking transpiration, and, if combined with a high temperature, leading to the development of large soft foliage ;

(7) too low a temperature, checking transpiration, assimilation, and growth ;

(8) drying winds, causing too great an amount of evaporation.

The following particulars will show which of these conditions obtained during the period in question.

Taking the several points in the order given above, we find, in the first place, that the average rainfall during the months from October to May inclusive at Wisley is about 15 inches, and the actual rainfall during these months in 1906–7 was 18·03 inches. The soil was there-fore not deficient in moisture.

(2) Neither, bearing in mind the well-drained condition of the Wisley apple plantation and the light nature of the soil, can the soil have been water-logged.

(3) The mean soil temperature at the depth of one foot during the period in question was over 51° and never fell, as the accompanying temperature chart (fig. 90) shows, below 47°. Such a temperature would not adversely act upon the power of absorbing water by the root-hairs, and does not vary appreciably from the normal for the period. In 1906 the mean at a depth of one foot was 51·8, and in 1905 53·4.

(4) The amount of bright sunshine recorded during the period was 208·5 hours, which compares with 223·7 hours in 1906, and 291·7 hours in 1905 for the same period. An excess of bright sunshine could scarcely have been a contributory cause ; rather it would appear

(5) there was a deficiency. Indeed, on each of eighteen days there was less than three hours of bright sunshine, compared with thirteen such days in 1906, and eight in 1905.

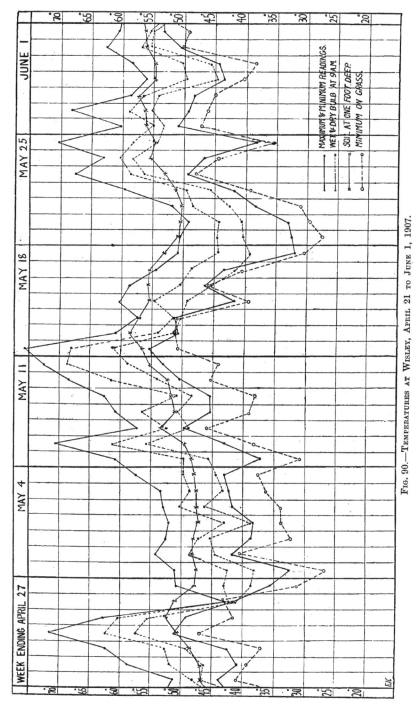

Fig. 90.—Temperatures at Wisley, April 21 to June 1, 1907.

MAXIMUM & MINIMUM READINGS.
WET & DRY BULB AT 9 A.M.
SOIL AT ONE FOOT DEEP.
MINIMUM ON GRASS.

WEEK ENDING APRIL 27   MAY 4   MAY 11   MAY 18   MAY 25   JUNE I

T T

(6) This lack of bright sunshine, together with the excess of rainfall for the period (3·64 inches, against 2·76 in 1906, and 0·96 inch in 1905), would have the effect of keeping the atmosphere more moist than usual and of checking transpiration. That a very considerable amount of water vapour was held in the air during a great part of the period may be seen by comparing the temperatures recorded by the wet- and dry-bulb thermometers in the accompanying temperature chart (fig. 90).

(7) Although, as shown above, the minimum temperature never fell low enough to cause the leaves to die, yet the thermograph record shows that during this period of forty-two days the temperature was below 42° (a temperature that may be regarded as one at which growth and assimilation may proceed but very slowly, and below which little activity is manifest) for more than 154 hours, that is, nearly one-sixth of the whole time. This checking of the growth for so long a time must have resulted in the somewhat abnormal development of the leaves.

(8) Cold, dry northerly and easterly winds, especially when blowing at a rapid rate, often do more harm to vegetation than many frosts unaccompanied by wind. Unfortunately for our purpose the anemometer at Wisley is not constructed to make graphic records of the rate and direction of the wind so that these may be known for any period of the day. Only the direction of the wind at 9 A.M. is recorded, together with the distance registered by the anemometer for the twenty-four hours. These data are insufficient for an examination into the particular point under discussion, and may be misleading. However, so far as they go, they do not show any prevalence of strong, dry winds from these points of the compass. The strongest winds came from the south-west, and these were generally accompanied by rain.

Thus it appears that some of the weather conditions were such as to lead to abnormal development of the foliage, viz., a deficiency of bright sunlight, a considerable deposition of moisture, a high relative humidity, and a continued period during which low temperatures prevailed, and certain of the vital processes were almost at a standstill. These combined seem to have altered the leaf, so that it was open to the attack of a fungus.

The Fungus implicated.—As stated above, a fungus was found in every case of leaf spotting of the type described, and the fungus in every case was *Cladosporium herbarum*. This fungus is exceedingly common upon dead vegetable matter of various kinds, growing as a saprophyte. But, like several of the fungi that usually grow upon dead vegetable matter, it has the power, in certain circumstances, of becoming a parasite and causing the death of living tissues. Thus, not infrequently, this fungus has been the cause of a leaf-spot and pod-spot of peas ; poppy capsules have been attacked ; Kosmahl [*] has attributed the death of seedlings of *Pinus rigida* to this species ; Cavara has found it as a harmful parasite on raspberries (on which host I have also found it doing considerable damage), Cycas, Agave, and other garden plants. Delacroix and Prillieux [†] have described it as injuring apples, and it is

---

[*] *Ber. d. deutsch. bot. Ges.* x. p. 442.

[†] *Bull. de la Soc. Mycol. de France*, vi. (1890), p. 136.—These investigators say : " Le cas le plus important est celui des pommiers, qui, il y a deux ans surtout, en

frequently the cause of what is called the 'black' disease of wheat. In the last case Lopriore * has proved its capability of infecting living wheat plants; while Janczewski † has shown that the attack depends largely upon climatic conditions.

In infection experiments carried out at Wisley during the past season, by applying living spores of the fungus to the surface of the leaf of the apple and protecting the infected leaves from outside infection, it was proved that the fungus was capable of attacking healthy leaves of at least some varieties (the majority of those experimented with) and producing upon them the typical spots as described above, and later (in the course of about five or six weeks) the fruiting form of the fungus. Infection probably takes place mainly through the stomata, since the germ tubes of the fungus have been seen making their way into the leaf by these openings. In one case, however, infection occurred when the spores were applied only to the upper surface of the leaf, but a slight

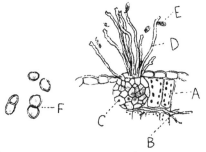

FIG. 91.—CLADOSPORIUM HERBARUM IN APPLE LEAF.

A, Cells of leaf (upper surface); B, mycelium of fungus; C, microsclerotium; D, conidiophores; E, F, spores. A–E, much magnified; F, more highly magnified.

injury to the epidermis of the leaf in this case may·have given the opportunity for the fungus to gain an entrance. The dark mycelium of the fungus grows through the tissues of the leaf causing the death of the cells, and after a time forms several compact masses of almost spherical shape, measuring about ·12mm. in diameter. These bodies, which are known as microsclerotia, are of a black colour, and are formed just below the epidermis of the leaf (fig. 91, A, B, C). They may be seen

bien des points de l'ouest et du centre de la France, et l'an dernier encore, ont perdu de bonne heure une grande partie de leur feuilles qui se desséchaient sur leur bords et tombaient. Les fruits mal nourris étaient arrêtés dans leur développement et ne donnaient qu'une récolte des plus médiocres. Nous avons récolté, reçu et examiné de nombreux échantillons de ces feuilles malades, à demi-desséchées, provenant surtout de la Normandie, du Maine, du Perche et de la Bretagne, toujours sur les places desséchées nous avons trouvé en abondance des touffes de *Cladosporium* [*herbarum*]. . . . Nous poursuivons des essais de culture de ces *Cladosporium*, sur le contrôle de l'expérience est nécessaire pour établir d'une façon certaine si le *Cladosporium*, ou une des formes s'y rapportant, envahit, comme nous le pensons, les feuilles vivantes du pommier . . . et est la cause des altérations que nous venons de signaler."

* "Die Schwarze des Getreides," *Landwirtsch. Jahr.* xxiii. 1894, &c.

† "Recherches sur le *Cladosporium herbarum* et ses compagnons habituels sur les céréales" in *Bull. de l'Acad. des Sci. de Cracovie*, 1894.

by means of a lens, forming minute black spots on the affected areas on the upper surface of the leaf (fig. 89, B). I have only once seen these microsclerotia just within the lower epidermis, and in that case the lower side of the leaf had curved over and was directed upwards. From the microsclerotia later arise the fertile hyphae, or conidiophores, in little tufts of black or dark brown, erect or somewhat spreading, branches. The conidiophores are unbranched and sparingly septate, and bear at their tips several conidia. As the hyphae which form these tufts are somewhat rigid, they may be seen standing up from the surface of the leaf, by the aid of a lens (fig. 91, D). Conidiophores, occurring singly, are occasionally found emerging from the lower surface. The conidia (fig. 91, E, F) are dark in colour and very variable in form, size, and number of cells, sometimes being unicellular, but more frequently consisting of two or three cells. The conidia are capable of reproducing the disease spots upon other apple leaves.

The Origin of the Parasitism.—The fungus is, as has already been stated, a very common saprophyte on dead vegetable matter, and it can, furthermore, be grown with ease on an ordinary culture medium such as beef-tea jelly. It is interesting to note that several of the allied species of the genus are normally active parasites. For example, *Cladosporium fulvum* is a species too well known upon the cultivated tomato, while *C. elegans* is the cause of a "scab" on oranges, and so on. How is it that this species is also capable of becoming a parasite? Considerable light has recently been thrown upon this interesting question by various workers among the fungi. In 1894 Miyoshi* showed that the hyphae of fungi are attracted through small openings in a membrane, such as the stomata in the epidermis, by the presence of sugar on the other side. Massee † has further shown that it is possible so to train a saprophytic fungus, by attracting it to grow in and fruit upon a plant, that after a certain number of generations it acquires the power of spontaneously infecting the plant upon which it has been enticed to grow. Many fungi are capable of adapting themselves to their environment in a very marked manner, for certain forms quite indistinguishable from one another in appearance are able to infect one plant only of a number of allied forms or species, while other forms of the same fungus are restricted to other of the allied species of host plant. These "biologic forms" have been carefully investigated, particularly by the late Professor Marshall Ward and by E. S. Salmon, and it has been shown that there are often certain hosts that can be infected by several of the "biologic forms" of a parasite, though these forms are otherwise restricted to one or two hosts, and do not invade each other's territory; but, after growing upon the common host, they are able to infect other hosts indiscriminately. These facts go to show that the food relations of a fungus are often not fixed, but that they are able to adapt themselves to altered circumstances, and even to acquire what appear to be new powers, such as the power of attacking living plants when they have hitherto been growing only upon dead matter. The species *Cladosporium herbarum* is a case in point. A possible explanation of the fact that this species has

* *Bot. Zeit.* part i. (1894).
† *Phil. Trans. Roy. Soc.* Ser. B, 197, p. 7 (1904).

been attracted to grow in the leaves of the apple, in much the way shown by Massee, and alluded to above, is afforded by the fact that in certain plants, when they are exposed to the action of low temperatures for a time, other substances than those produced when the temperature is at the optimum for development are produced. It is well known, for instance, that starch may be converted into fatty oils in plants placed under these conditions, these oils being reconverted into starch when the more appropriate temperature recurs. In many conifers red drops of oil are produced in the leaves only during the cold weather, and the leaves therefore acquire a reddish tint, regaining their normal green colour when the oil disappears in the next growing season. When starch is the form of food stored, this food is frequently converted into glucose when the temperature falls to about 36°, and remains in that form until the recurrence of higher temperatures. This is well seen in the potato, which becomes quite sweet when stored at a temperature between 32° and 42°, owing to the production of sugar ; but when the temperature is raised above 50° this sugar is reconverted into starch.*

Whether a similar accumulation of sugar occurs in the leaf of the apple is not yet known, but this seems probable when the leaves are exposed to a low temperature for a length of time. If so, the fungus is no doubt attracted to the leaf on this account, as most fungi have been shown to be attracted by the presence of sugar. In any case the reason of the attack is probably that, owing to the unusual climatic conditions under which they were growing, some substance has been formed in the leaves which in normal years is not formed at all, or at any rate to a very small extent, or that, from the same cause, some substance which has the power of repelling the entrance of the germ tubes of the fungus has failed to be formed.

Other Conditions contributing to the Attack.—It seems probable that other conditions besides unfavourable weather may at times lead to the attack of this fungus. For instance, in one case the apple 'Stirling Castle' has been attacked two or three years in succession and had, apparently, previously been weakened by excessive cropping, little growth having been made in each year. A correspondent says that year after year the apple 'Cox's Orange' and other *thin-leaved* varieties have been attacked. Another correspondent (Mr. Spencer Pickering, F.R.S.) says that both at Ridgmont and at Harpenden any tree that is in a weakly condition (such, for instance, as those recently transplanted) has been "so bad that the whole of the foliage is absolutely brown. . . . We are never entirely without this trouble."

Varieties Attacked.—It is very instructive to observe the difference in the amount of damage sustained by different varieties growing under identical conditions. In all districts 'Cox's Orange' appears to have suffered the most severely, and in some gardens this variety was the only one to suffer to any considerable extent. It was not, however, by any means the only one to be attacked in other places. At Wisley some 175 varieties of apples are planted, and of these very few escaped. 'Cellini Pippin,' 'Cox's Pomona,' 'Diamond Jubilee,' 'Endsleigh Beauty,' 'Foster's Seedling,' 'Grantonian,' 'Hormead Pearmain,'

* See Pfeffer, *Physiology of Plants*, i. p. 512.

'Margil,' 'Mrs. Barron,' 'Leopold de Rothschild,' 'Lane's Prince Albert,' 'Kerry Pippin,' 'James Grieve,' 'Pott's Seedling,' 'Prince Edward,' 'The Queen,' 'Rambour Papelen,' 'Reinette du Canada,' 'Ard Cairn Pearmain,' 'Winter Majetin,' 'Sure Crop,' and 'Tamplin' were quite, or almost, free from attack, while among the worst were 'Claygate Pearmain,' 'Cockle Pippin,' 'Cox's Orange,' 'Golden Spire,' 'Graven-stein,' 'Lord Burghley,' 'Melon Apple,' 'Mother,' 'Northern Greening,' 'Seaton House,' 'Scarlet Pearmain,' and 'William's Favourite'; many others were very badly attacked. Various correspondents mention and generally send specimens of the varieties 'Lord Hindlip,' 'Allington Pippin,' 'Peasgood's Nonsuch,' 'James Grieve,' 'Lane's Prince Albert,' 'Blenheim Orange,' 'Worcester Pearmain,' 'Frogmore Prolific,' 'Malster,' 'Northern Dumpling,' 'Bedfordshire Foundling,' 'Lord Grosvenor,' 'Grenadier,' 'Old Nonsuch,' 'Keswick Codlin,' 'Mank's Codlin,' 'Old Hawthornden,' 'Gold Medal,' 'Duchess of Oldenburg,' &c., affected with the same spot.

Are some Varieties immune ?—Certain varieties, growing among others badly affected, were quite free from the trouble, and there appear to be considerable differences in the degree of susceptibility to the attack. At Wisley no disease was observed on the varieties 'Diamond Jubilee,' 'Leopold de Rothschild,' 'Lane's Prince Albert' (but this was attacked in some other gardens), 'Kerry Pippin,' 'Pott's Seedling,' 'Ard Cairn Pearmain,' 'Winter Majetin,' 'Sure Crop,' 'Endsleigh Beauty,' and 'Tamplin'. Others were very slightly attacked. This raises the question whether or not some varieties may be immune. More extended observations are necessary before this question can be decided, but it is interesting to observe that while certain varieties, such as 'Charles Ross,' 'Lord Hindlip,' 'Wealthy,' &c., were easily infected by artificial means, others like 'Warner's King' could not be so infected.

Methods of Prevention.—So far no exhaustive series of experiments have been carried out with preventive measures for this disease, but the only methods that appear to offer any likelihood of success are those whose object is to prevent the germination of the spores of the fungus on the leaves. There is little doubt that at present the best material for the purpose when dealing with apple trees is Bordeaux mixture, a recipe for which has been given many times in this journal; and this must be applied to the trees so that all parts are covered with a thin covering of it, otherwise the good effects that should follow its use will not be apparent. The damage that may follow the attacks of various fungi on the leaves and on the fruits of the apple is so great, and the attacks are so frequent, that spraying with Bordeaux mixture should form part of the routine work in every orchard. Spraying should not be looked upon merely as a remedy, but as an insurance against the incidence of disease due to fungi. This disease depends indirectly upon weather conditions for its increase, but is directly due to the fungus, and therefore efforts should be directed to checking the growth of the fungus, since it is impossible to alter the weather. Apple-scab and the brown rot of fruit are both abundant in many orchards, and attack not only the fruit but the leaves as well. Spraying with Bordeaux mixture, though it may not entirely prevent these fungi from attacking the trees, will reduce the damage done to a very considerable extent, and at the same time it may be used against this fungus with hope of success. The spraying should· be done at least three times—once after the buds burst' but before the flowers open, once after the petals are shed, and a third time about three weeks later. The Bordeaux mixture should be only half the strength used in spraying potatos. It is evident also that clean culture will reduce the number of spores floating in the air ready to attack the leaves.

SUMMARY.

1. The blotching and " scorching " of apple leaves has been extremely prevalent during the season of 1907.

2. In almost every case examined the scorched spot has been produced by the fungus *Cladosporium herbarum.*

3. The presence of the spots offers a menace to the health of the tree, since the effective leaf area is very greatly diminished by their presence.

4. Various causes have been suggested to account for the spotting of the leaves, but it is shown that it could not have been directly due to the influence of the weather, since none of the climatic factors capable of causing the spotting differed materially from those of the preceding years when the spotting was not prevalent.

5. The weather had been such, however, as to cause somewhat abnormal growth, and to lay the foliage open to the attack of certain fungi.

6. Some varieties of apple are apparently more liable to the attack than others.

7. The best method of prevention lies in the direction of checking the germination of the fungus spores by means of such a spray as dilute Bordeaux mixture.

II. A DISEASE OF THE CINERARIA.

By FRED. J. CHITTENDEN, F.L.S.

Unlike the majority of plants cultivated on an extensive scale in this country, whether under glass or in the open, the Cineraria has so far been remarkably free from the attacks of fungi. Dr. Cooke in his " Fungoid Pests of Cultivated Plants," p. 52, alludes to only one, *Aecidium Cinerariae,* as attacking the Cineraria, and that " has [recently] been detected in Austria on leaves " of that plant. A second fungus is reported in Tubeuf and Smith's "Diseases of Plants," viz. *Bremia lactucae* Reg. As the last fungus is common on lettuce and sow-thistles, as well as on some other native plants, we ·may expect to find it on Cinerarias from time to time. Massee in his " Text Book of Plant Diseases," p. 242, in discussing the Chrysanthemum rust, suggests that " there is no reason why the fungus (*Puccinia hieracii*) should not, in course of time, attack other cultivated composite plants, as Cinerarias, Dahlias, &c.," and this is the only mention made in that useful work of a fungus even probably to be found on the Cineraria. It may be worth pointing out that the *Puccinia* on Chrysanthemum is now regarded by most mycologists as a distinct species, *P. chrysanthemi* Roze, probably restricted to the Chrysanthemum.

Recently, however, we have received from different localities specimens of Cineraria leaves attacked by one of the rust fungi, for which growers would do well to be on the watch, particularly as the fungus in question is one that is extremely common on one of our most abundant weeds, the groundsel (*Senecio vulgaris*), and is distributed in all the districts of our island and the continent of Europe, wherever both the groundsel and the Scots pine are found. The fungus is known as *Coleosporium senecionis*, and in addition to the groundsel other species of *Senecio* (*S. Jacobaea, S. viscosus, S. sylvaticus, S. palustris, S. vernalis, S. pulchrum,* and perhaps *S. doronicum*) are subject to its attacks. It is not, therefore, surprising that a plant so nearly related to these Senecios as Cineraria should at last fall a victim.

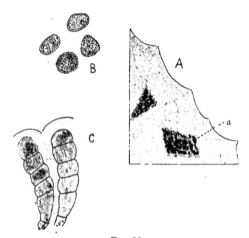

Fig. 92.

A, Cineraria with fungus (*Coleosporium senecionis*); B, uredospores; C, teleutospores.
(B and C much magnified.)

The attack is characterized in all cases by the appearance on the under surface of the leaves of orange-yellow, waxy-looking patches (fig. 92, A) covering areas varying from about ¼ inch in diameter to almost the whole of the lower surface of the leaf. The leaf, when the attack is a slight one, shows scarcely any injury on the upper surface; but as the disease spreads it may become blackish in colour. The yellow patches appear in September, and consist of masses of one-celled yellow spores (fig. 92, B), known as uredospores, capable of immediate germination and of infecting fresh leaves of the Cineraria and of the species of *Senecio* mentioned above. Later the patches become red, and then consist of large numbers of the winter form of spore, the three- or four-celled teleutospores (fig. 92, C). On the germination of the teleutospore in the spring another form of spore is produced at the end of the short hyphae which proceed from the teleutospore cells. This third form of spore is called a sporidium, and is incapable of reproducing the disease upon the

Cineraria or any of its allies. As in so many of the "rusts," it now attacks a plant of a totally distinct family, and produces disease either on the Scots pine (*Pinus sylvestris*) or on *P. austriaca*, these two species forming the hosts for the spring form of the fungus. The spores of this spring form of the fungus on the pine needles are formed in little white cups (aecidia) with torn white edges. Before they ripen these cups appear like pale blisters upon the leaves. They are to be found in May and June, and each contains large numbers of the aecidiospores, capable of immediate germination and of attacking the Cineraria or one of the species of *Senecio*, but not the pine. The fungus, as it occurs upon the pine needles (fig. 93), is so different in appearance from that on the Cineraria that it has been described under a different name and placed in a different genus, being formerly called *Peridermium pini* forma *acicola*, but there is no doubt that it is only a stage in the life-history of a very remarkable group of fungi.

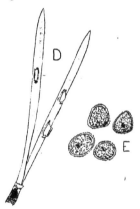

FIG. 93.—COLEOSPORIUM SENECIONIS ON LEAF OF PINUS SYLVESTRIS.
D, Aecidia; E, Aecidiospores. (E much magnified.)

Several other species of *Coleosporium* attacking other plants, *e.g.*, *Sonchus*, *Euphrasia*, and *Campanula*, have a form on pine needles which cannot be distinguished from that belonging to *C. senecionis* by mere examination even with the microscope; but the aecidiospores of these forms will attack only the plant from which the teleutospore, through which the infection of the pine needles occurred, was derived. Thus the aecidia produced as a result of infecting pine needles by the teleutospores from *Sonchus* contain spores which only infect *Sonchus*, but not *Senecio*, *Euphrasia*, *Campanula*, and so on.

The injury to the plant arises from the fact that a certain amount of the food manufactured for itself is withdrawn for the nourishment of the fungus, and thus the whole plant suffers while at the same time the leaves are disfigured.

The fungus may be prevented from spreading by spraying the leaves with a rose-red solution of potassium permanganate, and if watch is kept, and this remedy applied as soon as any sign of the fungus appears, little damage need be feared.

REPORT OF THE SOCIETY'S CONSULTING CHEMIST.

By Dr. J. AUGUSTUS VOELCKER, M.A., F.I.C., F.L.S.

THE samples submitted for analysis during 1907 were not as many in number as in 1906, there only being twelve samples analysed as against twenty-seven. In addition to these, however, there were several miscellaneous inquiries on matters about which I was consulted by letter.

The list of samples is as follows :—

Bone meal	2
Waters	4
Soils	4
Sand	1
Miscellaneous	1
	12

Bone Meal.—One of the two samples sent me gave the following results :—

Phosphate of lime . . .	48·72 per cent.
Ammonia	4·67 ,, ,,

The price of this was stated to be £6 10s. per ton. This is rather a high price if bone meal be bought in any quantity, and for cash payment.

A second sample, which was stated to have been bought as " Bone Meal," turned out, on examination, to be not bone meal but " Steamed Bone Flour," a material of less value because of the partial removal of the nitrogenous matters.

Waters.—Of the four samples of water submitted, one was distinctly polluted by drainage water, and the other three were quite suitable for drinking use and general purposes. Among the latter was a water which contained only the small amount of 7·56 grains per gallon of total solid residue. It was, accordingly, a water such as would be particularly useful for horticultural purposes.

A water of somewhat peculiar composition gave the following analytical results :—

	Grains per gallon.
Total solid residue	48·16
Oxidisable organic matter . .	·11
Nitric acid	None
Chlorine	11·91
Equal to chloride of sodium . .	19·62
Free ammonia	·055
Albuminoid ammonia . . .	Trace

The residue, 48·16 grains per gallon, was distinctly alkaline in nature, and was found to consist mainly of magnesia and other alkaline salts, and not of lime salts. Chlorides were especially prominent, and the water partook somewhat of the character of a slightly saline or mineral water.

The sample referred to above as being impure gave the following results :—

Grains per gallon.

Total solid residue	20·44
Oxygen absorbed	·225
Equal to oxidisable organic matter	1·80
Nitric acid as nitrates	2·97
Chlorine	1·52
Equal to chloride of sodium	2·50
Free ammonia	Trace
Albuminoid ammonia	·018

The water was of a yellowish colour and contained somewhat much deposit. There was a considerable amount of dissolved organic matter and ammonia, besides which the water contained nitrates to some marked extent. It would seem to me likely that this was a supply that was affected by land-drainage water such as might proceed from garden or similarly manured land.

Soils.—A sample of soil was sent me in respect of which a complaint was made by the gardener that it was in a bad state, and that he could not get Celery or Brassicas to grow satisfactorily in it.

A partial analysis gave the following results :—

Soil dried at 212° F.

Organic matter and loss on heating	16·96
Oxide of iron and alumina	8·91
Lime	5·27
Alkalies, magnesia, carbonic acid, &c.	3·45
Phosphoric acid	·87
Insoluble siliceous matter	64·54
	100·00

It will be seen that the soil contained a large amount of vegetable matter. Indeed, I consider that it was overcharged with manure, in consequence of which a bad physical state of the soil had been produced, and moisture was too readily retained by it. It was to this cause, rather than to any lack of the necessary elements of fertility, that I consider failure was due.

I have not unfrequently met with cases where soils have been spoiled in this way through being "over-dosed" with stable-manure and the like, and in such cases the best remedy is to be found in bringing about an alteration of the physical condition of the soil by mixing it with soil of different texture.

A soil was sent to me with a request that, among other points, I would indicate whether it was in need of liming. The analysis was as follows :—

Soil dried at 212° F.

* Organic matter and loss on heating	5·43
Oxide of iron	6·01
Alumina	3·81
Lime	·17
Magnesia	·33
Potash	·53
Soda	·46
Phosphoric acid	·45
Sulphuric acid	·18
Insoluble siliceous matter	82·63
	100·00
* Containing nitrogen	·168

It will be noticed that the soil was very poor in lime, but particularly rich in phosphoric acid, being also well supplied with potash.

On the other hand, there was comparatively little vegetable matter, and the soil was poor in nitrogen, so that the application of farmyard manure and other vegetable matter would probably be good for it.

It having been mentioned to me that the intention was to grow daffodils, I pointed out that this plant, like Ericas, Rhododendrons, &c., does not do well on soils where lime is abundant, and hence, for the purpose of such plants, the poverty in lime would be beneficial rather than otherwise.

For general purposes, however, the soil, being poor in lime, would undoubtedly be benefited by the application of lime.

A soil was sent to me for the purpose of ascertaining its suitability for the purposes of fruit-growing.

The following were the analytical results :—

Soil dried at 212° F.

Organic matter and loss on heating . .	9·70
Oxide of iron and alumina . .	12·37
Lime	·26
Magnesia, alkalies, &c. . . .	1·80
Insoluble silicates and sand . .	75·87
	100·00

The soil, as indicated in measure by the foregoing analysis, was one of heavy clay nature. Indeed, on examination I found it to contain very little fine top-soil, but to have clay running throughout it in lumps. The subsoil also was marked by streaks of yellow clay, and it was clear to me that such soil wanted a good deal of cultivation, and that the opening of it out was necessary before it could be considered at all a suitable soil for fruit-growing.

When one has to deal with cold clay, such as the above, the use of ashes or similar material to open out the soil is frequently advisable.

Sand.—A Fellow of the Society sent me a sample of Bude sea-sand, inquiring especially whether it contained sufficient salt to render it unsuitable for garden use. The analysis which I made, and which is appended, shows that the quantity of salt was extremely small, and that there was no occasion to apprehend any harm being done by the use of the sand.

Percentage of :—

Water	5·74
Lime	27·10
Equal to carbonate of lime . .	48·40
Silica	39·40
Chlorine	·0015
Equal to chloride of sodium (common salt)	·0025

Miscellaneous Inquiries.—These were of varied nature and included not only ordinary horticultural questions, but also such exceptional subjects as the preparation of an " Essence of onion " for flavouring purposes, and the preparation of a " Food for infants and invalids " from the sweet potato. Though asked to advise on these, it seemed to me that the subjects hardly came within my duties as consulting chemist to the Royal Horticultural Society.

REPORT ON THE METEOROLOGICAL OBSERVATIONS MADE AT THE SOCIETY'S GARDEN AT WISLEY IN 1907.

By R. H. CURTIS, F.R.Met.Soc.

THE observations at the Society's Climatological Station at Wisley continued to be made daily without break throughout the year. The instruments were as usual examined and verified in the Spring, and were all found to be in good order, whilst a detailed inspection of the observations themselves show them to have been very carefully made. During the year the instrumental equipment of the station was further improved by the addition of a mercurial barometer.

The principal features of the year's weather are as follows: ·

January.—During the first three weeks of the month a fairly steady type of mild, open, and generally dry weather was experienced, with relatively warm nights; but during the last week a spell of cold easterly winds, which sometimes blew with considerable strength, set in, and in most parts of the kingdom produced bitterly cold weather. There were a few thunderstorms, and a slight amount of snow; and over Great Britain rather more than the average amount of sunshine, but rather less than the average amount in Ireland. Slight earthquake shocks were reported at the beginning, and again in the middle of the month. During the last week of the month the barometer rose to a remarkable height over Western Europe, and exceeded 31 inches over the North of England and over Scotland. The month was generally free from very strong winds and gales.

Observations made at Wisley:

Mean temperature of the air in shade	... ...	38°·0		
Highest ,, ,, ,,	... ...	51°·3	on the	1st
Lowest ,, ,, ,,	... ...	20°·9	,,	24th
Lowest ,, on the grass	... ...	10°·9	,,	27th

	At 1 ft. deep.	At 2 ft. deep.	At 4 ft. deep.
Mean temperature of the soil at 9 a.m.	38°·4	40°·6	43°·0
Highest ,, ,, ,, ...	41°·9	43°·0	44°·0
Lowest ,, ,, ,, ...	34°·2	37°·5	41°·1

Mean relative humidity of the air at 9 a.m. (complete saturation being represented by 100) 86%

Rain fell on 7 days to the total depth of ... ... 0·64 in.
(Equivalent to about 3 gallons of water per square yard.)

Heaviest fall on any day ... ... 0·34 in. on the 1st

The prevailing winds were westerly.

The average velocity of the wind was 7¼ miles per hour.

There were 58·7 hours of bright sunshine, equal to 23 per cent. of the greatest possible amount. There were 13 days on which no sunshine was recorded.

February.—The weather throughout this month was generally quiet and dry, with temperature rather below the average, and with frequent ground frosts which very much retarded the progress of vegetation, and by keeping the grass from growing caused the pasture lands to look very bare, although the land was in good condition for corn sowing. The rainfall was deficient all over the kingdom, and the amount of bright sunshine was generally in excess of the average, notwithstanding the fact that fogs were somewhat frequently experienced. Over the South of Ireland the weather was remarkably dry.

Observations made at Wisley :

						At 1 ft. deep.	At 2 ft. deep.	At 4 ft. deep.
Mean temperature of the air in shade	...	...	...	...	37°·0			
Highest ,, ,, ,,	...	...	...	...	52°·3 on the 28th			
Lowest ,, ,, ,,	...	...	...	...	21°·1 ,, 3rd			
Lowest ,, on the grass	...	...	...	...	13°·8 ,, 3rd			
Mean temperature of the soil at 9 a.m.	...	...	...		36°·9	38°·7	40°·6
Highest ,, ,, ,,	...	...	...		41°·7	41°·8	41°·8
Lowest ,, ,, ,,	...	...	...		33°·8	36°·4	39°·7

Mean relative humidity of the air at 9 a.m. (complete saturation being
represented by 100) 88%
Rain fell on 13 days to the total depth of... ... ... 1·26 in.
(Equivalent to about 6 gallons of water per square yard.)
Heaviest fall on any day ... ... 0·37 in. on the 10th
The prevailing winds were from the westward.
The average velocity of the wind was 7 miles per hour.
There were 84·9 hours of bright sunshine, equal to 31 per cent. of the greatest
possible amount. There were 8 days on which no sunshine was recorded.

March.—This was a month of generally quiet weather, the only exception being a spell of rather boisterous weather lasting for a few days, near the middle of the month. Early morning fogs were somewhat frequent, and thunderstorms were experienced in some parts of the kingdom ; but the temperature was above the average for the month, and bright sunshine was unusually abundant, the total for the month being in some districts nearly equal to the average duration for May. At night, too, the sky was usually very clear, and the strong nocturnal radiation which resulted from this led to the formation of the morning mist already mentioned. The amount of rainfall was below the average over the southern half of the kingdom, the fall over some districts in the south being less than half an inch ; but in Scotland, the North of Ireland, and North-West England more than the average fell.

Observations made at Wisley :

						At 1 ft. deep.	At 2 ft. deep.	At 4 ft. deep.
Mean temperature of the air in shade	...	...	...	...	43°·7			
Highest ,, ,, ,,	...	...	...	...	68°·2 on the 31st			
Lowest ,, ,, ,,	...	...	...	...	25°·4 ,, 5th			
Lowest ,, on the grass	...	...	...	...	18°·0 ,, 12th			
Mean temperature of the soil at 9 a.m.	...	...	...		41°·7	42°·9	42°·8
Highest ,, ,, ,,	...	...	...		45°·9	46°·0	44°·5
Lowest ,, ,, ,,	...	...	...		38°·3	40°·5	41°·4

Mean relative humidity of the air at 9 a.m. (complete saturation being
represented by 100) 80%
Rain fell on 12 days to the total depth of ... ... 0·88 in.
(Equivalent to about 4 gallons of water per square yard.)
Heaviest fall on any day ... ... 0·23 in. on the 12th

The prevailing winds were westerly.

The average velocity of the wind was 7½ miles per hour.

There were 199·4 hours of bright sunshine, equal to. 55 per cent. of the greatest possible amount. There were only 2 days on which no sunshine was recorded.

April.—The weather of this month was very unlike that of March, the exceptionally brilliant character of which now became changed into an unusually wet, cold, and ungenial period. Over the northern half of the kingdom, however, the rainfall did not reach the average amount, but elsewhere the average was exceeded. Thunderstorms occurred in several parts of the kingdom and occasionally did considerable damage, especially in those instances in which they were accompanied by heavy falls of hail. In one which occurred on the 7th, in Northamptonshire, the hail accumulated in drifts to a depth of from four to five inches. On the night of the 6th-7th, there was also over the south-eastern counties a very heavy fall of snow, which, on the North Downs, amounted to a depth of six inches. There was, however, an absence of very strong winds, but fog was more prevalent than usual, especially in the west and south-west. On the whole the weather was favourable to vegetation, the rain doing much good notwithstanding the cold and the somewhat scanty amount of sunshine.

Observations made at Wisley :

Mean temperature of the air in shade ... ... 46°·8

Highest „ „ „ ... ... 71°·5 on the 24th

Lowest „ „ „ ... ... 29°·4 „ 19th

Lowest „ on the grass ... ... 25°·3 „ 1st

	At 1 ft. deep.	At 2 ft. deep.	At 4 ft. deep.
Mean temperature of the soil at 9 a.m.	47°·0	47°·7	46°·5
Highest „ „ „	52°·4	50°·8	48°·1
Lowest „ „ „	45°·1	46°·2	44°·8

Mean relative humidity of the air at 9 a.m. (complete saturation being represented by 100) 79%

Rain fell on 19 days to the total depth of ... ... 3·55 in.

(Equivalent to about 16½ gallons of water per square yard.)

Heaviest fall on any day ... ... 0·72 in. on the 6th

The winds were variable in direction.

The average velocity of the wind was 6¼ miles per hour.

There were 145·7 hours of bright sunshine, equal to 35 per cent. of the greatest possible amount. There were only 4 days on which no sunshine was recorded, and on two occasions the amount for the day reached 11 hours.

May.—The weather of this month was very variable in character, with considerable range of temperature between the maximum in the day and the minimum at night ; it was often cold, dull, and rainy, with occasional hail, sleet or snow, and not infrequently thunderstorms, which in some instances were very severe. The fall of rain was generally in excess, and the amount of sunshine below the average, the total duration of the latter being in many instances less than that recorded in April; the temperature was also in most parts of the kingdom below the average. The sudden changes of temperature were not good for the fruit trees, and the cold winds checked the growth of pastures and of plant life generally, but the rains were beneficial, and at the close of the month the general outlook as regards crops was good.

Observations made at Wisley :

Mean temperature of the air in shade ... ... 52°·5
Highest ,, ,, ,, ... 75°·3 on the 12th
Lowest ,, ,, ,, ... 32°·8 ,, 19th
Lowest ,, on the grass ... ... 27°·6 ,, 19th

	At 1 ft. deep.	At 2 ft. deep.	At 4 ft. deep.
Mean temperature of the soil at 9 a.m.	53°·0	52°·8	50°·4
Highest ,, ,, ,, ...	58°·7	56°·1	52°·7
Lowest ,, ,, ,, ...	46°·3	47°·8	47°·7

Mean relative humidity of the air at 9 a.m. (complete saturation being
    represented by 100) 73%
Rain fell on 16 days to the total depth of... ... ... 2·05 in.
    (Equivalent to about 9½ gallons of water per square yard.)
Heaviest fall on any day ... ... 0·66 in. on the 31st
The prevailing winds were northerly and easterly.
The average velocity of the wind was 6 miles per hour.
There were 160·6 hours of bright sunshine, equal to 34 per cent. of the greatest
    possible amount. There were only 4 days on which no sunshine was recorded.

June.—The cold and wet weather which characterised the months of
April and May continued throughout June. The weather was almost
continuously unsettled, with frequent high winds, low temperature for the
time of the year, less than the usual amount of bright sunshine, and an
excess of rain. Thunderstorms were not infrequent, and at a few places
in the north snow fell on midsummer day. Generally speaking there was
less sunshine in June than in March, and at Wisley the amount recorded
in the later month was only 82 per cent. of that recorded in March.

Observations made at Wisley :

Mean temperature of the air in shade ... ... 56°·6
Highest ,, ,, ,, ... 72°·6 on the 9th
Lowest ,, ,, ,, ... 43°·1 ,, 17th
Lowest ,, on the grass ... ... 37°·0 ,, 29th

	At 1 ft. deep.	At 2 ft. deep.	At 4 ft. deep.
Mean temperature of the soil at 9 a.m.	57°·2	57°·0	54°·3
Highest ,, ,, ,, ...	59°·0	58°·4	55°·4
Lowest ,, ,, ,, ...	53°·4	54°·5	52°·8

Mean relative humidity of the air at 9 a.m. (complete saturation being
    represented by 100) 76%
Rain fell on 19 days to the total depth of... ... ... 1·86 in.
    (Equivalent to about 8¾ gallons of water per square yard.)
Heaviest fall on any day ... ... 0·50 in. on the 1st
The prevailing winds were south-westerly and westerly.
The average velocity of the wind was 9 miles per hour.
There were 163 hours of bright sunshine, equal to 33 per cent. of the greatest
    possible amount. There was only 1 day on which no sunshine was recorded.

July.—The weather of this month showed a distinct improvement
upon that of the three which immediately preceded it. There were no
very high winds, the rainfall was on the whole less than the average
amount, and in the western half of the kingdom the amount of bright
sunshine was in excess of the normal. The temperature was, however,
still somewhat low, and there were no very high readings of the thermometer obtained. There were several thunderstorms, and in some instances

they were accompanied by heavy falls of hail; in places fogs were of some-what frequent occurrence.

Observations made at Wisley:

Mean temperature of the air in shade ... ...   59°·0

Highest   ,,   ,,   ,, ...   78°·3 on the 20th

Lowest   ,,   ,,   ,, ...   39°·3 ,,   11th

Lowest   ,,   on the grass ... ...·   34°·1 ,,   11th

	At 1 ft. deep.	At 2 ft. deep.	At 4 ft. deep.
Mean temperature of the soil at 9 a.m.	60°·2	60°·1	57°·0
Highest ,, ,, ,, ...	63°·6	62°·5	59°·0
Lowest ,, ,, ,, ...	56°·2	57°·6	55°·5

Mean relative humidity of the air at 9 a.m. (complete saturation being represented by 100) 75%

Rain fell on 13 days to the total depth of ... ...   1·11 in.

(Equivalent to about 5¼ gallons of water per square yard.)

Heaviest fall on any day ... ...   0·24 in. on the 21st

The prevailing winds were from south-west and west, but north-east winds were not infrequent.

The average velocity of the wind was 5¼ miles per hour.

There were 197·5 hours of bright sunshine, equal to 40 per cent. of the greatest possible amount. There was no day on which bright sunshine was not recorded.

August.—This was another month of cool changeable weather with an absence of anything in the way of hot summer temperature. The fall of rain was in excess of the average in the north, but below it over the rest of the kingdom, and the record of bright sunshine was less than the normal everywhere. Fogs were again rather frequent in places, and the winds were not very strong.

Observations made at Wisley:

Mean temperature of the air in shade ... ...   59°·9

Highest   ,,   ,,   ,, ...   75°·0 on the 4th

Lowest   ,,   ,,   ,, ...   44°·2 ·,,   28th

Lowest   ,,   on the grass ... ...   36°·1 ,,   1st

	At 1 ft. deep.	At 2 ft. deep.	At 4 ft. deep.
Mean temperature of the soil at 9 a.m.	60°·8	61°·4	58°·9
Highest ,, ,, ,, ...	63°·2	62°·7	59°·2
Lowest ,, ,, ,, ...	58°·7	60°·3	58°·5

Mean relative humidity of the air at 9 a.m. (complete saturation being represented by 100) 76%

Rain fell on 13 days to the total depth of ... ...   2·82 in.

(Equivalent to about 13 gallons of water per square yard.)

Heaviest fall on any day ... ...   1·06 in. on the 17th

The prevailing winds were south-westerly and westerly.

The average velocity of the wind was 6½ miles per hour.

There were 190·3 hours of bright sunshine, equal to 43 per cent. of the greatest possible amount. There was but 1 day on which no sunshine was recorded.

September.—The weather of this month presented a very marked but welcome contrast to the dull · and cool weather which had prevailed throughout the five months which preceded it. The temperature was upon the whole rather above the average; the rainfall was everywhere small, and in many districts no rain fell for periods varying from fifteen to twenty-five days; the amount of bright sunshine recorded was generally in excess of the usual amount; and as there were no high winds the weather of the month was the most genial which had been experienced for a long time.

Observations made at Wisley :

Mean temperature of the air in shade	...	...	...	...	57°·9
Highest „ „ „	...	...	...	...	77°·8 on the 25th
Lowest „ „ „	...	...	...	...	33°·0 „ 23rd
Lowest „ on the grass	..	...	...	...	29°·0 „ 23rd

	At I ft. deep.	At 2 ft. deep.	At 4 ft deep.
Mean temperature of the soil at 9 a.m.	58°·9	60°·2	58°·5
Highest „ „ „	61°·8	62°·6	59°·1
Lowest „ „ „	55°·4	58°·5	57°·7

Mean relative humidity of the air at 9 a.m. (complete saturation being represented by 100) 86%

Rain fell on 7 days to the total depth of ... ... 0·63 in.
  (Equivalent to about 3 gallons of water per square yard.)
Heaviest fall on any day ... ... 0·23 in. on the 3rd
The winds were from all points of the compass, but calms were very prevalent.
The average velocity of the wind was 3½ miles per hour.
There were 152 hours of bright sunshine, equal to 41 per cent. of the greatest possible amount. There was only 1 day on which no sunshine was recorded.

October.—With the commencement of this month the weather again became unsettled and breezy, although the wind did not as a rule reach the strength of a gale. Rainfall was somewhat unequal in its distribution, some districts having more than the average, whilst others received less. About the middle of the month some exceptionally large falls occurred ; an inch was exceeded at a great many places, and at Lincoln the fall amounted to three inches in the twenty-four hours ending at 9 A.M. on the 17th. At Wisley 0·96 inch was measured at 9 A.M. on the 15th. The temperature was generally in excess of the normal, and at some places considerably so. Bright sunshine was somewhat irregular in its distribution.

Observations made at Wisley :

Mean temperature of the air in shade	...	...	...	...	50°·8
Highest „ „ „	...	...	...	...	64°·7 on the 1st
Lowest „ „ „	...	...	...	...	30°·2 „ 25th
Lowest „ on the grass	..	...	...	...	28°·7 „ 25th

	At 1 ft. deep.	At 2 ft. deep.	At 4 ft. deep.
Mean temperature of the soil at 9 a.m.	52°·3	54°·8	55°·3
Highest „ „ „	58°·4	59°·1	58°·0
Lowest „ „ „	47°·6	51°·1	52°·4

Mean relative humidity of the air at 9 a.m. (complete saturation being represented by 100) 89%

Rain fell on 24 days to the total depth of ... ... 4·56 in.
  (Equivalent to about 21¼ gallons of water per square yard.)
Heaviest fall on any day ... ... 0·96 in. on the 14th
The prevailing winds were from between south-west and east, through south.
The average velocity of the wind was 5½ miles per hour.
There were 92 hours of bright sunshine, equal to 28 per cent. of the greatest possible amount. There were 6 days on which no sunshine was recorded.

November.—This was a month of quiet weather, but for the greater part of the time it was extremely mild and at the same time humid, the mean temperature being well above the average. During the last week the weather became very rainy, and in places snow and hail fell, whilst thunderstorms were reported from a few districts. Fogs were of rather frequent occurrence throughout the month. On the whole the month was a dry one; slightly colder than usual in the west but warmer than usual elsewhere; and with a somewhat irregular distribution of sunshine.

Observations made at Wisley:

Mean temperature of the air in shade	·	...	...	...	...		44°·7	
Highest ,, ,, ,,		...	...	...	...		60°·5 on the 9th	
Lowest ,, ,, ,,		...	...	...	...		27°·1 ,, 22nd	
Lowest ,, on the grass	...	...	...	...	...		22°·0 ,, 30th	

	At 1 ft. deep.	At 2 ft. deep.	At 4 ft. deep.
Mean temperature of the soil at 9 a.m.	46°·3	49°·0	50°·5
Highest ,, ,, ,, ...	49°·7	51°·4	52°·3
Lowest ,, ,, ,, ...	41°·7	45·3	48°·0

Mean relative humidity of the air at 9 a.m. (complete saturation being represented by 100) 92%
Rain fell on 13 days to the total depth of ... ... 1·83 in.
   (Equivalent to about 8½ gallons of water per square yard.)
Heaviest fall on any day ... ... 0·38 in. on the 26th
The winds were distributed pretty evenly round the compass.
The average velocity of the wind was 4½ miles per hour.
There were 41¼ hours of bright sunshine, equal to 16 per cent. of the greatest possible amount. There were 16 days on which no sunshine was recorded.

December.—The weather of the closing month of the year was of an unsettled character, but up to Christmas it was comparatively warm, frost being rarely experienced, with a good deal of rain. During the last week, however, the winds shifted from the westward to the eastward, and with the change the air became very dry, and although the temperature was not particularly low, yet the winds were very bitter and unpleasant, and there was very little increase of warmth during the day. Snow was experienced at various times, but generally the falls were only slight. Over the south-eastern counties there was a fair amount of sunshine, but generally speaking the month was not a bright one, and the sunshine was very variable in its distribution.

Observations made at Wisley:

Mean temperature of the air in shade	...	...	...	...		42°·2	
Highest ,, ,, ,,	...	...	...	...		57°·0 on the 8th	
Lowest ,, ,, ,,	...	...	...	...		28°·4 ,, 16th	
Lowest ,, on the grass	...	...	...	...		23°·1 ,, 16th	

	At 1 ft. deep.	At 2 ft. deep.	At 4 ft. deep.
Mean temperature of the soil at 9 a.m.	42°·1	44°·4	46°·4
Highest ,, ,, ,, ...	45°·8	46°·1	47°·9
Lowest ,, ,, ,, ...	37°·5	41°·0	44°·6

Mean relative humidity of the air at 9 a.m. (complete saturation being represented by 100) 88%
Rain fell on 13 days to the total depth of ... ... 2·70 in.
   (Equivalent to about 12½ gallons of water per square yard.)
Heaviest fall on any day ... ... 0·43 in. on the 13th
The prevailing winds were south-westerly, and then easterly.
The average velocity of the wind was 9½ miles per hour.
There were 56 hours of bright sunshine, equal to 23 per cent. of the greatest possible amount. There were 9 days on which no sunshine was recorded.

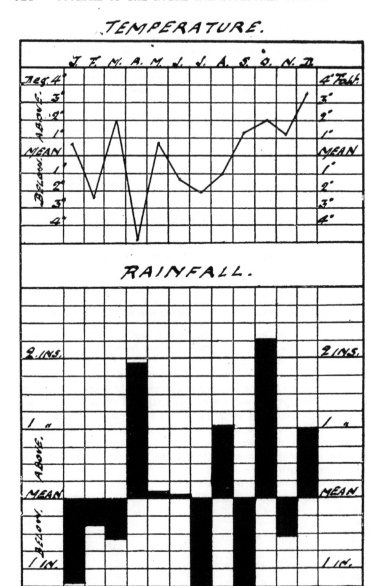

Fig. 94.—Difference from the Average of the Mean Monthly Temperature and Fall of Rain at Wisley during the Year 1907.

Regarding the year as a whole it was colder and drier than the average, with a deficiency of sunshine and an unusual amount of cold unseasonable wind, but without any other feature which differed markedly from the average. There were three periods of exceptionally dry weather, one

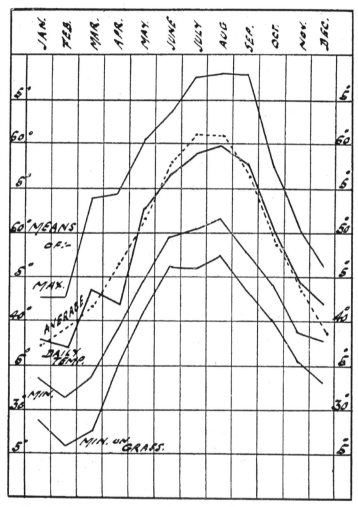

Fig. 95.—Mean Temperature of the Air for each Month of the Year compared with the Average; also the Means of the Highest and Lowest recorded each Day, and the Lowest Temperature registered on the Grass.

early in January, the second beginning in the latter part of March, and the third in September, this last being the most marked of the three. The amount of rainfall recorded at Wisley was 23·89 inches, and the number of days on which rain fell to a measurable amount was 169. The amount of bright sunshine recorded at Wisley was 1,542 hours, or 35 per cent. of the total possible amount for the year, and generally speaking there was more sunshine in March than there was in June. The mean temperature for the year was 49·1, which was only half a degree below the average, and the range of the thermometer was from 21° to 78°. There was very little snow at any time throughout the year.

The principal features of the year as regards temperature and rainfall are shown in the accompanying diagrams, figs. 94 and 95.

Fig. 94 shows graphically the departures from the average of the monthly means of temperature and falls of rain. As regards the first element, it will be seen that the year was generally cold right up to August, March being the only month in which the monthly mean exceeded the average to any noticeable extent. In the lower part of the diagram, April and October are shown to be the only months in which the total rainfall greatly exceeded the average, the departure amounting in each case to about two inches; in both August and December there was an excess of about one inch.

Fig. 95 exhibits the annual march of temperature, and shows the departure from the average of the mean for each month. The range of temperature is shown to have been small, and the near approach to each other of the curves of mean daily temperature and of the maximum and minimum temperatures agrees with the persistently cool character of the year, which was its most noticeable feature.

ANOTHER PEACH PEST.

By M. C. Cooke, M.A., LL.D., A.L.S., F.R.H.S., V.M.H.

We have lately (August 1907) received for examination some ripe peaches which were suffering from a presumably new parasitic disease. A brief examination was sufficient to remind us of a record of a like nature by the Rev. M. J. Berkeley more than forty years ago. Turning to this we were soon convinced that the same disease was under our hands. The record is in the "Gardeners' Chronicle" of October 1864, page 938, with a woodcut, and the account is mainly as follows :—" We have met in the garden of Sir Hugh Williams, in Wales, with a disease confined to a single variety of peach, the Barrington, produced by a mould which we have never seen before.

" Shallow pits, about half an inch in diameter, appear on the surface of the fruit, the centre of which is occupied by a dark mould bearing a profusion of spores. The mycelium penetrates deeply into the fruit, which, if not gathered in good time, becomes useless. The mycelium consists of more or less waved, articulated threads, which give off here and there stouter erect flocci with shorter joints, branched slightly above, and producing at the tip of each joint a large spore. The spores are at first oblong and pale, showing one or two transverse septa. These rapidly acquire a dark tint, elongate, become more or less linear, and consist of from seven to eleven swollen divisions, of which the terminal one is mostly apiculate. Each division contains a few minute oil globules (the length varies from 40 to 60 mm.).

" After the spores have fallen they frequently split in the centre and give out a globular body, which is in all probability reproductive. The mould apparently belongs to the genus *Macrosporium*, and may be named *M. rhabdiferum*."

Thus much for the original account. The species was recorded in "Cooke's Handbook" in 1871 under the name of *Helminthosporium rhabdiferum*, but we have failed to discover any specimen or any record of its appearance since 1864, and began to look upon it so much in the light of a myth that it was excluded from our "Pests of the Fruit Garden," recently published by the Royal Horticultural Society.

After more than forty years this same mould reappears, on the same host, answering in every particular to the original description, and long after it had become forgotten, and without a single record of its appearance in this country or any other during the interval.

Technically it must be stated that it is not a species of *Macrosporium* at all, for the spores are not muriform ; nor is it *Helminthosporium*, for the mycelium is delicate and uncoloured, and, moreover, there are no dark or carbonised sterile flocci, and the mature spores are only a pale delicate brown.   What it should be called is of less importance than the fact of the reappearance of what may prove to be an injurious pest.

Hitherto we have not seen any dehiscence of the cells, or extrusion of a globular body, but the spores are very *prdfuse,* and for a long time hyaline, at first cylindrical and without septum, then triseptate, and finally with five to seven septa, not being constricted at the joints until mature.   As a mould it is very curious and interesting, and rather abnormal ; but as a pest we are not anxious for its dissemination.

REPORT ON CELERY AT WISLEY, 1907–08.

FORTY-EIGHT stocks of Celery were sent for trial, all of which were sown on March 15, and planted out in trenches on May 29. In addition to the manure in the trenches, the plants received two applications of Peruvian guano at the rate of 1 oz. to the yard run of trench on each occasion. All the stocks made excellent growth, but in September there was the most persistent attack of Celery-fly we have ever known, and it was only by constant "picking" and the dressing of guano that the crop was saved from ruin. The Committee examined the whole collection in midwinter, after it had passed through sharp frost.

F.C.C. = First-class Certificate.
A.M. = Award of Merit.

1. A 1 (Sutton).—A very early variety; outer leaf stalks pink or red, inside white, faintly tinged with pink ; dwarf; thick. Very good as an early variety.

2. All-heart Pink (Nutting). — An early or midseason variety, irregular in growth ; outer leaf stalks pink, inside white. This variety was badly injured by frost.

3. Brydon's Prize White (Hurst).—A late variety ; tall, strong, thick ; fine solid heart ; leaf stalks white, crisp. Stood frost well.

4. Brydon's Prize Red (Hurst).—A late variety; short, thick ; very crisp, fine flavour; outer leaf stalks dull red, inside pale pink. Stood frost well.

5. Champion Solid White, A.M. December 18, 1900 (Barr).—A midseason or late variety ; short, thick, very solid ; excellent crisp flavour very white. Stood frost well. One of the best white varieties.

6, 7. Clayworth Prize Pink (Hurst, Massey).—A late variety ; tall very thick, heavy, solid hearts ; outer leaf stalks pink, inside nearly white. Stood frost well. This variety is much liked and largely grown in the North of England.

8. Covent Garden Dwarf White (Barr). —An early variety ; short thick, rather loose; moderate heart. Injured by frost.

9. Covent Garden Tall White (Barr).—A taller form of No. 8.

10. Covent Garden Tall Red, A.M. December 18, 1900 (Barr).—A late variety ; tall, thick, heavy, solid heart, good flavour ; outer leaf stalks bright pink or red, inner ones nearly white. Did not stand frost well.

11. Covent Garden Dwarf Red (Barr).—A dwarf form of No. 10.

12. Dobbie's Invincible White (Hurst).—A midseason or late variety rather tall ; thick, solid heart; crisp, fine flavour ; outer leaf stalks green, inside white. Stood frost well. Excellent stock.

13. Dwarf White Gem (Hurst).—A midseason or late variety ; moderately tall, somewhat loose and coarse, very thick. Stood frost well.

14. Earliest White (Daniels).—An early variety; growth moderate; thick, solid heart, good shape. Stood frost well. A very useful variety.

15. Early Perfection Pink (Toogood).—Tall, strong grower; hearts of medium size, distorted and twisted; outer leaf stalks pink, inside pale pink. Injured by frost.

16. Early Perfection White (Toogood).—A white form of No. 15.

17. Early Rose, **A.M.** December 18, 1900 (J. Veitch).—A midseason or late variety; tall, thick, solid hearts; crisp, nutty flavour; outer leaf stalks pink, inside pure white. Stood frost well, and resisted " fly " very well.

18. Grove Pink, **A.M.** December 18, 1907 (Nutting).—A midseason or late variety; tall, thick, heavy; crisp, fine flavour; outer leaf stalks bright pink, inside slightly tinged pink. Stood frost well. An excellent variety.

19. Incomparable Crimson (Carter).—A late variety; moderately tall, strong; thick, solid heart, good flavour; outer leaf stalks deep red, inside pinkish white. Stood frost well.

20. Improved White Solid (Hurst).—An early or midseason variety; moderate growth, thick, heavy hearts of fine flavour. Stood frost well. Excellent stock.

21. Ivery's Nonsuch Pink, **A.M.** December 18, 1900 (J. Veitch).—An early variety; moderate growth, thick, solid, compact, good flavour; outer leaf stalks pink inside. Much injured by frost.

22. Loseley Pink (Staward).—A late variety; moderate growth, medium and rather loose heart; leaf stalks a dull pink, inside white; fair flavour. Stood frost fairly well.

23. Loseley White (Staward).—A late variety; tall, loose, moderate heart, poor flavour, stringy. Did not stand frost well.

24. New Solid Pink, **A.M.** December 18, 1907 (Barr).—A midseason variety; moderate length, very thick, solid heart, nutty crisp flavour; outer leaf stalks pink, nearly white inside. Stood frost well.

25. Pink Beauty, **A.M.** December 18, 1907 (Barr).—A late variety; tall, strong, thick, solid heart, good flavour; outer leaf stalks dark pink, inside nearly white. Stood frost well.

26. Pink Beauty (Johnson).—A variety distinct from No. 25, equally tall, but not such a good heart, paler in colour, and did not stand frost well.

27. Pink Nut (Jones).—An early variety; distinct; moderate length; thick, compact hearts; outer leaf stalks salmon-pink, inside white. Stood frost well. A very promising variety.

28. Prize White (Nutting).—An early or midseason variety; tall, thick, but rather loose; good flavour. Did not stand frost well, and was severely attacked by " fly."

29, 30. Sandringham White (Carter, J. Veitch).—See No. 39.

31, 32, 33. Sulham Prize (Sutton, Carter, Hurst).—A midseason or late variety; rather tall, thick, solid, compact, fine flavour; outer leaf stalks red, inside tinged with pink. Stood frost and " fly " well.

34. Solid White, **A.M.** November 23, 1897 (Sutton).—A midseason variety; moderate length, very thick, solid heart, excellent nutty flavour. Stood frost well. A very fine variety.

35. Solid Ivory (Carter).—An early variety. Medium size and thickness, crisp, good flavour. A useful early variety, but will not stand much frost.

36. Superb Pink (Sutton).—A main crop variety of somewhat similar form and character to Nos. 31, 32, 33, standing frost equally well.

37. Superb White (J. Veitch).—An early variety; moderate length, thick but rather loose heart, good flavour, severely attacked by " fly."

38. Standard Bearer, **A.M.** December 18, 1900 (Carter).—Midseason or late variety; tall, very thick, solid hearts of first-rate flavour; outer leaf stalks red, with prominent red ribs, inside tinged with bright pink. Stood both frost and " fly " well. An excellent variety.

39. Turner's Incomparable White, **A.M.** December 18, 1907 (Nutting).—An early variety; moderate length, thick, solid heart of excellent flavour. Stood frost well. A very fine early variety. 'Sandringham White' is synonymous with 'Turner's Incomparable White,' and as the latter was first in commerce we have used it as the correct name.

40. White Gem (Sutton).—A very early variety; short, thick, solid hearts of a crisp, nutty flavour.

41, 42. White Plume (J. Veitch, Carter).—A pretty ornamental variety with white foliage, but otherwise not worth growing when compared with other early varieties.

43. Williams' Matchless Red, **A.M.** December 18, 1907 (J. Veitch).—A main crop or late variety; tall, thick, solid, very heavy hearts of first-rate flavour; outer leaf stalks red, inside white tinged with pale red. Stood frost and "fly " well. A splendid variety.

44. Wright's Grove Giant White (Carter).—A main crop variety; very tall and coarse in habit, and scarcely worth growing except for cooking purposes. Stood frost well.

CELERIAC.

45. Giant Prague (Hurst).—Bulbs large and nearly smooth, with moderate foliage. A very good variety. Stood frost fairly well.

46. Large-rooted (Carter).—Very similar to No. 45. Stood frost fairly well.

47. Large Smooth, **A.M.** December 18, 1907 (J. Veitch).—This was the largest rooted and smoothest of all the varieties, with a moderate spread of foliage.

48. Turnip-rooted (J. Veitch).—Very similar to No. 45.

We would commend Celeriac to the notice of all for its excellence for use both cooked and as a salad. It is delicious in either way, and very easily grown.

REPORT ON MISCELLANEOUS VEGETABLES AT WISLEY, 1907.

Artichoke seed (Mrs. Williamson).—A variety from Buenos Ayres. The seeds germinated well, and the seedlings were planted out in the Gardens; but the winter of 1907–8 killed all the plants.

Beet ' Lockyer's Perfection ' (Chittenden).—Roots of fine shape, deep colour, and excellent colour and flavour when cooked, but requires a little more selection.

Brussels Sprouts, Improved (Harrison).—A fair strain, with small, hard sprouts abundantly produced, dwarf habit, and a moderate spread of foliage.

Brussels Sprouts × Cabbage (Ridgewell).—A hybrid between a Brussels Sprout and Cabbage. The habit of the plant is that of the former, with huge sprouts on the stems, surmounted by a fair-sized cabbage at the apex. The Brussels Sprout flavour predominates.

Cabbage ' McGredy's Earliest ' (McGredy).— Stock not fixed.

Cabbage ' McGredy's Market Favourite ' (McGredy).—A promising variety, but requires a little more selection.

Cabbage ' McGredy's Winter ' (McGredy).—Raised from Drumhead × Flat Dutch. This resembles a small Christmas Drumhead, having the same flat, round head, with a moderate spread of foliage.

Cabbage, Savoy, ' Giant Green Curled ' (McGredy).—A very large variety, with firm, heavy heads and a large spread of outer leaves. Requires plenty of space.

Cauliflower ' Eclipse,' **A.M.** September 11, 1903 (Harrison).—Heads of medium size, firm, good shape, nice colour; plant of moderate size, very sturdy, and compact habit.

Egg Plant—*Berengena violeta larga* (Williamson).—This may be better known as ' Aubergine.' A very large variety from Buenos Ayres, many of the fruits being 9 inches long and freely produced on sturdy plants.

Kale ' Selected Hearting ' (Harrison).—A dwarf, sturdy stock of Kale, beautifully curled, and very true.

Lettuce ' Electric Cos ' (Harrison).—A self-folding variety, with very dark foliage; hearts large, crisp, and of good flavour.

Lettuce ' Cannell's First ' (Cannell).—A small cabbage variety, with a close, hard, compact heart of excellent quality. Very early in coming into use.

Parsley ' Exquisite Curled ' (Kent & Brydon).—A beautifully curled variety, but requires a little more selection.

Parsnip ' Ideal ' (Cannell).—A very fine form of ' Hollow-crown.'

Pea :—

(1) ' Essex Wonder,' **A.M.** July 4, 1905 (Hobday).—Pods in pairs, long, handsome, averaging eight large, delicious peas in a pod. Height 5 feet. Seeds wrinkled.

(2) 'Langley Gem' (J. Veitch).—Pods in pairs, rather short, averaging six very dark green, sweet peas in a pod. Height 18 inches. Seeds wrinkled.

(3) 'Mayor of Leicester' (Harrison).—Pods in pairs, long, handsome, dark green, averaging eight fine, sweet peas in a pod. Height 3 feet. Seeds wrinkled. Excellent crop.

(4) 'Mona's Pride' (Poland). — Pods single, long, pale green, averaging nine large, pale, good-flavoured peas in a pod. Seeds wrinkled.

(5) 'Mummy' Pea (Barr).—A useless variety, and only grown as a curiosity. It is also known as the 'Crown' Pea.

(6) 'Ideal Dwarf Marrow' (Cannell).—Pods in pairs, long, dark green, averaging seven large peas in a pod; of good flavour. Height 18 inches. Seeds wrinkled.

(7) 'Reliable' (Harrison).—Pods in pairs, medium size, dark green, averaging eight large peas in a pod. Height 3 feet. Seeds wrinkled.

(8) 'Supreme' (Cannell).—Pods in pairs, very long, handsome, pale green, averaging eight peas in a pod. Height 5 feet. Seeds wrinkled.

Sweet Pepper—*Pimiento dulce de Calahorra* (Williamson).—This proved to be the Capsicum 'Bull's Nose,' a variety of great size, and resembling a bull's nose in shape.

Radish 'Scarlet Globe' (Harrison).—Failed.

Turnip 'Early Market' (Harrison).—Bulb a flattish round white, but requires a little more selection.

Turnip 'New Marble' (Harrison).—Bulbs round yellow, coming quickly into use.

Vegetable Marrow (North-Row).—Three varieties of unnamed marrows were received : one had large yellow fruit, one large green fruit, and one was a bush variety with greenish fruit ; but all were too large, and rather coarse.

REVIEWS OF BOOKS.

"The Trees of Great Britain and Ireland." By H. J. Elwes and A. Henry. Privately printed at Edinburgh.

It is a pleasure to welcome this stately work, great alike in its conception and in its execution. It is the product of two men who have travelled much and observed carefully, and who unite in their persons unusual perseverance and scientific acumen. Moreover, the matter is handled in a fine literary spirit that is very attractive.

The reader may, perhaps, at first be repelled by the entire lack of systematic order that pervades the volumes, but there is much to be said for publishing material as it comes to hand, and a thoroughly exhaustive index will do much to make everything straight. One must therefore not complain if Ginkgo is sandwiched in between the Araucarias and the Tulip Tree, or if Taxodium follows directly after Pyrus; but perhaps a mild protest may be permitted where pictures of the western hemlock and of beeches are divided between two volumes.

The first tree to be described is the beech, to which, in its various species, twenty-seven pages of letterpress and fourteen full-page illustrations are devoted. This tree is claimed, and rightly, as a true native of England, and the authors evidently believe that it is also indigenous to Scotland and Ireland, although there is no evidence to substantiate the claim. They are, perhaps, hardly fair to the splendid work accomplished by F. J. Lewis in the Scottish bogs, when they say that "scarcely any scientific work has yet been done" in that country. But although Lewis and others have discovered no remains of the beech in post-glacial deposits, it is possible the authors may yet prove to be right in their suggestion that the common beech is a Scottish tree, for, as is well known, this species grows on dry calcareous uplands, which do not lend themselves to the accumulation of vegetable deposits.

The liability of this tree to injury when young by spring frost is emphasised, and yet, two pages later, it is suggested that better returns would be got from the beech woods of the Chilterns if the present shelter-wood selection system were abandoned in favour of clear-felling, with a rotation of sixty to one hundred years. It is not clear how, in the latter case, the necessary seed for regeneration would be obtained, nor is it shown how the destruction of the seedlings by late frosts would be avoided.

A considerable paragraph is devoted to the beech coccus, but this must not lead one to expect that other special (monophagous) insects will be similarly dealt with, as insects and also diseases are, for the most part, left untouched.

It is rather unexpected to find special stress laid on the hardiness of *Sophora japonica*, which, according to the experience of others, is specially liable to be frosted back in early life. In giving hints as to its cultivation, it might have been well to advise careful treatment of its roots in the nursery, which, if unchecked, develop in such a way as to make transplantation a matter of much difficulty.

The non-fastidious character, as regards soil, of the yew is rightly emphasised, and even the reservation in respect of wet clay might have been omitted, for the largest specimen in Britain, which grows in the churchyard of Crowhurst, has attained its gigantic girth of 33 feet on perhaps the purest clay in England—the Weald. It is not generally known that the yew possesses curious spiral thickenings in the wood cells, and these microscopic springs, amounting to millions in a cubic inch, are the cause of the wonderful elasticity and resilience that have placed the yew in the first position as a bow wood.

It would have been interesting to have had the authors' opinion as to the period of the introduction into England of the common walnut. Is this a species we owe to the Romans? or did it die out after they introduced it? or did they fail to bring with them a source of food that they must often have utilised by the shores of the Mediterranean? But the authors are quite explicit as to the year of introduction (1656) of the black walnut, one of the most valuable of our hardy exotics. This is a tree that should be extensively cultivated where the conditions are suitable, and now that the seed can be purchased for about 20s. per cwt. (enough for half an acre), there is every encouragement to do so. If the land can be ploughed and cleaned this should be done, and the nuts should subsequently be planted at intervals of 3 feet, in rows 4 feet apart. But it is a mistake to set out the nuts till they have sprouted, seeing that in this way we can be sure that every seed will produce a plant. A shallow trench, 3 feet wide, is made in the nursery, and the nuts, as soon as they arrive, are placed therein to a depth of a foot. Old manure bags are laid on the top, and on this stable dung is placed. In May the nuts will start to germinate, when the dung can be thrown off, and every week the nuts should be looked over, and those showing signs of life removed to their permanent quarters. It sometimes happens that many of the nuts remain dormant for a year, in which case they will start to grow as early as March of the following year. The spaces between the lines should be kept horse-hoed for two or three years, by which time the young trees will be well established. The authors' advice to grow the plants for the first year in boxes, at least 2 feet deep, would probably be modified by further experience. Much better roots will be got by using boxes only 9 inches deep, and the best root system of all is obtained by placing the nuts in flower-pots about 8 inches deep, though clearly, on a large scale, this is hardly practicable.

The section dealing with the British oaks is worthy of its subject. Never previously have such a mass of valuable information and so many interesting statistics been brought together. The authors have most generously made a wide distribution of a special reprint of this section, and those are fortunate who have been favoured with a copy.

As was to be expected, the larch comes in for exhaustive treatment. Mr. Robertson, the forester at Chatsworth, is quoted in support of Scottish as against Tyrolese larch, but it would be possible to cite an equally high authority on the other side, namely the Commissioner to his Majesty at Balmoral. Such difference of opinion may be due to the fact that the term " Tyrolese " covers all larch seed that is not British, and that it is not all alike suitable for our insular conditions goes without saying. Considerable doubt is thrown upon the suitability of the Japanese larch to act as a substitute for the European species, but those who have seen every European larch diseased, and every Japanese larch sound, in a mixed wood of the two species, will have more confidence in the value of the latter. It seems only to contract the disease when badly mauled by deer, or severely crippled in some other way.

It is to be regretted that the remark regarding the fine tree *Thuja plicata*, that it is ' rarely blown down,' cannot be justified by the experience at Kilmun, where hundreds of beautiful specimens have recently been levelled with the ground.

In the first sentence of the Introduction it is stated that " The object of this work is to give an account of all the trees which grow naturally or are cultivated in Great Britain, and which have attained, or seem likely to attain, a size which justifies their being looked on as timber trees, but does not include those which are naturally of shrubby or bushy habit." It would appear that those limitations are overstepped in the case of the first species to be discussed, namely *Fagus ferruginea*, regarding which it is said: " In no case do these [presumably the largest specimens in England] attain more than 15 feet in height. . . . It is very probable that . . . it will never reach timber size in this climate."

Perhaps the authors would be glad to have their attention called to a few slips that have been noticed in a cursory glance through the pages. Although the section on the Distribution of the Beech is initialled " A. H. and H. J. E.," one finds references on p. 13 to " my friend," and to what " I saw." On the other hand, the Introduction, which is uninitialled, contains the editorial " We," but from internal evidence it would appear to require " H. J. E." at the end. The note facing plate 58 is in the first person singular, but bears no initials. The plate between 68 and 70 is neither numbered nor described. On p. 6 the hazel is said to possess aerial cotyledons. There is a mistake in punctuation in the first foot-note on p. 213 that somewhat alters the sense. " Jagdwesen," on p. 186, is misspelt, and three pages later Monreith is said to be in Dumfriesshire. But these trifling blemishes hardly affect the value of these fine volumes, of which three have already appeared, with two or three more in prospect. The price is not stated, but it is understood to be somewhat beyond the means of all but the well-to-do.

" Practical Agricultural Chemistry." By F. D. S. Robertson, F.C.S. 8vo., 210 pp. (Baillière, Tindall, & Cox, London.) 7s. 6d. net.

This book should prove very useful to the student of agricultural chemistry, as it contains concise, generally clear, and accurate directions for the analysis of a considerable number of substances—such as soils, manures, milk, water, and so on—with which the agricultural chemist has to deal. One misses some of the more frequently used methods of analysis, but, on the whole, the work thoroughly covers the special ground required. Only a student who had already had a good training in chemical manipulation, and had gained a good knowledge of the use of chemical apparatus, could undertake the bulk of the work, and, for him, the opening chapters on these points appear somewhat super-fluous; and perhaps a little of the space occupied by them might have been devoted with profit to lengthening the directions for the carrying out of the special manipulations further on in the book. A few points will require revision in a second edition. For example, on p. 51 the student is told that a normal solution of sulphuric acid contains 49 grammes of the acid to 100 c.c. of water; while on p. 63 directions for the estimation of water in soils are given under the heading "Reaction," the mode of ascertaining the reaction of the soil being altogether omitted. These slight errors, however, the student sufficiently advanced to undertake the work would at once detect. A large number of useful tables are given at the end of the book, and add considerably to its value.

"Physiography." By Rollin D. Salisbury. 8vo., 770 pp. (John Murray, London.) 21s.

Though written by an American for American students, and having—as it should—practically all its illustrations drawn from America, yet the work is so excellent, and the principles of the science are so clearly enunciated, that the English reader is bound to profit greatly by its perusal. At first sight, perhaps, the subject matter of the book would appear to have little to do with horticulture—and certainly much it contains touches horticulture directly but very little—but it is equally certain that if every landscape gardener, and every builder of a rock garden, gave the attention to the subject that it deserves, there would occur fewer incongruities in his work. Physiography includes the study of all those forces that have worked towards the sculpturing of the earth's surface in large areas and in small, and all are dealt with in this work in a masterly way, and illustrated by numerous maps, diagrams, and reproductions from photographs of various places, mostly in North America. Nearly half the book is taken up with a consideration of the work of the atmosphere, of ground and running water, and of snow and ice in moulding the earth's surface; then follows a consideration of lakes and shores, of volcances and allied phenomena, of movements of the earth's crust, and so on. A chapter is also devoted to the consideration of the relation of the earth to other parts of the solar system, while the third part is devoted to another factor upon which the horticulturist's successes and failures so much depend—the weather and the climate. The last part deals with the ocean. The publisher has done his work well; the book is well printed on good paper with an ample margin, the numerous illustrations and maps are admirably reproduced, and a full index greatly enhances the value of the work.

"Agricultural Geology." By J. E. Marr, M.A., F.R.S. 8vo., 318 pp. (Methuen & Co., London.) 6s. net.

One of the subjects required to be studied by candidates for the International Diploma of Agriculture is geology, and this little work has been written to cover the ground required. There is, perhaps, little in the book to specially merit the term "agricultural," but as an introduction to the study of geology it has much to commend it. Little attention is paid to fossils, but much to the forces that have been at work in moulding the land. Notes upon the distribution of the various strata according to age throughout England and Wales are given, and a general statement is frequently made as to the fertility of the overlying soil or the reverse. A useful chapter is that on Water Supply. A large number of diagrammatic illustrations are given, together with a geological map of England and Wales, and a good index.

"Vegetable Physiology." By Professor J. Reynolds Green, F.R.S. 8vo., 459 pp. (Messrs. J. & A. Churchill, London.) 10s. 6d. net.

This is the second edition of one of those text-books upon a part of the science of botany that play such a useful part at the present day, when the whole subject has become so great that no one man can deal adequately with its several parts, and no one text-book can, unless it reaches unwieldy proportions, contain an outline of the several parts with due regard to the importance of each. To the student who desires to supplement the usually meagre account of this most important branch of botany contained in the average text-book, this book can be cordially recommended. The account is written in a clear and accurate manner, and the author insists upon the essential similarity between plants and animals so far as their physiology is concerned. The book is well illustrated, clearly printed on good paper, and well and neatly bound. It will serve to give that grounding in the fundamental facts of vegetable physiology necessary to a full appreciation of the more advanced text-books of Sachs, Vines, and Pfeffer, and itself contains sufficient to give the power of interpreting with accuracy the ecological observations that the student may make from time to time. In so far that a knowledge of vegetable physiology is as necessary to the gardener as a knowledge of animal physiology is to the doctor who has to prescribe foods, and settle the environment of his patients so far as he can, this book should prove of great benefit to the gardener, although it does not touch upon some of the points in vegetable physiology with which the gardener is brought into very close contact.

"Mendelism." By R. C. Punnett, M.A. 16mo., 85 pp. (Macmillan & Bowes.) 2s. net.

So great has been the advance in the study of the laws of inheritance that the first edition of this little book on "Mendelism" had become out of date though published as lately as May 1905. This second edition contains a brief account of Mendel and his work, and of the experiments which have been carried out subsequently along the lines laid down by Mendel. The author points out how that recent work has made clear the reason why two white sweet peas crossed together should sometimes give a purple, and why two hairless stocks should revert to the hairy form, and these reasons are worked in with the account of dihybridism in its various aspects. He shows how the new combinations of characters that are possible give the "novelties" the horticulturist craves, and how a stock may be fixed in, at furthest, the third generation, or rather how the fixed form may be with certainty isolated from the forms which still have a mixed gametic constitution. Lastly he considers the bearing of Mendel's discoveries upon current biological conceptions ; and here if we follow the laws to their logical conclusion we are bound to assume that new characters have not arisen by small fluctuating variations, but by mutation ; and when once a mutation has arisen selection alone can eliminate it. How and why these mutations arise is a problem that remains to be solved. All interested in the progress of what may prove to be one of the most far-reaching investigations man has ever entered upon should read this little essay.

"Introduction to Elementary Botany." By Charlotte L. Laurie. 8vo., 84 pp. (Allman & Son, London.) 1s. net.

This little book is intended for children, and the structure of plants, so far as can be made out without the aid of a microscope, is dealt with in simple language, the author having wisely drawn upon the commonest plants for her illustrations. There are interesting chapters on " The Use Plants make of Animals," " The Work of Wind in Plant Life," and " The Homes of Plants." The chapter on " Protective Structures of Plants " seems to need revision : coltsfoot is not typical of dry soils, but rather of damp, heavy soils, and protection through mimetic resemblance in the case of the dead nettle and the stinging-nettle requires proof. The illustrations by Miss Boys-Smith are for the most part excellent and really illustrate the text. We, however, miss the barren node of the strawberry-runner (fig. 9), and should not have recognised the insect with the humorous expression depicted in fig. 26 as a bee. There is a good index. The book is one that can be trusted to awake and maintain interest in the common plants of field and wood, and to lead to a desire for greater knowledge.

" Elementary Botany." By M. A. Liversidge. 8vo., 128 pp. (Blackie & Son.) 1s. 6d. net.

Nearly all teachers of botany appear to think it incumbent upon them to produce a text-book. It is probably true that no teacher finds a text-book exactly suited to his needs, and this is a good sign. We suppose it is indicative of a vastly increased study of plant life that so many publishers are found willing to issue new botany books, and for this we are thankful. This book is no better and no worse than many that have gone before. We could have wished to find in an elementary course for children, to be spread over three years, something more of the modern spirit of teaching and something of the ecological point of view. We think, too, that the intricacies of the microscopic structure of roots and stems might well be left to a later period in such a course than the first year. Some of the illustrations are new.

" Plant Biology." By Professor F. Cavers, D.Sc. 8vo., 460 pp. (W. B. Clive, London.) 3s. 6d.

It is refreshing to take up a book on elementary botany that presents any new features of value. By following the dictates of modern methods of teaching, and combining the heuristic with the didactic methods, the author has produced a text-book, with abundant practical exercises, that should have a large vogue among students of that phase of nature knowledge comprised under the above title. Like many teachers he has found the knowledge of elementary physics and chemistry possessed by the average beginner in botany to be very vague, and he has introduced the necessary simple experimental exercises in these subjects, a knowledge of which is so essential to an accurate understanding of the life of a plant in connection with its environment, with good effect. He has followed out the same idea of the connection between organism and environment to the end in some excellent chapters on plant ecology and on the biology of the soil, dealing finally with " Some Problems in Plant Biology." All the more commonly met with modifications in plant form are dealt with practically, and the physiology of plants is treated in the same way ; and the practical exercises are of such a nature that they may be carried out by any student of average ability who is provided with little more than the apparatus commonly used in the teaching of elementary chemistry. The book may be confidently recommended to the notice of any teacher of botany, who does not object to the trouble involved in this method of teaching, as a class-book ; to the isolated student the book will not be quite so useful, as some of the apparatus required is only to be found in a well-equipped laboratory ; but even he will be greatly benefited by using it honestly. Very few misprints are to be found, the first part of the book is well illustrated, a good index is given, and four useful appendices add considerably to the value of the book.

" The Flowers and their Story." By Hilderic Friend. 8vo., 300 pp. (Robert Culley, London.) 5s. net.

A book written for children with the idea of interesting them in nature, the illustrations being mainly drawn from native plants, but including some garden plants, and some not likely to be met with by the majority of children. It is couched somewhat in the form of a monologue, and introduces many of the more striking facts of plant life under such " popular " titles as " Dame Nature's Tuck-shop " (fleshy fruits) ; " Acrobats and Steeple Jacks " (climbing plants) ; " Fairy Gold " (pollen), and so on. The information it is sought to impart is accurate, though some of the verbal illustrations are a little difficult to follow, and it is doubtful whether an attempt to explain the structure of a daisy head in the first chapter will be understood by any who have not examined many flowers before. The 154 illustrations from photographs on plate paper are a feature of the book, and are, for the most part, pleasing, and there are in addition eight coloured plates. The printing is well done, on good paper, and the book is neatly bound. As a gift book for children it should find a hearty welcome.

" Insect Life." By F. V. Theobald, M.A. 8vo., 235 pp. (Methuen & Co., London.) 2s. 6d.

The first edition of this little work was published in 1896, and now a revised edition has appeared. A short and easily understood account of insects in general, and of each family of insects, is given, and fuller notes upon the habits of those which are useful or injurious in any human industries. A chapter on insecticides and the methods of applying them is given at the end, and a second appendix provides lists of useful entomological works. Figures of several insects illustrating the different orders help to give some idea of the great diversity of form found among these creatures and assist the reader in identifying the forms under discussion. The book may be heartily recommended to all cultivators of plants who are interested in insect life or its suppression—and who of those who grow plants is not?

"Agricultural Zoology." By J. Ritzema Bos. Translated by J. R. Ainsworth Davis, M.A. 8vo., 312 pp. (Methuen & Co., London.) 3s. 6d.

That this book has reached a third edition proves that it has met a want. The main subdivisions of the animal kingdom are passed in review, greatest attention being naturally directed to the animals of the farm. The parts most interesting to horticulturists are undoubtedly those dealing with birds and with insects and eelworms, and at times one wishes that the accounts given of some of the creatures might have been longer. The large number of illustrations (155) materially assist in an understanding of the text and allow of more brief verbal treatment. Probably the most interesting part of the book to the general reader interested in questions of economic zoology is to be found in the appendix, where an essay on "Conditions which determine the appearance of harmful animals," followed by an account of the "General principles regulating the means to be employed against harmful animals" is to be found. Both of these show the hand of a master of his subject and are alone worth the price charged for the book. A copious index adds greatly to the value of the book.

"The Plants of the Bible. Their ancient and mediaeval history popularly described." By the Rev. Professor G. Henslow, M.A., F.L.S. 8vo., 294 pp. (Masters, London.) 6s. net.

The venerable author has so long been before the public as an authority on botanical and horticultural subjects, and brings so much originality to bear upon anything that he takes in hand, that there is always a certainty of finding in his publications much of interest and instruction. Being also a Hebrew scholar and a clergyman, no one could be better fitted to deal with the botanical problems of the Bible. Although there are several works on the subject, as well as articles in encyclopaedias, the author has still something fresh to say about the almug, apple, melon, borith, cockle, chalamoth, the red dye, the rose, saffron, the unfading plant, and the wild vine. In other cases, where he has nothing new to add to previous knowledge, he has brought so much collateral information to bear that the articles are full of interest, and make very pleasant reading.

In the speculative portions of the work in which philology is utilised, it is difficult for those who are not familiar with Hebrew to follow the author. Philology is too much like a will-o'-the-wisp to be safely followed in botanical matters; thus, when the author states that the Hebrew name of Coriander (gad) is possibly given because of the way the fruit naturally splits, it seems a little improbable because Coriander is one of the few umbelliferous fruits that *do not readily split*, and usually comes into commerce in the globular form as the author states on p. 117. Nor can one follow the author without some degree of hesitation in his remarks on the spices and drugs of Scripture, especially when he follows Pliny rather than such modern authors as Hanbury. On p. 183 it is stated that Carpobalsamum is Balm of Gilead derived from the fruits, Xylobalsamum from the branches, and Opobalsamum from the trunk. This is certainly a mistake. The balsam (Opobalsamum) and the twigs (Xylobalsamum) and the fruit (Carpobalsamum) each formed a distinct article of materia medica. The fruits are so small that it would be almost impossible to procure balsam from them in any quantity. The chapter on Aloes is not very clear. The Aloes mentioned in connection with Myrrh and Cassia was undoubtedly a perfume, but probably one produced by fumigation, for which purpose the wood of several species of Aquilaria imported from the East was employed, and is still. The Myrrh still exported to China for use in joss sticks and in medicine is the perfumed Myrrh known as Bissabol and Habaghadu in the East, and is used also for perfuming by fumigation. But the Aloes brought by Nicodemus, to the extent of 100 lbs., was more probably the Socotrine Aloes used for embalming, and the Myrrh was probably the true Myrrh. The author seems to think that Cassia should be translated Costus, and quotes Pliny that it has a burning taste in the mouth and most exquisite odour; but Costus has only a faint violet odour, too often disguised by that of camel's hide; it was more probably the true Cassia to which Pliny's description would apply. If the Hebrew word means to peel off, as the author tells us on p. 190, it would be applicable to a bark, but not to a root, and Costus is a cylindrical root, not a thin bark. It is very doubtful if the Cinnamon of the Bible is that of the present day; since Cinnamon is not known to have been a product of Ceylon before the end of the thirteenth century A.D., it was probably some other of the barks of species of *Cinnamomum* imported from the East. Under Galbanum the author says "not having a sweet odour"; but, as a matter of fact, Galbanum of good quality has a distinctly musky odour by no means unpleasant. Concerning Onycha, the author agrees with most writers that it was the operculum of a shellfish; but it is difficult to class that with sweet spices, since when burning it gives off a disagreeable odour like burnt horn or burnt feathers. It seems to the reviewer that Benzoin, which has been in use from time immemorial as a chief ingredient in incense, of which the tears present a nail-like opacity and colour, might well be intended, the chief argument against it being that Benzoin does not appear to be described by the old Greek and Roman writers, although it has been found in the tombs of an ancient Greek colony in Egypt. On the other hand, Stacte or liquid Myrrh, of which Moses was instructed to take 500 shekels, must have been a well-known drug at that period, but no liquid Myrrh is known at the present day, unless Balm of Gilead (*Balsamodendron opobalsamum*) be so understood. The author states on p. 242 that the fruit of *Atropa Mandragora* has been described as of the size of a small apple, "exceedingly ruddy and of a most agreeable odour." But in this country it is yellowish when mature, and possesses no marked odour, and is smaller than any edible apple, being no larger than the Dartmouth crab. But the subject is beset with difficulties, and it is almost impossible in the present state of our knowledge to identify many of the plants and drugs mentioned by ancient writers. Professor Henslow's work must rank as the most recent on the subject, containing much fresh material and worthy of consultation by all interested in the plants of the Bible, although it is quite possible that in the course of time still further light may be thrown upon points that must be regarded as undetermined at present.

"Food from the Tropics." By T. M. Macknight. Small 8vo., 116 pp. (Thacker, London.) 3s. 6d.

Under this title Mr. Macknight, who has had experience as a produce merchant in tropical countries, has brought together much useful information concerning tropical plants, vegetables, edible roots, and cereal produce which should serve a very useful purpose, since so many foreign fruits and vegetables are gradually entering commerce in this country. At present few, except those who have lived abroad, know how such fruits as the mango, Avocado pear, egg fruit, &c., and such vegetables as yams, choco, and aubergines, should be eaten or cooked. Mr. Macknight gives full directions how to prepare all the foreign produce he describes for table use, and in an appendix gives a table of their comparative food values. The vernacular names are mentioned as well as the botanical names.

Information about tropical produce is so scattered in the literature of different countries that a handy little work like the present should be exceedingly convenient and ought to have a ready sale. In a future edition a little more information about the varieties of the banana would add to its value; for although the mango is given in three classes not even one variety of banana is mentioned nor one of the pineapple. The author also requires to correct the synonyms given to the East African cardamom.

The Korarima cardamom (*Amomum Korarima*) is quite a different plant from the Longozy of Madagascar (*Amomum angustifolium*), and Habselia (*Habzelia ethiopica*) is quite a different plant from Melagueta pepper (*Amomum Melagueta*). But no perfect book has ever yet been published, and these small errata detract but little from the general usefulness of the work, of which every fruiterer and greengrocer in the country ought to obtain a copy.

"A Treatise on Mango." By Probodh Chundra De, F.R.H.S. Second edition, 12mo., 141 pp. (Dass, Calcutta.) 1 rupee.

This little treatise contains all that a grower of mangos could desire to know. In England the knowledge of this fruit is very limited, although in India it is probably more grown and more generally used than any other fruit. Very little is exported, partly because it does not bear carriage well, and partly because it is so largely used where it is grown. The varieties in cultivation are exceedingly numerous and vary in size from 3–4 oz. to 2 lb. in weight. From Murshedabad alone the author enumerates and describes 103 varieties. The coarsest are fibrous and inferior, and have been likened to "turpentine and tow," but the finest are fibreless, juicy, and very fragrant, and vary much in flavour, from that of the rose to that of champacá flowers, sandal-wood, musk-melon, &c. The methods of cultivation, and the insect and plant parasites and the means of preventing them, are mentioned in detail. Two species of mistletoe are stated to grow on the mango tree. Mr. De is a horticulturist, and the information given is therefore practical and not merely theoretical, but the work will be more useful in the colonies than in this country.

"Roses: their History, Development, and Cultivation." By the Rev. J. H. Pemberton. 8vo., 336 pp. (Longmans & Co., London.) 10s. 6d. net.

As might be expected from such a well-known grower, exhibitor, and judge, Mr. Pemberton has produced a work that should be read by every rose grower, even by those who have studied and grown roses all their lives. Not only is the information given thoroughly practical, but it is imparted in a pleasing and interesting form. Besides chapters upon the history, development, and botany of the rose, we have others upon soil, treatment, manures, planting, pruning, budding, and other methods of propagation, including raising from seed, hybridising, growing for exhibition, exhibiting, judging, growing under glass, pests, varieties recommended for cultivation, &c. We are glad to see the author dealing so emphatically with the treatment of soils and manures. Many a gardener, and still more frequently the amateur, kills or ruins roses by zeal or mistaken kindness, and, as the author so justly says, "there is a limit to even the strongest digestion; and although the rose, like the pig, is a gross feeder, nevertheless it is possible to overfeed it, and that is why it is positively harmful to plant the rose in contact with strong manure." This applies to many, many other plants besides roses, and because a moderate amount does good, many imagine much will do still more good—and thus they kill the plants. Again, how many thin out the shoots after pruning, i.e., the young growths made directly after pruning? Very few, indeed; and yet this is nearly always advisable, even when flowers are not wanted for exhibition purposes, as there are always in both bush or standard plants a number of weakly shoots that it is evident cannot produce a flower, and only serve to crowd the growth and provide a harbour for insect or fungoid foes. In fact all through this valuable, well-written, and well-printed book important hints on rose growing that it is most advisable should be borne in mind are given. The book is provided with a capital index.

"Flower Decoration in the House." By Miss Gertrude Jekyll. 8vo., 98 pp. ("Country Life," London.) 6s. net.

A well-written book, with good letterpress and freely illustrated. The book supplies a long-felt want, for it shows garden owners what a wealth of material may be obtained for house decoration from a garden of moderate size, even in midwinter, by the judicious selection of foliage and berried plants. Full particulars are supplied of what plants, flowers, and foliage are available for all the months of the year, and useful advice is given on their decorative arrangement. Table decoration is very lightly touched upon, and we should like to have seen this important subject dealt with more fully; but still it is an excellent book, and will be much appreciated by ladies· who take an interest in this fascinating form of house decoration. The book has an excellent index.

"The Flower Garden."· By T. W. Sanders. 8vo., 454 pp. (Collingridge, London.) 7s. 6d. net.

We cannot speak too highly of this work, as it is crammed full of varied and valuable information for the amateur gardener, whether he own a large or a small garden. The book is divided into three parts, and in the first part we have plain instructions on the formation and management of the flower garden, including the making of lawns, paths, beds, borders, shrubberies, pergolas, arches, &c.; the draining and preparation of the soil, planting, pruning, pests, and diseases of the flowers; tools, appliances, &c. In the second part we have particulars of hardy and half-hardy plants for the flower garden, including annuals, biennials, perennials, rock plants, climbers, &c.; and in the third part hardy trees and shrubs are exhaustively dealt with under their botanical and common or English names. The cultural instructions are thoroughly practical. The printing is plain, illustrations very good, and a capital index is given at the commencement of the work. We can strongly recommend this book.

"The Book of Fruit-bottling."· By Miss Edith Bradley and Miss May Crook. 8vo., 99 pp. (Lane, London.) 2s. 6d. net.

This excellent little book should be in the hands of everyone who has a garden. It is only of late years that the bottling of fruit has received attention, but thirty years ago every lady, and most farmers' wives, used to bottle fruit—with appliances primitive compared with modern ones it is true, but with really first-rate results. But for some reason or other the bottling of fruit almost died out, and we welcome the renewed interest in this very important household matter. Not only is the bottling of all kinds of fruit gone into carefully, but drying fruit, jam-making, jelly-making, marmalade-making, candying, and other modes of preserving fruit, and the making of wines and cider. The book finishes up with some quaint ancient recipes, of more interest than practical value at the present day. The instructions are so clear, and the whole book is packed so full of sound, practical information, that we heartily commend it to all.

"Alphabet of Gardening."· By T. W. Sanders. 8vo., 182 pp. (Collingridge, London.) 1s. 6d. net.

A very handy little book, and useful for the student, as it treats on sowing seeds, striking cuttings, layering, grafting, budding, pruning, planting, watering, hybridising, and upon soils and manures, while at the end of the book is a chapter on heating apparatus. All the subjects are ably treated by the author, and, in spite of the multitude of gardening books, this is one that the student will find very helpful.

"Fruit Recipes." By Riley M. Fletcher Berry. 8vo., 341 pp. (Constable, London.) 7s. 6d. net.

This is a most elaborate book, beautifully printed, well illustrated, and with a very good index. The author "Dedicates [it] to all men and all women interested in fruits : as scientists, whether in the laboratory, the kitchen, or the garden ; as artists by profession, or those who unprofessionally have artistic appreciation of this type of earth's beauty ; and to those who claim neither special training in science nor art, but simply and thoroughly enjoy good, wholesome cookery." We may say that in this book there are many dainty recipes, so far as we know quite new to this country, and some that, though excellent in the author's country—Florida—could not be used here. With such a mass of recipes (and there are literally hundreds of them) it is impossible to particularise : fruit-soups, fruit-dressings, mayonnaise, biscuits, cakes, scones, pastry, icing, fruit-butter, fruit-fritters, puddings, fruit-junket, omelet, fruit-candy, syrups, &c.—all are described. The apple, pear, peach, apricot, cherry, plum, berries, melons, grapes, and oranges are very fully dealt with ; and hundreds of simple ways of using these fruits are given, and as these are within reach of most householders in this country we can commend this book. We often hear the lament that there is so little change in fruit and its use, but here we have abundance of variation. Many other fruits are mentioned, too numerous to even touch upon ; we need only say, "Get the book, and try them."

"The Book of Vegetables and Garden Herbs." By Allen French. 8vo., 312 pp. (Macmillan, New York and London.) 7s. 6d. net.

This book is by an American author, and some of the vegetables he names could not very well be grown in this country ; but the great value of the book to gardeners here lies in the information on the chemical manures most suitable for each kind of vegetable or salad, and the description of, and best means of eradicating, the insect pests attacking them.

"Seaside Planting of Trees and Shrubs." By Alfred Gaut, F.R.H.S. 8vo., 101 pp. ("Country Life," London.) 5s. net.

This book supplies a long-felt want. Much time and money have been wasted in seaside planting through the use of unsuitable trees. The locality most largely dealt with is the Yorkshire coast—probably as cold and windy as any part of the British coast—and we are glad to see the author states that *Pinus austriaca* is without exception the hardiest of all evergreen trees for the eastern coast, confirming our own experience in other parts of the country. We have found this pine makes a really splendid screen in very exposed positions, and though it may sometimes become browned on the exposed side it always looks well on the inner and non-exposed side, providing a capital shelter for less hardy trees. We should also mention two other trees specially hardy for seaside planting—viz., the common sycamore and the white poplar. Both succeed famously as seaside trees, especially the former; and for wet places on the coast Mr. Gaut recommends the common alder (*Alnus glutinosa*). Quite a number of other trees and shrubs for coast planting are named, and we can confirm what the author claims for the majority of them. If one tree more than another stands out as specially suitable for exposed places, and to act as an outer screen, we should advocate the sycamore. Hedges, fences, &c., are all dealt with. We strongly advise all who have property by the coast to study this excellent, well-printed, and well-illustrated work.

"Everyman's Book of the Greenhouse (Unheated)." By Walter Irving. 12mo., 247 pp. (Hodder & Stoughton, London.) 5s. net.

This useful book deals with a vast number of plants that can be easily grown in an unheated greenhouse. As there is such a house as the one described in the Royal Gardens, Kew, there is little doubt that Mr. Irving has there proved all the plants he describes as a success in such a structure. We have seen the house at Kew at various seasons of the year, and have always found in it very much to interest and call for admiration, and undoubtedly the unheated house serves to give protection to many plants which, although hardy, are the better for shelter such as can be afforded by its means. The book is divided into chapters dealing with different subjects connected with the unheated house, but we think its value would have been increased by an index.

"The Unheated Greenhouse." By K. L. Davidson. 8vo., 248 pp. ("Country Life," London.) 8s. 6d. net.

In this we have another book on the "Unheated Greenhouse" on a rather larger scale than that by Mr. Irving. It is well printed and nicely illustrated. Quite a host of plants, bulbs, trees, and shrubs are named for the cool house. Many references are made to Kew Gardens, and in a large private or public garden such a house as the author describes is of immense value, for there is such a large number of plants that, though not actually requiring heat, are spoiled if left to the tender mercies of the weather. In a private garden, too, an unheated house is always serviceable to the gardener for gradually hardening off plants, retarding others, &c.; but to keep the house always ornamental requires a big reserve of plants to draw upon. Much interesting and valuable information and many useful hints are given, making the book one that the garden-lover may peruse with pleasure, gaining a good deal of useful knowledge at the same time.

"A Concise Handbook of Garden Annual and Biennial Plants." By C. M. A. Peake. 8vo., 176 pp. (Methuen, London.) 3s. 6d. net.

A very concise book indeed, dealing with the class of plants named in a masterly manner. It is a book that will be full of help to the amateur, for whom it is specially compiled. The botanical and common names, the synonyms, the time of flowering, the native habitat, the cultural details, &c., are all carefully worked out. In fact, the author has written the book in a remarkably clear style ; and although some perennial plants are included, they are such as are usually best treated as biennials.

"Practical Fruit Culture." By John Whitehead. 8vo., 116 pp. (Greening, London.) 6d. net.

A very handy little book, containing some useful information for the intending grower of fruit for market. We do not quite agree with the author in his selection of varieties for commercial purposes ; for instance, we should not plant jargonelle pear or Blenheim orange apple for market purposes, as both would require root-pruning—which is expensive—to make them fruit, and we question if they would pay even then. However, there is much sound advice in the book, and intending fruit-growers may read the work with profit.

"Glass Culture." By James Cheal. 8vo., 112 pp. (Greening, London.) 6d. net.

A useful little book dealing with the growing of tomatos, cucumbers, roses, ferns, chrysanthemums, carnations, mushrooms, grapes, &c., under glass for commercial purposes. It is a very practical treatise on the subject, and will be of great assistance to the intending grower.

"Rock and Alpine Gardening." By H. Hemsley. 8vo., 81 pp. (Cheal, London.) 3s. 6d. net.

All who have a rock garden, or contemplate making one, should read this very interesting book. The printing and the illustrations are good, and the advice is that of a man who has had great experience, not only in the making of rockeries, but also in their management. Wall-gardening, too, is dealt with in a practical manner. The advice given on how stones should be placed when forming a rockery is important, as this often means all the difference between success and failure afterwards ; if the water runs " off," or, in other words, outwards instead of inwards, a vast number of plants will die from drought, and others will simply exist, not flourish. Suitable plants for shady positions as well as for more open situations are named. Marsh and bog plants are described, and the whole subject from all points is ably dealt with by the author.

"Flower Grouping in English, Scotch, and Irish Gardens." By various authors. 8vo., 237 pp. (Dent, London.) 21s. net.

A charming book, admirably printed and beautifully illustrated. The illustrations are lovely pictures of garden colour taken from actual effects in various gardens, and each forms a delightful object lesson upon what can be done by a judicious selection of plants, bulbs, &c., for producing colour effect. The information contained in the book is not only practical and valuable, but is written in an exceedingly interesting style. It makes a good companion to the other popular book from the same source, viz. " Garden Colour," which has already run into four editions. We predict similar popularity for this volume on " Flower Grouping."

"London Parks and Gardens." By the Hon. Mrs. Evelyn Cecil, with illustrations by Lady Victoria Manners. 8vo., 384 pp. (Constable, London.) 21s. net.

We read this comprehensive and valuable work with much interest, and all who are at all familiar with the London parks, gardens, and open spaces will be equally fascinated by this truly delightful work. No other book deals with the history of all the parks, squares, and gardens of London as this does; for here all are fully described and most interesting sketches of their history, associations, and origin are given. Many of the places mentioned are little known, and some probably not known at all, by many who know their London well, and we confess that it was a surprise to us to read of so many squares and gardens we had never heard about before. It is most interesting to find such a great· number of plants, trees, and shrubs thriving in fog-laden London, and the book will be of immense value to those in charge of parks and open spaces in other smoky towns. Many, too, who are not interested in horticulture will peruse the book with pleasure.

"Grapes, and How to Grow Them." By J. Lonsdell, F.R.H.S. Edited by T. W. Sanders. 8vo., 118 pp. (Collingridge, London.) Paper boards 1s. net; cloth 1s. 6d. net.

For the amateur this will prove a valuable little book, and contains all the information he will require on grape culture, from the making of the border onwards. Insect pests are treated of, and reference is made to the phylloxera; but this dread pest is, we believe, fortunately very rarely found in this country. We can confidently recommend this little book as a· thoroughly practical one for the amateur or professional gardener.

"The Country Month by Month." By J. A. Owen and Professor G. S. Boulger, F.L.S., F.G.S. 8vo., 492 pp. (Duckworth, London.) 6s. net.

To lovers of natural history this will prove a most welcome volume, as it teems with information on plant, bird, and animal life, and tells what one may expect to find in the country every month in the year. The book is of handy size, well printed on good paper, and has a very complete index. It is a book that should be read and carefully studied by everyone dwelling in the country.

"My Rock Garden." By Reginald Farrer. 8vo., 303 pp. (Arnold, London.) 7s. 6d. net.

A well-written and well-printed book, dealing briefly with the making of the rock garden, and very fully with the plants for it. We are glad to see the author gives prominence to English alpine plants, many of which are rarely seen on our rockeries. Valuable hints are given on the management of species and varieties that are considered difficult to grow. Mr. Farrer has evidently studied the plants and their requirements in their native habitats, and all who have a rock garden will be able to gain much serviceable information by reading this book.

"The Art of Landscape Gardening." By Humphrey Repton. Edited by J. Nolen. 8vo., 252 pp. (Constable, London.) 12s. 6d. net.

This book has an introduction by Mr. John Nolen, Cambridge, Mass., and in this introduction he makes the following statement : " It is to the period of Repton and the work of Repton himself that we must look for the sound and rational development of the so-called landscape school of England, a school whose influence spread rapidly to the continent of Europe, and whose principles still control the treatment of large areas in the informal or naturalistic style." As we had scarcely heard of Repton, we turned to Loudon, and that great authority speaks of Repton as follows : "His published observations on these subjects are valuable, though we think otherwise of his remarks on landscape gardening, which we look upon as puerile, wanting depth, often at variance with each other, and abounding too much in affectation and arrogance." We fully agree with Loudon, for although there is much to be admired in his plans and ideas of laying out a large or small garden, it is greatly discounted by the stilted style, and we are often puzzled as to the exact meaning of his description of places. Welbeck may be taken as a case in point (p. 18). Under the chapter of "Buildings" he quotes Saracenic, Saxon, Norman, Gothic, Grecian, and Roman models, but we fail to understand whether he means that Welbeck belongs to one or all of these styles. Again, in his landscape effects, Repton appears to be particularly fond of introducing cottages or other buildings on hill sides or near woods in full view of the mansion, and we cannot quite see why, for, although they may give life to the scene, they are by no means ornamental when the weekly—sometimes daily—washing is hung out. In our opinion one of the great charms of a country mansion is its privacy and peaceful surroundings; plenty of life can always be obtained by deer, Scotch or Hereford cattle, horses, &c., all of which are in harmony.

"The Art and Craft of Garden-making." By Thomas H. Mawson, Hon. A.R.I.B.A. Third edition. 4to. 310 pp. (Batsford, London.) 35s. net.

We are not surprised that this beautiful work has run into its third edition. The printing and illustrations are excellent, and the whole book is full of clear, concise information of great value for those possessing a garden, or intending to make one. If there is a fault at all we think it is in the formality and the architecture of the gardens near the mansion; though, in the majority of the illustrations, we admit the whole is in harmony with the building. However, this is a matter of taste, and what is beautiful to one may be the opposite to another. The chapters on "Gardens, Old and New," and "The Site and its Treatment," are particularly interesting and instructive, and the way in which striking and beautiful features may be introduced with good taste are well indicated. In the chapter on "Gates and Fences for Garden and Park" the difficult problem of the best boundary is thoroughly treated upon, and will be read with attention by all troubled on this important subject. Again the chapter on "Lawns and Garden Walks" is one that shows a master hand, for often do we find both to the highest degree unsatisfactory. The best kinds of grass seeds are given, and the quantities to be used to the acre to make a good green sward, following, of course, thorough preparation of the soil. The importance of properly making both lawns and walks is well described, and should be carefully read by all garden lovers. The subject of water-gardening is so great that a whole volume could easily be filled with it; but in a limited space the author deals practically with all the most important features; and although it is impossible to get water in quantity in some gardens, it is shown how in many, lovely lakes and streams may be made at a comparatively light cost. The advice on the arrangement of hot-houses is excellent, and Mr. Mawson lays special stress on the compactness of these structures; for, as he truly says, the loss caused by the hot-houses being far apart is very great; we are also glad to see he does not recommend lofty houses. Not only are lofty houses more costly, but they are not so suitable for plant or fruit culture. Excellent descriptive lists of trees, shrubs, hardy flowering perennials, &c., in fact, nearly every subject that comes under the title chosen for the book is comprehensively and ably treated. The book has a first-rate index.

" Sweet Peas and their Cultivation for Home and Exhibition." By Charles H. Curtis, F.R.H.S. 8vo. 90 pp. (Collingridge, London.) 1s. net; cloth, 1s. 6d. net.

Although there are a number of books on sweet peas this is the most practical and best we have seen, and the most ignorant novice could scarcely fail to be a successful grower if he followed out the directions so clearly and ably set forth. We are very glad Mr. Curtis writes so emphatically on the importance of thin sowing. A very fine example is shown on page 21 of what single seeds will do, provided they have an opportunity to develop properly. Plants are shown well over seven feet high and at least two feet through, raised from single seeds. Many will be surprised at the author recommending thinning out the seedlings a foot apart in the rows, but experience has shown for some years that this is the correct thing to do: not only are finer flowers produced, and more of them, but they are far more vigorous, and continue to blossom for a longer period. The Cupid section is only faintly praised by the author, for though a few may grow this class well, the great majority of people who have tried them soon give them up. They are disappointing things, and seldom worth the space they occupy. Excellent chapters on Watering, Manuring, Pests, and Diseases are given, and we have nothing but praise for this valuable little book, which is well printed and has a very good index.

" The Art of Garden Designs in Italy." By H. Inigo Triggs, A.R.I.B.A. Imp. 4to. 131 pp. Illustrated by 73 photographic plates reproduced in collotype, 27 plans, and numerous sketches in the text taken from original surveys and plans, specially made by the author, and 28 plates from photographs. By Mrs. Aubrey Le Blond. (Longmans, London.) £3 13s. 6d. net.

This is a really magnificent work: the printing is bold and very clear, and the numerous plates are quite works of art. Gardens and their formation are always subjects of intense interest, and anyone possessing a garden would not have to go far in this book without getting ideas and inspiration, and although architecture is strongly in evidence in all, or nearly all, the plates of these Italian gardens, it is in beautiful harmony with the whole of the surroundings. The author mentions the fact that Livy alluded to the garden of Tarquinius Superbus in the year 534 B.C., adjoining the Royal Palace, which abounded in lilies, roses, and poppies, and tells of other early writers like Varro, Columella, and Pliny the younger giving an interesting description of Pliny's garden. The head gardener in those days was a great personality in the Italian gardens, and was chief of all the slaves ; and the author tells us that conservatories and hot-houses for the protection of the more tender plants against cold, and for the cultivation of early melons and grapes out of season, are mentioned as early as the first century. The love of gardening amongst the ancient Romans must have been very great, for we read of Hadrian's country villa, south of Tivoli, occupying a space of over seven square miles. We cannot do better than quote the author on these gardens : " A Roman garden was the image of the Roman genius, and the love of order and symmetry was everywhere displayed. Laid out by line and rule, with straight alleys and well-trimmed hedges, an extravagant display of priceless statuary attested a wealthy nation. The luxury and display must not, however, be attributed to a spirit of laziness or inactivity ; for, as a rule, the senator or business man led a busy life. The town houses were used mostly during the winter months or during the Roman season, whilst, as Pliny says, the appearance of spring was a signal for the aristocracy to disperse to their country seats, many of which were conveniently situated within 'easy reach of the metropolis.'" How little we have altered in nearly 2,000 years ! The illustrations of Pompeian gardens are stiff and formal, but still there is good taste combined with due regard to proportions admirably shown. In another illustration we have good examples of balcony gardening, with ornamental plants in vases, &c., showing how deep the love of gardening had become. It is of interest to know that the first public botanic garden was formed, about 1545, by the Senate of Venice, at Padua, and the first private botanic garden was made by Gaspar di Gabriel, at Padua, in 1525, twenty years earlier than the public one. Isola Bella, Lake Maggiore, is a wonderful piece of work, and the plan given is easily read. Probably no finer effect has ever been produced by the hand of man, and it is only in a country like Italy that one could expect to find anything like it. The luxuriant vegetation, the beautiful terraces one above another, the fine architecture, the parterre, and the lovely water make it perfectly unique, and there is little wonder that all lovers of the beautiful, whether in gardens or scenery, make a point of visiting this place. Scores of other exquisite gardens are admirably shown, and, although we must confess we do not usually admire a formal garden, we are full of admiration for the splendour, good taste, and beauty of the Italian gardens so well depicted in the illustrations. Some are on a magnificent scale, while others are quite small, but all are wonderful, and all compel a feeling of the highest respect for the designers of such charming places. There are 128 plates, besides smaller illustrations ; and, although the book is so big, few are more worthy of a place on the bookshelves of the garden lover than this.

"Our Woodlands, Heaths, and Hedges." A popular description of British Trees, Shrubs, Wild Fruits, &c., with Notices of Insect Inhabitants. By W. S. Coleman, illustrated by the Author. 8vo., 140 pp. (Routledge, London.) 1s.

This little book is one of many adapted to encourage observations in plant and animal life. It contains brief but interesting descriptions of many plants. We note one slip. It was not about maple wood tables, but those made of *Citrus* (*Callitris quadrivalvis* of N. Africa) that Pliny speaks of as extravagant. An appendix of British lepidopterous insects, the caterpillars of which feed on the trees mentioned, and eight excellent plates of trees and shrubs are included. We can commend this little book as a good companion on a country walk.

"Plant Physiology and Ecology." By F. E. Clements, Professor of Botany in the University of Minnesota. 8vo., 315 pp. (Constable, London.) 10s. 6d. net.

This exhaustive treatise is the result of the methods of study first advanced in the author's "Research Methods in Ecology." "The plant is first considered as an individual with respect to factor, function, and form, and then as a member of a plant group or formation." The work contains fifteen chapters. The first discusses the nature of "stimuli and response." Physiological adaptation without change of form is called "adjustment." If structure changes, then the word "adaptation" is used. Chapters II. and III. deal with effects of water treated experimentally; while modifying factors, as of soil, influences of locality, &c., are exhaustively discussed.

The adjustment to water includes all the ordinary physiological functions of absorption, diffusion, transpiration, &c. Next comes the influences of light and shade; then adjustments to temperature. Chapters VII. and VIII. deal with adaptations to water and light in changes of structure. Chapter IX. deals with the "origin of new forms," and the author, instead of retaining Darwin's terms "indefinite" and "definite" variations, limits the word "variation" to the former and "adaptation" to the latter. He also still retains "natural selection" in the Darwinian sense; but if there be *no* "indefinite" variations, by which Darwin meant many "injurious" non-adaptive changes, together with a few "favourable" and adaptive, neither "indefinite" variations nor "natural selection" in "originating" species have any place in evolution.

Chapter X. is devoted to "Methods of Studying Vegetation," Chapter XI. to "Plant Formation," with illustrations of different kinds. The last two chapters suggest "invasion and succession" and "alternation and zonation" as the causes of change and distribution of habitats. It is a valuable book, and no teacher of advanced botany can well do without it. England is still far behind the world in the matter of ecology!

"The Essentials of Cytology." By C. E. Walker. 8vo., 139 pp. (Constable, London.) 7s. 6d. net.

This is a very important up-to-date work on the cell. It deals with the structure and division of the cell in all its phases, both vegetative and reproductive, and of the male and female, fertilisation of uni- and multi-cellular forms. The tenth chapter deals with the probable individuality of the chromosomes, and the eleventh is on the morphological aspect of the transmission of hereditary characters. Every student or teacher of botany will find this a most comprehensive treatise, abounding with illustrations.

"The Lesson of Evolution." By F. W. Hutton, F.R.S. 8vo., 101 pp. (Duckworth, London.) 2s. net.

This little book consists of three essays on "The Lesson of Evolution" and "The Progress of Life," commencing with a short account of the growth of natural philosophy. The author gives an outline of evolution, both inorganic and organic. He takes it for granted that living organisms *first* "appeared on the surface of the ocean; then increased in size, varied in many directions, and in time discovered the bottom of the sea, . . . changing from swimming to crawling creatures; . . . they finally became land plants and animals." It is as well to emphasise the fact that this is a *pure assumption* without a particle of evidence, the earliest rocks revealing nothing of the sort. It is quite as likely that the first organism rose on moist ground, then spread to the sea, and so in time gave rise to fishes, &c. "Evolution is evidently due to the action of mind." Here we quite agree with the author, but he does not appear to have heard of "directivity" or the "director of forces" in all animals and plants, which brings about "adaptive response" to new conditions of life; consequently the sentence, "We now are compelled to assume as First Cause a power [rather a Director] outside of Nature, without which the material universe could never have come into existence," should be altered to embrace the most modern view— viz., that the creative power is *immanent* rather than external. He holds to the Darwinian sense of natural selection in evolution, now quite discarded by ecological botanists at least. Ecology supplied the correction to the author's statement, "There is no general law either for development or for extinction." *Response with adaptation to changed conditions of life* is the first, and *the struggle for existence* is the second.

"Darwinism and Lamarckism, Old and New." Four Lectures. By F. W. Hutton, F.R.S., &c. 8vo., 169 pp. (Duckworth, London.) 3s. 6d. net.

Though published in England, these lectures were delivered in New Zealand, which may account for the total absence of all reference to ecology, pursued vigorously in the United States, England, and on the Continent. One hundred and thirty-three pages are devoted to Darwinism and sixty-six only to Lamarckism. The author is in favour of natural selection, for he says: "It is natural selection, working with other forms of isolation, which has brought about the main progress of life."

Ecology, however, shows that, while the struggle for life goes on every-where between different organisms, it has nothing to do with evolution. He also says : " Natural selection has no doubt developed that part of man's intellect which makes him cunning in devising means to ensnare his prey and to get the better of his fellow-men." This is probably correct, but it has not brought about a new variety of *Homo*. Speaking of useless structures in plants and animals he says : " I do not see how we can escape from the conclusion that all these so-called useless structures, all that give us beauty and variety, have been specially designed for his [man's] education." Spines give us " variety," but they are perfectly useless on desert plants, and are merely the result of drought ; one does not see what they have to do with education. " Evidently variation is the result of very complicated conditions, and is not to be explained by one overmastering principle." Response, with or without adaptations to the influences of changed conditions of life, is as nearly a universal principle as we are likely to reach—coupled with the principle of " directivity " within the organism itself.

The book gives a good account of Darwinism, both " new " and " old," and of Lamarckism ; but it is deficient, as stated above, in the latest application of the latter.

" Outlines of Biology." By P. Chalmers Mitchell. 8vo., 297 pp. (Methuen, London.) 6s.

This book " has been determined by the syllabus of the conjoint Examining Board of the Royal Colleges of Physicians and Surgeons of England, issued for the guidance of candidates preparing for the examination in Elementary Biology." It is a description of the usual types required, with an abundance of illustrations.

" Trees and their Life Histories." By Percy Groom. Large 8vo., 407 pp. (Cassell, London.) 25s. net.

Whether for accuracy of illustrations or text this is probably the most valuable book that has yet appeared on the subject of our woodland trees. Certainly much more might have been said regarding each species that has been treated of, but for the purpose intended a wise discrimination has been shown, while the analytical method adopted has much to recom-mend it. The distinctive features of each tree and shrub—for we can hardly call the buckthorn, bullace, hazel, and Euonymus trees—are well chosen, and give just sufficient clear points for purposes of ready recognition. The differences between *Pinus Laricio* and the variety *P. austriaca* are—from a purely commercial point at least—not well defined, for the timber of the former is far preferable to that of the variety, while the latter is more readily uprooted in stormy weather. But these are minor matters, especially as the book is written for the lover of trees, or, rather, to guide the interested observer of Nature, rather than to attract the book lover, and with a view to concentrate the reader's attention upon the tree itself, rather than to lure him from the woodland to his book-room.

"Forage Crops." By Edward B. Voorhees, D.Sc. 8vo., 884 pp. (Macmillan, New York and London.) 6s. 6d. net.

An excellent book on the subject with which it deals, although the English reader will regret that many of the plants treated of are not those extensively grown here. Forage crops are not of great interest to gardeners generally, but immensely so to those interested in green manures as a means of supplementing dung where the amount is inadequate. Still more interesting is the subject to those who have to feed stock, whether as small holders or otherwise. To such we may heartily recommend this work as probably the best one dealing with the subject.

It deals with all the cereals, and, of course, maize figures largely. Field peas and vetches, and suitable combinations of these with other plants, are dealt with very fully, and this section is the most valuable part of the book. Various root crops are enlarged upon, and the book also contains a useful chapter on composition, fertiliser, and coefficient tables. There are many good plates, chiefly from photographs.

BURNHAM BEECHES.

[At the request of the Right Hon. the Lord Mayor and the Corporation of the City of London the Council on August 20, 1907, appointed a small Committee to examine and report upon the condition of the trees at Burnham Beeches. The Committee devoted considerable attention to the matter, and in September issued their report to the Corporation, a copy of which is given below.]

The Royal Horticultural Society,
Vincent Square, Westminster:
September 5, 1907.

Report on the Beeches at Burnham.

In pursuance of a request contained in two letters from Mr. Thomas Harvey Hull, dated August 16 and 29, 1907, on behalf of the Corporation of the City of London, requesting the Royal Horticultural Society to appoint a small Committee of Experts to visit the Burnham Beeches and advise, the President and Council of the Society had much pleasure in acceding to such request, and appointed Mr. F. J. Chittenden, Director of the Society's Laboratory at Wisley and Secretary of the Scientific Committee; Mr. A. D. Webster, Superintendent of Regent's Park, a skilled expert in trees; Mr. Harry J. Veitch, who has had as varied and widespread experience in such matters as any man in the kingdom; and the Rev. W. Wilks, M.A., Secretary of the Society, who has for the last ten years been drawing special attention to the disease in beeches.

These four gentlemen visited the Beeches on Thursday, September 5, and report as follows :—

Roughly speaking the whole of the trees are attacked by an insect known as *Cryptococcus fagi*, some only slightly, others very badly, and that without any apparent reference to the age of the trees, some of the younger ones being more affected than some of the older.

At "Wheeler's Corner" is a very bad example, the comparatively young growths of a spreading tree being densely covered with the insects, and the quite young trees near by being almost invariably affected more or less.

In "Egypt" all the old trees are affected, but most of them only moderately. In the "Victoria Drive" the old pollarded trees are almost invariably, but slightly, whilst many of the younger ones are badly stricken.

We are of opinion that the greater thickness and rugosity of the bark is the reason of the comparatively fewer insects living on the older trees, it being only in the cracks in the bark that the insects can in these old specimens obtain the juices of the tree on which they live. No argument, therefore, can be based on the fact that the densest insect population is found on the younger trees.

The Committee ordered one of the younger trees to be dug up in order that they might examine its roots and the soil about them. This has been done, but without any direct suggestion occurring as to the very great and recent increase in the insect. It was, however, noticeable that almost all the roots lay close to the surface, and they would, therefore, more immediately feel the influence of rainfall and drought, especially of the latter.

The Committee were present at the felling of the " Queen " beech, and some of them were strongly of opinion that its death had been caused by this insect, as the splitting and peeling of the bark is very characteristic of the final stage of the insect's work of destruction.

Cryptococcus fagi was noticed in Germany about 1849. It is also reported, about the same date, as abundant in Bohemia, and casual notices of it appear from that time onward. In 1862 it is reported at Tyningehame, in Scotland, and Dr. Balfour remarks : " In many cases the trees are so covered as to look as if painted white " ; " when once it appears in a wood . it spreads rapidly " ; and " in every case where seen the tree dies "—a remark which must not be taken too strictly. Dr. Balfour also mentions that it had destroyed trees in Edinburgh Botanic Gardens, and that it appeared to him to attack quite healthy trees.

Since the above date it has been noticed all over Scotland and all over England ; and in 1867 a discussion took place as to whether the insect attacked healthy trees or only fastened on to those whose bark had been injured by severe frost ; but it has since been clearly seen that the insects are quite independent of the help they may nevertheless occasionally receive from exceptional frosts. Reports from all parts of the country unite in describing its rapid increase, its destructive effects, and the practical inutility of all hitherto suggested remedies except in the case of individual specimen trees.

In the " Land Agents' Society's Journal," vol. ii. 1903, p. 167, it is said that the insects never make any headway unless the tree is dying from other causes. It seems to be a symptom and not a cause of ill-health ; but this, again, is a statement to be received with much caution.

Professor Theobald remarks that the insect increases most rapidly in dry weather.

The insect is now one of the commonest of the group called " scale " insects, although, like the well-known " mealy-bug " (which belongs to the same group) it does not form scales, but protects itself instead by throwing out from its body a multitude of minute threads of a white waxy substance, somewhat like . cotton-wool, which gradually forms itself into a sort of white felt which shields it effectually and constitutes the main difficulty in applying any effective remedies.

The insect is furnished with a sort of proboscis, which it inserts into the bark of the tree and through which it sucks up its juices, the result being that the foliage becomes thin, the smaller branches die back, and eventually the bark splits and flakes off in sheets, and the tree dies. But this may take many years in process—indeed, individual trees have been known to withstand it altogether, without any assignable reason. Whether the death of the tree is attributable to the *Cryptococcus* alone, or whether it is brought about by the joint action of the insect and a fungus (*Polyporus spumeus*) which has been found on the dying trees, is not clearly known.

On removing the overlying white felty substance the insect may be clearly seen with the help of an ordinary magnifying glass, and appears as an almost globular, semitransparent, yellow body. It appears to be particularly free from natural enemies, and the birds do not seem to eat it. It is practically impossible to deal with it in woods or in extensive plantations, but individual trees may be freed from its infestation or greatly assisted in withstanding it and throwing it off by the following treatment :—

1. When the stem of a tree is thickly coated with the insect, spread sacking or other material on the ground round the trunk and scrape off as much of the white felt-like substance as possible, and then scrub the tree from the highest point you can reach downwards with a stiff brush dipped in paraffin emulsion, working it well into the cracks and crevices of the bark and burning all the *débris* that falls on the sacking.

This should be done twice or three times during the summer and autumn.

2. In winter a tree that has been partially cleaned by the last method should be sprayed or syringed with caustic alkali wash. The operator should wear protecting spectacles, thick leather gauntlet gloves, and be careful to spray or syringe with the way of the wind, as the wash is very burning to hands, eyes, or face. It must only be used in winter, *i.e.* any time after the leaves have all fallen, up to the end of the second week in February. It should be repeated twice, at intervals of a week.

3. A member of the Committee thought that those trees whose roots were somewhat exposed seemed to be more liable to the attack than others. It could certainly do no harm, and might be productive of much good to the general health of such a tree, to give it a mulching of soil sufficient to cover the now exposed roots to a depth of four or six inches.

These remedies are, as we said, impracticable for a beech wood or large plantation such as at Burnham, but they would be useful for individual trees specially desired to be saved.

Regretting that we cannot give a more promising and more hopeful report on this beautiful beech forest,

(Signed)   FRED. J. CHITTENDEN,   *Members*
                 HARRY J. VEITCH,   *of the*
                 A. D. WEBSTER,   *Committee.*
                 W. WILKS,

P.S.—*To Make Paraffin Emulsion.*—Mix equal portions of soft-soap dissolved in boiling water and paraffin and churn them up with a syringe. When required for use add twenty times its bulk of warm water and churn it up together again.

To Make Caustic Alkali.—Dissolve one pound of caustic soda in water; also dissolve one pound of crude potash in water. When dissolved mix the two well, add three-quarters of a pound of soft-soap, stir up together, and add enough water to make ten gallons.

COMMONPLACE NOTES.

By the Secretary, Superintendent, and Editor.

Exhibition of Nature Study.

A Fellow inquires how to set about getting up an exhibition of Nature Study.

Well, it is very difficult to suggest a scheme for an exhibition in Nature Study, as Nature Study is not a subject, but a point of view; or, in other words, a method of teaching; having for its object the training of the observing and reasoning powers of the pupils, by the use of the commonest things they meet with in their everyday life. This being the case, almost everyone who has given attention to the matter has a different conception of the meaning of the term "Nature Study," and the drawing up of a syllabus tends rather to the destruction of the idea than to the furtherance of a desirable method of teaching, which, in its essence, must be original with the teacher and the taught, and very frequently quite informal. However, there are a few directions in which the methods of Nature Study may form good subjects for exhibition.

For scholars in Elementary and Secondary Schools:

Nature Calendars, containing the pupil's own observations, and notes. These are of further value if, at the end of the year, the compiler has extracted a gardener's year, a bird year, a flower year, or any other record of the sequence of natural events in any direction. These calendars should always contain notes on the weather.

Drawings, in outline or in wash, of natural objects made in connection with the object-lessons in school or as records of things seen.

Essays upon things observed during a school excursion.

Diaries of work and method in school gardens, with notes on weather, growth of crops, mode of germination of seeds, and so on.

Collections of plants to illustrate some particular point:

For instance, methods of climbing found in wild plants or garden plants. Collections of plants from special kinds of soil, as limestone formation, sandy soil, and so on, to illustrate the vegetation of special formations common in the neighbourhood; or this might be restricted in an agricultural neighbourhood to grasses found growing in particular situations, as shade, open common, pastures on clay or sand, meadows, mountains, &c. Collections of weeds, to illustrate kinds peculiar to particular crops, means of distribution, habit of growth, manner in which they interfere with the growth of the crop, by, e.g., diminishing the cropped area, appropriating earth salts from the soil, preventing access of light to the developing crop, interfering with root-breathing, checking development of crop by twining or climbing over it, interfering with the seed produce, or by actual consumption of the crop as with the dodder. Collections showing the form of leaf, mode of branching, character of winter twigs, flowers and fruit of the common trees and shrubs and similar things to these. These may be illustrated either by dried specimens or fresh, according to the time of year at which the exhibition is held. The collections should be the sole work of the pupil, without "touching up" by the teacher, and the plants comprising them should be such as are quite common in the neighbourhood. The making of collections of plants that are rare serves no good purpose, and should be discouraged.

Where such collections as the foregoing are out of the question collections of the common flowering plants of the neighbourhood might be made and exhibited fresh, or of fruits in the autumn, and named by the children. But it would seem that, for children of eleven or twelve and upwards, the special collections would have more educational value.

Collections of insects found in the garden; and these are better if they show the life histories of the insects to as great a degree as possible, and they should be accompanied with notes as to food, habits, &c.

Plans of the school garden showing method of cropping, rotation followed, &c. Maps of the neighbourhood of the school, either on the flat or in relief. These, with the older children, might show sections and geological formations, as well as the more usual features.

In districts where mining or quarrying are important industries the nature of the rocks would naturally claim more attention than the plants and the animals of the neighbourhood, but in no case should one group be the exclusive object of attention, as it seems of importance to emphasise the dependence of the various forms of life upon one another and upon their inanimate environment.

The exhibition of the produce from school gardens in the neighbourhood might also be encouraged at times, provided that school is not pitted against school, but rather pupil against pupil. It sometimes happens that when school is pitted against school an unhealthy rivalry is created, instead of, as one might have expected, a proper spirit of emulation. These exhibits are better entered in special classes than in open ones.

For schools of a higher grade, where attention is given to the natural history of the neighbourhood, and where the acquisition of Nature knowledge has become more systematised and has been raised to the dignity of a scientific subject, such exhibits as those of simple experiments illustrating the main facts in the manner of life of plants and animals, and maps of the district showing plant formations and associations, with notes and drawings illustrating the manner in which plants are fitted to live where they are found, would form suitable subjects for exhibition.

As to Forestry—photographs showing the making of a natural woodland, specimens illustrating the structure and life history of forest trees from the seed to maturity, specimens of insect and fungoid pests, plans for planting, and for subsequent treatment, examples illustrating the results of skilful and unsuitable methods of pruning, and similar things might all be exhibited and would be of great educational value.

Many other points similar to the foregoing would suggest themselves; but local conditions must always govern to a very large extent the exact nature of such an exhibition.

The points that seem most promising might be picked out by anyone who had sufficient local knowledge, and others might be added if it were necessary.

Cannas for Winter Decoration.

The canna is well known as a summer denizen of our gardens, but it may be somewhat surprising to many to learn that it is equally valuable for room, conservatory, and greenhouse decoration in winter. Cannas were among the plants tried at Wisley during the summer and autumn of 1907, and as some of the varieties arrived late in the season, and were in comparatively small pots, it was decided to pot these, and some others already in large pots, into pots of larger size and grow them on, in a light and only moderately warm greenhouse, where the temperature often dropped to 45° at night. All grew vigorously, and threw up flower spikes almost as freely as in the summer months. When the pots became full of roots a little chemical manure was given, but really very little aid in this respect was supplied. All the varieties, in over one hundred pots, succeeded equally well, and surprised many by their clean healthy growth and handsome flowers in December and January. As the house was wanted in March for other purposes they were gradually " rested " in February and dried off, otherwise they promised to go on growing and flowering indefinitely. The trial proved very emphatically the use and value of these stately and beautiful plants for winter, and where big, bold plants are required for halls, corridors, and other somewhat draughty places, these will be found more suitable than most, particularly when used in conjunction with palms. The only pest troubling the plants was aphis to a slight extent, but this was easily eradicated by fumigation.

Raw Manure and Tree Roots.

We have seen in several places recently both fruit trees and ornamental shrubs badly injured by the bringing of fresh manure into direct contact with the roots when planting. The jobbing gardener is a great sinner in this respect, and though his intentions may be excellent, the results of such procedure are usually deplorable, as all new roots emitted by the trees are poisoned by coming in contact with the manure. If any manure at all is used it should be well decayed and thoroughly mixed with the soil, or used as a mulch after planting.

Japanese Iris.

In the course of an interesting communication from Mr. Kenkichi Okubo, of Osaka, Japan, he tells us that over three hundred varieties of the Japanese Iris (*Iris laevigata* or *I. Kaempferi*) are known in Japan. In order to obtain large flowers the plants are divided after flowering and the old roots removed, the plants being planted in rows and two or three in a clump in soil covered by water. After growth has started fertiliser is supplied, night-soil or oil-cake being considered the best. The more fertiliser is supplied the better the plants respond, but " to put a handful or two of soja beans at the roots before blooming is the secret of getting large flowers." When new varieties are desired recourse is had to seed sowing, "and the seed is harvested before the seed-pods are yellowed and broken. Early in the next spring the seed is sown on the prepared seed-bed on the land and watered every morning. When the plants have attained a few inches in height a little weak fertiliser is supplied, and on a cloudy day in the rainy season they are transplanted. The flowers are produced by this method in two years, fertiliser being given twice in the spring before the flower stalks come up, but if the management is not good the flowers are not produced until the third year."

SEED GERMINATION.

Probably many pots and pans of seeds are annually thrown away because, after the lapse of several months, there is no sign of any germination, and it is concluded that the seed was bad. Even practical gardeners sometimes lose patience and throw them out. In many cases it is the correct thing to do, as most kinds of seed will germinate quickly after sowing, and if they do not, it is useless to keep them; but, on the other hand, some seeds will be months before they germinate. For instance, *Primula japonica* often remains dormant eighteen months, *Gunnera manicata* seldom germinates in less than eight months, *Helleborus* usually takes the same length of time, *Lilium giganteum* sown November 1906 commenced germinating very freely in February 1908, while *L. Grayi* and *Camassia esculenta* were each a year in starting. Some of the Gentianas, Ericas, &c., are equally slow in moving, and we would suggest more patience with such seeds than is usually exercised; in many instances patience will meet with its due reward.

COLCHICUMS.

The question whether any special treatment is given to the Colchicums at Wisley is often asked, as they are always so fine. The answer is: "Nothing is done." Both in the border and in short and comparatively long grass in the Gardens they grow and flower profusely every year without any manure, and they are never disturbed. We believe it is a mistake to lift or disturb the bulbs, as those which have been planted for many years are always finer than newly planted ones. For the wild garden few bulbs are so useful, as their blossoms are produced when outdoor flowers are becoming scarce. The end of July or early in August is the best time to plant the bulbs; if left later, root action has commenced, and they are not so fine in flower or foliage in the first year. *Colchicum speciosum* (fig. 96) has the largest flower, and seems to be far the best for growing in masses in grass or in the border, as it thrives equally well in heavy or light soil, loose or hard ground, and in almost any position. Its variety *album* is one of the most beautiful and striking of all autumn flowers. Colchicums like a damp spot, but not one actually wet.

CELERIAC, OR TURNIP-ROOTED CELERY.

It is strange that this delicious vegetable is not more generally grown, as it is easy of cultivation, is excellent both as a vegetable or as a salad, and is highly esteemed by the cook for flavouring soups, &c. It is a valuable introduction, and we believe has but to be better known to be more widely cultivated. The treatment is exactly the same as for ordinary celery—that is, it is to be grown in well-manured trenches, or on the flat, planted the usual distance apart, and supplied with water when necessary, but earthing-up or blanching is not called for. When well grown, the root attains the size of a moderate Swede turnip, and some,

FIG. 96.—COLCHICUM SPECIOSUM IN THE WISLEY GARDEN.

particularly Prague celeriac and one or two other varieties of that type, are almost as free from rootlets as is the turnip. The root in these varieties is globular, even in shape, and has rootlets on the under side only. The 'Tom Thumb' variety is not worth growing, as it is so very small and possesses no merit in flavour over other varieties. Where the gardener is expected to supply large quantities of celery for flavouring purposes, he will find celeriac a great acquisition.

PETITION TO THE RAILWAY COMPANIES.

A NUMBER of Fellows having urged the Council to again approach the Railway Companies with a view to securing reduced fares, the Council having twice before urged the matter on the attention of the Directors unsuccessfully, it was thought better that the Petition should be signed by the Fellows themselves, in the hope of the weight of numbers succeeding where the influence of the Council had failed. A petition was therefore drafted and sent out for signature to all the Fellows. It was signed by nearly 3,000 of them, and forwarded with the following letter to the Companies.

Royal Horticultural Society,
Vincent Square, Westminster, S.W.
September 17, 1907.

To the Committee of British Railways,
    The Railway Clearing House,
        Seymour Street.

MY LORDS AND GENTLEMEN,—We, the President and Council of the Royal Horticultural Society, having received a Petition signed by 2,725 Fellows of our Society requesting us to approach the Railway Companies of Great Britain asking that reduced fares be granted to Fellows visiting the fortnightly Flower and Fruit Shows of the Society held in London, beg to formulate this request on their behalf.

We would point out that the Fellowship of the Society numbers about 10,000, representing all classes of Horticulturists, including the Horticultural trade and Working Gardeners besides Amateurs.

The Shows are exceedingly popular and attract a large number of visitors, but existing railway charges preclude a very appreciable proportion of our Fellows at a distance from attendance except on rare occasions. We are confident that by a reduction of railway fare such as you already allow to some Societies, the attendance of our Provincial Fellows would be very greatly stimulated, and an enormous benefit conferred on working gardeners throughout the country, and on the Horticultural trade.

Further than this, the great educational value of our Shows, at which all new fruits, flowers and vegetables make their first appearance in public, makes such increased attendance highly desirable for the improvement of the produce of the country, and for the maintenance of its pre-eminence in the quality of its fruit and market garden produce. And we would point out that the orders given to the trade on these fortnightly occasions cause considerable Goods traffic on the lines.

We are informed that special reduced rates are allowed (for example) to the Royal Agricultural Society, the Bath and West of England Society, and other Associations, bringing benefit to the Public and increased traffic to the Railways; also to such other Societies as that for the "Promotion of Christian Knowledge," and to individuals attending the May Meetings in London. You have also, we understand, for several years permitted reduced tickets for such purposes as Fishing and Golf, so that we feel that we are not without considerable precedence in urging the petition of our Fellows upon you.

The 2,725 signatures of our Fellows are filed at the office of the Society, and will at once be forwarded for your inspection if it is your wish.

A complete list of the Fellows of the Society is enclosed.

May we express the hope that your Committee will consider with favour this application from which so large a community will benefit, and which we cannot but believe will react in benefit to the Companies ?

The Secretary of the Society will be pleased to meet you at any time if you desire it to discuss the details of how this matter can be carried out, or we will appoint a deputation to wait upon you.

Signed on behalf of the Royal Horticultural Society,-

TREVOR LAWRENCE.
President.

Railway Clearing House,
Seymour Street, Euston Square, London, N.W.
October 29, 1907.

Royal Horticultural Society.

DEAR SIR,—Your letter of the 17th September last, asking that reduced fares be granted to Fellows of the Royal Horticultural Society visiting the fortnightly Flower and Fruit Shows of the Society held in London, has been considered by the Railway Superintendents in conference, and I am desired to inform you that they regret they are unable to see their way to accede to the application.

Yours truly,
T. MANSFIELD.

Sir Trevor Lawrence, Bart., K.C.V.O.
Royal Horticultural Society,
Vincent Square, Westminster, S.W.

BOOKS PRESENTED, PURCHASED, OR REVIEWED DURING THE YEAR
1907, AND DEPOSITED IN THE LIBRARY.

1 = Sent for review.
2 = Purchased.
3 = Presented by The Director, Royal Gardens, Kew.
4 =   ,,   ,, Messrs. Francis Barker & Son.
5 =   ,,   ,, The Bentham Trustees.
6 =   ,,   . ,, The Rev. W. Wilks, M.A.
7 =   ,,   ,, Lieut.-Col. F. W. Lambton.
8 =   ,,   ,, W. H. Read, Esq., C.M.G.
9 =   ,,   ,, Howard Payn, Esq.
10 =   ,,   ,, Mrs. E. M. Taylor.

ADAMS, H. I., "Wild Flowers of the British Isles." London, 1907, 8vo. (1).
ADAMS, J., "Guide to the Principal Families of Flowering Plants." Dublin, 1906, 8vo. (1).
ATKINSON, G. F., "First Studies of Plant Life." Boston, 1901, 8vo. (2).
AVEBURY, Lord, "Scientific Lectures," ed. 3. London, 1906, 8vo. (1).
BAILEY, L. H., "Plant Breeding," ed. 4. New York, 1906, 8vo. (2).
BARDSWELL, F. A., "Notes from Nature's Garden." London, 1906, 8vo. (1).
BERGEN, FANNY D., "Glimpses at the Plant World." Boston, 1898, 8vo. (2).
BERGER, ALWIN, "Sukkulente Euphorbien." Stuttgart, 1907, 8vo. (2).
BETTANY, G. T., "First Lessons in Practical Botany." London, 1899, 8vo. (1).
BLYTT, AXEL, "Haandbog i Norges Flora." Kristiania, 1906, 8vo. (2).
BONNIER, GASTON, "Le Monde végétal." Paris, 1907, 12mo. (2).
BOULGER, G. S., "Familiar Trees," new ed. London, &c., 1906, 8vo. (1).
BOWER, F. O., & GWYNNE-VAUGHAN, D. T., "Practical Botany for Beginners." London. 1905, 8vo. (1).
BRANDIS, Sir DIETRICH, "Indian Trees." London, 1906, 8vo. (1).
BRIQUET, J., "Règles internationales de la Nomenclature botanique." Jena, 1906, 8vo. (2).
BROTHERSTON, R. P., "The Book of Cut Flowers." Edinburgh & London, 1906, 8vo. (1).
BURBIDGE, F. W., "The Book of the Scented Garden." London & New York, 1905, 8vo. (1).
BURNAT, E., "Flore des Alpes Maritimes," 4 vols. Genève & Bale, 1892–1906, 8vo. (2).
"CASSELL's Popular Gardening," edited by WALTER P. WRIGHT, 2 vols. London, 1905, 8vo. (1).
CASTLE, R. LEWIS, "The Book of Market Gardening." London & New York, 1906, 8vo. (1).
CLOAG, M. R., "A Book of English Gardens." London, 1906, 8vo. (1).
CONN, H. W., "The Story of Germ Life : Bacteria." London, 1905, 8vo. (2).
DAWSON, Sir J. W., "The Geological History of Plants." London, 1905, 8vo. (2).
DE VRIES, HUGO, "Plant Breeding." London & Chicago, 1907, 8vo. (2).
DICKSON, H. N., "Meteorology : the Elements of Weather and Climate." London, 1893, 8vo. (2).
DUVAL, L., "Traité de Culture Pratique des *Cattleya.*" Paris, 1907, 8vo. (2).
EDMONDS, H., "Botany for Beginners." London, 1899, 8vo. (2).
ELLIOT, G. F. SCOTT, "The Romance of Plant Life." London, 1907, 8vo. (1).
ELY, HELENA RUTHERFURD, "Another Hardy Garden Book." New York and London, 1905, 8vo. (1).
EVANS, ERNEST, "Botany for Beginners." London, 1906, 8vo. (1).
EWART, A. J., "First Stage Botany." London, 1905, 8vo. (1).
FARRER, R., "My Rock Garden." London, 1907, 8vo. (2).
FISH, D. S., "The Book of the Winter Garden." London and New York, 1906, 8vo. (1).
FITZGERALD, H. P., "A Concise Handbook of Climbers, Twiners, and Wall Shrubs." London, 1906, 8vo. (1).
"Flora Capensis," iv, sect. 1, pt. 4. London, 1907, 8vo. (3).
FOLSOM, J. W., "Entomology, with Special Reference to its Biological and Economic Aspects." London, 1906, 8vo. (1).

GANONG, W. F., " The Teaching Botanist." New York, 1905, 8vo. (1).
"Garden Colour." Spring, by Mrs. C. W. EARLE ; Summer, by E. V. B. ; Autumn,
    by ROSE KINGSLEY ; Winter, by the Hon. VICARY GIBBS. London, 1905, 4to. (1).
GATTY, Mrs. ALFRED, " The Book of Sun-Dials," re-edited by H. K. F. EDEN and
    ELEANOR LLOYD. London, 1900, 8vo. (4).
GRAY, ASA, " Botanical Text-Book," vol. 2 : " Physiological Botany," by G. L. GOODALE.
    New York and Chicago, 1885, 8vo. (1).
HALL, A. D., " The Book of the Rothamsted Experiments." London, 1905, 8vo. (1).
HARRIS, M. O'BRIEN, " Seasonal Botany." London, 1906, 8vo. (1).
HARWOOD, W. S., " New Creations in Plant Life." New York and London, 1905,
    8vo. (1).
HENNESEY, J. E., " The School Garden." London, 1906, 8vo. (1).
HENSLOW, Rev. G., " Introduction to Plant Ecology." London, 1907, 8vo. (1).
HILGARD, E. W., " Soils : their Formation, Properties, Composition, and Relations to
    Climate and Plant Growth in the Humid and Arid Regions." New York, 1906,
    8vo. (1).
HILL, M. D., and WEBB, W. M., " Eton Nature-Study and Observational Lessons,"
    pts. 1 & 2. London, 1903-4, 8vo. (1).
HOOKER's " Icones Plantarum," ix., pts. 1 & 2. London, 1906-7, 8vo. (5).
JACKSON, B. D., " A Glossary of Botanic Terms, with their Derivation and Accent,"
    ed. 2. London, 1905, 8vo. (1).
JOHNS, Rev. C. A., " Flowers of the Field," revised throughout and edited by CLARENCE
    ELLIOTT. London, 1907, 8vo. (1).
JOHNSTONE, W. W., " Gardening : a Guide for Amateurs in India." Mussoorie, 1903,
    8vo. (1).
JOST, Dr. LUDWIG, " Lectures on Plant Physiology," translated by R. J. HARVEY
    GIBSON. Oxford, 1907, 8vo. (1).
KELLOGG, V. L., " Darwinism To-day." London and New York, 1907, 8vo. (2).
KERRIDGE, ALBERT A., " Early Lessons in Cottage Gardening." London, n.d., 8vo. (1).
KING, F. H., " The Soil." New York, 1906, 8vo. (2).
LASLETT, T., " Timber and Timber Trees : Native and Foreign," ed. 2, completely
    revised by H. MARSHALL WARD. London and New York, 1894, 8vo (1).
LEWIS, B. M. GWYN, " A Concise Handbook of Garden Shrubs." London, 1906,
    8vo. (1).
LOCK, R. H., " Recent Progress in the Study of Variation, Heredity, and Evolution."
    London, 1906, 8vo. (1).
LODGE, Sir OLIVER, " Life and Matter," ed. 4. London, 1907, 8vo. (1).
LOTSY, J. P., " Vorträge über botanische Stammesgeschichte," Bd. 1, Algen und Pilze.
    Jena, 1907, 8vo. (2).
LUCAS, C. P., " A Historical Geography of the British Colonies," vol. ii. : " The West
    Indies," ed. 2, revised and brought up to date by C. ATCHLEY. Oxford, 1905,
    8vo. (1).
MACDOUGAL, D. T., " The Nature and Work of Plants." New York and London, 1900,
    8vo. (1).
MCFARLAND, J. HORACE, " Getting Acquainted with the Trees." New York, 1904,
    8vo. (1).
MARSHALL, C., " A Plain and Easy Introduction to the Knowledge and Practice of
    Gardening, with Hints on Fish-Ponds," ed. 5. London, 1813, 8vo. (6).
MASSEE, G., " Text-Book of Fungi." London, 1906, 8vo. (1).
    „   " A Text-Book of Plant Diseases," ed. 3. London, 1907, 8vo. (1).
MILNE, COLIN, " A Botanical Dictionary." London, 1770, 8vo. (7).
MORLEY, W. M., " Little Wanderers." Boston, 1902, 8vo. (2).
NISBET, JOHN, " British Forest Trees." London and New York, 1893. 8vo. (1).
OLIVER, J. W., " The Student's Introductory Handbook of Systematic Botany," ed. 4.
    London, 1903, 8vo. (2).
PARKER, T. JEFFREY, " Lessons in Elementary Biology." London, 1905, 8vo. (1).
PHILLPOTTS, EDEN, " My Garden." London, 1906, 8vo. (1).
POBÉGUIN, H., " Essai sur la Flore de la Guinée française." Paris, 1906, 8vo. (2).
" PROGRESSUS rei botanicae," ... Redigiert von Dr. J. P. LOTSY, Bd. i., heft 1, and Bd.
    ii., heft 1. Jena, 1907, 8vo. (2).
REID, G. A., " The Principles of Heredity." London, 1906, 8vo. (1).
RICHMOND, I. L., " Flowers and Fruit for the Home." Edinburgh & London, 1904,
    8vo. (1).
ROBINSON, W., " The English Flower Garden," ed. 8. London, 1900, 8vo. (2).
    „   " The Garden Beautiful." London, 1906, 8vo. (1).
SACHS, J. VON, " History of Botany, 1530-1860." Oxford, 1890, 8vo. (2).
SIM, T. R., " Tree Planting in Natal." Pietermaritzburg, 1905, 8vo. (1).
SIMPSON, JOHN, " Game, and Game Coverts." Sheffield, 1907, 8vo. (1).
STENHOUSE, ERNEST, " An Introduction to Nature Study." London, 1906, 8vo. (1).

STEP, EDWARD, "Wayside and Woodland Blossoms," new edition, series 1 & 2 London and New York, 1905, 8vo. (1).

THEOBALD, F. V., "A Text-Book of Agricultural Zoology." Edinburgh & London, 1899, 8vo. (2).

VAN NOOTEN, MADAME B. H., "Fleurs, Fruits et Feuillages choisis de l'Ile de Java peints d'après nature," 3me edition. Bruxelles, 1880, fol. (8).

VIENNA, "Résultats scientifiques du Congrès international de botanique Vienne, 1905.' Jena, 1906, 8vo. (2).

VILMORIN-ANDRIEUX, "The Vegetable Garden." London, 1905, 8vo. (1).

WATKINS, W. E., & SOWMAN, A., "School Gardening." London, 1905, 8vo. (1).

WEBB, W. M., "The Principles of Horticulture." London, 1907, 8vo. (1).

WEYHE, M. F., WOLTER, J. W., & FUNKE, P. W., "Plantae medicinales oder Sammlung offizineller Pflanzen mit . . . Abbildungen von A. HENRY und Beschreibungen von M. F. WEYHE, J. W. WOLTER, P. W. FUNKE, fortgesetzt von T. F. L. NEES v. ESENBECK," 2 vols. Düsseldorf, 1828, fol. (9).

WEYHE, M. F., WOLTER, J. W., & FUNKE, P. W., "Plantae medicinales oder Sammlung offizineller Pflanzen mit . . . Abbildungen und Beschreibungen von T. F. L. NEES v. ESENBECK." Erster Supplement-Band. Düsseldorf, 1833, fol. (9).

WISHART, R. S., "The Self-Educator in Botany," edited by JOHN ADAMS. London 1900 (1).

WOODVILLE, W., "Medical Botany," 3 vols. London, 1790–93, 4to. (10).

WRIGHT, W. P., "Pictorial Practical Carnation Growing." London, 1906, 8vo. (1).

„   "School and Garden." London, 1906, small 8vo. (1).

WRIGHT, W. P., & CASTLE, E. J., "Pictorial Practical Flower Gardening." London, 1905, 8vo. (1).

WRIGHT, W. P., & CASTLE, E. J., "First Steps in Gardening." London, 1906, 8vo. (1).

WRIGHT, W. P., & CASTLE, P. W., "Pictorial Practical Potato Growing." London. 1906, 8vo. (1).

WYTHES, G., & ROBERTS, H., "The Book of Rarer Vegetables." London, 1906, 8vo. (1).

DONORS OF BOOKS, APPARATUS, AND SPECIMENS TO THE
LABORATORY AT WISLEY DURING THE YEAR 1907.

BOARD OF AGRICULTURE, Journal, Pamphlets, and Leaflets.
DOUGLAS, J., "Flora Nigritana," "British Ferns," Herbarium of British Plants.
GLENDENNING, R., British Flora (Bentham).
LEWIS, Mrs. HORNBY, Complete Photographic Outfit.
MASSEE, G., "Textbook of Fungi," "Textbook of Plant Diseases," and a number of
    Pamphlets.
VOSS, Messrs. WALT., Specimens of Manures, Insecticides, and Fungicides.
WILLMOTT, Miss, "Rock and Alpine Gardening."

————————

DONORS OF SEEDS, PLANTS, TREES, &c., TO THE SOCIETY'S GARDENS
AT WISLEY DURING THE YEAR 1907.

ALDENHAM, Lord, Elstree. Pentstemons. See p. 313.
ALLAN, W., Thorpe Market, Norwich. Raspberry 'Alexandra.' Planted in the
    collection.
ALLIN, G., Finsbury Park. Tomato seed. See p. 306.
ARBUTHNOTT, Miss, Paignton, South Devon. Seeds and plants of *Romneya Coulteri*.
    Planted in the Gardens.
ASHWORTH, A., Gresford. Double variegated Arabis and *Polygonum baldschuanicum*.
    Planted in the Gardens.
BABINGTON, C. H., Coulsdon, Surrey. *Calceolaria violacea* and Rose 'Adèle Prévost.'
    Planted in the Gardens.
BALLARD, E., Colwall, near Malvern. Aster. See p. 184.
BANNERMAN, J. M., Wyastone Leys, Monmouth. *Hymenanthera crassifolia* berries.
    Failed to germinate.
BARNES, Mrs., Fox Holm, Cobham. *Lilium sulphureum* bulbils. Growing on.
BARR & SONS, Covent Garden, W.C. Varieties for trial of aster (see p. 184), celery
    (p. 529), dwarf French beans (p. 288), lemon cucumber (p. ccii), melon (p. 281),
    pea (p. 533), and tomato (p. 306). Collections of seeds from Mallorca and
    Vancouver, the former of no value, but many of the latter have been raised
    and planted in the Gardens. Valuable collections of *Crocus, Eryngium,
    Gentiana,* and *Papaver.* Planted in the Gardens.
BASHAM, J., Bassaleg, Mon. Apple 'Chas. Ross.' Added to the collection.
BATES, H., Robertsbridge. Tomato seed. See p. 306.
BAXTER, W., Woking. Dahlias. See p. 223.
BECKTON, G. L., Sherborne, Dorset. Seed of *Ipomoea* sp. Failed.
BELL, ROBERT, M.D., Ewell. Potatos. See p. 299.
BENNETT-POË, J. T., Holmwood, Cheshunt. Collection of Narcissus. Planted in
    the Gardens. Cypripediums, Dracaenas, and Phyllocactus. In part distributed
    to Fellows, and in part growing in the Gardens.
BIDE & SONS, S., Farnham. Rose 'Queen of Spain.' Planted in the Gardens.
BILNEY, W. A., Weybridge. Orchids and *Primula japonica.* Added to the collections.
BLYTH, Lord, Stansted, Essex. French-grown roses. Planted in the Gardens.
BONAVIA, GEO., M.D., Richmond Road, Worthing. Hippeastrums and *Lilium
    Alexandrae roseum.* Growing in the Gardens.
BOON, L. G., Weybridge. Fertiliser. See p. 311. Calcium cyanamide. Will be
    reported on in 1908.
BOSCAWEN, Hon. JOHN, Perranwell, Cornwall. *Embothrium coccineum* seed. Not yet
    germinated.
BOVILL, LAURA U., Holmwood, Surrey. *Nandina domestica* seed. Failed to germinate
BOWERS, E. H., Roscommon. Carnations. Will be tried in 1908.
BOWLES, E. A., Myddelton House, Waltham Cross. Rock plants, &c. Planted in the
    Gardens.
BOYD, Mrs. A. H., Westward Ho, North Devon. *Crinum* sp. from India (?). Growing
    in the Gardens.
BRADFORD, O. G., Lustleigh, Newton Abbot. *Holboellia latifolia* seed. Not yet
    germinated.
BRAGGE, FLORENCE, Sadborow, Chard. Spores of tufted and frilled male fern and
    hart's tongue. Plants have been raised and will be planted in the wild garden.

BRITISH NICOTINE Co., Bootle. "Necrotine" insecticides and vaporising compounds. See p. 311.

BRODIE OF BRODIE, Forres, N.B. *Gladiolus primulinus* seed. Growing on.

BULLEN, L. M., Fleet, Hants. Seeds of *Acacia, Casuarina, Eucalyptus,* &c. Plants raised and distributed to Fellows.

BUNYARD, GEO., Maidstone. Apples, Pears, Plums, and Vines. Added to the collections.

BURRELL, J., Cambridge. Dahlias. See p. 223.

CANNELL & SONS, Loddon, Norwich. Seeds for trial of lettuce (see p. 532), parsnip (p. 532), pea (p. 533), and tomato (p. 306).

CAPE TOWN, CORPORATION OF THE CITY OF. A collection of Cape bulbs. Growing in the Gardens.

CARTER & Co., High Holborn. Varieties of celery (see p. 529), dwarf French bean (p. 288), onion (p. 296), potato (p. 299), and tomato (p. 306). Patent wormkiller. See p. 312.

CATON, E. S., Tobacco Trade Exhibition, Monument Station Buildings. Seed of varieties of tobacco. Grown on for the annual Tobacco Exhibition.

CHAMBERLAIN, Mrs. WALTER, Cobham. *Papaver orientale* seed. Not yet germinated.

CHAMBERS, B. E. C., Haslemere. Collection of trees and shrubs. Planted in the Gardens.

CHARLESWORTH & Co., Bradford, Yorks. Orchids. Added to the collection.

CHITTENDEN, F. J., Chelmsford. Beet seed. See p. 532.

CLARK, G. & A., Dover. *Gilia coronopifolia.* Growing in the Gardens.

CLARK, J. E., Purley, Surrey. Plants raised from seeds from the Cape. Not yet flowered.

CLEMENTI-SMITH, Rev. P., Doctors' Commons, E.C. *Aleurites Fordii* seeds. Not yet germinated.

CLIFTON-VAUGHAN, R., Knebworth, Herts. Seeds of a New Zealand conifer. Not yet germinated.

COLMAN, Sir J., Gatton Park. Orchids. Added to the collection. Crotons. Stocks raised and distributed to Fellows.

COMPACT MANUFACTURING COMPANY, Ludgate Hill, E.C. Syringes. See p. 312.

COOPER & NEPHEWS, Berkhampstead. V. 1 & V. 2 spray fluids. Will be reported on in 1908.

COOPER, TABER, & Co., Ltd., Southwark Street, S.E. Potato (see p. 299), onion (p. 296), and tomato (p. 306).

COUTTS, J., Killerton Gardens, Exeter. Seed of *Mutisia decurrens.* Not yet germinated.

CREAK, A. E., Creak Manufacturing Co., King Street, Hammersmith. Tree clips. See p. 312.

CRIPPS & SON, Ltd., Tunbridge Wells. Trees and shrubs. Planted in the Gardens.

CRUMP, W., Madresfield Court, Malvern. Eyes of vine 'Black Morocco.' Failed.

DANIELS BROS., Ltd., Norwich. Varieties of celery (see p. 529), dwarf kidney bean (p. 288), onion (p. 296), potato (p. 299), and tomato (p. 306).

DE LUCA, M., Long Lane, E.C. Frame raisers. See p. 311.

DE LUZY FRÈRES, Camberwell, S.E. National Knapsack Sprayer. See p. 311.

DENIS, FERNAND, Balaruc-les-Bains, Hérault. Iris vars. and *Narcissus dubius.* Planted in the Gardens. Cosmos seed. Will be tried in 1908.

DERHAM, W., Ham, Richmond. Collection of hardy ferns. Planted in the wild garden.

DOBBIE & Co., Rothesay. Varieties of cannas (see p. 212), dahlias (p. 223), sweet peas (p. 314), kidney beans (p. 288), and potatos (p. 299). Chrysanthemums will be reported on in 1908.

DODGE, Miss, Loseley Park, Guildford. Beans (see p. 288), celery (p. 529), dahlias (p. 223), onions (p. 296), potatos (p. 299), and tomatos (p. 306). Chrysanthemums. Will be reported on in 1908. Seed of *Chamaerops Fortunei.* Plants raised and distributed to Fellows.

DOUGLAS, J., Great Bookham. Seed of carnations and pinks. Not yet flowered.

DREER, H. A., Philadelphia, U.S.A. Gladiolus 'Golden West.' See p. 313. *Stokesia cyanea alba.* Failed.

DUKE, W., Wealdstone S.O., Middlesex. Potato. See p. 299.

EDMUNDS, Mrs., Finchley. *Asparagus acutifolius* and *Primula nivalis.* Planted in the Gardens.

ELLINGTON, W., Mildenhall, Suffolk. Potatos. See p. 299.

ELLIOT, SCOTT, Dumfries, N.B. Miscellaneous seeds. Plants raised and distributed to Fellows.

EMLYN, Lady, Frensham Hall, Haslemere. *Arundinaria* sp., and Canadian rice. Planted in the Gardens. Golden tench. Placed in ponds. Berries of red mistletoe. Failed.

FITZGERALD, H. PUREFOY, Wellington College. Collection of seeds from North America. In part growing in the Gardens, in part distributed to Fellows.

FORBES, J., Hawick, N.B. Flower seeds. See p. 313.

FORSTER, R. J., Brasted, Sevenoaks. Patent flower supports. See p. 311.

FOWLER, J. GURNEY, Glebelands, South Woodford. Epidendrum cuttings. Plants raised and distributed to Fellows.

FOX, W. L., Falmouth. Seedling Dracaenas. Distributed to Fellows.

GASKELL, A. J., Westminster. Collection of seeds from Australia, New Zealand, &c. Plants raised and distributed to Fellows.

GODDARD, Mrs. J. M., Crawley, Sussex. Seed of *Aristolochia elegans.* Plants raised and distributed to Fellows.

GOULD, H. H., Bursledon, Hants. Potato. See p. 299.

GOWIE, W. & C., Bloemfontein, Cape Colony. Seed of Cosmos var. Failed to flower before frosts.

GREG, Mrs., Coles, Herts. Seed of *Isatis tinctoria.* Seed and plants distributed to Fellows.

HALES, W., Curator, Chelsea Physic Garden. Collection of seeds. Plants raised and distributed to Fellows.

HALL, W. H., Goldsworth Lodge, Woking. *Azolla caroliniana.* Placed on ponds in the Gardens.

HANBURY, Sir THOMAS, La Mortola, Italy. Collections of seeds. Plants raised and distributed to Fellows

HARRIS, J., Blackpill, Swansea. Potato. See p. 299.

HARRISON & SONS, Leicester. Seeds of miscellaneous vegetables. See p. 532.

HARTLAND & SONS, Ard Cairn, Cork. *Tropaeolum.* See p. 315.

HARVEY, Mrs. ENOCH, Englefield Green. *Coriaria nepalensis.* Planted in the Gardens. Seed of *Arbutus Menziesii.* Not yet germinated.

HASELWOOD, C. T., Tufnell Park, N. *Funkia Sieboldiana major* seed. Not yet germinated.

HENRY & SON, Winchfield, Hants. Acha-Kut. See p. 311.

HILL, DANIEL, Herga, Watford. Alpines and rock plants. Planted in the Gardens.

HINDMARSH, W. J., Alnwick. Melon ' Brodé de Poche.' Will be tried in 1908.

HINTON BROS., Warwick. Sweet pea. See p. 314.

HOBBIES, LTD., Dereham. Dahlias. See p. 223.

HOBDAY, G., Havering Road, Romford. Pea. See p. 532.

HOMAN & SONS, H., Noordwijk, Holland. Collection of Spanish Iris. Planted in the Gardens.

HORN, W. J., Woldingham, Surrey. Seed of *Tacsonia* × *Passiflora.* Failed to germinate.

HOUGHTON, H. E., Nungumbakam, Madras. *Chamaedorea* sp. Growing on.

HUMPHRIES. T., Edgbaston, Birmingham. *Thunia Marshalliana.* For stock and distribution to Fellows.

HURST & SON, Houndsditch. Varieties of celery (see p. 529), dwarf French bean (p. 288), melon (p. 281), onion (p. 296), potato (p. 299), and tomato (p. 306).

ILCHESTER, Lady, Abbotsbury. Collections of seeds and Eucalyptus plants. Distributed to Fellows.

JANNOCH, T., Dersingham, King's Lynn. Lily of the valley crowns. Planted in the wild garden.

JOHNSON & SONS, Ltd., W. W., Boston. Celery for trial. See p. 529.

JONES, H. J., Ryecroft Nursery, Lewisham. Chrysanthemums. Will be reported on in 1908.

JONES, H. L., Congleton, Cheshire. Celery. See p. 529.

KEMMIS, Mrs. W., Easebourne, Midhurst. Seeds unnamed. Not yet germinated.

KENT & BRYDON, Darlington. Parsley and strawberry for trial. See pp. 285, 532.

KEW (ROYAL BOTANIC) GARDENS, Director of. Set of Kew Hand-lists. Added to the library. Collections of seeds. Plants raised and distributed to Fellows.

KIRK, A., Norwood Gardens, Alloa, N.B. Potatos. See p. 299.

LADHAMS, LTD., Shirley Nurseries, Southampton. *Anchusa* ' Opal.' Planted in the wild garden.

LANSDELL, J., Llandaff, Worcester. Tomatos. See p. 306.

LAWRENCE, Sir TREVOR, Bart., Burford, Dorking. Anthuriums, *Cassandra,* and miscellaneous orchids. Added to the collections in the Gardens, but in part distributed to Fellows. Seed of *Campanula longistyla* and *Kennedya rubicunda.* Plants raised and distributed.

LAXTON BROS., Bedford. Tomatos. See p. 306.

LENOX, J., Ashtead. *Ornithogalum lacteum.* Growing in the Gardens.

LILFORD, Lady, Oundle, Northants. *Ononis Natrix.* Specimens raised and planted in the Gardens.

LINDSAY, R., Edinburgh. *Antirrhinum majus Peloria, Erica Mackayi* fl. pl., *Fragaria vesca muricata.* Growing in the Gardens.

LODER, Sir EDMUND, Leonardslee, Horsham. Potato. See p. 299. Miscellaneous seeds. Plants raised and distributed to Fellows.
Low & Co., H., Bush Hill Park. Strawberry. See p. 285.
LYE, R., The Gardens, Sydmonton Court, Newbury. Tomato. See p. 306.
LYNCH, R. I., Botanic Gardens, Cambridge. Collection of seeds. Plants raised and distributed to Fellows.
McGREDY & SON, Portadown, Ireland. Varieties of cabbage and savoy for trial. See p. 532.
MAJOR, Miss E. M., Duppas Hill Terrace, Croydon. Hybrid Cacti and *Peristeria elata*. Growing in the Gardens. Collection of books : added to the Library.
MASON, Miss, Vincent Square Mansions, S.W. *Anemone sulphurea* and plants and seeds from Aix-les-Bains. Planted in the Gardens.
MASSEY, Spalding. Celery (see p. 529), potatos (p. 299), and potato fertiliser (p. 312).
MATTHEWS, Mrs., Belsite, Purley. Seeds of an unnamed shrub. Not yet germinated.
MAY & SONS, H. B., Edmonton. Collection of *Nephrolepis*. Growing in the Gardens.
MILNE-REDHEAD, G. B., Frome. Seed of *Antirrhinum majus*. Will be planted out.
MOORE, Ltd., J. W., Rawdon, Leeds. Collection of Dendrobiums and Vandas. Growing in the Gardens.
MORRIS, C. E., Carmarthen, South Wales. Potato. See p. 299.
MORTIMER, S., Farnham, Surrey. Dahlias. See p. 223.
MUNRO, Miss E., Fairfield, Lyme Regis. Small-leaved myrtle. Growing in the Gardens.
NEWMAN, T. P., Hazelhurst, Haslemere. Montbretias. Planted in the Gardens.
NICHOLSON, G, V.M.H., Larkfield, Richmond. Seed of *Geranium Robertianum album*. Plants raised in the Gardens.
NORTHCLIFFE, Lady, Sutton Place, Guildford. Seed of *Meconopsis racemosa*. Plants raised and distributed to Fellows.
NORTH-ROW, W., Tiverton. *Vanilla* sp. and Violet ' Emperor William.' Growing in the Gardens. Marrows. See p. 533.
NORTH-WESTERN CYANAMIDE Co., Winchester House, Old Broad Street, E.C. (Sun Gas Co., Ltd., Westminster). Calcium cyanamide. Trial will be continued in 1908.
NOTCUTT, R. C., Woodbridge. Asters. See p. 184.
NUTTING & SONS, Southwark Street, S.E. Celery (see p. 529), dwarf French beans (p. 288), onions (p. 296), and tomatos (p. 306).
O'BRIEN, JAMES, Edenderry, King's Co. Potatos. See p. 299.
OWEN, H., Penrhyndeudraeth, North Wales. Striped bean. See p. 288.
PATENT NEBULA SPRAY Co., St. Mary-at-Hill, E.C. Nebula sprayer with flexible metallic tube. See p. 311.
PEARSON & SONS, Lowdham, Notts. Beans. See p. 288.
PERRY, AMOS, Enfield. Papaver ' Mrs. Perry.' Planted in the Gardens.
PHILLIPS, J. W., College Hill, Cannon Street, E.C. Seeds of pitcher-plant. Not yet germinated.
PHILLPOTTS, EDEN, Eltham, Torquay. Luffa seed. Will be tried in 1908.
PIRIE, Miss, Ripley, Surrey. Seeds of *Anemone* sp. from the Rockies, *Dryas Drummondii*, and *Pancratium maritimum*. Plants will be raised and distributed.
POLAND, GEO., Onchan, Isle of Man. Pea. See p. 533.
PRICHARD, M., Christchurch, Hants. *Lathyrus filiformis*. Planted on the rockery.
RALLI, P., Cranleigh. Orchids. Added to the collection.
RAYNBIRD & Co., Ltd., Basingstoke. Wheat. See p. 312.
RICHMOND-POWELL, W. W., Canterbury. *Verbascum* sp. from Bosnia. Planted in the Gardens.
ROCHFORD & SONS, Turnford Hall, Broxbourne. *Nephrolepis todeaoides*. Added to the collection.
ROEMER, F., Quedlinburg, Germany. *Gladiolus praecox*. Its hardiness to be tested.
ROGERS, A., Commander, R.N., Carwinion, Falmouth. Seed of *Arundinaria nobilis*. Failed to germinate. Seed of *Pittosporum eugenioides*. Plants raised and distributed to Fellows.
ROGERS, R. B., Launceston, Cornwall. Seed of *Pittosporum*. Plants distributed to Fellows. *Momordica Morkorra*. Growing in the Gardens.
ROSS, C., Welford Park, Newbury. Melon (see p. 281) and potato (p. 299).
ROTHSCHILD, LEOPOLD DE, Gunnersbury House. Cuttings of figs ' Violette Sepor' and ' Grosse Verte.' Rose ' Richmond.' Growing in the Gardens.
ROTHSCHILD, Lord, Tring. Seedling Hippeastrums. Distributed to Fellows.
RUDGE, Mrs., The Whins, Camberley. *Crassula* sp. Growing in the Gardens.
SALWEY, T. J., Old Charlton, Kent. Avocado pear and unnamed seed. Growing on.
SANDEMAN, J. G., Hayling Island, Havant. Seeds from Burmah. Plants growing on.
SAUNDERS, Mrs. CARR, Milton Heath, Dorking. *Daphne Cneorum variegata*. Planted on the rockery.
SAVAGE, G. H., Devonshire Place, W. *Trifolium stellatum*. Planted in the Gardens.

SCBASE-DICKINS, C., Achill, Co. Mayo. Hardy Gladiolus and *Lilium bulbiferum.* Planted in the Gardens. Seed of *Alstroemeria.* Not yet germinated.

SEALE, M. V., Sevenoaks. Dahlias. See p. 223.

SEDGWICK, T., Acton. Freesias from the Cape. Planted in the Gardens.

SELLMAN, W., High Street, Dorking. Insecticide-fertiliser. Will be tried in 1908.

SHEPHERD, V., East Hill, Oxted. Seed of *Eccremocarpus scaber.* Plants distributed. *Sedum spectabile.* For stock.

SHIACH, N. C., Cemetery Nursery, Helensburgh. *Solanum* sp. Plants raised.

SHOESMITH, H., Westfield, Woking. Dahlias. See p. 223.

SINCLAIR, M. H., Union Street, Aberdeen. Potato. See p. 299.

SKELTON, R. T., Ugley Green, Essex. Ansellias, Cacti, Echeverias, &c., from the Transvaal Colony. Growing in the Gardens.

SMITH, H. HAMEL (Tropical Life), Fenchurch Street, E.C. 'Chrystophene.' Will be reported upon in 1908.

SMITH & Co., F., Woodbridge. Tomato. See p. 306.

SPARKES, J., Ewhurst, Guildford. Orchids. Added to the collection.

SPOONER & SONS, Arthur's Bridge Nursery, Woking. *Daboecia polifolia,* dark-flowered variety. Planted in the Gardens.

STANDARD MANUFACTURING Co., Irongate, Derby. Handy-Andy Hoes. See p. 311.

STARK & SON, Great Ryburgh, Norfolk. Sweet Peas and Tropaeolums. See p. 314. Hybrid dwarf beans. Will be tried in 1908.

STEPHENSON, J., Sutton Scarsdale, Chesterfield. Potato. See p. 299.

STOOP, F. C., West Hall, Byfleet. *Ceropegia Woodii.* Growing in the Gardens. Chrysanthemums. Will be reported on in 1908.

STREDWICK & SON, J., St. Leonards. Dahlias. See p. 223.

STURGIS, H. P., Givons, Leatherhead. Asters. See p. 184.

SUTTON & SONS, Reading. Dwarf beans (see p. 288), celery (p. 529), melons (p. 281), onions (p. 296), potatos (p. 299), and tomatos (p. 306).

SYDENHAM, R., Birmingham. Beans (see p. 288), melons (p. 281), Schizanthus (p. 314), and sweet peas (p. 314). Gladioli: planted in the Gardens.

THURLOW, Major E. H., Uckfield, Sussex. *Nymphaea stellata* and *Tropaeolum speciosum.* Planted in the Gardens.

TINNE, B., Aigburth. Seeds of *Clitoria* sp. Plants raised and distributed to Fellows.

TOD & SON, H. M., Seething Lane, E.C. Cuttings of outdoor vines. Vines raised and planted in the vineyard.

TOMLINSON, THOS., Tower House, Streatham. Seedling Caladiums. Growing on.

TOOGOOD & SONS, Southampton. Varieties of bean (see p. 288), celery (p. 529), onion (p. 296), potato (p. 299), and tomato (p. 306) for trial.

TURNER, A., Chelmsford. Seed of *Pinus flexilis* and seedlings of *Ulmus glabra.* Growing on.

TURNER, CHAS., Royal Nurseries, Slough. Dahlias. See p. 223.

UPTON, A. R., Guildford Hardy Plant Nursery. Collection of *Sedum* and *Semper-vivum.* Planted on the rockery.

VEITCH & SON, Ltd., Chelsea. Varieties of bean (see p. 288), cabbage (p. 532), celery (p. 529), melon (p. 281), onion (p. 296), pea (p. 533), potato (p. 299), tomato (p. 306), and miscellaneous flowering plants (p. 313). Orchids, trees and shrubs, and strawberry 'Veitch's Perfection.' Added to the collections. Veitch's horticultural manure (p. 312) and secateurs (p. 312).

VEITCH, R., Exeter. Varieties of dwarf bean (see p. 288) and potato (p. 299).

VOSS & Co., Ltd., Carlton Works, Millwall. Fruit tree banding grease, green sulphur, phospho-nicotyl, sulphide of potassium. See pp. 311, 312. Miscellaneous fertilisers. Will be tried in 1908.

WAKELEY BROS. & Co., Honduras Wharf, S.E. Hop manure. See p. 311.

WAKELY, C., Chelmsford. *Cirrhopetalum gracillimum, Coronilla glauca, Mitraria coccinea,* and *Parnassia palustris.* Growing in the Gardens.

WALTON, J., Wilsey Park, Bradford, Yorks. Potato. See p. 299.

WARE, W. T., Inglescombe, Bath. Tulip 'Walter T. Ware.' Planted in the collection.

WATTS, W. A., Bronwylfa, St. Asaph. Carnation 'Mrs. Kearley.' Will be reported on in 1908.

WELLS & Co., Merstham. Chrysanthemums. Will be reported on in 1908.

WELLSON & Co., Kirkstall Road, Leeds. Wellson's manure. See p. 312.

WETTSTEIN, Prof. Dr. R., Director, Botanic Garden, Vienna. Collection of seeds. Plants raised and distributed to Fellows.

WHITE, C. A., Nairobi, British East Africa. Orchids from Londiani. Growing in the Gardens.

WHITELEY, H., St. Marychurch, Torquay. Apples 'Endsleigh Beauty' and 'Wolf River Maiden.' Planted in the collection. Seeds of Manitoba maple. Not yet germinated.

WILES, E. S., Downe, Kent. Potatos. See p. 299.

WILKS, Rev. W., Shirley Vicarage, Croydon. Crinums and ornamental vines. Distributed to Fellows.

WILLIAMSON, J. F., Mallow, Co. Cork. Potatos. See p. 299.

WILLIAMSON, Mrs., St. George's Avenue, Weybridge. Seeds of miscellaneous vegetables. See p. 532. *Telopea speciosissima.* Not yet germinated.

WILLIS, A. P. R., High Elms, Leatherhead. Patent tree-fasteners. See p. 311.

WILLIS, HENRY, Ewell, Surrey. New Zealand seeds. Not yet germinated.

WILLMOTT, Miss, V.M.H., Warley. Verbenas. Failed. Collection of seeds. Plants raised and distributed to Fellows.

WINN, A., Cromwell Road, Grimsby. Potato. See p. 299.

WOOD, E. W., St. Botolph's Road, Worthing. Hippeastrum seed. Plants growing on.

WOOLLERTON, Dr., Wendover, Bucks. Potatos. See p. 299.

WORMALD, W. H., Town Office, East London, South Africa. Seed of *Tecoma Smithii.* Plants raised and distributed to Fellows.

WORSLEY, A , Mandeville House, Isleworth. *Agapanthus* and *Phyllocactus.* Growing on.

WRIGHT, Mrs. KENTISH, Newcastle Drive, Nottingham. White *Polemonium.* Planted on the rockery.

NATURAL SELECTION.

(A Reply.)

I do not think this JOURNAL is a fitting place for a controversy; but, as the late Editor has inserted Mr. Druery's criticism of my statements, I would ask to be allowed to reply, but as briefly as possible. As my paper on " The True Darwinism " is also published (p. 1), the reader can judge for himself between us.

Mr. Druery alludes to the many individual variations among ferns found in a comparatively limited area, and infers (I presume) that such arise from congenital causes within the spores. But, as De Vries has pointed out, you may make a border as uniform as possible, but it is impossible to prevent slight differences, which seedlings find out for themselves and which influence their growth; and there is no proof that such is not the case in nature. The fact that plants *do* at once adapt themselves to changes in the conditions of life is a generalisation from the widest induction, as all ecologists know, as well as from experimental proof.

Such variations as he found amongst the ferns, or as occur abundantly in cultivation *after* a wild plant has once " broken " (as gardeners say), may be called " indefinite," but not in the sense in which Darwin uses the term, implying that comparatively *few* only would survive, but the majority would die, not *because* of the struggle for life, but because they have " injurious " or " inadaptive " characters, which are supposed to be " mortal." Gardeners' varieties, on the other hand, would *all live* if they be not starved.

Mr. Druery regards " dwarfs " and " depauperates " as having " injurious " structures, and appeals to General Tom Thumb. But it all depends upon circumstances. Nanism *per se* is not " injurious "; nor even is a depauperate state of the plant if it be left alone, and can have enough to live upon. Thus *Ranunculus sceleratus* will grow five feet high in water, but only a foot or so in damp soil, and only three inches in the very dry ground, rarely inundated by the Nile, close to the Great Pyramid ; yet it persists there, year after year. Tom Thumb, as a son of ordinary-sized people, was an " abnormal monstrosity," and would probably not have had much chance of surviving in a severe struggle for life. But Mr. Druery forgets the Pigmies, which get on very well at home. Similarly a depauperate variety of a plant, by constant response to poor conditions, may actually become a fixed variety, as has occurred in many genera; some species are actually called *depauperata*. It is often said you cannot draw a hard-and-sharp line between monstrosities and varieties, because many of the former are hereditary and quite healthy. But as they, by far the oftener, arise under cultivation, the induction is that they are due to unnatural conditions of life. But, whether their malformations are "injurious" or "inadaptive," and therefore "mortal," can only be found by experiment.

It must be understood that the conclusion of present-day ecologists, which has so completely corroborated Darwin's letter to Wagner, is not based on the study of a single group of plants, whether ferns or others, but upon the geographical distribution of the whole vegetable world—as Dr. Schimper has shown—and as, perhaps I may add, my own books in the "International Scientific Series" also demonstrate.

GEORGE HENSLOW.

FIG. 97.—DAFFODIL 'HOMESPUN.'

A large, finely proportioned, deep yellow *Incomparabilis* of unusual beauty, unanimously recommended an Award of Merit, April 2, 1907.   (See page lxix.)

Exhibited by Mr. Chas. Dawson, Gulval, Penzance.

NOTES ON RECENT RESEARCH

AND

SHORT ABSTRACTS FROM CURRENT PERIODICAL LITERATURE, BRITISH AND FOREIGN,

AFFECTING

HORTICULTURE

AND

HORTICULTURAL AND BOTANICAL SCIENCE.

JUDGING by the number of appreciative letters received, the endeavour commenced in volume xxvi. to enlarge the usefulness of the Society's Journal, by giving an abstract of current Horticultural and Botanical periodical literature, has met with success. It has certainly entailed vastly more labour than was anticipated, and should therefore make the Fellows' thanks to those who have helped in the work all the more hearty.

The Editor desires to express his most grateful thanks to all who co-operate in this work, and he ventures to express the hope that they will all strictly adhere to the general order and scheme of working, as the observance of an identical *order* can alone enable the Editor to continue to cope with the work. The order agreed on was as follows :—

1. To place first the name of the plant, disease, pest, &c., being noticed ; and in this, the prominent governing or index word should always have precedence.

2. To place next the name, when given, of the author of the original article.

3. Then, the abbreviated form of the name of the journal, &c., in which the original article appears, taking care to use the abbreviation which will be found on pp. 581, 582.

4. After this, a reference to the number, date, and page of the journal in question.

5. If an illustration be given, to note the fact next, as " fig.," " tab.," or " plate."

6. After these preliminary necessities for making reference to the original possible for the reader, the abstract or digest should follow, ending up with the initials of the contributor affixed at the close of each Abstract or Note.

NAMES OF THOSE WHO HAVE KINDLY CONSENTED TO HELP IN THIS WORK.

Baker, F. J., A.R.C.S., F.R.H.S.
Boulger, Professor G. S., F.L.S., F.R.H.S.
Bowles, E. A., M.A., F.L.S., F.E.S., F.R.H.S.
Chapman, H., F.R.H.S.
Chittenden, F. J., F.L.S., F.R.H.S.
Cook, E. T., F.R.H.S.
Cooke, M. C., M.A., LL.D., A.L.S., F.R.H.S., V.M.H.
Cotton, A. D., F.L.S.
Cox, H. G., F.R.H.S.
Druery, C. T., V.M.H., F.L.S., F.R.H.S.
Farmer, Professor J. B., M.A., D.Sc., F.R.H.S.
Goldring, W., F.R.H.S.
Groom, Professor Percy, M.A., D.Sc., F.L.S., F.R.H.S.
Hartog, Professor Marcus, D.Sc., M.A., F.L.S., F.R.H.S.
Hawes, E. F., F.R.H.S.
Henslow, Rev. Professor Geo., M.A., F.L.S., F.R.H.S., V.M.H.
Hodgson, M. L., F.R.H.S.
Hooper, Cecil H., M.R.A.C., F.R.H.S.
Houston, D., F.L.S., F.R.H.S.
Hurst, C. C., F.L.S., F.R.H.S.
Kent, A. H., A.L.S., F.R.H.S.
Long, C. H., F.R.H.S.
Massee, Geo., F.L.S., F.R.H.S., V.M.H.
Mawley, Ed., F.M.S., F.R.H.S.
Moulder, Victor J., F.R.H.S.
Newstead, R., A.L.S., F.E.S., F.R.H.S.
Rendle, A. B., M.A., D.Sc., F.L.S., F.R.H.S.
Reuthe, G., F.R.H.S.
Saunders, Geo. S., F.L.S., F.E.S., F.R.H.S.
Scott-Elliot, G. F., M.A., B.Sc., F.L.S., F.R.H.S., F.R.G.S.
Shea, Charles E., F.R.H.S.
Shinn, C. H., F.R.H.S.
Smith, William G., B.Sc., Ph.D., F.R.H.S.
Veitch, Harry J., F.L.S., F.Z.S., F.R.H.S.
Webster, A. D., F.R.H.S.
Welby, F. A., F.R.H.S.
Worsdell, W. C., F.L.S., F.R.H.S.

JOURNALS, BULLETINS, AND REPORTS

from which Abstracts are made, with the abbreviations used
for their titles.

Journals, &c.	Abbreviated title.
Agricultural Gazette of New South Wales . . .	Agr. Gaz. N.S.W.
Agricult. Journal, Cape of Good Hope	Agr. Jour. Cape G.H.
Annales Agronomiques	Ann. Ag.
Annales de la Soc. d'Hort. et d'Hist. Naturelle de l'Hérault	Ann. Soc. Hé.
Annales de la Soc. Nantaise des Amis de l'Hort. .	Ann. Soc. Nant. des Amis Hort.
Annales des Sciences Naturelles	Ann. Sc. Nat.
Annales du Jard. Bot. de Buitenzorg	Ann. Jard. Bot. Buit.
Annals of Botany	Ann. Bot.
Boletim da Real Sociedade Nacional de Horticultura .	Bol. R. Soc. Nac. Hort.
Boletim da Sociedade Broteriana	Bol. Soc. Brot.
Botanical Gazette	Bot. Gaz.
Botanical Magazine	Bot. Mag.
Bulletin de la Société Botanique de France . .	Bull. Soc. Bot. Fr.
Bulletin de la Soc. Hort. de Loiret	Bull. Soc. Hort. Loiret.
Bulletin de la Soc. Mycologique de France .	Bull. Soc. Myc. Fr.
Bulletin Department of Agricult. Brisbane . . .	Bull. Dep. Agr. Bris.
Bulletin Department of Agricult. Melbourne .	Bull. Dep. Agr. Melb.
Bulletin of the Botanical Department, Jamaica .	Bull. Bot. Dep. Jam.
Bulletin of Bot. Dep. Trinidad	Bull. Bot. Dep. Trin.
Bulletino della R. Società Toscana d' Orticultura .	Bull. R. Soc. Tosc. Ort.
Canadian Reports, Guelph and Ontario Stations .	Can. Rep. G. & O. Stat.
Centralblatt für Bacteriologie	Cent. f. Bact.
Chronique Orchidéenne	Chron. Orch.
Comptes Rendus	Comp. Rend.
Department of Agriculture, Victoria . . .	Dep. Agr. Vict.
Department of Agriculture Reports, New Zealand .	Dep. Agr. N.Z.
Dictionnaire Iconographique des Orchidées .	Dict. Icon. Orch.
Die Gartenwelt	Die Gart.
Engler's Botanische Jahrbücher	Eng. Bot. Jah.
Gardeners' Chronicle	Gard. Chron.
Gardeners' Magazine	Gard. Mag.
Gartenflora	Gartenflora.
Journal de la Société Nationale d'Horticulture de France	Jour. Soc. Nat. Hort. Fr.
Journal Dep. Agricult. Victoria	Jour. Dep. Agr. Vict.
Journal Imperial Department Agriculture, West Indies .	Jour. Imp. Dep. Agr. W.I.
Journal of Botany	Jour. Bot.
Journal of Horticulture	Jour. Hort.
Journal of the Board of Agriculture . . .	Jour. Bd. Agr.
Journal of the Linnean Society	Jour. Linn. Soc.
Journal of the Royal Agricultural Society . .	Jour. R.A.S.
Journal S.E. Agricultural College, Wye . . .	Jour. S.E. Agr. Coll.
Kaiserliche Gesundheitsamte	Kais. Ges.
Le Jardin	Le Jard.
Lindenia	Lind.
Naturwiss. Zeitschrift Land und Forst . . .	Nat. Zeit. Land-Forst.
Notizblatt des Königl. Bot. Gart. und Museums zu Berlin .	Not. Königl. Bot. Berlin.
Orchid Review	Orch. Rev.
Proceedings of the American Pomological Society .	Am. Pom. Soc.
Queensland Agricultural Journal	Qu. Agr. Journ.
Reports of the Missouri Botanical Garden . .	Rep. Miss. Bot. Gard
Revue de l'Horticulture Belge	Rev. Hort. Belge.
Revue générale de Botanique	Rev. gén. Bot.
Revue Horticole	Rev. Hort.

Journals, &c.	Abbreviated title.
The Garden	Garden.
Transactions Bot. Soc. Edinburgh	Trans. Bot. Soc. Edin.
Transactions of the British Mycological Soc.. .	Trans. Brit. Myc. Soc.
Transactions of the Massachusetts Hort. Soc. .	Trans. Mass. Hort. Soc.
U.S.A. Department of Agriculture, Bulletins . .	U.S.A. Dep. Agr.*
U.S.A. Experimental Station Reports . . .	U.S.A. Exp. Stn.†
U.S.A. Horticultural Societies' publications . .	U.S.A. Hort. Soc.†
U.S.A. State Boards of Agriculture and Horticulture .	U.S.A. St. Bd.†
Woburn Experiment Farm Report	Woburn.

* The divisions in which the U.S.A. Government publish Bulletins will be added when necessary.
† The name of the Station or State will in each case be added in full or in its abbreviated form.

NOTES AND ABSTRACTS.

Aconitum gymnandrum. By O. Stapf (*Bot. Mag.* tab. 8113).—
Nat. ord. *Ranunculaceae*; tribe *Helleboreae*; Tibet and W. China.
Annual; leaves uniform, tripartite; sepals violet to deep blue, upper
helmet-shaped, lateral clawed.—*G. H.*

Aconitum Napellus, var. eminens. By O. Stapf (*Bot. Mag.*
tab. 8152).—Nat. ord. *Ranunculaceae*; tribe *Helleboreae*; Rhenish
Prussia. Herb, often 7–9 feet high; panicle very large, 3–5 feet long;
flowers intensely purplish-blue or variegated.—*G. H.*

Agriculture, Historical Sketch of U.S. Department of. By
C. H. Greathouse (*U.S.A. Dep. Agr., Bur. of Publications, Bull.* 3;
1907; 2 plates and 9 figs.).—A history of the inception and growth of
this department, with an account of its objects and present organisation.
A history of the wise administration of a great national organisation for
the furtherance of a national industry and of a great expenditure amply
justified. The appropriations for the department have from 1839–1906
totalled $65,438,391.49, that for 1906 being $7,175,690 (more than
double that for 1901) while from 1839–1843, the appropriation was
$2,000.—*F. J. C.*

**Alkali, Reclamation of White-ash Lands affected with, at
Fresno, California.** By W. W. Mackie (*U.S.A. Dep. Agr., Bur. of
Soils, Bull.* 42; July 1907).—The extent of lands containing too great a
quantity of alkaline salts is enormous in some parts of the States, and
this bulletin goes thoroughly into the question of the areas affected in
this district, and describes the origin of the excessive quantities of alkali
in the soil. The effect of the alkali on the plants is that the " root
crowns " of young plants become seared, and the tender rootlets become
corroded, carbonates and chlorides of sodium being specially injurious;
while when the alkali enters the plant the outer portions of the leaves
blacken, the leaves may become yellow and drop prematurely, so
weakening the growth. The leaves may also be caused to form yellowish
rosettes at the tips of the branches, particularly in such plants as apple,
pear, apricot, nectarine, and peach. Certain crops are adapted to alkali
soils, palms and eucalyptus growing particularly well; while among fruits
pomegranate, fig, olive, and pear are very resistant. The methods which
produce the best results in improving the soil are under-drainage and
flooding (the bulletin should be consulted for details); but other methods
are in use, such as the use of gypsum (this does not appear to be
invariably successful in accomplishing the desired purpose, but generally
improves the texture of the soil); constant tillage, which checks evaporation and so prevents the rapid rise of alkali; use of farmyard manure, a
method largely and successfully used by Italian and Chinese gardeners;

destruction of hardpan (but this gives poor results) ; surface flushing so as to remove the surface deposit of alkali ; flooding without under-drainage.   An appendix gives a list of native plants which indicate the presence of too great a quantity of alkali for successful cultivation.   The plants named are *Suaeda* sp., *Allenrolfea occidentalis*, *Atriplex* sp., *Frankenia grandiflora campestris*, *Bigelowia veneta*, *Centromedia pungens*, *Pluchea sericea*, *Distichlis spicata*, *Hordeum murinum*, and *Leptochloa imbricata*. —*F. J. C.*

Aloe campylosiphon.   C. H. Wright (*Bot. Mag.* tab. 8134).—Nat. ord. *Liliaceae* ; tribe *Aloineae* ; Tropical Africa.   Leaves 15 inches, bright green with whitish spots ; flowers coral-red.—*G. H.*

Aloe nitens.   By W. Watson (*Bot. Mag.* tab. 8147).—Nat. ord. *Liliaceae* ; tribe *Aloineae* ; South Africa.   Stem 12 feet high ; panicle with about 7 spikes, densely many-flowered ; perianth green ; filament red-orange.—*G. H.*

Aloe pallidiflora.   By A. Berger (*Bot. Mag.* tab. 8122).—Nat. ord. *Liliaceae* ; tribe *Aloineae* ; South Africa (?).   A stemless plant.   Leaves tapering to a long point, 14 inches long, dull green but marbled with long whitish marks, margin with strong, deltoid spines ; inflorescence 2½–4 feet high ; perianth pale flesh-colour, yellowish within.—*G. H.*

Angraecum infundibulare.   By R. A. Rolfe (*Bot. Mag.* tab. 8153).—Nat. ord. *Orchidaceae* ; tribe *Vandeae* ; Tropical Africa.   This has large white and pale yellow fragrant flowers, the lip broadly elliptical-ovate, with a slender curved spur. —*G. H.*

Aphides.   By J. Barsacq (*Le Jardin*, vol. xxi. No. 498, p. 348 ; November 20, 1907 ; 8 figs.).—Much confusion exists as to the species and habits of the Aphidia.   M. Barsacq classifies some species of the genus *Schizoneura*, pointing out at the same time that they are apt to migrate from one plant, or part of a plant, to another, which has caused mistakes in classification.   *Schizoneura ulmi* L. lives in spring on the tender leaves of the elm ; when these get tough it descends to the roots of currant and gooseberry bushes, where it has been distinguished by the name of *Schizoneura fodiens*, and even mistaken for the redoubtable *S. lanigera*, although in reality comparatively harmless.—*F. A. W.*

Apospory and Apogamy in Ferns, Studies in.   By J. Bretland Farmer and L. Digby (*Ann. Bot.* vol. xxi. April 1907, pp. 161–197 ; 5 plates).—The cytological features of seven species of ferns are first recorded.   This is followed by a general discussion on the phenomena of apogamy and apospory, and includes a suggested table for the classification of the different types that are known to occur.

The authors believe that, though alternation of generations is *normally associated* with the periodic reduction in the number of chromosomes, no necessary correlation exists between the two phenomena, and therefore the problem of alternation must be settled by evidence other than that derived from the facts of meiosis.—*A. D. C.*

Apple Orchards, Suggestions upon the Care of. By E.

Walker (*U.S.A. Exp. Stn. Arkansas, Bull.* 91; 1906).—Cultivation and cover-cropping are discussed, 10 lb. crimson clover being sown with 1½ lb. of turnip seed. Fertilisers, drainage, pruning—the latter more especially—are carefully described, with diagrams. The chief pests are apple-scab, bitter-rot, rust, fly-speck fungus, sooty blotch; and, of insects, codling-moth, plum weevil, a narrow-winged katydid, and apple maggot. Carbon bisulphide is used for killing sassafras sprouts. Protection against rabbits is gained by using paint made of pure white lead and linseed oil without turpentine. Spraying formulas, pumps, and nozzles are discussed.—*C. H. H.*

Apple Pests, Spraying for. By W. M. Scott and A. L.

Quaintance (*U.S.A. Exp. Stn. Illinois, Farm. Bull.* 283).—Bitter-rot, caused by *Glomerella rufomaculans*, is described. It is a disease of hot, showery weather. The thorough application of Bordeaux mixture is an almost complete protection against it. Ten-year-old trees sprayed three times, at a total cost of 5¼d., yielded upwards of four barrels to a tree.

Apple-blotch, caused by a fungus (*Phyllosticta*), is described, and like bitter-rot it is controlled by four applications of Bordeaux mixture.

Leaf-spot and apple-scab are similarly controlled. Leaf-spot is due to several fungi, perhaps the most prominent of which is a species of *Phyllosticta*. A species of *Hendersonia* and the ordinary black-rot fungus (*Sphaeropsis malorum*) are found in connection with some of these spots, and may be responsible for the injury in some cases. Other fungi are also frequently present in the dead areas, and it is not always clear which are the real parasites.

Beside the good effect of spraying, say four times, with Bordeaux mixture in preventing these diseases, the foliage of sprayed trees keeps on long after unsprayed trees are defoliated.

Apple-scab, which is the most serious disease the apple is subject to in the U.S.A., is caused by *Venturia inaequalis*.

A careful description follows of the codling-moth; the character of the injury; how it passes the winter; moth, egg, larva, pupa; generations of the insect, whether one or two generations in the year, according to latitude.

Spray immediately after the petals fall, so that a particle of the poisoned spray shall be in the calyx cavity of every apple; spray from above, directing the spray downward; use long extension-rods with an elbow fitted between the end of the rod and the nozzle to better deflect the spray. Some growers spray a second time, to further ensure that the calyx of each apple shall contain a particle of poison; another application may be made three or four weeks after dropping of the petals; another at ten weeks, and still another two or three weeks later. Of the arsenicals used arsenite of soda was found the cheapest, and quite efficient: 1 lb. white arsenic, boiled for a few minutes with 4 lb. sal soda (crystals) in 1 gallon of water, 1 pint of this stock solution being used to forty or fifty gallons of water or Bordeaux mixture. Paris green answers well with Bordeaux mixture; if used alone, add lime.

Arsenate of lead is more expensive, but is preferred by some experimenters. As to equipment, the hose should be of sufficient length, say 25 to 30 feet, with an 8- to 12-foot bamboo extension-rod. The Vermorel type of nozzle is recommended. In order to have a fine spray the pressure at the pump should be good, not less than 75 lb. for a hand pump, 125 to 150 lb. for a power pump.—*C. H. H.*

Arctostaphylos Manzanita. By O. Stapf (*Bot. Mag.* tab. 8128).— Nat. ord. *Ericaceae*; California. A shrub or tree growing 30 feet high; leaves ovate, 1½–1¾ inch long; panicle corymbose; corolla white or pinkish, ¼ inch long.—*G. H.*

Arctotis decurrens. By W. Watson (*Bot. Mag.* tab. 8162).— Nat. ord. *Compositae*; tribe *Arctotideae*; South Africa. Herbaceous perennial, 2–3 feet high, pilose; leaves lyrate, upper sessile; flower heads solitary, 3 inches diameter; ray white above, purple below disc; teeth dark purple; tube yellow.—*G. H.*

Astilbe Davidii. By S. Mottet (*Rev. Hort.* January 16, 1907, pp. 39–41; coloured plate and woodcut).—The plate depicts a very charming flower spike, bright rose and mauve flowers, very distinct.

C. T. D.

Azara microphylla. By S. Mottet (*Le Jardin*, vol. xxi. No. 492, p. 244; August 20, 1907; 1 fig.).—An attractive flowering shrub, 4 to 6 feet high, half-hardy near Paris. Small shiny evergreen leaves, abundance of tiny flowers with an aromatic scent, apetalous, but appearing yellow from the colour of the anthers. Flowers in April. Small orange berries, ripening in autumn. Native of Chili. Other species are *A. dentata, A. Gilliesii,* and *A. integrifolia.* Of the last there is also a pretty but exceedingly rare variety with variegated leaves.—*F. A. W.*

Bag Method of Keeping Grapes. By F. Charmeux (*Le Jardin*, vol. xxi. No. 489, p. 196; with 4 figs.; July 5, 1907).—Covers much the same ground as the previous articles, but the figures are useful as showing how the bags are to be applied. Will be followed by further details in a later number.—*F. A. W.*

Barium Chloride as Insecticide. By J. Barsacq (*Le Jardin*, vol. xxi. No. 490, p. 214; July 20, 1907).—Barium chloride infallibly destroys grubs such as *Gastrophysa raphani,* and is perfectly innocuous to man. As the solution is colourless and leaves no trace, it is advisable to colour it with a little flour or other inert substance, so as to see which parts of the affected plant have been treated.—*F. A. W.*

Beans, Garden, American Varieties of. By W. W. Tracy (*U.S.A. Dep. Agr., Bur. Pl. Ind., Bull.* 109, 1907; 24 plates).—Another of the series of volumes in course of preparation by the U.S. Department of Agriculture, attempting to substitute the precision of scientific method and classification for the looseness and uncertainty hitherto prevailing in the description of the varieties of garden vegetables, with a view to the simplification and reduction of varietal names and the establishment of a standard of excellence. Of over 400 named varieties of beans grown in the States at least 185 are regarded as distinct. The bulletin contains a simple natural classification, with an artificial key, of 165 of these, with descriptions based on a series of tests of seeds from various sources, carried out in a number of the States during the period 1897–1906, and notes on the history of the varieties, list of confusing and synonymous names, &c. The varieties tested are almost wholly of American origin, and comprise 137 varieties of *Phaseolus vulgaris* (kidney bean), twenty-two of *P. lunatus* (Lima bean), four of *P. multiflorus* (runner bean), and one each of *Vicia faba* (broad bean) and *Dolichos sesquipedalis* (asparagus bean). The localisation of varieties is at present unimportant, as most of the seed is obtained from a few well-known localities. Accurate definitions are included of terms employed, which receive added precision from an extensive series of photographic reproductions of typical forms of seeds, pods, and leaves.—*R. W.*

Begonia 'Gloire de Chatelaine.' By Gaston Vallerand (*Jour. Soc. Nat. Hort. Fr.*; 4th Series, vol. viii.; July 1907).—M. Vallerand gives enthusiastic praise to a new Begonia of the 'semperflorens' group produced by M. Platel, Director of the École d'Horticulture de Chatelaine (Switzerland). The plant recalls the 'Gloire de Lorraine.'—*M. L. H.*

Bigelowia graveolens. By W. B. Hemsley (*Bot. Mag.* tab. 8155). — Nat. ord. *Compositae*; tribe *Asteroideae*; North America. Shrubby plant, 6–8 feet high; leaves crowded, linear, 1–3 inches long; heads numerous, yellow, all tubular.—*G. H.*

Biology of the Soil in its Relation to Fertilisation. By J. L. Hills and C. H. Jones (*U.S.A. Exp. Stn. Vermont, Bull.* 130; 6/1907).—While adding nothing new to our knowledge of the part bacteria play in the soil, this bulletin yet gives an extremely interesting, reliable, and readable introduction to the subject, dealing with the manner of life and growth of bacteria, the part they play in the soil in decomposing various substances, nitrification, nitrogen fixation, nitrogen and Leguminosae, and so on, in a comprehensive way.—*F. J. C.*

Bitter-rot : Can it be Controlled by Spraying ? By Professor J. C. Blair (*Trans. Hort. Soc. Illinois*, 1905, p. 573).—The results of experimental work show with certainty that bitter-rot is controllable, and is no more to be dreaded than apple-scab, codling-moth, and curculio, if proper materials are properly used at the proper time.—*C. H. L.*

Bitter Rot of Apples. By Thomas J. Burrill (*U.S.A. Exp. Stn. Illinois, Bull.* 118, September 1907 ; 10 plates).—Bitter rot of apples, an exceedingly destructive disease attacking fruit on the tree, is due to a specific fungus called *Glomerella rufomaculans* (formerly *Gloeosporium rufomaculans*), which though sometimes found on other fruits, and which can be artificially grown upon many substances, is in Illinois practically confined to apples and to apple-tree limbs. On the latter the affected spots are called *cankers*. There are two forms of spores, but they appear to be alike in function, neither of them being specialised to

3 A 2

survive the winter. It is the mycelium in the cankers and in old infected fruits that does this.

Limbs of apple trees become infected only in spots where the bark has been previously injured mechanically or by some other parasite. Cankers may originate as late as the time of the apple harvest and in wounds made at this time.

The spores are very easily destroyed by copper sulphate. It seems impossible to kill the fungus in the limb cankers by any permissible external application. They must be destroyed by cutting off the affected limbs.

Outbreaks of the disease usually begin in July or August, but may start as early as June 1 in N. lat. 38°.

The spores are to some extent distributed by flies, but no insects are largely instrumental in the distribution or development of the disease. The spores are readily washed from cankers and infected fruits to fresh fruits hanging below in the tree. Light showers most effectively aid infection. Spores and spore masses are distributed by wind sometimes to considerable distances.

New apples are first infected only by spores produced in limb cankers, or in infected apples (mummies) of the previous year, which have hung during the winter on the trees. Neither the fungus nor its spores live over winter in the ground or in anything upon the ground.

The absolute eradication of the disease from an orchard is entirely possible by careful collection and destruction of the cankers and mummies, faithfully supplemented by effective spraying with Bordeaux mixture and the prompt removal of early infected fruit.—*M. C. C.*

Blaniulus guttulatus. By Dublesel and J. Béziat (*Le Jardin,* vol. xxi. No. 492, p. 247 ; August 20, 1907).—A minute myriapod, like a white maggot, with red spots on each side of its body, pernicious in the kitchen garden. It attacks seeds, *e.g.,* peas, beans, haricots ; the fleshy parts of vegetables, *e.g.,* carrots, turnips, beetroot, and potato tubers ; ripe strawberries, and even bulbs of tulips, hyacinths, &c. The best way to eliminate this pest is to pull up the affected plants and treat the ground with a solution of copper sulphate and lime.—*F. A. W.*

Blepharocalyx spiraeoides. By O. Stapf (*Bot. Mag.* tab. 8123).— Nat. ord. *Myrtaceae*; tribe *Myrteae*; Brazil. A much-branched shrub 9 feet high ; leaves lanceolate, $\frac{1}{2}$–$\frac{3}{4}$ inch long ; flowers in panicles ; petals pale yellow ; berry red or violet black.—*G. H.*

Bordeaux Mixture. By Spencer Pickering, F.R.S. (*Gard. Chron.* No. 1078, p. 150, August 24, 1907).—This fungicide is admitted by most cultivators to be the most effective agent known for the destruction of fungoid parasites. It is essential, however, that it should be applied of the proper strength, otherwise it will either injure the plant or not kill the fungus. This paper explains the process of manufacture and the action of this fungicide in a very clear and interesting manner.—*G. S. S.*

Bordeaux Injury. By U. P. Hendrick (*U.S.A. Exp. Stn. New York,* 287; March 1907).—It has long been known that, under some conditions, Bordeaux mixture injures the leaves and fruit of the apple. Different species of plants are injured in different degrees. The injury on the fruit first appears as small, round, black or brown specks; later the injured specimens become rough and russeted. Such fruit does not keep well. Affected leaves first show dead brown spots of various shapes and sizes. Quickly following the appearance of these spots, the leaf turns yellow and the leaves fall. Some varieties of apples are injured much less than others by Bordeaux mixture, and there is a wide range in this variation. Wet weather seems to give the favouring atmospheric condition for this trouble. Experiments with varying quantities of lime and copper sulphate showed that the more copper sulphate the greater the injury.

Practical suggestions for spraying are: " Use less copper sulphate; give the following formula for Bordeaux mixture a good trial:— 3 lb. copper sulphate, 3 lb. lime, fifty gallons water. Spray in moderation; spray to cover the foliage and fruit with a thin film and yet not have the trees drip heavily. So far as possible the Bordeaux mixture should only be used in dry weather. Use equal amounts of lime and copper sulphate."

Bordeaux mixture is the best fungicide known to the apple grower. Its use cannot be given up in fighting apple-scab, even though it does cause some injury. Apple-scab causes a far greater loss than Bordeaux mixture.—*C. H. H.*

Breeding of Plants. By Ed. Griffon (*Jour. Soc. Nat. Hort. Fr.*; 4th Series, vol. viii.; August 1907).—According to a review by E. Griffon, a work by M. Constantin, called " Le Transformism appliquée à l'Agriculture," is a good and useful handbook on the principles of natural and artificial selection in plants, and an instructive guide to the causes of variation from the point of view of the horticulturist.

M. L. H.

Bruckenthalia spiculifolia. By W. J. Bean (*Bot. Mag.* tab. 8148).—Nat. ord. *Ericaceae*; tribe *Ericeae*; Transylvania, Balkan Peninsula, and Northern Asia Minor. A much-branched shrublet, ½ foot high; corolla rose-coloured.—*G. H.*

Bulbophyllum dichromum. By R. A. Rolfe (*Bot. Mag.* tab. 8160).—Nat. ord. *Orchidaceae*; tribe *Epidendreae*; Annam. Epiphyte; flowers deep yellow with a dark purple lip.—*G. H.*

Bulbophyllum longisepalum. Anon. (*Gard. Chron.* No. 1082, p. 210, September 21, 1907; fig. 89).—The flowers of this plant are among the most extraordinary of those of orchids. The figure shows the peculiarity of the blossoms very clearly.—*G. S. S.*

Cacao Industry (West Indies) (*Journ. Imp. Dep. Agr. W.I.* 1907, 2).—This bulletin contains reprints of papers read at the West Indian Agricultural Conference, 1907, including the following : By H. A. Ballon, M.Sc.
Results of the Recent Experiments with Cacao in the West Indies.
Yield of Cacao in Trinidad.
Thrips on Cacao.—*M. C. C.*

Caesalpinia vernalis. By T. A. Sprague (*Bot. Mag.* tab. 8132).—
Nat. ord. *Leguminosae*; tribe *Caesalpineae*; China. A tall, climbing,
prickly shrub; leaves bipinnate; racemes 6 inches long; petals lemon-
yellow.   *G. H.*

Caiophora coronata. By T. A. Sprague (*Bot. Mag.* tab. 8125).—
Nat. ord. *Loasaceae*; tribe *Loaseae*; the Andes. A perennial herb; stems
several, decumbent; petals white, 1½ inch long.—*G. H.*

Calathea angustifolia. By C. H. Wright (*Bot. Mag.* tab. 8149).—
Nat. ord. *Scitamineae*; tribe *Maranteae*; Central America. Leaves
4 feet high, narrowly oblong, green above, purple beneath; flowers pale
yellow.—*G. H.*

Calibanus caespitosa Rosc. By C. Sprenger (*Bull. R. Soc. Tosc.
Ort.* 4, 1907, p. 104).—Dr. C. A. Purpus discovered this quite new and
unpublished genus last year on the high and arid mountains of Northern
Mexico. Seeds, along with a shoot collected on the rocks of that country,
were sent to the writer, who now has plants of it growing freely at
Naples. The new genus stands midway between *Dasylirion* Zucc. and
Nolina Mich., with which is reunited *Beaucarnea* of Lemaire; *Nolina*
is a synonym of *Roulinia* of Brongniart.

Nolina bears polygamo-dioecious, and *Dasylirion* simply dioecious,
flowers. The flowers of *Calibanus* have not yet been examined.

C. caespitosa grows on rocks exposed to the burning sun. It grows
at a height where snow regularly rests, and where the thermometer falls
below 10° R. It forms very dense colonies and often covers the entire
mountain with its rigid leaves. The greater part of the stem is above
ground; it is very broad and hard, and grey like the rocks on which it
grows; it is woody, dense in texture, and bears numerous tufts of leaves.
The stem bears thirty or more tufts of leaves, which are channelled,
rough, acute, veined, and glaucous, with a purplish-pink base. The
smallest plants have the aspect of, and resemblance to, some of the
Asphodelus of Asia Minor. The plant is quite hardy. The long peduncle
rises to a height of seven or eight feet, and is simple; it is only slightly
branched at the top and bears myriads of ivory-coloured flowers. It is
visited by thousands of insects, especially bees. Its culture is of the
simplest, and its hardiness in Naples is a proved fact.—*W. C. W.*

Calliandra portoricensis, var. **major.** By T. A. Sprague (*Bot.
Mag.* tab. 8129).—Nat. ord. *Leguminosae*; tribe *Mimoseae*; Mexico and
Central America. Small tree with bipinnate leaves, two to seven pairs of
pinnae; heads 2 inches diameter; flowers white; stamens 1 inch long.
                                                          G. H.

Campanula grandiflora (Platycodon grandiflorum). By
S. Mottet (*Rev. Hort.* February 16, 1907, pp. 88, 89; coloured plate
and 1 woodcut).—The plate represents extremely fine forms, white and
blue, of this species; flowers very large, resembling somewhat *Clematis
Jackmannii*, the bell form being flattened and deeply cut.—*C. T. D.*

Carnations and Pinks. By Le Texnier (*Le Jardin*, vol. xxi.
Nos. 489, 492, 493, 498, pp. 202, 253, 266, 346, and to be continued;

July 5, August 20, September 5, November 20).—A valuable series of historical articles giving the names of all varieties of pinks, picotees, and carnations, with their origin and culture in different countries.-- *F. A. W.*

Cassia alata. By R. Pampanini (*Bull. R. Soc. Tosc. Ort.* 10, 1907, p. 291).—In the summer of 1905 appeared suddenly in the botanic garden at Florence a plant which appeared to come from seed which had in some previous year emanated from Penang. On being cultivated it grew vigorously, and flowered in October of the following year; it was then seen that it was *Cassia alata*, an annual from the tropics of America and Asia. Some authors describe it as biennial, but the specimen in question showed itself to be perennial. Its spikes of large golden-yellow flowers open at a time of year when the stoves are poor in flowers. Its large pinnate leaves, 15-25 inches long, with broad leaflets, render the plant ornamental. Not suspecting it to be perennial the plant was allowed to grow about 10 feet high, without branching at the base, and so it had to be bent for admission to the stove; only the upper part is provided with leaves, of which the lower fall in October as the new shoot-tip is formed; hence the plant has not an elegant aspect at present.

It will probably be possible to multiply it by cuttings, not by seeds, for these, apparently, are not perfected. If so, the production of a good foliage plant will be possible. *Cassia alata* is usually neglected on account of the brief duration of its life, and the consequent impossibility of pruning it, and thus rendering it more compact. But this defect is eliminated in the case of the present perennial plant.—*W. C. W.*

Castanea pumila (Chincapin). By S. Mottet (*Le Jardin*, vol. xxi. No. 500, p. 372; December 20, 1907; 1 fig.).—A dwarf species of the edible chestnut. The fruit is smaller than that of *C. vesca*, but the tree is more decorative, and it thrives better in poor soil, where it can be used for coppices. It will grow from seed, but is better grafted on the stock of the common chestnut.—*F. A. W.*

Chicory, Witloof. By P. Rolit (*Le Jardin*, xxi. No. 495, p. 297; No. 496, p. 316; Oct. 5 and 20, 1907; 4 figs.).—The writer gives minute directions for cultivating and forcing chicory for the market, with round white heads. Sow in June or July, in good rich soil. Thin out into groups of two or three, subsequently keeping only the finest. Water with liquid manure, or a solution of two to three grammes nitrate of soda to the litre of water. The leaves should never be cut during the growing period, otherwise a rank vegetation is produced. In October dig up the roots, cutting the leaves down to 3 or 4 cm., and the roots to 25 cm. Prepare a very rich soil, and plant in trenches—along a south wall if possible. In a light soil such as that of Brussels, which is the most favourable, cover with 10 cm. of earth; in a damp soil the collar should be just above the ground. When ready to force, water with liquid manure, or solution of sodium nitrate. Cover with earth and stable manure, if necessary with planks and straw besides, to keep the temperature constant, at 15-20° C.

Too much heat scalds the heads, which then rot off. In three weeks to a month pull up the plants, turning the manure over to the row next in succession for forcing. Cut off the heads for market : they will keep fresh for two or three days. The roots can be used to feed cattle or pigs, but are apt to taint the milk of dairy cows. Or they may be laid by the heels in a cellar, or planted out again, when they throw up fresh leaves, which form an excellent salad. The main points for the gardener are to select the best seed ; not to sow before July, so as to check root development; and to force by moderate top heat, never from the bottom.

F. A. W.

Chlorophyll in the Young Shoots of Woody Plants, On the Distribution of. By Daisy G. Scott (*Ann. Bot.* vol. xxi. July 1907, pp. 437-489).—A brief note on the distribution of chlorophyll in young shoots of *Jasminum nudiflorum.* In the stem of this plant chlorophyll is found in the palisade layer, many cortical cells, pericyclic parenchyma, the medullary rays, and some of the medullary cells bordering on the protoxylem. A table is also given showing the distribution of chlorophyll in the shoots of some thirty of our common trees and shrubs.—*A. D. C.*

Chloroplast considered in Relation to its Function, The Structure of the. By J. H. Priestly and Annie A. Irving (*Ann. Bot.* vol. xxi. July 1907, pp. 407-413).—Plants of *Selaginella Martensii, S. Kraussiana,* and *Chlorophytum elatum* were selected for investigation on account of the large size of the chloroplasts. The chloroplasts of *Chlorophytum* consisted of a network with chlorophyll in the meshes. In optical section a distinct peripheral layer was observable which contained the colouring matter. These points were discernible in either living or fixed material. In the case of *Selaginella* living material was unsatisfactory, but when frozen in gum and glycerin, or when properly fixed, showed a microscopic structure in agreement with that of *Chlorophytum.*

The authors agree with Timiriazeff, who showed that the energy-transformation taking place in the chloroplast required that the chlorophyll should be distributed in a very thin layer, and that the thinner the layer in which a definite amount of chlorophyll is disposed the greater the amount of energy set free.—*A. D. C.*

Chrysanthemums : French Introductions, 1906-7. By G. Clement (*Rev. Hort.* January 1, 1907, pp. 18-21 ; and January 16, 1907, pp. 49-51 ; 1 woodcut).—A descriptive list of a large number of varieties with their raisers.—*C. T. D.*

Cicada, The Periodical. By C. L. Marlatt, M.S. (*U.S.A. Dep. Agr., Bur. of Entom., Bull.* 71 ; July 1907 ; 6 plates and 68 figs.).— A monograph of over 180 pages dealing exhaustively with the periodical cicada, and giving a summary of the habits and characteristics of the insect, the races, broods and varieties, and the distribution of the various broods. Then follow detailed accounts of structure, habits in all stages, and the natural enemies of the cicada, the best preventive and remedial measures, and a complete bibliography of the insect.—*F. J. C.*

Cochylis. By F. Charmeux (*Le Jardin*, vol. xxi. No. 493, p. 268 ; 2 figs.).—One of the most redoubtable pests in French vineyards is the cochylis, a minute nocturnal moth, yellow in colour, with black bars on the wings. The caterpillar, 8 mm. in length, is a dull purple or brown with dark-red head. This insect produces two generations a year ; the first in the flowering season destroys the stamens and ovaries by smothering clusters and leaves in its silky threads ; the second in August attacks the grapes, piercing every berry and causing them to rot. It is possible to destroy the insects in both generations, but a more efficacious remedy is to pick off the cocoons in October or November, burning all infected wood. It is to be noted that these insect pests increase in proportion as the insectivorous birds are destroyed.—*F. A. W.*

Codlin Moth Investigations in 1903 and 1904. By Fabián García (*U.S.A. Dep. Agr. New Mexico, Bull.* 65 ; May 1907).—A brief outline of the life-history and appearance of this pest is given. The question as to the number of broods and the influence of the weather upon this point has been investigated, and the result is here recorded. The caterpillars were caught in haybands after they left the apples, and these bands were daily examined. The conclusion is that the first brood of larvae matures about the end of May, the second about the end of July, and the third (often a partial brood) about the second week in September. The weather appears to have very little effect upon the time of appearance of the larvae.—*F. J. C.*

Coelogyne cristata. By C. Sprenger (*Bull. R. Soc. Tosc. Ort.* 7, 1907, p. 188).—According to Bentham and Hooker, *Coelogyne* belongs to the sub-genus *Epidendrum*. Ninety-seven good species are known, which occur exclusively in the Old World. They are all perennial and epiphytes, living on trees and shrubs, amongst ferns, on lichen-covered rocks, and along the sides of streams ; occasionally they are semi-epiphytic. In the Himalayas they grow as far up the mountains as 10,000 feet, and more. Hooker says of them : "Herbae epiphyticae, caespitosae vel longe repentes." He also says, which is interesting to cultivators : "Flores majusculi vel speciosi, in pedunculo vel scapo solitarii, vel plures laxe racemosi." *C. cristata* Lindl. occurs up to 10,000 feet on the Himalayas on old trees, such as Laurineae, *Quercus*, or Conifers, amongst epiphytic ferns, humus and lichens, and sometimes close to the ground. It is one of the easiest plants to grow.—*W. C. W.*

Coelogyne Lawrenceana. By R. A. Rolfe (*Bot. Mag.* tab. 8164).—Nat. ord. *Orchidaceae* ; tribe *Epidendreae* ; Annam. Epiphyte ; sepals 2–2¾ inches long, greenish-yellow ; petals 2–2¾ inches long, yellow ; lip 3-lobed, 2–2½ inches long, bright brown with yellow tip.—*G. H.*

Cotton Cultivation in Barbados. By J. D. Bovell, F.L.S., F.C.S. (*Journ. Imp. Dep. Agr. W.I.* 1907, 2).—Chiefly detailing the results of experiments in cotton cultivation, and especially manurial experiments and their cost, mainly of local interest.—*M. C. C.*

Cotton (Sea Island) Cultivation in St. Vincent. By W. N. Sands (*Journ. Imp. Dep. Agr. W.I.* 1907, 2).—Showing how the exports in Sea Island cotton have increased from the value of £475 in 1902 to £7,674 in 1905-6.—*M. C. C.*

Cotton Wilt. By H. R. Fulton (*U.S.A. Exp. Stn. Louisiana, Bull.* 96 ; September 1907 ; 3 plates).—Cotton wilt is due to the fungus *Neocosmospora vasinfecta* (Atk.) Erw. Sm.   The fungus lives in the soil and gains access to the plant through the small roots ; the mycelium grows upwards and soon fills the water-carrying ducts in the stem, causing the leaves to wither and drop off and producing a discoloration of the walls of the vessels, so that the wood appears brown.   Injury to the root by insects, &c., causes a more rapid spread of the disease. The spores are of a pinkish colour, and are produced on the outer surface of the dead cotton stalks, and may be spread by the wind, carrying earth from the field on tools, &c., or even on the lint, &c.   The fungus attacks only okra in addition to cotton, and is a facultative saprophyte. The methods of control are (1) the immediate destruction of affected plants, (2) rotation of crops, (3) manuring with stable manure, (4) the use of wilt-resistant varieties of cotton.   The method of selection is described.—*F. J. C.*

Cranberry Diseases. By C. L. Shear (*U.S.A. Dep. Agr., Bur. Pl. Ind., Bull.* 110 ; 10/07 ; 7 plates).—This bulletin gives the first full account of the fungi attacking the American cranberry (*Vaccinium macrocarpum*) and the diseases they produce. (See also JOURN. R.H.S., xxxii. [1907], p. 257.)   The losses annually arising from fungus diseases amount to 10 per cent. of the annual value, and are estimated at $200,000.   The greatest loss occurs in the southern part of the area in which the plant is cultivated.   An account is given of previous investigations, and then each of the diseases is dealt with in detail.   The disease commonly known as "scald" includes "scald" (*Guignardia vaccinii* Shear), "rot" (*Acanthorhynchus vaccinii* Shear), and " anthracnose " (*Glomerella rufomaculans vaccinii* Shear).   These and *Exobasidium oxycocci* Rostr., which causes hypertrophy of the axillary buds, are the most important diseases, but the following are also referred to : *Synchytrium vaccinii* Thomas, attacking the leaf, young stems, flowers, and fruit ; *Pestalozzia guepini vaccinii* Shear, occurring on leaves and fruits ; *Helminthosporium inaequalis* Shear, *Gloeosporium minus* Shear, *Arachniotus trachyspermus* Shear, *Septoria longispora* Shear, *Sphaeronema pomorum* Shear, *Phyllosticta putrefaciens* Shear, *Penicillium glaucum* Link., and *Leptothyrium pomi* (Mont.) Sacc. ? occasionally found on the fruits and sometimes on the leaves ; while the leaves and stems have been attacked by *Venturia compacta* Peck., *Sclerotinia oxycocci* Wor. (?), *Discosia artocreas* (Tode) Fr., *Plagiorhabdus oxycocci* Shear, *Sporonema pulvinatum* Shear, *Rhabdospora oxycocci* Shear, *Leptothyrium oxycocci* Shear, *Ceutospora* (?) *lunata* Shear, *Valsa delicatula* C. & E., *Cladosporium oxycocci* Shear, *Plectrothrix globosa* Shear, *Chondrioderma simplex* Schroet., *Epicoccum* sp., *Diplodia* sp., *Chaetomium* sp., *Oospora* sp., and *Macrosporium* sp.   Field studies have shown beyond a doubt that the physiological condition of the plants, as well as their environment, has much to do with their susceptibility to disease, and it would appear that the control of the water supply is a very important factor in the prevention of the occurrence of disease. This and the destruction of diseased plants, the selection of resistant plants, and the application of fungicides, such as Bordeaux mixture, offer the best means open to the grower in dealing with the diseases. Full descriptions of the fungi and the diseases they produce are given, and the fungi are figured.

F. J. C.

Cucumbers. By L. C. Corbett (*U.S.A. Dep. Agr., Bull.* 254).— Cucumbers in the States are grown for market, much as in England, in the open, in cold frames, in hot-houses, and also for pickling. The American type of cucumber is short and somewhat triangular in cross-section. It is marketed when about 10 inches long and 2 inches in diameter, and is especially useful for early slicing, and for pickling purposes. The larger "English" type is almost exclusively grown in forcing-houses. Bordeaux mixture (3 lb. copper sulphate to 6 lb. fresh lime to fifty gallons of water) is used against mildew and other diseases.

C. H. L.

Cymbidium erythrostylum. By R. A. Rolfe.—Nat. ord. *Orchidaceae*; tribe *Vandeae*; Annam. Erect epiphyte, 1½ foot high; sepals 1¾ inch long, white; petals white; lip broadly obovate, three-lobed, yellowish-white, with red-purple lines.—*G. H.*

Delphinium candidum. By W. B. Hemsley (*Bot. Mag.* tab. 8170).—Nat. ord. *Ranunculaceae*; tribe *Helleboreae*; Tropical Africa. A dwarf perennial; leaves palmately 5-lobed; flowers pure white, with purple anthers, 2½ inches across; spur cream-coloured.—*G. H.*

Delphinium macrocentron. By W. B. Hemsley (*Bot. Mag.* tab. 8151).—Nat. ord. *Ranunculaceae*; tribe *Helleboreae*; mountains of East Tropical Africa. Stems 5 feet high; flowers hairy, blue and green or yellowish and green, 2 inches long.—*G. H.*

Dendrobium Ashworthiae. By R. A. Rolfe (*Bot. Mag.* tab. 8141). Nat. ord. *Orchidaceae*; tribe *Epidendreae*; New Guinea. Epiphyte 1 foot high; flowers cream-white with purple streaks at base of lip; sepals 1¼ inch long; petals obovate, ¾ inch broad.—*G. H.*

Deutzias : New Species. By Hort. (*Le Jardin,* vol. xxi. No. 497, p. 325; November 5, 1907; 1 fig.).—*Deutzia discolor carnea* (hybrid from *D. scabra* and *D. discolor grandiflora*), with beautiful rose-red blooms; *D. discolor lactea* (from *D. scabra* and *D. discolor grandiflora*), milky-white flowers; *D. gracilis candelabra* (from *D. gracilis* and *D. Sieboldiana*), remarkably graceful, flowers creamy-white, with bright yellow stamens.—*F. A. W.*

Dioscorea Batatas. By l'Abbé Meuley (*Jour. Soc. Nat. Hort. Fr.*; 4th Series, vol. viii.; May 1907).—A complete account of the best method of cultivating the Sweet Potato (*Dioscorea Batatas*), which is described as a valuable vegetable, giving more trouble in cultivation than the potato, but superior to it in nourishment, more delicate in flavour,

and with the conspicuous advantage of far greater freedom from disease.
It is said to have been introduced into France in 1843 by M. de Montigny,
French Minister Plenipotentiary in China.—*M. L. H.*

Diospyros kaki. By W. B. Hemsley (*Bot. Mag.* tab. 8127).—
Nat. ord. *Ebenaceae*; E. India, China and Japan. A small dioecious
tree; leaves 8-10 inches long; male flowers in threes; female larger,
green and yellow, 1½-2 inches diameter; fruit globose, 3½ inches
diameter.—*G. H.*

Drugs, Plants furnishing American Root. By Alice Henkel
(*U.S.A. Dep. Agr., Bur. Pl. Ind., Bull.* 107; 10/07; 25 figs. and
7 plates).—An account of all the American official root drug-plants,
giving the names, habitat and range, description of the plant and of the
part used as a drug, method of collection, prices and uses. Fifty plants
are so dealt with, and figures are given of each.—*F. J. C.*

Education : Plant Production. By Dick J. Crosby (*U.S.A.
Dep. Agr., Office of Exp. Stn., Bull.* 186; May 1907; 40 figs.).—
An outline syllabus of instruction in elementary agriculture (equally
applicable to horticulture) for use in "rural common schools" is given,
and followed by an excellent series of suggestive experiments illustrating
the life of plants and the influence of environment, so simple as to be
easily understood by children.—*F. J. C.*

Eria longispica. By W. Watson (*Bot. Mag.* tab. 8171).—Nat. ord.
Orchidaceae; tribe *Epidendreae*; Borneo. An epiphytic herb without
pseudo-bulbs; racemes slender, 10-16 inches long, densely many-flowered;
flowers ¾ inch long, yellow spotted, tipped with crimson.—*G. H.*

Eupatorium deltoideum, Jacq. By C. Sprenger (*Bull. R. Soc.
Tosc. Ort.* 1-2, 1907, p. 18).—Woody evergeen shrub with long-stalked
leaves, which are triangular, almost cordate, with denticulate and serrate
bases, green above, pale green below, with opposite veins; large flowers
in elegant rose-purple umbels and of great value for our gardens and
markets. The species was found and described by Dr. Jacquin, who died
at Vienna in 1817, but it had never been introduced alive into European
gardens. Last year, however, among many seeds collected by the traveller
C. A. Purpus in Mexico, in the vicinity of Salto d'Agua, about 1,000 metres
above sea-level, were those of this marvellous *Eupatorium*, which flowered
in the writer's garden at Vomero for the first time in Europe uninterruptedly from October to December, and in the first year after sowing,
as if it were an annual. It is hardy there, but loses its leaves. The
plant is very graceful, and can be used in all sorts of ways for decoration,
&c. It can be propagated by seed and cuttings, which latter strike
readily; its cultivation is easy. The seeds are sown in April, and the
seedlings transplanted early and frequently. The treatment is much
the same as that for autumn chrysanthemums, when it will yield an
abundance of flowers in autumn. Light but substantial soil must be
used and plenty of manure applied. Jacquin preserved shoots of it in
his herbarium, and has a figure of it in his work "Icones Plant.
Var."—*W. C. W.*

Eupatorium glandulosum. By W. B. Hemsley (*Bot. Mag.* tab. 8189).—Nat. ord. *Compositae*; tribe *Eupatoriaceae*; Mexico. A shrub, 6–8 feet high; flower-heads numerous, corymbose, ½ inch diam., white and fragrant.—*G. H.*

Exoascus deformans. By G. Zauli (*Bull. R. Soc. Tosc. Ort.* 11, 1907, p. 325).—Professor Vittorio Peglion, after showing that *Exoascus* is the prime cause of the peach-tree disease, gives an account of some experiments which he performed. The time at which the fungicide can be most beneficially applied corresponds with that of the opening of the buds. The washing should be applied before this period, at least a week or two before vegetation begins. In moderately rainy regions a single washing is enough, in very rainy regions two or more. Where two washings are applied, it should be done when the tree is resting. The mixture advised to be used is composed as follows:

Copper sulphate	2	kilos.
Quicklime	1	,,
Ammonia chloride	·200	,,
Water	100	

The Professor treated a tree so far gone in disease that it had been ordered to be cut down; the tree had, as a result, retained nearly all its foliage, whereas, in others not so treated the *Exoascus* caused all the leaves to fall; plants only half-treated showed the complete efficiency of the treatment. Those treated fruited most prolifically, while the accustomed falling of the fruit did not occur.—*W. C. W.*

Fastigiate Trees. By W. J. Bean (*Gard. Chron.* No. 1054, p. 148, March 9, 1907; figs. 66–69; and No. 105, March 23, p. 184; figs. 81 and 82; and p. 200; fig. 89).—In this interesting article on "Fastigiate Trees," the writer gives a short account of the fastigiate varieties of the Oak, Beech, Elm, Birch, Robinia, Poplar, Hornbeam, Tulip tree, Hawthorn, Pyrus, Ptelea, Horse Chestnut, and Aralia.—*G. S. S.*

Ferula communis, var. brevifolia. By W. Watson (*Bot. Mag.* tab. 8157).—Nat. ord. *Umbelliferae*; tribe *Peucedaneae*; Mediterranean countries. A herb 10 feet high; stem 4 inches thick at base; leaves much dissected; umbels in a thyrse, 3 or more feet long; flowers yellow.—*G. H.*

Forestry: State Nursery for Forest Tree Seedlings. (*U.S.A. Exp. Stn. Vermont, Bull.* 127; 4/1907).—A nursery for the raising of forest trees to be grown in Vermont has been established by Act of the Legislature, and . the bulletin gives suggestions as to what trees to plant.—*F. J. C.*

Freesias, New Hybrid. By G. T. Grignan (*Rev. Hort.* October 1, 1907, pp. 448–9; coloured plate).—The plate shows a very pretty group of coloured *Freesia refracta*, light-mauve, yellow, orange-red and mauve, warm rose, &c., obtained by hybridising *F. refracta*, *F. Leichtlinii*, and *F. Armstrongii.*—*C. T. D.*

Fruit Growers' Associations. By W. Paddock (*U.S.A. Exp. Stn. Colorado, Bull.* 122; 4/1907).—Much of the Colorado fruit is disposed of through Associations. The many advantages of this method of trading are clearly set out, and a copy of the by-laws of one of the Associations is given as a guide to others. Not only is the selling done on the co-operative system, but the buying of supplies is carried out through the same channels, with the resulting lightening of freights and the benefit to small growers of buying at wholesale prices.—*F. J. C.*

Fruits, Summary of Results with. By E. J. Watson (*U.S.A. Exp. Stn. Louisiana, Bull.* 90; January 1907).—Summarises cultivation, varieties most successful, length of time of growth, yield and return of a number of fruits. In the strawberries the results showed that nitrogenous manure (cotton-seed meal) produced a rank growth and abundance of large fruits, but the three important elements—texture, colour, and flavour—were lacking. Phosphoric acid supplied both colour and flavour ; potash supplied texture and firmness, but neither of these appreciably added to the size or quality of the fruit. A large number of trials of peaches were carried on for five years, including representative varieties from Persia, North China, Spain, South China, or Honey and Puento strains. Records were kept of date of full bloom, date of last killing frost, percentage of blooms killed, percentage of full crop. The frost injury depends on the stage of the blossom, while the atmospheric condition is sometimes an important factor in deciding the result. If frost occurs immediately after or during the period of full bloom, prior to the flowers being fertilised, the results are usually disastrous ; severe rain or windstorms during this period are more injurious than frost. After the flowers have been fertilised, before the calyx drops, the fruit is capable of withstanding considerable frost. It was found that the late bloomers are more apt to be injured than those blooming earlier. In apples the varieties of northern origin were shorter lived and more subject to fungus disease.—*C. H. H.*

Fungi, Edible, Treatment of. By M. Maziman (*Jour. Soc. Nat. Hort. Fr.*; 4th Series, vol. viii. ; April 1907).—Sugar, and more particularly glucose, is said to have a great effect upon the vigour of the lower orders of vegetation, and M. Maziman records his experiments in watering beds of *Tricholoma nudum* occasionally with slightly sweetened water ; a practice which he considers was attended with good results.

M. L. H.

Gentiana ornata. By J. Hutchinson (*Bot. Mag.* tab. 8140).—Nat. ord. *Gentianaceae* ; tribe *Swertieae* ; Alpine Central and Eastern Himalaya. An herb, 6 inches high ; leaves linear, ½ inch long ; corolla blue, striated, with greenish-yellow stripes outside.—*G. H.*

Geraniums. By A. Pucci (*Bull. R. Soc. Tosc. Ort.* 5, 1907, p. 125).—As ornamental plants they have been largely neglected. The author mentions those most adapted to gardens as ornamental plants. One of the finest is *G. armenum* of Boissier, native of Asia Minor, a very vigorous, hardy plant, about three feet high, with flowers 2 inches across and of a brilliant red. It flowers from May to August, bearing a constant succession of flowers. It prefers deep, light, and fresh soil. André received it from Switzerland under the name of *G. Gerardi*; the "Belgique Horticole" wrote in 1878 that Backhouse had sent it out under the name of *Lambertianum*; Regel described it as *Backhouseanum*. The plant can be propagated by division in autumn or spring. *G. ancmonaefolium* Hérit. is suited to warmer places and is a native of Madeira and Teneriffe; its synonyms are: *G. laevigatum* Burm., *G. palmatum* Cav., and *G. rutilans* Ehrh. It branches so as to attain more than two yards in width, with very numerous dark pink flowers. Easily multiplied by seed. *G. cinereum* Cav., from the Pyrenees, has greyish-white flowers veined and streaked with a darker tint; flowers in June and July. Increased by division at the end of the winter. Its compatriot *G. Endressi* J. Gay is taller; its bright pink flowers, streaked and veined with deeper pink, open from May to July.

G. ibericum Linn. is a native of Georgia: it is suited to many situations. Over two feet high, it bears large flowers of a violet-turquoise hue, which expand continuously from May to September. It is highly probable that *G. platypetalum* Fisch. and Mey. (*G. gymnocaulon*) is a variety of this species; it also is from Georgia, and bears broad, expanded flowers, of an intense violet-turquoise colour, with darker reddish streaks; flowers from May to June. *G. sanguineum* var. *lancastriense* is found in Walney Island, Lancashire. It creeps over the ground, forming carpets, and is about six inches high, with hairy leaves, solitary pale pink flowers streaked with darker veins. It is one of the most elegant plants for borders and rockwork.

G. macrorrhizum L. is a native of the Alps and Apennines, growing on rocks and in woody places. It forms compact little shrubs; flowers from May to July with purplish-pink flowers. It is especially adapted for rockwork.

Van Geert in 1878 recommended a variety of *G. molle* L., called *aureum*, with golden-yellow leaves, adapted for borders and mosaics.

G. palustre L. is suitable for damp places: it forms in the beginning of summer numerous brilliant flowers. *G. phaeum* L. occurs wild in several parts of Europe: its only merit is in having flowers of a blackish or chestnut violet. Vilmorin cites two varieties: *G. lividum* Willd. with veined flowers, and the other (*G. roseum* Desf.) with pink flowers. Greatly to be recommended for gardens is *G. pratense*, as well as its varieties—viz. those with double, white, and bicoloured flowers.

The "Gardeners' Chronicle" in 1894 described a new species from New Zealand, *G. sessiliflorum* Cav., remarkable for its large leaves, and its white flowers veined with purple, which are sessile; the plant is acaulescent. Of the species *G. tuberosum*, indigenous in Southern Europe, the var. *grandiflorum* is worth cultivating, as are *G. Charlesi*, of Afghanistan, with pale pink flowers veined with purple and *G. Wallichianum*, a dwarf and prostrate form from the Himalayas, with leaves covered with bristly hairs and brilliant purple flowers.—*W. C. W.*

Gesnera cardinalis. By W. Watson (*Bot. Mag.* tab. 8167).—Nat. ord. *Gesncraceae*; tribe *Gesnereae*; Brazil. A velvety herb, 9 inches high; leaves broadly ovate, 4–6 inches long; flowers one to four together; corolla 2½–3 inches long, scarlet.—*G. H.*

Gipsy Moth in Maine. By E. F. Hitchings (*Maine Dep. Agr., Quart. Bull.*; March 1907; 2 plates and 5 figs.).—Contains the text of an Act providing for "the Protection of Trees and Shrubs from the introduction and ravages of dangerous insects and diseases," and an account of the life-history and habits of this pest, already alluded to several times in these abstracts. The principal points provided for in the Act are the declaration of the gipsy and brown tail moths in their various stages as public nuisances; the inspection of all nurseries and issue of certificates certifying absence of pests and notices of prohibition to sell without fumigation if pests are present; all stock imported must have been duly inspected or bear a certificate of fumigation; all importations infested with pests, whether with or without a certificate, shall be seized and an order shall be made for their destruction; persons suspecting the presence of certain pests anywhere are to report to the Commissioner of Agriculture to that effect, and he shall cause them to be inspected and take such further steps as are necessary for the destruction of the pests; the inspectors, &c., have the right to enter both public and private grounds for the purpose of inspection; vehicles coming from other States, &c., may be stopped and examined; provision for the State to reimburse to every town money above one-twentieth of 1 per cent. of its assessable value expended in administering the law; fines up to a hundred dollars may be inflicted for infringement of the law.—*F. J. C.*

Hardiness in Trees, Relation of Early Maturity to. By R. A. Emerson (*U.S.A. Exp. Stn. Nebraska*, 19th Report; August 1906).—The trees that can best resist cold in winter are those that have the habit of ripening their new growth perfectly in the fall, the earliest to ripen their wood being the hardiest. Young trees are more susceptible to severe winter weather than older trees of the same kind, except in case of trees that are so old as to be feeble from age. Young, vigorously growing trees ripen their wood later in the fall than older trees, and this is at least in large part responsible for their lack of hardiness. Trees growing on high land mature their twigs and buds earlier than those on low land. A cover-crop, by stopping growth, causes the new wood to ripen earlier than in trees on land receiving late summer cultivation, the effect of which is that the former stand the winter with less ill effect than the latter. The trees on which these observations are based were plums, apples, peaches, black walnut, and honey-locust, in which it was found that their relative hardiness was influenced by the locality in which the seed from which they sprang was grown.—*C. H. H.*

Helianthus decapetalus as a Food Plant. By R. de Noter (*Rev. Hort.* March 16, 1907, pp. 136–140; and April 16, 1907, pp. 186–7; 3 woodcuts).—The long tuberous roots of this species are described as being very nutritious as a culinary vegetable. The woodcuts representing the plant, the tuber system, and individual tubers resemble strongly *H. rigidus* of our gardens, but the average weight of the tuber clusters—some 8 or 9 lb.—produced by single spring-planted tubers appears extraordinary. In the second article numerous cooking recipes are given.—*C. T. D.*

Hoodia Currori. By N. E. Brown (*Bot. Mag.* tab. 8136).—Nat. ord. *Asclepiadaceae* ; tribe *Stapelieae* ; Angola.

A bushy succulent perennial, 2–2½ feet high ; stem with 13 rows of spine-tipped tubercles ; flowers 2–4 or more together ; corolla 3½–5 inches diameter, saucer-shaped, pinkish-red with ochreous-tinted rays on the central part.—*G. H.*

Hypodermic Injection in Plants. Anon. (*Gard. Chron.* No. 1045, January 5, 1907).

—Experiments have been made by M. J. M. Simon, with a view of restoring vigour to decaying fruit trees, by injecting certain nutritive fluids into their tissues, with considerable success. The method of procedure is to place a vessel containing the fluid, about 6 feet from the ground, near the tree : from this a pipe connects with a tube which is forced into the tree just above the level of the soil. By this means the liquid is subjected to a certain amount of pressure. It mingles with the sap, and is carried to all parts of the tree. Cabbages, cauliflowers, and potatos have been treated much in the same way with similar results.—*G. S. S.*

Incuspidaria dependens. By T. A. Sprague (*Bot. Mag.* tab. 8115).

—Nat. ord. *Tiliaceae* ; tribe *Elaeocarpeae* ; Central Chile. A small tree, 20–30 feet high. Leaves obovate or elliptic ; flowers 1–3 inches in the axils ; petals oblong, three-toothed, white.—*G. H.*

Indigofera arrecta, On the Cause of "Hardness" in the Seeds of. By G. Bergtheil and D. L. Day (*Ann. Bot.* vol. xxi. January 1907, pp. 57–60 ; 1 plate).

—Certain members of the Leguminosae are known to possess seeds provided with an excessively hard coat, which does not allow of the penetration of water, and consequently prevents germination from taking place. The authors have investigated the case of *Indigofera arrecta*, and find that the outermost covering of the seed consists of a substance which is probably intermediate in nature between cellulose and cuticle, and which is impermeable to water.

An increased percentage of germination can be obtained by scarifying the seeds or by treating them with a solution of concentrated sulphuric acid. The action of the scarifying is doubtless to remove a portion of the resistant covering, and thus to allow penetration of water.—*A. D. C.*

Insecticides, Results of Experiment Station Work with. By E. V. Wilcox (*U.S.A. Dep. Agr., Office of Exp. Stn., Rep.* 1905 ; pp. 239–280).

—An account is given of work in the various experiment stations with insecticides. The lime-sulphur-salt wash, frequently referred to in these abstracts, is most used against scale insects with almost uniformly good results, and is recommended in some cases against the attacks of some fungi, such as apple scab, &c. The results of experiments with crude oils and kerosene, diluted and mixed with other substances, are much more at variance than those obtained with the lime-sulphur-salt wash. Fumigation with hydrocyanic acid gas has been very effective in practically all experiments against scale insects. Arsenical poisons, such as Paris green and arsenate of lead, and arsenite of soda in combination with Bordeaux mixture, are recommended for use by most stations against leaf-eating caterpillars. In some of the experiments dust-spraying was found very effective, as, *e.g.*, a mixture of pulverised copper sulphate, slaked lime, and either Paris green or arsenate of lead was found very effective in Delaware, 2 lb. of the dry mixture being required to spray an amount of foliage which could be covered with four gallons of liquid mixture. Codlin moth and apple scab were satisfactorily controlled by dust spraying. The use of whale-oil soap as an insecticide has met with varying results, probably owing to variations in the composition of the soap. The New York Station recommends that the soap be made at home from 6 lb. caustic soda, 22 lb. fish oil, and 1½ gallon of water. This will make 40 lb. of soap, which may be used at the rate of .1 lb. in seven gallons of water.

An interesting summary of the work carried on against various insects is given ; but as most of horticultural interest has already been referred to in these abstracts under the various experiment stations, it need not be further dealt with now.—*F. J. C.*

Insects and Fungus Pests in Illinois, Fifty Years' Progress in Control of. By S. A. Forbes (*Trans. Hort. Soc. Illinois*, 1905, pp. 219–227).—Paris green was first used in the early 'sixties as a potato-beetle poison. By 1877 its use in orchards for canker-worm was fairly general. In 1878 London purple began to be used against the codling-moth. But a serious bar to the use of these arsenical poisons was their caustic action, which induced Professor Gillette, of Iowa, to add lime. The use of hellebore and pyrethrum dates from 1858 and 1879. Kerosene was first used in 1865. The author's experiments with lime and sulphur washes caused their adoption as recently as 1902. Bisulphide of carbon against weevils in mills and granaries, hydrocyanic gas for fumigation, Bordeaux mixture as a fungicide, and ammoniacal carbonate of copper for the same purpose, have all been introduced in the last fifty years.—*C. H. L.*

Ipomoea murucoides (*Rev. Hort.* February 1, 1907, p. 55).— A Mexican tree convolvulus of the habit of the elder, but with long sarmentous roots. As it withstands fairly hard frosts, it would probably succeed in Cornwall and other places where mild winter conditions prevail.
C. T. D.

Iris verna. By W. Watson (*Bot. Mag.* tab. 8159).—Nat. ord. *Iridaceae*; tribe *Moraeae*; United States. Leaves 6–8 inches long, veined ; perianth purple ; falls pale violet with orange claws.—*G. H.*

Irises, American. By G. B. M. (*Gard. Chron.* No. 1070, June 29, 1907, p. 417 ; No. 1071, July 6, p. 6).—The American irises are, according to the author, not so well known in this country as they ought to be, and he gives the names and descriptions of twenty-three species and varieties, with directions as to their cultivation. In conclusion the author says :

"Of all the irises it is my pleasure to know, those from America appeal to the artistic sense the most. They have not the stature of *I. aurea* or *I. Monnieri*, neither have they the huge flowers of *I. laevigata*, but they have refinement, beauty of form, and artistic schemes of colour that equal, if they do not surpass, any other irises in these respects."

' *G. S. S.*

Kennedya retrorsa. By W. B. Hemsley (*Bot. Mag.* tab. 8144).— Nat. ord. *Leguminosae*; tribe *Phaseoleae*; Eastern Australia. Twining shrub; leaves trifoliate, 3–6 inches long; flowers ⅗ inch diameter, rose-purple.—*G. H.*

Laelio-Cattleya Hybrids (*Rev. Hort.* January 16, 1907, p. 31).— *Cattleya* 'Eldorado alba,' pure white, crossed with *Laelia Perrini alba*, also pure white, yielded offspring bearing pink flowers; but *C. Mossiae alba*, crossed with another form of same name with yellow throat, yielded a pure-white variety.—*C. T. D.*

Lead Arsenate and Paris Green. By J. P. Street and W. E. Britton (*U.S.A. Exp. Stn. Conn., Bull.* 157; 9/1907).—Lead arsenate is now usually recommended as a spray in place of Paris green against leaf-eating insects, because it has greater adhesive powers and is harmless to foliage, while it lacks nothing in effectiveness. It is recommended that the lead arsenate be made at home, since the freshly precipated arsenate appears to keep in suspension better than even the best commercial preparations. To make it 24 oz. of lead acetate (or 20 oz. of lead nitrate) are dissolved in a gallon of cold water; 10 oz. of sodium arsenate are dissolved in another vessel in three quarts of water, and both solutions are poured into 100 to 150 gallons of water to use as a spray fluid. The solutions should be made in wooden vessels. It is recommended that Paris green solution for spraying should be made by taking Paris green 1 lb., fresh quicklime 3 lb., and water 100 gallons. Either may be used in connection with Bordeaux mixture, when the Paris green need have no lime added; but the lead arsenate is rendered insoluble by the Bordeaux mixture, and is therefore not so effective as when used alone.—*F. J. C.*

Legume Inoculation, Conditions affecting. By Karl F. Kellerman and T. R. Robinson (*U.S.A. Bur. Plant Industry, Bull.* 100, pt. viii., 1906).—An interesting paper which for the most part corroborates the most careful records on the subject. The decided benefit of lime in obtaining successful inoculations of legumes in some soils is clearly indicated. "At least during the first season's growth no general cross-inoculation takes place. Bacteria from one host may, however, inoculate a physiologically related species." "Heavy inoculation by a pure culture increases nodule formation if the soil solution is enriched by the excess of the culture medium; however, in a favourable soil, a light inoculation, well distributed, is as effective."

"Thorough aëration is favourable to nodule formation." This is a fact of greatest importance, and fully endorses the practical methods of our best English cultivators.—*F. J. B.*

Legumes, A Test for Commercial Cultures for. By Geo. C. Butz (*U.S.A. Exp. Stn. Penn. State Coll., Bull.* 78 ; July 1906).—Nitro-culture on absorbent cotton prepared by the National Nitro-culture Company, when scientifically tested, gave the following results :

Alfalfa (Lucerne).—Pot and field experiments showed no decided advantage from inoculation with nitro-culture.

Vetch.—Pot experiments gave one improved plant. In field experiments no strong development of nodules occurred.

Cow-pea.—The slight difference in favour of pot inoculation alone cannot support the great claims made for nitro-culture on cotton. The medium in which the bacteria had grown had a great effect upon the formation of nodules, being greatest in the field experiments, less in the greenhouse soil, and least of all in the sterilised sand supplied with mineral plant food.—*F. J. B.*

Lilac, New Varieties of. By G. T. Grignan (*Rev. Hort.* January 1, 1907, pp. 13–16; coloured plate and 2 woodcuts).—The illustrations show four very fine double varieties and one single—viz. 'Étoile de Mai,' rich red lilac, double ; 'Édouard André,' delicate rose-pink, large double flowers ; 'René Jarry-Desloges,' similar, but pale blue slightly suffused with pink; 'President Loubet,' deep rose, double, very large flowers ; and 'Pasteur,' remarkable for the length of the inflorescence, lilac-red, single.—*C. T. D.*

Lily, White (*Rev. Hort.* January 1, 1907, p. 9).—In Florence, grown under extremely starved conditions in a vase with an *Agave americana*, this lily has produced annually a number of seed pods containing perfect seed. This is attributed to the check in the production of reproductive scales, the ovules consequently resuming their function.—*C. T. D.*

Lomatia ferruginea. By S. A. Skan (*Bot. Mag.* tab. 8112).—Nat. ord. *Proteaceae*; tribe *Embothrieae* ; Chili and Patagonia. A much-branched shrub, 9 feet high and 27 feet in circumference ; very hardy. Leaves bipinnatisect ; flowers ½ inch long, golden yellow and scarlet without, and bright scarlet with a yellow base within.—*G. H.*

Lopezia hirsuta, Jacq. By C. Sprenger (*Bull. R. Soc. Tosc. Ort.* 1–2, 1907, p. 22).—This genus is allied to *Fuchsia.* Twenty-three good species are known. They are perennial and shrubby, rarely annual; almost all from Mexico ; only a few belong to Guatemala. All are mountain-lovers, found in moist meadows, on the margins of woods and copses, near streams and springs, loving open places and sun. This species was known to Jacquin, doctor, botanist, and traveller, who possessed it at Vienna at the beginning of last century—whether alive or not is not known. It was refound last year at Salto di Agua, in Mexico, and the seeds were sent to the writer by Dr. C. A. Purpus. The elegant plant is woody, perennial, evergreen, and distantly resembles a *Fuchsia.* It flowers in the first year after sowing, from October uninterruptedly until January. The young shoots are red-purple, the old, chestnut-colour. The alternate leaves are oval, acute, slightly pubescent, those nearest the inflorescence are a lovely pink edged with green, like some *Euphorbiaceae*. The flowers occur in long branched spikes, and are of a quite peculiar reddish-orange colour, stalked, and soon followed by globose fruits containing very numerous tiny seeds. The plant is naturally much branched, and forms towards the flowering period a broad and compact shrub. The plant has a branching rhizome and throws up a quantity of very short shoots, which at once begin to flower if the cold does not prevent them. It will form, therefore, a useful plant in the greenhouse. There it flowers at the beginning of February. The soil for it must be light but rich, manured, and mixed with sand. It can be used largely for cut flowers, which would have a good market sale. It will be quite hardy throughout Italy—at least along the coast.—*W. C. W.*

Magnolias with Deciduous Leaves. By A. Pucci (*Bull. R. Soc. Tosc. Ort.* 6, 1907, p. 162).—The strongest and oldest is *M. Yulan* Desf. or *M. conspicua* Salisb., from China, which has fine, white, odorous flowers, opening a little before the leaves come out. The Chinese make it the symbol of whiteness. The young flower-buds are used in vinegar as capers. It may attain about 50 feet in height, but in Italy reaches only 25 or 30 feet. It flowers in temperate climes in March; if the flowering shoots are pruned in February, and placed in a pot full of water in a warm house, the flowers open earlier. The species has an important variety, viz. *Alexandrina*, which flowers later and has large white flowers tinged with violet-purple : there is also a variety with leaves variegated with gold.

M. Campbelli Hook. f. & Toms is a native of Bhutan, where it grows at a height of 8,000 or 9,000 feet ; it was discovered by Griffith. It is about 90 or 100 feet high ; flowers in April, before leaves come out ; the flowers are the largest in the genus, measuring about a foot in diameter.

M. stellata Hook., also called *Halleana* Robins and *Halleana stellata*, is a low shrub, compact and fairly vigorous ; flowers freely in March. Comes from Japan, and was introduced into Europe in 1862 ; it was first described under the name of *Burgeria stellata* Sieb. & Zucc.

M. hypoleuca, from the mountains of Japan, is a majestic tree, with leaves about a foot long ; the flowers are white and odorous ; the wood is prized by the natives, and its ash is used for polishing and in lacquer-work ; the wood is used for basket-work. *M. Kobus* is also from Japan : it is very hardy and flowers at an early age. *M. parviflora* is a small tree from the alps of Nippon. *M. Thurberi* was introduced with *M. stellata*. *M. Watsoni* Hook. comes from Japan and is allied to *M. hypoleuca* ; has large flowers with pink sepals and creamy-white petals. A little-known species is *M. Wieseneri*, which was sold to the grower Wiesener, of Fontenay-aux-Roses, by Tokada, a Japanese grower ; it figured at the Paris Exhibition of 1889, under the erroneous name of *M. parviflora*. It is a dwarf, bushy shrub with oval-oblong, glaucescent leaves, and solitary, erect, pure-white flowers.

M. umbrella Lamk. is a beautiful tree from Virginia and Carolina. *M. auriculata* (*M. tripetala* L. and *Fraseri*) comes from the mountains of Carolina : it was discovered by Bartram and introduced into France by

Michaux. It has large leaves with auricles at base, and white odorous flowers.

M. acuminata is a native of Pennsylvania, where Bartram discovered it, and it was introduced into Europe by Collinson in 1736. It attains a height of 80 feet with a very straight stem, and compact, hard wood, which is used for various purposes. *M. cordata* is from Upper Georgia, about 50 feet high, and resembles the last one, with small yellow flowers.

M. macrophylla Mich. has leaves about 1½ foot long; flower white tinged with purple at the base; it comes from Carolina, where Michaux discovered it. Some regard it as a form of *M. auriculata*.

M. glauca Linn. is 15 or 20 feet high, with glaucous leaves. The small, cream-white flowers exhale a delicate perfume. It flowers from the middle of May onward through the summer. It comes from the low, damp territory of Virginia, Carolina, and other regions, and was introduced into Europe in 1688. The leaves and wood have an aromatic odour and were once used as a remedy for rheumatism. There is a variety *sempervirens* and another *longifolia* ; other varieties are *arborea*, *pumila*, and *Thompsoniana*.

M. Lennéi, a supposed hybrid between *Yulan* and *purpurea*. No one knows if it is a distinct species, a variety, or a natural variation. It is of Italian origin, coming from the Salvi Garden at Vicenza about 1850; thence it went to Topf at Erfurt, who called it after Lenné, director of the Potsdam Garden, and afterwards director-general of the Royal Gardens of Prussia. The large flowers are white inside, and a lovely violet-pink without ; they are very odorous. *M. Soulangeana* appears to be a natural hybrid introduced more than fifty years ago by Soulange-Bodin ; the flowers are pink tinged with white. A variety of this is *speciosa*. *Norbertiana* is a garden form ; *odoratissima* is a hybrid between *Yulan* and *Lennéi*. *M. praecox* 'Louis van Houtte' is a variety which flowers in the spring and again at the end of summer. The variety *rosea grandiflora* sprang from seed from *Lennéi*, and is one of the best varieties. All the deciduous species are hardy and prefer a loose, porous soil; they abhor lime. Many ripen seeds under cultivation and can be easily multiplied therefrom. Those which do not set seed may be grafted by three different methods, using *purpurea* as a stock, this last being propagated by seed or layering.—*W. C. W.*

Mango in Hawaii, The. By J. E. Higgins (*Agr. Exp. Stn. Hawaii, Bull.* 12 ; illustrated).—The mango will undoubtedly become an important article of export from the Sandwich Islands when it becomes better known and appreciated in temperate climates. At present it is regarded more or less as a curiosity, and the taste for it has to be acquired. Cultivation and cross-breeding will no doubt improve it and remove the fibre, which is present in so many varieties, as well as a marked turpentine flavour. The best varieties come from India, where the mango is supposed to have originated. Its varieties are almost innumerable, 500 having been collected in India by Watt, and forty distinct forms exist in Hawaii. It can be propagated by seed, grafting, and inarching, and requires little pruning. The "chutney" mango is a class rather than a variety, and has an acid sweet flavour.—*C. H. L.*

Manure, Effect of Feeding on, Value of. By J. M. Bartlett (*U.S.A. Exp. Stn. Maine, Ann. Rep.* 1906; pp. 44–48).—It is shown that the kind of food supplied has a marked effect on the composition and monetary value of the manure produced, *e.g.*, from hay the total value was represented by 8·63, and from cotton-seed meal by 118·30. Potash was found to be most abundant in the urine.—*F. J. C.*

Meconopsis bella. By D. Prain (*Bot. Mag.* tab. 8130).—Nat. ord. *Papaveraceae*; tribe *Eupapavereae*; Himalaya. Perennial herb; leaves radical, 2–4 inches long, pinnatisect; flowers pale blue; stamens deep blue filaments with yellow anthers.—*G. H.*

Meconopsis punicea. By D. Prain (*Bot. Mag.* tab. 8119).—Nat. ord. *Papaveraceae*; tribe *Eupapavereae*; Tibet and W. China. Flowers pendulous, very dark pink, 4 inches long.—*G. H.*

Minnesota, Notes from. Edited by the Secretary (*U.S.A. Stn. Bd. Hort. Minn.* 1905; plates).—As a preventive of black rot in cabbage the seeds should be soaked for fifteen minutes before sowing in a 1-1000 corrosive sublimate solution, or in formalin 1 lb. to thirty gallons. This would not prevent root infection from infected soils, but it would do away with all danger from infected seed. It is not only in propagating by seed that the principle of selection is of value. With accurate records the stability of any desirable characters may be safely shown. To the horticulturist it is often a question of securing the best scions or stocks. A certain plum tree or a certain apple tree may carry the inherited power of bearing more, or more perfect, fruit than its neighbours of the same variety, or a certain branch may always have better fruit than other branches of the same tree. Scions from such a tree, or from such a branch, should be sought for and made the foundation for an entire stock.

In speaking on chemical manures for horticultural purposes Professor Snyder laid stress upon the fact that plants, like animals, do best on a perfectly balanced ration. In a soil in which there is an excess of available nitrogen, for instance, in proportion to the mineral food, the plants will produce a healthy crop of leaves, but fail to fruit well. Until the particular needs of any special soil are discovered by experiment, it is best to keep to a complete fertiliser, that is, one containing nitrogen, phosphoric acid, and potash. The maturity of a crop can be influenced by fertilisers. An excess of nitrate of soda, particularly during a wet season, causes prolonged growth and retards maturity. A good supply of phosphoric acid and a medium supply of nitrogen, on the other hand, generally hastens maturity. Hardiness, also, it is believed, can be increased by a judicious use of fertilisers. The paper adds the formula of a hygienic manure suitable for use in a living-room, which may be applied to house plants two or three times a month at the rate of half a teaspoonful dissolved in about a quart of water. Nitrate of soda 8 oz., sulphate of potash 6 oz., lime phosphate (mono-calcium phosphate) 18 oz. If the ingredients are pure the mixture will practically all dissolve in water.

Two different washes were prescribed to keep rabbits and field mice from destroying the bark of trees and shrubs. One is whitewash, the lime thinned with a solution of glue and enough carbolic acid added to make the mixture smell strong. The other is a mixture of lime, sulphur, and Cayenne pepper. The first of these mixtures will also destroy any eggs of insects that may have been laid on the bark.

To prevent the spread of orchard pests it was strongly advised to collect all fallen apples, or to allow pigs and chickens to run in the orchard and help themselves. The eggs or spores of the blight remain in the rotting apples and are ready for dissemination, according to their kind, in the spring.

Dust spraying was the subject of one discussion, and the number in its favour, as against liquid spraying, was small.—*M. L. H.*

Montanoa mollissima. By J. Hutchinson (*Bot. Mag.* tab. 8143).— Nat. ord. *Compositae*; tribe *Helianthoideae*; Mexico. A shrub 6 feet high; leaves sessile, 4–7 inches long; capitula 1½ inch diameter; ray flowers white; disk yellow.—*G. H.*

Montbretias, Hybrid. By G. T. Grignan (*Rev. Hort.* May 1, 1907, p. 208; coloured plate).—The plate shows four very fine varieties: 'Grand Moulin,' large, petals half-yellow merging into deep orange-red; 'Bicolor,' three petals deep orange-red and three bright yellow, flowers smaller; 'Chrysis,' bold, broad-petalled, bright yellow flowers; and 'Flamboyant,' very large, rich red.—*C. T. D.*

Mulching Garden Vegetables, Experiments in. By R. A. Emerson (*Agr. Exp. Stn. Nebraska, Bull.* 80).—The results are given of mulching *versus* thorough cultivation. The experiments were tried with ordinary garden vegetables, and would seem to show that those vegetables benefit most from mulching which require a long season of growth and frequent cultivation, an advantage being that the mulch can be applied before the rush of summer work begins. Tomatos, cucumbers, and cabbage benefited most by mulching.—*C. H. L.*

Mutation, Induced (*Rev. Hort.* March 1, 1907, p. 199; and July 1, 1907, p. 205).—It is stated in the "Journal d'Agriculture Pratique," in a report on experiments by MM. Blaringhem and Bonnier, that by means of transverse or longitudinal stem wounds, or by bending the plant concerned, especially maize, permanent and inherited sports or mutations have arisen possessing agricultural value. See also L. Daniel (*Rev. Hort.* August 1, 1907, pp. 356–7), similar experiments with roses and results through graft disturbance.—*C. T. D.*

Naming Plants. Anon. (*Gard. Chron.* No. 1046, p. 17, January 22, 1907). — A condensed account of the rules, &c., of nomenclature of plants adopted at the International Congress of Botany held at Vienna in 1905 is given. The rules are published in three languages (French, English, and German), bound together in a paper cover: they may be obtained from any foreign-bookseller.

G. S. S.

Nepenthes Pauli (*Rev. Hort.* January 1, 1907, p. 9).—A new form raised by M. Jarry-Desloges. The pitcher, slightly flattened, measures about a foot in length by about three inches in width, light green, spotted reddish brown; the wings are very large, undulated, and markedly ribbed; the throat is very large, expands horizontally, and is of a reddish brown; leaves upright, greenish, and red-spotted.

C. T. D.

Nerine Bowdeni. By W. Watson (*Bot. Mag.* tab. 8117).—Nat. ord. *Amaryllidaceae*; tribe *Amarylleae*; Cape Colony. Leaves 6 inches to 1 foot long; perianth segments 2-3 inches long, rose-pink.—*G. H.*

Nymphaeas. By Eugène Boullet (*Jour. Soc. Nat. Hort. Fr.*; 4th Series, vol. viii.; April 1907).—M. Boullet reviews favourably a work by M. G. Guernier called "Les Nymphéas dans l'ornamentation des Jardins," and quotes his opinion that one essential to success in growing these plants is water of a minimum temperature of 20° to 25° C. for the Nupbar varieties, and slightly higher for the varieties of Nelumbium.

M. L. H.

Odontioda Heatonensis, ×. By R. A. Rolfe (*Bot. Mag.* tab. 8183). Nat. ord. *Orchidaceae*; tribe *Vandeae*. Garden hybrid between *Odontoglossum cirrhosum* ♀ and *Cochlioda sanguinea*. Plant 1 foot high; sepals oblong-lanceolate, 7 inches long; petals shorter, both having a white ground suffused at apex and spotted below with rosy purple.—*G. H.*

Odontoglossum Hybrids. By G. T. Grignan (*Rev. Hort.* May 16, 1907, p. 230; coloured plate).—The plate shows five very charming varieties raised by Ch. Vuylsteke—viz. *O. Vuylstekei, O. Vuylstekeae, O. percultum, O. Rolfae,* and *O. ardentissimum* 'Espérance.' The letter-press gives description and pedigree fully.—*C. T. D.*

Odontoglossum Leeanum. By R. A. Rolfe (*Bot. Mag.* tab. 8142). Nat. ord. *Orchidaceae*; tribe *Vandeae*; Colombia. A natural hybrid between *O. gloriosum* and *O. triumphans,* an epiphyte; flowers bright yellow blotched with brown.—*G. H.*

Oldenlandia dolichantha. By W. Watson (*Bot. Mag.* tab. 8165).—Nat. ord. *Rubiaceae*; tribe *Hedyotideae*; East Tropical Africa. Annual, 1 foot high; leaves sessile, lanceolate, 1-2 inches long; flowers 4-merous; corolla white above green below, but with white margins, 1½ inch across.—*G. H.*

Olearia speciosa. By J. Hutchinson (*Bot. Mag.* tab. 8118).—Nat. ord. *Compositae*; tribe *Asteroideae*; Australia. A shrub about 3 feet high; leaves coriaceous, 1½-2½ inches long; ray flowers, five to six, white; heads 1 inch in diameter.—*G. H.*

Orange Industry of the West Indies. By Dr. H. A. Alford Nicholls, C.M.G. (*Journ. Imp. Dep. Agr. W.I.* 1907, 2).
How to Encourage Orange Trees to Bear Early in Jamaica, by Hon. T. H. Sharp, Jamaica.—*M. C. C.*

Orchard Culture: a Comparison of different Methods as Applied in the Case of the Apple Orchard. By W. J. Green and F. H. Ballou (*U.S.A. Exp. Stn. Ohio, Bull.* 171; March 1906).— The cover-crop method is excellent while the orchard is young : it consists of disking or ploughing the orchard early in the spring, followed during the season by spring tooth-harrow, fine-tooth cultivator or weeder. Cultivation is continued until the middle of July, or even to the middle of August, when some crop—such as soy beans, cow-peas, with or without rye, and winter vetches—is sown. A good cover-crop holds the leaves and snow, thereby lessening the depth of alternate freezing and thawing ; turning under the crop makes the soil spongy and friable, increases its moisture-holding capacity, and renders it better able to resist drought. The continuous clean-culture method exhausts the humus and is unsuited to sloping and steep ground. Cultivation should cease in early autumn, the soil lying undisturbed and uncovered till the next spring. In the sod-culture method the apple trees were planted in generous excavations directly in the sod. Immediately following the planting of the trees a circular area of ground, three or four feet in diameter, was spaded or dug about each tree, and the spaces were annually kept clean and mellow by frequent use of hoe or rake throughout the growing seasons. The grass was cut three or four times each season, keeping the surface smooth and sightly. The grass as cut is allowed to lie where it falls, thereby adding a mulch to the entire surface through which the new growth pushes up with increased vigour. No fertiliser has been added to the circular cultivated spaces, which are gradually enlarged to equal the diameter of the head of the respective trees. Sod culture is the most expensive and laborious plan of culture of the four methods tested : it may be utilised to advantage upon small, very rough, or stony areas where mulching material is not available, and about the home grounds where neatness and sightliness of the grounds and lawn are desired. In the sod-mulch method the trees are planted in grass, but instead of keeping a circular area about each tree cultivated these spaces of similar size are at once heavily mulched with straw ; fine-meshed wire-screen cylinders are placed round the trees to prevent injury by mice and other rodents ; the grass, as in the former method, is mown three or four times each season, but instead of allowing it to lie where it falls it is raked up, divided, and used to maintain the mulch about the trees. This method is well adapted to orchards on sloping or steep ground, but is also well suited for well-drained and level ground, is sightly, and the ground at all seasons allows carting on. Continuous clean cropping was discontinued as the soil commenced to be depleted of fertility and washed away ; this method cannot, therefore, be recommended. The grass-mulch gave even a better result after six years than the cover-crop ploughed in, the sod-culture plot, in which the soil immediately round the tree was cultivated, being third. An examination of the soil with regard to roots was made, and photographs show the amount of root: in top two inches ; next four inches ; and next six inches of soil.—*C. H. H.*

Orchids, Hybridisation of. By Léon Duval (*Jour. Soc. Nat. Hort. Fr.*; 4th series; vol. viii.; June 1907).—An interesting paper in which the author deprecates the unscientific practice of some amateurs, who cross species chosen apparently at random just to " see what will happen." Given a complete acquaintance with the ancestry of the parent plants, the production of fresh varieties of orchids of increasing value should be a matter of almost scientific certainty. Method is, however, essential, and each successive cross should be made with some definite object in view. Nothing less than perfection should be aimed at, but one point only should be considered at a time, first form and then colour being the most correct order. That is to say, having produced a flower of the desired size or beauty of form, the hybrid must be recrossed with the colour parent several times if necessary to reach the greatest attainable perfection of colour. M. Duval looks forward to the appearance of varieties of orchids of surprising beauty and perfection, produced by the intercrossing of already improved hybrids. A study of the nature of colour and of the chemical composition of pigments in flowers is recommended to the serious worker in the hybridisation of orchids.

M. L. H.

Oryctes nasicornis. By J. Vercier (*Le Jardin*, vol. xxi. No. 497, p. 330 ; November 5, 1907 ; 1 fig.).—The larva of this insect is fatal to the green vegetables it attacks. It resembles the cockchafer grub, being white and similar in shape, but is much larger—3 to 4 cm. long. It inhabits, and is doubtless introduced by, manure and leaf-mould, whence it ravages the roots and stems of vegetables. The larvae should be sought out and destroyed in autumn, after which the ground must be disinfected with formol to destroy the survivors.—*F. A. W.*

Paeonia Cambessedesii. By W. Watson (*Bot. Mag.* tab. 8161).— Nat. ord. *Ranunculaceae* ; tribe *Paeonieae* ; Balearic Islands and Corsica. Perennial, 1½ feet high ; flowers deep rose-pink, 3½ inches diameter ; carpels 5–7, purple.—*G. H.*

Paeony, Yellow (*Le Jardin*, vol. xxi. No. 496, p. 306 ; October 20, 1907).—*Paeonia lutea* ' Mme. Louis Henry', hybrid from *P. lutea* and *P. Moutan* var. ' Elisabeth.' A beautiful new variety, striped pink and yellow, with marked characteristics (absence of shoots and woody stems) from both parents.—*F. A. W.*

Palm Seed, Germination of. By E. Draps-Dom (*Le Jardin*, vol. xxi. No. 497, p. 325 ; November 5, 1907).—Palm seeds often take several years to germinate, but M. Draps-Dom finds that by placing them on arrival in hot, almost boiling water, and leaving them to soak for twenty-four hours they can be made to germinate in a fortnight.

F. A. W.

Palms, Branching in. By H. N. Ridley (*Ann. Bot.* vol. xxi. July 1907, pp. 415–422).—Previous writers have considered that palms are normally unbranched, and that growth takes place by the continuous development of a single monopodial bud. The author of this paper believes that the greater number of palms are really branched, at all events at the base, and that cases in which there is but one axis produced are a departure from the normal. He shows that soboliferous palms have a distinct tendency to emit axillary buds above the base of the main stems, and that in cases of apparent bifurcation one of the branches is a lateral bud. A list is given of about twenty species in which branching is known to occur. Numerous other points of interest are touched upon in connection especially with the palms of the Singapore Botanic Garden and the Malay Peninsula.—*A. D. C.*

Paphiopedilum villosum, var. annamense. By R. A. Rolfe (*Bot. Mag.* tab. 8126).—Nat. ord. *Orchidaceae*; tribe *Cypripedieae*; Annam. Plant 1 foot high; upper sepal erect, 2 inches long, cream-coloured, veined, and suffused with dark purple; petals light yellow veined and suffused with brown.—*G. H.*

Pecan Culture, Report on. By H. Harold Hume (*Agr. Exp. Stn. Florida, Bull.* 85; plates).—A complete and detailed account of the culture of the pecan, a tree belonging to the walnut family, which is native in the alluvial bottoms of the Mississippi. Its cultivated area corresponds closely with that of the cotton plant, though the pecan has the slightly wider range of the two. In Florida the work of producing new varieties of pecan of known parentage is being systematically taken up.—*M. L. H.*

Pelargonium, Diseases of. By M. J. Chifflot (*Jour. Soc. Nat. Hort. Fr.*; 4th Series, vol. viii.; June 1907).—A detailed account of all the diseases which may attack the Pelargonium divided into—

1. Diseases caused by vegetable parasites;
2. Diseases caused by animal parasites;
3. Organic diseases;

with their appropriate cure and methods of prevention in each case.

M. L. H.

Phosphates, Test of Nine, with different Plants. By H. J. Wheeler and G. E. Adams (*U.S.A. Exp. Stn. Rhode I., Bull.* 118; 1906).—The results of tests with nine different phosphates on various plants are given, and the following results are typical of the majority, and show, in a remarkable degree, the value of lime when used in combination with the phosphates.

Phosphate applied	Yield of peas in pod (pounds)	
	Limed 1894	Not limed
Dissolved bone-black	29	15
Dissolved bone	32	20
Dissolved phosphate rock	27	19
Fine ground bone	29	21
Basic slag meal	26	24
Floats	17	18
Redondite (raw)	11	8
Redondite (roasted)	22	9
No phosphate	15	6
Double superphosphate	29	12

The quantity of phosphoric acid applied before the crop was sown varied, but in every case the total of phosphoric acid applied since the beginning of the experiment is the same, and amounted to an average of 67·12 lb. per acre per annum for the past ten years.—*F. J. C.*

Phyllodoce Breweri. By W. Watson (*Bot. Mag.* tab. 8146).—Nat. ord. *Ericaceae*; tribe *Phyllodoceae*; California. A shrublet, 9 inches high; leaves ½–⅔ inch long; flowers bright rose colour or purple, wide, campanulate; petals 5; stamens 10, exserted.—*G. H.*

Picea morindoides. By O. Stapf (*Bot. Mag.* tab. 8169).—Nat. ord. *Coniferae*; tribe *Abietineae*; Eastern Himalaya. A tree with rose-coloured male strobili and oblong-cylindric cones, 2–3½ inches long, 1 inch diameter.—*G. H.*

Pineapple Culture. By K. K. Miller and A. W. Blair (*U.S.A. Exp. Stn. Florida, Bull.* 83–84; 1906; figs.).—These bulletins give the results of fertiliser experiments on pineapples, with recommendations for the use of certain manures based on these results, particulars as to packing-houses, field equipment, packing, grading, and everything connected with the marketing of the fruit.—*C. H. H.*

Pineapple, Fungus Diseases of. By F. A. Stockdale, B.A. (*Journ. Imp. Dep. Agr. W.I.* 1907, 2).

Tangle Root, not traced to any fungus as its cause, but probably due to poor preparation of the land.

Blight. The fungus that accompanies the discoloration and softening of the roots has not been identified.

Black Heart, or Core Rot. The fungus causing this disease is attributed to the Mucedines, but has not yet been identified.

Disease of Stored Pineapples. The commonest fungus in this connection is the fungus of the sugar-cane, *Trichosphaeria sacchari*, together with a species of *Diplodia* and some moulds of the genera *Penicillium* and *Aspergillus*.

A subsequent note on pineapple disease in Hawaii determines that disease to be caused by *Thielaviopsis ethaceticus*.

Cane cuttings can be protected from this disease by the application of Bordeaux mixture to the ends.—*M. C. C.*

Pinks. By Le Texnier (*Le Jardin,* vol. xxi. No. 489, p. 202; July 5, 1907).—Part I. of an interesting historical article on pinks in general.—*F. A. W.*

Plant Breeding in its Relation to American Pomology. By W. M. Munson (*U.S.A. Exp. Stn. Maine, Ann. Rep.* 1906; pp. 149–176).—A very interesting account of the methods of work heretofore used in the raising of new varieties, beginning with that of Van Mons with pears, begun in 1785, and Thomas Andrew Knight, and later in America, where Russian, Chinese, Japanese, and native fruits have been freely crossed with European, giving varieties suited to the various special conditions obtaining in that country. The various common fruits are then dealt with individually.—*F. J. C.*

Podophyllum versipelle. By J. Hutchinson (*Bot. Mag.* tab. 8154).—Nat. ord. *Berberidaceae*; tribe *Berbereae*; China. Perennial rhizome; leaves two, peltate, the upper covering inflorescence; flowers deep crimson.—*G. H.*

Potatos, Cultivation and Care of. By A. W. Gilman (*Maine Dep. Agr., Quart. Bull.*; September 1907).—A short general outline of potato culture is given by two or three growers, together with directions for spraying with Bordeaux mixture and Paris green (1 lb. Paris green to 50 gallons Bordeaux mixture). Thorough spraying with a proper mixture at the right time is insisted upon.—*F. J. C.*

Potato-spraying Experiments in 1906. By F. C. Stewart, H. G. Eustace, G. T. French, and F. A. Sirrine (*U.S.A. Exp. Stn. New York, Bull.* 290; June 1907; 3 figs.).—This is a continuation of the experiments started in 1902 and previously referred to in these abstracts (JOURN. R.H.S. xxxi. p. 343). Eighty experiments are reported. At Geneva five sprayings increased the yield by 63 bushels per acre, and three sprayings increased it 31·75 bushels; while at Riverhead the gain due to five sprayings was 53¼ bushels per acre, and to three sprayings 21½ bushels. In fifteen farmers' experiments, including 225½ acres, the average gain was 42½ bushels, the cost of the spraying being $5.18 per acre, and the average cost of each spraying 98.5 cents per acre, yielding an average net profit of $13.89 per acre. Sixty-two volunteer experiments are also reported, the average gains over 598 acres being 44·5 bushels per acre. The main trouble was late blight (*Phytophthora infestans*), but the flea-beetle and early blight (*Alternaria*) did some damage. It is recommended to commence spraying when the plants are 6 to 8 inches high, and repeat at intervals of ten to fourteen days, making in all five or six applications. When flea-beetles are troublesome Paris green should be added to the Bordeaux mixture; but otherwise the latter may be used alone.—*F. J. C.*

Preserving Native Fruits and Vegetables, Practical Directions for. By Mrs. L. H. Adams and E. P. Sandsten (*U.S.A. Exp. Stn. Wisconsin, Bull.* 136; April 1906).—A small pamphlet, intended to encourage the more general use of the wild apples and plums of the State. It contains notes and directions for making preserves.—*C. H. L.*

Prickly Pear and other Cacti. By D. Griffiths and R. F. Hare (*U.S.A. Exp. Stn. New Mexico, Bull.* 60; November 1906; 7 plates with 13 figs.).—Very complete analyses of various *Opuntias*, &c., were carried out with the object of ascertaining their value as food for stock, and the results are given in this bulletin, which runs to 136 pages. Descriptions of the species and varieties analysed accompany the analyses. The use of the cacti as cattle feed is only of secondary importance in Mexico, as the fruit is of great value as human food and the dry plants are used for fuel.—*F. J. C.*

Primula deorum. By W. B. Hemsley (*Bot. Mag.* tab. 8124).—Nat. ord. *Primulaceae*; tribe *Primuleae*; Bulgaria. Perennial; leaves six to twelve in a rosette, spathulate-lanceolate ; scape 7–9 inches high, fifteen to twenty flowered ; corolla violet-purple.—*G. H.*

Primula muscarioides. By W. B. Hemsley (*Bot. Mag.* 8168).— Nat. ord. *Primulaceae* ; tribe *Primuleae* ; Western China. Leaves rosulate, obovate-spathulate, 4–5 inches long ; flowers numerous, densely turned downwards ; calyx purple ; corolla deep purple-blue.—*G. H.*

Primula orbicularis. By W. B. Hemsley (*Bot. Mag.* tab. 8135).— Nat. ord. *Primulaceae* ; tribe *Primuleae* ; China. A mealy perennial. Scape 6 inches ; flowers 1–1¼ inch diameter, clear yellow, fragrant.—*G. H.*

Prunus Besseyi. By W. J. Bean (*Bot. Mag.* tab. 8156).—Nat. ord. *Rosaceae* ; tribe *Pruneae* ; North-West United States. Dwarf, sometimes prostrate, shrub, 2–4 feet high ; leaves 1–2½ inches long ; flowers ⅝ inch diameter, white.—*G. H.*

Prunus Mume, Sieb. and Zucc. By C. Sprenger (*Bull. R. Soc. Tosc. Ort.* 3, 1907, p. 71).—A tree about 25 feet high, native of Japan, but, according to Siebold, imported thither from China originally. *Amygdalus nanus* of Thunberg is synonymous with this plant, which is not a peach, but more nearly allied to the apricot. The leaves are oval-round, acuminate, pubescent below, and doubly serrate ; flowers solitary or in twos ; fruit round, soft, and not much in vogue with European taste. It is quite hardy throughout Italy, produces bright white and pink flowers, very strong-smelling, and is recommended specially on account of its early flowering. There are two varieties —*alba* and *rubra plena*, with double or pure white or bright and lively carmine flowers, both equally lovely. The plants do well in pots. Those described are two years from the graft, much shortened by pruning and well branched ; each slender last year's twig is completely covered with large sweet-scented flowers. They flower easily without any special attention.—*W. C. W.*

Raspberries and Blackberries, Varieties of, with Cultural Directions. By O. M. Taylor (*Exp. Stn. New York, Bull.* 278 ; May 1906).—A description of the varieties, tested for a series of years, with notes as to their relative hardiness, earliness, and desirability. One hundred and four different varieties are described. The most important topics dealing with their cultivation are discussed, and suggestions are given in regard to some of the methods followed by successful growers.—*C. H. H.*

Raspberries and Brambles. By J. G. Baker (*Gard. Chron.* No. 1047, p. 33, January 29, 1907).—This article gives an interesting account of the different species of raspberries, their hybrids, and hybrids between raspberries and brambles, the various species of brambles and their hybrids. The distinguishing character between raspberries and brambles "is that in the former the fruit can easily be pulled away from the long receptacle, but in the latter it adheres firmly and cannot be separated."—*G. S. S.*

Red Gum (*Liquidambar styraciflua*), **Sap Rot, and other Diseases.**
By Hermann von Schrenk (*U.S.A. Dep. Agr., Bur. Pl. Ind., Bull.* 114,
December 1907 ; 8 plates).—The sap-wood of the red gum is destroyed
with great rapidity by several sap-rotting fungi. The decay caused by
these fungi may be called " sap-rot." They grow most rapidly during
the spring and summer months, and enter mainly through the ends of
logs piled on the banks of rivers.

Sap-rot may be prevented by shortening the drying period in the
woods, either by hauling logs by rail or by reducing the moisture in the
log. This may possibly be accomplished by felling the gum trees without
sawing them into logs and leaving them in the forest until the leaves are
thoroughly dry. The amount of water evaporated by the leaves before
they dry may be sufficient to permit of floating the logs cut from such
leaf-seasoned trees.

The sap-rot may likewise be almost entirely prevented by coating the
ends immediately after the logs are cut with hot coal-tar creosote. The
cost of this treatment is about 8 cents per 1,000 feet.

Wherever possible all freshly cut logs, particularly such as are cut
during the spring and summer months, should be peeled.

The heart-wood of the red gum is comparatively resistant against
decay.

Sap-rots similar to those which are found in the red gum are found
in the tupedo gum, swamp oak, and maple.

The fungi responsible for sap-rot in the red gum are chiefly *Polyporus
adustus*, sometimes with *Polystictus livesutus* and *Poria subacida.* A
few other fungi of minor importance cause decay of the sap-wood of the
red gum.—*M. C. C.*

Renanthera annamensis. By R. A. Rolfe (*Bot. Mag.* tab. 8116).—
Nat. ord. *Orchidaceae*; tribe *Vandeae*; Annam. A dwarf epiphyte,
8–12 inches high ; flowers yellow spotted with crimson ; lat. sepals
spathulate, ¾ inch long ; petals oblong, ¼ inch long.—*G. H.*

Rhododendron Delavayi. By W. B. Hemsley (*Bot. Mag.* tab.
8137).—Nat ord. *Ericaceae*; tribe *Rhodoreae*; China. A small tree;
leaves 3–6 inches long ; flowers crimson with black spots at base of
corolla.—*G. H.*

Rhododendron intricatum. By W. J. Bean (*Bot. Mag.* tab.
8163).—Nat. ord. *Ericaceae*; tribe *Rhodoreae*; China. Dwarf shrub,
4–6 feet high ; leaves ⅙–⅓ inch long, white beneath ; trusses 5-flowered ;
corolla violet or lilac ; anthers orange-coloured.—*G. H.*

Ribes mogollonicum. By S. A. Skan (*Bot. Mag.* tab. 8120).—
Nat. ord. *Saxifragaceae*; tribe *Ribesieae*; S.W. United States. A
robust shrub, 10 feet high ; leaves five-lobed ; petals white ; berry
purplish or bluish-black.—*G. H.*

Rice Cultivation in British Guiana. By Hon. B. Howell Jones
(*Journ. Imp. Dep. Agr. W.I.* 1907, 7).—Returns made to the Board
of Agriculture have shown that the acreage under rice had increased
from about 6,000 acres in 1900 to about 24,000 acres in 1906.—*M. C. C.*

Ringing Herbaceous Plants. By U. P. Hedrick, O. M. Taylor, and R. Wellington (*U.S.A. Exp. Stn., Geneva, New York, Bull.* 288 ; 4/1907).—The cutting through or removal of a ring of bark from the stem of a tree is frequently resorted to in order to induce productiveness, to increase the size of the fruit, and to hasten maturity ; and the practice is often attended with the desired result. Similar experiments are here recorded with tomatos and chrysanthemums, but with very different results. With tomatos the height of the stems was not affected, but swellings occurred just above the wounds, the average number of fruits was reduced, and the fruits weighed less ; the colour and flavour of the fruit were not affected, but the foliage of the ringed plants took a curved and pendent position, and had warty growths upon it, becoming at the same time somewhat yellow. The roots were less developed, fewer in number, and smaller in size. With chrysanthemums the foliage took on a yellowish tinge, with portions reddish-purple ; the stems became more or less swollen, but not so tall ; when the ringing was done just as the buds appeared, the buds failed to open, while in other cases the period of maturity was slightly hastened ; the size of the blossoms was reduced and the roots lacked vigour ; the ringed plants produced almost no suckers. The authors think that possibly the deleterious effect noted in herbaceous plants may also in the end be evident in woody plants.

F. J. C.

Roman Hyacinths. By M. de Mazières (*Le Jardin*, xxi. 495, p. 298 ; October 5, 1907).—Roman hyacinths are cultivated in Provence with the sole object of multiplying bulbs, which have become an important export. A light porous soil is required, permeable to air and water, and prepared in June or July (*i.e.* two or three months before planting) by digging in farm manure or oil-cake mixed with a little potash, in the proportion of 20,000 kilogrammes to 1 hectare. In September or October plant in rows 30 cm. apart, with a distance of 4 to 6 cm. between the bulbs. Each square metre will thus hold sixty to eighty bulbs. Trench up the ground, so that rain-water will run off into the furrows. Water if necessary during and after the flowering season. When the leaves are dry and yellow in June the bulbs should be taken up and dried in the shade, after which the roots are cleared off and the bulbs stored in a dry, well-ventilated shed. They have no commercial value till after the second year's growth, when they should be 12 to 15 cm. in circumference (gauged by a zinc sieve), and these are sold, the smaller ones being replanted. The large bulbs when taken up are surrounded with bulbils, which are removed and subsequently planted to make their first year's growth. When sold in June the large bulbs are worth 60 to 80 francs (£2 to £3) per 1000.—*F. A. W.*

Rosa rugosa Hybrids, New (*Rev. Hort.* March 1, 1907, pp. 101-2).—Two forms described as very fine : ' Madame René Gravereaux ' (' Conrad Ferdinand Meyer ' × ' Safrano '), very large odorous flowers, pale rose, slightly tinged lilac ; and ' Monsieur Bienvêtu ' (' Pierre Notting ' × ' Safrano ' × ' Conrad Ferdinand Meyer '), bright salmon-rose flowers, very large.—*C. T. D.*

3 c

Rosa Soulieanae. By W. J. Bean (*Bot. Mag.* tab. 8158).—Nat. ord. *Rosaceae*; tribe *Roseae*; Western China. Robust, suberect shrub, 8 feet high; flowers ivory-white; fruit orange-vermilion.— *G. H.*

Roses, Autumn-flowering. By A. Pirlot (*Le Jardin*, vol. xxi. No. 490, p. 220; July 20, 1907; 3 figs.).—M. G. Tuffaut obtains superb autumn roses in the open air by the following simple method. Plant out suitable varieties (*e.g.* 'Mme. Bonnaire,' 'Captain Christy,' 'Frau Karl Druschki,' 'Paul Neyron') in the garden, and treat as usual. In August prune severely, leaving only three or four shoots on each tree, and fork in some fertiliser in the following proportions: 125 grammes biogene to the square metre. A vigorous growth ensues; rust, &c., should be guarded against by a fortnightly dressing with flowers of sulphur, three or four grammes to the litre. In October protect the roses with a frame, of the kind used for chrysanthemums. Disbud rigorously, leaving only one terminal bud, which will produce magnificent blooms in November.—*F. A. W.*

Roses, Manures for. By Georges Truffaut (*Jour. Soc. Nat. Hort. Fr.*; 4th Series, vol. viii.; March 1907).—From careful chemical and cultural experiments made by the author, and several well-known rose growers under his instructions, with the rose 'Mme. Ulrich Brunner' it is concluded that the following is the most perfect system of manuring roses out of doors. In the autumn give a little cow manure, and in the spring sow on each square metre 50 grammes precipitated bone phosphate, 30 grammes burnt horn, 10 grammes dried meat, 10 grammes dried blood. Fork this in. From June 15 water the plants with a solution of 1 gramme per litre of the following mixture:—50 per cent. phosphate of ammonia, 50 per cent. nitrate of ammonia.—*M. L. H.*

Roses, New Hybrid (*Le Jardin*, vol. xxi. No. 499, p. 355; December 5, 1907).—M. Cochet-Cochet has listed four new hybrids of *Rosa rugosa*, produced by M. Gravereaux at the Roseraie de L'Haye.

1. 'Madeleine Fillot' ('Reine des Iles Bourbon' × 'Perle des Jardins' × *Rugosa germanica*). Extremely vigorous growth; pink flowers.

2. 'Madame Tiret' ('Pierre Notting' × 'Cardinal Pattrizi' × *Rugosa germanica*). Vigorous reddish-purple shoots, crimson flowers, silvery-pink on the reverse.

3. 'Madame René Gravereaux' ('Conrad Ferdinand Meyer' × 'Safrano'). Very vigorous grower; flowers highly scented; delicate rose-tinged lilac.

4. 'Monsieur Bienvêtu' ('Pierre Notting' × 'Safrano' × 'Conrad Ferdinand Meyer'). Very vigorous; a superb hybrid; bright salmon-pink flowers, with deeper shades recalling the colouring of its ancestors.

F. A. W.

Roses: Wichuraiana Hybrids (*Rev. Hort.* January 16, 1907, p. 31).—Barbier & Co., Orleans, have obtained five fine forms: (*W.* × 'Madame Laurette Messimy'), very vigorous and floriferous; flowers double, milk white, 3½-4 inches diameter; 'Jean Guichard' (*W.* × 'Souvenir de Catherine Guillot'), of similar habit; flowers 3-3½ inches across, very double carmine-salmon turning to carmine (a new colour in this section); 'Joseph Billard' (*W.* × 'Madame Eugène Resal'), vigorous,. flowers 3-3½ inches diameter, dazzling carmine; 'François Jauranville' (*W.* × 'Madame Laurette Messimy'), very large double flowers, bright rose; and 'Joseph Lamy' (same cross), flowers semidouble, porcelain white, slightly pink when opening.—*C. T. D.*

Rubber Cultivation in the West Indies (*Journ. Imp. Dep. Agr. W.I.* 1907).

—The records of the rubber industry reported to the West Indian Agricultural Conference, 1907, include the following:

Rubber Cultivation in Jamaica. By Hon. T. H. Sharp, Jamaica (*Journ. Imp. Dep. Agr. W.I.* 1907, 2).—Being suggestions as to soils, species of rubber-plants, &c., consequent on rubber cultivation being taken up seriously in Jamaica by several planters.

Progress of Rubber Industry in Trinidad. By J. H. Hart, F.L.S. (*Journ. Imp. Dep. Agr. W.I.* 1907, 2).—After noting that in 1901 there were six different kinds of rubber plants in experimental cultivation, it proceeds to record that since that period Castilloa rubber planting had steadily continued, and had done well in all parts of Trinidad, and appears to suit the conditions of soil and climate.

Other notices are given of Hevea or Para rubber and other kinds, ending with the statement that the rubber industry is now well established in Trinidad, and there is a prospect of abundant success.

Rubber in British Guiana. By Hon. B. Howell Jones (*Journ. Imp. Dep. Agr. W.I.* 1907, 2).—Chiefly indicating the species of rubber trees which are indigenous, such as species of the genus *Sapium*, and to some extent of *Hevea*, with suggestions that the only rubber trees of the colony worth consideration are certain species of *Sapium*. This genus belongs to that large family of plants, the *Euphorbiaceae*, to which *Hevea, Manihot*, &c., also belong.

Summary of Results of Tapping Rubber Trees in Dominica and St. Lucia.

These experiments chiefly have reference to trees of *Castilloa*, and three questions are proffered to form the basis of future experiments.

1. Which system of tapping will give the maximum yield of rubber for the labour employed?

2. Can *Castilloa* be repeatedly tapped by successively paring the lower edges of the original incisions, as is practised on *Hevea* in Ceylon?

3. How frequently this or any other method of tapping may be safely and profitably employed?—*M. C. C.*

Rusts, The Cereal. i. The Development of their Uredo mycelia.

By J. B. Pole Evans (*Ann. Bot.* vol. xxi. October 1907, pp. 441–463; 4 plates).—The author has undertaken a comparative histological study of the rust fungi (*Uredineae*) which attack cereals. In the present communication he brings forward his observations on the uredo stage of the parasites.

He distinguishes three phases in the development of a uredine: (1) the attack by the parasite on its host, or the first phenomenon of occupation; (2) the course taken after occupation by the further growth

3 c 2

of the parasite; and (3) the reaction of the host after occupation, and the subsequent reciprocal action of host and parasite. The present paper deals chiefly with the first of these stages. In infection two steps are recognised—entry or inoculation and infection. *Inoculation* includes the entry of the germ tube through the stomatal opening, and the formation under the latter of the substomatal vesicle. *Infection* is the production of infecting hyphae from the substomatal vesicle which apply themselves closely to the internal cells of the host plant and send into them their haustoria. Thus a plant may be inoculated by a fungus spore, but infection may not follow.

The author gives details of the histology of nine species of rusts and sums up his results at the end in tabular form. He finds considerable variation displayed by the germ-tube, appressorium, substomal vesicle haustoria, and hyphae, but he shows at the same time that each set of infection phenomena is of a very definite nature for each species of uredo.—*A. D. C.*

Saccolabium rubescens.   By R. A. Rolfe (*Bot. Mag.* tab. 8121).— Nat. ord. *Orchidaceae*; tribe *Vandeae*; Annam. Erect epiphyte, 1 foot high; flowers ¾ inch long, light rose-purple; spur ½ inch long.—*G. H.*

Salvia splendens 'Surprise.'   By G. T. Grignan (*Rev. Hort.* June 16, 1907, pp. 279–281; coloured plate and 1 woodcut).—The plate represents three Salvias, one of which, *S. splendens*, is of an extremely vivid scarlet and very floriferous, while *S. s.* 'Surprise' is similar, with pinnatifid, finely variegated leaves, centre yellow, edges green.—*C. T. D.*

San José Scale.   By H. T. Fernald (*U.S.A. Exp. Stn. Mass., Bull.* 116; March 1907).—An outline of the life-history of this pest and the injuries caused by it, together with a summary of experimental work in other stations. At this station a variety of caustic washes, crude petroleum, emulsified kerosene, and lime-sulphur-salt wash have been tried, and, all things considered, the last gave the best results. The crude oil and kerosene emulsions killed the scale, but injury was caused to the trees after a few sprayings. The chemical composition of the lime-sulphur-salt spray is given as follows :—

Substances	Per cent. in fresh wash	Per cent. after 12 hours	Per cent. after 120 hours
Calcium monosulphide, CaS, and calcium hydrosulphide, $Ca(SH)_2$	25–30		21–26
Calcium polysulphides, CaS_3, CaS_4, CaS_5 . .	3–5		2–3
Calcium hydrate, $Ca(OH)_2$	9	8·5	7
Calcium carbonate, $CaCO_3$	1·8	2·3	2·8
Calcium sulphite, $CaSO_3$	0	1	2
Calcium thiosulphate, CaS_2O_3 . . .		0·5	0·8
Calcium sulphate, $CaSO_4$			0·2

With the exception of the hydrate, carbonate, and sulphate, which have no insecticidal value, each of the other compounds was tried separately. The experiments were not conclusive, as they were not tried upon a sufficiently extensive scale; but the calcium monosulphide and calcium sulphite failed to improve the condition of the trees, and the hydrosulphide gave little better results ; the weak thiosulphate gave fair results, the strong thiosulphate better, and the polysulphides are about equal to the thiosulphate in insecticidal power. None of the compounds singly gave such good results as the complete mixture.—*F. J. C.*

Seaside Planting. By H. W. Trevince (*Gard. Chron.* No. 1084, p. 242, October 5, 1907.)—The author enumerates various plants which are suitable for exposed positions near the sea. He says : " In almost all cases the plants should be thoroughly hardened before being planted in their permanent quarters ; the more exposed the position the more necessary it is to carefully prepare the soil before planting."—*G. S. S.*

Selaginellas. By G. T. Grignan (*Rev. Hort.* November 16, 1907, pp. 515–18 ; 6 illustrations).—An interesting list of this genus, with cultural advice.—*C. T. D.*

Shortia uniflora. By W. Watson (*Bot. Mag.* tab. 8166).—Nat. ord. *Diapensiaceae* ; tribe *Galacineae* ; Japan. Evergreen, creeping undershrub, 3–6 inches high ; leaves petiolate, orbicular, cordate ; scapes numerous, 1-flowered ; flowers $1\frac{1}{2}$–$1\frac{3}{4}$ inch diameter ; corolla broadly campanulate, pink, toothed.—*G. H.*

Smudge Fires. By Mr. Handly (*Trans. Hort. Soc. Illinois*, 1905, p. 111).—To lessen danger from severe spring frosts what are called "smudge fires" are made in Missouri and Florida—trimmings of trees piled up with straw on top and manure above that, lighted and burnt slowly, have saved apple and orange crops from destruction.—*C. H. L.*

Solanum Commersonii. By Paul Vincey (*Jour. Soc. Nat. Hort. Fr.*, 4th Series, vol. viii. ; February 1907).—*Solanum Commersonii*, lately discovered wild in Uruguay, has been by some people identified with the potato of the French variety ' Géante Bleue.' Experiments have, however, been made with *Commersonii* and two varieties of potato, ' Géante Bleue ' and ' Richter Imperator ' on the sewage farm at Achère, with the result that *Commersonii* proves to be a distinct plant, to be useful in itself, unusually resistant to mildew, and able to support great extremes of wet and drought.—*M. L. H.*

Soy Bean Varieties. By C. R. Ball (*U.S.A. Exp. Stn., Bur. Pl. Ind., Bull.* 98 ; May 1907 ; 5 plates).—The soy bean (*Glycine hispida* Maxim.), an annual leguminous plant, is becoming more and more cultivated in the States, while it forms the principal crop of its kind in China and Japan. This well-illustrated bulletin gives detailed descriptions and a classification of the known varieties based primarily upon the seed, which varies in colour considerably. Other points considered of differential value are the length of time taken to reach maturity, the height of the plant, and the size of the seed. Those varietal names that are synonymous are indicated.—*F. J. C.*

Spiraeas, Herbaceous. By G. B. Mallett (*Gard. Chron.* No. 1084, p. 243, October 5, 1907, and p. 260, October 12).—A large number of species belonging to this genus are described and commented on.

G. S. S.

Spraying. By Albert Dickens and Robt. E. Eastman (*U.S.A. Exp. Stn. Kansas, Bull.* 145; April 1906; 7 figs.).—The various materials used in spraying are briefly discussed, and it is found that the most satisfactory combination of insecticide and fungicide is Bordeaux mixture and arsenate of lead. The various means of operating the pump are described—viz., spray-pumps operated by hand, air-pressure, carbonic gas, gasolene engine. Preparations for spraying should be made sufficiently early in the year in order to ensure the obtaining of materials of guaranteed quality. The effect of spraying is shown to result in a large increase of sound fruit, and the sprayed orchards have suffered no injury from insect or fungoid pests. A spray calendar is then given, with formulas for the preparation of the principal insecticides and fungicides.—*C. H. H.*

Spraying. By A. V. Schermerhorn (*Trans. Hort. Soc. Illinois*, 1905, p. 333).—Spraying is essential in apple and peach orchards. The Bordeaux mixture should be used, plus Paris green, as insecticide, and the 4-4-4 formula has been found most satisfactory, viz., 4 lb. lime, 4 lb. copper sulphate, and 4 oz. of Paris green to fifty gallons of water. To get a perfect mixture, dissolve the lime and copper sulphate separately, each in twenty-five gallons of water. Then pour together into a third receptacle and add poison. This ensures thorough mechanical mixture and better suspension.

It is best that the lime should be newly slaked (not a stock solution), the Paris green should be pure, and the copper sulphate dissolves most rapidly when suspended in the water and barely covered by it. Spray three times at least, first in " the pink of the bloom," when buds are just showing pink before they open. This is for apple-scab and fungoid diseases. Secondly, when the petals first begin to fall. Thirdly, ten days later, when the petals fall readily. The two latter are against codling-moth. It should be done steadily year after year, as much in private orchards as in commercial, and is equally beneficial for peach-leaf curl.

Anything under forty acres can be done with a hand-pump, but for larger areas a power-engine of some sort will be required.—*C. H. L.*

Spraying Apples : Relative Merits of Liquid and Dust Applications. By Charles S. Crandall (*U.S.A. Exp. Stn. Illinois, Bull.* 106; February 1906; 11 figs.).—The results of experiments have shown that Bordeaux mixture, applied with arsenites as a dust spray, have only two advantages over liquid spray: (i.) that it is about 50 per cent. cheaper; (ii.) is easier to transport about the orchard. Beyond this it has no advantages whatever, it being absolutely ineffective as a preventive of the attacks of fungi—notably apple-scab and fruit-blotch —and is much less effective as an insecticide than is the liquid method of applying arsenites. The workmen employed were unanimous in choosing liquid spraying, as being less disagreeable than the dust spray.

C. H. H.

Spraying Experiments. By Professor C. S. Crandall (*Trans. Hort. Soc. Illinois*, 1905, pp. 251-266).—Foliage injury following the use of Bordeaux mixture, either alone or in combination with Paris green, is of rather common occurrence in commercial practice.

All care having been taken in mixing and application, the injury in these cases may probably be attributable to atmospheric conditions and mostly to showers of rain.

It not infrequently happens that leaves thoroughly coated with Bordeaux mixture will remain healthy for several weeks, when all at once, following a shower, serious injury will develop. It is supposed that the carbon dioxide in the atmosphere has been at work, slowly converting the insoluble copper hydroxide upon the leaves into the normal soluble copper sulphate, which upon the addition of moisture is absorbed by the leaves with resulting poisonous action.—*C. H. L.*

Spray, Liquid and Dust, Relative Merits of. By Professor C. S. Crandall (*Trans. Hort. Soc. Illinois*, 1906. p. 547).—Experiments seem to show that liquid spraying is superior to dust. The latter does not arrest apple-scab, which develops freely on dust-sprayed trees ; the same is observed with fruit-blotch.

The percentage of windfalls is also highest when dust spraying is resorted to, and the leaves fall early, thus arresting development.

C. H. L.

Sterilisation of Soil. By G. Abbey (*Gard. Chron.* No. 1053, p. 129, March 2; No. 1054, March 9 ; and No. 1056, March 23, 1907).—Sterilisation of the soil is a very interesting but not a very simple matter, for all the organisms in soils are not injurious to crops, but some are very beneficent, and without them the soil would indeed be sterile. In this article the matter is fully discussed, and the conclusion come to is that, while steam is the best means for the destruction of various animal and vegetable pests in the soil, care must be taken not to raise the temperature above 140° or 160° F., for fear of killing the useful micro-organisms. Worms, insects, millipedes, mites, woodlice, slugs and snails, are unable to withstand a temperature above 125° F. and most fungi are killed at a temperature 10° higher.—*G. S. S.*

Stewartia Malachodendron. By W. B. Hemsley (*Bot. Mag.* tab. 8145).—Nat. ord. *Ternstroemiaceae* ; Eastern North America. Branching shrub, 6–14 feet high ; leaves 2–4 inches long ; flower solitary, $3\frac{1}{2}$–4 inches diameter ; petals white.—*G. H.*

Strawberry-bed after First Fruiting. By J. Friend (*Trans. Hort. Soc. Illinois*, 1905, p. 345).—When grown on a large scale, as soon as the last berries are gathered, the beds should be mown, then raked and cleared of rubbish. The ground should then be well stirred between the rows and thoroughly harrowed.

The bed will look bare at first, but strong growth soon follows. The beds are only kept three years, and are well manured before planting.

C. H. L.

Strawberry, New Hybrid. By A. P. (*Le Jardin*, vol. xxi. No. 490, p. 221 ; July 20, 1907 ; 1 fig.).—'Mme. Charles Moutot,' from 'Docteur Morère' and 'Royal Sovereign.' Specially recommended for forcing.

F. A. W

Streptocarpus Holstil. By W. Watson (*Bot. Mag.* tab. 8150).—
Nat. ord. *Gesneraceae*; tribe *Cyrtandreae*; East Tropical Africa. A
slender branching herb, 18 inches high; flowers mauve-purple, with a
white throat, 1–1⅓ inch long.—*G. H.*

Sugar-cane Experiments in West Indies (*Journ. Imp. Dep.
Agr. W.I.* 1907, 1).—This bulletin contains Reports of the West Indian
Agricultural Conference, 1907, with reprints of papers read, chiefly of
local interest, including—
    Seedling Canes in Jamaica. By the Hon. H. H. Cousins, M.A.,
F.C.S.
    Sugar-cane Experiments in the Leeward Islands. By the Hon.
Francis Watts, C.M.G., D.S., F.C.S.
    Sugar-cane Experiments in Barbados. By J. R. Bovell, F.L.S.,
F.C.S.
    Breeding Hybrid Sugar-canes. By F. A. Stockdale, B.A.
    The Rational Use of Manures for Sugar-cane in Jamaica. By
Hon. H. H. Cousins, M.A., F.C.S.
    Selective Cane-reaping in Jamaica. By Mrs. A. Charley, Jamaica.
    The Polarimetric Determination of Sucrose. By Hon. Francis Watts
C.M.G., D.S., F.C.S., and H. A. Tempany, B.Sc., F.I.C., F.C.S.
    Jamaica Rum. By Hon. H. H. Cousins, M.A., F.C.S.

                                                    M. C. C.

Tamarix pentandra. By O. Stapf (*Bot. Mag.* tab. 8138).—Nat ord.
Tamaricaceae; tribe *Tamariceae*; South-Eastern Europe and Orient.
Flowers in panicles, rose-coloured or white.—*G. H.*

Tampico Fibre. By A. Ravaioli (*Bull. R. Soc. Tosc. Ort.* 9,
1907, p. 265).—This fibre, known also as *istle* or *ixtle*, is obtained
principally from certain varieties of Agave. The name *istle* is the
native name, while the former name is due to its being exported, at
least in part, from Tampico, on the Gulf of Mexico. It is obtained
from four or five different species of plants growing on the arid region
of Southern Mexico—viz., in the western part of the State of Tamanlipas
(from 1,500 to 4,000 feet above the sea), in sterile, calcareous soils.
Three kinds are known in commerce: the Jaumave, the Tula, and the
Palma. The Jaumave is the best quality, and is obtained from *Agave
lophantha.* The part of the plant yielding the fibre is the central apical
mass of youngest leaves. The leaves are transported by mules two
days' journey across country to Vittoria. This quality of *istle* is
20–40 inches long, whitish in colour, flexible, and strong like *sisal* or
hemequen, also from a species of Agave, but with which the *istle*
must not be confused. The Tula *istle* is from *Agave Lechuguilla,*
which abounds not only in Mexico but also in Texas and New Mexico;
it is white, but only 12–20 inches long, and hence not so highly prized
as the former kind. A third variety, whose commercial value is about
that of the last-named, is obtained from a plant called in Mexico a
palm (*Samuella carncrosana*), one of the Liliaceae. It has a stem
6–15 inches in diameter and a bundle of pointed leaves 20–80 inches
long. Another plant producing this same variety of fibre is *Yucca*

Treculeana, found at Cohanila and Nueva Leon. The fibre is obtained from the young leaves, which are boiled from two to four hours in order to extract the pulp. These fibres are 15–25 inches long. Almost all of it is exported to the United States, where the importation has increased from 4,000 tons in 1900 to 14,597 tons in 1906, to the value of 1,327,352 dollars. The cost per ton is 91 dollars.

The actual prices on the New York market are :—

Jaumave istle	$5\frac{5}{8}$ to $5\frac{3}{4}$ cents per lb.
Tula istle.	5 ,, $5\frac{1}{4}$,,
Palma istle	$5\frac{3}{8}$,, $5\frac{1}{2}$,,

Tampico fibre has long been used in place of animal bristles for making brushes. It is also largely used for pack-thread and cordage.

W. C. W.

Tchihatchewia isatidea, Bois. Anon. (*Gard. Chron.* No. 1089, p. 325, November 9, 1907 ; figs. 129 and 130).—This curious plant is a native of the mountains at the source of the Euphrates. It was awarded a botanical certificate by the Scientific Committee of the Royal Horticultural Society on April 20, 1907, when a fine specimen was shown in flower by Viscountess Emlyn. It belongs to the order Cruciferae, but might easily, it is said, be mistaken for a member of the Boragineae. It is a dwarf-growing perennial plant, up to 10 inches in height, with a corymb of red-rose flowers 4 inches in diameter, which are distinctly fragrant. Directions are given for pronouncing the name of this plant, which most persons will find useful.—*G. S. S.*

Thalictrum, The Species of. By G. B. Mallett (*Gard. Chron.* No. 1032, February 23, 1907). The author gives descriptions of the different species and varieties of this genus, some of which are "confidently recommended for the flower border, rock garden, waterside, and woodland."—*G. S. S.*

Tobacco Plants (Nicotiana) (*Rev. Hort.* February 1, 1907, p. 53).—Culture of *N. affinis* and other ornamental flowering Nicotianas interdicted by Customs law relating to dutiable tobaccos, no discrimination being specified.—*C. T. D.*

Tuna as Food for Man, The. By D. Griffiths and R. F. Hare (*U.S.A. Dep. Agr., Bur. Pl. Ind., Bull.* 116 ; December 1907 ; 6 plates ; and *Exp. Stn., New Mexico, Bull.* 64 ; April 1907 ; 7 plates).—The former of these two bulletins is practically a reprint of the latter. A very full account of the species of *Opuntia* which produce edible fruits is given. 'Tuna' is the Spanish American synonym of the English 'Indian fig,' the American and Australian 'prickly pear,' the 'Barbary fig' of the French and the 'higos chumbos' of Spain. In Mexico, Texas, and Sicily the plant is regarded with great favour, but it is reviled in Australia, South Africa, and India. The following note, in view of various magazine articles on "spineless" cacti, is worth quoting. "All the so-called spineless forms (the fruit of which is not spineless, however) concerning which there is definite knowledge, are less hardy, especially under conditions of drought, than spiny native forms." And again : " The spineless forms . . . require considerable precipitation at some time during the year, and economic species are not known which thrive under a minimum temperature of less than 10° F." It is evident that the spineless forms have a very limited range of cultivation. The plants in Mexico are propagated, when any attempt at cultivation is made at all, by cuttings of two and a half or three joints, and from these a crop of fruit is produced in three years. Not only are they planted in orchards, but the most prickly forms on the hillsides. The fruits are sold and eaten in the markets after being peeled. The price varies according to locality and variety, but sometimes as many as twenty fruits are to be bought for a cent. The fruits are fully described and chemical analyses given of the different portions. The mode of harvesting is also alluded to, and a description given of the machinery used in making tuna products. The products described are 'Miel de Tuna,' a sort of fruit syrup ; 'Melcocha,' somewhat like the foregoing, but becoming candied more quickly ; 'Queso de Tuna,' or tuna cheese ; 'Colonche,' a fermented drink which will not keep ; and dried tunas, the thinly peeled fruits dried in the sun. The principal varieties are described in simple language, and for the botanical descriptions the reader is referred to Bulletin 60 of the New Mexico Exp. Stn. (see ' Prickly Pear,' above). The species of which the fruit is used are *Opuntia Larreyi* Weber ; *O. robusta* Wendl. ; *O. streptacantha* Lem. ; *O. leucotricha* DC. ; *O. Lindheimeri* Engelm. ; *O. Engelmannii* var. *cycloides* E. & B. ; *O. Engelmannii* var. *cuija* G. & H. ; *O. laevis* (?) Coulter ; *O. phaeacantha* Engelm. ; *O. macracantha* Engelm. ; *O. imbricata* DC., and some other species at present undetermined. The fruit of *Echinocereus stramineus* Engelm. is also described under the name of Mexican strawberry, and this also is edible.—*F. J. C.*

Vegetables for the Table, Preparation of. By Maria Parloa (*U.S.A Dep. Agr., Bull.* 256).—A collection of recipes for cooking, which seem practical and good, together with the nutritive value of vegetables as food and the changes undergone in cooking. Some appetising recipes for vegetable soups are included, as well as salads and salad dressing. Amongst the vegetables enumerated are green peppers, okra, egg-plant, squash, and green corn.—*C. H. L.*

Vegetable Growing in Porto Rico. By H. C. Henricksen (*Agr. Exp. Stn. Porto Rico, Bull.* 7 ; illustrated).—European methods of cultivation applied to vegetables in Porto Rico are not always successful, and have to be modified ; but this necessity once recognised and acted upon, vegetables of very good quality can be produced, climatic and soil conditions being on the whole favourable.—*C. H. L.*

Viburnum Carlesii. By W. B. Hemsley (*Bot. Mag.* tab. 8114).— Nat. ord. *Caprifoliaceae* ; tribe *Sambuceae* ; Corea. A dwarf shrub ; leaves ovate rotundate ; cymes dense, 2–3 inches diameter ; corolla pink and white.—*G. H.*

Vines, Experiments in Pruning. By Gustave Rivière (*Jour. Soc. Nat. Hort. Fr.* ; 4th Series, vol. viii. ; July 1907).—The following table represents the results, in sugar content of the must, of some experiments made by M. Bailhache and the author. Grapes were chemically analysed from canes of the variety 'Golden Chasselas,' which had been pinched off above the first, second, third, and fourth leaf respectively, after the second bunch of grapes.

Grammes of	0 leaf.	1 leaf.	2 leaves.	3 leaves.	4 leaves.
Sugar per litre of must	70 grs.	100 grs.	131·2 grs.	141·9 grs.	145·8 grs.
Acidity expressed in sulphuric acid, H_2So_4, per litre of must	60·5 grs.	55 grs.	49·5 grs.	43 9 grs.	36·3 grs.

M. L. H.

Vitality of Seed. By E. H. Jenkins (*U.S.A. Exp. Stn. Conn., Rep.* 1906, pp. 395–397).—The average vitality of onion seeds for thirteen consecutive years was 77·7 per cent., that in 1903 being only 62 per cent. owing to the wet and cold summer. Californian seed gives a higher percentage of vitality than Connecticut seed, and the vitality decreases with age, as shown in the following table :—

Alleged age of seed.	Connecticut grown.		California grown.	
	No. of samples.	Per cent. sprouted.	No. of samples.	Per cent. sprouted.
1 year	573	75·38	215	89·55
2 years . . .	122	61·81	128	79·08
3 years . . .	24	21·90	20	57·53
4 years . . .	1	59·50	1	10·00

F. J. C.

Woburn Wash, The. By Spencer Pickering (*Gard. Chron.* No. 1051, February 16, 1907).—This wash, which is a caustic one, containing paraffin, is the result of many experiments made with a view of obtaining such a wash in which the paraffin will not separate from the other ingredients. This has been effected, and the wash may be made as follows :—" Take sulphate of iron (copperas), or sulphate of copper (blue vitriol), 1½ lb. ; quicklime, 6 oz. ; paraffin, 5 pints ; caustic soda, 2 lb. ; water, 9½ gallons. Dissolve the sulphate of iron or copper in the water by suspending it in a bag of sacking over night ; at the same time put the lime into a jar with enough water to not quite cover it ; next day, when the sulphate is dissolved and the lime slaked, add a little more water to the latter to make it into a milk, and pour it into the sulphate solution ; add the paraffin and churn the mixture with a garden syringe ; one or two strokes of the syringe are sufficient to produce a perfect emulsion. The soda may then be added and the whole mixed well together ; if the soda is in the powdered form, it may be added while solid to the water ; if it be in large lumps, it should be dissolved separately in a little water reserved for that purpose." An account is then given of how this wash may be modified to suit certain circumstances.

G. S. S.

Wood Ashes and Acid Phosphates, Effect of, on Yield and Colour of Apples. By U. P. Hedrick (*U.S.A. Exp. Stn. New York, Bull.* 289 ; 4/1907). A record of experiments on this point extending over twelve years is given, but the results are inconclusive, since it is evident that the soil of the orchard was not deficient in the food substances supplied, despite the fact that the trees had been planted forty-three years before the experiment began.—*F. J. C.*

Yews, Golden and Variegated. By J. C. (*Gard. Chron.* No. 1087, p. 289, October 26, 1907).—The yew almost rivals the common holly in the number of its cultivated varieties; some forty varieties are now in cultivation, and twenty having coloured foliage are here described. Most of these varieties are increased by grafting on the common yew; cuttings, as a rule, do not grow freely, and the plants remain dwarf and stunted for years. Full information is given as to the best means for their cultivation.—*G. S. S.*

EXTRACTS FROM THE PROCEEDINGS

OF THE

ROYAL HORTICULTURAL SOCIETY.

GENERAL MEETING.

JANUARY 8, 1907.

Sir ALBERT ROLLIT, LL.D., in the Chair.

Fellows elected (49).—John Angles, Miss Lily Antrobus, N. Baggesen, Miss Baker-Baker, A. Lister-Blow, F.R.M.S., Miss M. Brandreth, Joshua Brummitt, J. Bullock, J. Chinnery, W. Colson, Miss Crosse, G. S. Damsell, Mrs. Davidson of Dess, C. Day, J. Day, W. Fortescue, F. G. Graham, Reuben Gray, J. Gregory, Hon. A. Grosvénor, Mrs. Hammond, F. H. Harvey, Mrs. A. M. Henderson, Miss Hildyard, L. D. Hyland, Miss D. H. Kitson, Miss M. Lancaster, Capt. Liddon, Mrs. C. E. Lloyd, J. McAndrew, Mrs. A. Monsley, G. P. Mudge, A.R.C.S., Edmund Pelly, W. T. Phillips, Mrs. M. O. Pritt, Mrs. W. H. Purchase, Guy Repton, A. J. Robbins, S. Roberts, jun., T. E. Sedgwick, Miss Shreeve, N. W. Strong, Mrs. Tallent, A. Tatham, H. H. Trevithick, S. Turnbull, Mrs. A. S. Wellby, Mrs. C. H. Wray, Miss E. Wyndham.

Fellows resident abroad (4).—Capt. Archibald D. Campbell (Guernsey), P. C. Guha (India), H. J. Trimmell (British Columbia), H. Wartmann (Switzerland).

Associates (3).—Miss H. Colt, W. J. Fitzwater, J. W. Ward.

A lecture on "The Introduction of the American Gooseberry Mildew into England" was given by Mr. E. S. Salmon, F.L.S.

GENERAL MEETING.

JANUARY 22, 1907.

The late Dr. MAXWELL T. MASTERS, F.R.S., in the Chair.

Fellows elected (52).—John L. Angles, Miss Badcock, H. Blake, Miss L. N. Bovill, Miss H. B. Callander, A. Clout, Mrs. C. Cockroft, Miss E. Cole, Mrs. H. H. Coles, J. D. Colledge, Lady Compton-Thornhill, Miss Darwin, Miss B. Joubert de La Ferté, E. Duquesnoy, A. Evans, R. P. Evans, J.P., Mrs. F. Glennie, J. M. Gregg, Dr. E. T. Hale, Mrs. Hallward, Mrs. E. C. Hannen, Miss Heath, H. Hemus, Miss C. B. Henty,

z

Miss M. Howard, A. R. Hunt, Mrs. Jago, Percy P. Jordan, H. H. König, Miss Louise Legg, P. P. Leschallas, Mrs. Lescher, J. A. Marfell, W. Matthews, Mrs. F. Newman, Mrs. F. R. Pelly, Mrs. C. J. Pemberton, T. Power, Mrs. Lucy J. Radcliffe, Mrs. E. Seth-Smith, A. Skinner, H. F. Sleap, C. Soar, Mrs. C. M. Somerville, Mrs. Taylor, F. C. Tilley, Mrs. L. A. Tilley, R. L. Tucker, Mrs. F. Turle, Mrs. E. Whitmore, J. J. Williamson, G. U. Yule.

Societies affiliated (2).—New Romney Gardeners' Society, King William's Town and District.

A lecture on "Some Aspects of Fruit-growing in Japan," by Mr. N. Matsui, Director of Agriculture in Tokio, was read by the Secretary.

ANNUAL GENERAL MEETING.

FEBURARY 12, 1907.

Sir TREVOR LAWRENCE, Bart., K.C.V.O. (President of the Society), in the Chair.

Fellows elected (95).—Miss K. A. M. Adams, Miss Baird, Mrs. H. Beaumont, G. B. Behrens, C. Benger, Miss N. Benson, Mrs. F. G. Berkeley, C. M. Bevan, Lady Bickersteth, W. E. T. Bolitho, Mrs. F. W. Bovill, Dr. R. Boxall, Mrs. W. Briscoe, H. I. Bromilow, E. C. Brown, Miss M. Butler, J. Campbell, M.A., Mrs. I. Carson, Mrs. Chanter, Mrs. C. Charrington, P. S. Cleave, G. J. Cookson, Miss G. Cotton-Browne, Mrs. Crompton, Dr. H. D. Crook, Mrs. A. Cummins, W. Dennis, A. Dimmock, Miss C. M. Dixon, Mrs. Donaldson-Hudson, Mrs. Eley, George Evans, R. E. Evans, Miss M. J. Eve, Mrs. Evelyn, Miss M. A. Finnie, Major F. C. Fowler, Miss Gardiner, W. T. Gepp, Frank Giles, W. H. Goschen, Rev. Dr. J. Gow, Mrs. Greathead, Miss M. J. Hawkins, W. H. Hawthorne, W. Hewin, Miss A. K. Hincks, A. B. Hindmarsh, Mrs. How, Miss E. D. Hunt, Mrs. M. C. Jolliffe, W. Jordan, H. Kent, J. C. Kenward, Miss E. M. Kingdom, W. H. C. Lewis, J. J. MacDonald, Mrs. D. M. MacDonald, Mrs. G. Mair, H. Maugham, Mrs. R. Menzies, J. W. Mills, T. Case Morris, F. Mount, F. Mühlenkamp, H. W. Murfitt, Mrs. G. Norman, Mrs. Blackett-Ord, F. J. Patmore, Mrs. John Peel, Dr. J. H. Philpot, Mrs. A. Pilley, J. J. Pittman, P. J. Pankerd, H. Quare, A. Quarrell, Mrs. Rich, Mrs. Rogers, A. B. Sanderson, J. B. Seatle, Mrs. Shepherd, G. A. Spratt, H. C. Staples, Miss Swinscow, Miss Taylor, Miss M. M. Taylor, Mrs. Temple, Karl Therkildsen, H. Thomas, J. Vicary, A. Primrose Wells, L. Sackville West, Miss M. Wheeler, H. Wigfull, C. Williams.

Fellows resident abroad (2).—J. Burtt-Davy (Transvaal), J. Jarvis (New Zealand).

Associate (1).—J. P. Leadbetter.

Societies affiliated (3).—Harrow Weald Horticultural Society, Milton Park Horticultural Society, Seven Kings and Goodmayes Horticultural Society.

The President moved the adoption of the Report, which was seconded by Mr. J. Gurney Fowler and carried unanimously.

The following names of President, Vice-Presidents, Members of Council, and Officers having been duly proposed and seconded, and the list circulated in accordance with Bye-Law 74, and no alternative names having been proposed, were declared by the President to be duly elected, viz.—

As new members of Council.—Mr. W. A. Bilney, J.P., Mr. Harry J. Veitch, V.M.H., Mr. Arthur L. Wigan.

As Vice-Presidents.—The Right Hon. Joseph Chamberlain, M.P., the Right Hon. the Earl of Ducie, the Right Hon. Lord Rothschild, Sir John T. Dillwyn-Llewelyn, Bart., Baron Schröder, V.M.H., Sir Frederick Wigan, Bart.

As Officers.—Sir Trevor Lawrence, Bart., K.C.V.O., V.M.H. (President), J. Gurney Fowler, Esq. (Treasurer), Rev. W. Wilks, M.A. (Secretary), A. C. Harper, Esq. (Auditor).

Sir John T. Dillwyn-Llewelyn, Bart., moved a vote of thanks to the President, Sir Trevor Lawrence, Bart., which was seconded by the Rev. W. Wilks, and carried unanimously.

REPORT OF THE COUNCIL

FOR THE YEAR 1906.

1. The One Hundred and Third Year.—The year 1906 has been one of steady progress in every direction.

2. International Conference on Genetics.—The distinguishing mark of the year has been the very successful Conference on Genetics, when upwards of 120 scientific representatives of all nationalities gathered together as the Society's guests. The Council wish to express the very great pleasure which it gave them to welcome these distinguished persons. Special thanks are due, in the first place, to Mr. W. Bateson, F.R.S. V.M.H., for the most able and pleasant way in which he acted as President of the Conference ; and, in the second place, to the Horticultural Club and its President, Sir John Dillwyn-Llewelyn, Bart. ; to our own President, Sir Trevor Lawrence, Bart., K.C.V.O., V.M.H. ; and to Mr. Leopold de Rothschild, for the sumptuous manner in which they entertained the Members of the Conference, at dinner on July 31, and at luncheon on August 1 and 3 respectively. Nor must the kindness of Lieut.-Colonel Prain, F.R.S., the Director of the Royal Gardens, Kew, be forgotten in receiving the foreign guests and other representatives when they visited Kew. The authorities at the Natural History Museum were also very good in personally conducting the party through the galleries and drawing attention to the objects most likely to interest our visitors. One and all vied with each other in their endeavour both to honour our distinguished guests and also to make their visit to England a real pleasure to them ; and it gives the Council peculiar satisfaction to have been assured from all quarters that this endeavour was not in vain. Our foreign visitors went home to their distant countries carrying with them a most pleasant recollection of the geniality and hospitality of the friends and Fellows of the Royal Horticultural Society.

The Report of the Conference which is now almost ready for issue will not be sent to all Fellows as an ordinary volume of the JOURNAL, as its deeply scientific character would, it is thought, fail to interest many. As was stated in the " Notices to Fellows " in the JOURNAL issued soon after Christmas, it will be sent to all who took part in the Conference and to those Fellows who shall have made written request for it before February 1, 1907.

3. **Research Station and Laboratory at Wisley.**—Another feature of the past year has been the actual commencement of the Laboratory and Scientific Research Station at Wisley. The Council have long felt that such a building with a skilled Director and proper equipment was necessary, not only for the investigation of scientific problems practically affecting horticulture, but also in order that the large number of students attending the Gardens might receive a thorough grounding in elementary chemistry, biology, and other allied sciences as applied to the life-history and development of plant-life. The building and its equipment will, it is estimated, entail a capital expenditure of £1,250 to £1,500, and the Council appeal to all Fellows who recognise the great advantages which science can bestow on practical gardening to assist them in meeting this large outlay. In the United States these research stations are built and supported by the Government, but in Great Britain we are entirely dependent on voluntary effort. Mr. Arthur W. Sutton, V.M.H., has most generously promised £100 towards it, and the Council will be pleased to receive any other donations either of money or suitable instruments.

4. **The Finances.**—The very satisfactory Balance Sheet which the Treasurer is able to present proves the finances of the Society to be in a thoroughly sound condition.

5. **The President's Portrait.**—At the last Annual Meeting Sir Trevor Lawrence, Bart., K.C.V.O., V.M.H., completed his twenty-first year as President of the Society, and it was resolved to celebrate the event by inviting all the Fellows to subscribe towards having their President's portrait painted by Professor Herkomer, R.A., to place in the Society's new buildings ; and also by establishing in perpetuity a large gold medal to be called " The Lawrence Medal," to be awarded each year to exhibits of a specially meritorious character. In response to this invitation a sum of over one thousand guineas was received. The portrait has been already hung in the Council Chamber, and the execution of the medal is expected to be finished shortly.

6. **Retiring Members of Council.**—Under Bye-Law 60 Mr. W. A. Bilney, J.P., Mr. A. L. Wigan, and Mr. Harry J. Veitch, V.M.H., the three members of Council who have been longest in office, retire, but are proposed for re-election.

7. **Victoria Medal of Honour.**—During the past year six of the holders of the Victoria Medal of Honour in Horticulture have passed away, and the Council elected Mr. Edwin Beckett, Dr. Augustine Henry, Mr. R. Irwin Lynch, Mr. William Marshall, Mr. Thomas Smith (of Newry), and Mr. Harry J. Veitch, F.L.S., to fill the vacancies.

8. **Annual Progress.**—The following table will show the Society's progress in regard to numerical strength during the past year:—

Loss by Death in 1906.		£	s.	d.
Life Fellows .	. 19 .	. 0	0	0
4 Guineas .	. 3 .	. 12	12	0
2 „ .	. 32 .	. 67	4	0
1 „ .	. 49 .	. 51	9	0
	103	£131	5	0

Loss by Resignation &c.		£	s.	d.
4 Guineas .	. 2 .	. 8	8	0
2 „ .	. 70 .	. 147	0	0
1 „ .	. 544 .	. 571	4	0
Associates .	. 20 .	. 10	10	0
Affiliated Societies	18 .	. 18	18	0
	654	£756	0	0
Total Loss	757	£887	5	0

Fellows elected in 1906.		£	s.	d.
Hon. Members .	7 .	. 0	0	0
4 Guineas .	. 6 .	. 25	4	0
2 „ .	. 480 .	1,008	0	0
1 „ .	. 626 .	. 657	6	0
Associates .	.. 36 .	. 18	18	0
Affiliated Societies	36 .	. 39	18	0
Commutations	16 .}			
= £381 3s. 0d.	.}			
	1,207	£1,749	6	0
Deduct Loss .		. 887	5	0
Net Increase in Income		£862	1	1
New Fellows &c. . .		. 1,207		
Deduct Resignations and Deaths		757		
Numerical Increase during the year 1906		. 450		

The Council are pleased to record that the total number of Fellows, Members, Associates, and Affiliated Societies is now 9,467, which is believed to be the highest number of subscribing Fellows belonging to any Royal Society.

9. **Journal.**—The Report of the Conference of Fruit Growers, held under the joint auspices of the National Fruit Growers' Federation and the Society, in October 1905, was issued in April as a volume (vol. xxx.) of the Society's Journal. Volume xxxi. has been sent out more recently, and the preparation of volume xxxii. is already well advanced. It will be issued about April 1907, after which it is intended to publish the JOURNAL at regular intervals in three four-monthly parts every year.

10. **Handbook on Fungoid Pests.**—Another important publication was the issue last autumn of a monograph on "Fungoid Pests of Cultivated Plants," by Dr. M. C. Cooke, V.M.H., illustrated with coloured plates, and containing figures of 360 different fungoid attacks. Each pest is figured and described separately, and means for its prevention and checking are given, with directions for making the necessary washes and sprays. The volume is handsomely bound in half-calf, and will probably form the standard textbook on the subject for a great number of years. It may be obtained from the Society's Office, price 10s. 6d.

11. **Examinations.**—The Society continues to hold its three annual examinations:—one in General Horticultural Knowledge ; one, for School Teachers, in Cottage and Allotment Gardening ; and one specially for men employed in public parks and gardens. The Reports of the Examiners will be found in the JOURNAL.

12. **The Society's Hall.**—During the past year the Hall has been painted and decorated, and the porch has been enclosed with glass screens and revolving shutters for the prevention of draught. It will be the Council's constant endeavour to keep the building thoroughly up to date by the adoption of such alterations and improvements as may be required for the comfort of the Fellows.

13. Letting of the Hall.—The policy adopted by the Council of making moderate but inclusive charges for hiring the Hall has already been productive of most satisfactory results to the Society's finances, and they are glad to report that the bookings for 1907 are in excess of those for 1906, and several dates in 1908 are already engaged. The Fellows are particularly asked to continue to make known the fact of the Hall being thus available for hire, so as to reduce the pressure of the heavy charges for ground rent, rates, taxes, and other expenditure connected with the building.

14. Shows in 1906.—During the year thirty-three Exhibitions, covering forty-two days, have been provided for the benefit of the Fellows and their friends.

15. The Temple Show.—By the kindness of the Master and Benchers the Society was able to hold its great Show of Flowers for the nineteenth year in succession on May 29, 30, and 31 in the gardens of the Inner Temple, and, despite the unfavourable weather, both the exhibits and the attendance exceeded the average.

16. The Summer Show.—On July 10 and 11 a most successful Show was held in the Park of Holland House by the kindness of Dowager Countess of Ilchester, who has graciously consented to allow the Summer Show to be held there again on July 9 and 10, 1907.

17. Colonial Fruit Shows.—Three Shows of Colonial Fruit and Vegetable products have been held, and the Council have noticed with pleasure that the quality of the exhibits has this year greatly improved. It has been arranged to hold further exhibitions on June 13 and 14, and November 28 and 29, 1907. The object of fixing these dates is, if possible, to suit the season which is most likely to find the produce of Australia, Tasmania, and New Zealand, and of Canada, British Columbia, and the West Indies, in the greatest perfection in London. The policy of holding Shows of Colonial Fruit has been questioned by a few English fruit growers, but the Council ask them to remember that the Society is not for England alone, and that it possesses many Fellows already in Greater Britain over the seas, whose number it is hoped to increase.

18. Awards.—The Council are fully aware (as all Fellows who visit the Society's Shows must also be) how very meritorious the groups of Flowers, Fruits, and Vegetables have been, and how thoroughly, as a rule, they seem to deserve the medals and other awards recommended by the Committees. The Council, therefore, recognise fully the difficulty of the work of the Committees in decreasing the number of medals they recommend. At the same time they feel it their duty to urge very strongly upon all the Committees, and upon each individual member thereof, the necessity of gradually but continually raising the standard of excellence which they set before themselves in recommending awards. The number of awards recommended by the Committees have been :—In 1901, 983 ; in 1902, 1,025 ; in 1903, 1,180 ; in 1904, 1,169 ; in 1905, 1,254 ; in 1906, 1,337 ; and the Council cannot but feel that the continuance of this high and steadily progressing number detracts from, rather than adds to, both the prestige of the Society and the value of each individual award.

19. **Kindred Societies.**—The Council are anxious to place the Hall at the service of any kindred Horticultural Society at the least possible expense to the kindred Society. They think, however, that, considering that the kindred Society by its occupation of the Hall prevents the R.H.S. from making a remunerative letting, the kindred Society should at least defray the establishment expense of the day. They have, therefore, offered any kindred Society : (1) The sole use of the Hall for the sum of £5 5s. a day, which is in reality considerably less than one day's establishment cost; or, (2) The free use of· 600 square feet of tabling on one of the days of the Society's meetings, together with a number of free passes for that day equal to four for each £1 of the subscription income of the kindred Society.

In the former case (1) the Council will lend the kindred Society tabling and put it up and remove it for them free of charge, but the kindred Society must provide their own superintendent and doorkeepers as they take the whole gate money. In case of a kindred Society accepting this offer the Council make no claim for free entry for the R.H.S. Fellows.

Since the Fellows' Tickets for 1907 were printed the Potato Society's Show, announced for October 24 and 25, has been cancelled.

20. **Wisley.**—The new Garden, which was so generously presented to the Society by Sir Thomas Hanbury, V.M.H., K.C.V.O., is gradually getting into thorough working order. A good deal, however, still remains to be done. Various trials of flowers and vegetables have been carried out, and Mr. George Massee, V.M.H., has conducted some original research work.

A contribution of Orchids has been presented to the Gardens by W. A. Bilney, Esq., J.P., George Bunyard, Esq., V.M.H., Major Holford, C.I.E., C.V.O., Sir Trevor Lawrence, Bart., V.M.H., J. S. Moss, Esq., and F. Wellesley, Esq., J.P. It will form the nucleus of, it is hoped, a far larger collection in a few years to come.

The number of visitors to the Gardens admitted by Fellows' tickets during the year 1906 amounted to 8,147, as compared with 5,250 in 1905. This number is exclusive of Horticultural parties, which were admitted by special arrangement, and would bring up the total to over 9,000.

21. **Committees &c.**—The Society continues to be deeply indebted to the Members of the Committees, the Judges, the Lecturers, the Writers of Papers communicated to the JOURNAL, the Compilers of Abstracts, the Examiners, and others who by their self-denying work in its service have largely contributed to its present high position among the practical and scientific societies of the world.

22. **Conclusion.**—In concluding their Report for the past year the Council feel that they may justly congratulate the Fellows on the continued prosperity of the Society and on the indisputable fact that their

Дr.   ANNUAL REVENUE AND EXPENDITURE

						£ s. d.	£ s. d.
To ESTABLISHMENT EXPENSES—							
Ground Rent	...	...	...	...	...	690 0 0	
Rates and Taxes	...	...	...	...	609 0 7	
Water Rate	...	...	...	...	...	53 3 0	
Electric Lighting	...	...	...	...	167 7 9	
Gas	...	...	...	...	...	20 10 2	
Hall Expenses	...	...	...	...	...	31 17 9	
Insurances	...	...	...	...	...	47 18 8	
							1,619 17 11
Salaries and Wages	...	...	...	...	1,424 14 8	
Printing and Stationery	...	...	...	886 17 9	
Postages ...	...	...	...	...	...	375 17 0	
Fuel	...	...	...	...	...	45 19 8	
Audit Fee	...	...	...	...	...	42 12 10	
Repairs and Renewals ...	...	...	...	205 5 1	
Miscellaneous Expenses	...	...	...	328 19 6	
							3,310 6 6
							4,930 4 5
„ JOURNAL, PRINTING AND POSTAGE	...			2,123 17 4
„ DONATIONS TO KINDRED SOCIETIES	...			10 0 0
„ PAINTING ORCHID PICTURES...	...	...		57 19 0
„ LINDLEY LIBRARY	...	...	...	...		6 9 5
„ HYBRID CONFERENCE—							
Amount expended	...	...	...	...	524 17 0	
Less received ...	...	...	...	14 5 6	
							510 11 6
„ SHOWS and MEETINGS—							
Temple Show	...	...	...	...	669 15 6	
Holland Park Show	...	...	...	...	580 19 8	
Special Autumn Show ...	...	...	...	348 19 0	
Labour	...	...	...	...	...	163 11 8	
Expenses of Floral Meetings and Conferences	108 11 7	
							1,871 17 5
„ PRIZES and MEDALS—							
Committee Awards	...	...	...	...		440 10 1
„ WISLEY GARDENS—							
Rates, Taxes, and Insurance	...	...	...	86 15 5	
Superintendent's Salary	...	...	...	225 0 0	
Labour	...	...	...	...	...	755 1 8	
Garden Implements	...	...	...	...	58 3 2	
Loam and Manure	...	...	...	...	194 3 1	
Repairs	...	...	...	...	...	75 15 0	
Fuel	...	...	...	...	...	140 13 0	
Miscellaneous Expenses	...	...	...	213 18 10	
							1,749 10 2
„ COST of GROWING, PACKING, and DISTRIBU-							
TION of PLANTS to FELLOWS	...	...		302 15 8
„ DEPRECIATION—							
Hall Glass Roof, Furniture, Glass Houses,							
Wisley, and Plant and Materials	...	...		482 17 7
„ BALANCE, carried to Balance Sheet	...	...		5,820 4 4
							£18,306 16 11

ACCOUNT for YEAR ending DECEMBER 31, 1906.

Cr.

		£ s. d.	£ s. d.
By ANNUAL SUBSCRIPTIONS			12,313 5 0
„ ENTRANCE FEES			428 7 0
„ DIVIDENDS		572 8 11	
„ INTEREST ON DEPOSIT ACCOUNT		59 4 5	
			631 13 4
„ SHOWS AND MEETINGS—			
Temple Show		1,562 7 1	
Holland Park Show		668 18 1	
Special Autumn Show		121 9 2	
Takings at Hall Shows		268 0 0	
			2,620 14 4
„ JOURNALS—			
Advertisements		590 4 5	
Sale of Journals		120 0 11	
			710 5 4
„ HALL LETTINGS		1,333 2 0	
Less Labour Expenses		108 4 1	
			1,224 17 11
„ PRIZES AND MEDALS			107 15 3
„ EXAMINATIONS in HORTICULTURE—			
Amount received in Fees		104 15 0	
Less expended		68 3 3	
			36 11 9
„ LIFE COMPOSITIONS :			
Being amounts paid by Fellows now deceased			52 10 0
„ WISLEY GARDENS —			
Produce sold		5 9 6	
Students' Fees		42 0 0	
Inspection of Gardens		133 7 6	
			180 17 0

£18,306 16 11

Dr.   **BALANCE SHEET,**

		£ s. d.	£ s. d.

To CAPITAL FUND ACCOUNTS—
  New Hall Building Fund—
      As at December 31, 1905   £26,004 12 4
      Received Since 17 6 6
                                            ——————— 26,021 18 10
      Sale of Chiswick Lease'...   ...   . 4,673 0 0
      Donations, Wisley 39 19 6
      Life Compositions—
          As at December 31, 1905 ...£3,146 9 6
          Received since 381 3 0
                                        —————
                                        3,527 12 6
      Less Fees paid by Fellows
          now deceased 52 10 0
                                            ——————— 3,475 2 6
                                                    ——————— 34,210 0 10
„ SUNDRY CREDITORS 502 6 0
„ SUBSCRIPTIONS &c. paid in advance 368 13 1
„ WISLEY SCHOLARSHIP—
      Amount received 25 0 0
      Less expended 6 5 0
                                            ———————   18 15 0
„ DEPRECIATION AND RENEWALS RESERVE
      ACCOUNT 482 17 7
„ GENERAL REVENUE ACCOUNT—
      Balance, December 31, 1905 ...   . 29,449 9 4
          Less Bad Debts 17 8 3
                                                29,432 1 1
„ REVENUE FOR THE YEAR, as per annexed
      Account 5,820 4 4
                                            ——————— 35,252 5 0

                                            ——————
                                            £70,834 17 11

DECEMBER 31, 1906.   ₡r.

		£ s. d.	£ s. d.
By CAPITAL EXPENDITURE—			
„ NEW HALL AND OFFICES—			
As at December 31, 1905	38,924 5 2		
Expenditure since	1,219 15 6		
		40,144 0 8	
„ FURNISHING THE HALL AND OFFICES—			
As at December 31, 1905	1,760 17 2		
Expenditure since	270 2 10		
		2,031 0 0	
„ DWELLING HOUSES, WISLEY ... · ...		2,236 19 4	
„ GLASS HOUSES AND RANGES, WISLEY ...		3,295 15 2	
„ LABORATORY, WISLEY, on account		275 0 0	
(*Estimated cost* £1,500.)			
		47,982 15 2	
„ PLANT AND MATERIALS—			
Appliances for Shows	236 11 0		
Fittings, Wisley	58 8 6		
Horse and Cart, Wisley	37 0 0		
Fencing and Wire Netting, Wisley	36 15 0		
		368 14 6	
„ SUNDRY DEBTORS		462 14 0	
„ INVESTMENTS—			
2½ % Consols, £10,586 13s. 11d. ... *cost*	9,960 4 9		
(£2,022 8s. 9d. of this sum is held by the			
Society, subject to the provisions of the will			
of the late J. Davis, Esq.)			
3 % Local Loan, £5,800 ... ... *cost*	6,006 16 6		
Indian Rupee Paper, 37,000 Rupees ... „	2,462 14 4		
4 % Canadian Inscribed Stock £2,000 „	2,077 11 0		
		20,507 6 ɩ	
The approximate value of these Investments			
is £19,360.			
„ CASH—			
At Bank	495 9 4		
On Deposit	1,000 0 0		
In Hand	17 18 4		
		1,513 7 ȣ	
		£70,834 17 11	

I have audited the books from which the foregoing Accounts are compiled, and certify that they exhibit a true and correct statement of the position of the Society on December 31, 1906.

ALFRED C. HARPER, F.C.A., *Auditor* (HARPER BROTHERS),
Chartered Accountant, 10 Trinity Square, E.C.

January 15, 1907.

privileges are greater and more valuable than those of any similar institution in the kingdom. At the same time they feel that what has been done in the past will be surpassed in the future, provided the Fellows do not relax their exertions to complete the thorough equipment of Wisley, to increase the roll of Fellows, and otherwise to render such service as they can to the Society in the continued success of which all have an interest.

By Order of the Council,

W. WILKS, Secretary.

ROYAL HORTICULTURAL HALL,
VINCENT SQUARE, WESTMINSTER, S.W.
January 1, 1907.

GENERAL MEETING.

MARCH 5, 1907.

Sir TREVOR LAWRENCE, Bart., K.C.V.O. (President of the Society),
in the Chair.

Fellows elected (71).—S. W. Abbott, A. C. Allen, C. W. Ansdell, E. Arnold, Mrs. W. Barlow, Miss L. J. Barrett, Miss F. W. Barrett, J. E. Berrey, Miss Blacker, Miss Blake, Hon. Mrs. K. P. Bouverie, A. Bull, H. E. Burgess, F. E. Colenso, Mrs. W. E. Crum, J. B. Davies, Mrs. G. Dawber, Miss D. Graves, H. R. Dent, Mrs. E. A. de Paiva, Miss N. de Pass, Rev. G. E. Farran, Mrs. Fuller, W. W. Gott, Mrs. W. Gregory, Mrs. C. J. Gwyer, Mrs. L. Hardy, I. M. Hewlett, F. W. Hibbins, C. J. Holden, H. J. Horn, A. F. Houfton, Miss M. Hulton, Miss Hutchinson, Mrs. Stanley Keith, Mrs. Lawrence, W. L. S. Loat, Mrs. C. P. Markham, Mrs. Martin, J. R. Mattock, F. T. Medcalf, A. Miller, H. B. Munt, J. A. Ord, C. H. Pattisson, Miss M. D. Payne, E. J. E. Pilkington, J. Porter, Miss E. S. Price, Miss Richards, Lady Ripley, G. P. Rose, Mrs. H. A. Satchell, G. Saunders, J. Scouse, T. Scrimshaw, C. D. Seymour, A. D. Sharp, J. Shelton, Dr. Sherrard, Miss C. M. Swinton, Mrs. J. White Todd, Miss V. G. Toler, Miss A. M. Thornton, Miss M. W. Thornton, Mrs. Thorpe, Lady Wenlock, Mrs. H. A. Westmacott, Mrs. G. Wingfield, R. P. Winter, A. Worsley.

Fellows resident abroad (2).—B. Prokash (India), Miss J. C. J. de van Steenwijk (Holland).

Associates (12).—Miss J. Barlow, Miss D. Greaves, Miss N. Hunter, Miss K. K. Mouat, Miss H. Parsons, Miss H. White, Miss G. Richards, Miss N. Singard, W. H. Tanner, Miss M. Selocheur, Miss G. Watkin, H. Whiting.

Societies affiliated (5).—Cheshunt and Waltham Cross; Claygate Flower Show; Lyndhurst, Emery Down, and Bank; Ringwood and District Gardeners'; Storrington and District Horticultural Society.

A lecture on "The True Darwinism" was given by the Rev. Professor G. Henslow, M.A., V.M.H. (see p. 1). .

GENERAL MEETING.

MARCH 19, 1907.

Mr. ALEXANDER DEAN, V.M.H., in the Chair.

Fellows elected (37).—Mrs. Aldersey, Mrs. M. Baillie, J. Bayley, Mrs. M. Bland, W. Biggs, J. Black, Mrs. E. V. Bromley, Mrs. Carroll, A. Chalmers, F. Chambers, Mrs. Charlesworth, S. V. Clirehugh, Miss V. H. Cooper, Miss Cumberlye, R. Findlay, J. B. H. Goodden, Miss E. F. Goodhew, Mrs. W. A. Hill, Miss E. F. Hirst, Miss R. A. H. Hirst, Hon. Lady Keane, Lady Seymour King, Miss Longstaff, A. Masters, Lord Monson, I. Parish, E. Power, Mrs. G. U. Prior, J. Ricks, Mrs. Sanford, R. C. Savill, Mrs. F. Stoop, C. E. Strachan, Miss E. Tarrant, Mrs. E. Walsham, H. J. Wheeler, Mrs. E. A. Winterton.

Fellow resident abroad (1).—A. H. McVey (U.S.A.).

Societies affiliated (2).—Herefordshire Fruit and Chrysanthemum, Farningham Rose and Horticultural Society.

A lecture on "Horticulture in British Guiana" was given by Mr. J. A. Barbour James (see p. 8).

GENERAL MEETING.

APRIL 2, 1907.

The late Dr. MAXWELL T. MASTERS, F.R.S., in the Chair.

Fellows elected (50).—C. M. Allwood, Mrs. Angerstein, Mrs. F. Bayley, Mrs. K. Bentley, T. Bowyer, R. H. Caird, Miss E. Carter, Countess Cavan, Lady Cayley, J. Chappell, G. Cornwallis-West, Mrs. Dauber, J. Ellis, Mrs. E. Grove, Miss Hamilton, H. Hinde, W. R. Hobbs, Mrs. S. Horton, Dr. E. P. Hoyle, Miss Hull, Mrs. I. A. Jameson, M. Keyes, Lady Knightley, H. W. Lawrence, G. Leather-Culley, H. Lewis, R. A. D. Liebert, W. Lockyer, C. N. Marshall, Lady Monson, C. Moore, Miss H. Nightingale, M. Norman, Miss G. Ogle, Rev. E. C. Owen, Mrs. Pelham-Papillon, E. Price-Athelstan, Mrs. H. M. Ridley, Fritz Rock, Mrs. R. Smith, Mrs. T. M. Soper, Miss C. Spalding, S. Stokes, Miss Strong, W. B. Taylor, Mrs. J. Thompson, C. S. Tomes, Miss Turner, J. Westwood, Miss M. Wood.

Society affiliated.—Chorleywood and Chenies Horticultural Society.

A lecture on "Orchid Hybrids and their Parents" was given by Mr. H. J. Chapman, and was illustrated by lantern slides.

GENERAL MEETING.

APRIL 16, 1907.

Mr. ALEXANDER DEAN, V.M.H., in the Chair.

Fellows elected (65).—Miss Aird, C. H. Akroyd, Mrs. Anderson, Lt.-Col. E. W. D. Baird, A. J. Barber, E. Bayley, Mrs. Beddington,

J. Berlein, A. Broake, Miss G. Brooke, P. Burdett-Cunningham, Mrs.
O. Courage, H. Cresswell, H. J. Criddle, G. Edelsten, H. Edlmann,
H. S. Gee, J.P., Mrs. Greatheed, R. Halsey, Mrs. A. G. V. Harrison,
P. S. W. Hemsley, W. Hennell, E. J. Horncastle, T. Howard, J. G.
Howlett, Mrs. Hutchinson, Mrs. F. A. M. Jennings, Miss Kendall,
J. R. Knight, Lady T. T. Laing, Mrs. Lambert, H. Lewis, Mrs. V.
Llewelyn, Mrs. Lowndes, Mrs. MacDonald, I. D. McDougall, A. McNeill
Martin, Mrs. Martin, Lady Medlycott, Miss Miller, Mrs. Miller, W. T. Moore,
Mrs. A. Payne, C. J. Phillips, Col. W. F. Pilter, C.B., Mrs. M. Rea, Hon.
Mrs. Rowley, Miss H. W. Royds, Mrs. B. J. Samuel, W. H. Standwith,
Mrs. M. C. Smith, Mrs. H. C. Tuberville, J. C. Spencer Phillips,
F. C. H. Snead, Mrs. Snelgrove, Mrs. W. Stevens, Hon. Mrs. E. Strutt,
R. Thornton, R. T. Toope, P. S. Tudor, R. G. Upton, W. Walton, Mrs.
Whiteley, John Wort, Miss A. Young.

Societies affiliated (2).—Bargoed Horticultural Society, Ramsey (Isle
of Man) Horticultural Society.

A lecture on " Rainfall in its Relation to Horticulture," illustrated
by lantern slides, was given by Mr. R. H. Curtis, F.R.Met.Soc. (see
p. 12).

GENERAL MEETING.

April 30, 1907.

Mr. W. A. Bilney, J.P., in the Chair.

Fellows elected (50).—R. H. Anderson, Mrs. F. R. Balfour, H. Bed-
dington, G. C. Bond, Mrs. Bosville, H. C. Burnett, Mrs. S. Clucas,
H. Connell, Mrs. K. Corrie, P. Cox, Mrs. C. Dale, Mrs. J. Dickson,
R. Doake, Mrs. J. Duncan, A. G. Gamlin, Miss Garford, Mrs. Graham,
J. C. Gripper, Mrs. C. M. Heriot, Mrs. Hopton, Morris Hudson, Mrs.
Hutchison, A. B. Johnson, A. W. W. Jones, Lord Kesteven, C. Lanton,
C. E. Lyon, Miss A. H. Makant, A. T. Manger, H. R. Marsh, C. S.
Marshall, F. W. Martin, Lord Middleton, W. Mitchell, L. G. Moir, Miss
Morrish, P. Parker, Mrs. Pocock, W. H. Powell, Miss L. Power, Mrs.
B. Quincey, E. B. Sewell, W. Shackleton, M. Stephens, W. J. Stevens,
H. Taylor, H. H. Wallis, Mrs. W. C. Williams, Mrs. J. L. Wood,
A. Wright.

Fellow resident abroad (1).—P. C. Seth (Calcutta).

Associates (2).—F. Blackith, Miss King.

Society affiliated (1).—Exmouth Horticultural Society.

A lecture on " The Law in Relation to Horticulture " was given by
Mr. H. Morgan Veitch (see p. 20).

GENERAL MEETING.

May 14, 1907.

Mr. Harry J. Veitch, F.L.S., V.M.H., in the Chair.

Fellows elected (60).—Mrs. A. M. Arkwright, Lady Alice Ashley,
Col. E. Balfe, A. S. Banks, Mrs. W. A. Bevan, Rev. C. Boden, J. F.

Botterill, Victor Brown, Lady Bruce, L. J. Cook, Hon. H. A. Denison, C. E. Edlmann, H. W. T. Empson, T. Farthing, D. Field, Mrs. Howard Figgis, Hon. Alban G. H. Gibbs, Miss G. M. Gibson, Mrs. Gough, Miss K. Gray, Hon. Mrs. R. C. Grosvenor, W. Grove, Mrs. Hall, Mrs. E. H. Hanson, W. Hunter Hardy, D. S. Harvey, E. I. B. Harvey, Mrs. Haydock, Mrs. Jenkins, R. Jones, R. N. Kenyon, Sir Charles Knowles, Miss M. R. Lane, A. E. Shirley Leggatt, Mrs. L. McDonald, Austin Mackenzie, G. T. Mackley, Hon. Mrs. T. Monson, J. H. Mossop, A. W. Oke, Mrs. Hugh Paget, F. D. Pollard, Mrs. de l'Hoste Ranking, Miss N. C. Reid, Sir Clifton Robinson, Mrs. Scotland, Mrs. M. E. Shalless, Mrs. Shuttleworth, Lady Sitwell, Miss A. Skelton, Mrs. F. Stocker, Mrs. A. Swingler, J. Roberts Sykes, L. W. A. Keiffenheim-Trubridge, Miss A. Tweedie, H. J. Vollar, Miss C. R. Whitton, M. J. E. Williams, J. Willoughby, C. W. B. Wright.

Fellows resident abroad (2).—H. Graire (France), Ivor D. Lewis (S. Africa).

Associates (2).—F. Chatfield, J. Chatfield.

Societies affiliated (3).—Crimpleshaw and Bexwell Cottage Horticultural Society, Hemingford Grey Cottagers' Gardening Society, Walton and Felixstowe Adult School Horticultural Society.

A number of lantern slides showing groups of Plants, Domestic Animals, and Curios were shown by Mr. Henry Stevens.

THE TEMPLE SHOW, 1907.

MAY 28, 29, AND 30.

JUDGES.

ORCHIDS.

Bilney, W. A.
Chapman, H. J.
Fowler, J. Gurney
Little, H.

ROSES.

Jefferies, W. J.
Jennings, John
May, H. B.
Shea, C. E.

FRUIT AND VEGETABLES.

Bunyard, Geo., V.M.H.
Challis, T., V.M.H.
Poupart, W.

GROUPS IN OPEN AIR.

Chapman, A.
Crump, W., V.M.H.
Pearson, A. H.
Thomson, D. W.

HARDY HERBACEOUS PLANTS.

Beckett, E., V.M.H.
Lynch, R. Irwin, V.M.H.
Ware, W.

FOLIAGE PLANTS.

Bain, W.
Hudson, J., V.M.H.
Ker, R. Wilson
McLeod, J. F.

ROCK AND ALPINE PLANTS.

Bennett-Poë, J. T., V.M.H.
Mottett, S.
Nicholson, Geo., V.M.H.

FLOWERING PLANTS.

Fielder, C. R.
Howe, W.
Paul, G., V.M.H.
Salter, C. J.

MISCELLANEOUS.

Dixon, C.
Douglas, Jas., V.M.H.
Notcutt, R. C.
Odell, J. W.

SPECIAL AND VEITCHIAN CUP.

Bilney, W. A.
Fowler, J. Gurney
Gibson, Jas.
Lawrence, Sir Trevor, V.M.H.

Methven, J.
Veitch, P. C. M.
Whytock, Jas.

AWARDS GIVEN BY THE COUNCIL AFTER CONSULTATION WITH THE JUDGES.

The order in which the names are entered under the several medals and cups has no reference whatever to merit, but is purely accidental.

The awards given on the recommendation of the Floral and Orchid Committees will be found under their respective reports.

Veitchian Cup, value Fifty-five Guineas.

Major G. L. Holford, C.I.E., C.V.O., Westonbirt, Tetbury,. Glos. (gr. Mr. H. G. Alexander), for Orchids.

Gold Medal.

Lord Aldenham, Aldenham House, Elstree (gr. Mr. E. Beckett), for vegetables, Melons, and flowering shrubs.

Leopold de Rothschild, Esq., Gunnersbury House, Acton (gr. Mr. J. Hudson), for collection of Cherries.

J. Colman, Esq., Gatton Park, Reigate (gr. Mr. W. P. Bound), for Orchids.

J. Veitch & Sons, Royal Exotic Nursery, Chelsea, S.W., for stove and hardy plants.

Sutton & Sons, Reading, for Potatoes, Begonias, Calceolarias, Cinerarias, Gloxinias, &c.

Wm. Paul & Son, Royal Nurseries, Waltham Cross, N., for Roses.

H. B. May & Sons, Dysons Lane Nurseries, Upper Edmonton, for exotic and hardy Ferns &c.

F. Sander & Sons, St. Albans, for Orchids and new and rare plants.

W. Cutbush & Son, Highgate, N., for Roses, Carnations, rock plants, and clipped trees.

R. P. Ker & Sons, Aigburth Nursery, Liverpool, for Hippeastrums.

R. Wallace & Co., Colchester, for Lilies, Ixias, hardy Cypripediums, Gladioli, alpines, &c.

G. Mount, Rose Nurseries, Canterbury, for Roses.

Silver Cup.

Duke of Portland, K.G., Welbeck Abbey, Worksop (gr. Mr. J. Gibson), for Carnations and vegetables.

Major G. L. Holford, C.I.E., C.V.O., Westonbirt, Tetbury, Glos. (gr. Mr. A. Chapman), for Hippeastrums.

Barr & Sons, King Street, Covent Garden, W.C., for pigmy trees, hardy cut flowers, alpines, &c.

A. J. A. Bruce, Chorlton-cum-Hardy, near Manchester, for Sarracenias.

G. Bunyard & Co., Royal Nurseries, Maidstone, for Apples, Pears, and Herbaceous plants.

H. Cannell & Sons, Swanley, for Calceolarias, Streptocarpus, Phyllocactus, Cannas, Roses, &c.

J. Cant & Co., Braiswick Nursery, Colchester, for Roses.

Charlesworth & Co., Heaton, Bradford, for Orchids.

J. Cheal & Sons, Lowfield Nurseries, Crawley, for trees and shrubs, rock garden, and clipped trees.

T. Cripps & Sons, The Nurseries, Tunbridge Wells, for Japanese Acers and ornamental trees.

R. & G. Cuthbert, The Nurseries, Southgate, for *Azalea mollis, rustica,* Ghent, and *mollis* hybrids.

A. Dickson & Sons, 55 Royal Avenue, Belfast, for Darwin Tulips.

W. Fromow & Sons, Sutton Court Nursery, Chiswick, for Japanese Maples.

J. Hill & Son, Barrowfield Nursery, Lower Edmonton, for Ferns.

H. Low & Co., Royal Nurseries, Bush Hill Park, Enfield, for Orchids, New Holland Plants, and Carnations.

Paul & Son, The Old Nurseries, Cheshunt, for Roses, Lilacs, Azaleas, and Rhododendrons.

Amos Perry, Hardy Plant Farm, Enfield, for Hardy Herbaceous, Alpine, Bog, and Aquatic plants.

Maurice Prichard, Christchurch, Hants, for hardy herbaceous plants, alpines, &c.

G. Reuthe, Fox Hill Hardy Plant Nursery, Keston, for Tulips, rare herbaceous plants, and alpines.

D. Russell & Son, Essex Nurseries, Brentwood, for hardy ornamental trees and shrubs.

L. R. Russell, Richmond, Surrey, for hardy ornamental trees and shrubs, Clematis, &c.

R. Smith & Co., Worcester, for Clematis, herbaceous plants, ornamental trees and shrubs.

C. Turner, Royal Nurseries, Slough, for Roses, Carnations, and *Azalea indica.*

T. S. Ware (1902), Ltd., Ware Nurseries, Feltham, for Begonias, Carnations, Roses, and hardy flowers.

J. Waterer & Sons, Ltd., American Nursery, Bagshot, for hardy evergreens, shrubs, and Rhododendrons.

Silver-gilt Hogg Medal.

Thomas Rivers & Son, The Nurseries, Sawbridgeworth, for fruit trees in pots.

Silver-gilt Knightian Medal.

University College, Reading (instr. Mr. C. Foster), for fruit and vegetables.

Silver-gilt Flora Medal.

Sir Samuel E. Scott, Bart., D.L., Westbury, near Brackley, Northants, for Carnations.

H. L. Bischoffsheim, Esq., F.R.G.S., Warren House, Stanmore (gr. Mr. J. Doig), for Orchids.

H. S. Goodson, Esq., Fairlawn, West Hill, Putney (gr. Mr. G. E. Day), for Orchids.

Armstrong & Brown, Sandhurst Park, Tunbridge Wells, for Orchids.

J. Backhouse & Son, The Nurseries, York, for Miniature rock work.

Bakers, Wolverhampton, for Aquilegias, Dahlias, Pelargoniums, Violas, and rock garden.

R. H. Bath, Ltd., The Floral Farms, Wisbech, for Sweet Peas, Tulips, Carnations, and hardy flowers.

Bell & Sheldon, Castel Nursery, Guernsey, for Carnations.

W. Bull & Sons, 536 King's Road, Chelsea, for Orchids and foliage plants.

H. Burnett, St. Margaret's, Guernsey, for Carnations.

B. R. Cant & Sons, The Old Rose Gardens, Colchester, for Roses.

J. Carter & Co., 97 High Holborn, W.C., for Begonias, Calceolarias, Cinerarias, Gloxinias, &c.

Craven Nursery Co., Clapham, Lancaster, for alpines.

J. Cypher & Sons, Exotic Nurseries, Cheltenham, for Orchids.

Dobbie & Co., Rothesay, N.B., for Pansies, Violas, Aquilegias, Sweet Peas, and Anemones.

A. F. Dutton, Iver, Bucks, for Carnations.

Hobbies, Ltd., Norfolk Nurseries, Dereham, for Roses.

Hogg & Robertson, Ltd., 22 Mary Street, Dublin, for Tulips.

G. Jackman & Son, Woking Nurseries, Surrey, for Herbaceous Plants and Clematis.

J. Laing & Sons, Forest Hill, S.E., for Caladiums, Begonias, and Streptocarpus.

S. Mortimer, Swiss Nursery, Farnham, Surrey, for Carnations.

John Peed & Son, West Norwood, S.E., for Caladiums, Gloxinias, and hardy plants.

Pulham & Son, 71 Newman Street, Oxford Street, W., for Rock Work planted with Rock Plants.

T. Rochford & Sons, Ltd., Broxbourne, for Ferns.

A. R. Upton, Guildford Hardy Plant Nursery, Guildford, for herbaceous and alpine plants.

Silver-gilt Banksian Medal.

Blackmore & Langdon, Twerton Hill Nursery, Twerton-on-Avon, for Begonias.

C. W. Breadmore, High Street, Winchester, for Sweet Peas.

G. & A. Clark, Ltd., Dover, for hardy herbaceous, alpine and rock plants.

B. R. Davis & Son, Yeovil, for Begonias.

Henry Eckford, Wem, Salop, for Sweet Peas.

C. Engelmann, Saffron Walden, for Tree Carnations.

W. J. Godfrey, Exmouth, for Oriental Poppies, Pelargoniums, Verbenas, &c.

A. Ll. Gwillim, New Eltham, Kent, for Begonias.

W. Iceton, Putney, S.W., for foliage and other plants, and Lilies of the Valley.

T. Jannoch, Dersingham, Norfolk, for Lilacs and Lilies of the Valley.

B. Ladhams, Ltd., Shirley, Southampton, for hardy flowers.

R. C. Notcutt, Woodbridge. Suffolk, for hardy plants.

W. H. Page, Tangley Nurseries, Hampton-on-Thames, for Carnations.

Silver Knightian Medal.

J. & F. Chatfield, Southwick, Sussex, for Strawberries.

W. Godfrey, Colchester, for Asparagus.

Laxton Bros., High Street, Bedford, for Strawberries.

R. Stephenson, Esq., J.P., Burwell, near Cambridge, for Asparagus.

Silver Flora Medal.

Frank Lilley, Guernsey, for hardy herbaceous plants, Irises, &c.

H. C. Pulham, Elsenham, Essex, for alpine and rock plants.

W. H. Rogers & Son, Red Lodge Nursery, Southampton, for Rhododendrons, &c.

R. Sydenham, Tenby Street, Birmingham, for Sweet Peas and Lilies of the Valley.

Silver Banksian Medal.

E. Ascherson, Esq., Charing, Kent (gr. Mr. J. Pitts), for Pelargoniums, Phyllocacti, Cannas, &c.

H. H. Crane, Highgate, N., for Pansies.

Wickham Noakes, Selsdon Park, Croydon (gr. Mr. Howarth), for herbaceous Calceolarias.

Mrs. Stanyforth, Kirk Hammerton Hall, York (gr. Mr. Millington), for *Dendrobium thyrsiflorum.*

John R. Box, West Wickham, Kent, for Begonias.

J. Garaway & Co., Clifton, Bristol, for Schizanthus.

A. J. Harwood, Colchester, for Asparagus.

Heath & Son, Cheltenham, for Regal and Show Pelargoniums.

Misses Hopkins, Barming, near Maidstone, for alpines.

Kelway & Son, Langport, Som., for Paeonies and Pyrethrums.

Levavasseur & Sons, Orleans, France, for Rose ' Maman Levavasseur.'

E. Neubert, Wandsbek, Hamburg, for Ferns.

C. F. Waters, Balcombe, Sussex, for Carnations.

GENERAL MEETING.

JUNE 11, 1907.

Mr. G. S. SAUNDERS, F.L.S., in the Chair.

Fellows elected (133).—Major-General H. R. Abadie, C.B., Mrs. Alexander, F. J. A. Arch, W. G. Arkwright, D. V. Bacon, Mrs. J. H. Ball, T. Barton, C. Black, Mrs. E. F. Brandreth, Lady Brinkman, F. Bridges, jun., Miss E. Brooks, Miss Barbara Brough, Dr. Gordon Brown, Mrs. F.

R. Brown, Miss Bulkeley, B. Bulkeley Campbell, E. C. Caton, R. C. Cart-
wright, Miss Chambers, W. R. Chaplin, F. Chatfield, Seton Christopher,
R. Collyer, Mrs. Cooper, Mrs. H. Corlette, Miss Money Coutts, F.
J. Crowder, W. Currie, Mrs. Dakeyne, Miss K. Dalton, Mrs. Donne,
Countess of Drogheda, John Drury-Lowe, A. Duffield, H.H. Princess
Duleep Singh, G. Edwards, Mrs. A. V. P. Evans, Mrs. Ewart, Mrs. Eyre,
Mrs. Fleischmann, Mrs. F. Ford, Mrs. C. Fox, G. R. Fraser, J.P., Capt.
H. Fulton, G. Gardner, W. Gibson, Gordon Godseff, Mrs. A. E. Gordon,
H. J. Greenwood, J. D. Gregory, Hon. Mrs. H. Grosvenor, E. Habben,
Mrs. M. Hare, Austin E. Harris, Mrs. C. Harvey, Mrs. Humbert, Mrs.
H. Illingworth, T. W. H. Inskip, C. F. Kearley, E. F. Kelly, J. King, jun.,
John K. King, Mrs. H. F. Kingdom, J. B. Knowles, Mrs. Lascelles, Max.
Lindlar, C. P. Little, Mrs. H. R. Little, Miss A. M. Lyle, Mrs. E. M. M.
McKenne, H. D. McLaren, Mrs. R. McVitie, Mrs. H. Mansfield, F.
Marshall, J. S. Marshall, Mrs. F. J. Matthews, Mrs. Metcalf, G. M. Mid-
wood, W. H. Mills, Lord Monk Bretton, W. Morris, Miss Musgrave, Mrs.
A. M. Nathan, Mrs. Neill, Mrs. K. F. Nix, Miss L. Noll, W. Ogilvie, H. S.
Paul, G. Pascon, Mrs. Payne, Miss C. A. Prater, E. E. Pearson, Mrs. J.
Philipps, Mrs. Pudgron, C. Pitt-Taylor, J. T. Powell, T. H. Prater, J. V.
Pryor, Dr. Frank Riley, F. H. Roberts, Mrs. A. Roche, Miss N. Ronaldson,
W. Rowlands, A. F. Ruxton, Mrs. Dudley Scott, Miss D. Salaman, Mrs.
Smee, T. Spence, Miss T. M. Stenning, W. Stephens, Mrs. G. G. Stevens,
E. C. Street, Earl of Suffolk, J. H. Swanton, J. T. Sydenham, R. A.
Tatton, A. D. Thompson, T. C. M. Thompson, Mrs. M. Tomlin, L. E.
Traherne, G. Treherne, R. Tringrouse, F. Trussell, W. J. Unwin, Mrs.
C. R. Vallance, Rev. R. J. Walker, L. O. Walter, Miss M. Walton, Mrs.
Watson, Mrs. C. H. Watson, Mrs. White, Hon. Mrs. Wilson.

Fellows resident abroad (5).—B. N. Bonnerjee (India), F. Cooper
(New Zealand), L. W. Koning (Holland), A. Nonin (France), L. M.
Shoobridge (Tasmania).

Associates (4).—H. Broadbent, G. Eggleton, C. V. Fells, G. Hillman.

Societies affiliated (2).—Trowbridge Horticultural Society, Westmeon
Horticultural Society.

A lecture on " Arches, Pillars, and Pergolas " was given by Mr. Walter
P. Wright (see p. 49).

SHOW OF COLONIAL-GROWN FRUIT, VEGETABLES, AND PRESERVED FRUITS.

June 13 and 14, 1907.

JUDGES.

George Bunyard, V.M.H.	M. J. Garcia
George F. Butt	George Monro, V.M.H.
C. R. Fielder	Rev. W. Wilks, M.A.

LIST OF AWARDS.

Gold Medal.

L. M. Shoobridge, Esq., Tasmania, for Apples, Pears, and Quinces.
The Government of South Australia, for Apples and Pears.

The Permanent Exhibition Committee of Dominica, 15 Seething Lane, London, E.C., for Citrus fruits.

The West Indian Produce Association, Ltd., 4 Fenchurch Buildings, London, E.C., for Colonial preserves.

Silver-gilt Knightian.

The Natal Orchard Association, Durban, Natal, for Citrus fruits.

Silver-gilt Banksian.

Messrs. R. Jackson & Co., c.o. Trades Commissioner for Cape of Good Hope, 98 Victoria Street, S.W., for bottled and dried fruits.

Messrs. J. Clark & Co., Renmark, South Australia, for Colonial-grown and dried fruits.

Mr. J. Stuart, Hillside, Australia, for Victorian Apples.

Mr. W. S. Shoobridge, Tasmania, for Tasmanian Apples.

Silver Knightian.

Mr. H. Vick, Harcourt, Australia, for Victorian Apples.

Mr. B. Goldberg, Durban, Natal, for Cape Pine-apples.

Mr. M. G. Anderson, Adelaide, Australia, for Pears.

Silver Banksian.

Mr. J. B. Mills, Harcourt, Australia, for Victorian Apples.

Messrs. G. S. Yuill & Co., Melbourne, Australia, for Victorian Apples.

Hon. H. A. Alford Nicols, Kingsland House, Dominica, for Limes.

Mr. F. L. White, Durban, Natal, for Citrus fruits.

Mr. H. Balcombe, Stanger, Natal, for Oranges.

Mr. T. R. Wellington, Bluff, Natal, for Naartjes.

Rev. Oxley Oxland, Hill Crest, Natal, for *Lilium Harrisii* bulbs.

Bronze Banksian.

Mr. C. Craike, Portland, Australia, for Victorian Apples.

Mr. T. J. Smith, Victoria, Australia, for Victorian Apples.

Mr. H. Rock, Malvern, Natal, for Naartjes.

GENERAL MEETING.

June 25, 1907.

Professor G. S. Boulger, F.Z.S., in the Chair.

Fellows elected (36).—J. H. Addinsell, Miss A. M. Allen, Mrs. L. S Allen, Evelyn Lady Alington, Mrs. C. J. Birch, Miss Bradford, Miss H. M. Brown, A. G. Catesby, H. C. Chad, Miss H. M. Chubb, H. W. Clinton Baker, J.P., Mrs. Donkin, C. P. Dunlan, E. B. Fielden, W. Fowler, Viscountess Goschen, J. W. Harrison, Lieut.-Colonel F. A. Irby, Miss M. B. Jones, Miss Keele, E. Knowldin, A. Merck, T. G. Mellors, Miss Nicholson, F. J. Pullen, J. P. Rudolf, Baroness von Schroeder, Dr. A. Senior, R. S. Smallman, Hon. M. Stanley, H. Tatton Sykes, Mrs. A. G.

Theed, Mrs. J. H. Todd, Mrs. Tristram-Valentine, D. Watson, J. H. Welch.

Fellows resident abroad (2).—J. Balme, jun. (Mexico), T. G. Ellery (Australia).

Society affiliated (1).—Ingateston and District Rose and Horticultural Society.

A lecture on " Peculiarities of Leaf Arrangements " was given by the Rev. Prof. G. Henslow, M.A., V.M.H. (see p. 36).

SCIENTIFIC COMMITTEE.

JANUARY 8, 1907.

Mr. G. S. SAUNDERS, F.L.S., in the Chair, and four other members present.

Pleurothallis sp.—Mr. R. A. Rolfe reported that the *Pleurothallis* shown at the meeting on November 20, 1906, by R. I. Measures, Esq., could not be identified at Kew, but may be one of several described by Reichenbach, still only known from description. It is near *P. velaticaulis* Reichb.

Grapes shanking.—Some shoots of vines, the fruit of which had shanked, were received from Basingstoke. From the description of the border that accompanied the specimens it was thought that the trouble was undoubtedly due to unhealthy root action, and that renovation of the border would probably result in improvement in the growth of the fruit.

Magnolias and Mealy Bug.—Some shoots of magnolia affected with mealy bug were received from Horsham. The shoots were from plants growing on the south side of a wall 200 feet long and 15 feet high, and, although various insecticides had been tried upon the plants no good results had followed. The scale insects were, curiously enough, not found in the houses built on the south side of the wall. Mr. Saunders reported as follows :—"The mealy bug attacking the magnolias is *Dactylopius longispinus*. Of course it is very difficult, if not impossible, to properly cleanse the leaves with an insecticide, as the plants are growing against a wall. It might, however, be possible to destroy them with hydrocyanic acid gas if some comparatively air-tight covering could be constructed over the plants, *e.g.* a tarpaulin or a rick cloth might be fastened with a batten against the wall above the plants and allowed to fall down in front of them to the ground. The sides might be fastened to the wall in the same manner as the top. The gas is generated by pouring sulphuric acid over cyanide of potassium. The method of procedure is as follows : Place 4 ounces of water in an earthenware jar, pour slowly into it $1\frac{1}{2}$ fluid ounces of sulphuric acid (specific gravity 1·84), then in a shallow earthenware dish put 1 ounce of potassium cyanide (98 per cent. strength), and arrange the jar of acid so that its contents can be slowly poured over the cyanide without any chance of the fumes reaching the operator, *as they are most poisonous.* Or the cyanide may be wrapped up in a piece of blotting paper and placed on a piece of board laid on the top of the jar, but not closing the mouth, and by means of a stick or string it may be dropped into the jar containing the acid, and then every aperture should be tightly closed. The above recipe gives the quantities for use in a space containing 150 cubic feet of air ; if the space be larger, the quantities must be increased in proportion. The plants should remain exposed to the fumes for above three hours. Means must be devised to remove the covering, or at least to open it, so that all fumes escape without any person breathing them, *as they are very deadly*. It is curious that the insects do not infest the plants in the houses on the other side of the wall. Mealy bugs do not breed in the ground, but usually on the plants; they may, however, do so at times in cracks &c. in the walls. They lay their eggs in masses covered with a cotton-like secretion in convenient positions on the plant."

Plants for naming.—Shoots of *Sophora tetraptera, Clianthus puniceus,* and another, of which the material was insufficient, were received from Stockton.

Malformed Cypripedium.—Dr. Masters, F.R.S., reported that he had examined the curious *Cypripedium* shown at the last meeting by Mr. Bennett-Poë, and found that there were three sepals, two lateral and one anterior, and three petals, one posterior and two lateral. The lip was normal; the column had two staminodes, the stigma was obliquely two-lobed, and the axis of the flower was diagonal, the ovary being normal with one cell, and three parietal two-lobed placentae. The following diagram represents the arrangement of the floral organs :—

S   S

P

C C

P   O   P

L

S

Monœcious Mistletoe.—Dr. Masters showed a specimen of this rarely occurring form on behalf of Mr. Corderoy, of Didcot, and a variety of the common mistletoe having thick, leathery leaves about four times larger than usual.

Christmas Roses diseased.—Mrs. Squarey, F.R.H.S., sent leaves of the Christmas Rose which had turned brown and died; the flowers appeared, but showed little above the surface of the soil. Mr. Bennett-Poë said that he had found a similar thing to occur when the roots are attacked, as is frequently the case, by the grubs of the crane fly. Goosebery shoots, diseased cucumbers, and amaryllis bulbs were also received, and will be reported upon at the next meeting.

SCIENTIFIC COMMITTEE, JANUARY 22, 1907.

The late Dr. M. T. MASTERS, F.R.S., in the Chair, and ten other members present.

Mites in Amaryllis Bulb.—Mr. Saunders, F.L.S., reported that he had examined the bulb sent from Folkestone, and had found that it was undoubtedly attacked by the bulb mite, *Rhizoglyphus echinopus.* He could see no reason why this mite should not infest carnations, tomatoes, melons, pelargoniums, begonias, cyclamen, arum lilies, and cucumbers, which were also reported to be injured in a manner similar to that in the *Amaryllis.* "As to destroying the pest, he suggested sterilising the soil the plants are growing in, soaking the bulbs in hot water of a temperature of 125° Fahr. for about ten minutes to kill the mites in them. He also recommended bisulphide of carbon, and it might be well to try vaporite ; the latter is highly spoken of by some persons, but he did not know of any properly conducted experiments having been made with it."

Cucumbers "going off."—These, sent from Botley, were reported upon by Mr. Saunders as follows :—" I could find no sign of insects, worms, or mites in the cucumber plants, nor could I detect the mycelium of any fungus. The cellular tissue was much broken up in places, particularly near the nodes of the stems—a condition which looked very much like the work of eelworms—but I could not find any, either in the stems or roots. I cannot suggest any reason for the plants ' going off.' "

Diseased Gooseberry Shoots.—Mr. Chittenden reported that he had examined the gooseberry shoots shown at the last meeting, and had found upon them a few perithecia of the common gooseberry mildew, but none of the American gooseberry mildew.

Cypripedium malformed.—Mr. Saunders, F.L.S., exhibited a curious flower of *Cypripedium*, in which, in addition to other malformations, a second flower was growing in the axil of one of the floral segments. Mr. Worsdell will report more fully upon it at the next meeting.

Use of Destructor Refuse as Manure.—Mr. F. J. Baker said that he had found the refuse from a dust destructor in which condemned meat, infected clothing, &c. had been burnt very valuable as manure. It contained a considerable amount of phosphates, and its effects were discernible after having been applied four years ago, the crops raised having been vetches, rye, peas, and barley. It was pointed out that the composition of the refuse probably varied very greatly from different districts, and its value could only be ascertained by analysis or by actual trial. The sample shown was in the form of a fine powder, and Mr. Baker said he had found it very useful for mixing with potting soil.

Uncommon Coniferae.—Dr. Masters showed leaves, about nine inches long, of a pine, called in certain catalogues *Pinus Malleti*, a name which could not be found in any English list. The leaves enabled him, however, to identify the pine as one of the numerous forms of *Pinus ponderosa*. He also showed six probably seedling varieties of *Torreya Myristica* (= *T. californica*), which he had received from Messrs. Croux, of Chatenay, where it is quite hardy, although it is scarcely so in England. The variations were principally in the form, direction, colour, and length of the leaves, and in the habit of the trees. He also exhibited a shoot of the true *Abies lasiocarpa* of Hooker, the species usually grown under that name being a form of *A. concolor*.

Roses dying.—Specimens of leaves and roots of roses and the soil in which they were growing were received from Hoddesdon. The roses lost their leaves very early, the tea roses especially suffering. The trouble was probably attributable to the somewhat heavy soil containing too small a percentage of organic matter, and the addition of farmyard manure was recommended.

Stocks diseased.—Stocks with leaves dying were received from Yateley. They were attacked by the slime fungus, *Plasmodiophora Brassicae*, the cause of the club-root disease in turnips, cabbages, and all plants of the cabbage family.

Mildewed Apple Shoots.—Apple shoots were received from Gloucester-shire badly attacked by the mildew *Sphaerotheca Mali*, a trouble that appears to be spreading (see JOURNAL R.H.S. vol. xxvi. p. 736, vol. xxviii. p. 2). Other diseased twigs from Falmouth were taken by Mr. Massee for further examination.

Apples spotted.—Mr. Hooper showed several ' Cox's Orange Pippins ' spotted, which Mr. Massee took for further examination.

Gooseberry Caterpillars.—Some soil from under gooseberry bushes was received, and Mr. Saunders undertook to examine it in order to discover whether any chrysalids of the gooseberry sawfly were present or not.

SCIENTIFIC COMMITTEE, FEBRUARY 12, 1907.

The late Dr. M. T. MASTERS, F.L.S., in the Chair, and thirteen other members present, and T. S. SIMS, Esq., of Natal, and J. BURTT-DAVY, Esq., of the Department of Agriculture, Transvaal, visitors.

Caterpillars on Gooseberries.—Mr. G. S. Saunders, F.L.S., reported that he had examined the soil from under gooseberry bushes sent to the last meeting, and had found no cocoons of the gooseberry sawfly ; he there-fore concluded that the caterpillars which had attacked the bushes were those of the "magpie moth," which do not pupate in the ground, " but in leaves which it attaches to the stem by threads, or in a light cocoon fastened to the stem under dead leaves, rubbish, &c. on the ground or on walls &c. These should be searched for and destroyed. Any leaves which hang on the bushes after the others have fallen should be collected and burnt, and the dead leaves, rubbish, &c. under the bushes should be treated in the same manner ; taking up the earth under the trees will be of no avail if the sample submitted was an average one."

Apple Twigs diseased.—Mr. Massee, V.M.H., reported that the apple twigs from Falmouth showed the presence of canker, *Nectria ditissima.* He recommended that similar appearances on other twigs should be removed and " green fly " &c. should be kept down, as they distribute the fungus and also cause wounds through which it gains an entrance. Referring to other twigs shown at the last meeting attacked by *Sphaero-theca Mali*, he said " diseased shoots should be cut off, as the mycelium hibernates in the bark and appears year after year. Good drainage checks the development of the parasite."

Apples spotted.—Mr. Massee also reported that the pitting and internal discoloration of the apples shown at the last meeting by Mr. Hooper were due to the exceptional heat of last season, and were not in any way influenced by fungi or insects.

Cypripedium malformed.—Referring to the *Cypripedium* shown at the last meeting, Mr. Worsdell, F.L.S., wrote :—" It is a case of fasciation two flowers being concerned in the make-up of the whole. Taking the large flower first, the whole has become twisted out of the ordinary position, due to the *untwisting* of the ovary. The sepals are normal, but the lower, by the notch at its apex, shows signs of its true compound nature. Only one of the petals, viz. one of the *lateral* ones, is normal ; both the others are curiously constituted, each being half labelliform and half sepaloid. As regards the column, the usual staminode (of the outer whorl of the androecium) is present ; there is a petaloid outgrowth which I interpret as belonging also to the outer whorl, while the two (usually fertile) stamens of the inner whorl are represented by a normal fertile and a more or less petaloid stamen. The ovary is straight, and consists of two carpels. The second flower has its stalk intimately fused with the ovary of the first ; its bract is carried up so as to occur immediately below the first flower, as. if forming one of the floral leaves of the latter : it subtends the bicarpellary ovary of the second flower, which is as yet unexpanded, but the remaining parts of which were seen on dissection to be normal. A considerable number of *Cypripedium* and other orchid sports are due to fasciation, in which two or more flowers are concerned ; as, for example, in the last case reported on at the Scientific Committee by Dr. Masters. If this were more often borne in mind much of the difficulty of unravelling these complex structures would be avoided. The two flowers are often much more intimately blended than in the case described above."

Fasciated Bramble.—A curiously fasciated and contorted shoot of bramble was received from Mrs. M. S. Nicol, of King's Langley.

Amaryllis Spike withering.—A spike of *Amaryllis* was received from Twyford in a withered condition. It had been growing well, but suddenly growth stopped, and the leaves and stem became weak and flabby. The roots appeared healthy and the bulb firm. The plant had been started about three weeks, and was plunged in a bottom heat of about 60° to 65°. It was thought that the trouble was probably due to encouraging too great an amount of aërial growth before the roots were sufficiently developed to provide a proper supply of water.

Forest Journeys.—Dr. Henry gave a brief outline of his recent travels in the Western States of America, Spain, Italy, Corsica, and Algiers, commenting particularly upon some of the forest trees he had met with, and speaking in appreciative terms of the forest service of the States, which in a few years has done a great amount of valuable work. The forests of the United States, he thought, were being rapidly exhausted, and this would greatly enhance the value of the woods of Canada. Mr. Worsley, who had recently been travelling in Portugal, remarked upon a dwarf variety of *Quercus Suber* which covered considerable areas near Cintra, and said similar barrenness of the soil was following the destruction of woodlands in Portugal to that Dr. Henry had described as occurring in other parts of the world. Mr. J. Burtt-Davy, the director of the Department of Agriculture of the Transvaal, spoke of the species of *Widdringtonia* growing wild in South Africa, saying there was at least one species occurring wild in the Transvaal, and others were cultivated ; while Mr. Sim, of Natal, remarked upon the great variability of the species of this genus, one growing in the mountains merely in the form of bushes, but when transplanted to the valleys below attaining the size of a considerable tree. There appear to be many forms of this genus which are as yet not well known.

Daffodil flowering without Roots.—Mr. E. H. Jenkins sent an example of a double-flowered daffodil which had grown well, but had produced few and badly developed roots, illustrating the well-ascertained fact that flowers are produced from properly formed bulbs when they are supplied with sufficient water and warmth, the former being able to pass apparently through the base of the bulb.

SCIENTIFIC COMMITTEE, MARCH 5, 1907.

The late Dr. M. T. MASTERS, F.R.S., in the Chair, and sixteen other members present.

Potato : Species and Varieties.—Mr. A. W. Sutton, V.M.H., showed, an interesting series of potato plants and tubers as follows :—

1. Plant of *Solanum Commersonii* (' the potato of Uruguay '), belonging to the same stock as seen by the Committee at Reading last July. The flowers of this species are white and sweet-scented, while the fruit is cordiform.

2. Three plants grown from tubers received this winter direct from Uruguay, the tubers being collected from plants growing in a perfectly wild condition. The collector states that there are *two* wild types in Uruguay—one bearing white flowers, the other violet flowers.

3. Tubers just received, supposed to be of the same species as the last, bearing violet flowers, but found in another district at a great distance from the last. The tubers were of a considerable size, some measuring over 2 inches in length by 1½ inches across. It will be interesting to notice later on (*a*) whether the last two are one and the same species, and (*b*) what relation, if any, there may be between these last two and the type *Solanum Commersonii*, now so well known and recognised. Possibly this violet-flowered Uruguay potato may prove to be an unknown species.

4. Two plants of *Solanum Magli* grown from single eyes.

5. One plant of *Solanum Commersonii* violet (Labergerie), and one of the ' blue giant potato ' (Paulsen).

Nos. 4 and 5 were grown from single eyes (with a large number of others), under the same treatment under glass, in order to test the assertion of Labergerie that a greater tendency to "mutation" is seen when single eyes are removed from a potato tuber and submitted to a system of intense culture. None of the plants under this treatment at present show any tendency to mutate.

Mr. Sutton kindly promised to bring these again before the Committee when growth had proceeded further.

Intumescence in Viburnum.—Mr. A. E. Bowles, F.L.S., showed some shoots of *Viburnum Tinus* var., upon which small blisters were developed, which later grew larger, until corky growths of considerable size were developed. These were recognised as similar to growths described by Dr. Sorauer under the name of "intumescences" arising from over-turgidity of the tissues, and similar in origin to the warts on vine leaves &c.

Curiously coloured Seeds.—Mr. Bowles also showed seeds of *Ravenala madagascariensis*, the traveller's tree, and of *Trichilia indica*. The seeds of the former are of a blue-green colour, and have a metallic lustre, being similar in form and appearance to some of the tropical *Buprestideae*, and the latter red and black, mocking in appearance some of the *Coccinellidae*. The marked likeness to these beetles was thought to be possibly connected with the distribution of the seeds by birds who might be deceived into carrying them some distance before they found their mistake.

Fungus on Oak.—Mr. Douglas, V.M.H., showed dead branches from oak trees in the neighbourhood of Great Bookham covered with a parasitic fungus. Mr. Douglas said that large numbers of oak branches were being killed by the fungus.

Malformed Cypripedium.—Mr. Douglas also drew attention to a flower of *Cypripedium Dayanum* in which the dorsal and one of the lateral sepals were coherent, showing a normal flower for comparison with it.

Malformed Cyclamen.—Dr. Masters showed a malformed *Cyclamen* flower sent by Mr. Pettigrew which had an adventitious bud in the axil of one of the sepals, a not uncommon malformation in flowers of the *Cyclamen*.

Lenticels in Laburnum.—Professor Henslow showed a piece of the bark of *Laburnum*, and drew attention to the enormous number of lenticels present in that plant, particularly in the inner bark.

Cabbage in Patagonia.—Professor Henslow also showed a specimen of *Brassica oleracea* collected by Charles Darwin at Port Desire in Patagonia when on his memorable journey, and others collected on the Kentish coast of the same species. It would be interesting to know how that species came to be growing in Patagonia so long ago.

Cotyledon macrantha (Berger).—A specimen of this fine plant shown by Sir Trevor Lawrence was discussed, and Dr. Masters promised to examine it and report further upon it at the next meeting.

Diseased Gladiolus Corms.—Some diseased *Gladiolus* corms of the variety 'Princeps,' imported from America in 1905, having the interior partly eaten away and so injured that after lifting the corms rot completely away, were received. Mr. Güssow reported that he found they were attacked by the fungus *Botrytis parasitica*, a common fungus on certain bulbous plants. The flies that had been noticed in the corms had evidently been attracted by the decaying tissues, and were feeding upon those.

SCIENTIFIC COMMITTEE, MARCH 19, 1907.

The late Dr. M. T. MASTERS, F.R.S., in the Chair, and twelve other members present, and Messrs. J. BURTT-DAVY, of the Transvaal, and B. JAMES, of British Guiana, visitors.

Spots on Rhododendron Leaves.—Mr. Saunders, F.L.S., reported that he had carefully examined the rhododendron leaves shown at the last meeting, but had been unsuccessful in detecting any cause for the holes and notches in them. "Leaves of various plants with very similar perforations &c. are frequently passing through my hands, and they have often been before the Scientific Committee, but I have never been able to satisfy myself as to the cause of the injury. Our mycologists assure us that they are not caused by fungi. As there is so much mystery about as to the cause of these holes, it would be very desirable if some experiments could be made in order to try to throw some light on the subject. The holes being of such different sizes make one think that they probably increase in size. If they do, this would certainly be against the theory of their being caused by insect agency. If someone who has access to plants attacked in this way would make some observations on this point it would help in the elucidation of the mystery."

Malformed Carnation.—Mr. Saunders also reported that the carnation shoots from Stuckly Castle had been examined by him, but no trace of insect, mite, eelworm, or fungus could be discovered in them. Perhaps if the entire plant was examined something might be found.

Diseased Violets.—Mr. Massee, V.M.H., reported that the violets sent to the last meeting were attacked by the fungus *Phyllosticta Violae.* "This and the disease due to *Cercospora Violae* are indistinguishable in their mode of attack, and can only be identified under the microscope. The primary cause of both diseases is excess of moisture and lack of proper ventilation during cultivation."

Diseased Tulips.—Mr. Massee also reported that the diseased tulips were attacked by the fungus *Botrytis parasitica.* The disease had appeared when ventilation was deficient, plants growing in similar soil in the open not being attacked.

Gall on Oak.—Mr. Holmes, F.L.S., showed a gall from the common oak which Mr. Saunders reported to be formed by the grubs of one of the hymenopterous gallflies, probably by *Aphilotrix Globuli,* one of the gallflies with alternating generations; these galls would produce *Andricus inflator,* whose grubs would form green globular galls surrounded at their base by the scales of the buds. *Aphilotrix Globuli* is the sexual generation.

Curious Swelling on Stem.—Thos. Sharp, Esq., F.R.H.S., of Westbury, Wilts, sent a stem of sloe (?) having at its upper end a curious knob-like swelling, about 3½ inches in length and over 2 inches in diameter, marked very similarly to 'bird's-eye maple.' This was evidently formed as the result of a wound, the healing tissue having given rise to a large number of adventitious buds, the small shoots from which had disappeared.

Cotyledon macrantha.—Dr. Masters reported that he had examined this plant shown at the last meeting, and found that it had been described and figured some time since, and showed no remarkable deviations from other plants of its genus. The proposal to award it a botanical certificate therefore fell through.

Thibaudia sp.—A remarkable shrub with large red tubular flowers was shown by Mr. J. T. Bennett-Poë, which appeared to be a hitherto undescribed species of *Thibaudia.* Its native home was not known, as the plant had been found by Mr. Poë in the greenhouse, and there was no record of its original source. The question of awarding it a botanical certificate was deferred until the plant should be named.

Malformed Cyclamen.—Mr. Worsdell, F.L.S., reported that he had examined the cyclamen shown at the last meeting, and had found small adventitious flower buds in the axils of the sepals with their parts greatly aborted. Mr. Chittenden had sent him one showing similarly malformed growths, but in that the adventitious flowers had become well developed, although stamens were missing from some of them, and so on. Although the buds were probably really axillary to the sepals, they had become laterally displaced owing to lack of room, so that they stood between the sepals. The whole presented the appearance of a large double flower.

Hybrid Orchid.—Mr. James Douglas, V.M.H., showed an interesting hybrid raised by crossing the hybrid *Cymbidium eburneum* × *Lowianum* with *C. eburneum*. The resulting plant had flowers closely approaching *C. eburneum* in appearance and colour, but showing traces of *C. Lowianum*, particularly in the tinting of the column, the suffusion of yellow on the labellum, and the form of the double crest which runs down the labellum.

Asparagus Kale dying.—Mr. S. T. Wright sent specimens of asparagus kale from Wisley which showed, on cutting sections across the stem, lattice-like openings in the woody tissue. These had been destroyed by the attacks of the bacterium *Pseudomonas campestris*, well known in some parts of the Continent and in America. It is reported that the spores may be carried with the seed, and the disease so propagated.

SCIENTIFIC COMMITTEE, APRIL 2, 1907.

The late Dr. M. T. MASTERS, F.R.S., in the Chair, and twelve other members present.

Botanical Certificates.—Dr. Masters reported on the plant shown by Mr. Bennett-Poë at the last meeting under the name of *Thibaudia* sp. (?). The plant proved to be a hitherto-undescribed species of *Agapetes*, and the name *Agapetes speciosa* had been given it. On the motion of Mr. Bowles, seconded by Mr. Worsdell, a botanical certificate was recommended to this plant by seven votes to one on the ground of its novelty and botanical interest.

Narcissus from Chili.—Mr. Worsley showed the flower of a variety of *N. Tazetta*, the bulb of which he had received from Chili, to which country it had evidently been introduced and had escaped. Mr. Elwes, F.R.S., said that he had been struck by the large number of South European plants which had found a congenial home in various parts of South America.

Hybrid Vallota and Hippeastrum.—Mr. H. J. Chapman showed a plant which he stated to be raised from seed produced by *Vallota purpurea* crossed with pollen from a purple-flowered *Hippeastrum*. The foliage was only just beginning to develop, and was stated to be very similar to the *Vallota* in appearance. The flowers were large and white with a rather broad greenish median vein. About two hundred seedlings of this cross had been raised, all of similar habits, and all but three bore scarlet flowers ; the plant shown and two others, however, had white flowers. Mr. Chapman promised to show the plant again when in full foliage. The reverse cross did not result in the production of any seed.

Pollen of Phaius Hybrids.—Mr. Chapman observed that when two species of *Phaius* were crossed the pollen of the resulting plant was infertile, but the hybrids produced seed when pollinated with pollen from either of the parents. The pollen of the hybrids resulting from these second crosses was fertile.

Colletia spinosa.—Dr. Masters drew attention to two plants of this species shown by Mr. Smith, of Worcester, which illustrated the great variation in the form of the spinous leaves with which the branches are furnished. So great is the difference that the various forms had been described under the names *Colletia spinosa* and *C. cruciata*, but Mr. Barnes, of Bicton, had long ago pointed out to Dr. Lindley that one plant bore shoots of both types. The present examples illustrated this fact, proving that the two species were really one and the same.

Diseased Potatoes.—Mr. John Coutts, of Killerton Gardens, sent tubers of potatoes he had received from a cottager showing in some cases watery black marks throughout the flesh and in others hollowed spaces. These appearances were recognised as due to the attacks of the winter rot fungus, *Nectria Solani.*

Effect of Environment in a Primrose Leaf.—Dr. Masters showed drawings of a primrose leaf collected in Jersey, where the plant has been growing on rocks by the seacoast. It was of the normal length and breadth, but about a quarter of an inch in thickness, and showed many of the anatomical characters common to seaside plants.

Axial Proliferation in Carnation.—Mr. G. Reid, of Oxshott, sent a specimen of carnation having a well-developed bud growing from the middle of the flower, a well-known phenomenon frequently illustrated.

Numerous specimens of diseased plants were received and reported upon.

SCIENTIFIC COMMITTEE, APRIL 16, 1907.

The late Dr. M. T. MASTERS, F.R.S., in the Chair, and twelve other members present.

Green Wood.—Rev. W. Wilks exhibited a dead branch having the wood of a deep verdigris-green colour. All the fallen branches in a certain wood in Sussex became of this green colour. Such wood is used in making "Tunbridge ware," and owes its colour to the presence of a fungus, *Chlorosplenium aeruginosum.*

Plants exhibited.—A species of *Megaclinium* with the curiously flattened rachis was shown by J. B. H. Gooden, Esq., F.R.H.S., of Sherborne, Dorset; another orchid, under the name of the "beetle" orchid of Australia, with flowers curiously simulating a beetle with long antennae, shown by Mrs. Whitlaw, of Amerden, Taplow, and an interesting bigeneric hybrid between *Diacrium bicornutum* and *Epidendrum Ellisii*, with flowers of a pinkish colour, shown by Jeremiah Colman, Esq., of Gatton Park. The terrestrial orchid, *Satyrium coriifolium* ("Bot. Mag." tab. 2172), was shown by Messrs. Ware. It has a long spike of yellow flowers, having the labellum at the upper part of the flower, since the ovary is not twisted as in most orchids. A vote of thanks was unanimously proffered to the exhibitors.

Tchihatchewia isatidea (Boiss.).—The Viscountess Emlyn, Frensham Hall, Haslemere, exhibited this very curious cruciferous plant, a native of the mountains of Asia Minor, where it grows at an altitude of between 5000 and 6000 feet. The habit of the plant is exactly that of an *Echium*. A botanical certificate was unanimously awarded to the plant. It is figured in *Bot. Mag.* tab. 7608.

New Break in Auricula.—Mr. Douglas, V.M.H., showed an alpine auricula having golden stripes running through the edges of the petals. Mr. Douglas stated that this was the first time he had seen this remarkable variation in colour.

African Crinums.—Mr. Elwes, F.R.S., showed inflorescences of crinums, one having white flowers with a very curious and somewhat unpleasant scent, which Mr. Worsley recognised as a form of *Crinum giganteum* ; the other flowers had a pinkish tint, and the plant sold under the name of *C. Macowani*. Mr. Worsley regarded this as a form of *C. latifolium* from the most southern part of the range of that species.

Hybrid Japanese Plum and Peach.—Mr. Laxton showed an interesting hybrid raised between the Japanese plum ♀ and the peach ' Sea Eagle ' ♂. The foliage of this hybrid is illustrated at fig. 131 in Rept. International Conference (1906) on Genetics. This year the hybrid has flowered for the first time, the flowers being white with the faintest tinge of pink in the bud stage, the filaments of the stamens white and stouter than those of the Japanese plum, the anthers well developed, and pollen apparently properly formed, the flower as large as that of the peach. No pistil was present in any of the flowers shown, but a photograph showed the style and stigma developed in some of the flowers. No fruits have, however, been so far perfected, the ovary being frequently absent even when the style and stigma are present.

Pruning and Protection of Gooseberry Bushes.—Mr. J. F. Baker showed a branch completely furnished with blossom throughout its entire length of over three feet from a gooseberry bush. It had been regularly summer-pinched every June, but not otherwise pruned. Several snags left at the last pinching were still present, and at the base of each one or two blossoms showed that the pinching of the young shoot had induced fruit formation. Each autumn the bush was bound up with string, so that the branches were brought near together and kept as upright as possible to prevent disbudding by birds, which abound in the district. The string was removed each spring. He stated that as a result of his experiments, extending over several years, he had for the last two or three years adopted these methods extensively, very little trouble or expense being involved, and the results were excellent. A branch from a bush treated and left in the ordinary way, growing in the same plot, was also shown, and this was almost denuded of buds.

SCIENTIFIC COMMITTEE, APRIL 30, 1907.

The late Dr. M. T. MASTERS, F.R.S., in the Chair, and thirteen other members present.

African Crinums.—Mr. Worsley reported that the crinums shown at the last meeting by Mr. Elwes were *C. giganteum* and *C. Macowani*.

Some years since Messrs. Bull sent out a pink variety of the former as *C. nobile*, so that *C. nobile* var. *album* would, under this nomenclature, represent the type. The finest varieties of this species have widely expanded flowers, such as var. *Rattrayi* &c. They are all fragrant, and some of them (as in the case of the form now shown by Mr. Elwes) are very fragrant. On this account the name 'vanilodorum' was given to a form of this species. *C. Macowani* has been the subject of much confusion. The plant figured under this name in "Bot. Mag.," tab. 6381, is *C. Moorei*; *C. Macowani* is the southernmost representative of a widely distributed species which spreads northwards at least as far as the equator, and passes by indiscernible gradations into forms of *C. latifolium*. The form shown by Mr. Elwes is practically sessile, and in this respect is not identical with the forms originally described by Mr. Baker under *C. Macowani* ("Handbook of Amaryllideæ," p. 94).

Fungus on Retinospora.—Mr. Saunders, F.L.S., showed a specimen of *Retinospora* (immature form of *Juniperus chinensis*) attacked by the fungus *Gymnosporangium* sp., which forms jelly-like masses on the shoots.

Auricula with Petaloid Stamens.—Mr. J. Douglas, V.M.H., showed an auricula in which the stamens of most of the flowers had become petaloid ; in some they were well developed, in others quite minute.

Ceropegia Woodi.—Mr. Worsley showed seeds of this plant, which, like so many of the family to which it belongs, is provided with a parachute arrangement for the distribution of the seed. Mr. Worsley said that the hairs appeared to be sticky. He also showed a shoot which had been hanging down quite freely, bearing little tuberous growths upon it. The formation of these small tubers had been attributed to contact of trailing shoots with damp earth, but that could not have been the exciting cause in this case. He thought that possibly irritation by insects might have excited their formation. Not all shoots bear these tubers when hanging freely down.

Genetics.—Mr. Worsley thought that the Committee should by some means or other be kept informed of the progress made in the investigation in progress into the laws of inheritance, and it was left to the Secretary to ascertain from members what could be done in this direction.

Coloration of Hawthorn Leaves.—Mr. Holmes, F.L.S., showed leaves of hawthorn bearing crimson patches, and remarked that these coloured spots followed as the result of injury by insects, in the case in point apparently by aphides. These colours so produced are not, it has recently been shown, due to anthocyanin, but to bodies allied to the phenols. Mr. Holmes stated that "M. Armand Gautier has shown ('Comptes Rendus,' cxiv. p. 624) that an injury done to the petiole of a vine-leaf causes the formation in the leaf of a red colouring matter, similar to that produced in autumn, and he now states ('Comptes Rendus,' cxliii. p. 490) that the colouring matter produced by injury or not, as previously supposed concerning anthocyanin or erythrophyll, a uniform colouring matter derived from chlorophyll, from which it differs in containing neither nitrogen nor phosphorus, but belongs to the coloured phenol acids, is crystallisable, and of the nature of tannin. These pigments vary with each kind of plant, and those of fruits are not identical with those of leaves, although related to them. According to M. Mirande, the lesions produced by various fungi on leaves, e.g. *Ramularia, Cercospora, Septoria, Ovularia, Coryneum,* and *Gloeosporium,* have the same effect in producing the red colouring matter." The exciting cause in the case of the hawthorn leaves shown appears to have been the attack of aphides.

Geaster fornicatus.—Mr. Mawley showed an excellent specimen of this curious fungus found growing by the roadside at Berkhamsted.

Contortion in Carnation.—Dr. Masters showed a specimen of carnation having a curiously contorted stem, similar in appearance to the fasciated and contorted stems often seen in the teasel. It was referred to Mr. Worsdell, who promised to report upon it at the next meeting.

Pelargonium Sport.—Dr. Masters also showed specimens of flowers taken from a show pelargonium which normally produced irregular single flowers with purple blotches upon the upper petals. A lateral branch from this sported, so that it bore regular flowers and had the stamens replaced by petals. This sport was reproduced by cuttings.

SCIENTIFIC COMMITTEE, MAY 14, 1907.

Mr. G. MASSEE, V.M.H., in the Chair, and fifteen members present.

Contorted Carnation.—Mr. Worsdell F.L.S., said he had further examined the curious carnation plant shown by Dr. Masters at the last meeting, and remarked that De Vries had suggested that such contorted growths were the result of a reversion to a spiral arrangement of leaves, departing from the opposite decussate arrangement usual in the plant. Dissection of the bud appeared to support this view. In the specimen shown the leaves were also curiously rolled back.

Fungus on Retinospora.—Mr. Massee, V.M.H., said that the fungus shown at the last meeting by Mr. Saunders on *Retinospora* was *Gymnosporangium clavariiforme.*

Growth of Fern in Bottle.—Mr. Druery, V.M.H., showed the result of placing a small half-inch piece of the base of a frond of *Scolopendrium vulgare* on a layer of well-washed silver sand, one inch deep, thoroughly moistened, at the bottom of a pickle jar. The severed piece bore an incipient bud. The pickle jar was then tightly closed by means of a glass stopper, provided with a rubber ring. The exhibit represented the result of two years' growth without the admission of any air, the stopper having been wired on. The fern had a number of fronds about six inches in length, and new ones were rising; there were also one or two seedlings, believed to be Lastreas. A mass of filamentous algæ covered the sand and part of the bottle. The whole of this vegetative growth had been developed under the presumed air-tight conditions described. Members pointed out, however, the possibility of the diffusion of air even under the conditions described, and the fact that, as tap water had been used in washing and moistening the sand, a certain quantity of soluble earth salts had been originally admitted into the bottle.

Picea orientalis.—Mr. Bowles, F.L.S., showed, on behalf of Canon Ellacombe, inflorescences and cones of this beautiful conifer.

Coloration of Apple Flowers and Fruit.—Mr. H. J. Veitch, V.M.H., showed a long series of flowers of apples, some having white or only very slightly tinged flowers, while others had deeply coloured flowers. He remarked that in each case the pale-flowered apple trees bore very brightly coloured fruits, while those with deeply coloured flowers produced pale fruits. Mr. Cuthbertson said he had observed a similar thing in turnips, as in the 'Golden Tankard,' a turnip with yellow flesh, that produced white flowers. Mr. Bowles said that the rule was not without exception, as in *Pyrus Niedzwetzkyana* both the flowers and the fruits are very deeply coloured.

Richardias.—Mr. Chas. Woodbridge sent an inflorescence of *Richardia Elliottiana*, having a leaf arising close below the yellow spathe and coloured like the spathe, except that the margin and tip were green. Mr. Veitch showed R. × 'Mrs. Roosevelt' having a leaf arising from the base of the plant, as is usual, coloured very pale green except at the tip, which was similar in colour to the spathe.

Double Ribes.—A branch with very much doubled flowers of *Ribes sanguineum*, from Sir E. Loder (gr. Mr. W. A. Cook), of Leonardslee, was referred to Mr. Worsdell.

Potatoes.—Mr. A. W. Sutton, V.M.H., showed a very extensive and exceedingly interesting series of plants of tuberous Solanums. Particularly interesting were those of 'Papa Silvestre' (*Solanum Commersonii*), the wild potato of Uruguay. The examples had been grown from tubers received direct from Montevideo. Five separate consignments of these tubers have reached Mr. Sutton from his correspondent, who had himself collected the tubers in several different localities. The separate lots of tubers were found growing under very different conditions as regards soil and locality, but in no case near cultivated land. In each instance, so far as the plants have as yet developed, there is every reason to think that each lot of tubers represents one and the same species. With the last consignment Mr. Sutton received a certificate from Señor Arechavaleta, Curator of the Botanical Gardens, Montevideo, certifying that the tubers then sent were the true *Solanum Commersonii*, agreeing in all respects with the plant introduced by Commerson in 1767. Señor Arechavaleta further stated that all the wild potatoes found in Uruguay were one and the same type, and that they all bore violet-coloured flowers. Mr. Sutton produced Mons. Roze's book entitled " Histoire de la Pomme de Terre," in which there is an illustration and description of Commerson's original plants fully confirming Señor Arechavaleta's statement concerning the wild types of potato in Uruguay. In connection with the exhibit Mr. Sutton called attention to the fact that, so far as his information went, all the plants hitherto grown in Europe under the name *Solanum Commersonii* were of the white-flowered type, and it was certainly the white-flowered type which Mons. Labergerie had experimented with. The white-flowered plant was apparently introduced to Europe (Marseilles) between 1895 and 1901, and has since been cultivated under the name *Solanum Commersonii*.

Mr. Sutton also exhibited the following :—

1. "*Solanum tuberosum*, wild species," grown from tubers raised from seed received from Vermont Agricultural Experiment Station, 1906. This seed was collected in Mexico.

1a. "*Solanum tuberosum*, wild species," from seed saved from the foregoing at Reading in 1906.

1b. "*Solanum tuberosum*, wild species." Seedling plants raised from seed received from Vermont in 1907.

These three lots of seedlings so far exhibit no variations, but promise to come quite true from seed, and to be uniform in character.

1c. Seedlings raised by crossing No. 1 with pollen from white-flowering *Solanum Commersonii* at Reading in 1906.

1d. Seedlings from No. 1 crossed with pollen of *Solanum etuberosum*.

2. "*Solanum tuberosum (new* wild species)" collected in Mexico. Grown from seeds saved at Vermont in 1906.

3. *Solanum Maglia.* Grown from tubers received from Mr. Baker of Kew in 1886.

4. *Solanum verrucosum.* Grown from tubers raised from seed received from Vermont Agricultural Experiment Station, 1906.

4a. *S. verrucosum* seedlings from seed saved from No. 4 at Reading in 1906.

4b. *S. verrucosum* raised from seed received direct from Vermont, 1906.

5. *S. polyanthemum* from seed received from Vermont in 1906.

5a. *S. polyanthemum* from seed saved at Reading from tubers raised from No. 5.

It is remarkable that seedlings of all the above wild types appear to come true and quite uniform, when it is remembered that in the case of no cultivated potato do the seedlings come either uniformly true to each other or to the parent.

A hearty vote of thanks was accorded to Mr. Sutton for his very interesting and comprehensive exhibit.

SCIENTIFIC COMMITTEE, JUNE 11, 1907.

Sir J. T. D. LLEWELYN, Bart., in the Chair, and seventeen other members present.

The late Dr. M. T. Masters, F.R.S.—The Chairman, Sir J. T. D. Llewelyn, after referring in sympathetic terms to the loss the Committee had sustained in the death of Dr. Masters, who had for so long presided over the deliberations of the Committee, a loss which would be felt not only by them, but by the whole Society, and by the whole horticultural world, moved that a letter of condolence should be sent to his family. Dr. Cooke, V.M.H., seconded the motion, and it was carried by all the members of the Committee upstanding in their places.

Genetics.—Mr. Chittenden reported that he had received a communication from Mr. Bateson concerning the proposed meetings for the special consideration of the progress in the study of Genetics, brought forward at a recent meeting by Mr. A. Worsley. Mr. Bateson expressed himself in sympathy with the scheme. Mr. Chittenden also announced that Mr. Biffen would, at the next meeting, show a series of hybrid sweet peas to illustrate the Mendelian laws of inheritance.

British Plants.—Mr. Druery, V.M.H., showed some plants of *Senecio squalidus*, collected by Mr. C. B. Green, of Acton, on the railway bank near Southall, Middlesex. Mr. Worsdell said he had found it near the same place. The same gentleman sent the orchids, *Aceras anthropophora*, *Orchis Morio*, *Habenaria conopsea*, and *Orchis maculata*, collected near Harefield, in Middlesex.

Fern Distribution.—Mr. Druery also showed, on behalf of Mr. A. Dean, a fern, *Adiantum Capillus-Veneris*, enclosed in a bottle, one of many others growing in similar situations (but not all of the same species). A newly formed garden in Surbiton was edged with these bottles forced neck downwards into the soil, and the spores from which the ferns had grown must have been present in the soil. As Mr. Druery remarked, this illustrated well the ubiquity of the spores of ferns.

Fruit of Carum nigrum.—Mr. E. M. Holmes, F.L.S., showed the fruit of this Indian plant. The fruit possesses a distinct odour of cummin.

Spurless Aquilegia.—Mr. Empson, of North Walsham, sent flowers of a seedling *Aquilegia* which possesses no spurs. The form is not at all uncommon.

Injured Pistachio Nuts.—Cecil Whitaker, Esq., sent a number of pistachio nuts, grown in Sicily, which had been rendered completely useless owing to the attacks of some insects.

Malformation of Miltonia vexillaria.—Baron Schröder, V.M.H., sent a curious spike of this orchid, which bore four apparently double flowers. The spike was produced on a small and not very vigorous plant, taken from a larger plant, which had previously borne only single flowers of the ordinary type.

Spirally twisted Cedar.—Mr. Chittenden showed photographs and shoots from a cedar, *Cedrus atlantica*, the trunk and branches of which appeared to be spirally twisted, so that a corkscrew-like groove ran down them. Many of the young shoots upon the tree showed the same curious character. The tree is growing in the garden of Miss Seabrook, Springfield, Chelmsford, and appears to be unique.

Ribes sanguineum, Double.—Mr. Worsdell, F.L.S., reported that he had examined the double *Ribes* shown at the last meeting by Sir E. Loder, and found that each " flower " was not only doubled, but was at the same time of a compound structure, representing a rudimentary phase of splitting up into a number of flowers. No fungi or insects could be found in the flowers or twigs, although one or other of these may have occurred at an early stage in the plant's growth. A plant bearing similar flowers occurs at Kew.

SCIENTIFIC COMMITTEE, JUNE 25, 1907.

Mr. A. E. BOWLES, M.A., in the Chair, with fifteen other members present, and Mr. and Mrs. BIFFEN visitors.

The late Dr. Masters.—The Chairman read the following letter from Mrs. Maxwell Masters :—" Mrs. Maxwell Masters and her daughters wish to thank the members of the Scientific Committee for their very kind and much valued sympathy with them in their irreparable loss. The Scientific

Committee and its work were always of the deepest interest to its Chairman, and the fortnightly meetings formed one of the most agreeable interludes in his busy life."

New Vice-Chairman.—Rev. W. Wilks announced that the Council had that day resolved to appoint Messrs. J. T. Bennett-Poë, M.A., V.M.H., and E. A. Bowles, M.A., F.L.S., to fill the vacant places caused by the loss the Committee and the Society had sustained through the lamented death of Dr. M. T. Masters, F.R.S., and of Professor Michael Foster, F.R.S. The announcement was received with great pleasure by the Committee.

Sweet Peas and the Mendelian Laws.—Mr. R. H. Biffen showed a very interesting series of sweet peas to illustrate the discoveries so far made in regard to the laws of inheritance as exhibited in these plants. The great majority of crosses and so on had been made by Mrs. Biffen. The following were included in the series.

(1) Cream crossed with white gave all white (*i.e.* white dominant over cream). In the second generation from these whites self-fertilised, white and cream varieties were produced in the proportion of three white to one cream. The cream breeds true in the following generation, but only one in three of the whites is pure, the remaining two again producing creams.

(2) White crossed with white in the first generation gave a sweet pea approaching 'Painted Lady' in type. The seeds of this, by self-fertilisation, gave 'Painted Lady' and white in the proportion of nine of the former to seven of the latter, showing that one white parent carries a certain factor, the other another, which meeting, produce the red colour. In the third generation the whites and one of the reds breed true.

(3) White . × blue in the first generation gave purple, and in the following generation purple, blue, white, and 'Painted Lady.' The parents thus carry the two red-producing factors whose existence is demonstrated in the cross between the two white peas mentioned above. Where these meet in the presence of the blue colour, purple is formed, but in its absence 'Painted Lady.' Seeds of the purple varieties may reproduce the whole colour series again, those of the 'Painted Lady,' white and 'Painted Lady' only. The white varieties breed true, but blue may throw white.

(4) Cream with purple picotee edge × Mont Blanc (white) gave purple and in the second generation cream, white, cream with picotee edge, white with blue edge, 'Painted Lady' and purple. The character producing the picotee is dominant over the non picotee. The parents carry the factors for red demonstrated in the case of the cross between the two white varieties, which on meeting give 'Painted Lady.' In addition to these characters there are yellow and white, the former being recessive to the latter. Non-picotees breed true to this character. Picotees breed true in the proportion of one to three. Thus a picotee white may throw picotee white, picotee cream, plain white and plain cream, but a plain cream will breed true from the outset.

(5) 'Eric Hinton' (pink, with waved standard) × 'Hon. F. Bouverie' (pink, with buff tinge due to the presence of yellow chromoplasts, standard not waved). In the first cross the colour of the flowers was deep rose, similar to 'Prince of Wales,' and all had flat standards ; in the second the

flowers were yellow, pink, and buff with flat standards, and yellow and pink with waved standards. Waved forms had not so far occurred in buff colours.

(6) 'Bouverie' (pink and cream) × 'Navy Blue' gave in the first generation purple. In the following generation segregation into purple, pink, pink with cream, cream and tinged white occurred, and each of these types may or may not be flaked.

(7) If this be compared with the results obtained by crossing another pink with 'Navy Blue,' the same colours are produced, but no flaking occurs owing to the absence of the determining factor in one of the parents.

The series demonstrated the possibility of predicting the colour of the offspring in the second generation of any particular cross with great certainty, and showed the facility with which any particular two characters may be combined in any plants. In answer to questions, Mr. Biffen said that it was impossible to say beforehand in the case of two whites whether or not they carried the colour-producing factors. This could only be determined by experimental crossing. Several members remarked upon the desirability of trying the effect of crossing the wild sweet pea of Sicily with some of those known at present. A hearty vote of thanks was accorded to Mr. Biffen for his exhibit and explanatory remarks.

So-called Improved Clover.—Rev. Professor Henslow showed on behalf of Mr. A. G. Leighton, of Newcastle, Staffs, specimens of Mr. Leighton's improved clover. Mr. Leighton wrote :—"The form which I have produced assumes a more permanent character than the commercial plant. This qualification of permanency was the condition required ; for that derived from commercial seed appeared to run through the cycle of life during one summer ; this having been brought about by the system of producing seed for sale during the first year, the consequence being an annual tendency which by this continued selection becomes fixed and hereditary. I find that the period of life may be shortened in *Trifolium medium*, which brings with it more seeding capabilities combined with succulency and size of foliage. In like manner I find that *T. pratense* can be made more permanent, and this permanency brings with it a more procumbent habit, less succulency and size." The matter of clover standing over the first winter becomes a question of national importance ; farmers appeared to have a good plant at autumn, but the following spring all the clover had gone. This was attributed to clover sickness, but the fungus which is said to produce the trouble accompanies the death of most annuals ; therefore we may rightly say clover sickness was merely a fungus which accompanied the death of the plant.

The experiment conducted at Harpur Adams College, Newport, proves the truth of our investigations. A six-acre field was divided into three sections of two acres each.

Two acres, plot 1 : ordinary commercial seed from seedsman No. 1.

Two acres, plot 2 : seed of plants referred to above.

Two acres, plot 3 : ordinary commercial seed from seedsman No. 2.

At harvest, the first autumn after sowing, when the cereals were cut, and for some weeks after on plots Nos. 1 and 3, a good amount of clover was present. On plot No. 2, although the plant could be seen, it was small (not advanced in growth), but during December, January, and February, plots 1 and 3 appeared to lose plants with a black mould prevalent upon the plant. No. 2, as growing weather came along, showed evidence of great vitality, and produced a magnificent crop of red clover. In the other plots, although the same quantity of seed was used, clover almost entirely died out during the winter months. Several members demurred to the statement that the fungus (*Sclerotinia trifoliorum*), which so frequently appears connected with dying clover, accompanied the death of most annuals, and the Committee desired to hear the result of other experiments upon the plants. A hearty vote of thanks was accorded to Mr. Leighton.

Abnormal Cabbage.—W. Marshall, Esq., V.M.H., sent a cabbage from the leaves of which numerous cup-shaped growths had arisen, many upon long stalks taking their origin in the midrib of the leaf. The monstrous condition of mignonette referred to by Professor J. Henslow ("Trans. Camb. Phil. Soc." vol. v.) appears to present a similar phenomenon.

Carnation Flowers rotting.—Flowers of carnation were received which had rotted at the base of the petals, and had large black masses (sclerotia) among the decayed portions. The trouble was due to the growth of the fungus *Botrytis cinerea*, which had found congenial conditions for its development between the closely packed petals of the flower.

Double Miltonia vexillaria.—In reference to this flower, shown at the last meeting from Baron Schröder, Mr. Worsdell, F.L.S., reported that it was a good case of true doubling in which the column was split up ; the stamens and carpels had become petaloid so as to form three or four extra whorls of petals (labella on one side of the flower, ordinary petals on the other side), while the outer whorls of the flower were quite normal.

Sporting Coleus.—Mr. Divers showed a large *Coleus* having branches bearing at least five variations in the markings and coloration of the leaf different from those appearing in the first formed shoot. It is rarely that so many sports are to be seen upon one plant.

Plane diseased.—Shoots of plane (*Platanus acerifolia*) were shown from Romsey by Mr. Odell, which looked as though they had been injured by frost, but which had been attacked by the fungus *Gloeosporium nervisequum*, and this had caused the destruction of the shoots.

FLORAL COMMITTEE.

JANUARY 8, 1907.

Mr. H. B. MAY in the Chair, and twenty-four members present.

Awards Recommended :—

Silver-gilt Banksian Medal.

To Messrs. May, Edmonton, for Ferns &c.

Silver Flora Medal.

To Messrs. Cutbush, Highgate, for Carnations and hardy plants.

To Rev. H. Buckston, Etwall, Derby (gr. Mr. Shambrook), for Cyclamens.

To Messrs. J. Veitch, Chelsea, for winter-flowering plants and *Buddleia asiatica.*

Silver Banksian Meda .

To Lord Aldenham, Elstree (gr. Mr. Beckett, V.M.H.), for *Euphorbia jacquiniaeflora.*

To Messrs. Low, Enfield, for Carnations and Cyclamens.

To F. Galsworthy, Chertsey, for flower paintings.

Other Exhibits.

Messrs. Bull, Chelsea, staged miscellaneous stove plants.

Messrs. Hopkins, Barming, Maidstone, sent hardy flowers.

Messrs. Peed, Streatham, brought alpine plants.

Mr. L. R. Russell,.Richmond, sent *Buddleia asiatica.*

Messrs. Cannell, Swanley, staged Begonias and *Moschosma riparum.*

Mr. H. Whateley, Kenilworth, sent Chrysanthemum, ' Kenilworth Castle.'

Mr. G. Reuthe, Keston, Kent, brought hardy flowers.

A. Kingsmill, Esq., Harrow Weald, sent very fine *Pernettya mucronata.*

Mrs. Mann Thomson, Donkeith, Kilmarnock, N.B. (gr. Mr. Dewar), sent Chrysanthemums.

FLORAL COMMITTEE, JANUARY 22, 1907.

Mr. H. B. MAY in the Chair, and twenty-two members present.

Awards Recommended :—

Silver-gilt Banksian Medal.

To Messrs. Cutbush, Highgate, for Carnations, Oranges, &c.

Silver Flora Medal.

To Messrs. May, Edmonton, for Ferns.

To Messrs. J. Veitch, Chelsea, for winter-flowering plants.

Silver Banksian Medal.

To Messrs. Sutton, Reading, for Cyclamens.
To Mrs. S. Miller, Marlow, for paintings of flowers.
To Messrs. Low, Bush Hill Park, for Carnations, Cyclamens, &c.
To Mr. G. Lange, Hampton, for Carnations.

Bronze Flora Medal.

To C. F. Raphael, Esq., Porter's Park, Shenley (gr. Mr. Grubb), for cut Malmaison Carnations.

Other Exhibits.

Messrs. Barr, Covent Garden, sent hardy flowers.
Miss Hopkins, Hillside, Barming, brought hardy flowers.
Messrs. Peed, Streatham, sent Primulas and alpine plants.
Mr. L. R. Russell, Richmond, staged hardy shrubs.
Miss F. Farmer, sent paintings of flowers.
Mr. G. Reuthe, Keston, Kent, brought bulbous plants.
Messrs. Low, Bush Hill Park, sent *Nephrolepis Whitmonii*, which the Committee asked to see again.

FLORAL COMMITTEE, FEBRUARY 12, 1907.

Mr. MARSHALL, V.M.H., in the Chair, and twenty-six members present.

Awards Recommended :—

Silver-gilt Flora Medal.

To Messrs. Cutbush, Highgate, for Magnolias, Carnations, Crocus, &c.
To Messrs. Cuthbert, Southgate, for forced shrubs.
To Messrs. Sutton, Reading, for Primulas.

Silver-gilt Banksian Medal.

To Messrs. J. Veitch, Chelsea, for winter-flowering plants and Carnations.
To Mr. W. Seward, Hanwell, for Cyclamens.
To Messrs. W. Paul, Waltham Cross, for Camellias.
To Lady Tate, Park Hill, Streatham (gr. Mr. Howe), for forced bulbs.
To Messrs. Hill, Edmonton, for Ferns.
Messrs. Cannell, Swanley, for Primulas.

Silver Flora Medal.

To Lord Aldenham, Elstree (gr. Mr. Beckett, V.M.H.), for Cyclamens.
To C. F. Raphael, Esq., Shenley, Herts (gr. Mr. Grubb), for Malmaison Carnations.

Silver Banksian Medal

To Sir E. Loder, Bart., Leonardslee, Horsham (gr. Mr. Cook), for evergreen shrubs and Saracenias.
To Messrs. May, Edmonton, for winter-flowering plants and Ferns.

Bronze Flora Medal.

To Messrs. Low, Enfield, for Carnations, Cyclamens, &c.

To Mr. G. Reuthe, Keston, for alpine plants and shrubs.

To Messrs. Ware, Feltham, for alpine plants and Carnations.

Award of Merit.

To *Kalanchæ Dyeri* (votes, 15 for, 3 against), from Messrs. J. Veitch, Chelsea. A beautiful new species from Nyassaland (Central Africa). The plant has the usual succulent leaves, with a stout flower-stem about 2 feet high and a large truss of pure white flowers, each flower being 2 inches long, and ½ inch across, somewhat resembling a very large white Bouvardia bloom.

To *Nephrolepis Whitmonii* (votes, 17 for, 1 against), from Messrs. May and Messrs. Low. A perfectly charming variety, said to be a sport from *N. Fosterii*, which was a sport from *N. exaltata*. The variety under notice is somewhat like *N. todeaoides*, but sturdier in the fronds, and forms a beautiful mass of elegant fronds, about 15 inches long, and 8 inches wide at the base, tapering to a fine point.

Other Exhibits.

Messrs. Brooks, Basingstoke, staged Primula, 'Orange King.'

Miss M. H. Dodge, Losely Park, Guildford, sent a remarkably fine bunch of seeds, *Chamaerops Fortunei*.

Mr. A. F. Dutton, Iver, sent Carnations.

Mr. R. Mountford, Norton Priory Gardens, Runcorn, sent a plant of Begonia, 'Gloire de Lorraine,' bearing seed-pods freely.

Messrs. Barr, Covent Garden, sent bulbous flowers.

Mr. C. Englemann, Saffron Walden, staged Carnations.

Mrs. B. Gregory, Shoreham, sent some very fine Freesias.

Miss Hopkins, Barming, brought hardy flowers.

Messrs. Peed, Streatham, staged rock plants.

Mr. L. R. Russell, Richmond, sent forced flowering shrubs.

Mr. R. Sydenham, Birmingham, staged Lily of the Valley, &c.

Messrs. Felton, Hanover Square, W., brought Carnations.

FLORAL COMMITTEE, MARCH 5, 1907.

Mr. W. MARSHALL, V.M.H., in the Chair, and twenty-eight members present.

Awards Recommended :

Silver Banksian Medal.

To Lord Zouche, Barham Park, Pulborough (gr. Mr. Spillard), for Cyclamens.

First-class Certificate.

To *Cyrtomium Rochfordii* (votes, 15 for), from Messrs. T. Rochford, Turnford. This is much the finest form of *Cyrtomium falcatum* we have seen ; the long fronds are divided into numerous leaflets, each leaflet being deeply and beautifully serrated. The habit is strong and graceful. A charming acquisition.

Award of Merit.

To *Azalea amoena Hexe* (votes, 11 for, 5 against), from Messrs. J. Veitch, Chelsea. This variety was said to be raised from *A. indica* × *A. amoena*; the flowers are about the size of *A. indica*, of a very bright reddish-purple colour, and produced so freely as to hide the foliage, which is shorter and more rounded than that of *A. indica.* Quite small plants were covered with flowers.

To Rose 'Richmond' (votes, unanimous), from Mr. W. E. Wallace, Eaton, Bray. A deliciously scented H. T. Rose of brilliant colour, some-what resembling 'Liberty,' on which it is said to be an improvement, and larger in size. An American variety.

To Iris 'Aspasia' (votes, 16 for, 1 against), from Mr. F. H. Chapman, Guldeford Lodge, Rye. A glorified form of *I. reticulata*, and finer than *I. reticulata major*, the largest of the type.

To Iris 'Melusine' (votes, 12 for), from Mr. F. H. Chapman. A beautiful little variety of a pretty pale-blue colour, with bright yellow blotches on the falls, and indicating *I. reticulata* parentage on one side, with another dwarf variety for the other. Both the above varieties were raised by Herr Max Leichtlin, of Baden-Baden.

To *Freesia Chapmanii* (votes, unanimous), from Mr. F. H. Chapman, Rye. A remarkably fine variety, with five to eight flowers on each stem. The flowers are a pale yellow, with orange at the base of each segment, with a deep-orange blotch on the lower segment; the flower stems of unusual strength.

To the strain of *Primula stellata* 'The Lady,' from Messrs. Cannell, Swanley. A very fine strain of this type, the colours ranging from pure white to intense crimson.

To Lachenalia 'May Crosbie' (votes, unanimous), from Mr. F. W. Moore, V.M.H., Botanic Gardens, Glasnevin. A strong-growing variety, with large flowers of a beautiful soft-yellow colour.

Other Exhibits.

Mr. T. Avery, The Gardens, Loudwater, Rickmansworth, staged *Primula obconica.*

Messrs. Barr, Covent Garden, brought hardy flowers.

Messrs. Brooks, Basingstoke, sent Primulas.

Mr. F. H. Chapman, Rye, staged Iris.

Miss Hopkins, Barming, sent hardy flowers.

Messrs. H. B. May, Edmonton, staged flowering plants.

Mr. G. Reuthe, Keston, Kent, brought Crocus, Iris, &c.

Mr. R. Sydenham, Birmingham, sent Lily of the Valley.

Messrs. J. Veitch, Chelsea, staged flowering plants.

Messrs. Wallace, Colchester, brought bulbous flowers.

Messrs. Low, Enfield, staged Carnations.

Mr. J. Belland, Newton Abbot, sent a double-flowered Cyclamen.

Sir Trevor Lawrence, Bart., V.M.H., Burford, Dorking, sent *Cotyledon macranthum.*

Mr. F. Bedford, Straffan House Gardens, Straffan, Ireland, sent two varieties of Galanthus.

FLORAL COMMITTEE, MARCH 19, 1907.

Mr. MARSHALL, V.M.H., in the Chair, and twenty-six members present.

Awards Recommended :

Gold Medal.

To Messrs. J. Veitch, Chelsea, for Hippeastrums, Azaleas, &c.
To Messrs. Cutbush, Highgate, for forced shrubs and alpine plants.

Silver-gilt Flora Medal.

To Messrs. Cuthbert, Southgate, for forced shrubs.

Silver-gilt Banksian Medal.

To E. A. Hambro, Esq., Hayes Place, Kent (gr. Mr. Grandfield), for hardy plants.

Silver Flora Medal.

To Mr. H. Burnett, Guernsey, for Carnations.
To Messrs. Cannell, Swanley, for Pelargoniums and Primulas.
To Messrs. T. Rochford, Broxbourne, for *Nephrolepis todeaoides.*
To Messrs. Sutton, Reading, for Cactus-flowered Cinerarias.
To Mr. W. E. Wallace, Eaton, Bray, for Roses and Carnations.

Silver Banksian Medal.

To Lord Aldenham, Elstree, Herts (gr. Mr. Beckett, V.M.H.), for *Thyrsacanthus rutilans* and cut shrubs.
To Mr. A. F. Dutton, Iver, for Carnations.
To Messrs. May, Edmonton, for Clematis.
To Mr. G. Mount, Canterbury, for Roses.
To Messrs. W. Paul, Waltham Cross, for Peaches and Almonds in blossom.
To Mr. G. Reuthe, Keston, for alpine plants and Rhododendrons.
To Messrs. Ware, Feltham, for hardy plants.

Bronze Flora Medal.

To Mr. L. R. Russell, Richmond, for forced shrubs.
To Mr. R. Gill, Penryn, for cut Rhododendrons.

Bronze Banksian Medal.

To Mrs. Bischoffsheim, The Warren House, Stanmore (gr. Mr. Doig), for Lachenalias.

Award of Merit.

To *Magnolia Soulangiana nigra* (votes, unanimous), from Messrs. Cuthbert, Southgate. A very striking variety, similar to the type, except that the back of each petal is a dark-plum colour, covered with a purplish sheen.
To Rhododendron 'Duke of Cornwall' (votes, unanimous), from Mr. R. Gill, Tremough, Penryn. Flower and truss of the largest size and of a rich-crimson colour, with a beautiful sheen ; the upper petals

are marked with minute dark dots.   Raised from *R. barbatum* ×
R. arboreum.

To Rhododendron ' Kewensi' (votes, unanimous), from Messrs. Paul,
Cheshunt. Flowers large, broad, and in moderate-sized clusters, and a
lovely shade of pale rosy-pink ; it is said to be raised from *R. Griffithianum*
× *Hookeri.*

To *Saxifraga Burseriana gloria* (votes, 17 for, 4 against), from Mr.
R. J. Farrer, Clapham, Lancaster. A splendid form of *Saxifraga
Burseriana*, having flowers over 1 inch across, pure white, and much
finer than any of the other forms.

Other Exhibits.

Mr. F. Hamilton, Craighlaw, Kirkcowan, sent Violets.

Arthur R. Goodwin, Esq., The Elms, Kidderminster, brought
Galanthus Imperati, var. *Atkinsii.*

Messrs. Jarman, Chard, staged *Cineraria stellata.*

J. T. Bennett-Poë, Esq., V.M.H., sent a new and unrecognised
Thibaudia.

Sir E. Loder, Bart., Leonardslee, sent *Stauntonia latifolia.*

Sir Trevor Lawrence, Bart., V.M.H., Burford, sent several stove and
greenhouse plants of interest.

Mr. J. H. Pollock, Wandsworth, brought a curious Hyacinth.

Mr. W. A. Cull, Edmonton, staged *Pteris Wimsettii* 'Distinction.'

Messrs. Barr, Covent Garden, brought hardy flowers.

Messrs. Bloom, Haarlem, sent bulbs and forced shrubs.

Messrs. Cheal, Crawley, staged hardy-plants.

Miss Hopkins, Maidstone, sent spring flowers.

Messrs. Peed, Streatham, brought alpine plants, &c.

Mr. G. Redman, Clapham, Lancaster, staged spring flowers.

Mr. R. Sydenham, Birmingham, sent Lily of the Valley.

Mrs. Williams, Caerhay Castle, Gerron, sent Violets.

FLORAL COMMITTEE, APRIL 8, 1907.

Mr. MARSHALL, V.M.H., in the Chair, and thirteen members present.

Awards Recommended :—

Silver-gilt Flora Medal.

To Messrs. Cutbush, Highgate, for Carnations, alpine plants, &c.

To Messrs. Cuthbert, Southgate, for Hyacinths.

To Messrs. Veitch, Chelsea, for flowering plants.

To W. James, Esq., West Dean Park, Chichester (gr. Mr. Smith), for
Tree Paeonies.

Silver-gilt Banksian Medal.

To Messrs. Cannell, Swanley, for Pelargoniums and Cinerarias.

To Messrs. Low, Bush Hill Park, for hard-wooded plants and
Carnations.

Silver Flora Medal.

To Messrs. May, Edmonton, for hardy Ferns and Cinerarias.

To Messrs. Smith, Worcester, for Clematises.

FIG .21.—RHODODENDRON INTRICATUM. (*Gardeners' Chronicle.*)

Silver Banksian Medal.

To Hon. Walter Rothschild, Tring Park, for *Doryanthus excelsa.*

To Messrs. F. Cant, Colchester, for Roses.

To Sir E. Loder, Bart., Leonardslee, Horsham (gr. Mr. Cook), for Rhododendrons *Magnolia Campbellii.*

To Mr. G. Reuthe, Keston, Kent, for hardy plants.

To Mr. L. R. Russell, Richmond, for forced flowering shrubs.

Bronze Flora Medal.

To Miss M. Dodge, Loseley Park, Guildford (gr. W. Staward), for Violets.

First-class Certificate.

To *Rhododendron intricatum* (votes, 9 for), from Messrs. J. Veitch, Chelsea. A new species introduced by Messrs. J. Veitch from China. The plants exhibited were quite small and covered with neat little trusses of pretty small rosy-lilac blossoms and with foliage somewhat resembling that of *Azalea amoena,* but of a greyer shade of colour. The plant is said to be perfectly hardy and to blossom twice a year. A charming and distinct plant.

Award of Merit.

To Hippeastrum 'Lady Howick' (votes, 8 for, 1 against), from Major Holford, C.V.O., C.I.E., Westonbirt, Tetbury (gr. Mr. Chapman). A new and distinct treat in colour ; the flower is of medium size, good shape, and a lovely Malmaison carnation colour, flaked with white.

To Hippeastrum 'Vulcan' (votes, 8 for, 3 against), from Major Holford, C.V.O., C.I.E, Westonbirt. An immense flower of excellent form and of an intense crimson colour, shading to a darker colour at the base of the petals.

Cultural Commendation.

To Mr. Smith, gr. to W. James, Esq., West Dean Park, Chichester, for Tree Paeonies.

Other Exhibits.

Messrs. Cheal, Crawley, staged hardy plants.

Messrs. Dobbie, Rothesay, brought Violas and Violets.

Miss Hopkins, Barming, sent hardy flowers.

Messrs. Paul, Cheshunt, brought Rhododendrons &c.

Messrs. Peed, Streatham, staged alpine plants.

The Horticultural College, Swanley, sent Primulas.

Messrs. Manger, Guernsey, sent Anemone 'His Excellency.'

N. C. Cookson, Esq., Oakwood, Wylam-on-Tyne, sent *Hippe-Vallota Oakwoodiense album.* A very pretty flower raised from white-flowered *Hippeastrum* × *Vallota purpurea.* The colour of the flower is pure white, with a shade of green down the midrib of each petal.

The Earl of Onslow, Clandon Park, Guildford, sent Wistaria 'Countess of Onslow,' a pretty pink-flowered variety.

Messrs. Barr, Covent Garden, sent hardy plants.

W. Cobb, Esq., Rusper, Horsham, brought a curiously formed flower of *Richardia Elliottiana.*

FLORAL COMMITTEE, APRIL 16, 1907.

Mr. MARSHALL, V.M.H., in the Chair, and twenty-six members present.

Awards Recommended :—

Gold Medal.

To Mr. G. Mount, Canterbury, for magnificent Roses.

Silver-gilt Flora Medal.

To Messrs. J. Veitch, Chelsea, for miscellaneous flowering plants.

Silver-gilt Banksian Medal.

To Messrs. Sutton, Reading, for Cinerarias.
To Messrs. Cannell, Swanley, for Pelargoniums, Begonias, &c.

Silver Flora Medal.

To J. A. Kenrick, Esq., Edgbaston, for Hippeastrums.
To Messrs. Low, Bush Hill Park, for New Holland and greenhouse plants.
To Messrs. W. Paul, Waltham Cross, for pillar Roses.

Silver Banksian Medal.

To Messrs. Hill, Lower Edmonton, for Ferns.
To Sir E. Loder, Bart., Leonardslee, Horsham (gr. Mr. Cook), for Camellias, Magnolias, &c.
To Mr. L. R. Russell, Richmond, for Clematis and flowering shrubs.
To Mr. W. E. Wallace, Dunstable, for Roses.

Bronze Flora Medal.

To Messrs. Cragg, Harrison, & Cragg, Heston, for Cacti and succulent plants.
To Messrs. Cutbush, Highgate, for Carnations, alpines, &c.
To Mr. M. Prichard, Christchurch, for hardy flowers.
To Mr. G. Reuthe, Keston, Kent, for alpine plants &c.
To Messrs. Ware, Feltham, for herbaceous and alpine plants.

Bronze Banksian Medal.

To Messrs. Cripps, Tunbridge Wells, for Acers, Roses, &c.
To Messrs. Cuthbert, Southgate, for Azaleas.

First-class Certificate.

To *Agapetes speciosa* (votes, unanimous), from J. T. Bennett-Poë, Esq., V.M.H. A beautiful new species, with bright-red tubular flowers about 1 inch long. A warm greenhouse plant seldom seen, and of which there are only a few varieties.

Award of Merit.

To *Freesia Tubergeni* Amethyst (votes, 16 for, 2 against), from Mr. C. G. van Tubergen, jun., Haarlem, Holland. A large-flowered variety, with light lilac-coloured flowers. Raised from *F. refracta alba* × *F. Tubergeni*.

To *Primula Cockburniana* (votes, 17 for), from Messrs. J. Veitch, Chelsea. A new and very dwarf species from Western China. Foliage small and greyish, serrated at the margins, flower stalk slender, with a small truss of deep orange-red flowers, rather less than 1 inch across.

To Rose ' Pharisaer ' (votes, 20 for, 2 against), from Mr. W. E. Wallace, Eaton Bray, Dunstable. A very pretty pink rose, valuable for bedding, and well known.

To Auricula ' Miss Berkeley ' (votes, unanimous), from Mr. J. Douglas, V.M.H., Great Bookham. An alpine variety of large size with a clear white eye surrounded by intense dark purple.

To Auricula ' Brightness ' (votes, 10 for, 5 against), from Mr. J. Douglas, V.M.H., Great Bookham. A very handsome alpine variety with rosy-purple flowers.

Cultural Commendation.

To Mr. S. Kevan, gr. to Lady Emlyn, Frensham Hall, Haslemere, for *Tchihatchewia isatidea.* A very rare and difficult plant to grow, and said to succeed best on the rockery. Flowers rosy-lilac or shading to red on a much-branched corymb ; leaves 3 inches long, linear and hairy. Perennial. The plant exhibited was admirably grown

Other Exhibits.

Messrs. F. Cant, Colchester, staged Roses.

Messrs. Dobbie, Rothesay, brought Violas, Pansies, &c.

Mr. J. Douglas, V.M.H., Great Bookham, staged Auriculas.

Miss Hopkins, Barming, sent hardy flowers.

Messrs. Jackman, Woking, brought alpine plants.

Lady Hindlip, Hindlip, Worcester, sent Sweet Peas.

Mr. G. Kerswill, Exeter, staged *Gentiana acaulis.*

Miss Kipping, Hutton, Essex, brought alpine plants.

Messrs. H. B. May, Edmonton, sent flowering plants and Ferns.

Messrs. Peed, Streatham, sent alpine plants.

Mr. A. Quarrell, Brecon, staged Asters and Chrysanthemums.

Mr. G. Redman, Clapham, Lancaster, brought alpine plants.

Mr. R. Sydenham, Birmingham, sent Lilies-of-the-Valley.

Mr. A. R. Upton, Millmead, Guildford, staged alpine plants.

Messrs. Wallace, Colchester, brought hardy flowers.

Messrs. Barr, Covent Garden, sent Daisies &c.

Mrs. Brocklehurst, Sudeley Castle, Gloucester, sent *Tritonia crocata* ' Prince of Orange.'

Lady Montagu of Beaulieu, Brockenhurst, Hants, sent *Epimedium rubrum.*

Lady Tress Barry, Windsor, sent Camellias.

Mr. E. M. Holmes, Ruthven, Sevenoaks, brought *Oxalis acetosella.*

The Countess of Bathurst, Cirencester, sent Clivia ' Countess of Bathurst.'

Mr. T. Leslie, Trinity Cottage, Edinburgh, staged Rhododendron seedlings.

Mr. C. E. Wilkins, South Croydon, brought zonal Pelargonium ' Coral.'

FLORAL COMMITTEE, APRIL 30, 1907.

Mr. MARSHALL, V.M.H., in the Chair, and seventeen members present.

Awards Recommended :—

Silver-gilt Lindley Medal.

To Hon. Walter Rothschild, Tring Park (gr. Mr. Dye), for splendidly grown and flowered plants of *Gloriosa Rothschildiana.*

Silver-gilt Flora Medal.

To C. F. Raphael, Esq., Porter's Park, Shenley (gr. Mr. Grubb), for admirably grown ' Malmaison ' Carnations.

To Messrs. J. Veitch, Chelsea, for greenhouse plants and flowering shrubs.

Silver Flora Medal.

To Lord Aldenham, Elstree (gr. Mr. Beckett, V.M.H.), for flowering shrubs.

To Messrs. Cannell, Swanley, for Pelargoniums and Primulas.

To Messrs. B. Cant, Colchester, for Roses.

To Messrs. Cutbush, Highgate, for Carnations and herbaceous plants.

To Mr. L. R. Russell, Richmond, for flowering shrubs and Clematises.

Silver Banksian Medal.

To Messrs. Cheal, Crawley, for rock plants.

To Messrs. Cripps, Tunbridge Wells, for Acers.

To Messrs. Dobbie, Rothesay, for Violas and Anemones.

To Hobbies, Ltd., Dereham, for Roses.

To Messrs. May, Edmonton, for flowering greenhouse plants.

To Mr. G. Mount, Canterbury, for Roses.

To Messrs. Paul, Cheshunt, for shrubs.

To Messrs. W. Paul, Waltham Cross, for Roses.

To Messrs. Peed, Streatham, for Gloxinias and Acers.

To Messrs. Carter, High Holborn, for Cinerarias.

Bronze Flora Medal.

To Mr. Upton, Guildford, for hardy plants.

To Mr. G. Reuthe, Keston, Kent, for hardy plants.

Award of Merit.

To Cydonia japonica Simonii (votes, unanimous), from Lord Aldenham, Elstree. A very fine free-flowering variety, with intense crimson-scarlet flowers. A decided acquisition for its splendid colour.

To Carnation 'Jessica ' (votes, 12 for), from Messrs. Cutbush, Highgate. A winter-flowering variety with large very well-shaped flowers ; colour white striped with deep red, sweet-scented.

Other Exhibits.

Messrs. Gauntlett, Chiddingfold, staged Japanese Azaleas.

Messrs. Gilbert, Dyke, Bourne, brought Anemones.

J. Tremayne, Esq., Heligon, sent Rhododendron blooms.

Miss Hopkins, Barming, staged hardy plants.

Lord Howard de Walden, Audley End, Saffron Walden (gr. Mr. Vert), sent Schizanthus.

Messrs. Jackman, Woking, brought hardy plants.

Misses Kipping, Hutton, staged hardy plants.

B. Levett, Esq., 39 Wilton Crescent, S.W., sent *Iris tingitana*.

Messrs. Low, Bush Hill Park, brought New Holland plants &c.

Mr. A. Perry, Enfield, staged hardy plants.

Mr. M. Prichard, Christchurch, staged hardy plants.

The Duke of Rutland, Belvoir Castle (gr. Mr. Divers), sent flowering shrubs.

Mr. R. Sydenham, Birmingham, brought Lilies &c.

Messrs. R. Veitch, Exeter, sent flowering shrubs.

Messrs. Ware, Feltham, brought hardy plants.

Mr. W. E. Wallace, Dunstable, staged Roses.

Messrs. Bide, Farnham, sent Rose 'Queen of Spain.'

Mr. Wilson, gr. to Lady Lilford, Lilford Hall, Oundle, brought a seedling form of *Primula rosea*.

Mr. Murray Thomson, Edinburgh, sent double Primulas.

H. A. Mangles, Esq., Littleworth Cross, Seale, sent some charming Rhododendron flowers.

FLORAL COMMITTEE, MAY 14, 1907.

Mr. MARSHALL, V.M.H., in the Chair, and twenty-five members present.

Awards Recommended :—

Gold Medal.

To Mr. J. Douglas, V.M.H., Edenside, Great Bookham, for a magnificent collection of Auriculas.

Silver-gilt Flora Medal.

To Messrs. J. Veitch, Chelsea, for Carnations, flowering plants, and shrubs.

To Messrs. J. Waterer, Bagshot, for Rhododendrons.

Silver-gilt Banksian Medal.

To Mr. A. F. Dutton, Iver, for Carnations.

To Mr. L. R. Russell, Richmond, for Clematises and shrubs.

To Messrs. Ware, Feltham, for hardy plants.

Silver Flora Medal.

To Messrs. Cannell, Swanley, for Pelargoniums &c.

To Messrs. B. R. Cant, Colchester, for Roses.

Messrs. J. Carter, High Holborn, for Cinerarias.

To Messrs. Cutbush, Highgate, for Ericas, Carnations, shrubs, &c.

To Messrs. Peed, Streatham, for Gloxinias, Maples, &c.

To Messrs. Turner, Slough, for Azaleas and Lilacs.

Silver Banksian Medal.

To Messrs. Dobbie, Rothesay, for Violas and Polyanthuses.

To Mr. G. Jackman, Woking, for alpine plants &c.

To Sir E. Loder, Bart., Leonardslee, Horsham, for rare flowering plants.

To Messrs. Low, Enfield, for Carnations and New Holland plants.

To Messrs. May, Edmonton, for Ferns and Verbenas.

To Messrs. Paul, Cheshunt, for hardy shrubs.

To Messrs. W. Paul, Waltham Cross, for Roses.

To the Marquis of Salisbury, Hatfield House (gr. Mr. Prime), for *Saintpaulia ionantha.*

Bronze Flora Medal.

To Messrs. James, Farnham Royal, for Calceolarias.

To Messrs. Tubergen, Haarlem, for Irises.

Bronze Banksian Medal.

To Misses Hopkins, Barming, for alpine plants.

To J. A. Young, Esq., Stone House, Putney (gr. Mr. Street), for Schizanthuses &c.

Award of Merit.

To Aubrietia ' Henry Marshall ' (votes, 15 for), from Mr. M. Prichard, Christchurch. A remarkably floriferous variety with medium-sized rich purple flowers with a whitish eye.

To *Gladiolus atroviolaceus* (votes, 17 for), from Messrs. Wallace, Colchester. A rather peculiar species from Palestine, with a flower spike about 18 inches long, somewhat twisted, with deep violet-coloured flowers, the lower segments being striped with white. The foliage is narrow, and of a beautiful glaucous green colour.

To Iris ' Luna ' (votes, unanimous), from Mr. C. G. van Tubergen, Haarlem. The ground colour of this handsome flower is a delicate mauve, with regular veins of dark purple ; on the falls is a very large purple, almost black, blotch. The flower is of good size and perfect form, and is one of the *I. Onco-Regelia* section.

To *Haberlea rhodopensis virginalis* (votes, unanimous), from Mr. R. Farrer, Clapham, Yorks. A very pretty hardy herbaceous perennial, imported from the Balkans two years ago. The flowers are borne singly on slender stalks, about 6 inches long, and are a pure white with a lemon blotch at the base of the lower segment. The foliage resembles that of the Ramondia.

To *Hydrangea arborescens grandiflora* (votes, unanimous), from Messrs. Paul, Cheshunt. A very fine variety with pure white flowers, larger than those of *H. arborescens.* An excellent hardy plant.

To *Clivia miniata citrina* (votes, 9 for, 8 against), from the Hon. Mrs. Evelyn Cecil, 10 Eaton Place, S.W. A pure yellow-flowered form of the well-known *C. miniata,* and was found growing wild near Eshowe, Zululand, by Lady Saunders.

Other Exhibits.

Messrs. Bees, Liverpool, sent Mimulus.

Mr. C. Breadmore, Winchester, staged Sweet Peas.

Messrs. Bunyard, Maidstone, brought herbaceous plants.

Mr. F. Cant, Colchester, brought Roses.

Messrs. Carter Page, London Wall, E.C., staged Fuchsias, Sweet Peas, &c.

Messrs. Cheal, Crawley, sent flowering shrubs &c.

Messrs. Clark, Dover, sent alpine plants.

Messrs. Gilbert, Bourne, brought Anemones.

Misses Kipping, Hutton, staged alpine plants &c.

Mr. C. S. Layton, Harrow Weald, sent Calceolarias.

Sir James W. Mackay, Dublin, staged Anemones.

Mr. A. Perry, Enfield, brought hardy plants.

Mr. M. Prichard, Christchurch, brought rock plants.

Mr. H. C. Pulham, Stansted, sent alpine plants.

Mr. G. Reuthe, Keston, staged Rhododendrons &c.

Mr. A. R. Upton, Guildford, brought alpine plants.

Mr. H. Hedges, Sydenham, staged Pelargonium ' Kirkdale Scarlet.'

TEMPLE SHOW.

FLORAL COMMITTEE, MAY 28, 1907.

Mr. H. B. MAY in the Chair, and twenty-seven members present.

The list of Cups and Medals will be found on pp. xvi–xix.

Awards Recommended :—

Award of Merit.

To *Saxifraga Aizoon rosea* (votes, unanimous), from The Craven Nursery, Clapham, Lancs. A charming plant for the rockery, with encrusted foliage and pretty rose-coloured flowers. A lovely acquisition.

To Azalea 'Madame Anthony Koster' (votes, 13 for, 1 against), from Messrs. Cuthbert, Southgate. An exquisite variety with large trusses of flowers of a rich apricot-colour, with a decided tinge of rose at the margin of the petals. Raised from *A. mollis* × *A. sinensis.*

To *Verbena Aubletia compacta* (votes, 8 for, 4 against), from Messrs. Dobbie, Rothesay. A very compact form of the old *V. Aubletia*, with rosy-lilac flowers. It is said to come true from seed.

To Begonia 'Mrs. J. C. Gwillim' (votes, unanimous), from Mr. A. L. Gwillim, New Eltham. A tuberous variety with large shapely flowers of a salmon-red ; double flowers. (Fig. 22.)

To Begonia 'Rhoda Pope' (votes, unanimous), from Messrs. Ware, Feltham. A tuberous variety with large handsome flowers of pale pink colour.

To Begonia 'William Marshall' (votes, unanimous), from Messrs. Ware, Feltham. Flowers double, deep scarlet, and of fine form. A very fine tuberous variety.

To Begonia 'Lady Cromer' (votes, unanimous), from Messrs. Ware, Feltham. An immense double-flowered tuberous variety. The flowers are of good form and a rich coral-pink colour.

To Rose 'Dr. William Gordon' (votes, unanimous), from Messrs. W. Paul, Waltham Cross. A H.P. variety with beautifully formed pink flowers with recurved petals. The growth is upright and very sturdy.

To Primula 'Unique' (votes, unanimous), from Messrs. J. Veitch, Chelsea. Raised from *P. pulverulenta* × *P. Cockburniana*. The flower resembles the former more than the latter, but shows very distinct

FIG. 22.—BEGONIA 'MRS. J. C. GWILLIM.'

indications of *P. Cockburniana*. The flowers are a deep reddish-purple, and produced in whorls on stout flower-stems about 18 inches high.

To *Cytisus Andreanus* 'Firefly' (votes, unanimous), from Messrs. Wallace, Colchester. A very pretty variety with flowers of yellow and crimson, the latter colour predominating.

To Tulip 'Gorgeous' (votes, unanimous), from Messrs. A. Dickson, Belfast. This is one of the Darwin class, and the shapely flowers are a very deep orange-red, borne on strong stems.

To *Actinidia chinensis* (votes, 11 for), from Messrs. J. Veitch, Chelsea. A very beautiful hardy climber from China, and should prove a most valuable plant for pergolas or pillars. The growth resembles that of the vine, and the foliage is of ovate form, reddish, and the under side of the leaves and the young stems are covered with shining red hairs. It is stated to produce handsome yellow flowers, 1½ inch in diameter, followed by fruits the size of a walnut and the flavour of a gooseberry.

To Caladium 'Thomas Tomlinson' (votes, unanimous), from Messrs. J. Veitch, Chelsea. A very striking large-foliaged variety. The leaves are crimson margined with deep green.

To Papaver 'Princess Ena' (votes, unanimous), from Mr. A. Perry, Enfield. A handsome large-flowered herbaceous variety with lovely pale salmon-coloured flowers.

To Carnation 'Marmion' (votes, unanimous), from Mr. H. Burnett, Guernsey. A beautiful sweet-scented variety of the Tree type, with flowers of bright crimson and the petals margined with white.

FLORAL COMMITTEE, JUNE 11, 1907.

Mr. MARSHALL, V.M.H., in the Chair, and thirty members present.

Awards Recommended : —

Silver-gilt Flora Medal.

To Messrs. May, Edmonton, for a splendid collection of Nephrolepis.
To Mr. G. Mount, Canterbury, for Roses.

Silver-gilt Banksian Medal.

To Messrs. Cutbush, Highgate, for Carnations &c.
To Messrs. Low, Enfield, for Carnations &c.
To Mr. A. Perry, Enfield, for Poppies, Pyrethrums, &c.
To Mr. C. F. Waters, Balcombe, for Carnations.
To Messrs. J. Veitch, Chelsea, for Gloxinias, shrubs, &c.

Silver Flora Medal.

To Messrs. Cannell, Swanley, for Cannas and Gloxinias.
To Messrs. B. R. Cant, Colchester, for Roses. .
To Messrs. Paul, Cheshunt, for Roses.
To Mr. M. Prichard, Christchurch, for hardy plants.
To Messrs. Wallace, Colchester, for hardy plants.
To J. A. Young, Esq., Stone House, Putney (gr. Mr. Street), for Calceolarias and Gloxinias.

Silver Banksian Medal.

To Mr. C. W. Breadmore, Winchester, for Sweet Peas.
To Messrs. F. Cant, Colchester, for Roses.
To Messrs. Gilbert, Bourne, for Anemones.
To Messrs. Kelway, Langport, for Paeonies, Delphiniums, &c.
To Mr. G. Reuthe, Keston, for hardy plants.

Bronze Flora Medal.

To Messrs. Barr, Covent Garden, for hardy plants.

To Messrs. Bunyard, Maidstone, for hardy plants.

To Lady Northcliffe, Sutton Place, Guildford (gr. Mr Goatley), for herbaceous flowers.

To Messrs. Ware, Feltham, for hardy plants.

Bronze Banksian Medal.

To Messrs. Clark, Dover, for hardy flowers.

Award of Merit.

To *Meconopsis racemosa* (votes, 19 for), from Lady Northcliffe, Sutton Place, Guildford (gr. Mr.. Goatley). A Chinese species, with purplish-blue flowers, with a distinct sheen on the petals ; the flowers are about 3 inches across, produced singly up the stems, which are 15 to 18 inches high. The leaves are about 4 inches long, and both foliage and stem are covered with stiff grey prickles.

To *Davallia braziliensis* (votes, 14 for), from Messrs. May, Edmonton. A new species from Brazil. A very distinct plant with long smooth fronds and attenuated pinnules. As it comes from the temperate regions, and is found on mountain sides, it should thrive well in a cool greenhouse.

To Iris 'Caterina' (votes, unanimous), from Messrs. Barr, Covent Garden. A hybrid raised from *I. cypriana × I. pallida.* Flowers light mauve with white "fall" marked with brown and conspicuous yellow anthers. Stems tall and handsome, and evidently a vigorous grower.

To Iris 'Paracina' (votes, unanimous), from Messrs. Barr, Covent Garden. Raised from *I. paradoxa × I. sambucina.* The flower is of medium size, purple, with the "falls" nicely marked with white. The stems were about 18 inches long.

To *Syringa Josikaea eximia* (votes, unanimous), from Sir Trevor Lawrence, Bart., Burford, Dorking (gr. Mr. Bain). This is valuable chiefly for its lateness, flowering after most lilacs are over. Flowers are pale red, almost pink, and deliciously scented.

To Hippeastrum 'Mrs. Carl Jay' (votes, unanimous), from Mrs. Carl Jay, Blendon Hall, Bexley (gr. Mr. Humphrey). A very distinct variety, producing its scapes of flowers remarkably freely. The flowers are of medium size, good form ; the ground of the flower is white, heavily marked and netted with rose-pink. The leaves are broader than the type, with a bold white band down the centre of each leaf.

To *Lonicera Maackii* (votes, unanimous), from Messrs. J. Veitch, Chelsea. A beautiful hardy shrubby variety with pure white flowers, freely produced, and rather lance-shaped foliage.

Other Exhibits.

Messrs. Baker, Codsall, Staffs, staged Aquilegias.

Messrs. Boyes, Leicester, brought Carnations.

Messrs. Bull, Chelsea, sent miscellaneous plants.

Messrs. Carter Page, London Wall, sent Fuchsias and Dahlias.

Messrs. Dobbie, Marks Tey, staged Aquilegias.

Miss Wilshire, The Frythe, Welwyn (gr. Mr. Fitt), sent flowers of Double Rocket.

Mr. A. R. Upton, Guildford, brought hardy plants.

Messrs. Gunn, Olton, staged Phlox.

Hobbies, Ltd., Dereham, sent Roses.

Miss Hopkins, Barming, brought hardy plants.

Messrs. Jackman, Woking, staged hardy plants.

Mr. H. Jones, Lewisham, sent Sweet Peas.

Messrs. W. Paul, Waltham Cross, staged Rhododendrons.

Messrs. Peed, Streatham, brought hardy plants.

Mr. G. Prince, Oxford, sent Roses.

Mr. L. R. Russell, Richmond, staged stove plants.

Messrs. Turner, Slough, sent Carnations.

Mr. J. H. Blandford, Hill Brow, Farnborough, sent *Melia Azedarach* var. *umbraculifera*.

P. P. G. Ferguson, Esq., Weybridge, sent *Iris bracteata*.

Hon. Mrs. Evelyn Cecil, 10 Eaton Place, S.W., sent several interesting plants collected in Rhodesia.

FLORAL COMMITTEE, JUNE 25, 1907.

Mr. MARSHALL, V.M.H., in the Chair, and twenty-two members present.

Awards Recommended :—

Silver-gilt Flora Medal.

To Messrs. J. Veitch, Chelsea, for miscellaneous flowering plants, Paeonies, &c.

To Messrs. Paul, Cheshunt, for *Lilium giganteum*, Roses, and Paeonies.

To Mr. A. Perry, Enfield, for hardy cut flowers.

Silver-gilt Banksian Medal.

To Mr. C. W. Breadmore, Winchester, for Sweet Peas.

Silver Flora Medal.

To Messrs. Barr, Covent Garden, for Paeonies &c.

To Messrs. Bunyard, Maidstone, for herbaceous flowers, Roses, &c.

To Messrs. Cannell, Swanley, for Begonias, Gloxinias, &c.

To Messrs. Cutbush, Highgate, for hardy plants.

To Mr. M. Prichard, Christchurch, for hardy cut flowers.

To Mr. G. Reuthe, Keston, for shrubs, alpine plants, &c.

To J. A. Young, Esq., Putney (gr. Mr. Street), for Pelargoniums.

Silver Banksian Medal.

To Messrs. B. R. Cant, Colchester, for Roses.

To Messrs. H. B. May, Edmonton, for Ferns and flowering plants.

To Mr. L. R. Russell, Richmond, for stove and greenhouse foliage plants.

To Messrs. R. Wallace, Colchester, for hardy flowers.

To Messrs. Ware, Feltham, for Paeonies.

Bronze Flora Medal.

To Messrs. Clark, Dover, for herbaceous flowers.

To Messrs. Homan, Noordwijk, Holland, for Spanish Iris.

To Mr. Upton, Guildford, for hardy plants.

Award of Merit.

To Iris ' King of the White ' (votes, unanimous), from Messrs. Homan, Noordwijk, Holland.   An *I. hispanica* with large pure white flowers and a bright yellow blotch on the falls.

To Iris 'L'Unique' (votes, unanimous), from Messrs. Homan, Holland.   Another *I. hispanica* with large upright blue standards and blue-and-white falls.   A very fine variety.

To Iris 'Mr. Walter T. Ware' (votes, unanimous), from Messrs. Homan, Holland.   A charming *I. hispanica,* having large pale-yellow flowers with a rich orange blotch on the falls.

To Coleus ' Cordelia ' (votes, unanimous), from E. Mocatta, Esq., Woburn Place, Addlestone.   A very large fine-foliaged variety, the colour being a yellow ground, nearly covered with bright-red shading to orange in the younger leaves.

To Calceolaria 'Veitch's Hardy Hybrid' (votes, unanimous), from Messrs. R. Veitch, Exeter.   A perfectly hardy variety raised from *C. herbacea* × *C. plantaginea* ; flowers pure yellow, remarkably freely produced on stems about a foot high, and continuing in blossom a long time.   In the Society's Gardens at Wisley this stood without any protection all through the trying winter of 1906–1907 and received no injury.   (Fig. 23.)

To *Papaver orientale* ' Jennie Mawson ' (votes, 18 for), from Messrs. Mawson, Windermere.   Flowers very large and of a rosy-salmon shade of colour, with a bold dark blotch at the base of each segment.   The flowers are of much substance and should stand well.

To *Amphicome Emodi* (votes, 19 for), from Messrs. J. Veitch, Chelsea. An old and somewhat delicate plant, with pale rosy flowers, produced and similar in form to *Incazvillea Delavayii,* but smaller and distinct from that plant.

To *Lathyrus filiformis,* under the name *Ervum gracile* (votes, unanimous), from Mr. M. Prichard, Christchurch.   A lovely perennial Leguminous plant with dark purplish-blue flowers borne in a cluster of nine or ten blossoms.   The leaves are about 9 inches long, narrow, and grass-like.   A very effective plant for the rockery.

To Sweet Pea 'Paradise Carmine' (votes, unanimous), from Miss Hemus, Upton-on-Severn.   A large finely formed flower of a deep carmine colour.

To Sweet Pea 'Evelyn Hemus ' (votes, unanimous), from Miss Hemus. A very large, strong-growing variety with shapely creamy-white flowers margined with rosy-pink.

To Carnation 'The Squire' (votes, 15 for, 2 against), from Mrs. Berkeley, Spetchley Park, Worcester.   A perfectly formed, handsome flower of rosy-heliotrope colour, sweet-scented, and non-splitting calyx.

Other Exhibits.

R. H. Biffen, Esq., Histon, Cambridge, sent Hybrid Sweet Peas.
Messrs. Bull, Chelsea, staged English and Spanish Irises.
Messrs. Carter, High Holborn, brought Gloxinias.
Messrs. Cripps, Tunbridge Wells, staged Acers and Clematises.

Fig. 23.—Calceolaria ' Veitch's Hardy Hybrid.'

Mr. W. J. Godfrey, Exmouth, sent Solanums, Carnations, Poppies, &c.
Messrs. Hopkins, Barming, brought hardy flowers.
Messrs. Jackman, Woking, staged alpine plants.
Messrs. Kelway, Langport, sent Paeonies.
Messrs. Kipping, Hutton, brought herbaceous flowers.
Messrs. Laing, Forest Hill, staged Begonias.

Mr. Page, Hampton, sent Ivy-leaved Geraniums.

Miss Hemus, Upton-on-Severn, staged Sweet Peas.

Messrs. Peed, Streatham, brought alpine plants.

Mr. Lee, Clevedon, sent Violets.

Messrs. Cheal, Crawley, staged Lupins.

Mr. A. J. Swanson, Barton-on-Humber, sent Begonias.

Mrs. Scott Elliott, Hawick, sent Aquilegias.

H. S. Bartleet, Esq., Shooters Hill, staged Lychnis ' Bartleet.'

· R. Gill, Esq., Penryn, sent *Rhododendron cinnabarinum*.

Mr. J. Vert, Saffron Walden, brought Carnations.

The Hon. Lady Victoria Welby, Harrow, sent Paeonies.

J. W. Marshall, Esq., Godalming, staged *Iris carthusiana*.

The Marquis of Normanby, Whitby, sent Carnations.

The Duke of Rutland, Belvoir Castle, sent Coleuses.

FRUIT AND VEGETABLE COMMITTEE.

JANUARY 8, 1907.

Mr. BUNYARD, V.M.H., in the Chair, and twenty-one members present.

Awards Recommended :—

Silver-gilt Knightian Medal.

To Messrs. Cannell, Swanley, for 110 dishes of Apples.

Silver Knightian Medal.

To Messrs. J. Veitch, Chelsea, for seventy dishes of Apples.

Silver Banksian Medal.

To Sir Weetman D. Pearson, Bart., M.P., Paddockhurst, Sussex (gr. Mr. Wadds), for a collection of fruit.

Award of Merit.

To Pear 'Blickling' (votes, unanimous), from Mr. W. Allan, Gunton Park, Norwich. Fruit large, pyramidal or obovate, rather uneven in its outline. Skin pale yellow, covered with spots of russet; eyes small and open, set in a wide, deepish basin; stalks 1 inch long, thin, set in a deep cavity surrounded with deep russet. Flesh whitish, melting, full of juice, and of delicious flavour. Mr. Allan wrote: "It is one of the very best January pears. I obtained it from an old tree at Blickling. No one that I have shown it to knows the variety. It is very distinct in its growth from other varieties; it has a small leaf of a darker shade of green than other varieties."

Cultural Commendation.

To Mr. J. Crook, Forde Abbey Gardens, Chard, for exceedingly fine fruits of Pear 'Glou Morceau.'

Other Exhibits.

Mr. J. Stephenson, Sutton Scarsdale, Chesterfield, sent a seedling Potato, which the Committee wished to be tried at Wisley.

Mr. G. Maynard, Wymondham, sent Apple 'Bill-sticker.'

Mr. W. Bull, Billericay, sent Apples 'The Welcome' and 'Dolly Varden.' The former the Committee wished to see again earlier next year.

Mr. W. Voss, Rayleigh, Essex, staged Apple 'Lemon Russet.'

Mr. Wallace, Dunstable, brought Apples 'King of all Apples,' and a seedling variety which the Committee wished to see again earlier.

Mr. E. Steward, Lenton Boulevard, Notts, sent Potatoes.

FRUIT AND VEGETABLE COMMITTEE, JANUARY 22, 1907.

Mr. J. CHEAL in the Chair, and eighteen members present.

Awards Recommended :—

Silver-gilt Banksian Medal.

To Lord Stanhope, Chevening Park, Sevenoaks (gr. Mr. Sutton), for Grapes and Apples.

Other Exhibit.

Messrs. Cannell, Swanley, sent some very fine Onions.

FRUIT AND VEGETABLE COMMITTEE, FEBRUARY 12, 1907.

Mr. BUNYARD, V.M.H., in the Chair, and twenty-four members present.

Awards Recommended :—

Gold Medal.

To Messrs. Rivers, Sawbridgeworth, for a superb collection of Oranges.

Silver Banksian Medal.

To C. P. Serocold, Esq., Taplow Hill, Taplow, for a collection of Apples.

Award of Merit.

To Orange 'Excelsior' (votes, unanimous), from Messrs. Rivers, Sawbridgeworth. A large round fruit of deep colour, thin skin, and fine flavour. A remarkably prolific variety. A comparatively small branch exhibited had over thirty large ripe fruit on it.

Other Exhibits.

Miss M. H. Dodge, Loseley Park, Guildford, sent Rhubarb and Chicory.

Mr. W. Crump, V.M.H., Madresfield Court Gardens, Malvern, sent Grape 'Black Morocco.'

Mr. J. Garland, Broadclyst, Exeter, staged Apple 'Star of Devon.'

The Duke of Wellington, Stratfieldsaye, sent Apple 'Waterloo.' A variety resembling 'Wadhurst Pippin.'

Messrs. Veitch, Chelsea, brought Pear 'John Seden,' which the Committee desired to see earlier next year.

Mr. W. H. Divers, Belvoir Castle Gardens, Grantham, staged Pear 'Orchard Baker.' A medium-sized cooking variety, and said to be an enormous bearer.

Mr. James Page, Landford, Salisbury, sent Apple 'Bismarck.'

Thatcham Fruit and Flower Farm, Thatcham, staged a large collection of jams.

FRUIT AND VEGETABLE COMMITTEE, MARCH 5, 1907.

Mr. J. CHEAL in the Chair, and eighteen members present.

Award Recommended :—

Silver Banksian Medal.

To T. J. Charlesworth, Esq., Nutfield Court, Surrey (gr. Mr. Herbert), for thirty-four dishes of Apples.

Other Exhibits.

Mr. W. Poupart, Twickenham, staged Apple 'Barrack Beauty.'

Mr. Turton, Sherborne Castle Gardens, Dorset, sent two dishes of Apples.

FRUIT AND VEGETABLE COMMITTEE, MARCH 8, 1907.

Mr. W. BATES in the Chair, and eight members present.

Awards Recommended :—

Award of Merit.

To Kale 'Chou de Russie' (votes, unanimous), from Messrs. J. Carter, High Holborn, W.C.

To Kale 'Dwarf Moss Curled' (votes, unanimous), from Messrs. J. Carter.

To Kale 'Cottagers' (votes, unanimous), from Messrs. Barr, Covent Garden, Messrs. J. Carter, High Holborn, and Messrs. J. Veitch, Chelsea.

To Kale 'Selected Dwarf Curled' (votes, unanimous), from Messrs. Kent & Brydon, Darlington.

To Kale 'Tall Green Curled' (votes, unanimous), from Messrs. J. Veitch, Chelsea.

FRUIT AND VEGETABLE COMMITTEE, MARCH 19, 1907.

Mr. A. H. PEARSON in the Chair, and fifteen members present.

Awards Recommended:—

Silver Knightian Medal.

To Mark Firth, Esq., Wiston Hall, Leicester (gr. Mr. Clark), for a very fine collection of Onions.

Silver Banksian Medal.

To Messrs. Rivers, Sawbridgeworth, for a collection of Oranges.

First-class Certificate.

To Kale 'Chou de Russie' (votes, unanimous), from Messrs. Carter, High Holborn, W.C. This is a very old variety and known as Russian Kale, and in the trying winter of 1906–7 it stood the winter at Wisley better than any other variety in the Kale trials there. Plant about 20 inches high ; stem short and sturdy ; foliage a greyish green, much cut and divided, and fringed at the margins. Habit very compact. In the spring a great mass of tender sprouts are produced that are of excellent flavour when cooked. In our opinion this is one of the most valuable of all Kales, because of its hardiness, productiveness, and freedom from disease.

Other Exhibits.

Mr. G. W. Miller, Wisbech, sent a dish of Apples found growing near Lynn, which the Committee could not recognise.

FRUIT AND VEGETABLE COMMITTEE, APRIL 2, 1907.

Mr. G. BUNYARD, V.M.H., in the Chair, and thirteen members present.

Exhibits.

Mr. W. Strugnell, Rood Ashton Gardens, Trowbridge, sent twelve dishes of Apples.

Mr. R. Smith, Brickendonbury, Herts, staged Apple ' Smith's Late Keeping,' which the Committee wished to see again next meeting with more particulars as to cropping qualities, &c.

FRUIT AND VEGETABLE COMMITTEE, APRIL 16, 1907.

Mr. J. CHEAL in the Chair, and nineteen members present.

Exhibits.

Miss Dodge, Loseley Park, Guildford (gr. Mr. Staward), sent eighteen dishes of vegetables.

Mr. P. Cornu, Jersey, sent Apple ' Sunny Jersey.'

Messrs. H. Low, Bush Hill Park, staged Apple ' Gibbons Russet.'

Mr. F. Collis, Bollo Lane, Chiswick, brought Rhubarb ' Collis's Ruby.'

A. W. Sutton, Esq., V.M.H., Bucklebury Place, Woolhampton, sent ripe Strawberries.

FRUIT AND VEGETABLE COMMITTEE, APRIL 30, 1907.

Mr. G. BUNYARD, V.M.H., in the Chair, and nineteen members present.

Award Recommended :—

Cultural Commendation.

To Messrs. Ledsham, 40 Foregate Street, Chester, for exceedingly fine ' Royal Sovereign ' Strawberries, eighteen fruits weighing 2 lbs.

Other Exhibits.

Mr. Ross, gr. to Colonel Archer Houblon, Newbury, staged Apple ' Encore.'

Mr. Orchard, Hemel Hempstead, sent a dish of unnamed Apples.

Mr. S. Mortimer, Rowledge, Farnham, brought Tomato ' Sunrise.'

Mr. W. Munt, Stagenhoe Park Gardens, Welwyn, sent seedling Apples.

Mr. F. Collis, Chiswick, brought Rhubarb ' Collis's Ruby.'

FRUIT AND VEGETABLE COMMITTEE, MAY 14, 1907.

Mr. G. BUNYARD, V.M.H., in the Chair, and sixteen members present.

Awards Recommended :—

Silver Banksian Medal.

To the Marquis of Salisbury, Hatfield House, Herts (gr. Mr. Prime), for very fine ' Royal Sovereign ' Strawberries.

Cultural Commendation.

To Messrs. Lane, Berkhampstead, for exceedingly large, well-coloured fruits of ' Prince Albert ' Apples from the original tree of this variety.

To Messrs. Sutton, Reading, for Pea ' World's Record ' raised from Harbinger × Early Giant. It was requested that seeds be sent to Wisley for trial.

To Mr. Hobday, Romford, for Rhubarb ' Hobday's Giant.'

Other Exhibits.

From the Society's Gardens at Wisley came a collection of Rhubarb. The Committee considered Daw's Champion the best.

FRUIT AND VEGETABLE COMMITTEE, JUNE 11, 1907.

Mr. G. BUNYARD, V.M.H., in the Chair, and sixteen members present.

Awards Recommended :—

Silver-gilt Knightian Medal.

To Lady Northcliffe, Sutton Place, Guildford (gr. Mr. Goatley), for a collection of Melons.

Silver Banksian Medal.

To Miss C. M. Dixon, Westergate, Chichester, for Melons.

Other Exhibits.

Mr. S. Mortimer, Rowledge, Farnham, sent Cucumber ' Rival.'

Mr. H. Parr, Trent Park Gardens, New Barnet, brought Melons.

Mr. Cook, gr. to Sir E. Loder, Bart., Leonardslee, staged an unnamed Melon.

Mr. French, gr. to J. R. Yorke, Esq., Forthampton Court, Tewkesbury, sent Apple ' Reliable,' which the Committee wished to see again next year.

FRUIT AND VEGETABLE COMMITTEE, JUNE 25, 1907.

Mr. G. BUNYARD, V.M.H., in the Chair, and eighteen members present.

Awards Recommended :

Silver Hogg Medal.

To Lord Llangattock, The Hendre, Monmouth (gr. Mr. Coomber), for magnificent ' Queen ' Pineapples.

Silver Banksian Medal.

To Messrs. Dobbiè, Rothesay, for a collection of early Potatoes.

Award of Merit.

To Strawberry ' Kentish Favourite ' (votes, 8 for, 1 against), from Messrs. Low, Enfield. Fruit very large, mostly wedge-shaped ; colour dark crimson with prominent red seeds ; flesh red, firm, with a very pleasant flavour. The plant is a great bearer, and said to be first-rate for forcing.

To Melon 'Eminence' (votes, unanimous), from Mr. A. McKellar, Royal Gardens, Windsor. Fruit rather large, roundish oval ; skin bright yellow, and beautifully netted ; flesh white, thick, very melting, and of delicious flavour. Raised from St. Patrick × Hero of Lockinge.

Other Exhibits.

Mr. W. Treseder, Cardiff, sent Cabbage 'Treseder.' The Cabbages shown had been grown at Wisley.

Mr. C. Ross, Welford Park Gardens, Newbury, staged Melon 'Advance' not quite in condition.

Mr. T. A. Cook, Barnett Hill, Wonersh, brought Melon 'Barnett Hill Favourite,' which the Committee desired to see again.

Messrs. Veitch, Chelsea, sent Tomato 'New Dwarf Red.' A variety that received an Award of Merit at Wisley in 1905.

NARCISSUS AND TULIP COMMITTEE.

MARCH 19, 1907.

Mr. H. B. MAY in the Chair, and fifteen members present.

Three new varieties were placed before the Committee, but no awards were granted to them.

Award Recommended :—

Silver-gilt Flora Medal.

To Messrs. Wm. Cutbush & Son, Highgate, London, N., for a large and interesting group of forced Daffodils and Tulips, in pots.

NARCISSUS AND TULIP COMMITTEE, APRIL 2, 1907.

Mr. H. B. MAY in the Chair, and twenty-four members present.

Ten new Daffodils and five groups were considered by the Committee.

Arising out of a discussion initiated by Mr. P. D. Williams, a motion proposed by the Rev. Eugene Bourne, and seconded by the Rev. Canon Fowler, " That after the 1907 season not fewer than eight blooms of a new Daffodil be submitted for an Award of Merit," was carried without dissent.

Following on this proposal came one from the Rev. Canon Fowler and Mr. P. D. Williams, " That after the 1907 season not fewer than twelve blooms of a Daffodil shall be necessary to secure a First-class Certificate." This was adopted unanimously.

Awards Recommended :—

Silver Flora Medal.

To Mr. Chas. Dawson, Gulval, Penzance, for a group of new and rare varieties of Daffodils, admirably arranged.

To Sir Josslyn Gore-Booth, Bart., Lissadell, Sligo, for a group of Irish-grown Daffodils, chiefly popular varieties.

Award of Merit.

To Daffodil ' Homespun ' (votes, unanimous), from Mr. Chas. Dawson, Gulval, Penzance. A largely, finely proportioned, deep golden-yellow *Incomparabilis* variety of unusual beauty.

Other Exhibits.

Messrs. J. Pope & Son, King's Norton, showed a small group of Daffodils.

S. B. Kendall, Esq., Newton Poppleford, Devon, submitted some wonderfully well-grown flowers of Daffodil ' King Alfred.'

Messrs. Wm. Cutbush & Son, Highgate, N., showed Tulips in pots.

NARCISSUS AND TULIP COMMITTEE, APRIL 16, 1907.

Mr. H. B. MAY in the Chair, and twenty-seven members present.

A unanimous vote of thanks was accorded the Hon. Sec. for his work in the preparation of the list of Daffodil names.

Thirty Daffodils and two Tulips were placed before the Committee, and fourteen groups of Daffodils and Tulips were staged, the latter forming the leading feature of the exhibition.

Awards Recommended:—

Silver-gilt Flora Medal.

To Mr. Chas. Dawson, Gulval, Penzance, for a group of new Daffodils.

Silver-gilt Banksian Medal.

To Mr. F. H. Chapman, Guldeford Lodge, Rye, for a group of Daffodils.

To Miss F. W. Currey, Lismore, Ireland, for a large group of Daffodils.

Silver Flora Medal.

To Messrs. R. H. Bath, Ltd., Wisbech, for a group of Daffodils.

To Messrs. Barr & Sons, Covent Garden, for a group of Daffodils.

To Sir Josslyn Gore-Booth, Lissadell, Sligo, for a group of Daffodils.

Silver Banksian Medal.

To Messrs. J. Pope & Son, Kings Norton.

Award of Merit.

To Daffodil 'Queen of the West' (votes, 17 for, 3 against), from Messrs. Walter T. Ware, Ltd., Inglescombe, Bath. A handsome 'Ajax' Daffodil with frilled trumpet and elegant perianth segments, all bright golden yellow.

To Daffodil 'Atalanta' (votes, 16 for, none against), from Miss F. W. Currey, Lismore, Ireland. A large 'Ajax' Daffodil with cream-white, lightly frilled trumpet, and white perianth segments.

Cultural Commendation.

To Mr. F. H. Chapman, Rye, for some extra fine flowers of Daffodil 'Virgil,' a *Poeticus* variety.

Other Exhibits.

The Rev. G. Engleheart, V.M.H., Dinton, Hants, set up a group of new seedling Daffodils.

Mrs. Backhouse, Sutton Court, Hereford, showed a few new Daffodils.

Messrs. William Bull & Sons, King's Road, Chelsea, exhibited a group of Daffodils.

Messrs. R. & G. Cuthbert, Southgate, N., showed a group of Daffodils and Tulips.

Messrs. Hogg & Robertson, Mary Street, Dublin, showed Daffodils and Tulips.

Mr. Robert Sydenham, Tenby Street, Birmingham, showed various bulbs grown in moss fibre.

Barr Daffodil Cup Competition.

There was but one entry for the Barr Daffodil Cup, and this, from the Rev. G. P. Haydon, Westbere, Canterbury, was considered worthy of the award. Miss Willmott, V.M.H., Mr. James Walker, and Mr. Walter T. Ware, acted as judges.

Tulip Trials at Wisley.

The following members were elected to form the Sub-Committee to inspect the Tulip Trials at the Society's Gardens, Wisley :—Miss Willmott, V.M.H., Rev. J. Jacobs, Messrs. E. A. Bowles, J. T. Bennett-Poë, V.M.H., James Walker, Walter T. Ware, Wm. Poupart, P. R. Barr, R. Wallace, and R. Sydenham, with the Chairman, Mr. H. B. May, and the Hon. Sec., Mr. Chas. H. Curtis.

NARCISSUS AND TULIP COMMITTEE, APRIL 30, 1907.

Mr. H. B. MAY in the Chair, and twenty-three members present.

Fifteen new Daffodils and eight new Tulips were placed before the Committee, and twelve groups of Tulips and Daffodils were staged.

Awards Recommended :—

Gold Medal.

To Miss Willmott, V.M.H., Warley Place, Great Warley, Essex, for an exceptionally fine and interesting group of new and rare Daffodils.

Silver-gilt Flora Medal.

To Messrs. J. R. Pearson & Sons, Lowdham, Notts, for a group of well-grown Daffodils, including some new varieties.

To Mr. A. M. Wilson, East Keal, Spilsby, for a group of Daffodils, finely set up.

Silver Flora Medal.

To Messrs. Hogg & Robertson, Mary St., Dublin, for a group of Tulips.

To Messrs. Barr & Sons, Covent Garden, for an exhibit of Daffodils and Tulips.

Silver Banksian Medal.

To Messrs. R. H. Bath, Ltd., Wisbech, for a group of Daffodils and Tulips.

To Messrs. R. Wallace & Co., Colchester, for a group of Tulips.

To Messrs. James Veitch & Sons, Ltd., Chelsea, for a group of Daffodils and Tulips.

Award of Merit.

To Daffodil ' Miss Willmott' (votes, unanimous), from Messrs. Walter T. Ware, Ltd., Inglescombe, Bath. A fine variety of *Poeticus* type ; very large flowers ; perianth pure white ; cup larger than in *Narcissus Poeticus*, orange-yellow, with orange rim.

To Daffodil 'Ailsa' (votes, 14 for, 8 against), from Mr. E. M. Cross-field, Little Acton, ¡Wrexham. A beautiful 'Ajax' variety, with bold, frilled trumpet; pale soft yellow. (Fig. 24.)

To Tulip 'La Grandeur' (votes, 15 for, none against), from Messrs. Walter T. Ware, Ltd., Inglescombe, Bath. A rather early flowering Tulip; flowers big and substantial; crimson-scarlet, with yellow base and black anthers.

Fig. 24.—Daffodil 'Ailsa.' (*Journal of Horticulture.*)

Other Exhibits.

Mr. F. H. Chapman, Guldeford Lodge, Rye, showed a small set of the newer Daffodils.

Mr. John Walker, High St., Thame, showed Daffodils.

The Rev. G. H. Engleheart, V.M.H., Dinton, Hants, submitted new seedling Daffodils.

NARCISSUS AND TULIP COMMITTEE, MAY 14, 1907.

Mr. H. B. MAY in the Chair, and seventeen members present.

Twelve varieties of Tulips and eight of Daffodils were placed before the Committee, and nine groups of Tulips and Daffodils were staged.

Awards Recommended :—

Silver-gilt Flora Medal.

To Messrs. R. Wallace & Co., Colchester, for a splendid group of ' Cottage,' ' Darwin,' and other Tulips.

Silver-gilt Banksian Medal.

To Messrs. R. H. Bath, Ltd., Wisbech, for a group of fine Tulips.

To Messrs. Alex. Dickson & Sons, Ltd., Newtownards, co. Down, Ireland, for a group of large Irish-grown Tulips.

Silver Flora Medal.

To Mr. A. M. Wilson, East Keal, Spilsby, for a group of Tulips.

To Messrs. Barr & Sons, Covent Garden, for a group of Tulips.

Silver Banksian Medal.

To Messrs. James Veitch & Sons, Ltd., Chelsea, for a group of Tulips.

Other Exhibits.

Messrs. Walter T. Ware, Ltd., Inglescombe, Bath, set up a few very fine flowers of new and rare Tulips.

Messrs. Wm. Bull & Sons, King's Road, Chelsea, staged a small group of Tulips.

Miss Katherine Spurrell, Bessingham, Hanworth, Norwich, sent a few late Daffodils.

ORCHID COMMITTEE.

JANUARY 8, 1907.

Mr. J. GURNEY FOWLER in the Chair, and nineteen members present.

Awards Recommended.

Silver Flora Medal.

To Messrs. Charlesworth & Co., Heaton, Bradford, for a fine group of hybrid Odontoglossums &c.

Silver Banksian Medal.

To Messrs. Jas. Cypher & Sons, Cheltenham, for a group of Cypripediums and other Orchids.

First-class Certificate.

To *Odontioda* × *Bradshawiae* (*Cochlioda Noezliana* × *Odontoglossum crispum*) (votes, unanimous), from Messrs. Charlesworth. & Co., Heaton, Bradford. A charming hybrid with flowers formed like *O. crispum*, but of a cinnabar-scarlet colour.

Award of Merit.

To *Odontoglossum* × *Aliceae* (*Edwardii* × *Harryano-crispum*) (votes, unanimous), from J. Gurney Fowler, Esq., Glebelands, South

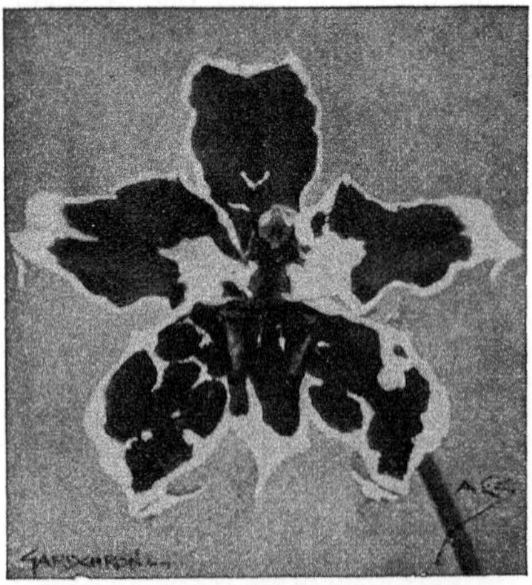

FIG. 25.—ODONTOGLOSSUM × ALICEAE. (*Gardeners' Chronicle.*)

Woodford (gr. Mr. J. Davis). A singular hybrid near to *O. Thompsonianum.* Flowers pale lilac, heavily blotched with claret colour. (Fig. 25.)

To *Brasso-Cattleya* × ' Pluto ' (*Brassavola Digbyana* × *Cattleya granulosa*) (votes, unanimous), from Major G. L. Holford, C.I.E., C.V.O.

(gr. Mr. Alexander). Flowers partaking strongly of *C. granulosa*, green with whitish, distinctly trilobed lip which is striped with purple, and has both the front and side lobes fringed.

To *Cattleya* × ' Maggie Raphael' *alba* (*Trianaei alba* × *Dowiana aurea*) (votes, unanimous), from Major G. L. Holford. Sepals and petals white, lip rose-crimson veined with gold.

To *Phaio-Calanthe* × *Colmanii* Phaius × (' Norman ' × *Calanthe Regnieri Stevensi*) (votes, unanimous), from Jeremiah Colman, Esq., Gatton Park (gr. Mr. Bound). Flowers white with a slight green tint on the sepals, and a few purple lines at the base of the lip.

Other Exhibits.

Francis Wellesley, Esq., Westfield, Woking, showed *Cypripedium Aeson giganteum* in fine condition, and other hybrids.

Major G. L. Holford showed several new hybrids.

De B. Crawshay, Esq., sent *Odontoglossum crispum Poultoni* and *O.* × ' Queen Alexandra.'

J. Wilson Potter, Esq., sent *Laelia cinnabarina* × *Jongheana*.

Mr. H. A. Tracy showed *Cypripedium xanthimum* (*Leeanum* × *insigne* variety).

Messrs. Hugh Low & Co. staged a group.

Messrs. Heath & Sons, Cheltenham, showed hybrid Cypripediums.

J. Gurney Fowler, Esq., sent Cypripedium × ' Ernest Read ' (parentage unrecorded).

Messrs. Linden, Brussels, showed two beautiful blotched forms of *Odontoglossum crispum* raised from seeds.

M. Jules Hye de Crom, Ghent, sent Cypripedium × *Lathamianum primatum*.

M. Mertens, Ghent, showed various Orchids.

Messrs. Sander & Sons sent three fine forms of *Vanda Sanderiana*.

ORCHID COMMITTEE, JANUARY 22, 1907.

Mr. J. GURNEY FOWLER in the Chair, and twenty-four members present.

Awards Recommended.

Silver Flora Medal.

To Major G. L. Holford, C.I.E., C.V.O., Westonbirt, Tetbury (gr. Mr. H. G. Alexander), for an elegant arrangement of White *Laelia anceps*.

To F. Du Cane Godman, Esq., South Lodge, Horsham, for a group of fine specimens of *Lycaste Skinneri*.

To Messrs. Jas. Cypher & Sons, Cheltenham, for a group of Cypripediums &c.

To Messrs. Charlesworth & Co., Bradford, for a group of hybrid Orchids.

To Messrs. Sander & Sons, St. Albans, for a group of hybrids and interesting species.

To Monsieur Chas. Vuylsteke, Ghent, for a selection of hybrid Odontoglossums.

Silver Banksian Medal.

·To Messrs. Jas. Veitch & Sons, Chelsea, for a group.

To G. Singer, Esq., Coventry (gr. Mr. Collyer), for cut spikes of *Phalaenopsis* and hybrid Cypripediums.

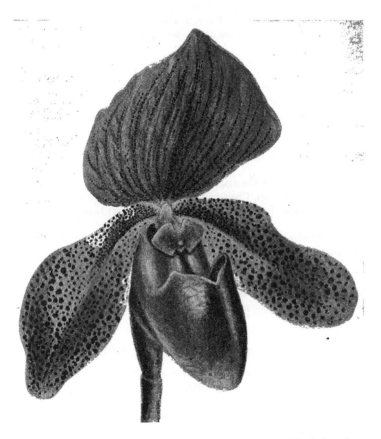

FIG. 26.—CYPRIPEDIUM TAUTZIANUM NIGRICANS. (*Journal of Horticulture.*)

To Messrs. J. McBean & Son, Cooksbridge, for Odontoglossums and *Laelia anceps.*

To Messrs. Armstrong & Brown, Tunbridge Wells, for hybrid Cypripediums.

To Mr. F. C. Young, St. Albans, for hybrid Cypripediums.

Award of Merit.

To *Cypripedium × Tautzianum nigricans* (*barbatum nigrum × niveum*) (votes, unanimous), from Francis Wellesley, Esq., Westfield,

Woking (gr. Mr. Hopkins). Dorsal sepal ruby-red, with a slight white margin and dark claret lines. Petals reddish rose, profusely spotted with chocolate-purple ; lip claret-coloured. (Fig. 26.)

To *Odontoglossum × caloglossum* (*crispum* × 'Vuylstekeae') (votes unanimous), from M. Chas. Vuylsteke. Flower of fine shape ; the broad lilac-tinted sepals and petals almost covered with large claret-coloured blotches ; lip white, blotched with dark rose. (Fig. 27.)

To *Odontoglossum* × 'Ruby' (parentage unrecorded) (votes, 14 for, 3 against), from M. Chas. Vuylsteke. Flowers claret colour on the inner two-thirds of the segments, pale lilac on the outer portion. (Fig. 28.)

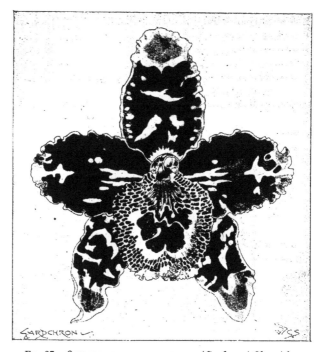

Fig. 27.—Odontoglossum caloglossum. (*Gardeners' Chronicle.*

To *Laelia anceps Schröderae* 'Grace Ruby' (votes, unanimous), from Messrs. J. McBean & Son, Cooksbridge. Sepals and petals white, brightly tinted with magenta-crimson, especially on the petals ; front and side lobes of the lip deep maroon colour.

To *Maxillaria grandiflora* (votes, unanimous), from F. Du Cane Godman, Esq., Horsham. The fine species allied to 'M. venusta.' Flowers white with purple and yellow markings on the lip.

Cultural Commendation.

To Norman C. Cookson, Esq., Oakwood, Wylam (gr. Mr. Chapman), for a fine specimen of *Cypripedium Leeanum Clinkaberryanum.*

To F. Du Cane Godman, Esq., for a fine pair of specimens of *Maxillaria grandiflora*, each with over fifty flowers.

Other Exhibits.

Francis Wellesley, Esq., Westfield, Woking (gr. Mr. Hopkins), showed several good hybrids.

Norman C. Cookson, Esq., Oakwood, Wylam (gr. Mr. Chapman), sent hybrid Calanthes, Cattleyas, &c.

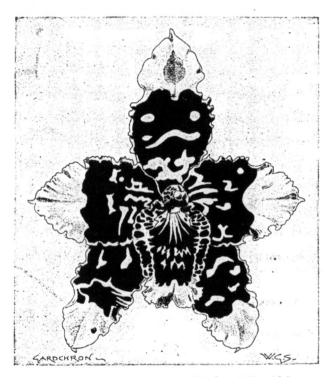

FIG. 28.—ODONTOGLOSSUM 'RUBY.' (*Gardeners' Chronicle*.)

Messrs. Hugh Low & Co. staged a small group.

Jeremiah Colman, Esq., sent *Cattleya × Miranda*, 'Gatton Park' variety.

H. T. Pitt, Esq., sent *Lycaste × Balliae*, 'Rosslyn' variety.

Mr. Robson, Altrincham, showed two hybrid Cypripediums.

M. Mertens, Ghent, staged a small group.

ORCHID COMMITTEE, FEBRUARY 12, 1907.

Mr. J. GURNEY FOWLER in the Chair, and twenty-one members present.

Awards Recommended.

Silver-gilt Flora Medal.

To J. Bradshaw, Esq., The Grange, Southgate (gr. Mr. Whitelegge), for a group of Cattleyas &c.

To Messrs. Charlesworth & Co., Heaton, Bradford, for a group of hybrid Orchids.

Silver Flora Medal.

To Messrs. Jas. Veitch & Sons, Chelsea, for Cattleya Trianaei and hybrid Cypripediums.

To H. S. Goodson, Esq., Putney (gr. Mr. G. E. Day), for a collection of Orchids.

To Messrs. Sander & Sons, St. Albans, for a group.

. To Messrs. Jas. Cypher & Sons, Cheltenham, for a group of Cypripediums &c.

Silver Banksian Medal.

To Messrs. Hugh Low & Co., Enfield, for a group.

To Messrs. Armstrong & Brown, Tunbridge Wells, for a selection of hybrid Cypripediums.

To Mr. F. G. Young, St. Albans, for Cypripediums.

To Messrs. J. & A. A. McBean, Cooksbridge, for a group of the scarlet *Epiphronitis* × *Veitchii.*

First-class Certificate.

To *Odontoglossum* × *Lambeauianum* 'Idol' (*Rolfeae ardentissimum* × *crispum* var.) (votes, unanimous), from M. A. A. Peeters, Brussels. Flowers large ; sepals and petals broad, rose-colour, with large claret-coloured blotches ; lip white with violet markings in front of the yellow crest. (Fig. 29.)

Award of Merit.

To *Odontoglossum* × *venustulum* ' Apollo ' (*crispo-Harryanum* × *ardentissimum*) (votes, unanimous), from J. Bradshaw, Esq., Southgate (gr. Mr. Whitelegge). Flowers cream-white blotched with purple.

To *Coelogyne* × *Colmanii* (*speciosa major* × *cristata alba*) (votes, unanimous), from Jeremiah Colman, Esq., Gatton Park (gr. Mr. W. P. Bound). A very interesting hybrid raised at Gatton, and having large whitish flowers with reddish-orange crest to the lip.

Cultural Commendation.

To Messrs. McBean, Cooksbridge, for finely flowered *Epiphronitis* × *Veitchii.*

Other Exhibits.

J. Gurney Fowler, Esq., Glebelands, South Woodford (gr. Mr. Davis), sent *Odontoglossum* × ' Othello Fowler's ' variety, and *O.* × *Lobbiae* (*amabile* × *Pescatorei*).

Francis Wellesley, Esq., Westfield, Woking (gr. Mr. Hopkins), showed the very handsome *Cypripedium* × *Aeson giganteum, C.* × *Tracyanum, C.* × 'Ville de Paris' *magnificum, C.* × *aureo-Spicerianum,* and *Cattleya chocoensis* 'Mrs. Francis Wellesley.'

Messrs. Linden, Brussels, sent *Odontoglossum crispum* 'Gloire de Moortebeek,' *O. c.* 'Bijou de Moortebeek,' and *O.* × *auriferum (Halliixanthum* × *crispum).*

M. A. A. Peeters, Brussels, showed varieties of *Odontoglossum* × *Lambeauianum* and *Cypripedium* × *Leeanum laekenense.* De B. Crawshay, Esq., Rosefield, Sevenoaks (gr. Mr. Stables), sent the fine White *Laelia anceps* 'Holliday,' and variety 'Theodora,' and two Odontoglossums.

Fig. 29.—Odontoglossum Lambeauianum 'Idol.' (*Journal of Horticulture.*)

R. I. Measures, Esq., Camberwell (gr. Mr. Smith), showed various interesting Orchids.

F. Menteith Ogilvie, Esq., Oxford (gr. Mr. Balmforth) showed *Cypripedium* × *aureum Hyeanum.*

G. Jessop, Esq., Rawdon, sent *Cypripedium Fairrieanum* 'Lucifer.'

Elijah Ashworth, Esq., Wilmslow, sent *Vanda teres albens.*

Dr. Hodgkinson, Wilmslow, showed *Cypripedium insigne* 'MacNabianum.'

Messrs. Heath & Sons, Cheltenham, showed Cypripediums.

Sir Frederick Wigan, Bart. (gr. Mr. W. H. Young), showed several *Cymbidium* × *Holfordianum,* and the parents *C. grandiflorum* and *C. eburneum.*

M. Mertens, Ghent, showed a small group.

H. J. Bromilow, Esq., Rainhill (gr. Mr. Morgan), sent *Cypripedium* × *fulshawense*, 'Bromilow's' variety.

Messrs. J. W. Moore, Rawdon, staged a group.

ORCHID COMMITTEE, MARCH 5, 1907.

Mr. J. GURNEY FOWLER in the Chair, and twenty members present.

Awards Recommended :—

Gold Medal.

To Jeremiah Colman, Esq., Gatton Park (gr. Mr. Bound), for a very fine group of Dendrobiums and other Orchids.

Silver Flora Medal.

To Canon the Hon. K. F. Gibbs, Aldenham Vicarage, Watford (gr. Mr. Lazzall), for six splendid specimens of *Coelogyne cristata*.

Silver Banksian Medal.

To Messrs. Charlesworth & Co., Bradford, for a selection of hybrid Orchids.

To Messrs Jas. Cypher & Sons, Cheltenham, for a group of Dendrobiums, Cypripediums, &c.

To Messrs. Hugh Low & Co., Enfield, for a group.

First-class Certificate.

To *Cymbidium insigne*, 'Glebelands variety' (votes, unanimous), from J. Gurney Fowler, Esq., Glebelands, South Woodford (gr. Mr. Davis). A very large variety with white flowers, having rose-purple spotting at the bases of the petals and on the lip.

To *Lycaste* × *Balliae*, 'South Lodge variety' (votes, unanimous), from F. Du Cane Godman, Esq., South Lodge, Horsham. Flowers reddish-rose, with light ruby-crimson lip.

To *Odontoglossum crispum Mossiae* (votes, unanimous), from J. S. Moss, Esq., Wintershill Hall, Bishops Waltham (gr. Mr. Kench). A very handsome variety, with white flowers evenly blotched with claret-red.

To *Cattleya Trianaei* 'The Premier' (votes, unanimous), from J. Bradshaw, Esq., The Grange, Southgate (gr. Mr. Whitelegge). Flowers large, segments broad; sepals and petals silver-white, tinged with rose-pink; lip broad, crimson-purple in front, and with an orange disc.

Award of Merit.

To *Brasso-Cattleya* × 'H. G. Alexander' (votes, unanimous), from Major G. L. Holford, C.I.E., C.V.O., Westonbirt (gr. Mr. Alexander). A singular hybrid with yellowish-green flowers, the labellum being fringed.

To *Odontoglossum* × 'Lady Howick' (parentage unrecorded) (votes, unanimous), from Major G. L. Holford. Flowers of good form, French-white, with large chocolate-purple blotches.

To *Cypripedium* × *Vill-exul* (votes, unanimous), from Major G. L. Holford. Flowers similar to *C. exul* but larger.

E E

To *Spathoglottis* × *Colmanii aurea* (*aureo-Veillardii* × *aurea* (votes, unanimous), from Jeremiah Colman, Esq., Gatton Park (gr. Mr. Bound). Flowers larger than *S. aurea*; clear yellow.

To *Cypripedium* × 'Mrs. Francis Wellesley' (*Sanderianum* × *Gowerianum*) (votes, unanimous), from Francis Wellesley, Esq., West-field, Woking (gr. Mr. Hopkins). A beautiful hybrid with the dark colour of *C. Sanderianum*. Dorsal sepal greenish, tinged with rose, and bearing many blackish-chocolate lines ; petals extended and having raised lines of dark chocolate, the margins ciliate ; lip reddish-rose on the face.

To *Cypripedium* × *Dicksonianum* (*villosum aureum* × *Hera-Euryades*) (votes, unanimous), from Francis Wellesley, Esq. Dorsal sepal rosy-crimson, with a broad snow-white band on the upper part ; petals and lip honey-yellow, tinged with mahogany-red.

Cultural Commendation.

To Mr. Lazzall, gr. to Canon the Hon. K. F. Gibbs, for six finely flowered *Coelogyne cristata*.

To Mr. H. G. Alexander, orchid-grower to Major G. L. Holford, C.I.E., C.V.O., for a specimen of *Sophro-Laelia* × 'Psyche' with eighteen reddish-scarlet flowers.

Other Exhibits.

Messrs. Armstrong & Brown, Tunbridge Wells, showed a selection of Cypripediums &c.

The Curator of the Royal Botanic Gardens, Glasnevin, Dublin, sent two spikes of the handsome *Cymbidium grandiflorum* 'Glasnevin variety.'

De B. Crawshay, Esq., sent *Odontoglossum* × *waltoniense rose-fieldense*.

Francis Wellesley, Esq., showed *Cypripedium* × 'Mons. de Curte,' 'Westfield variety.'

ORCHID COMMITTEE, MARCH 19, 1907.

Mr. J. GURNEY FOWLER in the Chair, and twenty-four members present.

Awards Recommended:—

Silver-gilt Flora Medal.

To Messrs. Charlesworth & Co., Heaton, Bradford, for a fine group of hybrid Odontoglossums, Cattleyas, &c.

Silver Flora Medal.

To Messrs. Jas. Veitch & Sons, Chelsea, for an effective group of Dendrobiums.

To Messrs. Jas. Cypher & Sons, Cheltenham, for a good group of Cypripediums, Dendrobiums, &c.

To Messrs. Sander & Sons, St. Albans, for a group in which were fine forms of *Cattleya Trianaei*.

To Messrs. Armstrong & Brown, Tunbridge Wells, for a selection of hybrid Cypripediums &c.

Award of Merit.

To *Odontoglossum crispum* ' Rosemary ' (votes, unanimous), from Major G. L. Holford, C.I.E., C.V.O., Westonbirt (gr. Mr. Alexander). A very large form with flowers nearly 5 inches across, white, tinged with rose colour. (Fig. 30.)

FIG. 30.—ODONTOGLOSSUM CRISPUM ' ROSEMARY.'   (*Gardeners' Chronicle*.)

To *Odontoglossum crispum* ' Lily Bourdas ' (votes, unanimous), from H. S. Goodson, Esq., Fairlawn, Putney (gr. Mr. Day). A handsome variety with white flowers of good shape, heavily blotched with claret-red.

To *Cymbidium* × *Colmanae*, ' Edenside variety ' (*eburneum* × *eburneo-Lowianum*), from Mr. Jas. Douglas, Edenside, Great Bookham. Flowers ivory-white, several on a spike.

Cultural Commendation.

To Mr. Warrington, gr. to Miss M. E. Ruston, Monks Manor, Lincoln, for a large specimen of *Cypripedium Rothschildianum* with eight spikes, bearing altogether twenty-seven flowers.

Other Exhibits.

Major G. L. Holford, C.I.E., C.V.O., showed *Laelio-Cattleya* × 'Olivia' (*L. Jongheana* × *C. Schröderae*).

Francis Wellesley, Esq., sent *Laelio-Cattleya* × 'Mrs. R. A. H. Mitchell' (*C. Warscewiczii* × *L.-C. Martinetii*).

C. J. Lucas, Esq., showed several hybrid Orchids.

Jeremiah Colman, Esq., showed *Dendrobium* × 'Othell Colossum.'

M. Florent Claes, Brussels, showed a finely blotched *Odontoglossum crispum.*

G. F. Moore, Esq., sent *Cypripedium* × 'Chas. Lucas' (*Beekmanii* × *Swinburnei magnificum*).

ORCHID COMMITTEE, APRIL 2, 1907.

Mr. J. GURNEY FOWLER in the Chair, and seventeen members present.

Awards Recommended :—

Silver-gilt Flora Medal.

To Norman C. Cookson, Esq., Oakwood, Wylam (gr. Mr. Chapman), for a fine group of Odontoglossums, Phaius, &c.

To J. Bradshaw, Esq., The Grange, Southgate (gr. Mr. Whitelegge), for a group of White *Cattleya Trianaei* &c.

To Messrs. Armstrong & Brown, Tunbridge Wells; for a group of *Dendrobium nobile virginale.*

Silver Flora Medal.

To Messrs. Sander & Sons, St. Albans, for a group of hybrid and other Orchids.

To Messrs. Charlesworth & Co., Bradford, for a group, principally hybrids.

Silver Banksian Medal.

To Messrs. Jas. Veitch & Sons, Chelsea, for a group of hybrid Cypripediums &c.

To Messrs. Moore, Ltd., Rawdon, Leeds, for a group.

First-class Certificate.

To *Laelio-Cattleya* × 'Baroness Schröder,' 'Westonbirt variety' (*L. Jongheana* × *C. Trianaei*) (votes, unanimous), from Major G. L. Holford, C.I.E., C.V.O., Westonbirt, Tetbury (gr. Mr. Alexander). Flower as large as that of *C. Trianaei* and finely formed, light rose-pink, the petals veined with a darker shade of the same colour ; lip deep-orange, with broad pink margin.

Award of Merit.

To *Laelio-Cattleya* × 'Lawrie' (*L.-C. warnhamensis* × *C. Lawrenceana*) (votes, 14 for, 1 against), from C. J. Lucas, Esq., Warnham Court (gr. Mr. Duncan). Flowers bright mauve-purple with maroon lip.

To *Odontoglossum crispum* 'Roi d'Angleterre' (votes, 12 for, 3 against), from Messrs. Linden, Brussels, obtained by crossing two blotched forms of *O. crispum.* Flowers light purple with an orange shade; margin and intersecting lines between the blotches silver-white.

To *Odontoglossum crispum album,* 'Orchid Villa variety' (votes, 14 for, 0 against), from Monsieur Theodore Pauwels, Ghent. A snow-white flower with orange-coloured spots on the lip.

To *Cattleya Trianaei Mooreana* (votes, unanimous), from J. Bradshaw, Esq., The Grange, Southgate (gr. Mr. Whitelegge). Flower rosy-lilac with ruby-claret lip.

Other Exhibits.

J. Gurney Fowler, Esq., Glebelands, South Woodford (gr. Mr. Davis), showed a pretty unnamed hybrid Òdontoglossum with pale-yellow flowers blotched with red-brown.

Baron Sir H. Schröder, The Dell, Egham (gr. Mr. Ballantine), sent the fine *Odontoglossum Wilckeanum Schröderianum.*

The Rev. D. J. Stather Hunt, Tunbridge Wells (gr. Mr. Baker), showed *Laelia* × *Statherae (purpurata* × *flava).*

F. Menteith Ogilvie, Esq., Oxford (gr. Mr. Balmforth), sent *Odontoglossum crispum* 'Fergus,' a distinctly blotched form, flowering for the first time.

W. Waters Butler, Esq., Edgbaston, sent a fine *Cymbidium insigne* and *Odontoglossum Wilckeanum* 'King of Spain.'

Messrs. Linden, Brussels, showed several hybrid Odontoglossums.

Monsieur Mertens, Ghent, showed a selection of Odontoglossums.

ORCHID COMMITTEE, APRIL 16, 1907.

Mr. J. GURNEY FOWLER in the Chair, and twenty-four members present.

Awards Recommended :—

Silver-gilt Flora Medal.

To Messrs. Charlesworth, Heaton, Bradford, for a group of hybrid Odontoglossums &c.

Silver Flora Medal.

To J. Gurney Fowler, Esq., Glebelands, South Woodford (gr. Mr. Davis), for a fine group of *Cattleya Schröderae* of excellent quality, some of the plants bearing eighteen flowers.

To Messrs. Jas. Veitch & Sons, Chelsea, for a group of hybrid and other Orchids.

To H. S. Goodson, Esq., Putney (gr. Mr. Day), for a group.

To C. J. Lucas, Esq., Horsham (gr. Mr. Duncan), for a group of Odontoglossums &c.

To Messrs. Armstrong & Brown, Tunbridge Wells, for a group, principally Dendrobiums.

First-class Certificate.

To *Sophro-Laelia × Phroso superba* (*S.-L. × laeta Orpetiana × L. Jongheana*) (votes, unanimous), from Major G. L. Holford, C.I.E.,

FIG. 31.—SOPHRO-LAELIA × PHROSO SUPERBA. (*Gardeners' Chronicle.*)

C.V.O., Westonbirt (gr. Mr. Alexander). Habit dwarf and compact. Flower large and of a uniform mauve-crimson colour. (Fig. 31.)

To *Brasso-Catt-Laelia* × *Veitchii* (*L. purpurata* × *B.-C.* × *Digbyano-Mossiae*) (votes, unanimous), from Messrs. J. Veitch & Sons, Chelsea. A very fine hybrid, comparable to a good *Laelio-Cattleya* × *callistoglossa*, with a fringed lip ; sepals and petals silver-white, tinged with rosy-lilac ; · lip large, deep rose-purple, with a chrome-yellow disc ; margin deeply fringed. (Fig. 32.)

To *Odontoglossum* × *ardentissimum* ' Herbert Goodson ' (*Pescatorei* × *crispum*) (votes, unanimous), from H. S. Goodson, Esq., Fairlawn, Putney (gr. Mr. Day). Flower large and well formed, white, tinged with rose colour, and heavily blotched with purple. (Fig. 33.)

FIG. 33.—ODONTOGLOSSUM ARDENTISSIMUM ' HERBERT GOODSON.'
(*Journal of Horticulture.*)

Award of Merit.

To *Odontoglossum* × ' Othello ' (*Harryanum* × *Adrianae*) (votes, unanimous), from C. J. Lucas, Esq., Warnham Court, Horsham (gr. Mr. Duncan). Resembling *O. Harryanum* in its dark colour, but with larger and more openly expanded flower, yellowish, heavily blotched with chocolate colour.

Cultural Commendation.

To Mr. H. G. Alexander, orchid-grower to Major G. L. Holford, C.I.E., C.V.O., for a, grand specimen of *Cattleya Mendelii*, ' Westonbirt variety,' with sixteen flowers.

To Mr. H. G. Alexander, for *Odontoglossum* × *Adrianae* ' Lady Wantage,' grown from a single pseudo-bulb and now bearing six spikes, having together 105 flowers.

To Mr. W. H. White, orchid-grower to Sir Trevor Lawrence, Bart., Burford, for two fine spikes of *Phalaenopsis amabilis* (*grandiflora*), the one with twenty-one and the other with three branches, bearing forty-five fine white blooms.

Other Exhibits.

J. Gurney Fowler, Esq. (gr. Mr. Davis), showed the fine white *Cattleya Lüddemanniana Stanleyi* and the large cream-white *Cymbidium* × 'J. Gurney Fowler.'

Francis Wellesley, Esq. (gr. Mr. Hopkins), sent *Laelio-Cattleya* × *stellata* (*L. xanthina* × *C. intermedia alba*).

Major G. L. Holford showed *Brasso-Cattleya* × 'Cordelia' (*C. intermedia* × *B. Digbyana*).

Messrs. Sander & Sons sent the handsome *Cymbidium Parishii Sanderae*.

Messrs. Hugh Low & Co. staged a group.

Messrs. Stanley & Co. showed a selection of Oncidiums &c.

J. T. Bennett-Poë, Esq. (gr. Mr. Downes), sent *Cymbidium* × *Colmanae flavescens*.

De B. Crawshay, Esq. (gr. Mr. Stables), showed *Odontoglossum* × 'Iago' (*Harryanum* × *Hunnewellianum*) and the fine *O. triumphans* 'Imperator' and 'Theodora.'

R. I. Measures, Esq., sent *Cymbidium Lowgrinum*.

ORCHID COMMITTEE, APRIL 30, 1907.

Mr. J. GURNEY FOWLER in the Chair, and twenty-four members present.

Awards Recommended :—

Silver-gilt Flora Medal.

To Sir Trevor Lawrence, Bart., Burford, for a large and interesting group of rare Orchids.

Silver Flora Medal.

To Messrs. Jas. Veitch & Sons, Chelsea, for a group of Odontoglossums and hybrid Orchids.

To Messrs. Sander & Sons, St. Albans, for a group in which were several new Odontoglossums.

To Messrs. Jas. Cypher & Sons, Cheltenham, for an excellent group.

Silver Banksian Medal.

To R. I. Measures, Esq., Camberwell (gr. Mr. Smith), for a selection of Orchids.

To Messrs. Moore, Ltd., Rawdon, Leeds, for Orchids.

First-class Certificate.

To *Brasso-Laelio-Cattleya* × *Fowleri* (*Cattleya Schröderae aurantiaca* × *Brasso Laelia* × 'Mrs. M. Gratrix') (votes, unanimous), from J. Gurney Fowler, Esq., Glebelands, South Woodford (gr. Mr. Davis). Flowers of good shape and equal to those of *C. Schröderae* in size; yellow, with the whole surface tinged and veined with salmon-rose colour, the large disc of the lip being buttercup-yellow. (Fig. 34.)

To *Brasso-Cattleya* × *Digbyano-Schröderae*, 'Fowler's variety' (*B. Digbyana* × *C. Schröderae*) (votes, unanimous), from J. Gurney Fowler,

Esq. (gr. Mr. Davis). A finely formed blush-white flower with primrose disc to the fringed lip.

To *Odontoglossum* × 'Prince Edward of Wales' (*Rolfeae*, × *crispo-Harryanum*) (votes, 18 for, 2 against), from Messrs. Sander & Sons,

FIG. 34.—BRASSO-LAELIO-CATTLEYA × FOWLERI. (*Journal of Horticulture.*)

St. Albans. Flowers large, white, with heavy transverse bars of purple colour on the sepals and blotches of the same tint on the petals. (Fig. 35.)

Award of Merit.

To *Brasso-Laelia* × 'Gipsy' (*L. cinnabarina* × *B.-L.* 'Helen') (votes, unanimous), from Major G. L. Holford, C.I.E., C.V.O., Westonbirt (gr. Mr. Alexander).   Sepals and petals reddish copper-colour tinged with rose ; lip fringed, yellow in the centre and with a rose-coloured margin.

To *Laelio-Cattleya* × 'Ganymede' (*L.* × *Latona* × *C. Schröderae*) (votes, unanimous), from Major G. L. Holford.   Sepals and petals blush-white tinged with orange ; lip claret-purple with large orange-coloured disc.

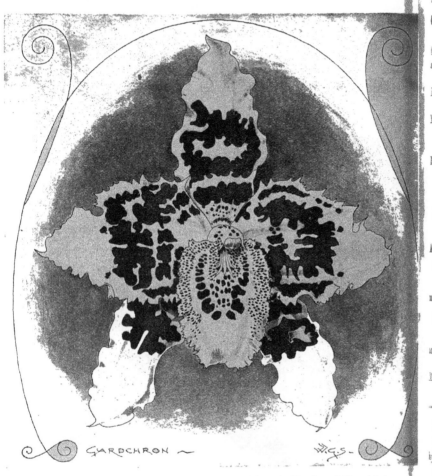

FIG. 35.—ODONTOGLOSSUM 'PRINCE EDWARD OF WALES.'   (*Gardeners' Chronicle.*)

To *Dendrobium chryseum giganteum* (votes, unanimous), from Messrs. Sander & Sons.   Flowers large, bright yellow, solitary.

Botanical Certificate.

To *Dendrobium Wilsoni*, from Messrs. Jas. Veitch & Sons.   A floriferous species with a resemblance to *D. moniliforme* but taller and more slender ; flowers pink.   China.

To *Acineta Humboldtii* (var. *Colmani*), from Jeremiah Colman, Esq. (gr. Mr. Bound). Flowers in pendulous racemes, whitish, spotted with purple.

Cultural Commendation.

To Mr. W. H. White, orchid-grower to Sir Trevor Lawrence, Bart., for *Cattleya Schröderae* with twenty-nine flowers.

Other Exhibits.

J. Bradshaw, Esq., The Grange, Southgate (gr. Mr. Whitelegge), sent *Odontoglossum* × *Rolfeae*, var. ' Kathleen,' a very sparsely spotted form, and a good variety of *Cattleya Trianaei.*

Henry Little, Esq., Twickenham (gr. Mr. Howard), showed the white *Laelia purpurata* ' Miss Little.'

Jeremiah Colman, Esq. (gr. Mr. Bound), sent *Cattleya* × ' Wm. Murray,' variety ' Gatton Queen.'

Monsieur Mertens, Ghent, showed hybrid Odontoglossums.

E. Roberts, Esq. (gr. Mr. Carr), sent *Cypripedium* × ' Mrs. Herbert Druce.'

ORCHID COMMITTEE, MAY 14, 1907.

Mr. J. GURNEY FOWLER in the Chair, and twenty-two other members present.

Awards Recommended :—

Silver-gilt Flora Medal.

To Norman C. Cookson, Esq., Oakwood, Wylam (gr. Mr. H. J. Chapman), for a fine group of rare Odontoglossums and other Orchids.

Silver Flora Medal.

To Messrs. Jas. Veitch & Sons, Chelsea, for a group of Odontoglossums and hybrid Orchids.

To Messrs. Hugh Low & Co., Enfield, for a group of *Cattleya Mendelii* &c.

To De B. Crawshay, Esq., Rosefield, Sevenoaks (gr. Mr. Stables), for rare Odontoglossums.

Silver Banksian Medal.

To Messrs. Sander & Sons, St. Albans, for a group of Dendrobiums, hybrid Odontoglossums, &c.

To Messrs. J. Cypher & Sons, Cheltenham, for fine varieties of *Miltonia vexillaria* &c.

To R. I. Measures, Esq., Camberwell (gr. Mr. Smith), for a group containing about forty species and varieties of Orchids.

Award of Merit.

To *Odontoglossum crispum xanthotes* ' White Lady ' (votes, unanimous), from F. Menteith Ogilvie, Esq., The Shrubbery, Oxford (gr. Mr. Balmforth). A pure white variety with an occasional orange-coloured spot on some of the sepals, and orange-coloured disc to the lip.

To *Oncidium leucochilum* 'Mrs. F. J. Hanbury' (votes, unanimous), from F. J. Hanbury, Esq., Stainforth House, Upper Clapton. Sepals and petals almost entirely of a chocolate-purple colour ; lip white.

Other Exhibits.

Major G. L. Holford, C.I.E., C.V.O., Westonbirt (gr. Mr. H. G. Alexander), sent *Laelio-Cattleya* × 'Ganymede' var. *illustre.*

J. Gurney Fowler, Esq., Glebelands, South Woodford (gr. Mr. J. Davis), showed *Odontoglossum* × *Ossulstonii,* 'Glebelands variety.'

W. A. Bilney, Esq., Fir Grange, Weybridge (gr. Mr. Whitlock), showed *Cattleya Mossiae* 'Mrs. W. A. Bilney.'

Messrs. Charlesworth & Co., Heaton, Bradford, sent *Cattleya Schröderae* 'The Bride' and other Orchids.

Mr. H. A. Tracy, Twickenham, showed *Cattleya Mossiae* 'Mrs. H. Rider Haggard.'

Monsieur Mertens, Ghent, showed four hybrid Odontoglossums.

TEMPLE SHOW.

ORCHID COMMITTEE, MAY 28, 1907.

Mr. HARRY J. VEITCH in the Chair, and twenty-nine members present.

(The list of Cups and Medals will be found on pp. xvi–xix.)

First-class Certificate.

To *Laelio-Cattleya* × 'Golden Glory' (*L.-C.* × 'Zephyra' × *C. Mossiae Reineckiana*) (votes, unanimous), from Major G. L. Holford, C.I.E., C.V.O., Westonbirt, Tetbury (gr. Mr. H. G. Alexander). A pretty hybrid with golden-yellow flowers, having the front of the lip rose-crimson. (Fig. 36.)

To *Miltonia vexillaria* 'Westonbirt' variety (votes, unanimous), from Major G. L. Holford. Very near to the variety 'Memoria G. D. Owen.' Flowers white tinged with rose-pink, disc of the lip deep crimson-maroon.

To *Odontoglossum crispum* 'Solum' (votes, unanimous), from Messrs. Sander & Sons. A very remarkable variety with white flowers, having the whole of the labellum dark ruby-purple.

To *Odontoglossum crispum xanthotes* 'White's variety' (votes, unanimous), from Messrs. Sander & Sons. Flowers white with orange-coloured crest to the lip and an occasional orange spot on the sepals.

To *Cypripedium tibeticum* (votes, unanimous), from Messrs. Jas. Veitch & Sons. A hardy species from China, with large flowers, the sepals and petals tesselated with chocolate, the globose labellum chocolate-purple. (Fig. 37.)

To *Odontoglossum* × *ardentissimum Robsonae* (*Pescatorei* × *crispum*) (votes, unanimous), from Mr. J. Robson, Altrincham. A fine white flower with the inner two-thirds of each segment of a crimson tint.

To *Odontoglossum* × *gandavense* (*ardentissimum* × *Vuylstekeae*) (votes, unanimous), from Monsieur Chas. Vuylsteke, Loochristi, Ghent. Flowers rose-purple, the margins and tips white.

FIG. 36.—LAELIO-CATTLEYA × ' GOLDEN GLORY.' *(Gardeners' Chronicle.)*

(To face page xcii.)

To *Odontoglossum* × *eximium* ' King of England' (*ardentissimum* × *crispum*) (votes, unanimous), from Monsieur Chas. Vuylsteke. Sepals and petals white, with the inner parts of the segments claret colour.

To *Odontoglossum caeruleum* (parentage unrecorded) (votes, unanimous). Flowers white, heavily blotched with light violet. (Fig. 38.)

Award of Merit.

To *Cattleya Mossiae* 'Princess of Wales' (votes, unanimous), from Major G. L. Holford, C.I.E., C.V.O. (gr. Mr. H. G. Alexander). A noble form of typical *C. Mossiae* with very large flowers of fine colour.

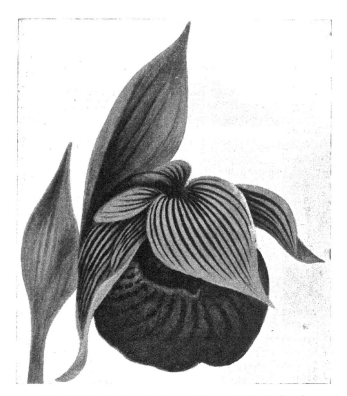

Fig. 37.—Cypripedium tibeticum. (*Journal of Horticulture.*)

To *Odontoglossum Thompsonianum superbum* (*Edwardii* × *crispum*). Flowers claret-colour edged and tipped with rose. From W. Thompson, Esq.

To *Brasso-Laelio-Cattleya* × ' Lido' (*B. Digbyana* × *L.-C.* 'Henry Greenwood') (votes, unanimous), from Monsieur Chas. Maron, Brunoy, France.

Cultural Commendation.

To Mrs. Stonyforth, Kirk Hammerton Hall, Yorkshire, for an enormous plant of *Dendrobium thyrsiflorum* with over fifty spikes.

To Mr. W. P. Bound, gr. to Jeremiah Colman, Esq., Gatton Park, for Odontoglossum crispum 'Mary Colman,' with three spikes.

To Messrs. Armstrong & Brown, Tunbridge Wells, for a finely flowered Odontoglossum naevium.

Other Exhibits.

Major G. L. Holford, C.I.E., C.V.O., staged one of the finest groups ever seen at the Temple Show, and secured the Veitchian Cup.

Messrs. Sander & Sons had a group covering 200 square feet.

Messrs. Charlesworth & Co. staged a similar group.

Jeremiah Colman, Esq. (gr. Mr. Bound), staged an extensive group.

Messrs. William Bull & Sons had a group of Cattleyas, Laelias, &c.

Messrs. Hugh Low & Co., Enfield, staged an effective group.

Fig. 38.—Odontoglossum caeruleum. (Journal of Horticulture.)

H. S. Goodson, Esq., Putney (gr. Mr. Day), had a select group.

Messrs. Jas. Cypher & Sons, Cheltenham, staged a fine group of Miltonia vexillaria and other Orchids.

Mr. Robson, Altrincham, showed a selection of Odontoglossums.

J. Rutherford, Esq., Beardwood, Blackburn (gr. Mr. Lupton), showed white Cattleyas.

Francis Wellesley, Esq. (gr. Mr. Hopkins), sent Cattleya Mossiae 'Miss Mary Knollys,' a fine variety.

Messrs. Jas. Veitch & Sons showed two of their new Brasso-Catt-Laelia × Veitchii and the fine white C. Mossiae 'Rosalind.'

H. L. Bischoffsheim, Esq. (gr. Mr. Doig), had a fine display of Cattleya Mossiae and Laelia purpurata.

R. Ashworth, Esq., Manchester (gr. Mr. Pidsley), staged a selection of Odontoglossum crispum.

ORCHID COMMITTEE, JUNE 11, 1907.

Mr. J. GURNEY FOWLER in the Chair, and twenty members present.

Awards Recommended :—

Silver-gilt Flora Medal.

To Messrs. Jas. & A. A. McBean, Cooksbridge, for a fine group of Odontoglossums, *Oncidium maranthum*, &c.

Silver Flora Medal.

To De B. Crawshay, Esq., Rosefield, Sevenoaks (gr. Mr. Stables), for a selection of hybrid Odontoglossums.

To Messrs. Sander & Sons for a group of rare species and hybrids.

To Messrs. Charlesworth & Co. for a varied collection of Orchids.

To Messrs. Hugh Low & Co. for a group of *Cattleya Mendelii* and *C. Mossiae.*

To Messrs. Stanley & Co. for a group of *Cattleya Mossiae.*

Silver Banksian Medal.

To R. I. Measures, Esq., Camberwell (gr. Mr. Smith), for a group.

First-class Certificate.

To *Miltonia vexillaria chelsiensis superba* (votes, unanimous), from Major G. L. Holford, C.I.E., C.V.O., Westonbirt, Tetbury (gr. Mr. Alexander). A large-flowered form of a rosy-lilac colour, the base of the lip having confluent radiating lines of deep purple, the central being the longest.

Award of Merit.

To *Cattleya Mendelii* 'Francis Wellesley' (votes, unanimous),. from Francis Wellesley, Esq., Westfield, Woking (gr. Mr. Hopkins). A very distinct, large-flowered blush-white variety with broad crimped labellum which has a chrome-yellow disc and a freckling of light purple in front.

Other Exhibits.

Francis Wellesley, Esq., sent *Cypripedium Lawrenceanum* 'Purple Emperor.' A very fine dark-coloured variety.

Major G. L. Holford showed *Cattleya Mendelii delicata.*

H. S. Goodson, Esq., showed *Cattleya Mossiae* 'King Edward VII.,' *Cymbidium Huttonii*, and *Laelia purpurata* 'Fair Lawn.'

Messrs. Jas. Veitch & Sons showed plants of *Brasso-Laelia* × *Digbyano-purpurata*, and *Sobralia* × *Veitchii.*

G. D. Bailey, Esq., Burgess Hill, sent *Bifrenaria Harrisoniae eburnea.*

ORCHID COMMITTEE, JUNE 25, 1907.

Mr. J. GURNEY FOWLER in the Chair, and twenty-one members present.

Awards Recommended :—

Silver-gilt Flora Medal.

To Messrs. Charlesworth & Co. for a fine group of Laelio-Cattleyas and other Orchids.

Silver Flora Medal.

To Major G. L. Holford, C.I.E., C.V.O., Westonbirt (gr. Mr. Alexander), for a selection of rare Orchids.

Silver Banksian Medal.

To Messrs. Hugh Low & Co. for a group of Cattleyas &c.

To Messrs. Moore, Ltd., Rawdon, Leeds, for a group.

To R. I. Measures, Esq., Cambridge Lodge, Camberwell (gr. Mr. Smith), for a collection of interesting species of Orchids.

First-class Certificate.

To *Lissochilus giganteus* (votes, unanimous), from the Hon. Walter Rothschild, M.P., Tring Park, Tring (gr. Mr. A. Dye). A remarkable species from the Congo, with bright green plicate leaves and stout spikes seven feet or more in height, and bearing over thirty flowers and buds on the upper part; sepals greenish tinged with purple and reflexed, inconspicuous; petals and lip showy, over three inches across, bright rose-pink with a slight violet shade and some rose-purple lines on the lip. Treated as a swamp plant while growing.

Award of Merit.

To *Cirrhopetalum gracillimum* (votes, unanimous), from Sir Trevor Lawrence, Bart., Burford (gr. Mr. W. H. White). An elegant slender species with umbels of Indian-red flowers, the thread-like lateral sepals curved downward.

To *Coelogyne asperata* (votes, unanimous), from Messrs. Moore, Ltd., Rawdon, Leeds. A Bornean species of strong growth. Inflorescence 1 foot, and bearing a dozen large cream-white flowers with brownish-orange markings on the lip.

Botanical Certificate.

To *Plocoglottis Lowii* (votes, unanimous), from the Hon. Walter Rothschild, M.P. Pseudo-bulbs and leaves tinged with purple. Inflorescence erect, one foot or more. Flowers cream-white tipped with brown, the curious lateral sepals connivent.

To *Hartwegia purpurea* (votes, unanimous), from Sir Trevor Lawrence, Bart. A dwarf plant with fleshy leaves and slender inflorescence bearing a cluster of rose-coloured flowers.

Cultural Commendation.

To Mr. H. G. Alexander (gr. to Major G. L. Holford, C.I.E., C.V.O.), for a fine specimen of *Odontoglossum crispum* with twelve spikes bearing together eighty-eight flowers. The specimen was grown from a single pseudo-bulb.

Other Exhibits.

Francis Wellesley, Esq., showed *Laelio-Cattleya* × *Hippolyta* 'Prince of Orange' and other Orchids.

Miss Willmott sent *Sobralia* × *Veitchii*, 'Warley variety.'

J. Gurney Fowler, Esq., sent *Laelio-Cattleya* × 'C. G. Roebling,' 'Glebelands variety.'

H. S. Goodson, Esq., showed *Odontoglossum Wilckeanum* 'H. S. Goodson.'

Messrs. J. & A. A. McBean sent white varieties of *Cattleya Mossiae* and *Odontoglossum crispum*.

W. Thompson, Esq., showed *Odontioda × Bradshawiae*.

R. G. Thwaites, Esq., sent *Odontoglossum Pescatorei* 'Grand Duchess.'

Messrs. Stanley & Co. showed a selection of varieties of *Cattleya Mossiae*.

EXAMINATION IN HORTICULTURE.

APRIL 10, 1907.

THE Annual Examination in the Principles and Practice of Horticulture was held on April 10, 1907, when 150 candidates entered.

Three hundred marks were allotted as a maximum. Twenty candidates, or nearly 14 per cent. of the whole number, were placed in the First Class.

Fifty-nine, or about 40 per cent. of the whole, were placed in the Second Class.

Sixty-three, or a little over 44 per cent., were placed in the Third Class.

It is noticeable that the successes of the First Class are nearly double those of 1906—13·8 per cent. (1907), 7 per cent. (1906)—while the Second Class has decreased from 50 to 40 per cent. The Third Class is nearly stationary.

With regard to the papers on the Principles of Horticulture. Many of the answers were extremely good: but too many candidates gave an account of *Assimilation* in error for *Respiration*; and in replying to the question in the *Divisions*, gave merely the distinctions between the *Classes* of Dicotyledons and Monocotyledons, which was not asked for. It is to be regretted that Darwin's mistake as to the "injuriousness" of self-fertilisation still holds its ground, though it was shown to be not true to nature thirty years ago.

With regard to the Practice of Horticulture, with a few exceptions the candidates answered the questions fairly well. None of them obtained the maximum number of marks. Many candidates started well and obtained the maximum number of marks in the first or second questions, but fell off towards the third and fourth. There are about 26 minutes allowed for each question, and if the eight questions were apportioned into 26 minutes each, a more uniform degree of merit would be obtained. Allusion has been made in previous years to the candidates introducing irrelevant matter into their answers, but there is not much reason for comment on this point in the present examination. The main cause of failure has been the spending of too much time on the first questions and failing for want of time towards the end. In two or three instances three questions were answered well, and then a very poor attempt indeed made at a fourth, evidently owing to want of time.

GEORGE HENSLOW.
JAMES DOUGLAS.

June 1907.

First Class.

1. { Price, G., Studley Horticultural College, Studley.
   { Sherris, G. E. M., The Horticultural College, Swanley.

3. { Brown, M. K., The Horticultural College, Swanley.
   { Sherris, D., The Horticultural College, Swanley.

5. Kitson, D. H., School of Gardening, Bredon's Norton, Tewkesbury.

6. { Cayley, D. M., University College, Reading.
   { Lelacheur, M. M., The Horticultural College, Swanley.
   { Stanion, A. E., University College, Reading.

9. { Legg, M. L., The Horticultural College, Swanley.
   { Marshall, W. H., Muston, Filey, Yorks.

11. { Brown, J. M., Park Gardens, Drumoak, Aberdeenshire.
    { Dixon, J. E., 184 West Hill, Putney, S.W.
    { Dyson, D. A. E., University College, Reading.
    { Morrell, G., Wanngach Cottage, Beaufort, Mon.

15. { Dyer, F. I., Studley Horticultural College, Studley.
    { Hodgkins, E. C., School House, Franche, Kidderminster.
    { Jones, D. R., The Horticultural College, Swanley.
    { Kay-Mouat, K., The Horticultural College, Swanley.
    { Pollard, G. E., The Horticultural College, Swanley.
    { Rackham, W. F., Ridgway Road, Farnham, Surrey.

Second Class.

21. { Burnicle, J. W., 8 The Knoll, Sunderland.
    { Ford, R. E., 21 St. Fillan's Road, Catford, S.E.
    { Whitaker, W. S., The Warrens, Camelford, Cornwall.
    { Williams, B., Essex County School of Horticulture, Chelmsford.

25. { Bridger, E. N., Studley Horticultural College, Studley.
    { D'Ombrain, E., Studley Horticultural College, Studley.
    { Douglas, A. V. E., School of Gardening, Bredon's Norton, Tewkesbury.
    { Kennedy-Bell, M., Studley Horticultural College, Studley.
    { Meeke, B. D., University College, Reading.
    { Parsons, H., The Horticultural College, Swanley.
    { Webb, J., Technical School, Marple, near Stockport.

32. { Cooke, A. M., Horticultural School, Glynde, Sussex.
    { Crisp, W. C., Upper Vobster, Coleford, near Bath.
    { Ford, A. P., Countess of Warwick's School, Dunmow.
    { Hunter, N., The Horticultural College, Swanley.
    { Mitchell, J. W., Finsthwaite, Newby Bridge, near Ulverston.
    { Poffley, A. T., 11F Peabody Buildings, Herne Hill, S.E.
    { Sadler, H., University College, Reading.
    { Towsey, G. M., The Horticultural College, Swanley.
    { Turner, A., Essex County School of Horticulture, Chelmsford.

41. { Gray, G. J. J., Foulden, Stoke Ferry, Norfolk.
    { Moles, F., Essex County School of Horticulture, Chelmsford.
    { Ricardo, M. F., The Horticultural College, Swanley.
    { Saunders, W., The Horticultural College, Swanley.
    { Warner, P. E., Ringwood School, Yarmouth, Isle of Wight.
    { Whitaker, W., London and County Bank, 263 Strand, W.C.

47. {
Macey, A., Home Farm, Saint Hill, East Grinstead.
Pollard, F. D., Elmwood Nursery, Cosham.
Wooderson, W., Sunny Bank, Upper Bourne, Farnham, Surrey.
Yandell, W., Hatfield House Gardens, Hatfield, Herts.
}

51. {
Braithwaite, H., Normanby Park Gardens, Doncaster.
Brown, C. H., The Horticultural College, Swanley.
Downie, I., Studley Horticultural College, Studley.
Moore, H. J., 35 Alexandra Road, Richmond, Surrey.
Norwood, T. E., 25 Petersham Street, Lenton, Notts.
Walsh, E. C., Studley Horticultural College, Studley.
}

57. {
Barrie, M. L., Elmwood Nursery, Cosham.
Fugler, R. G., Whitford, Holywell, N. Wales.
Irvine, H., Horticultural School, Glynde, Sussex.
Sharland, F., Nunnery Gardens, Douglas, Isle of Man.
Widgery, T. W., School House, Petham, Canterbury.
}

62. {
Allsopp, D., Elmwood Nursery, Cosham.
Gardiner, C. L., Church Street, Saffron Walden.
Goldring, D. M., Horticultural School, Glynde, Sussex.
Hodgson, E., Essex County School of Horticulture, Chelmsford.
Jackson, W., University College, Reading.
Lloyd, J. R., The Gardens, Brewood, Staffs.
}

68. {
Arnold, E., Sandwell View, Church Vale, West Bromwich.
Comer, J., Countess of Warwick's School, Dunmow.
Hammett, M., Studley Horticultural College, Studley.
Parks, W., School House, Ightham, Sevenoaks.
Townshend, R., Horticultural School, Glynde, Sussex.
}

73. {
Bridger, D. C., Studley Horticultural College, Studley.
Harris, J., Inverleith Public Park, Edinburgh.
Lipson, M., Essex County School of Horticulture, Chelmsford.
Savage, A. A., University College, Reading.
Taylor, K. W., Studley Horticultural College, Studley.
Willard, E. J., 1 Forest View, Forest Road, Leytonstone.
Wright, F. L., Far Hills, Somerset County, New Jersey, U.S.A.
}

Third Class.

80. {
Bartlett, W., 5 Westgrove Terrace, Melverton, Leamington Spa.
Best, H. T., Devonia, Ripley, Woking, Surrey.
Bransden, H., Essex County School of Horticulture, Chelmsford.
Day, F., Blithfield, Rugeley, Staffs.
McKay, D. R., Slains Castle Gardens, Port Erroll, N.B.
Meacock, G. H., Countess of Warwick's School, Dunmow.
Ridley, J., Essex County School of Horticulture, Chelmsford.
Spalding, C., Elmwood Nursery, Cosham.
}

88. {
Blench, G. S., Technical School, Marple, near Stockport.
Cornelius-Wheeler, L., Elmwood Nursery, Cosham.
Dickson, H., 37 Dahomey Road, Streatham, S.W.
Grey, E. E., Aske Hall Gardens, Richmond, Yorks.
Tweedie, A., Elmwood Nursery, Cosham.
Whitby, G. C., Countess of Warwick's School, Dunmow.
}

94. {
Eastwood, J. R., 1 Neville Street, Skipton, Yorks.
Glendinning, R., R.H.S. Gardens, Wisley, Ripley, Surrey.
Ronaldson, N., Elmwood Nursery, Cosham.
Sharland, F. P., The Nunnery Gardens, Douglas, Isle of Man.
}

98. {
Atkins, H. W., Cross Lane Nursery, Gravesend.
Gould, T. W., The Lodge, Moorfield, Glossop, Derbyshire.
Salmon, R., White Oak School, Swanley.
}

101. {
Corby, C. W., Orchard Mains Gardens, Hildenboro', Tonbridge.
Peter, H., Studley Horticultural College, Studley.
Rye, B., Horticultural School, Glynde, Sussex.
Senior, A., The Gardens, Newbold Revel, near Rugby.
}

105. {
Day, W. G., Galloway House Gardens, Garlieston, N.B.
Gardner, L. W., Essex County School of Horticulture, Chelmsford.
}

107. {
Burgess, J., Technical School, Marple, near Stockport.
Larking, A., Stapleton Park Gardens, near Pontefract.
Shepherd, F. W., The Gardens, Searles, Fletching.
}

110. {
Abrahams, W., Papworth Hall Gardens, Papworth Everard.
Casement, C. M., The Horticultural College, Swanley.
Darrington, G. M., Essex County School of Horticulture, Chelmsford.
Hill, W., St. Bernards, Upper Caterham, Surrey.
Little, W. B., 286 Kew Road, Kew, Surrey.
Lorriman, W. H., Thorpe Common, Pontefract.
McCarrell, W., Aberlour House Gardens, Aberlour, Banffshire.
Parsons, E. T., St. Johns, Clarence Street, Egham.
}

118. Brine, G., The Gardens, Bearwood, Wokingham.

119. {
Cambray, F. A., Syon House Gardens, Brentford, Middlesex.
Figgis, G., 115 Upper Thrift Street, Northampton.
Hodgson, C., Essex County School of Horticulture, Chelmsford.
}

122. {
Blench, G., Junr., Technical School, Marple, near Stockport.
Blundell, R., Essex County School of Horticulture, Chelmsford.
Clouston, I. O., Horticultural School, Glynde, Sussex.
Cockin, D., The Horticultural College, Swanley.
Whitton, C. R., Elmwood Nursery, Cosham.
}

127. {
Fuller, C. M., Horticultural School, Glynde, Sussex.
Swinbank, J. G., South View, Kirk Hammerton, York.
}

129. {
Alder, G. R., Essex County School of Horticulture, Chelmsford.
Broyd, O. E., Essex County School of Horticulture, Chelmsford.
Crow, T., Essex County School of Horticulture, Chelmsford.
Kennedy, S., Countess of Warwick's School, Dunmow.
Poole, W. C., 16 Slatey Road, Cloughton, Birkenhead.
Westby, W., Long Lane, Aughton, near Ormskirk, Lancs.
}

135. Philips, D. R., Ross Priory Lodge, Balloch, N.B.

136. {
Green, H., 40 Swanfield Road, Waltham Cross.
Smith, W. C., Essex County School of Horticulture, Chelmsford.
Stringer, E., Countess of Warwick's School, Dunmow.
}

139. Stobbo, J., Pinhay, Lyme Regis.

140. Walker, G., Countess of Warwick's School, Dunmow.

141. {
Brennan, W., White Oak School, Swanley.
Osmond, A. J., Park Hill Gardens, Streatham Common, S.W.
}

EXAMINATION OF SCHOOL TEACHERS
IN COTTAGE AND ALLOTMENT GARDENING.

APRIL 24, 1907.

EXAMINERS' REPORT.

ONE HUNDRED AND FORTY-FIVE candidates entered for the Examination, as against 166 last year. Of these 36 have won a first class, 41 a second, 45 a third, and 23 have failed to satisfy us; but, notwithstanding these failures, we are glad to be able to report a general advance all along the line, the improvement since the first establishment of this Examination being well maintained.

The following criticisms may be of use to those who have failed this year and to intending candidates in future :—

Whilst the best papers showed a proper appreciation of the common term " Cabbage," and dealt solely with that section of plants, many candidates wandered into long dissertations on various other members of the Brassica family.

Generally the deterioration of Potatoes was ascribed to absence of needful constituents in the soil, especially through excessive cropping. Free dilating on chemical manures was common. The most practical papers, however, mentioned the importance of good winter storing of tubers and frequent interchange of them for planting purposes.

The selections of vegetables for exhibition at rural Shows were generally excellent, and the culture of Vegetable Marrows, though variously described, still evidenced fair practical knowledge. The same might be said of garden herbs, their propagation, culture, and uses; but some candidates included salads and other unlooked-for subjects with them.

A knowledge of hardy plants suitable for rock-work or garden edgings caused a good deal of stumbling, very many including both tall and tender plants in their lists; the best papers, however, furnished excellent lists.

When dealing with garden flowers for cutting and sale, candidates generally were more at home, some lists being of exceptional merit. These flowers, apart from their decorative value, have good market value also for cottagers.

Reference to Apple stocks caused some tripping, but, all the same, many candidates thoroughly understood the diverse uses of Crab and Paradise stocks, and described their peculiarities and adaptabilities. Very few of the candidates seemed to realise the value of the " Bramble " type of fruit for garden culture, and dwelt solely on the Raspberry, some even dwelling largely on Gooseberries and Strawberries.

The appearance of what is known as " big bud " on Black Currants, and the true nature of the insect causing it, and the best recognised remedies, were properly described by some, whilst others showed great ignorance.

All those candidates who come low on the list or have failed should acquire wider and more practical knowledge before another Examination takes place.

The Examiners wish again to impress upon the candidates the importance of reading the regulations prior to commencing, thereby saving trouble afterwards. Several candidates devoted too much time to the first half of the questions answered, and had thereby no time left to do justice to the later ones.

In conclusion, we are pleased to note that practical knowledge in the replies was abundantly manifested in the majority of the papers. The knowledge thus shown must, if properly directed, be the means of imparting to those whom they are called upon to teach a vast amount of good and most serviceable information.

JAMES HUDSON, V.M.H.

ALEXANDER DEAN, V.M.H.

August 1907.

First Class.

1. { Cornall, W. J., Chilham, Canterbury.
   { Whitaker, W. S., The Warrens, Camelford, Cornwall.
3. Smith, W., The School House, Henham, Wangford, R.S.O.
4. Cook, J., The School House, Areley Kings, Stourport.
5. { Cook, T. H. P., Biggin, Hartington, Buxton.
   { Jeavons, J. T., County Technical School, Stafford.
7. Bache, W., County Technical School, Stafford.
8. Jackson, F., School House, Kirk Burton, Huddersfield.
9. Apse, J., County Technical School, Stafford.
10. Tinley, W., School House, Malmesbury, Wilts.
11. { Best, H. T., Devonia, Ripley, Woking, Surrey.
    { Legge, C. D., School House, Great Tew, Enstone, Oxon
13. Tyson, N., Edenhall School House, Langwathby, R.S.O.
14. Westbrook, J., Blagdon School, near Bristol.
15. { Ford, R. E., 21 St. Fillans Road, Catford, S.E.
    { Kirk, C. G., 6 Woodfield Road, Cheadle Hulme, Stockport.
    { Warner, P. E., Ringwood School, Isle of Wight.
18. Randell, R., London Road Boys' School, Burgess Hill, Sussex.
19. { Ancill, A. C., 35 Broad Street, Stratford-on-Avon.
    { Thompson, J. C., Endowed School, Leybourne, Maidstone.
21. Gray, G. J. J., School House, Foulden, Stoke Ferry, Norfolk.
22. { Johnson, A. E., 18 Gladstone Terrace, Brighton.
    { Parks, W., School House, Ightham, Sevenoaks.
    { Williams, E., Havelock House, High Street, Prestatyn, R.S.O.
25. Burbridge, R. H., Middlesex County School of Gardening.
26. { Dutton, E. W., Essex County School of Horticulture, Chelmsford.
    { Matthews, L., Essex County School of Horticulture, Chelmsford.
28. Sadler, G. H. J., Ilketshall St. Andrews, Bungay.
29. Harris, H. J., School House, South Hornchurch, Romford.

30. { Good, W., Broomknowe Cottage, Kilmalcolm, N.B.
     { Stubbs, H., County Technical School, Stafford.

32. { Dunt, R. C., 12 Frederick's Place, Beccles, Suffolk.
     { Fell, W. J., Council Schools, Claydon, Ipswich.
     { Graham, J., Middlesex County School of Gardening.
     { Laming, C., Park Lane, Birchington, Thanet.
     { Stenning, A., Friston, Saxmundham, Suffolk.

Second Class.

37. Knowles, T. A., The School House, Fritwell, Banbury.
38. Atkin, J. D., Coneysthorpe, Malton, Yorks.
39. { Cartwright, C., Western Road, Lower Hagley, Stourbridge.
     { Gilbert, K., Belvoir Castle Gardens, Grantham.
     { Smith, T., School House, Wood-Ditton, Newmarket.
42. Woodward, G., Old Newton, Stowmarket.
43. Harrison, R. F., School House, Barsham, Beccles.
44. { Glover, H. J., St. Katherine's, Westham, near Hastings.
     { Wilks, W. J., The Hollies, Charfield, R.S.O., Glos.
46. Fugler, R. G., Whitford, Holywell, North Wales.
47. { Blainey, E. E., The School House, Churchill, Kidderminster.
     { Heaton, W. G., Sutton and Bignor School, Pulborough.
     { Morgan, J. L., 43 Thorpe Road, Walsall, Staffs.
50. { Joy, D. G., School House, Sand Hutton, York.
     { Underwood, J. P., County Technical School, Stafford.
52. Howes, A., County Technical School, Stafford.
53. { Hunt, H., Foresters' Convalescent Home, Clent.
     { Stevens, G., The Laurels, Wetherden, Stowmarket.
     { Taylor, G., The Council School, East Stockwith, Gainsborough.
56. { Hibbs, F. E., County Technical School, Stafford.
     { Jackson, W., County Technical School, Stafford.
58. Marfell, J. A., Plump Hill Council School, Mitcheldean.
59. { Bonnick, C., Frederick Bird School, Coventry.
     { Farthing, C. W., Terra Cotta House, Hanham Road, Kingswood.
     { Homer, J. J., Beecher Road, Cradley, Staffs.
     { Witham, H. W., Old Newton Schools, Stowmarket.
63. { Cook, A., School House, Broome, Stourbridge.
     { Ferber, W., The School House, Shuttington, Tamworth.
     { Stewart, J. W., County Technical School, Stafford.
     { Stokes, G. W., Hulver, Wangford, Suffolk.
67. Huke, E. T., Fairview, Hayway Road, Rushden.
68. { Routledge, H., Stanford Bridge, Worcester.
     { Thompson, E., Ickburgh School, Mundford, S.O., Norfolk.
70. { Barton, J. E., School House, Charlbury, Oxon.
     { Wixey, F. G., 2 Cromwell Terrace, Hanham, Bristol.
72. Wall, W. H., The School House, Great Witley, Stourport.
73. James, A. E., Cutnall Green School, near Droitwich.
74. { Crooks, W., Biggin Hill, Westerham, Kent.
     { Hunt, A. R., Essex County School of Horticulture, Chelmsford.
     { Jones, T. O., 184 High Street, Cymmer, Porth, Glam.
     { Shier, W. E., Middlesex County School of Gardening.

Third Class.

78. { Evans, A. L. A., The School House, Onehouse, Stowmarket.
{ Lancaster, J., School House, Yarpole, Leominster.

80. { Bond, E., School House, Welton, Daventry.
{ Edwards, E., Albion Villas, Cradley, Staffs.

82. Harvey, J. H., Technical School, Stafford.

83. Stace, W. H. S., 5 Izane Road, Bexley Heath, Kent.

84. Heywood, J. H., Hagley, Stourbridge.

85. { Clark, R. W., Bamburgh, Northumberland.
{ Fullwood, A. D., Technical School, Stafford.
{ Laight, R., Middlesex County School of Gardening.
{ Webster, E. D., Essex County School of Horticulture, Chelmsford.

89. Kipping, M., Whitehaven, Hutton, Essex.

90. Stevens, J. G. J. D., Hawkesbury Upton, Badminton, S.O.

91. { Dobson, W., 9 Institute Street, West Sleekburn, Morpeth.
{ Hargett, H., School House, Chippenham, Soham, Cambs.
{ Massey, F., Worlingham, Beccles, Suffolk.
{ Perry, F. T., Forward Green, near Stowmarket.

95. Langford, J., County Technical School, Stafford.

96. { Archbold, J. E., St. Philip's Boys' School, Arundel.
{ Holland, H. J., County Technical School, Stafford.

98. Dennison, J. E., Elmside, Wootton-under-Edge, Glos.

99. { Gibbins, W. A., Essex County School of Horticulture, Chelmsford.
{ Lack, B., Essex County School of Horticulture, Chelmsford.
{ Williams, J. E., Albert Street, Leeswood, near Mold.

102. { Brown, H. E., Middlesex County School of Gardening.
{ Howe, J. W., County Technical School, Stafford.
{ Postgate, T., Fell View, Cockermouth.
{ Roberts, T., Essex County School of Horticulture, Chelmsford.

106. David, W. R., School House, Ivington, Leominster.

107. Williams, G., County Technical School, Stafford.

108. { Collins, J., Ivy Cottage, Field Lane, Alvaston, Derby.
{ Graham, E. E., County Technical School, Stafford.
{ Roper, C. A., Furlong Lane, Cradley, Staffs.

111. Parsons, E. T., Clarence Street, Egham.

112. { Drury, G. H., County Technical School, Stafford.
{ Longley, W., 1 Queen's Row, Walworth, S.E.
{ Teece, R., West Hyde Schoolhouse, Rickmansworth.

115. { Buckham, C. F., Ingoldisthorpe, King's Lynn.
{ Woodhouse, S., County Technical School, Stafford.

117. { Goodchild, J. R., The School House, Staunton-on-Arrow.
{ Sales, J. E., Council School, Wenhaston, Suffolk.

119. Barker, F. H., County Technical School, Stafford.

120. Kinnaird, E., Dunstan School, Lesbury, R.S.O.

121. { Beddall, G., County Technical School, Stafford.
{ Brecknell, T. F., County Technical School, Stafford.

ROYAL HORTICULTURAL SOCIETY'S EXAMINATIONS, 1908.

GENERAL EXAMINATION.

WEDNESDAY, APRIL 8, 1908.

THE Society's Annual Examination in the Principles and Practice of Horticulture will be held on Wednesday, April 8th, 1908.

The Society is willing to hold an Examination wherever a magistrate, clergyman, schoolmaster, or other responsible person accustomed to Examinations will consent to supervise one on the Society's behalf, and in accordance with the rules laid down for its conduct.

A copy of the Syllabus, covering both Examinations, will be sent to any person on receipt of a stamped and directed envelope.

SCHOLARSHIPS.

A Scholarship of £25 a year for two years is offered by the Worshipful Company of Gardeners to be awarded after the 1908 examination, to the student who shall pass highest, if he is willing to accept the conditions attaching thereto. The main outline of these conditions is that the holder must be of the male sex, and between the ages of 18 and 22 years, and that he should study gardening for one year at least at the Royal Horticultural Society's Gardens at Wisley, conforming to the general rules laid down there for Students. In the second year of the Scholarship he may, if he like, continue his studies at some other place at home or abroad which is approved by the Council of the Royal Horticultural Society. In case of two or more eligible students being adjudged equal, the Council reserve to themselves the right to decide which of them shall be presented to the Scholarship.

Similar Scholarships have been presented by :—

Sir TREVOR LAWRENCE, Bart., K.C.V.O., V.M.H., in 1894.

Baron SCHRÖDER, V.M.H., in 1895.

The Worshipful Company of Gardeners, 1896.

N. N. SHERWOOD, Esq., V.M.H., 1897.

G. W. BURROWS, Esq., 1898.

The Right Hon. the Lord AMHERST, 1899.

HENRY WOOD, Esq., 1900.

F. G. IVEY, Esq., 1901.

Sir WILLIAM FARMER, 1902.

E. A. STRAUSS, Esq., 1903.

The Worshipful Company of Gardeners, 1906.

Royal Horticultural Society, 1907.

Copies of the Questions set at the Examinations 1893-1907 (price 2/-) may be obtained at the R.H.S. Office, Vincent Square, London, S.W.

SCHOOL TEACHERS' EXAMINATION IN COTTAGE AND ALLOTMENT GARDENING.

WEDNESDAY, APRIL 29, 1908.

The Royal Horticultural Society will hold its Fifth Examination in Cottage and Allotment Gardening on Wednesday, April 29, 1908.

This Examination is intended for and will be confined to Elementary and Technical School Teachers. It has been undertaken in view of the increasing demand in Country districts that the School Teachers shall be competent to teach the elements of Cottage and Allotment Gardening, and of the absence of any test whatever of such capacity.

The Society is willing to hold an Examination wherever a magistrate, clergyman, or other responsible person accustomed to Examinations will consent to supervise one on the Society's behalf; but for obvious reasons no school teacher should act as Supervisor at this Examination.

A capitation fee of 5s. will be charged for every Candidate in order to partially defray the expenses of the Examination.

The time allowed for the Examination is three hours and a half, the hour fixed being generally from 6.30 to 10 P.M.

A Silver-gilt Flora Medal will be awarded to the Candidate gaining the highest number of marks, and each successful Candidate will receive a Certificate of the Class in which he has passed.

The general conduct of this Examination will be on similar lines to that of the more general Examination.

OUTLINE SYLLABUS.

(1) Some knowledge of the formation or nature of soils, not necessarily Scientific, but such as is essential to cultivators.

(2) Information as to the best average sizes of cottage gardens and allotments such as men engaged in diverse vocations can cultivate in spare time.

(3) Preparation of soils for the reception of crops of all descriptions to ensure successful results.

(4) Renovating Neglected Gardens.

(5) Manuring soils for diverse crops, with some knowledge in practical form of the nature of manures and their constituents.

(6) Spring Vegetable crops, varieties and method of cropping, times for manuring, planting, &c.

(7) Summer Crops—successional.

(8) Autumn or Winter crops for successional purposes.

(9) General treatment to secure best results for all seasons.

(10) Suitable fruits for cottage gardens. Varieties, methods of culture, pruning and training. General treatment.

(11) Fruits suitable for allotment culture.

(12) Flowers for cottage gardens, seasons of flowering, methods of propagation, &c.

(13) Flowers suited for allotments, varieties and general culture.

(14) Window gardening, inside and out.

N.B.—School Teachers who have passed this Examination, if they subsequently wish to become Fellows of the Society, may do so on payment of a subscription of One Guinea per annum. A list of privileges relating to Fellowship may be obtained from the Society's Offices, Vincent Square, London, S.W.

School Teachers may also sit for the General Examination on Wednesday, April 8, 1908. A copy of the Syllabus may be obtained from the Society's Offices, Vincent Square, Westminster, S.W.

Each applicant should enclose a stamped envelope ready addressed to himself.

SCHOOL TEACHERS' EXAMINATION IN COTTAGE AND ALLOTMENT GARDENING.

BOOKS RECOMMENDED FOR STUDY.

Agricultural Botany, by John Percival, F.L.S. (Duckworth, 3 Henrietta Street, W.C.), 7/6.

Elementary Botany, by J. W. Oliver (Blackie & Son, 50 Old Bailey, E.C.), 2/-.

Primer of Botany, by Sir J. D. Hooker, K.C.S.I. (Macmillan & Co., St. Martin's Street, W.C.), 1/-.

Structural Botany (Flowering Plants), by Dr. D. H. Scott (A. & C. Black, Soho Square, W.), 3/6.

The Chemistry of the Garden, by H. H. Cousins (Macmillan & Co.), 1/-.

The Forcing Book, by Prof. L. H. Bailey (Macmillan & Co.), 4/-

Profitable Fruit Growing, by J. Wright, V.M.H. (" City Press " Office, Aldersgate, E.C.), 1/3.

The Principles of Fruit Growing, by Prof. L. H. Bailey (Macmillan & Co.), 5/-.

Thompson's Gardeners' Assistant, New Edition by W. Watson, 6 vols. (Gresham Publishing Co., 34 Southampton Street, Strand), £2/8/-.

Garden Flowers and Plants, by J. Wright, V.M.H. (Macmillan & Co.), 1/-.

Paxton's Calendar of Garden Operations (" Gardeners' Chronicle " Office, 41 Wellington Street, W.C.), 7½d.

Pictorial Flower Gardening
Pictorial Greenhouse Management ⎫ By Walter P. Wright
Pictorial Vegetable Growing ⎬ (Cassell & Co.)
Pictorial Fruit Growing ⎭ 1/- each.
Pictorial Practical Gardening

Primer of Horticulture, by J. Wright, V.M.H. (Macmillan & Co.), 1/-.

Farm and Garden Insects, by W. Somerville, D.Sc. (Macmillan & Co.), 1/-.

Natural History of Plants, 2 vols., by Kerner & Oliver (Blackie & Son), 30/-.

Nature Teaching, by Francis Watts, B.Sc., and W. G. Freeman, B.Sc. (John Murray), 3/6.

Plant Life, by Dr. M. T. Masters, F.R.S. (Vinton & Co., 9 New Bridge Street, E.C.), 2/6.

Plant Breeding, by Prof. L. H. Bailey (Macmillan & Co.), 4/ .

The Pruning Book, by Prof. L. H. Bailey (Macmillan & Co.), 5/-.

The Soil, by A. D. Hall, M.A. (John Murray), 3/6.

The Spraying of Plants, by E. G. Lodeman (Macmillan & Co.), 4/-.

Vegetable Culture, by A. Dean (Macmillan & Co.), 1/-.

The Principles of Vegetable Gardening, by Prof. L. H. Bailey (Macmillan & Co.), 4/-.

Lessons in Cottage Gardening, by A. A. Kerridge, 51 St. Mary Street, Chippenham, Wilts. Bound in cloth, 2/6 ; in paper cover, 1/-.

EXAMINATION PAPERS, 1893-1907.

The SOCIETY'S QUESTIONS, set at the various Examinations —from 1893 to 1907—are now published in book form, and will —————— prove very useful to intending candidates. ——————

TO BE OBTAINED FROM THE SOCIETY'S OFFICES,

VINCENT SQUARE, WESTMINSTER. Price 2s.

SCHOOL TEACHERS' EXAMINATION IN COTTAGE AND ALLOTMENT GARDENING.

WEDNESDAY, APRIL 29, 1908.

ENTRY FORM.

Intending Candidates are requested to fill in this form, and return it (with Postal Order for 5s.) to the Secretary, Royal Horticultural Society, Vincent Square, London, S.W., at least three weeks before the Examination takes place, but before if possible (*see* Syllabus on page cvii).

*Name** Mr.
in full Mrs. ⎱———
Miss ⎰

Address

*Age*_____

*Name of Supervisor*___ __ _

Address of Supervisor __

*Place of Examination*_____

* Scratch out two of the words " Mr.," " Mrs.," or " Miss."

The Examination will be held simultaneously in as many different centres in Great Britain and Ireland as circumstances may demand.

If any Candidate desires to sit in London for this Examination he must say so on his entry form, and the Society will then make arrangements for him to attend at their Hall in Vincent Square, Westminster, S.W.

When this form, duly filled up, has been returned, the Society assumes that the Candidate has already made all necessary arrangements with his Supervisor as to the place where the Examination will be held, &c. ; therefore no further notice will be sent to him, except a postcard to acknowledge receipt of entry form and capitation fee. The questions will be sent direct to the Supervisor.

SCHOOL TEACHERS' EXAMINATION IN COTTAGE AND ALLOTMENT GARDENING.

DUTIES OF A SUPERVISOR.

(a) To satisfy himself that the room proposed for the Examination is a suitable one for the purpose, and to see that a sufficient quantity of foolscap paper, *all of one size*, is provided for the use of the Candidates.

(b) To satisfy himself that all Candidates belonging to his centre have been duly acquainted with the place, day, and hour of Examination. This may be done by communicating with the Lecturer or with the Secretary of the County Council, &c.

(c) To receive the sealed parcel of Papers which will be posted to him from London seven clear days before the Examination. N.B.—If the Papers do not arrive by the fourth day before the Examination, he should *immediately* telegraph to the Secretary of the Society, Vincent Square, London, S.W. Telegraphic address : " Hortensia, London."

(d) To preserve the seals of the parcel *unbroken*, until he opens it *in the presence of the Candidates*, at the hour fixed for the Examination to commence.

(e) To distribute one copy of the Examination Paper, one copy of Form X, and an envelope bearing the Society's address and space for Candidate's number to each Candidate. It is better that the Candidates should be seated not too closely together.

(f) The Supervisor will then *immediately* read aloud the directions printed at the head of the Paper of Questions, make a note of the exact time, and inform Students distinctly of the exact hour at which all Papers must be handed in.

(g) To tell each Candidate to number every sheet of his Paper with the number printed on the top of his Question-paper, and not to write his name and address on any of them, but to send it separately in an envelope which is sent for the purpose, on the outside of which *the Candidate must also be sure to write his distinctive number.*

(h) To collect from the Candidates the envelopes containing their names and addresses, and see that they are numbered outside with the corresponding number of the Question-paper of each.

(i) To see the following rules are strictly observed :—

1. Three and a half hours are allowed for the Paper.
2. Students are not allowed to bring any books, paper, notes, &c., into the Examination-room ; nor to ask any questions whatever, save of the Supervisor, who must exercise his judgment as to whether such question is one he should answer or not.
3. Students are not allowed to leave the Examination-room on any pretext whatsoever after each Paper has been distributed. In case of unavoidable illness, the Student must be content either to hand in what he has already done or to wait till another Examination takes place.
4. Any Student leaving the room before the full time allowed has expired must first give up to the Supervisor his written Papers.
5. The Papers of any Students breaking these rules or found copying should at once be destroyed.

(k) The allotted time having expired, the Supervisor will call on the Students to fold up and hand in their Papers, which should then be *at once* (before leaving the room) properly secured, either with string or paper-fasteners. They should be posted to the Secretary, R.H.S., Vincent Square, London, S.W., by the earliest possible post.

(l) The supervisor will, of course, not himself leave the room during the time of Examination.

The Supervisor is requested to sign the following form and return it with the Students' Papers to the Secretary, R.H.S., Vincent Square, London, S.W.

I hereby certify that the Examination held at ＿＿＿＿＿＿＿ has been conducted strictly according to the rules and regulations of the Royal Horticultural Society.

Supervisor's Signature＿＿＿＿＿＿＿＿＿＿＿＿

Supervisor's Address＿＿＿＿＿＿＿＿＿＿＿＿

Date

⁎ The Council of the Royal Horticultural Society reserve to themselves the right to modify the application of these Regulations as they may consider necessary, and all disputed questions of interpretation and procedure must be referred to them for final decision.

ESTABLISHED
1804.

INCORPORATED
1809.

TELEGRAMS:
" HORTENSIA, LONDON."

TELEPHONE :
5863 WESTMINSTER.

ROYAL HORTICULTURAL SOCIETY,

VINCENT SQUARE, WESTMINSTER, S.W.

NOTICES TO FELLOWS.

1. NOTICE TO FELLOWS.

NOTICE IS HEREBY GIVEN that the **ONE HUNDRED AND FOURTH ANNUAL GENERAL MEETING** of the Fellows of the Society will be held at the **Royal Horticultural Hall, Vincent Square, Westminster,** on Tuesday, February 11, 1908, at 3 P.M. precisely, for the purpose of receiving the Report of the Council for 1907, electing a President, Vice-Presidents, Treasurer, Secretary, Auditor and four Members of Council for the ensuing year. ·

A few pages of Notices to Fellows are always added at the end of each number of the JOURNAL, immediately preceding the Advertisements, and also at the beginning both of the "Book of Arrangements" and of the "Report of the Council." Fellows are particularly requested to consult these Notices, as it would often save them and the Secretary much needless correspondence.

2. LETTERS.

All letters on *all* subjects should be addressed—The Secretary, Royal Horticultural Hall, Vincent Square, Westminster, S.W.

3. TELEPHONE AND TELEGRAMS.

Telephone Number: **5363, WESTMINSTER.**
"**HORTENSIA, LONDON,**" is sufficient address for telegrams.

4. JOURNALS WANTED.

The Secretary would be very greatly obliged for any of the following back numbers :—Vol. V., Part 1 ; Vol. VII., Part 2 ; Vol. X. ; Vol. XIII., Part 1 ; Vol. XVI., Parts 2 and 3 ; Vol. XVII., Parts 1 and 2 ; Vol. XVII., Parts 3 and 4 ; Vol. XIX., Part 1 ; Vol. XIX., Part 2 ; Vol. XX., Part 3 ; Vol. XXII., Part 3 ; Vol. XXII., Part 4 ; Vol. XXV., Part 3 ; Vol. XXVI., Part 4 ; Vol. XXVII., Part 1 ; Vol. XXVII., Part 4 ; Vol. XXVIII., Parts 3 and 4 ; and Vol. XXIX., Parts 1, 2, and 3. Also the return to the Society of ANY NUMBERS of the JOURNAL which may be of no further use or interest to Fellows would be appreciated, as applications for back numbers are repeatedly received.

5. SUBSCRIPTIONS.

All Subscriptions fall due on January 1 of each year. To avoid the inconvenience of remembering this, Fellows can *compound* by the payment of one lump sum in lieu of all further annual payments ; or they can, by applying to the Society, obtain a form of instruction to their bankers to pay for them every January 1. It may be a week or more before the Tickets reach the Fellow, owing to the very large numbers, nearly 20,000, having to be despatched within the first month of the year. Fellows who have not already given an order on their bankers for the payment of their subscriptions each year are requested to do so, as this method of payment is preferred, and saves the Fellows considerable trouble. Forms for the purpose may be obtained from the R.H.S. Offices at Vincent Square, Westminster, S.W. Fellows whose subscriptions remain unpaid are debarred from all the privileges of the Society ; but their subscriptions are nevertheless recoverable at law, the Society being incorporated by Royal Charter.

In paying their subscriptions, Fellows often make the mistake of drawing their cheques for Pounds instead of for Guineas. Kindly note that in all cases it is Guineas and not Pounds. Cheques and Postal Orders should be made payable to "The Royal Horticultural Society" and crossed "London and County Bank, Westminster."

6. FORM OF BEQUEST.

I give and bequeath to the Treasurer for the time being of the Royal Horticultural Society, London, the sum of £   , to be paid out of such part of my personal estate as I can lawfully charge with the payment of such legacy, and to be paid free of legacy duty, within six months of my decease ; the receipt of such Treasurer to be a sufficient discharge for the same. And I declare that the said legacy shall be applied towards [the general purposes of the Society].*

7. PRIVILEGES OF CHEMICAL ANALYSIS.

Instructions are contained in the "Book of Arrangements," 1908.

8. LIST OF FELLOWS.

A list of all the Fellows of the Society is sent out in January. Fellows are requested to look at their own names in it, and if in any way these are incorrect, or the addresses insufficient, they are requested to inform the Secretary at once. Another use which all Fellows might make of this list is to consult it with reference to their friends' names, and if any of them are not found recorded therein they might endeavour to enlist their sympathies with the Society, and obtain their consent to propose them as Fellows forthwith. Forms of Nomination, and of the Privileges of Fellows, are bound in with every number of the JOURNAL and the "Book of Arrangements."

9. NEW FELLOWS.

On March 6 next the Society completes its 104th year, and before that day arrives, will all the Fellows do their best to extend the usefulness of the Society by enlisting the sympathy of all their friends and persuading them to join the ranks of the Society? A list of the privileges of Fellows will be found at page 14 in the "Book of Arrangements," and just a line addressed to the Secretary R.H.S., Vincent Square, Westminster, containing the name and address of the proposed new Fellow will suffice. Should it be preferred, the Secretary will, upon receipt of a postcard or letter giving the name and address of any persons likely to join the Society, write direct and invite them to allow their names to be proposed for election.

10. AN APPEAL.

What has been accomplished for the Society since 1887 is largely due to the unwearied assistance afforded by a small proportion of the Fellows ; but as all belong to the same Society, so it behoves each one to do what he or she can to further its interests, especially in :—

* Any special directions or conditions which the testator may wish to be attached to the bequest may be substituted for the words in brackets.

G G

1. Increasing the number of Fellows.

2. Contributing towards the Masters' Memorial Fund for establishing Foundation Lectures on the Application of Science to Horticulture.

3. Helping to swell the Fund started by Mr. A. W. Sutton, V.M.H., for providing Prizes for the Students at Wisley.

4. Books are required to fill the gaps in the Library both at Vincent Square and at Wisley.

5. New and rare Plants are wanted for the Garden and surplus roots for distribution to the Fellows.

Thus there is plenty for all to do according to their individual liking : personal effort, money, plants, books, are all alike needed. The Secretary, therefore, asks those who read these lines to do their best to help in any of the methods above indicated.

11. THE SOCIETY'S GARDENS AT WISLEY.

The Gardens are open daily to Fellows and others showing Fellows' Transferable Tickets from 9 A.M. till sunset, except on Sundays, Good

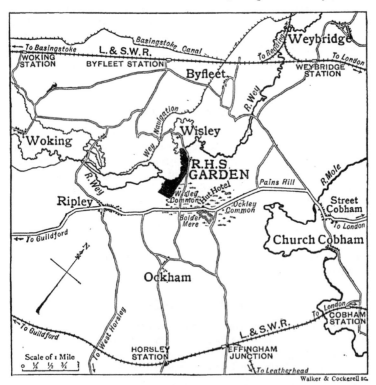

POSITION OF THE SOCIETY'S GARDENS.

Friday, and Christmas Day. Each Fellow's ticket admits three to the Gardens. The Public are not admitted. There is much of interest to be seen at Wisley throughout the year. The late Mr. G. F. Wilson's garden included a wild wood-garden, a bank of flowering shrubs, a series of ponds and pools, and a fine collection of Japanese Iris, Primulas, Lilies, Rhododendrons, &c. The Society has added a fine collection of the best varieties of fruit trees, of bamboos, of roses, and of ornamental trees and flowering shrubs, for the most part kindly given by the leading nurserymen. A very large sum of money has also been spent in the erection of a first-rate Meteorological Station, and a fine series of glass-houses ; a dwelling-house for the Superintendent ; a Cottage for the Fruit Foreman ; and in establishing a complete system of water supply ; on drainage works, and on road-making.

The Gardens are situated at Wisley, about 2 miles from Ripley in Surrey, and about $3\frac{1}{2}$ miles from Horsley and $5\frac{1}{2}$ miles from Weybridge, both stations on the South-Western Railway, with frequent trains from Waterloo and Clapham Junction. Carriages to convey four persons can be obtained by writing to Mr. D. White, fly proprietor, Ripley, Surrey ; the charge being, to and from Weybridge,. waiting two hours at the Gardens, 8s. ; or waiting three hours, 10s. ; or to and from Horsley, 7s. ; Effingham Junction, 7s. ; Byfleet, 7s. Visitors should in all cases be careful to state the trains they intend to arrive by and leave by. Carriages can also be obtained at Weybridge for 8s. by writing to Mr. Trembling, New Road, Weybridge. Excellent accommodation and re-freshments can be had at the Hut Hotel, close to the Gardens, and also at the Hautboy at Ockham.

12. THE· WISLEY RESEARCH STATION.

The new Research Station and Laboratory at Wisley is now com-pleted and work is in progress there. Mr. F. J. Chittenden ·has been appointed Director of the Research Work on Scientific Matters affecting Practical Horticulture, and Lecturer to the Students. By the completion of this station a long-felt want has been met. In the United States, where so much good work has been done in this direction, all is paid for by the Government, but in this country we have to fall back on private individuals or on Societies.

13. STUDENTS AT WISLEY.

The Society admits a limited number of young men, not exceeding 22 years of age, to study Gardening at Wisley, where the training has been recently further developed by the erection of the Laboratory and Research Station. The curriculum now includes not only practical garden work in all the main branches of Horticulture, but also lectures, demonstrations, and elementary Horticultural Science in the Laboratory, whereby a practical knowledge of simple Garden Chemistry, Biology, &c. may be obtained. The Laboratory is equipped with the best apparatus procurable for Students. The training extends over a period of two years, with a progressive course for each year. Students can only enter at the end of September and at the end of March. Selected

Students have also the advantage of attending certain of the Society's Shows and Lectures in London. It is generally easy to find these young men employment on the completion of their training; in fact, the Council are quite unable to meet the demands for energetic, trustworthy young men; but they *must all* be workers.

14. DISTRIBUTION OF SURPLUS PLANTS.

In a recent Report the Council drew attention to the way in which the annual distribution of surplus plants has arisen. In a large garden there must always be a great deal of surplus stock which must either be given away or go to the waste heap. A few Fellows, noticing this, asked for plants which would otherwise be discarded; and they valued what was so obtained. Others hearing of it asked for a share, until the Council felt they must either systematise this haphazard distribution or else put a stop to it altogether. To take the latter step seemed undesirable. Why should not such Fellows have them as cared to receive such surplus plants? It was therefore decided to keep all plants till the early spring, and then give all Fellows alike the option of claiming a share of them by ballot.

Fellows are therefore particularly requested to notice that only waste and surplus plants raised from seeds or cuttings are available for distribution. Many of them may be of very little intrinsic value, and it is only to avoid their being absolutely wasted that the distribution was established. The great majority also are of necessity *very small*, and may require careful treatment for a time.

Fellows are particularly requested to note that a Form of Application and list to choose from of the plants available for distribution is sent in January *every year* to every Fellow, enclosed in the "Report of the Council." To avoid all possibility of favour, all application lists are kept until the last day of February, when they are all thrown into a Ballot; and as the lists are drawn out, so is the order of their execution, the plants being despatched as quickly as possible after March 1.

Of some of the varieties enumerated the stock is small, perhaps not more than twenty-five or fifty plants being available. It is therefore obvious that when the Ballot is kind to any Fellow he will receive all the plants exactly as he has selected, but when the Ballot has given him an unfavourable place he may find the stock of the majority of plants he has chosen exhausted. A little consideration would show that all Fellows cannot be first, and some must be last, in the Ballot. Application forms received after March 1 and before April 30 are kept till all those previously received have been dealt with, and are then balloted in a similar way. Fellows having omitted to fill up their application form before April 30 must be content to wait till the next year's distribution. The work of the Gardens cannot be disorganised by the sending-out of plants at any later time in the year. All Fellows can participate in the annual distribution *following* their election.

The Society does not pay the cost of packing and carriage. The charge for this will be collected by the carriers on delivery of the plants, which will be addressed exactly as given by each Fellow on his application form. It has been found impracticable to despatch plants by post owing to the lack of Post Office facilities at Wisley and Ripley.

Fellows residing beyond a radius of thirty-five miles from London are permitted to choose double the number of plants to which they are otherwise entitled.

Plants cannot be sent to Fellows residing outside the United Kingdom, owing either to length of time in transit or to vexatious regulations in some foreign countries; but the Council will at any time endeavour to obtain for Fellows living abroad any unusual or rare seeds which they may have been unable to procure in their own country.

15. POPPY SEED.

The Secretary will be pleased to send a packet of his 1907 crop of Shirley Poppy Seed to any Fellows who like to send to Rev. W. WILKS, Shirley Vicarage, Croydon, a stamped envelope ready addressed to themselves. The seed should be sown as early as possible in March. This is an offer made by the Secretary in his private capacity, and it causes much inconvenience when requests for seed are mixed up with letters sent to the office in London instead of as above directed.

16. THE SOCIETY'S HALL AND OFFICES.

The Royal Horticultural Hall and Offices are situated in Vincent Square, which lies straight through Ashley Gardens from Victoria Street, Westminster, and is about five minutes' walk from the Victoria and St. James's Park Stations.

17. LETTING OF HALL.

Fellows are earnestly requested to make known among their friends and among other institutions that the ROYAL HORTICULTURAL HALL is available, twelve days in each fortnight, for Meetings, Shows, Exhibitions, Concerts, Conferences, Lectures, Balls, Banquets, Bazaars, Receptions, and other similar purposes. The Hall has a floor surface of 13,000 square feet. It is cool in summer and warm in winter. For a Concert it will seat 1,500, or for a public meeting 1,800. It is undoubtedly the lightest Hall in London, and its acoustic properties are pronounced excellent by some of our greatest authorities. The charges, which are very moderate, include lighting, warming in winter or cooling the air in summer, seating, and the use of trestle-tabling and platform. The first floor, consisting of four fine rooms, may also be hired for similar purposes, either together with or separately from the Great Hall. This accommodation can also be divided up if desired. Ample cloakrooms for ladies and for gentlemen are available. In fact, the Hall is not only the most suitable Hall in London for special Shows of a high-class character, but it is also second only to the Queen's Hall and the Royal Albert Hall for the purposes of Concerts and Meetings. Reduction is made to Charities, and there are special terms for Societies kindred or allied to Horticulture. The regulations &c. for hiring the Hall are printed in the "Book of

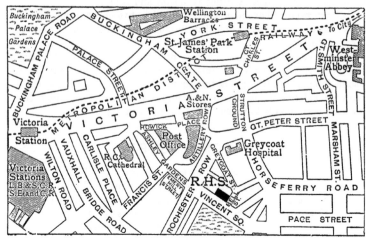

POSITION OF THE SOCIETY'S HALL.

Arrangements," and full particulars may be obtained on application to the Secretary R.H.S., Vincent Square, Westminster, S.W., with whom dates may be booked.

18. EXHIBITIONS, MEETINGS, AND LECTURES IN 1908.

A full programme for 1908 will be found in the "Book of Arrangements," 1908. It will be noticed that an Exhibition and Meeting is held in the Royal Horticultural Hall practically every fortnight throughout the year, and a short lecture on some interesting subject connected with Horticulture is delivered during the afternoon. Special Shows have also been arranged on days other than those of the Society's own Exhibitions. See No. 23.

A reminder of every Show will be sent in the week preceding to any Fellow who will send to the R.H.S. Offices, Vincent Square, S.W., a sufficient number (33) of halfpenny cards *ready addressed* to himself.

19. THE TEMPLE SHOW, 1908.

The twentieth great annual Flower Show in the Inner Temple Gardens, Thames Embankment, will be held, by the kind permission of the Treasurer and Benchers of the Inner Temple, on Tuesday, Wednesday, and Thursday, May 26, 27, and 28. Fellows are requested to note that there will be a **Private View** of the Show on Wednesday, May 27, from 7 A.M. till noon, at which only transferable and non-transferable Fellows'

Annual Tickets will admit. Day-tickets will not be purchasable or passed during these particular hours of Private View. See "Book of Arrangements," 1908.

20. HOLLAND HOUSE SHOW, 1908.

By the kind permission of Mary, the Countess of Ilchester, the Summer Show will be held at Holland House on July 7 and 8, particulars of which will be found in the "Book of Arrangements," 1908. The rules for the Temple Show apply as far as possible to Holland House, but there is sufficient space to allow of an extra Tent for Horticultural Sundries.

21. BRITISH-GROWN FRUIT SHOW, 1908.

The Great Autumn Show of British-grown Hardy Fruits, which the Society has held for so many years past, has become as much a thing to be regularly looked for by fruit-growers as the Show at the Temple in May is looked for by growers of flowers.

The fifteenth of these Shows will be held on October 15 and 16, 1908, in the Society's Hall.

22. COLONIAL-GROWN FRUIT SHOWS, 1908.

The President and Council of the Royal Horticultural Society have again arranged to hold Exhibitions of Colonial-grown Fruits and Vegetables on March 5 and 6, June 11 and 12, November 26 and 27.

In fixing such dates the object aimed at is to suit the seasons which are most likely to find the produce of the Cape and India, of Australia, Tasmania, and New Zealand, and of Canada, British Columbia, and the West Indies, in the greatest perfection in London. Opportunity is afforded for each Colony to make Collective Exhibits in addition to the exhibits of individual growers or firms. These Exhibitions were originally organised in 1904, and have been the means of bringing before the British Fruit Merchants and fruit-consuming public the wonderful resources of the Fruit Markets of Great Britain quite independently of the foreigner. The Society's sole object is the advancement of the interest of the Colonies (a) by stimulating the production of better fruits ; (b) by giving advice and assistance in the difficulties ever confronting Fruit Growers ; and (c) by helping to inform the home market. The results have been encouraging ; for even in so short a time as the last three years a distinctly better quality of fruit has been sent, those recently shown being of an improved appearance, less blotched by fungus, scale and other defects, and better packed. At the same time the Council are disappointed at the backwardness of Exhibitors and the smallness of their exhibits. Fruit Growers in the Colonies are therefore asked to assist their own future competition in the market by sending exhibits to these Exhibitions, invitations to which will be given to the Colonial and Government Offices, the Embassies, the leading London Fruit Merchants, Colonials on furlough, and many others.

The Agents-General and other authorities are most kindly rendering every assistance, and we trust that both growers and shippers will do their best to send in Exhibits worthy of our Colonies, and to show what can be produced for the Home markets. No entrance fee or charge for space is made, and Tabling is also provided free of expense.

If desired any produce may be consigned direct to the Society and it will be stored in the cellars at Vincent Square and staged by the Society's officials ; but the Society cannot undertake to repack and return any exhibits.

Particulars of the Shows can be obtained from the Secretary R.H.S., Vincent Square, Westminster, S.W., by enclosing one penny stamp in order to cover the cost of postage.

23. SHOWS OF KINDRED SOCIETIES IN 1908.

The following dates have been fixed on which R.H.S. Fellows' tickets will admit :—

April 1.—Winter Flowering Carnation Society.

April 28.—Auricula and Primula Society.

July 22.—Carnation and Picotee Society.

July 24.—Sweet Pea Society.

September 3.—Dahlia Society.

September 17.—Rose Society.

Copies of the Schedules for these Shows may be obtained from the Honorary Secretary of each Society.

24. SPECIAL PRIZES, 1908.

(1) For Hyacinths.

The Royal Dutch Bulb-growers' Society at Haarlem have offered to present—and the Royal Horticultural Society has accepted—the undermentioned prizes for forced Hyacinths, to be competed for at the R.H.S. Show, at Vincent Square, on Tuesday, March 31, 1908. Each bulb must be in a separate pot (size optional), and all must have been forced entirely in Great Britain or Ireland. No exhibit may contain more than two specimens of any one variety, and no exhibitor may exhibit in more than one class.

Division I.

For Amateurs and Gentlemen's Gardeners.

Class 3.	18 Hyacinths.	First prize £8 8s.	Second £4 4s.
„ 4.	12 „	„	£6 6s.	„	£3 3s.
„ 5.	6 „	„	£4 4s.	„	£2 2s.

Division II.

For Nurserymen.

Class 6.	24 Hyacinths.	First prize £8 8s.	Second £4 4s.
„ 7.	18 „	„	£6 6s.	„	£3 3s.
„ 8.	12 „	„	£4 4s.	„	£2 2s.

(2) THE BARR CUP FOR DAFFODILS.

Messrs. Barr & Sons have again presented to the Society a £7 7s. Silver Cup to be awarded on April 28, 1908, for a group of Daffodils See "Book of Arrangements," 1908.

(3) THE VEITCHIAN CUP.

The Veitchian Cup was offered to the President and Council of the Royal Horticultural Society in the year 1903, in commemoration of the fiftieth anniversary of the establishment of the Chelsea house by Mr. James Veitch, the Nurseryman. The Cup is of silver-gilt of the Georgian period, with traces of the Greek.

The object of the gift is to recognise in an exceptional degree exhibits of the highest order, the greatest advance in Horticulture—either a single plant, a group, or series of groups being equally eligible—in the opinion of seven specially chosen and eminent judges at the Temple Show. In 1903 it will be given to an amateur.

The judge's decision is final, and the Cup may be withheld at their discretion.

The judges will not award this high distinction unless satisfied and assured that the exhibit is, in the main, due to the work and capability of the exhibitor or his legitimate employés; on this point the judges may consult any expert not eligible to win the Cup.

The judges need not give a decision till the third day of the Show.

(4) THE SHERWOOD CUP.

The £10 10s. Silver Cup which N. N. Sherwood, Esq., V.M.H., has for the past ten years given to the Society will be awarded at the Holland House Show on July 7, 1908, for twenty-four bunches of Roses with their own foliage shown in vases by amateurs. A background of other foliage will be allowed.

25. LECTURES.

The new Lecture Room is fitted with an electric lantern of the most modern construction; electric current, gas, and water are laid on, and every provision has been made for the due illustration and delivery of Lectures.

Any Fellows willing to Lecture, or to communicate Papers on interesting subjects, are requested to communicate with the Secretary.

26. EXAMINATIONS, 1908.

1. The Society held an examination on Monday, January 13, 1908, specially intended for gardeners employed in Public Parks and Gardens belonging to County Councils, City Corporations, and similar bodies. This examination was conducted in the Royal Horticultural Society's Hall, Vincent Square, Westminster, S.W. The entries closed on January 1, 1908.

2. The Society's Annual Examination in the Principles and Practice of Horticulture will be held on Wednesday, April 8, 1908. Candidates should send in their names not later than March 18. Full particulars may be obtained by sending a stamped and directed envelope to the Society's offices. Copies of the Questions set from 1893 to 1907 (price 2s. post free) may also be obtained from the Office. The Society is willing to hold an examination wherever a magistrate, clergyman, schoolmaster, or other responsible person accustomed to examinations will consent to supervise one on the Society's behalf.

In connection with this examination a Scholarship of £25 a year for two years is offered by the Society to be awarded after the 1908 examination to the student who shall pass highest, if he is willing to accept the conditions attaching thereto. The main outline of these conditions is that the holder must be of the male sex, and between the ages of 18 and 22 years, and that he should study gardening for one year at least at the Royal Horticultural Society's Gardens at Wisley, conforming to the general rules laid down there for Students. In the second year of the Scholarship he may, if he like, continue his studies at some other place at home or abroad which is approved by the Council of the Royal Horticultural Society. In case of two or more eligible Students being adjudged equal, the Council reserve to themselves the right to decide which of them shall be presented to the Scholarship.

3. The Society will hold an Examination in Cottage Gardening on Wednesday, April 29, 1908. This examination is intended for, and is confined to, Elementary and Technical School Teachers. It is undertaken in view of the increasing demand in country districts that the Schoolmaster shall be competent to teach the elements of Cottage Gardening, and the absence of any test whatever of such competence. The general conduct of this examination will be on similar lines to that of the more general examination. Questions on Elementary Chemistry and Biology will in future be added to this examination. This year they will be optional, but in subsequent years they will form an integral part of the examination.

4. In 1908, on March 25, a fourth examination is to be commenced for Juniors under 19 years of age in elementary horticulture.

Medals and Certificates are awarded and Class Lists published in connection with these examinations, and the Syllabus may be obtained on application to the Secretary R.H.S., Vincent Square.

27. INFORMATION.

Fellows may obtain information and advice free of charge from the Society as to the names of flowers and fruit, on points of practice, insect and fungoid attacks, and other questions by applying to the Secretary R.H.S., Vincent Square, Westminster, S.W. Where at all practicable, it is particularly requested that letters and specimens may be timed to reach Vincent Square by the first post on the mornings of the Fortnightly Meetings, so as to be laid before the Scientific or other Committees at once.

28. INSPECTION OF FELLOWS' GARDENS.

The Inspection of Gardens belonging to Fellows is conducted by a thoroughly competent Inspector from the Society, who reports and advises at the following cost, viz. a fee of £3. 3s. for one day (or £5. 5s. for two consecutive days), together with all out-of-pocket expenses. No inspection may occupy more than two days, save by special arrangement. Fellows wishing for the services of an Inspector are requested to give at least a week's notice and choice of two or three days, and to indicate the most convenient railway station and its distance from their Gardens. Gardens can only be inspected at the *written* request of the *owner*.

29. AFFILIATION OF LOCAL SOCIETIES.

One of the most successful of the many new branches of work undertaken since the reconstruction of the Society in 1887 is the unification of all local Horticultural, Floral, and Gardening Societies by a scheme of affiliation to the R.H.S. Since this was initiated, no less than 200 Societies have joined our ranks, and that number is steadily increasing.

To the privileges of Affiliated Societies have recently been added all the benefits accruing under the scheme recently introduced for the Union of Horticultural Mutual Improvement Societies.

Secretaries of Affiliated Societies can obtain on application a specimen copy of a Card which the Council have prepared for the use of Affiliated Societies wishing to have a suitable Card for Certificates, Commendations, &c. It can be used for Fruit or Flowers or Vegetables. Price 3s. 6d. for 10 copies, 5s. 6d. for 20, 11s. 6d. for 50, 20s. for 100.

The Council have also struck a special Medal for the use of Affiliated Societies. It is issued at cost price in Bronze, Silver, and Silver-gilt— viz. Bronze, 5s. 6d., with case complete ; Silver, 12s. 6d., with case complete ; Silver-gilt, 16s. 6d., with case complete. Award Cards having the Medal embossed in relief can be sent with the Medal if ordered—price 6d. each.

30. UNION OF HORTICULTURAL MUTUAL IMPROVEMENT SOCIETIES.

This Union has recently been established for the encouragement and assistance of Horticultural Mutual Improvement Societies, the object being to strengthen existing Mutual Improvement Societies, to promote interchange of lecturers, to provide printed lectures, and if possible to increase the number of these useful Societies, and thus generally to advance the aims and objects of horticulture.

The Secretary of the Society will be very glad to hear from any competent lecturers who are willing to lecture to such Societies that he may enrol them in the Register of Lecturers and bring them into touch with Societies requiring assistance. Others may like to send to him written lectures (with or without lantern slides), that he may have them printed for circulation among these Societies.

Lantern slides on horticultural topics are urgently needed, and their gift will be very much appreciated.

31. MONOGRAPH ON FUNGOID PESTS.

The attention of Fellows is directed to a handsome volume just published by the Society on Fungoid Pests of Cultivated Plants, by Dr. M. C. Cooke, V.M.H. It consists of 280 pages of letterpress, and is illustrated with 24 coloured plates, containing figures of 360 different fungoid attacks, and 23 woodcuts. The work is divided under the headings of Pests of the Flower Garden, of Vegetables, of Fruit, of the Vinery and Stove, of the Ornamental Shrubbery, of Forest trees, and of Field Crops. These are followed by a Chapter on Fungicides, which explains very clearly how to make the different washes and sprays, and also gives the proportions in which the various ingredients should be used.

Each pest is described separately, and means for its prevention or eradication are given, and the whole work is written so as to interest and instruct the cultivator in the simplest and most practical manner. The volume, as published, is half-bound in calf, as it was considered probable that it would form the text-book on the subject for very many years to come; and it thus makes an admirable school prize or gift to a gardener or student of nature. Price 10s. 6d., R.H.S. Office, Vincent Square.

"No one whose plants are subject to fungoid attacks—and whose are not?—should be without this book; for not only can they by its use identify the disease at once, but they are also told both how to treat it and overcome it, and also how to make the different washes and sprays which the different classes of fungoid attacks require."

32. RULES FOR JUDGING.

The "Rules for Judging, with Suggestions to Schedule Makers and Exhibitors" have been revised and considerably modified from the experience gained during the last few years. The Secretaries of Local Societies are therefore strongly advised to obtain a fresh copy. It will be sent post free on receipt of a postal order for 1s. 6d. addressed to the Secretary, Royal Horticultural Society, Vincent Square, Westminster, S.W.

33. VARIETIES OF FRUITS.

Many people plant Fruit trees without a thought of what Variety they shall plant, and as a result almost certain disappointment ensues, whilst for an expenditure of 2d. they can obtain from the Society a little 16-page pamphlet which contains the latest expert opinion on Apples,

Pears, Plums, Cherries, Raspberries, Currants, Gooseberries, and Straw-berries, together with Notes on Planting, Pruning, and Manuring, which for clearness of expression and direction it would be impossible to surpass. It has in fact been suggested that no other 16 pages in the English language contain so much and such definite information. At the end of the pamphlet are given the names of some of the quite new varieties of Fruits, which promise well, but are not yet sufficiently long proved to be recommended for general planting.

Copies of this most valuable little pamphlet for distribution may be obtained at the Society's Office, Vincent Square, Westminster. Price, post free: single copy, 2*d*., or 25, 2*s*.; 50, 3*s*.; 100, 4*s*.

34. ADVERTISEMENTS.

Fellows are reminded that the more they can place their orders with those who advertise in the Society's Publications the more likely others are to advertise also, and in this way the Society may be indirectly benefited.

35. MASTERS MEMORIAL FUND.

The Council are very anxious that the memory of the late Dr. Masters, F.R.S., should be fittingly perpetuated in connection with the Society. It is hardly necessary to indicate the invaluable work Dr. Masters did for Horticulture by drawing constant attention to the various ways in which Scientific Discovery and Research might be made useful to Gardening. A letter appeared in the *Times* after his death, from which the following passages are quoted:—

> "Dr. Masters was a man with a combined capacity, willingness, and aptitude for instructing gardeners in the bearing and applica-tion of Science to gardening . . . . He could present a natural law or a scientific discovery, and their bearing on the Art of Horti-culture, in such simple every-day language as to be easily understood. . . . He combined the capacity to instruct with the willingness to impart, and, best of all, with the aptitude of *how* to instruct; and he never minded condescending to explain in the most simple words. . . . A fitting Memorial is suggested by this. Just as there are Foundation Lectures in Law, in Medicine, and in Theology, so let us establish 'The Masters Memorial Lectures' on the ap-plication of Science to Horticulture. Let us raise a fund sufficient to provide an adequate fee acceptable to the most renowned scientists among us, to deliver a series of three or five Lectures annually, the Lectures to be delivered in the first instance before the Royal Horticultural Society, and to be afterwards printed and circulated amongst all the Gardeners' Mutual Improvement and similar societies throughout the land. In this way we should not only perpetuate the memory of our friend, but also his work—a point which he himself, with his habitual modesty of demeanour, would have considered of far greater importance."

To carry out the suggestion here made a sum of about £1,000 would be required, help in raising which would be greatly appreciated. £320 has been received. It is earnestly hoped that further donations will be forthcoming in order that the " Lectures " may be " Founded " at once.

Subscriptions have been received from the following Fellows, to whom the Council tender their hearty thanks :—

Avebury, The Rt. Hon. Lord ; Adam, F. J.; Alderson, Mrs. ; Allen, A. C.; Armstrong & Brown ; Arnott, S.; Apthorpe, W. H.; Ashton, B.

Bateson, W.; Bowles, E. A.; Baker, J. G.; Butler, W. W.; Barr, Peter; Bennett, Mrs. F. W.; Bain, W.; Barrymore, The Rt. Hon. Lord ; Blackburn, H. R.; Browne, Mrs.; Balfour, I. Bayley; Bishop, Mrs. E. W.; Berry, Mrs. S.; Beckett, E.; Ballantine, H.; Beatson, Miss ; Bonavia, Dr.; Brooman-White, R.; Barr & Sons ; Barnes, N. F.; Boulger, Prof. G. S.

Crawshay, de Barri; Cama, D. P.; Cookson, N. C.; Church, Prof. A. H.; Crompton, T. E.; Clark, G. & A.; Clibran, J. H.; Cheal, J., & Sons; Churcher, J.; Caselton, G. L.; Chittenden, F. J.; Carter, J. & Co.; Cove, H. G.; Coomber, T.; Clarke, Harvey.

Douglas, Jas.; Davies, Mrs.; Davis, Norman; Druery, C. F.; Doncaster, S.; Davis, Miss M. J.; Dean, Alex.; Dickson & Robinson; Davison, G. D.; Dobbie & Co.; Darwin, F.

Elwes, H. J.; Earle, Mrs.; Edwards, W.; Ellacombe, Rev. Canon ; Earp, W.

Farmer, Prof. J. B.; Fremlin, R. H.

Gumbleton, W. E.; Goodyear, E.

Hanbury, C.; Henslow, Rev. G.; Hall, Mrs. E. S.; Hindmarsh, W. T.; Hillier, E. L.; Humphery, F. W.; Haldeman, D. C.; Hanbury, F. J.; Harrison, T. F.; Haslett, G.; Honess, W. H.; Hughes, H. E.

Ince, Surg.-Maj. J.

Jacob, Rev. J.; Jewell, C.; Johnson, Miss A.

Lawrence, Sir Trevor, Bart.; Llewelyn, Sir John Dillwyn-, Bart.; Larmor, J., D.Sc.; Lindley, Miss ; Lindley, Lady ; Low, Hugh, & Co.; Lynch, R. Irwin ; Lindley, R. S.; Lovatt, Mrs.; Lange, G.

Mellish, Miss ; Macmillan, G. A.; McBean, J. & A. A.; Monro, G.; Musgrave, Jno.; McDonald, D.; Mackay, R. J.; Moore, F. W.; Marchant, Mrs. M.; Mitchell, W.; Malcolm, Col. E.; McDonald, F. W.; Mayne, J.; Mackellar, A.

Norman, Mrs. H.; Nicholson, G.; Nevitt-Bennett, Mrs.

Osmaston, Mrs.; O'Brien, Jas.

Pawle, F. C.; Preston, Mrs. R.; Pitman, Miss E.; Paul, Wm. & Son; Page, W. H.; Prain, Mrs.; Prime, H.; Pickering, Spencer ; Protheroe & Morris ; Parkin, J.; Packe, Miss G. F.; Pearson, R. Hooper ; Pulham & Sons.

Rothschild, Leopold de ; Rothschild, The Rt. Hon. Lord ; Rawes, Rev. F. Russell, Ramsay, Miss E. L.; Roberts, W. R.; Ransom, A.; Rogers, W. F.; Ross, Chas.; Rutherford, John ; Russell, Dr.

Schröder, Baron Sir Henry, Bart.; Sutton & Sons; Shea, C. E.; Somerville, Dr.; Sweet, Jas.; Smith, Martin R.; Sutherland, Dr. G. S.; Stephens, J. W.; Smith, T.; Sharman, Mrs. M.; Sydenham, R.; Simpson, T.; Sulivan, Miss ; Stirling, Sir J.; Salter, C. J.; Scott, Prof. D. H.; Shaw-Stewart, Lady Alice.

Topping, R.; Thomas, Owen ; Treseder, F. G. and R. W.; Tidy, W.; Turton, T.; Thomson, D. W.; Thomson, W. P.

Veitch, P. C. M.

Worsdell, W. C.; Walker, A. O.; Ware, W. T.; Wilson, Mrs.; Woodgate, Geo.; Wells, Miss M. J.; Williams, P. D.; Willmott, Miss Ellen ; White, E.; Woodward, Geo.; Willard, Jesse ; Woodall, E. H.; Weston, J. G.; Witty, J. H.

Young, Mrs. J. C.

MASTERS MEMORIAL FUND.

To the Rev. W. WILKS,
      Royal Horticultural Society,
          Vincent Square,
             Westminster, S.W.

...............................1908.

Sir,
      I shall be happy to subscribe............................... to the Masters
Memorial Fund, and herewith enclose you my cheque for that amount.

Faithfully yours,

Name ....

Address..

[This Form can be easily detached for use.

THE ROYAL HORTICULTURAL SOCIETY.

**Established
A.D. 1804.**

**Incorporated
A.D. 1809.**

VINCENT SQUARE, WESTMINSTER, S.W.

Telegrams: "HORTENSIA, LONDON." Telephone No.: 5363, Westminster.

Form of Recommendation for a FELLOW of the ROYAL HORTICULTURAL SOCIETY.

Name ....

Description ....

Address ....

....

being desirous of becoming a FELLOW of the ROYAL HORTICULTURAL SOCIETY, we whose Names are underwritten beg leave to recommend him (her) to that honour ; he (she) is desirous of subscribing * .... Guineas a year.

Proposed by ....

Seconded by ....

* Kindly enter here the word *four* or *two* or *one*.

would be a convenience if the Candidate's Card were sent at the same time.

Signed on behalf of the Council, this ....day of .... 190......

....   CHAIRMAN.

EXTRACTS FROM THE PROCEEDINGS

OF THE

ROYAL HORTICULTURAL SOCIETY.

HOLLAND HOUSE SHOW, 1907.

JULY 9 AND 10.

JUDGES.

ORCHIDS.

Bilney, W. A.
Chapman, H. J.
Fowler, J. Gurney
Little, H.

ROSES.

Goodwin, A. R.
Philbrick, Miss
Willmott, Miss, V.M.H.

FRUIT AND VEGETABLES.

Challis, T., V.M.H.
McIndoe, J., V.M.H.
Pearson, A. H.
Poupart, W.

GROUPS IN OPEN AIR.

Chapman, A.
Douglas, J., V.M.H.
Jennings, John

HARDY HERBACEOUS PLANTS.

Bennett-Poë, J. T., V.M.H.
Charrington, Mrs. A. C.
Divers, W. H.
Shea, Chas. E.
Thatcher, A. E.

ALPINE AND ROCK PLANTS.

Nicholson, G., V.M.H.
Pearson, C. E.
Ware, W. T.

FOLIAGE PLANTS.

Bain, W.
Fielder, C. R.
Ker, R. Wilson
McLeod, J.

FLOWERING PLANTS.

Bates, W.
Howe, W.
Reynolds, G.
Turner, Arthur

MISCELLANEOUS.

Dixon, C.
Notcutt, R. C.
Turner, T. W.

IMPLEMENTS AND SUNDRIES.

Beckett, E., V.M.H.
Gibson, Jas.
Mortimer, S.

3 D

AWARDS GIVEN BY THE COUNCIL AFTER CONSULTATION WITH THE JUDGES.

The order in which the names are entered under the several medals and cups has no reference whatever to merit, but is purely accidental.

. Other awards given on the recommendation of the Fruit, Floral, and Orchid Committees will be found under their respective reports.

Gold Medal.

Sir Jeremiah Colman, Bart., Gatton Park, Reigate (gr. Mr. W. P. Bound), for Orchids.

Messrs. W. Cutbush, Highgate, N., for flowering plants, Carnations, Roses, herbaceous and bulbous plants, clipped trees, &c.

Messrs. Alexander Dickson, Newtownards, Co. Down, for Roses.

Messrs. H. B. May, Upper Edmonton, for Exotic Ferns, hardy Ferns, and flowering plants.

Messrs. Paul, Cheshunt, Herts, for Roses, Paeonies, and herbaceous plants.

Mr. Amos Perry, Enfield, for Aquatics, Delphiniums, florist's flowers, and herbaceous plants.

Messrs. F. Sander, St. Albans, for Orchids.

Messrs. T. S. Ware, Feltham, for Begonias, herbaceous plants, and cut flowers.

Messrs. R. Wallace, Colchester, for hardy herbaceous and bulbous plants.

Messrs. J. Veitch, Chelsea, S.W., for Carnations, stove and green-house plants, new hardy plants, and Figs in pots.

Sherwood Cup.

J. Bradshaw, Esq., The Grange, Southgate (gr. Mr. G. G. Whitelegg), for a collection of herbaceous and bulbous plants grown in pots.

Silver Cup.

S. Heilbut, Esq., Holyport, Maidenhead (gr. Mr. G. Camp), for fruit trees in pots.

R. I. Measures, Esq., Cambridge Lodge, Camberwell, S.E. (gr. Mr. J. Smith), for Orchids and pitcher plants.

Messrs. W. Artindale, Sheffield, for herbaceous and bulbous plants grown in pots, Violas, &c.

Messrs. Barr, Covent Garden, for herbaceous flowers, alpines, and Japanese pigmy trees.

Messrs. Blackmore & Langdon, Twerton-on-Avon, for Begonias and Delphiniums.

Mr. C. W. Breadmore, Winchester, for Sweet Peas.

Messrs. G. Bunyard, Maidstone, for fruit trees in pots and herbaceous plants.

Messrs. Frank Cant, Colchester, for Roses.

Messrs. H. Cannell, Swanley, for Cannas.

Messrs. Charlesworth, Heaton, Bradford, for Orchids.

Messrs. T. Cripps, Tunbridge Wells, for Japanese Maples.

Messrs. R. & G. Cuthbert, Southgate, N., for flowering and foliage plants.

Messrs. Dobbie, Rothesay, N.B., for Pansies, Violas, and Sweet Peas.

Messrs. Hobbies, Dereham, for Roses, &c.

Messrs. J. Laing, Forest Hill, S.E., for Begonias, Caladiums, and Gloxinias.

Messrs. H. Low, Enfield, for Orchids, fruit trees in pots, Carnations, and new Ferns.

Mr. Frank Lilley, Guernsey, for Gladioli.

Mr. R. C. Notcutt, Woodbridge, for Roses and hardy flowers.

Mr. M. Prichard, Christchurch, Hants, for Aquatics and hardy herbaceous plants.

Mr. L. R. Russell, Richmond, S.W., for hardy ornamental trees and shrubs.

Mr. C. Turner, Slough, for Roses.

Silver-gilt Flora Medal.

J. Gurney Fowler, Esq., Glebelands, South Woodford (gr. Mr. J. Davis), for Selaginellas.

Messrs. R. H. Bath, Wisbech, for Carnations, herbaceous plants, Roses, and Sweet Peas.

Messrs. J. Carter, High Holborn, W.C., for Begonias, Gloxinias, Garden Peas, Sweet Peas, and Japanese trees.

Messrs. J. Cheal, Crawley, for hardy herbaceous plants, trees, and shrubs.

Messrs. G. & A. Clark, Dover, for flowering shrubs, Sweet Peas, alpine and rock plants.

Messrs. Fromow, Chiswick, W., for hardy plants, Japanese Maples, and Bamboos.

Messrs. G. Jackman, Woking, for Roses and hardy herbaceous flowers.

Messrs. E. W. King, Coggeshall, for Sweet Peas.

Messrs. Kelway, Langport, for Paeonies.

Messrs. B. Ladhams, Shirley, Southampton, for hardy flowers.

Messrs. W. Paul, Waltham Cross, N., for Roses.

Messrs. J. Peed, West Norwood, S.E., for Begonias, Caladiums, Carnations, Gloxinias, alpines, and herbaceous plants.

Mr. G. Reuthe, Keston, for hardy herbaceous plants and flowering shrubs.

Silver-gilt Knightian Medal.

Messrs. Laxton, Bedford, for Strawberries.

Silver-gilt Banksian Medal.

Sir Geo. Faudel-Phillips, Balls Park, Hertford (gr. Mr. Fitch), for Malmaison Carnations.

E. E. Grimson, Esq., York House, Sutton, for Roses and Sweet Peas.

Messrs. B. R. Cant, Colchester, for Roses.

Mr. A. F. Dutton, Iver, for Carnations.

Messrs. Sutton, Reading, for Gloxinias and Nemesias.

Mr. A. R. Upton, Millmead, Guildford, for hardy plants.

Silver Flora Medal.

Lieut.-Col. C. Heseltine, 196 Queen's Gate, S.W., for Roses.

Messrs. W. Bull, Chelsea, S.W., for foliage plants and cut flowers.

Messrs. Gunn, Olton, Birmingham, for new hardy Phlox.

Mr. A. Ll. Gwillim, Eltham, for Begonias.

Mr. J. Forbes, Hawick, N.B., for Phloxes, Pentstemons, and Pyrethrums.

Mr. W. Iceton, Putney, S.W., for Lilies of the Valley.

Mr. W. H. Page, Hampton-on-Thames, for Carnations.

Messrs. T. Rochford, Broxbourne, for *Nephrolepis todeaoides.*

Silver Knightian Medal.

Mr. A. J. Harwood, Colchester, for Asparagus.

Silver Banksian Medal.

H. T. Burroughes, Esq., Ketton Cottage, Stamford, for *Lilium colchicum.*

H. H. Crane, Esq., Archway Road, Highgate, for Violas and Pansies.

Mrs. Ernest Hills, Redleaf, Penshurst (gr. Mr. Ringham), for *Miltonia vexillaria.*

Messrs. S. Bide, Farnham, Surrey, for Roses.

Mr. W. R. Chaplin, Waltham Cross, for Roses.

Mr. W. J. Godfrey, Exmouth, for Ivy-leaved and other Pelargoniums, Oriental Poppies, and *Solanum Wendlandii.*

Mr. T. Jannoch, Dersingham, for Lilies of the Valley.

Misses Hopkins, Barming, Maidstone, for herbaceous plants and alpines.

Messrs. Merryweather, Southwell, Notts, for Roses.

Mr. H. C. Pulham, Elsenham, for alpine and rock plants.

Mr. Vincent Slade, Taunton, for Zonal and Ivy-leaved Pelargoniums.

Messrs. G. Stark, Great Ryburgh, for Sweet Peas and Tropaeolums.

Messrs. Stanley, Southgate, N., for Orchids.

HORTICULTURAL SUNDRIES.

Silver-gilt Flora Medal.

Mr. G. W. Riley, Herne Hill, S.E., for rustic summer-houses, seats, arches, &c.

Messrs. W. Wood, Wood Green, N., for horticultural sundries.

Silver-gilt Banksian Medal.

Messrs. Merryweather, Greenwich Road, S.E., for watering appliances, pumps, sprinklers, &c.

Messrs. Inmans, Stretford, Manchester, for rustic summer-houses, tables, garden seats, vases, &c.

Messrs. T. Green, New Surrey Works, Southwark Street, S.E., for motor and other lawn mowers, garden rollers, &c.

Messrs. Ransomes, Sims & Jefferies, Ipswich, for motor and pony lawn mowers, edge trimmers, &c.

Silver Flora Medal.

Messrs. Headly & Edwards, Corn Exchange Street, Cambridge, for garden seats, chairs, arches, weather vanes, tents, hose reels, &c.

Castle's, Baltic Wharf, Millbank, S.W., for Castle's Man-o'-War teak-wood garden furniture.

Messrs. H. Scott, Woodside, South Norwood, S.E., for rustic work and summer-houses.

Messrs. Liberty, Regent Street, W., for terra-cotta garden pottery, sundials, flower vases, &c.

Messrs. A. Shanks, Bush Lane House, Cannon Street, E.C., for lawn mowers.

Messrs. W. Duncan Tucker, South Tottenham, N., for conservatory garden seats, trellis-work, &c.

Messrs. Pulham, 71 Newman Street, W., for "Pulhamite Stone" vases and other garden objects.

Messrs. T. J. Syer, 45 Wilson Street, Finsbury, E.C., for garden tools, ladders, &c.

The Potters' Arts Guild, Compton, Guildford, for terra-cotta garden furniture.

Mr. James George, 14 Redgrave Road, Putney, for horticultural sundries.

Silver Banksian Medal.

Incorporated Soldiers' and Sailors' Help Society, 122 Brompton Road, S.W., for baskets.

Messrs. Champion, 115 City Road, E.C., for tubs for shrubs.

Messrs. D. Dowel, Hammersmith, W., for Orchid pottery and horti-cultural requisites.

Messrs. W. Herbert, 2 Hop Exchange, S.E., for garden sundries.

Messrs. J. Stiff, High Street, Lambeth, S.E., for terra-cotta vases and pedestals, and stoneware garden edgings.

Bronze Banksian Medal.

Messrs. Abbott, Southall, W., for garden tables, table trays, fruit-preserving bottles, and modern beehives and appliances.

Mr. G. H. Sage, 71 Manor Road, Richmond, S.W., for garden sundries, flower holders, and Wakeley's hop manure.

Messrs. W. Voss, Glengall Road, Millwall, for insecticides.

Messrs. Gillard, Walthamstow, for Menager's sauce, pickle, and chutney.

Messrs. W. Walters, 16 Water Lane, E.C., for artistic wood arches, trellis, seats, &c., and greenhouse blinds.

Mr. J. Williams, 4A Oxford Street, Ealing, for flower-holders for table decorations.

GENERAL MEETING.

JULY 23, 1907.

The Rev. W. WILKS, M.A., in the Chair.

Fellows elected (73).—Mrs. F. M. à Court, Mrs. R. Alford, E. Allday, J. H. Annear, Lady Beaumont, C. A. Bloomfield, Miss E. Bowles, H. H. Brown, Mrs. A. Cairn, S. R. Chesterton, H. E. Cooper, Mrs. R. Copland-

Sparkes, Mrs. Coulson, Mrs. F. Creagh-Osborne, Mrs. Cull, A. Davey, Mrs. Davidson, Mrs. G. H. Dawson, Mrs. H. Dewhurst, G. Duffus, Rev. S. Dugdale, Mrs. Dugdale, Miss K. Duncombe, Miss D. J. Ellis, J. Emberson, Miss H. C. Everett, Trevor Eyton, Mrs. Fabling, Mrs. M. Field, Miss M. Fisher, T. Fisher, G. A. FitzGerald, Lady Fox, S. A. Frech, Ewan C. Galton, J. Garton, Mrs. Grant Meek, F. W. Green, Miss Greet, Mrs. Ground, H. Grylls, W. G. Hanburg, Mrs. Hamar, Mrs. Hay, Mrs. Hogge, E. J. Jervis-Smith, W. H. Johns, L. F. Lee, Hon. Mrs. Malcolm, Mrs. C. Miller, T. C. Moberley, G. Morrell, Lady Mostyn, R. M. Neill, Lady Osborne, L. Pendred, Dr. Pratt, F. D. Samuel, Sir H. B. Samuelson, I. Shield, Mrs. S. Stephen, R. Teece, Miss Thornely, Mrs. Tully, Mrs. Upcher, Mrs. Vaughan, Mrs. Walters, Miss Waterston, W. H. Wells, J. S. White, W. S. Whitaker, E. Willett, W. White.

Fellows resident abroad (6).—W. Bradley (Australia), F. de Courcey (South Africa), F. Herzog (Germany), L. T. Homan (Holland), J. Nelson (Las Palmas), H. Prasad (India).

A lecture on "Rare Trees and Shrubs in the Open Air" was given by the Hon. Vicary Gibbs (see p. 847).

GENERAL MEETING.

August 6, 1907.

Mr. John T. Bennett-Poë, M.A., V.M.H., in the Chair.

Fellows elected (32).—I. N. Arbery, Ven. Archdeacon Bevan, H. B. Blackburn, D. S. Carson, R. Carter, Mrs. E. Chance, Mrs. Cloudsley, Dr. R. Crawfurd, F. Davies, Mrs. Dobbing, Mrs. M. Elgood, C. W. Groves, Lady M. Hamilton-Russell, H. Hooper, A. P. Keep, Mrs. R. Kennard, J. Klitgaard-May, H. J. Lange, Hon. Mrs. C. Lawrence, Dr. H. H. Mills, Hon. Mrs. Monckton, Mrs. F. Noel, A. J. Paine, Mrs. F. Ponsonby, H. R. Poole, R. Randell, S. Savill, Mrs. J. T. Smithes, W. G. Stevenson, Mrs. Tillotson, J. Todhunter, W. T. Wilkinson.

Fellow resident abroad (1).—Gerald L. Parker (British Columbia).

A lecture on "Water-lilies" was given by Mr. Arthur Bedford (see p. 864).

GENERAL MEETING.

August 20, 1907.

The Rev. W. Wilks, M.A., in the Chair.

Fellows elected (15).—Richard Q. Amer, C. R. E. Bell, W. F. Burford, Mrs. Kenneth M. Clark, Mrs. C. A. Edes, Mrs. Allen Fergusson, Lady Hopton, Lady Hornby, Mrs. E. W. Hussey, Mrs. Insole, J. Stanley James, Mrs. Walter Leaf, Miss Pearce-Serocold, R. S. Scholfield, Miss Waldron.

Fellow resident abroad (1).—A. R. Ragg (New Zealand).

A lecture on "Terrace-garden Plants," illustrated by lantern slides, was given by Mr. James Hudson, V.M.H. (see p. 869).

GENERAL MEETING.

SEPTEMBER 3, 1907.

Mr. HARRY J. VEITCH, F.L.S., V.M.H., in the Chair.

Fellows elected (8).—W. Astor, R. H. Barran, A. D. Carr, Lady Croft, Mrs. W. Dudgeon, Lieut.-Col. R. England, Miss R. R. Greaves, Alfred James.

A lecture on "Lesser Known Orchids," illustrated by lantern slides, was given by Mr. F. W. Moore, V.M.H. (see p. 378).

GENERAL MEETING.

SEPTEMBER 17, 1907.

The Rev. W. WILKS, M.A., in the Chair.

There were no candidates for election.

A paper on "Grasses," written by Mr. Walter Smyth, was read (see p. 107).

GENERAL MEETING.

OCTOBER 1, 1907.

Mr. G. S. SAUNDERS, F.L.S., in the Chair.

Fellows elected (62).—F. C. Annesley, Mrs. E. P. M. Appleton, Miss M. L. Barrie, Mrs. C. Bell, Mrs. F. Black, Campbell Boyd, Col. M. C. Brackenbury, Mrs. J. A. Bragge, G. Britton, E. H. Brown, Lady F. Bruce, Sir Charles Cave, H. D. Cory, Lady Collins, Hon. Mrs. S. H. Collins, John Collins, Mrs. S. Courtauld, Mrs. Hilgrove Coxe, Mrs. Weston Crocker, Mrs. Teanne de la Rive, Mrs. J. Drysdale, Mrs. Dunlop, Miss Ethel Elwes, W. Farquharson, A. G. Fenn, W. Fisher, R. E. Ford, J. J. French, J. Geddes, Rev. Canon W. Grane, Miss I. F. Green, D. W. Hampshire, A. H. Hannay, J. N. Harvey, Mrs. H. Hutton, Fred Jowett, C. G. Kirk, R. Laight, O. Lamont, B. H. Lane, Olga Lindemann, Mrs. F. McAdam, Mrs. C. L. Methuen, W. J. Middleton, H. E. Molyneux, K. P. V. Morgan, Mrs. Ogilvy, Miss G. T. Ridley, Rev. H. Robins, T. D. Savill, G. Siggs, A. Stenning, J. W. Stevens, T. H. Tailby, James Taylor, S. W. Thomas, Miss T. M. Wells, John B. White, E. H. Wilding, H. Willis, E. J. Woodhouse, E. A. Young.

Fellows resident abroad (3).—A. Bathgate, E. E. Berry, B. Nathan.

Associates (2).—R. Barton, Miss E. M. Birtill.

Societies affiliated (3).—Queenstown Horticultural Society, Transvaal Horticultural Society, Upminster and District Horticultural Society.

A lecture on "Electric Cultivation in relation to Horticulture," illustrated by lantern slides, was given by Mr. B. H. Thwaite (see p. 401).

GENERAL MEETING.

OCTOBER 15, 1907.

The Rev. W. C. HOWELL in the Chair.

Fellows elected (28).—Marquis of Ailsa, Mrs. Bell, Sir F. D. Blake, Bart., A. E. Burdon, J. A. Clutton-Brock, Miss Coates, James Gray, Lieut.-Col. H. P. Greenwood, Mrs. A. Heath, Rev. W. G. Johnston, M.A., Hon. J. A. Joicey, F. Longster, Mrs. C. E. Lugard, Mrs. Mainwaring, Mrs. W. Mappin, Sir C. S. Milburn, Bart., Hon. Mrs. R. Parker, Stephen Sanderson, Lady Sargood, Mrs. H. L. Savory, James Parker Simpson, Ernest Smith, Henry H. Smith, Edward Spurge, Miss E. Steel, H. A. Strickland, John Vicarage, Mrs. Violet York.

A lecture on ".The Origin and Present Distribution of the British Flora" was given by the Rev. Professor G. Henslow, M.A., V.M.H. (see p. 417).

FOURTEENTH ANNUAL EXHIBITION OF BRITISH-GROWN FRUIT.

HELD AT THE SOCIETY'S HALL, VINCENT SQUARE, S.W., OCTOBER 17 AND 18, 1907.

Mrs. McLaren, 56 Ashley Gardens, kindly sent £1. 1*s.* towards the Prize Fund for this Show.

The Council awarded an extra medal—Silver-gilt Hogg—to Messrs. James Veitch, of Chelsea, for an excellent exhibit of Apples and Pears which was withheld from competition.

THE JUDGES.

The following gentlemen kindly acted as Judges, and deserve the best thanks of the Society for their oftentimes very difficult work, viz.—

Allan, W., Gunton Park Gardens, Norwich.
Arnold, T., Cirencester Park Gardens, Gloucester.
Bacon, W. H., Mote Park Gardens, Maidstone.
Barnes, N. F., Eaton Gardens, Chester.
Barnes, W., Bearwood Gardens, Wokingham.
Basham, J., Bassaleg, Newport, Mon.
Bates, W., Cross Deep Gardens, Twickenham.
Beckett, E., V.M.H., Aldenham House Gardens, Elstree.
Blick, C., Warren House Gardens, Hayes, Kent.
Bowerman, J., Hackwood Park Gardens, Basingstoke.
Challis, T., V.M.H., Wilton House Gardens, Salisbury.
Cheal, J., Crawley, Sussex.
Coomber, T., The Hendre Gardens, Monmouth.
Cornford, J., Quex Park Gardens, Birchington.
Crump, W., V.M.H., Madresfield Court Gardens, Malvern.
Dean, Alex., V.M.H., 62 Richmond Road, Kingston.
Divers, W. H., Belvoir Castle Gardens, Grantham.

Doe, J., Rufford Gardens, Ollerton, Notts.
Douglas, J., V.M.H., Great Bookham, Surrey.
Earp, W., Bayham Abbey Gardens, Lamberhurst.
Fielder, C. R., North Mymms Park Gardens, near Hatfield.
Foster, C., University College, Reading.
Fyfe, W., Lockinge Park Gardens, Wantage.
Gibson, J., Welbeck Abbey Gardens, Worksop.
Goodacre, J. H., Elvaston Castle Gardens, Derby.
Jaques, J., Grey Friars, Chorley Wood, Herts.
Lyne, J., Foxbury Gardens, Chislehurst.
McIndoe, J., V.M.H., 8 Hythe Street, Dartford.
Markham, H., Wrotham Park Gardens, High Barnet.
Molyneux, E., V.M.H., Swanmore Gardens, Bishop's Waltham.
Mortimer, S., Rowledge, Farnham, Surrey.
Parr, H., Trent Park Gardens, New Barnet.
Paul, G., J.P., V.M.H., Cheshunt, Herts.
Pearson, A. H., The Hut, Lowdham, Nottingham.
Poupart, W., Marsh Farm, Twickenham.
Rivers, H. Somers, Sawbridgeworth.
Ross, C., Welford Park Gardens, Newbury.
Salter, C. J., Normanhurst Gardens, Rusper, Horsham.
Shoobridge, L. M., Tasmania.
Veitch, P. C. M., J.P., New North Road, Exeter.
Vert, J., Audley End Gardens, Saffron Walden.
Walker, J., The Farm, Ham Common, Surrey.
Ward, A., Godinton Gardens, Ashford.
Weston, J. G., Eastwell Park Gardens, Ashford.
Woodward, G., Barham Court Gardens, Teston.

THE REFEREES.

The following gentlemen very kindly held themselves at the disposal of the Society to act in conjunction with any of the Judges as Referees if required, viz.—

Bunyard, G., V.M.H., Royal Nurseries, Maidstone.
Hudson, James, V.M.H., Gunnersbury House Gardens, Acton, W.
Thomas, Owen, V.M.H., 25 Waldeck Road, West Ealing.

OFFICIAL PRIZE LIST.

The address and the Gardener's name are entered on the first occurrence, but afterwards only the Owner's name is recorded.)

Division I.

Fruits grown under Glass or otherwise.

Open to Gardeners and Amateurs only.

Note.—Exhibitors can compete in one Class only of Classes 1, 2 and of Classes 3, 4.

Class **1.**—Collection of 9 dishes of Ripe Dessert Fruit:—6 kinds at least ; only 1 Pine, 1 Melon, 1 Black and 1 White Grape allowed ; not more than two varieties of any other kind, and no two dishes of the same variety.

First Prize, Silver Cup and £5; Second, £5; Third, £3.
1. The Earl of Harrington, Derby (gr. J. H. Goodacre).
2. Hon. Mr. Justice Swinfen Eady, Weybridge (gr. J. Lock).
3. C. R. Adeane, Esq., Cambridge (gr. R. Alderman).

Class 2.—Collection of 6 dishes of Ripe Dessert Fruit :—4 kinds at least; only 1 Melon, 1 Black and 1 White Grape allowed; not more than two varieties of any other kind, and no two dishes of the same variety. Pines excluded.

First Prize, Silver Cup and £3; Second, £3; Third, £2.
1. The Earl of Londesborough, Market Weighton (gr. J. C. McPherson).
2. M. W. Price, Esq., Welwyn (gr. T. Pateman).
3. Sir Charles Hamilton, Bart., Sandy (gr. T. W. Birkenshaw).

Class 3.—Grapes, 6 distinct varieties, 2 bunches of each; both Black and White must be represented.

First Prize, Silver Cup and £3; Second, £3.
1. J. W. Fleming, Esq., Romsey (gr. W. Mitchell).
2. H. J. King, Esq., Eastwell Park (gr. J. G. Weston).

Class 4.—Grapes, 4 varieties, selected from the following : ' Madresfield Court,' ' Mrs. Pince,' ' Muscat Hamburgh,' ' Muscat of Alexandria ' or ' Canon Hall ' (not both), ' Mrs. Pearson,' and ' Dr. Hogg,' 2 bunches of each.

First Prize, Silver Cup and £3; Second, £3; Third, £2.
No award.

Class 5.—Grapes ' Black Hamburgh,' 2 bunches.
First Prize, £1. 10s.; Second, £1; Third, 10s·
1. J. W. Fleming, Esq.
2. The Earl of Harrington.
3. No award.

Class 6.—Grapes ' Mrs. Pince,' 2 bunches.
First Prize, £1. 10s.; Second, £1.
1. J. Edmonds, Esq., Arnold.
2. O. E. Avigdor-Goldsmid, Esq., Tonbridge (gr. C. Earl).

Class 7.—Grapes ' Alicante,' 2 bunches.
First Prize, £1. 10s.; Second, £1; Third, 10s.
1. W. G. Raphael, Esq., Englefield Green (gr. H. H. Brown).
2. Sir Walpole Greenwell, Bart., Marden Park (gr. W. Lintott).
3. Col. Hon. Chas. Harbord, Norwich (gr. W. Allan).

Class 8.—Grapes ' Madresfield Court,' 2 bunches.
First Prize, £1. 10s.; Second, £1; Third, 10s.
1. J. W. Fleming, Esq.
2. Lord Savile, Ollerton (gr. J. Doe).
3. F. R. Rodd, Esq., Launceston (gr. F. A. Billings).

Class **9.**—Grapes, any other Black Grape, 2 bunches.
First Prize, £1. 10s.; Second, £1; Third, 10s.
1. The Earl of Londesborough.
2. Col. Hon. Chas. Harbord.
3. Earl Stanhope, Sevenoaks (gr. J. C. Sutton).

Class **10.**—Grapes 'Muscat of Alexandria,' 2 bunches.
First Prize, £2; Second, £1. 5s.; Third, 15s.
1. J. W. Fleming, Esq.
2. W. G. Raphael, Esq.
3. Col. Hon. Chas. Harbord.

Class **11.**—Grapes, any other White Grape, 2 bunches.
First Prize, £1. 10s.; Second, £1; Third, 10s.
1. A. Benson, Esq., Merstham (gr. W. Mancy).
2. Lady Tate, Streatham Common (gr. W. Howe).
3. Lord Savile.

Class **12.**—Grapes, 2 bunches of any Frontignan varieties.
First Prize, £1. 10s.; Second, £1.
No entry.

Class **13.**—Collection of Hardy Fruits, in a space not exceeding 12 × 3:—30 dishes distinct, grown entirely in the open; not more than 12 varieties of Apples or 8 of Pears.
First Prize, The Hogg Medal and £3; Second, £2; Third, £1.
1. Lieut.-Col. Borton, Hunton (gr. J. Whittle).
2. G. T. Bates, Esq., Whitfield (gr. R. Grindrod).
3. Major Powell-Cotton, Birchington (gr. J. Cornford).

DIVISION II.
Open to Nurserymen only.

Nurserymen and Market Growers must exhibit as individuals or as firms. *They must have actually grown all they exhibit.* Combinations of individuals or firms are not allowed, nor collections of produce from districts.

Nurserymen and Market Growers desiring to exhibit at this Show must make application for space as under Class 14 or 15; 16; 17 or 18; 19. No other spaces but the above can be allotted. Exhibitors can only enter in one of Classes 14 and 15; or in one of 17 and 18; and Exhibitors in 17 and 18 may not show in Class 19.

Nurserymen and Market Growers may adopt any method of staging they desire, subject to the following reservations: (a) The number of fruits is not limited, but the baskets or dishes must not exceed 15 inches in diameter if circular, or 19 × 15 if rectangular, unless they be sieves or half-sieves; (b) Duplicate trees are permitted in Class 16, but *not duplicate baskets or dishes* of fruit in any of the Classes; (c) No trees are admissible in Classes 14 and 15; (d) The fruit in Exhibits under Classes 14 and 15, 17 and 18, must in no case be raised higher than 3 feet above the table. The use of berries and foliage plants is allowed for decoration but not flowers.

No awards of any sort will be made to Nurserymen and Market Growers who do not conform to the above regulations.

IMPORTANT.—Nurserymen and Market Growers having entered and finding themselves unable to exhibit are *particularly* requested to give four days' notice to the Superintendent, R.H.S. Gardens, Wisley, Ripley, Surrey. Telegraphic Address— "Hortensia, Ripley."

Allotment of table-space will be made on the following scales:—

For Fruit grown entirely out of doors.

Class **14.**—24 feet run of 6 feet tabling.
First Prize, Gold Medal; Second, Silver-gilt Banksian Medal.
1. Messrs. G. Bunyard, Maidstone.
2. Messrs. H. Cannell, Eynsford.

Class **15.**—16 feet run of 6 feet tabling.
First Prize, Silver-gilt Knightian Medal ; Second, Silver-gilt Banksian
Medal ; Third, Silver Knightian Medal.
1. King's Acre Nurseries, Hereford.
2. Messrs. J. Peed, West Norwood.
3. Messrs. Paul & Son, Cheshunt.

For Orchard-house Fruit and Trees.

Class **16.**—24 feet by 6 feet of stage.   Grapes excluded.
First Prize, Gold Medal ; Second, Silver-gilt Knightian Medal.
1. Messrs. G. Bunyard.
2. Messrs. T. Rivers, Sawbridgeworth.

DIVISION III.

Open to Market Growers only.

Allotment of Table Space will be made on the following scales :—

Class **17.**—18 feet run of 6 feet tabling.
First Prize, £2 ; Second, £1. 10s. ; Third, £1.
1. Mr. W. Poupart, Twickenham.
2. Mr. W. H. Press, Hereford.
3. No award.

Class **18.**—12 feet run of 6 feet tabling.
First Prize, £2 ; Second, £1. 10s. ; Third, £1.
1. Horticultural College, Swanley.
2. ⎫
3. ⎭ No awards.

Class **19.**—Apples, 12 dishes distinct, 6 Cooking, 6 Dessert ;
Exhibitors in Classes 17 and 18 not admissible.
First Prize, £2 ; Second, £1. 10s. ; Third, £1.
1. Mr. H. T. Mason, Hampton Hill.
2. ⎫
3. ⎭ No awards.

DIVISION IV.

Fruits grown entirely in the Open Air—except Class 32.

Open to Gardeners and Amateurs only.   Nurserymen and Market
Growers excluded.

Exhibitors of Apples or Pears in Division IV. are excluded from Division VI.

NOTE.—Exhibitors can compete in one Class only of the Classes 20, 21, 22 ; or
of 25, 26, 27, 28.

Class **20.**—Apples, 24 dishes distinct, 16 Cooking, 8 Dessert.   The
latter to be placed in the front row.
First Prize, £3 and Silver Medal awarded by the Court of Fruiterers ;
Second, £3 ; Third, £2.
1. Lieut.-Col. Borton.
2. Sir Marcus Samuel, Bart., Maidstone (gr. W. H. Bacon).
3. J. G. Williams, Esq., Tring (gr. F. G. Gerrish).

Class **21.**—Apples, 18 dishes distinct, 12 Cooking, 6 Dessert. The latter to be placed in the front row.

First Prize, £3 ; Second, £2 ; Third, £1.

1. Major Powell-Cotton.
2. E. Ascherson, Esq., Charing (gr. J. Pitts).
3. Earl De Grey, Kingston (gr. J. Smith).

Class **22.**—Apples, 12 dishes distinct, 8 Cooking, 4 Dessert. The latter to be placed in the front row.

First Prize, £2 ; Second, £1 ; Third, 15s.

1. { C. R. Adeane, Esq.
   { F. A. Bevan, Esq., New Barnet (gr. H. Parr) } equal.
3. Rt. Hon. W. H. Long, Trowbridge (gr. W. Strugnell).
4. O. E. Avigdor-Goldsmid, Esq.

Class **23.**—Cooking Apples, 6 dishes, distinct.

First Prize, £1 ; Second, 15s.

1. Lieut.-Col. Borton.
2. Sir Marcus Samuel, Bart.

Class **24.**—Dessert Apples, 6 dishes, distinct.

First Prize, £1 ; Second, 15s.

1. Lieut.-Col. Borton.
2. Sir Marcus Samuel, Bart.

Class **25.**—Dessert Pears, 18 dishes, distinct.

First Prize, £2 and Silver-gilt Medal awarded by the Court of Fruiterers ; Second, £2 ; Third, £1.

1. Sir Marcus Samuel, Bart.
2. Lieut.-Col. Borton.
3. Major Powell-Cotton.

Class **26.**—Dessert Pears, 12 dishes, distinct.

First Prize, £2 ; Second, £1 ; Third, 15s.

1. Rev. O. L. Powels, Weybridge (gr. A. Basile).
2. F. A. Bevan, Esq.
3. Rt. Hon. W. H. Long.

Class **27.**—Dessert Pears, 9 dishes, distinct.

First Prize, £1. 10s. ; Second, 17s. 6d.

1. J. R. Brougham, Esq., Carshalton (gr. W. Jones).
2. No award.

Class **28.**—Dessert Pears, 6 dishes, distinct.

First Prize, £1 ; Second, 15s.

1. C. A. Morris-Field, Esq., Tunbridge Wells (gr. J. R. Allan).
2. { C. A. Morris-Field, Esq., Sevenoaks (gr. R. Edwards) } equal.
   { R. E. Phillips, Esq., Sittingbourne.

Class **29.**—Stewing Pears, 3 dishes, distinct.

First Prize, 15s. ; Second, 10s.

1. R. E. Phillips, Esq.
2. Major Powell-Cotton.

Class **30.**—Peaches grown entirely out of doors, 1 dish of one variety.
First Prize, 10*s.* ; Second, 7*s.*
1. The Marquis of Northampton, Castle Ashby (gr. A. R. Searle).
2. C. R. Adeane, Esq.

Class **31.**—Nectarines grown entirely out of doors, 1 dish of one variety.
First Prize, 10*s.* ; Second, 7*s.*
1. C. R. Adeane, Esq.
2. H. A. Attenborough, Esq., Daventry (gr. A. Child).

Class **32.**—Plums grown under Glass, 3 dishes, distinct.
First Prize, £1 ; Second, 10*s.*
1. Lord Howard de Walden, Saffron Walden (gr. J. Vert).
2. The Marquis of Northampton.

Class **33.**—Plums, 3 dishes, distinct.
First Prize, 15*s.* ; Second, 10*s.*
1. The Earl of Ashburnham, Battle (gr. G. Grigg).
2. Lord Howard de Walden.

Class **34.**—Plums, 1 dish of Coe's Golden Drop.
First Prize, 7*s.* ; Second, 5*s.*
1. Lord Howard de Walden.
2. H. P. Sturgis, Esq., Leatherhead (gr. W. M. Peters).

Class **35.**—Plums, 1 dish of any other Dessert variety.
First Prize, 7*s.* ; Second, 5*s.*
1. E. S. Hanbury, Esq., Ware (gr. F. W. Church).
2. The Marquis of Northampton.

Class **36.**—Plums, 1 dish of Cooking of one variety.
First Prize, 7*s.* ; Second, 5*s.*
1. The Marquis of Northampton.
2. Sir Jeremiah Colman, Bart., Reigate (gr. W. P. Bound).

Class **37.**—Damsons, or Bullaces, 3 dishes, distinct.
First Prize, 10*s.* ; Second, 7*s.* 6*d.*
No entry.

Class **38.**—Morello Cherries, 50 fruits.
First Prize, 7*s.* ; Second, 5*s.*
1. Lieut.-Col. Borton.
2. J. G. Williams, Esq.

Class **39.**—Grapes grown out of doors, Basket of about 6 lb. weight.
First Prize, £1 ; Second, 10*s.*
1. No award.
2. H. M. Tod, Esq., Seething Lane, E.C.

DIVISION V.

Special District County Prizes.

Open to Gardeners and Amateurs only.

(In this Division all Fruit must have been grown in the Open.)

N.B.—Exhibitors in Division V. must not compete in Divisions II. or III., or in Classes 1, 2, 3, 4, 13, 20, 21, 22, 25, 26, 27.

Class **AA.**—Apples, 6 dishes, distinct, 4 Cooking, 2 Dessert.

1st Prize, £1 and 3rd class Single Fare from Exhibitor's nearest railway station to London ; * 2nd Prize, 15s. and Railway Fare as above.*

Class **BB.**—Dessert Pears, 6 dishes, distinct.

1st Prize, £1. 10s. and Railway Fare as above ; * 2nd Prize, £1 and Railway Fare as above.*

The above two classes, Nos. AA and BB, are repeated eleven times as follows, and Exhibitors must enter for them thus : "Class AA 41 " or "BB 42," and so on, to make it quite clear whether they mean Apples or Pears.

* In the event of the same Exhibitor being successful in both classes AA and BB only one Railway Fare will be paid.; and no Railway Fare will be paid if the fruit is sent up for the Society's officers to unpack and stage.

Class **40.**—Open only to Kent Growers.

AA. { 1. W. E. S. E. Drax, Esq., Wye (gr. J. Bond).
{ 2. H. G. Kleinwort, Esq., Maidstone (gr. B. J. Mercer).

BB. { 1. Dowager Lady Hillingdon, Sevenoaks (gr. J. Shelton).
{ 2. R. E. Phillips, Esq.

Class **41.**—Open only to Growers in Surrey, Sussex, Hants, Dorset, Somerset, Devon, and Cornwall.

AA. { 1. B. H. Hill, Esq., Crediton (gr. G. Lock).
{ 2. F. J. B. W. Digby, Esq., Sherborne (gr. T. Turton).

BB. { 1. Sir E. G. Loder, Bart., Horsham (gr. W. A. Cook).
{ 2. B. H. Hill, Esq.

Class **42.**—Open only to Growers in Wilts, Gloucester, Oxford, Bucks, Berks, Beds, Herts, and Middlesex.

AA. { 1. Lord Hillingdon, Uxbridge.
{ 2. Mrs. Coney, Maidenhead (gr. A. Tidy).

BB. { 1. Lord Hillingdon.
{ 2. Mrs. H. Ames, Westbury-on-Trym (gr. W. H. Bannister).

Class **43.**—Open only to Growers in Essex, Suffolk, Norfolk, Cambridge, Hunts, and Rutland.

AA. { 1. Major Petre, Norwich (gr. G. D. Davidson).
{ 2. N. R. Page, Esq., Clacton-on-Sea.

BB. { 1. Major Petre.
{ 2. Col. Hon. Chas. Harbord.

Class **44.**—Open only to Growers in Lincoln, Northampton, Warwick, Leicester, Notts, Derby, Staffs, Shropshire, and Cheshire.

AA. { 1. John Lee, Esq., Higher Bebington.
{ 2. The Duke of Rutland, Grantham (gr. W. H. Divers).

BB. { 1. The Marquis of Northampton.
{ 2. The Duke of Rutland.

Class **45.**—Open only to Growers in Worcester, Hereford, Monmouth, Glamorgan, Carmarthen, and Pembroke.

AA. { 1. F. P. Norbury, Esq., Malvern.
{ 2. G. H. Hadfield, Esq., Ross.

BB. { 1. G. H. Hadfield, Esq.
{ 2. G. T. Bates, Esq.

Class **46.**—Open only to Growers in the other Counties of Wales.

AA. { 1. Sir George Meyrick, Bart., Anglesey (gr. W. Pilgrim).
{ 2. P. Yorke, Esq., Wrexham (gr. G. Aitken).

BB. { 1. Sir George Meyrick.
{ 2. P. Yorke, Esq.

Class **47.**—Open only to Growers in the Six Northern Counties of England, and in the Isle of Man.

AA. { 1. J. Brennand, Esq., Thirsk (gr. J. E. Hathaway).
{ 2. No award.

BB. { 1. J. Brennand, Esq.
{ 2. No award.

Class **48.**—Open only to Growers in Scotland.

AA. { 1. Mr. J. Day, Garlieston.
{ 2. No award.
{ Extra Prize to Col. Gordon, Castle Douglas (gr. J. Duff).

BB. { 1. Mr. J. Day.
{ 2. No award.

Class **49.**—Open only to Growers in Ireland.

AA. { 1. C. B. Broad, Esq., Conna.
{ 2. T. O'Donnell, Esq., Piltown.

BB. { No entry.

Class **50.**—Open only to Growers in the Channel Islands.
No entry.

Division VI.

Single Dishes of Fruit grown in the Open Air.

Six Fruits to a Dish.

Open to Gardeners and Amateurs only.   Nurserymen and Market Growers excluded.

Prizes in each Class except 70, 85, 86, 92, 93, 102, 134.
1st Prize, 7*s.*; 2nd Prize, 5*s.*

Choice Dessert Apples.

N.B.—Quality, Colour, and Finish are of more merit than Size.

Class **51.**—Adams' Pearmain.
1. Lord Poltimore, Exeter (gr. T. H. Slade).
2. H. St. Maur, Esq., Newton Abbot (gr. G. Richardson).

Class **52.**—Allington Pippin.
1. F. P. Norbury, Esq.
2. Major Petre.

Class **53.**—American Mother.
1. John Wootton, Esq., Byford.
2. F. J. B. W. Digby, Esq.

Class **54.**—Ben's Red.
1. J. B. Fortescue, Esq., Maidenhead (gr. C. Page).
2. John Wootton, Esq.

Class **55.**—Blenheim Orange.
1. Lord Foley, Claygate (gr. H. C. Gardner).
2. Sir Jeremiah Colman, Bart.

Class **56.**—Claygate Pearmain.
1. G. H. Hadfield, Esq.
2. A. Saunders, Esq.

Class **57.**—Cockle's Pippin.
1. G. C. D. Weddell, Esq.
2. No award.

Class **58.**—Cox's Orange Pippin.
1. F. P. Norbury, Esq.
2. H. G. Wadlow, Esq., Peterborough.

Class **59.**—Egremont Russet.
1. W. E. S. E. Drax, Esq.
2. A. Saunders, Esq.

Class **60.**—James Grieve.
1. F. P. Norbury, Esq.
2. Col. Archer-Houblon, Bishops Stortford (gr. W. Harrison).

Class **61.**—King of the Pippins.
1. H. J. King, Esq.
2. Lord Foley.

Class **62.**—King of Tomkins County.
1. { J. Brennand, Esq. / J. Wootton, Esq. } equal.
3. Col. Archer-Houblon (gr. W. Harrison).

Class **63.**—Lord Hindlip.
1. H. J. King, Esq.
2. John Wootton, Esq.

Class **64.**—Margil.
1. G. H. Hadfield, Esq.
2. Dowager Lady Hillingdon.

Class **65.**—Ribston Pippin.
1. The Earl of Ashburnham.
2. Lord Howard de Walden.

Class **66.**—Rival.
1. Col. Archer-Houblon, Newbury (gr. C. Ross).
2. F. J. B. W. Digby, Esq.

Class **67.**—Scarlet Nonpareil.
1. Mr. J. McIndoe, V.M.H., Dartford.
2. J. B. Fortescue, Esq.

Class **68.**—St. Edmund's Pippin.
1. J. B. Fortescue, Esq.
2. No award.

Class **69.**—Wealthy.
1. G. H. Hadfield, Esq.
2. Sir Jeremiah Colman, Bart.

Class **70.**— Any other variety not named above.
Four Prizes : 7*s.*, 6*s* , 5*s.*, 4*s.*

An Exhibitor may only enter one variety in Class 70, in which Class eight Fruits must be shown to a dish for the Judges to be able to taste two of them.
1. E. A. Ross, Esq., Winchester.
2. Earl Stanhope.
3. Lord Howard de Walden.
4. F. P. Norbury, Esq.

CHOICE COOKING APPLES.

N.B.—Quality and Size are of more merit than Colour.

Class **71.**—Alfriston.
1. John Lee, Esq.
2. No award.

Class **72.**—Annie Elizabeth.
1. F. J. B. W. Digby, Esq.
2. Col. Archer-Houblon (gr. W. Harrison).

Class **73.**—Beauty of Kent.
1. Sir Jeremiah Colman, Bart.
2. John Lee, Esq.

Class **74.**—Bismarck.
1. F. P. Norbury, Esq.
2. T. O'Donnell, Esq.

Class **75.**—Bramley's Seedling.
1. Major Petre.
2. H. St. Maur, Esq.

Class **76.** — Dumelow's Seedling (*syn.* Wellington, Normanton Wonder).
1. Sir Jeremiah Colman, Bart.
2. Hon. Mr. Justice Swinfen Eady.

Class **77.**—Edward VII.
1. No award.
2. J. Wootton, Esq.

Class **78.**—Emneth Early (*syn.* Early Victoria).
No entry.

Class **79.**—Emperor Alexander.
1. F. Edenborough, Esq., Rayleigh.
2. W. E. S. E. Drax, Esq.

Class **80.**—Gascoyne's Scarlet.
1. H. J. King, Esq.
2. W. E. S. E. Drax, Esq.

Class **81.**—Golden Noble.
1. Mrs. Coney.
2. F. J. B. W. Digby, Esq.

Class **82.**—Golden Spire.
1. G. T. Bates, Esq.
2. Earl Stanhope.

Class **83.**—Grenadier.
1. J. B. Fortescue, Esq.
2. John Lee, Esq.

Class **84.**—Hambling's Seedling.
1. H. St. Maur, Esq.
2. W. E. S. E. Drax, Esq.

Class **85.**—Hector Macdonald.
First Prize, 20*s.*; Second, 10*s.*; Third, 5*s.*

Prizes presented by Messrs. J. R. Pearson & Sons, Lowdham, Notts.

Open only to Exhibitors living in Cardigan, Radnor, Shropshire, Stafford, Warwick Northampton, Bedford, Cambridge, Essex, or counties further north.

No entry.

Class **86.**—Hector Macdonald.
First Prize, 20*s.*; Second, 10*s.*; Third, 5*s.*

Prizes presented by Messrs. J. R. Pearson & Sons, Lowdham, Notts.

Open only to Exhibitors living south of before-named counties.

1. Col. Archer-Houblon (gr. C. Ross).
2.
3. } No awards.

Class **87.**—Hormead Pearmain.
1. G. H. Hadfield, Esq.
2. No award.

Class **88.**—Lady Henniker.
1. F. J. B. W. Digby, Esq.
2. J. B. Fortescue, Esq.

Class **89.**—Lane's Prince Albert.
1. F. P. Norbury, Esq.
2. Earl Stanhope.

Class **90.**—Lord Derby.
1. F. P. Norbury, Esq.
2. John Lee, Esq.

Class **91.**—Mère de Ménage.
1. F. J. B. W. Digby, Esq.
2. John Lee, Esq.

Class **92.**—Newton Wonder.
First Prize, 20s. ; Second, 10s. ; Third, 5s.
Prizes presented by Messrs. J. R. Pearson & Sons, Lowdham, Notts.
Open only to Exhibitors living in Cardigan, Radnor, Shropshire, Stafford, Warwick, Northampton, Bedford, Cambridge, Essex, or counties further north.
1. Major Petre.
2. Mr. F. J. Lansdell.
3. F. Edenborough, Esq.

Class **93.**—Newton Wonder.
First Prize, 20s. ; Second, 10s. ; Third, 5s.
Prizes presented by Messrs. J. R. Pearson & Sons, Lowdham, Notts.
Only open to Exhibitors living south of the before-named counties.
1. F. P. Norbury, Esq.
2. B. H. Hill, Esq.
3. W. E. S. E. Drax, Esq.

Class **94.**—Norfolk Beauty.
1. Col. Hon. Chas. Harbord.
2. J. B. Fortescue, Esq.

Class **95.**—Peasgood's Nonesuch.
1. W. E. S. E. Drax, Esq.
2. Mrs. Coney.

Class **96.**—Potts' Seedling.
1. F. W. Platt, Esq., Highgate (gr. C. Turner).
2. F. J. B. W. Digby, Esq.

Class **97.**—Royal Jubilee.
1. J. B. Fortescue, Esq.
2. Col. Archer-Houblon (gr. C. Ross).

Class **98.**—Royal Late Cooking.
1. Earl Stanhope.
2. No award.

Class **99.**—Stirling Castle.
1. Col. Archer-Houblon (gr. C. Ross).
2. John Wootton, Esq.

Class **100.**—Tower of Glamis.
1. F. J. B. W. Digby, Esq.
2. J. B. Fortescue, Esq.

Class **101.**—Warner's King.
1. A. P. Brandt, Esq.
2. H. J. King, Esq.

Class **102.**—Any other variety not named above.

Four Prizes : 7*s.*, 6*s.*, 5*s.*, 4*s.*

An Exhibitor may only enter one variety in Class 102, in which Class eight fruits must be shown to a dish for the Judges to be able to taste two of them.

1. Sir Jeremiah Colman, Bart.
2. F. J. B. W. Digby, Esq.
3. John Lee, Esq.
4. John Wootton, Esq.

Choice Dessert Pears.

Class **103.**—Belle Julie.
1. Dowager Lady Hillingdon.
2. No award.

Class **104.**—Beurré Alexander Lucas.
1. F. J. B. W. Digby, Esq.
2. The Earl of Ashburnham.

Class **105.**—Beurré d'Amanlis.
1. Col. Archer-Houblon (gr. W. Harrison).
2. Col. Hon. Chas. Harbord.

Class **106.**—Beurré d'Anjou.
1. J. T. Charlesworth, Esq., Nutfield (gr. T. W. Herbert).
2. Mrs. H. Ames.

Class **107.**—Beurré d'Avalon (*syn.* Porch's Beurré and Glastonbury).
No entry.

Class **108.**—Beurré Bosc.
1. The Earl of Ashburnham.
2. Sir Walpole Greenwell, Bart.

Class **109.**—Beurré Dumont.
1. Lord Hillingdon.
2. F. J. B. W. Digby, Esq.

Class **110.**—Beurré Hardy.
1. Sir E. G. Loder, Bart.
2. G. H. Hadfield, Esq.

Class **111.**—Beurré Superfin.
1. F. J. B. W. Digby, Esq.
2. Dowager Lady Hillingdon.

Class **112.**—Charles Ernest.
1. Lord Poltimore.
2. N. R. Page, Esq.

Class **113.**—Comte De Lamy.
1. Dowager Lady Hillingdon.
2. J. T. Charlesworth, Esq.

Class **114.**—Conference.
1. Sir Jeremiah Colman, Bart.
2. Col. Hon. Chas. Harbord.

Class **115.**—Doyenné du Comice.
1. F. Leverton-Harris, Esq., Dorking (gr. J. MacDonald).
2. Major Petre.

Class **116.**—Durondeau.
1. Lord Hillingdon.
2. Major Petre.

Class **117.**—Emile d'Heyst.
1. Rev. H. A. Bull, Westgate-on-Sea (gr. F. King).
2. Major Petre.

Class **118.**—Fondante d'Automne.
1. Lord Hillingdon.
2. Col. Hon. Chas. Harbord.

Class **119.**—Fondante de Thiriot.
1. M. W. Price, Esq.
2. Sir E. G. Loder, Bart.

Class **120.**—Glou Morceau.
1. F. E. Croft, Esq., Ware (gr. G. Longhurst).
2. Major Petre.

Class **121.**—Josephine de Malines.
1. F. J. B. W. Digby, Esq.
2. Dowager Lady Hillingdon.

Class **122.**—Le Brun.
1. F. R. Rodd, Esq.
2. No award.

Class **123.**—Le Lectier.
1. The Earl of Ashburnham.
2. Lord Howard de Walden.

Class **124.**—Louise Bonne of Jersey.
1. W. E. S. E. Drax, Esq.
2. Sir Jeremiah Colman, Bart.

Class **125.**—Marie Benoist.
1. F. J. B. W. Digby, Esq.
2. Lord Poltimore.

Class **126.**—Marie Louise.
1. G. H. Hadfield, Esq.
2. Col. Hon. Chas. Harbord.

Class **127.**—Nouvelle Fulvie.
1. Col. Hon. Chas. Harbord.
2. Lord Howard de Walden.

Class **128.**—Pitmaston Duchess.
1. Rev. H. A. Bull.
2. A. P. Brandt, Esq.

Class **129.**—President Barabé.
1. Col. Hon. Chas. Harbord.
2. Dowager Lady Hillingdon.

Class **130.**—St. Luke.
1. J. B. Fortescue, Esq.
2. No award.

Class **131.**—Thompson.
1. Lord Hillingdon.
2. Col. Hon. Chas. Harbord.

Class **132.**—Triomphe de Vienne.
1. Lord Hillingdon.
2. Major Petre.

Class **133.**—Winter Nelis.
1. H. G. Kleinwort, Esq.
2. Dowager Lady Hillingdon.

Class **134.**—Any other variety not named above.

Four Prizes : 7s., 6s., 5s., 4s.

An Exhibitor may only enter one variety in Class 134, in which Class eight fruits must be shown to a dish for the Judges to be able to taste two of them.

1. W. A. Voss, Esq., Rayleigh.
2. Sir Jeremiah Colman, Bart.
3. H. P. Sturgis, Esq.
4. J. T. Charlesworth, Esq.

"NOTE UPON THE AWARD OF PRIZES IN CLASS I."

DEAR SIR,—Having noticed our decision in the above class questioned in the public Press, we, in courtesy to the parties interested, sent a copy of the following letter to them, briefly stating the grounds on which our decision was based :—

" The awards of the four judges, whose names are appended, having been publicly questioned, we, in courtesy to the parties interested, briefly state the facts as follows :—Three collections of fruit were very carefully ' pointed ' through, and in doing so we were very suspicious that two bunches of White Grapes, by their appearance, were not true Muscat of Alexandria, although named as such. Ultimately we decided to exercise our right to taste the Grapes. This test of quality fully confirmed our previous doubts, for, in addition to the suspicious shape of the berries, there was a total absence of Muscat flavour, and an unusual thickness of skin. As this was the unanimous opinion of all four judges, and in order to render perfect justice to all concerned, there was no alternative but to reduce the number of points awarded to these said Grapes previous to tasting, which, of course, very materially altered the position of the exhibit in question. It may be added that we accept no responsibility for any naming of Mr. Lock's Grapes by other persons, nor for any previous awards that may have been made to his ' Muscats.'—N. F. BARNES, WILLIAM CRUMP, JOHN DOE, C. R. FIELDER (Judges in Class I.)."

This we considered was all that we were called upon to do as servants (for the time being) of the Royal Horticultural Society, and we purpose to take no further notice whatever of what has appeared, or may appear, upon the matter in the public Press.

We feel, however, that it is our duty to the Council of the Royal Horticultural Society, and to ourselves, to place on record with you the following facts, to be used publicly or otherwise, as the Council may deem expedient, and thereby maintain our own *bona fides* and impartiality :

I.—The collections of fruit were judged by points, as adopted and authorised by the Royal Horticultural Society.

II.—We unanimously and emphatically record that in our opinion the Grapes shown by Mr. Lock, and labelled "Muscat of Alexandria," were not true to that name ; but, whether our opinion was correct or not, our award was entirely based, not upon wrong naming, but upon the bad flavour of his white Grapes when tasted.

III.—We did not attach the name of "Chasselas Tokay" to these so-called "Muscats," nor do we accept any responsibility for so naming of them.

IV.—We did not disfigure these bunches by eating a quantity of the berries (*vide* public Press).

V.—We submit that Mr. Lock could easily have had our decision on his Muscats (?) confirmed, or upset, by showing them at once before the Royal Horticultural Society's Fruit Committee. Your judges would welcome this arrangement at any time, if they could have *a guarantee* that Grapes from the *same vine* as that of the ones shown, and in dispute, would be forthcoming.

VI.—Your judges beg leave to suggest that the Royal Horticultural Society should have a rule inserted in its schedule whereby all disputed kinds or varieties could be at once impounded until the point or points in dispute had been settled.

We are your obedient servants, the judges in Class I.,

N. F. BARNES, Eaton Hall.
J. DOE, Rufford.
WILLIAM CRUMP, Madresfield Court.
C. R. FIELDER, North Mymms.

To the Rev. W. Wilks, M.A.

GENERAL MEETING.

OCTOBER 29, 1907.

Mr. A. H. PEARSON in the Chair.

Fellows elected (34).—Col. T. H. Anstey, Rev. T. C. V. Bastow, Mrs. W. C. Bond, Major A. G. Boscawen, C. F. Buckham, H. Butler, Mrs. J. G. Clark, S. H. Cotton, W. Crowfoot, Mrs. Kynaston Cross, W. Dannreuther, Mrs. Denny, H. L. de Putron, Lady Emily Digby, Miss S. P. Ely, Miss Annie Epps, Mrs. A. S. Gladstone, W. F. Jeeves, Mrs. S. Kiddle, F. Livingstone, R. E. Longfield, L. J. Longmead, Mrs. McBain, A. Medcalf, W. Michell, W. Mitchell, F. Nash, Mrs. P. Nelke,

Hon. Mrs. C. Portman, Miss P. Ratcliff, S. G. Sale, J. Spink, Dr. G. Walker, A. S. Williams.

Associate (1).—Miss Tinckler.

Society affiliated (1).—Kenley and District Horticultural Society.

A lecture on "The Birds of our Gardens," illustrated by lantern slides, was given by Mr. Cecil H. Hooper, M.R.A.C., F.S.I. (see p. 427).

GENERAL MEETING.

NOVEMBER 12, 1907.

Mr. E. A. BOWLES, M.A., F.L.S., F.E.S., in the Chair.

Fellows elected (27).—R. Alexander, W. S. Birch, Mrs. S. A. Cheale, J. Cunningham, W. S. Goodridge, C. Head, Mrs. Rufus D. Isaacs, Lady Lawrance, Lady Lyall, Mrs. Booth H. Lynes, G. Lang Macfarlan, Mrs. Manning, Miss Anne Newton, N. J. Nielsen, Lady Oldknow, O. C. J. G. L. Overbeck, Dr. Edmund Owen, E. Dalman Page, Mrs. H. C. Paget, Col. A. Plant, Miss G. Price, J. H. Rewcastle, Mrs. Russell, Mrs. F. Smith, Mrs. Alice Sonnenthal, J. G. Wainwright, Miss M. Wilson.

Fellows resident abroad (3).—H. E. Brown (Transvaal), José d'Almeida Pereira (Singapore), C. de B. Tayler (Jersey).

Society affiliated (1).—Chislehurst Gardeners' Mutual Improvement Association.

A lecture on "Succulent Plants," illustrated by lantern slides, was given by Mr. R. Irwin Lynch, A.L.S., V.M.H. It was further illustrated by two interesting exhibits of Cacti sent by Monsieur Franz de Laet and Herr H. Zeissold. A Silver Banksian Medal was awarded to each exhibit. (See p. 451.)

GENERAL MEETING.

NOVEMBER 26, 1907.

Mr. F. J. CHITTENDEN in the Chair.

Fellows elected (34).—C. Adamson, Dr. R. L. Bowles, A. P. Brandt, Lady D'Oyly Carte, Mrs. Rowland Cox, Dr. R. W. Cunningham, Charles Daborn, Lieut. A. T. Dawson, Martinez de Hoz, Lady Dent, Edwin A. Extence, Mrs. H. S. Fenwick, Hon. Mrs. Howard, Thomas O. Jones, W. B. Keen, Mrs. K. Kibblewhite, Mrs. D. H. Kyd, Hon. Emily Lawless, Hon. Mrs. E. Lyttlelton, T. Matthison, A. Maudslay, Major A. B. Murray, Mrs. Nevill, Mrs. M. Robson, T. Roper, Wm. Rowell, G. Sadler, S. E. Saunders, C. Stewart Sharp, Mrs. C. Stewart Sharp, Mrs. G. Stracey, Mrs. J. Tabor, Mrs. Truman, W. Willett.

Fellows resident abroad (2).—C. M. Swynnerton (Rhodesia), H. F. Bray (Japan).

Associates (2).—W. Allen, Miss E. M. Powell.

Society affiliated (1).—Bickley and District Horticultural Society.

A lecture on "Garden Experiments" was given by Mr. F J. Baker, A.R.C.S. (see p. 482).

EXHIBITION OF COLONIAL-GROWN FRUITS, VEGETABLES, AND PRESERVES, AND OF HOME BOTTLED AND PRE-SERVED BRITISH FRUITS AND VEGETABLES.

NOVEMBER 28 AND 29, 1907.

JUDGES OF COLONIAL FRUIT.

Bunyard, Geo., V.M.H.
Butt, George
Fielder, C. R.
Hudson, Jas., V.M.H.

Monro, Geo., V.M.H.
Simons, C.
Walker, A. M.

JUDGES OF PRESERVED FRUITS.

Marshall, W., V.M.H.
Senn, C. Herman
Worth, Emile

Wilkin, C.
Wilks, Rev. W.

Gold Medal.

The Government of the Province of British Columbia (Agent-General : Hon. J. H. Turner, Salisbury House, Finsbury Circus, London, E.C.), for a collection of Apples and Pears.

The West Indian Produce Association (Manager : Mr. A. C. Philip, 4 Fenchurch Buildings, London, E.C.), for Colonial-grown Fruits and Vegetables, Colonial Preserves, &c.

The West India Committee (Secretary : Mr. Algernon E. Aspinal, 15 Seething Lane, London, E.C.), for Citrus Fruits, Colonial Preserves, &c., contributed by Grenada, Jamaica, and Trinidad.

Silver-gilt Lindley Medal.

The Royal Mail Steam Packet Company, 18 Moorgate Street, London, E.C., for Colonial-grown Fruit and Vegetables and Colonial Preserves.

Silver-gilt Knightian Medal.

The Government of Nova Scotia (Agent-General : Hon. John Howard, 57A Pall Mall, London, S.W.), for a collection of Apples.

Silver-gilt Banksian Medal.

Mr. T. G. Earl, Lytton, British Columbia, for Apples.
Mr. J. R. Blanchard, Nova Scotia, for Apples.
Mr. F. A. Parker, Berwick, Nova Scotia, for Apples.

Silver Knightian Medal.

The Department of Agriculture, Ontario, Canada, for a collection of Apples and Pears contributed by the Fruit Growers' Association of Ontario.

The Nelson Fruit Growers' Association, Nelson, British Columbia, for Apples.

Messrs. Stirling & Pitcairn, Kelowna, British Columbia, for Apples.
Mrs. J. Smith, Spence's Bridge, British Columbia, for Apples.

Mr. J. R. Brown, Summerland, British Columbia, for Apples.
Mr. A. L. Morse, Berwick, Nova Scotia, for Apples.
Mr. R. J. Messenger, Tupperville, Nova Scotia, for Apples.
Mr. J. A. Kinsman, Lakeville, Nova Scotia, for Apples.
Mr. J. E. Smith, Wolfville, Nova Scotia, for Apples.

Silver Banksian Medal.

Messrs. Oscar Brown & Co., Vernon, British Columbia, for Apples.
Mr. A. Unsworth-Chilliwack, British Columbia, for Apples.
The Kaslo Fruit Growers' Association, Kaslo, British Columbia,
for Apples.
Mr. E. E. Archibald, Wolfville, Nova Scotia, for Apples.
Mr. T. W. Forster, North Kingston, Nova Scotia, for Apples.
Mr. F. C. Johnson, Bridgetown, Nova Scotia, for Apples.
Mr. W. Woodwork, Nova Scotia, for Apples.
Messrs. Jackson, 172 Piccadilly, London, W., for Cape Preserves,
including Jams, Tinned and Bottled Fruits.

Bronze Knightian Medal.

Mr. A. C. Starr, Starr's Point, Nova Scotia, for Apples.
Mr. J. A. Ritchie, Summerland, British Columbia, for Apples.
Grand Forks District, Grand Forks, British Columbia, for Apples.
Mr. F. R. Gartrell, Summerland, British Columbia, for Apples.
Salmon Arms Farmers' Exchange, Salmon Arms, British Columbia,
for Apples.

Bronze Banksian Medal.

The Committee of St. Helena (Secretary: Mr. A. G. Wise, Caxton
Hall, Westminster, London, S.W.), for Jams.
Mr. H. Hamel Smith, 112 Fenchurch Street, E.C., for Cacao Beans.
Mr. A. H. Evans, 72 Victoria Street, London, S.W., for Cape Preserves.

This exhibition of Colonial-grown fruits and vegetables afforded
ample justification for the confidence so often expressed that British
Colonies can supply Great Britain with apples at least equal or even
superior to those hitherto imported from the United States. Visitors
to the Hall cannot fail to have been most favourably impressed with
the encouraging display of fruits, raw and preserved; and never, we
believe, has a similar exhibition in London, or elsewhere, shown equal
excellence with this. Every inch of available space in the Society's
large hall was utilised; in fact, late entries had of necessity to be
refused. Though apparently very late in the year, the Show was fixed
specially to meet the requirements of Canada, British Columbia, &c.,
and of the West Indies.

The most impressive exhibit was that of the British Columbia
Government, which was very attractively staged, and displayed a
remarkably high standard of apples. They were shown in boxes, as
packed for commercial purposes, and consisted of 275 cases from
thirty growers and fifteen packers, representing the best orchards of
the colony. The fruits, from standard trees growing in the open, were

a wonderful testimony to the valuable fruit resources of British Columbia, the quality, colour, and packing each competing in attractiveness.

Apples from Nova Scotia were also to be seen in (1) a Government exhibit and (2) a composite exhibit from fifteen growers. This colony was thus more largely represented than it has formerly been at the Society's Shows. It must be very gratifying to Nova Scotians that their apple crop has been so exceptionally good this year, as proved by the 150 cases and thirty barrels sent for exhibition. It is estimated that three-quarters of a million barrels have been produced in the colony, and the estimated return is £400,000.

A late arrival was that of sixty cases of apples and pears from Ontario, sent by and at the cost of the Fruit Growers' Association of Ontario, and previously exhibited at the recent Ontario Horticultural Exhibition, from which the fruits were immediately transported to London, and arrived only on the morning of the Show. Unfortunately the fruit had suffered severely in transit, and the award secured was, consequently, not so high as it would have been had they arrived in better condition; but they showed evidence of having at one time been of great excellence.

The West Indies were very strongly represented. Their interesting and attractive fruits had been magnificently staged by the West Indian Committee on behalf of the Exhibition Committee of Trinidad, Jamaica, and Grenada; also by the Royal Mail Steam Packet Company and the West India Produce Association. These exhibits included Avocado pears, mangos, claret bananas, citrus fruits of many varieties, sapodillas, golden apples, good specimens of soursop, and a particularly good collection of vegetables—such as eddoes, yams, red sweet potatos, and white sweet potatos. Arrowroot, from St. Vincent, and sugar-canes were also shown.

Nor should the colonial preserves—jellies, syrups, and bottled fruits—pass entirely unmentioned; for though at present they cannot truthfully be said to compare very favourably with the home produce, yet at the same time they evidence what the Colonies can do, and hold out the promise of a far better production in the near future. Amongst them was a small impromptu exhibit sent by the St. Helena Committee, which was most interesting as being probably the first time this little colony has been thus represented at a great London Fruit Show, and from the fact that his Excellency the Governor requested that an unbiassed report might be made upon them for the information and instruction of the islanders. This report was as follows:—

REPORT ON A SMALL PARCEL OF JAMS FROM ST. HELENA.

It would not be kind to speak of these jams in such a way as to encourage the islanders to embark on their manufacture on a large scale, only to meet with subsequent disappointment. True kindness consists in pointing out faults and suggesting how they may be corrected in future, and a really saleable article produced.

First of all, however, let me say that I know nothing whatever of the cost of carriage or of materials, so that I leave that entirely out of my consideration. But if these be insignificant, then I am sure the islanders can manufacture a good saleable article if they will make certain absolutely necessary alterations in their methods.

Bottles.—These are of a very awkward pattern, making it very difficult to get the jam out. One-pound or two-pound pots, or wide-mouthed bottles, or seven-pound jars must be adopted.

Bungs.—The ones at present used, of soft pappy wood, are most unsatisfactory. A corkscrew refuses to pull them out, but comes away through them. If the use of bottles is continued a glass stopper or a cork bung is essential.

Texture and Quality.—Referring to the jams generally, they are more of the nature of confections than jams. They are all, without exception, much too sweet and much too sticky. They have probably been cooked far more than is necessary, dispersing the liquid juices of the fruit and leaving far too much sugar, which at once begins to crystallise and candy. Less sugar must be used, and they must be less cooked.

Blackberry.—Far too sweet; all the fruit juice gone; all flavour cooked away. The individual fruits are dried up and hard, and the whole a mass of unpalatable pips. It must have less sugar, be less cooked, and the hard fruits and pips be strained out—in fact made into jelly.

Loquat.—This would be excellent if less sugar had been used, and if a little less cooked.

Raspberry.—Called " raspberry " on the bottles, but really strawberry (probably made of very small wild strawberries), and consisting almost wholly of small pips in sugar. It might, however, prove good if less sugar were used and if less cooked. The minuteness of the pips might be disregarded if the jam were less sticky and more flavoursome.

Guava.—This, like the loquat, might be excellent if a little less sugar were used, and if the large hard pips were strained out. This last point is *absolutely* necessary. It must be positively dangerous for human beings to swallow such a number of hard stony pips—actually inviting appendicitis.

General Remarks.—If there is an abundance of fruit—particularly of loquat and guava—in the island, and if the jam can be made and can find a market to give a good profit, it would be worth while sending out some-one who knows what jam is, and how it should be made, to take out pots and jars and other necessary appliances, just for one fruit season, to teach the islanders exactly what is wanted for British consumption.

                    (Signed)   W. WILKS.

Note.—The intensely sweet confections on which this brief report is founded might suit the markets of the United States, where they appear to disregard the flavour of jams so long as they can get the sweetness and stickiness which these present samples possess, but they will never sell in Great Britain.

A letter has been received from the Governor of St. Helena, from which the following sentences are taken :—

                    THE CASTLE, ST. HELENA :
                              February 26, 1908.

Sir,—His Excellency the Governor desires me to acknowledge receipt of your letter dated the 20th ultimo, and to thank you for sending him a duplicate copy of the medal card awarded to St. Helena jams at your last Colonial Fruit Show.

Regarding your report on the island jams exhibited at your last Show, his Excellency is much obliged to you for the useful advice contained therein; and the community generally is indebted to you for the kindly interest you take in the Colony's welfare. His Excellency does not consider your criticism to be in any sense too candid. You stated facts, which are what one always prefers.

I have the honour to be, Sir,
Your obedient servant,
A. HANDS, *Chief Clerk.*

To the Rev. W. Wilks, M.A.

Home Bottled Fruits and Vegetables.

Class **1.**—Home Bottled Fruits. *Open.* This exhibit must not occupy a space greater than 10 feet by 3 feet. All must be British-grown and British-prepared.

1. *Silver Knightian Medal.*

Mr. W. Poupart, Jun., Fernleigh, Belmont Road, Twickenham.

2. *Silver Banksian Medal.*

Messrs. W. Miles, 16 Church Road, Hove.

3. *Bronze Knightian Medal.*

Horticultural College, Swanley.

Class **2.**—18 bottles of British-grown Fruits (including six different kinds at least), bottled and shown by exhibitors who do not sell their produce or in any way work for the trade.

1. £3.—Mrs. V. Banks, 102 Park Street, Grosvenor Square, W.
2. £2.—Miss Alice Smith, The Bungalow, Barnham, Bognor.
3. £1.—Mr. W. Poupart, Jun., Fernleigh, Belmont Road, Twickenham.

Class **3.**—12 bottles of British-grown Fruits (including four different kinds at least), bottled and shown by exhibitors who do not sell their produce or in any way work for the trade.

Equal £1. 10s. { Mr. G. Hobday, Havering Road, Romford, Essex.
Mrs. W. H. Plowman, 16A Chapter Street, London, S.W.

Class **4.**—Home Dried or Evaporated Fruits. No entries.

Class **5.**—Home Preserved Vegetables (Bottled or Dried).

Silver-gilt Knightian Medal.

Messrs. McDoddies, Sharsted Works, Kennington, S.E.

Class **6.**—Home Bottled Vegetables. *Amateurs.* Eight bottles, including four different kinds at least.

1. 30s.—Mrs. V. Banks, 102 Park Street, Grosvenor Square, W.
2. 15s.—Miss A. Smith, The Bungalow, Barnham, Bognor.
3. 10s.—Miss G. B. Weddall, Park House, Teddington.

Class **7.**—Home Tinned Vegetables. *Open.* No entries.

Class **8.**—Foreign Bottled Fruits, Jams, &c. No entries.

MISCELLANEOUS EXHIBITS.

Silver-gilt Knightian Medal.

To Messrs. Wilkin, Tiptree, Essex, for Bottled Fruits.

Silver Knightian Medal.

To Messrs. Gillard, Walthamstow, for Chutney, Pickles, &c.
To Hereford Preserves, Aubrey Street, Hereford, for Bottled Fruits.
To Messrs. C. Lunn, Kirkburton, for Bottled Fruits.
To Mrs. W. H. Plowman, 16A Chapter Street, London, S.W., for Bottled Fruits, Jams, and Jellies.
To Swanley Horticultural College (Principal, Miss Wilkinson), for Jams, Jellies, and Marmalade.

Silver Banksian Medal.

To Messrs. Abbot Bros., Southall, for Preserving Bottles with glass tops.
To Miss Edith Bradley, Bredon's Norton, Tewkesbury, for Steriliser.
To the Studley Horticultural College, Studley, Warwickshire, for Home-made Jams.
To the Thatcham Fruit and Flower Farm, Henwick, near Newbury, for Home-made Jams.

The show of Home-bottled British Fruits exceeded any similar show previously held by the Society in the number and extent of the exhibits, and in the quality of bottling. It gave promise of a coming success for these shows hitherto unanticipated, and it is hoped that ere many years pass the demand for space in this section will be so great as to induce the Council to dissever the show from that for Colonial Fruits, and to give it an exclusive occupation of the Hall. It is believed that these efforts will do much to revive the taste for this domestic but skilful and tasteful old-time occupation for ladies, an occupation at once economical, profitable, and enjoyable. The ancient processes of half a century ago have given place to more skilful, scientific, and effective methods, which are, however, still perfectly easy and simple, as demonstrated by Miss Edith Bradley's most interesting lectures on fruit-bottling and sterilisation with her Mercia patent steriliser. These lectures were much appreciated by those attending them, and the Council accord their very sincere thanks to Miss Bradley for them.

The attention of exhibitors is specially drawn to a perfectly new feature in the Schedule for 1908, contained in Class 29, for three bottles of British-grown Fruits (of which one must be Raspberries), bottled and shown by amateurs, " To be shown on November 26, 1908, and *left in the Society's care until a corresponding date in* 1909, when they will be tested and the prizes awarded."

GENERAL MEETING.

DECEMBER 10, 1907.

The Rev. JOSEPH JACOB in the Chair.

Fellows elected (28).—G. R. Alderon, Mrs. R. Bence-Jones, T. Bucker-field, Mrs. Newton Chichester, Mrs. J. S. Constauld, Mrs. R. Davey, Miss L. Devas, C. J. D. Eveleigh, H. Gething, J.P., Mrs. Gibbon, Mrs. L. Harding, A. E. Jenner, R. F. Leake, Miss A. Martin, Mrs. H. F. Maxwell, Mrs. Mudie-Cooke, A. A. Myers, Mrs. D. Nicoll, Mrs. Playfair, Miss A. R. Pomfret, H. L. Roberts, W. Sarel, Mrs. J. R. Severn, Mrs. Sperling, P. C. Thornton, Mrs. J. M. Vickers, W. H. Whiter, Lady Wiseman.

Fellow resident abroad (1).—R. Seller (Cape Colony).

Societies affiliated (2).—Gosport and Alverstoke Gardeners' Association, Wood Green Horticultural Society.

A lecture on "Fungoid Pests and how to Combat them" was given by Mr. E. S. Salmon, F.L.S.

GENERAL MEETING.

DECEMBER 31, 1907.

Sir TREVOR LAWRENCE, Bart., K.C.V.O., V.M.H. (President of the Society), in the Chair.

Fellows elected (59).—P. Anthos, Mrs. H. Arbuthnot, G. Shorland Ball, F. H. Barker, Mrs. Oliver P. Behrens, Mrs. J. I. Boswell, Mrs. Campbell, Thomas Collinson, C. S. Cooper, L. H. de B. Crawshay, Countess of Denbigh, Com. L. A. de Sausmarez, R.N., E. S. Enoch, J. E. Finch, Miss Goldsmid, M. Herrod, Mrs. Hetherington, P. W. Heyes, Mrs. A. Hicks, Mrs. H. Hobhouse, R. J. Hope, Mrs. L. N. Hutchison, H. S. Johnson, Mrs. Kirk, Mrs. Kynrett, Miss Langley, C. D. Langworthy, H. Longster, Miss N. Luxmoore, W. McPherson, Rev. F. H. Manley, A. Courland Marshall, Mrs. H. W. Massingham, Miss Menzies, Miss Monck, Thomas Nicholson, Alfred Norton, W. Pearman-Clarke, Miss N. Pollock, Mrs. Pym, Miss E. W. Rayner, F. A. Roscoe, R. Saul, Edmund Saunders, R. W. Schultz, W. Sewell, Col. Shepper, Mrs. E. J. W. Slade, Miss M. A. Smart, W. H. Taylor, R. E. S. Thomas, F. W. Troup, J. Turnbull, Jun., F. A. Wallroth, S. A. Whitmore, Mrs. J. W. Wilson, Mrs. A. F. Winter, Mrs. Cornwallis Wykeham-Martin.

Fellows resident abroad (8).—A. B. Haggit (New Zealand), Frank Lilley (Guernsey), Wm. J. Maskell (Transvaal), M. Midzuno (Japan), R. K. Shaw (India), W. W. Smith (New Zealand), H. Vacherot (France), R. B. Whyte (Canada).

Associate (1).—J. Floate.

Societies affiliated (6).—Griqualand West Horticultural Society, Haywards Heath Horticultural Society, Mansfield (Notts) Horticultural Society, Purley Rose and Horticultural Society, Shepshed Horticultural Society, Sudbury (Middlesex) Allotment Association.

SCIENTIFIC COMMITTEE.

JULY 23, 1907.

Mr. E. A. BOWLES, M.A., F.L.S., in the Chair, and fourteen members present.

Dying Beech Trees.—Mr. Güssow reported that he had examined the wood of the Beech sent to the last meeting and found the mycelium of a *Polyporus* growing in it. He had little doubt that the death of the tree was due to this parasite.

Fuchsia, Vine, and Aucuba.—Messrs. Massee, V.M.H., and Güssow reported that no fungi could be found in the tissues of either of these sent to the last meeting.

Memorial of Dr. Masters.—Rev. W. Wilks repeated a suggestion he had already brought forward in the Press concerning the establishment of a permanent memorial of the late Dr. Masters, to take the form of a series of lectures to be delivered annually before the Royal Horticultural Society by some eminent scientific man upon some phase of the relationship between science and horticulture, the lectures to be subsequently published. The suggestion met with the cordial approval of the Committee, and Mr. Wilks undertook to bring the matter before the Council.

Germination of Seeds in Sterilised Soil.—Mr. Spencer Pickering, F.R.S., raised the question of the germination of bacillus-free seeds in sterilised soil, stating that he had found that the heating of soil to 60° C. and upwards retarded the germination of the seeds to a very marked extent, just as he had found the growth of trees in soil which had been heated to be retarded. The seeds (Ryegrass and Mustard) had been sterilised with carbon bisulphide, and had germinated after treatment quite freely in ordinary soil. Different members of the Committee mentioned sources of information upon this point.

Galls on Willow.—Professor Boulger, F.L.S., showed some galls upon Willow, similar to those shown last year by Mr. Chittenden, due to the attacks of a mite. The galls were this year very common around Loughton and Buckhurst Hill, in Essex, and formed large masses of short shoots with crowded, much shortened leaves.

Fasciated Lilium candidum.—Mr. Bowles showed on behalf of Mr. Hyde, of Enfield Highway, a fasciated stem of this Lily. The stem was about 3½ inches broad, and bore a very large number of small flowers.

Lueddemannia Pescatorei.—Mr. Bowles also exhibited a large spike of this remarkable species, which had already received a Botanical Certificate.

Chlorosis in Fruit Trees.—Specimens of Apples on the Paradise stock, Pears on the Quince, Peaches, Nectarines, Plums, Raspberries, and Vines were received from near Glastonbury, all with their leaves showing

3 F

yellow spots or being wholly yellow. A variety of causes may bring about this condition, such as lack of iron, lime, or· potash in the soil, and at times insufficient drainage, combined with lack of sun, &c., may produce similar results.

SCIENTIFIC COMMITTEE, AUGUST 6, 1907.

Mr. E. A. BOWLES, M.A., F.L.S., in the Chair, with six members present, and Mr. C. E. GROSVENOR, of Berkeley, California, U.S.A., visitor.

Chlorosis in Fruit Trees.—Mr. Spencer Pickering, F.R.S., wrote as follows regarding this subject, which was before the Committee at their last meeting :—" In one district where the trouble is very prevalent the soil contains as much as 10 per cent. of lime. Deficiency of lime, therefore, cannot be the cause of the disease."

"Yellow Stripe" in Narcissus.—Some bulbs of ' Sir Watkin.' Narcissus were received, the foliage and flowers having been affected with the well-known " yellow stripe." The cause of this disease is still obscure, but it appears to follow from too heavily manuring the soil in which the plants are grown. Mr. Bennett-Poë, V.M.H., and Mr. Douglas, V.M.H., stated that if the plants were cultivated in soil not manured for a time they would recover, but only after a considerable period, and the attempt to cure the plants was hardly worth while with the cheaper varieties.

Curious Growth on Broom.—Mr. Holmes, F.L.S., showed a branch of Broom which had been drooping downwards, and had sent out from its tip numerous thin shoots much crowded together and growing almost erect. The parent branch had become thickened just at the point at which the branches had been produced.

Crinum augustum.—A splendid inflorescence with foliage of this *Crinum* was shown by Sir Trevor Lawrence, Bart. The plant is figured in *Bot. Mag.* 1823, tab. 2397.

Plymouth Strawberry.—Mr. Chittenden showed, on behalf of Mr. R. Lindsay, a specimen of the ' Plymouth Strawberry ' from the gardens of Mr. Fraser, Comely Bank Nurseries, Edinburgh. This curious Strawberry, in which the carpels are replaced by small leafy growths, was first described by Tradescant, and is referred to in Johnson's edition of Gerarde's " Herbal"; it was figured by John Parkinson. Dr. Masters refers to it in " Vegetable Teratology " as "a kind of Botanical Dodo," as it was not heard of for about a century, but was afterwards discovered again at Bitton, in Canon Ellacombe's garden, and by Mr. G. F. Wilson at Wisley.

Peloric Antirrhinum. — Mr. Chittenden showed, also from Mr. Lindsay, a specimen of Antirrhinum with regular flowers, the peloric condition being complete in all the lower flowers of the spike, while some of the upper flowers were returning to the irregular condition. The peloric condition has now become fixed, but the form cannot be depended upon to come true from seed.

SCIENTIFIC COMMITTEE, AUGUST 20, 1907.

Mr. E. A. BOWLES, M.A., F.L.S., in the Chair, and six members
present.

Tomato Disease caused by Septoria Lycopersici.—Mr. Güssow
showed specimens of Tomato leaves from Gloucestershire having brown
spots. These quickly cover the whole leaf, which dies in the course of a
very few days after the infection commences. The disease does not seem
to have been recorded in this country hitherto, although it was found in
Argentina as long ago as 1881. There seems to be no remedy after the
plants are once attacked, since the progress of the trouble is so rapid,
but plants attacked should be burned immediately.

Neobenthamia gracilis, Rolfe.—A spike of this very pretty Orchid from
Zanzibar was shown by Mr. Bennett-Poë, V.M.H. It was awarded a
Botanical Certificate in 1900, and is described by Mr. Rolfe in the
Gardeners' Chronicle, 1891, ii. p. 272, and figured in *Bot. Mag.* 1900,
tab. 7221.

Aphides on Palm Roots.—Mr. Gordon, V.M.H., showed portions of
the root of *Kentia Forsteriana* upon which were large numbers of a
species of woolly aphis. The plant from which the specimen had been
taken did not appear to have suffered to any extent from the attacks
of the insects. They were referred to Mr. Saunders for further
examination.

Reappearance of a Peach Pest.—Dr. M. C. Cooke, V.M.H., showed
figures of a pest of Peaches which " the late Rev. M. J. Berkeley recorded
and figured in the *Gardeners' Chronicle* for 1864, p. 938. This mould
Berkeley discovered on ripe Peaches in Wales, where he found it to be a
pest producing a great profusion of large spores. He named the fungus
Macrosporium rhabdiferum; but as the spores were not muriform
it could not be *Macrosporium*. In the 'Handbook' I called it
Helminthosporium rhabdiferum, but now that I have seen it I find it
is not *Helminthosporium*. In the interim it appears not to have been
met with anywhere, until last week it turned up on Peaches again—after
everyone had given it up as a mystery, and it was excluded from all
consideration as a pest. There can be no doubt of its being Berkeley's
species; it agrees so well with the description and the figure. The
spores are so profuse that it would be dangerous as a pest were it to
obtain a foothold." (See p. 527.)

Plum Anthracnose.—Dr. Cooke also said: " Some Plums have
recently been submitted to me which were evidently suffering from the
attacks of a new pest. The surface of the nearly ripe fruit exhibited
one or two concave depressions, about a quarter of an inch in diameter,
and of a pale tan colour, contrasting strongly with the deep purple of
the fruit. These depressions were lined with the minute receptacles of
species of Anthracnose, as the Americans term this form of disease,
produced by species of the genus *Gloeosporium*. In this instance the
spores were abundant in the depressions, hyaline, but comparatively very
small for the genus, not more than 10 to 12 mm. long, and about
one-fourth as broad. Hitherto I have found no described species to

correspond with the present, so that for the purpose of identification I have called it *Gloeosporium prunorum*." Dr. Cooke showed sketches and specimens of this disease.

Ceropegia hybrida.—Mr. E. A. Bowles showed a flowering specimen of this hybrid, which was described and figured in the *Gardeners' Chronicle* for December 1906, p. 383. It was raised from seed of *C. Sandersoni*, which species had been crossed with pollen of *C. similis*. Mr. Bowles also showed a flower of *C. Sandersoni* for comparison.

Fruit of Pyrus Malus floribunda.—Dr. Bonavia sent some large fruits of this Japanese variety of Apple, which he had not before seen producing seed. Several members of the Committee remarked on the large size of the fruit produced by this variety this year.

Variation in Beech Foliage.—Mr. A. Hosking sent specimens of the foliage of the fern-leaved Beech (*Fagus sylvatica asplenifolia*), and branches from near the top of the same tree bearing leaves intermediate between the fern-leaved type and the normal type, which he sent for comparison. The specimens were from the garden of W. Fitzherbert-Brockholes, Esq., of Claughton Hall, Preston. Mr. Hosking had since noticed the same variation on a Beech in Avenham Park, Preston. The branches bearing the intermediate foliage were intermixed with the ordinary branches, and did not arise from the base of the tree. Mr. Hosking suggested that this was another case of graft hybridisation somewhat similar to that seen in *Cytisus Adami* and in *Crataego-Mespilus*.

Effect of Lightning on Elm.—Mr. C. H. Hooper sent specimens illustrating the effect of lightning on an Elm tree which had been struck during a storm on August 17. "The tree, which is about 100 yards from a tall church tower, was struck about 40 feet from the ground, and shows no damage till within 6 feet of the ground, where on one side the bark with the wood has been gouged out, and on the other side the bark only has been cut and stripped as if with a knife." The extent of the damage caused to trees in this manner seems to depend on the amount of water in the wood.

Effect of Light on Direction of Growth.—Mr. Sutton, through Mr. Bennett-Poë, called attention to a letter from Mr. J. B. Wallis in the *Times*, who described a curious growth in an Elder in a thicket near Wirksworth, Derbyshire. He writes : " So great was the tangle of brushwood that the branches of this tree had been forced to bend over and grow towards the ground, after the manner of the Weeping Willow. To grow normally the leaves would have appeared with their under sides uppermost, but to avoid this the stalk had grown spirally, making a complete revolution of the axis, thus bringing the leaf right way up, the whole presenting a peculiar appearance. Such is the power of sunlight and the faculty of adaptation to environment."

Twin Apples.—Mr. G. F. Hooper, of Croft Fruit Farm, Pershore, sent an excellent specimen of this not very uncommon phenomenon. In the present instance the two fruits were on quite distinct stalks, and the fruits had become coherent in the upper parts.

SCIENTIFIC COMMITTEE, SEPTEMBER 3, 1907.

Mr. E. A. BOWLES, M.A., F.L.S., in the Chair, and ten members present.

Mildew on Maple.—Mr. H. T. Güssow showed leaves of a species of *Acer* attacked by the conidial form of the fungus *Uncinula Aceris*, so frequent on *Acer campestre*.

Currant Leaves diseased.—Mr. Saunders, F.L.S., showed leaves of Currant attacked by the fungus *Gloeosporium Ribis*, which Mr. Gussow stated had recently been found to be a stage in the life-history of the fungus *Pseudopeziza Ribis*.

Propagation of Potato Diseases.— Mr. Cuthbertson showed the produce of two tubers of Potato which had been sent to the Committee last year attacked by the fungus causing "winter-rot." Both tubers had grown normally, and had produced a fair crop. He proposed to keep these tubers through the winter in order to discover whether or not the disease would appear in them. Mr. Sutton observed that in certain experiments carried out by him at Reading this year it was found that tubers of Potato attacked by the fungus *Phytophthora infestans*, and employed as sets, yielded about 70 per cent. of normal plants free from disease.

Mendelian Laws of Inheritance.—Mr. Worsley brought up this question with reference to the colours of certain Bean flowers which he exhibited, and the need for further extended careful experiment was insisted upon.

Fig Leaves diseased.—Mr. Bowles showed Fig leaves much disfigured by irregular brown and yellow-brown patches of variable size. The appearance is due to the attacks of a fungus, *Cercospora Bolleana*, which develops its fructification on the dead leaves, and hibernates in the stem of the plant, so that it is carried over from one year to the next.

Malformation of Myosotis.—Mr. Bowles also exhibited a specimen of *Myosotis palustris*, which he had collected in Suffolk, near Ipswich, having the calyx lobes much enlarged and the spike somewhat lengthened. Each inflorescence on the plant had exhibited the same structure.

Mint-rust.—Plants of Peppermint from near Dorking were sent badly attacked by the Mint-rust, or "snuff," as the trouble is locally called. The small reddish spots which occur on the leaves in abundance at this season of the year are the uredo form of the fungus *Puccinia Menthae*, and the mycelium of the fungus hibernates in the underground portions of the plant, so that no cure can be suggested. If external conditions are favourable, the disease is sure to make itself evident in the succeeding year.

Galls on Walnut Leaf.—Mr. W. C. Worsdell, F.L.S., sent from Westmorland leaves of *Juglans regia* having rather large swellings on the upper surface of the leaf, with corresponding hollows on the lower surface. These malformations, which are frequent on Walnut leaves, are due to the attack on the leaf of a mite, *Eriophyes tristratus* var. *erinea*.

Gooseberry-mildew.—Dr. C. B. Plowright sent shoots of Gooseberry badly attacked by the mildew *Microsphaera Grossulariae,* the well-known European " Gooseberry-mildew," with the following note : " These shoots were gathered from a garden which a friend of mine planted some years ago with fruit trees and Gooseberry bushes. The latter became affected with a mildew so badly that they had to be destroyed because they bore no fruit ; and if by any chance they did so it never ripened. When the American fungus appeared in this county (Norfolk) one naturally suspected it had been the cause. It so happened that a score or two bushes had been left in the garden ; for although they never ripened fruit, yet they bore a sufficient quantity to pay for gathering whilst still green. On specimens of the bushes examined during last winter no traces of the winter state of *Sphaerotheca mors uvae* were to be found, nor is it present now. The moral is : Do not despise old enemies. Here is an instance in which hundreds of young bushes in the fruit-bearing stage were destroyed because they were affected by a fungus with which I was acquainted as a boy. One is inclined to ask, Would it not have paid to have sprayed them ? "

Change of Colour in Germinating Acorns.—Dr. Plowright also sent specimens illustrating the following observations : " The colour which germinating Acorns often assume is frequently considerable. The specimens sent herewith were gathered near King's Lynn in the spring of the present year. A deep reddish tint more than usually distinct was the cause of their being examined more carefully, when it was seen that not only was the external surface coloured red, but that in some places distinct yellow and greenish shades were observable. The coloration is external, and is possibly due to some form of oxidisation." The coloration referred to was still very distinct, showing that it is persistent for many months.

British Dye-plants.—Dr. Plowright also sent skeins of worsted dyed with British wild plants : (1) Bore a delicate shade of light green produced from the young flower-heads of *Phragmites communis,* the common Reed, mordanted with alum. Previous experiments with other flower-heads gave a much darker colour. (2) Was of a dark green colour (olive), the result of treatment with iron sulphate following the treatment of No. 1. (3) *Bidens tripartita* is not mentioned by Linnæus as a dye-plant, but it gives a yellow more approaching orange than that given by other British dye-plants. (4) *Chrysanthemum segetum* gives a yellow more like that of other dye-plants, but it is not noted by Linnæus as a fast colour.

Malformed Inflorescence.—An interesting specimen of *Sempervivum spinulosum* came from the Hon. Walter Rothschild, in which the inflorescence bore only a few flowers, and was crowned by a rosette of foliage leaves quite like the rosettes at the base of the plant. The lower leaves of the rosette bore flower-buds in their axils.

SCIENTIFIC COMMITTEE, SEPTEMBER 17, 1907.

Mr. J. T. BENNETT-POË, M.A., V.M.H., in the Chair, and eight members present.

Runner Bean Flower-colour.—Mr. Cuthbertson wrote, concerning the Runner Beans similar in flower-colour to those of the 'Butterfly' Bean shown by Mr. Worsley at the last meeting, that Herr Benary, the introducer of that Bean, informed him that it was found as a sport among 'Painted Lady' Runners some five or six years ago, and by careful selection it was fixed. Herr Benary had never made any crossings between red and white Runner Beans, and could not, therefore, say what the result of such crossing would be likely to be.

Hybrid between Pear and Quince.—Mr. H. J. Veitch, V.M.H., showed fruit and foliage from two trees raised from seed, the result of a cross made by Mr. Seden, in 1895, between the Pear 'Bergamotte Esperen' ♀ and the Portugal Quince ♂. The seeds were both obtained from one fruit, and it was seen that, whilst one of the seedlings was very similar to the Pear, the other much more resembled the Quince. The fruits were immature, so that the flavour could not be tested. Mr. Veitch, however, promised to send further specimens if they should ripen (see p. clxxi).

Double Aster.—Mr. Veitch also showed flowers of a double Aster sp. (Michaelmas Daisy).

Leaf Diseases.—Mr. A. O. Walker showed leaves of *Clerodendron trichotomum* with brown spots, and remarked upon the prevalence of leaf diseases during the past season, with particular reference to the death of Black Currant leaves. This, the Committee thought, was probably due to the fungus *Gloeosporium Ribis*, which had been particularly prevalent during the past season. Mr. Walker said that he had found young trees free from the disease, while older trees were badly affected.

Potato Disease.—Mr. Güssow showed specimens of tubers of Potato badly attacked by a disease having something of the appearance of a bad attack of "scab." He found, however, that the appearance was not associated with any of the fungi which had been previously observed in Holland and in Ireland. The present specimens came from Lincoln. The scabby spots have an olive-green tint when the spores are still attached to the rind of the Potato, but the spores frequently become detached and are left in the soil. The organism appears to be unable to grow in any but an acid medium.

Red-fleshed Pear.—Mr. E. Burrell, of Claremont Gardens, Esher, sent Pears having the flesh of a deep red colour, with the following note: "A Pear I take to be 'Sanguinole,' with several synonyms, among which is Parkinson's 'Blood-red Pear,' a variety said to have been grown in France over 350 years ago. The tree from which the specimens exhibited were taken is a standard, between 15 feet and 20 feet in height, growing in a garden at Claygate, Surrey. The tree has the appearance of having been twice 'worked.' The Pear is naturally of no value in these days, but is of interest on account of its rarity."

Carrot malformed.—Mr. E. Stone sent from Hayes, Kent, a curiously malformed Carrot, which had a mass of ten roots, of somewhat small size, springing from the base of the crown, but joined together at that end for a short distance. One of the thickest roots appeared to have been injured or checked in growth in its early stages, and this had perhaps induced the curious formation.

Dark-red-fleshed Peach.—Mr. W. A. Carey sent a Peach gathered from a tree raised from seed by himself, the stone having come from one of the varieties (name unknown) commonly grown outdoors. Mr. Carey stated that, when ripe, the fruit was of very good flavour, but differed from other commonly grown Peaches in the remarkable colour, which was black until a few days before the fruit was ripe, when it gradually became lighter, till it was a deep red colour. The fruit agreed well in its characters with that described in French works under the name 'Sanguinole,' and known in this country as 'Blood Peach,' and it is curious that the variety (or something very nearly approaching it) should have been raised from the stone of an ordinary Peach.

SCIENTIFIC COMMITTEE, OCTOBER 1, 1907.

Mr. E. A. BOWLES, M.A., F.L.S., in the Chair, and fifteen members present.

Diseased Plants.—Mr. Güssow reported on diseased Sweet Peas. He said they were attacked by a fungus, but there was no fruit present, so the fungus could not be determined. He also reported that the leaves of *Clerodendron trichotomum* had been attacked by *Botrytis cinerea*, and the Blackberry leaves by *Phyllosticta Rubi*.

Uncommon Fungi.—Mr. Odell showed specimens of *Mutinus caninus*, a fungus belonging to the *Phalloideae*, appearing somewhat erratically. The specimens were collected in Middlesex. Mr. Saunders, F.L.S., showed a specimen of *Tuber aestivum*, one of the truffles.

Bulbils on Stem of Lilium candidum.—Mr. Saunders also showed one of two similar plants of *Lilium candidum* grown in a garden at Tunbridge Wells. One of the plants had been growing in rather a damp border, and had not been moved for a long time; the other was in a very dry position, and was moved two years ago. One plant bore three, the other four spikes, each beset with small bulbils in every leaf axil. The foliage was similar to that of other plants of *L. candidum* growing near by. It was suggested that possibly injury to the apex of the stem had caused the formation of these bulbils.

'Wheat-ear' Dianthus.—Mr. Bowles showed, from the Rev. Canon Ellacombe's garden, an inflorescence of a *Dianthus* raised from seed gathered from *Dianthus superbus*, but the plant was evidently a hybrid, being very dissimilar from that species. No normal flowers had been produced, but the bracts had been repeated again and again in the manner seen in the 'Wheat-ear' Carnation, and at times also in the Sweet William.'

Calycanthus Fruits.—Mr. Chittenden showed fruits of *Calycanthus laevigatus* from the R.H.S. Gardens, Wisley.

Bud on Cotyledon.—Mr. Chittenden also showed a seedling of *Bryophyllum* sp. having a small shoot bearing two leaves growing from the petiole of the cotyledons, and another in the notch of the apex of the same cotyledon, being produced in much the same way as buds are in the angles of the crenations of the ordinary leaves.

SCIENTIFIC COMMITTEE, OCTOBER 15, 1907.

Mr. E. A. BOWLES, M.A., F.L.S., in the Chair, with twelve members present and numerous visitors.

The Up-country Tea-root Disease of Ceylon.—Dr. C. B. Plowright sent specimens of bark and roots of tea plants, illustrating the following note: "Mr. T. Petch, the Government mycologist of Ceylon, sends specimens of this disease. It is due to *Polyporus hypolateritia* of Berkeley, a species which is now allocated to the genus *Poria*. It is most prevalent above 4,000 feet, and is easily distinguished from the disease caused by *Rosellinia*. If a dying bush be uprooted, the roots are seen to be covered with small white raised patches or knobs of mycelium about one-twelfth of an inch in diameter with reddish raised margins. From these nodules a mycelium spreads to other roots, white at first, but subsequently forming a thick cord with a tough red coat, while the mycelium between the bark and the wood forms a thin continuous white sheet. The fructification (the *Poria*) is generally formed on the stem just above the ground, but it may be formed on the surface of the soil. In one experimental culture it was produced on the under side of a flower-pot, an illustration of the travelling power of the fungus. The fungus is white with a red edge and under-surface; hence the specific name which was given by Berkeley to specimens from India. Its life-history as a parasite has been worked out by Mr. Petch."

Hybrid Orchids.—Mr. F. W. Moore, V.M.H., made some interesting remarks upon two hybrid Orchids sent by Mr. H. J. Chapman. The first was the result of intercrossing the two albinos *Cattleya intermedia alba* and *C. Schröderae alba*. The flowers of the cross had the three sepals and two of the petals with a rosy tinge, while the lip was at the edges of the basal portion a little deeper in colour, and had the terminal portion magenta with a stripe of the same colour running towards the throat, the only portion of the flower that was pure white being the inner part of the throat on each side of this stripe. The colour, therefore, showed reversion to the typical form; the shape, however, of the flowers showed traces of both parents.. The second flower was the result of a cross between the so-called albino forms, *Cypripedium insigne Sanderae* and *C. callosum Sanderae*. This, like the first, showed distinct traces of the coloration of the typical forms of both parent species, thus again reverting. These two specimens seem to illustrate in another group of plants that phenomenon which has been pointed out by the Mendelian workers with Sweet Peas, where the colour-producing factors that were present separately in the two parents, so that they were albinos, meet in the offspring and produce colour. As Mr. Moore pointed out, not all albino Orchids when crossed produced coloured flowers, but albinos may be produced. The Orchids were from the collection of N. C. Cookson, Esq., of Oakwood, Wylam-on-Tyne.

Injury to Apple Twigs.—Mr. F. J. Baker, A.R.C.Sc., showed some Apple twigs that had been injured by too tightly binding the shoots together. The shoots had been washed in May with a somewhat strong solution of paraffin, and the result had been that the injuries to the stems appeared very like cankered spots. The wounds were now beginning to callus over.

Cup-shaped Leaves of Pelargonium.—Mr. W. C. Worsdell, F.L.S., showed some leaves of *Pelargonium zonale* from Kew which had grown in a cup-shaped manner. Each of these was terminal, a fact that accounted for the form. One of the cup-like leaves bore a second springing from its outer surface. These leaves probably took the place of the flowering shoots, which would have been developed in the same position in a normal season.

Summer Pruning of Fruit Trees.—A discussion upon this subject took place (see page 487).

SCIENTIFIC COMMITTEE, OCTOBER 29, 1907.

Mr. E. A. BOWLES, M.A., F.L.S., in the Chair, and ten members present.

Cup-shaped Leaves of Saxifraga.—Mr. W. C. Worsdell, F.L.S., showed leaves of *Saxifraga ligulata* which had grown in a cup-shaped manner, so that the leaf had the appearance of an inverted cone on the top of the leafstalk. The plant on which they had been produced each year formed similar leaves in October and November, but not in the early part of the year. Not all the leaves were so far developed as to assume the cup-shape completely, but all stages from the normal to this form were to be found. Mr. Worsdell suggested that the cause of the malformation might have been the lack of vigour in the plants.

Malformed Cattleya.—Mr. Bennett-Poë, V.M.H., showed two flowers of *Cattleya labiata*, each of which had but two petals and two sepals, the labellum in each case being completely suppressed as well as one of the sepals. Mr. Worsdell took the flowers for further examination.

Calycanthus Fruits.—Mr. Bowles showed fruits of *Calycanthus occidentalis* from his garden for comparison with those of *C. laevigatus* shown at the meeting on October 1 (p. clxviii).

Marrow Cabbage.—Messrs. Cooper, Taber & Co. sent specimens of the Marrow Cabbage (' Chou Mcëllier ') grown at Witham, Essex. The Cabbages were about 5 feet in height, the stem being between 4 inches and 5 inches in diameter in the middle. The central part of the stem is filled with soft tissue, and forms the chief edible portion of the plant. The Cabbage is grown largely in France, where it is pulped and used for cattle food in districts where Swedes and Turnips will not grow. It is an exceedingly interesting example of a variation of the Cabbage, where the reserve food is stored in an elongated, thickened stem instead of in a barrel-shaped stem, as in Kohl Rabi.

Kale with Leaflike Growth from Midrib.—W. J. Maitland, Esq., of Witley, sent leaves of a purple Kale having leaflike outgrowths from the midrib. This kind of hypertrophy is common in Kales, and has become fixed, so that such forms come true from seed.

Hybrid Pear and Quince.—Messrs. James Veitch & Sons sent further specimens of the hybrid fruits borne on the two plants raised from seeds from a single fruit of the Pear 'Bergamotte Esperen,' the result of crossing that Pear with the Portugal Quince. Immature fruits were shown at the meeting of September 3, and, as was then observed, the fruits of one tree approached the Pear in character, those of the other the Quince. The Pear-like hybrid, for which Messrs. Veitch propose the name × *Pyronia* 'John Seden' was practically ripe, and had a distinct Bergamotte flavour. 'Bergamotte Esperen' ripens much later. The Quince-like fruits were still quite hard.

Crocus.—Mr. Bowles showed specimens of a Crocus which he believes to be a hybrid between *Crocus speciosus* and *C. pulchellus*. In 1904, and each season since, he has found a corm or two among seedlings of *C. speciosus* from seeds saved from plants growing near *C. pulchellus* that show characters intermediate between these two species, and which may be tabulated as follows :—

	C. speciosus.	C. pulchellus.	Supposed hybrid.
Throat	White	Orange	Yellow shading to white
Anther	Orange	White	Cream colour
Filament	White	Orange	Yellow
	Glabrous	Pubescent	With scattered hairs
Corm tunic	Membranous	Coriaceous	A thick stiff membrane

Iu colour the perianth segments are somewhat variable, and most nearly resemble *C. speciosus*, but are paler and less distinctly veined, except on the inner surface of the inner segments, where the characteristic purple veins of *C. pulchellus* are clearly defined.

SCIENTIFIC COMMITTEE, NOVEMBER 12, 1907.

Mr. J. T. BENNETT-POË, V.M.H., in the Chair, and nine members present.

Malformed Orchids.—Mr. W. C. Worsdell, F.L.S., said that the flowers shown at the last meeting showed only two sepals and two petals, the lip being entirely absent; he also showed specimens of *Cattleya Loddigesii* (?) with double lips, and a *Cypripedium* with the same malformation. The last two specimens came from Gurney Wilson, Esq., Glenthorne, Haywards Heath.

"*Low Country*" *Tea-root Disease of Ceylon.*—Dr. C. B. Plowright sent specimens illustrating this disease, which Mr. T. Petch attributes to an undescribed species of *Ustulina*. "The fructification occurs in two forms, conidial and ascigerous. The former consists of flattened, rounded, disc-like growths upon the lower part of the stems, which are covered with a copious growth of greyish conidia. The ascospores follow in due course upon these plate-like growths, and can easily be recognised by their minute black concentric openings. The mycelium is white or yellowish, but becomes black when it comes to the surface in a crack in the bark of the root and forms irregular black lines in the wood."

The specimen sent showed the disease in its typical state. There was also a specimen of an unusually well-developed ascophore. " This disease resembles very closely in many ways *Ustulina vulgaris* Tul., which grows in our own country, and this, in the light of Mr. Petch's specimen, is doubtless also a pyrenomycetous parasite upon Beech trees." Specimens both in the conidial and ascigerous conditions, gathered this autumn near Narford Hall, King's Lynn, accompanied the notes. " It has hitherto been regarded as a saprophyte, but we must now regard it rather as a parasite on this tree." Mr. Petch says of this disease : " In low-country districts nearly all root disease in Tea appears to be caused by this species of *Ustulina*. The indications on the dying root are not so clear as those of *Poria* or *Rosellinia*, but there is no difficulty in finding them once they have been pointed out. The roots show small black nodules or warts, which probably give rise to underground mycelium, though this has not been clearly established. The mycelium between the wood and the bark spreads in white or yellowish fan-shaped patches, which acquire a black edge when they meet a crack in the bark. Irregular black lines are seen in a cross-section of the root. The fructification appears on the lower part of the stem, emerging through a crack in the bark in the form of a white swollen cushion. This spreads over the surface as a more or less flattened white plate, which finally becomes grey and concentrically zoned. When quite ripe it is a grey, concentrically zoned plate marked with minute black dots ; it lies close to the surface of the stem, but is only attached at one point. The under surface is black, and the whole surface hard and brittle. Two kinds of spores are produced : the first are borne on the outer surface, when the fungus is wholly white ; the second are produced when the fungus is ripe, in minute chambers, whose openings are the black points previously mentioned. On Tea bushes in the field the fructification often takes a different shape, springing from a very thin base to a height of about half an inch and widening out to a flat, circular top. In one instance this disease began on *Grevillea* stumps, and spread to the adjoining Tea by contact."

Hybrid Pear and Quince.—Mr. Worsley wrote that he had examined two of the fruits of the hybrid between ' Bergamotte Esperen ' ♀ and the Portuguese Quince ♂ ; in the small fruits he had found no perfect seeds, but merely husks. " The skin was smoother than in the female parent, and not so notably spotted with dark brown spots. The colour of the flesh was greenish, and both in this and in the amount of grit it resembled the female parent. The time of ripening was synchronous with that of the Quince, and more than three months earlier than that of the ' Bergamotte Esperen.' The flesh was sweet and exceedingly aromatic, in both of which respects it excelled the female parent and in the former the male. I could discern no trace of either the acidity, roughness, or special flavour of the Quince. . . . The quality of this hybrid entitles it to be placed in the highest rank of dessert fruits if sizable fruits can be obtained after grafting. It is interesting to note that the Pear I have under the name of ' Conseiller de la Cour ' is ripe at the end of October, that the fruits vary greatly in size and shape, that fertile seeds are rarely if ever borne, that the flesh is yellow and in flavour very close to Mr. Veitch's example. It is at least possible that these characters attach to Pears crossed with Quince pollen.''

Fungus beneath Beech Bark.—Mr. Druery, V.M.H., showed specimens of fungus mycelium taken from beneath the bark of a Beech, and these, with diseased fronds of *Todea*, were referred to Mr. Massee for further investigation.

Wheat-ear Carnation, &c.—From Messrs. J. Peed, of Streatham, came specimens of the Wheat-ear Carnation, and of fasciated and contorted stems of Broom.

SCIENTIFIC COMMITTEE, NOVEMBER 27, 1907.

Mr. E. A. BOWLES, M.A., F.L.S., in the Chair, with ten members present, and Mr. GURNEY WILSON, visitor.

Hybrid Orchids.—Mr. Chapman showed the result of a cross between *Cypripedium insigne Sanderae* and *C. callosum Sanderae* having coloured flowers. Over one hundred plants of this cross had flowered, and each of them had borne coloured flowers, although the parents were albinos. The cross had been effected both ways with the same result. The two albinos breed true from seed. The flower of the particular specimen exhibited was coloured much in the same way as those of the type forms of the species, and bore great resemblance to *C. Leoniae* (*C. insigne* × *C. callosum*). He also showed a plant with a coloured flower, the result of crossing the albino forms *C. callosum Sanderae* and *C. bellatulum album*; about twenty-five plants of this cross had flowered, and all had borne coloured flowers. A third plant bore a great resemblance to *C. insigne Sanderae*, and had been raised by crossing that form with *C. Leeanum giganteum* (= *C. insigne* × *C. Spicerianum*); of the offspring of this cross some reverted to the *insigne* type, but one was much lighter and was crossed again with *C. insigne Sanderae*, giving *C.* × *San-Actaeus*. This was again crossed with *C. insigne Sanderae*, and the plant under notice was the result. The continued crosses had almost brought back the original *C. insigne Sanderae*. This form had in its composition, said Mr. Chapman, 14–16 *C. insigne Sanderae*, 1–16 normal *C. insigne*, and 1–16 *C. Spicerianum*.

Orchids and Fungi.—Mr. Gurney Wilson referred to the theory brought forward by Professor Noel Bernard concerning symbiosis between the Orchids and certain fungi (see Genetic Conference Report, p. 392). He, working in conjunction with Dr. Fulton, had not been able to verify the observations Professor Noel Bernard had made. He had recently placed a large number of imported *Odontoglossum crispum* in contact with some Oak leaves which had been thoroughly dried for some months; a fungus had certainly developed upon them, but it had turned out to be the common Mushroom, and the mycelium had undoubtedly been on the Oak leaves.

Saxifraga Cotyledon.—Mr. Saunders, F.L.S., showed from Mr. A. O. Walker, F.R.H.S., a specimen of this plant in which the flowers had been replaced by terminal rosettes of foliage leaves, somewhat similar to the plant sent some time since by Mr. Jenkins.

Ergot on Ryegrass.—Mr. Baker drew attention to the remarkably frequent occurrence of this fungus in this and the past few years, in North Kent, on Ryegrass and some other wild Grasses. Mr. Odell said that close feeding, and the cleaning of ditches and headlands, was the best means of eradicating the fungus.

Malformed Orchids.—Mr. Odell showed a specimen of the Orchid *Selenipedium × calurum*, in which the lateral petals were completely suppressed, while the dorsal sepal was much reduced and malformed. A similar condition is frequently seen in *S. × Sedeni*.

Chrysanthemum indicum Hybrids.— Mr. Smith, of Weybridge, exhibited flowers of·hybrids between *C. indicum* and cultivated forms. These were retained for further examination.

Diseased Fern.—Mr. Massee, V.M.H., reported that he found abundance of mycelium on the brown spots on the *Todea* leaves, but no fruit ; the fungus was therefore indeterminable. The rhizomorphs from Beech shown at the last meeting were those of *Armillaria mellea.*

SCIENTIFIC COMMITTEE, DECEMBER 10, 1907.

Mr. E. A. BOWLES, M.A., F.L.S., in the Chair, and thirteen members present.

Grubs in Gooseberry Stem.—Mr. G. S. Saunders, F.L.S., reported that he had examined the Gooseberry stem shown by Mr. Odell, and had found it to be attacked by a number of small red grubs, which were hidden under the loose outer bark near the bud. They evidently feed on the cells immediately under the bark. They belong to the *Diptera*, and probably to the family *Cecidomyidae*. They are very small, being scarcely one-tenth of an inch in length. Mr. Saunders suggested that as the insect probably pupates under the bark, some shoots should be inclosed in muslin sleeves so that later the fly might be identified.

Chrysanthemum indicum Varieties and Crosses.—Mr. Chittenden reported that he had examined the Chrysanthemums shown by Mr. Smith at the last meeting. They were divisible into two sets. In the first the result of sowing seed from *C. indicum* which had been pollinated with pollen from a rose-coloured variety : all the plants bore yellow flowers, but there was considerable variation in the depth of colour, the length and breadth of the corollas, the arrangement of the flowers, and the hardiness of the foliage. It is, however, scarcely safe to argue from this instance that the colour of *C. indicum* is dominant over rose, in view of the facts that (1) considerable variation from seed is probable in *C. indicum* ; (2) there is difficulty in ensuring the pollination of the flowers of Chrysanthemums (as of most other composites) with foreign pollen to the exclusion of pollen from the same flower or neighbouring flowers in the head ; and (3) the absence of any precautions to prevent insect pollination. The second . series, *C. indicum*, crossed with an almost magenta flower, showed considerable variation in colour from almost white to deep rose, as well as in form, &c. Altogether it would appear that Chrysanthemums were unsuitable flowers with which to attempt the elucidation of any laws regarding hybridisation. Mr. Worsley had also examined the flowers, and had arrived at similar conclusions.

Californian Galls.—Mr. C. O. Waterhouse, of the British Museum, reported upon some large Californian galls which had been sent for identification, and said that they were formed by a species of *Cynips*, which could nòt, however, be named. The galls were similar to the English Oak marble galls, but much larger, measuring, indeed, fully 2 inches in diameter. They were of a pale brown colour, and, unlike the Oak marble gall, contained, originally, more than one grub. The perfect insects had, however, emerged.

Quince with Fungus.—Mr. Güssow reported that he found no fungus on the Quinces shown by Mr. Worsley, but *Botrytis cinerea*, which had evidently followed the ripening of the fruit.

Grub in Crassula falcata.—Mr. Druery, V.M.H., showed a stem of *Crassula falcata* containing the larva of the " Garden Swift Moth " (*Hepialus lupulinus*), which had burrowed up into the stem, a most unusual place for the larva of this insect to feed, as it is usually found feeding underground.

Temperature Variations.—Mr. Curtis showed several sets of thermograph records, showing the enormous variation found in the temperatures taken at different levels above the surface of the ground, and illustrating the erroneous notions as to the temperatures to which vegetation is exposed through radiation; gathered by merely taking the records in an ordinary screen.

Seedless Apple.—Mr. Worsdell, F.L.S., showed a photograph of a seedless Apple which had five very small Apples growing out at the "eye" end. He suggested that the seedlessness was possibly brought about by the energies of growth being diverted from the seeds to the formation of these small growths.

" Sport " in a Fungus.—Mr. Worsdell also showed a specimen of a species of *Tubaria* in which the gills were developed upon both surfaces of the pileus instead of upon the lower surface only.

Brassica Crosses.—Mr. A. W. Sutton, V.M.H., showed crosses between a Savoy and Brussels Sprout, and between a Cabbage and Brussels Sprout, each of which bore a good heart and a large number of small hearts up the stem, somewhat after the manner of a Brussels Sprout. The condition, said Mr. Sutton, was now fixed.

Summer Pruning.—Mr. C. Wakely, of Chelmsford, Essex, communicated the results of a series of experiments in summer pruning (see p. 497).

Fruits of Akebia lobata.—Miss Ethel Webb sent fruits of this plant from Newstead, Notts, where it fruits freely every year. The plant is on a south wall, and has reached a height of about 14 feet. The fruits are freely disposed about the plant in groups of two to four, and, though now past their best, form with the foliage a very ornamental feature. Birds do not touch the fruit until frost has split the skin and exposed the contents, when they devour the black seeds embedded in the white, jelly-like pulp. Bluebottles are also partial to the fruit. The skin has a bitter flavour, which doubtless protects the fruit from birds and insects until it is split by the frost.

High-frequency Currents and Plant Life.—Mr. C. E. Shea gave an interesting and suggestive account of the action of high-frequency electrical currents upon various forms of life, dealing especially with their action upon Phylloxera. He considered that, while a short time ago the destruction of minute organisms by means of the electrical current was within the realms of possibility, it had now become extremely probable that in the near future the application of high-frequency currents would prove a useful method of destroying many pests which were only with difficulty able to be dealt with at present.

SCIENTIFIC COMMITTEE, DECEMBER 31, 1907.

Mr. E. A. BOWLES, M.A., F.L.S., in the Chair, and four members present.

Cankered (?) *Rose Roots.*—A report was received from Mr. Güssow concerning the Rose roots shown by Mr. Jenkins, as follows:—" I find the trouble with the Rose roots is not canker, and cannot be transferred from one plant to another. It is generally accepted that canker is caused (*a*) by frost; (*b*) by fungus; (*c*) by any other mechanical injury which fungi have infested. In the present case there is no fungus present, and if the root in the attacked plant (when repotting) is cut away, no injury will be done to the plant. The growth is nothing but a continuous formation of adventitious roots, especially where the root is bent or injured. New callus is formed, and from that callus rootlets are everywhere sent out; but as the plant depends on the root system of the Manetti, no use is made of these roots, and they develop but little."

Grease Bands and Winter Moth.—Messrs. W. Voss, of Millwall, showed specimens of grease bands taken from trees on Mr. Michell's fruit farm, Enfield Highway, covered with both male and female specimens of winter moth (*Cheimatobia brumata*). The bands had been placed on the trees in the middle of November, and no other insects but these had been caught, with the exception of two or three weevils. The Chairman remarked that the time of appearance of wingless moths varied greatly with the seasons, some being found as early as the beginning of October. Grease banding to be thoroughly efficient should be commenced then, and the bands should be kept sticky until near the end of March in order to capture other species of a similar nature.

Seed and Soil Inoculation.—Mr. Chittenden gave some account of his experiments with seed and soil inoculation of leguminous crops.

Double Anemone blanda.—Rev. Canon Ellacombe sent buds of this beautiful form, which has occurred in his garden, remarking that it is the first Anemone to show buds this season.

FLORAL COMMITTEE.

JULY 9, 1907, AT HOLLAND HOUSE.

Mr. MAY in the Chair, and twenty-five members present.

[A list of the Cups and Medals awarded by the Council will be found at p. cxxix.]

Awards Recommended :—

First-class Certificate.

To *Crinum Mearsii* (votes, unanimous), from Col. Beddome, West Hill, Putney. A new and beautiful species from Upper Burma. Plant very dwarf, not more than one foot high ; leaves narrow, channelled, pointed, about one foot long, and of a glaucous green. Flower stems about six inches long, each carrying six pure white flowers. A floriferous and lovely plant.

Award of Merit.

To *Crinum* × ' H. J. Elwes ' (votes, unanimous), from H. J. Elwes, Esq., Colesborne, Cheltenham. Raised from *C. americanum* ♂ × *C. Moorei* ♀. A remarkably fine spike without foliage was exhibited. The spike bore fourteen flowers and buds. The expanded flowers were of moderate size, sweet-scented, and of a lovely shade of deep rose. Not quite hardy.

To Delphinium ' Alake ' (votes, 14 for, 1 against), from Messrs. Clark, Dover. Flowers semi-double, deep violet, suffused with bronze, and of large size.

To Delphinium ' Rev. E. Lascelles ' (votes, unanimous), from Messrs. Walters, Bath. A bold, distinct variety, with large double blue flowers, having a prominent, clear white eye. (Fig. 98.)

To *Hedera dentata variegata* (votes, unanimous), from Mr. L. R. Russell, Richmond. A valuable much-variegated form of the well-known strong-growing *H. dentata*. This should prove one of the best of all the variegated Ivies.

To Rose ' Goldfinch ' (votes, unanimous), from Messrs. Paul, Cheshunt. A lovely Rambler variety, with large clusters of soft yellow blooms. It is evidently a free bloomer and good grower, and should be a useful addition to this beautiful class.

To Rose ' Joseph Lowe ' (votes, unanimous), from Messrs. Lowe & Shawyer, Uxbridge. A magnificent Hybrid Tea variety that sported from ' Mrs. W. J. Grant.' The flower is of moderate size, perfect form, fragrant, and of a rich rosy pink colour.

To Rose ' Lady Helen Vincent ' (votes, unanimous), from Messrs. Dickson, Newtownards. A wonderfully beautiful Hybrid Tea variety, with rather large perfectly formed flowers of a charming shade of salmon, slightly tinged with rose, and sweetly scented.

To Rose 'Mrs. Harold Brocklebank' (votes, 12 for, 3 against), from Messrs. Dickson, Newtownards. Another handsome Hybrid Tea variety, of a creamy white colour, of good size and shape, delicate scent, and moderate size.

Fig. 98.—Delphinium 'Rev. E. Lascelles.'

To Rose 'Mrs. Munt' (votes, unanimous), from Messrs. Dickson, Newtownards. A remarkably fine Hybrid Tea variety, with large, handsome, well-formed flowers of a creamy-white colour, with petals of much substance, inclined to reflex. Fragrant.

To Rose 'Souvenir of Stella Gray' (votes, **11** for, **2** against), from Messrs. Dickson, Newtownards. Flowers of medium size, good shape, and a pale yellow colour shading to a bronzy tint ; sweet-scented. Hybrid Tea.

To Sweet Pea 'Elsie Herbert' (votes, **7** for, **3** against), from Mr. C. W. Breadmore, Winchester. A pretty white variety suffused with pinkish-red.

To Sweet Pea 'Princess Victoria' (votes, **12** for, **2** against), from Messrs. Dobbie, Rothesay. A very fine soft pink variety.

To Sweet Pea 'St. George' (votes, **10** for, **4** against), from Messrs. Hurst, Houndsditch. A handsome bold flower of a rosy-carmine colour.

Other Exhibits.

Messrs. Charlton, Tunbridge Wells : *Alyssum* and Begonias.

Mr. A. Young, Elgin : Pelargonium ' Queen Alexandra.'

Claydon Nursery Co., Bucks : *Bothriocline longipes.*

A. C. de Lafontaine, Esq., Dorchester : Delphiniums.

Messrs. Bunting, New Oxford Street, W.C. : Sweet Peas.

G. Ferguson, Esq., Weybridge : a new *Mimulus*, named *M. cupreus aurantiacus*, raised from *M. cupreus luteus* × *M. cupreus* 'Brilliant.'

FLORAL COMMITTEE, JULY 23, 1907.

Mr. MAY in the Chair, and twenty-two members present.

Awards Recommended :—

Gold Medal.

To Mr. A. Perry, Enfield, for aquatic and hardy flowers.

Silver-gilt Flora Medal.

To Lord Aldenham, Elstree (gr. Mr. E. Beckett, V.M.H.), for cut shrubs and *Streptocarpus.*

To Messrs. Cutbush, Highgate, for Carnations.

Silver-gilt Banksian Medal.

To Mr. A. F. Dutton, Iver, for Carnations.

Silver Flora Medal.

To Mr. J. Douglas, V.M.H., Great Bookham, for Carnations.

To the Dowager Lady Hillingdon, Wildernesse, Sevenoaks (gr. Mr. Shelton), for Malmaison Carnations.

To Mr. H. B. May, Edmonton, for flowering plants.

To Mr. S. Mortimer, Farnham, for Carnations.

To Messrs. W. Paul, Waltham Cross, for Roses.

To Mr. M. Prichard, Christchurch, for hardy flowers.

To Messrs. Ware, Feltham, for hardy flowers.

Silver Banksian Medal.

To Miss Alexander, Seal, Sevenoaks (gr. Mr. Tubb), for Sweet Peas.

To Messrs. Bide, Farnham, for Roses.

To Messrs. Bunyard, Maidstone, for hardy flowers.

To Mr. J. Forbes, Hawick, for Delphiniums.

To Messrs. Gunn, Birmingham, for Phlox.

To Messrs. Ladham, Southampton, for Gaillardias.

To Mr. G. Reuthe, Keston, Kent, for Lilies, shrubs, &c.

Fig. 99.—Rose 'Hugo Roller.' (*Journal of Horticulture.*)

Bronze Banksian Medal.

To Messrs. Gauntlett, Chiddingfold, for Irises.

Award of Merit.

To *Campanula persicifolia* 'William Lawrensen' (votes, 11 for, 5 against), from W. Lawrensen, Esq., Egglescliffe. This is a seedling from Backhouse's variety, with flowers of a pretty shade of pale blue; otherwise it is similar to the type.

To Delphinium 'Mrs. G. Ferguson' (votes, unanimous), from G. Ferguson, Esq., The Hollies, Weybridge (gr. Mr. Smith). This is much the finest white variety we have seen. Both flowers and spike are very large and shapely.

To Rose 'Hugo Roller' (votes, unanimous), from Messrs. W. Paul, Waltham Cross. A very decorative Hybrid Tea variety, with medium-sized flowers, each having a pale yellow centre, with a soft, rosy-peach colour over all the outer petals (fig. 99).

To *Spiraea camtschatica rosea* (votes, unanimous), from Mr. A. Perry, Enfield. A very fine bold sub-aquatic plant, growing 6 or 7 feet high, with fine spikes of rosy-pink flowers.

Other Exhibits.

Messrs. Artindale, Sheffield : hardy flowers.

Messrs. Barr, Covent Garden : Eucalyptus.

Mr. J. Bruckhaus, Twickenham : Stocks.

Messrs. Cannell, Swanley : Stocks and Antirrhinums.

Messrs. Charlton, Tunbridge Wells : *Alyssum.*

Messrs. Cheal, Crawley : Sweet Peas, &c.

Miss Easterbrook, Fawkham : a basket of wild flowers.

Messrs. J. King, Coggeshall : Sweet Peas.

Messrs. Peed, Streatham : Gloxinias.

Messrs. J. Veitch, Chelsea : flowering plants.

Mr. L. R. Russell, Richmond : hardy Ericas.

Messrs. Dobbie, Rothesay : Godetia and Sweet Williams.

G. Yeld, Esq., York : Hemerocallis Hybrids.

Mrs. Curle, Melrose : Rose 'Christian Curle.'

Mr. J. Wheeler, Seven Kings : Carnations.

Mr. W. H. Gardiner, St. Osyth : *Eschscholtzia* 'Coral Queen.'

Miss Jones, Exton : Sweet Peas.

Messrs. Firth, Leeds : Pelargoniums.

Mr. Frank Lilley, Guernsey : Gladiolus.

Mr. J. H. Virgo, Clevedon : *Adiantum virginicum.*

Major Dent, Wetherby : white Delphiniums.

R. Montague, Esq., Brixton : Pelargonium 'R. Montague.'

A. Kingsmill, Esq., Harrow Weald : *Carpenteria californica platy-petala.*

Messrs. Pearson, Lowdham : Delphinium 'Mrs. C. Pearson.'

FLORAL COMMITTEE, AUGUST 6, 1907.

Mr. MARSHALL, V.M.H., in the Chair, and eighteen members present.

Awards Recommended :—

Silver-gilt Flora Medal.

To Messrs. Kelway, Langport, for Gladiolus.

Silver Flora Medal.

To Messrs. Clark, Dover, for herbaceous flowers and annuals.

To Messrs. Charlton, Tunbridge Wells, for hardy flowers.

To Mr. A. Perry, Enfield, for herbaceous flowers.

To Leopold de Rothschild, Esq., Gunnersbury House, W. (gr. Mr. Hudson, V.M.H.), for Nymphaeas.

To Mr. L. R. Russell, Richmond, for hardy foliage plants.

To Mr. George Arends, Ronsdorf, for hybrid Astilbes.

Silver Banksian Medal.

To H. W. Perry, Esq., Hillthorp, Upper Norwood (gr. Mr. Buckingham), for Gloxinias.

To Mr. H. H. Crane, Highgate, N., for Violettas.

To Messrs. Dobbie, Marks Tey, for *Dianthus*.

Bronze Flora Medal.

To Mr. J. Douglas, V.M.H., Edenside, Great Bookham, for Carnations.

To Mr. G. Reuthe, Keston, Kent, for hardy flowers.

First-class Certificate.

To *Eucalyptus ficifolia* (votes, unanimous), from W. North-Row, Esq., Cove House, Tiverton. Flowers a brilliant scarlet, about two inches across, and specially attractive by having a creamy-white calyx. The heads or clusters are large, consisting of about twenty flowers and buds. The foliage is large, leathery, and very dark green. Mr. North-Row stated that the plant was raised from seed ten years ago, and was grown in a cool conservatory, only heated in winter, and after being twice cut down the plant was now about fifteen feet high. A native of Australia.

To *Nymphaea atropurpurea* (votes, unanimous), from Lord Hillingdon, Uxbridge (gr. Mr. Allan). A very large flower of an intense purple-red colour, with golden stamens.

Award of Merit.

To *Campanula longistyla* (votes, unanimous), from Sir Trevor Lawrence, Bart., V.M.H., Burford, Dorking. A free-growing species, with medium-sized purplish-blue flowers very freely produced. A handsome herbaceous plant (fig. 100).

To Carnation 'King Edward VII.' (votes, unanimous), from Mr. J. Douglas, V.M.H., Great Bookham. An immense flower with a white ground, marked and striped with dark crimson. A 'fancy' border variety.

To Gladiolus 'Duke of Richmond' (votes, 12 for, 2 against), from Messrs. Kelway, Langport. A remarkably fine variety with the upper petals of pale rose, marked with a darker shade; the lower petal is white, with a yellow blotch, and spotted with rose.

To *Matricaria inodora* 'Bridal Robe' (votes, unanimous), from Messrs. Titt, Windsor. A beautiful pure white variety, with flowers nearly three inches across, very double, and evidently freely produced. A decided acquisition.

Other Exhibits.

Messrs. J. Veitch, Chelsea : flowering shrubs.

Mr. F. J. C. Patmore, Lymington : Carnations.

Mr. W. Gladwish, Tunbridge Wells : a climbing variegated Tropaeolum, which arrived too late for the Committee's inspection.

FIG. 100.—CAMPANULA LONGESTYLA. (Gardeners' Chronicle.)

Messrs. Mawson, Windermere : Chrysanthemum 'Gladys Mawson.'
Mr. T. W. Cowburn, Tring : *Acalypha musaica* 'Mrs. Marc.'
Mr. G. Kent, Dorking : Carnation 'Charming Bride.'
Miss V. Fellowes, Shotesham Park, Norwich : Rambler Rose 'Robert
Fellowes.'   The Committee asked to see a plant.
Mr. C. M. Humphreys, Birchanger : Sweet Peas.
Mr. J. Vert, Saffron Walden : Delphiniums.
Messrs. Barr, Covent Garden : Phlox.

<h2 style="text-align:center">FLORAL COMMITTEE, AUGUST 20, 1907.</h2>

Mr. MARSHALL, V.M.H., in the Chair, and thirteen members present.

Awards Recommended :—

Silver-gilt Flora Medal.

To Messrs. Kelway, Langport, for Gladioli.
To Messrs. J. Veitch, Chelsea, for rare or newly introduced hardy
plants.

Silver-gilt Banksian Medal.

To Messrs. Cannell, Swanley, for annuals.

Silver Flora Medal.

To Mr. A. Ll. Gwillim, New Eltham, for Begonias.
To Messrs. H. B. May, Upper Edmonton, for flowering plants.

Silver Banksian Medal.

To Messrs. Bull, Chelsea, for a collection of economic plants.
To Mr. A. Bullock, Epping, for Ixoras.
To Messrs. A. Charlton, Tunbridge Wells, for hardy flowers.
To Mr. G. Prince, Longworth, for Roses.

Bronze Flora Medal.

To Messrs. Paul, Cheshunt, for new Roses.
To Messrs. T. S. Ware, Feltham, for hardy flowers.

Award of Merit.

To *Streptocarpus* 'Burdett's Strain' (fig. 101) (votes, unanimous), from
Mr. F. Burdett, Sunningdale.   Finely grown specimens of a large flowered
and floriferous variety were exhibited.   Flowers purplish-blue, blotched
and rayed at the throat with reddish-purple, 3 inches across, rather rough
in form, on stout stalks 15 inches long.   The Award was to the strain,
and slight variations in the form and shade of colour of the flowers were
evident in the plants exhibited.

Botanical Certificate.

To *Rubus bambusarum* (votes, 7 for), from Messrs. J. Veitch, Chelsea.
An interesting hardy bramble from North China.   The flowers and fruits
will add little to the decoration of the garden, but the long trailing shoots,
reaching 10–15 feet, with the three-parted leaves green above, very white

below, the segments linear-lanceolate, render the plant a valuable one for trial in the wild garden or against a wall.

Cultural Commendation.

To Mr. J. Hudson, V.M.H., gr. to Leopold de Rothschild, Esq., Gunnersbury House, W., for finely flowered × *Cyrtanthus hybridus*, with four to six flowers to a stem. The plant, a bigeneric hybrid between *C. sanguineus* and *Vallota purpurea*, received a First-class Certificate when shown by Sir Trevor Lawrence in 1885, and is still very rare.

Fig. 101.—Streptocarpus 'Burdett's Strain.' (*Gardeners' Chronicle.*)

Other Exhibits.

Messrs. J. Cheal, Crawley, showed their rose-coloured form of *Lupinus polyphyllus*.

Messrs. W. Cutbush, Highgate : *Chrysanthemum maximum* var. ' The Speaker.'

Miss Dodge (gr. Mr. R. Staward), Loseley Park : Stocks.

Leopold de Rothschild, Esq. (gr. Mr. J. Hudson, V.M.H.), Gunnersbury House, W. : scented-leaved Pelargonium ' Countess of Devon.'

Mr. G. Reuthe, Keston : a collection of Alpines, Lilies, and other hardy plants.

Mr. A. Wyatt, Wallington : Petunia blooms.

Messrs. Brown, Stamford : Ageratum ' Director Berner.'

Mr. F. Cole, Hertford : a seedling Carnation.

Mrs. Lloyd Edwards, Llangollen : a seedling border Carnation.

Messrs. Stredwick, St. Leonards : new varieties of Cactus Dahlias.

Messrs. Hurst, Houndsditch : *Chrysanthemum carinatum* ' Silver Queen.'

is
th
Fl
fl
be

T
re
m

p
se
sp

FLORAL COMMITTEE, SEPTEMBER 3, 1907.

Mr. MARSHALL, V.M.H., in the Chair, and thirteen members present.

Awards Recommended :—

Gold Medal.

To Messrs. J. Veitch, Chelsea, for Bamboos.

Silver-gilt Flora Medal.

To Lord Aldenham (gr. Mr. Beckett), Elstree, for Pentstemons.
To Messrs. Carter Page, London Wall, E.C., for Dahlias.
To Messrs. Kelway, Langport, for Gladioli.
To Messrs. W. Paul, Waltham Cross, for Roses.

Silver-gilt Banksian Medal.

To Messrs. Gunn, Olton, for Phloxes.
To Messrs. H. B. May, Edmonton, for flowering plants.
To Mr. Amos Perry, Enfield, for herbaceous plants.

Silver Flora Medal.

To Messrs. Cutbush, Highgate, for Carnations.
To Mr. A. Ll. Gwillim, New Eltham, for Begonias.

Silver Banksian Medal.

To Messrs. Bull, Chelsea, for stove plants.
To Messrs. G. Bunyard, Maidstone, for herbaceous plants.
To Messrs. Frank Cant, Colchester, for Roses.
To Messrs. Cheal, Crawley, for Dahlias.
To Mr. L. R. Russell, Richmond, for hardy shrubs.
To Messrs. T. S. Ware, Feltham, for herbaceous plants.

Bronze Flora Medal.

To Messrs. Jarman, Chard, for Centaureas.
To Mr. H. J. Jones, Lewisham, for *Fuchsia triphylla* hybrids.
To Messrs. Wells, Merstham, for early flowering Chrysanthemums.

Award of Merit.

To *Arctotis regalis* (votes, 10 for), from Sir Trevor Lawrence, Bart. (gr. Mr. Bain), Burford. Ray florets, silvery-white with a bluish tinge on the reverse side ; disc purplish-blue, surrounded by a narrow yellow band. Flowers 4 inches across. Said to be a hybrid between the orange-flowered *A. aureola* and the white *A. grandis*. *A. regalis* is a perennial, best propagated annually from cuttings. (Fig. 102.)

To Canna 'Mme. Louis Voraz' (votes, 6 for, 3 against), from Sir Trevor Lawrence, Bart. The flowers are orange-yellow richly netted with red ; petals large, regular ; truss close ; foliage glaucous green. The variety is unique in the reticulation of its petal.

To Carnation 'Mrs. T. Coulthwaite' (votes, unanimous), from Mr. P. Blair, Trentham. Flowers white, large, smooth-petaled, strongly clove-scented, of refined form. A free-flowering border variety, with non-splitting calyx.

To Dahlia 'Elsa Ellrich' (votes, 10 for), from Mr. H. Shoesmith, Westfield, Woking. A Cactus variety of excellent exhibition size and form. The flowers are blush-white, with long curled quill-petals.

To Dahlia ' Mauve Queen' (votes, 9 for), from Messrs. Cheal, Crawley. An exhibition Cactus variety, mauve-pink with creamy centre.

To Dahlia 'Peggy' (votes, 9 for), from Messrs. Cheal. A "single" variety with an unusual harmony of colour. Mauve-pink at the edge, suffused with orange towards the centre, a red band surrounding the disc.

To Dahlia 'The Bride' (votes, 9 for), from Messrs. Cheal. A decorative Cactus variety, white, of medium size, with very straight quill-petals and excellent long, stiff stalks.

To Fuchsia 'Coralle' (votes, 8 for, 1 against), from Mr. H. J. Jones, Lewisham. This is the best of a number of hybrids of *Fuchsia triphylla* which within the last year or two have been introduced from Germany. The flowers are of a light coral-red, about two inches long, with small calyx lobes and petals at the end of the tapering calyx-tube. The inflorescence is an elongated drooping raceme at the ends of the branches, bearing twenty or more flowers at a time, and lasting for several months.

To Gaillardia 'Lady Rolleston' (votes, 11 for), from Messrs. Harrison, Leicester. An excellent variety of *G. grandiflora*. Both ray and disc are of a uniform golden yellow, the rays broad, in two rows, and the flowers over four inches across.

To Gladiolus 'Purity' (votes, 13 for), from Messrs. Kelway, Langport. Flowers large, regular, pure white, with cream at the throat of the lower segments and touches of purple at the base of the flower.

To *Lychnis grandiflora* (votes, 11 for), from Mr. Amos Perry, Enfield. A species from China, allied to *L. fulgens* and *L. Haageana*, introduced long ago but still very rare in gardens. The flowers are variable, but, in the plant certificated, were of a rather dull red, 3 inches across, with broad smooth petals. A showy plant, 1–2 feet high.

To Pentstemons 'Beckett's strain' (votes, unanimous), from Lord Aldenham (gr. Mr. Beckett, V.M.H.), Elstree. A fine strain of named varieties of this favourite bedding plant, varying from white tinged with pink (' Virgin Queen'), white and pink (' Rosalba'), to rich shades of scarlet (' Firefly,' ' Rubicunda ') and purple.

Other Exhibits.

The Misses Kipping, Hutton : a small group of alpine and herbaceous plants.

Messrs. G. Stark, Gt. Ryburgh : variegated Tropaeolums and Sweet Peas.

Mrs. Greaves, Leicester : seedling Carnation.

Mr. Sarsfield-Winstan, Shenfield : seedling Violas.

Mr. J. Spence, Guildford : the original dwarf form of *Alyssum maritimum*.

Mr. Chas. Turner, Slough : seedling Pompon Dahlias.

Messrs. Paul, Cheshunt: Phlox ' General van Heutsky.'

FIG. 103.—VIBURNUM RHYTIDOPHYLLUM.

(*To face page* clxxxvii.

FLORAL COMMITTEE, SEPTEMBER 17, 1907.

Mr. MARSHALL, V.M.H., in the Chair, and twenty-three members present.

Awards Recommended :—

Silver-gilt Flora Medal.

To Messrs. Carter Page, London Wall, E.C., for Dahlias.

Silver-gilt Banksian Medal.

To Mr. J. Walker, Thame, for Dahlias and China Asters.
To Messrs. Wallace, Colchester, for Tritonias, &c.
To Messrs. Ware, Feltham, for Dahlias.

Silver Flora Medal.

To Messrs. Cannell, Swanley, for Dahlias.
To Messrs. Cutbush, Highgate, for Carnations.
To Mr. Perry, Enfield, for herbaceous plants.
To Mr. Prichard, Christchurch, for herbaceous plants.
To Lord Salisbury (gr. Mr. Prime), Hatfield, for *Clerodendron fallax.*
To Mr. Chas. Turner, Slough, for Dahlias.
To Messrs. Veitch, Chelsea, for hardy shrubs and greenhouse plants.

Silver Banksian Medal.

To Mr. Brazier, Caterham, for herbaceous plants.
To Messrs. Brown, Peterborough, for Roses.
To Messrs. Cheal, Crawley, for Dahlias, &c.
To Messrs. Hobbies, Dereham, for Dahlias.
To Messrs. May, Upper Edmonton, for Bouvardias, &c.
To Mr. West, Brentwood, for Dahlias.

Bronze Flora Medal.

To Messrs. Bull, Chelsea, for stove plants.
To Messrs. Wells, Merstham, for Chrysanthemums.

First-class Certificate.

To *Viburnum rhytidophyllum* (votes, unanimous), from Messrs. Veitch, Chelsea. This " wrinkle-leaved " Viburnum, introduced by Mr. Wilson from Western China, forms a very fine addition to our perfectly hardy evergreen shrubs. The leaves are from six to nine inches long by two to three inches broad, very rugose, dark green above, white-tomentose (hairs stellate) below. The leaf stalks and young stems are covered with rusty down. The cream-white flowers, in large clusters, of which the buds are evident in early autumn, open about June, and are succeeded by bright scarlet berries, blackening as they ripen. (Fig 103.)

Award of Merit.

To Dahlia ' C. E. Wilkins ' (votes, 15 for), from Messrs. Stredwick, St. Leonards. An exhibition Cactus variety ; quills numerous, narrow, curled ; dominating colour coral-pink, but the petals are cream-tipped and yellow-based.

To Dahlia ' Cynthia ' (votes, 9 for, 3 against), from Messrs. Ware, Feltham. An exhibition Cactus variety ; petals rather broad, the outer ones reflexing to form a flower of good depth ; outer florets salmon-red, yellow-tipped, inner yellow, scarcely quilled.

To Dahlia 'Dorothy' (votes, 16 for, 1 against), from Messrs. Stredwick. An exhibition Cactus variety ; much twisted sharp-pointed quills ; bright mauve-pink, creamy-white centre.

[NOTE.—The names 'Cynthia' and 'Dorothy' have already been applied to single-flowered varieties of Dahlia.]

To Dahlia 'Flame' (votes, unanimous), from Mr. Shoesmith, Woking. An exhibition Cactus variety ; flowers large, with much twisted long quill petals ; rich orange-scarlet.

To Dahlia 'Ivernia' (votes, 15 for, 1 against), from Messrs Stredwick. An exhibition Cactus variety ; flowers large, quills much twisted ; general colour salmon, but the bases of the florets are orange and yellow.

To Dahlia 'Rev. Arthur Bridge' (votes, 11 for, 2 against), from Messrs. Stredwick. An exhibition Cactus variety ; the outer florets rose-pink, tipped yellow ; inner florets bright yellow, a little touched with pink.

To Tritonia (Montbretia) 'King Edmund' (votes, 15 for, 6 against). Orange, a little crimson at the throat, strong-branching, vigorous, early.

To Tritonia 'Lady Hamilton' (votes, unanimous). Orange, with a shading of deeper orange, later than the preceding.

To Tritonia 'Lord Nelson' (votes, unanimous). Reddish-orange, with a small clear yellow centre, quite red outside, dark stems. This variety takes after *T. Pottsii* in failing to fully expand its flowers.

These fine hybrid Montbretias from Major Petre, Norwich, were raised by his gardener, Mr. George Davison. In size of flower and richness of colour they are not superior to the varieties 'Germania,' 'George Davison,' and 'Prometheus,' already certificated, but their vigorous branching habit renders them valuable additions to the flower borders.

Other Exhibits.

Mr. H. J. Jones, Lewisham : Michaelmas Daisies.

Sir Edmund Loder (gr. Mr. Cook), Leonardslee : blue Hydrangea.

Messrs. Low, Bush Hill Park : Ferns and Carnations.

Mr. G. Miller, Wisbech: a new Tropaeolum.

Messrs. Paul, Cheshunt : Dahlias and shrubs.

Mr. Russell, Richmond : hardy evergreens.

Mrs. Wakefield, Uxbridge : *Rudbeckia hirta* var. *superba*.

FLORAL COMMITTEE, OCTOBER 1, 1907.

Mr. MARSHALL, V.M.H., in the Chair, and nineteen members present.

Awards Recommended :—

Gold Medal.

To Messrs. Veitch, Chelsea, for a unique collection of hardy specie of Vitis.

Silver-gilt Flora Medal.

To Messrs. Gunn, Olton, for Phloxes.

To Messrs. W. Paul, Waltham Cross, for Roses.

To Messrs. T. S. Ware, Feltham, for Dahlias.

NORAH PETERS

SARDCHRON

FIG. 104.— ASTER 'NORAH PETERS.' (*Gardeners' Chronicle.*)　(*To face page* clxxxix.)

Silver-gilt Banksian Medal.

To Messrs. Cutbush, Highgate, for Asters and Carnations.
To Messrs. Cannell, Swanley, for Dahlias.

Silver Flora Medal.

To Messrs. Dobbie, Rothesay, for Scabious and Montbretias.
To Messrs. May, Edmonton, for Veronicas and hardy ferns.
To Mr. Perry, Enfield, for Asters.

Silver Banksian Medal.

To Mr. Frank Cant, Colchester, for Roses.
To Messrs. Bath, Wisbech, for Chrysanthemums.
To Messrs. Prior, Colchester, for Roses.
To Mr. West, Brentwood, for Dahlias.

Bronze Flora Medal.

To Messrs. Barr, Covent Garden, for hardy plants.
To Mr. Brazier, Caterham, for hardy plants.
To Messrs. Bull, Chelsea, for stove plants.
To Mr. Prince, Longworth, for Roses.
To Mr. Notcutt, Woodbridge, for hardy plants.
To Mr. Seale, Sevenoaks, for Pompon-Cactus Dahlias.
To Messrs. van Waveren, Sassenheim, for Paeony-flowered Dahlias.

First-class Certificate.

To *Aspidium* (*Polystichum*) *aculeatum pulcherrimum Drueryi* (votes, unanimous), from C. T. Druery, Esq., V.M.H., Acton. There are but few forms of *A. aculeatum* grown, and this, which was raised by Mr. Druery from spores of the type, is undoubtedly the finest. The pinnules are much elongated, slightly laciniate, and rather distantly placed on the rachis. With its light, graceful, arching fronds this is one of the most beautiful hardy ferns.

To strain of Annual Scabious (votes, unanimous), from Messrs. Dobbie, Rothesay. A very fine strain of taller forms of *Scabiosa atropurpurea.* The range of colour includes flesh, rose, mauve, pale china blue, black (dark crimson), and black purple and white.

Award of Merit.

To Aster ' Norah Peters ' (votes, unanimous), from Mr. Peters, Leatherhead. One of the best white Michaelmas daisies. Disc large, pale yellow; rays very narrow, numerous and Erigeron-like, pure white. Flowers 1½ inch across, flat. Panicle pyramidal, pointed, dense-flowered. (Fig. 104.)

To *Cotoneaster applanata* (votes, unanimous), from Messrs. Veitch, Chelsea. A new decorative hardy shrub from Central China. Leaves ovate, acute, about an inch long, glossy dark green above, downy below ; twigs downy, shoots forming long arching sprays. Berries scarlet, in close clusters of from two to ten or more on the leafless growths of the preceding year.

To Phlox ' George A. Strohlein ' (votes, 12 for, 6 against), from Messrs. Gunn, Olton. A fine-trussed variety with large, smooth, flat, round pip. Colour carmine-scarlet, with crimson-purple eye.

To *Vitis inconstans Lowii* (votes, unanimous), from Messrs. Low, Bush Hill Park. A very slender, graceful seedling form of *V. inconstans* (*Ampelopsis Veitchii*). Leaves generally trifoliate, leaflets small, sessile, round, coarsely toothed, tendrils clinging. The foliage takes the rich reds of the type in autumn.

To *Vitis leeoides* (votes, 12 for), from Messrs. Veitch, Chelsea. A new hardy ornamental vine from Western China. Leaves compound, with three or five leaflets, glossy above, purple below.

To Cactus Dahlias. The following show Cactus Dahlias were recommended Awards of Merit by a joint committee of the Royal Horticultural and the National Dahlia Societies :—

'Chas. H. Curtis,' from Mr. Shoesmith, Woking. Flower intense orange-crimson, large, with long, much-twisted, incurved, narrow quill-petals.

'Clara,' from Messrs. Stredwick, St. Leonards. Mauve-pink, yellow-tipped, narrow incurved petals.

'Etruria,' from Messrs. Stredwick. Terra-cotta red, with spirally twisted narrow quill-petals.

'Harold Peerman,' from Messrs. Stredwick. Flowers very large, lemon-yellow, with much-twisted petals.

'Helium,' from Messrs. Stredwick. Fawn with centre and tips of yellow, broad twisted petals.

'Saturn,' from Messrs. Stredwick. Pink, creamy-pink at the centre, with light crimson splashings.

Other Exhibits.

J. T. Bennett-Pöe, Esq., V.M.H., Cheshunt : a new *Nerine*.
Mr. Chapman, Camberley : single Dahlias.
Lady Alice Dundas, Middleton Tyas : seedling Carnations.
Mr. Draps-Dom, Brussels : *Dracaena tricolor.*
Mr. Langdon, Hucclecote : a seedling Carnation.
Mr. Mortimer, Farnham : a new Cactus Dahlia.
Messrs. Peed, Mitcham Lane : alpines, &c.
Mr. Reuthe, Keston : hardy plants.
Mr. Riddell, Filey : a new Carnation.
Messrs. Wells, Merstham : early Chrysanthemums.

FLORAL COMMITTEE, OCTOBER 15, 1907.

Mr. MARSHALL, V.M.H., in the Chair, and twenty-six members present.

Awards Recommended :—

Gold Medal.

To Messrs. Veitch, Chelsea, for Nepenthes and groups of shrubs an greenhouse plants.

Silver-gilt Flora Medal.

To Mr. Jones, Lewisham, for Chrysanthemums.
To Messrs. Cheal, Crawley, for trees and shrubs.

Silver Flora Medal.

To Mr. Brazier, Caterham, for Asters.

To Messrs. Cutbush, Highgate, for Asters.

To Messrs. May, Edmonton, for Adiantums.

To C. F. Raphael, Esq. (gr. Mr. Grubb), Shenley, for Malmaisons.

To Mr. Such, Maidenhead, for Chrysanthemums.

Fig. 105.—Berberis Wilsonae. (*The Garden*

Silver Banksian Medal.

To Mr. Reuthe, Keston, Kent, for hardy plants.

To Messrs. Wells, Merstham, for Chrysanthemums.

Bronze Flora Medal.

To Messrs. Clark, Dover, for hardy plants.

To Messrs. Cuthbert, Southgate, for *Lilium tigrinum Fortunei.*

To Mr. Russell, Richmond, for berried shrubs.

First-class Certificate.

To *Berberis Wilsonae* (votes, unanimous), from Messrs. Veitch, Chelsea. A newly introduced species from China, with small narrow leaves shorter than the spines within which they are clustered ; unique among the cultivated barberries by reason of the dense, almost sessile, clusters of globular berries, which, white when unripe and glaucous coral-red when ripe, make the 2–4 feet shrub a very handsome one. Mr. Wilson reports the foliage to be handsomely tinted in autumn, but this is not yet evident in England. (Fig. 105.)

Award of Merit.

To Aster ' Miss Southall ' (votes, unanimous). An exceptionally fine Michaelmas daisy from Wisley, where plants had been sent by Mr. Davies, Ross-on-Wye. Height over five feet, stems stiff, wiry ; panicle long, open ; flowers lilac-mauve, full-rayed, about two inches in diameter.

To Chrysanthemum ' Esme Reed ' (votes, unanimous), from Mr. Ladds, Swanley. A decorative white sport from ' Mrs. Winkfield,' especially valuable from its dwarf growth and free-flowering habit.

To Chrysanthemum ' H. J. Jones, 1908 ' (votes, unanimous), from Mr. Jones, Lewisham. A fine addition to the incurved Japanese section. Flowers golden-yellow, large ; petals broad, long, twisted.

To Nepenthes ' Ruby ' (votes, unanimous), from Messrs. Veitch, Chelsea. A seedling from *N. sanguinea* × *N. Curtisii superba*; pitchers broad and deep, dark-red in colour ; habit robust.

To Solidago ' Golden Wings ' (votes, 17 for, 4 against), from Mr. Such, Maidenhead. A very elegantly and loosely branched Golden Rod with almost horizontally spreading golden-yellow plumes. Said to be a seedling from *S. latifolia*, the plant bore a much closer resemblance to *S. Shortii*, the handsomest of the introduced species.

Other Exhibits.

Mr. W. Appleton, Bradenhurst : a seedling Chrysanthemum.
Messrs. Barr, Covent Garden : herbaceous plants.
Messrs. Bull, Chelsea : stove plants.
Mr. Dutton, Iver : new Carnations.
Captain Kemp, Arundel : a flower of a seedling Hippeastrum.
Messrs. Lane, Berkhamstead : Conifers.
The executrix of the late George May : a new Tree Carnation.
Messrs. Peed, West Norwood : Chrysanthemums and Begonias.
Sir Wm. Smith-Marriott, Bart., Blandford : new Carnations.
Messrs. Ware, Feltham : hardy flowers.

FLORAL COMMITTEE, OCTOBER 29, 1907.

Mr. MARSHALL, V.M.H., in the Chair, and twenty-six members present.

Awards Recommended :—

Gold Medal.

To Mr. Norman Davis, Framfield, for Chrysanthemums.

Silver-gilt Flora Medal.

To Messrs. May, Edmonton, for Davallias.
To Mr. H. J. Jones, Lewisham, for Chrysanthemums.
To Messrs. Rochford, Turnford Hall, for Crotons (Codiaeums).

Silver-gilt Banksian Medal.

To Messrs. Veitch, Chelsea, for greenhouse plants and dwarf Conifers.

Silver Flora Medal.

To Messrs. Cannell, Swanley, for Pelargoniums.
To Messrs. Cutbush, Highgate, for retarded plants.
To Mr. Lange, Hampton, for Carnations.

Silver Banksian Medal.

To Mr. Brazier, Caterham, for Asters and Chrysanthemums.
To Mr. Mortimer, Farnham, for Carnations.
To Mr. Spink, Walthamstow, for Chrysanthemums.
To Messrs. Wells, Merstham, for Chrysanthemums.

Bronze Banksian Medal.

To Messrs. Russell, Richmond, for berried shrubs.

Award of Merit.

To Aster ' H. J. Cutbush ' (votes, 18 for, 3 against), from Mr. Beckett, Elstree. A variety of *A. Amellus*, free and late flowering; flowers not large, but full-rayed, of a rosy-purple colour ; height 2 feet.

To Carnation 'Beacon' (votes, unanimous), from Messrs. Dutton, Iver ; Messrs. Lange, Hampton ; and Messrs. Paul, Cheshunt. An American winter-flowering tree variety. Colour dark scarlet ; form good ; calyx rigid, non-bursting ; habit dwarf, sturdy ; scentless.

To Carnation ' Rose Pink Enchantress ' (votes, unanimous), from Messrs. Dutton, Iver, and Messrs. Lange, Hampton. An American variety with the vigorous habit, stiff stems, and good calyx of 'Enchantress,' from which it is a sport. Colour rose-pink ; scentless.

To Carnation ' Winsor ' (votes, unanimous), from Messrs. Dutton, Iver, and Messrs. Lange, Hampton. An American variety. Colour a warm salmon-pink, with the characteristically good calyx and vigour of the tree varieties ; habit dwarf ; scentless.

To Chrysanthemum ' Clara Vurnum ' (votes, unanimous), from Messrs. Wells, Merstham. A fine decorative variety, with florets of a rich crimson, bronze on the reverse.

To Chrysanthemum ' Clara Wells ' (votes, 18 for), from Messrs. Wells, Merstham. An incurved variety of large size and great substance ; florets rather narrow, pale yellow, the outer florets shading with buff.

3 H

To Chrysanthemum 'F. W. Lever' (votes, unanimous), from Mr. Mileham, Leatherhead. A huge white Japanese variety with broad florets and of fine form.

To Chrysanthemum 'Mrs. G. F. Coster' (votes, unanimous), from Mr. Silsbury, Shanklin, Isle of Wight. A large flowered Japanese variety; colour rich old gold.

To Chrysanthemum 'Mrs. Wakefield' (votes, 14 for, 4 against), from Mr. Jones, Lewisham. A fine, free, decorative variety. Colour claret-red, bronzy-orange at the centre.

To Chrysanthemum 'Romance' (votes, 17 for), from Mr. Godfrey, Exmouth. An incurved variety of medium size, but great substance. Colour golden-yellow.

To Chrysanthemum 'Splendour' (votes, unanimous), from Mr. Silsbury, Shanklin, Isle of Wight. An incurved Japanese variety. Florets broad, finely curled ; colour light crimson, bronzy-gold on the reverse.

To *Cyclamen persicum fimbriatum giganteum*, strain of (votes, 16 for, 6 against), from Mr. Jannoch, Dersingham. Flowers large, saucer-shape, drooping, with fringed margin ; colour ranging from lilac- to purplish-rose. The light graceful appearance of *C. persicum* was lost, but the individual flowers would make good "buttonholes."

To *Nerine* 'F. D. Godman' (votes, 11 for, 2 against), from F. D. Godman, Esq., F.R.S., Horsham. Colour pink ; form and habit good ; segments a little waved at the extremities ; umbels ten-flowered.

Other Exhibits.

Messrs. Barr, Covent Garden : hardy plants.
Messrs. Bull, Chelsea : stove foliage plants.
Mr. Cole, Peterborough : a new Chrysanthemum.
Messrs. Peed, Streatham : winter flowering Begonias.
Mr. Reuthe, Keston : hardy plants.
Mr. Staward, Loseley Park : a seedling Violet.
Mr. Triscott, Sidmouth : a new Chrysanthemum.

FLORAL COMMITTEE, NOVEMBER 12, 1907.

Mr. MAY in the Chair, and twenty-three members present.

Awards Recommended :—

Gold Medal.

To Messrs. Veitch, Chelsea, for stove and greenhouse plants.

Silver-gilt Flora Medal.

To Messrs. Hill, Edmonton, for Gleichenias.

Silver-gilt Banksian Medal.

To F. A. Bevan, Esq., Trent Park (gr. Mr. Parr), for Begonias.
To Messrs. Cutbush, Highgate, for trees and shrubs and Carnations.

Silver Flora Medal.

To Rev. H. Buckston, Etwall (gr. Mr. Shambrook), for Cyclamen.
To Messrs. Cannell, Swanley, for Cacti and Pelargoniums.

To Messrs. May, Edmonton, for flowers and Ferns.

To Mr. Page, Hampton, Middlesex, for Carnations.

Silver Banksian Medal.

To Messrs. Clibrans, Altrincham, for Begonias.

To F. L. Davis, Esq., Potters Bar (gr. Mr. May), for Chrysanthemums.

Fig. 106.— Nephrolepis superbissima. (*Journal of Horticulture.*)

First-class Certificate.

To *Nephrolepis superbissima* (votes, unanimous), from Messrs.
F. R. Pierson, Tarrytown, New York. This is a "seedling" from
N. exaltata Piersonii. The fronds are densely plumose, very firm in
texture, vigorous in growth, and of a deep green colour. The plants

exhibited had just arrived from New York, and their fine condition after having been packed for a fortnight speaks well for the constitution and hardiness of the variety. (Fig. 106.)

Award of Merit.

To Begonia 'Miss Clibran' (votes, unanimous), from Messrs. Clibrans, Altrincham. A winter flowering variety raised from a tuberous variety × *B. socotrana.* The flowers are of a rich pink, very double, 3 inches across, and borne loosely on arching sprays of 3–5 flowers together.

To Chrysanthemum 'Foxhunter' (votes, unanimous), from Messrs. Wells, Merstham. A "decorative" or market variety; petals deep chestnut-red, markedly incurved towards the centre, where the pale bronze of the reverse gives distinction to the colouring.

To Chrysanthemum 'Frank Payne' (votes, 11 for, 2 against), from Messrs. Wells. A seedling Japanese exhibition variety; colour a pale silvery-pink; petals a little fringed at the tips.

To Chrysanthemum 'Freda Bedford' (votes, unanimous), from Messrs. Wells. A rather large-flowered "decorative" or market variety; petals apricot or warm bronze above, and light bronze yellow on the reverse.

To *Nerine* 'Purple Princess' (votes, 9 for, 1 against), from H. J. Elwes, Esq., Colesborne (gr. Mr. Walters). Raised from Purple Prince × Novelty. Colour light crimson; flowers large, of good form, the perianth segments lightly curled at the tip. The bulb bore eight flowers on the scape.

Other Exhibits.

Mr. Cooper, Colney Hatch Lane : a single Chrysanthemum.

Mr. L. Currie, Kingston-on-Thames : a Chrysanthemum sport.

Miss Emmeline Crocker : water-colour drawings of Rhododendrons.

Mr. Davis, Potters Bar : a Chrysanthemum sport.

Mr. Dutton, Iver, Bucks : new Carnations.

Mr. Glanville, Cudworth, Dorking : a double Petunia.

Mr. Heath, Newmarket : new Chrysanthemums.

Messrs. Low, Enfield : Carnations.

Messrs. Paul & Son, Cheshunt : *Crataegus melanocarpa.*

Messrs. Peed, Mitcham Lane : alpines.

Mr. Reuthe, Keston : Himalayan Rhododendrons.

L. de Rothschild, Esq. (gr. Mr. Hudson, V.M.H.) : Begonias.

Mr. L. R. Russell, Richmond : berried shrubs.

Mr. Simpson, Chelmsford : Chrysanthemums.

FLORAL COMMITTEE, NOVEMBER 26, 1907.

Mr. MARSHALL, V.M.H., in the Chair, and twenty-three members present.

Awards Recommended :—

Silver-gilt Flora Medal.

To Lord Howard de Walden (gr. Mr. Vert), Saffron Walden, for Begonias. The decorative arrangement of this group was highly commended.

To Messrs. Hill, Edmonton, for Ferns.

Silver-gilt Banksian Medal.

To Mr. Jones, Lewisham, for Chrysanthemums.

To Messrs. May, Edmonton, for Ferns.

To Messrs. Waterer, Bagshot, for Conifers.

Silver Flora Medal.

To Mr. Ladds, Swanley, for market Chrysanthemums.

To Messrs. Veitch, Chelsea, for Begonias, Jacobinias, &c.

To Frank Galsworthy, Esq., Chertsey, for pictures of flowers.

Silver Banksian Medal.

To Messrs. Cannell, Swanley, for Pelargoniums, &c.

To Messrs. Cutbush, Highgate, for Astilbes, &c.

To Messrs. Low, Bush Hill Park, for Carnations and Cyclamen.

To Mr. Russell, Richmond, for berried shrubs, &c.

Award of Merit.

To Chrysanthemum 'Edith Jameson' (votes, unanimous), from Mr. Norman Davis, Framfield. A Japanese variety of exhibition size and form ; colour mauve-pink, a little yellowish at the centre where the reverse of the petals becomes visible.

To *Juniperus chinensis nana aurea* (votes, 6 for), from Messrs. Waterer, Bagshot. Three new dwarf forms of the Chinese juniper were shown—*nana, nana glauca,* and *nana aurea*—of which the last was considered the most ornamental. It is a dwarf, globose, evergreen shrub, admirably suited for the rockery, brownish-gold in general colour, and its form lightened by small tasselled shoots springing from the mass.

Other Exhibits.

G. Ferguson, Esq., Weybridge : Chrysanthemums.

R. Foster, Esq., Lindfield : a seedling Chrysanthemum.

A. Kingsmill, Esq., Harrow Weald : *Pernettya mucronata.*

Sir Trevor Lawrence, Bart., Burford : a new Begonia.

Mr. Mileham, Leatherhead : a new Chrysanthemum.

Mr. Oliver, Ashford : a seedling Chrysanthemum.

J. Weller Poley, Esq., Bury St. Edmunds : *Impatiens Cooperi.*

Mr. Reuthe, Keston : hardy flowering plants.

Mr. Ridley, King's Lynn : a Chrysanthemum sport.

The Duke of Rutland (gr. Mr. Divers) : Chrysanthemums.

Messrs. Wells, Merstham : Chrysanthemums.

Mr. Wood, Lichfield : a Chrysanthemum sport.

FLORAL COMMITTEE, DECEMBER 10, 1907.

Mr. MAY in the Chair, and twenty-one members present.

Awards Recommended :—

Silver-gilt Flora Medal.

To Mrs. Nell Lugard, Battersea Park, for floral studies in water-colour.

Silver-gilt Banksian Medal.

To C. F. Raphael, Esq. (gr. Mr. Grubb), Shenley, for Carnations.
To Messrs. Veitch, Chelsea, for greenhouse flowering plants.

Silver Flora Medal.

To Messrs. Cannell, Swanley, for Zonal Pelargoniums.
To Messrs. Low, Bush Hill Park, for Carnations.
To Messrs. May, Edmonton, for Euphorbias.

Silver Banksian Medal.

To Messrs. Bull, Chelsea, for stove plants.
To Messrs. Cutbush, Highgate, for berried shrubs.
To H. J. King, Esq. (gr. Mr. Weston), Ashford, for Carnations.

Award of Merit.

To *Montañoa bipinnatifida* (votes, 14 for, 7 against), from Messrs.
Paul & Son, Cheshunt. Introduced some sixty years ago, this is still a
rare plant, though its large loose panicles of white-rayed flower-heads
make a valuable addition to the cool greenhouse in winter. Height
4–8 feet; leaves large, rough and strong, opposite, coarsely pinnatifid
or bipinnatifid; flower-heads about 3 inches across. It is a good
foliage plant for the sub-tropical bed in summer. It should be lifted
and placed in the greenhouse about the end of September to flower.

Other Exhibits.

Messrs. Chatfield, Southwick : a new Chrysanthemum.
Mr. H. J. Jones, Lewisham : a new Chrysanthemum.
Messrs. Lancashire, Guernsey : a new Carnation.
Sir Trevor Lawrence, Bart. (gr. Mr. Bain), Burford : a new Amaryllid
from the Cape.
Messrs. Wells, Merstham : Chrysanthemums.

FLORAL COMMITTEE, DECEMBER 31, 1907.

Mr. MARSHALL, V.M.H., in the Chair, and twenty members present.

Awards Recommended :—

Silver-gilt Flora Medal.

To Messrs. J. Veitch, Chelsea, for winter-flowering plants.

Silver-gilt Banksian Medal.

To Messrs. Cannell, Swanley, for Zonal Pelargoniums.
To Messrs. Cutbush, Highgate, for Carnations and berried shrubs.

Silver Flora Medal.

To Messrs. Low, Bush Hill Park, for Carnations and foliage plants.
To Messrs. May, Edmonton, for Poinsettias.

Silver Banksian Medal.

To Messrs. Peed, Streatham, for alpines, &c.

Bronze Flora Medal.

To Sir E. Loder, Bart., Leonardslee (gr. Mr. Cook), for *Sarracenia purpurea.*

Award of Merit.

To strain of *Primula obconica grandiflora* 'Hayes Place double' (votes, 18 for), from E. A. Hambro, Esq., Hayes (gr. Mr. Grandfield). The best double variety of this species yet exhibited. The flowers are large, varying in colour from lilac to mauve, and the strain comes true from seed.

Other Exhibits.

Mr. McAinsh, Maidstone : *Moschosma riparium.*

Mrs. Stephen Marshall, Ambleside : a valuable winter-flowering Rhododendron, derived from *R. arboreum.*

FRUIT AND VEGETABLE COMMITTEE.

July 9, 1907, at Holland House.

Mr. Bunyard, V.M.H., in the Chair, and nineteen members present.

[For Cups and Medals awarded by the Council see page cxxix.]

There was no business before the Committee.

––––––––––

Fruit and Vegetable Committee, July 23, 1907.

Mr. Bunyard, V.M.H., in the Chair, and seventeen members present.

Awards Recommended :—

Silver-gilt Knightian Medal.

To Messrs. Carter, High Holborn, W.C., for 250 dishes of Peas.
To Messrs. Sutton, Reading, for a collection of edible Peas.
To Messrs. Rivers, Sawbridgeworth, for a collection of Cherries.

Silver Banksian Medal.

To Messrs. G. W. King, Coggeshall, for a collection of Peas.
To Mr. W. Deal, Kelvedon, for a collection of Peas.

Award of Merit.

To Strawberry 'Fillbasket' (votes, unanimous), from Messrs. Laxton, Bedford. Fruit medium size, bright red, conical in form ; flesh firm, very juicy, nice, agreeable flavour, and a prodigious bearer. It was one of the heaviest croppers, and one of the latest varieties in the trial of Strawberries at Wisley.

Other Exhibits.

Mr. G. Goddard, Norwood Green, Southall : a variety of Black Currant, which the Committee wished to be tried at Wisley.

Mr. Thomas, Eden Park Gardens, Beckenham : Tomatos.

Messrs. Laxton, Bedford : Strawberries and a Japanese Plum named 'First,' which the Committee desired to see from the open air.

Mr. S. Attrell, Chailey, Sussex : Raspberries.

Mr. C. J. Simpson, Chelmsford : a Tomato, which the Committee wished to be tried at Wisley.

––––––––––

Fruit and Vegetable Committee, August 6, 1907.

Mr. A. H. Pearson in the Chair, and ten members present.

Award Recommended :—

Gold Medal.

To Messrs. J. Veitch, Chelsea, for a superb collection of fruit trees in pots and a magnificent collection of Gooseberries.

Other Exhibits.

Messrs. Sutton, Reading : a collection of Cabbages and Savoys.

Mr. Stillwell, Goring : a Cucumber.

Messrs. Spooner, Hounslow : a small collection of fruit.

Mr. H. Walter, Hayward's Heath : Tomato ' Walter's Ideal.'

Messrs. Barr, Covent Garden : 'Marrowfat Mars ' Pea.

Mrs. Hargreaves, Arborfield Cross (gr. Mr. Plumb) : Melons.

Mr. R. Smith, Brickendonbury : Apple ' Smith's Early,' which the Committee desired to see later.

FRUIT AND VEGETABLE COMMITTEE, AUGUST 9, 1907, AT WISLEY.

Mr. BUNYARD, V.M.H., in the Chair, and ten members present.

Awards Recommended :—

First-class Certificate.

To Melon ' Sutton's Scarlet ' (votes, unanimous), from Messrs. Sutton, Reading.

To Melon ' Diamond Jubilee ' (votes, unanimous), from Messrs. Hurst, 152 Houndsditch, E.C.

Award of Merit.

To Melon ' Eastnor Castle ' (votes, unanimous), from Messrs. Barr, Covent Garden.

To Melon ' The Empress ' (votes, unanimous), from Mr. R. Sydenham, Birmingham.

To Melon ' Chas. Ross ' (votes, unanimous), from Mr. C. Ross, Welford Park, Newbury.

To Potato 'The Colleen ' (votes, unanimous), from Mr. J. F. Williamson, Sumner Hill, Mallow, Cork.

FRUIT AND VEGETABLE COMMITTEE, AUGUST 20, 1907.

Mr. BUNYARD, V.M.H., in the Chair, and fifteen members present.

Awards Recommended :—

Hogg Medal.

To Messrs. Rivers, Sawbridgeworth, for a collection of Apricots in pots.

Silver-gilt Knightian Medal.

To Messrs. W. Paul, Waltham Cross, for fruit trees in pots.

Silver Knightian Medal.

To Messrs. Spooner, Hounslow, for fruit.

Award of Merit.

To Melon ' Perfection ' (votes, unanimous), from Messrs. Sutton, Reading.

To Melon 'Duchess of York' (votes, unanimous), from Messrs. Hurst, Houndsditch.

To Potato 'Favourite' (votes, unanimous), from Messrs. Dobbie, Rothesay.

Both the Melons and the Potato had been grown at Wisley.

Other Exhibits.

A large collection of Melons came from the Society's Gardens at Wisley.

Mrs. Collingwood, Lilburn Tower, Alnwick : Melon 'Lilburn Favourite.'

G. A. McLean Buckley, Esq., Worth Hall. Sussex : a promising Melon, which the Committee wished to be tried at Wisley.

Mrs. M. Nicholls, St. Clere, Sevenoaks : a Melon.

Mr. G. Bond, High Ashurst, Dorking : Melon 'Ashurst Beauty.'

Mr. R. Smith, Brickendonbury : Apple 'Smith's Early.'

Miss Dodge, Loseley Park, Guildford : Melons and Peas.

Rev. C. Shepherd, Trosley, Maidstone : a Nectarine.

Fruit and. Vegetable Committee, September 3, 1907.

Mr. Bunyard, V.M.H., in the Chair, and sixteen members present.

Awards Recommended :—

Silver-gilt Hogg Medal.

To the King's Acre Nursery Co., Hereford,.for fruit trees in pots.

Silver-gilt Knightian Medal.

To Messrs. Bunyard, Maidstone, for a collection of fruit.
To Messrs. Cannell, Swanley, for a collection of fruit.
To Messrs. J. Veitch, Chelsea, for fruit trees in pots.

Silver Knightian Medal.

To Mrs. Brace, Doveridge Hall, Derby, for a collection of fruit.

Other Exhibits.

Mr. G. Jones, Evesham : Plum 'Evesham Purple Egg.'

Mr. G. Scott, Gladstone Gardens, Yorks : a Pea that had sported from 'Alderman.' The Committee asked for it to be tried at Wisley.

Miss Dixon, Chichester : two Melons.

Mr. W. Howard, Worksop : Tomato 'Howard's Dukeries.'

Messrs. Laxton, Bedford : a Plum very similar to 'Prince of Wales.'

Mr. A. Huckfield, Pershore : a Plum similar to 'Evesham Purple Egg.'

From the Society's Gardens : Melons and Lemon Cucumber, the fruit of which resembles a Lemon in shape and appearance, with a Cucumber flavour and Cucumber growth and foliage. A curiosity without any great garden value.

FRUIT AND VEGETABLE COMMITTEE, SEPTEMBER 17, 1907.

Mr. A. H. PEARSON, J.P., in the Chair, and eighteen members present.

Awards Recommended :—

Silver-gilt Banksian Medal.

To the University College, Reading, for a collection of fruit.

Silver Knightian Medal.

To Messrs. Spooner, Hounslow, for a collection of fruit.

Silver Banksian Medal.

To Mr. B. Lockwood, Low Hills, Lindley, Huddersfield, for a collection of Peas.

Other Exhibits.

From the Society's Gardens : a collection of lesser known varieties of Apples.

Mr. S. Mortimer, Rowledge, Farnham : Cucumber 'Market Rival.'

Sir E. G. Loder, Bart., Leonardslee, Horsham (gr. Mr. Cook) : Apple 'Worcester Pearmain' and Pear 'Williams' Bon Chrétien.'

Mr. F. W. Thomas, Burgess Hill : Tomato 'Southern Beauty.' .

Miss Evézard, Thornton Heath : a seedling Apple.

J. Railton, Esq., Gadsden, Hayes : a curious malformed Carrot.

Messrs. J. Veitch, Chelsea : Melon 'Supreme.'

Rev. A. Carter, Thrussington Vicarage, Leicester : a seedling Apple.

Mr. W. Carey, 2 Devonshire Road, Bexhill-on-Sea : the old 'Blood' Peach, said to have been raised from a stone of a pale-fleshed variety.

Mr. G. W. Miller, Wisbech : Apple 'Red Victoria.' An early, highly coloured Apple that should probably sell well.

Mr. E. Burrell, The Gardens, Claremont : fruits, and branches of the very old scarlet-fleshed Pear known as 'Sanguinole.'

FRUIT AND VEGETABLE COMMITTEE, OCTOBER 1, 1907.

Mr. BUNYARD, V.M.H., in the Chair, and sixteen members present.

Awards Recommended :—

Silver-gilt Knightian Medal.

To Messrs. J. Veitch, Chelsea, for fruit trees in pots.

Silver Knightian Medal.

To the R.H.S. Gardens, Wisley, for a collection of Pears.

Other Exhibits.

Mr. G. W. Robinson, Forton, Garstang : Pear 'Tongue's Seedling.'

Mr. Hudson, V.M.H., gr. to Leopold Rothschild, Esq., Gunnersbury House, Acton : remarkably fine perpetual fruiting Strawberries 'La Perle' and 'Merveille de France.'

R. Bell, Esq., Stoneleigh, Ewell : three varieties of Potatos, which the Committee wished to be tried at Wisley.

H. M. Roberts, Esq., Ivinghoe, Tring : Apple 'Ivinghoe Beauty.'

FRUIT AND VEGETABLE COMMITTEE, OCTOBER 15, 1907.

Mr. J. CHEAL in the Chair, and fifteen members present.

Awards Recommended :—

Silver-gilt Knightian Medal.

To Miss M. H. Dodge, Loseley Park, Guildford (gr. Mr. Staward), for 100 varieties of Potatos.

To Messrs. Dobbie, Marks Tey, for eighty varieties of Onions.

Silver Banksian Medal.

To Mr. W. Turnham, Culham Court, Henley, for Onions.

To Messrs. Low, Enfield, for Apples.

To Messrs. Massey, Spalding, for Potatos.

Bronze Banksian Medal.

To R. H. Comyns, Esq., Heath Farm House, Watford (gr. Mr. Waterton), for Onions.

Award of Merit.

To Potato ' The Provost ' (votes, unanimous), from Messrs. Dobbie, Rothesay.

To Potato ' Longkeeper ' (votes, unanimous), from Messrs. Carter, High Holborn.

Both these varieties of Potato had been grown at Wisley.

Other Exhibits.

Mr. R. Johnston, Wakefield Lodge Gardens, Stony Stratford: Peach ' Lady Frederick,' which proved to be the old ' Blood Peach,' having dark red flesh.

Mr. J. C. Tallack, Shipley Hall Gardens, Derby: Melons ' Shipley Scarlet ' and ' Shipley White,' which the Committee wished to see again next year.

Mr. R. H. Weller, Hawthorn, Station Road, N.: a seedling Apple.

Mr. J. W. Onion, Sidmouth: Potato ' Cheltonia.'

Mr. W. Harrison, Heston; a magnificent dish of Apples grown on an irrigation fruit farm in Colorado.

H. H. Jones, Esq., Shelbrook Hill, Ellesmere: a seedling Apple.

FRUIT AND VEGETABLE COMMITTEE, OCTOBER 17, 1907.

Mr. G. BUNYARD, V.M.H., in the Chair, and twenty-seven members present.

Awards Recommended :—

Award of Merit.

To Raspberry ' The Alexandra ' (votes, unanimous), from Colonel the Hon. C. Harbord, Gunton Park, Norwich (gr. Mr. Allan). A very fine autumn-fruiting variety, with large dark red fruits of excellent flavour, very sweet, and produced in great profusion.

Cultural Commendation.

To J. N. Arbery, Esq., London House, Wantage, for 'Calebasse Grosse' Pears.

Other Exhibits.

Colonel Archer Houblon, Welford Park, Newbury (gr. Mr. C. Ross): Pear 'Margaretha' and Apples 'Richard' and 'Redwing.'

Messrs. Merryweather, Southwell: Damson 'Merryweather,' a large variety. The Committee instructed the Secretary and Superintendent to cook the fruit and report to them on its qualities (see below).

S. J. Squibbs, Esq., Whittlebury Lodge, Towcester: a box of Plums.

Sir John Thornycroft, Eyot Villa, Chiswick: three seedling Apples, one of which, named 'Blanche,' the Committee desired to see again.

Mr. W. Peters, Givons Gardens, Leatherhead: Apple 'Hairy Pring,' very similar to 'Grantonian.'

FRUIT AND VEGETABLE COMMITTEE, OCTOBER 29, 1907.

Mr. BUNYARD, V.M.H., in the Chair, and sixteen members present.

Awards Recommended :—

Silver-gilt Knightian Medal.

To Messrs. Bunyard, Maidstone, for a collection of Pears.

Silver Knightian Medal.

To Mr. R. W. Green, Wisbech, for a collection of Potatos.

Silver Banksian Medal.

To Miss Dixon, Westergate, Chichester, for Melons.
To Messrs. Low, Enfield, for a collection of Apples and Pears.

Bronze Banksian Medal.

To R. H. Ling, Esq., The Braes, Berkhampstead (gr. Mr. Bedford), for Onions.

Award of Merit.

To Damson 'Merryweather' (votes, unanimous), from Messrs. Merryweather, Southwell, Notts. A seedling Damson of great size, fine dark colour, pleasant flavour; the fruiting branches sent were laden with fruit. The tree is evidently a strong grower, with thick leathery foliage, and a free bearer. The Secretary and Superintendent had some of the fruit cooked, and reported to the Committee that the flavour was excellent.

Other Exhibits.

Miss M. H. Dodge, Loseley Park, Guildford (gr. Mr. Staward): Vegetables.

Miss Williams, Fairfield, Walton-by-Clevedon: Apple 'Kenn Seedling.'

Mrs. Tyler, Ashby-de-la-Zouch: an Apple; a seedling from Alfriston, somewhat similar to the parent.

Mr. E. Lane, Kentchurch Court, Hereford : a seedling Apple raised apparently from ' Gravenstein.'

Miss Roberts, Rose Hill House, Ipswich : an Apple similar to ' Hereford Beaufin.'

Mr. H. G. Wadlow, Marylands, Peterborough : an Apple raised from ' Barnack Beauty '; of very marked acidity.

P. Edie, Esq., Willow Cottage, Bexley : a seedling Apple.

Messrs. Cannell, Swanley : Apple ' Abundance.'

Messrs. Cooper, Tabor, 90 Southwark Street, S.E. : Marrow Cabbage (Chou Moëllier).

Messrs. J. Veitch, Chelsea : Pyronia (*Pyrus × Cydonia*), a hybrid between a Pear and a Quince. The fruit was small and of very good flavour, and the Committee asked to see it again next year. Two seeds were produced from the cross, one producing a Quince and the other a Pear.

FRUIT AND VEGETABLE COMMITTEE, NOVEMBER 12, 1907.

Mr. J. CHEAL in the Chair, and thirteen members present.

Awards Recommended :—

Silver Knightian Medal.

To Messrs. Dobbie, Rothesay, for Potatos.

Silver Banksian Medal.

To Messrs. Cheal, Crawley, for Vegetables.

Other Exhibits.

Mr. J. Toogood, Fulmodeston, East Dereham : Parsley ' Ostrich Plume,' which the Committee wished tried at Wisley : and Apple ' Autumn Glory,' very similar to ' Margil.'

Messrs. Low, Enfield : Apples.

Mr. A. Faulkner, Inkpen, Hungerford : Nut ' Faulkner's Prolific.'

Messrs. Cooling, Bath : Pear ' November Favourite.'

FRUIT AND VEGETABLE COMMITTEE, NOVEMBER 26, 1907.

Mr. BUNYARD, V.M.H., in the Chair, and eighteen members present.

Awards Recommended :—

Silver-gilt Hogg Medal.

To the Duke of Rutland, Belvoir Castle, Grantham (gr. Mr. Divers), for a collection of fruit.

Silver Banksian Medal.

To Mrs. Thornhill, Stanton Hall, Bakewell (gr. Mr. Harvey), for home-grown Oranges and Lemons.

To Messrs. Low, Enfield, for Apples and Oranges.

Other Exhibits.

Mrs. E. Massey, Finchingfield, Braintree : Apple, 'Prince Olaf,' raised from 'Newton Pippin.' A promising variety which the Committee desired to see again.

Mr. Philip Le Cornu, Jersey : Apple 'Lansdowne Seedling,' closely resembling ' Mère de Ménage.'

FRUIT AND VEGETABLE COMMITTEE, DECEMBER 10, 1907.

Mr. BUNYARD, V.M.H., in the Chair, and twenty members present.

Awards Recommended :—

Silver-gilt Knightian Medal.

To Lord Llangattock, The Hendre, Monmouth (gr. Mr. Coomber), for ' Charlotte Rothschild ' Pine Apples.

Silver Knightian Medal.

To the Earl of Harrington, Elvaston Castle, Derby (gr. Mr. Goodacre), for Grapes.

To Viscount Enfield, Wrotham Park, Barnet (gr. Mr. Markham), for a collection of fruit.

Silver Banksian Medal.

To Messrs. Massey, Spalding, for Potatos.

Award of Merit.

To Pear 'Beurré de Naghan' (votes, unanimous), from Messrs. Cheal, Crawley. Fruit rather large, pyriform, broad at the middle ; stalk 1 inch long, prominently inserted and wrinkled at the base ; eyes set in a broad and rather deep basin ; segments erect and inclined to close over the eye ; skin pale yellow, and covered with minute russety dots ; flesh white, melting, and of delicious flavour. Parentage unknown, supposed to have been brought over from a French monastery. (Fig. 107.)

Other Exhibits.

Mr. Challis, Wilton House Gardens, Salisbury : an Apple of no special merit.

Mr. C. Ross, Welford Park Newbury : seedling Apples and Pears.

Messrs. Sutton, Reading : hybrids between Brussels Sprouts and Cabbage, and between Brussels Sprouts and Savoys. They were referred to the Scientific Committee.

Miss E. Webb, Newstead Abbey, Notts : fine fruits of *Akebia lobata.*

Sir Weetman Pearson, Bart., M.P. (gr. Mr. Wadds) : Tomato 'Lye's Early Prolific,' which the Committee wished tried at Wisley.

FRUIT AND VEGETABLE COMMITTEE, DECEMBER 31, 1907.

Mr. BUNYARD, V.M.H., in the Chair, and eleven members present.

Awards Recommended :—

Gold Medal.

To Messrs. Veitch, Chelsea, for a superb collection of Apples and Pears.

FIG. 107.—PEAR 'BEURRÉ DE NAGHAN.' (*Journal of Horticulture.*)

Silver Banksian Medal.

To Sir E. Loder, Bart., Leonardslee, Horsham, for Apples and Pears.

First-class Certificate.

To Potato 'Favourite' (votes, unanimous), from Messrs. Dobbie, Rothesay. A handsome, round, white variety with a russety skin, shallow eyes, and free from disease. This variety produced a heavy crop at Wisley; and, after cooking on two occasions, the last being on the above date, the Committee considered the quality so excellent that they unanimously recommended the highest award.

Cultural Commendation.

To Mr. Allan, Gunton Park Gardens, Norwich, for remarkably fine and deliciously flavoured fruit of Pear ' President Barabé.'

Other Exhibits.

Mr. H. Fletcher, Annesley, Notts : a seedling Apple.

Mr. Divers, Belvoir Castle Gardens, Grantham : Pear 'St. Stephen,' raised from ' Madame Millet ' × ' Marie Louise.' The fruit resembled the latter variety in shape, but the flesh was somewhat gritty, as the fruits were from a bush tree. The Committee asked to see fruit from a wall tree.

Messrs. Veitch, Chelsea : Apple 'Langley Favourite,' raised from ' Bismarck ' × ' Cornish Gilliflower.' The fruits resembled the latter in shape but the former in flavour.

ORCHID COMMITTEE.

ORCHID COMMITTEE, JULY 9, 1907, AT HOLLAND HOUSE.

Mr. J. GURNEY FOWLER in the Chair, and twenty-three members present.

[For Cups and Medals awarded by the Council see p. cxxix.]

Awards Recommended :—

First-class Certificate.

To *Laelio-Cattleya* × ' Clive,' 'Lambeau's variety' (*L. pumila praestans* × *C. Dowiana aurea*) (votes, 22 for, 2 against), from Mons. Lambeau, Brussels. A remarkable variation, much taller in growth and larger in flower than other forms. Sepals and petals deep purplish rose, the finely displayed lip ruby-crimson, with thin gold lines from the base to the centre.

Award of Merit.

To *Cymbidium Humblotii* (votes, unanimous), from Mons. A. A. Peeters, Brussels. Flowers bearing a resemblance to those of *Coelogyne pandurata* ; pale apple-green, with blackish markings on the bases of the petals and the lip (Botanical Certificate, June 7, 1892).

To *Brasso-Cattleya* × ' Mary ' (*B. nodosa grandiflora* × *C. Lawrenceana*) (votes, unanimous), from Sir Jeremiah Colman, Bart., Gatton Park (gr. Mr. W. P. Bound). Flowers shaped nearer to those of the Brassavola parent, but larger, cream white, spotted with rose-purple. (Fig. 108.)

Other Exhibits.

Sir Jeremiah Colman, Bart., Gatton Park : a group of Orchids, including British species.

Messrs. Sander, St. Albans : rare species and hybrids.

Messrs. Charlesworth, Bradford : group in which the various Laelio-Cattleyas and hybrid Cattleyas were effectively displayed.

Messrs. Hugh Low, Enfield : group of Oncidiums, Odontoglossums, &c.

Messrs. Stanley, Southgate : group of Cattleyas.

Mrs. Ernest Hills, Redleaf, Penshurst (gr. Mr. Ringbam) : a group of *Miltonia vexillaria.*

R. I. Measures, Esq., Camberwell (gr. Mr. Smith) : group of over fifty species, varieties, and hybrids.

Messrs. Jas. Veitch, Chelsea : a group.

Francis Wellesley, Esq. (gr. Mr. Hopkins) : *Cattleya Warscewiczii* ' Mrs. Francis Wellesley,' a large light-coloured flower of good shape.

Walter Cobb, Esq. (gr. Mr. C. J. Salter) : *Odontoglossum* × *Cobbianum.*

W. P. Burkinshaw, Esq., Hessle, Hull : *Cattleya Mossiae Reineckiana.*
J. W. Jessop, Esq., Rawdon, Leeds (gr. Mr. Wilkinson) : *Aerides multiflorum Lobbii.*

Fig. 108.—Brasso-Cattleya × 'Mary.' (*Journal of Horticulture.*)

Mons. A. A. Peeters, Brussels : *Odontoglossum crispum* 'La Dame Blanche.'

Orchid Committee, July 23, 1907.

Mr. J. Gurney Fowler in the Chair, and eighteen members present.

Awards Recommended :—

Gold Medal.

To Major G. L. Holford, C.V.O., C.I.E., Westonbirt, Tetbury (gr. Mr. H. G. Alexander), for a fine group chiefly of hybrids raised at Westonbirt.

Silver Flora Medal.

To Messrs. Charlesworth, Heaton, Bradford, for a group of Orchids.
To Messrs. Cripps, Tunbridge Wells, for *Disa grandiflora.*

Silver Banksian Medal.

To Messrs. Sander, St. Albans, for a group containing several curious species of Orchids.
To Messrs. Jas. Veitch, King's Road, Chelsea, for Orchids.
To. R. I. Measures, Esq., Camberwell (gr. Mr. Smith), for a group.

Award of Merit.

To *Cattleya* × 'Waldemar' (× *Whitei* × *Dowiana aurea*) (votes, unanimous), from Major G. L. Holford, C.V.O., C.I.E. (gr. Mr. Alexander). Sepals and petals cream colour tinged with rose ; labellum broad and crimped, blush-white veined and marbled with rose-purple.

To *Cattleya* × 'Maecenas,' var. 'Thor' (*Warscewiczii* × *superba*) (votes, unanimous), from Major G. L. Holford. Inflorescence erect, bearing six flowers ; sepals and petals blush-rose colour ; front of the labellum ruby-purple, the disc and throat white with a yellow zone.

To *Miltonia vexillaria*, 'Lambeau's variety' (votes, unanimous), from Mons. Lambeau, Brussels. Sepals and petals bright rose with white margin ; lip 4 inches across, bright purplish-rose with darker rose veining ; disc white with several red lines.

To *Dossinia marmorata* (votes, unanimous), from R. I. Measures, Esq., Camberwell. The fine Bornean species, often named *Anaectochilus Lowii*, in gardens.

Other Exhibits.

J. Gurney Fowler, Esq. (gr. Mr. J. Davis) : *Cattleya Warscewiczii saturata* and *Laelio-Cattleya* × 'Henry Greenwood,' 'Glebelands variety.'

Francis Wellesley, Esq. (gr. Mr. Hopkins) : *Laelio-Cattleya* × *Clonia gigantea*, a fine magenta-purple flower.

Messrs. Charlesworth : *Odontoglossum Pescatorei* 'Golden Gem.'

H. T. Pitt, Esq. (gr. Mr. Thurgood) : *Oncidium pumilum* and *Dendrobium ciliatum annamense.*

F. W. Moore, Esq., Royal Botanic Gardens, Glasnevin, Dublin : an inflorescence of the rare *Lueddemannia Pescatorei.*

Messrs. Hugh Low : Cattleyas.

ORCHID COMMITTEE, AUGUST 6, 1907.

Mr. HARRY J. VEITCH in the Chair, and fifteen members present.

Awards Recommended :—

Silver Flora Medal.

To Messrs. Charlesworth, Heaton, Bradford, for a group of Orchids.

Silver Banksian Medal.

To H. S. Goodson, Esq., Putney (gr. Mr. G. E. Day), for a group.

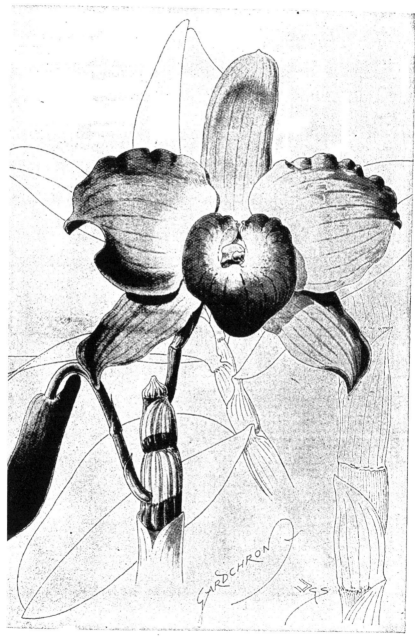

FIG. 109.—DENDROBIUM REGIUM. (*Gardeners' Chronicle.*)

First-class Certificate.

To *Dendrobium regium*, Prain (votes, unanimous), from Sir Trevor Lawrence, Bart., and Messrs. Charlesworth. A pretty and distinct species allied to *D. nobile*, and recorded as native of Lower Hindustan. Flowers clear rose colour, the base of the lip being white, the disc yellow, and without the dark blotch usually seen in *D. nobile*. (Fig. 109.)

To *Cattleya × Germania superba* (*granulosa Schofieldiana × Hardyana*) (votes, unanimous), from Major G. L. Holford, C.V.O., C.I.E. (gr. Mr. H. G. Alexander). Sepals and petals purplish-rose; lip ruby-crimson.

Award of Merit.

To *Miltonia vexillaria Lambeauiana* (votes, unanimous), from Mons. Jules Hye de Crom, Ghent (gr. Mr. Coen). A pure white variety with yellow crest, and without the reddish lines usually seen on the lip of this species.

Cultural Commendation.

To Mr. H. G. Alexander, Orchid grower to Major G. L. Holford, for *Cattleya × Germania superba*, with four spikes bearing together thirty-two flowers.

To Mr. H. Ballantine, gr. to Baron Sir H. Schröder, for *Cypripedium × 'W. R. Lee,' var. 'Lord Derby,'* with eleven spikes having an aggregate of thirty-four flowers.

Other Exhibits.

J. Gurney Fowler, Esq. (gr. Mr. Davis): *Aerides Houlletianum,* 'Fowler's variety,' for which **F.C.C.** was awarded July 17, 1906.

Major G. L. Holford: *Miltonia vexillaria,* 'Hardy's variety,' with forty-six flowers; and the very handsome *Laelio-Cattleya × elegans* 'King Edward.'

Francis Wellesley, Esq. (gr. Mr. Hopkins): hybrid Orchids.

De B. Crawshay, Esq. (gr. Mr. Stables): hybrid Odontoglossums.

Sir Jeremiah Colman, Bart. (gr. Mr. Bound): *Epi-Laelia × longiciliare* (*Laelia longipes × Epidendrum ciliare*).

Sir Trevor Lawrence, Bart. (gr. Mr. W. H. White): *Laelia × 'Purple May'* (*majalis × purpurata*).

ORCHID COMMITTEE, AUGUST 20, 1907.

Mr. J. GURNEY FOWLER in the Chair, and nineteen members present.

Awards Recommended:—

Silver-gilt Lindley Medal.

To Major G. L. Holford, C.V.O., C.I.E., Westonbirt, Tetbury (gr. Mr. H. G. Alexander), for a noble specimen of *Laelio-Cattleya × elegans*, with thirty spikes bearing together 230 fine rose-purple flowers.

Silver Flora Medal.

To Messrs. Sander, St. Albans, for a group.

To Messrs. Charlesworth, Bradford, for a group.

To Mrs. Temple, Leyswood, Groombridge (gr. Mr. Bristow), for a fine selection of *Disa grandiflora.*

To Messrs. Armstrong & Brown, Tunbridge Wells, for a group.

Silver Banksian Medal.

To Sir Trevor Lawrence, Bart. (gr. Mr. W. H. White), for a group of twenty-four plants of the light scarlet *Habenaria rhodocheila* and other Orchids.

To Major G. L. Holford, for six new hybrid Orchids.

Award of Merit.

To *Miltonia Schröderiana,* 'Heaton variety' (votes, unanimous), from Messrs. Charlesworth, Heaton, Bradford. Flowers larger than in the ordinary form. Sepals and petals whitish, closely barred with chocolate colour; lip white with a magenta-rose base.

Botanical Certificate.

To *Polycycnis Charlesworthii,* from Messrs. Charlesworth. Pseudo-bulbs ovate; leaves stalked, ovate-acuminate; inflorescence decurved, and bearing about fifty flowers, each 1 inch across; sepals broad, yellowish, densely spotted with red brown; petals linear and curiously curved, yellow with a few red spots at the base; lip narrow, brownish, studded with white hairs.

To *Bulbophyllum longisepalum,* from Sir Trevor Lawrence, Bart. (gr. Mr. W. H. White). Sepals inclined forward, forming a beak-like flower some 6 inches in length, whitish, heavily netted and tinged with claret-colour (*B. grandiflorum* of *Lindenia* III.).

Cultural Commendation.

To Mr. W. H. White, Orchid grower to Sir Trevor Lawrence, Bart., for a fine specimen of *Bulbophyllum longisepalum,* with fourteen flowers.

Other Exhibits.

Baron Sir H. Schröder, The Dell, Egham (gr. Mr. Ballantine): a new *Cypripedium* × *dellense (Mastersianum* × *Rothschildianum).*

Sir Jeremiah Colman, Bart. (gr. Mr. Bound): *Cattleya* × 'Adula' (*bicolor* × *Hardyana*).

Messrs. Jas. Veitch: *Cypripedium* × 'Jas. H. Veitch' (*Curtisii* × *Stonei platytaenium*).

Messrs. Hugh Low: a selection of Orchids.

Messrs. McBean, Cooksbridge: *Oncidium macranthum nanum* and *Odontoglossum Harryanum grande.*

ORCHID COMMITTEE, SEPTEMBER 3, 1907.

Mr. J. GURNEY FOWLER in the Chair, and seventeen members present.

Awards Recommended :—

Silver-gilt Lindley Medal.

To the Hon. Walter Rothschild, M.P., Tring Park, Tring (gr. Mr. A. Dye), for a group of *Lissochilus giganteus.* each plant bearing one or two stout spikes, 7 feet in height, and furnished with rose-coloured flowers, each 3 inches across. The plants, which were imported from the Congo, were grown as marsh plants.

Silver Flora Medal.

To Messrs. Jas. Veitch, Chelsea, for hybrid Cattleyas and Laelias.

To Messrs. Charlesworth, Heaton, Bradford, for a group.

To Messrs. Sander, for a group.

Fig. 110.—Brasso-Laelio-Cattleya × 'Rowena.' (*Journal of Horticulture.*)

Silver Banksian Medal.

To Messrs. Hugh Low, Enfield, for a group.

First-class Certificate.

To *Brasso-Laelio-Cattleya* × 'Rowena' (*L.-C.* 'Doris' × *B. Digbyana*) (votes, unanimous), from Major G. L. Holford, C.V.O., C.I.E.,

Westonbirt, Tetbury (gr. Mr. Alexander). A large-flowered variety of clear light-yellow colour and with fringed lip. (Fig. 110.)

To *Cattleya* × Iris ' His Majesty ' (*bicolor* × *Dowiana aurea*) (votes, unanimous), from Messrs. Jas. Veitch, Chelsea. Flowers of the largest of its class. Sepals and petals bronzy-orange shading to sulphur-yellow at the margin ; lip ruby-crimson.

Award of Merit.

To *Stanhopea platyceras* (votes, unanimous), from the Hon. Walter Rothschild (gr. Mr. A. Dye). A very handsome species from Colombia. Sepals and petals cream-white dotted with purple ; lip large and fleshy, the boat-shaped base heavily marked with blackish-purple, the remaining portion white, spotted with purple.

To *Cattleya* × *Hardyana* var. ' Madame Valcke ' (votes, unanimous), from Mons. A. A. Peeters, Brussels. Sepals and petals white ; lip light rose-colour with a broad pale lilac margin.

To *Sophro-Laelio-Cattleya* × ' Phyllis ' (*Sophro-Laelio* × *laeta* × *Cattleya Lawrenceana*) (votes, unanimous), from Major G. L. Holford. A dwarf plant bearing comparatively large bright purple flowers.

Botanical Certificate.

To *Eulophia ensata*, from the Hon. Walter Rothschild. A singular South African species, with pale yellow flowers, having a hairy, orange-coloured crest to the lip.

Other Exhibits.

Major G. L. Holford (gr. Mr. Alexander) : hybrid Orchids.

J. Gurney Fowler, Esq. (gr. Mr. Davis), *Cypripedium* × *Massaianum* and *C.* × *calloso-Rothschildianum* for comparison.

Messrs. Armstrong & Brown : hybrid Orchids.

Sir Jeremiah Colman, Bart. : several interesting species.

H. T. Pitt, Esq.: *Cattleya Hardyana* ' Countess of Derby.'

ORCHID COMMITTEE, SEPTEMBER 17, 1907.

Mr. J. GURNEY FOWLER in the Chair, and twenty members present.

Awards Recommended :—

Silver Flora Medal.

To Messrs. Charlesworth, Heaton, Bradford, for hybrids and rare species.

To Messrs. Jas. Veitch, Chelsea, for hybrid Cattleyas and Laelio-Cattleyas.

To Messrs. Sander, St. Albans, for a group.

To Messrs. Armstrong & Brown, Tunbridge Wells, for a group of *Cattleya* × Iris and other Orchids.

To Messrs. Moore, Rawdon, Leeds, for a group.

Award of Merit.

To *Sophro-Laelia* × *Gratrixae* (*S. grandiflora* × *L. tenebrosa*) (votes, unanimous), from F. Menteith Ogilvie, Esq., The Shrubbery, Oxford (gr.

Mr. Balmforth). Resembling a very dwarf *L. tenebrosa.* Sepals and petals reddish-buff; lip rose, marked with claret-colour.

To *Sophro-Cattleya* × 'Antióchus' (*C. Warscewiczii* × *S.-C.* × 'Cleopatra') (votes, unanimous), from Messrs. Charlesworth. Flowers formed like *C. Warscewiczii,* but smaller. Sepals and petals bright purplish-rose on a yellowish ground-colour; disc of the lip chrome-yellow, the tips of the side lobes and the front ruby-crimson.

Botanical Certificate.

To *Epidendrum campylostalix,* from Sir Trevor Lawrence, Bart., Burford (gr. Mr. W. H. White). Pseudo-bulbs and leaves greyish-green; inflorescence bearing smallish green flowers tinged with purple; lip white. •

Other Exhibits.

Sir Trevor Lawrence, Bart.: the handsome *Cattleya* × *Hardyana marmorata,* several Catasetums and hybrid Orchids.

Major G. L. Holford, C.V.O., C.I.E. (gr. Mr. Alexander): hybrid Orchids.

Francis Wellesley, Esq., Westfield, Woking (gr. Mr. Hopkins): *Cattleya* × 'Mrs. Frederick Knollys' (*granulosa Buyssoniana* × *Bowringiana*) and *C.* × Adula 'Mrs. Francis Wellesley' (*bicolor* × *Hardyana*).

F. Menteith Ogilvie, Esq.: *Laelio-Cattleya* × 'W. Balmforth' (*C. Warnerii* × *L.-C.* × *callistoglossa*).

Mons. Mertens, Ghent: varieties of *Miltonia vexillaria.*

ORCHID COMMITTEE, OCTOBER 1, 1907.

Mr. J. GURNEY FOWLER in the Chair, and twenty members present.

Awards Recommended :—

Silver Flora Medal.

To Sir Jeremiah Colman, Bart., Gatton Park, Reigate (gr. Mr. W. P. Bound), for a group of hybrid Orchids raised at Gatton Park.

To Messrs. Charlesworth, for a group of hybrids.

To H. S. Goodson, Esq., Putney (gr. Mr. Day), for a group.

To Messrs. Cypher, Cheltenham, for *Cypripedium Fairrieanum.*

To Messrs. Armstrong & Brown, Tunbridge Wells, for a group of hybrid Cattleyas.

To Messrs. Hugh Low, for a group.

Award of Merit.

To *Laelio-Cattleya* × 'The Duchess' (*C.* × *Hardyana* × *L.-C.* × 'Hippolyta') (votes, unanimous), from Messrs. Sander, St. Albans. In form and habit similar to *L.-C.* × *Cappei,* but with larger flowers; sepals and petals light orange faintly tinged with rose; lip ruby-purple.

To *Odontoglossum Pescatorei ornatum* (votes, unanimous), from Messrs. McBean, Cooksbridge. A fine form with white sepals and petals, and large white labellum blotched with violet colour.

Botanical Certificate.

To *Catasetum laminatum*, from J. Gurney Fowler, Esq., Glebe-lands, South Woodford (gr. Mr. J. Davis). The plant bore two many-flowered spikes, the flowers being pale green with a thin cream-white keel up the middle of the labellum.

Other Exhibits.

Major G. L. Holford, C.V.O., C.I.E. (gr. Mr. Alexander) : new hybrid Orchids.

J. Gurney Fowler, Esq. (gr. Mr. Davis) : *Cattleya* × ' Prince Edward,' with seven flowers on a spike, and *Cymbidium erythrostylum*.

Messrs. Sander : a group.

Messrs. Jas. Veitch : a very fine *Cattleya* × *Davisii* (*velutina* × *Hardyana*).

C. J. Lucas, Esq. (gr. Mr. Duncan) : *Cattleya* × Iris ' Warnham Court variety.'

Francis Wellesley, Esq. (gr. Mr. Hopkins) : *Laelio-Cattleya* × ' Lady Leese ' (*L.-C.* × *callistoglossa* × *L. xanthina*).

ORCHID COMMITTEE, OCTOBER 15, 1907.

Mr. HARRY J. VEITCH in the Chair, and twenty-two members present.

Awards Recommended :—

Silver Flora Medal.

To Leopold de Rothschild, Esq., Gunnersbury House, Acton (gr. Mr. J. Hudson), for a group of *Cattleya labiata*, *Vanda coerulea* and other showy Orchids.

To Messrs. Charlesworth : for a group.

To Messrs. Jas. Veitch : for hybrid Orchids.

To Messrs. Sander : for a group of *Cattleya labiata* and hybrids.

Silver Banksian Medal.

To Norman C. Cookson, Esq., Oakwood, Wylam (gr. Mr. Chapman), for hybrid Cypripediums, Cattleyas.

To Messrs. Hugh Low, for a group.

To Messrs. McBean, Cooksbridge, for a collection of varieties of *Cattleya Dowiana aurea*, hybrid Cypripediums, and Odontoglossums.

To Messrs. Moore, Rawdon, Leeds, for a group.

To Messrs. Stanley, Southgate, for *Cattleya labiata*.

First-class Certificate.

Arachnanthe Rohaniana (*Renanthera Rohaniana* Rchb. f., *Xenia*, vol. i. p. 89) (votes, unanimous), from J. Gurney Fowler, Esq., Glebe-lands, South Woodford (gr. Mr. J. Davis). Plant in its broad leaves and erect habit differing considerably from the curved-leafed *Arachnanthe Lowii*, to which, however, in its flowers it bears a general resemblance, the chief differences being in the structural arrangement of the lip and the brighter colour of the dimorphic flowers. The inflorescence bore three large yellow basal flowers, slightly spotted with purple, and after an interval of 9 inches twenty fine cream-white flowers, heavily barred with dark red. The plant is a portion of the type specimen from the collection of Prince Camille de Rohan. (Fig. 111.)

Fig. 111.—Arachnanthe Rohaniana. (*The Garden.*)

To *Cattleya × Hardyana*, 'Westonbirt variety' (*Warscewiczii × Dowiana aurea*) (votes, unanimous), from Major G. L. Holford, C.V.O., C.I.E., Westonbirt (gr. Mr. H. G. Alexander). A grand variety with fine flowers, 8 inches across, and of a bright rosy-mauve colour mottled with white; lip dark ruby-purple with gold lines.

Award of Merit.

To *Cattleya labiata* 'Daphne' (votes, unanimous), from J. Bradshaw, Esq., The Grange, Southgate. Flowers pure white with a small violet spot on the lip in front of the yellow disc.

To *Cypripedium × Nandii* 'Low's variety' (*callosum × Tautzianum*) (votes, 9 for, 3 against), from Norman C. Cookson, Esq. (gr. Mr. Chapman). Flowers white, delicately tinged with rose.

Other Exhibits.

The Right Hon. the Earl of Onslow, Clandon Park, Guildford (gr. Mr. Blake) : a fine six-flowered inflorescence of *Cattleya labiata.*

Messrs. Linden, Brussels : two home-raised spotted forms of *Odontoglossum crispum.*

Messrs. Jas. Cypher, Cheltenham : Cypripediums and Cattleyas.

Messrs. Armstrong & Brown, Tunbridge Wells : the pretty *Cattleya × Armstrongiae magnifica* and the singular *Bulbophyllum Dayanum.*

J. Forster Alcock, Esq. : a hybrid Cypripedium, with the lower sepals developed as in the upper.

Henry Little, Esq. : *Cypripedium × 'Winifred Little.'*

ORCHID COMMITTEE, OCTOBER 29, 1907.

Mr. J. GURNEY FOWLER in the Chair, and nineteen members present.

Awards Recommended :—

Gold Medal.

To Major G. L. Holford, C.V.O., C.I.E., Westonbirt (gr. Mr. Alexander), for a magnificent group of Orchids, principally hybrids raised at Westonbirt, and occupying a space of 200 square feet.

Gold Lindley Medal.

To Major G. L. Holford, for the excellence of the cultivation of all the Orchids in his group.

Silver Flora Medal.

To H. S. Goodson, Esq., Fairlawn, Putney (gr. Mr. Day), for a group.

To Messrs. Jas. Cypher, Cheltenham, for a group of *Cypripedium Fairrieanum* and other Cypripediums.

Silver Banksian Medal.

To Sir Jeremiah Colman, Bart., Gatton Park, Reigate (gr. Mr. Bound), for a collection of hybrid Cattleyas and Laelio-Cattleyas raised at Gatton Park.

To Messrs. Jas. Veitch, for hybrid Orchids.

To Messrs. Charlesworth, for a group.

To Messrs. Hugh Low, for a group.

To Messrs. Armstrong & Brown, Tunbridge Wells, for hybrid Cattleyas, &c.

First-class Certificate.

To *Cattleya × Fabia gigantea (labiata × Dowiana aurea)* (votes, unanimous), from Major G. L. Holford, C.V.O., C.I.E., sepals and petals deep rosy-mauve colour; labellum ruby-crimson with orange centre and deep gold veining.

FIG. 112.—CATTLEYA × FULVESCENS. (*Journal of Horticulture.*)

To *Cattleya labiata alba* 'Purity' (votes, unanimous), from Major G. L. Holford.

To *Cattleya × fulvescens,* 'Westonbirt variety' (*Forbesii × Dowiana aurea* (votes, unanimous), from Major G. L. Holford. A large and finely formed flower with yellowish buff sepals and petals and orange-coloured lip changing to yellow at the margin and blotched and tinged with rose-colour. (Fig. 112.)

To *Odontioda × Devossiana* (*O. Edwardii × Cochlioda Noezliana*) (votes, unanimous), from Mons. H. Graire, Amiens. Inflorescence 2 feet, the upper half bearing a four-branched head of blood-red flowers with yellow crest, and each about an inch across.

Award of Merit.

To *Sophro-Laelio-Cattleya × Medea* (*C. bicolor ∕ S.-L. × laeta Orpetiana*) (votes, 10 for, 5 against), from Major G. L. Holford. Plant dwarf; flowers in shape resembling *C. bicolor*, purplish, with violet-purple lip.

To *Laelio-Cattleya × Epicasta* 'The Premier' (*L. Pumila ∕ C. Warscewiczii*) (votes, 7 for, 0 against), from Sir Jeremiah Colman, Bart., Gatton Park (gr. Mr. Bound). A large flower with white sepals and petals tinged with rose-pink; lip deep purplish-crimson.

To *Cattleya × Aliciae* (*labiata × Iris*) (votes, 13 for, 2 against), from H. S. Goodson, Esq. (gr. Mr. Day). Flowers rosy-lilac with elongated rosy-crimson lip.

To *Cattleya labiata angusta* (votes, 10 for, 0 against), from J. Bradshaw, Esq., The Grange, Southgate. A clear white variety with chrome-yellow centre to the lip, which has a slight tinge of pink in front.

Other Exhibits.

J. Gurney Fowler, Esq. (gr. Mr. Davis): *Odontoglossum × Duvivierianum* and the pure white *Laelia pumila alba*.

De B. Crawshay, Esq. (gr. Mr. Stables): the handsomely blotched *Odontoglossum crispum* 'Boadicea,' and *O. crispum* 'Imperatrix.'

Miss Willmott, Warley Place, Great Warley: a very fine variety of *Cattleya ∕* 'Minucia.'

J. Shepherd, Esq., Twyford: a large specimen of *Laelio-Cattleya ∕* 'Tiresias.'

F. Du Cane Godman, Esq.: *Cypripedium Phaedra superba*.

ORCHID COMMITTEE, NOVEMBER 12, 1907.

Mr. J. GURNEY FOWLER in the Chair, and twenty-six members present.

Awards Recommended :—

Silver Banksian Medal.

To H. Spicer, Esq., Aberdeen Park, Highbury (gr. Mr. Lovegrove), **for a group of** *Cypripedium Spicerianum*.

To Messrs. Sander, St. Albans, for a group.

Messrs. Cypher, Cheltenham, for Cypripediums.

To Messrs. Hugh Low, Enfield, for Cattleyas.

To Mons. Mertens, Ghent, for hybrid Odontoglossums.

Bronze Banksian Medal.

To Messrs. Armstrong & Brown, Tunbridge Wells, for hybrid Cypripediums and Cattleyas.

First-class Certificate.

To *Cypripedium* × *nitens-Leeanum* var. 'Hannibal' (*Leeanum-giganteum* × *nitens magnificum*) (votes, unanimous), from Major G. L. Holford, C.V.O., C.I.E. (gr. Mr. H. G. Alexander). Dorsal sepal apple-green at the base, spotted with purple, the upper half white ; petals and lips honey-yellow tinged with reddish-purple.

Award of Merit.

To *Habenaria ugandae* (votes, unanimous), from Sir Trevor Lawrence, Bart., Burford (gr. Mr. W. H. White). A fine species from Uganda. Allied to *Habenaria Bonatea.*

Cultural Commendation.

To Mr. W. H. White, Orchid grower to Sir Trevor Lawrence, Bart., for a specimen of *Habenaria ugandae,* with a stout stem, 4 feet in height, furnished with fleshy light green leaves on the lower half and an inflorescence of twenty-five white and green flowers, with spurs 6 inches in length on the upper part.

Other Exhibits.

Sir Jeremiah Colman, Bart., Gatton Park (gr. Mr. W. P. Bound) : the pretty *Brasso-Cattleya* × 'Mary' and *Coelogyne Colmanii.*

Major G. L. Holford, C.V.O., C.I.E.: *Laelio-Cattleya* × 'Priam' (*C. Harrisoniana* × *L.-C. callistoglossa*) ; and *L.-C.* × 'Golden Beauty' (*L.-C. Ernestii* × *C. Dowiana*).

Francis Wellesley, Esq. (gr. Mr. Hopkins) : *Cypripedium* × 'Emperor of India.'

J. Forster Alcock, Esq., Northchurch : *Cypripedium* × *nobile,* of unrecorded parentage.

Mr. H. A. Tracy: a fine form of *Cypripedium* × 'Fred. Hardy.'

Messrs. Jas. Veitch : *Cypripedium* × 'Diomede' ('Niobe' × *Leeanum*).

ORCHID COMMITTEE, NOVEMBER 26, 1907.

Mr. J. GURNEY FOWLER in the Chair, and twenty members present.

Awards Recommended :—

Silver-gilt Flora Medal.

To Messrs. Cypher, Cheltenham, for Cypripediums.

Silver Flora Medal.

To Francis Wellesley, Esq., Westfield (gr. Mr. Hopkins), for rare hybrid Cypripediums.

To Messrs. Charlesworth, for Laelio-Cattleyas.

Silver Banksian Medal.

To Messrs. Jas. Veitch, for Laelio-Cattleyas and Cypripediums.

To Messrs. Hugh Low, for a group.

To Mons. Mertens, Ghent, hybrid Odontoglossums.

To Mr. H. A. Tracy, Twickenham, for a group.

To W. M. Appleton, Esq., Weston-super-Mare, for a group.

First-class Certificate.

To *Odontoglossum* × 'John Clarke' (parentage unrecorded) (votes, unanimous), from Baron Sir H. Schröder, The Dell, Egham (gr. Mr. Ballantine). A fine hybrid allied to *O. Lambeauianum*. Colour white, tinged with mauve and heavily blotched with mauve-purple. (Fig. 113.)

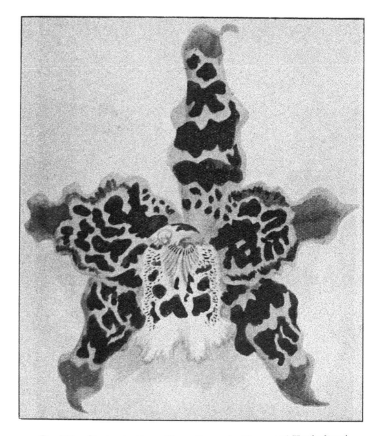

Fig. 113.—Odontoglossum × 'John Clarke.' (*Journal of Horticulture.*)

Award of Merit.

To *Laelio-Cattleya* × 'Ortrude' (*L. anceps* × *C. Dowiana aurea*) (votes, unanimous), from Major G. L. Holford, C.V.O., C.I.E., Westonbirt (gr. Mr. Alexander). Flower retaining the form of *L. anceps*, but much larger; sepals and petals blush-rose colour; lip broad, crimson, with gold lines at the base.

To *Cypripedium* × 'Ernest Read' (parentage unrecorded) (votes unanimous), from J. Gurney Fowler, Esq., Glebelands, South Woodford

3 k

(gr. Mr. J. Davis). A large flower of light colour and a model in shape ; cream-white delicately tinted with rose and slightly marked with emerald-green.

To *Angraecum Buyssonii* (votes, unanimous), from Messrs. Charlesworth. A fine species with inflorescence resembling *A. articulatum* and *A. Ellisii*, but of scandent habit of growth, the stems bearing sixteen to eighteen leaves each. Flowers white, the long spurs tinged with pale reddish-brown.

FIG. 114.—CYPRIPEDIUM × SANACDERAE SUPERBUM. (*Journal of Horticulture.*)

To *Cypripedium* × 'Winifred Hollington,' 'Cookson's variety' (*C. niveum* × *callosum Sanderae*) (votes, 13 for, 3 against), from Norman C. Cookson, Esq. (gr. Mr. Chapman). Flowers white, effectively tinged and spotted with rose-colour.

To *Cypripedium* × *Sanacderae superbum* (*San-Actaeus* × *insigne Sanderae*) (votes, 8 for, 2 against), from Norman C. Cookson, Esq. (gr. Mr. Chapman). A very close approach to *C. insigne Sanderae*, but with lip slightly darker yellow and more white in the dorsal sepal. (Fig. 114.)

Botanical Certificate.

To *Cirrhopetalum Makoyanum*, from Sir Trevor Lawrence, Bart. An elegant species, with slender stems, bearing on the top an equally rayed umbel of yellow flowers slightly tinged with red and arranged like the spokes of a wheel.

Other Exhibits.

Norman C. Cookson, Esq. (gr. Mr. Chapman) : Cypripediums.

Messrs. Sander : an effective group.

Messrs. Hugh Low : a group.

H. Spicer, Esq., Highbury (gr. Mr. Lovegrove) : a group of *Cypripedium Spicerianum.*

J. Craven, Esq., Keighley : *Cypripedium Daltonianum.*

H. S. Goodson, Esq., Putney (gr. Mr. Day) : *Cypripedium* × 'Lily Blanche' (*C. Charlesworthii* × 'Niobe').

Messrs. Heath, Cheltenham : a group of Cypripediums.

H. J. Bromilow, Esq., Rann Lea, Rainhill, Lancashire (gr. Mr. Morgan) : hybrid Cypripediums.

ORCHID COMMITTEE, DECEMBER 10, 1907.

Mr. J. GURNEY FOWLER in the Chair, and twenty-three members present.

Awards Recommended :—

Gold Medal.

To G. F. Moore, Esq., Chardwar, Bourton-on-the-Water (gr. Mr. Page), for a large group of Orchids, Cypripediums predominating.

Silver Flora Medal.

To Messrs. Cypher, Cheltenham, for a group.

To F. Du Cane Godman, Esq., South Lodge, Horsham (gr. Mr. Moody), for a group of Calanthes and *Laelia anceps.*

Silver Banksian Medal.

To Messrs. Charlesworth, Bradford, for many interesting species.

To Messrs. Hugh Low, for a group.

To Messrs. Armstrong & Brown, for hybrid Cypripediums.

First-class Certificate.

To *Sophro-Cattleya* × *eximia* 'Fowler's variety' (*S. grandiflora* × *C. Bowringiana*) (votes, unanimous), from J. Gurney Fowler, Esq., Glebelands, South Woodford (gr. Mr. J. Davis). A beautiful hybrid, of dwarf habit and bearing comparatively large mauve-crimson flowers, with yellow base to the lip. (Fig. 115.)

Award of Merit.

To *Laelio-Cattleya* × 'Berthe Fournier' var. *tigrina* (*L.-C.* × *elegans* × *C. Dowiana aurea* (votes, unanimous), from Major G. L.

3 к

Holford, C.V.O., C.I.E., Westonbirt, Tetbury (gr. Mr. H. G. Alexander). Flowers like those of *C. Dowiana aurea*, golden-yellow, delicately flushed with reddish rose, lip carmine-crimson, with gold lines at the base.

To *Brasso-Cattleya* × 'Siren' (*B. Digbyana* × *C. Skinneri*) (votes, unanimous), from Major G. L. Holford. Growth resembling *C. Skinneri*; flowers bright rose, with white base to the fringed labellum.

To *Cypripedium* × 'Beryl' ('Mrs. Wm. Mostyn' × *Beeckmanii*) (votes, unanimous), from Major G. L. Holford. Flower closely approaching *C. Beeckmanii*, and of fine shape; dorsal sepal emerald-green, with white margin and heavy blackish blotches; petals and lip greenish-yellow, tinged and marked with mahogany-red.

Fig. 115.—Sophro-Cattleya × eximia, 'Fowler's Var.' (*Journal of Horticulture.*)

To *Cypripedium Fairrieanum* 'Black Prince' (votes, unanimous), from Messrs. Sander, St. Albans. A very remarkable variety, having the greater part of the dorsal sepal covered with broad reticulated bands of dark purple, the rest of the flower being also of a very dark hue.

To *Cypripedium insigne* 'Gwynedd' (votes, 10 for, 2 against), from Drewett O. Drewett, Esq. (gr. Mr. Renwick). A seedling of the *C. insigne Chantinii* class.

Botanical Certificate.

To *Cirrhopetalum retusiusculum*, from Sir Jeremiah Colman, Bart. Gatton Park, Reigate (gr. Mr. W. P. Bound). A singular little species with one-sided heads of orange-coloured flowers tinged with red.

Other Exhibits.

Major G. L. Holford : *Cypripedium* × 'Earl of Tankerville' (*exul* × *nitens*) and *Cattleya* × 'Cyril' (*Harrisoniana* × *Percivaliana*).

Francis Wellesley, Esq., Westfield (gr. Mr. Hopkins) : *Cypripedium insigne* 'Francis Wellesley,' a close ally of *C. insigne* 'Harefield Hall.'

Drewett O. Drewett, Esq., Riding Mill-on-Tyne (gr. Mr. Renwick): a selection of Cypripediums.

Sir Jeremiah Colman, Bart. : *Cirrhopetalum rəfractum* and *Phaio-Calanthe* × *Colmanii rosea.*

H. W. Perry, Esq., Upper Norwood (gr. Mr. Buckingham) : a group.

Messrs. Heath, Cheltenham : Cypripediums.

H. S. Goodson, Esq. (gr. Mr. Day) : four hybrid Cypripediums.

H. J. Bromilow, Esq., Rainhill (gr. Mr. Morgan) : Cypripediums.

F. Menteith Ogilvie, Esq., Oxford (gr. Mr. Balmforth): two hybrid Cypripediums.

ORCHID COMMITTEE, DECEMBER 31, 1907.

Mr. J. GURNEY FOWLER in the Chair, and seventeen members present.

Awards Recommended :—

Silver Flora Medal.

To Messrs. Cypher, Cheltenham : for Cypripediums, *Laelia anceps*, &c.

Silver Banksian Medal.

To Messrs. Moore, Rawdon, Leeds, for a group.
To Messrs. Hugh Low, Enfield, for a group of Cypripediums.

First-class Certificate.

To *Cypripedium* × 'Moonbeam' (*Thompsoni* × *Sallieri Hyeanum*) (votes, unanimous), from Major G. L. Holford, C.V.O., C.I.E., Weston-birt, Tetbury (gr. Mr. H. G. Alexander). A large and perfectly formed flower with white dorsal sepal, having a greenish base and purple central band with shorter purple lines ; petals and lip yellowish tinged with purple. (Fig. 116.)

Award of Merit.

To *Odontioda* × *Craveniana* (*Cochlioda Noezliana* × *Odontoglossum cordatum*) (votes, unanimous), from Messrs. Charlesworth, Heaton, Bradford. Flowers bearing a resemblance to those of *O.* × *Bradshawiae*, but with broader lip ; colour red with orange crest to the lip. The only indications of *O. cordatum* are the distinctly keeled sepals and a slight indication of freckling in the colour of the inner parts of the petals.

To *Cypripedium* × *Troilus Cravenianum* (*insigne* 'Harefield Hall' × *nitens magnificum*) (votes, 10 for, 4 against), from J. H. Craven, Esq., Beeches, Keighley, Yorks. A large flower resembling *C. insigne* 'Harefield Hall,' but with the dorsal sepal more flat and bearing more and smaller spots than that variety.

Other Exhibits.

Major G. L. Holford, C.V.O., C.I.E.: *Laelia anceps* 'Theodora' and the new *Cypripedium* × 'Bellerophon' (*nitens* 'Mrs. Tautz' × 'Calypso').

Mons. Mertens, Ghent: hybrid Odontoglossums.

Fig. 116.—CYPRIPEDIUM · 'MOONBEAM.' (*Journal of Horticulture.*)

J. Gurney Fowler, Esq., Glebelands, South Woodford (gr. Mr. J. Davis): *Cypripedium insigne Arnoldii.*

Messrs. Jas. Veitch: two forms of *Cypripedium* × 'Countess of Carnarvon.'

Messrs. Sander, St. Albans: a finely blotched home-raised *Odontoglossum crispum.*

ESTABLISHED
1804.

INCORPORATED
1809.

TELEGRAMS:
"HORTENSIA, LONDON."

TELEPHONE:
5363 WESTMINSTER.

ROYAL HORTICULTURAL SOCIETY,

VINCENT SQUARE, WESTMINSTER, S.W.

NOTICES TO FELLOWS.

1. NOTICE TO FELLOWS.

A few pages of Notices to Fellows are always added at the end of each number of the JOURNAL, immediately preceding the Advertisements, and also at the beginning both of the "Book of Arrangements" and of the "Report of the Council." Fellows are particularly requested to consult these Notices, as it would often save them and the Secretary much needless correspondence.

2. LETTERS.

All letters on *all* subjects should be addressed—The Secretary, Royal Horticultural Hall, Vincent Square, Westminster, S.W.

3. TELEPHONE AND TELEGRAMS.

Telephone Number: **WESTMINSTER, 5363.**
" **HORTENSIA, LONDON,**" is sufficient address for telegrams.

4. JOURNALS WANTED.

The Secretary would be very greatly obliged for any of the following back numbers :—Vol. V., Part 1 ; Vol. VII., Part 2 ; Vol. X. ; Vol. XIII., Part 1 ; Vol. XVI., Parts 2 and 3 ; Vol. XVII., Parts 1 and 2 ; Vol. XVII., Parts 3 and 4 ; Vol. XIX., Part 1 ; Vol. XIX., Part 2 ; Vol. XX., Part 3 ; Vol. XXII., Part 3 ; Vol. XXII., Part 4 ; Vol. XXV., Part 3 ; Vol. XXVI., Part 4 ; Vol. XXVII., Part 1 ; Vol. XXVII., Part 4 ; Vol. XXVIII., Parts 3 and 4 ; and Vol. XXIX., Parts 1, 2, and 3. Also the return to the Society of ANY NUMBERS of the JOURNAL which may be of no further use or interest to Fellows would be appreciated, as applications for back numbers are repeatedly received.

5. SUBSCRIPTIONS.

All Subscriptions fall due on January 1st of each year. To avoid the inconvenience of remembering this, Fellows can *compound* by the payment of one lump sum in lieu of all further annual payments ; or they can, by applying to the Society, obtain a form of instruction to their bankers to pay for them every January 1st. It may be a week or more before the Tickets reach the Fellow, owing to the very large numbers, nearly 20,000, having to be despatched within the first month of the year. Fellows who have not already given an order on their bankers for the payment of their subscriptions each year are requested to do so, as this method of payment is preferred, and saves the Fellows considerable trouble. Forms for the purpose may be obtained from the R.H.S. Offices at Vincent Square, Westminster, S.W. Fellows whose subscriptions remain unpaid are debarred from all the privileges of the Society ; but their subscriptions are nevertheless recoverable at law, the Society being incorporated by Royal Charter.

In paying their subscriptions, Fellows often make the mistake of drawing their cheques for Pounds instead of for Guineas. Kindly note that in all cases it is Guineas and not Pounds. Cheques and Postal Orders should be made payable to " The Royal Horticultural Society " and crossed " London and County Bank, Westminster."

6. FORM OF BEQUEST.

I give and bequeath to the Treasurer for the time being of the Royal Horticultural Society, London, the sum of £   , to be paid out of such part of my personal estate as I can lawfully charge with the payment of such legacy, and to be paid free of legacy duty, within six months of my decease ; the receipt of such Treasurer to be a sufficient discharge for the same. And I declare that the said legacy shall be applied towards [the general purposes of the Society].*

7. PRIVILEGES OF CHEMICAL ANALYSIS.

Instructions are contained at page 70 in the " Book of Arrangements," 1908.

8. LIST OF FELLOWS.

A list of all the Fellows of the Society is sent out in January. Fellows are requested to look at their own names in it, and if in any way these are incorrect, or the addresses insufficient, they are requested to inform the Secretary at once. Another use which all Fellows might make of this list is to consult it with reference to their friends' names, and if any of them are not found recorded therein they might endeavour to enlist their sympathies with the Society, and obtain their consent to propose them as Fellows forthwith. Forms of Nomination, and of the Privileges of Fellows, are bound in with every number of the JOURNAL and the " Book of Arrangements."

9. NEW FELLOWS.

On March 6 last the Society completed its 104th year. Will all the Fellows do their best to extend the usefulness of the Society by enlisting the sympathy of all their friends and persuading them to join the ranks of the Society? A list of the privileges of Fellows will be found at page 16 in the " Book of Arrangements," and just a line addressed to the Secretary R.H.S., Vincent Square, Westminster, containing the name and address of the proposed new Fellow will suffice. Should it be preferred, the Secretary will, upon receipt of a postcard or letter giving the name and address of any persons likely to join the Society, write direct and invite them to allow their names to be proposed for election.

10. AN APPEAL.

What has been accomplished for the Society since 1887 is largely due to the unwearied assistance afforded by a small proportion of the Fellows ; but as all belong to the same Society, so it behoves each one to do what he or she can to further its interests, especially in :—

1. Increasing the number of Fellows.

2. Contributing towards the Masters' Memorial Fund for establishing Foundation Lectures on the Application of Science to Horticulture.

3. Helping to swell the Fund started by Mr. A. W. Sutton, V.M.H., for providing Prizes for the Students at Wisley.

---

* Any special directions or conditions which the testator may wish to be attached to the bequest may be substituted for the words in brackets.

4. Lectures with lantern slides.

5. Books are required to fill the gaps in the Library both at Vincent Square and at Wisley.

6. New and rare Plants are wanted for the Garden and surplus roots for distribution to the Fellows.

Thus there is plenty for all to do according to their individual liking : personal effort, money, plants, books, are all alike needed. The Secretary, therefore, asks those who read these lines to do their best to help in any of the methods above indicated.

11. THE SOCIETY'S GARDENS AT WISLEY.

The Gardens are open daily to Fellows and others showing Fellows' Transferable Tickets from 9 A.M. till sunset, except on Sundays, Good Friday, and Christmas Day. Each Fellow's ticket admits three to the Gardens. The Public are not admitted. There is much of interest to

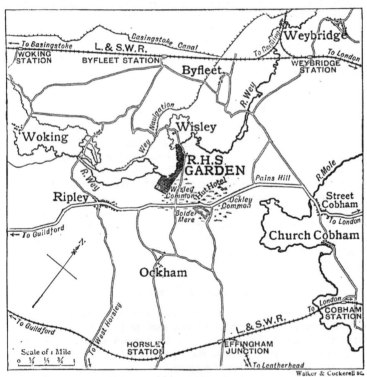

POSITION OF THE SOCIETY'S GARDENS.

be seen at Wisley throughout the year. The late Mr. G. F. Wilson's garden included a wild wood-garden, a bank of flowering shrubs, a series of ponds and pools, and a fine collection of Japanese Iris, Primulas, Lilies, Rhododendrons, &c. The Society has added a fine collection of the best varieties of fruit trees, of bamboos, of roses, and of ornamental trees and flowering shrubs, for the most part kindly given by the leading nurserymen. A very large sum of money has also been spent in the erection of a first-rate Meteorological Station, and a fine series of glass-houses; a dwelling-house for the Superintendent; a Cottage for the Fruit Foreman; and in establishing a complete system of water supply; on drainage works, and on road-making.

The Gardens are situated at Wisley, about 2 miles from Ripley in Surrey, and about 3½ miles from Horsley and 5½ miles from Weybridge, both stations on the South-Western Railway, with frequent trains from Waterloo and Clapham Junction. Carriages to convey four persons can be obtained by writing to Mr. D. White, fly proprietor, Ripley, Surrey; the charge being, to and from Weybridge, waiting two hours at the Gardens, 8s.; or waiting three hours, 10s.; or to and from Horsley, 7s.; Effingham Junction, 7s.; Byfleet, 7s. Visitors should in all cases be careful to state the trains they intend to arrive by and leave by. Carriages can also be obtained at Weybridge for 8s. by writing to Mr. Trembling, New Road, Weybridge. Excellent accommodation and refreshments can be had at the Hut Hotel, close to the Gardens, and also at the Hautboy at Ockham.

12. THE WISLEY RESEARCH STATION.

The new Research Station and Laboratory at Wisley is now completed and work is in progress there. Mr. F. J. Chittenden has been appointed Director of the Research Work on Scientific Matters affecting Practical Horticulture, and Lecturer to the Students. By the completion of this station a long-felt want has been met. In the United States, where so much good work has been done in this direction, all is paid for by the Government, but in this country we have to fall back on private individuals or on Societies.

13. STUDENTS AT WISLEY.

The Society admits a limited number of young men, not exceeding 22 years of age, to study Gardening at Wisley, where the training has been recently further developed by the erection of the Laboratory and Research Station. The curriculum now includes not only practical garden work in all the main branches of Horticulture, but also lectures, demonstrations, and elementary Horticultural Science in the Laboratory, whereby a practical knowledge of simple Garden Chemistry, Biology, &c., may be obtained. The Laboratory is equipped with the best apparatus procurable for Students. The training extends over a period of two years, with a progressive course for each year. Students can only enter at the end of September and at the end of March. Selected Students have also the advantage of attending certain of the Society's Shows and Lectures in London. It is generally easy to find these young men employment on the completion of their training; in fact, the Council are quite unable to meet the demands for energetic, trustworthy young men; but they *must all be workers.*

14. DISTRIBUTION OF SURPLUS PLANTS.

In a recent Report the Council drew attention to the way in which the annual distribution of surplus plants has arisen. In a large garden there must always be a great deal of surplus stock which must either be given away or go to the waste heap. A few Fellows noticing this, asked for plants which would otherwise be discarded; and they valued what was so obtained. Others hearing of it asked for a share, until the Council felt they must either systematise this haphazard distribution or else put a stop to it altogether. To take the latter step seemed undesirable. Why should not such Fellows have them as cared to receive such surplus plants? It was therefore decided to keep all plants till the early spring, and then give all Fellows alike the option of claiming a share of them by ballot.

Fellows are therefore particularly requested to notice that only waste and surplus plants raised from seeds or cuttings are available for distribution. Many of them may be of very little intrinsic value, and it is only to avoid their being absolutely wasted that the distribution was established. The great majority also are of necessity *very small*, and may require careful treatment for a time.

Fellows are particularly requested to note that a Form of Application and list to choose from of the plants available for distribution is sent in January *every year* to every Fellow, enclosed in the " Report of the Council." To avoid all possibility of favour, all application lists are kept until the last day of February, when they are all thrown into a Ballot; and as the lists are drawn out, so is the order of their execution, the plants being despatched as quickly as possible after March 1.

Of some of the varieties enumerated the stock is small, perhaps not more than twenty-five or fifty plants being available. It is therefore obvious that when the Ballot is kind to any Fellow he will receive all the plants exactly as he has selected, but when the Ballot has given him an unfavourable place he may find the stock of the majority of plants he has chosen exhausted. A little consideration would show that all Fellows cannot be first, and some must be last, in the Ballot. Application forms received after March 1 and before April 30 are kept till all those previously received have been dealt with, and are then balloted in a similar way. Fellows having omitted to fill up their application form before April 30 must be content to wait till the next year's distribution. The work of the Gardens cannot be disorganised by the sending-out of plants at any later time in the year. All Fellows can participate in the annual distribution *following* their election.

The Society does not pay the cost of packing and carriage. The charge for this will be collected by the carriers on delivery of the plants, which will be addressed exactly as given by each Fellow on his application form. It is impracticable to send plants by post owing to the lack of Post Office facilities for despatch without prepayment of postage.

Fellows residing beyond a radius of thirty-five miles from London are permitted to choose double the number of plants to which they are otherwise entitled.

Plants cannot be sent to Fellows residing outside the United King-dom, owing either to length of time in transit or to vexatious regulations in some foreign countries; but the Council will at any time endeavour to obtain for Fellows living abroad any unusual or rare seeds which they may have been unable to procure in their own country.

15. THE SOCIETY'S HALL AND OFFICES.

The Royal Horticultural Hall and Offices are situated in Vincent Square, which lies straight through Ashley Gardens from Victoria Street,

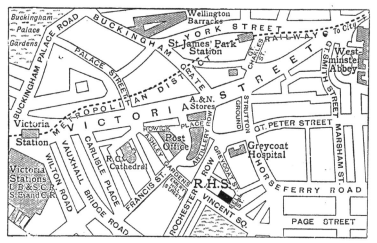

POSITION OF THE SOCIETY'S HALL.

Westminster, and is about five minutes' walk from the Victoria and St. James's Park Stations.

16. LETTING OF HALL.

Fellows are earnestly requested to make known among their friends and among other institutions that the ROYAL HORTICULTURAL HALL is available, twelve days in each fortnight, for Meetings, Shows, Exhibitions, Concerts, Conferences, Lectures, Balls, Banquets, Bazaars, Receptions, and other similar purposes. The Hall has a floor surface of 13,000 square feet. It is cool in summer and warm in winter. For a Concert it will seat 1,500, or for a public meeting 1,800. It is undoubtedly the lightest Hall in London, and its acoustic properties are pronounced excellent by some of our greatest authorities. The charges, which are very moderate, include lighting, warming in winter or cooling the air in summer, seating, and the use of trestle-tabling and platform. The first floor, consisting of four fine rooms, may also be hired for similar pur-poses, either together with or separately from the Great Hall. This accommodation can also be divided up if desired. A long-felt want has now been met by the construction of a convenient kitchen in the basement, with lift connections to the eastern annexe and lecture room. For serving luncheons, &c., this will prove a great boon. Ample cloak-rooms for ladies and for gentlemen are available. In fact, the Hall is not only the most suitable Hall in London for special Shows of a high-class character, but it is also second only to the Queen's Hall and the Royal Albert Hall for the purposes of Concerts and Meetings. Reduction is made to Charities, and there are special terms for Societies kindred or allied to Horticulture. The regulations, &c., for hiring the Hall are printed in the "Book of Arrangements," and full particulars may be obtained on application to the Secretary R.H.S., Vincent Square, Westminster, S.W., with whom dates may be booked.

17. EXHIBITIONS, MEETINGS, AND LECTURES IN 1908.

A full programme for 1908 will be found at pages 41 to 63 in the "Book of Arrangements" for 1908. It will be noticed that an Exhibition and Meeting is held in the Royal Horticultural Hall practically every fortnight throughout the year, and a short lecture on some interesting subject connected with Horticulture is delivered during the afternoon. Special Shows have also been arranged on days other than those of the Society's own Exhibitions. See page ccxl.

A reminder of every Show will be sent in the week preceding to any Fellow who will send to the R.H.S. Offices, Vincent Square, S.W., a sufficient number (33) of halfpenny cards *ready addressed* to himself.

18. THE TEMPLE SHOW, 1908.

The twentieth great annual Flower Show in the Inner Temple Gardens, Thames Embankment, will be held, by the kind permission of the Treasurer and Benchers of the Inner Temple, on Tuesday, Wednesday, and Thursday, May 26, 27, and 28. Fellows are requested to note that there will be a **Private View** of the Show on Wednesday, May 27, from 7 A.M. till noon, at which only transferable and non-transferable Fellows' Annual Tickets will admit. Day-tickets will not be purchasable or passed during these particular hours of Private View. See pages 47 to 52 in the "Book of Arrangements," 1908.

19. HOLLAND HOUSE SHOW, 1908.

By the kind permission of Mary, the Countess of Ilchester, the Summer Show will be held at Holland House on July 7 and 8, particulars of which will be found in the "Book of Arrangements," 1908. The rules for the Temple Show apply as far as possible to Holland House, but there is sufficient space to allow of an extra Tent for Horticultural Sundries. See page 54 in the "Book of Arrangements," 1908.

20. BRITISH-GROWN FRUIT SHOW, 1908.

The Great Autumn Show of British-grown Hardy Fruits, which the Society has held for so many years past, has become as much a thing to be regularly looked for by fruit-growers as the Show at the Temple in May is looked for by growers of flowers.

The fifteenth of these Shows will be held on October 15 and 16, 1908, in the Society's Hall.

21. BOTTLED BRITISH FRUITS, &c., SHOW.

The Annual Exhibition of British Bottled Fruits will be held on November 26 and 27, 1908, when it is hoped to see a still larger number of exhibits than last year. This is an Exhibition which should prove particularly attractive in domestic circles. Money Prizes and Medals are offered, and this year a new Class (No. 29 in the Schedule) has been added for bottled fruits to be shown in November 1908, and retained by the Society for a corresponding Show in 1909, when they will be tested by the Judges. The first prize is a Silver Cup. See "Book of Arrangements," page 63.

22. COLONIAL-GROWN FRUIT SHOWS, 1908.

The President and Council of the Royal Horticultural Society have again arranged to hold Exhibitions of Colonial-grown Fruits and Vegetables on June 11 and 12, November 26 and 27.

In fixing these dates the object aimed at is to suit the seasons which are most likely to find the produce of Australia, Tasmania, and New Zealand, and of Canada, British Columbia, and the West Indies, in the greatest perfection in London. Opportunity is afforded for each Colony to make Collective Exhibits in addition to the exhibits of individual growers or firms. These Exhibitions were originally organised in 1904, and have been the means of bringing before the British Fruit Merchants and fruit-consuming public the wonderful resources of the Fruit Markets of Great Britain quite independently of the foreigner. The Society's sole object is the advancement of the interest of the Colonies (a) by stimulating the production of better fruits ; (b) by giving advice and assistance in the difficulties ever confronting Fruit Growers ; and (c) by helping to inform the home market. The results have been encouraging ; for even in so short a time as the last three years a distinctly better quality of fruit has been sent, those recently shown being of an improved appearance, less blotched by fungus, scale and other defects, and better packed. At the same time the Council are disappointed at the backwardness of Exhibitors and the smallness of their exhibits. Fruit Growers in the Colonies are therefore asked to assist their own future competition in the market by sending exhibits to these Exhibitions, invitations to which will be given to the Colonial and Government Offices, the Embassies, the leading London Fruit Merchants, Colonials on furlough, and many others.

The Agents-General and other authorities are most kindly rendering every assistance, and we trust that both growers and shippers will do their best to send in Exhibits worthy of our Colonies, and to show what can be produced for the Home markets. No entrance fee or charge for space is made, and Tabling is also provided free of expense.

If desired any produce may be consigned direct to the Society and it
will be stored in the cellars at Vincent Square and staged by the Society's
officials ; but the Society cannot undertake to repack and return any
exhibits.

Particulars of the Shows can be obtained from the Secretary R.H.S.,
Vincent Square, Westminster, S.W., by enclosing one penny stamp in
order to cover the cost of postage.

23. SHOWS OF KINDRED SOCIETIES IN 1908.

The following dates have been fixed on which R.H.S. Fellows' tickets
will admit :—

April 1.—Perpetual Flowering Carnation Society.
April 28.—Auricula and Primula Society.
July 22.—Carnation and Picotee Society.
July 24.—Sweet Pea Society.
September 8.—Dahlia Society.
September 17.—Rose Society.
December 9.—Perpetual Flowering Carnation Society.

Copies of the Schedules for these Shows may be obtained from the
Honorary Secretary of each Society.   For names and addresses see above
dates in programme on pages 41 to 63, "Book of Arrangements," 1908.

24. SPECIAL PRIZES, 1908.

(1) THE VEITCHIAN CUP.

The Veitchian Cup was offered to the President and Council of the
Royal Horticultural Society in the year 1903, in commemoration of the
fiftieth anniversary of the establishment of the Chelsea house by Mr.
James Veitch, the Nurseryman.   The Cup is of silver-gilt of the Georgian
period, with traces of the Greek.

The object of the gift is to recognise in an exceptional degree exhibits
of the highest order, the greatest advance in Horticulture—either a
single plant, a group, or series of groups being equally eligible—in the
opinion of seven specially chosen and eminent judges at the Temple
Show.   In 1908 it will be given to an amateur.

The judge's decision is final, and the Cup may be withheld at their
discretion.

The judges will not award this high distinction unless satisfied and
assured that the exhibit is, in the main, due to the work and capability
of the exhibitor or his legitimate employés ; on this point the judges
may consult any expert not eligible to win the Cup.

The judges need not give a decision till the third day of the Show.

(2) THE SHERWOOD CUP.

The £10 10s. Silver Cup which N. N. Sherwood, Esq., V.M.H., has
for the past ten years given to the Society will be awarded at the Holland
House Show on July 7, 1908, for twenty-four bunches of Roses with
their own foliage shown in vases by amateurs.   A background of other
foliage will be allowed.

(3) MEDALS AND PRIZES—VEITCH MEMORIAL TRUSTEES.

The following Medals and Prizes are offered by the Trustees of the
" Veitch Memorial " at the Autumn Fruit Show :—

For five distinct varieties of Grapes, three bunches of each, of which
two at least must be white :—First Prize, a Silver Medal and £10 ;
Second, Bronze Medal and £5 ; Third, Bronze Medal. *Amateurs.*

Also at the Society's Fortnightly Meeting on December 8, a Medal
and £5 is offered for the best group of winter-flowering Carnations (either
in pots or as cut flowers, or a combination of both), grown by the
exhibitor, and occupying a space of 100 square feet. *Amateurs.*

A similar prize is again to be offered for Carnations at the Society's
first Exhibition in April 1909.

25. LECTURES.

The new Lecture Room is fitted with an electric lantern of the most
modern construction ; electric current, gas, and water are laid on, and
every provision has been made for the illustration and delivery of
Lectures.

Any Fellows willing to Lecture, or to communicate Papers on interesting subjects, are requested to communicate with the Secretary.

26. EXAMINATIONS, 1909.

1. The Society will hold an examination on Monday, January 11,
1909, specially intended for gardeners employed in Public Parks and
Gardens belonging to County Councils, City Corporations, and similar
bodies. This examination will be conducted in the Royal Horticultural
Society's Hall, Vincent Square, Westminster, S.W. The last day for
receiving entries is January 1, 1909.

2. The Society's Annual Examination in the Principles and Practice
of Horticulture will be held on Wednesday, April 21, 1909. The
examination has two divisions, viz., (*a*) for Candidates of eighteen years
of age and over, and (*b*) for Juniors *under* eighteen years. Candidates
should send in their names not later than March 31. Full particulars may
be obtained by sending a stamped and directed envelope to the Society's
offices. Copies of the Questions set from 1893 to 1907 (price 2*s.* post
free) may also be obtained from the Office. The Society is willing to
hold an examination wherever a magistrate, clergyman, schoolmaster,
or other responsible person accustomed to examinations will consent to
supervise one on the Society's behalf.

In connection with this examination a Scholarship of £25 a year for
two years is offered by the Society to be awarded after the 1909
examination to the student who shall pass highest, if he is willing to
accept the conditions attaching thereto. The main outline of these conditions is that the holder must be of the male sex, and between the
ages of 18 and 22 years, and that he should study gardening for one
year at least at the Royal Horticultural Society's Gardens at Wisley,
conforming to the general rules laid down there for Students. In the

second year of the Scholarship he may, if he like, continue his studies at some other place at home or abroad which is approved by the Council of the Royal Horticultural Society. In case of two or more eligible Students being adjudged equal, the Council reserve to themselves the right to decide which of them shall be presented to the Scholarship.

3. The Society will hold an Examination in Cottage Gardening on Wednesday, April 28, 1909. This examination is intended for, and is confined to, Elementary and Technical School Teachers. It is undertaken in view of the increasing demand in country districts that the Schoolmaster shall be competent to teach the elements of Cottage Gardening, and the absence of any test whatever of such competence. The general conduct of this examination will be on similar lines to that of the more general examination. Questions on Elementary Chemistry and Biology are now added to this examination.

Medals and Certificates are awarded and Class Lists published in connection with these examinations, and the Syllabus may be obtained on application to the Secretary R.H.S., Vincent Square.

27. INFORMATION.

Fellows may obtain information and advice free of charge from the Society as to the names of flowers and fruit, on points of practice, insect and fungoid attacks, and other questions by applying to the Secretary R.H.S., Vincent Square, Westminster, S.W. Where at all practicable, it is particularly requested that letters and specimens may be timed to reach Vincent Square by the first post on the mornings of the Fortnightly Meetings so as to be laid before the Scientific or other Committees at once.

28. INSPECTION OF FELLOWS' GARDENS.

The Inspection of Gardens belonging to Fellows is conducted by a thoroughly competent Inspector from the Society, who reports and advises at the following cost, viz., a fee of £3. 3s. for one day (or £5. 5s. for two consecutive days), together with all out-of-pocket expenses. No inspection may occupy more than two days, save by special arrangement. Fellows wishing for the services of an Inspector are requested to give at least a week's notice and choice of two or three days, and to indicate the most convenient railway station and its distance from their Gardens. Gardens can only be inspected at the *written* request of the *owner*.

29. AFFILIATION OF LOCAL SOCIETIES.

One of the most successful of the many new branches of work undertaken since the reconstruction of the Society in 1887 is the unification of all local Horticultural, Floral, and Gardening Societies by a scheme of affiliation to the R.H.S. Since this was initiated, no less than 200 Societies have joined our ranks, and that number is steadily increasing.

To the privileges of Affiliated Societies have recently been added all the benefits accruing under the scheme recently introduced for the Union of Horticultural Mutual Improvement Societies.

Secretaries of Affiliated Societies can obtain on application a specimen copy of a Card which the Council have prepared for the use of Affiliated Societies wishing to have a suitable Card for Certificates, Commendations, &c. It can be used for Fruit or Flowers or Vegetables. Price 3s. 6d. for 10 copies, 5s. 6d. for 20, 11s. 6d. for 50, 20s. for 100.

The Council have also struck a special Medal for the use of Affiliated Societies. It·is issued at cost price in Bronze, Silver, and Silver-gilt— viz., Bronze, 5s. 6d., with case complete ; Silver, 12s. 6d., with case complete ; Silver-gilt, 16s. 6d., with case complete. Award Cards having the Medal embossed in relief can be sent with the Medal if ordered—price 6d. each.

30. UNION OF HORTICULTURAL MUTUAL IMPROVEMENT SOCIETIES.

This Union has recently been established for the encouragement and assistance of Horticultural Mutual Improvement Societies, the object being to strengthen existing Mutual Improvement Societies, to promote interchange of lecturers, to provide printed lectures, and if possible to increase the number of these useful Societies, and thus generally to advance the aims and objects of horticulture.

A list of lecturers and their subjects, and also a list of typewritten lectures, with or without lantern slides, prepared by the Society, may be obtained from the Secretary R.H.S., price 3d.

The Secretary of the Society will be very glad to hear from any competent lecturers who are willing to lecture to such Societies that he may enrol them in the Register of Lecturers and bring them into touch with Societies requiring assistance. Others may like to send to him written lectures (with or without lantern slides), that he may have them printed for circulation among these Societies.

Lantern slides on horticultural topics are urgently needed, and their gift will·be very much appreciated.

31. MONOGRAPH ON FUNGOID PESTS.

The attention of Fellows is directed to a handsome volume recently published by the Society on Fungoid Pests of Cultivated Plants, by Dr. M. C. Cooke, V.M.H. It consists of 280 pages of letterpress, and is illustrated with 24 coloured plates, containing figures of 360 different fungoid attacks, and 23 woodcuts. The work is divided under the headings of Pests ·of the Flower Garden, of Vegetables, of Fruit, of the Vinery and Stove, of the Ornamental Shrubbery, of Forest Trees, and of Field Crops. These are followed by a Chapter on Fungicides, which explains very clearly how to make the different washes and sprays, and also gives the proportions in which the various ingredients should be used.

Each pest is described separately, and means for its prevention or eradication are given, and the whole work is written so as to interest and instruct the cultivator in the simplest and most practical manner.

The volume, as published, is half-bound in calf, as it was considered probable that it would form the text-book on the subject for very many years to come; and it thus makes an admirable school prize or gift to a gardener or student of nature. Price 6s., R.H.S. Office, Vincent Square.

"No one whose plants are subject to fungoid attacks—and whose are not?—should be without this book; for not only can they by its use identify the disease at once, but they are also told both how to treat it and overcome it, and also how to make the different washes and sprays which the different classes of fungoid attacks require."

32. RULES FOR JUDGING.

The "Rules for Judging, with Suggestions to Schedule Makers and Exhibitors," have been revised and considerably modified from the experience gained during the last few years. The Secretaries of Local Societies are therefore strongly advised to obtain a fresh copy. It will be sent post free on receipt of a postal order for 1s. 6d. addressed to the Secretary, Royal Horticultural Society, Vincent Square, Westminster, S.W.

33. VARIETIES OF FRUITS.

Many people plant Fruit trees without a thought of what Variety they shall plant, and as a result almost certain disappointment ensues, whilst for an expenditure of 2d. they can obtain from the Society a little 16-page pamphlet which contains the latest expert opinion on Apples, Pears, Plums, Cherries, Raspberries, Currants, Gooseberries, and Strawberries, together with Notes on Planting, Pruning, and Manuring, which for clearness of expression and direction it would be impossible to surpass. It has in fact been suggested that no other 16 pages in the English language contain so much and such definite information. At the end of the pamphlet are given the names of some of the quite new varieties of Fruits, which promise well, but are not yet sufficiently long proved to be recommended for general planting.

Copies of this most valuable little pamphlet for distribution may be obtained at the Society's Office, Vincent Square, Westminster. Price, post free: single copy, 2d., or 25, 2s.; 50, 3s.; 100, 4s.

34. ADVERTISEMENTS.

Fellows are reminded that the more they can place their orders with those who advertise in the Society's Publications the more likely others are to advertise also, and in this way the Society may be indirectly benefited.

THE ROYAL HORTICULTURAL SOCIETY.

Established
A.D. 1804.

Incorporated
A.D. 1809.

VINCENT SQUARE, WESTMINSTER, S.W.

Telegrams: "HORTENSIA, LONDON." Telephone No.: 5363, Westminster.

Form of Recommendation for a FELLOW of the ROYAL HORTICULTURAL SOCIETY.

Name ....

Description ....

Address ....

....

being desirous of becoming a FELLOW of the ROYAL HORTICULTURAL SOCIETY, we whose Names are underwritten beg leave to recommend him (her) to that honour; he (she) is desirous of subscribing * .... Guineas a year.

Proposed by ....

Seconded by ....

* Kindly enter here the word *four* or *two* or *one*.

It would be a convenience if the Candidate's Card were sent at the same time.

Signed on behalf of the Council, this .... day of .... 190......

.... CHAIRMAN.

THE ROYAL HORTICULTURAL SOCIETY.

Privileges of Fellows.

1.—Anyone interested in Horticulture is eligible for election, and is invited to become a Fellow.
2.—Candidates for election are proposed by two Fellows of the Society.
3.—Ladies are eligible for election as Fellows of the Society.
4.—The Society being incorporated by Royal Charter, the Fellows incur no personal liability whatsoever beyond the payment of their annual subscriptions.
5.—Forms for proposing new Fellows may be obtained from the Offices of the Society, Vincent Square, Westminster, S.W.
6.—If desired, the Secretary will, on receipt of a letter from a Fellow of the Society suggesting the name and address of any lady or gentleman likely to become Fellows, write and invite them to join the Society.

FELLOWS.

A Fellow subscribing Four Guineas a year (or commuting for Forty Guineas) is entitled—

1.—To ONE Non-transferable (personal) Pass and FIVE Transferable Tickets admitting to all the Society's Exhibitions, and to the Gardens.

> *N.B.*—Each Transferable Ticket or Non-transferable personal Pass will admit three persons to the Gardens at Wisley on any day *except* days on which an Exhibition or Meeting is being held, when each Ticket or Pass will admit One Person only. The Gardens are closed on Sundays, Good Friday, and Christmas Day.

2.—To attend and vote at all Meetings of the Society.
3.—To the use of the Libraries at the Society's Rooms.
4.—To a copy of the Society's JOURNAL, containing the Papers read at all Meetings and Conferences, Reports of trials made at the Gardens, and descriptions and illustrations of new or rare plants, &c.
5.—To purchase, at reduced rates, such fruit, vegetables, and cut flowers as are not required for experimental purposes.
6.—To a share (in proportion to the annual subscription) of such surplus or waste plants as may be available for distribution. Fellows residing beyond a radius of 35 miles from London (by the A B C Railway Guide) are entitled to a double share.
7.—Subject to certain limitations, to obtain Analysis of Manures, Soils, &c., or advice on such subjects, by letter from the Society's Consulting Chemist, Dr. J. A. Voelcker, M.A., F.I.C.
8.—To have their Gardens inspected by the Society's Officer at the following fees:—One day, £3. 3s.; two days, £5. 5s.; *plus* all out-of-pocket expenses.
9 —To exhibit at all Shows and Meetings, and to send seeds, plants, &c., for trial at the Society's Gardens.
10 —To recommend any ladies or gentlemen for election as Fellows of the Society.

A Fellow subscribing Two Guineas a year (or commuting for Twenty-five Guineas) is entitled—

1.—To ONE Non-transferable Pass and Two Transferable Tickets.
2.—To the same privileges as mentioned in Nos. 2, 3, 4, 5, 6, 7, 8, 9, 10, as above.

A Fellow subscribing One Guinea a year, with an Entrance Fee of £1. 1s. (or commuting for Fifteen Guineas), is entitled—

1 —To ONE Transferable Ticket (in lieu of the non-transferable personal Pass), and the privileges mentioned in Nos. 2, 3, 4, 5, 6, 7, 8, 9, 10, as above.

> [*Bonâ fide* Gardeners earning their living thereby, and persons living permanently abroad, are exempt from the payment of the Entrance Fee.]

ASSOCIATES.

An Associate subscribing 10s. 6d. a year is entitled—

1.—To ONE Non-transferable Pass, and to privileges as mentioned in Nos. 3, 4, and 9.

> *N.B.*—Associates must be *bonâ fide* Gardeners, or employés in a Nursery, Private or Market Garden, or Seed Establishment, and must be recommended for election by Two Fellows of the Society.

Local Horticultural and Cottage Garden Societies may be Affiliated to the Royal Horticultural Society, particulars as to which may be had on application.

INDEX No. I.

FIGURES AND ILLUSTRATIONS.

INDEX No. II.

GENERAL INDEX.

———◆———

Lightning Source UK Ltd.
Milton Keynes UK
UKHW021602030219
336610UK00007B/906/P